Dear Reader: We welcome your comments!

RE: The Olympic Factbook: A Spectator's Guide to the Summer Games and NBC Interactive Viewer's Guide to the 1996 Olympic Games CD-ROM

We would like to know what you think of The Olympic Factbook and what would make it even more useful for you.
Please take a few minutes to fill out and return this card. Thanks for your interest!

Where did you purchase this book? _____

How did you become aware of this book? _____

What feature of the book do you like the most? _____

What feature do you like the least? _____

How would you improve this book? _____

Other subject areas of interest _____

☐ Please send me information on other Visible Ink Press titles.

Name _____ Phone (_____) _____

Street Address _____

City _____ State _____ Zip _____

Age _____ M _____ F _____ Do you own a PC? _____ Do you own a CD-ROM Player? _____

Visible Ink Press

In U.S. and Canada: 1-800-776-6265   Fax: (313) 961-6637

THE
OLYMPIC
FACTBOOK

A SPECTATOR'S GUIDE
TO THE
SUMMER GAMES

Also from Visible Ink Press

Hot Dogs, Heroes & Hooligans
The Story of Baseball's Major League Teams

"Monumental."—*Washington Post*

A wide-screen view of the teams, the leagues, the lore, and the red-blooded legends of "America's National Pastime."

Michael L. LaBlanc, 11" x 8-1/2", paperback, 593 pages, 300 photos and sports statistics tables, ISBN 0-8103-9748-X, $16.95

Look for new editions of these sports books, coming soon!

The Complete Encyclopedia of Hockey,
5th edition

Marv Albert raves that the "fourth edition is better than a hat trick." Sports editor Zander Hollander expands coverage and gives the complete update on hockey, including pro, college, and Olympic play in this new edition.

Due out Fall 1996

The Olympic Factbook
A Spectator's Guide to the Winter Games

The world's attention turns to Japan as the Olympic Games get under way in February of 1998. This edition of the *Factbook* provides viewers with the whole scoop on the XVII Winter Games.

Due out Fall 1997

Visit our web site

For more information on other titles from Visible Ink Press, visit our home page: http://www.thomson.com/vip.html

THE
OLYMPIC
FACTBOOK

A SPECTATOR'S GUIDE
TO THE
SUMMER GAMES

Edited by
Rebecca Nelson
and
Marie J. MacNee

DETROIT • NEW YORK • WASHINGTON D.C. • TORONTO

CONTENTS

Equestrian

Profiles

Michael and Leslie Marx 238

Peter Westbrook 241

Fencing

Field Hockey

Gymnastics

Judo

Modern Pentathlon

Rowing

Shooting

Soccer

INTRODUCTION

This is the first edition of *The Olympic Factbook* that is exclusively devoted to those games we play in warm weather—or indoors. *The Olympic Factbook* was first published in 1992, the last time the Winter and Summer Olympic Games were held in the same year. The International Olympic Committee (IOC) moved to alternate the winter and summer events, which is good news: Now we get to enjoy the Games every other year. And enjoy them we do.

Every two years the Olympics capture our attention like no other sporting event. The Games make front page news, magazine covers, and prime-time television. An estimated 35 billion people will watch the 1996 Olympics on television worldwide while another 2 million make the trip to Atlanta to cheer from the sidelines while sports history is made. Television and radio will provide more than 3,000 hours of live coverage during the Atlanta Olympics, where nearly 11,000 athletes from around the world will participate in the events. With the addition of three new sports (Mountain Biking, Softball, and Beach Volleyball) to an already bulging Summer program, the Olympics are a smorgasbord of athletic delight for both the ardent and casual spectator.

About 50 weeks before the Games in Atlanta began, ticket sales were brisk for the Opening Ceremonies, many of the gymnastics and diving events, and for the finals for American favorites baseball and basketball. But these sports, along with swimming and track & field, are always the big draws: What about modern pentathlon? (It's considered to be one of the ultimate tests of athleticism.) Badminton? (It's the world's fastest racket sport.) Archery? (It may well be man's [and woman's] oldest sport.) Fencing? (It's one of only four sports to have been included in every Olympic Games.) There are fascinating facts behind all the events that make up the Games of the Summer Olympiad. Where do you turn to find the facts? To understand the rules of the game? To learn about which athletes and which teams you should keep your eye on?

The Olympic Factbook is your companion to the Games— whether you're watching from box seats or a Barcalounger™. In these pages each sporting event gets its due: From Archery through Yachting, you can brush up on the sport's history (in the **Warm-up** section that opens each chapter), the rules and regulations (in the **Spectator's Guide**), who the hot competitors are (in the **Hopefuls** section), when the competitions for each event are slated to take place (**Schedule**), what glorious and inglorious moments the sport has produced in past Olympic Games (**Highlights**), and who has taken home Olympic gold, silver, and bronze in years past (**Medalists**). When that's all done, you can test your knowledge by stepping up to the challenge of the **Trivia Quiz** that closes each chapter.

There's more, too: Sprinkled throughout these pages you'll find facts and quotes that give you the inside scoop on the Olympic events. Armed with these tantalizing tidbits of information, you'll be asking friends, family, and colleagues, "Did you know that . . . ?" or "Have you heard that . . . ?"

You'll recognize these asides because they announce themselves like this:

FACT: With a 30-medal harvest from Barcelona, U.S. track and field athletes scored their highest total in a non-boycotted Games since 1956.

And like this:

Of course the interest in the Games often centers on the people who participate in them. In addition to profiling the athletes to watch in 1996, *The Factbook* also reports on athletes who have passed into Olympic legend: British runners Abrahams and Liddell (their rivalry inspired the movie *Chariots of Fire*), Johnny Weissmuller (regarded as the best swimmer of the first half of the 20th century, he went on to Hollywood fame as the star of 19 Tarzan movies), super swimmer Matt Biondi (who captured a total of 11 medals in swimming events during the 1984, 1988, and 1992 Olympic Games), John Smith (arguably the greatest wrestler in American history, he became the first American to win four world titles in the tough sport), and others!

The Factbook is your guide to the Games—one convenient reference source to turn to before, during, or after the competitions, or whenever you feel like looking up the facts.

Acknowledgments

These pages are only as good as the many writers who have contributed their knowledge, research, and passion for the Olympics to them: Thanks to Eric Kinkopf, Mark Kram, George Cantor, Steve Carey, Anne Janette Johnson, Les Stone, and Michelle Kaufman. These contributors—some of them returning to work on this new edition and others who are new to *The Factbook*—have worked hard to make this an informative resource for the interested spectator. After all, there's a lot to know about 100 years of the Olympics, the thousands of athletes who participate each year, and the 33 sporting events that now make up the Summer Games. Zeroing in on the athletes who might be contenders in 1996 has been a challenge indeed. But the writers remained stalwart in their quests to do just that. Naturally many of the hopefuls who are profiled in these pages are U.S. athletes, since much of the news we read and heard focused on the American teams. But wherever possible, we have tried to call out those athletes from around the globe who are worth keeping an eye in Atlanta. And there will be many of them.

Also thanks to the contributors to the first edition whose work lives on in these pages—Harvey Dickson and Paul Green.

Many others have worked tirelessly on this new edition of *The Factbook:* Dean Dauphinais provided fact-checking and proofreading; Leslie Norback and Judy Galens also proofread; Andy Malonis helped with the research; Michelle DiMercurio created a winning look for our pages and redesigned our cover; Margaret McAvoy Amoto and Kim Smiley secured permissions; Barbara Yarrow and Pam Hayes readied the photos for publication; and Kevin Hillstrom and Laurie Collier of Northern Lights Writers Group compiled the index. Additionally, a debt of gratitude is owed the editors of the previous editions for their insights and thoughts on the book—Diane L. Dupuis, Marty Connors, and Christa Brelin.

We would also like to thank the following organizations and, in particular, their media and communications people for so cooperatively accommodating our requests for information:

National Archery Association
U.S. Badminton
USA Baseball
USA Basketball
USA Boxing
US Canoe and Kayak Team
U.S. Cycling Federation
United States Diving
U.S. Equestrian Team
U.S. Fencing Association
U.S. Field Hockey Association
USA Gymnastics
United States Judo
U.S. Modern Pentathlon Association

U.S. Rowing Association
U.S. Sailing
USA Shooting
U.S. Soccer Federation
U.S. Swimming
U.S. Synchronized Swimming
USA Table Tennis
U.S. Team Handball Federation
U.S. Tennis Association
USA Track & Field
USA Volleyball
United States Water Polo
US Weightlifting Federation
USA Wrestling

Our thanks especially to the International Olympic Committee (IOC) and the U.S. Olympic Committee (USOC).

CONTRIBUTORS

George Cantor

Currently a journalist for *The Detroit News,* George began his career with another Detroit paper, the *Free Press,* in 1963, where he worked the baseball beat and served as travel editor. He later became a sports columnist at the *News* before moving on to write feature articles for the paper. George is the author of several books, including *Pop Culture Landmarks: A Traveler's Guide.*

Steve Carey

Steve is a freelance designer and writer and a homemaker with an avid interest in boats with paddles, boats with oars, and boats with sails. He claims to be inspired by Phil Bolger (who designs and writes about boats) and composed most of the boating articles in these pages while two-year-old daughter Fiona trimmed the sails.

Anne Janette Johnson

A freelance writer based in New Jersey, Anne's sportswriting credits include contributions to *Hotdogs, Heroes & Hooligans: The Story of Baseball's Major League Teams* and *Professional Sports Teams Histories.* On September 6, 1995, Anne's hero, Cal Ripken, Jr., played in his 2,131st consecutive game, breaking Lou Gehrig's record, which many (except for Anne) thought would never be broken.

Michelle Kaufman

Michelle is a sports writer for the *Detroit Free Press,* and more than one year before the opening of the Games in Atlanta, Michelle was already on the beat, tracking the progress of Olympic hopefuls.

Eric Kinkopf

A two-time Pulitzer Prize nominee, Eric currently makes his living as a freelance writer in Shaker Heights, Ohio. He is also the author of a novel, *Shooter*, based on his experiences as a police reporter for the *Detroit Free Press*.

Mark Kram

Mark is a sportswriter for the *Philadephia Daily News* and a frequent contributor to *Philadelphia Magazine*. He has written pieces that have appeared in the *Sporting News* and in the *SN* anthologies *Best Sports Stories*. From 1983 to 1987, Mark wrote sports features for the *Detroit Free Press*, and covered the Olympic Games in Los Angeles in 1984.

Marie MacNee

An avid cyclist, Marie is a freelance writer and editor who has worked on every edition of *The Olympic Factbook*, earning co-editor status with this volume. She has contributed to *Sports Illustrated for Kids* and in 1995 co-edited *Hoaxes!* Sunny summer afternoons find her logging miles on her bike, attending mountain bike competitions in northern Michigan, or, in Olympic years, in front of the TV, monitoring the events for the next edition of *The Factbook*.

Les Stone

Les is an Ann Arbor, Michigan-based freelance writer who has contributed to several reference books, including *The World Encyclopedia of Soccer* and *VideoHound's Golden Movie Retriever*. In his spare time, Les enjoys motion pictures (particularly those with subtitles) and backyard soccer with son Cal.

NOW LET THE REAL GAMES BEGIN
by Mitch Albom

Editors' note: This article appeared in The Detroit Free Press *on August 9, 1992. While some of the references are to world events taking shape at that time, columnist Mitch Albom's observations on the Olympic Games and the athletes who participate in them are timeless.*

BARCELONA, Spain   Once every four years, they build a Disneyland out of swimming pools and stadiums. They hand out E tickets and give athletes the ride of their lives.

But once every four years the clock also strikes midnight, and they have to close Disneyland. The pools are drained. The stadiums are locked. And the question that no one asks about the Olympics is today the one that all its participants are wondering: Where do we go now?

The answers can be humbling. In the Olympic Village, a group of Bosnians, who had the simple joy these past two weeks of sleeping without the sound of gunfire, prepare to go home. They ask, "Is our airport still standing?" And they are serious.

Meanwhile, a Russian gymnast packs his suitcase and smiles grimly at its weight. Six gold medals are inside. Six? In many countries, he would never have to work again. Instead, Vitaly Scherbo plans to move to Germany or the United States, because back home, in his crumbling nation, he simply cannot cash in.

Not far away, the South African team checks under the beds one last time. For two blessed weeks, they have lived together as brothers and sisters in this Olympic Village apartment, black athletes and white athletes, same showers, same toilets. Now they return to a country where that thought still stirs people to kill.

"You are eligible to run here in the Olympics," a reporter said to a black South African, "but you are not eligible to vote in your own country. How do you feel about that?"

The black athlete thought for a moment, then said it would be best if he did not answer that question.

Disneyland is closing. There is a Dr. Seuss book on the best-seller list these days called "Oh, The Places You'll Go." The stories of these 1992 Games would fit nicely into two similar works: "Oh, The Places You've Been" and "Oh, The Places You'll Go Back To."

By no means would they all be grim. Shannon Miller came to Barcelona as an "also-featured" American gymnast, behind the celebrated Kim Zmeskal, yet it is Miller who goes home to parades, a 40-city tour and the talk-show circuit.

Gail Devers came as a little-known sprinter, taking medication for Grave's disease, an illness that almost caused her to lose her feet. Now she leaves Barcelona with a gold medal and the title "Fastest Woman in the World." When she lands at a U.S. airport, she'll see her picture on the cover of *Sports Illustrated*.

Israeli athletes arrived in Barcelona with only one real Olympic memory: the massacre of 11 athletes in the Munich Games of 1972. Tomorrow they go home with something much better: their first Olympic medals. Two of them. In Judo. A man and a woman. Nice.

Some go home in shame: The Egyptian soccer team, early losers, was booed by fans and forced to wait in line at the Cairo airport "like regular people" as punishment. A British athlete named Jason Livingston began these Games as his country's hottest sprinter. He ends them in disgrace, having failed a drug test and not even running.

There are those who performed for one country but go home to another. Swimmer Martin Lopez Zubero, born and raised in Jacksonville, Fla., won a gold medal for Spain, his father's homeland, and then made his acceptance speech in Spanish, even though his Spanish is not much better than a high school senior's. Now he returns to Florida, where people may understandably ask, "Whose side are you on?"

Tomorrow means recovery for many Olympians, injured in the line of duty. Dave Johnson will certainly nurse the stress fracture that he says cost him his gold medal in the decathlon. But he's the picture of health compared with British judo competitor Karen Briggs, who dislocated her shoulder twice during a match and tried to pop it back in and continue. Pop it back in? This is the same woman who, five years ago, broke her leg in three places during a match and tried to straighten it and keep going.

She's got a right to sing the blues.

Homeland and Heartbreak

For some Olympians, tomorrow actually means a return to the good life. The Dream Team basketball players finally check out of their measly $900-a-night hotel and get back to their multi-million-dollar homes in the States. Top tennis stars such as Boris Becker, Jim Courier and Steffi Graf get to drop the team bus and . . . control of these Olympics and resume the more familiar limousine and personal-hairdresser routine.

And don't forget the Spanish sailor who happens to be Spain's future King.

Talk about a secure future.

But for every Carl Lewis, Stefan Edberg or Prince of Spain who did a bit of slumming at these Olympics, there were many more athletes for whom the Games were a pure gust of luxury in an otherwise acrid existence.

A Bosnian weight lifter named Mehmed Skender trained for Barcelona on one meal a day, rice and macaroni, due to the shortage of food in his country. He did not perform well here. But at least he performed. It is a kinder fate than that of his teammate, Vinko Samrlic, a judo specialist. Three weeks before the Opening Ceremonies, Samrlic was killed by sniper fire as he tried to help a wounded man out of the street.

"We cannot let the world forget what is happening to us," said Mladan Talic, a Bosnian Olympic Committee member. "We are here to show the world that we are still alive." What a statement. Wasn't it eight years ago that we were in Sarajevo, raising the Olympic flag for the Winter Games?

Todays. Tomorrows.

Did you notice the woman who won the 1,500 meters race Saturday night? Her name is Hassiba Boulmerka, the daughter of an Algerian truck driver. She is a great talent. And yet every time she runs, Muslim fundamentalists in her country are furious, claiming a woman should not expose her bare legs to strangers. Some preachers have denounced her as "scandalous."

She returns to Algeria tomorrow, gold medal in hand.

Will it be different?

Rewriting History

There was a fascinating scene at the boxing Saturday afternoon. A young Irish welterweight, a Dublin kid with short, red hair, upset his Cuban rival and won his country's first gold medal of these

Games—and first ever in boxing. A mob of Irish fans banged a drum and sang "Ireland! Ireland!"

When the kid heard his name announced as winner, he ran to his corner and leapt into the arms of his coach—a black man from Cuba named Nickolas Hernandez Cruz.

Funny. You don't look Irish. "These boxers have become my boxers," said Cruz, a former Cuban athlete who has been hired out by his nation to work with the Irish lads. "I feel very comfortable here. You see how I have learned to speak English."

Not only that. He spoke with an Irish brogue!

Funny? And yet this is post-Olympic life for many athletes and coaches. Cuba is already the Kelly Girl Services of sports. At these Games alone there were Cubans coaching the Venezuelan wrestling team, the Spanish volleyball team, the Mexican track team and the Italian baseball team. Not to mention the boxing teams of China, India, Mexico, Pakistan, Spain, Tanzania, Thailand and Uganda.

Half the money received goes to the coach. The other half goes to Cuba to fund its own sports system. Pretty clever, huh?

And Cuba is not the only one. Many former East German coaches are working in China and having plenty of success, particularly with the swimmers. And how about the biggest medal winners of the Olympics, the Unified Team? Here is one of the finest assemblies of athletes and coaches in history and, as of tomorrow, they are history. Gone. Dust. Never again will they dominate in such a fashion. Back in what used to be the Soviet Union, gymnasiums are dark, lacking heat. Pools are dry. Tracks are empty. When there is little money for food, few worry about sport.

So instead of a hero's welcome and a parade back in Russia, swimmer Aleksandr Popov, two gold medals, returns to a dormitory in Volograd. He has no phone. He has no car. He is hoping someone out there sees him as valuable and "wants to make a commercial." The Unified basketball team? Gone. Those iron-hand gymnastics coaches? Looking for work. Going to the highest bidder.

The Olympics are ending. Where do we go now? Some will get rich. Some will need psychiatrists. Some will fall into a funk, wondering why things seem so unexciting. Others will have no time for that, needing to worry, once again, about bullets and bread.

They are a marvelous exercise, these Olympic Games, not only for what they create over 16 days but for what they are able to erase. Unfortunately, no amusement park lasts forever, and the time has come for this one to end. Last call at the Village. Closing time at Disneyland. A return to real life for the winners and the losers, for better or worse.

FROM ATHENS TO ATLANTA:
100 YEARS IN A NUTSHELL

The ancient Greeks loved a good contest. Every four years, beginning sometime around 900 BC, tens of thousands of sandal-wearing spectators descended on Olympia to cheer (or jeer) their favorite runners, wrestlers, and bare-skinned boxers. But the Olympic games weren't the only show in town. Three other festivals—the Isthmian games at Corinth, the Nemean games, and the Pythian games at Delphi—alternated with the Olympic festival to form the *periodos,* or "circuit," which guaranteed sports fans the opportunity to attend an athletic festival every year.

Ancient athletes were required to register to compete, and rumors of Herculean opponents sometimes prompted competitors to withdraw. The reason: Winning was everything. Take the pancratium, for instance. The sport's only interdictions prohibited opponents from eye-gouging and biting; strategically placed knee thrusts, strangulation, and sand-throwing, on the other hand, were all considered to be part of the fun—at least for the spectators.

The creed of the modern Olympics is: "The important thing in the Games is not winning but taking part. The essential thing is not conquering but fighting well." The fact is that couldn't be further from the spirit of the original Games. Winning and conquering were tantamount: Victory at the ancient Olympic festivals was rewarded with a crown of olive leaves, while second- and third-place finishers returned home undecorated. Today's three-tiered winners' podiums had no place in Olympia: You either won or lost, and losing wasn't pretty.

Nor was winning always pretty, for that matter. The rules of the brutal pancratium—which, freely translated, means to make mince meat of your opponent—didn't specify that the winner had to live to collect his shrubbery. Arrichion, a sixth-century (BC) pancratium competitor, might have had the Ancient Games' shortest tenure as Olympic victor: He died, records indicate, moments after his opponent admitted defeat. To say that he "took part" and "fought well," we can assume, would have been faint praise, indeed.

A Little Man with a Big Dream

Some 1,500 years after the Ancient Games were abolished by imperial edict, a 5′3″-tall Frenchman decided the time was ripe to revive—or, more accurately, revise—the Olympic ideal. Not That Pierre de Fredi, Baron de Coubertin (an erstwhile fencer and visionary) was the first to state a revival of the Games. As early as 1636, the Cotswold Olympic Games celebrated the ancient festival; in the 1830s, Sweden halfheartedly mounted the Jeux Olympiques Scandinaves; during the second half of the nineteenth century, the Brits staged four decades of Olympian Games in Shropshire, complete with track and field events, cricket, and cultural competitions; and between 1859 and 1889, Greece held its own Panhellenic contests—open only to Hellenic athletes.

But Coubertin, who had been commissioned by the French government to form a universal sports association in 1889, had a grander global vision. Convinced that athletic competition built moral fiber, he was determined to foment a social movement based on what he considered to be the Olympic ideal.

Peace, harmony, and internationalism were to be the cornerstones of the Modern Olympic movement. In Paris, on November 25, 1892, the Baron publicly proposed resurrecting the Olympic Games, and by 1894, the International Olympic Committee had become a veritable who's who of international movers and shakers. Within two years' time, the Olympic Games were resurrected from their Athenian ashes: In April of 1896, 40,000 spectators pressed into the Panathenean Stadium, which had been reconstructed on the site of an ancient stadium in Athens, to witness the athletic feats of the first Modern Olympic heroes; and the rest—the mind-blowing performances and sometimes tragic defeats, the politics of inclusion, and the poetry of it all—is history.

— *Marie J. MacNee*

1896—Athens
The First Summer Olympic Games
Attendance: 13 nations
Master of Ceremonies: King George I
Guys: 311 • Gals: 0
Most-Medaled Country: Greece (47)
U.S.A.'s Rank: 2nd

To Parisians' dismay—and Athenians' delight—the first Games are held in Athens, funded by a gift from architect Georgios Averoff and the sale of Olympic stamps and medals. 311 athletes from 13 countries compete in a stadium with room for 50,000 spectators, with the *USS San Francisco* anchored just offshore. Although Greek and American college athletes dominate the events, performances are mediocre and athletes benefit from next to no athletic organization. The new cinder track (based on the ancient design of two straight-aways with two hairpin turns) has too much cinder and too little clay, making it a slow surface; 1896 records are soon broken.

- Expecting to train for twelve days before the Games, American athletes find they have to compete the day after their arrival: no one had taken into account the difference between the Greek and American calendars.

- Harvard student exchanges Ivy League for crown of laurels: refused a leave of absence from school, James Connolly hops, steps, and jumps to the first Olympic victory in 1500 years, as track and field events inaugurate the Modern Olympics.

- Greek shepherd Spyridon Louis runs 42km to victory on the course first run by the Greek courier Pheidippides from the battlefield of Marathon.

1900—Paris
The Second Summer Olympic Games
Attendance: 22 nations
Guys: 1319 • Gals: 11
Most-Medaled Country: France (102)
U.S.A.'s Rank: 2nd

The 1900 Games—held in Coubertin's native Paris—are marked by studious insouciance: more athletes than spectators (fewer than 1000) attend the five-day carnival, thanks to the unfortunate coincidence of the Paris exposition. No cinder tracks or pits are provided for the track and field athletes, a grassy field is the venue for the field events, and surrounding trees catch the hammer and discus throwers' shots. Nonetheless, records are set in all track and field events—which isn't saying much after the 1896 performances—and Americans win 17 of 23 events (still without national uniforms). "Valuable artifacts," rather than wreaths or medals, are awarded to the Games winners.

- Archery becomes an official event—the original Games having been founded by well-known archer Hercules. Without standardized rules, the 1904, 1908, and 1920 Games feature various rounds and rules; archery goes on hiatus from 1924 until 1972.

- Marathon-winning bakery deliveryman Michel Theato (France) is accused of taking a shortcut to victory.

- Margaret Abbott scores U.S.'s first female Olympic championship in the nine-hole women's golf event.

- Alvin Kraenzlein sets a never-surpassed record of four individual golds in track and field in a single Olympics, and introduces the leg-extended hurdling style.

- Live pigeon-shooting event makes its only Olympic appearance; after a Belgian sharpshooter slays 21 birds, the event is barred from future Games.

- Australia's Frederick Lane beats a circuitous path to the gold in the never-repeated swimming obstacle race.

- Cricket and croquet make their only Olympic appearance.

1904—St. Louis
The Third Summer Olympic Games
Attendance: 12 nations
Guys: 681 • Gals: 6
Most-Medaled Country: U.S.A. (238)

Originally slated for the Windy City; President Roosevelt sides with St. Louis to hold the Games in conjunction with the Louisiana Purchase exhibition. Upstaged again, the Games take a backseat to the St. Louis World's Fair: a Hungarian Olympic official describes the 1904 Games as "a fair where there are also sports." European participation is negligible—no athletes from England, France, or Sweden attend—and even Coubertin stays home. Eighty-four of the medals go to the U.S., which represents 85 of the competitors.

- American George Sheldon's 10m platform dive victory is contested by the Germans, who argue that final entry should not be figured into the diver's score.

- George Poage, the first black to compete in the Games, hurdles to the bronze in the 400m event.

- American J. Scott Leary is declared the winner of the 50m freestyle after finishing one foot behind Hungarian Zoltan Halmay, who strokes to gold in the rematch.

- The U.S. dominates the team title in the second and last appearance of golf at the Games. Reason for its omission: lack of general appeal.

- Roque, a form of croquet, enjoys its moment in the sun in its singular Olympic appearance. American Charles Jacobus hits gold.

- Two teams enter official lacrosse in 1904 and 1908; lacrosse reappears as a demo sport in 1928, 1932, and 1948.

1906—Athens
The Intercalated Olympic Games
Attendance: 20 nations
Guys: 877 • Gals: 7
Most-Medaled Country: France (40)
U.S.A.'s Rank: 4th

Dismayed by the waning enthusiasm for the Games, Coubertin proposes a new four-year cycle to be held in Athens beginning in 1906. Record crowds attend and the first official Olympic teams participate in the second Games at Athens, but political strife causes officials to cancel further intercalated Games. The IOC does not recognize the 1906 results as official.

- Fencing includes the three-cornered sabre event, which will never again be included on the Olympic roster.

- Track and field athlete Meyer Prinstein (U.S.A.), 1900's second-place finisher and 1904's first-place finisher in the long jump, goes on to win the event in these unofficial 1906 Games; but he does not better his 1904 jump, which set an Olympic record (7.34).

- In rowing, a 2,000-meter six-man naval boat event and a 3,000-meter sixteen-man naval boat race are run — and are never again contested at the Olympics.

- The women from Greece sweep singles tennis: Esmee

Simiriotou, Sophia Marinou, and Euphrosine Paspati win the top three places in the women's event.

- The Swedish men sweep the javelin throw: Eric Lemming, sets a world record with 53.90; teammates Knut Lindberg (45.17) and Bruno Soderstrom (44.92) take second and third place.

- American runner James Lightbody, who led a U.S. sweep of the 800-meter race in 1904, places second, after teammate Paul Pilgrim (who does not better Lightbody's Olympic Record from 1904).

- Lightbody also collects top honors in the 1,500-meter race in these intercalated Games, but does not better his world record in that event (set in 1904, in St. Louis).

- Swimmer Charles Daniels (U.S.A.) sets a world record in the men's 100-meter freestyle event with a time of 1:13.4.

1908—London
The Fourth Summer Olympic Games
Attendance: 23 nations
Master of Ceremonies: King Edward VII
Guys: 1999 • Gals: 36
Most Medaled Country: Britain (145)
U.S.A.'s Rank: 2nd

Forced to give up the Games for financial reasons, Rome sits out another 52 years before becoming an Olympic host city. Reassigned to London, the Games are held in newly constructed Shepherd's Bush stadium (68,000 capacity), complete with cycling and running tracks, soccer field, pool, and a platform for wrestling and gymnastics. Only entries by nations — rather than individuals — are permitted in competition lasting from April to October, with events in 21 sports. Run entirely by Brits, the 1908 Games are rife with conflicts: other nations protest the prejudicial British rules, the erstwhile redcoats and colonists are at each others' throats, the English attempt to prevent the Irish flag from flying, and the Russians attempt to ground the Finnish colors.

- The Olympic committee decides to award medals to the top three winners, and the first official report is compiled.

- Figure skating makes its first Olympic appearance, with four events. Swedish skater Ulrich Salchow claims the first title, lending his name to a much performed jump.

- In a photo opportunity, Forest Smithson protests Sunday competition by leaping, Bible in hand to high, hurdles victory.

- The standard marathon distance is established when the 25 mile distance is revised to start the race at the royal nursery on Windsor Castle grounds. The 26-mile, 385-yard distance remains a worldwide standard.

- *Jeu de paume* enjoys official status in one Games, reappearing in 1928 as a demo sport, and rackets and motor boating appear in their oneandonly Games.

- John Taylor, the second black to compete in the Games, runs a 1600m relay to fame as a gold medalist.

1912—Stockholm
The Fifth Summer Olympic Games
Attendance: 28 nations
Master of Ceremonies: King Gustav V
Guys: 2490 • Gals: 57
Most-Medaled Country: Sweden (65)
U.S.A.'s Rank: 2nd

The Games come of age in Stockholm, on the eve of World War I. Counted among the two or three best-ever Olympics, these Games initiate the modern age of Olympic competition. The Stockholm Organizing Committee prepares a comprehensive list of official events, officials are thoroughly trained, and modern paraphernalia—including electric timing devices and a public address system—are introduced. A 22,000-spectator stadium and a new swimming pool are built, as is housing for athletes and officials; the 400m dash is run in lanes for the first time in the Games. Jim Thorpe, lauded by King Gustav as "the greatest living athlete," becomes the Games' first real individual star, although his victory is soon eclipsed.

- IOC issues rule limiting power of local organizing committees after Swedes refuse to hold boxing matches.

- Japan enters the Games for the first time, sending 14 athletes. Japanese athletes first enter the Winter Games in 1928.

- A West Point lieutenant—the only American to enter the Military Pentathlon—outscores much of his competition in four events, but drops to fifth overall with poor shooting scores. Thus ends George S. Patton's Olympic career.

- In a blazing $10\frac{3}{4}$ hours, South African Rudolph Lewis pedals to the medal in the Games' longest road race ever: the 320km event.

- University of Michigan sprinter Ralph Craig dashes to double victory in the 100m and 200m sprints, and returns 36 years later to compete in a yachting event.

- King Gustav proclaims Native American pentathlon and decathlon gold medalist Jim Thorpe the "greatest living athlete." Thorpe's medals are stripped and his name erased from the records in 1913 when the IOC discovers he had accepted a token sum for summer baseball. His medals are eventually reinstated.

1916 Canceled

The ancient Games, held every four years for almost 1200 years during what ultimately developed into the Peloponnesian War, protected antagonistic participants with the "Truce of God," violators of which were severely penalized. The modern Games have no such truces; World War I cancels all performances.

1920—Antwerp
The Seventh Summer Olympic Games
Attendance: 29 nations
Master of Ceremonies: King Albert
Guys: 2453 • Gals: 64
Most-Medaled Country: U.S.A. (96)

Eighteen months after the armistice is signed, the Games resume under a new flag—five interlocked colored rings on a white background—symbolizing the fraternity of nations. Austria, Germany, Hungary, and Turkey are not invited, but the number of participating countries nevertheless reaches a record high. Crowds, however, are at a near-record low, and performances suffer from the lack of preparation and impromptu nature of the Antwerp Games . . . the inevitable result of the Games' eight-year hiatus.

- Brit Albert Hill double-golds in the 800m and 1500m . . . a feat not repeated for 44 years.
- Hockey makes its first Olympic appearance.
- The States medal for the first time in fencing, in the third team foil.
- The U.S. Olympic rugby team—the only rugby team in the U.S.—trounces France in a surprise victory.

1924—Paris
The Eighth Summer Olympic Games
Attendance: 44 nations
Master of Ceremonies: President Gaston Doumergue
Guys: 2956 • Gals: 136
Most-Medaled Country: U.S.A. (99)

Convinced that practice makes perfect, Paris claims the thirtieth anniversary Games (after a successful lobbying attempt by

Coubertin to transfer the Games from Amsterdam), this time taking care to overcome the ennui that marked the 1900 Games. The Colombes Stadium is enlarged to accommodate 60,000 rapt spectators, and record-breaking abounds in track and field—where runner Paavo Nurmi strains the limits of endurance—and in the pool, as soon-to-be-Tarzan Johnny Weissmuller swims record-breaking laps. The Games are becoming more organized: the IOC prohibits host countries from adding events at will (could it have been the 1900 pigeon shoot?), Juries of Appeal are introduced, and all sports are organized by their international governing bodies. Germany, no bosom buddy to France, is still absent from the Games.

- America's Carl Osburn nails 11 medals in three Olympics: 1912–1924 . . . more than any rifleman in the history of the Games.
- Finnish runner Paavo Nurmi finishes with the first five-gold performance in Games' history, winning the 1500m and 5000m within $1\frac{1}{2}$ hours of each other.
- DeHart Hubbard (U.S.) long-jumps to fame as the first black to win an individual gold.
- Helen Wills, one of history's greatest female tennis players, adds two golds to her volley of victories. The U.S. medals 15 times from 1896 until 1924, when the sport is sidelined from the Games until Seoul.
- Near riot follows another American upset rugby victory; rugby is dismissed from the Games. (Only two countries competed in 1920, three in 1924.)
- Johnny Weissmuller—a.k.a. Tarzan—makes a splash in Paris, claiming three golds in freestyle swimming and a bronze in water polo.

1928—Amsterdam
The Ninth Summer Olympic Games
Attendance: 46 nations
Master of Ceremonies: Prince Hendrik
Guys: 2724 • Gals: 290
Most-Medaled Country: U.S.A. (56)

Although unable to provide appropriate facilities for the Winter Games, the Dutch—after three unsuccessful applications—finally host the Summer Games. Record participation and superlative competition mark the Amsterdam Games, held in a newly built 40,000-spectator stadium. The Dutch Games introduce an easily read results board, a soon-to-be-standard 400m running track, and flocks of pigeons symbolizing peace. Germany, after a 16-year absence, returns to compete.

- The Olympic flame is introduced and continues to burn from start to finish of Games thereafter.

- The first Indian field hockey team to enter the Olympics captures the gold, a trend in the making.

- Algerian marathon winner Mohamed El Ouafi—although running for France—is the first of the great distance runners from Africa.

- Not without great consternation, women are allowed to compete in five track and field events. The 800m, held first in 1928; is subsequently omitted until 1960.

1932—Los Angeles
The Tenth Olympic Games
Attendance: 37 nations
Master of Ceremonies: Vice President Charles Curtis
Guys: 1281 • Gals: 127
Most-Medaled Country: U.S.A. (104)

Despite worldwide depression, the Los Angeles Olympic Committee—with nine years to prepare for the fun and Games— is well financed and organized. Transportation and room and board subsidies woo athletes from abroad, persuading them to overcome an apparent European phobia concerning the California climate. LA leaves a lasting mark on the Games: ring-inside referees for boxing bouts, tri-level winners' stands, and photo-finish paraphernalia debut in 1932, not to mention the first Olympic Village (albeit for men only). Crowds are sizeable, if not always manageable; announcer Bill Henry admonishes unruly American spectators, "Remember please, these people are our guests."

- 20-year-old Argentinean Juan Zabala is the youngest athlete ever to run away with the marathon gold.

- Mildred (Babe) Didriksen medals in high-jumping, hurdle-running, and javelin-tossing, the only athlete ever to medal in all three events. (Babe is said to have been miffed that she was allowed to enter only three events.)

- American track athletes Louise Stokes and Tydia Pickett are the first black women to compete in the Games.

- Two U.S. teams bump shoulders in an exhibition game of American football.

1936—Berlin
The Eleventh Summer Olympic Games
Attendance: 49 nations
Master of Ceremonies: Chancellor Adolph Hitler
Guys: 3738 • Gals: 328
Most-Medaled Country: Germany (89)
U.S.A.'s Rank: 2nd

Not for the last time, the Games are highly politicized: the Olympic village is rife with swastikas and goose-stepping uniformed soldiers, and Hitler attends daily. Five thousand athletes from 49 countries compete in front of more than one million spectators in what the Nazi party intends as a paean to the blond 'n' blue Aryan superman. In the ranks, however, is American track athlete Jesse Owens, who the previous year had—over the course of 45 minutes—broken three world records and tied a fourth. Superman appears at the Games, but he doesn't have blond hair and he's not from Germany.

- The torch relay—to bring the Olympic flame from the Temple of Zeus—is run for the first time: 3000 runners trek over seven countries.

- Jesse Owens owns the 1936 Games, picking up four golds as he ties the 100m world record and sets records in the 200m dash, the broad (long) jump, and the 400m relay. Tuesday, August 4, is affectionately dubbed "Black Tuesday."

- Mathew (Mack) Robinson—Jackie Robinson's brother— earns silver in the 200m, three yards behind Owens.

- Germany's hopes for fencing gold are foiled when Helene Mayer—Germany's only Jewish competitor (who was promised "Aryan" classification so she would return from America in order to compete)—crosses swords with Hungarian Ilona Elek—also Jewish.

- The Games are televised for the first time, albeit on closed-circuit.

- Athletes paddle and shoot hoops for the first time at the Games: basketball and canoeing gain official status.

1940 & 1944 Canceled

Games scheduled for Sapporo and Tokyo are canceled when Japan invades China. Winter Games are rescheduled for Garmisch-Partenkirchen (the 1936 site), but are canceled upon Germany's invasion of Poland, less than five months before the Games' scheduled starting date. The Summer Games, rescheduled for Helsinki, are canceled again when Finland is invaded by Soviet troops. The ancient "Truce of God" is again disregarded.

1948—London

The Fourteenth Summer Olympic Games
Attendance: 59 nations
Master of Ceremonies: King George VI
Guys: 3714 • Gals: 385
Most-Medaled Country: U.S.A. (84)

Housed in RAF and Army camps, athletes from a record 59 countries inhabit a post-war Olympic Village modeled—in form—after the Berlin Village of 1936. Radio coverage makes itself heard for the second time at the Olympics: 250 broadcasters narrate the Games in 40 languages. Germany and Japan sit home again, but the IOC determines—with less-than-unanimous support—not to rescind their records.

- China sends its last team to the Summer Games . . . until 1984.
- Communist nations participate in the Games for the first time; athletes defect in the Olympic venue, not for the last time.
- Holland's 30-year-old "Fanny" Blankers-Koen quadruples her gold in athletics, setting a women's record.
- At 17, London's youngest individual athletics golden boy (and later-to-be-U.S. Congressman), Bob Mathias dominates the decathlon.
- American fencer Janice Lee Romary enters her first Games on her way to compete in more Olympics than any woman in history. Her career ends in 1968, sans a single medal.
- Audrey (Mickey) Patterson finishes third in the 200m run, the first black woman to medal. Later in the Games, Alice Coachman high-jumps to an Olympic record, for the first gold awarded to a black woman.

1952—Helsinki

The Fifteenth Summer Olympic Games
Attendance: 69 nations
Master of Ceremonies: President Juho Paasikivi
Guys: 4407 • Gals: 518
Most-Medaled Country: U.S. (76)

A state-of-the-art Olympic complex on the outskirts of Helsinki houses athletes from 69 countries: yet another attendance record-breaker. The Soviet Union enters its first Games, historically having sat them out because Lenin believed the Games to be decadent. A second Olympic Village, with high fences and low profile, is constructed for the Soviet bloc athletes.

- Nina Romaschkova captures the first Soviet gold, out-hurling her discus competition by 14 feet.

- Czech Emil Zatopek runs away with triple gold in the 5000m, 10,000m, and marathon. 60 minutes after Zatopek's 5000m finish, his wife Dana throws the javelin for gold.

- Barbara Jones runs on the winning U.S. relay team. At 15 years of age, Jones is the youngest track and field gold medalist.

- Luxembourger Josy Barthel upsets the competition—and the band—finishing the 1500m first. No one had foreseen the need to provide the music for Luxembourg's national anthem.

1956—Melbourne
The Sixteenth Summer Olympic Games
Attendance: 67 nations
Master of Ceremonies: The Duke of Edinburgh
Guys: 2958 • Gals: 384
Most-Medaled Country: U.S.S.R. (98)
U.S.A.'s Rank: 2nd

The 1956 Summer Games—the first to be held in the Southern Hemisphere—run from November 22 to December 8, because seasons are reversed Down Under. The international scene is rife with bad karma: the Soviets invade Hungary and there's trouble with a capital "T" in the Suez. A number of no-shows protest Soviet acceptance, and Communist China sits home because Nationalist China participates. Nonetheless, 67 countries attend.

- American diver Pat McCormick double-dips for gold . . . for the second time.

- Perennial contender Laszlo Papp punches out his third boxing victory for Hungary.

- Soviet water polo players pummel Hungarian competition, forcing Swedish referee to intervene in "boxing match under water."

- Al Oerter tosses the discus a record distance, earning his first of four golds.

- Amateur Aussie teams play exhibition game of Australian rules football.

1960—Rome
The Seventeenth Summer Olympic Games
Attendance: 83 nations
Master of Ceremonies: President Giovanni Gronchi
Guys: 4738 • Gals: 610
Most-Medaled Country: U.S.S.R. (103)
U.S.A.'s Rank: 2nd
TV Rights: CBS / $394,000 / 20 hrs

Planning for the Games since 1908, the Italians make an Olympic venue of something old and something new. Ancient ruins and brand-new stadia, not to mention an Olympic Village complete with banks and post office, entice 5400 athletes from 83 nations to compete in Rome. The temperature is scorching, the competition fervid: records fall daily, and standards are so high that previous Games medalists don't always qualify in the finals.

- Hungarian Aladar Gerevich medals in his sixth consecutive Games—taking his sixth gold in the team sabre—an Olympic record.

- Lance Larson (U.S.) places second to Aussie John Devitt in the 100m in the pool . . . even though timed as 1/10 second faster. Full electronic timing is used in subsequent Games.

- Wilma Rudolph basks in Roman gold for both the 100m and 200m dash, as well as the 400m relay.

- Cassius Clay stings the boxing competition to earn gold in the light heavyweight category; later he claims to have thrown his gold medal off an Ohio River bridge; Later still, becomes "The Greatest," Muhammad Ali.

- Denmark's cyclist Knut Jensen collapses and dies—not from sunstroke, but from a drug overdose.

- South Africa competes in its last Olympics until 1992; ten years later, the IOC bans South Africa because of its racial apartheid laws.

1964—Tokyo
The Eighteenth Summer Olympic Games
Attendance: 93 nations
Master of Ceremonies: Emperor Hirohito
Guys: 4457 • Gals: 683
Most-Medaled Country: U.S.A. (90)
TV Rights: NBC / $1.5 mil / 14 hrs

The IOC awards the 1964 Summer Olympics to Tokyo—the world's largest city—in 1959. Five years and $2 billion later, Tokyo convinces skeptics that it has sufficiently recovered from the war to be a good host. The Summer of '64 is a runner-up in the best-ever Games contest, with a seventeen-story hotel, a new expressway for the occasion, and a precision-built Olympic Village. Originally slated to host the 1940 Olympics, Tokyo is the first Asian Games site: Emperor Hirohito opens the ceremonies, and a 19-year-old, born near Hiroshima the day the bomb dropped, carries the Olympic flame.

- Joe Frazier socks his way to Tokyo gold and heavyweight fame.

- Soon-to-be Dallas Cowboy Bob Hayes—the aureate 100m sprinter—spurs his team to the gold in the 400m relay.

- Italy's Klaus Dibiasi, a.k.a. *angelo biondo* (blond angel), takes a dive for silver in 1964 and later rips for gold in three more Games.

- Gargantuan Dutchman Anton Geesink floors Tokyo by taking the open class judo title.

- Ethiopian marathoner Abebe Bikila is the first man to defend the marathon title successfully; he wears shoes only for his second victory.

- Budo—Japanese wrestling, fencing, and archery—is demonstrated.

1968—Mexico City
The Nineteenth Summer Olympic Games
Attendance: 112 nations
Master of Ceremonies: President Gustavo Diaz Ordaz
Guys: 4750 • Gals: 781
Most-Medaled Country: U.S.A. (107)
TV Rights: ABC / $4.5 mil / 44 hrs

The first Games to be held in Latin America bring the Olympics to a new high . . . 7573 feet above sea level, to be exact (658 feet is the highest elevation to date). Reports of possible deaths turn out to be greatly exaggerated, although exhaustion is a problem among athletes who train low at sea level. The political climate is again torrid: Czechoslovakia is fraught with turmoil, student riots in Mexico City are soundly squelched just before the Games' start, and the IOC's initial readmission of South Africa meets with the promise of boycott by some African nations (the IOC repents). A victory-stand photo opportunity turns controversial: two black-socked American track medalists raise gloved-and-clenched fists in support of Black Power, earning suspension and expulsion from the Olympic Village.

- Al Oerter throws his fourth consecutive discus gold, the only athlete to win the same track and field event four times running.

- Heavyweight pugilist George Foreman proves there's gold in them there gloves.

- Bob Beamon astonishes the world by soaring to a record-breaking 29 feet, 2½ inches in the long jump, while teammate Dick Fosbury sets an Olympic record for the running high jump.

- Fosbury's flop is a winner: American athlete scores gold and revolutionizes high jump with unique "flop" style.

- The U.S. dominates the Summer Games for the last time until 1984.

- Pelota Basque is demonstrated for the first time since 1924.

1972—Munich
The Twentieth Summer Olympic Games
Attendance: 122 nations
Master of Ceremonies: President Gustave Heinemann
Guys: 5848 • Gals: 1299
Most-Medaled Country: U.S.S.R. (99)
U.S.A.'s Rank: 2nd
TV Rights: ABC / $7.5 mil / 63 hrs

The television age officially arrives, as millions and millions of people—1000 million, to be precise—watch the opening ceremonies via satellite, a new record in Olympic voyeurism. One week before the Games start, the IOC rescinds its invitation to Rhodesia to prevent a boycott, and the Munich Games are beset by false starts and *faux pas*. Athletes now have 195 chances to medal, thanks to the addition of new sports and events, and the edge-cutting gutter design of the Munich pool sets the stage for piscine history. But Black September, an Arab terrorist group, kills eleven Israeli athletes held captive in the Olympic Village. The Games are suspended the following morning for a memorial service, after which, with the approval of the Israelis, they reconvene.

- Pool shark Mark Spitz swims in gold—medals, that is, gold medals—setting an Olympic record for the most medals at a single Games.

- Soviet gymnast Olga Korbut tumbles into the limelight to take the gold for the balance beam and combined team exercises.

- 400m freestyle winner Rick DeMont (U.S.) is DQ'd for a positive drug test—because team officials failed to inform the IOC of his asthma treatment.

- Archery—now with standardized rules set by the FITA— reappears as an Olympic sport.

- Valery Borzov reels in the first Soviet golds in the 100m and 200m dash.

- Soviets score gold when a court-long pass nets the winning points in the final three seconds of a basketball face-off with the U.S. Twice the final three seconds are played, permitting the Soviets to capitalize on second chance.

- 36 competitors don boards in water skiing exhibition, while 11 countries go to the net in badminton demonstration.

1976—Montreal
The Twenty-first Summer Olympic Games
Attendance: 92 nations
Master of Ceremonies: Queen Elizabeth II
Guys: 4834 • Gals: 1251
Most-Medaled Country: U.S.S.R. (125)
U.S.A.'s Rank: 3rd
TV Rights: ABC / $25 mil / 77 hrs

The Soviets and the States bid for the 1976 Summer Games, but, in a compromising decision, the IOC awards the Games to Montreal. A slight miscalculation underestimates the cost of financing the Games ... to the tune of $1090 million more than the initial $310 million estimate. Security continues to be a major concern: 16,000 military and police patrol the Games, not for free (but for $100 million). Taiwan refuses to participate because Canada won't recognize them as the Republic of China, and at the eleventh hour, 20 Third World nations boycott the Games in protest of New Zealand's participation (because their rugby team had been to South Africa).

- Edwin Moses hurdles to victory, winning the gold for 400m hurdles (and again in 1984).

- America KO's the competition with the best U.S. boxing team in history, including Leo Randolph, Howard Davis, Sugar Ray Leonard, and the brothers Spinks. Middleweight Michael Spinks knocks the wind out of Soviet Rufat Riskiev's bid for the gold with a blow to the stomach.

- A record 18,000 spectators watch as Romanian gymnast Nadia Comaneci scores perfect 10s seven times.

- Cuban Alberto Juantorena, a.k.a. *El Caballo* (the horse), trots to the rare victory of double gold in the 400m and the 800m.

1980—Moscow
The Twenty-second Summer Olympic Games
Attendance: 81 nations
Master of Ceremonies: President Leonid Brezhnev
Guys: 4265 • Gals: 1088
Most-Medaled Country: U.S.S.R. (195)
U.S.A.'s Rank: U.S. boycotted Games

The Soviets—who had staged alternate games, a.k.a. "Workers Olympics," for the socialist world during Lenin's tenure—argue that their participation and performance in the Games since 1952 earns them the right to their turn as Olympic host. Refused for the previous Games, Moscow's approval in 1974 for the summer of 1980 is met with little disapproval. But the 1979 invasion of Afghanistan turns the tide, and the Games, again politicized, are boycotted by the United States and as many as 62 other non-communist countries, including Japan and the Federal Republic of Germany.

- Britain's Daley Thompson goes gold in "nine Mickey Mouse events and a 1500m"; he wins every decathlon he enters from 1977 to 1984.

- Swimmers from East Germany net 26 of the 35 women's swimming medals.

- Brit Allan Wells dashes the competition in the 100m in the closest finish in 28 years; countrymen Sebastian Coe and Steve Ovett confuse the crowds by winning each other's events (the 1500m and 800m, respectively).

- Pentathlon silver medalist Olga Rukavishnikova finishes first in the last 800m, making her a world record holder—but only for 0.4 seconds, the shortest tenure ever.

- Soviet gymnast Aleksandr Ditiatin earns a record eight golds and the first maximum score given to a male gymnast.

1984—Los Angeles
The Twenty-third Summer Olympic Games
Attendance: 141 nations
Master of Ceremonies: President Ronald Reagan
Guys: 5458 • Gals: 1620
Most-Medaled Country: U.S.A. (174)
TV Rights: ABC / $225 mil / 180 hrs

A number of countries refuse to make the Olympian pilgrimage to the showbiz mecca of the Western world. The Soviet Union and 16 sympathizers boycott the Games, as do two independent prefer-not-to's. Officially, the Soviets decline for reasons of "fear," while skeptics are more specific: fear of drug testing. Libya withdraws from the Games at the last minute when two Libyan journalists are refused entry to the U.S. on suspicion of terrorism. Nevertheless, LA 1984 is the biggest bash in the history of the Games, with 7000 athletes from 141 nations. Northern Ireland and the Republic of Ireland compete as one, and the two Koreas consider—briefly—doing the same. Despite cries of medal inflation due to Soviet-et-al absenteeism, the 630 U.S. athletes are hailed as the best American team in Olympic history. Many are first-crop beneficiaries of the 1978 Amateur Sports Act, which is responsible for an Olympic job program, the Olympic Training Center in Colorado Springs, and biomechanical technology improvements.

- Communist China enters its first Games, with 353 competitors. Japan and Australia send their biggest, most expensive teams ever.

- Carl Lewis strikes gold four times—in the 100m, 200m, long jump, and 4 × 100m relay—the first such haul since Jesse Owens'.

- Hard-luck American track-and-field athlete Mary Decker, hoping to medal, tumbles to the agony of defeat.

- With no competition from the "Leningrad tomboy" Elena Shoushounova, Mary Lou Retton's gymnastic pixiehood is unchallenged, earning her precious medals (gold, silver, and bronze), and Wheaties box fame.

- Greg Louganis dives for gold in both the platform and the springboard, becoming the first Olympian to win both since 1928.

- Cyclist Connie Carpenter-Phinney sprints to the gold in the first Olympic women's road race. Having speed skated in Sapporo in 1972, she was the first woman to have competed in both the Summer and Winter Games.

- Eleven athletes are inducted into the Olympic Hall of Shame for positive drug tests.

1988—Seoul
The Twenty-fourth Summer Olympic Games
Attendance: 159 nations
Guys: 6983 • Gals: 2438
Most-Medaled Country: U.S.S.R. (132)
U.S.A.'s Rank: 3rd
TV Rights: ABC / $300 mil / 180 hrs

The 1988 why-do-you-think-they-call-it-dope Summer Games begin with the IOC president's claim that "doping equals death";

the list of banned substances now numbers in the hundreds. The lengthening list of suspected drug abusers is the talk of the town. Though scarred by the drug-test debacle, Seoul nevertheless stages a spectacular show, primarily using facilities already in place for the 1986 Asian Games. Threats of boycott precede the Games, but only North Korea—and their unfathomable ally Cuba—follow through on the threat; North Korea insists, without IOC support, that it has the right to host half of the Games. Fears of terrorism at the Games prove unjustified, but rah-rah Yankee nationalism sometimes strains the host country's hospitality. The number of medal events climbs to 237, to be dominated again by the Soviets, followed by East Germany and the U.S. Amateurism is again the talk of the town, and governments and Olympic committees promise for the first time—publicly, at least—to award cash prizes for medals.

- 1936's marathon winner, Japanese team member Sohn Kee Chung, carries the torch into the Olympic stadium . . . this time under the aegis of his own country, South Korea.

- Aussie surfer-swimmer Duncan Armstrong—ranking 46th in the world at the Games' start—strongarms Biondi et al in the men's 200m freestyle.

- American Arlene Limas blocks South Korea's sweep of Tae kwon do medals, winning the demonstration sport's welter-weight title.

- Greg Louganis dives for gold again, becoming the first man to repeat double springboard and platform wins.

- Diminutive Janet Evans (U.S.) performs swimmingly in the pool: three golds, one world record, and one Olympic record.

- Ben Johnson blazes past Carl Lewis et al to win the 100m; unfortunately, his victory is short-lived as he tests positive for steroids. He trades his gold medal for a place in the Hall of Shame. Besides Johnson, two other gold medalists, one silver, and one bronze are stripped of their wins.

- Daley Thompson's hopes of thrice gold-medaling in the decathlon splinter as his pole-vault breaks in half, causing an old injury to flare.

- Tennis returns to the Games after a 64-year hiatus, while China and South Korea horde the gold when table tennis makes its first Olympic appearance.

1992—Barcelona
The Twenty-fifth Summer Olympic Games
Attendance: 172 nations
Guys: 7,555 • Gals: 3,008
Most-Medaled Team: The Unified Team (112)
U.S.A.'s Rank: 2nd
TV Rights: NBC / $401 mil / 161 hrs

July 25—the Feast of Saint James of Compostela, the Patron Saint of Spain—marks the opening of the first Olympic Games ever to be hosted by Spain. Once slated to sponsor the aborted 1936 Peoples' Olympics, host city Barcelona—"the Great Enchantress"—vows to wow the world with the best Olympics ever. Bar none. With $9 billion to burn, and an IOC president in their cheering section, Barcelona's Olympic officials stage one spectacular show. Even before the first athlete toes the starting line, Olympic records begin to tumble. Almost eleven thousand athletes compete, representing 172 nations and shards of nations—more athletes and more nationalities than have ever graced a single Games. And an unprecedented number of nations share in the spoils.

At the twenty-fifth Summer Olympics, Barcelona, Spain's second-largest city, revels in its 2,000-year history: Ancient Roman ruins, weathered castles, historic statues, and cobblestone streets sprawl against the backdrop of the Mediterranean Sea. Opening the festivities is King Juan, whose Catalan greeting—"Benvinguts tots a Barcelona" ("Welcome, everyone, to Barcelona")—sets the tone of things to come. There's no mistaking: These are the Catalan Games, a paean to the people of the port capital of Catalonia. Full of myth and whimsy, the opening and closing ceremonies tap the same creative well that nurtured the likes of Salvador Dali, Joan Miró, and Antonio Gaudi. Everywhere, banners and buttons proclaim "Freedom for Catalonia," and the striking Catalan flag—blood red and incendiary yellow—swells from every plausible perch.

Awarded to Barcelona in 1986, the year that Spain nestled its way into the European Community, these Games are global Games, marked by record attendance, first-time appearances, and the return of prodigal nations. South Africa, the Games' erstwhile pariah, is welcomed back to the Olympic fold in recognition of the 1991 moratorium on apartheid. Nelson Mandela—a former amateur boxer—surveys from the stands. Namibia, independent from South Africa since 1990, sends its first representatives to the Games; the Croats and the Slovenes march in the Olympic pro-

- Sixteen-year-old U.S. gymnast Kim Zmeskal—the 1991 all-around champion and former world champion—inexplicably falls in her first Olympic competition, devastating her chances of medaling in the women's all-around.
- The Unified Team's Tatiana Goutsou trumps Shannon Miller's bid to add the all-around gold to the U.S. team's medal haul.
- Romanian gymnast Lavinia Milosovici and China's Lu Li dazzle Olympic judges, scoring 10s in the floor exercise and uneven bars, respectively.
- The Unified Team co-opts the men's gymnastic events, claiming four of the five top spots. Competing as rivals in the individual all-around competition, three Unified teammates share the spoils among them; Belarus's golden boy Vitaly Scherbo clinches the title, and—with six gold medals—becomes the most-gilded gymnast at a single Games.
- The home-court favorite, Spain's Arantxa Sanchez Vicario, suffers defeat twice as King Juan Carlos and Queen Sofia look on. Tying in the singles event, she shares the bronze with U.S. player Mary Joe Fernandez, and, with doubles partner Conchita Martinez, adds a silver to the host country's medal count.
- The U.S. volleyball team has a bad hair day when Japan is awarded a controversial win by appeal. Expressing their solidarity with bald-headed Bob Samuelson, who received two yellow cards for poor etiquette, the U.S. team members all shave their heads.

Olympic Village
(sailing events depart from the Olympic port)

- Prince Felipe, son of Spanish King Juan Carlos, rolls up his sleeves to compete in yachting's Soling event. The royal follows in the wake of father Juan Carlos, who competed in the 1972 Munich Games; sister Cristina, who competed in the 1988 Games; and mother and uncle, who both sailed in the Rome Games (where the latter, King Constantine of Greece, pocketed a gold medal in the Dragon class).

ON THE ROAD TO ATLANTA
by George Cantor

When the world comes to Atlanta for the 1996 Olympic Games it will not be arriving as a stranger. Although the Georgia capital doesn't rank as one of America's top tourist destinations for foreign travelers, there are certain aspects of Atlanta life that will be immediately familiar.

Coca-Cola. Everyone has guzzled one, especially those from sultry climes where it is more dependable than water.

CNN. Cable News Network is now the most widely-watched television news service on the globe and an international standby in times of crisis.

Gone with the Wind. Even those who never read the novel probably had the image of this city burned into their memory by the filmed depiction of it, going up in flames.

Those who never have been in the city itself, surely passed through the airport. As the old saying goes: When you die in the South, on the way to heaven you have to change planes in Atlanta.

The images of this southern metropolis are an intrinsic part of America's face to the world.

It will be the third city in the United States to host the summer Olympics, but in many ways, the city most representative of life in this country—moreso than Los Angeles, which hosted in 1984 and before that in 1932, and St. Louis, which hosted in 1904, so long ago that it belongs to the realm of misty nostalgia.

But in 1996, Atlanta will give visitors a taste of how the country lives now, for better or worse. Because this will be a downtown Olympics. The

FACT: The Atlanta Games are going to be the biggest and most expensive ever, with a bill totaling approximately $1.6 billion

In the 20th century, the city has been most closely associated with the careers of four remarkable men: Dr. Martin Luther King, Jr., President Jimmy Carter, Robert Woodruff, and Ted Turner. A trip to Atlanta isn't complete without a visit to one of the places tied to their lives.

- Martin Luther King, Jr., National Historic Site, which includes his birthplace, grave, and commemorative center, is just east of downtown, in the historic black neighborhood of Auburn. Restoration efforts have tried to bring back the ambience of the area as it appeared at the time of Dr. King's birth, in 1929. The birthplace is a 14-room house built in 1895. One block away is his tomb, which adjoins a museum of his life in the Center for Non-Violent Social Change. And one more block over, along Auburn Street, is the Ebenezer Baptist Church, where Dr. King was co-pastor with his father.

- The Carter Presidential Center and Museum is about 2 miles northeast of downtown, reached from the Highland Avenue exit of interstates 75 and 85. The museum examines the major events of Carter's term in office, including his decision to boycott the 1980 Olympic Games in Moscow because of the Soviet Union's invasion of Afghanistan. In retaliation, the U.S.S.R. did not participate in the 1984 Games in Los Angeles. So Atlanta will be the first time Russian athletes have appeared in an American-held summer Olympics

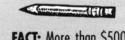

FACT: More than $500 million is being spent on new construction for the Atlanta Olympic Games.

- Woodruff is credited with building Coca-Cola from a regional soft drink firm into a global colossus. The company was born in Atlanta in 1892. But not until Woodruff became its president in 1923 did it adopt the advertising and marketing strategies that turned it into a major force. World of Coca-Cola explores the history of the company and the variety of its products. It has become one of the city's top tourist attractions. It is located downtown, at Central Avenue and Martin Luther King Drive.

- Turner has turned Atlanta into the cable capital of television. One of the first people to grasp the communications potential of cable, Turner took an obscure local TV station with no network news affiliation and created a news empire. His CNN and affiliated cable services have become major players in international journalism and entertainment. Tours are offered at the downtown studios, located next to The Omni.

Those with an interest in Civil War history will want to visit Grant Park and its Cyclorama, a 360-degree painting of the battle, siege, and burning of Atlanta. Stone Mountain, just east of the city (which will also be an Olympics venue) is the site of the Confederate Memorial, a shrine depicting Generals Robert E. Lee and Stonewall Jackson, as well as President of the Confederacy Jefferson Davis, carved in stone and riding into history.

Many of the top spectator events of the Olympics, including the opening and closing ceremonies, basketball and baseball, swimming and track and field, gymnastics and wrestling, will go on at sites located within the downtown Atlanta loop.

But yachting will be held clear across the state in Savannah. Canoe and kayak events will go on across the state line, on a new course along Tennessee's Ocoee River. The city of Columbus, Georgia, about 100 miles to the southwest, gets the softball events. Preliminary soccer matches will be played in Miami, Orlando, Washington, D.C., and Birmingham (Ala.), before the finals are held at Sanford Stadium, at the University of Georgia, in Athens, 65 miles east of Atlanta.

Biggest of the venues built especially for the Games is the 85,000-seat Olympic Stadium. This is located immediately to the south of Atlanta-Fulton County Stadium, home of baseball's Braves since they moved here in 1966. After the Olympics, the new stadium will be modified and become the home field for the ball club.

Its brick facade will remind many spectators of the nostalgia-inspired baseball parks recently built in Baltimore, Maryland, Cleveland, Ohio, and Arlington, Texas. But the fast track is supposed to represent the last word in surface engineering. The opening and closing ceremonies will be held here, as will the track and field events. This was scheduled to be the last of the Olympic sites to be topped off. It was completed too late to be tested during the Atlanta Sports '95 competition, during which most of the other venues made their debut. A huge electronic clock over the adjacent freeway ticked off the days remaining until the opening of Olympic Stadium, just to remind the workmen inside that time was not on their side.

The other major new facility in Atlanta is the Aquatic Center, on the Georgia Tech campus, at the northern edge of downtown. The

FACT: 10,800 athletes, representing 197 countries, will participate in the Atlanta Olympics. Track and field has the most competitors (2,076) and modern pentathlon the least (32).

university is also the site of the Olympic Village that will house the athletes and later be used for college dormitories. The Aquatic Center, completed the summer of 1995, seats 15,000 at the main pool area, which will be used for the swimming and diving events. A smaller pool area, seating 4,000, will be the site of the synchronized swimming and water polo competitions.

The University of Atlanta complex will be used for several events. New stands at the Clark University stadium will accommodate 5,000 spectators for the field hockey competition. Field hockey will also be played at the Morris Brown stadium. Some preliminary basketball games will be held at the Morehouse College field house. The campus sites are on the western edge of downtown.

The other downtown venues already existed. Atlanta-Fulton County Stadium will have 52,000 seats for the baseball events. The Omni Coliseum, home of the National Basketball Association's Atlanta Hawks, will be the site of the volleyball matches. It can accommodate 16,400 spectators.

FACT: Events for the Atlanta Olympics will take place at 25 athletic sites.

While The Omni is fine for the NBA, the Olympics will move Dream Team III down the block, to a stadium with a capacity twice as large, for its defense of America's basketball gold medal. Most games are scheduled for the Georgia Dome, which can seat 32,000 for basketball. Gymnastics, the other indoor event with the greatest interest for American crowds, will also be held in the Dome.

In the same vicinity is the Georgia World Congress Center, usually used for trade shows and conventions. Its two main exhibit halls can seat up to 7,500, and will be the venues for fencing, team handball, judo, table tennis, weightlifting and wrestling.

Boxing matches will be held at Georgia Tech's Alexander Coliseum, which can seat 9,500. Finally, the Georgia State University Coliseum, yet another downtown facility, will host the badminton competition.

FACT: The minimum cost to be an official 1996 Olympic Games sponsor is $20 million.

Stone Mountain Park, which is situated 19 miles east of the city, is a long-established recreation area for Atlantans. It will benefit from three permanent new facilities built especially for the Olympics: a tennis complex, an archery field, and a cycling velodrome.

Another 13 miles beyond Stone Mountain, in the town of Conyers, is the Georgia International Horse Park. Completed in 1995, it is described as the most complete equestrian facility in the country. It will seat almost 30,000 for the riding events, and a slightly smaller number for the mountain bike competition.

Lake Lanier, a 38,000-acre body of water created by damming the Chattahoochee River, is 45 miles northeast of the city. Rowing and all the speed events in the canoe and kayak competitions will go on here.

Suburban Atlanta Beach will be the site of beach volleyball. The Wolf Creek Trap and Skeet Range, in southwestern Fulton County, will host the shooting events.

While Savannah is a 250-mile interstate highway haul from Atlanta, the old colonial port cashed in on the Olympics building boom, too. A sailing course on Warsaw Sound, in the Atlantic Ocean, south of the city, was the first of the new Olympic sites to open, hosting its first regatta in July 1995. The yachting competitions will be held here.

Even Tennessee felt the impact of these games. On the Ocoee River, 150 miles northeast of Atlanta, a new slalom course for the canoe and kayak events also opened during the summer of 1995.

Besides all this, Atlanta is creating a 12-acre Olympic Centennial Park in the heart of a formerly decrepit area of downtown. Organizers saw a similar set-up in Barcelona, a place where spectators could relax, stroll through exhibits set up by sponsors of the Games, and attend free concerts and cultural attractions. They decided to make such a park a feature of these games, too. Centennial Park will serve as a gateway to the downtown venues situated all around it.

Atlanta's preparations have not gone off without a hitch. While a major reason for the city's successful bid for the Games was the promise by organizers that all facilities would be built with private funds, they forgot to mention a few items. New roads and other infrastructure around the new venues had to be paid for by a local government bond issue. This caused a bit of a furor around Atlanta among those who had taken the organizers at their word.

FACT: There are 55,000 hotel rooms located within one hour of Atlanta.

Twelve months before the games began, the Atlanta Committee for the Olympic Games (ACOG) announced that tickets to the top events already were oversold and a lottery system would be necessary to sort things out. Almost every hotel room within a 90-mile radius of Atlanta was already sold out, with Olympic officials and corporate sponsors glomming onto everything within the city itself. A few hotels as far away as Birmingham and Chattanooga, two hours from Atlanta in the best conditions, were also sold out early.

Then there is the question of heat. Atlanta gets a lot of it in mid-July and those accustomed to mild European summers may have a problem dealing with a succession of high-80- and 90-degree days with humidity to match.

FACT: The average high temperature in Atlanta in late July is 88 degrees Fahrenheit.

Still, there is always Izzy, the cheery blue symbol of the Games; a creature of indeterminate species, whose bug-eyed countenance looks out from every corner of the city. Who could be churlish in the face of Izzy? The boosters of Atlanta mirror his manic joy. They have come too far in burnishing the image of their town to let down now, with its greatest moment at hand.

ARCHERY

Warm-up

William Tell's aim was true, his arrow piercing the apple atop his son's head. Cupid does his romantic work with bow in hand, arrow at the ready. One of history's most popular legends, Robin Hood, was an archer. In fact, a "Robin Hood" is part of the archery jargon: it occurs when an archer drives the tip and shaft of one arrow deep into the end of another arrow already in the bulls eye; this is the archery equivalent of a hole-in-one.

Invented some 100,000 years ago, archery has been called one of the four most important inventions in human history, next to fire, language, and microwave ovens. For prehistoric humans, archery was a means toward an end, that end being survival.

Legend has it that the ancient Olympic Games, held from 776 BC to 395 AD, were founded by Hercules, an archer. Back then, the games featured tethered doves as the targets. During the heat of the competition, ancient broadcasters were fond of saying, "Now the feathers are really flying," thus giving birth to a valuable cliché.

But several thousand years before the Olympics, Egyptians were using bows as tall as themselves and arrows with flint arrowheads, later replaced by bronze. In 1800 BC, the Assyrians developed the shorter recurve bow, which provided more power and easier handling. The skill of shooting from moving chariots, so popular in cinematic tales, was developed by the Hittites around 1200 BC. In 500 AD, the Romans, known as second-rate archers, began drawing the arrow to the face rather than the chest, improving their accuracy dramatically.

FACT: Belgium's Hubert van Innis holds the most Olympic gold medals in archery. Between 1900 and 1920, he captured six gold medals — four of which were for the now-discontinued moving bird target event.

Archery

Archery as a sport traces its heritage back to 17th-century England, as part of community festivals. In the U.S., the National Archery Association was founded in 1879 by two brothers, J. Maurice and William H. Thompson. The brothers Thompson, like other Confederate soldiers, were not allowed firearms after the Civil War. Naturally, they took to bow and arrow instead. The National Archery Association belongs to FITA (Fédération Internationale de Tir à Arc), the international governing federation for archery.

In 1900, the sport became an official event in the modern Olympics, and was featured in the 1904, 1908, and 1920 games.

FACT: Olympic-style target archery, also known as FITA style, is the most widely practiced archery discipline.

For lack of interest, the sport was dropped for nearly 50 years, returning in 1972. That year, John Williams and Doreen Wilber won the men's and women's gold medals for the U.S. In 1992, Sebastien Flute of France won the men's individual championship, while the women's individual gold was taken by Cho Youn-Jeong of South Korea. Spain won the men's team competition and the South Koreans captured the women's team title.

Spectator's Guide

Olympic archery competition uses the recurve bow, featuring limbs that curve away from the archer to increase power. The lever effect created can propel arrows in excess of 150 miles per hour.

The average draw weight of a man's bow is 50 pounds. In a typical tournament, the bow is lifted and drawn more than 312 times for a total of 15,500 pounds, or nearly eight tons, pulled over four days. Women pull more than five tons with their 34-pound bows.

The bows are generally constructed of wood, fiberglass, and graphite or carbon composites. Most strings are made of Fast Flight, a hydrocarbon product, while some still are made of kevlar, the material used to make bullet-proof vests. The arrows are either of aluminum, which is more uniform in weight and shape, or carbon graphite, which flies faster.

At the 1996 Olympic Games, each country is allowed to enter three men and three women in separate events. The format of the Olympic competition consists of a Ranking Round followed by the FITA Olympic Round.

In the Ranking Round, archers shoot 72 arrows at 70 meters in ends (groupings) of six arrows each. A score of 720 is a perfect score. The FITA Olympic Round is divided into the Elimination Round and the Finals Round.

The top 64 competitors in the men's and women's events will advance to the Elimination Round, a single-elimination, match-play style of competition. Six ends of three arrows (18 arrows total) are shot at 70 meters. Winners of each match move on to the next matches.

The Finals Round is held when the field has been narrowed to eight archers. It begins with the quarterfinals and continues with the semifinals and bronze-medal match. The round ends with the gold-medal match. Archers shoot four ends of three arrows (12 arrows total) in each finals match.

The top 16 nations (based on scores from the Ranking Round) compete for team medals. Three archers per country will each shoot nine arrows from 70 meters in each elimination match between two countries. The Finals Round in the team event will consist of the four top teams.

In 1996, 128 athletes will compete in archery events at Stone Mountain Park.

FACT: The Barcelona Games introduced major scoring changes in archery events. A direct elimination round decided the 32 qualifiers while a knock-out competition established the medalists. The old system determined winners by compiling totals.

Hopefuls

Jay Barrs

The first sentence in a 1988 *Sports Illustrated* story on Jay Barrs captured the essence of the Salt Lake City archer.

"In a sport of straight arrows," the story began, "Jay Barrs is slightly warped."

Barrs, 34 (b. July 17, 1962), the Olympic gold medalist in 1988—with a team silver—and a top U.S. medal hopeful in Atlanta, is just that. The Salt Lake City resident, who can shoot an aspirin off a golf tee at 10 yards—and Alka Seltzer tablets at 20—and whose archery exploits have won him the keys to four different cities—Jacksonville, Fla., Montrose, Colo., and Mesa and Gilbert, Ariz.—has been known to don earphones and play air guitar, drums, and keyboards to Sammy Hagar, Motley Crüe, AC/DC and Whitesnake during competitions.

"I play all the air instruments very well," he says with a grin.

He once embraced a lifestyle he called STAG—Sex, Taco Bell, Archery, and Golf. And some days, he would say, "You can't work archery in there."

He also has been known to crack wise at his Olympic success.

"When 2,000 white doves of peace are released at the Opening Ceremonies, it looks beautiful on television. But if you're standing underneath them, it's not as much fun."

Rimshot, please.

At the medal ceremonies in Seoul, Barrs was introduced as "Barrs, Jay, U.S.A." Says Barrs: "That's all right. In Venezuela, I was *Joy* Barrs. And in France I was *Gay* Barrs."

Another rimshot, please.

And, finally: "I was so proud of my gold medal from Seoul, that I had it bronzed."

The flip side of all this good humor is the disappointment Barrs experienced at the 1992 Games—and the subsequent drive he's making for Atlanta and 1996.

Barrs, a former basketball, ski racing, and tennis star, began shooting arrows at age six with his parents, but didn't totally embrace the sport until age 17, when he figured it was the only way a 6-foot, 145-pound athlete could earn a college scholarship. Ironically, he became so quickly infatuated with the sport that he dropped out of college to pursue it full-time.

As recently as 1992, he had been considered by many to be just the oddball, idiosyncratic, Billy-the-Kid gunslinger to succeed at the new Olympic archery format in Barcelona, which had been switched from hundreds of arrows over a period of days—the target versus the shooter; a real mental marathon—to a head-to-head, *mano a mano* competition.

In fact, the format seemed perfectly suited for the archer who eschewed the somnambulistically deadly pace of what he considered overly cautious competitors.

"The less I have to think about a shot, the better off I am," Barrs said after his winning performance in Seoul. "If you stand there and think about it, that's when you run into problems. If you can shut off your conscious mind, you can shoot fast."

Well, Jay Barrs finished fifth at Barcelona. The U.S. team ended up sixth.

Some saw the 1992 disappointment coming—Barrs included.

In fact, just a few years after his gold medal in Seoul, Barrs failed to make the 1991 national team for the world championships. His coach, Dick Tone, wondered then if Barrs wasn't concentrating too much on the S, T, and G, and ignoring the A.

"All athletes go through a period once they've won the gold medal of asking, 'What's next?' " Tone told *Olympian* magazine. "It's hard to get regrouped and focused. I don't know if it's so much how many hours you train as the direction you go in when you're training and what you're thinking about. If you're thinking about playing golf or going to a rock concert, you're not going to accomplish anything."

Said Barrs: "I wanted to take some time off. All I'd done was archery, full-blown, since 1985. I'd needed to devote myself to archery (for that time) and I did. I'd quit my job, found an apartment at half price, and my little brother moved in and paid most of the rent. I'd eat dinner at my mom and dad's, drive a '68 Karmann Ghia, skipped the phone bill to pay the electric bill, then skipped the electric bill the next month to pay the phone bill. At competitions, we'd sleep three or four in a room."

The day Barrs made the 1992 team, the *Arizona Republic* declared, "The Boss of Bows is back."

Barrs said, "A world of pressure has been lifted from my shoulders. What a relief. I missed the World team, and I just had to make this team."

Well, he wasn't quite all the way back. And, if anything, it seems that Barrs is coming back even stronger after Barcelona.

Barrs won the U.S. championships in 1994 and finished second at the World Target Trials in 1995.

After his success in Seoul, Barrs had said, "I knew I had the ability to win the gold medal. Whether I was successful or not was up to the gods."

This time it's a little different. This time, perhaps the gods are leaving it all up to the shooter. And maybe this time Jay Barrs realizes that.

No more STAG party line.

No more jokes.

— Eric Kinkopf

Denise Parker

Shortly after Denise Parker returned from the Seoul Olympics in 1988, the state of Utah lowered the age requirement for a bow-hunting license from the age of 16 to 14.

The best news is that the U.S. can count on Parker for years to come. Archers outlast most other Olympic competitors. Even early on, Parker, the *wunderkind,* was saying, "Archery is a lifetime sport. That's how I think of it."

There, of course, also is the present. Parker addresses that, too.

"I believe we have the potential for a strong team in 1996," Parker says. "We have the talent to win a medal in Atlanta. We just have to put it all together."

Today, she speaks as a veteran.

At the ripe old age of 22.

— Eric Kinkopf

Monday, July 29

Women's 1/32 eliminations
Women's 1/16 eliminations

Tuesday, July 30
Men's 1/32 eliminations
Men's 1/16 eliminations

Wednesday, July 31
Women's 1/8 eliminations
Women's final

Thursday, August 1
Men's 1/8 eliminations
Men's final

Friday, August 2
Women's & Men's team 1/8 finals, quarterfinals & semifinals
Women's & Men's team finals

Highlights

Archery was absent from the Summer Games for more than fifty years. In the early going, from 1900 through 1920, competing archers came mostly from the host countries, and the event was not considered to be of world champion caliber. In fact, none of the archery events held between 1904 and 1920 carried over to the present Olympic program. U.S. archers cleaned up all the medals in St. Louis in 1904, led by Will Thompson and Lyda Scott Howell, both long-time national champions. The British dominated in London in 1908, led by William Dod and Charlotte Dod; the latter was 36 when she took a silver in 1908. And the Belgians just happened to triumph in Antwerp in 1920, counting among their competitors Hubert van Innis, 54 years old in

1920, who added four gold and two silver medals to the two golds and one silver he'd won in 1900.

When archery returned to the Olympics in 1972, the U.S. was ready: John Williams and Doreen Wilber won the men's and women's golds that year, when Wilber was 42 years old and Williams was 18. In 1976 U.S. archer Darrell Pace took the men's gold, while Luann Ryon won the women's gold for the U.S. in Montreal; Ryon had never before competed at the international level. Tomi Poikolainen of Finland took the men's gold at the Moscow Games, with Keto Losaberidze of the Soviet Union capturing the women's gold. Pace repeated his gold-medal performance in 1984, while teammate Rick McKinney earned a silver medal. A 17-year-old North Korean archer, Hyang-Soon Seo, captured the women's title in 1984.

Fourteen-year-old Denise Parker made her debut on the U.S. women's team in 1988, but was met with a South Korean sweep of the women's event. The men's gold in Seoul went to U.S. archer Jay Barrs, also competing in 1992, ahead of two South Korean archers.

1984's silver medalist Rick McKinney led the 1992 U.S. men's team, and Parker again competed in 1992 as leader of the U.S. women's team.

FACT: Charlotte "Lottie" Dod, Great Britain's silver medalist in the 1908 National Round event, was more than just a good aim. A champion field hockey player and golfer, she won a total of five Wimbledon tennis titles—the first of which she captured in 1887, when she was only 15 years old.

Highlights from Barcelona

The Barcelona Games opened as Spanish archer Antonio Rebollo, a two-time medalist at the Paralympics, shot a flaming arrow above the crowd of spectators to set the Olympic fire ablaze. The home team would later claim that the Opening festivities were a harbinger of things to come: the men's team—comprised of Antonio Vazquez, Alfonso Menendez, and Juan Carlos Holgado—snared the team competition gold before a highly flammable hometown crowd at the Vall d'Hebron.

Ironically, none of the Spanish team victors claimed a medal in the individual event, where Frenchman Sebastien Flute edged out Korea's Jae-Hun Chung. U.S. hopes for a medal were dashed as master-technician Jay Barrs, the gold medalist in the 1988 Games, was knocked out of the running by Great Britain's Simon Terry in the bronze medal face-off.

"People who don't understand archery understand 'you versus me,'" Barr later explained. "If you lose you're a goner—or I'm a goner." Also a goner was Denise Parker, who, at the age of 14, had been a member of the 1988 silver-medaling U.S. team. "I'm very disappointed," she lamented. "I felt I was shooting well enough to bring home a medal."

But the South Korean women who were shooting well enough to bring home a fistful of medals. Twenty-five-year-old Cho Youn-Jeong (the oldest member of the Korean squad), finally upstaged her teammates, Chin-Ho Kim and Soo-Nyung Kim—both gold medalists from the LA and Seoul shootouts—setting three world records in the preliminaries on her way to nailing the first of the Korean women's three medals. With Soo-Nyung Kim installed as the silver medalist in the individual event, the heavily medaled Korean shooters took aim at the team gold, knocking out the Chinese team's shot at the title.

Medalists

Archery Men's Individual

1992* (70-meter)
1. Sebastian Flute, France
2. Chung Jae-Hun, South Korea
3. Simon Terry, Britain

1988
1. Jay Barrs, U.S.A., 338
2. Sung-soo Park, South Korea, 336
3. Vladimir Echeev, South Korea, 335

1984
1. Darrell Pace, U.S.A., 2616 (OR)
2. Richard McKinney, U.S.A. 2564
3. Hiroshi Yamamoto, Japan, 2563

1980
1. Tomi Poikolainen, Finland, 2455
2. Boris Isachenko, Soviet Union, 2452
3. Giancarlo Ferrari, Italy, 2449

1976
1. Darrell Pace, U.S.A., 2571 (OR, WR)
2. Hiroshi Michinaga, Japan, 2502
3. Carlo Ferrari, Italy, 2495

1972
1. John Williams, U.S.A., 2528 (WR)
2. Gunnar Jervill, Sweden, 2481
3. Kyosti Laasonen, Finland, 2467

1924–1968
Not held

Archery Men's Team

1992*
1. Spain, Juan Holgado Romero, Antonio Vazquez Megido, Alfonso Menendez Vallin
2. Finland, Ismo Falck, Jari Lipponen, Tomi Poikolainen
3. Britain, Richard Priestman, Steven Hallard, Simon Terry

1988
1. South Korea, 986, In-Soo Chun, Han-Sup Lee and Sung-Soo Park
2. U.S.A., 972, Jay Barrs, Rick McKinney and Darrell Pace
3. Great Britain, 968, Steven Hallard, Richard Priestman and Leroy Watson

Archery Women's Individual

1992* (70-meter)
1. Cho Youn-Jeong, South Korea
2. Soo-Nyung Kim, South Korea
3. Natalia Valeeva, Moldavia

1988
1. Soo-Nyung Kim, South Korea, 344
2. Hee-kyung Wang, South Korea, 332
3. Young-sook Yun, South Korea, 327

1984
1. Hyang-Soon Seo, Republic of Korea, 2568 (OR)
2. Lingjuan Li, People's Republic of China, 2559
3. Jin-Ho Kim, Republic of Korea, 2555

1980
1. Keto Losaberidze, Soviet Union, 2491
2. Natalia Butuzova, Soviet Union, 2477
3. Paivi Meriluoto, Finland, 2449

1976
1. Luann Ryon, U.S.A., 2499 (OR, WR)
2. Valentina Kovpan, Soviet Union, 2460
3. Zebiniso Rustamova, Soviet Union, 2407

*scores for 1992 not available

1972
1. Doreen Wilber, U.S.A., 2424 (WR)
2. Irena Szydlowska, Poland, 2407
3. Emma Gapchenko, Soviet Union, 2403

1912-1968
Not held

Archery Women's Team

1992*
1. South Korea, Lee Eun-Kyung, Cho Youn-Jeong, Soo-Nyung Kim
2. China, Wang Hong, Wang Xiaozhu, Ma Xiangjun
3. Unified Team, Natalia Valeeva, Lioudmila Arjannikova, Khatouna Kvrivichvili

1988
1. South Korea, 982, Soo-Nyung Kim, Hee-Kyung Wang and Young-Sook Yun
2. Indonesia, 952, Lilies Handayani, Nirfitriyana Saiman and Kusuma Wardhani
3. U.S.A., 952, Debra Ochs, Denise Parker and Melanie Skillman

Trivia Quiz

1. Legend has it that the Ancient Olympic Games were founded by
   a. Zeus   **b.** Hercules   **c.** Cupid

2. Archers in the Ancient Games shot at
   a. Each other   **b.** Politicians   **c.** Tethered doves

3. The U.S. National Archery Association was founded by
   a. Two Confederate soldier brothers   **b.** An NRA defector
   c. A boy scout

4. Archery first appeared in the Olympic Games
   a. In 1896   **b.** In 1992   **c.** In 1900

5. In archery jargon, a "Robin Hood" occurs
   a. When an archer impales a bystander
   b. When an archer shoots a perfect bullseye
   c. When an archer drives the tip and shaft of one arrow into the end of another

6. **Men's and women's team competition were added to the Olympic roster**
   a. In 1896   **b.** In 1988   **c.** They are not part of the Olympic program.

7. **The average draw weight of a man's bow is**
   a. 100 pounds   **b.** 75 pounds   **c.** 50 pounds

8. **Which material is *not* used in the bow strings?**
   a. Hydrocarbon products   **b.** Polyurethane   **c.** Kevlar

9. **The lever effect of a recurve bow can propel arrows**
   a. Faster than the speed of light   **b.** Over 150 mph   **c.** Up to 95 mph

10. **Since 1972, the U.S. team**
    a. Has captured six gold medals   **b.** Has swept the individual events
    c. Has never medaled

Answers: 1-b, 2-c, 3-a, 4-c, 5-c, 6-b, 7-c, 8-b, 9-b, 10-a

BADMINTON
Warm-up

Badminton became a full medal sport in 1992, a promotion from exhibition status in 1988 (in its other Olympic appearance in 1972, badminton was a demo sport). Badminton began on the Asian continent, although the exact circumstances are unknown. It may have began as *Ti Jian Zi*, or shuttlecock kicking, in China of the 5th-century BC. The modern version of badminton can be traced to India, where *poona* matches were contested during the 1800s.

British military officers stationed in the country during that time became interested in *poona* due to its similarities to lawn tennis. When they returned to their homeland, the Brits brought the game with them. In particular, the game became a popular pastime on the Gloucestershire estate of the Duke of Beaufort, where the sport was officially launched at a party given in 1873.

The estate's name was "Badminton" and participants were given to referring to the sport as "that game at Badminton." The name, as they say, stuck.

Until 1887, the sport was played in England under the *poona* rules, which, from the English point of view, were often contradictory and confusing. The first organized badminton association in England, the Bath Badminton Club, anglicized and standardized the rules. In 1895, the rules were further refined by the Badminton Association (of England), which assumed authority of the sport from the Bath club.

Badminton soon spread to the U.S., Canada, Australia, and New Zealand. Badminton was established in the U.S. in 1878,

FACT: An 1864 edition of *American Boy's Book of Sports and Games* contains a description of battledore shuttlecock. It's the earliest known reference to badminton in the United States.

be above the hand holding it at the moment of contact. Service is diagonal, right service court to right service court (even serves) and left service court to left service court (odd serves).

Badminton strategy is similar to that of tennis. In singles, the idea is to move the opponent primarily up and back and to minimize errors. In doubles play, the game becomes a flurry of frantic energy as teams constantly reposition to either attack the opposition or repel an attack. The offensive formation places one player at the net, the other smashing from the back court.

In the defensive position both players play side-by-side, each defending his or her side of the court.

In 1996, 192 athletes will compete in badminton at Georgia State University.

Hopefuls

Kevin Han

Kevin Han was born in Shanghai, emigrated to New York City, calls Palos Heights, Ill., his hometown, lives at the U.S. Olympic training center in Colorado Springs, and plays for a club team in Sweden.

Play badminton and . . . see the world?

For awhile there, Han, 23 (b. November 25, 1972) and 6-feet-1 and 180-pounds, the top U.S. hopeful in men's badminton in Atlanta, was seeing almost more than he could handle. Disarray is not conducive to championship play.

But everything comes at a price. And Han and his father, Liang, wanted freedom in the United States.

Han's discombobulation, if you will, began in 1990, when he and his father emigrated to the U.S. from China. The younger Han, who had played badminton professionally in China at age 13 and had long dreamed of becoming a U.S. citizen, had to give up his sport to take several jobs as a delivery man and busboy for Chinese restaurants. He didn't play badminton for 18 months.

"That's quite a layoff for an athlete with Olympic potential," said Steve Mann, of U.S. Badminton.

But things slowly began to change. As Han and his father adapted to life in the U.S. and their financial status became a little more solvent, Han found badminton partners in New York City clubs and at Columbia University, eventually getting back into shape, winning a few minor tournaments, attracting the attention of U.S. Badminton officials, and finally settling at the U.S. Olympic Training Center in Colorado Springs.

Soon, things were better than ever.

"Before I came to Colorado Springs, I would play maybe two or three times per week," Han says. "Now, I practice twice a day with the top players and great coaches and at a top facility with the best equipment. It really makes a difference to have the extra court time and have a constant schedule. It also helps just to be around other badminton players off the court."

Indeed, all of that has paid off. Han, ranked No. 119 in the world in January 1995, is projected to be near the top 50—and maybe even higher—by the time the 1996 Olympics roll around, where badminton will be a medal sport for the second time. (It was a demonstration sport in Munich in 1972 and Seoul in 1988, before being designated a medal sport in Barcelona.)

Says Mann: "Kevin's ultimate goal is, of course, to be the best in the world, but considering how far the U.S. is behind powerful Asian countries like Indonesia and China, he would definitely be satisfied to crack the top 25."

Obviously, the ultimate would be winning a gold medal in Atlanta.

"I've got a shot," says Han, whose room in Colorado Springs is decorated with an eight-foot American flag with red stitching on the border that reads: *Kevin Han, U.S. Citizen, 12-13-94.* "There are no guarantees, but I have the confidence to do it. I still have to improve my conditioning, and, hopefully, my game will improve with it."

Han's optimism notwithstanding, an American medal in Atlanta would be the longest of long shots. Most in the badminton world would consider an American player medaling in the Olympics as unlikely as India or Ireland beating the Dream Team in basketball.

Still, U.S. badminton is at its strongest in years, according to Jim Hadley, executive director of U.S. Badminton, who sees a comeback in U.S. fortunes.

And there is history to support optimism. Between 1949 and 1967, U.S. players won 23 individual world titles. Three times, U.S. women were world champs. *Sports Illustrated* featured the top U.S. player, Joe Alston, on its cover on March 7, 1955.

Says Hadley: "With our commitment to our younger players, I see us earning an Olympic medal in the year 2004, and being very competitive at World Championships by 2002. But it could happen in 1996. You never know."

A lot depends, of course, on Han, who has developed from being the U.S. team's shy, new-kid-on-the-block to a confident, assertive player and team leader.

"Kevin's got a lot of natural skills," says 1992 Olympian Tom Reidy, who pairs with Han in doubles. "He's definitely a good athlete. He's come a long way and he'll get better with experience."

"I've known Kev a long time," says another team member, Andrew Ibrahim. "When we first met, he was 19 and could barely speak English. It was hard for him. Then after a few years on the court, he came out of nowhere. You have to appreciate all he's done and admire his love for the game."

Adds Hadley: "Kevin's progress has raised some eyebrows and brought a focus on the U.S. program. The improvement is happening. We're getting stronger and growing, but we're still in the third tier of countries. You have Indonesia, Malaysia, China and Denmark at the top level. The next level includes Sweden, England and Canada. We're still a ways behind those countries, but I don't see it taking too long to get up to that point."

Hadley cited Han's performance at the 1995 World Championships as an example. Han reached the round of 32, before losing to second-ranked Ardy Wiranata of Indonesia, 15-3, 15-8. Wiranata was the silver medalist in Barcelona.

"That performance was huge for U.S. badminton," Hadley says. "I'm not going to say it put us on the map, but it could definitely help legitimize out program to many Americans, much like the World Cup did for soccer."

Han sees that, too. He understands what the Olympics mean, not only to him, but to the sport in his adopted country.

"I get nervous when I think about Atlanta," he says. "I can't wait."

—Eric Kinkopf

Erika von Heiland

Persistence.

When U.S. Badminton tried to double its 1992 Olympic strategy, a disappointed Erika von Heiland was forced to invest in a singular approach.

It paid off in a trip to Barcelona.

In January of 1991, U.S. Badminton officials chose von Heiland as one of its athletes to participate in Olympic qualifying tournaments around the world—18 months, 23 countries—with no guarantee that she would make the final 40-player international Olympic singles pool.

After a year, von Heiland's chances of reaching the Olympics looked so poor, that she lost her funding.

U.S. Badminton "decided to put all their energies and finances into the doubles players for one of the 56 doubles slots, which is very understandable," von Heiland told the *Orange County* [Calif.] *Register.*

Understandable, perhaps, but not acceptable.

At least not to von Heiland, 30 (b. December 24, 1965), a Philippine native who now lists Anaheim, Calif., as her hometown and who is one of the top U.S. women's badminton prospects in Atlanta. She'd already been through 12 grueling months of competition and she decided that she may as well go for the rest. She took out a loan from her bank and borrowed against her credit cards to raise the money she needed to support herself through the final six months of Olympic qualifying tournaments.

Perseverance.

It paid off.

But not immediately.

Because of the complicated computer-ranking system, von Heiland was never sure where she stood in the ratings. The days and weeks were full of emotional highs followed by lows.

"I came home from the tournaments and didn't think I had made it," she said. "I did my grieving and planned my next move," which would have been summer school at Northern Michigan University.

"I was 99.9 percent sure I wasn't going to make Barcelona," von Heiland told the *Los Angeles Times.* "I was already planning my comeback in 1996. (But) I made it as the highest-ranked women's singles player from the U.S. It was so ironic . . . really bizarre.

"I didn't quit," von Heiland said of her decision to try to make the Olympics on her own. "I never go into anything half-baked. Ever since I was a kid I wanted to play in the Olympics. It's the ultimate for any athlete."

When she received the announcement that she'd qualified for Barcelona, von Heiland says that her "hair stood on end."

Von Heiland, a nine-year member of the U.S. national team, has represented the U.S. at World Championships in 1989, 1991, and 1993, and won a silver medal in singles at the 1991 Pan Am Games and a bronze medal in doubles play with Linda French at the 1995 Pan Am Games. She is a 1994 *magna cum laude* criminal justice graduate of Arizona State University and worked three years in "loss prevention" as an undercover shopper for a string of convenience stores.

She also is a former member of the Philippine national junior tennis team. She took up badminton when she was 17.

"I was ranked 10th in the country in tennis and wasn't good enough to cut it," von Heiland says. "One day, a bunch of my friends got me to get on the badminton court."

After seeing her play, members of the group suggested that von Heiland try out for the national team. She did, and not only made the team, but represented the Philippines at international tournaments the next two years.

"There was a big difference between tennis and badminton," von Heiland told the *Los Angeles Times*. "The hand-eye coordination is the same, but badminton is in the wrist and tennis is in the arm."

What followed, shortly after von Heiland emigrated to the U.S., was three years of inactivity due to knee injuries—a cartilage tear in the right knee and a dislocated kneecap to the left.

"The doctors told me that my chances of competing again were very, very slim," von Heiland told the *Los Angeles Times*. "I was told my playing days were over. I needed to do something with a goal at the end, so I started to body build."

She even considered a competitive career in bodybuilding.

Then, she took a trip back to the Philippines.

"Of course, my old teammates and friends got me to pick up a racquet and play," she said. "Much to my surprise, I was pain-free. When I returned (to the U.S.), I started playing again."

Persistence *and perseverance*.

Von Heiland qualified for the U.S. national team, won a scholarship to Arizona State, and eventually moved into the top five rankings in the country, representing the U.S. in the 1989 World Championships.

U.S. coach Vicki Toutz says: "Erika's probably the fastest player we have in the women's events. If Erika is on, she can be competitive internationally."

FACT: South Korea's Park Joo-bong holds the most overall world championship titles, with five world titles—two in men's doubles and three in mixed doubles. China's Yang Yang is the only man to have captured two world singles titles. In women's singles, Chinese shuttlecock aficionados Han Aiping and Li Lingwei each have two titles to their credit.

Unfortunately, von Heiland's speed didn't help her get past the first round in Barcelona. She was defeated by Denyse Julien of Canada.

Von Heiland, who since has had two more knee surgeries, plans to do better in Atlanta.

Persistence.

Perseverance.

Von Heiland.

Good bets.

—*Eric Kinkopf*

Schedule

The tentative badminton schedule is:

Wednesday, July 24
Women's & Men's singles 1/32

Thursday, July 25
Women's doubles 1/16
Men's doubles 1/16
Men's singles 1/16

Friday, July 26
Women's singles 1/16
Men's singles octos
Mixed doubles 1/16

Saturday, July 27
Women's singles octos
Men's doubles octos
Mixed doubles octos
Women's doubles octos

Sunday, July 28
Men's & Women's doubles quarterfinals
Women's & Men's singles quarterfinals

Monday, July 29
Mixed doubles quarterfinal
Women's doubles semifinal
Women's & Men's doubles semifinal

Tuesday, July 30
Women's & Men's singles semifinal
Men's singles semifinal
Mixed doubles semifinal
Women's & Men's doubles bronze medal

Wednesday, July 31
Women's & Men's doubles gold medal
Women's & Men's singles bronze medal
Mixed doubles bronze medal

Thursday, August 1
Women's & Men's singles gold medal
Mixed doubles gold medal

Highlights

First a demonstration sport at Munich in 1972, and then an exhibition sport at the 1988 Games in Seoul, badminton made its first appearance as a full medal sport in Barcelona. Although no single player pocketed more than one medal, it was no surprise that Asian players walked away with the lion's share of medals. Eleven of the 12 top places fell to top-seeded players from South Korea, China, and Indonesia.

Badminton's Olympic debut did hold one surprise, however: beating the Chinese team to the men's doubles win, Eddy Hartono and Rudy Gunawan grabbed a second-place finish in the team event, landing Indonesia's first-ever Olympic medal. Winning the event in a tough neck-to-neck three-setter against the top-ranked Chinese team was the South Korean duo of Moon-Soo Kim and Joo-Bong Park, who entered the Games with a world-record claim to five world championship titles.

Indonesia fared well in both singles events, as Alan Budi Kusuma—who was second in the 1991 world championships—beat teammate Ardy Wiranata to the gold, and Susi Susanti clinched the women's title. Denmark's Thomas Stuer-Lauridsen, with a bronze medal in the men's singles event, was the only non-Asian to mount the victory stand at the Pavello de la Mar Bella.

FACT: Malaysia medaled for the first time ever at the Olympic Games when Lidek Razif and Sidek Jalani shared the men's doubles bronze with the Chinese team of Li Yongbo and Tian Bingyi in 1992.

Medalists

Badminton—Men's Singles

1992
1. Alan Budi Kusuma, Indonesia
2. Ardy Wiranata, Indonesia
3. Thomas Stuer-Lauridsen, Denmark
3. Hermawan Susanto, Indonesia

Badminton—Men's Doubles

1992
1. Kim Moon-Soo and Park Joo-Bong, South Korea
2. Eddy Hartono and Rudy Gunawan, Indonesia
3. Li Yongbo and Tian Bingyi, China
3. Sidek Razif and Sidek Jalani, Malaysia

Badminton—Women's Singles

1992
1. Susi Susanti, Indonesia
2. Bang Soo Hyun, South Korea
3. Huang Hua, China
3. Tang Jiuhong, China

Badminton—Women's Doubles

1992
1. Huang Hye Young and Chung So-Young, South Korea
2. Guan Weizhen and Nong Qunhua, China
3. Gil Young-Ah and Shim Eun-Jung, South Korea
3. Lin Yanfen and Yao Fen, China

Trivia Quiz

1. Badminton first appeared as an official sport in the Olympics

   a. In 1996, in Atlanta   **b.** In 1992, in Barcelona   **c.** In 740 BC, in Hellas

2. Modern badminton can be traced to

   a. *Poona*, a game from India

   b. *Jeu de paume*, the French predecessor to tennis

   c. Fly swatting, an American pastime

3. Badminton first appeared as a demonstration sport

   a. At the 1988 Seoul Games

   b. At the 1964 Tokyo Games

   c. At the 1972 Munich Games

4. The accuracy and speed of the shuttlecock can be adjusted

   a. By plucking some of the feathers

   b. By a turning a small metal screw hidden inside the bird

   c. By soaking the shuttlecock in resin

5. *Ti Jian Zi,* a 5th-Century Chinese predecessor of badminton, translates as

   a. "Shuttlecock kicking"

   b. "Bird dancing"

   c. "Too much leisure time"

6. The name "Badminton" comes from

   a. The name of a British estate where the sport became popular

   b. The name of the Duke who introduced the game to British military officers

   c. The name of the first company to manufacture shuttlecocks

7. In competitive badminton, the shuttlecock travels

   a. At speeds approaching 200 mph

   b. At speeds exceeding 75 mph

   c. At 300,000 km per second

8. In order for a shuttlecock to be "true," it must

   a. Be constructed of 16 goose feathers, taken from the identical wing of four different geese

   b. Pass a fly detector test

   c. Pass an IBA-approved wind tunnel test

9. International play first began
a. In 1908, after the London Games
b. In 1939, when national championships spread throughout the world
c. In 1956, after the Melbourne, Australia Games

10. Badminton first became popular in the U.S. in
a. 1988, after the Seoul Games
b. 1878, when the first club included Rockefeller, Roosevelt, Astor, and Vanderbilt
c. 1980, when it became the favorite White House lawn sport

Answers: 1-b, 2-a, 3-c, 4-b, 5-a, 6-a, 7-a, 8-a, 9-b, 10-b

BASEBALL

Warm-up

In 1992, almost 90 years after it was first introduced to Olympic competition, baseball finally became an official full-medal sport. "America's pastime," as it is affectionately called, is today played by an estimated 20 million people in approximately 60 countries.

Baseball was demonstrated in 1904 in St. Louis; in 1912 in Stockholm (where a makeshift team of U.S. track and field athletes banded together and bombed a Swedish team, 13–3); and became an official demonstration sport in 1936 in Berlin (where 125,000 watched a game between two U.S. teams); in 1952 in Helsinki; in 1956 in Melbourne; 1964 in Tokyo; 1984 in Los Angeles; and 1988 in Seoul.

The game we know—or some reasonable facsimile thereof— began in Hoboken, New Jersey, in 1846. There, umpire Alexander J. Cartwright, acting under the authority of rules he designed, supervised a game between the Knickerbockers and the New York Nine, which was won by the Nine, 23–1.

Thereafter the game developed. Leagues sprang up, teams evolved—in Cleveland, for example, the franchise was known variously as the Forest Cities, Spiders, the Blues, Bronchos, the Naps (for Hall of Famer Napoleon Lajoie), and now, the Indians (for Native American Louis Sockalexis, a former player)—and stars were born: Babe Ruth, Mickey Mantle, Jackie Robinson, Henry Aaron . . . Sadaharu Oh.

Oh? Exactly.

The Japanese slugger—in the Far East a Ruth and Aaron rolled into one—played in the Japanese Major League 22 years. Aaron hit 755 home runs; Ruth hit 714; Oh had 868. It wasn't long before Oh was more than an expression of surprise to U.S. baseball fans, who were slowly—and often reluctantly—learning that baseball wasn't just an American sport anymore.

because they are asked to go up against national teams that have played together for several years. Many of them have key performers who are in their 30s and used to a more aggressive style of play than the Americans are ready for.

Baseball U.S.A. has set out to change all that for the 1996 Games.

For the first time, candidates for the team were selected almost entirely from among college underclassmen, predominantly freshmen and sophomores. Moreover, the coaching staff, headed by Skip Bertman of Louisiana State, has signed on for a two-year commitment.

The team played a tough 35-game schedule in 1995 against some of the top international teams. Among them were the top three medalists in the 1992 Games—Cuba, Japan, and Chinese Taiwan—and a young Korean team regarded as the newest addition to the short list of international powers.

Korea was a surprising runner-up to Cuba in the 1994 World Championships and will be one of the big challenges for Team U.S.A. in Atlanta.

But everybody has to get by Cuba, which will once again be the overwhelming favorite in 1996. This team is the international equivalent of the New York Yankees of the 1950s. They not only expect to win, the possibility of defeat never seems to enter their minds.

No one who has watched them play doubts that the Cuban lineup is loaded with players who could start in the big leagues. Moreover, their skilled players have been together for a decade. They anticipate one another's moves, understand their roles, have developed a confidence in their teammates' abilities.

That last item has often been the undoing of U.S. teams. The players come to international competitions accustomed to being the star and leader of their own teams. They expect to fill the same role on this squad and don't grasp that every other player feels the same way.

Friction develops, players begin to press and take the entire weight of the team's performance on their shoulders.

But under the new system, the team will enter the Olympics after two seasons together. If the theory is correct, this should be a more confident and seasoned U.S. team than has taken the field in years.

Whether that will be enough to beat Cuba, however, remains to be seen.

One aspiring Olympian already has shown an ability to rise to the challenge on the big stage. Mark Kotsay came to Team U.S.A. direct from the 1995 collegiate champions, California State-Fullerton.

In the College World Series, all Kotsay did was:

- Hit .563 with a slugging percentage of 1.250.
- Slam two home runs in the championship game.
- Appear in two games as a relief pitcher and not allow a run.

For that performance, the sophomore was voted Most Outstanding Player. But some of his teammates felt that because he didn't get the College Player of the Year award for the full season, Kotsay was a driven player during the World Series.

The award went instead to a Tennessee player, with Kotsay as runner-up. In Fullerton's two tournament games with Tennessee, Kotsay went five for eight while his team won 11-1 and 11-0. That seemed to make a statement.

"He'd never say this out loud, but I think not winning that award did bother Mark a little," said his assistant coach, George Horton.

Since Kotsay hit .422 for the season, made just one error in the outfield, and gave up only one run in 17 relief appearances, some irritation may be justified. While collegiate officials are reluctant to hand out big awards to sophomores, he may have proven that such caution was unwarranted.

The left-handed Kotsay, who grew up outside of Los Angeles, seems able to do just about anything he wants on the diamond. He runs well, hits for power, strikes out only once every 20 at bats. In fact, in his sophomore year he had more home runs than strikeouts, an astonishing achievement for a younger player.

Given all that, however, his greatest asset may be his work ethic.

"I know it's going to take a lot of effort to get where I want to go," he says. "The Olympics has been a dream of mine and so is getting to the big leagues. Now that it's all so close, you can't let up."

The team also seems to have the ideal coach in Bertman. A 12-year veteran at LSU, he has won two national championships.

"As far as international competition, I think allowing the pros to play is something that should be looked into. But then again, how do you say to a major league owner that Roger Clemens is going to miss the next two weeks of the season to play on the Olympic team."

—*California Angels pitcher Brian Anderson, who was a member of the 1992 U.S.A. Baseball team*

Sixty of his players have gone on to sign professional contracts and his graduation rate is consistently above 90 percent.

Moreover, he is a masterful motivator.

"This team has the ability to win," he says. "Representing the United States has got to be the ultimate for anyone. But playing against teams like Cuba in the 1995 season will prepare them for what's ahead, give them the ability to conceptualize themselves as winners.

"There isn't going to be any surprises for them in Atlanta. Knowing what you're dealing with beforehand is a good part of what it takes to overcome it."

—*George Cantor*

Schedule

The tentative baseball schedule is:

Saturday, July 20
games 1–3

Sunday, July 21
games 4 & 5

Monday, July 22
games 6–8

Tuesday, July 23
games 9–11

Wednesday, July 24
games 12 & 13

Thursday, July 25
games 14–16

Saturday, July 27
games 17–19

Sunday, July 28
games 20–22

Monday, July 29
games 23–25

Tuesday, July 30
games 26–28

Thursday, August 1
semifinal games 1 & 2

Friday, August 2
bronze medal game
gold medal game

Highlights

Ex-Olympians who have gone on to the majors include Will "The Thrill" Clark, Andy Benes, Barry Larkin, Mark McGwire, Shane Mack, Greg Swindell, Ben McDonald, and California Angels lefty Jim Abbott, who won the gold-medal game against Japan for Team U.S.A. in Seoul.

Jim Abbott

The Olympics aren't just about sports. Equally important are such things as desire and politics and national pride and individuals struggling to overcome impossible odds. And those are the things that came together at Seoul in 1988 for an extraordinary young man named Jim Abbott.

National pride was on the line. The American baseball team had been defeated by Japan at the 1984 Games in Los Angeles—a shocking, almost unbelievable upset. The 1988 Olympics provided the perfect showcase for revenge: the U.S. would meet Japan once again for the gold medal, the final game to be pitched by Abbott.

The game was dramatic and filled with suspense. Abbott pitched the full nine innings and made a spectacular fielding play in the bottom of the eighth inning to kill a rally by Japan. The Americans came away with a 5–3 victory and Abbott was the hero of the day, swarmed by his team in an exuberant post-game celebration. He was awarded the 1988 Sullivan Award as the outstanding amateur athlete in the United States.

The Olympics capped an impressive amateur baseball career for the then 21-year-old Flint, Michigan, native. He was a Little League standout who threw a no-hitter in his first game, led his high school baseball, basketball, and football teams, and starred as a pitcher for the University of Michigan. While in college, he was selected for Team U.S.A. and became the first U.S. pitcher to beat the Cuban team in Cuba in 25 years, helping the team win a silver medal in 1987.

After his gold-medal performance in the Olympics, Abbott was drafted in the first round by the California Angels in 1988. He spent four years with the Angels before being traded to the New York Yankees after the 1992 season. On September 4, 1993, Abbott pitched a no-hitter for the Yankees, beating the Cleveland Indians 4–0. He was traded back to the Angels in 1995.

Just one of the amazing things about Abbott is the fact that he was born with no right hand. He refers to this as a "situation" but never a handicap. As he says: "Growing up, I always pictured myself as a baseball player, but I can't remember how many hands I had in my dreams." Abbott was born September 19, 1967, the son of Mike (a beer distributor sales manager) and Laura (an attorney) Abbott. From the beginning his parents stressed that Jim could do anything he wanted to do. What he wanted to do was play baseball.

He spent countless hours throwing a ball against a brick wall perfecting the move that allows him to field his position: he balances his glove on his right wrist, throws left-handed, slips on the glove in his follow-through, and is ready to field. It works so well that, watching him from a distance, it's practically impossible to tell he's one-handed; and, as many batters have found out, it's nearly impossible to bunt your way on base with Jim Abbott on the mound.

As former California Angels manager Doug Rader puts it: "Jim is the most *un*handicapped person I know. He's a singular human being."

—*Eric Kinkopf*

Highlights from Barcelona

Cuba once sent outstanding players to baseball's major leagues. Luis Tiant and Tony Oliva, Minnie Minoso and Tony Perez.

Now only a rare ballplayer filters through the Cuban barrier to the outside. Instead, they stay at home and beat everyone else's brains out. Fidel Castro, who once harbored dreams of glory in the big leagues, has made baseball success a top state priority.

The Cuban team is unquestionably the best amateur organization in the world. When baseball first became an Olympic sport, in 1988, the U.S.A. won the gold. But most observers conceded that was only because Cuba boycotted the Seoul Games for political reasons.

FACT: The U.S. team's 1992 game against Cuba set a record as the longest game in Olympic history. And it was just 18 minutes shy of the major league record as well.

With the Cubans back in action at Barcelona in 1992, they swept to the gold, ahead of Taiwan and Japan. The U.S. team finished fourth.

Some individuals on that U.S. team have made it to the majors. Most notable is Charles Johnson, now the starting catcher for the Florida Marlins. Jeffrey Hammonds has moved into the outfield of the Baltimore Orioles.

Still, the more experienced Cubans, many of whom were 10-year veterans of international competition, could not be seriously challenged.

"We just protested the game," said U.S.A. coach Ron Fraser, of the University of Miami. "My kids saw them take batting practice and they won't come out."

"To me, it is normal the U.S.A. is the first country in baseball," said Juan Antonio Samaranch, head of the International Olympic Committee at Barcelona. "Here, to win nothing, is not normal. My point of view is that we have to find a solution to this. They cannot play very young players from the United States against state players from Cuba."

But stating the problem is a long way from solving it. If baseball were transferred to the Winter Olympics and played, say, in a dome, there would be no question that the biggest names in the major leagues would participate and win the gold handily. That works for basketball.

Baseball, however, is not about to surrender its stars for several weeks in mid-season every four years—no matter how much badly needed good publicity the sport would receive.

> "The Cubans tied so many shoes that I went out to the umpires to offer them some of our shoelaces."
> —Ron Fraser, the 1992 U.S. team's manager, on Cuba's penchant for stalling for time

"Sure, I think a few of (the Cubans) could probably play in the majors," said Ricky Helling, a pitcher on the '92 U.S. team. "But I'd like to see them hitting against Roger Clemens."

As good as the Cubans were, however, the fact remains that the U.S.A. didn't measure up to Japan or Taiwan, either. In both of those countries, the sport has taken hold. It is well-played and seriously coached from a very young age. Taiwan, especially, has been dominant in the Little League World Series. So while it may be our National Pastime, Barcelona proved again that in international competition, it is just not the U.S.A.'s time.

—George Cantor

Medalists

1992
1. Cuba, Luis Alvarez, Alberto Perez, Lazaro Alvarez, Omar Izquierdo, German Fresnada, Juan Altonso, Lourdes Delgado, Jose Antonio Gonzalez, Osvaldo Rodriguez, Orlando Pedroso, Giorge Loren, Omar Iglesias, Victor Martinez, Jorge Luis Berriel, Jose Raul Diez, Rolando Avila, Orestes Olivares, Antonio Masso, Juan Carlos Rondon, Ermidelio Quiroga
2. Taiwan, Chao-Huang Lin, Kun-Han Lin, Kuang-Shih Wang, Wei-Chen Chen, Wen-Po Huang, Shih-Hsih Wu, Yaw-Teing Chang, Ming-Hsiung Liao, Kuo-Chong Lo, Chung-Yi Huang, Chen-Jung Lo, Chi-Hsin Chen, Tai-Chaun Chiang, Kun-Hong Pai, Chien-Fu Kuo Lee, Kuo-Chian Ku, Ming-Hung Tsai, Cheng-Hsien Chang, Wen-Chung Chang, Yeu-Jeng Jong
3. Japan, Koichi Oshima, Shigeki Wakabayashi, Masafumi Nishi, Koji Tokunaga, Akihiro Togo, Hirotami Kojima, Hiroki Kokubo,

Baseball

Hiroyuki Sakaguchi, Yasunori Takami,
Yasuhiro Sato, Kento Sugiyama, Katsumi
Watanabe, Kazutaka Nishiyama, Masahito

Kohiyama, Tomohito Ito, Masanori Sugiura,
Takashi Miwa, Shinichi Sato, Hiroshi
Nakamoto, Shinichiro Kawabata

Trivia Quiz

1. Baseball made its first official Olympic appearance
   a. In 1992, at Barcelona   **b.** In 1936, in Berlin   **c.** In 1900, in Paris

2. Baseball, or a facsimile of the sport, was first played in the U.S. in
   a. 1846, in Hoboken, New Jersey
   b. 1902, in Brooklyn, New York
   c. 1621, in Plymouth, Massachusetts

3. The designation of most career home-runs, at 868, belongs to
   a. Hank Aaron   **b.** Mickey Mantle   **c.** Sadaharu Oh

4. At the 1991 Pan American Games, the U.S. team finished
   a. Third   **b.** First   **c.** Fifth

5. Baseball was *not* played at the
   a. 1936 Berlin Games   **b.** 1900 Paris Games   **c.** 1952 Helsinki Games

6. The Soviet team that competed at the Intercontinental Cup in Barcelona in 1991
   a. Pitched a shut-out in the semi-finals
   b. Was comprised of wrestlers, javelin throwers, and team handball players
   c. Went on to win the gold medal in Barcelona

7. Olympic baseball follows International Baseball Association rules, which differ from professional rules by allowing
   a. Aluminum bats
   b. Opinion-sharing with the umpire
   c. Two pitches disallowed by professional rules

8. What team did *not* medal at the Barcelona Games?
   a. Japan   **b.** Chinese Taipei   **c.** United States

9. Jim Abbott pitched a no-hitter for
   a. The U.S. team   **b.** The California Angels   **c.** The New York Yankees

10. The 1988 Olympic championship went to
   a. Cuba   **b.** The U.S.   **c.** Wales

Answers: 1-b, 2-a, 3-c, 4-a, 5-b, 6-b, 7-a, 8-c, 9-c, 10-b

Basketball

Warm-up

The legend of Dr. James A. Naismith and his two peach baskets is fairly well known. In 1891, Naismith was given an assignment to devise an indoor game for a group of students at the International YMCA Training College (now Springfield College) in Springfield, Massachusetts.

After some brainstorming, Naismith derived the concept for a game that would not involve physical contact (basketball irony).

After drawing up 13 rules—many of which are still in effect—he organized the first game on January 20, 1892. He nailed two peach baskets on opposite ends of the YMCA balcony, 10 feet high, and divided up the 18 students into two teams of nine each.

With the aid of a soccer ball, the first basketball game was played.

And sports history was made.

Although Naismith was born and educated in Canada, basketball is the only major game created in the U.S. without roots deriving from another sport. At the turn of the century, basketball was well on its way to becoming a popular sport. The Organizing Committee for the 1904 St. Louis Games made it a demonstration sport, as did the Olympic committees in Paris (1924) and Amsterdam (1928).

But Los Angeles, site of the 1932 Olympics, ignored basketball.

The rejection of basketball on the sport's native turf galvanized basketball's proponents (which included the NCAA) into pushing for a 1936 Olympic berth in Berlin.

In 1936, playing outdoors due to a lack of indoor facilities, the U.S. prevailed and won the gold, beginning a 36-year stretch of Olympic game dominance. The first Olympic tournament was an interesting one: due to disqualifications and controversy resulting from the semi-professionalism of many U.S. players, the U.S. actually sent two teams: one from Universal movie studio and another known as the McPherson Globe Oilers. Universal played in games one and three and was to play the championship game, but a prior game was canceled, allowing McPherson to represent the U.S. in the finals. McPherson/U.S. defeated Canada, 19–8, in a driving rainstorm that filled the court with water and made dribbling impossible. Only two baskets were scored for each team in the last half on the gravel court.

The U.S.A. men have captured the gold in 10 of the last 12 Olympics. But from 1987 to 1991 the pickings were slimmer. The U.S.A. missed the gold at the 1987 Pan Am Games, the 1988 Seoul Olympics, the 1990 Goodwill Games, and the 1991 Havana Pan Am Games. All of these defeats were sustained by a group of college players against older international athletes. To offset this advantage, U.S. professional players were allowed to participate (along with top collegiate stars) in 1992. This, by the way, was not the first U.S. basketball squad to include professionals, but was the first which had to qualify to play in the Olympics. "The Dream Team," led by Michael Jordan, Magic Johnson, and other NBA greats, lived up to their billing as the world's greatest basketball team, capturing the gold medal at Barcelona.

Women's basketball was added as a medal sport in 1976. The Unified Team won the gold medal in 1992, ending the U.S. women's streak of two consecutive Olympic titles.

Spectator's Guide

For the men's tournament, 12 teams qualify, evenly divided into two groups of six teams. The host country gets an automatic berth, while qualifying tournaments held prior to the Games determine the other Olympic participants.

In addition to the United States, the countries qualifying for competition in Atlanta will include one team from the Oceania Zone, one team from the Africa Zone, two teams from the Asia Zone, three teams from the Americas Zone, and four teams from the Europe Zone.

The teams will play a round robin preliminary round, progressing to quarterfinals, semifinals, and medal-round games.

In 1996 the women's competition will feature a 12-team field for the first time. As host country, the U.S. team automatically qualifies, as does the Brazilian team, by virtue of its 1994 FIBA World Championship.

The remaining 10 berths are allocated by zones: one to the Oceania, one to Africa, two to the Americas, three to Asia, and three to Europe. As with the men's competition, pre-Olympic tournaments are held to determine the zone qualifiers.

Should the top two teams of the tournament wind up with the same won-lost records, the gold medal is awarded to the winner of their head-to-head meeting.

International rules vary somewhat from National Basketball Association regulations:

Time: A 30-second time clock (rather than 24-second) is in effect, during which span an offensive team must attempt a shot.

Generally, in international play a game consists of two 20-minute periods. Each team receives two one-minute timeouts per half. In the event of a tie at the end of regulation, the game resumes with a five-minute overtime following a two-minute break. Each team receives one time-out during an overtime period.

Throw-ins: The official is required to handle the ball for all sideline throw-ins that are made from the backcourt.

Fouling: The eighth team foul in each half, and all succeeding ones, will result in two free throws for the other team. The individual foul limit is five. No shots are awarded on offensive fouls.

Substitution: Substitution rules are somewhat different from the pro and college game. On a possession after a violation, the offense may substitute, and the defense may substitute only if the offense substitutes. After successful free throws, the shooter may be replaced if requested prior to the first free throw. The opponent is allowed one substitute if requested before the last free throw.

Lanes: The lanes on an international court flare out more deeply and are not box-like as in the U.S., creating more opportunities for three-second violations and driving lay-ups, since the lane is less congested.

Three-point play: Olympic marksmen shoot from a distance roughly midway between those of the college and professional sports. The three-point distance in the international game is a little over 20.5 feet, or 6.25 meters, compared to 22 feet in the NBA, and the NCAA's 19 feet, nine inches.

Hopefuls

Men's Basketball

It was probably too much to expect that the U.S.A. could get through the selection process for the 1996 version of basketball's Dream Team without a whiff of controversy.

The choice of Hakeem Olajuwon as one of its players took care of that.

No one could make a credible argument that Olajuwon doesn't deserve his place. He is quite probably the best basketball player in the world, leading his Houston Rockets to consecutive National Basketball Association championships. In the process, he dominated opposing centers David Robinson and Shaquille O'Neal in a way they have seldom been dominated before.

Robinson had been the 1994-95 season's Most Valuable Player in the NBA, and O'Neal was so chagrined by Houston's four-game sweep of his Orlando Magic that he took out full-page ads in several newspapers informing Hakeem that "It isn't over." Both Robinson and O'Neal were also named to the Dream Team.

No, what bothers the critics this time is that Olajuwon was born in Nigeria. Although he is now a citizen of the U.S.A., they argue that this smacks of recruiting on a global scale. Wasn't the American team going to be dominant enough without snaring Hakeem for it, too? Including him is overkill.

In the past, Olympic rules have permitted U.S. citizens to compete for other countries with which they have ties of birth or family. But, in every instance, they were athletes who would not have made the American team. Olajuwon could make any team he chose.

For those who felt the first Dream Team was just a bunch of big bullies, this looks like more of the same. To those who regard basketball as an esthetic experience, however, more is better.

"We are the Dream Team of another part of the world."
—Danko Cvjeticanin, a member of the 1992 Croatian team

Moreover, while Barcelona's Dream Team was stocked with legends, Dream Team III will also contain stars who are just gaining ascendancy—players like Detroit's Grant Hill and Milwaukee's Glenn Robinson, with just two pro seasons on their resumes. (Dream Team II, incidentally, was chosen in 1994 to compete in the World Championships in Toronto, where it won without breathing hard.) Two collegiate players will also be chosen for the 12-man Olympic roster.

There is, to be sure, a growing European presence in the NBA. Toni Kukoc, Dino Radja and others will again play for their national teams. But as brilliant as they are as individual performers, their supporting casts cannot begin to compare to the standard of the NBA's best.

So, once again, the U.S.A. is not only expected to win but to win huge. Any game decided by fewer than double digits would be regarded as an upset and any medal other than gold a failure of unimaginable proportions.

While Croatia may gain heroic stature by keeping it close for the first part of the first half, the U.S.A. has no options. In some contexts, this could engender pressure. But with a choice of the world's three best centers in the post, the only pressure in Atlanta will be in the Georgia Dome's water system.

There was no more logical choice for coach of the U.S.A. Olympic team than Lenny Wilkens. The man who has won more games than any other coach in the history of pro basketball is, after all, hardly a daring selection.

But Wilkens has gone about his business so quietly, with so few of the mannerisms and quirks that characterize the top coaches, that he sneaks up on people. No victory cigar or endless wardrobe or slicked-back hair or sideline histrionics. Wilkens just wins.

The only title he ever won, however, was with the 1979 Seattle SuperSonics, in a small market long ago. So the fact that Wilkens has overtaken the victory total of Red Auerbach, the guiding genius of the Boston Celtics in their greatest era, and will pass 1,000 wins sometime during the 1995-96 season, astonished many students of the game. Coaches who don't deliver championships usually run out of places to coach after a while. But Wilkens, always low key and in control, never hurts for work.

"I always felt you should be judged by what you do," he said, "but in our league it wasn't always that way. It was who got publicized the most. It used to bother me a bit, but I don't worry about it anymore. Besides, I'm getting the recognition now."

It wasn't until 1994 that Wilkens won his first Coach of the Year award. Ironically enough, the trophy is named after Auerbach, whose record he would break a few months later.

"The record meant a lot to me because I played against Red's team in their prime," he said. "He maximized his talent. He got the most from nine players every night. I always wanted to coach that kind of team." And now he shall.

Wilkens was the last full-time player-coach in the NBA, finishing up a three-year run in the double job with Seattle in 1972. He thinks that sort of duty is impossible in the current NBA. Even then, a player had to be assigned to watch Wilkens and remind him when to take himself out of the game.

A fine, penetrating point guard, he is still among the career leaders in assists, and was runner-up in that statistic in one of the years he also coached. But Wilkens believes that worked against him.

"I think the feeling was in the NBA that players couldn't coach," he said. "I don't say that only players can coach but it sure didn't hurt me. Bill Russell was a great player-coach. Of course, he had Bill Russell on his team."

Wilkens wasn't even invited to try out for the 1960 Olympic team, while a star at Providence College. Auerbach also passed up a chance to draft him because he doubted that Wilkens had an outside shot. But he averaged more than 16 points a game in a pro playing career that began in 1960-61 and lasted 15 seasons.

"Not many people realize just how good a coach he is," said Danny Manning, an Olympian in 1988, who played for Wilkens in 1994. "And he's even a better person. The way he carries himself with so much class, so much dignity. It was a joy to play for him."

The Olympic assignment will be a hometown gig for Wilkens, who now coaches the Atlanta Hawks. He is with a team that hasn't won a championship in almost four decades and again gets little media attention. But now he is about to step up to the world's biggest athletic stage. Hardly anyone thinks that he will miss a step.

—*George Cantor*

> "It has to be now; it's now or never. I really believe this is it. This is our chance to get everybody's attention by showing that we can play and it's fun to watch women's basketball. People in this country don't realize that the best women's basketball is played after college."
>
> —*1996 U.S. Olympic Team member Katrina McClain, who's been called the best female forward in the world*

Women's Basketball

In the spring of 1995, women's basketball in the U.S.A. came of age in the only place that really counts—the television ratings.

The NCAA finals, in which the University of Connecticut went on to complete its record-breaking perfect season against the University of Tennessee, shattered every viewing mark and cliche associated with women's sports.

Conventional wisdom advised that the viewing audience would not tune in for women's team events. Individual matches in tennis, skating, or gymnastics, yes. But basketball fans, accustomed to the bone-jarring slam dunks and three-point outer space launches of the men's game, would never settle for the women's version. The women had not even been carried on prime time TV from Barcelona.

But when UConn pulled in a 5.4 rating, or five times higher than some of the early rounds in hockey's Stanley Cup playoffs, TV took notice. Two networks quickly signed on to carry 10 games of the U.S. Women's National Team as it prepared for the 1996 Olympics. Even the corporate sponsors showed up, shoe contracts in hand. All this has helped give a new look and new life to women's basketball.

While the experience of playing overseas in tough professional leagues was supposed to have given the 1992 team an edge, it may have been its undoing. Unaccustomed to playing together on a long-term basis, the U.S.A. did not respond well when Unified Team strategy shredded their pressing defense. The result was a galling defeat and only a bronze medal. This was sandwiched between lackluster showings in the '91 Pan Am Games and '94 World Championships

This time around, the core of the team will have been together for more than a year. Many of the women passed up six-figure foreign pro contracts to make this the first full-time U.S.A. Women's National Team. The National Team salary is $50,000 a year per player. Tara VanDerveer also gave up her position at Stanford to become the team's full-time coach.

The payoff will come in closeness and familiarity with each other's games. That should make the U.S.A. the overwhelming favorite for the gold in Atlanta.

But there are other stakes involved in their success. Because if public interest grows as anticipated, and name-recognition of the top players develops, there are plans to organize a women's professional league in the United States. So the pressure on this team to succeed is even greater than usual. That is the x-factor.

FACT: Atlanta natives Teresa Edwards and Katrina McClain are the only former Olympians on the 1996 U.S. women's team.

Its personnel is more than good enough to win. But with the stakes this high will it fold up against the challenge of powers like China and Brazil?

Rebecca Lobo

Rebecca Lobo knows about high stakes.

College basketball's Player of the Year in 1995, she was the driving force in Connecticut's run to a championship. She has become an authentic sports hero in New England, and is regarded as the most marketable individual in the history of women's basketball. She is known for her accessibility and patience with fans. The only complaint her college coach had about her was that she was too nice.

In the middle of her junior year, however, she learned that her mother had breast cancer. An outstanding high school player herself, RuthAnn Lobo was her daughter's inspiration. She urged Rebecca to "take care of your business and I'll take care of mine." With her mother not missing a home game, wearing a wig to cover the effects of chemotherapy, Lobo went on to elevate her game and prepare herself for the even greater achievements of her senior year. Her mother's cancer also has been in a remission for a year. The two have co-authored a book, *The Home Team* (due out July 1996), about family and relationships.

"I won't trivialize the situation," says Rebecca, "and say that when I'm in a game I just have to look over at mom to get more energy. But it does feel good to see her sitting there."

Lobo grew up in Southwick, Mass., just over the Connecticut state line. She was a high school superstar, lettering in field hockey, track, and softball. And basketball, to be sure.

She broke the state high school scoring record and once had 62 points in a game. How does she recall that achievement?

"With embarrassment," she says. "I mean, it's a team game."

That's why her college coach, Geno Auriemma, had to constantly urge her to be more selfish. He wanted her to score up to her capabilities, and—with her physical dominance in the post—that meant, in Auriemma's mind, about 50 points a game.

"He thought I was a wussy suburban girl and wanted me to be more of a son of a bitch," she says. "But that's not my nature."

Her nature was reflected more by the hours she spent signing autographs at Syracuse after a game on Girl Scout Day. And the column the *Hartford Courant* was persuaded to run that enabled her to answer in one swoop the flood of mail she consistently received.

> "Little girls need big girls to look up to. They can dream about dribbling like Dawn (Staley), shooting like Sheryl (Swoopes), intimidating like Rebecca (Lobo)."
>
> — *Teresa Edwards, who, if she makes it to Atlanta, will be the first basketball player — male or female — to compete in four Olympics*

Many of Lobo's teammates have far more extensive experience in international competition, including several repeaters from the '92 team. For guard Katrina McClain, who made the biggest financial sacrifice, a guaranteed $300,000 to play in Hungary, it will be the third trip to the Games.

Other women have deferred their education, including Lobo, who was a Rhodes scholar candidate. And VanDerveer preaches team over individual. "Instead of focusing on who can dunk and who can't," she says, "I'd like people to say: 'They really lay it on the line. This is a team we're proud of.'" That fits in perfectly with Lobo's point of view.

"You're playing for yourself and your teammates, but also for your fans," she says. "It's not about finishing the game and running back to the bus."

When she was 10-years old, Lobo found out that her grandmother was going into Boston to see the Celtics play. Rebecca gave her a note to hand to general manager Red Auerbach. It promised that she would be the first women ever to play for the Celts.

"I was young and dumb," she says.

Maybe that will not come to pass. But if all goes according to plan, Lobo and the other talented women on Team U.S.A. may soon have a league of their own.

—George Cantor

Schedule

The tentative basketball schedule is:

Saturday, July 20
Men's preliminaries — games 1–6

Sunday, July 21
Women's preliminaries — games 1–6

Monday, July 22
Men's preliminaries — games 7–12

Tuesday, July 23
Women's preliminaries — games 7–12

Wednesday, July 24
Men's preliminaries — games 13–18

Thursday, July 25
Women's preliminaries — games 13–18

Friday, July 26
Men's preliminaries — games 19–24

Saturday, July 27
Women's preliminaries — games 19–24

Sunday, July 28
Men's preliminaries — games 25–30

Monday, July 29
Women's preliminaries — games 25–30

Tuesday, July 30
Men's classification — games 1 & 2
Men's quarterfinal — games 1–4

Wednesday, July 31
Women's classification — games 1 & 2
Women's quarterfinal — games 1–4

Thursday, August 1
Men's classification—games 3 & 4
Women's classification—games 3 & 4
Men's semifinals—games 1 & 2

Friday, August 2
Men's finals 5–6, 7–8, 9–10 & 11–12
   places
Women's semifinals—games 1 & 2

Saturday, August 3
Women's finals 5–6, 7–8, 9–10 &
   11–12 places
Men's bronze & gold medal games

Sunday, August 4
Women's bronze & gold medal games

Highlights

For years the U.S. men's basketball team has dominated Olympic competition, ever since its introduction to the Games in 1936.

The exception was in Munich, in 1972, when dubious officiating gave the gold to the Soviet team. The U.S.A. team refused the silver, and Cuba took the bronze. The first women's games were played at the Montreal Olympics in 1976; the U.S. took a silver medal behind the Soviet women that year, with Bulgaria claiming the bronze medal. In the 1980 games—boycotted by the U.S. and other Western nations—Yugoslavia, always a contender, captured the men's gold, and the Soviet team had to settle for a bronze behind Italy. Soviet women were able to bring in the gold in 1980 ahead of Bulgaria and Yugoslavia.

At the Los Angeles Games in 1984 basketball was a monotonous string of victories for the American teams. Spain played to the men's silver, led by Juan Antonio San Epifanio. Yugoslavia took the 1984 men's bronze. In 1984 the American men beat their opponents by an average margin of 32; the women by 33. American women Cheryl Miller and Lynette Woodard stood out among the women's teams; the Republic of Korea took the silver medal and Canada the bronze. In 1988 the Central African Republic fielded a team for the first time, and were jubilant when they beat South Korea. The Soviet men's team again captured the gold in 1988, Yugoslavia the silver, and the U.S. settled for bronze. For the women, U.S.A. took the 1988 gold ahead of Yugoslavia and the Soviet Union.

Congressional Olympians

A few former Olympians have gone on to work in the U.S. Congress.

An all-American player at Princeton, Bill Bradley was a member of the 1964
U.S. Olympic team that earned a gold medal. *AP/Wide World*

Senator Bill Bradley (D–New Jersey), elected to Congress in 1978, played on the 1964 gold-medal basketball team in Tokyo. Bradley, now 52, a three-time All-American at Princeton and a Rhodes scholar, went on to play for the NBA New York Knicks. He averaged 10.1 points per game for the U.S. team in 1964.

Bradley announced in August 1995 that he would not seek re-election to Congress the following year. Nevertheless, he is still mentioned as a future presidential candidate. In fact, as early as 1964, when Bradley was still at Princeton, Leonard Shecter of the *New York Post* began a column this way: "In twenty-five years or so our presidents are going to have to be better than ever. It's nice to know that Bill Bradley will be available."

Representative Tom McMillen (D–Maryland), was elected to Congress in 1986 and served six years in that office. McMillen, now 43, averaged 7.6 points and 4.3 rebounds for the 1972 silver-medal team that suffered that crushing, controversial last-second defeat to the Soviets, 51–50, in Munich. He played collegiately at Maryland, was a Rhodes scholar, and played an 11-year NBA career with Buffalo, New York, Atlanta, and Washington. While in Congress he served on the Energy and Commerce and Science, Space, and Technology committees. In 1992, his book *Out of Bounds*, a critique of professional and youth sports, was published by Simon & Schuster. And in 1993 he was named co-chairman of the President's Council on Physical Fitness, along with fellow Olympian Florence Griffith Joyner.

The third ex-Olympian who has gone on to Capitol Hill is Native American Ben Nighthorse Campbell (R–Colorado), who was elected to the House as a Democrat in 1986 and to the Senate in 1992. In 1995, he switched parties to become a Republican.

Campbell, a member of the Black Belt Hall of Fame in Burbank, California, captained the 1964—and first—U.S. Olympic judo team.

Campbell, who served on the Agriculture and Interior and Insular Affairs committees and whose great-grandfather fought at the Battle of the Little Bighorn—Custer's last stand—led the charge to rename the Custer Battlefield National Monument in Montana, the site of the battle; the new designation is the Little Bighorn Battlefield National Monument. It was an effort aimed at honoring the Native American warriors as well as the soldiers. "It's now time to tell the world that we made a mistake in denying American Indians equal and fair honor on the battlefield," Campbell says.

Campbell, 62, also made the news in March 1991, when he fought off a mugger while returning to his Capitol Hill apartment from a nearby grocery store. When the mugger warned he was wielding a .45, Campbell answered, "Let's see it." When the thug came up empty, Campbell dusted off his chops—the martial arts variety.

Sort of.

"I found out in one fell swoop that I wasn't a 28-year-old judo champ anymore," said Campbell, who chased after the mugger, tearing some ankle ligaments in the process. "I found out I'm a 58-year-old out-of-shape congressman. But he didn't get my peanut butter and jelly."

Then, in May 1991, Campbell finally received his high school diploma—40 years after his class had graduated. The teenage Campbell dropped out of Placer High in Auburn, California, his hometown, joined the Air Force, passed a high school equivalency test, and went on to earn a bachelor's degree at San Jose State University.

"There's been something missing," Campbell said.

He wasn't talking about a gold medal.

—*Eric Kinkopf*

Highlights from Barcelona—Men's

They were called the Dream Team. But according to their critics, and there were many, they only earned the title because they turned men's basketball in the 1992 Olympics into a snoozer.

The top players in the National Basketball Association, many of them already international sports legends, toyed with the competition. They were never seriously challenged beyond the first few minutes of any game and won the gold medal by a margin of 32 points over runner-up Croatia.

To their boosters, that's the way it should have been. The basketball loss to the 1988 Soviet Union team was an abberation, they said, an international humbling that never should have happened.

Taking advantage of newly-liberalized eligibility rules, the likes of Michael Jordan, Magic Johnson, and Larry Bird were permitted to play in Barcelona. The United States unarguably produces the finest basketball players in the world

"If somebody make violence with me, it is important that I not react to the violence. Sport is not violent. It is supposed to be friends forever."
—*Angola's Herlander Coimbra, upon being elbowed by Charles Barkley*

Now being dubbed Dream Team *I*, the U.S. Men's Basketball Team was an assembly of pros from NBA teams. Scottie Pippen (l.), Michael Jordan (c.), and Clyde Drexler (r.) with their gold medals after beating Croatia, 117–85, in Barcelona. *AP/Wide World*

and the Dream Team was simply allowed to validate that statement without qualification. It may well have been the greatest team ever assembled in any sport.

On the other hand, it turned what is supposed to be the apogee of athletic competition into kind of a joke.

"The greatest basketball I've ever been involved in was in Monte Carlo," said Johnson afterwards. That's when the Dream Team scrimmaged among themselves.

"I've cried at home when I've seen Americans win close races," added Bird. "There would have been a lot more emotion (on the medals stand) if we hadn't won every game by 50 points."

But many American journalists professed to be embarrased by the spectacle and called the players little better than overgrown bullies. There was a big flap over corporate logos. The official Olympics sponsor conflicted with some of the players' endorsement contracts and they attempted to conceal the brand name on their equipment. Charles Barkley threw a vicious elbow into the side of an Angolan player he outweighed by about 75 pounds; standard procedure in the NBA but an ugly scene in the Olympics.

Still, the subject was basketball, and the Americans gave a lesson to the world. Even the players they crushed seemed proud just to have been able to compete against them.

"Karl Malone pushed me across the court like I wasn't there," said Arturas Karnishovas, of Lithuania. "I told my coach there's a lot of guys he pushes like that."

Political developments between 1988 and 1992 also gave the Dream Team a much easier road. The formidable Soviet team no longer existed. Its players were divided between Lithuania, the bronze medalist, and the so-called Unified Team, representing the rest of the former U.S.S.R. Yugoslavia also had disintegrated as a nation. While Croatia, which took the silver, had been the backbone of the former national team, it still was a less forceful presence than in past Games.

Not that it would have made much difference against the Dreamers.

"Going back to college players would be a mistake," cautioned Johnson after the Games. "We may have dominated but those college guys would have a problem."

No problem in '92; none foreseen for the Dream Team edition for '96.

— George Cantor

FACT: At the Barcelona Games, the U.S. Dream Team won each of their eight games by an average margin of 44 points.

Chuck Daly

He was known in Detroit as the Prince of Pessimism. The slogan that instructed his life was: "Don't trust happiness." And yet Chuck Daly, coach of the 1992 U.S. Olympic basketball team, said flatly, "I expect to come back from Barcelona with the gold medal."

Daly was named to the position after guiding the Detroit Pistons to consecutive National Basketball Association championships. The selection committee said he was picked because he had demonstrated an ability to win at all levels of competition. But he may find that pessimism is the reasonable frame of mind to carry into the task ahead of him.

For the first time, the professional superstars of the NBA were eligible for the games. So Daly was faced with the job of melding some of the largest egos in athletics into a cohesive team.

Moreover, he was not the only one who anticipated gold at Barcelona. Americans always expect their basketball team to carry off the Olympic gold. When they fail, it is regarded as a national embarrassment, if not a scandal. Since 1936, when basketball was admitted to the Olympics, American teams have lost a total of two games, both of them to the Soviet Union. In the 1972 finals, the actions of the officials, who seemingly made blatantly favorable calls for the Soviets in the last few seconds, caused an international furor. And in 1988, a decisive loss in the semifinals sustained by an American team that lacked consistent outside scoring, brought down a torrent of criticism on coach John Thompson's selection process.

> "It [traveling with the Dream Team] is very much like traveling with 12 rock stars."
> — Chuck Daly, coach of the 1992 U.S. Dream Team

1992 was Daly's turn in the fire. It is recognized that America's success in the games is no longer a matter of course. European teams have achieved tremendous advances in basketball. Professional leagues thrive in several countries and the game is followed avidly. But with the players at his disposal, Daly was not only expected to win but to win easily. And win they did.

"Losing is not going to enter my mind," he said. "There will be pressure to win and I can accept the fact. Every one of the guys we play will not only have super physical ability but superior intelligence as far as basketball is concerned. I have every confidence that these guys can handle any challenge."

That's what Daly said publicly. What he really thought may have been far less upbeat.

Chuck Daly, coach of 1992's Dream Team: He expected to win the gold in Barcelona and did.
AP/Wide World

The clash of personalities, the fragile balancing of a dozen huge talents, the adjustment of men who make millions of dollars a year—and live like it—to the comfort level of amateur athletes was not a cakewalk.

Some of his players behaved as if they believe their own commercials. Some of them absolutely detested each other. Yet their talents were regarded as so superior to any other country's collection of players that losing was inconceivable. If they had lost, it would have been humiliating for both Daly and the NBA.

Daly calls himself "a lifer" in basketball.

"I'm very happy that I'll be representing all the coaches in this country who are lifers. This game has been a way of life for me. It is what I always wanted to do."

He has done very well at it, too. Starting as a high school coach in Kane, Pennsylvania, he worked his way up through seven years at the University of Pennsylvania, a brief and unsuccesful stint with Cleveland, and an assistant's job with Philadelphia before landing in Detroit as head coach in 1983. The Pistons had never experienced two consecutive winning seasons in Detroit. But Daly took them to the division finals in four years, the championship round in five, and the NBA title in six.

His emphasis on grinding defense has not been universally popular in the NBA. His Pistons teams were known as the "Bad Boys" and some of their members among the most hated individuals in the game's history. Eventually, however, his defensive style was copied by other successful teams and Daly was credited with changing the face of professional basketball.

He is known as a man with a wry, self-deprecating sense of humor and a wardrobe out of *Gentleman's Quarterly*. The players call him "Daddy Rich" and his clothes closet reputedly extends beyond the county line. But his defining genius with the Pistons was generally recognized as being in the same area that tested him with the Olympic team—handling disparate personalities and making them work as a team.

And handle them he did. The Dream Team swept the Olympics and when Daly returned from Barcelona, there were three messages on his answering machine—all of them from pro basketball teams offering him jobs. Daly went to New Jersey, where he coached the Nets until his retirement in 1994. He now does color commentary on TNT/TBS.

—George Cantor

Highlights from Barcelona—Women's

It was supposed to have been a mirror image of the Dream Team's romp to the gold. Instead, U.S. women's basketball was jolted in Barcelona by a ghost from Olympics past.

The same scenario that had tripped up the men's team at Seoul in 1988 shocked the women in 1992. Moreover, the architect of the upset was a member of the same family of Russian coaches who had masterminded the Seoul victory, Yevgeny Gomelsky.

The American women's team was billed as the best ever assembled. Eleven of its 12 members were professionals. Six of them had Olympics experience.

Katrina McClain, a tremendous rebounder and scorer, was playing in her third Olympic Games, winning golds on her first two tries. Guard Teresa Edwards was an outstanding ball-handler and defender.

The team was loaded with dependable, experienced gamers who knew how to play the sort of aggressive defense that bottled up and frustrated the opposition. It brought players off the bench that were better than the starters on most other national teams. It had won a women's Olympic record 15 games in a row.

Then it ran into the Unified Team from the former U.S.S.R. Just as big, almost as fast, and coached by a man with a plan.

Gomelsky had figured out how to beat the U.S. press. He in-bounded the ball to his bigger front court people then had them set screens for guards who fired long passes upcourt. The tactic seemed to baffle the Americans who abandoned the press altogether in the second half after falling behind by 11 points.

While the Americans rallied to take the lead with 12 minutes to go, the effort of catching up seemed to exhaust them. A succession of close-in shots and free throws were missed and they wound up losing 79-73.

The final result was a bronze for the United States, behind Cuba and China.

"We hadn't been in a close game," lamented Medina Dixon afterwards. "We questioned that. How would we act? How would we flow together?"

FACT: In a game against the Unified Team at the 1992 Games, China's best player, Ma Jian, sat on the bench for all but the final five minutes of the competition. Officials speculated that Ma's decision to leave the national team in order to enroll in UCLA might have prompted Coach Jiang Xingquan to use his star player as a benchwarmer.

U.S. women's basetball player Katrina McClain (c.) is overwhelmed on a rebound by members of the women's Unified basketball team in Barcelona. The Unified Team defeated the U.S. 79–73 and won the gold medal. *AP/Wide World*

"This will leave a scar for the rest of our lives," said Teresa Weatherspoon.

Gomelsky's older brother, Alexsandr, was a coach with the 1988 Russian team and had devised the same sort of strategy against the press in those Games. His mother, Nina, was the founder of the first Soviet women's team in 1924.

"U.S. players, very jumping, very individual good players," said Alexsandr Gomelsky after watching his game plan resurrected in the women's game. "Team, not so good."

It was only the fourth Games for U.S.A. women's basketball. In 1976, it lost twice on its way to a silver, including a 35-point drubbing at the hands of the championship Soviet team. Since then, only two teams had been able to come within 10 points of them and they had beaten the Soviets by 14 in 1988.

The bronze was a bitter letdown.

—George Cantor

Medalists

Basketball—Men's Team

1992

1. U.S.A., Christian Laettner, David Robinson, Patrick Ewing, Larry Bird, Scottie Pippen, Michael Jordan, Clyde Drexler, Karls Malone, John Stockton, Chris Mullin, Charles Barkley, Earvin Johnson
2. Croatia, Drazen Petrovic, Velimir Perasovic, Danko Cvjeticanin, Toni Kukoc, Vladan Alanovic, Franjo Arapovic, Zan Tabak, Stojko Vrankovic, Alan Gregov, Arijan Komazec, Dino Radja, Aramis Naglic
3. Lithuania, Valdemaras Chomicius, Alvydas Pazdrazdis, Arunas Visockas, Darius Dimavicius, Romanas Brazdauskis, Gintaras Krapikas, Rimas Kurtinaitis, Arvydas Sabonis, Arturas Karnisovas, Sarunas Marciulionis, Gintaras Einikis, Sergejus Jovaisa

1988

1. Soviet Union, A. Belostennyi, Valeri Goborov, V. Khomitchious, R. Kourtinaitis, R. Martchioulenis, Igor Migliniex, V. Pankrachkine, A. Sabonis, Tilt Sokk, S. Tarakanov, V. Tikhonenko, A. Volkov
2. Yugoslavia, Franjo Arapovic, Zoran Cutura, D. Cvjeticanin, Vlade Divac, Toni Kukoc, Z. Obradovic, Zarko Paspalj, Drazen Petrovic,

Dino Radja, Z. Radulovic, S. Vrankovic, Jurij Zdovc
3. U.S.A., Willie Anderson, Stacey Augmon, Vernell Coles, Jeffrey Grayer, Hersey Hawkins, Dan Majerle, Danny Manning, Herman "J.R." Reid, Mitch Richmond, David Robinson, Charles D. Smith, Charles E. Smith IV

1984

1. U.S.A., Steve Alford, Leon Wood, Patrick Ewing, Vern Fleming, Alvin Robertson, Michael Jordan, Joseph Kleine, Jon Koncak, Wayman Tisdale, Chris Mullin, Samuel Perkins, Jeffrey Turner
2. Spain, Jose Manuel Beiran, Jose Luis Llorente, Fernando Arcega, Jose Maria Margall, Andres Jimenez, Juan Antonio San Epifanio, Fernando Romay, Fernando Martin, Juan Antonio Corbalan, Ignacio Solozabal, Juan Domingo de la Cruz, Juan Maria Lopez I
3. Yugoslavia, Drazan Petrovic, Aleksandr Petrovic, Nibojsa Zorkic, Rajko Zizic, Ivan Sunara, Emir Mitapcic, Sabit Hadzic, Andro Knego, RAtko Radovanovic, Mihovil Nakic-Vojnovic, Drazen Dalipagic, Branko Vukicevic

1980

1. Yugoslavia, Andro Knego, Dragan Kicanovic, Rajko Zizic, Mihoril Nakic, Zeljko Jerkov,

Branko Skroce, Zoran Slavnic, Kresimir Cosic, Ratko Radovanovic, Duje Krstulovic, Drazen Dalipagic, Mirza Delibasic
2. Italy, Romeo Sachetti, Roberto Brunamonti, Michael Silvester, Enrico Gilardi, Fabrizio DellaFiori, Marco Solfrini, Marco Bonamico, Dino Meneghin, Renato Villalta, Renzo Vecchiato, Pierluigi Marzorati, Pietro Generali
3. Soviet Union, Stanislav Eremin, Valeri Miloserdov, Sergei Tarakanov, Aleksandr Salinikov, Andrey Lopatov, Nikolai Deruguin, Sergei Belov, Vladimir Tkachenko, Anatoli Myshkin, Sergei Yovaysha, Aleksandr Belostenny, Vladimir Zhiguily

1976

1. U.S.A., Phil Ford, Steven Sheppard, Adrian Dantley, Walter Davis, Quinn Buckner, Mitchell Kupchak, Ernie Grunfeld, Kenneth Carr, Scott May, Mike Armstrong, Thomas LaGarde, Philip Hubbard
2. Yugoslavia, Blagoje Georgijevski, Dragan Kicanovic, Vinko Jelovac, Rajko Zizic, Zeljko Jerkov, Andro Knego, Zoran Slavnic, Kresimir Cosic, Damir Solman, Zarko Varajic, Drazen Dalipagic, Mirza Delibasic
3. Soviet Union, Vladimir Arzamaskov, Aleksandr Salnikov, Valery Miloserdov, Alshan Sharmukhamedov, Andrei Makeev, Ivan Edeshko, Sergei Belov, Vladimir Tkachenko, Anatoly Myshkin, Mikhail Korkiya, Aleksandr Belov, Vladimir Zhigily

1972

1. Soviet Union, Anatoli Polivoda, Modestas Paulauskas, Zurab Sakandelidze, Alshan Sharmukhamedov, Aleksandr Boloshev, Ivan Edeshko, Sergei Belov, Mishako Korkia, Ivan Dvorni, Gennady Volnov, Aleksandr Belov, Sergei Kovalenko
2. U.S.A., Kenneth Davis, Douglas Collins, Thomas Henderson, Michael Bantom, Robert Jones, Dwight Jones, James Forbes, James Brewer, Tommy Burleson, Thomas McMillen, Kevin Joyce, Ed Ratleff
3. Cuba, Juan Domecq, Ruperto Herrera, Juan Roca, Pedro Chappe, Jose M. Alvarez Pozo, Rafael Canizares, Conrado Perez, Miguel Calderon, Tomas Herrera, Oscar Varona, Alejandro Urgelles, Franklin Standard

1968

1. U.S.A., John Clawson, Ken Spain, Joseph White, Michael Barrett, Spencer Haywood, Charles Scott, Bill Hoskett, Calvin Fowler, Michael Silliman, Glynn Saulters, James King, Donald Dee
2. Yugoslavia, Aljosa Zorga, Radivoje Korac, Zoran Maroevic, Trajko Rajkovic, Vladimir Cvetkovic, Dragoslav Raznatovic, Ivo Daneu, Kresmir Cosic, Damir Solman, Nikola Plecas, Dragutin Cermak, Peter Skansi
3. Soviet Union, Anatoli Krikun, Modestas Paulauskas, Zurab Sakandelidze, Vadim Kapranov, Yuri Selikhov, Anatoli Polivoda, Sergei Belov, Priit Tomson, Sergei Kovalenko, Gennady Volnov, Yaak Lipso, Vladimir Andreyev

1964

1. U.S.A., Jim Barnes, William Bradley, Lawrence Brown, Joe Caldwell, Mel Counts, Richard Davies, Walter Hazzard, Lucius Jackson, John McCaffrey, Jeffry Mullins, Jerry Ship, George Wilson
2. Soviet Union, Valdis Muischnieks, Nikolai Bagley, Armenak Alachachyan, Aleksandr Travin, Vyacheslav Khrynin, Yanis Kruminsch, Levan Mosechvili, Yuri Korneyev, Aleksandr Petrov, Gennady Voinov, Yaak Lipso, Yuris Kaininsch
3. Brazil, Amaury A. Pasos, Wlamir Marques, Ubiratan Pereira Maciel, Carlos Domingos Massoni, Friedrich Wilhelm Braun, Carmo de Souza, Jatyr Eduardo Schall, Edson Bispo dos Santos, Antonio Salvador Sucar, Victor Mirshawka, Sergio de Toledo Machado, Jose Edvar Simoes

1960

1. U.S.A., Jay Arnette, Walter Bellamy, Robert Boozer, Terry Dischinger, Burdette Haldorson, Darall Imhoff, Allen Kelley, Lester Lane, Jerry Lucas, Oscar Robertson, Adrian Smith, Jerry West
2. Soviet Union, Yuri Korneyev, Yanis Kruminsch, Guram Minaschvill, Valdis Muischnieks, Cesar Ozers, Aleksandr Petrov, Mikhail Semyonov, Vladimir Ugrekhelidze, Maigonis Valdmanis, Albert Valtin, Gennady Volnov, Viktor Zubkov
3. Brazil, Edson Bispo Dos Santos, Moyses Blas, Waldemar Blatkauskas, Zenny De Azevedo, Carmo De Souza, Carlos Domingos Massoni, Waldyr Geraldo Boccardo, Wlamir Marques, Amaury Antonio Pasos, Fernando Pereira De Freitas, Antonio Salvador Sucar, Jatyr Eduardo Schall

1956

1. U.S.A., Carl C. Cain, William Hougland, K.C. Jones, William Russell, James P. Walsh, William Evans, Burdette Haldorson, Ronald Tomsic, Richard J. Boushka, Gilbert Ford, Robert E. Jeangerard, Charles F. Darling
2. Soviet Union, Valdis Muischnieks, Maigonis Valdmanis, Vladimir Torban, Stassis Stonkus, Kazis Petkyavichus, Arkady Bochkaryov, Yanis Kruminsch, Mikhail Semyonov, Algirdas Lauritenas, Yuri Ozerov, Viktor Zubkov, Mikhail Studenetsky
3. Uruguay, Carlos Blixen, Ramiro Cortes, Hector Costa, Nelson Chelle, Nelson Demarco, Hector Garcia Otero, Carlos Gonzalez, Sergio Matto, Oscar Moglia, Raul Mera, Ariel Olascoaga, Milton Scaron

1952

1. U.S.A., Charles Hoag, William Hougland, Melvin D. Kelley, Robert Kenney, Clyde Lovellette, Marcus Frieberger, Victor W. Glasgow, Frank McCabe, Daniel Pippin, Howard Williams, Ronald Bontemps, Robert Kurland, William Lienhard, John Keller
2. Soviet Union, Viktor Vlassov, Styapas Butautas, Yvan Lysov, Kazis Petkyavichus, Nodar Dshordshikiya, Anatoli Konyev, Otar Korkiya, Ilmar Kullam, Yuri Ozerov, Aleksandr Moiseyev, Heino Kruus, Yustinas Lagunavichus, Maigonis Vladmanis, Stassis Stonkus
3. Uruguay, Martin Acosta y Lara, Enrique Balino, Victorio Cieslinskas, Hector Costa, Nelson Demarco, Hector Garcia Otero, Roberto Lovera, Adesio Lombardo, Tabare Larre Borges, Sergio Matto, Wilfredo Pelaez, Carlos Rossello

1948

1. U.S.A., Clifford Barker, Donald Barksdale, Ralph Beard, Lewis Beck, Vincent Boryla, Gordon Carpenter, Alex Groza, Wallace Jones, Robert Kurland, Raymond Lumpp, Robert Pitts, Jesse Renick, Robert Robinson, Kenneth Rollins
2. France, Andre Barrais, Michel Bonnevie, Andre Buffiere, Rene Chocat, Rene Derency, Maurice Desaymonnet, Andre Even, Maurice Girardot, Fernand Guillou, Raymond Offner, Jacques Perrier, Yvan Quenin, Lucien Rebuffie, Pierre Thiolon
3. Brazil, Zenny De Azevedo, Joao Francisco Braz, Marcus Vinicius Dias, Affonso Azevedo Evora, Ruy De Freitas, Alexandre Gemignani,

Alberto Marson, Alfredo Rodrigues Da Motta, Nilton Pacheco De Oliveira, Massinet Sorcinelli

1936

1. U.S.A., Ralph Bishop, Joe Fortenberry, Carl S. Knowles, Jack W. Ragland, Carl Shy, William Wheatly, Francis Johnson, Sam Balter, John H. Gibbons, Frank J. Lubin, Arthur O. Mollner, Donald A. Piper, Duane A. Swanson, Willard Schmidt
2. Canada, Gordon Aitchison, Jan Allison, Arthur Chapman, Charles Chapman, Douglas Peden, James Stewart, Malcolm Wiseman, Edward J. Dawson, Irving Meretsky
3. Mexico, Carlos Borja Morca, Victor H. Borja Morca, Raul Fernandez Robert, Francisco Martinez Cordero, Dr. Jesus Olmos Moreno, Greer Skousen Spilsbury, Luis I. de la Vega Leija, Rodolfo Choperena Irizarri, Jose Pamplona Lecuanda, Andres Gomez Dominguez, Silvio Hermandez del Valle

1904

1. U.S.A., A. W. Manweiler, A. A. Heerdt, G. L. Redlein, William Rhode, Ed Miller, Charles Monahan
2. U.S.A., J. A. Jardine, Axel Berggien, John Schominer, M. B. Indarius, Carl Watson, W. K. Armstrong, W. A. Williams, Seth Collins
3. U.S.A., James Donovan, C. B. Cleveland, James Kenny, J. S. Smith, J. Leitz, Frnak Craven, E. J. Koche, W. Herschel

1896–1900
Not held

Basketball — Women's Team

1992

1. Unified Team, Elena Jirko, Elena Baranova, Irina Guerlits, Elena Tornikidou, Elena Chvaibovitch, Marina Tkatchenko, Irina Minkh, Elena Khoudachova, Irina Soumnikova, Elen Bountatiants, Natalia Zassoulskaia, Sveltana Zaboloueva
2. China, Xuedi Cong, Xin Li, Jun Liu, Fang Wang, Dongmei Zheng, Jun He, Ping Peng, Haixia Zheng, Xiulin Zheng, Dongmei Li, Quing Liu, Shuping Zhan
3. U.S.A., Teresa Edwards, Daedra Charles, Clarissa Davis, Tammy Jackson, Teresa Weatherspoon, Vickie Orr, Vicky Bullett, Carolyn Jones, Katrina F. McClain, Medina Dixon, Cynthia Cooper, Suzie McConnell

1988

1. U.S.A., Teresa Edwards, Mary "Kamie" Ethridge, Cynthia Brown, Anne Donovan, Teresa Weatherspoon, Bridgette Gordon, Vicky Bullett, Andrea Lloyd, Katrina McClain, Jennifer Gillom, Cynthia Cooper, Suzie McConnell
2. Yugoslavia, A. Arbutina, Vesna Bajkusa, Polona Dornik, Sladjana Golic, K. Kvesic, Mara Lakic, Zana Lelas, B. Milosevic, R. Mujanovic, Danira Nakic, S. Vangelovska, Eleonora Wild
3. Soviet Union, Olessia Barel, Olga Bouriakina, Olga Evkova, Irina Guerlits, Olga Lakovleva, E. Khoudachova, A. Leonova, Irina Minkh, G. Savitskaia, I. Soumnikova, V. Touomaite, N. Zassoulskaia

1984

1. U.S.A., Teresa Edwards, Lea Henry, Lynette Woodard, Anne Donovan, Cathy Boswell, Cheryl Miller, Janice Lawrence, Cindy Noble, Kim Mulkey, Denise Curry, Pamela McGee, Carol Menken-Schaudt
2. Republic of Korea, Aei-Young Choi, Yang-Gae Park, Eun-Sook Kim, Kyung-Sook Lee, Kyung-Hee Choi, Mi-Ja Lee, Kyung-Ja Moon, Hwa-Soon Kim, Myung-Hee Jeong, Young-Hee Kim, Jung-A Sung, Chan-Sook Park
3. Canada, Lynn Poison, Tracie McAra, Anna Pendergast, Debbie Huband, Carol Jane Sealey, Alison Lang, Bev Smith, Sylvia Sweeney, Candi Clarkson-Lohr, Toni Kordic, Andrea Blackwell, Misty Thomas, Don McCrae

1980

1. Soviet Union, Angele Rupshene, Lyubov Sharmay, Vida Besselene, Olga Korosteleva,

Tatiana Ovevhkina, Nadezhda Olkhova, Iuliyana Semenova, Lyudmila Rogozina, Nelly Feriabnikova, Olga Sukharnova, Tatiana Nadyrova, Tatiana Ivinskaya
2. Bulgaria, Nadka Golcheva, Penka Metodieva, Petkana Makaveeva, Snezhana Mihailova, Vania Dermandzhieva, Krassimira Bogdanova, Angelina Mihailova, Diana Brainova, Evladia Zakatanova, Kostadinka Radkova, Silvia Germanova, Penka Stoyanova
3. Yugoslavia, Vera Djuraskovic, Mersada Becirspahic, Jelica Komnenovic, Mira Bjedov, Vukica Mitic, Sanja Ozegovic, Sofija Pekic, Marija Tonkovic, Zorica Djurkovic, Vesna Despotovic, Biljana Majstorovic, Jasmina Perazic

1976

1. Soviet Union, Angele Rupshene, Tatyana Zakharova, Raisa Kurvyakova, Olga Barisheva, Tatyana Ovechkina, Nadezhda Shubaeva, Iuliyana Semenova, Nadezhda Zakharova, Nelly Feriabnikova, Olga Sukharnova, Tamara Daunene, Natalya Klimova
2. U.S.A., Cindy Brogdon, Susan Rojcewicz, Ann Meyers, Luisa Harris, Nancy Dunkle, Charlotte Lewis, Nancy Liebermann, Gail Marquis, Patricia Roberts, Mary Anne O'Connor, Patricia Head, Julienne Simpson
3. Bulgaria, Nadka Golcheva, Penka Metodieva, Petkana Makaveeva, Snezhana Mihailova, Krassima Gyurova, Krassimira Bogdanova, Todorka Yordanova, Diania Dilova, Margarita Shturkelova, Maria Stoyanova, Girgina Skerlatova, Penka Stoyanova

Trivia Quiz

1. In its earliest form, basketball
a. Allowed no physical contact among players
b. Allowed pushing and shoving, unlike the modern game
c. Allowed pushing and shoving, like the modern game

2. The nineteenth-century version of basketball was played
a. Outdoors, using rusted-out buckets for hoops
b. Indoors, using peach baskets for hoops
c. In churchyards, using spokeless wagon wheels for hoops

3. James A. Naismith, the man credited with creating basketball, was born and educated in
    a. The U.S.   **b.** Canada   **c.** Australia

4. The three-point distance in international play is
    a. The same as the NBA: 22 feet
    b. The same as the NCAA: 19 feet, nine inches
    c. Unique, at just over 20.5 feet

5. Basketball is the only major game created in the U.S.
    a. Without roots deriving from another sport
    b. That doesn't allow pushing and shoving
    c. With roots that can be traced to Angola

6. Which of the following U.S. congressman did not play on an Olympic basketball team
    a. Ben Nighthorse Campbell   **b.** Bob Mathias   **c.** Bill Bradley

7. Basketball was first a demonstration sport at
    a. The 1932 Los Angeles Games   **b.** The 1904 St. Louis Games
    c. The 1972 Sapporo Games

8. The United States's domination of Olympic basketball began
    a. At the 1936 Berlin Games   **b.** At the 1972 Sapporo Games
    c. At the 1956 Melbourne Games

9. Women's basketball became part of the Olympic program
    a. In Barcelona, in 1992   **b.** In Atlanta, in 1996
    c. In Montreal, in 1976

10. An automatic berth in the Olympics is not awarded to
    a. The second-place finisher from the previous Games
    b. The host country
    c. The previous year's Pan American Games first-place finisher

Answers: 1-a, 2-b, 3-b, 4-c, 5-a, 6-b, 7-b, 8-a, 9-c, 10-c

Boxing

Warm-up

As long as people have held sway on the planet, they've employed fighting and fisticuffs as a means of settling debates. Boxing as an Olympic sport was introduced in 688 BC, during the 23rd Ancient Olympiad (the event in 776 BC is considered the first). The boxers wore headgear and wrapped their fists with long leather thongs known as *caestus* to protect their hands and increase the power of their punches. The fights were not divided into rounds; the boxers fought until one combatant dropped or conceded by raising a fist in the air.

Hard leather gloves, with cutting edges, later replaced the thongs. The Romans introduced a more brutal aspect to the sweet science, as boxers used gloves studded with spikes, knots, nails, and/or bits of metal. A fight often ended with a death, which is how many Roman events ended.

Famous boxers of the very distant past include Theagenes from Thassos, who won the boxing event during the 75th Olympiad in 480 BC, the boxing and pancratium (a combination of boxing and wrestling) events during the 76th and 77th Olympiads, and the boxing, pancratium, and wrestling events in the 78th games. Cleitomachus from Thebes, a famous boxer and pancratist, won both events during the 141st Olympiad in 216 BC. Another boxer of the period, Melagomas from Caria, Asia Minor, forced his opponents to admit their defeat without blows being exchanged, because, he said, "to hit, to wound and be wounded was not bravery." Mentally intimidated, his opponents would admit defeat and withdraw. Current ring psychology still draws on Melagomas's strategy; hence the stare-down during the pre-fight introductions.

With the fall of the Roman Empire, boxing's recorded history disappeared until the 17th century in England. James Figg was an early champion, using a mixture of bare knuckles and fencing tactics. A former fencer, Figg would hit, thrust, and parry, or float like a butterfly and sting like a bee. His style came to dominate the sport, as kicking, gouging, and wrestling were discouraged.

In the 1800s, the Marquis of Queensberry introduced a set of rules to further diminish the brutality of the sport. These rules remain the core of the sport: the use of gloves; three-minute rounds with a 60-second rest between rounds; a 24-foot square ring; and a 10-second count after each knockdown.

At the first modern Olympics in 1896, boxing was omitted from the program because it was considered too dangerous and ungentlemanly by the Athens committee. It was not until the third Olympic Games in St. Louis (1904) that boxing was included, due to its popularity in America. Women's boxing was also featured on the program as a demonstration event. The host of the 1912 Olympics, pacifistic Sweden, decided not to stage a boxing event in their Olympiad, since it was against national law. Following the war, boxing returned to the program in 1920, when some 25 countries competed for the gold. From that point, boxing took hold as an international amateur sport and one of the more popular Olympic pursuits.

In the U.S., an Olympic medal remains a passport to professional success, graduating fighters such as Floyd Patterson (1952, middleweight gold), Muhammad Ali, then known as Cassius Clay (1960, light heavyweight gold), Joe Frazier (1964, heavyweight gold), Sugar Ray Leonard (1976, light welterweight gold), Michael Spinks (1976, middleweight gold), brother Leon Spinks (1976, light heavyweight gold), Pernell Whitaker (1984, lightweight gold), Mark Breland (1984, welterweight gold), Virgil Hill (1984, middleweight silver), Evander Holyfield (1984, light heavyweight bronze), Riddick Bowe (1988, super heavyweight silver), and Oscar De La Hoya (1992, lightweight gold).

Spectator's Guide

Olympic boxing features 12 weight classes: light flyweight (up to 48 kg/106 lbs); flyweight (48 kg to 51 kg/112 lbs); bantamweight (51 kg to 54 kg/119 lbs); featherweight (54 kg to 57 kg/125 lbs); lightweight (57 kg to 60 kg/132 lbs); light welterweight (60 kg to 63.5 kg/139 lbs); welterweight (63.5 kg to 67 kg/147 lbs); light middleweight (67 kg to 71 kg/156 lbs); middleweight (71 kg to 75 kg/165 lbs); light heavyweight (75 kg to 81 kg/178 lbs); heavyweight (81 kg to 91 kg/201 lbs); and super heavyweight (more than 91 kg/201 lbs).

The boxing competition is a single elimination tournament, with the survivors of each match proceeding to the next level of competition. A bout consists of three, three-minute rounds, with a one-minute interval between rounds. The referee is the sole authority in the ring, needing only three words to maintain control: stop (boxing), box (begin again), and break (step back, used to break up clinches). Any boxer who does not obey immediately may be disqualified on the spot.

The bouts are judged by five judges, who award points to the fighters for legal blows landed. Three scoring blows are counted as one point; for example, a boxer landing 15 scoring punches would be awarded five points. A scoring blow must be clean, fair, unguarded, land on the front of the face or body, and carry the proper weight. Basically, the white part of the glove, covering the knuckles, must make contact to be a scoring blow. All legal blows are scored equally, including knockdown blows.

During each round, each judge will add up the scoring blows delivered by each boxer, awarding 20 points to the round's winner and a lesser number to the loser.

The judges award points after each round. When the bout is over, the scores are added to determine the winner. Fouls enter into the scoring, resulting in a point deduction. Fighters are usually cautioned before a point deduction occurs. Common fouls include hitting below the belt, kicking or head butting, lying against the ropes or using them unfairly, offensive language, not breaking on command, and behaving aggressively against the referee.

The referee can stop a bout if he thinks a boxer is totally outclassed or if a boxer is injured. The match is also stopped if one of the boxers receives an eight-count three times in one round or four times in a bout. Unlike in professional boxing, the bell cannot save a boxer from a stopped contest. The count continues to completion, regardless of when the bell rings, *except* in the finals of the tournament.

A boxer is considered "down" if he touches the floor with anything other than his feet (chin, knee, forehead, etc.). He is also down if he is dangling on the ropes or is wholly or partially outside the ropes as a result of a blow. If he is in a dazed condition, a boxer can be considered down even while standing. And, of course, the boxer's corner can literally "throw in the towel" and retire from the match.

For safety, thumb-less gloves are used. Boxers from 106 through 147 pounds use eight-ounce gloves, while 10-ounce gloves are used for the heavier categories. Headgear is mandatory.

A feature unique to boxing (and judo) among Olympic events is the awarding of two bronze medals, since the Olympic boxing elimination tournament dispenses with a consolation bout of the two semifinal losers. In Atlanta, 364 boxers will compete for Olympic gold.

Hopefuls

Carlos Navarro and Fernando Vargas

American boxers face tough competition on the international level, especially from the Cuban team. Among the U.S. challengers who hope to win gold at the Summer Games are Carlos Navarro and Fernando Vargas, both teenagers who have proven themselves against older, more experienced opponents.

Navarro, who was born September 11, 1976, in Los Angeles, has been boxing virtually since the day his father first took him to a gym in 1983. In fact, his father, Carlos Sr., was his first coach, "showing me little by little what to do," the fighter recalled in *USA Today* on March 16, 1995. Working primarily with his father throughout his career to date, Carlos Jr. has established himself as a U.S. champion bantamweight (119 pounds) with a history of facing the most grueling tournament schedule without complaint.

Navarro won his first major competition, the Junior Olympics, in 1991. He was 14 at the time. The following year he took two silver medals, in the Junior Olympics and the Junior Olympic Box-Offs. He has been national amateur champion at his weight since 1993, winning the gold medal at the U.S. Championships in 1993, 1994, and 1995. As with many American boxers, Navarro faces his toughest competition from the Cuban team. He settled for a silver medal at the 1994 Goodwill Games after being beaten on points by Cuba's Waldemar Font, and he came up short again in 1995 at the Pan American Games, this time losing on points to Juan Despaigne in a quarterfinal match.

Undaunted, Navarro plans to train hard for the 1996 Olympic team, both with his father in Los Angeles and with U.S. Olympic coach Tom Mustin. A high school graduate who lives in a two-bedroom house with his 11 brothers and sisters and four nieces and nephews, Navarro told *USA Today:* "I know what I want. To win the Olympics, go to school for awhile, then go pro and win two world titles, maybe more." Lofty ambitions, indeed.

Ambition and work ethic—two prerequisites for the Olympic boxer—have been sorely tested for Fernando Vargas. The youngest national amateur champion ever, light-welterweight Vargas won the title in 1994 as a 16-year-old. He was such a young champion, in fact, that he was barred from competing in the 1994 Goodwill Games—he was forced to settle for a gold medal at the U.S. Junior Championships instead. In 1995, Vargas was the youngest member of the U.S. boxing team sent to compete in the Pan American Games.

Age is the only thing tender about Vargas. He likes to work out in a t-shirt that reads: "I'M NOT SCARED, I'M NOT AFRAID, I'M TOUGH, I'M AN ANIMAL AND I WILL EAT YOU IF I HAVE TO." A native of Oxnard, California, where he was born on December 7, 1977, he began boxing at the age of ten at the local Boys and Girls Club. Legend has it that he would actually cry for more ring time after sparring through the afternoon. Today he works with coach Eduardo Garcia at La Colonia Boxing Club, often the center of a small universe of admirers.

The pace of international amateur boxing has taken a toll on Vargas's enthusiasm for the sport. In September of 1994 he fought abroad for the first time, at the World Junior Championships in Istanbul, where he lost on points in the quarterfinals to a fighter from Kazakhstan. He came back in 1995 to win the Pan American Trials in Portland, Oregon, and a U.S.A.-Russia meet in Jacksonville, Florida, but he lost a disputed decision at the Pan Am Games in a semifinal against Luis Peres of Puerto Rico. "I'm worried about my performance," Vargas admitted in a March 30, 1995, *Los Angeles Times* profile.

The worries seemed justified when Vargas was forced to miss the 1995 U.S. Championships in Colorado Springs due to a stomach virus. Although the U.S. Boxing coaches felt that another U.S. championship—and a visit to the World Championships—might have proven valuable to the young fighter, they concur that Vargas has not really risked his chances of making the 1996 U.S. Olympic team. David Lubs of U.S.A. Boxing told the *Los Angeles Times* on April 5, 1995, that Vargas "has established himself. . . . It's fair to say that he will be selected for the U.S. Olympic Festival."

> "[Being compared to 1992 Olympic gold medalist Oscar De La Hoya] is an accomplishment and I don't mind being mentioned in the same sentence as Oscar, but it isn't something that motivates me. Fernando Vargas is Fernando Vargas. I want to be known for what I have and will accomplish. I'm not being disrespectful, I just refuse to stand in the shadow of any other boxer or person."
> — 1996 U.S. Olympic hopeful Fernando Vargas

An Olympic gold medal is just one of Vargas's ambitions. The other—perhaps even more important—is a high school diploma. He tried to continue his high school studies independently while training in 1994 and 1995, but he has since re-enrolled at Channel Islands High School in Oxnard. Vargas told the *Los Angeles Times* that the thought of competing in the Olympics without having earned his degree is unacceptable. "If I win the gold medal," he concluded, "I don't want to tell the world I'm a dropout."

—Mark Kram

David Reid

He lives the *Rocky* story every day: boxer David Reid, born in Philadelphia and living in Philadelphia, hopes to be the welterweight champion at the 1996 Olympic Games. Reid, who trains at the Spartan ABC Boxing Club, is a two-time U.S. national amateur champion and was the gold medalist at the 1995 Pan American Games. He is a serious and hard-working individual, a high school graduate who earns a living as a stockroom assistant at JC Penney while dreaming of glory in Atlanta. "I want [an Olympic championship] more than anything in the world right now," the fighter told the *Philadelphia Inquirer* on July 16, 1995. "I want to be able to get that gold medal. Since I was 11 years old, I've been preparing for the Olympics."

Born on September 17, 1973 in Philadelphia, Reid grew up in one of America's toughest urban environments. He recalled in the *Philadelphia Inquirer* how he got started in boxing. "I had been suspended from school for fighting," he said. "And my mom was mad at me. She said, 'What you need to try is boxing if you like fighting so much.' That sounded good to me, so I asked around and everybody told me to go to the gym and find the guy with the glasses on. And [coach] Al Mitchell was standing right over there by the ring. I thought boxing people were mean, so I was shy. I asked if he could teach me to box, and he looked at me and he said, 'Yeah, come on in Monday.' And I did, and I've been coming ever since then."

The coach who took Reid under his wing, Al Mitchell, is the head coach for the 1996 U.S. Olympic boxing team. Even ten years ago, Mitchell knew a prospect when he saw one. As a youngster Reid listened, did what he was told, and showed considerable talent as a puncher. "You get tired of training little kids and then they go out and don't come back," Mitchell told the *Philadelphia Inquirer.* "You want a kid who is dedicated, and that was David. He'd come over to my house and watch tapes of fights. He just stuck with me, and he got right under me. I feel like he's a son."

Reid began his amateur career boxing in tournaments sponsored by local recreation centers. After just two years in the sport, he was routinely assigned fights with opponents who were a year or two older than he was. Mitchell recalled that when Reid began getting bored as a 15-year-old, "I turned him around and taught him to fight southpaw. Now, he can go either way." When Mitchell was assigned to the Olympic Training Center in Marquette, Michigan, Reid moved there to continue his training. Reid actually finished his high school education at Bi-County High in Marquette so that his work with Mitchell would not be interrupted. Then, in 1993, Reid returned to Philadelphia to train with Fred Jenkins, Mitchell's former partner and co-founder of the ABC Boxing Club.

"Since I was 11 years old, I've been preparing for the Olympics."
—David Reid

As early as 1991 Reid won his first national title, taking the gold medal at the U.S. Junior Championships. He appeared in his first Olympic Festival meet in 1993, winning a gold medal by stopping Jesse Briseno in the finals. The following year he won his first national championship at welterweight with a decision over David Palac in the finals. He was less successful at the 1994 Goodwill Games, where he lost on points to Cuban fighter Juan Hernandez in the quarterfinals.

Reid's gold medal at the 1995 Pan American Games wasn't easily won. In the final round he built a big early lead against a tough Puerto Rican boxer named Daniel Santos, but then was knocked down in the third round, barely escaping with a close decision. "He dazed me, and I was wondering whether I should try to get my points back right there or should I run," Reid explained in the *Philadelphia Inquirer*. "I heard the coaches outside the ring, and they were saying, 'Run, run, run.' So I thought I better run." That tactic proved quite unpopular with the crowd in Mar del Plata, Argentina, and when Reid's victory was announced he was soundly booed and pelted with cans, debris, and even chewing gum. The American took it all in stride. "I had come to Argentina and I had gotten what I came for," he said. "I didn't let it bother me inside, because I had that gold medal."

From 1993 through the summer of 1995 (as this book went to press) Reid remained undefeated in the United States through some 22 major bouts. He plans to keep his amateur status through 1996 and then turn professional, with the goal of winning undisputed titles in both the welterweight and junior-middleweight divisions. His coaches feel that Reid has the potential to do that and more—he spars with professionals and can last through ten rounds against them without becoming seriously winded. Trained in the simple, direct combinations that appeal most to amateur judges, Reid shows particular strength in his straight right hand and his jab. Jenkins told the *Philadelphia Inquirer* of his pupil: "Pound for pound, I think he's the best fighter in [Philadelphia]. He's one of the best to ever come through this gym."

Reid goes running in the mornings, works an eight hour shift at the department store, and then reports to the gym for afternoon workouts. He plans to take a year off to prepare for the 1996 Summer Games but is not certain whether he wants to do the bulk of his training at the U.S. Olympic site or at home in Philadelphia. At home, he told the *Philadelphia Inquirer,* he can serve a greater purpose. "There are young guys around, and they look up to me," he concluded. "I want to be kind of a role model for them. If I can do it, they can do it."

—Mark Kram

Antonio Tarver

Light heavyweight Antonio Tarver has waited a long time for his chance at an Olympic gold medal. In a sport where most athletes turn professional at 20, Tarver has kept his amateur status through his mid-20s, with his sights clearly set on the 1996 Summer Games. "I know what it takes to reach the gold," he told the *Washington Post* on March 25, 1995. "I'm going to put U.S. boxing back on top."

That boast is hardly idle. Tarver is the first American to beat a Cuban boxer at the Pan American Games since 1987. He won the gold medal at the 1995 Pan Ams in part by defeating Cuban light heavyweight Diosvany Vega in a preliminary round that was judged by observers to be the most exciting bout in the Games. Tarver and Vega also met in the 1995 World Championships, and the determined American again won the gold. Tarver is currently World Champion and U.S. Champion in his weight class and is a member of U.S.A. Boxing's National Select Team.

The road to the top has been tough for the Orlando, Florida, native. Born on November 21, 1968, Antonio Tarver daydreamed about being wealthy and famous even as a young child. *The Orlando Sentinel* reported on February 15, 1995 that Tarver informed his mother, "I'm going to be a rich man, Mom," as he headed off for his first grade class. He spent much of his spare time as a child at the Boy's Club of Southwest Orlando, gravitating to boxing at the age of ten. "I was one of the rougher kids, always getting into trouble, and boxing slowed me down," he recalled in the *Washington Post.*

When he entered Orlando's Boone High School, Tarver lost interest in boxing, even though he had won his share of junior tournaments. Instead he played football, baseball, and basketball for his high school team. Somewhere in those busy teen years he developed a cocaine addiction that became so serious that he sought treatment in a rehabilitation center. The six-month recovery program he undertook included motivational speeches by other recovering addicts. One of them was former world heavyweight champion Pinklon Thomas. After Thomas spoke to the group, he struck up a conversation with Tarver and convinced the young man to return to boxing. After a five-and-a-half year layoff, Tarver took up the sport again.

In 1987 Tarver joined the Frontline Outreach gym in Orlando and has worked there, with trainer Lou Harris, ever since. Tarver told the *Washington Post* that he was particularly inspired by the 1988 Olympics in Seoul, when he watched Roy Jones Jr. lose a very close—and controversial—match. "He was very talented, but we both were," Tarver said. "When I saw him fight in 1988, that fired me up. I knew I could accomplish what he had accomplished."

Tarver's effort has been nothing less than monumental, and he has suffered setbacks and moments of discouragement. He was stopped in 1992 by Richard Bonds, who defeated him in the U.S. Championship finals as well as the Eastern Olympic Trials. In 1993 Tarver roared back, winning the U.S. Championships with a decision over Frank Vassar and earning the silver medal in the World Championships after losing on points to Jacklord Jacobs. Then, in 1994, he faltered again. After a first-place finish at the U.S. Olympic Festival, he lost a quarterfinal match in the U.S. Nationals and watched as his top ranking was given to Benjamin McDowell. Tarver, who was 25 at the time, considered taking a hiatus from boxing. His coaches at the Frontline Outreach Center convinced him otherwise, and he returned to his training. "I was really down, but I came back," he told the *Orlando Sentinel*.

The ascendance of Antonio Tarver began in earnest at the Pan American Games in the early spring of 1995. The Cubans had dominated those games almost absolutely, year after year since the mid-1980s. Further, the tournament's location in Mar Del Plata, Argentina, was considered to be an environment friendly to the Cuban team and hostile to the American one. No controversy attended Tarver's match with Diosvany Vega, however. After the first round,

"I know what it takes to reach that gold. I'm going to put U.S. boxing back on top."
—Antonio Tarver

Tarver led the favored Cuban 6-1. He held on to win the bout 11-10. The game American achieved similar results in the World Championships, against Vega once more, this time in a final that may serve as a glimpse into the Olympic future.

His long layoff from the sport and personal problems as a teen make Tarver one of the older Olympic prospects, especially in the American field. He sees that as an asset, not a liability, describing himself as mature and capable of a leadership role. "You need one thing to beat the Cubans: intestinal fortitude," he explained in the *Washington Post*. "I [have] showed my teammates the way." In a Knight-Ridder wire service story on March 15, 1995, the boxer elaborated on his chances in Atlanta. "I feel I have the skills, the talent," he said. "I don't see how anyone can defeat me unless I beat myself. I'm really mentally prepared as well as physically."

FACT: Cuba dominated the boxing events at Barcelona, nailing seven out of 12 gold medals and two silvers—the best performance by any nation in a non-boycotted Games.

Physically Tarver does resemble his Cuban opponents more than the standard American boxers of his weight class. American boxers build their bodies in preparation for a professional career and tend to be short and stocky. At six-feet-two and 178 pounds, Tarver is tall and slender for his division, a fighter built for the speed and agility that counts in the amateur ranks. His ambition is nothing less than restoring U.S. amateur boxing to its place as the best in the world. "It's my lifelong dream to be in the Olympics," he told the *Orlando Sentinel*. "I still have regrets about taking that time off. I feel I would have been there by now, but it's not too late." He added: "I feel that going into this competition, I'm as good as anybody in the world."

—*Mark Kram*

Schedule

The tentative boxing schedule is:

Saturday, July 20
first round sessions 1 & 2

Sunday, July 21
first round sessions 3 & 4

Monday, July 22
first round sessions 5 & 6

Tuesday, July 23
first round sessions 7 & 8

Wednesday, July 24
first round sessions 9 & 10

Thursday, July 25
second round sessions 11 & 12

Friday, July 26
second round sessions 13 & 14

Saturday, July 27
second round sessions 15 & 16

Sunday, July 28
second round sessions 17 & 18

Tuesday, July 30
quarterfinal sessions 1 & 2

Wednesday, July 31
quarterfinal sessions 3 & 4

Thursday, August 1
semifinal session 1

Friday, August 2
semifinal session 2

Saturday, August 3
gold medal session 1

Sunday, August 4
gold medal session 2

Highlights

Perhaps not surprisingly, boxing has been the most contentious sport on the Olympic program. Throughout the years the sport has been riddled with questionable officiating, resulting in protests, grievances, dubious disqualifications, and reversed decisions.

It wasn't until the 1904 Games in St. Louis that boxing found its way onto the Olympic program. All of the gold medal winners that year were Americans, including Oliver L. Kirk, who won gold medals in two weight divisions (featherweight and bantamweight), back when the rules allowed such things. That year the program even included a demonstration of women boxing. Again in 1908 all the weight divisions were won by host-country boxers, including 37-year-old featherweight Richard Gunn, who had been Britain's amateur champion from 1894 to 1896 and came out of retirement for the Games. Also medaling in London were John Douglas, a renowned cricketer, and Reginald Baker, who also competed as a springboard diver at the 1908 Games.

Boxing was not part of the program in 1912, but after World War I the sport returned to the Olympic arena at the 1920 Games in Antwerp, with 25 nations competing. England and the U.S. dominated, but gold medalists hailed from South Africa, France, and Canada as well. Some of the first protested decisions and grievances emerged from these Games. Controversy again surfaced at the 1924 Games, over the match between Britain's Harry Mallin and France's Roger Brousse; Brousse initially got the decision, but Mallin demonstrated that he had been bitten vigorously several times on the chest. Brousse claimed the teeth marks were administered inadvertently, even though his previous opponent had also accused Brousse of biting; the decision was eventually reversed. In another bout, a U.S. boxer knocked out his Swedish opponent and was then declared the loser for a supposed infraction.

At the 1928 Games debatable decisions again arose; Argentinean fans fought Dutch police, the U.S. boxing team threatened to withdraw in protest over a decision in the flyweight category, and Czech fans accosted the judges. In 1932 no disputes emerged, and the U.S., South Africa, and Argentina claimed two titles apiece.

The Americans were shut out at the 1936 Games, where once again decisions were contested. At the 1948 Games, the Jury of Appeals was physically assaulted twice by outraged contingents protesting decisions. That year South African light heavyweight George Hunter was the outstanding contender; Argentina's flyweight champion, Pascual Perez, went on to win a professional title. The U.S. came back with five champions in 1952, including 17-year-old Floyd Patterson. At the Helsinki Games, Ireland won its first Olympic boxing medal with bantamweight silver medalist John McNally.

In 1956 Britain gained its first gold since 1924, winning two weight classes, and Soviet boxers scored their first gold in 1956, winning three weight classes, but boxing at the Melbourne Games is most remembered for the performance of László Papp of Hungary. The left-handed Papp had won the middleweight gold in 1948, came back for the light middleweight gold in 1952, and successfully defended the light middleweight title in 1956.

FACT: No protest of a scoring decision has ever been upheld in Olympic boxing history.

Italy came up with three champions in 1960, the year U.S. boxer Cassius Clay (later Muhammad Ali) claimed the light heavyweight gold. Half of the Olympic judges and referees were dismissed at the Rome Games.

The U.S.S.R. and Poland each won three titles in 1964, and Nigeria gleaned its first Olympic medal, a bronze in the light middleweight category. That year an incensed Korean flyweight, Don-Kih Choh, protested his disqualification during a quarterfinal bout by remaining in the ring for almost an hour. In another weight class, Spanish featherweight Valentin Loren punched a referee in the face and was banned from boxing for life. Argentinean light middleweight Jose Chirino also punched a referee at the Tokyo Games.

In 1968 Soviet light middleweight Boris Lagutin and Polish light welterweight Jerzy Kulej repeated their gold-medal performances of four years before. Eye injuries were down in 1968 due to the introduction of a new leather glove from Germany that was soft and seamless. That year more than a dozen referees and judges were dismissed for incompetence, and two officials had to follow British middleweight Christopher Finnegan to a restaurant to obtain a urine sample.

In 1972 the match between Soviet featherweight Boris Kusnetsov and Kenya's Philip Waruinge was widely disputed. That year Cuba brought three gold medalists to the Games, including Teofilo Stevenson, who won the heavyweight title from 1972 through 1980.

The 1976 U.S. team was rich with champions, including Sugar Ray Leonard, the Spinks brothers, and Howard Davis. A Thai boxer, Payao Pooltarat, took third place in the light flyweight class that year, winning his country's first Olympic medal. Cuban boxer Angel Herrera took the featherweight gold in 1976 and the lightweight gold in 1980; his countryman, Andrés Aldama was light welterweight silver medalist in 1976 and won the welterweight gold in 1980.

A record-setting American team won eleven medals in 1984, including a bronze for Evander Holyfield in the light heavyweight class. The competitions were once again shrouded in judging controversies that alienated almost every team competing. That year two Canadians entered the spotlight, light middleweight Shawn O'Sullivan and heavyweight Willie deWit. Protective headgear was introduced at the 1984 Games as well.

In Seoul boxing was again marred by ugly incidents. A U.S. boxer had to forfeit a match due to a mix-up in times, venues, and transportation; many felt the competitive South Koreans had deliberately led the American boxer astray. Then Keith Walker, a referee from New Zealand, was physically assaulted in the ring by angry South Korean boxing officials, including at least two coaches. A fellow referee tried to shield Walker from the attack, while South Korean security police moved slowly in to break up the melee. Residents of Seoul expressed embarrassment over the behavior of their countrymen.

Many U.S. boxers have used the Olympics as a springboard into professional boxing. One of the most intriguing Olympic champions in history was destined never to fight professionally. Cuba's Teofilo Stevenson, heavyweight gold medalist in 1972, 1976, and 1980, swore by his country's "amateur" system, which only added to his mystic presence, as boxing fans continue to speculate on how far his wondrous boxing skills would have taken him in the professional ring.

Sugar Ray Leonard

Born May 17, 1956, Ray Charles Leonard (he was named after the singer) was raised in the Washington suburb of Palmer Park, Maryland. Initially his parents, Cicero and Getha, were concerned that the quiet, introspective Ray enjoyed few interests outside of school work and the church choir, but then, at the age of fourteen, Ray discovered boxing.

As an amateur, Leonard amassed an impressive 145–5 record. He participated in the 1975 Pan American Games, where he won a gold medal, and then went on to capture the light welterweight gold at the 1976 Olympics in Montreal. In post-match interviews, the handsome and personable Leonard charmed the press, and a celebrity was born. He called himself "Sugar Ray" after the great Sugar Ray Robinson and started working with Muhammad Ali's former trainer, Angelo Dundee.

Leonard's first title fight took place in 1979, when he beat welterweight Wilfredo Benitez in the 15th round with a technical knock-out (TKO). To defend that title, Leonard entered the ring in 1980 with Panamanian Roberto Duran, who unseated Leonard in a brutal slugfest. Their famous rematch five months later showcased Leonard's speed and agility, rather than Duran's brute strength, and resulted in Duran's withdrawal ("no mas") in the eighth round.

Shortly thereafter, Leonard faced then-undefeated Thomas "Hit Man" Hearns, in what was one of the great fights of the decade. A battered and exhausted Leonard, behind on all the judges' cards, found something extra in the 14th round and flailed at Hearns along the ropes until the referee stepped in and ended the fight, giving Leonard the decision in a TKO.

During a training match in 1982, Leonard suffered a potentially blinding detached retina. He subsequently announced his retirement from the ring. But in 1984 he returned to boxing, intending to prepare for a long-awaited bout with "Marvelous" Marvin Hagler. Before that battle came about, though, Leonard retired again. In 1986 he returned to serious training, and challenged Hagler to a match. The match finally took place in 1987, and, miraculously, Leonard emerged victorious, dispatching the brutal Hagler in twelve rounds. He then went on to a rematch with Hearns in 1989, which ended in a draw (most in the fight community believe that Hearns won), and another fight with Duran that same year, which Leonard won.

In February 1991, Leonard, for the fourth time in his career, announced his retirement from the ring. On the heels of a bloody defeat at the hands of 23-year-old Terry Norris, Leonard declared: "I had a great career. It took this fight to show me it is no longer my time. . . . Now I am going to learn how to play golf."

1993 was a banner year for the retired boxer: he released his first exercise video, *Boxout,* and married model Bernadette Robi.

—Paul Green

Highlights from Barcelona

If the boxing bouts in Barcelona are remembered for anything, it will most likely be for the Olympic debacle that resulted from the new computerized scoring system that was introduced at the 1992 Games. U.S. co-captain Eric Griffin—a 5'3", 106-pound four-time amateur world champion—soundly pummeled Spain's unranked Rafael Lozano in their light flyweight bout. But, because the judges were unaccustomed to scoring hits on ringside computer pads, Lozano pilfered a 6-5 decision over Griffin. Never mind that the five-member scoring jury, who tallied hits the old-fashioned way, unanimously declared the 23-year-old American to be the unrefuted victor.

Griffin was robbed; the public, outraged; and the judges, perplexed. "It's like if you got a typewriter," U.S. coach Joe Byrd explained. "If you got a guy who don't know how to type, you don't have nothing." And Griffin, despite a clear win, had nothing.

Cuban fighters, on the other hand, had gilded gloves, claiming seven of the 12 gold medals, and two silvers. Unbeaten in competition since 1986, triple world champion Felix Savon surprised no one by rousting Nigeria's David Izonritei in his bid for the heavyweight title. In a quarterfinal bout, however, Danell Nicholson of the U.S. came startlingly close to upsetting the 6'5" 200-pound Cuban powerhouse. Leading the first round by a handsome 4-1 margin, the 24-year old held on to his lead in the second round, but was eventually stunned into submission by Savon's lethal right. Savon's

FACT: Capturing the 1992 Olympic flyweight title, Chol Su Choi of the People's Democratic Republic of Korea won his country's first boxing gold since Yong-Jo Gu medaled in 1976.

mighty fist came as no surprise to Nicholson, who had been advised by coach Byrd: "If you walk into that right hand, it'll be a short night."

The Barcelona Games also marked the first time that Cuba and the United States had met in the Olympic ring since 1976, when a stellar U.S. team grabbed five gold medals, leaving Cuba three. At the Pavello Club Joventut, however, the U.S. claimed only one gold, as 17-year-old national champ Oscar De La Hoya trumped Germany's world champion, Marco Rudolph, in the lightweight division.

Medalists

Boxing—106 lbs./48 kg
(Light Flyweight)

1992
1. Rogelio Marcelo, Cuba
2. Daniel Bojinov, Bulgaria
3. Jan Quast, Germany
3. Roel Velasco, Philippines

1988
1. Ivalio Hristov, Bulgaria
2. Michael Carbajal, U.S.A
3. Robert Isaszegi, Hungary
3. Leopoldo Serantes, Philippines

1984
1. Paul Gonzales, U.S.A
2. Salvatore Todisco, Italy
3. Jose Marcelino Bolivar, Venezuela
3. Keith Mwila, Zambia

1980
1. Shamil Sabyrov, Soviet Union
2. Hipolito Ramos, Cuba
3. Byong-Uk Li, Democratic People's Republic of Korea
3. Ismail Mustafov, Bulgaria

1976
1. Jorge Hernandez, Cuba
2. Byong-Uk Li, Democratic People's Republic of Korea
3. Orlando Maldonado, Puerto Rico
3. Payao Pooltarat, Thailand

1972
1. Gyorgy Gedo, Hungary
2. U Gil Kim, Democratic People's Republic of Korea
3. Ralph Evans, Great Britain
3. Enrique Rodriguez, Spain

1968
1. Francisco Rodriguez, Venezuela
2. Yong-ju Chi, Republic of Korea
3. Harlan Marbley, U.S.A
3. Hubert Skrzypczak, Poland

1886–1964
Not held

Boxing—112 lbs./51 kg
(Flyweight)

1992
1. Su Choi-Chol, North Korea
2. Raul Gonzalez, Cuba
3. Timothy Austin, U.S.A
3. Istvan Kovacs, Hungary

1988
1. Kwang-Sun Kim, South Korea
2. Andreas Tews, East Germany
3. Mario Gonzalez, Mexico
3. Timofel Skriabin, Soviet Union

1984
1. Steven McCrory, U.S.A
2. Redzep Redzepovski, Yugoslavia
3. Ibrahim Bilali, Kenya
3. Eyup Can, Turkey

1980
1. Petr Lesov, Bulgaria
2. Viktor Miroshnichenko, Soviet Union
3. Hugh Russell, Ireland
3. Janos Varadi, Hungary

1976
1. Leo Randolph, U.S.A
2. Ramon Duvalon, Cuba
3. Leszek Blazynski, Poland
3. David Torozyan, Soviet Union

1972
1. Georgi Kostadinov, Bulgaria
2. Leo Rwabwogo, Uganda
3. Leszek Blazynski, Poland
3. Douglas Rodriguez, Cuba

1968
1. Ricardo Delgado, Mexico
2. Artur Olech, Poland
3. Servilio Oliveira, Brazil
3. Leo Rwabwogo, Uganda

1964
1. Fernando Atzori, Italy
2. Artur Olech, Poland
3. Robert Carmody, U.S.A
3. Stanislav Sorokin, Soviet Union

1960
1. Gyula Torok, Hungary
2. Sergei Sivko, Soviet Union
3. Abdelmoneim Elguindi, United Arab Republic
3. Kiyoshi Tanabe, Japan

1956
1. Terence Spinks, Great Britain
2. Mircea Dobrescu, Romania
3. John Caldwell, Ireland
3. Rene Libeer, France

1952
1. Nathan Brooks, U.S.A
2. Edgar Basel, West Germany
3. Anatoli Bulakov, Soviet Union
3. William Toweel, South Africa

1948
1. Pascual Perez, Argentina
2. Spartaco Bandinelli, Italy
3. Su-an Han, Republic of Korea

1936
1. Willy Kaiser, West Germany
2. Gavino Matta, Italy
3. Louis Daniel Lauria, U.S.A

1932
1. Istvan Enekes, Hungary
2. Francisco Cabanas, Mexico
3. Louis Salica, U.S.A

1928
1. Antal Kocsis, Hungary
2. Armand Apell, France
3. Carlo Cavagnoli, Italy

1924
1. Fidel LaBarba, U.S.A
2. James McKenzie, Great Britain
3. Raymond Fee, U.S.A

1920
1. Frank Genaro, U.S.A
2. Anders Petersen, Denmark
3. William Cuthbertson, Great Britain

1906–1912
Not held

1904
1. George Finnegan, U.S.A
2. Miles Burke, U.S.A

1896–1900
Not held

Boxing—119 lbs./54 kg (Bantamweight)

1992
1. Joel Casamayor, Cuba
2. Wayne McCullough, Ireland
3. Li Gwang Sik, North Korea
3. Mohamed Achik, Morocco

1988
1. Kennedy McKinney, U.S.A
2. Alexandar Hristov, Bulgaria
3. Jorge Julio Rocha, Colombia
3. Phajol Moolsan, Thailand

1984
1. Maurizio Stecca, Italy
2. Hector Lopez, Mexico
3. Pedro J. Nolasco, Dominican Republic
3. Dale Walters, Canada

1980
1. Juan Hernandez, Cuba
2. Bernardo Jose Pinango, Venezuela
3. Michael Anthony, Guyana
3. Dumitru Cipere, Romania

1976
1. Yong-Jo Gu, Democratic People's Republic of Korea
2. Charles Mooney, U.S.A
3. Patrick Cowdell, Great Britain
3. Viktor Rybakov, Soviet Union

1972
1. Orlando Martinez, Cuba
2. Alfonso Zamora, Mexico
3. Ricardo Carreras, U.S.A
3. George Turpin, Great Britain

1968
1. Valeri Sokolov, Soviet Union
2. Eridari Mukwanga, Uganda
3. Kyu-chu Chang, Republic of Korea
3. Eiji Morioka, Japan

1964

1. Takao Sakurai, Japan
2. Sin-jo Chong, Republic of Korea
3. Juan Fabila Mendoza, Mexico
3. Washington Rodriguez, Uruguay

1960

1. Oleg Grigoryev, Soviet Union
2. Primo Zamparini, Italy
3. Brunon Bendig, Poland
3. Oliver Taylor, Australia

1956

1. Wolfgang Behrendt, East Germany
2. Sun-chun Song, Republic of Korea
3. Claudio Barrientos, Chile
3. Frederick Gilroy, Ireland

1952

1. Pentti Hamalainen, Finland
2. John McNally, Ireland
3. Gennady Garbusov, Soviet Union
3. Jun-ho Kang, Republic of Korea

1948

1. Tibor Csik, Hungary
2. Giovanni Battista Zuddas, Italy
3. Juan Venegas, Puerto Rico

1936

1. Ulderico Sergo, Italy
2. Jack Wilson, U.S.A
3. Fidel Ortiz, Mexico

1932

1. Horace Gwynne, Canada
2. Hans Ziglarski, Germany
3. Jose Villanueva, Philippines

1928

1. Vittorio Tamagnimi, Italy
2. John Daley, U.S.A
3. Harry Isaacs, South Africa

1924

1. William Smith, South Africa
2. Salvatore Tripoli, U.S.A
3. Jean Ces, France

1920

1. Clarence Walker, South Africa
2. Chris J. Graham, Canada
3. James McKenzie, Great Britain

1912

Not held

1908

1. A. Henry Thomas, Great Britain
2. John Condon, Great Britain
3. W. Webb, Great Britain

1906

Not held

1904

1. Oliver Kirk, U.S.A
2. George Finnegan, U.S.A

1896–1900

Not held

Boxing—125 lbs./57 kg
(Featherweight)

1992

1. Andreas Tews, Germany
2. Faustino Reyes, Spain
3. Hocine Soltani, Algeria
3. Ramazi Paliani, Unified Team

1988

1. Giovanni Parisi, Italy
2. Daniel Dumitrescu, Romania
3. Abdulahak Achik, Morocco
3. Jae-Hyunk Lee, South Korea

1984

1. Meldrick Taylor, U.S.A
2. Peter Konyegwache, Nigeria
3. Turgut Aykac, Turkey
3. Omar Catari Paraza, Venezuela

1980

1. Rudi Fink, East Germany
2. Adolfo Horta, Cuba
3. Krzysztof Kosedowski, Poland
3. Viktor Rybakov, Soviet Union

1976

1. Angel Herrera, Cuba
2. Richard Nowakowski, East Germany
3. Leszek Kosedowski, Poland
3. Juan Paredes, Mexico

1972

1. Boris Kuznetsov, Soviet Union
2. Philip Waruinge, Kenya
3. Andras Botos, Hungary
3. Clemente Rojas, Columbia

1968

1. Antonio Roldan, Mexico
2. Albert Robinson, U.S.A
3. Ivan Mihailov, Bulgaria
3. Philip Waruinge, Kenya

1964

1. Stanislav Stepashkin, Soviet Union
2. Anthony Villanueva, Philippines
3. Charles Brown, U.S.A
3. Heinz Schulz, East Germany

1960
1. Francesco Musso, Italy
2. Jerzy Adamski, Poland
3. Jormal Limmonen, Finland
3. William Meyers, South Africa

1956
1. Valdimir Safronov, Soviet Union
2. Thomas Nicholls, Great Britain
3. Pentti Hamalainen, Finland
3. Henryk Niedzwiedzki, Poland

1952
1. Jan Zachara, Czechoslovakia
2. Sergio Caprari, Italy
3. Leonard Leisching, South Africa
3. Joseph Ventaja, France

1948
1. Ernesto Formenti, Italy
2. Dennis Shepherd, South Africa
3. Aleksy Antkiewicz, Poland

1936
1. Oscar Casanovas, Argentina
2. Charles Catterall, South Africa
3. Josef Miner, Germany

1932
1. Carmelo Robledo, Argentina
2. Josef Schleinkofer, Germany
3. Allan Carlsson, Sweden

1928
1. Lambertus "Bep" van Klaveren, Netherlands
2. Victor Peralta, Argentina
3. Harold Devine, U.S.A

1924
1. John "Jackie" Fields, U.S.A
2. Joseph Salas, U.S.A
3. Pedro Quartucci, Argentina

1920
1. Paul Fritsch, France
2. Jean Gachet, France
3. Edoardo Garzena, Italy

1912
Not held

1908
1. Richard Gunn, Great Britain
2. C. W. Morris, Great Britain
3. Hugh Roddin, Great Britain

1906
Not held

1904
1. Oliver Kirk, U.S.A
2. Frank Haller, U.S.A

1896–1900
Not held

Boxing—132 lbs./60 kg
(Lightweight)

1992
1. Oscar De La Hoya, U.S.A
2. Marco Rudolph, Germany
3. Hong Sung Sik, North Korea
3. Namjil Bayarsaikhan, Mongolia

1988
1. Andreas Zuelow, East Germany
2. George Cramne, Sweden
3. Romallis Ellis, U.S.A
3. Nerguy Enkhbat, Mongolia

1984
1. Pernell Whitaker, U.S.A
2. Luis F. Ortiz, Puerto Rico
3. Chil-Sung Chun, Republic of Korea
3. Martin Ndongo Ebanga, Cameroon

1980
1. Angel Herrera, Cuba
2. Viktor Demianenko, Soviet Union
3. Kazimierz Adach, Poland
3. Richard Nowakowski, East Germany

1976
1. Howard Davis, U.S.A
2. Simion Cutov, Romania
3. Ace Rusevski, Yugoslavia
3. Vasili Solomin, Soviet Union

1972
1. Jan Szczepanski, Poland
2. Lazzlo Orban, Hungary
3. Samuel Mbugua, Kenya
3. Alfonso Perez, Colombia

1968
1. Ronald Harris, U.S.A
2. Jozef Grudzien, Poland
3. Calistrat Cutov, Romania
3. Zvonimir Vujin, Yugoslavia

1964
1. Jozef Grudzien, Poland
2. Velikton Barannikov, Soviet Union
3. Ronald Harris, U.S.A
3. James McCourt, Ireland

1960
1. Kazimierz Pazdzior, Poland
2. Sandro Lopopolo, Italy
3. Abel Laudonio, Argentina
3. Richard McTaggart, Great Britain

1956
1. Richard McTaggart, Great Britain
2. Harry Kurschat, Great Britain
3. Anthony Byrne, Ireland
3. Anatoli Lagetko, Soviet Union

1952
1. Aureliano Bolognesi, Italy
2. Aleksy Antkiewicz, Poland
3. Gheorghe Fiat, Romania
3. Erkki Pakkanen, Finland

1948
1. Gerald Dreyer, South Africa
2. Joseph Vissers, Belgium
3. Svend Wad, Denmark

1936
1. Imre Harangi, Hungary
2. Nikolai Stepulov, Estonia
3. Erik Agren, Sweden

1932
1. Lawrence Stevens, South Africa
2. Thure Ahlqvist, Sweden
3. Nathan Bor, U.S.A

1928
1. Carlo Orlandi, Italy
2. Stephen Halaiko, U.S.A
3. Gunnar Berggren, Sweden

1924
1. Hans Nielsen, Denmark
2. Alfredo Copello, Argentina
3. Frederick Boylstein, U.S.A

1920
1. Samuel Mosberg, U.S.A
2. Gotfred Johansen, Denmark
3. Clarence "Chris" Newton, Canada

1912
Not held

1908
1. Frederick Grace, Great Britain
2. Frederick Spiller, Great Britain
3. H. H. Johnson, Great Britain

1906
Not held

1904
1. Harry Spanger, U.S.A
2. James Eagan, U.S.A
3. Russell Van Horn, U.S.A

1896–1900
Not held

Boxing—139 lbs./63.5 kg
(Light Welterweight)

1992
1. Hector Vinent, Cuba
2. Mark Leduc, Canada
3. Jyri Kjall, Finland
3. Leonard Doroftei, Romania

1988
1. Viatcheslav Janovski, Soviet Union
2. Grahame Cheney, Australia
3. Reiner Gies, West Germany
3. Lars Myrberg, Sweden

1984
1. Jerry Page, U.S.A
2. Dhawee Umponmaha, Thailand
3. Mircea Fulger, Romania
3. Mirko Puzovic, Yugoslavia

1980
1. Patrizio Oliva, Italy
2. Serik Konakbaev, Soviet Union
3. Jose Aguilar, Cuba
3. Anthony Willis, Great Britain

1976
1. "Sugar" Ray Leonard, U.S.A
2. Andres Aldama, Cuba
3. Vladimir Kolev, Bulgaria
3. Kazimierz Szczerba, Poland

1972
1. Ray Seales, U.S.A
2. Angel Angelow, Bulgaria
3. Issaka Daborg, Niger
3. Zvonimir Vujin, Yugoslavia

1968
1. Jerzy Kulej, Poland
2. Enrique Regueiferos, Cuba
3. Arto Nilsson, Finland
3. James Wallington, U.S.A

1964
1. Jerzy Kulej, Poland
2. Yevgeny Frolov, Soviet Union
3. Eddie Blay, Ghana
3. Habib Galhia, Tunisia

1960
1. Bohumil Nemecek, Czechoslovakia
2. Clement Quartey, Ghana
3. Quincelon Daniels, U.S.A
3. Marian Kasprzyk, Poland

1956
1. Vladimir Yengibaryan, Soviet Union
2. Franco Nenci, Italy
3. Constantin Dumitrescu, Romania
3. Henry Loubscher, South Africa

1952
1. Charles Adkins, U.S.A
2. Viktor Mednov, Soviet Union
3. Erkki Mallenius, Finland
3. Bruno Visintin, Italy

1896–1948
Not held

Boxing—147 lbs./67 kg
(Welterweight)

1992
1. Michael Carruth, Ireland
2. Juan Hernandez, Cuba
3. Anibal Acevedo Santiago, Puerto Rico
3. Arkom Chenglai, Thailand

1988
1. Robert Wangila, Kenya
2. Laurent Boudouani, France
3. Jan Dydak, Poland
3. Kenneth Gould, U.S.A

1984
1. Mark Breland, U.S.A
2. Young-Su An, Republic of Korea
3. Luciano Bruno, Italy
3. Joni Nyman, Finland

1980
1. Andres Aldama, Cuba
2. John Mugabi, Uganda
3. Karl-Heinz Kruger, East Germany
3. Kazimierz Szczerba, Poland

1976
1. Jochen Bachfeld, East Germany
2. Pedro Gamarro, Venezuela
3. Reinhard Skricek, West Germany
3. Victor Zilberman, Romania

1972
1. Emilio Correa, Cuba
2. Janos Kajdi, Hungary
3. Dick Tiger Murunga, Kenya
3. Jesse Valdez, U.S.A

1968
1. Manfred Wolke, East Germany
2. Joseph Bessala, Cameroon
3. Mario Guilloti, Argentina
3. Vladimir Mussalimov, Soviet Union

1964
1. Marian Kasprzyk, Poland
2. Richardas Tamulis, Soviet Union
3. Silvano Bertini, Italy
3. Pertti Purhonen, Finland

1960
1. Giovanni Benvenuti, Italy
2. Yuri Radonyak, Soviet Union
3. Leszek Drogosz, Poland
3. James Lloyd, Great Britain

1956
1. Nicolae Linca, Romania
2. Frederick Tiedt, Ireland
3. Nicholas Gargano, Great Britain
3. Kevin Hogarth, Australia

1952
1. Zygmunt Chychla, Poland
2. Sergei Scherbakov, Soviet Union
3. Gunther Heidemann, Germany
3. Victor Jorgensen, Denmark

1948
1. Julius Torma, Czechoslovakia
2. Horace Herring, U.S.A
3. Alessandro D'Ottavio, Italy

1936
1. Sten Suvio, Finland
2. Michael Murach, Germany
3. Gerhard Petersen, Denmark

1932
1. Edward Flynn, U.S.A
2. Erich Campe, Germany
3. Bruno Ahlberg, Finland

1928
1. Edward Morgan, New Zealand
2. Raul Landini, Argentina
3. Raymond Smillie, Canada

1924
1. Jean Delarge, Belgium
2. Hector Mendez, Argentina
3. Douglas Lewis, Canada

1920
1. Albert "Bert" Schneider, Canada
2. Alexander Ireland, Great Britain
3. Frederick Colberg, U.S.A

1906–1912
Not held

1904
1. Albert Young, U.S.A
2. Harry Spanger, U.S.A
3. Jack Eagan, U.S.A
3. Joseph Lydon, U.S.A

1896–1900
Not held

Boxing—156 lbs./71 kg
(Light Middleweight)

1992
1. Juan Lemus, Cuba
2. Orhan Delibas, Netherlands
3. Gyorgy Mizsei, Hungary
3. Robin Reid, Britain

1988
1. Si-Hun Park, South Korea
2. Roy Jones, U.S.A
3. Raymond Downey, Canada
3. Richard Woodhall, Great Britain

1984
1. Frank Tate, U.S.A
2. Shawn O'Sullivan, Canada
3. Christophe Tiozzo, France
3. Manfred Zielonka, West Germany

1980
1. Armando Martinez, Cuba
2. Aleksandr Koshkin, Soviet Union
3. Jan Franek, Czechoslovakia
3. Detlef Kastner, East Germany

1976
1. Jerzy Rybicki, Poland
2. Tadija Kacar, Yugoslavia
3. Rolando Garbey, Cuba
3. Viktor Savchenko, Soviet Union

1972
1. Dieter Kottysch, West Germany
2. Wieslaw Rudkowski, Poland
3. Alan Minter, Great Britain
3. Peter Tiepold, East Germany

1968
1. Boris Lagutin, Soviet Union
2. Rolando Garbey, Cuba
3. John Baldwin, U.S.A
3. Gunther Meier, West Germany

1964
1. Boris Lagutin, Soviet Union
2. Joseph Gonzales, France
3. Jozef Grzesiak, Poland
3. Nojim Maiyegun, Nigeria

1960
1. Wilbert McClure, U.S.A
2. Carmelo Bossi, Italy
3. William Fisher, Great Britain
3. Boris Lagutin, Soviet Union

1956
1. Laszlo Papp, Hungary
2. Jose Torres, U.S.A
3. John McCormack, Great Britain
3. Zbigniew Pietrzykowski, Poland

1952
1. Laszlo Papp, Hungary
2. Theunis van Schalkwyk, South Africa
3. Eladio Herrera, Argentina
3. Boris Tischin, Soviet Union

1896–1948
Not held

Boxing—165 lbs./75 kg
(Middleweight)

1992
1. Ariel Hernandez, Cuba
2. Chris Byrd, U.S.A
3. Chris Johnson, Canada
3. Lee Seung Bae, South Korea

1988
1. Henry Maske, East Germany
2. Egerton Marcus, Canada
3. Chris Sande, Kenya
3. Hussain Shah Syed, Pakistan

1984
1. Joon-Sup Shin, Republic of Korea
2. Virgil Hill, U.S.A
3. Aristides Gonzales, Puerto Rico
3. Mohamed Zaoui, Algeria

1980
1. Jose Gomez, Cuba
2. Viktor Savchenko, Soviet Union
3. Jerzy Rybicki, Poland
3. Valentin Silaghi, Romania

1976
1. Michael Spinks, U.S.A
2. Rufat Riskiev, Soviet Union
3. Luis Martinez, Cuba
3. Alec Nastac, Romania

1972
1. Vyacheslav Lemeschev, Soviet Union
2. Reima Virtanen, Finland
3. Prince Amartey, Ghana
3. Marvin Johnson, U.S.A

1968
1. Christopher Finnegan, Great Britain
2. Aleksei Kisselyov, Soviet Union
3. Alfred Jones, U.S.A
3. Agustin Zaragoza, Mexico

1964
1. Valeri Popenchenko, Soviet Union
2. Emil Schulz, Great Britain
3. Franco Valle, Italy
3. Tadeusz Walasek, Poland

1960
1. Edward Crook, U.S.A
2. Tadeusz Walasek, Poland
3. Yevgeny Feofanov, Soviet Union
3. Ion Monea, Romania

1956
1. Gennady Schatkov, Soviet Union
2. Ramon Tapia, Chile
3. Gilbert Chapron, France
3. Victor Zalazar, Argentina

1952
1. Floyd Patterson, U.S.A
2. Vasile Tita, Romania
3. Boris Nikilow, Bulgaria
3. Stig Sjolin, Sweden

1948
1. Laszlo Papp, Hungary
2. John Wright, Great Britain
3. Ivano Fontana, Italy

1936
1. Jean Despeaux, France
2. Henry Tiller, Norway
3. Raul Villareal, Argentina

1932
1. Carmen Barth, U.S.A
2. Amado Azar, Argentina
3. Ernest Pierce, South Africa

1928
1. Piero Toscani, Italy
2. Jan Hermanek, Czechoslovakia
3. Leonard Steyaert, Belgium

1924
1. Harry Mallin, Great Britain
2. John Elliott, Great Britain
3. Joseph Beecken, Belgium

1920
1. Harry Mallin, Great Britain
2. Georges A. Prud-Homme, Canada
3. Moe H. Herscovitch, Canada

1912
Not held

1908
1. John Douglas, Great Britain
2. Reginald Baker, Australia
3. W. Philo, Great Britain

1906
Not held

1904
1. Charles Mayer, U.S.A
2. Benjamin Spradley, U.S.A

1896–1900
Not held

Boxing—178 lbs./81 kg
(Light Heavyweight)

1992
1. Torsten May, Germany
2. Rostislav Zaoulitchnyi, Ukraine
3. Zoltan Beres, Hungary
3. Wojciech Bartnik, Poland

1988
1. Andrew Maynard, U.S.A
2. Nourmagomed Chanavazov, Soviet Union
3. Henryk Petrich, Poland
3. Damir Skaro, Yugoslavia

1984
1. Anton Josipovic, Yugoslavia
2. Kevin Barry, New Zealand
3. Evander Holyfield, U.S.A
3. Mustapha Moussa, Algeria

1980
1. Slobodan Kacar, Yugoslavia
2. Pawel Skrzecz, Poland
3. Herbert Bauch, East Germany
3. Ricardo Rojas, Cuba

1976
1. Leon Spinks, U.S.A
2. Sixto Soria, Cuba
3. Costica Dafinoiu, Romania
3. Janusz Gortat, Poland

1972
1. Mate Parlov, Yugoslavia
2. Gilberto Carrillo, Cuba
3. Janusz Gortat, Poland
3. Isaac Ikhouria, Nigeria

1968
1. Dan Posnyak, Soviet Union
2. Ion Monea, Romania
3. Stanislaw Dragan, Poland
3. Georgi Stankov, Bulgaria

1964
1. Cosimo Pinto, Italy
2. Aleksei Kisselyov, Soviet Union
3. Aleksandar Nikolov, Bulgaria
3. Zbigniew Pietrzykowski, Poland

1960
1. Cassius Clay, U.S.A
2. Zbigniew Pietrzykowski, Poland
3. Anthony Madigan, Australia
3. Giulio Saraudi, Italy

1956
1. James Boyd, U.S.A
2. Gheorghe Negrea, Romania
3. Carlos Lucas, Chile
3. Romualdas Murauskas, Soviet Union

1952
1. Norvel Lee, U.S.A
2. Antonio Pacenza, Argentina
3. Anatoli Perov, Soviet Union
3. Harri Siljander, Finland

1948
1. George Hunter, South Africa
2. Donald Scott, Great Britain
3. Maurio Cia, Argentina

1936
1. Roger Michelot, France
2. Richard Vogt, Germany
3. Francisco Risiglione, Argentina

1932
1. David Carstens, South Africa
2. Gino Rossi, Italy
3. Peter Jorgensen, Denmark

1928
1. Victor Avendano, Argentina
2. Ernst Pistulla, Germany
3. Karel L. Miljon, Netherlands

1924
1. Harry Mitchell, Great Britain
2. Thyge Petersen, Denmark
3. Sverre Sorsdal, Norway

1920
1. Edward Eagan, U.S.A
2. Sverre Sorsdal, Norway
3. H. Franks, Great Britain

1896–1912
Not held

Boxing—201 lbs./91 kg
(Heavyweight)

1992
1. Felix Savon, Cuba
2. David Izonritei, Nigeria
3. Arnold Van Der Lijde, Netherlands
3. David Tua, New Zealand

1988
1. Ray Mercer, U.S.A
2. Hyun-Man Baik, South Korea
3. Andrzej Golota, Poland
3. Arnold Vanderlidje, Netherlands

1984
1. Henry Tillman, U.S.A
2. Willie Dewitt, Canada
3. Angelo Musone, Italy
3. Arnold Vanderlidje, Netherlands

1980
1. Teofilo Stevenson, Cuba
2. Pyotr Zaev, Soviet Union
3. Jurgen Fanghanel, East Germany
3. Istvan Levai, Hungary

1976
1. Teofilo Stevenson, Cuba
2. Mircea Simon, Romania
3. Clarence Hill, Bermuda
3. Johnny Tate, U.S.A

1972
1. Teofilo Stevenson, Cuba
2. Ion Alexe, Romania
3. Peter Hussing, West Germany
3. Hasse Thomsen, Sweden

1968
1. George Foreman, U.S.A
2. Ionas Chepulis, Soviet Union
3. Giorgio Bambini, Italy
3. Joaquin Rocha, Mexico

1964
1. Joe Frazier, U.S.A
2. Hans Huber, West Germany
3. Giuseppe Ros, Italy
3. Vadim Yemelyanov, Soviet Union

1960
1. Franco De Piccolo, Italy
2. Daniel Bekker, South Africa
3. Josef Nemec, Czechoslovakia
3. Gunter Siegmund, West Germany

1956
1. Peter Rademacher, U.S.A
2. Lev Mukhin, Soviet Union
3. Daniel Bekker, South Africa
3. Giacomo Bozzano, Italy

1952
1. H. Edward Sanders, U.S.A
2. Ingemar Johansson, Sweden (disqualified)
3. Ilkka Koski, Finland
3. Andries Nieman, South Africa

1948
1. Rafael Iglesias, Argentina
2. Gunnar Nilsson, Sweden
3. John Arthur, South Africa

1936
1. Herbert Runge, Germany
2. Guillermo Lovell, Argentina
3. Erling Nilsen, Norway

1932
1. Santiago Lovell, Argentina
2. Luigi Rovati, Italy
3. Frederick Feary, U.S.A

1928
1. Arturo Rodriguez Jurado, Argentina
2. Nils Ramm, Sweden
3. M. Jacob Michaelsen, Denmark

1924
1. Otto von Porat, Norway
2. Soren Petersen, Denmark
3. Alfredo Porzio, Argentina

1920
1. Ronald Rawson, Great Britain
2. Soren Petersen, Denmark
3. Xavier Eluere, France

1912
Not held

1908
1. A. L. Oldham, Great Britain
2. S. C. H. Evans, Great Britain
3. Frederick Parks, Great Britain

1906
Not held

1904
1. Samuel Berger, U.S.A
2. Charles Mayer, U.S.A
3. William M. Michaels, U.S.A

1896–1900
Not held

Boxing—over 201 lbs./over 91 kg
(Super Heavyweight)

1992
1. Roberto Balado, Cuba
2. Richard Igbineghu, Nigeria
3. Brian Nielsen, Denmark
3. Svilen Roussinov, Bulgaria

1988
1. Lennox Lewis, Canada
2. Riddick Bowe, U.S.A
3. Alexandre Mirochnitchenko, Soviet Union
3. Janusz Zarenkiewicz, Poland

1984
1. Tyrell Biggs, U.S.A
2. Francesco Damiani, Italy
3. Azis Salihu, Yugoslavia
3. Robert Wells, Great Britain

1896–1980
Not held

Trivia Quiz

1. Boxing first appeared as an Olympic sport
a. In 1896, in Athens   **b.** In 1912, in Stockholm
c. In 688 BC, during the 23rd Olympiad

2. The 1912 Olympics in Stockholm did not include boxing because
a. Boxing was against national law
b. Only three nations were prepared to compete
c. Boxers refused to compete against Great Britain's 1908 medalists

3. When boxing returned to the Olympic program in 1920
a. 25 countries competed   **b.** Three countries competed
c. The U.S. did not compete

4. Boxing in the Ancient Olympics
a. Was governed by precise rules that ensured fair play
b. Often included gloves that were spiked with knots, nails, and bits of metal
c. Often ended in death

5. Boxers in the Ancient Olympic Games

a. Fought in boxing rounds, like today's fighters

b. Fought until one combatant dropped or raised one fist in the air to admit defeat

c. Fought in matches that were limited to one hour

6. Today's boxing style was heavily influenced by James Figg, who had a background in

a. Wrestling   **b.** Hockey   **c.** Fencing

7. Boxing reappeared in the Modern Olympic Games

a. In 1896, in Athens   **b.** In 1900, in Paris   **c.** In 1904, in St. Louis

8. Women's boxing events

a. Have never been included on the Olympic roster

b. Will be included for the first time in 1996

c. Were included as a demonstration event at the 1904 Games in St. Louis

9. Which of the following boxers did not win a light heavyweight gold?

a. Cassius Clay   **b.** Evander Holyfield   **c.** Leon Spinks

10. A boxer is considered "down"

a. Only if his head touches the floor

b. If he touches the floor with anything other than his feet

c. If starts to impersonate Don King

Answers: 1-c, 2-a, 3-a, 4-b and c, 5-b, 6-c, 7-c, 8-c, 9-c, 10-b

Canoe/Kayak

Warm-up

The most primitive form of boat, the canoe is found in some form or other in most cultures with a yen for aquatic transportation.

The form these boats assumed in various parts of the world stemmed from the type of materials available locally and what the intended function of the canoe was to be.

In the Pacific Northwest of the United States, where large trees were plentiful, the Tlinget and Haida peoples carved dugout canoes out of whole trees. These sturdy craft could reach impressive proportions, sometimes carrying as many as 30 to 50 people, and with many paddlers the boats were swift and seaworthy. The boats were used for a wide spectrum of activities, including transportation, fishing, hunting of marine mammals, and, of course, waging war.

Farther north, tree populations dwindle, so the Aleuts and other Arctic peoples resorted to other methods of boat construction.

Their skin-on-frame kayaks (along with those of Greenland natives) represent a highly developed boatbuilding tradition.

The Eskimo's kayak was composed of a framework of whalebone and driftwood, lashed together to support a sea lion skin stretched taut and treated with whale fat for waterproofing. Extremely agile and seaworthy in the hands of a skilled paddler, the boats were used for fishing and for hunting everything from seals and sea otters to whales.

Facing an entirely different set of circumstances imposed upon them by their noncoastal environment, native peoples in the interior of North America invented a unique solution to water transportation. As with the dugout builders of the Pacific Northwest, wood was available as a building material. But their type of river travel forced them to have to carry their canoes overland; thus, lightness was an essential trait. The bark canoe, a wooden framework covered with the bark of a birch or other tree, was a nimble rivercraft that could navigate tricky river currents, carry large loads, and yet portage (be carried) easily. This canoe was used by European explorers of North America and was the standard mode of transportation for native and non-native fur traders, and so played an important role in the history of North America.

Other variations on the canoe are found throughout the world.

Polynesian cultures built their version of the dugout canoe with outriggers for stability and sails to power the boats on extended ocean crossings between islands. Dugouts are also found in rainforest cultures such as those of the Amazon.

Credit for the birth of canoeing as a recreational sport is given to an English barrister, John MacGregor, who designed a boat based on the Eskimo kayak that he called *Rob Roy*. Between 1845 and 1869 he took the boat on extended journeys on the rivers and lakes of Europe. During this period he wrote a popular series of books and delivered lectures detailing his canoeing adventures.

People were captivated by his tales of paddling a small boat in the wilderness, and soon many similar craft were being built by Englishmen. That particular type of canoe is still known as a Rob Roy.

In 1866, MacGregor founded the Royal Canoe Club to encourage interest in the new sport. The Prince of Wales became the first Commodore of the club and remained in that office until 1901, when he stepped down to assume another post (king of England).

In 1867 the club held its first regatta and was busy codifying a set of rules to govern competitive canoe racing. By 1868, the group had swelled to 300 enthusiastic paddlers, who traveled the waterways of Europe and North America, exposing the local populations to the thrills of canoeing. As the popularity of canoeing grew, clubs sprang up in Europe and North America; the New York Canoe Club was founded in 1871.

During this time the open birchbark type of canoe was gaining favor among canoeists. Earlier boat builders of the Penobscot, or Oldtown, tribe had substituted canvas for the birchbark covering material, and European settlers copied the design in an all-wood construction. These so-called "Canadian canoes," having been designed for river travel, were better suited to that medium than the Rob Roys, which were based on open-water Eskimo kayaks, and gradually replaced the Rob Roy in recreational paddling. During the 1880s, Canadian canoe builders found a ready market for their boat in Europe.

The rise in popularity of canoeing led to the proliferation of organizations. In 1880 the American Canoe Association was launched to establish racing rules for both sail- and paddle-propelled craft. In 1887 the British Canoe Association was founded, primarily as a cruising-oriented group. Regattas were held in North America and many countries, and by 1921 national associations had been established in Sweden, Bohemia, Germany, Austria, and Denmark. In 1924 delegates from the European paddling community met in Copenhagen and created the Internationella Representantskapet för Kanotidrott (IRK), an international body to formulate rules for competitive racing worldwide.

Another development in the sport occurred during the 1920s: the invention by German Alfred Heurich of the *falboot*, or folding boat. This type of kayak was a skin-on-frame boat like those of the Eskimos. Its fabric skin, however, could be removed and its framework dismantled, enabling a canoeist to pack her boat into one or two duffle bags and transport it as she would baggage. This facilitated making trips to far-away destinations and further widened the appeal of the sport. It also added a category of boats to the list of events in organized racing.

In 1924, the same year that the IRK was formed, an international regatta was mounted in Paris as an exhibition to coincide with the Olympic Games. The regatta was a success, and the IRK began setting its sights on acceptance by the IOC of canoeing as an official Olympic event. Their efforts, however, were not immediately rewarded. The IOC rejected their suit for the Amsterdam and Los Angeles Games of 1928 and 1932.

In order to gain legitimacy, the IRK staged a European championship in Prague in 1933. They redoubled their efforts to persuade the IOC to include canoeing in the 1936 Games in Berlin.

With the IRK headquartered in Munich and a strong national German canoeing organization lobbying as well, enthusiasts were optimistic that the German-hosted Games would include the paddle sports. Disappointed they were when, once again, the IOC rejected the application. However, the IRK appealed the ruling and canoe racing was finally admitted as an Olympic sport for the Berlin Games.

FACT: In Olympic years, the Games also serve as the world championship for canoeing and kayaking.

The 1936 program for canoe/kayak consisted of flatwater courses of 1000 and 10,000 meter lengths, to be raced by single and pairs kayaks, single and pairs folding canoes; and single and pairs Canadian canoes. The event was a great success, with 19 nations participating and the 27 medals divided between 8 countries. Hopes were high for the future of Olympic canoeing.

But as luck would have it, World War II intervened, disrupting (among other pursuits) canoeing as an international sport. Nevertheless, the boats still had a role during war time: folding kayaks performed effectively for Allied Special Forces missions. At the end of the war the situation for the sport was made worse by the Munich location of the IRK headquarters. The organization was in a shambles politically, as was the building that housed it, the target of Allied bombing during the war.

In 1946, Jonas Asschier, the pre-war vice president of the IRK, convened a meeting of the representatives of the worldwide paddling community to rebuild an international organization and prepare for the upcoming 1948 Olympics. The new organization was called the International Canoe Federation (ICF). The 1948 Olympics saw the sport of canoeing somewhat diminished, with only 17 countries participating. The program had changed also: folding boat events were eliminated and a women's event, the 500-meter kayak singles, was added.

With each Olympiad, the number of entrants has increased, and over the years the program has been tinkered with. In Rome in 1956, the 10,000m races were eliminated and a relay race (4 × 500m) for kayak singles was added. That year the practice of repêchage was instituted, allowing an entrant a second chance before elimination from competition. At the 1964 Tokyo Games, the relay race was replaced by a 1000m event for four-man kayaks.

A major innovation to the program occurred in 1972 when canoe slalom was introduced. This event is based on the kind of canoeing done on "whitewater"—torrential rivers coursing along in rapids and falls—making it fundamentally different from the flatwater events. Participants in kayak singles (and Canadian canoe singles and pairs) race down a course on the turbulent water, navigating through gates such as those found on a slalom ski course.

Spectator's Guide

A canoe is a long, narrow watercraft usually sharp at both ends and typically propelled by handheld paddles. The fact that the paddler sits facing forward and the paddle is unsupported distinguishes the sports of canoeing and kayaking from the rowing sports, where an *oar* pivots on a fixed fulcrum and the rower "pulls" the oar from a seated position facing backward.

The distinction between the terms *canoe* and *kayak* is somewhat hazy. The larger category of canoes includes the kayak (that is, all kayaks are canoes, but only some canoes are kayaks). The main thing that distinguishes kayaks from other canoes is the position of the paddler(s). In a kayak the paddler sits with her legs outstretched in front of her, whereas other canoeists paddle from a kneeling position. Also, a kayak is typically a decked or covered boat and is paddled with a double-bladed paddle, while a canoe is more often an open boat powered by a single-bladed paddle.

The 16 events on the Olympic program for canoe/kayak are classified first by the type of water paddled (flatwater or whitewater) and, second, by the type of boat (Canadian canoe or kayak, and number of paddlers). A shorthand system of nomenclature makes it easier to keep all the types of boats straight: the letter C for Canadian canoe and the letter K for kayak are followed by a digit representing the number of crew on board. For example, K-4 is a four-man/woman kayak, C-1 a single Canadian canoe.

The biggest distinction between any of the canoe events is whitewater versus flatwater. The two environments result in boat designs and paddling techniques that are vastly different. In flatwater sprint racing, the essential ingredient is flat-out straight-line speed. The boats, whether Canadian canoe or kayak, are long and narrow for high hull speed, and low in profile to reduce wind resistance. In profile the keel, or bottom edge of the hull, of a flatwater boat appears very straight. This straight keel-line enables the boat to track a straight course easily through flatwater. A whitewater boat, by contrast, is shorter, with a more curved keel profile, to enable it to turn quickly as it is maneuvered around gates. The whitewater boat's sides are higher, to keep the turbulent water at bay. In either type of whitewater boat the crew wears spray skirts, which attach around the cockpit and seal the paddler into the boat to prevent water from entering. The spray skirt is unnecessary in the calm conditions of the flatwater events.

Flatwater events: Twelve of the 16 events in the program are flatwater sprints. The men compete at 500m and 1000m in singles and doubles kayaks (K-1 and K-2) and singles and doubles Canadian canoes (C-1 and C-2). A 1000m race in fours kayaks (K-4) is also run as a men's event. Women compete at 500m in the three kayak types (K-1, K-2, and K-4). In the kayak events, racers sit in the traditional kayak posture, with legs forward, and use a double-bladed paddle. In the Canadian canoe events, a single-bladed paddle is wielded from a kneeling position.

Each boat paddles a straight course within a marked 9-meter-wide lane. Leaving one's lane or coming within 5 meters of a neighboring boat results in disqualification. The races, as the label indicates, are essentially sprints, in which paddlers go all-out from start to finish. Boat design is constrained by specifications set forth by the ICF, and so each boat will perform, to a large degree, the same, leaving it up to the strength and stamina of the athletes to make the winning difference.

To determine which nine competitors make it to the finals, a system of heats, repêchages (or second chances; in French, literally, "fishing again"), and semi-finals is used. The first three finishers of the heats move on to the semi-final races, while the others go to a repêchage. Through the repêchage stage competitors can get back into the semi-finals. The top three finishers in the semi-finals move on to the finals, where the medalists and fourth through sixth places are determined.

Whitewater slalom events: The four events in the whitewater slalom portion of the Olympic program are men's single kayak (K-1), men's single and pairs Canadian canoe (C-1 and C-2) and women's kayak (K-1W). In the whitewater events, boats are raced downstream on a course of rapidly moving water that can range in length from 400 to 1200 meters. Although patterned after a stretch of wilderness "wild water," the Olympic course is usually a man-made structure featuring particular hazards that are specially designed into the course. The specific path of the course to be run is marked off by a series of "gates" suspended above the waterway and reaching down to just above the water's surface.

Scoring is based on elapsed time to run the course, corrected for navigation errors. Touching a gate adds five seconds to a paddler's time, while missing a gate altogether tacks on 50 seconds. The gates themselves fall into two categories: upstream or downstream gates, depending on which direction the boat must pass through. Green-and-white striped gates are to be passed through in a downstream direction, while red-and-white striped gates are negotiated against the stream.

In paddling a whitewater slalom course, a competitor can choose to race cleanly, paddling fastidiously but conservatively to clear the gates without racking up the five-second penalties assessed for touching them. Or a paddler can sight a line down the course and power recklessly through whatever the water offers.

Canoe/Kayak Speak

Beam: The widest part of the canoe.

Blade: The wide part of the paddle; it is the part of the paddle that passes through the water.

Bow (rhymes with *plow):* The front of the boat.

Downstream Gate: A slalom gate that is negotiated in the same direction as the flow of the water; distinguished from an upstream gate by its green and white stripes.

Draw: A stroke pulling in toward the paddler at 90 degrees to the direction of travel; when executed by the bowman, the bow of the canoe will turn in the direction of the drawing side.

Gunwale (pronounced gun'l): The upper edge of the canoe's side.

"J" Stroke: A paddle stroke that ends in a rudder maneuver (see below).

Keel: The ridge running the length of the canoe on the bottom.

Petit-Final: Literally, in French, "small final"; used to determine final placement of athletes who do not earn a starting position in the finals of a sprint event.

Repêchage: French for "second chance," literally, fishing again; this stage of a sprint racing event permits athletes a second chance to earn a spot in the next round of competition (semi-finals).

River Left: The left side of the waterway as it would appear to a paddler facing downstream.

River Right: The right side of the waterway as it would appear to a paddler facing downstream.

Rudder: Dragging the paddle to create resistance; when executed by the sternsman the stern of the canoe turns in the direction of the rudder side.

Shaft: The narrow part of the paddle, gripped by the paddler.

Stern: The back of the boat.

Sweep: A stroke made in a broad curve; when executed by the sternsman, the canoe turns in the direction opposite the sweeping side.

Thwart: A supporting member of a canoe's structure, extending across the canoe from side to side between the gunwales.

Upstream Gate: A slalom gate that must be negotiated against the flow of the water; distinguished from a downstream gate by its red and white stripes.

Hopefuls

Flatwater Events

The 1996 flatwater sprint venue is located at Lake Lanier in Gainesville, Georgia, where Canada and Cuba will be floating strong flatwater teams, along with the traditional favorites, Germany, Hungary, and the Czech Republic. Nearly 500 competitors will compete for 16 gold medals.

U.S. flatwater paddler **Mike Herbert** was a cross-country star in junior high; a motorcycling accident that put him in a body cast for six months and kept him off his feet for nearly a year ultimately interfered with his growth and left one leg significantly shorter than the other. After learning to walk again, Herbert turned to a sport that relies more on the upper body. His kayaking ambitions were inspired by U.S. 1000m flatwater kayaker Greg Barton, who also has a lower-body disability and won two gold medals at the 1988 Games in Seoul and a bronze at the Barcelona Games in 1992. Herbert's odd adventures have been widely reported, and include the time he wrestled a bear in a bar in an attempt to win a Chevy, his barehanded by-the-gills scoop of a 65-pound catfish into his canoe, and the buck he bagged during deer season in a gunless contest that began with Herbert in a boat and ended with the paddler breaking the animal's neck from astride its back.

Herbert missed a flatwater 500m bronze in Seoul in 1988 by inches. He won the two-man 500m and the four-man 1000m at the 1987 Pan Am Games and took first in the one-man 1000m at the 1991 Pan Am Games. In Barcelona Herbert's hopes for a medal did not materialize, but Atlanta aspirations abound. Herbert is challenged by teammate Peter Newton, who won two gold medals and one silver at the 1995 Pan American Games; this total of three medals was the most ever by a canoe/kayak athlete at those games.

Flatwater paddler **Jim Terrell** returned to the U.S. team in 1995 after two years of retirement and promptly won the gold medal in the 500m solo canoe event at the Pan American Games. During his break from competitive sprint racing Terrell served as paddling director at the Newport Aquatic Center in California. In April, 1995, he began training with the Canadian National Team in Florida and now has his sights set on Atlanta victories.

Flatwater paddler **Traci Phillips**, a Honolulu native, will be competing in her third Games in 1996. In 1995 she earned the title "fastest kayak paddler in America" for the third straight year by winning the Champion International Canoe/Kayak Knockout competition.

—Steve Carey

Whitewater Events

The 1996 Olympic whitewater slalom canoe and kayak course is located on the Ocoee River in southeastern Tennessee. Strong whitewater performances will come from Great Britain and the Czech Republic. In fact, if British paddler Richard Fox competes in 1996, his will be the performance to beat on the whitewater course.

Dana Chladek, the daughter of two-time Czechoslovakian World Champion kayakers Stan and Ema Chladek, came to paddling prominence as the World Cup Champion in 1988. The 1992 Olympic bronze medalist in women's whitewater kayak, Chladek was ranked number nine in the world in 1995 but could turn in another medal-winning performance in Atlanta.

Scott Shipley competed for the United States in Barcelona, placing 27th in the men's whitewater kayak event. One year later he won the World Cup title and two years later he was ranked number one by the International Canoe Federation. In 1995 that ranking slipped to a sixth-place standing near the end of the 1995 competitive season. Shipley's predilection for paddling was not hard to come by. His father, Dick Shipley, was a member of the U.S. national team and a former national champion in doubles canoe. Shipley's first taste of the sport was in the bow of an aluminum canoe his great-grandmother had paddled. His interest developed during his youth on Puget Sound, where he discovered the power and speed of kayaks. Now living and training in North Carolina, Shipley is poised to shine in 1996. "I'll be there knowing I've done everything I can to take the gold medal," he told the *Olympian* in 1994. "Me coming out of the gate at the Olympics is going to be all or nothing, every last scrape of the fingernails to get that medal. If I don't get it, then that's the effort that I've lived for."

A whitewater favorite in Barcelona who went down in a stunning upset, American **Jon Lugbill** took the next three years off, returning to competitive paddling in 1995. His first-place finish at the whitewater slalom trials in May of that year convinced his teammates that Lugbill is once again a force to be reckoned with.

The Haller brothers, Fritz and Lecky, were ranked number two in the world in whitewater double canoe early in 1995, but later that year the pair missed two World Cup races after Fritz sustained bruised ribs in a freak practice collision.

"To win the Olympics, it's not enough to be prepared. You have to take a chance."
—*Fritz Haller*

The brothers dropped to a fourth-place standing but are nevertheless expected to figure prominently for the U.S. team in Atlanta. They are no strangers to the competitive paddling world. In fact, Fritz was a coach at Barcelona in 1992, where his brother competed for the U.S. team; the brothers' national and world slalom doubles titles date back to the early 1980s. They will both be nearing forty when the Atlanta Games begin, but, as Fritz comments, "What happens when you get older is that you get smarter."

—Steve Carey

Schedule

The tentative canoe/kayak schedule for slalom events is:

Friday, July 26
official training runs

Saturday, July 27
K-1 Women's finals
C-1 Men's finals

Sunday, July 28
C-2 Men's finals
K-1 Men's finals

The tentative canoe/kayak schedule for sprint events is:

Tuesday, July 30
K-2 Men's 1000 heats & reps
C-1 Men's 1000 heats & reps
K-4 Women's 500 heats & reps
K-1 Men's 1000 heats & reps
C-2 Men's 1000 heats & reps
K-4 Men's 1000 heats & reps

Wednesday, July 31
K-2 Men's 500 heats & reps
C-1 Men's 500 heats & reps
K-1 Women's 500 heats & reps
K-1 Men's 500 heats & reps
C-2 Men's 500 heats & reps
K-2 Women's 500 heats & reps

Thursday, August 1
K-2 Men's 1000 semifinal
C-1 Men's 1000 semifinal
K-4 Women's 500 semifinal
K-1 Men's 1000 semifinal
C-2 Men's 1000 semifinal
K-4 Men's 1000 semifinal

Friday, August 2
K-2 Men's & Women's 500 semifinal
C-1 Men's 500 semifinal
K-1 Women's & Men's 500 semifinal
C-2 Men's 500 semifinal

Saturday, August 3
K-2 Men's 1000 final
C-1 Men's 1000 final
K-4 Women's 500 final
K-1 Men's 1000 final
C-2 Men's 1000 final
K-4 Men's 1000 final

Sunday, August 4
K-2 Men's 500 final
C-1 Men's 500 final
K-1 Women's 500 final
K-1 Men's 500 final
C-2 Men's 500 final
K-2 Women's 500 final

Highlights

Americans and Canadians dominated in the early days of canoe/kayak before it was an official Olympic sport. At the Olympic debut of the sport in 1936, the medals clustered around Austrian, Dutch, German, Czech, and Swedish competitors, though Canada captured one gold, one silver, and one bronze. The U.S. team went home with a bronze medal.

After the war, Scandinavian, Czech, and French paddlers triumphed; Canada paddled to a silver and a bronze in 1948. That year the U.S. won a gold and two silver medals, on a team that included Frank Havens; Havens competed in 1952 for a gold in the C-1 10,000m event, and placed 8th in the same event four years later. Standout athletes in these years included Czech paddler Jan Brzak-Felix and Sweden's Gert Fredriksson, who ultimately won six gold medals, one silver, and one bronze, and went on to coach the 1964 Swedish team.

Europeans continued to dominate in the 1950s and 1960s, especially the U.S.S.R., Hungary, and Romania in the single-blade events. In 1964 the U.S. women captured additional medals for the U.S., taking a silver in the K-2 and a bronze in the K-1; that team featured the efforts of Marcia Jones Smoke. At the Tokyo Games, the three medalist crews in the men's K-4 event finished within one second of each other.

Altitude in Mexico City affected many of the crews in 1968, making the performances there something of a disappointment. In the late 1960s and early 1970s Hungary's Mihaly Hesz and Aleksandr Shaparenko of the U.S.S.R. made marks for themselves in the men's events, as did Soviet paddler Lyudmila Pinayeva-Khvedosyuk in the women's contests. Jamie McEwan earned the first U.S. whitewater Olympic medal with a bronze in C-1 slalom competition in 1972; the two Germanies dominated the slalom in Munich, while the Soviets practically swept the flatwater events. Canada was nosed out of a gold in the C-1 500m at Montreal in 1976, where Soviets and East Germans again showed strongly, including East German Rudiger Helm, the youngest competitor in 1976. At the Moscow Games, Eastern-bloc countries again triumphed, with Vladimir Parfenovich picking up three gold medals.

In 1984 New Zealand burst on the scene for four gold medals—three for Ian Ferguson alone—to Canada's two gold, two silver, and two bronze medals. The four-person kayak competition was added to the Olympics and U.S. kayaker Greg Barton won the bronze in the K-1 1000m event.

Barton was back in 1988 for a 0.005-second victory in the K-1 1000m event, then took a second gold with teammate Norman Bellingham in the K-2 1000m event, thus becoming the first athlete to win two Olympic kayaking golds at the same Games. In Seoul, New Zealand again showed strong, capturing one gold and two silver medals; Soviet paddlers claimed three gold, three silver, and one bronze medal.

Highlights from Barcelona

Strong teams paddling into the 1992 Games included Germany, Hungary, Bulgaria, Great Britain, and the Unified Team. Medal tallies confirmed some of the predictions, with men's events netting seven medals for Germany, four for France, three for Hungary, and three for Bulgaria. Women's events captured four more medals for Germany, three more for Hungary, and three for Sweden.

Competitors considered the 1992 Olympic slalom course in the Pyrenean mountain town of La Seu d'Ugell to be fairly easy, which meant that canoes were packed closely together in competition. Strategy and superb technique prevailed when two decided underdogs, Scott Strausbaugh and Joe Jacobi, became the first Americans ever to win gold medals in either whitewater canoeing or kayaking. Czechoslovakia took the silver in that two-man event and France the bronze.

Scott Shipley was expected to win the silver for the U.S. in the men's singles slalom, but was bested by Lukas Pollert of Czechoslovakia, Gareth Marriott of Britain, and Jacky Avril of France. Dana Chladek of the U.S. was the bronze-medal favorite in the women's solo whitewater slalom and rose to the task behind Elisabeth Micheler of Germany and Danielle Woodward of Australia. Two whitewater favorites, Great Britain's Richard Fox and U.S. paddler Jon Lugbill, were notable in their unexpected fourth-place finishes.

In 1992 Greg Barton was the top American in the 1000m one-man flatwater race. He was favored to win the silver in that event but had to settle for bronze behind Australia's Clint Robinson and Norway's Knut Holmann. U.S. paddler Norman Bellingham, who won the gold in the 1000m two-man flatwater event in Seoul in 1988, was expected to silver in the one-man 500m in Barcelona. But in that event Mikko Yrjoe Kolehmainen of Finland won the gold, Zsolt Gyulay of Hungary took the silver, and Norway's Knut Holmann medaled again for the bronze. Together Barton and Bellingham looked like possibilities for the silver in the two-man 1000m event in Barcelona. They were shut out by pairs from Germany, Sweden, and Poland.

U.S. flatwater paddler Mike Herbert looked likely to medal in the two-man 500m and the four-man 1000m. German paddlers took the gold in both those events. Poland and Italy also medaled in the doubles event, while Hungary and Australia took second and third in the four-man race. U.S. pair Lecky Haller and Jamie McEwan just barely missed a bronze in the two-man flatwater canoe event, placing behind the Unified Team, Germany, and Bulgaria.

—*Steve Carey*

Greg Barton

Greg "Buck" Barton says his upbringing helped him become the first American to win an Olympic gold medal in kayaking.

Barton was raised on a pig farm in the southern Michigan town of Homer. He says farm chores—early in the morning before work and late in the evenings after—developed the discipline necessary to succeed.

"I do the sport because I enjoy it, not because there is a lot of payoff," he told the *Detroit Free Press* at the 1988 Games in Seoul. "You don't see kayakers get rich or famous. It's a personal goal for myself to see if I can be the best in the world."

Barton is an engineering graduate of the University of Michigan. He learned to paddle on the streams, lakes, and rivers of his native state. His parents introduced him to the sport when he was young.

"It's always fun to be outside and to pull on the paddle and feel the boat accelerate under your body," says Barton, who is known for his precise paddling technique.

As a youth Barton, who now lives in Bellingham, Washington, and works as a mechanical engineer for a kayak design firm, wasn't solely a paddler. Despite being born with club feet, he wrestled and ran cross country in high school.

"I was born with this problem," he told *Olympian* magazine in the summer of 1989. "Ten years ago, I had some surgery, but instead of helping, my feet ended up a lot worse. The doctor fused the bones together—so I lost a lot of motion in my ankles; mostly my ankles and calves are messed up and one leg ended up shorter then the other. I'm in no hurry for surgery."

He knows, then, what it is to work and overcome obstacles—in life and in kayak racing.

"Towards the end of a race," he says, "your whole body is numb, in agony."

133

Barton was world champion in one kayaking event in 1985—the first American to win a world title in the sport—and champ in two events in 1987.

"To people who know the sport and really compete in it, the world championships are just as important as the Olympics," said Barton, whose bronze medal at the 1984 Games in Los Angeles is considered by most to be the catalyst for the development of competitive kayaking in the U.S. "But with the Olympics, there is so much more attention."

The bronze medal he won in LA was the first Olympic bronze won by a U.S. kayaker in more than 20 years.

Barton, who also was a member of the 1980 team that did not compete in Moscow, topped off his ascension by beating Australia's Grant Davies—3:55.27 to 3:55.28—in the singles 1000m event at Seoul.

The win didn't come without some extra, well, numbness. To Barton's amazement, Davies was proclaimed the winner on the venue's electronic scoreboard, even though it appeared as though Barton had eked across the finish line first.

Said Barton: "I looked up at the scoreboard and I said, 'Oh, man, I hope someone is up in the photo-finish room.'"

The judges were. Barton already had signed the finish sheet as the runner-up when the panel, after studying a freeze-frame film for 10 minutes, reversed the decision.

Charles Dambach, chairman of the U.S. team, said the finish might have been closer than 0.01 of a second.

"It was five 1,000ths of a second," he said. "But the official results don't go that far."

And just how close is that?

"They actually considered awarding two gold medals," Dambach said.

Barton said he felt happy, but "kind of bad for Grant."

"They must have slowed down the tape and studied it," Davies said. "It's pretty disappointing, but Greg won fair and square. If that's my biggest disappointment in life, I can handle that. It's an honor to be that close to Greg."

Before the event, Barton had said, "Two medals is a real possibility, but it's tough doing two in a day. It's a rare combination." But less than 90 minutes later, Barton competed in the 1000m pairs event with teammate Norman Bellingham, of Cambridge, Massachusetts, and finished ahead of New Zealand. Australia took the bronze.

Afterward, he said: "I've been kayaking for 18 years. I've worked a long time for this. Winning two golds is just the icing on the cake. I'm kind of basking in the glory."

Indeed.

Barton took a year off after the Seoul Games and returned to competition in 1990. He finished third in the 1000m singles in the 1991 World Championships at Paris, and first in the non-Olympic 10,000m singles. Finishing second in 1000m singles in the pre-Olympic Regatta in Barcelona, he was a favorite to repeat that performance at the Barcelona Games, but settled for bronze. With teammate Norman Bellingham, Barton was also favored to win a silver in the 1000m two-man event at the 1992 Games, but that was not to be.

In 1994 Barton competed professionally in the Finlandia Vodka Clean Water Challenge, a month-long endurance race that travels 1,000 miles through all weather conditions and traces a route from Chicago to New York City. Barton won that race and defended his title in the 1995 contest.

—*Eric Kinkopf*

Medalists

Canoe/Kayak — Men's Canadian Singles, 500 Meters

1992
1. Nikolai Boukhalov, Bulgaria, 1:51.15
2. Mikhail Slivinski, Ukraine, 1:51.40
3. Olaf Heukrodt, Germany, 1:53.00

1988
1. Olaf Heukrodt, East Germany, 1:56.42
2. Mikhail Slivinski, Soviet Union, 1:57.26
3. Martin Marinov, Bulgaria, 1:57.27

1984
1. Larry Cain, Canada, 1:57.01
2. Henning L. Jakobsen, Denmark, 1:58.45
3. Costica Olaru, Romania, 1:59.86

1980
1. Sergei Postrekhin, Soviet Union, 1:53.37
2. Liubomir Liubenov, Bulgaria, 1:53.49
3. Olaf Heukrodt, East Germany, 1:54.38

1976
1. Aleksandr Rogov, Soviet Union, 1:59.23
2. John Wood, Canada, 1:59.58
3. Matija Ljubek, Yugoslavia, 1:59.60

Canoe/Kayak — Men's Canadian Singles, 1,000 Meters

1992
1. Nikolai Boukhalov, Bulgaria, 4:05.92
2. Ivans Klementjevs, Latvia, 4:06.60
3. Gyorgy Zala, Hungary, 4:07.35

1988
1. Ivan Klementiev, Soviet Union, 4:12.78
2. Joerg Schmidt, East Germany, 4:15.83
3. Nikolai Boukhalov, Bulgaria, 4:18.94

1984
1. Ulrich Eicke, West Germany, 4:06.32
2. Larry Cain, Canada, 4:08.67
3. Henning L. Jakobsen, Denmark, 4:09.51

1980
1. Liubomir Liubenov, Bulgaria, 4:12.38
2. Sergei Postrekhin, Soviet Union, 4:13.53
3. Eckhard Leue, East Germany, 4:15.02

1976
1. Matija Ljubek, Yugoslavia, 4:09.51
2. Vassili Urchenko, Soviet Union, 4:12.57
3. Tamas Wichmann, Hungary, 4:14.11

1972
1. Ivan Patzaichin, Romania, 4:08.94
2. Tamas Wichmann, Hungary, 4:12.42
3. Detlef Lewe, West Germany, 4:13.63

1968
1. Tibor Tatai, Hungary, 4:36.14
2. Detlef Lewe, West Germany, 4:38.31
3. Vitali Galkov, Soviet Union, 4:40.42

1964
1. Jurgen Eschert, East Germany, 4:35.14
2. Andrei Igorov, Romania, 4:37.89
3. Yevgeny Penyayev, Soviet Union, 4:38.31

1960
1. Janos Parti, Hungary, 4:33.93
2. Aleksandr Silayev, Soviet Union, 4:34.41
3. Leon Rotman, Romania, 4:35.87

1956
1. Leon Rotman, Romania, 5:05.3
2. Istvan Hernek, Hungary, 5:06.2
3. Gennady Bukharin, Soviet Union, 5:12.7

1952
1. Josef Holecek, Czechosolavakia, 4:56.3
2. Janos Parti, Hungary, 5:03.6
3. Olavi Ojanpera, Finland, 5:08.5

1948
1. Josef Holecek, Czechoslovakia, 5:42.0
2. Douglas Bennett, Canada, 5:53.3
3. Robert Boutigny, France, 5:55.9

1936
1. Francis Amyot, Canada, 5:32.1
2. Bohuslav Karlik, Czechoslovakia, 5:36.9
3. Erich Koschik, Germany, 5:39.0

1896–1932
Not held

Canoe/Kayak—Men's Canadian Singles, Slalom

1992
1. Lukas Pollert, Czechoslovakia, 113.69
2. Gareth Marriott, Britain, 116.48
3. Jacky Avril, France, 117.18

Canoe/Kayak—Men's Canadian Pairs, 500 Meters

1992
1. Unified Team (Alexandre Masseikov, Dmitri Dovgalenok), 1:41.54
2. Germany (Ulrich Papke, Ingo Spelly), 1:41.68
3. Bulgaria (Martin Marinov, Blagovest Stoyanov), 1:41.84

1988
1. Soviet Union, 1:41.77. Victor Reneiski, Nikolai Jouravski
2. Poland, 1:43.61, Marek Dopierala, Marek Lbik
3. France, 1:43.81, Phillipe Renaud, Joel Bettin

1984
1. Yugoslavia, 1:43.67, Matija Ljub, Mirko Nisovic
2. Romania, 1:45.68, Ivan Potzaichin, Toma Simionov
3. Spain, 1:47.71, Enrique Miguez, Narcisco Suarez

1980
1. Hungary, 1:43.39, Laszlo Fultan, Istvan Vaskuti
2. Romania, 1:44.12, Ivan Patzaichin, Petre Capusta
3. Bulgaria, 1:44.83, Borislav Ananiev, Nikolai Ilkov

1976
1. Soviet Union, 1:45.81 Sergei Petrenko, Aleksandr Vonogradov
2. Poland, 1:47.77, Jerzy Opara, Andrzej Gronowicz
3. Hungary, 1:48.35, Tamas Buday, Oszkar Frey

Canoe/Kayak—Men's Canadian Pairs, 1,000 Meters

1992
1. Germany (Ulrich Papke, Ingo Spelly), 3:37.42
2. Denmark (Arne Nielsson, Christian Frederiksen), 3:39.26
3. France (Didier Hoyer, Olivier Boivin), 3:39.51

1988
1. Soviet Union, 3:48.36, Victor Reneiski, Nikolai Jouravski
2. East Germany, 3:51.44, Olaf Heukrodt, Ingo Spelly
3. Poland, 3:54.33, Marek Dopierala, Marek Lbik

1984
1. Romania, 3:40.60, Ivan Potzaichin, Toma Simionov
2. Yugoslavia, 3:41.56, Matija Ljubek, Mirko Nisovic
3. France, 3:48.01, Didier Hoyer, Eric Renaud

1980
1. Romania, 3:47.65, Ivan Patzaichin, Toma Simionov
2. East Germany, 3:49.93, Olaf Heukrodt, Uwe Madeja

3. Soviet Union, 3:51.28, Vassili Yurchenko, Yuri Lobanov

1976

1. Soviet Union, 3:52.76, Sergei Petrenko, Aleksandr Vinogradov
2. Romania, 3:54.28, Gheorghe Danilov, Gheorghe Simionov
3. Hungary, 3:55.66, Tamas Buday, Oszkar Frey

1972

1. Soviet Union, 3:52.60, Vladas Chessyunas, Yuri Lobanov
2. Romania, 3:52.63, Ivan Patzaichin, Serghei Covaliov
3. Bulgaria, 3:58.10, Fredja Damjanow, Iwan Burtschin

1968

1. Romania, 4:07.18, Ivan Patzaichin, Serahei Covaliov
2. Hungary, 4:08.77, Tamas Wichmann, Gyula Petrikovics
3. Soviet Union, 4:11.30, Naum Prokupets, Mikhail Zamotin

1964

1. Soviet Union, 4:04.64, Andrei Khimich, Stepan Oschepkov
2. France, 4:06.52, Jean Boudehen, Michel Chapuis
3. Denmark, 4:07.48, Peer Norrbohm Nielsen, John R. Sorensen

1960

1. Soviet Union, 4:17.94, Leonid Geischtor, Sergei Makarenko
2. Italy, 4:20.77, Aldo Dezi, Francesco La Macchia
3. Hungary, 4:20.89, Imre Farkas, Andras Toro

1956

1. Romania, 4:47.4, Alexe Dumitru, Simion Ismailciuc
2. Soviet Union, 4:48.6, Pavel Kharin, Gratsian Botev
3. Hungary, 4:54.3, Karoly Wieland, Ferenc Mohacsi

1952

1. Denmark, 4:38.3, Bent Peder Rasch, Finn Haunstoft
2. Czechoslovakia, 4:42.9, Jan-Felix Brzak, Bohumil Kudrna
3. Germany, 4:48.3, Egon Drews, Wilfried Soltau

1948

1. Czechoslovakia, 5:07.1, Jan-Felix Brzak, Bohumil Kudrna
2. U.S.A, 5:08.2, Stephen Lysak, Stephen Macknowski
3. France, 5:15.2, Georges Dransart, Georges Gandil

1936

1. Czechoslovakia, 4:50.1, Vladimir Syrovatka, Jan-Felix Brzak
2. Austria, 4:53.8, Rupert Weinstabl, Karl Proisl
3. Canada, 4:56.7, Frank Saker, Harvey Charters

1896–1932

Not held

Canoe/Kayak—Men's Canadian Pairs, Slalom

1992

1. U.S.A. (Scott Strausbaugh and Joe Jacobi), 122.41
2. Czechoslovakia (Miroslav Simek and Jiri Rohan), 124.25
3. France (Franck Adisson and Wilfrid Forgues), 124.38

Canoe/Kayak—Men's Kayak Singles, 500 Meters

1992

1. Mikko Yrjoe Kolehmainen, Finland, 140.34
2. Zsolt Gyulay, Hungary, 140.64
3. Knut Holmann, Norway, 140.71

1988

1. Zsolt Gyulay, Hungary, 1:44.82
2. Andreas Staehle, East Germany, 1:46.38
3. Paul MacDonald, New Zealand, 1:46.46

1984

1. Ian Ferguson, New Zealand, 1:47.84
2. Lars-Erik Moberg, Sweden, 1:48.18
3. Bernard Bregeon, France, 1:48.41

1980

1. Vladimir Parfenovich, Soviet Union, 1:43.43
2. John Sumegi, Australia, 1:44.12
3. Vasile Diba, Romania, 1:44.90

1976

1. Vasile Diba, Romania, 1:46.41
2. Zoltan Sztanity, Hungary, 1:46.96
3. Rudiger Helm, East Germany, 1:48.30

Canoe/Kayak—Men's Kayak Singles, 1,000 Meters

1992
1. Clint Robinson, Australia, 3:37.26
2. Knut Holmann, Norway, 3:37.50
3. Greg Barton, U.S.A., 3:37.93

1988
1. Greg Barton, U.S.A, 3:55.27
2. Grant Davies, Australia, 3:55.28
3. Andre Wohllebe, East Germany, 3:55.55

1984
1. Alan Thompson, New Zealand, 3:45.73
2. Milan Janic, Yugoslavia, 3:46.88
3. Greg Barton, U.S.A, 3:47.38

1980
1. Rudiger Helm, East Germany, 3:48.77
2. Alain Lebas, France, 3:50.20
3. Ion Birladeanu, Romania, 3:50.49

1976
1. Rudiger Helm, East Germany, 3:48.20
2. Geza Csapo, Hungary, 3:48.84
3. Vasile Diba, Romania, 3:49.65

1972
1. Aleksandr Shaparenko, Soviet Union, 3:48.06
2. Rolf Peterson, Sweden, 3:48.35
3. Geza Csapo, Hungary, 3:49.38

1968
1. Mihaly Hesz, Hungary, 4:02.63
2. Aleksandr Shaparenko, Soviet Union, 4:03.58
3. Erik Hansen, Denmark, 4:04.39

1964
1. Rolf Peterson, Sweden, 3:57.13
2. Mihaly Hesz, Hungary, 3:57.28
3. Aurel Vernescu, Romania, 4:00.77

1960
1. Erik Hansen, Denmark, 3:53.00
2. Imre Szollosi, Hungary, 3:54.02
3. Gert Fredriksson, Sweden, 3:55.89

1956
1. Gert Fredriksson, Sweden, 4:12.8
2. Igor Pissaryev, Soviet Union, 4:15.3
3. Lajos Kiss, Hungary, 4:16.2

1952
1. Gert Fredriksson, Sweden, 4:07.9
2. Thorvald Stromberg, Finland, 4:09.7
3. Louis Gantois, France, 4:20.1

1948
1. Gert Fredriksson, Sweden, 4:33.2

2. Johann F. Kobberup, Denmark, 4:39.9
3. Henri Eberhardt, France 4:41.4

1936
1. Gregor Hradetzky, Austria, 4:22.9
2. Helmut Cammarer, Germany, 4:25.6
3. Jacob Kraaier, Netherlands, 4:35.1

1896–1932
Not held

Canoe/Kayak—Men's Kayak Singles, Slalom

1992
1. Pierpaolo Ferrazzi, Italy, 106.89
2. Sylvain Curinier, France, 107.06
3. Jochen Lettmann, Germany, 108.52

Canoe/Kayak—Men's Kayak Pairs, 500 Meters

1992
1. Germany (Kay Bluhm, Torsten Rene Gutsche), 1:28.27
2. Poland (Maciej Freimut, Wojciech Kurpiewski), 1:29.84
3. Italy (Antonio Rossi, Bruno Dreossi), 1:30.00

1988
1. New Zealand, 1:33.98, Ian Ferguson, Paul MacDonald
2. Soviet Union, 1:34.15, Igor Nagaev, Victor Denissov
3. Hungary, 1:34.32, Attila Abraham, Ferenc Csipes

1984
1. New Zealand, 1:34.21, Ian Ferguson, Paul McDonald
2. Sweden, 1:35.26, Per-Inge Bengtsson, Lars-Erik Moberg
3. Canada, 1:35.41, Hugh Fisher, Alwyn Morris

1980
1. Soviet Union, 1:32.38, Vladimir Parfenovich, Sergei Chukhrai
2. Spain, 1:33.65, Herminio Menendez, Guillermo del Riego
3. East Germany, 1:34.00, Rudiger Helm, Bernd Olbricht

1976
1. East Germany, 1:35.87, Bernd Olbricht, Joachim Mattern, 1:35.87
2. Soviet Union, 1:36.81, Vladimir Romanovsky, Sergei Nagorny
3. Romania, 1:37.43, Laria Serghei, Policarp Malihin 37.43, Larion Serghei, Policarp Malihin

Canoe/Kayak—Men's Kayak Pairs, 1,000 Meters

1992
1. Germany (Kay Bluhm, Torsten Gutsche), 3:16.10
2. Sweden (Gunnar Olsson, Karl Sundqvist), 3:17.70
3. Poland (Grzegorz Kotowicz, Dariusz Bialkowski), 3:18.86

1988
1. U.S.A, 3:32.42, Greg Barton, Norman Bellingham
2. New Zealand, 3:32.71, Ian Ferguson, Paul MacDonald
3. Australia, 3:33.76, Peter Foster, Kelvin Graham

1984
1. Canada, 3:24.22, Hugh Fisher, Alwyn Morris
2. France, 3:25.97, Bernard Bregeon, Patrick Lefoulon
3. Australia, 3:26.80, Barry Kelly, Grant Kenny

1980
1. Soviet Union, 3:26.72, Vladimir Parfenovich, Sergei Chukhrai
2. Hungary, 3:28.49, Istvan Szabo, Istvan Joos
3. Spain, 3:28.66, Luis Ramos-Misione, Herminio Menendez

1976
1. Soviet Union, 3:29.01, Sergei Nagorny, Vladimir Romanovsky
2. East Germany, 3:29.33, Bernd Olbricht, Joachim Mattern
3. Hungary, 3:30.36, Istvan Szabo, Zoltan Balko

1972
1. Soviet Union, 3:31.23, Nikolai Gorbachev, Viktor Kratassyuk
2. Hungary, 3:32.00, Jozsef Deme, Janos Ratkai
3. Poland, 3:33.83, Wladyslaw Szuszkiewicz, Rafal Piszcz

1968
1. Soviet Union, 3:37.54, Aleksandr Shaparenko, Vladimir Morozov
2. Hungary, 3:38.44, Csaba Giczi, Istvan Timar
3. Austria, 3:40.71, Gerhard Seibold, Gunther Pfaff

1964
1. Sweden, 3:38.54, Sven-Olov Sjodelius, Gunnar Utterberg
2. Netherlands, 3:39.30, Antonius Geurts, Paul Hoekstra
3. West Germany, 3:40.69, Heinz Buker, Holger Zander

1960
1. Sweden, 3:34.73, Gert Fredriksson, Sven-Olov Sjodelius
2. Hungary, 3:34.91, Gyorgy Meszaros, Andras Szente
3. Poland, 3:37.34, Stefan Kaplaniak, Wladyslaw Zielinski

1956
1. West Germany, 3:49.6, Michel Scheuer, Meinrad Miltenberger
2. Soviet Union, 3:51.4, Mikhail Kaaleste, Anatoli Demitkov
3. Austria, 3:55.8, Max Raub, Herbert Wiedermann

1952
1. Finland, 3:51.1, Kurt Wires, Yrjo Hietanen
2. Sweden, 3:51.1, Lars Glasser, Ingemar Hedberg
3. Austria, 3:51.4, Max Raub, Herbert Wiedermann

1948
1. Sweden, 4:07.3, Hans Berglund, Lennart Klingstrom
2. Denmark, 4:07.5, Ejvind Hansen, Bernhard Jensen
3. Finland, 4:08.7, Thor Axelsson, Nils Bjorklof

1936
1. Austria, 4:03.8, Adolf Kainz, Alfons Dorfner
2. Germany, 4:08.9, Ewald Tilker, Fritz Bondroit
3. Netherlands, 4:12.2, Nicolaas Tates, Willem F. van der Kroft

1896–1932
Not held

Canoe/Kayak—Men's Kayak Fours, 1,000 Meters

1992
1. Germany (Mario Von Appen, Oliver Kegel, Thomas Reineck, Andre Wohllebe), 2:54.18
2. Hungary (Ferenc Csipes, Zsolt Gyulay, Laszlo Fidel, Attila Abraham), 2:54.82
3. Australia (Kelvin Graham, Ian Rowling, Steven Wood, Ramon Andersson), 2:56.97

1988
1. Hungary, 3:00.20, Zsolt Gyulag, Ferenc Csipes, Sandor Hodosi, Attila Abraham
2. Soviet Union, 3:01.40, Alexandre Motouzenko, Sergei Kirsanov, Igor Nagaev, Victor Denissov
3. East Germany, 3:02.37, Kay Bluhm, Andre Wohllebe, Andreas Staehle, Hans-Joerg Bliesener

1984

1. New Zealand, 3:02.28, Grant Bramwell, Ian Ferguson, Paul McDonald, Alan Thompson
2. Sweden, 3:02.81, Per-Inge Bengtsson, Tommy Karls, Lars-Erik Moberg, Thomas Ohisson
3. France, 3:03.94, Francois Barouh, Philippe Boccara, Pascal Boucherit, Didier Vavasseur

1980

1. East Germany, 3:13.76, Rudiger Helm, Bernd Olbricht, Harold Marg, Bernd Duvigneau
2. Romania, 3:15.35, Mihai Zafiu, Vasile Diba, Ion Geanta, Nicusor Eseanu
3. Bulgaria, 3:15.46, Borislav Borisov, Bozhidar Milenkov, Lazar Khristov, Ivan Manev

1976

1. Soviet Union, 3:06.69, Sergei Chukhrai, Aleksandr Degtiarev, Yuri Filatov, Vladimir Morozov
2. Spain, 3:08.95, Jose M. Esteban, Jose R. Lopez, Herminio Menendez, Luis G. Ramos
3. East Germany, 3:10.76 Rudiger Helm, Frank-Peter Bischof, Juergen Lehnert, Bernd Duvigneau

1972

1. Soviet Union, 3:14.02, Yuri Filatov, Yuri Stezenko, Vladimir Morozov, Valeri Didenko
2. Romania, 3:15.07, Aurel Vernescu, Mihai Zafiu, Roman Vartolomeu, Atanase Sciotnic
3. Norway, 3:15.27, Egil Soby, Steinar Amundsen, Tore Berger, Jan Johansen

1968

1. Norway, 3:14.38, Steinar Amundsen, Egil Soby, Tore Berger, Jan Johansen
2. Romania, 3:14.81, Anton Calenic, Dimitrie Ivanov, Haralambie Ivanov, Mihai Turcas
3. Hungary, 3:15.10, Csaba Giczi, Istvan Timar, Imre Szollosi, Istvan Csizmadia

1964

1. Soviet Union, 3:14.67, Nikolai Tschuschikow, Anatoli Grischin, Vyacheslav Ionovw, Vladimir Morozov
2. West Germany, 3:15.39, Gunther Perleberg, Bernhard Schulze, Friedhelm Wentzke, Holger Zander
3. Romania, 3:15.51, Simion Cuciuc, Atanase Sciotnic, Mihai Turcas, Aurel Vernescu

1896–1960

Not held

Canoe/Kayak—Women's Kayak Singles, 500 Meters

1992

1. Birgit Schmidt, Germany, 1:51.60
2. Rita Koban, Hungary, 1:51.96
3. Izabella Dylewska, Poland, 1:52.36

1988

1. Vania Guecheva, Bulgaria, 1:55.19
2. Birgit Schmidt, East Germany, 1:55.31
3. Izabela Dylewska, Poland, 1:57.38

1984

1. Agneta Andersson, Sweden, 1:58.72
2. Barbara Schuttpelz, West Germany, 1:59.93
3. Annemiek Derckx, Netherlands, 2:00.11

1980

1. Birgit Fischer, East Germany, 1:57.96
2. Vania Gecheva, Bulgaria, 1:59.48
3. Antonina Melnikova, Soviet Union, 1:59.66

1976

1. Carola Drechsler-Zirzow, East Germany, 2:01.05
2. Tatiana Korshunova, Soviet Union, 2:03.07
3. Klara Rajnai, Hungary, 2:05.01

1972

1. Yulia Ryabchinskaya, Soviet Union, 2:03.17
2. Mieke Jaapies, Netherlands, 2:04.03
3. Anna Pfeffer, Hungary, 2:05.50

1968

1. Lyudmila Pinayeva-Khvedosyuk, Soviet Union, 2:11.09
2. Renate Breuer, West Germany, 2:12.71
3. Viorica Dumitru, Romania, 2:13.22

1964

1. Lyudmila Khvedosyuk, Soviet Union, 2:12.87
2. Hilde Lauer, Romania, 2:15.35
3. Marcia Jones, U.S.A, 2:15.68

1960

1. Antonina Seredina, Soviet Union, 2:08.08
2. Therese Zenz, West Germany, 2:08.22
3. Daniela Walkowiak, Poland, 2:10.46

1956

1. Yelisaveta Dementyeva, Soviet Union, 2:18.9
2. Therese Zenz, West Germany, 2:19. 6
3. Tove Soby, Denmark, 2:22.3

1952

1. Sylvi Saimo, Finland, 2:18.4
2. Gertrude Liebhart, Austria, 2:18.8
3. Nina Savina, Soviet Union, 2:21.6

1948
1. Karen Hoff, Denmark, 2:31.9
2. Alida van der AnkerDoekans, Netherlands, 2:32.8
3. Fritzi Schwingl, Austria, 2:32.9

1896–1936
Not held

Canoe/Kayak—Women's Kayak Singles, Slalom
1992
1. Elisabeth Micheler, Germany, 126.41
2. Danielle Woodward, Australia, 128.27
3. Dana Chladek, U.S.A., 131.75

Canoe/Kayak—Women's Kayak Pairs, 500 Meters
1992
1. Germany (Ramona Portwich, Anke Von Seck), 140.29
2. Sweden (Susanne Gunnarsson, Agneta Andersson), 140.41
3. Hungary (Rita Koban, Eva Donusz), 140.81

1988
1. East Germany, 1:43.46, Birgit Schmidt, Anke Nothnagel
2. Bulgaria, 1:44.06, Vania Guecheva, Diana Paliiska
3. Netherlands, 1:46.00, Annemiek Derckx, Annemarie Cox

1984
1. Sweden, 1:45.25, Agneta Anderson, Anna Olsson
2. Canada, 1:47.13, Alexandra Barre, Sue Holloway
3. West Germany, 1:47.32. Josefa Idem, Barbara Schuttpelz

1980
1. East Germany, 1:43.88, Carsta Genauss, Martina Bischof
2. Soviet Union, 1:46.91, Galina Alekseyeva, Nina Trofimova
3. Hungary, 1:47.95, Eva Rakusz, Maria Zakarias

1976
1. Soviet Union, 1:51.15, Nina Popova, Galina Kreft
2. Hungary, 1:51.69, Anna Pfeffer, Klara Rajnai
3. East Germany, 1:51.81, Barbel Madhaus-Koester, Carola Drechsler-Zirzow

1972
1. Soviet Union, 1:53.50, Lyudmila Pinayeva-Khvedosyuk, Jekaterina Kuryshko

2. East Germany, 1:54.30, Ilse Kaschube, Petra Grabowski
3. Romania, 1:55.01, Maria Nichiforov, Viorica Dumitru

1968
1. West Germany, 1:56.44, Roswitha Esser, Annemarie Zimmermann
2. Hungary, 1:58.60, Anna Pfeffer, Katalin Rozsnyoi
3. Soviet Union, 1:58.61, Lyudmila Pinayeva-Khvedosyuk, Antonina Seredina

1964
1. West Germany, 1:56.95, Roswitha Esser, Annemarie Zimmermann
2. U.S.A, 1:59.16, Francine Fox, Gloriane Perrier
3. Romania, 2:00.25, Hilde Lauer, Cornelia Sideri

1960
1. Soviet Union, 1:54.76, Maria Chubina, Antonina Seredina
2. West Germany, 1:56.66 Therese Zenz, Ingrid Hartmann
3. Hungary, 1:58.22, Klara Fried-Banfalvi, Vilma Egresi

1896–1956
Not held

Canoe/Kayak—Women's Kayak Fours, 500 Meters
1992
1. Hungary (Eva Donusz, Kinga Czigany, Erika Meszaros, Rita Koban), 1:38.32
2. Germany (Katrin Borchert, Birgit Schmidt, Anke Von Seck, Ramona Portwich), 1:38.47
3. Sweden (Anna Olsson, Maria Haglund, Susanne Rosenqvist, Agneta Andersson), 1:39.79

1988
1. East Germany, 1:40.78, Birgit Schmidt, Anke Nothnagel, Ramona Portwich, Heike Singer
2. Hungary, 1:41.88, Erika Geczi, Erika Meszaros, Eva Rakusz, Rita Koban
3. Bulgaria, 1:42.63, Vania Guecheva, Diana Paliiska, Ogniana Petkova. Borislava Ivanova

1984
1. Romania, 1:38.34, Agafia Constantin, Nastasia Ionescu, Tecia Marinescu, Maria Stefan
2. Sweden, 1:38.87, Agneta Andersson, Anna Olsson, Eva Karlsson, Susanne Wiberg
3. Canada, 1:39.40, Alexandra Barre, Lucie Guay, Sue Holloway, Barb Olmsted

Canoe/Kayak

Trivia Quiz

1. A Rob Roy is
a. A difficult whitewater maneuver
b. A canoe design based on an eskimo kayak
c. The preferred sports drink of whitewater slalom experts

2. The "Canadian canoe" design—popular today among recreational paddlers—was first developed by
a. Penobscot boatbuilders   b. Members of the New York Canoe Club
c. The R&D department at Coleman, Inc.

3. The Tlinget people of the Pacific Northwest were renowned for
a. Beautiful strip canoes   b. Dugout canoes made from whole trees
c. Kevlar kayaks

4. Eskimos originally waterproofed their kayaks by treating sea lion skins with
a. Parrafin   b. Whale fat   c. Scotchguard

5. The first commodore of the Royal Canoe Club was
a. Rob Roy   b. Winston Churchill   c. The Prince of Wales

6. Folding kayaks were first developed
a. In 1982, in response to requests by weekend paddlers
b. In the 1920s, and were later used for Allied Special Forces missions during WWII
c. By the Wenonah tribe, who used them to move between settlements

7. Canoeing made its first Olympic appearance
a. As an exhibition regatta at the 1924 Paris Games
b. In 1960, at the Squaw Valley Games
c. In 1908, at the London Games

8. The first women's event, the 500-m kayak singles, was first added to the Olympic roster
a. In Montreal, in 1976   b. In Barcelona, in 1992   c. In London, in 1948

9. The 1964 Tokyo Games replaced the relay race with
a. A folding-boat event   b. A four-man kayak event
c. A whitewater slalom event

10. What U.S. athlete collected two canoe/kayak gold medals in 1988?
a. Dana Chladek   b. Greg Barton   c. Bo Jackson

Answers: 1-b, 2-a, 3-b, 4-b, 5-c, 6-b, 7-a, 8-b, 9-b, 10-b

142

Cycling — Mountain Biking

Warm-up

Sometime in the mid-1970s—just as northern California's tenure as the hotbed of hippie culture was beginning to wane—a fat-tire fraternity began to coalesce in the foothills of Marin County, not far from San Francisco. A handful of road racers, many of them members of Velo Club-Tamalpais, unwittingly—and irreversibly—changed the sport of cycling; and almost overnight.

Joe Breeze, Gary Fisher, Tom Ritchey—riders now revered as the Brahmin of mountain bike frame builders—together with a covey of like-minded adrenaline-junkies, began to make a regular pilgrimage to the base of Mount Tamalpais. Pushing their 50-pound balloon-tired steeds up Mount Tam—a 2,600-foot summit criss-crossed by trails and fireroads—they launched a kamikaze time trial from the top. The object was simple: To finish the two-mile, 1,300-foot descent first. And in one piece.

This required a bit of technical ingenuity. Having bought up most of the area's eligible frames—most of which had seen a paper route or two in a previous incarnation—the "Repack" racers, as they were dubbed, grafted parts from BMX bikes, tandems, and even motorbikes. The resulting hybrid creature—a "klunker"—had a derailleur system that allowed the rider to shift into a progressively bigger gear as the bike plummeted toward the base of the hill; and tenacious brakes. By the end of a run, the brakes were often smoking-hot, and riders had to pack the coaster

"Early in the going, we really just thought [the Repack, the first mountain bike race] was too radical for anyone to continue to do. I can't think of an immediate analogy, maybe snowshoe racing or something like it that very few people would care to continue to do for very long."
— Charlie Kelly, organizer of the Repack race

brake bearings in grease before attempting another breakneck descent (repack—get it?).

As this core group of proto-mountain bikers continued to experiment, bike frames and componentry became increasingly refined. In 1977, Joe Breeze crafted nine signature bikes, with custom frames and multiple gears. The following year, Tom Ritchey designed the first mountain bike to have a diamond-shaped frame—like a road-racing bike—rather than the cantilever frame design that was common to the Schwinn paper-route model. And in 1981, Mike Sinyard, the founder of Specialized Bicycle Components, rolled out the first mass-produced (and Far East-sourced) mountain bike. A seismic shift would soon rock the industry. Once a lark, mountain bicycling had caught on like a California fire: Today, industry experts estimate that mountain bike sales account for a whopping two-thirds of full-size bike sales.

The evolution of mountain bike racing has been no less mercurial. By 1987—a little over ten years after the first kamikaze descent down Mount Tam—a National Championship Series was already in place. Sponsored by the National Off-Road Bike Association (NORBA), the sport's governing body in the U.S., the series had no title sponsor—and therefore no purse. Undaunted by the lack of financial reward, a deep field of talented riders—among them Sarah Ballantyne, Lisa Muhich, Ned Overend, and John Tomac—competed for the national title. In 1989, riders vied for a piece of the first NCS cash purse, which, at $5,000, didn't buy many burritos.

"You've got to save a little something for the end. That's where it's won or lost."
—John Tomac

As corporate sponsors began to jump on the bandwagon, NCS funding—and television exposure—continued to grow. Meanwhile, mountain bike fever had been spreading through Europe. The 1986 Alpi Cup—an off-road series that staged races in Austria, France, Germany, Italy, and Switzerland—soon caught the eye of Grundig, a German electronics behemoth that was looking to revamp its corporate image. In 1988, the erstwhile Alpi Cup became the Grundig Challenge. A scant three years later, the Union Cycliste Internationale (UCI), bicycling's international governing body, sanctioned the event as a World Cup series, with individual races to be held on both sides of the Atlantic.

The International Olympic Committee looks for a number of things when considering whether to add a sport to the burgeoning Olympic menu. First, a sport must be "widely" played on three continents. As one of the fastest-growing leisure sports in the world, mountain biking was a shoo-in on this account: In the U.S. alone, 15 million people were riding mountain bikes in 1990. And elite competitions have a global draw: 45 countries competed in the 1994 World Cup championships. Next, a sport that's hoping to make the Olympic roster must call for what IOC poobahs deem to be "a high degree of athleticism." No problem there: It takes a high level of fitness to flirt with your anaerobic threshold one minute while maintaining the composure to navigate a screaming descent the next. All this makes for good spectating—and good TV.

Spectator's Guide

Mountain biking will debut at the Atlanta Games with two events: a men's and a women's cross-country race. NORBA defines cross country as "An individual or mass start competition which is held on a circuit course comprised of forest roads, forest or field trails and unpaved dirt or gravel roads (a minimal amount of paved road may be necessary). Downhiller Sue Fish, who eschews cross-country competitions, has her own definition: ". . . it's like getting four root canals all at once: long, drawn-out agony."

In some ways, mountain bike racing is the antithesis of road racing. Team strategy is seldom a factor. Aerodynamic considerations are nil. Obstacles are to be ridden over, and pack finishes are rare. At race's start, riders explode off the starting line to vie for a position at the head of the pack: Cross-country events are held largely on single-track, which makes it difficult—and at times impossible—to pass a rider who's blocking you.

Typically, courses consist of a circuit that's somewhere between 4 and 20 miles long. Gut-wrenching climbs, technical descents, roots, rocks, stumps, and stubble all test a rider's bike handling skills and moxy. This year's Olympic course—at the Georgia International Horse Park in Conyers, 35 miles east of Atlanta—will combine tight single-track trails, open Jeep trails, double-track, and short, steep climbs that will total over 1,000 feet per lap. A year before the Games, as the Olympic course was being constructed, the cycling community was bruit-

FACT: After much deliberation, the IOC granted mountain biking a permanent berth in the Olympics, but not without a catch: The total number of cyclists in the Olympic Games must stay the same. In order to add two dirt-bike events to the 1996 program, the team time trial—a television-unfriendly road event that included 20 teams of four riders each—was eliminated from the Atlanta Games.

ing rumors that the course would have few technical sections. If that's the case, the sport's inaugural Olympic race could have an unorthodox finish, with riders sprinting *en masse* for the line.

Knobby Talk

Bunny Hop: A technique for clearing small objects at speed.

Big Air: A term used to describe the amount of lift a rider gets by jumping or hitting a whoop-de-do.

Cannibalize: To replace bike parts during a race with components from another bike. Strictly verboten.

Endo: A graceful maneuver whereby a rider is catapulted from his or her bike as the rear wheel lifts off the ground. Similar to being bucked by a horse; always done deliberately.

Granny Gear: The smallest of a mountain bike's three chainrings, used in conjunction with the biggest sprocket. Also known as the "weeny gear," the pros use this low gear to defy physics.

On the Pegs: A technique for descending steep hills; the rider shifts her weight back, with feet positioned at 3:00 and 9:00. The term is borrowed from motorcycling argot.

Rainbow Jersey: The jersey awarded to world champions in road, track, and mountain cycling events. Highly difficult to attain.

Snake Bite: A flat tire caused by hitting an object so hard that the inner tube is punctured by the rim. The resulting two-holed puncture looks like a snake bite.

Suspension: A design feature that provides shock absorption.

Track: Said to another rider. Translation: "Outta my way or I'll leave tread marks on your back."

Hopefuls

As was befitting a sport that was spawned in the California foothills, U.S. riders were the dominant force in the early days of international mountain bike racing. In 1990, five out of the six men's, and three of the four women's first-place spots went to U.S.

riders. But sometime in the early 1990s, the tide began to shift. European riders—who enjoy races in such major cities as Rome and Berlin—began to score more of the top awards at international competitions.

In the men's cross country events, Denmark's Henrik Djernis and Switzerland's Thomas Frischknecht have defined themselves as forces to be reckoned with; among the women, Italy's Paola Pezzo has been gaining some impressive World Cup experience, and France's Jeannie Longo—a silver medalist in the Barcelona road race—has capitalized on her extensive racing background to become a potential threat in fat tire events. And then there's Canada's Alison Sydor, who's been challenging Juli Furtado's hegemony as the best women's off-road cyclist. Not that U.S. athletes haven't been turning in stunning performances; they have. But they're not alone any more.

The 1996 U.S. Olympic Mountain Bike racing squad will be selected through a series of six races, four of which will take place in 1995 and two of which are scheduled for early in the 1996 season. Among the probable contenders are six-time national champion Ned Overend, who will celebrate his forty-first birthday within a month of Atlanta's closing ceremony; David "Tinker" Juarez, the 1995 Pan Am Games gold medalist; Ruthie Matthes, 1993's World Cup runner-up; and two of the sport's winningest riders, John Tomac and Juli Furtado.

FACT: According to the International Mountain Bicycling Association, 90 percent of the 7.5 million bicycles sold in the U.S. in 1994 were fat-tire models.

Juli Furtado

It isn't easy to be labeled a Renaissance athlete in the sport of cycling. Connie Pareskevin-Young, who competed on the U.S. speedskating squad in 1980 and 1984, took home a bronze medal in cycling in the summer of 1988. Winter Games' wunderkind Eric Heiden turned his talents to the road bike, first as rider, then as coach. Even Greg LeMond—the first American ever to wear the coveted yellow jersey in the prestigious Tour de France—started out as an up-and-coming ski racer.

So it's not so astonishing that Juliana Furtado launched her athletic career as a promising youngster on the U.S. ski team. Five operations later, however, she was forced off the slopes and into physical therapy, which eventually included, among other things, riding a bike. This she did with gusto: in her first year of competitive riding, she reigned as the National Road Champion, having dispatched the field with a masochistic 60-mile solo break-away. "Skiing had come easy to me," she later told *Bicycling* magazine, "so I almost expected to excel in cycling. I never had to struggle."

Furtado's coach, David Farmer, sums her talents thus: "[She's a] natural—someone who would excel even on the tennis court. And she's extremely focused." Convinced that road racing in the U.S. was in a slump and that her "horrible sprint" would keep her from further success, Furtado turned not to the tennis courts but to the dirt trails near her Colorado homestead. There, she revealed herself to be a talented climber; an even more talented downhiller; and a consummate bike handler. In short, she was a natural. The first year of mountain biking's world cup—and Furtado's first full year off-road—the New Jersey-born phenom reigned as the world cross-country champ.

That inaugural championship title augured things to come. That same year, Furtado added a litany of NORBA first-place finishes to her resume, including the National Series overall title. Ditto the next year. What's more, she notched a World Championship victory in the downhill event, making her the first pro ever to wear the rainbow jersey in both the downhill *and* cross-country events.

FACT: Mountain biking's downhill event enjoys official status in the U.S. National Championships, the World Championships, and the World Cup. Decked in aerodynamic crash-proof garb, down-hillers sometimes reach speeds in excess of 50 miles per hour. If mountain biking organizations have their way, a downhill event will eventually be added to the Olympic program.

1993 was a year not to be believed; Furtado was unstoppable. "I felt sorry for the other girls," she admitted to *Bicycling* magazine. And with good reason. Reeling in one win after another, Furtado owned a tremendous psychological edge on the competition. She nailed every one of the six NORBA nationals *and* all but one of the ten Grundig World Cup skirmishes. In seven months' time, she collected 17 first-place finishes—out of 18 races entered.

And when Furtado won, she won big: In every World Cup victory but one, she scorched the field, winning by no less than sixty seconds. *Velo News* was impressed enough to name her 1993's Cyclist of the Year, making her the first woman to join a boys' club that includes such luminaries as Miguel Indurain, Greg LeMond, and Ned Overend.

The following year was less spectacular: Reigning for her fourth consecutive year as the NORBA women's national champion, Furtado placed *second* to Alison Sydor in the Grundig World Cup final. And—having announced in a pre-race press conference that she was off-form—she failed to place in the World Championships. The year ended with the tragedy of her mother's suicide.

Early in 1995, Furtado was "weathering the storm," although she confessed to *Velo News:* "My training has been lackadaisical. I've lacked motivation for it. But when the racing begins, I'll try my hardest—I always do." By mid-March—the eve of the Pan Am Games—she was coming out of her off-season (when she claims to train just enough to stay "sort of" in shape). The only U.S. entrant in the women's cross-country event, she worried, "Hopefully, I won't make a fool of myself and will be able to medal."

Entering the Olympic-style event with a 26-and-2 record for the previous two years, Furtado pocketed a silver medal at the Pan Am dirt fest—not bad for someone who wasn't at the top of her racing form. With her sights set for Atlanta, the GT rider should be in top form to vie for a spot on the U.S. Olympic team —and from there, for a place in history. Atlanta's winner will capture the first-ever women's Olympic mountain biking title—a feat that sounds like trademark Furtado.

> "I'm lucky that mountain biking wasn't around when I was 20, because I wouldn't have won the Tour de France."
> —Greg LeMond, 3-time Tour de France winner and 3-time world road champ

Tinker Juarez

"What I did to win the title—I still can't believe it," Tinker Juarez says of his 1995 NORBA national series victory. And with good reason. With two early season defaults, his chances of accumulating enough points at the Helen, Georgia, race to reclaim the national title looked as about as grim as the well-irrigated course did. But, as Volvo/Cannondale team manager, Josh Klein, puts it, Tinker is one dedicated rider: "He knows what he wants, and he's been learning how to put it all together for the big events. He's been able to pick the events that he wants to win."

The NORBA series final was apparently an event that Juarez wanted to win. Fresh from a comfortable victory at the penultimate NORBA showdown at Traverse City, Michigan, Juarez rousted the field at the rain-bogged Georgia course, winning by a whip-cracking seven-and-a-half minute margin. Netting enough points to grab his second consecutive national title, he did so with the maximum score possible for his best five races.

With his sights set on Olympic competition in '96, Tinker Juarez competes in a race in northern Michigan during the summer of 1995. *Marie J. MacNee*

But recapturing the national title wasn't the primary focus of Juarez's 1995 agenda. Having collected a Pan Am Games gold medal as an early-season prize, the 34-year-old Californian resolved to stake his claim to a spot on the U.S. Olympic squad. "The main thing is to build up the [Olympic selection] points," he explains, "to make it impossible to reach." Midway through the selection process, Juarez was already next-to-impossible to reach: after the third of six selection races, he led the men's Olympic point standings by a yawning forty-four point margin.

Known for years as a tactical rider who preferred to shadow race leaders, Juarez reinvented himself in the pre-Olympic season as a dominant—and relentless—race leader. "To be a leader is the main thing," he explains. "That's what they [U.S. Olympic coaches] want—a rider who will be aggressive to the end."

"[Tinker] used to never really just bolt off and lead a race," team manager Klein affirms. "He used to always race tactically. And I think just recently, his change in style is that he's just a lot stronger. It has to be. There's no other explanation. He's just killing everybody."

Stronger, undoubtedly, and more motivated. About his newfound murderous *modus operandi*, Juarez offers: "All of a sudden it just came on. I pretty much haven't changed any of my training; I've just gotten more focused because I want to be one of the chosen for the Olympics. And it's my only chance; I figure that in my career, it's the biggest thing that will ever happen, and you can't get any much bigger than this. I mean anyone that does a sport, and is competitive, like I am, the biggest thing is to make an Olympic team. And for the mountain biking to be in the Olympics, it's the perfect time in my career because I've done it long enough, and I have enough experience, so there's nothing that can hold me back from going for it. You know, there's no excuse: I mean either I do it, or I don't."

A former BMX racer, Juarez—who earned his nickname at the age of 13 because he tinkered incessantly with his bike—has had bicycling in his blood as long as he can remember. "We used to just meet every day after school and just fool around on this hill where we built jumps and did all kinds of neat things," he recalls. "When you're at a young age, BMX is acting sort of like a motorcross racer. Motorcross racers were always jumping and turning, and doing all that, and that's what I used to like doing —a lot of jumping and stuff like that. Sort of like a freestyle rider, but I was never into freestyle."

The appeal of racing was simple: "Trying to win trophies, that was the fun part," he says. "I collected a lot of trophies—probably over 1,000 trophies. I enjoyed it to the point where it just seemed like it was my life.

"I pretty much dedicated my whole life into the sport of biking," he continues, "and was kind of hoping to make a living out of cycling. My thoughts were pretty much BMX but it just kind of started slowing down—the sport itself. My career in BMX started going downhill, so to speak, after '82—just because the sport wasn't really going anywhere, sponsorships were hard to get, and you weren't making a lot. So it was kind of tough to make a career out of it if you weren't really going anywhere."

Juarez didn't discover mountain biking until 1986—at the age of 25, a veritable greybeard among BMX indigenes—when he entered a race near his mother's home on a lark—and on a cheap bike he picked up for less than $400. "I found it was really fun," he recalls. "It was like BMX, but it was more endurance. I just felt like this was a sport that I didn't know if it was going to go anywhere. It was just fun, and I was able to compete again. In '86 I was kind of like an older guy, so to speak, and it was a sport that was people my age.

"I thought that mountain biking was going to go somewhere, and it did," he continues. "I did it, it was fun—it was a weekend thing—and I was able to get a sponsor. And I was getting paid, so I was doing it as a job. At first it was enough to survive on. It wasn't much back in '86, but it was enough to make a living. And in the last few years [mountain biking has] just been a really competitive sport and it's gotten real serious. Road racing has been around for a long time and it's a competitive sport, and it's a job for the professionals that are doing it now—and that's what [mountain biking] is for me."

It's a job that Juarez takes seriously. "I look at it, when you're paid monthly . . . you've got to get between 10 and 20 hours of riding in every week. That may not sound like a lot, but on the trails, it is."

And he's not logging easy miles. "[I] make sure my riding is quality riding, not just going out with a bunch of guys and goofing off. [You've got to] go out and train hard, and focus [on] what you're doing, and keep track of what you're doing."

With his sights set on Atlanta, Juarez—who will be 35 when the Games commence—intends to plot his course to the Georgia International Horse Park carefully. "After this season," he says, "I just want to relax and put this all behind. . . . I have to focus on being ready early in the season."

Team manager Klein concurs: "He's got all winter to relax after the worlds. . . . All he has to do is do it over again. He just needs to remember to relax. He had an early goal this year—the Pan American Games—and he was going a lot faster and harder earlier than a lot of Americans. . . . I think the season next year will be ideal for him and his training techniques. There are a couple of gaps in there where I think everybody is going to sneak away and get horribly fit. And then it'll just be a big shootout."

Juarez presents a well-armed opponent. A gifted climber who attacks 16-percent grades in his big chainring, Juarez has become more confident and aggressive in his downhill technique. He has both technical and tactical savvy, and he can sprint with the best of the fast-twitch fraternity. And—something not to be underestimated in the balmy southern summer clime—he can tolerate the heat. "He's like a camel," Klein muses, "he seems to be able to go so long in the heat."

Juarez does, however, admit to a chink in his armor. "My biggest weakness," he divulges, "is racing in mud and rain." Haunted by a shoulder injury he sustained as a teenager, Juarez has trouble when it comes to shouldering the bike. "Ned [Overend and I]," he laments, "are probably the worst in the U.S. at carrying our bikes." Barring a deluge, however, the Atlanta course, which offers comparatively little climbing, should force no one to dismount—least of all an erstwhile BMX racer. And don't forget that the 1995 NORBA final, where Juarez dropped the pack with preternatural ease, was, by most mortals' reckoning, muddy.

> "[Coffee-drinking is] a big hobby for a lot of mountain bikers . . . I thought I drank a lot. But these guys [Juli Furtado and Alison Sydor, in particular] are professionals."
> —Tinker Juarez

A religiously well-prepared competitor, Juarez has a disarmingly mellow attitude toward competition. "If it's going to happen, it'll happen. You know, if you're going to have a good race, you're going to have a good race. It's just too much pressure otherwise. Your sponsor can put pressure on you, people around you can put pressure on you. You just gotta go in there and have fun and do the best you can. I mean, that's the bottom line."

Schedule

The tentative cycling schedule for mountain bike racing events is:

Tuesday, July 30
Women's & Men's individual cross country

1. The sport of mountain biking first appeared
   a. On ESPN, out of nowhere
   b. Near San Luis Obispo, in Southern California
   c. In Marin County, near San Francisco

2. This former mountain bike racer now manufactures mountain bike frames
   a. Eddy Merckx   **b.** Greg LeMond   **c.** Joe Breeze.
   d. Arnold Stumpjumper

3. The Repack race
   a. Is the most important Olympic qualifying race for the 1996 Games
   b. Is a cross-country event that begins with a time trial in which riders re-pack their brake bearings and true their wheels
   c. Was a downhill race held on Mount Tamalpais

4. The first mountain bike to have a diamond-shaped frame was designed by
   a. Neill Armstrong   **b.** Tom Ritchey   **c.** Gary Fisher

5. The first mass-produced mountain bike was manufactured by
   a. Huffy   **b.** Specialized   **c.** Gary Fisher

6. The Grundig Challenge, which was eventually sanctioned as a World Cup series, started out as
   a. The Alpine Cup   **b.** The Alpi Cup   **c.** The Alpo Cup

7. The 1996 Atlanta Games will include
   a. Downhill events only   **b.** Cross-country events only
   c. Downhill and slalom events.   **d.** Observed trials and a huffy toss

8. The first mountain biking National Championship was held in
   a. 1967   **b.** 1977   **c.** 1987

9. A rider who shouts "track" is warning another rider
   a. About an upcoming obstacle
   b. About an upcoming dismount that will require the rider to run with the bike
   c. To stay out of his or her way

10. Stage races
   a. Are the oldest form of mountain bike racing
   b. Are the only events contested in the World Cup
   c. Have not until recently been contested in mountain biking

Answers: 1-c, 2-c, 3-c, 4-b, 5-b, 6-b, 7-b, 8-c, 9-c, 10-c

Cycling — Track and Road

Warm-up

Bicycling is so familiar that we take it for granted. Cyclists, unlike street lugers, are nearly everywhere: The bike is both transportation and recreation. But though the wheel and human history are long intertwined, the bicycle is a relative newcomer.

One of the earliest bicycles—if you can call it that—was demonstrated by one Comte de Sivrac in the gardens of the Palais Royal in Paris in 1791. More of a caricature of the modern two-wheeler, the *célérifère,* as it was called, consisted of a wooden bar, with padded saddle, supported by two rather large wheels, but it didn't have pedals. These hobby horses, resembling an overgrown children's toy, moved when riders thrust their feet on the ground from side to side, while at the same time holding tightly to their dignity. The same sort of centaur-like creation is said to be pictured on a stained-glass window in Stoke Poges Church, near Windsor, England.

The riders of these contraptions formed a club and raced along the Champs Élysées. Since the front wheel was directly affixed to the frame and fork and could not swivel, racers had little control of their tenuous mounts. Straightaways were considered a blessing.

A more serious mode of transportation came in 1817 when Karl, Baron von Drais de Sauerbrun, of Mannheim, added the luxury of steering to his two-wheeler. After its public debut in the Luxembourg Gardens in 1818, the new-improved "dandy horse" or *draisienne* made quite an impression, and later became the preferred mode of transportation for some French rural postmen.

Later attempts included the tricycle and the high-wheeler, so called because the rear wheel outsized the front wheel five times over. Finally, in 1834, a Scottish blacksmith named Kirkpatrick

McMillan invented pedals with connecting rods, producing a vehicle recognizable as an early incarnation of the modern bicycle.

The first bicycle, made entirely of wood except for the iron-covered tires, was brought to the United States in 1866, where it received a lukewarm welcome. In 1868, rubber tires replaced wood and iron ones, and the first recorded bicycle race took place at Parc de Saint Cloud in France. An Englishman, James Moore, pedaled to the first official bicycle racing victory.

With the advent of the edge-cutting pneumatic tire in 1888, long-distance cycling—in these pre-automobile halcyon days— became the rage. It wasn't uncommon for bikers to trek from country to country on their trusty steeds. By the turn of the century, bicycling was a popular sport with an enthusiastic following, not least of all in the States. Racing was popular in the U.S. from the 1880s on, and grueling six-day races, held indoors at Madison Square Garden, became a national obsession in the 1920s and 1930s.

The first World Championships were held in Chicago in 1893, and cycling has been featured in the Olympics since the first Games in 1896—making cycling one of only a half-dozen sports to lay claim to a regular spot in the Olympic program. In 1903, the first Tour de France was held and soon became one of the most prestigious cycling events ever. Founded by Henri Desgranges, who set the first hour record in 1893, "Le Tour" turned bicycle racing in a new direction; no one had ever thought to stage races in sequence.

FACT: Three-time Tour de France winner Greg LeMond won't ever have a chance to fulfill his dream of capturing an Olympic medal. A rare muscle disease—mitochondrial myopathy— prevents him from competing at a high level.

Desgranges, a Parisian sports paper editor, made a sports marketing coup of the event. To this day, the Tour, dubbed "the ultimate bike race," is among the most revered cycling events.

Cycling's popularity continued to mount in Europe: France, Belgium, Italy, Switzerland, the Netherlands, Britain, and Luxembourg, in particular, took the sport to heart. Races of all sorts proliferated (and continue to thrive): the Tour of Italy tested rider's mettle in the hills, the Paris-Roubaix—christened the "tour d'enfer" or "tour of hell"—pushed the limits of the cyclists who rode over cobblestone streets.

In the States, however, the sport took a back seat to another wheeled vehicle: in the 1930s, enamored with the newly introduced automobile, America turned its back on cycling. While the sport became a national passion for a number of countries on the European continent, cycling in the U.S. finally hit its all-time low-point in the 1970s, when only a few thousand licensed racers competed. Six-day races—which had enjoyed such celebrity in the first decades of the century—ended in 1961.

In the 1980s, the sport enjoyed an about-face. Speedskating phenomenon Eric Heiden turned a few heads when he turned to cycling; a number of major corporations—such as 7 Eleven, Mohawk Carpets, and Lowenbräu Beer—sponsored cycling teams; and the energy crunch inspired many would-be couch potatoes to turn to the bike, for transportation if not for health. Add to this the success of Greg LeMond, the first American ever to win the Tour de France (he did so three times), and suddenly cycling as a competitive sport was enjoying a resurgence. By the end of the 1980s, more than 85 million cyclists were peddling in the U.S.—200,000 of whom raced their bikes, making cycling the fourth most popular weekend activity (with 21 million weekend warriors).

Spectator's Guide

Until fairly recently, the shape of the bicycle has not changed much; even now, despite ultra high-tech materials and "radical" innovations, the bike still consists of a frame, two wheels, moving contact points (the crank arms and pedals) and components for the transmission of motion (chain rings and chain).

FACT: Cycling is one of the world's most popular sports. Surpassed only by soccer, it has the second-largest number of participants in the world.

Fundamental design aside, secondary characteristics of the bike have been modified more significantly. Frame material, wheel design, and handlebar configuration (and consequently riding position) have undergone more than a few changes in recent years.

Aerodynamics—the motion of air acting on bodies in motion—is a major factor in bike racing; the less wind resistance a rider encounters, the less effort it takes to go fast.

Aerodynamic "funny bikes" debuted at the 1984 Olympic Games. With frames that often weigh as little as seven pounds, they are usually constructed of fiberglass and a synthetic composite called kevlar. Kevlar—also used in airplanes, bulletproof clothing, canoes, and other high-tech objects—is a pricey material: the 1988 Olympic bicycles each carried a $45,000 pricetag. Best suited to the pursuit and time-trial events, "funny bikes" lack the maneuverability required in pack-riding situations.

Disc wheels add to the aerodynamic efficiency of track and time-trial bikes. The wheels, which lessen the amount of wind resistance the bike encounters as it rolls, are usually made of fiberglass or kevlar, and are laminated. Heavier than standard wheels, discs are normally not desirable for events in which it is important to make sudden jumps, or increases in speed.

"Bullhorn" handlebars, another aerodynamic innovation, originated when a track racer turned his standard Maes-bend bars upside down and cut off the "drops," or what is normally the lowest part of the handlebar. Various "aero" bars, widely used among triathletes at first, later were accepted within the ranks of conservative cyclists. With this new configuration, the rider can lower the stem (the part that holds the handlebars intact with the bike frame) to ride leaning closer to the front wheel; this position decreases the amount of wind resistance created by the rider's body.

And speaking of wind resistance created by the rider's body, high-tech cycling clothing is more than a fashion statement. In 1976, the West German team was not allowed to wear their one-piece silk bodysuits, but 1981 marked a new fashion era when so-called Darth Vader helmets and rubberized skin suits were allowed in competition. And do riders shave their legs for that aerodynamic advantage? Not really; it's just that shaved legs are easier to massage, and in the event of a crash, are more easily cleaned.

The Events

Cycling consists of two distinct categories of racing: track and road. Bikes used in track events are single-geared, with no brakes. Road bikes vary among events, and are highly specialized; they can have up to 14 gears, and are built with aerodynamic qualities. While track events take place on banked tracks called velodromes, road races—as you might have guessed—take place on paved roadways.

In addition to strength, fitness, and endurance, bike racing requires strategy. A smart rider knows his or her own strengths and weaknesses, as well as those of his or her opponents. The rider must plan and use tactics that take these elements into account.

Track Competitions

Women first competed in Olympic track events in 1988, when the women's match sprint was added to the program.

Match Sprint: Riders are seeded based on 200m time trials: each cyclist is given a lap to gain momentum, and is then timed for the final "flying 200." A fast time is important because it keeps the rider from competing against the top-seeded opponents until later in the game.

In the match sprint itself, riders meet in a best-of-three competition. With no lane markings, riders use the entire width of the track, often diving from the top of the embankment to gain momentum. Often called a cat-and-mouse game, the race usually starts out at a slow pace (though it must be at least a walking pace). One rider is required to lead the first lap. A drawing takes place prior to the first sprint to determine which rider will take the inside position during the first lap, and riders switch position each race thereafter. Riders constantly jockey for position during the second lap, attempting to position themselves in front of or behind their competitors, depending on their preference and how they've read the competition. Sometimes the riders use a "track stand"—where both remain motionless and balanced on the track—to attempt to force another rider into the lead. The third and final lap, the "bell lap," is a sprint to the finish; the final 200 meters of the race is timed.

Individual Pursuit: Two riders, positioned exactly opposite to each other on the track, chase each other in circles . . . sort of.

A rider can win the race in one of two ways: by passing the other rider, or by recording the fastest time. Times are posted when the rider reaches each half lap: each rider may have one—and only one—person announce his or her times. If both riders post the same time at the finish, they are placed according to the better time at the end of the previous lap.

Both endurance and speed are important in the individual pursuit, and riders' strategies vary. Some start out slow, lulling the competition into a false sense of security, to come on strong at the end; others go out fast, to rattle the opponent's confidence. Women competed in this event for the first time at the 1992 Games.

Team Pursuit: The team pursuit follows the same guidelines as the individual, except that a team of four rides as a unit. The winner of the race is determined when the third member of the fastest team crosses the finish line, at which point the time is recorded. A team is considered caught when the third rider of one team draws even with the third member of the team that has been overtaken. If both teams post the same time at the finish, they will be placed according to the faster time at the end of the previous lap.

The racers ride in a single file, known as a pace line, taking turns leading the team around the track. At each turn the lead rider moves up the embankment, allowing the other three riders to proceed, and then moves to the back of the pace line. The lead rider is responsible for maintaining the pace, while the other cyclists work with the draft to keep their speed. Precision and cooperation among team members are essential in the team pursuit.

Points Race: One of the most difficult races to understand, the points race can be a lot of fun to watch. It's unusual to see this one on TV because the race is long, and conveying the action to viewers is difficult.

In a nutshell, riders cover a distance of 40 kilometers, or 100 laps, and the rider who accumulates the most points, or the rider who laps the field—regardless of his total points—wins the race. Points are awarded during lap sprints, which occur every fifth lap. Five points are awarded to the sprint winner, three to the second, two to the third, and one to the fourth. The fiftieth lap and the final lap are bonus laps, and the points awarded are doubled. When a rider laps the field, he must maintain this advantage throughout the race in order to be awarded the victory without having the highest point total. If more than one rider laps the field the one with the most points is declared the winner.

Kilometer Time Trial: The "kilo" or "killermeter" is perhaps one of the most demanding track events. An all-out race, the cyclist rides as fast as possible for 1000 meters. It's easy to call this one: the fastest time wins.

Alone on the track, riders compete *contre la montre* (against the clock) in this "race of truth." The rider's greatest challenge is to pace throughout the race, going fast enough to turn in a best-possible time, but not so fast as to "blow up," losing momentum before the end of the race. Some cyclists use a technique called "floating," which incorporates a soft-pedaled stroke at intervals in order to prevent muscular burnout.

The best riders ride a tight line on the inside of the track—particularly in the turns—shaving those hundredths of seconds that make or break the finish.

Road Competitions

Women first competed in Olympic cycling in 1984, when the women's road race was added to the program.

Individual Road Race: Mass-start events, road races can be point-to-point races or long loops of five to 25 miles in length. The 1996 road race takes place on a 15km course through the neighborhoods of Atlanta.

Although teamwork is essential in the Olympic road race, riders are nonetheless seeking individual victory. Teamwork in Atlanta should be interesting to watch. Pros will be allowed to compete for the first time at the Games, which means that professional adversaries may well become national allies. Again, the concept is simple: first across the finish wins.

What goes on in the pack, however, is not so simple. Because of the staying power required in a long road race, drafting—riding close behind another rider—is important. A rider who "grabs a wheel" saves about 25 percent of his or her effort. Riders who break away most often take turns drafting in order to stay away from the pack.

Strong, aggressive riders often attempt solo breaks. The solo rider risks being caught by the field, allowing a sprinter who has been "sitting in"—riding protected to conserve energy—to jump to the finish line.

Watch for teammates taking turns setting the pace, allowing others to rest by drafting. Most teams feature strong sprinters, and may work together to protect the sprinter and position him or her for the final sprint to the finish. You may also see riders in the front of the chasing pack blocking—that is, deliberately slowing down the pace of the pack to prevent them from chasing the breakaway riders.

Individual Time Trial: Riders compete individually, at timed intervals, against the clock; the rider with the best time wins. Riders begin the race from a launching ramp; an assistant holds the rider in place, releasing him or her at the end of the starting countdown. Men's races vary from 45–55 km, while women ride a 25–35 km course.

Team Time Trial: In this race against the clock, team members work together to cover a designated distance in as short a time as possible. Included as a men's-only event from 1960–88, the event has been dropped to make way for the two mountain biking events (*see* page 143).

VeloTalk

Break/breakaway: A rider or group of riders that leaves the main group behind.

Bridge: To leave one group of riders to join another group that is farther ahead.

Contre la Montre: A French term meaning "against the clock"; a time trial.

Drafting: Riding in a slipstream—a pocket of moving air—created by the rider in front, in order for the drafting rider to maintain speed with less effort. You might hear a number of expressions that refer to drafting; "grab a wheel," "jump on a wheel," and "get a wheel" all refer to drafting.

Echelon: A staggered line of riders in a paceline, each downwind of the rider ahead. This formation is often used in cross-winds.

Field: The main group of riders, also known as the "pack" or "peloton."

Field Sprint: To sprint to the finish among the main group of riders.

Force the pace: When one rider presses harder than the pack to increase the tempo.

Gap: The distance between individuals or groups of riders. Not a clothing store.

Hammering: An all-out, go-for-broke effort.

Jam: An extended chase.

Jump: A quick acceleration that usually develops into a sprint.

Mass Start: Any race in which all riders start at the same time.

Pace Line: A string of riders who take turns at the front and sitting in.

Pole Line: The innermost line on the velodrome, used to measure the length of the track (usually 333.33 meters).

Pull: To take a turn at the front of the group, maintaining a constant speed.

Sitting in: To ride protected, in the draft of other riders.

Take a flyer: To suddenly sprint off the front of a pack.

Wind-up/Wind-out: A gradual acceleration that develops into a sprint. Usually initiated with more than a lap to go.

Hopefuls

Barcelona had its Dream Team, Wimbledon alumni, and a host of well-endorsed athletes. The Atlanta Games, for the first time ever, will welcome professional cyclists to the Olympic fold.

But will they come?

It's hard to say. An Olympic medal has a certain cachet; but then, so does a stage win in the Tour de France. It so happens the two will coincide. And then there's money: Olympic gold tends to pale in comparison to a well-padded purse. Nevertheless, the Union Cycliste Internationale confirms that Miguel Induráin—and many other heavyweight pros—are "very interested to compete in the Olympics."

The U.S. team, in any case, is determined to stage a coup on home turf. The U.S. Cycling Federation's Project '96 has a single objective: To mount an all-out assault in Atlanta. That requires revolutionary methods of athlete preparation, world-class coaching, and technical innovation. "Project '96 is a complete package," bicycle design coordinator Chester Kyle told the *Olympian*. "We were way ahead of the rest of the world in 1984 in terms of bicycle design, but in the past decade we have lost that technical advantage. Project '96 will change that. Everything the rider touches, feels or pedals will be specifically designed for the project. Each bike will be built around an individual rider's specific biomechanic and aerodynamic needs."

So far, generation-'96 has posted standout results. Grabbing eight medals at the 1994 World Championship, U.S. riders turned in their best world's performance since 1993. And the Pan Am Games yielded more precious medals, as U.S. cyclists snared 9 of the 14 gold medals.

In short, Atlanta could prove to be the U.S. team's best Olympic showing since LA, 1984, when the stars-and-stripes squad, with no competition from Soviet riders, nailed seven medals —four of them gold.

FACT: Averaging 52.35 kilometers per hour in the 1992 Tour de France's 50-km race against the clock, Miguel Induráin rode the time trial faster than any rider in the ninety-one year history of the Tour.

—*Marie MacNee*

Lance Armstrong

Ballyhooed as the U.S. cycling team's goldenboy at the 1992 Games, Lance Armstrong reeled in a disappointing 14th-place finish in the 115-mile Barcelona road race. Things didn't improve. The next week—in his official coming-out as a pro rider—Armstrong finished Spain's San Sebastian race in 111th place: Dead last, with nowhere to go, he thought, but far, far away from driving rains and booing spectators.

Heeding the advice of both his mother and coach, the erstwhile triathlete decided not to ditch his until-then promising cycling career. It was a good move. In 1993, just old enough to buy a legal beer, Armstrong posted a banner season. He reigned as the indefatigable U.S. National Road champ. He grabbed a stage win in the Tour de France, making him the third-youngest rider ever to win a stage in that prestigious race. He nailed the Thrift Drug Triple Crown, for which he pocketed a cool million to be divvied among his teammates—winning the final stage by the fattest margin in the race's star-addled history.

And in August, not even Spain's Miguel Induráin—fresh from a three-peat at the Tour de France—could keep the young Motorola monster from adding a rainbow jersey to his wardrobe (making him the second-youngest man to win the professional bicycle road racing championship).

Armstrong's 1994 season, although far from pedestrian, didn't herald the manifestation of a latter-day Greg LeMond (a comparison to which the ever-humble Armstrong routinely replied: "I'm not the next Greg LeMond—I'm the first Lance Armstrong"). The burden of being a world champion began to weigh heavily on the young rider, who, with only two years' experience as a pro, was still wet behind the ears. "If you're a world champion in this sport, you're a marked man," he later recounted.

FACT: There's more to a world champion than great legs and a will to win: Lance Armstrong—a.k.a. the Motorola monster—has a lactate tolerance that permits him to pedal for hours at heart rates in excess of 190 beats per minute.

The peloton clocked his every move, and Armstrong—who seemed not to be at the top of his game—was frustrated in every attempt to stage a second hurrah. He was bridesmaid again at the Tour DuPont, having also placed second the previous year. And worst of all, posting only a seventh-place finish in the 1994 worlds, he was forced to surrender his *maillot arc en ciel*—the coveted rainbow jersey—without even mounting a protest.

With experience came hindsight: "When I won the jersey it was a surprise," he told *The New York Times*, "and I took it and wore it for a year and you don't realize at a young age, at a young point in your career, what you have. Then when you lose the jersey, you see another person wearing it, you realize exactly what it was that you achieved. And what an honor it was."

By the end of 1994, Armstrong realized what he had had. And he wanted *more*. "I don't want to disappoint myself, my teammates, or my fans," he told *Bicycling* magazine. "I have to carry the sport in this country, and the best way to do that is to win and win big."

And that's exactly what he did. Entering his fifth Tour DuPont since 1991 (when he placed 73rd), Armstrong effused, "I feel real strong, superstrong." Superman couldn't have stopped him. Relentlessly dominating the entire race, he nailed three stage wins en route to an overall victory. No other U.S. rider—except, dare we say it, Greg LeMond—had ever captured the nation's most prestigious title.

"Lance Armstrong is still a new name to a lot of people," the Lonestar phenom presaged the summer before the big win. "The only way to get around that is longevity. I can't just do well in '93. I've got to do it in '94, '95, and '96. And I plan on doing that."

"That feeling," he told *Bicycling*, ". . . the finish line, the last couple of meters—is what motivates me. If I could bottle that up and sell it I'd be the richest man in the world." If all goes according to plans, in the year leading up to the Olympics, Armstrong will snag a one-day classic (something no American has done), and he'll hang with the Euro-boys to finish the Tour de France. And he's aiming to leave Atlanta a richer man—with the Olympic medal LeMond never had the chance to contest.

Like the man said: He's the first Lance Armstrong.

—*Marie MacNee*

Rebecca Twigg

Los Angeles, 1984, Olympic cycling history was made, and Rebecca Twigg was there. Nipped at the line by teammate Connie Carpenter, she locked a second-place finish in the first Olympic women's road race—the only distaff cycling event that year.

The 1988 Games added women's track events—in which the four-time national and world champion excelled—but illness, crashes, and fatigue prevented Twigg from qualifying for the U.S. squad that year. Disenchanted, disenfranchised, and twenty-five years old, she retired from the sport of cycling.

A steady nine-to-fiver, Twigg worked as a computer programmer, Jazzercising regularly to keep her girlish figure. Then came the news that a women's 3,000m individual pursuit—Twigg's best event—would be added to the Barcelona program.

"These other guys that win the rainbow jerseys [for world championship victories] are gods in their respective European countries. They spend the majority of their off-season flying here and there, doing commercial this and commercial that, and they forget about their biking. Well, I'm real fortunate that I'm an American and nobody wants me."
—*Lance Armstrong, 1993 World Road Champion*

"She's a lady that if she likes, she can do," says Eddie Bory-sewicz. And he should know: During his ten-year tenure as the head coach at the United States Cycling Federation, he groomed riders whose résumés include nine Olympic medals, 12 Pan Am Games placings, almost 30 world championship medals, and a host of other impressive credentials. "There are not many like her," he explains to the *Olympian*. "Every 50 years there's born one. Age is no main factor. Mind, dedication, health are main factors. And she can do it, no problem."

Well, maybe a *little* problem. Having been off the bike for three years, Twigg discovered she had the legs of a tourist: her spin was gone, her muscles, leaden. But mind, dedication, and health she had, and, after a month and a half of serious training, she began to recover her racing form. "It's hard to say what's age and what's just being away from it," she told *Women's Sports and Fitness*. "It takes longer to recover from workouts and races."

Her hard work paid off; in spades. First was Barcelona, where she collected a bronze medal in the first Olympic women's pursuit. Next stop: the World Championships in Hamar, Norway, where she co-opted her fourth 3,000m individual pursuit. This she did with a certain panache, posting a record time of 3 minutes, 37.347 seconds; almost .8 of a second faster than the previous record. Added to the mix were a dozen or so miscellaneous victories scattered throughout the year.

Back under the watchful tutelage of Borysewicz—who is both coach and director sportif of the new Montgomery/Bell pro team—Twigg gives little thought to her second retirement. After all, her longtime coach has big plans for her—including a trip to Atlanta.

"Let me say this," Eddie B. told *Winning* magazine, "I believe in Rebecca Twigg."

—Marie MacNee

Schedule

The tentative cycling schedule for road events is:

Sunday, July 21
Women's road race

Saturday, August 3
Women's & Men's individual time trial

Wednesday, July 31
Men's road race

The tentative cycling schedule for track events is:

Wednesday, July 24
Men's individual pursuit qualifying &
  quarterfinal
Women's sprint qualifying (200m time
  trial)
Men's 1 km time trial final
Men's sprint qualifying (200m time
  trial), round 1 & repechages

Thursday, July 25
Women's individual pursuit qualifying
Men's individual pursuit semifinal
Men's sprint round 2
Women's sprint octos final
Men's & Women's sprint repechage
Men's individual pursuit final

Friday, July 26
Men's team pursuit qualifying
Women's sprint quarterfinal
Men's sprint octos final

Men's sprint repechage
Women's sprint quarterfinal TB
Men's team pursuit quarterfinal

Saturday, July 27
Men's sprint quarterfinal
Women's individual pursuit semifinal
Men's team pursuit semifinal
Men's & Women's sprint final
Men's sprint quarterfinal tie break
Women's sprint final tie break
Men's sprint semifinal & semifinal tie
  break
Men's sprint 5-8 final
Men's team pursuit final

Sunday, July 28
Women's & Men's points race final
Men's sprint final
Women's individual pursuit final

Highlights

The Games have seen a lot of jockeying among nations leading the cycling competition. The first Olympic cyclist to win the gold, Leon Flameng, circled a 333.33m cement track 300 times to out-pedal his weary competitors. Flameng was the first of a host of Frenchmen to turn cycling into a golden opportunity: to date, France has taken a total of 64 medals—27 of them gold. (Italy, in second place, has taken 49 medals, of which 28 were gold, while the U.S. has dipped four of 12 medals in gold.) In the 1960s, a number of new arrivals started to turn heads at the Games: the traditional European dominance was challenged by competitors from Poland, the German Democratic Republic, Romania, and the U.S.S.R.

Although cycling has been an Olympic constant, a number of events have come and gone: the 12-hour race, oddly, was never held again after the 1896 Games, a one-lap (603.49m) race appeared in 1908 only, the 5000m, the 10km, 20km, 50km, and 100km track races have all bitten the dust, and the last 2000m tandem race was held in 1972. And the Barcelona Games bid adieu to the team time trial event.

The women's match sprint was added to the program in 1988, allowing Connie Paraskevin-Young to earn a bronze—the only medal the U.S. took in cycling in Seoul. *AP/Wide World*

In 1976, a few cycling events went indoors for the first time at the Games, a year that also marked the Czechoslovakian team's unfortunate loss of the team wheels to a garbage compressor. The U.S., which hadn't medaled in cycling in the Olympics since 1912, dusted the competition in LA at the 1984 Games, where four golds, three silvers, and a bronze were awarded to riders wearing the stars and stripes. Women, long ignored by the Games, first competed in 1984 when a women's road race was added to the program; Americans Connie Carpenter-Phinney and Rebecca Twigg took the gold and silver.

In 1988, a women's track event was added, allowing Connie Pareskevin-Young to earn the only medal the U.S. took in cycling in Seoul.

The faster you go, the harder it gets. To increase from 18 kph to 25 kph, a rider must double her strength; to reach 40 kph, six times the effort is required.

The individual road race, which has missed only three Games, has given rise to its share of memorable—and sometimes forgettable—trivia. The 1896 course ran from Athens to Marathon, where riders had to sign their names and turn around. The winner, Aristidis Konstantintidis, from Greece, rode three bikes in the race, although not all at the same time.

Three Games later, an imbroglio developed over the race results: the course was intersected at six points by railway crossings that produced a number of delays, and guards posted at the crossings recorded the delays. The first cyclist into the stadium, Henry Kaltenbrun, was greeted as the winner. A little arithmetic, however, revealed that Harry Stenquist, who had waited four minutes at a railway crossing, was the first-place finisher.

And then there's the story of meals on wheels during the 1932 Games. According to the press, Italian first-place winner Attilio Pavesi carried a bucket of water, soup, spaghetti, sweet rolls, cheese sandwiches, jam—and two spare tires.

Just how fast do these guys go, anyway? In the altitudinous velodrome in Mexico City, Daniel Morelson and Pierre Trentin, from France, blazed through the final 200 meters of the tandem race in 9.83 seconds; that's 73.24 kph or 45.51 mph. At the 1980 Moscow Games, Soviet rider Sergey Kopylov clocked the last 200 meters of the 1000m time-trial at 10.47 seconds, setting the then-fastest individual speed record at 68.76 kph or 42.73 mph. But that was before Chris Boardman hit the board track at Barcelona.

Lore has it that drugs were an integral part of grueling stage races, such as the Tour de France, in the early days of the sport. The 1960 Rome Games produced tragic results for the Danish team. When two Danish teammates collapsed during the arduous 100km road race, everyone believed that they had been struck by sunstroke in the 93-degree Roman summer. One of the two Danes, Knut Enemark Jensen, fractured his skull in the fall, and died en route to the hospital; he became the first athlete to die in Olympic competition since the 1912 marathon. Later, a postmortem revealed that Jensen had taken a large overdose of the blood circulation stimulant Ronicol.

Spurred by Jensen's death, the International Cycling Federation (UCI) became the first to institute drug control, well before the International Olympic Committee Medical Commission issued mandatory drug testing for all sports in 1968. In 1989, the USCF established a stringent drug policy, stiffening the penalties for athletes who fail the test. Anyone testing positive—subject to random testing—suffers a two-year suspension for the first offense, and four years for the second. Riders refusing to be tested are automatically suspended for one year.

Nevertheless, despite international dope policing, cycling has contributed its share of inductees to the Hall of Shame. In the

In Barcelona, Erika Salumae, who won a gold medal in 1988 for the Soviet team, turned in another gold-medal performance, this time for Estonia. *(Courtesy of K. A. Hugelier)*

1972 Games, Spain's third-place medalist in the individual road race and Holland's third-place medalist in the team road race were both disqualified for ergogenic cheating.

Eddy Merckx

Better known for his total domination of the Tour de France (five wins), and for having set the hour record (later smashed by Francesco Moser), Eddy Merckx—one of the most famous cyclists in the world—competed in the 1964 Olympics.

A mere 19 years old in Tokyo in 1964, Merckx stayed at the front throughout the road race, until just several hundred meters from the finish.

There, a crash left him behind the pack, but the Belgian diehard jammed to the finish, within hundredths of a second behind Mario Zanin, the Italian winner. Sounds close, but he finished twelfth.

Merckx retired at age 33 to much fame and fortune, the attainment of an Olympic medal out of reach. Wonder if he knew the oldest Olympic cycling gold medalist was 38?

—*Marie MacNee*

FACT: Erika Salumae, winner of the 1992 match sprint event, is only the second cyclist to win back-to-back golds in individual events.

Highlights from Barcelona

It was a proud day for Estonia at the Barcelona Games when Erika Salumae—the Soviet Union's gold medalist in the inaugural women's match sprint in 1988—turned in another gold-medal performance, this time as a member of the Estonian team. With Salumae installed on the top step of the podium, Olympic officials raised the Estonia flag—albeit upside-down—for the first time since 1948, when the Baltic Republic became part of the Soviet Union. In second place was Germany's Annett Neumann, forcing 1991 world champion Ingrid Haringa of the Netherlands to settle for the bronze.

Only the second Olympics to include women's track cycling events, the 1992 Games marked the introduction of the women's 3,000m pursuit. Convinced to come out of retirement to compete in her favorite event, twenty-nine-year-old Rebecca Twigg—the 1984 road race silver medalist who failed in 1988 to make the U.S. team—managed a stunning comeback by outpacing Denmark's Hanne Malmberg. En route to the bronze medal, Twigg eliminated France's heavily favored Jeannie Longo in the quarterfinals, outsprinting the four-time world champion record holder by .04 seconds.

The home team scored the first-ever Spanish cycling gold as José Moreno Periñan broke the Olympic record on the wooden boards of the Horta Velodrome in the Vall d'Hebron on the first day of track competition. In third place in that event, Erin Hartwell nailed the first of the U.S. team's two medals.

No less spectacular was Christopher Boardman's total domination of the 4,000m individual pursuit. Riding a tricked-out aerodynamic bike designed by Mike Burrows, the British rider set two world's-best times in the heats. Then he got serious. With a lap to go, Boardman caught world champion Jens Lehmann—something no other cyclist had ever done in an Olympic final.

FACT: Fabio Casartelli, the winner of the 1992 Olympic road race, died in a crash in the 1995 Tour de France.

In the road events, Italy, too, had its moment in the sun—a punishing 93-degree scorching sun, to be exact. By race's end, almost half of the field's 159 riders had dropped out because of the staggering heat. Finishing two bike lengths ahead of Hendrik Dekker at the 194km mark, Fabio Casartelli became the first Italian to win the Olympic road race title since Pierfranco Vianelli nailed a high-altitude victory in Mexico in 1968. Adding to the Italian team's medal harvest, Giovanni Lombardi picked up a gold in the 50km points race.

Medalists

Cycling—Men's 100-Kilometer Team Time Trial

1992
1. Germany (Bernd Dittert, Christian Meyer, Uwe Peschel, Michael Rich), 2:01.39
2. Italy (Flavio Anastasia, Luca Colombo, Gianfranco Contri, Andrea Peron), 2:02.39
3. France (Herve Boussard, Didier Faivre-Pierret, Philippe Gaumont, Jean-Louis Harel), 2:05.25

1988
1. East Germany, 1:57:44.7, Uwe Ampler, Mario Kummer, Maik Landsmann, Jan Schur
2. Poland, 1:57:47.3, Joachim Halupczok, Zenon Jaskula, Marek Lesniewski, Andrzej Sypytkowski
3. Sweden, 1:59:47.3, Bjorn Johansson, Jan Karlsson, Michel Lafis, Anders Jarl

1984
1. Italy, 1:58:28, Marcello Bartalini, Marco Giovannetti, Eros Polis, Claudio Vandelli
2. Switzerland, 2:02:38, Alfred Acherman, Richard Trinkler, Laurent P. Vial, Benno Wiss
3. U.S.A, 2:02:46, Ronald Kiefel, Roy Knickman, Davis Phinney, Andrew Weaver

1980
1. Soviet Union, 2:01:21.7, Yuri Kashirin, Oleg Logvin, Sergei Shelpakov, Anatoli Yarkin
2. East Germany, 2:02:53.2, Falk Boden, Bernd Drogan, Olaf Ludwig, Hans-Joachim Hartnick
3. Czechoslovakia, 2:02:53.9, Michal Klasa, Vlastibor Konecny, Alipi Kostadinov, Jiri Skoda

1976
1. Soviet Union, 2:08:53.0, Anatoli Chukanov, Valeri Chaplygin, Vladimir Kaminsky, Aavo Pikkuus
2. Poland, 2:09:13.0, Tadeusz Mytnik, Myeczyslaw Nowicki, Stanislaw Szozda, Ryszard Szurkowski
3. Denmark, 2:12:20.0, Verner Blaudzin, Gert Frank, Jorgen Emil Hansen, Jorn Lund, Niels Fredborg

1972
1. Soviet Union, 2:11:17.8, Boris Chuchov, Valeri Iardi, Gennady Komnatov, Valeri Likhachov
2. Poland, 2:11:47.5, Lucjan Lis, Edward Barcik, Stanislaw Szozda, Ryszard Szurkowski
3. 3rd place team was Netherlands, but disqualified due to drug use.

1968
1. Netherlands, 2:07:49.06, Fedor den Hertog, Jan Krekels, Marinus Pijnen, Henk Zoetemelk
2. Sweden, 2:09:26.60, Erik Pettersson, Gosta Pettersson, Sture Pettersson, Tomas Pettersson
3. Italy, 2:10:18.74, Giovanni Bramucci, Vittorio Marcelli, Mauro Simonetti, Pierfranco Vianelli

1964
1. Netherlands, 2:26:31.19, Evert G. Dolman, Gerben Karstens, Johannes Pieterse, Hubertus Zoet
2. Italy, 2:26:55.39, Sverino Andreoli, Luciano Dalla Bona, Pietro Guerra, Ferrucio Manza
3. Sweden, 2:27:11.52, Sven Hamrin, Erik Pettersson, Gosta Pettersson, Sture Pettersson

1960
1. Italy, 2:14:33.53, Antonio Bailetti, Ottavio Cogliati, Giacomo Fornoni, Livio Trape
2. East Germany, 2:16:56.31, Gustav-Adolf Schur, Egon Adler, Erich Hagen, Gunter Lorke
3. Soviet Union, 2:18:41.67, Viktor Kapitonov, Yevgeni Klevzov, Yuri Melichov, Aleksei Petrov

1896–1956
Not held

Cycling—Men's One-Kilometer Time Trial

1992
1. Jose Moreno Perinan, Spain, 1:03.342 (OR)
2. Shane Kelly, Australia, 1:04.288
3. Erin Hartwell, U.S.A., 1:04.753

1988
1. Alexander Kirichenko, Soviet Union, 1:04.499
2. Martin Vinnicombe, Australia, 1:04.784
3. Robert Lechner, West Germany, 1:05.114

1984
1. Fredy Schmidtke, West Germany, 1:06.104
2. Curtis Harnett, Canada, 1:06.436
3. Fabrice Colas, France, 1:06.649

1980
1. Lothar Thoms, East Germany, 1:02.955 (WR)
2. Aleksandr Panfilov, Soviet Union, 1:04.845
3. David Weller, Jamaica, 1:05.241

1976
1. Klaus Juergen Gruenke, East Germany, 1:05.927
2. Michel Vaarten, Belgium, 1:07.516
3. Niels Fredborg, Denmark, 1:07.617

1972
1. Niels Fredborg, Denmark, 1:06.44
2. Daniel Clark, Australia, 1:06.87
3. Jurgen Schutze, East Germany, 1:07.02

1968
1. Pierre Trentin, France, 1:03.91 (WR)
2. Niels Fredborg, Denmark, 1:04.61
3. Janusz Kierzkowski, Poland, 1:04.63

1964
1. Patrick Sercu, Belgium, 1:09.59
2. Giovanni Pettenella, Italy, 1:10.09
3. Pierre Trentin, France, 1:10.42

1960
1. Sante Gaiardoni, Italy, 1:07.27 (WR)
2. Dieter Gieseler, West Germany, 1:08.75
3. Rostislav Vargashkin, Soviet Union, 1:08.86

1956
1. Leandro Faggin, Italy, 1:09.8 (OR)
2. Ladislav Foucek, Czechoslovakia, 1:11.4
3. Alfred J. Swift, South Africa, 1:11.6

1952
1. Russell Mockridge, Australia, 1:11.1 (OR)
2. Marino Morettini, Italy, 1:12.7
3. Raymond Robinson, South Africa, 1:13.0

1948
1. Jacques Dupont, France, 1:13.5
2. Pierre Nihant, Belgium, 1:14.5
3. Thomas Godwin, Great Britain, 1:15.0

1936
1. Arie van Vliet, Netherlands, 1:12.0 (OR)
2. Pierre Georget, France, 1:12.8
3. Rudolf Karsch, Germany, 1:13.2

1932
1. Edgar Gray, Australia, 1:13.0
2. Jacobus van Egmond, Netherlands, 1:13.3
3. Charles Rampelberg, France, 1:13.4

1928
1. Willy Falck Hansen, Denmark, 1:14.4
2. Gerard Bosch van Drakestein, Netherlands, 1:15.2
3. Edgar Gray, Australia, 1:15.6

1908–1924
Not held

1906
1. Francesco Verri, Italy, 22.8
2. H. Crowther, Great Britain, 22.8
3. Menjou, France, 23.2

1900–1904
Not held

1896
1. Paul Masson, France, 24.0
2. Stamatios Nikolopoulos, Greece, 25.4
3. Adolf Schmal, Austria, 26.6

Cycling—Men's 4,000-Meter Individual Pursuit

1992
1. Chris Boardman, Britain, NA
2. Jens Lehmann, Germany, NA
3. Gary Anderson, New Zealand, 4:31.061

1988
1. Gintaoutas Umaras, Soviet Union, 4:32.00
2. Dean Woods, Australia, 4:35.00
3. Bernd Dittert, East Germany, 4:34.17

1984
1. Steve Hegg, U.S.A, 4:39.35
2. Rolf Golz, West Germany, 4:43.83
3. Leonard Nitz, U.S.A, 4:44.03

1980
1. Robert Dill-Bundi, Switzerland, 4:35.66
2. Alain Bondue, France, 4:42.96
3. Hans-Henrik Orsted, Denmark, 4:36.54

1976
1. Gregor Braun, West Germany, 4:47.61
2. Hermann Ponsteen, Netherlands, 4:49.72
3. Thomas Huschke, East Germany, 4:52.71

1972
1. Knut Knudsen, Norway, 4:45.74
2. Xavier Kurmann, Switzerland, 4:51.96
3. Hans Lutz, West Germany, 4:50.80

1968
1. Daniel Rebillard, France, 4:41.71
2. Mogens Frey Jensen, Denmark, 4:42.43
3. Xavier Kurmann, Switzerland, 4:39.42

1964
1. Jiri Daler, Czechoslovakia, 5:04.75
2. Giorgio Ursi, Italy, 5:05.96
3. Preben Isaksson, Denmark, 5:01.90

1896–1960
Not held

Cycling—Men's 4,000-Meter Team Pursuit

1992
1. Germany (Michael Gloeckner, Jens Lehmann, Stefan Steinweg, Guido Fulst), 4:08.791
2. Australia (Brett Aitken, Stephen McGlede, Shaun O'Brien, Stuart O'Grady), 4:10.218
3. Denmark (Ken Frost, Jimmi Madsen, Jan Bo Petersen, Klaus Kynde Nilsen), 4:15.860

173

1988
1. Soviet Union, 4:13.31, Viatcheslav Ekimov, Artouras Kaspoutis, Dmitri Nelubine, Gintaoutas Umaras
2. East Germany, 4:14.09, Steffen Blochwitz, Roland Hennig, Dirk Meier, Carsten Wolf
3. Australia, 4:16.02, Brett Dutton, Wayne McCarney, Stephen McGlede, Dean Woods

1984
1. Australia, 4:25.99, Michael Grenca, Kevin Nichols, Michael Turtur, Dean Woods
2. U.S.A, 4:29.85, David Grylls, Steve Hegg, R. Patrick McDonough, Leonard Nitz
3. West Germany, 4:25.60, Reinhard Alber, Rolf Golz, Roland Gunther, Michael Marx

1980
1. Soviet Union, 4:15.70, Viktor Manakov, Valeri Movchan, Vladimir Osokin, Vitali Petrakov
2. East Germany, 4:19.67, Gerald Mortag, Matthias Wiegand, Volker Winkler, Uwe Unterwalder
3. Czechoslovakia, 4:32.68, Teodor Cerny, Martin Penc, Jiri Pokorny, Igor Slama

1976
1. West Germany, 4:21.06, Gregor Braun, Hans Lutz, Gunther Schumacher, Peter Vonhof
2. Soviet Union, 4:27.15, Vladimir Osokin, Aleksandr Perov, Vitali Petrakov, Viktor Sokolov
3. Great Britain, 4:22.41, Ian Banbury, Michael Bennett, Robin Croker, Ian Hallam

1972
1. West Germany, 4:22.14, Jurgen Colombo, Gunther Haritz, Udo Hempel, Gunther Schumacher
2. East Germany, 4:25.25, Thomas Huschke, Heinz Richter, Herbert Richter, Uwe Unterwalder
3. Great Britain, 4:23.78, Michael Bennett, Ian Hallam, Ronald Keeble, William Moore

1968
1. Denmark, 4:22.44, Gunnar Asmussen, Per Lyngemark, Reno B. Olsen, Mogens Frey Jensen
2. West Germany, 4:18.94, Udo Hempel, Karl Link, Karlheinz Henrichs, Jurgen Kissner
3. Italy, 4:18.35, Lorenzo Bosisio, Cipriano Chemello, Luigi Roncaglia, Giorgio Moribiato

1964
1. West Germany, 4:35.67, Lothar Claesges, Karlheinz Henrichs, Karl Link, Ernst Streng

2. Italy, 4:35.74, Luigi Roncaglia, Vincenzo Mantovani, Carlo Rancati, Franco Testa
3. Netherlands, 4:38.99, Gerard Koel, Hendrik Cornelisse, Jacob Oudkerk, Cornelis Schurring

1960
1. Italy, 4:30.90, Luigi Arienti, Franco Testa, Mario Vallotto, Marino Vigna
2. East Germany, 4:35.78, Siegfried Kohler, Peter Groning, Manfred Klieme, Bernd Barleben
3. Soviet Union, 4:34.05, Stanislav Moskvin, Viktor Romanov, Leonid Kolumbet, Arnold Belgardt

1956
1. Italy, 4:37.4, Leandro Faggin, Valentino Gasparella, Antonio Domenicali, Franco Gandini
2. France, 4:39.4, Michel Vermeulin, Jean-Claude Lecante, Rene Bianchi, Jean Graczyk
3. Great Britain, 4:42.2, Donald Burgess, Michael Gambrill, John Geddes, Thomas Simpson

1952
1. Italy, 4:46.1, Marino Morettini, Guido Messina, Mino De Rossi, Loris Campana
2. South Africa, 4:53.6, Thomas F. Shardelow, Alfred J. Swift, Robert G. Fowler, George Estman
3. Great Britain, 4:51.5, Ronald C. Stretton, Alan Newton, George A. Newberry, Donald C. Burgess

1948
1. France, 4:57.8, Charles Coste, Serge Blusson, Ferdinand Decanali, Pierre Adam
2. Italy, 5:36.7, Arnaldo Benfenati, Guido Bernardi, Anselm Citterio, Rino Pucci
3. Great Britain, 4:55.8, Alan Geldard, Thomas Godwin, David Ricketts, Wilfred Waters

1936
1. France, 4:45.0, Robert Charpentier, Jean Goujon, Guy Lapebie, Roger Le Nizerhy
2. Italy, 4:51.0, Bianco Bianchi, Mario Gentili, Armando Severino Rigoni
3. Great Britain, 4:53.6, Harry Hill, Ernest A. Johnson, Charles King, Ernest Mills

1932
1. Italy, 4:53.0, Marco Cimatti, Paolo Pedretti, Alberto Ghilardi, Nino Borsari
2. France, 4:55.7, Amede Fournier, Rene Legreves, Henri Mouillefarine, Paul Chocque
3. Great Britain, 4:56.0, Ernest A. Johnson, William Harvell, Frank W. Southall, Charles Holland

1928
1. Italy, 5:01.8, Luigi Tasselli, Giacomo Gaioni, Cesare Facciani, Mario Lusiani
2. Netherlands, 5:06.2, Adriaan Braspenninx, Jan Maas, Johannes Pijnenburg, Piet van der Horst
3. Great Britain, Frank Wyld, Leonard Wyld, Percy Wyld, M. George Southall

1924
1. Italy, 5:15.0, Angelo De Martino, Alfredo Dinale, Aleardo Menegazzi, Francesco Zucchetti
2. Poland, Jozef Lange, Jan Lazarski, Tomasz Stankiewicz, Franciszek Szymczyk
3. Belgium, Leonard Daghelinckx, Henri Hoevenaers, Fernand Saive, Jean van den Bosch

1920
1. Italy, 5:20.0, Franco Giorgetti, Ruggero Ferrario, Arnaldo Carli, Primo Magnani
2. Great Britain, Albert White, Horace Thomas Johnson, William Stewart, Cyril A. Alden
3. South Africa, James Walker, William Smith, Henry J. Kaltenbrun, Harry W. Goosen

1912
Not held

1908
1. Great Britain, 2:18.6, Leon Meredith, Benjamin Jones, Ernest Payne, Charles Kingsbury
2. Germany, 2:28.6, Hermann Martens, Max Gotze, Karl Neumer, Rudolf Katzer
3. Canada, 2:29.6, William Morton, Walter Andrews, Frederick McCarthy, William Anderson

1896–1906
Not held

Cycling—Men's Match Sprint

1992
1. Jens Fiedler, Germany, NA
2. Garry Neiwand, Australia, NA
3. Curtis Harnett, Canada, NA

1988
1. Lutz Hesslich, East Germany
2. Nikolai Kovche, Soviet Union
3. Gary Neiwand, Australia
3. Gary Niewand, Australia

1984
1. Mark Gorski, U.S.A, 10.49
2. Nelson Vails, U.S.A, 10.95
3. Tsutomu Sakamoto, Japan, 11.03

1980
1. Lutz Hesslich, East Germany
2. Yave Cahard, France
3. Sergei Kopylov, Soviet Union

1976
1. Anton Tkac, Czechoslovakia
2. Daniel Morelon, France
3. Hans-Juergen Geschke, East Germany

1972
1. Daniel Morelon, France, 11.25
2. John M. Nicholson, Australia
3. Omar Pchakadse, Soviet Union

1968
1. Daniel Morelon, France, 10.68
2. Giordano Turrini, Italy
3. Pierre Trentin, France

1964
1. Giovanni Pettenella, Italy, 13.69
2. Sergio Bianchetto, Italy
3. Daniel Morelon, France

1960
1. Sante Gaiardoni, Italy, 11.1
2. Leo Sterckx, Belgium
3. Valentino Gasparella, Italy

1956
1. Michel Rousseau, France, 11.4
2. Guglielmo Pesenti, Italy
3. Richard Ploog, Austria

1952
1. Enzo Sacchi, Italy, 12.0
2. Lionel Cox, Australia
3. Werner Potzernheim, Germany

1948
1. Mario Ghella, Italy, 12.0
2. Reginald Harris, Great Britain
3. Axel Schandorff, Denmark

1936
1. Toni Merkens, Germany, 11.8
2. Arie van Vliet, Netherlands
3. Louis Chaillot, France

1932
1. Jacobus van Egmond, Netherlands, 12.6
2. Louis Chaillot, France
3. Bruno Pellizzari, Italy

1928
1. Roger Beaufrand, France, 13.2
2. Antoine Mazairac, Netherlands
3. Willy Falck Hansen, Denmark

1924
1. Lucien Michard, France, 12.8 (last 200 m)

2. Jacob Meijer, Netherlands
3. Jean Cugnot, France

1920
1. Maurice Peeters, Netherlands, 1:38.3
2. Horace Thomas Johnson, Great Britain
3. Harry Ryan, Great Britain

1912
Not held

1908
Final was declared void because the time limit was exceeded

1906
1. Francesco Verri, Italy, 1:42.2
2. H. C. Bouffler, Great Britain
3. Eugene Debongnie, Belgium

1904
Not held

1900
1. Georges Taillandier, France, 2:52.0 (last 200 m 13.0)
2. Fernand Sanz, France
3. John Henry Lake, U.S.A

1896
1. Paul Masson, France, 4:56.0
2. Stamatios Nikolopoulos, Greece, 5:00.2
3. Leon Flameng, France

Cycling—Men's Individual Points Race

1992
1. Giovanni Lombardi, Italy, 44
2. Leon Van Bon, Netherlands, 43
3. Cedric Mathy, Belgium, 41

1988
1. Dan Frost, Denmark, 38
2. Leo Peelen, Netherlands, 26
3. Maral Ganeev, Soviet Union, 46 (one lap down)

1984
1. Rogers Ilegems, Belgium, 37
2. Uwe Messerschmidt, West Germany, 35
3. Jose Manuel Youshimatz, Mexico, 29

Cycling—Men's Individual Road Race

1992
1. Fabio Casartelli, Italy, 4:35.21
2. Erik Dekker, Netherlands, 4:35.22
3. Dainis Ozols, Latvia, 4:35.24

1988
1. Olaf Ludwig, East Germany, 4:32.22

2. Bernd Groene, West Germany, 4:32.25
3. Christian Henn, West Germany, 4:32.46

1984
1. Alexi Grewal, U.S.A, 4:59:57
2. Steve Bauer, Canada, 4:59:57
3. Dag Otto Lauritzen, Norway, 5:00:18

1980
1. Sergei Sukhoruchenkov, Soviet Union, 4:48:28.9
2. Czeslaw Lang, Poland, 4:51:26.9
3. Yuri Barinov, Soviet Union, 4:51:29.9

1976
1. Bernt Johansson, Sweden, 4:46:52.0
2. Giuseppe Martinelli, Italy, 4:47:23.0
3. Mieczyl Nowicki, Poland, 4:47:23.0

1972
1. Hennie Kuiper, Netherlands, 4:14:37.0
2. Kevin C. Sefton, Australia, 4:15:04.0

1968
1. Pierfranco Vianelli, Italy, 4:41:25.24
2. Leif Mortensen, Denmark, 4:42:49.71
3. Gosta Pettersson, Sweden, 4:43:15.24

1964
1. Mario Zanin, Italy, 4:39:51.63
2. Kjeld Rodian, Denmark, 4:39:51.65
3. Walter Godefroot, Belgium, 4:39:51.74

1960
1. Viktor Kapitonov, Soviet Union, 4:20:37.0
2. Livio Trape, Italy, 4:20:37.0
3. Willy van den Berghen, Belgium, 4:20:57.0

1956
1. Ercole Baldini, Italy, 5:21:17.0
2. Arnaud Geyre, France, 5:23:16:0
3. Alan Jackson, Great Britain, 5:23:16.0

1952
1. Andre Noyelle, Belgium, 5:06:03.4
2. Robert Grondelaers, Belgium, 5:06:51.2
3. Edi Ziegler, West Germany, 5:07:47.5

1948
1. Jose Beyaert, France, 5:18:12.6
2. Gerardus P. Voorting, Netherlands, 5:18:16.2
3. Lode Wouters, Belgium, 5:18:16.2

1936
1. Robert Charpentier, France, 2:33:05:0
2. Guy Lapebie, France, 2:33:05.2
3. Ernst Nievergelt, Switzerland, 2:33:05.8

1932
1. Attilio Pavesi, Italy, 2:28:05.6

2. Guglielmo Segato, Italy, 2:29:21.4
3. Bernhard Britz, Sweden, 2:29:45.2

1928
1. Henry Hansen, Denmark, 4:47:18.0
2. Frank W. Southall, Great Britain, 4:55:06.0
3. Gosta Carlsson, Sweden, 5:00:17.0

1924
1. Armand Blanchonnet, France, 6:20:48.0
2. Henri Hoevenaers, Belgium, 6:30:27.0
3. Rene Hamel, France, 6:30:51.6

1920
1. Harry Stenqvist, Sweden, 4:40:01.8
2. Henry J. Kaltenbrun, South Africa, 4:41:26.6
3. Fernand Canteloube, France, 4:42:54.4

1912
1. Rudolph Lewis, South Africa, 10:42:39.0
2. Frederick Grubb, Great Britain, 10:51:24.2
3. Carl Schutte, U.S.A, 10:52:38.8

1908
Not held

1906
1. B. Vast, France, 2:41:28.0
2. M. Bardonneau, France, 2:41:28.4
3. Luguet, France, 2:41:28.6

1900–1904
Not held

1896
1. Aristidis Konstantinidis, Greece, 3:22.31
2. August Goedrich, Germany, 3:42.18
3. F. Battel, Great Britain

Cycling—Women's Match Sprint

1992
1. Erika Salumae, Estonia
2. Annett Neumann, Germany
3. Ingrid Haringa, Netherlands

1988
1. Erika Salumae, Soviet Union
2. Christa Rothenburger-Luding, East Germany
3. Connie Paraskevin-Young, U.S.A.

Cycling—Women's Individual Road Race

1992
1. Kathryn Watt, Australia, 2:04.42
2. Jeannie Longo-Ciprelli, France, 2:05.02
3. Monique Knol, Netherlands, 2:05.03

1988
1. Monique Knol, Netherlands, 2:00.52
2. Jutta Niehaus, West Germany, 2:00.52
3. Laima Zilporitee, Soviet Union, 2:00.52

1984
1. Connie Carpenter-Phinney, U.S.A., 2:11.14
2. Rebecca Twigg, U.S.A., 2:11.14
3. Sandra Schumacher, West Germany, 2:11.14

3,000 Individual Pursuit

1992
1. Petra Rossner, Germany, 3:41.753
2. Kathryn Watt, Australia, 3:43.438
3. Rebecca Twigg, U.S.A., 3:52.429

Trivia Quiz

1. The first early bicycle to include pedals was
   a. The eighteenth-century célérifère
   b. The "Draisienne," which debuted in 1818
   c. A vehicle built by Kirkpatrick McMillan in 1834

2. In 1868, rubber tires replaced
   a. All-wood tires   **b.** Iron-covered wood tires   **c.** Plastic tires

3. The first recorded bicycle race at Parc de Saint Cloud in France was won by
   a. Eddy Merckx   **b.** Laurent Fignon   **c.** James Moore

4. Six-day races
a. Were held indoors at Madison Square Garden in the 1920s and 1930s
b. Were held on automotive proving grounds in Detroit in the 1950s
c. Were never popular in the United States

5. U.S. cyclist Lance Armstrong started out as
a. A BMX racer   **b.** A triathlete   **c.** A speedskater

6. Women's cycling events first appeared in the Olympics
a. In Athens, in 1896   **b.** In LA, in 1984   **c.** In Montreal, in 1976

7. Women's track events
a. Have never been included in the Olympics
b. Were included at the same time as women's road events
c. Were first included in Seoul, in 1988

8. The first World Championships were held
a. In Chicago in 1893   **b.** As part of the Olympics, in 1956
c. In Turin, Italy, in 1938

9. American legend Greg LeMond won
a. Five Tour de France overall titles, matching the records of Bernard Hinault, Jacques Anquetil and Eddy Merckx
b. An Olympic bronze medal in 1976 and the 1985 Tour de France
c. Three Tour de France victories, beginning in 1986

10. Which of the following riders did not compete in the Olympic Games?
a. Eddy Merckx   **b.** Davis Phinney   **c.** Francesco Moser

Answers: 1-c, 2-b, 3-c, 4-a, 5-b, 6-b, 7-c, 8-a, 9-c, 10-c

DIVING

Warm-up

F lying through the air with the greatest of ease, spiraling downward before slipping into the water with barely a splash, divers participate in one of the more elegant and breathtaking Olympic events. Few would disagree that the grace, beauty, and form inherent in a near flawless dive is unmatched in competitive athletics.

Diving dates back to the 17th century when gymnasts in Sweden and Germany would practice their sport over water on equipment set up on the beaches during the summer months. The activity became popular, eventually branching away from gymnastics in the late 19th century to form the new acrobatic sport of diving. As late as the 1920s, however, it was often included in gymnastic competitions.

Diving was first introduced in England in 1893 with a plunging championship, and two years later the Royal Life Saving Society of Great Britain initiated a nationwide graceful diving competition, which continued in various forms until 1961.

Diving was included in the Olympic program at the 1904 Games in St. Louis, when a men's springboard competition was held. Men's 10-meter platform was added for the 1908 Games in London, while women's platform began at the following Olympics. Women's springboard was added in 1920.

Since the introduction of diving to the Olympic Games, the U.S. divers have enjoyed extraordinary success. The American team has won 46 of 74 gold medals and 124 of 222 total medals, including 16 of 20 gold medals in men's and 11 of 17 in women's three-meter springboard. In the platform, U.S. divers have taken 11 of 19 gold medals in the men's competition and eight of 17 in the women's event.

Spectator's Guide

The Olympic diving competition consists of the men's and women's platform (10 meters or 33 feet high—about equal in height to a three-story building) and springboard (3 meters or almost 10 feet) events. The springboard is an adjustable diving board that regulates "springiness." Like slalom ski racing, springboard diving requires both agility and timing as the diver uses the flex of the board, timing the dive to catch maximum spring. The platform is a stationary, nonbending board that is at least 20 feet long and six and a half feet wide. Platform diving is like downhill ski racing, a dangerous, breathless plunge that seems like folly to spectators and sometimes to divers.

In each of the four events, a preliminary round is held to bring the number of divers down to 18 semifinalists, from which the top 12 advance to the final round where they dive in reverse order of their prelim finish. In the springboard preliminary, the men perform a series of 11 dives and the women 10, a sequence that is repeated in the finals and semifinals. In the platform events, the men perform 10 dives and the women eight in each round.

FACT: The judges mark each of the 11 Olympic dives on a scale from 0 to 10, and then multiply the sum by a number that indicates the dive's degree of difficulty. An elite diver is usually comfortable in the 1.5 to 2.5 range. Athletes who attempt dives with a 3.0 degree of difficulty are flirting with the possibility of a failed dive.

The springboard event requires that the men perform five required dives with a total degree of difficulty not exceeding 9.5, and six optional dives without limit. The women's springboard is similar except they execute five optional dives without limit.

On the platform, both men and women perform four required dives with a total degree of difficulty not exceeding 7.6, while the men execute six optional without limit and the women four.

Olympic diving contests are judged by a crew of seven. After each dive, each judge determines the point total for the dive on a scale of 0 (lowest) to 10 (highest), in half or whole point increments.

The seven point scores are displayed, with the highest and lowest eliminated. The remaining five scores are totalled and then multiplied by the degree of difficulty. The **degree of difficulty** is a rating for executing a specific dive, ranging from 1.1 to 3.5. (And new diving rules will be in place in 1996: Divers no longer have to choose their dives off a list that had set degrees of difficulty, instead they can create their own dives using the different categories — forward, reverse, or twisting. With the new dives, competitors can potentially raise their scoring ability since they are choosing as much difficulty as they desire. Some observers say this will scramble the medal race.) The result is reduced by ⅗ (0.6), in keeping with the tradition that a diver's score comes from three judges.

For example: a dive earns scores of 6–5–5–5–5–5–4. The sum, after high (6) and low (4) scores are eliminated, is 25. Let's say the degree of difficulty is 2.0, so 25 multiplied by 2 is 50. Fifty multiplied by 0.6 is 30, the score for the dive.

At the beginning of a dive, the diver's body should be straight, head erect, heels together and arms straight to the sides. Once the diver stands on the front end of the board to perform a standing dive, the judges assume the dive has begun. In judging a dive, the parts of each dive must be analyzed and evaluated, and an overall award obtained.

Parts of a Dive

Approach: In forward dives, the starting position is assumed when the diver is ready to take the first step. The forward approach must be smooth, straight, and forceful. It should be comprised of no fewer than three steps before the hurdle (the jump to the end of the board in which both feet contact the end of the board simultaneously). If a diver takes fewer than three steps, the referee deducts two points off the award of each judge.

Takeoff: The takeoff should be forceful and confident, show control and balance, and proceed without delay. In running dives, the takeoff from the springboard must be from both feet simultaneously. The final segment of a diver's approach to the takeoff is called the **hurdle**, and consists of a spring to the end of the board, taking off from one foot, and landing on two feet at the end of the board.

In **back takeoffs**, the diver is not allowed to lift his feet from the board before actual takeoff, but may use his own method of arm swings. During a back dive, a diver is not allowed to excessively rock the board before taking off. A violation costs two points from each judge's score. Divers also use armstand takeoffs in platform diving.

Elevation: The amount of spring or lift a diver receives from the takeoff greatly affects the appearance of the dive. Since more height means more time, a higher dive generally permits greater accuracy and smoothness of movement. If, on any dive, the diver touches the end of the board or dives to the side of the direct line of flight, the judges may deduct points at their discretion.

Execution: As important as the dive itself. A judge watches for proper mechanical performance, technique, form, and grace.

Entry: The entry is very significant because it is the last element of the dive the judges see, and is probably the one they will remember best. The two criteria to be evaluated on entry are the angle, which should be near vertical with toes pointed, and the amount of splash, which should be as little as possible. In a head-first entry, arms should be stretched above the head in line with the body and hands close together. In feet-first entries, the arms should be held close to the body, without bending the elbows. Divers aiming for a clean entry into the water are encouraged to think of aiming for the bottom of the pool instead of the surface of the water.

From the 10-meter platform, a diver is traveling about 35 miles per hour at entry. A **rip** is an entry into the water that makes a "ripping" sound and leaves little splash.

Types of Dives

For the springboard event, one dive from each of the first five groups listed below is required. The platform event requires four of the six to be performed (including the armstand).

Forward: The diver faces the front of the board and rotates toward the water. Dives in this group vary from the simple front dive to the extremely difficult forward four and one-half somersault.

Back: At the beginning of the dive, the diver is at the end of the board with his or her back toward the water. The direction of rotation is away from the board.

Reverse: These dives (formerly called "gainers") begin with the diver facing the front of the board (using a forward approach) and rotating toward the board.

Inward: The diver stands on the end of the board, back toward the water, and rotates toward the board (opposite of back dives). Formerly called "cutaways."

Twisting: Includes any forward, back, inward, or reverse dive with a twist. This group includes the greatest number of dives because of all the possible combinations.

Armstand: Used only in platform diving, these dives begin with the diver assuming a handstand position on the edge of the platform before executing the dive.

Body Positions

The official dive chart lists 87 basic dives. With body positions of straight, pike, tuck, or free, 348 dive variations exist.

Straight: No bending at the waist or the knees. The arm placement is either by the diver's choice or defined by the dive performed.

Pike: Legs are straight with the body bent at the waist. Again, arm position is either decided by the diver or dictated by the dive.

Tuck: The body is bent at both the waist and the knees. The thighs are drawn to the chest while the heels are kept close to the buttocks.

Free: This is the diver's option of using a combination of the other three positions, with the most common combination being straight and pike. The free position is only used in dives that include twists.

Hopefuls

At the 1996 Olympic Team Trials for Diving (June 19–23, 1996), a maximum of four men and four women qualify for the Olympic Team.

Mary Ellen Clark

Diver Mary Ellen Clark will try to repeat as an Olympics participant in 1996 even though her recent career has been severely hampered by vertigo. Clark—who won a bronze medal in the 10-meter platform competition at Barcelona—is an eight-time national diving champion and, at 32, a veritable senior citizen in the ranks of world class diving. She knows that the 1996 Summer Games will be her last chance to win recognition in her sport, but first she has to battle past a baffling ailment to get there.

Vertigo, which is marked by dizziness and disorientation, occurs when crystals imbedded in the inner ear get knocked loose. Doctors have speculated that Clark may have injured herself sometime during her long years of practice, causing bouts of vertigo that begin and end mysteriously. She suffered her first episode in 1988—and did not qualify for the Olympics that year. The condition reappeared in 1990 and again in 1995. Clark described her condition in a July 8, 1995, *Philadelphia Inquirer* profile. She explained that when she dives with vertigo she needs her own personal lifeguard. "I need someone to make sure I swim to the top and not down to the bottom," she said. "It can happen."

Diving was not always so difficult for the lively Clark. The youngest of seven children, she began her sport at the age of seven, following her older sisters and brothers into the pool. Her father,

Gene, had been a diving team captain at the University of Pennsylvania, and he taught all of his children what he had learned as a collegian. Mary Ellen was a particularly apt pupil, especially on the springboard dive. After graduating from Radnor High School near Philadelphia in 1981, she earned a scholarship to Penn State, and there she began working on the 10-meter platform. In her first year of competition on the 10-meter platform, she finished fifth in the national championships.

> "My parents always told me that I should get out of diving when it wasn't fun anymore. But I've always had fun. It's always been a challenge."
> — Mary Ellen Clark

In 1987, Clark won her first national championship in an upset victory over Michele Mitchell. Needless to say, the championship encouraged Clark to believe she would be one of the two American divers to represent the U.S. in the event at the 1988 Olympics. Instead she finished a disappointing seventh in the 1988 Olympic Trials and—worse—injured her left shoulder at the meet. After that she began to question her future in the sport. "I wondered whether I had it in me to keep going," she told the *Philadelphia Inquirer* on June 20, 1991. "I had some time off. I had to go through rehabilitation, which was painful and tedious. But I decided to give it four more years after 1988."

Clark earned her master's degree in physical education from Ohio State University in 1989 and then moved to Fort Lauderdale, Florida, to train with Ron O'Brien, the coach behind Olympic champion Greg Louganis. Having supported herself by selling Cutco Cutlery door-to-door, Clark was delighted when she received a grant from the Women's Sports Foundation and a public relations job with the McDonald's Olympic Job Opportunities Program. Freed from financial worries, she trained five hours a day, six days a week and quickly regained her national championship form.

At the 1992 Olympic Trials, Clark finished second to Ellen Owen, thereby earning a trip to Barcelona. Her chance at an Olympic medal came at a time when her father had just undergone bypass surgery, so she was doubly determined to win. Clark finished second in the platform diving preliminaries and trailed only Chinese sensation Fu Mingxia in the finals after six dives. Then she made a crucial mistake: looking ahead to a possible medal, she over-rotated her seventh dive and dropped into fifth place with only one dive to go. "It felt like hours before my last dive," she recalled in a March, 1993, *Women's Sports & Fitness* profile. When the "hours" finally passed, Clark went out and nailed her final dive for a third-place finish and a bronze medal.

After the 1992 Olympics, most observers expected Clark to retire. For years she had told the press that the 1992 Summer Games were her goal and that she would retire afterwards. She changed her mind after her bronze-medal performance. "I felt I still had better diving in me, that I was still learning about the sport and about myself," she explained in the *Philadelphia Inquirer.* "There was no reason to quit." Elsewhere in the *Philadelphia Inquirer* she stated: "My parents always told me that I should get out of diving when it wasn't fun anymore. But I've always had fun. It's always been a challenge." Since 1993 she has continued to train, facing ever younger competitors who also want to savor an Olympic moment. In 1994, for instance, she lost her national championship to 17-year-old Becky Ruehl, but she still competed in the Goodwill Games and the World Championships.

Clark's vertigo re-surfaced in 1995 and literally kept her out of the pool for months. Before she had trained right through the vertigo, but this time she decided to take a rest, try some alternative treatments, and hope that the condition would improve in time for the 1996 Olympic Trials. "I have to look at this as a real grounding experience, to maybe slow down, refocus, then charge into next year and finish my career in Atlanta," she told the *Philadelphia Inquirer.* The 32-year-old diver added: "I don't have to prove anything, but it's a personal challenge for me. I set my own goals and this is a goal. I want to overcome this."

—Anne Janette Johnson

Scott Donie

Scott Donie won't need an Olympic medal in platform diving to measure his success at the Atlanta Games.

Competing will be enough to bring out the kid in him.

Donie (pronounced *Doe-knee*), 27 (b. October 10, 1968), of Miami, Florida, is a Southern Methodist University graduate, an All-American, and a U.S. diving hopeful in both springboard and platform events. Like teammate Mark Lenzi, Donie is fashioning a comeback. But unlike Lenzi, Donie is battling demons, not rust.

Donie, who won a silver medal in platform diving at the 1992 Olympics, suffered bouts of deep depression following his triumphant experience in Barcelona.

At his lowest point, Donie, who froze during a dive at the 1993 Olympic Festival in San Antonio, considered climbing a diving tower and taking a final, killing leap.

His mother, Judy, the vice president of senior diving for U.S. Diving, admits that she actually feared the worst. She actually asked him once if he was going to harm himself.

"You live with this dream in your mind, such a bright and vivid picture, that just *going* to the Olympics would be so great," Donie told the *Dallas Morning News.* "You think your life would change and everything would be so beautiful. Then you go, win a medal, and life doesn't change at all. After that, you start questioning everything."

Psychologists estimate that as many as one-third of all U.S. Olympians—divers, gymnasts, skiers, sprinters, winners, *and* also-rans—suffer through some sort of post-Olympics emotional crisis. For some, it is no more serious than a bad case of the blues, or withdrawal. For others, it can lead to alcoholism, eating disorders, drug abuse, or clinical depression.

Donie knew that he finally had to address the problem when he froze during a handstand before that dive in San Antonio. The dive, termed "easy" by Donie, was officially an "arm stand cut-through, reverse one-and-a-half." It was to be Donie's sixth dive. He was leading the competition as he went into his position. He froze.

"I just flipped out," said Donie, whose struggle was reported on *Dateline NBC* in 1994. "I was thinking, 'What are you gonna do, Scott? What are you gonna do?' It was ridiculous. I was torturing myself."

After 30 seconds or so, Donie came out of the handstand, climbed down the ladder, walked across the deck, and told the judges that he was retiring from the competition.

He said later that he had simply lost the joy of diving, that he had misplaced the wonder he felt as a nine-year-old seeing famed Olympic decathlete Bruce Jenner take his victory lap after winning the gold medal in Montreal in 1976. He said that he had lost the thrill he felt as a 12-year-old, doing diving tricks for fun, spontaneously and unencumbered by unrealistic hopes and fears of failure.

Of the depression, Donie says: "If it happened to me, it can happen to anyone. The chemicals in your brain change. Your body feels terrible. It's like being hung over all the time. It was terrible, just terrible."

To make things worse, Donie resisted help, which is not an unusual reaction, psychologists say, by elite athletes who by nature and training can be self-reliant to a fault.

"San Antonio was the first time I admitted to myself that I wasn't happy," Donie says. "I think that's where I started to heal."

Ironically—or perhaps naturally—it was through children that Donie rediscovered the child in himself. That too, was a big step, he says, on the way to recovery.

That began when Donie was hired as a teacher's assistant at a private school in Miami and was assigned to a class of 6- and 7-year-olds with learning disabilities including hyperactivity, attention-deficit disorders, and dyslexia.

Working with the children, he says, helped him reestablish his perspective, to understand diving for what it is—a sport.

"These kids . . . they'll never have the chance I did," he told the *Morning News.* "It really makes you remember that diving is just a sport. (They've) helped me control my own childishness. When I was having trouble with my diving, it was like the little kid in me was saying, 'C'mon, let's break out of this serious stuff and do something fun'. I was so scared of this kid in me and how powerful it was I didn't trust the adult in me enough to control him.

"Once I started learning how to control the kids," he told *USA Today,* "I think I started learning how to control the kid in me."

Donie began his diving comeback on the 1-meter springboard. To that, he has begun to add platform dives—and competitions.

The latter have not come without some minor setbacks, however.

In April of 1995, Donie scratched himself from the platform final at the indoor championships in Midland, Texas. He began warming up for the final, but couldn't get through the final practice dives.

"I got caught in a bad loop," he said. "Like returning from any other injury, I may have rushed it a bit. I'm pleased with my progress. I achieved my goal of coming back and competing, so I'm not going to look at it as a negative, but a positive. I've come a long way, but I've got some more work to do. I want to get back to enjoying what it is I do just for the sake of what it is. Not just for the competition. I want to enjoy practice."

Like a kid, again. Scott Donie is getting there. His destination is Atlanta. The platform. The medal platform would just be a plus.

—*Eric Kinkopf*

Mark Lenzi dives his way to a gold medal in the men's 3-meter springboard final in Barcelona. He should be a contender again in 1996. *AP/Wide World*

Mark Lenzi

Veteran diving coach Dick Kimball was speaking about Mark Lenzi before the 1992 Olympic Games in Barcelona.

"This summer could be the start of something great. Mark's going to do some really amazing things that people will remember."

Well, almost.

Mark Lenzi, Huntsville, Alabama, native and Bloomington, Indiana, resident, *did* win an Olympic springboard gold medal in 1992.

Then came the things people would remember—Lenzi's post-Olympics retirement, his flirtation with a movie career, and his attempt to finance commercial pilot training by considering, publicly, the sale of his gold medal.

Now, of course, they're talking about Mark Lenzi's comeback.

It was, naturally, a big splash. A bit bigger than expected, actually, because Lenzi, 28 (b. July 4, 1968), who'd avoided pools during his retirement as though they were crawling with alligators, was some 25 pounds overweight when he returned.

Still, U.S. Diving was hopefully optimistic. After all, Lenzi, a true Yankee Doodle Dandy—born on the 4th of July—was the athlete the federation had been counting on to take up where Greg Louganis left off—in performance *and* leadership.

"I felt like God gave me a talent and an opportunity to dive, and I made the most of it," Lenzi told Steve DeShazo, of the *Fredricksburg* [Va.] *Free Lance-Star* about his decisions to retire, then unretire. "But then I ran away from it. The problem wasn't diving, it was everything else. I came to the conclusion that I was running away from something that I was meant to do. I was wasting my talent. I can put off flight school, and it will be OK. But diving, I can't put off. This is the last go-round for me."

At the time Lenzi considered hocking his gold, he told DeShazo: "I really don't want to do it. But if worse comes to worst, I'll have to. A lot of people ask me what it's like to be rich and famous. Well, I'm not rich."

Lenzi says he finally came to his senses when he visited the pool at a Florida apartment.

"The smell of chlorine brought back memories," he said, adding: "I needed the time away."

When Lenzi returned, he could hardly bend over to touch his toes.

"He was way out of shape," Kimball says.

"I hadn't stretched in two years," Lenzi said. "I could barely touch my head to my knees."

Not that anyone, if really pressed, would have expected a whole lot different from Mark Lenzi, a free spirit from the word go. He got into diving on an impulse, giving up a promising high school wrestling career to train with a diving club a two-hour round trip from home. The switch irked his father, Bill, a Navy physicist, for more reasons than gas money. Lenzi Sr. was counting on Mark, one of four of his and Mary Ellen's children, winning a college scholarship in wrestling. It was the only way he could figure on financing his kid's education. Mark and Bill were at loggerheads for a long time over the decision to dump wrestling. The situation became so difficult that Mark even moved in with neighbors for a short time.

What happened? Lenzi ended up winning a college scholarship in diving, instead—after diving for less than a year.

Mark and Bill went at it again, when Mark threw in his Speedo after the 1992 Games.

At that time, Bill Lenzi said: "I don't know what to say. Before, I couldn't keep him from going into diving and that worked out. All I can do is hang loose and support him the best I can."

Lenzi's short-lived retirement included the possibility of a movie career in a *Caddyshack*-styled movie called *Pumphouse,* a slapstick comedy about a community pool manager—Lenzi—who would foil a Las Vegas crime boss's attempt to buy pool property for a development complex.

Pumphouse never materialized, though its writer, De Miller, saw loads of potential stuffed inside Lenzi's 5-foot-5 frame.

"He has those Paul Newman eyes that are so photogenic on film," Miller said. "The fact that he's a diver and the movie centers around a swimming pool made me think of shades of Johnny Weissmuller." Weissmuller, of course, was the 1924 and 1928 Olympic swimming champion, who later starred in the Tarzan movies.

Kimball wasn't sure about Lenzi's celluloid possibilities, but he has been impressed with Lenzi's comeback effort.

"I was really surprised, but not surprised, because I'd seen him dive in practice," Kimball said, after Lenzi won the 1- and 3-meter events at the Kimball Classic in Ann Arbor in June of 1995. "He's the kind of guy that when he sets his mind to doing something, he does it. He knows what kind of dedication it will take to get there."

Hobie Billingsley, Lenzi's college coach at Indiana University, said, "Mark can do harder dives than Louganis did because he spins faster. There will never be another Louganis—but there'll never be another Mark Lenzi, either."

Now, Lenzi chases Louganis, trying to become the only man to win springboard golds in consecutive Games. Which is only apropos. After all, Louganis is the athlete who switched Lenzi's attention from the mat to the springboard. Lenzi switched to diving in 1984, after watching Louganis on TV at the Los Angeles Games.

"I always watched the Olympics, from the time I was a little kid," Lenzi said. "Winning a medal was something I always wanted to do, and I *knew* I was going to do it. I'm the kind of person that, if I see something I want to do, nine times out of ten, I'll make it happen."

That exception, being, perhaps, being the star of *Pumphouse,* which could have, perhaps, been—excuse the temptation—a springboard to a different career.

And U.S. Diving officials would probably say that nine out of ten for Mark Lenzi is just fine.

At least for the time being.

—*Eric Kinkopf*

Schedule

The tentative diving schedule is:

Friday, July 26
Women's platform preliminaries

Saturday, July 27
Women's platform semifinal
Women's platform final

Sunday, July 28
Men's springboard preliminaries

Monday, July 29
Men's springboard semifinal
Men's springboard final

Tuesday, July 30
Women's springboard preliminaries

Wednesday, July 31
Women's springboard semifinal
Women's springboard final

Thursday, August 1
Men's platform preliminaries

Friday, August 2
Men's platform semifinal
Men's platform final

MEN'S DIVING EVENTS

Highlights

The U.S.A.'s own G.E. Sheldon won the first Olympic diving event in 1904. Sweden's Hjalmar Johansson was 34 when he took the gold in 1908, and captured a silver four years later. From 1920 the U.S. had mounted the most consistent diving performances. The long string of U.S. gold medals in the men's springboard event that began in 1920 has only been broken in 1972 and 1980; U.S. men also captured the springboard silver every Olympiad from 1920 to 1968. In that period, in fact, the U.S. swept the springboard event at every Games except four. Platform divers Richmond Eve of Australia in 1924, and Joaquin Capilla Pérez of Mexico in 1956, were among those divers who broke the American stranglehold on diving titles.

The first two men to win two gold medals in diving in the same Games were both Americans, Albert White in 1924 and Peter Desjardins—a native Canadian—in 1928. Michael Galitzen of the U.S. won a springboard silver and a platform bronze in 1928 and a springboard gold and platform silver in 1932; he later married diver Georgia Coleman. Richard Degener headed the U.S. sweep of the springboard in 1936.

U.S. diver Dr. Sammy Lee won golds in platform diving in 1948 and 1952; he continued his diving career as coach to the phenomenal American diver Greg Louganis from 1974 to 1977. Bob Clotworthy won a springboard bronze in 1952, claiming the gold in that event four years later. Bob Webster of the U.S. was a double gold winner in the platform event in 1960 and 1964. Italy's *angelo biondo* (blond angel), Klaus Dibiasi, was a master of the rip entry. He won a platform silver medal in the 1964 Olympics, a springboard silver in 1968, and platform golds in 1968, 1972, and 1976. Soviet diver Vladimir Vasin took the springboard gold from the Americans in 1972, claiming the first diving medal for the U.S.S.R.

A protegé of Sammy Lee, U.S. diver Greg Louganis took up the diving mantle from Dibiasi, winning a silver in 1976, then, after missing the 1980 Games due to the boycott, pulling in two golds in 1984, the first two-gold male since 1928. Louganis had won by record-setting margins over the silver medalists. His teammate Bruce Kimball won the platform silver, ahead of China's Kongzheng Li. On the springboard in 1984, Louganis's teammate Ronald Merriott captured the bronze behind China's Liangde Tan.

Some thought Louganis would retire after 1984, but he continued to refine his sport, gaining eight pounds of muscle in the four years between Olympiads.

Louganis seemed a shoo-in to double-gold in the 1988 Games as well. But in the springboard preliminaries Louganis cracked his head on the board performing a reverse $2^1/_2$ in the pike position.

With four temporary sutures in place he finished the preliminaries, then sported five mattress stitches and a waterproof patch in the finals. He faced creditable competition from veteran Chinese diver and 1984 silver medalist Tan Liangde, but by round seven had opened up a 20-point lead. When it came time for Louganis to execute the reverse $2^1/_2$, the crowd was hushed, then roared when the dive was performed to scores between 8.0 and 9.0. He aced his final and most difficult dive to claim the gold. Tan Liangde settled for silver once more, ahead of his compatriot, Li Deliang. In the platform event Louganis took the title ahead of Chinese silver medalist Xiong Ni and Mexican bronze medalist Jesus Mena, clinching the second double-gold performance of his Olympic career.

Greg Louganis

His record-breaking two gold medals in each of two successive Olympic diving competitions, his unprecedented platform score of more than 700 points, and his gold-medal success in every major national and international diving event he entered during the 1980s—not to mention his classically good looks and charming, modest personality—have made Greg Louganis an American legend.

Louganis, of Samoan and European ancestry, was adopted a few months after his birth in 1960 by American parents who recognized early his athletic ability. He took dance classes with his sister, gymnastics to combat childhood asthma, and—after his family noticed him performing acrobatic leaps into the backyard pool—diving lessons. By the time he arrived at a Junior Olympics competition in 1971, where he scored a "perfect ten," he was well known by coaches nationwide and attracted the attention of Olympic gold-medal diver Dr. Sammy Lee. When Louganis was fifteen, Lee volunteered to be his personal coach, charging the family nothing for his services except that Louganis clean Lee's pool. A year after that, Louganis won a silver medal at Montreal in his first Olympic diving competition.

Though he couldn't compete in the 1980 Olympics in Moscow, which the United States and other Western nations boy-

Greg Louganis in the platform diving preliminaries in Los Angeles. The U.S. diver picked up men's gold medals there in 1988 as well as in Seoul, in 1984. With the publication of his autobiography in 1995, Louganis continued to make headlines after the Olympics were over. *AP/Wide World*

cotted to protest the Soviet invasion of Afghanistan, he had already begun building his reputation as the greatest diver in the world. Having won twenty-six U.S. championships, four Pan American events, and three world championships, Louganis was clearly favored to win the platform and springboard diving events in the 1984 Olympic Games.

Not only did Louganis win gold medals in both events (becoming the first man to do so in fifty-six years), he won the springboard competition by more than ninety points over the silver medalist, and he set a record for points scored in the platform event.

Four years later, at the Summer Olympics in Seoul, Louganis's competitive edge was complicated by physical problems, including an injured wrist, a fever, and a three-inch head wound he'd sustained by striking the springboard during a preliminary competition dive. Nonetheless, Louganis finished the springboard event and won the gold, and he performed a superior final platform dive, which ensured him that gold medal, too. For his gutsy performance at the 1988 Olympics, Louganis was also granted the Olympic Spirit Award.

In March 1995, with the publication of his autobiography, *Breaking the Surface,* the retired diver made headlines when he revealed that he has AIDS. Louganis also disclosed that he was HIV-positive when he was competing in Seoul, which shed new light on his reaction to the head injury he sustained during the springboard preliminaries: He agonized over the injury because he had lost blood in the pool and was concerned for the safety of the other divers. His worries proved unfounded. The gold medalist has taken on a second career—this time as a stage actor in New York City.

Highlights from Barcelona

Like the women's diving events, the men's 10m event was also co-opted by a young Chinese diver. Sixteen-year-old Sun Shuwei easily dismissed American Scott Donie's bid for the gold, racking up one of the highest scores in Olympic history: out of 10 dives, Sun managed seven perfect 10s. Finishing with a $3\frac{1}{2}$ somersault tuck, he garnered top marks from four of the seven judges, for a final score nearly 40 points ahead of Greg Louganis's 1988 tally.

With arch-nemesis Greg Louganis retired from competition, Tan Liangde entered the Games with gilded aspirations. But U.S. newcomer Mark Lenzi thwarted the Chinese veteran's bid for the 3m springboard title. Increasing the degree of difficulty with every dive, Lenzi—dubbed the latter-day Louganis—moved inexorably to a set of perfect 10s in his ninth dive, a forward $3\frac{1}{2}$ somersault in a pike position. With a lock on the title by the time he reached his last dive, Lenzi could have won with a first-year face-plant, but chose instead a difficult 3.5 as his final hurrah.

Not so spectacular was the seventh dive of 10m medal long-shot Matt Scoggin, whose back $3\frac{1}{2}$ somersault tuck turned into one of the most painful-to-watch failed dives in all of Olympic history. Tumbling out of control through most of the three-story dive, the 28-year-old Scoggin slammed into the pool back first, with a deafening thud. Sprinting out of the pool in an attempt to run off the pain, he received a "failed dive" for his effort. Scoggin later summarized the experience: "It was definitely agony and it was definitely defeat."

"I think Matt will make the new 'Agony of Defeat' poster."
—U.S. coach Mike Brown, on Matt Scoggins's painful dive in 1992

Medalists

Diving—Men's Platform

1992
1. Sun Shuwei, China, 677.31
2. Scott Donie, U.S.A., 633.63
3. Xiong Ni, China, 600.150

1988
1. Gregory Louganis, U.S.A., 638.61
2. Xiong Ni, People's Republic of China, 637.47
3. Jesus Mena, Mexico, 594.39

1984
1. Gregory Louganis, U.S.A., 710.91
2. Bruce Kimball, U.S.A., 643.50
3. Kongzheng Li, China, 638.28

1980
1. Falk Hoffmann, East Germany, 835.650
2. Vladimir Aleynik, Soviet Union, 819.705
3. David Ambartsumyan, Soviet Union, 817.440

1976
1. Klaus Dibiasi, Italy, 600.51
2. Gregory Louganis, U.S.A., 576.99
3. Vladimir Aleynik, Soviet Union, 548.61

1972
1. Klaus Dibiasi, Italy, 504.12
2. Richard Rydze, U.S.A., 480.75
3. Franco Cagnotto, Italy, 475.83

1968
1. Klaus Dibiasi, Italy, 164.18
2. Alvaro Gaxiola, Mexico, 154.49
3. Edwin Young, U.S.A., 153.93

1964
1. Robert Webster, U.S.A, 148.58
2. Klaus Dibiasi, Italy, 147.54
3. Thomas Gompf, U.S.A, 146.57

1960
1. Robert Webster, U.S.A, 165.56
2. Gary Tobian, U.S.A, 165.25
3. Brian Phelps, Great Britain, 157.13

1956
1. Joaquin Capilla Perez, Mexico, 152.44
2. Gary Tobian, U.S.A, 152.41
3. Richard Connor, U.S.A, 149.79

1952
1. Dr. Samuel Lee, U.S.A, 156.28
2. Joaquin Capilla Perez, Mexico, 145.21
3. Gunther Haase, West Germany, 141.31

1948
1. Dr. Samuel Lee, U.S.A, 130.05
2. Bruce Harlan, U.S.A, 122.30
3. Joaquin Capilla Perez, Mexico, 113.52

1936
1. Marshall Wayne, U.S.A, 113.58
2. Elbert Root, U.S.A, 110.60
3. Hermann Stork, Germany, 110.31

1932
1. Harold Smith, U.S.A, 124.80
2. Michael Galitzen, U.S.A, 124.28
3. Frank Kurtz, U.S.A, 121.98

1928
1. Peter Desjardins, U.S.A, 98.74
2. Farid Simaika, Egypt, 99.58
3. Michael Galitzen, U.S.A, 92.34

1924
1. Albert White, U.S.A, 97.46
2. David Fall, U.S.A, 97.30
3. Clarence Pinkston, U.S.A, 94.60

1920
1. Clarence Pinkston, U.S.A, 100.67
2. Erik Adlerz, Sweden, 99.08
3. Harry Prieste, U.S.A, 93.73

1912
1. Erik Adlerz, Sweden, 73.94
2. Albert Zurner, Germany, 72.60
3. Gustaf Blomgren, Sweden, 69.56

1908
1. Hjalmar Johansson, Sweden, 83.75
2. Karl Malmstrom, Sweden, 78.73
3. Arvid Spangberg, Sweden, 74.00

1906
1. Gottlob Walz, Germany, 156.00
2. Georg Hoffmann, Germany, 150.20
3. Otto Satzinger, Austria, 147.40

1904
1. Dr. George Sheldon, U.S.A, 12.66
2. Georg Hoffmann, Germany, 11.66
3. Alfred Braunschweiger, Germany, 11.33
3. Frank Kehoe, U.S.A, 11.33

1896 – 1900
Not held

Diving—Men's Springboard

1992
1. Mark Lenzi, U.S.A., 676.530
2. Tan Liangde, China, 645.570
3. Dmitri Saoutine, Russia, 627.780

1988
1. Gregory Louganis, U.S.A., 730.80
2. Liangde Tan, People's Republic of China, 704.88
3. Li Deliang, People's Republic of China, 665.78

1984
1. Gregory Louganis, U.S.A., 754.41
2. Liangde Tan, China, 662.31
3. Ronald Merriott, U.S.A., 661.32

1980
1. Aleksandr Portnov, Soviet Union, 905.025

2. Carlos Giron, Mexico, 892.140
3. Franco Cagnotto, Italy, 871.500

1976
1. Philip G. Boggs, U.S.A., 619.05
2. Franco Cagnotto, Italy, 570.48
3. Aleksandr Kosenkov, Soviet Union, 567.24

1972
1. Vladimir Vasin, Soviet Union, 594.09
2. Franco Cagnotto, Italy, 591.63
3. Craig Lincoln, U.S.A., 577.29

1968
1. Bernie Wrightson, U.S.A., 170.15
2. Klaus Dibiasi, Italy, 159.74
3. James Henry, U.S.A., 158.09

1964
1. Kenneth Sitzberger, U.S.A., 159.90
2. Francis Gorman, U.S.A., 157.63
3. Larry Andreasen, U.S.A., 143. 77

1960
1. Gary Tobian, U.S.A., 170.00
2. Samuel Hall, U.S.A., 167.08
3. Juan Botella, Mexico, 162.30

1956
1. Robert Clotworthy, U.S.A., 159.56
2. Donald Harper, U.S.A., 156.23
3. Joaquin Capilla Perez, Mexico, 150.69

1952
1. David Browning, U.S.A., 205.29
2. Miller Anderson, U.S.A., 199.84
3. Robert Clotworthy, U.S.A., 184.92

1948
1. Bruce Harlan, U.S.A., 163.64
2. Miller Anderson, U.S.A., 157.29
3. Dr. Samuel Lee, U.S.A., 145.52

1936
1. Richard Degener, U.S.A., 163.57
2. Marshall Wayne, U.S.A., 159.56
3. Al Greene, U.S.A., 146.29

1932
1. Michael Galitzen, U.S.A., 161.38
2. Harold Smith, U.S.A., 158.54
3. Richard Degener, U.S.A., 151.82

1928
1. Peter Desjardins, U.S.A., 185.04
2. Michael Galitzen, U.S.A., 174.06
3. Farid Simaika, Egypt, 172.46

1924
1. Albert White, U.S.A., 696.4
2. Peter Desjardins, U.S.A., 693.2
3. Clarence Pinkston, U.S.A., 653.0

1920
1. Louis Kuehn, U.S.A, 675.4
2. Clarence Pinkston, U.S.A, 655.3
3. Louis Balbach, U.S.A, 649.5

1912
1. Paul Gunther, Germany, 79.23
2. Hanns Luber, Germany, 76.78
3. Kurt Behrens, Germany, 73.73

1908
1. Albert Zurner, Germany, 85.5
2. Kurt Behrens, Germany, 85.3
3. George Gaidzik, U.S.A, 80.8
3. Gottlob Walz, Germany, 80.8

1896–1906
Not held

WOMEN'S DIVING EVENTS

Highlights

Diving events for women commenced with the 1912 Games in Stockholm. Aileen Riggin won a springboard gold for the U.S. in 1920 and a springboard silver in 1924; she also captured a bronze in the backstroke at the 1924 Games. U.S. diver Elizabeth Becker was the first woman to win two diving titles, capturing the springboard gold in 1924 and, after marrying men's diving champion Clarence Pinkston, adding a platform gold in 1928.

Georgia Coleman of the U.S. won a platform silver and a springboard bronze in 1928 and a springboard gold and platform silver in 1932; later married to diver Michael Galitzen, she was the first woman to perform a 2 1/2 forward somersault. Her teammate, Katherine Rawls, took silvers in the springboard event in 1932 and 1936, and added a bronze as a member of the U.S. freestyle relay team. Dorothy Poynton brought the U.S. two golds, capturing the platform in both 1932 and, as Dorothy Poynton Hill, 1936; she had won a springboard silver in 1928 at age 13, and took the springboard bronze eight years later. Marjorie Gestring of the U.S. was also only 13 when she took the springboard gold in 1936. Another U.S. diver, Vickie Draves, swept both events in 1948, the first woman to do so.

French diver Madeleine Moreau was the first woman to prevent U.S. divers from sweeping the springboard event; she captured the silver medal in 1952. Pat McCormick was a four-time Olympic champion for the U.S., sweeping springboard and platform golds in 1952 and 1956. Her compatriot, Paula Myers-Pope, won a platform silver in 1952 and 1960, a platform bronze in 1956, and a springboard silver in 1960.

Until 1980, the only non-American to win the women's springboard event was East German diver Ingrid Krämer, who tri-

U.S. diver Pat McCormick was a four-time Olympic champion for the U.S., sweeping springboard and platform golds in 1952 and 1956. *AP/Wide World*

umphed in springboard and platform in 1960 and repeated for the springboard gold in 1964 as Ingrid Engel-Krämer. She also competed in Mexico City as Ingrid Gulbin.

The springboard title came back to the U.S. in 1968, with a victory by Sue Gossick. U.S. diver Micki King broke her arm when she hit the board in Mexico City at the 1968 Games, but returned in 1972 to capture the springboard gold; as Micki Hogue she was team manager for the U.S. divers in 1988. Czech diver Milena Duchková enjoyed the crowd's support in Mexico City when she bested Soviet Natalya Lobanova (Kuznetsova) for the platform gold; Duchková took the silver in the platform event in Munich. Jennifer Chandler claimed the springboard gold in 1976, the last time a U.S. woman triumphed in the event. The women's platform event has eluded American women since 1964, although Michele Mitchell took silvers in the event in 1984 and 1988, behind divers from China.

Kelly McCormick, daughter of U.S. champion Pat McCormick, earned a springboard silver in 1984, ceding to the Canadian gold medalist, Sylvie Bernier, and a bronze in 1988, behind Chinese divers Gao Min and Li Quing.

The Diving McCormicks

If diving fans feel any disappointment prior to the 1996 Games, it is that America will probably have to wait at least a generation for another McCormick diver.

That will be too long—though probably well worth the wait.

Pat McCormick was 22 when she won the springboard and platform gold medals at the 1952 Helsinki Games. In 1956, just months after giving birth to her first child, a son, she won the same pair at Melbourne.

Twenty-eight years later, her daughter, Kelly, then 24, won the silver medal in the springboard competition at the Los Angeles Games; four years later, she won the bronze medal in Seoul.

Pat McCormick was years ahead of her time. She perfected dives seldom attempted by men—dives outlawed by the Olympic committee before her appearance at the Helsinki Games as too dangerous for women. An oft-told tale features McCormick visiting a doctor. After examining her accumulation of cracked bones and scars from practicing 100 dives a day six days a week, he remarked, "I've seen worse casualty cases, but only where a building caved in."

It has also been said that if Pat McCormick had competed in front of today's amassed media, America would have done a half-gainer over her. As it was, when McCormick returned home from the Helsinki Games, a puzzled neighbor asked her if she had been away on vacation.

It's not that Pat McCormick didn't receive her due from her peers. She was named AP Athlete of the Year and Sullivan Award winner in 1956 and was the first woman inducted into the International Swimming Hall of Fame. It was just that Pat didn't really enjoy the spotlight until Kelly came along.

It helped, of course, that Kelly had a good portion of the free spirit her mother had—pumping herself up with a boom box in rooms between dives during competitions and once evaluating her performance this way: "If you land on your head 10 times, you should be happy."

My mother "showed me her medal when I was a little girl," Kelly told *Sports Illustrated* before the 1984 Games. "I made a bet with her that someday I'd make an Olympic team and win [a gold medal]. The bet's for a Porsche and either an ocelot or a cheetah."

Kelly got the car—but not the cat. She finished three points shy of the gold at the LA Games. After those Games and after surviving the intense pressure to match her mother's performances, Kelly said: "It's a relief to me it's over. But [my mother] told me that she's really proud of me and that she loves me."

Kelly's style, which emphasized her gymnastic ability—she studied as a gymnast for 8 years, then gave it up, saying she just couldn't stand being cooped up indoors—was described as "eerily similar" to her mother's. She showed the same stunning grace and strength, though was hounded by a lack of consistency.

She is remembered by others for more than her diving. When a teammate clinched an Olympic berth then cried, wishing that her father, who had died a few months earlier, had been there to see her, Kelly stopped her interview with a reporter, turned away and assured her friend. "He's here," Kelly whispered. "You know that."

Kelly McCormick retired from competitive diving and went on to coach diving in Federal Way, Washington.

Diving fans take heart: another family of divers—this time siblings—may be on the Olympic scene in year 2000: Justin and Troy Dumais, 16 and 15 years old, of Ventura, Calif., are two bright prospects for the future of diving.

—*Eric Kinkopf*

Highlights from Barcelona

The diving events at the Municipal Pool on Montjuic were without a doubt the best all-around ticket at Barcelona. Played

Diving

out on the springboard and platform stages were the full repertoire of Olympic sentiments: the ecstasy of perfect execution, the agony of defeat, the precocity of youth, and darn good diving.

Chinese divers outperformed all others, grabbing three of the four men's and women's golds. Way outclassing her older opponents, Fu Mingxia—a 92-pound slip of a girl —snagged a gold medal in the 10m platform with a devastating 50-point margin over the Unified Team's Yelena Miroshina. Managing picture-perfect dives with a progressively higher degree of difficulty, Fu, at the age of 13 years and $11\frac{1}{2}$ months, became the second-youngest person in Olympic history to win an individual gold medal. (American springboard medalist Marjorie Gestring, who was two-and-a-half months younger than Fu at the 1936 Games, is still the youngest individual gold medalist in any sport.)

> "We train by the seas. And where we train there are storms. If you can dive in the middle of a rainstorm, then you can dive anywhere."
> — Yu Fen, the coach of 1992 women's platform gold medalist Fu Mingxia

Medalists

Diving — Women's Platform

1992
1. Fu Mingxia, China, 461.43
2. Elena Mirochina, Unified Team, 411.63
3. Mary Ellen Clark, U.S.A., 401.91

1988
1. Yanmei Xu, People's Republic of China, 445.20
2. Michele Mitchell, U.S.A., 436.95
3. Wendy Williams, U.S.A., 400.44

1984
1. Jihong Zhou, China, 435.51
2. Michele Mitchell, U.S.A., 431.19
3. Wendy Wyland, U.S.A., 422.07

1980
1. Martina Jaschke, East Germany, 596.250
2. Servard Emirzyan, Soviet Union, 576.465
3. Liana Tsotadze, Soviet Union, 575.925

1976
1. Elena Vaytsekhovskaya, Soviet Union, 406.59
2. Ulrika Knape, Sweden, 402.60
3. Deborah Wilson, U.S.A., 401.07

1972
1. Ulrika Knape, Sweden, 390.00
2. Milena Duchkova, Czechoslovakia, 370.92
3. Marina Janicke, East Germany, 360.54

1968
1. Milena Duchkova, Czechoslovakia, 109.59
2. Natalia Lobanova, Soviet Union, 105.14
3. Ann Peterson, U.S.A, 101.11

1964
1. Lesley Bush, U.S.A, 99.80
2. Ingrid Engel-Kramer, East Germany, 98.45
3. Galina Alekseyeva, Soviet Union, 97.60

1960
1. Ingrid Kramer, East Germany, 91.28
2. Paula Jean Pope-Myers, U.S.A., 88.94
3. Ninel Krutova, Soviet Union, 86.99

1956
1. Patricia McCormick, U.S.A., 84.85
2. Juno Irwin-Stover, U.S.A., 81.64
3. Paula Jean Myers, U.S.A., 81.58

1952
1. Patricia McCormick, U.S.A., 79.37
2. Paula Jean Myers, U.S.A., 71.63
3. Juno Irwin-Stover, U.S.A., 70.49

1948
1. Victoria Draves, U.S.A., 68.87
2. Patricia Elsener, U.S.A., 66.28
3. Birte Christoffersen, Denmark, 66.04

1936

1. Dorothy Hill-Poynton, U.S.A, 33.93
2. Velma Dunn, U.S.An, 33.63
3. Kathe Kohler, West Germany, 33.43

1932

1. Dorothy Poynton, U.S.A, 40.26
2. Georgia Coleman, U.S.A, 35.56
3. Marion Roper, U.S.A, 35.22

1928

1. Elizabeth Pinkston-Becker, U.S.A, 31.60
2. Georgia Coleman, U.S.A, 30.60
3. Lala Sjoquist, Sweden, 29.20

1924

1. Caroline Smith, U.S.A, 33.2
2. Elizabeth Becker, U.S.A, 33.4
3. Hjordis Topel, Sweden, 32.8

1920

1. Stefani Fryland-Clausen, Denmark, 34.6
2. Eileen Armstrong, Great Britain, 33.3
3. Eva Ollivier, Sweden, 33.3

1912

1. Greta Johanson, Sweden, 39.9
2. Lisa Regnell, Sweden, 36.0
3. Isabelle White, Great Britain, 34.0

1896–1908

Not held

Diving — Women's Springboard

1992

1. Gao Min, China, 572.40
2. Irina Lachko, Russia, 514.14
3. Brita Pia Baldus, Germany, 503.07

1988

1. Min Gao, People's Republic of China, 580.23
2. Qing Li, People's Republic of China, 534.33
3. Kelly McCormick, U.S.A, 533.19

1984

1. Sylvie Bernier, Canada, 530.70
2. Kelly McCormick, U.S.A, 527.46
3. Christina Seufert, U.S.A, 517.62

1980

1. Irina Kalinina, Soviet Union, 725.910
2. Martina Proeber, East Germany, 698.895
3. Karin Guthke, East Germany, 685.245

1976

1. Jennifer Chandler, U.S.A, 506.19
2. Christa Koehler, East Germany, 469.41
3. Cynthia McIngvale, U.S.A, 466.83

1972

1. Micki King, U.S.A, 450.03
2. Ulrika Knape, Sweden, 434.19
3. Marina Janicke, East Germany, 430.92

1968

1. Sue Gossick, U.S.A, 150.77
2. Tamara Pogoscheva, Soviet Union, 145.30
3. Keala O'Sullivan, U.S.A, 145.23

1964

1. Ingrid Engel-Kramer, East Germany, 145.00
2. Jeanne Collier, U.S.A, 138.36
3. Mary Willard, U.S.A, 138.18

1960

1. Ingrid Kramer, East Germany, 155.81
2. Paula Jean Pope-Myers, U.S.A, 141.24
3. Elizabeth Ferris, Great Britain, 139.09

1956

1. Patricia McCormick, U.S.A, 142.36
2. Jeanne Stunyo, U.S.A, 125.89
3. Irene MacDonald, Canada, 121.40

1952

1. Patricia McCormick, U.S.A, 147.30
2. Mady Moreau, France, 139.34
3. Zoe Ann Jensen-Olsen, U.S.A, 127.57

1948

1. Victoria Draves, U.S.A, 108.74
2. Zoe Ann Olsen, U.S.A, 108.23
3. Patricia Elsener, U.S.A, 101.30

1936

1. Marjorie Gestring, U.S.A, 89.27
2. Katherine Rawls, U.S.A, 88.35
3. Dorothy Hill-Poynton, U.S.A, 82.36

1932

1. Georgia Coleman, U.S.A, 87.52
2. Katherine Rawls, U.S.A, 82.56
3. Jane Fauntz, U.S.A, 82.12

1928

1. Helen Meany, U.S.A, 78.62
2. Dorothy Poynton, U.S.A, 75.62
3. Georgia Coleman, U.S.A, 73.38

1924

1. Elizabeth Becker, U.S.A, 474.5
2. Aileen Riggin, U.S.A, 460.4
3. Caroline Fletcher, U.S.A, 436.4

1920

1. Aileen Riggin, U.S.A, 539.9
2. Helen Wainwright, U.S.A, 534.8
3. Thelma Payne, U.S.A, 534.1

1896–1912

Not held

Trivia Quiz

1. **Early diving events were included as part of**
   a. Swimming competitions **b.** Gymnastic competitions
   c. Bungee-jumping competitions

2. **Diving first appeared on the Olympic roster**
   a. In Athens in 1896 **b.** In St. Louis in 1904 **c.** In Rome in 394

3. **The men's and women's platform is**
   a. 33 feet high **b.** 38 feet high **c.** Way high

4. **More than half of the Olympic medals awarded for diving have gone to**
   a. Chinese divers **b.** Eastern bloc divers **c.** U.S. divers
   d. Greg Louganis

5. **Women's events were added to the Olympics**
   a. In 1912, when women's platform was added
   b. In 1904, when women's springboard was added
   c. In 1936, when women's platform and springboard were added

6. **A dive's degree of difficulty is rated on a scale of**
   a. 1 to 5 **b.** 1.1 to 3.5 **c.** 1.1 to 10.0

7. **From the 10m platform, a diver is traveling**
   a. about 22 mph **b.** about 35 mph **c.** Way too fast

8. **What used to be called a "gainer" is now known as**
   a. A reverse dive **b.** A back dive **c.** An inward dive

9. **Greg Louganis was nearly beaten out of a fourth gold medal at Seoul by Chinese diver**
   a. Xiong Ni **b.** Yanmei Xu **c.** Chow Yun Fat

10. **The official dive chart lists**
    a. 42 basic dives with 168 variations
    b. 28 basic dives with 112 variations
    c. 87 basic dives with 348 variations

Answers: 1-b, 2-b, 3-a (and c), 4-c, 5-a, 6-b, 7-b (and c), 8-a, 9-a, 10-c

EQUESTRIAN

Warm-up

The first known use of the horse as a domesticated animal in prehistoric times was for pulling or dragging loads. Horse back riding evolved through the centuries as the horse did, —the prehistoric equine were dramatically smaller than the animal we are familiar with today. The Scythians, residents of what is now south-central Russia, are believed to be the earliest innovators in horseback riding, developing types of equipment still in use today.

Writings and artwork from around 365 BC document some of the Greek methods of selecting and training horses based on their education by the Scythians. Records of the ancient Olympic Games of 688 BC show that competitions for four-horse chariot racing were included, and horseback riding competitions were included in the following Olympiad of 648 BC.

Modern equestrian competition began developing in the 16th century when classical riding schools opened in Naples, Vienna, and Saumer. The training, movements, and equipment have changed little since those days. Yet as recently as the 1900s seemingly rudimentary changes in horseback riding *techniques* have been made. For example, the elementary development of the "forward seat," that is to say, leaning forward (not backward) with the body when the horse is jumping, came about in 1902, introduced by Federico Caprilli of Italy.

With the mechanization of transportation, equestrian pursuits fell to sporting events, foxhunting, wagering, and the military. Prior to World War II most international equestrian competitions were the exclusive showplace of cavalry officers and their mounts. Though civilians participated on occasion, from their first inclusion in 1912 (Stockholm) until the 1952 Helsinki Games—when the forty-year monopoly in show jumping competitions was broken by Frenchman Pierre Jonqueres d'Oriola—the military dominated the majority of international competitions. In fact, it is because of the strong influence of the cavalry in equestrian sports that three-day eventing was developed. And even today, some of the top show jumpers hail from their nation's cavalry.

The real origins of show jumping can be traced to the 1800s when "leaping" contests were held over a single high fence. International show jumping competitions were held before the turn of the century and the birth of the Grand Prix style show jumping took place in Paris in 1866. In 1906 Swedish count Baron von Rosen proposed to the IOC that equestrian sports be included on a permanent basis in the Games. The 1912 Olympics saw the introduction of the three equestrian events still in competition today. But the Baron's legacy extends beyond this: three von Rosens have been among the equestrians who have competed in the Games—in the first half of the twentieth century, Hans and Clarence von Rosen took medals back to Sweden with them when the Olympic Games were finished and in 1972, a Maud von Rosen was among the Swedish riders who earned the bronze in team dressage in 1972.

With the formation of the FEI (Fédération Equestre Internationale) in 1921, the rules and standards of international and Olympic show jumping and other equestrian disciplines became regulated. Military—as well as male—domination prevailed in Olympic show jumping until the 1956 Stockholm Games when women were first allowed to compete.

> "The so-called elite sports, like equestrian, add a dimension to the Games that we must be careful not to lose. If we are only about popular, low-cost sports, we will become homogenized and hardly be able to tell one sport from another."
> — IOC vice president Kevan Gosper

The word dressage (pronounced *dress-AHGE*) comes from the French verb *dresser*, which means "to train." As a training method, it prepares the horse for a number of disciplines. As a sport, dressage is a challenge for horse and rider to achieve precision and harmony. The event has its roots in Greek horsemanship and was influenced by the knights of the Middle Ages, but it was not until the Renaissance that it became an important equestrian pursuit. The riding masters of that time developed a training system that has changed little since. Introduced as an Olympic sport in 1912, the event was open only to military riders until 1952. The military recognized the value of dressage as a training method for the cavalry, but the participation of the civilian riders since the Games in Helsinki is thought to have raised the standards of competition. Competitors pursue perfection—100 percent—and in so doing pay meticulous attention to detail.

Three-day eventing emerged as a sport after World War II, prior to which it had been a part of cavalry training. Competitions are based on and descended from the French Championship for Military Horses. Eventing appeared along with the other equestrian disciplines in the 1912 Olympics as a competition for military officers to demonstrate their preparedness and as a comparison of breeds and cavalry training techniques. The events test horse and rider for skill and all-around ability. Many equestrians consider it the ultimate test of teamwork. The triathlon event is patterned after the demands of the military, which required a horse to be precise, elegant, obedient (dressage); possess stamina, versatility, and courage (the cross-country race); and possess jumping ability (jumping).

Spectator's Guide

Show Jumping: Of all the Olympic equestrian events, show jumping is the most televised, the easiest to understand and score by armchair judges, and arguably the most thrilling. Horse and rider teams set out to tackle an imposing course of 15–20 obstacles at breakneck speed. The courses are designed with colorful jumps intended to blend in with the background or to draw the horses' attention away from the top rail—which is set over five feet high (often over the head of the horse) and lightly balanced in a slight cup. Courses are designed to challenge both the technical ability of the rider to control the horse, regulate its speed, and, at the same time calculate the best as well as the quickest approach to each fence. Traversing the course sight-unseen, the horse demonstrates his sheer athletic power, confidence, and complete trust in the rider.

The team competition, also called the Nations' Cup, is run in two rounds over the same course, with only the best of three scores of the four-person national team counting in each round. Faults are incurred for each rail (or "fence") a horse knocks down with either its front or back feet, putting a foot in the water or on the tape that marks the edge of a water jump, refusing a fence (called balking), and finally, for exceeding the time allowed to navigate the course. Time is a crucial factor in show jumping because if horses/riders go around faultless, the fastest times determine the placings. The times are calculated in thousandths of a second, and decisions often come down to this increment. After the two rounds, if there is a tie in faults, a jump-off over a shortened course is held, with an increase in faults as well (just to up the ante).

Jumping includes a first qualifying round and the team competition serves as the second and third qualifying rounds, with the top 45 riders advancing to the individual semifinal round. Competition between fellow teammates is not uncommon here, as demonstrated in 1984 when the U.S. swept up the gold and silver individual medals in addition to the team gold.

Dressage: This event is often regarded as the stuffy stepsister of other equestrian events. Horses and riders perform in silence, executing the exact same movements (called a "test") one after another. To many viewers, dressage lacks the thrills that show jumping or the three day event provide, but the beauty and exacting perfection of Grand Prix dressage is winning more viewers each Olympics.

Olympic dressage competitions showcase a series of movements natural to the horse. Unlike the popular Lipizzaners from the Spanish Riding School in Vienna, Olympic dressage riders perform none of the exciting "airs above the ground," or unnatural circus-like movements designed with military usage in mind (a foot soldier's nightmare: to have a horse leap in the air and kick him one). The goal is to perform a test that showcases the horse's training as well as its calmness, submissiveness, flexibility, athletic power, the rider's position, and the use of often invisible prompts known in the horse business as "aids."

In dressage, warmbloods and warmblood crosses are favored for their even temperament and big, expressive, fluid gaits. Event riders can be seen competing on thoroughbred/warmblood crossed horses. This combination seems to offer the best of the thoroughbred speed and agility with the warmbloods temperament and endurance capabilities. Show jumpers ride a wide variety of crossbred horses, but the most popular are again the warmblood/thoroughbred crosses.

Two different tests are used for the Olympic Games. The first is the FEI Grand Prix team competition, which is comprised of 38 moves, followed by the Grand Prix Special individual medal competition, with of 32 movements. The seven to seven-and-a-half minute tests are ridden from memory in an arena marked with letters around the outside (as well as imaginary ones down the center). Each movement is performed at or in between these letters for five judges that are seated at three vantage points. Scoring in both competitions ranges from 0 (a movement not executed) to 10 (excellent), with movements that are especially difficult counting double. The Grand Prix Special test is a qualifying round for the Grand Prix freestyle, with individual medals awarded for the best combined special and freestyle scores. The team competition also serves as a qualifying round for individual competition.

Watch for advanced movements like passage (elegant, bouncy suspended trot), half pass (sideways trot or canter where legs completely cross), flying or tempi changes (skips in midair at the canter to switch legs every 2 steps and every other step), canter pirouette (hind legs stay almost in place while front move around small circle), and piaffe (trot completely in place).

Three-Day Event: Logistically, three-day eventing is a difficult sport to televise as well as watch. It is the "combined" event in the equestrian, a test of endurance and versatility for both the horse and rider in three distinct competitions. Though the cross-country phase is the heart (and heart-stopper) of the competition, horse and rider must be competitive in the other phases to contend for a medal. Winners are determined by converting the dressage scores to penalties (a high score resulting in a low number of penalties), and adding to that the penalties incurred in the endurance and jumping competitions. In the individual competition, the winner is the person with the lowest combined score for the three tests. In the team competition, the lowest three scores of each four-member team determine the winner.

Each day's competition holds a vastly different challenge, beginning with the **dressage** competition. Though still called three-day eventing, the dressage phase actually takes two days to run. The "test" is a series of prescribed movements performed within a confined area. Three judges award marks for each movement, ranging from 0 to 10. The judges are looking for the versatility, general obedience, flexibility, rhythm, and training of the horse and the ability of the rider. The test is executed from memory. Errors or incorrect sequences of movements are penalized by subtraction of points. A winning dressage performance is fluid, balanced, and accurate—the picture of grace and harmony.

The **speed and endurance test** is the real heart of three-day eventing. It is made up of four parts: two sessions of Road & Tracks, a Steeplechase, and a Cross Country test consisting of as many as 30 obstacles set in varied terrain. Some obstacles may include four or five separate jumps, and the horse and rider should jump boldly and with speed. Jumps include ditches, banks, drops, and (scariest for the horse) water. As in show jumping, the horses have not seen the course before the competition, and therefore the trust between horse and rider is put to the test with every obstacle.

It is not unusual to lose a quarter of the competitors at this phase, and mandatory veterinary check points are set up to insure no competitor is in distress. The challenge often becomes keeping the horse fit enough simply to complete the last day of competition.

The final day of competition for those who survived consists of **stadium show jumping**. Though not a standard jumping competition, considering the challenges of the previous day, the ten to twelve fences are nonetheless challenging. Show jumping faults or penalties are given for knocking down rails and for a horse refusing. The final placings, as in show jumping, often come down to split-second timing and surefooted execution.

In 1996, 225 athletes will compete in six medal events at the Georgia International Horse Park in Conyers, Georgia.

Horse Sense (A Glossary)

AHSA: American Horse Show Association; membership organization founded in 1917 that determines, regulates and enforces uniform rules and procedures, official licenses and standings, recognizing shows and events.

Aids: Prompts given to the horse by a rider using body weight, legs, hands, or voice.

Canter: Gait in which the legs move in vertical pairs.

Course: Series of fences to be negotiated by horse/rider; riders are allowed to view the course prior to each event to plan a strategy.

Dressage: French word that means training.

Distance: Refers to the space between or in front of a fence or obstacle, usually stated in the number of strides.

Fault: Penalty point incurred for a fall, knockdown, or disobedience; the amount depends on the equestrian event.

FEI: Fédération Equestre Internationale; Swiss-based organization formed in 1921 to regulate the standards, rules, and judging of international equestrian competitions.

Fence: In **show jumping**, an obstacle some five feet high and some breadth (usually not to exceed height), typically constructed of colorful poles, planks, flowers, hedges, fake stone/brick, water, and other materials designed to test the skill of team. In **three-day eventing**, cross-country phase, a fixed obstacle (no more than 3'11") designed in conjunction with the surrounding terrain, usually of natural materials, which tests the skill of the team; two approaches are available (safer/slow or harder/fast).

Grand Prix Dressage: The highest level of dressage competition.

Grand Prix Jumping: Highest level, two-round show jumping event that awards the most prize money in non-Olympic contests.

Hazard: In combined driving, a maze-like obstacle of fixed construction with two options of approach (easy/slow or hard/fast) that the team must negotiate within an allotted time.

On the flat (or flat work): Term referring to riding, training or performance done at the walk, trot, canter, gallop without obstacles.

Stride: The natural distance each horse covers with each step. Riders must be able to regulate this distance to negotiate obstacles without knockdown or falling, or to exhibit a horse's obedience and athletic ability on the flat.

Test: In dressage, the execution of a series of movements, performed from memory in all higher-level competitions.

Trot: Gait in which legs move in diagonal pairs (faster than walk, slower than canter).

USET: United States Equestrian Team; a nonprofit membership organization who officially represents the United States in FEI and international equestrian competition. The U.S.ET is responsible for the selection, training, equipping, and financing of the representative equestrian teams that compete in the Olympic Games.

Walk: Gait in which legs move individually in diagonal pattern.

Walking the course: Only chance for riders to view and pace out the distance between fences or obstacles and plan an approach prior to negotiating it.

Hopefuls

The biggest concern Olympic equestrian competitors will have entering the 1996 Games in Atlanta is not how to beat the other riders but how to beat the heat.

One U.S. three-day event horse suffered heat exhaustion and dehydration at the 1992 Olympics in Barcelona, and all indications are it will be hotter and more humid in Atlanta. Every precaution is being taken to ensure that the 350 horses that will be at the Olympics are kept as cool as possible.

The average high temperature in Atlanta for the period of July 19 to August 4 is 88 degrees, higher than any Olympic host in history. Typical Julys and Augusts in Atlanta have an average of 23 days above 90 degrees. Add to that a relative humidity of 55 percent, and an urban heat index of 12 degrees, and Olympic horses and riders might be looking at 100-plus degree afternoons.

"In one word, the biggest concern with everybody around the world is the heat," U.S. jumping rider Greg Best, who won a silver medal in 1992, told the *Atlanta Journal-Constitution.* "It's unique in that we're dealing with a whole separate entity (a horse) that can't talk, that can't say, 'Listen, I'm not feeling well, listen, I'm thirsty.' It's of great concern, especially for people coming from the cooler climates."

Olympic organizers and the University of Georgia conducted studies of 500 horses in competition in hot weather to determine ways to help the animals perform in that kind of environment.

The research convinced the Fédération Equestre International to make some changes for the 1996 Olympic Games:

1. Equestrian events will begin at 7 a.m., an hour earlier than usual.

2. Distances in the three-day endurance phase will be shortened by about 15 percent.

3. A 10-minute break will be added between events.

4. Whenever possible, tracks and trails will be in shady areas.

5. Horses will be held in a cool area. Also, several teams plan to train in Atlanta for a month prior to the Olympics in order to acclimate their horses.

The other big concern in the equestrian community is an international epidemic of a horse disease called Piroplasmosis. U.S. agriculture officials will not allow any horse that has been diagnosed with the disease to enter the country. Riders are hoping that epidemic doesn't hamper the event.

"For 30 years I have dreamed of this. When they told me I was going to the Games, I could not open my mouth for three hours. I could not even move my jaw. This is something I will never forget."
— Enos Mafokate, the only black member of the South African equestrian squad

Assuming all the top riders' horses stay healthy, the **dressage** competition will probably come down to the Germans, the Swiss, and the French. The disciplined Germans win many of the most prestigious competitions, and the 1996 Olympics should be no different.

U.S. dressage riders include three-time Olympian Robert Dover, who won two show jumping silver medals at the 1988 Olympics. Dover won a bronze medal atop Dutch warmblood Devereaux at the 1994 World Equestrian Games, but he had to give up the horse in 1995, and isn't sure any new ride will be as good as Devereaux. (The owner of the horse was pregnant when she got him, so she allowed Dover to compete on him, but she has taken the prize horse back.)

Up-and-coming rider Michelle Gibson, of Roswell, Georgia, finished 7th at a 1995 Grand Prix event in Germany, the best finish of any American at a major competition that year.

The other big story in U.S. dressage this Olympic year is the status of George Lindemann, Jr., son of Cellular One magnate, George, Sr. Lindemann was indicted in July 1994 for conspiring to electrocute a horse to collect $250,000 of insurance. Lindemann was convicted in September 1995 and has filed an appeal. The American Horse Shows Association is seeking to ban him from competition.

In **show jumping**, the U.S. team is led by veteran rider Lisa Jacquin, whose horse For the Moment has helped her to numerous national titles. Jacquin won a silver medal at the 1988 Olympics, and her horse was named 1991 Horse of the Year.

The best show jumpers are expected to come from France and Germany, where courses are generally tougher than the television-friendly courses in the United States.

The U.S. Equestrian Team has one of the world's top riders in the **three-day event**. Bruce Davidson of Unionville, Pa., is a five-time Olympian. The 46-year-old won team gold medals in 1976 and 1984, and a team silver in 1972. More recently, he won the 1995 Badminton competition in England, a four-star event.

New Zealand, Great Britain, and Germany traditionally field good riders in three-day, as well.

—*Michelle Kaufman*

Schedule

The tentative equestrian schedule for dressage events is:

Saturday, July 27
team dressage session 1

Sunday, July 28
team dressage session 2 & finals

Wednesday, July 31
individual dressage final

Saturday, August 3
individual dressage freestyle final

The tentative equestrian schedule for jumping events is:

Monday, July 29
jumping first qualifier

Thursday, August 1
team jumping preliminary & final

Sunday, August 4
individual jumping final

The tentative equestrian schedule for three day events is:

Sunday, July 21
team dressage session 1

Monday, July 22
team dressage session 2

Tuesday, July 23
team speed & endurance
individual dressage session 1

Wednesday, July 24
team jumping
individual dressage session 2

Thursday, July 25
individual speed, endurance

Friday, July 26
individual jumping

DRESSAGE

Highlights

Olympic dressage competition was not only exclusively military from 1912 to 1952, it was also strictly an enforced competition for commissioned officers. (In 1948 the Swedes, who would have taken home the team gold and had earned an additional individual sixth, were disqualified after it was discovered that team member Gehnall Persson was ineligible to compete based on his lack of rank. France was awarded the gold instead.) The rules in this equestrian event underwent some radical changes before the competition reached today's level. Most notably, team competitions were not even included until 1928, and were not held at the Rome Games of 1960.

1952 was a landmark year, as the Games were opened to women and civilians in all levels of equestrian competition. Four women represented their countries in this event, and the silver medal was won by Lis Hartel of Denmark, though her legs from the knee down remained paralyzed from polio.

FACT: Germany has traditionally dominated Olympic equestrian events. German riders have captured a total of 64 medals, of which 27 were gold.

In the 1956 Games Henri Saint Cyr of Sweden became the only person to win the individual gold twice when he took the last of his four gold medals. Cyr won individual and team golds in both 1952 and 1956, and had also been a member of the disqualified gold medalist 1948 team.

After 1956 the Swedish and Dutch domination swayed in favor of the German teams. Beginning in 1964, Dr. Reiner Klimke of West Germany began an incredible Olympic career that includes team golds in 1964, 1968, 1976, 1984, and 1988, the individual bronze in 1968 and 1976, and the individual gold in 1984. In 1972, the only time in a 24-year span Dr. Klimke was not an Olympic medalist, countrywoman Liselott Linsenhoff became the first female individual gold medalist (also 1956 bronze individual medalist behind Denmark's Lis Hartel and Sweden's Cyr, as well as 1956 team silver, 1968 team gold, and 1972 team silver).

The U.S. team has won medals in dressage competition on only four occasions. In 1932 and 1976 it won the team bronze and in 1948 the team silver. The lone individual medal (the bronze) was taken by Hiram Tuttle in 1932.

Highlights from Barcelona

Not since 1912, when the Swedes outclassed their rivals, had any nation swept the individual dressage medals. At least, not until the German team swept into the Real Polo Club in Barcelona. Leading the German assault on the medals was Nicole Uphoff, who, with her mount, Rembrandt, collected a second gold medal in consecutive Games—the best equestrian performance in the history of the Olympics.

Trailing behind Uphoff was teammate Isabelle Regina Werth, on Gigolo, with only 1551 points to the twice-gilded Uphoff's 1626. Completing the German grand slam were Klaus Balkenhol and Goldstern, both of whom were on sabbatical from the Dusseldorf police. Although German riders only barely stayed in the medals in the Three-day Team event, they galloped to top honors in the dressage team competition—in which three of their four competitors were individual medalists. And Ludger Beerbaum, on Classic Touch, reined in his opponents in the individual jumping competition.

FACT: China, which entered 261 athletes in the Barcelona Games, did not compete in any equestrian events: The nation has no dearth of riders, but cannot afford to train and prep horses.

Matthew Ryan won the gold medal in the individual Three-Day Event and helped his Australian teammates win the same for the team Three-Day Event in Barcelona. *Duomo Photography*

Matthew Ryan took the gold for the Australian team in two events—individual three-day event and the team three-day event. U.S. riders took home two surprise bronze medals from Barcelona, one of which landed with the dressage team of Carol Lavell, Michael Pulin, Charlotte Bredahl, and Robert Dover.

Medalists

Equestrian—Individual Dressage

1992
1. Nicole Uphoff, Germany, Rembrandt, 1,626
2. Isabelle Werth, Germany, Gigolo, 1,551
3. Klaus Balkenhol, Germany, Goldstern, 1,515

1988
1. Nicole Uphoff, West Germany, Rembrandt 24, 1,521
2. Margitt Otto-Crepin, France, Corlandus, 1,462
3. Christine Stueckelberger, Switzerland, Gauguin de Lully Ch., 1,417

1984
1. Dr. Reiner Klimke, West Germany, Ahlerich, 1,504
2. Anne Grethe, Denmark, Marzog, 1,442
3. Otto J. Hofer, Switzerland, Limandus, 1,364

1980
1. Elisabeth Theurer, Austria, Mon Cherie, 1,370
2. Yuri Kovshov, Soviet Union, Igrok, 1,300
3. Viktor Ugriumov, Soviet Union, Shkval, 1,234

1976
1. Christine Stueckelberger, Switzerland, Granat, 1,486.0
2. Harry Boldt, West Germany, Woycek, 1,435.0
3. Reiner Klimke, West Germany, Mehmet, 1,395.0

1972
1. Liselott Linsenhoff, West Germany, Piaff, 1,229
2. Yelena Petushkova, Soviet Union, Pepel, 1,185
3. Josef Neckermann, West Germany, Venetia, 1,177

1968
1. Ivan Kisimov, Soviet Union, Ichor, 1,572
2. Josef Neckermann, West Germany, Mariano, 1,546
3. Dr. Reiner Klimke, West Germany, Dux, 1,537

1964
1. Henri Chammartin, Switzerland, Woermann, 1,504
2. Harry Boldt, West Germany, Remus, 1,503
3. Sergei Filatov, Soviet Union, Absent, 1,486

1960
1. Sergei Filatov, Soviet Union, Absent, 2,144.0
2. Gustav Fischer, Switzerland, Wald, 2,087.0
3. Josef Neckermann, West Germany, Asbach, 2,082.0

1956
1. Henri St. Cyr, Sweden, Juli, 860.0
2. Lis Hartel, Denmark, Jubilee, 850.0
3. Liselott Linsenhoff, West Germany, Adular, 832.0

1952
1. Henri St. Cyr, Sweden, Master Rufus, 561.0
2. Lis Hartel, Denmark, Jubilee, 541.5
3. Andre Jousseaume, France, Harpagon, 541.0

1948
1. Hans Moser, Switzerland, Hummer, 492.5
2. Andre Jousseaume, France, Harpagon, 480.0
3. Gustav-Adolf Boltenstern, Jr., Sweden, Trumf, 477.5

1936
1. Heinz Pollay, Germany, Kronos, 1,760.0
2. Freidrich Gerhard, Germany, Absinth, 1,745.5
3. Alois Podhajsky, Austria, Nero, 1,721.5

1932
1. Xavier Lesage, France, Taine, 343.75
2. Charles Marion, France, Linon, 305.42
3. Hiram Tuttle, U.S.A., Olympic, 300.50

1928
1. Carl Friedrich Freiherr von Langen, Germany, Draufganger, 237.42
2. Charles Marion, France, Linon, 231.00
3. Ragnar Olson, Sweden, Gunstling, 229.78

1924
1. Ernst Linder, Sweden, Piccolomini, 276.4
2. Bertil Sandstrom, Sweden, Sabel, 275.8
3. Xavier Lesage, France, Plumard, 265.8

1920
1. Janne Lundblad, Sweden, Uno, 27.937
2. Bertil Sandstrom, Sweden, Sabel, 26.312
3. Hans von Rosen, Sweden, Running Sister, 25.125

1912
1. Carl Bonde, Sweden, Emperor, 15
2. Gustav-Adolf Boltenstern, Sr., Sweden, Neptun, 21
3. Hans von Blixen-Finecke, Sr., Sweden, Maggie, 32

1896–1908
Not held

Equestrian—Team Dressage
1992
1. Germany, 5,224, Nicole Uphoff, Monica Theodorescu, Isabelle Werth, Klaus Balkenhol
2. Netherlands, 4,742, Anky Van Grunsven, Annemarie Sanders, Tineke Bartels, Ellen Bontje
3. U.S.A., 4,643, Charlotte Bredahl, Michael Poulin, Robert Dover, Carol Lavell

1988
1. West Germany, 4,302, Reiner Klimke, Ann Kathrin Linsenhoff, Monica Theodorescu, Nicole Uphoff
2. Switzerland, 4,164, Otto J. Hofer, Christine Stueckelberger, Daniel Ramseier, Samuel Schatzmann
3. Canada, 3,969, Cynthia Ishoy, Eva Maria Pracht, Gina Smith, Ashley Nicoll

1984
1. West Germany, 4,955, Reiner Klimke, Uwe Sauer, Herbert Krug
2. Switzerland, 4,673, Otto J. Hofer, Christine Stueckelberger, Amy Catherine De Bary
3. Sweden, 4,630, Ulla Hakansson, Ingamay Bylund, Louise Nathhorst

1980
1. Soviet Union, 4,383, Yuri Kovshov, Viktor Ugriumov, Vera Misevich
2. Bulgaria, 3,580, Petr Mandadzhiev, Svetoslav Ivanov, Georgi Gadzhev
3. Romania, 3,346, Anghelache Donescu, Dumitru Veliku, Petre Rosca

1976
1. West Germany, 5,155.0, Harry Boldt, Reiner Klimke, Gabriela Grillo
2. Switzerland, 4,684, Christine Stueckelberger, Ulrich Lehmann, Doris Ramseier
3. U.S.A., 4,647, Hilda Gurney, Dorothy Morkis, Edith Master

1972
1. Soviet Union, 5,095, Yelena Petushkova, Ivan Kisimov, Ivan Kalita

2. West Germany, 5,083, Liselott Linsenhoff, Josef Neckermann, Karin Schluter
3. Sweden, 4,849, Ulla Hakansson, Ninna Swaab, Maud von Rosen

1968
1. West Germany, 2,699, Josef Neckermann, Dr. Reiner Klimke, Liselott Linsenhoff
2. Soviet Union, 2,657, Ivan Kisimov, Ivan Kalita, Yelena Petushkova
3. Switzerland, 2,547, Gustav Fischer, Henri Chammartin, Marianne Gossweiler

1964
1. West Germany, 2,558, Harry Boldt, Reiner Klimke, Josef Neckermann
2. Switzerland, 2,526, Henri Chammartin, Gustav Fischer, Marianne Gossweiler
3. Soviet Union, 2,311, Sergei Filatov, Ivan Kisimov, Ivan Kalita

1960
Not held

1956
1. Sweden, 2,475, Henri St. Cyr, Gehnall Persson, Gustav-Adolf Boltenstern, Jr.
2. West Germany, 2,346, Liselott Linsenhoff, Hannelore Weygand, Anneliese Kuppers
3. Switzerland, 2,346, Gottfried Trachsel, Henri Chammartin, Gustav Fischer

1952
1. Sweden, 1,597.5, Henri St. Cyr, Gustav-Adolf Boltenstern, Jr., Gehnall Persson
2. Switzerland, 1,579.0, Gottfried Trachsel, Henri Chammartin, Gustav Fischer
3. Germany, 1,501.0, Heinz Pollay, Ida von Nagel, Fritz Thiedemann

1948
1. France, 1,269.0, Andre Jousseaume, Jean Saint-Fort Paillard, Maurice Buret
2. U.S.A., 1,256.0, Robert Borg, Earl Thomson, Frank Henry
3. Portugal, 1,182.0, Fernando Pais, Francisco Valadas, Luiz Mena e Silva

1936
1. Germany, 5,074.0, Heinz Pollay, Freidrich Gerhard, Hermann von Oppeln-Bronikowski
2. France, 4,846.0, Andre Jousseaume, Gerrard de Ballore, Daniel Gillois
3. Sweden, 4,660.5, Gregor Adlercreutz, Sven Colliander, Folke Sandstrom

1932
1. France, 2,818.75, Xavier Lesage, Charles Marion, Andre Jousseaume
2. Sweden, 2,678.00, Thomas Bystrom,

Gustav-Adolf Boltenstern, Jr., Bertil
Sandstrom
3. U.S.A., 2,576.65, Hiram Tuttle, Isaac Kitts,
Alvin Moore
1928
1. Germany, 669.72, Carl Friedrich Freiherr von
Langen, Hermann Linkenbach, Eugen Freiherr

von Lotzbeck
2. Sweden, 650.86, Ragnar Olson, Janne
Lundblad, Carl Bonde
3. Netherlands, 642.96, Jan H. van Reede,
Pierre M. R. Versteegh, Gerard W. Le Heux

1896–1924
Not held

SHOW JUMPING

Highlights

At the first individual show jumping competition in 1912, the gold medal went to French military officer Jean Cariou and his mount Mignon, a hard-fought win considering that they competed in all three equestrian events. Cariou also helped his team to the silver in show jumping, took home a bronze in the individual three-day event, and, with his teammates, just missed collecting the team three-day bronze.

For the next forty years military riders dominated Olympic competition and medal placings. A civilian first captured a medal in 1952, when Frenchman Pierre Jonqueres d'Oriola took the individual gold. He returned to recapture the individual gold and helped his team win the silver in Tokyo in 1964 and then remained an Olympic competitor through 1968.

1956 proved to be an interesting year for the Olympic equestrian events. A restrictive six-month quarantine on horses made it financially impossible to hold the equestrian events at the Melbourne, Australia, site. Olympic equestrians competed instead in Stockholm, Sweden. In Stockholm, not only were civilians and women allowed to compete for the first time, but the show jumping team bronze went to Great Britain, whose team included Patricia Smythe. Other women competitors soon were distinguishing themselves and their teams. In 1968, Great Britain's Marion Coakes and her incredible mount, a 14.2-hand (that's only 57 inches tall) pony named Stroller, took the individual silver medal.

From 1956 to 1968 the German team dominated show jumping with famous riders like Hans Gunter Winkler, who earned the

FACT: Halla—who was ridden by Hans-Gunter Winkler, the most-medaled Olympian ever— holds title as the most successful horse in Olympic competition. Halla carried his mount to individual and team wins in 1956, and a team win in 1960.

distinction of winning the most gold medals in Olympic equestrian history. His incredible career includes five gold medals: individual gold in 1956, team gold in 1956, 1960, 1964, and 1972, as well as the team bronze in 1968, and the team silver in 1976.

After 1952 the United States began to stake its own claim on show jumping medals, but only Bill Steinkraus has matched Winkler's impressive twenty-year medal winning span with the 1952 team bronze, 1960 team silver, the individual gold in 1968 (on the famous jumper Snowbound), and the 1972 team silver.

After the boycotted 1980 Moscow Olympics (where, not surprisingly, five gold medals went to the Russian team) the 1984 show jumping events proved to be a U.S.-dominated competition. The individual gold and silver medals as well as the first-ever team gold were taken home to Gladstone, New Jersey, home of the USET. The strong finish by individual silver medalist Greg Best and his mount Gem Twist helped the USET take home the team silver in 1988.

Highlights from Barcelona

Norman Dello Joio and Irish mustered an impressive third-place finish in Individual Show Jumping on an exceedingly difficult rainwater-logged course that included the dreaded Liverpool fence—said to turn reliable mounts into insubordinate mules. The bronze was one of two the American team brought home—the other for dressage.

Medalists

Equestrian—Individual Show Jumping

1992
1. Ludger Beerbaum, Germany, Classic Touch, 0.00
2. Piet Raymakers, Netherlands, Ratina Z, 0.25
3. Norman Dello Joio, U.S.A., Irish, 4.75

1988
1. Pierre Durand, France, Jappeloup, 1.25
2. Greg Best, U.S.A., Gem Twist, 4.00 (won jump-off)
3. Karsten Huck, West Germany, Nepomuk 8, 4.00

1984
1. Joe Fargis, U.S.A., Touch of Class, 4.00
2. Conrad Homfeld, U.S.A., Abdullah, 4.00
3. Heidi Robbiani, Switzerland, Jessica V, 8.00

1980
1. Jan Kowalczyk, Poland, Artemor, 8.00
2. Nikolai Korolkov, Soviet Union, Espadron, 9.50
3. Oswaldo Mendez Herbruger, Guatemala, Pampa, 12.00
3. Joaquin Perez de la Heras, Mexico, Alymony, 12.00

1976
1. Alwin Schockemoehle, West Germany, Warwick Rex, 0.00
2. Michel Vaillancourt, Canada, Branch County, 12.00
3. Francois Mathy, Belgium, Gai Luron, 12.00

1972
1. Graziano Mancinelli, Italy, Ambassador, 8/0
2. Ann Moore, Great Britain, Psalm, 8/3
3. Neal Shapiro, U.S.A., Sloopy, 8/8

1968
1. William Steinkraus, U.S.A., Snowbound, 4
2. Marion Coakes, Great Britain, Stroller, 8
3. David Broome, Great Britain, Mister Softee, 12

1964
1. Pierre Jonqueres d'Oriola, France, Lutteur, 9
2. Hermann Schridde, West Germany, Dozent, 13.75
3. Peter Robeson, Great Britain, Firecrest, 16

1960
1. Raimondo D'Inzeo, Italy, Posillipo, 12
2. Piero D'Inzeo, Italy, The Rock, 16
3. David Broome, Great Britain, Sunsalve, 23

1956
1. Hans-Gunter Winkler, West Germany, Halla, 4
2. Raimondo D'Inzeo, Italy, Merano, 8
3. Piero D'Inzeo, Italy, Uruguay, 11

1952
1. Pierre Jonqueres d'Oriola, France, Ali Baba, 8/0
2. Oscar Cristi, Chile, Bambi, 8/4
3. Fritz Thiedemann, Germany, Meteor, 8/8

1948
1. Humberto Mariles Cortes, Mexico, Arete, 6.25
2. Ruben Uriza, Mexico, Harvey, 8/0
3. Jean F. d'Orgeix, France, Sucre de Pomme, 8/4

1936
1. Kurt Hasse, Germany, Tora, 4/4/59.2
2. Henri Rang, Romania, Delfis, 4/4/72.8
3. Jozsef von Platthy, Hungary, Sello, 8/0/62.6

1932
1. Takeichi Nishi, Japan, Uranus, 8
2. Harry Chamberlin, U.S.A., Show Girl, 12
3. Clarence von Rosen, Sweden, Empire, 16

1928
1. Frantisek Ventura, Czechoslovakia, Eliot, 0/0/0
2. Pierre Bertran de Balanda, France, Papillon, 0/0/2
3. Chasimir Kuhn, Switzerland, Pepita, 0/0/4

1924
1. Alphonse Gemuseus, Switzerland, Lucette, 6
2. Tommaso Lequio, Italy, Trebecco, 8.75
3. Adam Krolikiewicz, Poland, Picador, 10

1920
1. Tommaso Lequio, Italy, Trebecco, 2
2. Alessandro Valerio, Italy, Cento, 3
3. Gustaf Lewenhaupt, Sweden, Mon Coeur, 4

1912
1. Jean Cariou, France, Mignon, 186
2. Rabod W. von Krocher, Germany, Dohna, 186
3. Emanuel de Blommaert de Soye, Belgium, Clonmore, 185

1904–1908
Not held

1900
1. Aime Haegeman, Belgium, Benton II, 2:16.0
2. Georges van de Poele, Belgium, Windsor Squire, 2:17.6
3. de Champsavin, France, Terpischore, 2:26.0

1896
Not held

Equestrian—Team Show Jumping

1992
1. Netherlands, 12.00, Piet Raymakers, Bert Romp, Jan Tops, Jos Lansink
2. Austria, 16.75, Boris Boor, Joerg Muntzner, Hugo Simon, Thomas Fruhmann
3. France, 24.75, Herve Godignon, Hubert Bourdy, Michel Robert, Eric Navet

1988
1. West Germany, 17.25, Ludger Beerbaum, Wolfgang Brinkmann, Dirk Hafemeister, Franke Sloothaak
2. U.S.A., 20.50, Greg Best, Lisa Jacquin, Anne Kursinski, Joe Fargis
3. France, 27.50, Bourdy Hubert, Frederic Cottier, Michel Robert, Pierre Durand

1984
1. U.S.A., 12.00, Joe Fargis, Conrad Homfeld, Leslie Burr, Melanie Smith
2. Great Britain, 36.75, Michael Whitaker, John Whitaker, Steven Smith, Timothy Grubb
3. West Germany, 39.25, Paul Schockemohle, Peter Luther, Franke Sloothaak, Fritz Ligges

1980
1. Soviet Union, 20.25, Viacheslav Chukanov, Viktor Poganovski, Viktor Asmaev, Nikolai Korolkov
2. Poland, 56.00, Marion Kozicki, Jan Kowalczyk, Wieslaw Hartman, Janusz Bobik
3. Mexico, 59.75, Joaquin Perez de la Heras, Jesus Gomez Portugal, Gerardo Tazzer Valencia, Alberto Valdes Lacarra

1976

1. France, 40.00, Hubert Parot, Marc Roguet, Marcel Rozier, Michel Roche
2. West Germany, 44.00, Alwin Schockemoehle, Hans-Gunter Winkler, Sonke Soenksen, Paul Schockemoehle
3. Belgium, 63.00, Francois Mathy, Eric Wauters, Edgar-Henri Cuepper, Stanny Van Paeschen

1972

1. West Germany, 32, Fritz Ligges, Gerhard Wiltfang, Hartwig Steenken, Hans-Gunter Winkler
2. U.S.A., 32.25, William Steinkraus, Neal Shapiro, Kathy Kusner, Frank Chapot
3. Italy, 48, Vittorio Orlandi, Raimondo D'Inzeo, Graziano Mancinelli, Piero D'Inzeo

1968

1. Canada, 102.75, Jim Elder, Jim Day, Tom Gayford
2. France, 110.50, Janou Lefebvre, Marcel Rozier, Pierre Jonqueres d'Oriola
3. West Germany, 117.25, Alwin Schockemoehle, Hans-Gunter Winkler, Hermann Schridde

1964

1. West Germany, 68.50, Hermann Schridde, Kurt Jarasinski, Hans-Gunter Winkler
2. France, 77.75, Pierre Jonqueres d'Oriola, Janou Lefebvre, Guy Lefrant
3. Italy, 88.50, Piero D'Inzeo, Raimondo D'Inzeo, Graziano Mancinelli

1960

1. West Germany, 46.50, Hans-Gunter Winkler, Fritz Thiedemann, Alwin Schockemoehle
2. U.S.A., 66.00, Frank Chapot, William Steinkraus, George Morris
3. Italy, 80.5, Raimondo D'Inzeo, Piero D'Inzeo, Antonio Oppes

1956

1. West Germany, 40, Hans-Gunter Winkler, Fritz Thiedemann, Alfons Lutke-Westhues
2. Italy, 66, Raimondo D'Inzeo, Piero D'Inzeo, Salvatore Oppes
3. Great Britain, 69, Wilfred H. White, Patricia Smythe, Peter Robeson

1952

1. Great Britain, 40.75, Wilfred H. White, Douglas Stewart, Harry M. Llewellyn
2. Chile, 45.75, Oscar Cristi, Cesar Mendoza, Ricardo Echeverria

3. U.S.A., 52.25, William Steinkraus, Arthur J. McCashin, John Russel

1948

1. Mexico, 34.25, Humberto Mariles Cortes, Ruben Uriza, Alberto Valdes Lacarra
2. Spain, 56.50, Jaime Garcia Cruz, Jose Navarro Morenes, Marcelino Gavilan y Ponce de Leon
3. Great Britain, 67, Harry M. Llewellyn, Henry M. V. Nicoll, Arthur Carr

1936

1. Germany, 44, Kurt Hasse, Martin von Branekow, Heinz Brandt
2. Netherlands, 51.5, Johan J. Greter, Jan A. de Bruine, Henri L. M. van Schaik
3. Portugal, 56, Jose Beltrao, Luiz Marques do Funchal, Luiz Mena e Silva

1932

No nation completed the course with three riders.

1928

1. Spain, 4, Jose Navarro Morenes, Jose Alvarez de los Trujillos, Julio Garcia Fernandez
2. Poland, 8, Kazimierz Gzowski, Kazimierz Szosland, Michal Antoniewicz
3. Sweden, 10, Karl Hansen, Carl Bjornstjerna, Ernst Hallberg

1924

1. Sweden, 42.25, Ake Thelning, Axel Stahle, Age Lundstrom
2. Switzerland, 50, Alphonse Gemuseus, Werner Stuber, Hans Buhler
3. Portugal, 53, Antonio Borges de Almeida, Helder de Souza Martins, Jose Mousinho de Albuquerque

1920

1. Sweden, 14, Hans von Rosen, Claes Konig, Daniel Norling
2. Belgium, 16.25, Henri Lamme, Andre Coumans, Herman de Gaiffier d'Hestroy
3. Italy, 18.75, Ettore Caffaratti, Giulio Cacciandra, Alessandro Alvisi

1912

1. Sweden, 25, Gustaf Lewenhaupt, Gustaf Kilman, Hans von Rosen
2. France, 32, Michel d'Astafort, Jean Cariou, Bernard Meyer
3. Germany, 40, Sigismund Freyer, Wilhelm Graf von Hohenau, Ernst-Hubertus Deloch

1896–1908

Not held

THREE-DAY EVENT

Highlights

The U.S. squad has fared best in the three-day event. Though no member has yet to capture an individual gold, Americans have earned a total of four silver and two bronze individual medals. In the team competition the U.S. has won three gold, four silver (including a three time/twelve year streak—1964 through 1972—of silver medals), as well as the initial bronze medal in 1912. The original powerhouse dressage team, Sweden, began fading in the 1950s. Sweden has won seven individual medals (including three gold in 1912, 1920, and 1956) and five team medals (gold in 1912, 1920, and 1952; silver in 1924 and 1948).

The Netherlands also were a dominant force in three-day eventing in the 1920s and early 1930s, taking seven medals: three individual golds in 1924, 1928, and 1932, as well as team gold in 1924 and 1928. Great Britain and New Zealand have remained competitive, with the British capturing the team silver in 1988 and 1984, as well as the individual bronze in 1988 (Virginia Leng) and 1984 (Virginia Holgate). New Zealand's Mark Todd captured the gold on Charisma in the 1984 and 1988 individual events and also helped his team to the 1988 bronze.

In 1988, possibly for the first time in the history of the Olympic Games, a winner's wife presented him with his medal; England's Princess Anne, who was then president of the Fédération Equestre Internationale, bestowed the team silver on Mark Phillips, who was part of the British team and was married to HRH Anne at the time.

Highlights from Barcelona

Repeating their 1988 gold-medal performance in the Three-day Team Event, the Australian team followed the lead of Matt Ryan and Kibah Tic Toc, who, at the ripe old age of 15 horse-years, flashed through the cross-country course at lightning speed. In second place, lamenting their barn full of old gray mares, were the New Zealanders, who collected several penalties along with the silver medal.

Mark Todd (c.) medaled in 1984, 1988, and 1992. The New Zealand equestrian is shown here with Great Britain competitors Ian Stark (l.) and Virginia Leng (r.) in 1988, who took the silver and bronze, respectively. *AP/Wide World*

Medalists

Equestrian—Individual Three-Day Event

1992
1. Matthew Ryan, Australia, Kibah Tic Toc, 70.00
2. Herbert Blocker, Germany, Feine Dame, 81.30
3. Robert Tait, New Zealand, Messiah, 87.60

1988
1. Mark Todd, New Zealand, Charisma, 42.60
2. Ian Stark, Great Britain, Sir Wattie, 52.80
3. Virginia Leng, Great Britain, Master Craftsman, 62.00

1984
1. Mark Todd, New Zealand, Charisma, 51.60
2. Karen Stives, U.S.A., Ben Arthur, 54.20
3. Virginia Holgate, Great Britain, Priceless, 56.80

1980
1. Federico Euro Roman, Italy, Rossinan, 108.60
2. Aleksandr Blinov, Soviet Union, Galzun, 120.80
3. Yuri Salnikov, Soviet Union, Pintset, 151.60

1976
1. Edmund Coffin, U.S.A., Bally-Cor, 114.99
2. J. Michael Plumb, U.S.A., Better and Better, 125.85
3. Karl Schultz, West Germany, Madrigal, 129.45

1972
1. Richard Meade, Great Britain, Laurieston, 57.73
2. Alessandro Argenton, Italy, Woodland, 43.33
3. Jan Jonsson, Sweden, Sarajevo, 39.67

1968
1. Jean-Jacques Guyon, France, Pitou, 38.86
2. Derek Allhusen, Great Britain, Lochinvar, 41.61
3. Michael Page, U.S.A., Foster, 52.31

1964
1. Mauro Checcoli, Italy, Surbean, 64.40
2. Carlos Moratorio, Argentina, Chalan, 56.40
3. Fritz Ligges, West Germany, Donkosak, 49.20

1960
1. Lawrence Morgan, Australia, Salad Days, 7.15
2. Neale Lavis, Australia, Mirrabooka, 16.50
3. Anton Buhler, Switzerland, Gay Spark, 51.21

1956
1. Petrus Kastenman, Sweden, Illuster, 66.53
2. August Lutke-Westhues, West Germany, Trux v. Kamax, 84.87
3. Frank Weldon, Great Britain, Kilbarry, 85.48

1952
1. Hans von Blixen-Finecke, Jr., Sweden, Jubal, 28.33
2. Guy Lefrant, France, Verdun, 54.50
3. Wilhelm Busing, Germany, Hubertus, 55.50

1948
1. Bernard Chevallier, France, Aiglonne, 4
2. Frank Henry, U.S.A., Swing low, 21
3. Robert Selfelt, Sweden, Claque, 25

1936
1. Ludwig Stubbendorf, Germany, Nurmi, 37.70
2. Earl Thomson, U.S.A., Jenny Camp, 99.90
3. Hans Mathiesen-Lunding, Denmark, Jason, 102.20

1932
1. Charles F. Pahud de Mortanges, Netherlands, Marcroix, 1,813.83
2. Earl Thomson, U.S.A., Jenny Camp, 1,811.00
3. Clarence von Rosen, Jr., Sweden, Sunnyside Maid, 1,809.42

1928
1. Charles F. Pahud de Mortanges, Netherlands, Marcroix, 1,969.82
2. Gerard de Kruijff, Netherlands, Va-t-en, 1,967.26
3. Bruno Neumann, Germany, Ilja, 1,944.42

1924
1. Adolph van der Voort van Zijp, Netherlands, Silver piece, 1,976.00
2. Frode Kirkebjerg, Denmark, Meteor, 1,853.50
3. Sloan Doak, U.S.A., Pathfinder, 1,845.50

1920
1. Helmer Morner, Sweden, Germany, 1,775.00
2. Age Lundstrom, Sweden, Yrsa, 1,738.75
3. Ettore Caffaratti, Italy, Traditore, 1,733.75

1912
1. Axel Nordlander, Sweden, Lady Artist, 46.59
2. Friedrich von Rochow, Germany, Idealist, 46.42
3. Jean Cariou, France, Cocotte, 46.32

1896–1908
Not held

Equestrian—Team Three-Day Event

1992
1. Australia, 288.60, David Green, Gillian Rolton, Andrew Hoy, Matthew Ryan
2. New Zealand, 290.80, Andrew Nicholson, Victoria Latta, Robert Tait, Mark Todd
3. Germany, 300.30, Matthias Baumann, Cord Mysegaes, Ralf Ehrenbrink, Herbert Blocker

1988
1. West Germany, 225.95, Claus Erhon, Matthias Baumann, Thies Kaspareit, Ralf Ehrenbrink
2. Great Britain, 265,80, Mark Phillips, Karen Straker, Virginia Leng, Ian Stark
3. New Zealand, 271.20, Mark Todd, Marges Knighton, Andrew Bennie, Tinks Pottinger

1984
1. U.S.A., 186.00, J. Michael Plumb, Karen Stives, Torrance Fleischmann, Bruce Davidson
2. Great Britain, 189.20, Virginia Holgate, Ian Stark, Diana Clapham, Lucinda Green
3. West Germany, 234.00, Dietmar Hogrete, Bettina Overesch, Burkhard Tesdorpf, Claus Erhom

1980
1. Soviet Union, 457.00, Aleksandr Blinov, Yuri Salnikov, Valeri Volkov, Sergei Rogozhin
2. Italy, 656.20, Federico Euro Roman, Anna Casagrande, Mauro Roman, Marina Sciocchetti
3. Mexico, 1,172.85, Manuel Mendivil, David Barcena, Soto Jose Luis Perez, Fabian Vazquez

1976
1. U.S.A.,, 441.00, Edmund Coffin, J. Michael Plumb, Bruce Davidson, Mary Anne Tauskey
2. West Germany, 584.60, Karl Schulz, Herbert Bloecker, Helmut Rethemeier, Otto Ammerman
3. Australia, 599.54, Wayne Roycroft, Mervyn Bennett, William Roycroft, Denis Piggott

1972
1. Great Britain, 95.53, Richard Meade, Mary Gordon-Watson, Bridget Parker, Mark Phillips
2. U.S.A., 10.81, Kevin Freeman, Bruce Davidson, J. Michael Plumb, James Wofford
3. West Germany, 18.00, Harry Klugmann, Ludwig Gossing, Karl Schultz, Horst Karsten

1968
1. Great Britain, 175.93, Derek Allhusen, Richard Meade, Reuben Jones
2. U.S.A., 245.87, Michael Page, James Wofford, J. Michael Plumb
3. Australia, 331.26, Wayne Roycroft, Brian Cobcroft, William Roycroft

1964
1. Italy, 85.80, Mauro Checcoli, Paolo Angioni, Giuseppe Ravano
2. U.S.A., 65.86, Michael Page, Kevin Freeman, J. Michael Plumb
3. West Germany, 56.73, Fritz Ligges, Horst Karsten, Gerhard Schulz

1960
1. Australia, 128.18, Lawrence Morgan, Neale Lavis, William Roycroft
2. Switzerland, 386.02, Anton Buhler, Hans Schwarzenbach, Rudolf Gunthardt
3. France, 515.71, Jack Louis Le Goff, Guy Lefrant, Jean R. Le Roy

1956
1. Great Britain, 355.48, Frank Weldon, Arthur L. Rock, Albert E. Hill
2. West Germany, 475.91, August Lutke-Westhues, Otto Rothe, Klaus Wagner
3. Canada, 572.72, John Rumble, James Elder, Brian Herbinson

1952
1. Sweden, 221.94, Hans von Blixen-Finecke, Jr., Olof Stahre, Folke Frolen
2. Germany, 235.49, Wilhelm Busing, Klaus Wagner, Otto Rothe
3. U.S.A., 587.16, Charles Hough, Walter Staley, John Wofford

1948
1. U.S.A., 161.50, Frank Henry, Charles Anderson, Earl Thomson
2. Sweden, 165.00, Robert Selfelt, Olof Stahre, Sigurd Svensson
3. Mexico, 305.25, Humberto Mariles Cortes, Raul Campero, Joaquin Solano Chagoya

1936
1. Germany, 676.65, Ludwig Stubbendorf, Rudolf Lippert, Konrad Van. Wangenheim
2. Poland, 991.70, Henryk Rojcewicz, Zdzislaw Kawecki, Serweryn Kulesza
3. Great Britain, 9,195.50, Alec Scott, Edward Howard-Vyse, Richard Fanshawe

1932
1. U.S.A., 5,083.083, Earl Thomson, Harry Chamberlin, Edwin Argo

2. Netherlands, 4,689.083, Charles F. Pahud de Mortanges, Karel J. Schummelketel, Aernout v. Lennep

1928
1. Netherlands, 5,865.68, Charles F. Pahud de Mortanges, Gerard de Kruijff, Adolph van der Voort van Zijp
2. Norway, 5,395.68, Bjart Ording, Arthur Quist, Eugen Johansen
3. Poland, 5,067.92, Michal Antoniewicz, Jozef Trenkwald, Karol de Rommel

1924
1. Netherlands, 5,297.5, Adolph van der Voort van Zijp, Charles F. Pahud de Mortanges, Gerard de Kruijff
2. Sweden, 4,743.5, Claes Konig, Torsten Sylvan, Gustaf Hagelin
3. Italy, 4,512.5, Alberto Lombardi, Alessandro Alvisi, Emanuele Di Pralorma

1920
1. Sweden, 5,057.50, Helmer Morner, Age Lundstrom, Georg von Braun
2. Italy, 4,735.00, Ettore Caffaratti, Garibaldi Spighi, Giulio Cacciandra
3. Belgium, 4,560.00, Roger Moeremans d'Emaus, Oswald Lints, Jules Bonvalet

1912
1. Sweden, 139.06, Axel Nordlander, Nils Adlercreutz, Ernst Casparsson
2. Germany, 138.48, Friedrich von Rochow, Richard Graf von Schaesberg-Tannheim, Eduard v. Lutcken
3. U.S.A., 137.33, Benjamin Lear, John Montgomery, Guy Henry

1896–1908
Not held

Trivia Quiz

1. The "forward seat" technique, in which the rider leans forward while the horse is jumping, was first introduced
   a. In the third century AD, by a Roman general
   b. In 1902, by an Italian
   c. During the French and Indian war

2. Horseback riding competitions were first included in the Olympics
   a. In Antwerp in 1920   **b.** In Berlin in 1944   **c.** In 648 BC

3. The first forty years Olympic equestrian events were dominated by
   a. British riders   **b.** Swiss riders   **c.** Military riders

4. Women were first allowed to compete in Olympic show jumping
   a. In Montreal in 1976   **b.** In Stockholm in 1956   **c.** In 648 BC

5. Dressage events favor
   a. Thoroughbred horses   **b.** Warmblood horses
   c. Clydesdales and shetland ponies

6. If, after two rounds, there is a tie in faults in Olympic show jumping
   a. A jump-off is held on a shortened course
   b. The two riders repeat their routines exactly
   c. The two riders toss horseshoes to determine who gets the gold medal

7. Horses are most intimidated by

a. Bank jumps   **b.** Water jumps   **c.** Overweight riders

8. In the Olympic Games, women equestrians

a. Are allowed to compete in only two of the six events

b. Compete on equal footing with men

c. Are allowed to compete in team events only

9. Equestrian events in the 1956 (Melbourne) Olympics were held

a. In Sydney, Australia   **b.** In Stockholm, Sweden

c. In Lexington, Kentucky

10. The following West German rider medaled in every Olympics from 1964 to 1988, except for the 1972 Games

a. Dr. Reiner Klimke   **b.** Dr. Franz Bibfeldt   **c.** Dr. Wilbur Post

Answers: 1-b; 2-c; 3-c; 4-b; 5-b; 6-a; 7-b; 8-b; 9-b; 10-a

FENCING

Warm-up

Like several other Olympic sports—archery and javelin, to name two—fencing traces its roots to armed combat. Swords evolved out of the daggers that were first made during the Bronze Age (4000 to 3000 BC), although nothing really practical for fighting turned up until the early Iron Age (some time prior to 1000 BC).

A decorative relief depicting practice swordplay with knobs on the ends of the weapons, dating back at least to 1190 BC, has been found in Egypt. The relief shows the fencers wearing face protection and earflaps, and it also includes umpires, tournament organizers, and spectators, so presumably this was not just a military exercise but an actual sporting event. And, in fact, fencing was one of the earliest sports to be regulated by theoretical and practical rules—necessary to ensure safety as well as to make the sport follow as closely as possible the pattern of a real sword fight.

Although the sword was the main weapon of battle from these early times until the introduction of gunpowder, little is known about the technique of swordsmanship prior to 1400. The Romans and Greeks favored a short, wide sword that would seem to capitalize on speed and agility. During the age of chivalry, the long, heavy two-handed broadsword used by the knights to crack heavy armor would suggest slower action, large movements, and the need for a great deal of strength on the part of the combattant.

With the advent of firearms in the fifteenth century, armor became obsolete, and the sword was permanently replaced as the primary weapon of the military. Lighter and better-balanced swords came into vogue, and they became the standard sidearm for the European gentleman. Cutting an opponent with the honed edge of the weapon, which was considered the most effective technique until about 1500, gradually diminished as the width of the blade decreased. The rapier, a very narrow, straight, two-edged sword, became popular, and with it came the style of fighting familiar to fans of swashbuckling movies, in which thrusting with the point of the weapon is favored. The rapier was primarily an offensive sword, defense being the province of a dagger held in the other hand.

The next major advance in technique was the use of the same weapon for both offense and defense, which resulted in the development of the smallsword in about 1650. This period heralded the arrival of modern fencing technique with a single, light, highly maneuverable weapon being held in one hand.

The Italians, Spanish, and French all claim to have created modern fencing, with plenty of available evidence supporting each country. Throughout Europe, swordplay took on the aura of a mystical high art, and fencing masters jealously guarded their secret techniques, conducting instruction behind locked doors and charging handsome fees for their wisdom. This changed in the sixteenth century when the publication of several illustrated fencing books allowed comparison of the techniques of the various masters. It quickly became apparent that the differences between the techniques were few: all stressed concentration, economy of movement, surprise, and timing—the basic elements that are still essential to win a fencing bout.

Fencing as we know it, with its distinctive rules and scoring system, can be traced back to the eighteenth century with the publication of treatises on the subject by G. Danet and D. Angelo. The equipment they describe includes the foil, originally designed as a practice weapon for the smallsword, a metal mask with a horizontal eye slit, and a protective vest or jacket. The rules they set up were intended to simulate real combat and ensure the safety of the combatants. A "convention" was adopted that limited the target to the trunk of the body, a safety factor but also probably a throwback to the time when a killing thrust to this area by a rapier or smallsword was highly desirable.

Another convention provided for an orderly and realistic alternation of play by stating that an attack had the "right of way" until it was parried, or neutralized; then the defender's counterattack had the right of way until it was parried, and so forth. This convention served two obvious purposes: first, it had the practical use of allowing an official to clearly determine which fencer had scored a legal touch, rather than trying to ascertain split-second timing; and, second, it provided for realistic sword-fighting action (in a real fight a defender would never leave himself exposed to a sharp blade while cutting into an attack; he would always parry his opponent's thrust first, then counterattack).

No discussion of fencing history would be complete without some mention of dueling. After the sword was rendered obsolete as a combat weapon by the introduction of firearms, it remained for many centuries a favored method by which gentlemen settled differences of opinion. Dueling to the death proved to be a fairly drastic way to resolve disputes—not every point of honor is worth dying for. Instead, differences of opinion were settled by seeing who could draw first blood in a sword fight. A poke in the arm or shoulder could decide the argument—with the added advantage that both opponents survive the duel, perhaps even to enjoy a glass of wine together after. The modern épée, the second of fencing's three weapons, had its origins with swords that were specifically developed for dueling purposes. (Its name comes from the French term for dueling sword, *épée de terrain*.)

The third modern fencing weapon, the sabre, is a direct descendant of the cavalry sabre used for centuries by mounted troops, although clearly its origins go back even further to ancient times, to the first flat-bladed swords with a honed edge. It is the only one of the three that may be used with a cutting motion in addition to the thrusting moves of the foil and épée.

FACT: The 1906 Athens Games included the three-cornered sabre—the event has never again been included on the Olympic roster.

At the time of the first modern Olympics, in 1896, fencing was a clear choice to be included in the program. For one thing, the sword was still an important military weapon, with students at all respectable military academies taking instruction in swordsmanship. And, of course, sword fighting was by that time a well established European tradition with centuries of history behind it. Also, French Baron Pierre de Coubertin, who initiated the Modern Games, was himself a fencer. Since that time, fencing has been one of only six sports to have been featured in every modern Olympic Games.

Needless to say, Europeans dominated the sport from the beginning, with champions in the thrusting weapons emerging from a variety of countries, including France, Italy, Spain, Great Britain, the former Soviet Union, and the Netherlands; Hungary became the traditional leader in the sabre competition. Following World War II, however, state support of athletes in the socialist countries allowed them to make remarkable strides in Olympic fencing competition, and the Eastern European nations became the leaders for many years. The 1960 Olympics in Rome marked the end of an era: for the first time in 48 years neither a French nor an Italian fencer won the foil event, the gold medal being taken that year by the U.S.S.R.

In the 1970s and 1980s, a considerable realignment took place in international fencing. The Poles broke the Hungarian stronghold in the sabre, while the Hungarians asserted themselves in the thrusting weapons, especially épée. Then came several years of Soviet domination. In 1992, Hungary and France did well in the sabre competitions, as did Italy and the Unified Team. The French also had a strong presence in the épée events, where they shared their medal-winning status with the Unified Team, Germany, and Hungary.

FACT: Hungary's Aladar Gerevich holds the most Olympic gold medals, with seven—all in sabre.

Spectator's Guide

Fencing has been called "chess with muscles," an indication of the complicated strategy, the moves, counter-moves, and counter-counter-moves, that make up a fencing bout. Even determining when a hit has taken place (at one time merely a matter of seeing who was bleeding, or, later, relying on an honorable opponent to mention a hit scored against himself by acknowledging, "I was touched," or "touché") is complicated by the flashing blades and lightning-quick movements of the competitors. Modern fencing, with its emphasis on agility, quickness, and subtlety of movement, can be difficult to follow without at least a brief explanation of its fundamentals.

The key to fencing is distance and timing. The goal is to deliver the business end of the weapon on target by getting close enough to your opponent to score the touch at a time when he or she is out of position to block the attack. The basic attack move is the **lunge**, in which the body is propelled forward by straightening the back leg while the front leg is advanced and the blade is extended toward the target. This may be countered by a recovery from a lunge on the part of the opponent (if he or she is already in a lunge position) or by a retreat, in which the defender moves backward several paces.

Occasionally, an attacker will choose to employ the **flèche,** or running attack. This is a very dramatic and flamboyant movement (especially when employed in a sabre bout), in which the fencer actually runs at his or her opponent. It is also incredibly risky, as it sacrifices balance, limits the types of recoveries available, and generally exposes the fencer to a variety of counterattacks. Nevertheless, the flèche can be an effective strategy, and it never fails to impress onlookers.

Ten fencing events are held at the Olympics, six for men (individual and team events in each of the three weapons) and four for women (individual and team foil and individual and team épée). Through the years, other fencing events have come and gone, some of them rather strange—for example, outdoor fencing—and some a bit less bizarre—such as three-weapon events (in which entrants competed in all three weapons). One other Olympic event, the modern pentathlon, features fencing, along with running, swimming, riding, and shooting.

The Weapons

The **foil** is the sword of choice for the majority of fencers. Designed as a training weapon, the foil still serves as the introductory weapon for virtually all fencers. That does not mean, however, that it should be regarded only as a beginner's weapon. On the contrary, the foil is often said to be the most difficult of the three to master.

A foil may be up to 1100 millimeters (43.307 inches) in total length and up to 500 grams (17.637 ounces) in weight, although with the modern emphasis on quickness, it is often much lighter. Foils feature four-sided blades, rectangular in cross-section, a circular hand guard, and a handle that can vary according to the preference of the individual fencer. Traditionally, the French preferred a relatively straight grip, about eight inches in length, while the Italian version added a cross bar about two inches behind the guard. Today, however, rather oddly shaped orthopedic grips, specially designed for comfort and precise control, have become commonplace.

Although the foil is, of course, blunted, it is in theory a pointed sword capable of inflicting a puncture wound only; the blade is not presumed to be honed along its edge. A touch in a foil event is scored only when the point of the blade hits a valid target area. And the valid foil target is the torso only, from the collar to the groin lines in front, and from the collar to the hips in back. Since this is, historically, a training event for combat, only those hits that would inflict potentially fatal wounds are counted. (Notice, however, that the head is not a valid target, a holdover from the days before masks, when even a blunted weapon could cause severe damage to the face.)

Off-target hits don't count against a fencer but result in the bout being temporarily stopped, then re-started. The bout is also stopped if either competitor steps off the fencing "strip," a narrow rectangle 2 meters wide by 14 meters long on which matches in all three weapons take place; a fencer who goes off the side of the strip is penalized by the loss of ground, and one who retreats more than a limited distance is penalized by having a touch scored against him or her. A match is ended when a fencer has been touched five times in a men's bout or four times in a women's event.

FACT: Fencers wear white uniforms because in the early days of fencing, hits were determined by an ink spot left on the uniform by the weapon. Wily competitors would dip their uniforms in vinegar so that when the weapon hit their uniform, no mark was left.

Foil fencing is characterized by a group of "conventions," rules that have evolved from the desire to make the sport resemble as closely as possible a real sword fight. Once an attack has been started, the defender must neutralize, or "parry" the thrust before beginning a counterattack. If a defender attacks into an attack (a very dangerous and foolhardy move that could, in a real duel, result in the death of both opponents), that defender does not score a legal touch. The determination of "right of way" is made by a tournament official called the president or director.

To assist the director in making these judgments, electrical scoring was introduced to foil fencing in 1955. (It had been in use in épée events since 1935.) Lights come on to signal hits—usually a colored light for a touch on a valid target, white on an invalid target. Before electricity, fencers were expected to do the sportsmanlike thing and acknowledge valid hits scored upon themselves by saying "touché," French for "I was touched." Competitors wear metallic vests that delineate the valid target area; a wire running up the back and down the sleeve connects to a button at the tip of the weapon; simply pushing in the button against any surface other than the vest results in signalling an invalid hit, while the button's contact with the metal in the vest signals a good touch. But in watching a foil bout, bear in mind that the timing of the hits is crucial, and even though lights may go on simultaneously, the official may award a point to one fencer based on the right-of-way convention.

The **épée** (pronounced *eh*-pay in English, or eh-*pay*, if you insist on proper French) is similar to the foil in that it is a thrusting weapon only and is the same length as the foil. But the épée is considerably heavier, weighing up to 770 grams (27.16 ounces).

The blade of an épée is triangular in cross section, making it quite a bit stiffer than a foil, and its hand guard is significantly larger.

Since the épée evolved from dueling weapons, and since the object of many duels was to draw first blood and not necessarily deliver a fatal thrust, the épée has no invalid target. Hits from head to toe count as touches. It is, therefore, the simplest of the three weapons to follow in a bout. And it was the first of the three to be electrified in the 1930s; all that was required was a rudimentary plunger on the end of the blade.

The only thing remotely sophisticated about electric épée equipment is its ability to "lock out" a second light within a split second, thus eliminating constant simultaneous touches and, incidentally, making this the easiest type of fencing for the novice viewer to understand: The light signals a point.

The **sabre** is the only weapon that can score points by cutting, or slicing, in addition to thrusting. Its blade is V-shaped and narrow, fairly stiff when used with a cutting motion but quite flexible in the flat plane (that is, when moved side to side). The maximum overall length of the sabre is 1050 millimeters (41.338 inches), and it has the same maximum weight as the foil. While in the *en guard*, or "ready," position, a foil or épée fencer's arm is generally in line with the blade, while the sabre is held roughly perpendicular to the arm. As a result, the sabre's handguard sweeps around the back of the hand to the pommel, so that it protects the fencer's knuckles against cuts.

Having evolved from the cavalry sabre, the fencing sabre takes as its target area the entire body above the waist, the most logical targets for a mounted warrior. As in foil competition, sabre bouts are regulated by conventions, with the same right-of-way rule in effect. Unlike foil and épée bouts, however, sabre matches until very recently were officiated manually, since this weapon proved to be the most complicated to electrify. The director presided over the bout with four judges watching for touches. But new advances in technology have finally allowed the sabre to catch up with the other weapons, and in 1992 (for the first time), Olympic sabre matches were officiated with the aid of electrical equipment.

Sabre fencing is often considered the most exciting of the three weapons to watch. Since the sabre offers a wider variety of targets than the foil, as well as cutting attacks not possible with either the foil or the épée, sabre movements tend to be noisier and more flamboyant. The movements are also larger than the tiny, quick maneuvers of the other weapons, making sabre bouts easier for casual fans to enjoy.

No matter which weapon is being used, some movements are common to all fencing bouts. The action begins at the center of the strip with the opponents facing each other, masks in hand. They salute the director first, then each other, by raising their weapons, guard level with the chin, then snapping them down smartly.

At the command "*en guard*" from the director, the competitors put on their masks and assume the ready position, standing sideways to each other (to present the smallest possible target), the weapon held out in front of the body, the empty hand raised behind the body to help provide balance (except in sabre fencing, in which the empty hand is rested on the hip), with the weight evenly distributed, ready to move either backward or forward. At the command "fence," they are free to engage each other, trying to touch and avoid being touched.

FACT: In the days when contestants dueled in armor, the competitors were required to show their faces to prove their identities before the bout. It is in this tradition that fencers still salute with their masks off.

Although, ultimately, a time limit is imposed on all fencing bouts, the action generally continues until a hit is made, either valid or invalid, or until one of the contestants steps off the strip. If a legal touch is scored, the fencers return to the center of the strip to begin the next point. If an invalid hit occurs, the action picks up at that point. And if a fencer leaves the strip, the director may assess a penalty against the violator by resuming the action closer to that competitor's end of the strip, causing him or her to "lose ground," or give up maneuvering room.

A few final points on viewing fencing matches: Do not expect to hear competitors screaming "Touché" after scoring points; this would be considered extremely gauche, even for beginners. However, traditionally, before the advent of electrical scoring, the competitor upon whom a touch was scored was expected to acknowledge the touch by uttering a "touché," to avoid any unseemly argument that would mar the battle. Disarming an opponent counts for nothing; if a fencer should lose his or her weapon, the director stops the bout until both competitors are ready to resume.

Glossaire d'Escrime

Advance: A short step forward.

Armorer: Checks, verifies, and fixes equipment for competitions.

Attack: A series of movements by which a fencer tries to score a touch.

Beat: A sharp tap made on the opponent's blade to deflect it.

Black Card: Given for extreme penalties; results in exclusion from competition.

Bout: Each pair of fencers.

Closing in (or corps à corps): Occurs when blade guards or fencers' bodies come in contact with each other; results in a penalty in foil or sabre.

Composite attack: An attack in more than one movement.

Corps-a-Corps: Physical contact between two fencers. The referee halts the action when this occurs.

Counterattack: An attack by a fencer who has just defeated—or "parried"—an attack by an opponent.

Counter-parry (or circular parry): A defensive movement executed by making a small circle with the point of the weapon around the opponent's blade.

Counter-riposte: A riposte that follows the parry of an opponent's riposte.

Coupé: An attack made by passing the blade over an opponent's blade.

Director: The primary (or, in most cases, the only) official presiding over a fencing bout.

Disengage: Any break of contact between blades; term commonly used to indicate any avoidance of contact.

Double touch: Both fencers being hit at the same time; if one has the right of way, in foil or sabre, a touch is counted against the other; in épée, both fencers have a touch scored against them.

Engagement: Contact of blades.

En guard (or on guard): The position taken before the fencers begin a bout; also, a command given by the director to warn the fencers that the bout is about to begin.

Enveloppement: A continuous binding movement so that the opponent's blade is carried for at least one complete circle.

Feint: A false attack, intended to cause the opponent to move his or her guard, thus opening a new line for attack.

Flèche: A running attack; literally, "arrow" or "dart."

Glide: A gentle forward action in contact with the opponent's blade.

Guard: The part of the weapon that protects the hand.

Invitation: Any movement intended to tempt an opponent into an attack.

Jump: An advance in which both feet move at the same time.

Fencing

Lunge: The most common and basic attack, characterized by a straightening of the back leg and the advancing of the front leg as the weapon is thrust forward.

Parry: A defensive action that blocks an attacking blade to keep it off target.

Piste: The French term (meaning "path") for the fencing strip.

Pommel: A nut at the butt-end of the weapon that holds it together.

President: Another name for the director.

Recover: Return to the *en guard* position after lunging.

Red Card: Penalty for second offense (penalty touch).

Remise (or replacement): Immediately attacking again after an initial attack.

Riposte: The defender's counterattack after a parry.

Simple: An action completed in one movement (as opposed to a composite).

Stop thrust: A counterattack against an opponent's attack or riposte, intended to land with sufficient time advantage over an opponent's action to score a touch.

Strip: The fencing area, 2 meters wide by 14 meters in length.

Taking: Controlling an opponent's blade.

Thrust: Extending the arm and threatening the target with the tip of the weapon.

Yellow Card: Penalty for the first offense (warning).

Hopefuls

Michael and Leslie Marx

Some could call it a marriage of convenience.

When U.S. fencers—and marriage partners—Michael and Leslie Marx need workout partners, they need to look no further than across the dinner table.

The Marxes?

Duck soup?

"At home, alone, sometimes we will practice against each other," Leslie Marx told *USA Today*. And, as might be expected, sometimes things get a little personal.

"That time comes when we're practicing something, and he has to correct me," Leslie says. "It's hard to take correction. It's irrational, but I feel like he doesn't like me, he doesn't love me anymore. But he's just trying to make me be better."

If that's the case, he's been doing a pretty good job.

Michael Marx, 38 (b. July 7, 1958), a native of Portland, Ore., and the vice-president of the U.S. Fencing Association, is the former coach of the University of Notre Dame fencing team. At 17, he was the youngest fencer to win a Division 1 National Championship at Indiana University—South Bend in the men's foil. He currently coaches at the Rochester (N.Y.) Fencing Centre and teaches physical education to home-schooled children.

Michael was a member of U.S. Olympic teams from 1980 through 1992. Leslie, 29 (b. April 24, 1967), was a gold medalist at the 1995 Pan Am games.

Each was ranked No. 1 in the U.S. in 1995 in épée, the descendent of the dueling sword. (The foil descends from the dueling rapier; the sabre, from the Calvary sword.)

Michael Marx has been fencing for more than two decades. Leslie came to the sport almost by accident much later.

Leslie Marx was a freshman at Duke University when she chose fencing over volleyball, racquetball, and tennis as a physical education elective. She was subsequently recruited out of that class by Duke fencing coach Alex Beguinet, who later introduced Leslie to Mark.

Leslie spent her junior year practicing with the Duke varsity, then earned Academic All-American honors as valedictorian of her class as a senior.

In June 1993, in what the Marxes hope is a portent of things to come, Leslie, a native of Houston, won a national championship in épée and Michael, who will also compete in épée at the Olympics, won a national championship in sabre.

The blade of the épée is triangular, about 36 inches long and 27 ounces in weight. Fencers score by recording electronic "touches" on opponents. The épée is wired with a spring-loaded tip which completes an electrical circuit when depressed to 750 grams of pressure or more. Closing the circuit causes the scoring machine to light. Unlike the foil, where the target area is comprised only by the torso, the target area in the épée is the entire body.

"The blade is a bit different than others," Leslie says. "So are the rules. But mainly, it's the target area."

Leslie, with her slim, 5-foot-11 frame is more suited for épée than foil, she says.

"I'm tall and not fast enough for the foil," she says. "My height helps in épée and I've had a lot of success in it."

Why did she choose fencing in the first place?

She says it was because the sport seemed more "brainy." (Indeed, the title of a *Cosmopolitan* magazine article, no less, called fencing *The sexy, cerebral sport.*)

"The part I like best is trying to understand your opponent," says Leslie, who teaches business at the W.E. Simon School of Business at the University of Rochester. "You have to figure out what they're going to do next. Why are they closer to you? Why are they farther away? Then you have to think about how you want to counter that. The strategic part is the most challenging."

For Michael, who finished 36th out of 59 competitors in the men's foil at Barcelona in 1992, competing on the same team with his wife will complete a rather unique trifecta.

He has competed on the same Olympic team with his brother, Robert, a three-time Olympian, who finished 24th in the épée out of 70 at Barcelona in 1992. He has also competed on the same Olympic team as a student of his, Molly Sullivan, who placed 39th in women's foil at Barcelona.

"Now, I want to go with my wife," he says.

Michael Marx says that making the 1996 team in Atlanta satisfies only a first goal for the husband-wife team.

"We both want a result," he says. "We both want a medal."

That might be a tall order. The U.S. has had only 11 medalists in Olympic fencing history. Its last medalist was Peter Westbrook in the boycott-tainted LA Olympics in 1984; Westbrook took a bronze in the men's individual sabre.

If lightning were to strike, the hope is that it might do so twice.

Medals.

Plural.

It would be a great story, sure.

It also might keep things a lot simpler, safer and more harmonious during some of those homey Marx practice sessions.

—Eric Kinkopf

Peter Westbrook

Peter Westbrook's mother bribed him into take fencing lessons.

At 15, Westbrook, who is black, was running with a bad crowd in a Newark housing project. Mariko Westbrook, a native of Japan with a family history of Samurai warriors, offered her son $5 for every fencing class he would take. She figured the lessons would get him off the street.

"My mother saw that if I got involved in basketball, the clientele of people I would be mingling with would be the same as the environment I was already in," Westbrook told *The New York Times*. "In her mind, that was a no-win situation."

Westbrook took one lesson.

"Then I would say that I was going to quit and she would give me another $5," he says. "I did that a few times to get some pocket money, but after awhile, I loved it. It was great. It was a sport where you could hit people like a fighting sport. As an inner city youth, we always used to fight each other anyway. It was a very natural transition for an inner city youth."

As for the $5?

He laughs. "When people ask me if I would like to see fencing become a professional sport, I laugh and tell them I started as a pro."

Westbrook went on to win a rare fencing scholarship to New York University, where he earned a degree in marketing, and became not only the nation's first black fencing champion, but the top American fencer of the century, winning spots on five U.S. Olympic teams, including the 1992 squad in Barcelona. He also became the only American to win a sabre medal at an Olympics, when he won a bronze in 1984 in Los Angeles, the first U.S. fencer, at that time, to win a medal in 24 years.

His list of accomplishments are far too long to mention. Suffice it to say, in a brief update, that, at 44 (b. April 16, 1952), Westbrook was the 1995 U.S. national champion in sabre—his 13th national title in sabre—and 1995 gold medalist at the Pan Am Games.

None of that, however, will be his legacy.

Or should be.

Westbrook's legacy, most believe, will be the Peter Westbrook Foundation, which he formed in 1991 to teach the art of fencing to disadvantaged and inner-city youngsters.

"We're giving kids discipline and helping them cope with their anxieties," says Westbrook, who carries a warm, quick smile and a contagious enthusiasm. "We're accomplishing what we set out to do—building the self-esteem in these inner-city kids. We're using fencing as a vehicle to teach kids how to win and lose, deal with stress and control emotions. Fencing can help these kids to think creatively."

Westbrook, who carried the U.S. flag at the closing ceremonies in Barcelona, started the foundation with $2,000 of his own money and has placed ads in fencing publications to seek donations. Along the way, he attracted several high-profile black athletes, such as the late Arthur Ashe and Wilma Rudolph to join the foundation's board of directors.

"The fencing experience enriches the mind not only through the discipline of athletic training, but also through exposure to the various cultures that have practiced the sport through the centuries," he says. "I want these kids to have a cross-cultural experience, and I want them to develop the skills and self-control necessary to channel their emotions into positive outlets."

Indeed, after only four years of existence, the Foundation sent two fencers to the World Junior Olympic Championships in Paris and had three others nationally ranked.

Westbrook told *The New York Times* about his sport: "It's an esoteric sport, a white, elitist sport. There is a white aristocracy in fencing in this country. When I started, blacks were not allowed to become members of the New York Athletic Club. Now, they ask me to join. I was able to overcome barriers because of my God-given talent."

"But I still get two things when I tell people that I'm a fencer. They say, 'You fence? What do you fence?' Like I'm stealing things or something (and selling them). Or, I hear, 'What kind of fences do you put up?' "

Still, the kid who dressed like TV's Zorro on a Halloween before he took up the sport and who once carved the black-caped hero's name as Z-O-R-O ("I left the other R out," he says; "I wasn't a great speller at 10) doesn't let his anonymity bother him.

"I could get more notoriety and more money in other sports, but it doesn't bother me at all," he says. "It's just the nature of fencing. I just feel very fortunate and I want to give back what I can."

So, he has.

Still, there is a matter of the 1996 Olympics. To succeed there, Westbrook, who has lost some of his lightning-quick ability, must rely on his defensive strategy and experience.

After his 1995 Pan Am gold medal, Westbrook said, "I prepared myself as much as any 42-year-old could competing against opponents half my age."

Just being in Atlanta, of course, is something special.

"The Olympics are an addiction," Westbrook said about the 1992 Games in Barcelona. "First, you're trying just to go once. Then, it's two and three and four and five. An addiction is an addiction. But if I'd go to the next one in Atlanta, it would be neurosis."

Consider him so diagnosed.

—Eric Kinkopf

Schedule

The tentative fencing schedule is:

Saturday, July 20
Men's individual épée 1/32, 1/16, 1/8 & quarterfinals
Men's individual épée semifinals 1 and 2, bronze & gold

Sunday, July 21
Women's individual épée 1/32, 1/16, 1/8 & quarterfinals
Men's individual sabre 1/32, 1/16, 1/8 & quarterfinals
Women's individual épée semifinals, bronze & gold
Men's individual sabre semifinals, bronze & gold

Monday, July 22
Women's & Men's individual foil 1/32, 1/16, 1/8 & quarterfinals
Women's & Men's individual foil semifinals, bronze & gold

Tuesday, July 23
Men's team épée 1/8, quarterfinals, 5-12 places & semifinals
Men's team épée bronze & gold

Wednesday, July 24
Women's team épée 1/8, quarterfinals, 5-12 places & semifinals
Men's team sabre 1/8, quarterfinals, 5-12 places & semifinals
Women's & Men's team épée bronze & gold
Men's team sabre bronze & gold

Thursday, July 25
Women's & Men's team foil 1/8, quarterfinals, 5-12 places & semifinals
Women's & Men's team foil bronze & gold

Highlights

Fencing has been a part of every modern Olympics, one of only six sports able to make this claim. Men's events have been featured since the first modern Games in 1896, while women began competing in Olympic competition in 1924.

Interestingly (and, perhaps, fittingly), Jean Georgiadis of Greece took the gold medal in the sabre competition at the 1896 games, the last time the Greeks ever won that event. In the early years, amateur and professional fencers (fencing masters) competed against each other. In 1900, in a joint foil-épée contest, professional Albert Ayat of France came in first, defeating Cuban champion Ramon Fonst. Fonst was Ayat's pupil. And one of the greatest masters of the time, Italo Santelli, competed along with the amateurs. A generation of Santelli-trained Hungarian sabre fencers began a period of Hungarian domination of that weapon that started with the London Olympics in 1908 and lasted sixty years.

FACT: Sweden's Kerstin Palm, who finished twenty-ninth in the women's individual foil at the 1988 Games, became the first woman in any sport to compete in seven Olympics.

The United States won its first fencing medal in Antwerp in 1920, a bronze in team foil. (American Albertson Van Zo Post won a gold in team foil in 1904, the only American ever to receive a gold medal in Olympic fencing, but he was teamed with Cubans Fonst and Manuel Diaz at the time.) The first American individual medalist was George C. Calnan, a Navy lieutenant who took the bronze in épée at the 1928 Olympics. In the first post-World War II Olympics, held in London in 1948, the U.S. sabre team took the bronze, and the foil team finished fourth; Maria Cerra Tishman finished fourth in women's foil, while George V. Worth was the best male finisher with a fifth place in sabre.

At the 1960 Rome Olympics, Albert Axelrod took third place in individual foil, and the U.S. sabre team finished fourth. Peter Westbrook's bronze medal in individual sabre capped the 1984 Olympics. The best overall U.S. Olympic performance ever was probably 1932 in Los Angeles, when the American fencers took third place in team foil, third in team épée, and fourth in team sabre, while George Calnan finished sixth in sabre, Norman Armitage was ninth in sabre, and Marion Lloyd Vince took ninth place in women's foil.

West Germany won numerous fencing medals in 1976, 1984, and 1988—many of them could be traced to the Tauberbischofsheim fencing club, situated in a town of 12,000 residents.

Highlights from Barcelona

Fencing victories in Barcelona had a bittersweet edge, as

everyone, including Olympic officials, wondered whether the sport had a future in Games to come. "People think of 'Captain Blood' and 'Scaramouche,' George Lucas's 'Star Wars,'" U.S. team captain Carl Borack explained. But the truth is, even though fencing has been around since the first modern Games, few people understand the subtle beauty of the sport.

In an effort to punch up their chances of remaining on the Olympic roster, officials and competitors at latter-day Games have begun to consider how they might make their thrusts and parries more palatable to the paying public: "You could make clear masks, so people could see the faces," Borack, for one, speculated. "You could put colored lights on the jacket itself, so people could see where the hit was."

The French, who have a long and romantic history of the sword, scored quite at hit at the Barcelona Games. At the age of 32, Philippe Omnes had several French champion titles, a world title, and a score to settle from his disappointing experience at Seoul. Having shared in only a team bronze in LA, Omnes made the 1992 French team by the skin of his teeth. Once ensconced in Barcelona, he lived up to his reputation as the best foil fencer of his generation,

FACT: The Soviet Union's Yelena (Belova) Novikova holds the most Olympic gold fencing medals of any woman, with four, all in foil. At the 1976 Games, she captured her final victory of the Montreal Olympics on her 29th birthday.

Caitlin Banos-Bilodeaux (U.S.) faces her opponent, Jie E (China), during the Women's Team Foil event in Barcelona. Though Bilodeaux is the most-titled U.S. woman fencer, she earned no medals in 1992. *U.S. Fencing Association*

eventually beating the Ukraine's Serguei Goloubitski (who is ten years his junior) in the final. Then, outdueling Russia's Pavel Kolobkov, Eric Srecki notched a second gold for the French team in the individual, while Jean-Michel Henry collected a bronze in the same event.

Not to be out-parried by the French, the Italian team clinched two gold medals, thanks to the stylish engagements of their women fencers. Having beaten China's Juifeng Wang to the individual foil title, Giovanna Trillini scored a second gold as the Italian women's foil team outscored a very disappointed German team. In a taut battle for the bronze medal, Romania dominated the Unified Team, whose only medal came in a third-place finish in the women's individual foil.

"I wish people could understand the beauty of my sport— you have to think, you have to be strong, you have to be quick."
—U.S. fencer Caitlin Banos-Bilodeaux

Meanwhile, no U.S. athlete stepped up to challenge Albertson Van Zo Post's title as the only U.S. fencer to capture an Olympic title (in 1904). Collecting no medals for their troubles, Caitlin Banos-Bilodeaux (the most-titled U.S. woman fencer) placed 29th in the women's foil, while Michael Lofton managed a 21st-place finish in men's sabre.

Medalists

Fencing—Men's Individual Épée

1992
1. Eric Srecki, France
2. Pavel Kolobkov, Russia
3. Jean-Michel Henry, France

1988
1. Arnd Schmitt, West Germany
2. Philippe Riboud, France
3. Andrei Chouvalov, Soviet Union

1984
1. Philippe Boisse, France
2. Bjorne Vaggo, Sweden
3. Philippe Riboud, France

1980
1. Johan Harmenberg, Sweden
2. Erno Kolczonay, Hungary
3. Philippe Riboud, France

1976
1. Alexander Pusch, West Germany
2. Juergen Hehn, Great Britain
3. Gyozo Kulcsar, Hunary

1972
1. Dr. Csaba Fenyvesi, Hungary

2. Jacques Ladegaillerie, France
3. Gyozo Kulcsar, Hungary

1968
1. Gyozo Kulcsar, Hungary
2. Grigori Kriss, Soviet Union
3. Gianluigi Saccaro, Italy

1964
1. Grigori Kriss, Soviet Union
2. Henry Hoskyns, Great Britain
3. Guram Kostava, Soviet Union

1960
1. Giuseppe Delfino, Italy
2. Allan Jay, Great Britain
3. Bruno Khabarov, Soviet Union

1956
1. Carlo Pavesi, Italy
2. Giuseppe Delfino, Italy
3. Edoardo Mangiarotti, Italy

1952
1. Edoardo Mangiarotti, Italy
2. Dario Mangiarotti, Italy
3. Oswald Zappelli, Switzerland

1948
1. Luigi Cantone, Italy
2. Oswald Zappelli, Switzerland
3. Edoardo Mangiarotti, Italy

1936
1. Franco Riccardi, Italy
2. Saverio Ragno, Italy
3. Giancarlo Cornaggia-Medici, Italy

1932
1. Giancarlo Cornaggia-Medici, Italy
2. Georges Buchard, France
3. Carlo Agostoni, Italy

1928
1. Lucien Gaudin, France
2. Georges Buchard, France
3. George Calnan, U.S.A.

1924
1. Charles Delporte, Belgium
2. Roger Ducret, France
3. Nils Hellsten, Sweden

1920
1. Armand Massard, France
2. Alexandre Lippmann, France
3. Gustave Buchard, France

1912
1. Paul Anspach, Belgium
2. Ivan Osiier, Denmark
3. Philippe Le Hardy de Beaulieu, Belgium

1908
1. Gaston Alibert, France
2. Alexandre Lippmann, France
3. Eugene Olivier, France

1906
1. Georges de la Falaise, France
2. Georges Dillon-Kavanagh, France
3. Alexander van Blijenburgh, Netherlands

1904
1. Ramon Fonst, Cuba
2. Charles Tatham, Cuba
3. Albertson Van Zo Post, Cuba

1900
1. Ramon Fonst, Cuba
2. Louis Perree, France
3. Leon See, France

1896
Not held

Fencing—Men's Team Épée

1992
1. Germany, Elmar Borrmann, Robert Felisiak, Arnd Schmitt, Uwe Proske, Vladimir Reznitchenko
2. Hungary, Ivan Kovacs, Krisztian Kulcsar, Ferenc Hegedus, Erno Kolczonay, Gabor Totola
3. Unified Team, Pavel Kolobkov, Andrei Chouvalov, Serguei Kravtchouk, Serguei Kostarev, Valeri Zakharevitch

1988
1. France, Frederic Delpla, Jean Michel Henry, Olivier Lenglet, Philippe Riboud, Eric Srecki
2. West Germany, Elmer Borrmann, Volker Fischer, Thomas Gerull, Alexander Pusch, Arnd Schmitt
3. Soviet Union, Andrei Chouvalov, Pavel Kolobkov, Vladimir Reznitchenko, Mikhail Tichko, Igor Tikhomirov

1984
1. West Germany, Elmer Borrmann, Volker Fischer, Gerhard Heer, Rafael Nickel, Alexander Pusch
2. France, Philippe Boisse, Jean-Michel Henry, Olivier Lenglet, Philippe Riboud, Michel Salesse
3. Italy, Stefano Bellone, Sandro Cuomo, Cosimo Ferro, Roberto Manzi, Angelo Mazzoni

1980
1. France, Philippe Riboud, Patrick Picot, Hubert Gardas, Philippe Boisse, Michel Salesse
2. Poland, Piotr Jabikowski, Andrzej Lis, Leszek Swornowski, Ludomir Chronowski, Mariusz Strzalka
3. Soviet Union, Ashot Karagian, Boris Lukomski, Aleksandr Abushakhmetov, Aleksandr Mozhaev

1976
1. Sweden, Carl von Essen, Hans Jacobson, Rolf Edling, Orvar Jonsson, Goran Flodstrom
2. West Germany, Alexander Pusch, Juergen Hehn, Hanns Jana, Rheinhold Behr, Volker Fischer
3. Switzerland, Jean-Blaise Evequoz, Michel Poffet, Daniel Giger, Christian Kauter, Francois Suchanecki

1972
1. Hungary, Sandor Erdos, Gyozo Kulcsar, Dr. Csaba Fenyvesi, Pal Schmitt, Istvan Osztrics
2. Switzerland, Guy Evequoz, Peter Lotscher, Daniel Giger, Christian Kauter, Francois Suchanecki
3. Soviet Union, Viktor Modsalevsky, Georgi Saschitski, Sergei Paramonov, Igor Valetov, Grigori Kriss

1968
1. Hungary, Csaba Fenyvesi, Zoltan Nemere, Pal Schmitt, Gyozo Kulcsar, Pal Nagy
2. Soviet Union, Grigori Kriss, Yosif Vitebsky, Aleksei Nikanchikov, Yuri Smoliakov, Viktor Modzelevsky

3. Poland, Bogdan Andrzejewski, Michal
Butkiewicz, Bogdan Gonsior, Henryk
Nielaba, Kazimierz Barburski

1964

1. Hungary, Gyozo Kulcsar, Zoltan Nemere,
Tamas Gabor, Dr. Istvan Kausz, Arpad Barany
2. Italy, Gianluigi Saccaro, Giovanni Battista
Breda, Gianfranco Paolucci, Giuseppe
Delfino, Alberto Pellegrino
3. France, Claude Brodin, Yves Dreyfus, Claude
Bourquard, Jack Guittet, Jacques Brodin

1960

1. Italy, Giuseppe Delfino, Alberto Pellegrino,
Carlo Pavesi, Edoardo Mangiarotti, Fiorenzo
Marini, GianLuigi Saccaro
2. Great Britain, Allan Jay, Michael Howard,
John Pelling, Henry Hoskyns, Raymond
Harrison, Michael Alexander
3. Soviet Union, Guram Kostava, Bruno
Khabarov, Arnold Chernushevich, Valentin
Chernikov, Aleksandr Pavlovsky

1956

1. Italy, Giuseppe Delfino, Alberto Pellegrino,
Edoardo Mangiarotti, Carlo Pavesi, Giorgio
Anglesio, Franco Bertinetti
2. Hungary, Jozsef Sakovics, Bela Rerrich,
Lajos Balthazar, Ambrus Nagy, Jozesf
Marosi, Barnabas Berzsenyi
3. France, Armand Mouyal, Claude Nigon, Daniel
Dagallier, Yves Dreyfus, Rene Queyroux

1952

1. Italy, Dario Mangiarotti, Edoardo
Mangiarotti, Franco Bertinetti, Carlo
Pavesi, Giuseppe Delfino, Roberto Battaglia
2. Sweden, Bengt Ljungquist, Berndt-Otto
Rehbinder, Sven Fahlman, Per Carleson, Carl
Forssell, Lennart Magnusson
3. Switzerland, Otto Rufenacht, Paul Meister,
Oswald Zappelli, Paul Barth, Willy Fitting,
Mario Valota

1948

1. France, Henri Guerin, Henri Lepage, Marcel
Desprets, Michel Pecheux, Edouard Artigas,
Maurice Huet
2. Italy, Luigi Cantone, Antonio Mandruzzato,
Dario Mangiarotti, Edoardo Mangiarotti,
Fiorenzo Marini, Carlo Agostoni
3. Sweden, Per Carleson, Frank Cervell, Carl
Forssell, Bengt Ljungquist, Sven Thofelt,
Arne Tollbom

1936

1. Italy, Saverio Ragno, Alfredo Pezzana, Giancarlo
Cornaggia-Medici, Edoardo Mangiarotti, Franco
Riccardi, Giancarlo Brusati

2. Sweden, Hans Granfelt, Sven Thofelt, Gosta
Almgren, Gustaf Dyrssen, Hans Drakenberg,
Birger Cederin
3. France, Michel Pecheux, Bernard Schmetz,
Georges Buchard, Henri Dulieux, Paul
Wormser, Philippe Cattiau

1932

1. France, Philippe Cattiau, Georges Buchard,
Bernard Schmetz, Jean Piot, Fernand
Jourdant, Georges Tainturier
2. Italy, Carlo Agostoni, Giancarlo Cornaggia-
Medici, Renzo Minoli, Franco Riccardi,
Saverio Ragno
3. U.S.A., George Calnan, Gustave Heiss, Frank
Righeimer, Tracy Jaeckel, Curtis Shears,
Miguel De Capriles

1928

1. Italy, Carlo Agostoni, Marcello Bertinetti,
Giancarlo Cornaggia-Medici, Renzo Minoli,
Giulio Basletta, Franco Riccardi
2. France, Armand Massard, Georges Buchard,
Gaston Amson, Emile Cornic, Bernard
Schmetz, Rene Barbier
3. Portugal, Paulo d'Eca Leal, Mario de
Noronha, Jorge Paiva, Frederico Paredes,
Joao Sassetti, Henrique da Silveira

1924

1. France, Lucien Gaudin, Georges Buchard,
Roger Ducret, Andre Labatut, Lionel Liottel,
Alexandre Lippmann, Georges Tainturier
2. Belgium, Paul Anspach, Joseph De Craecker,
Charles Delporte, Fernand de Montigny,
Ernest Gevers, Leon Tom
3. Italy, Giulio Basletta, Marcello Bertinetti,
Giovanni Canova, Vincenzo Cuccia, Virgilio
Mantegazza, Oreste Moricca

1920

1. Italy, Nedo Nadi, Aldo Nadi, Abelardo Olivier,
Tullio Bozza, Giovanni Canova, Andrea
Marrazzi, Dino Urbani, Antonio Allocchio,
Tommaso Costantino, Paolo Thaon de Revel
2. Belgium, Ernest Gevers, Paul Anspach, Felix
Goblet d'Alviella, Victor Boin, Joseph De
Craecker, Leon Tom, Maurice De Wee,
Philippe Le Hardy de Beaulieu
3. France, Armand Massard, Alexandre Lippmann,
Gustave Buchard, Georges Trombert, S.
Casanova, Gaston Amson, E. Moreau

1912

1. Belgium, Paul Anspach, Henri Anspach, Robert
Hennet, Fernand de Montigny, Jacques Ochs,
Francis Rom, Gaston Salmon, Victor Willems
2. Great Britain, Edgar Seligman, Edward
Amphlett, Robert Montgomerie, John Blake,
Percy Davson, Arthur Everitt, Sydney

Martineau, Martin Holt
3. Netherlands, Adrianus E. W. de Jong, Willem P. Hubert van Blijenburgh, Jetze Doorman, Leo Nardus, George van Rossem

1908
1. France, Gaston Alibert, Bernard Gravier, Alexandre Lippmann, Eugene Olivier, Henri-Georges Berger, Charles Collignon, Jean Stern
2. Great Britain, Edward Amphlett, C. Leaf Daniell, Cecil Haig, Robert Montgomerie, Martin Holt, Edgar Seligman
3. Belgium, Paul Anspach, Fernand Bosmans, Fernand de Montigny, Francis Rom, Victor Willems, Desire Beaurain, Ferdinand Feyerick

1906
1. France, Pierre d'Hugues, Georges Dillon-Kavanagh, Mohr, Georges de la Falaise
2. Great Britain, William H. Desborough, Cosmo E. Duff-Gordon, Charles N. Robinson, Edgar Seligman
3. Belgium, Constant Cloquet, Fernand de Montigny, Edmond Crahay, Philippe Le Hardy de Beaulieu

1896–1904
Not held

Fencing—Men's Individual Foil
1992
1. Philippe Omnes, France
2. Serguei Goloubitski, Ukraine
3. Elvis Gregory Gil, Cuba

1988
1. Stefano Cerioni, Italy
2. Udo Wagner, East Germany
3. Aleksandr Romankov, Soviet Union

1984
1. Mauro Numa, Italy
2. Matthias Behr, West Germany
3. Stefano Cerioni, Italy

1980
1. Vladimir Smirnov, Soviet Union
2. Aleksandr Romankov, Soviet Union
3. Pascal Jolyot, France

1976
1. Fabio dal Zotto, Italy
2. Aleksandr Romankov, Soviet Union
3. Bernard Talvard, France

1972
1. Witold Woyda, Poland
2. Dr. Jeno Kamuti, Hungary
3. Christian Noel, France

1968
1. Ion Drimba, Romania

2. Dr. Jeno Kamuti, Hungary
3. Daniel Revenu, France

1964
1. Egon Franke, Poland
2. Jean-Claude Magnan, France
3. Daniel Revenu, France

1960
1. Viktor Zhdanovich, Soviet Union
2. Yuri Sissikin, Soviet Union
3. Albert Axelrod, U.S.A

1956
1. Christian d'Oriola, France
2. Giancarlo Bergamini, Italy
3. Antonio Spallino, Italy

1952
1. Christian d'Oriola, France
2. Edoardo Mangiarotti, Italy
3. Manlio Di Rosa, Italy

1948
1. Jehan Buhan, France
2. Christian d'Oriola, France
3. Lajos Maszlay, Hungary

1936
1. Giulio Gaudini, Italy
2. Edward Gardere, France
3. Giorgio Bocchino, Italy

1932
1. Gustavo Marzi, Italy
2. Joseph Levis, U.S.A
3. Giulio Gaudini, Italy

1928
1. Lucien Gaudin, France
2. Erwin Casmir, Germany
3. Giulio Gaudini, Italy

1924
1. Roger Ducret, France
2. Philippe Cattiau, France
3. Maurice van Damme, Belgium

1920
1. Nedo Nadi, Italy
2. Philippe Cattiau, France
3. Roger Ducret, France

1912
1. Nedo Nadi, Italy
2. Pietro Speciale, Italy
3. Richard Verderber, Austria

1906
1. Georges Dillon-Kavanagh, France
2. Gustav Casmir, Germany
3. Pierre d'Hugues, France

Fencing

1904
1. Ramon Fonst, Cuba
2. Albertson Van Zo Post, Cuba
3. Charles Tatham, Cuba

1900
1. Emile Coste, France
2. Henri Masson, France
3. Jacques Boulenger, France

1896
1. Emile Gravelotte, France
2. Henri Callot, France
3. Perikles Mavromichalis-Pierrakos, Greece

Fencing—Men's Team Foil
1992
1. Germany, Udo Wagner, Ulrich Schreck, Thorsten Weidner, Alexander Koch, Ingo Weissenborn
2. Cuba, Elvis Gregory Gil, Guillermo Betancourt, Oscar Garcia, Tulio Diaz, Hermenegildo Garcia
3. Poland, Marian Sypniewski, Piotr Kielpikowski, Adam Krzesinski, Cezary Siess, Ryszard Sobczak

1988
1. Soviet Union, Aleksandr Romankov, Ilgar Mamedov, Vladimir Aptsiaouri, Anvar Ibraguimov, Boris Koretski
2. West Germany, Mathias Gey, Thorsten Weidner, Matthias Behr, Ulrich Schreck, Thomas Endres
3. Hungary, Zsolt Ersek, Pal Szekeres, Istvan Szelei, Istvan Busa, Robert Gatai

1984
1. Italy, Mauro Numa, Andrea Borella, Stefano Cerioni, Angelo Scuri
2. West Germany, Matthias Behr, Mathias Gey, Harald Hein, Frank Beck
3. France, Philippe Omnes, Patrick Groc, Frederic Pietruszka, Pascal Jolyot

1980
1. France, Didier Flament, Pascal Jolyot, Bruno Boscherie, Philippe Bonin, Frederic Pietruszka
2. Soviet Union, Aleksandr Romankov, Vladimir Smirnov, Sabirzhan Ruziev, Ashot Karagian, Vladimir Lapitsky
3. Poland, Adam Robak, Boguslaw Zych, Lech Koziejowski, Marian Sypniewski

1976
1. West Germany, Matthias Behr, Thomas Bach, Harald Hein, Klaus Reichert, Erk Sens-Gorius
2. Italy, Fabio Dal Zotto, Attilio Calatroni, Carlo Montano, Stefano Simoncelli, Giovan Battista Coletti

3. France, Daniel Revenu, Christian Noel, Didier Flament, Bernard Talvard, Frederic Pietruszka

1972
1. Poland, Witold Woyda, Lech Koziejowski, Jerzy Kaczmarek, Marek Dabrowski, Arkadiusz Godel
2. Soviet Union, Vassili Stankovitsch, Anatoli Kotescev, Vladimir Denissov, Leonid Romanov, Viktor Putyatin
3. France, Daniel Revenu, Christian Noel, Bernard Talvard, Jean-Claude Magnan, Gilles Berolatti

1968
1. France, Daniel Revenu, Gilles Berolatti, Christian Noel, Jean-Claude Magnan, Jacques Dimont
2. Soviet Union, German Sveshnikov, Yuri Scharov, Vassili Stankovitsch, Viktor Putyatin, Yuri Sissikin
3. Poland, Witold Woyda, Ryszard Parulski, Egon Franke, Zbigniew Skrudlik, Adam Lisewski

1964
1. Soviet Union, German Sveshnikov, Yuri Sissikin, Mark Midler, Viktor Zhdanovich, Yuri Scharov
2. Poland, Zbigniew Skrudlik, Witold Woyda, Egon Franke, Ryszard Parulski, Janusz Rozycki
3. France, Daniel Revenu, Jacky Courtillat, Pierre Rodocanachi, Christian Noel, Jean-Claude Magnan

1960
1. Soviet Union, Viktor Zhdanovich, Mark Midler, Yuri Sissikin, German Sveshnikov, Yuri Rudov
2. Italy, Alberto Pellegrino, Luigi Carpaneda, Mario Curletto, Aldo Aureggi, Edoardo Mangiarotti
3. West Germany, Jurgen Brecht, Tim Gerrescheim, Eberhard Mehl, Jurgen Theuerkauff

1956
1. Italy, Edoardo Mangiarotti, Giancarlo Bergamini, Antonio Spallino, Luigi Carpaneda, Manlio Di Rosa, Vittorio Lucarelli
2. France, Christian d'Oriola, Bernard Baudoux, Claude Netter, Jacques Lataste, Roger Closset, Rene Coicaud
3. Hungary, Jozsef Gyuricza, Jozsef Sakovics, Mihaly Fulop, Endre Tilli, Lajos Somodi, Jozsef Marosi

1952
1. France, Jehan Buhan, Christian d'Oriola, Adrien Rommel, Claude Netter, Jacques Noel, Jacques Lataste
2. Italy, Giancarlo Bergamini, Antonio Spallino,

250

Manlio Di Rosa, Giorgio Pellini, Renzo
Nostini, Edoardo Mangiarotti
3. Hungary, Endre Tilli, Aladar Gerevich, Endre
Palocz, Lajos Maszlay, Tibor Berczelly,
Jozsef Sakovics

1948
1. France, Andre Bonin, Rene Bougnol, Jehan
Buhan, Jacques Lataste, Christian d'Oriola,
Adrien Rommel
2. Italy, Renzo Nostini, Manlio Di Rosa,
Edoardo Mangiarotti, Giuliano Nostini,
Giorgio Pellini, Saverio Ragno
3. Belgium, Georges DeBourguignon, Henri
Paternoster, Edouard Yves, Raymond Bru, Andre
van de Werwe de Vorsselaer, Paul Valcke

1936
1. Italy, Giulio Gaudini, Gioacchino Guaragna,
Gustavo Marzi, Giorgio Bocchino, Manlio Di
Rosa, Ciro Verratti
2. France, Jacques Coutrot, Andre Gardere,
Rene Lemoine, Rene Bougnol, Edward
Gardere, Rene Bondoux
3. Germany, Siegfried Lerdon, August Heim,
Julius Eisenecker, Erwin Casmir, Stefan
Rosenbauer, Otto Adam

1932
1. France, Philippe Cattiau, Edward Gardere, Rene
Lemoine, Rene Bondoux, Jean Piot, Rene Bougnol
2. Italy, Giulio Gaudini, Gustavo Marzi, Ugo
Pignotti, Giorgio Pessina, Gioacchino
Guaragna, Rodolfo Terlizzi
3. U.S.A., George Calnan, Joseph Levis, Hugh
Allesandroni, Dernell Every, Richard Steere,
Frank Righeimer

1928
1. Italy, Ugo Pignotti, Oreste Puliti, Giulio
Gaudini, Giorgio Pessina, Giorgio Chiavacci,
Gioacchino Guaragna
2. France, Lucien Gaudin, Philippe Cattiau,
Roger Ducret, Andre Labatut, Raymond
Flacher, Andre Gaboriaud
3. Argentina, Roberto Larraz, Raul Anganuzzi, Luis
Lucchetti, Hector Lucchetti, Carmelo Camet

1924
1. France, Lucien Gaudin, Philippe Cattiau, Jacques
Coutrot, Roger Ducret, Henri Jobier, Andre
Labatut, Guy de Luget, Joseph Peroteaux
2. Beligum, Desire Beaurain, Charles Crahay,
Fernand de Montigny, Maurice Van Damme,
Marcel Berre, Albert De Roocker
3. Hungary, Laszlo Berti, Sandor Posta, Zoltan
Schenker, Odon Terstyanszky, Istvan
Lichteneckert

1920
1. Italy, Baldo Baldi, Tommaso Costantino, Aldo
Nadi, Nedo Nadi, Abelardo Olivier, Oreste
Puliti, Pietro Speciale, Rodolfo Terlizzi
2. France, Lionel Bony de Castellane, Gaston
Amson, Philippe Cattiau, Roger Ducret,
Andre Labatut, Georges Trombert, Marcel
Perrot, Lucien Gaudin
3. U.S.A., Henry Breckinridge, Francis Honeycutt,
Arthur Lyon, Harold Rayner, Robert Sears

1906–1912
Not held

1904
1. Cuba, Ramon Fonst, Albertson Van Zo Post,
Manuel Diaz
2. International Team, Charles Tatham, Cuba;
Charles Townsend, U.S.A; Arthur Fox, U.S.A.

1896–1900
Not held

Fencing—Men's Individual Sabre

1992
1. Bence Szabo, Hungary
2. Marco Marin, Italy
3. Jean-Francois Lamour, France

1988
1. Jean-Francois Lamour, France
2. Janusz Olech, Poland
3. Giovanni Scalzo, Italy

1984
1. Jean-Francois Lamour, France
2. Marco Marin, Italy
3. Peter Westbrook, U.S.A

1980
1. Viktor Krovopuskov, Soviet Union
1. Viktor Krovopuskov, Soviet Union
2. Mikhail Burtsev, Soviet Union
2. Mikhail Burtsev, Soviet Union
3. Imre Gedovari, Hungary
3. Imre Gedovari, Hungary

1976
1. Viktor Krovopuskov, Soviet Union
2. Vladimir Nazlymov, Soviet Union
3. Viktor Sidiak, Soviet Union

1972
1. Viktor Sidiak, Soviet Union
2. Peter Maroth, Hungary
3. Vladimir Nazlymov, Soviet Union

1968
1. Jerzy Pawlowski, Poland
2. Mark Rakita, Soviet Union
3. Tibor Pezsa, Hungary

1964
1. Tibor Pezsa, Hungary
2. Claude Arabo, France
3. Umar Mavlikhanov, Soviet Union

1960
1. Rudolf Karpati, Hungary
2. Zoltan Horvath, Hungary
3. Wladimiro Calarese, Italy

1956
1. Rudolf Karpati, Hungary
2. Jerzy Pawlowski, Poland
3. Lev Kuznyetsov, Soviet Union

1952
1. Pal Kovacs, Hungary
2. Aladar Gerevich, Hungary
3. Tibor Berczelly, Hungary

1948
1. Aladar Gerevich, Hungary
2. Vincenzo Pinton, Italy
3. Pal Kovacs, Hungary

1936
1. Endre Kabos, Hungary
2. Gustavo Marzi, Italy
3. Aladar Gerevich, Hungary

1932
1. Gyorgy Piller, Hungary
2. Giulio Gaudini, Italy
3. Endre Kabos, Hungary

1928
1. Odon Terstyanszky, Hungary
2. Attila Petschauer, Hungary
3. Bino Bini, Italy

1924
1. Dr. Sandor Posta, Hungary
2. Roger Ducret, France
3. Janos Garay, Hungary

1920
1. Nedo Nadi, Italy
2. Aldo Nadi, Italy
3. Adrianus E. W de Jong, Netherlands

1912
1. Dr. Jeno Fuchs, Hungary
2. Bela Bekessy, Hungary
3. Ervin Meszaros, Hungary

1908
1. Dr. Jeno Fuchs, Hungary
2. Bela Zulavszky, Hungary
3. Vilem Goppold von Lobsdorf, Bohemia

1906
1. Jean Georgiadis, Greece

2. Gustav Casmir, West Germany
3. Federico Cesarano, Italy

1904
1. Manuel Diaz, Cuba
2. William Grebe, U.S.A
3. Albertson Van Zo Post, Cuba

1900
1. Georges de la Falaise, France
2. Leon Thiebaut, France
3. Fritz Flesch, Austria

1896
1. Jean Georgiadis, Greece
2. Telemachos Karakalos, Greece
3. Holger Nielsen, Denmark

Fencing—Men's Team Sabre

1992
1. Unified Team, Grigorij Kirienko, Alexandre Chirchov, Gueorgui Pogossov, Vadim Gouttsait, Stanislav Pozdniakov
2. Hungary, Bence Szabo, Csaba Koves, Gyorgy Nebald, Peter Abay, Imre Bujdoso
3. France, Jean-Francois Lamour, Jean-Philippe Daurelle, Franck Ducheix, Herve Granger-Veyron, Pierre Guichot

1988
1. Hungary, Gyorgy Nebald, Bence Szabo, Laszlo Csongradi, Imre Bujdoso, Imre Gedovari
2. Soviet Union, Serguei Mindirgassov, Mikhail Bourtsev, Gueorgui Pogossov, Andre Alchan, Serguei Koriajkine
3. Italy, Giovanni Scalzo, Marco Marin, Gianfranco Dalla Barba, Ferdinando Meglio, Massimo Cavaliere

1984
1. Italy, Marco Marin, Gianfranco Dalla Barba, Giovanni Scalzo, Ferdinando Meglio, Angelo Arcidiacono
2. France, Jean-Francois Lamour, Pierre Guichot, Herve Granger-Veyron, Philippe Deirieu, Franck Ducheix
3. Romania, Marin Mustata, Ioan Pop, Alexandru Chiculita, Corneliu Marin

1980
1. Soviet Union, Mikhail Burtsev, Viktor Krovopuskov, Viktor Sidiak, Vladimir Nazlymov, Nikolai Alekhin
2. Italy, Michele Maffei, Mario Aldo Montano, Marco Romano, Ferdinando Meglio, Giovanni Scalzo
3. Hungary, Imre Gedovari, Rudolf Nebald, Pal Gerevich, Ferenc Hammang, Gyorgy Nebald

1976

1. Soviet Union, Eduard Vinokurov, Viktor Krovopuskov, Mikhail Burtsev, Viktor Sidiak, Vladimir Nazlymov
2. Italy, Mario Aldo Montano, Michele Maffei, Angelo Arcidiacono, Tommaso Montano, Mario Tullio Montano
3. Romania, Dan Irimiciuc, Ioan Pop, Marin Mustata, Corneliu Marin, Alexandru Nilca

1972

1. Italy, Michele Maffei, Aldo Montano, Rolando Rigoli, Tullio Montano, Cesare Salvadori
2. Soviet Union, Vladimir Nazlymov, Eduard Vinokurov, Viktor Sidiak, Viktor Bajenov, Mark Rakita
3. Hungary, Pal Gerevich, Tamas Kovacs, Peter Maroth, Tibor Pezsa, Dr. Peter Bakonyi

1968

1. Soviet Union, Vladimir Nazlymov, Eduard Vinokurov, Viktor Sidyak, Mark Rakita, Umar Mavlikhanov
2. Italy, Wladimiro Calarese, Cesare Salvadori, Michele Maffei, Pier-Luigi Chicca, Rolando Rigoli
3. Hungary, Tamas Kovacs, Miklos Meszena, Dr. Janos Kalmar, Peter Bakonyi, Tibor Pezsa

1964

1. Soviet Union, Yakov Rylsky, Nugsar Asatiani, Mark Rakita, Umar Mavlikhanov, Boris Melnikov
2. Italy, Wladimiro Calarese, Cesare Salvadori, Giampaolo Calanchini, Pier-Luigi Chicca, Mario Ravagnan
3. Poland, Emil Ochyra, Jerzy Pawlowski, Ryszard Zub, Andrzej Piatkowski, Wojciech Zablocki

1960

1. Hungary, Zoltan Horvath, Rudolf Karpati, Tamas Mendelenyi, Pal Kovacs, Gabor Delneky, Aladar Gerevich
2. Poland, Andrzej Piatkowski, Emil Ochyra, Wojciech Zablocki, Jerzy Pawlowski, Ryszard Zub, Marek Kuszewski
3. Italy, Wladimiro Calarese, Giampaolo Calanchini, Pier-Luigi Chicca, Mario Ravagnan, Roberto Ferrari

1956

1. Hungary, Rudolf Karpati, Aladar Gerevich, Pal Kovacs, Attila Keresztes, Jeno Hamori, Daniel Magay
2. Poland, Jerzy Pawlowski, Wojciech Zablocki, Marek Kuszewski, Zygmunt Pawlas, Ryszard Zub, Andrzej Piatkowski
3. Soviet Union, Lev Kuznyetsov, Yakov Rylsky, Yevgeny Cherepovski, David Tyschler, Leonid Bogdanov

1952

1. Hungary, Pal Kovacs, Aladar Gerevich, Tibor Berczelly, Rudolf Karpati, Laszlo Rajcsanyi, Bertalan Papp
2. Italy, Vincenzo Pinton, Mauro Racca, Roberto Ferrari, Gastone Dare, Renzo Nostini, Giorgio Pellini
3. France, Jacques Lefevre, Jean Laroyenne, Maurice Piot, Jean Levavasseur, Bernard Morel, Jean-Francois Tournon

1948

1. Hungary, Aladar Gerevich, Rudolf Karpati, Pal Kovacs, Tibor Berczelly, Laszlo Rajcsanyi, Bertalan Papp
2. Italy, Gastone Dare, Carlo Turcato, Vincenzo Pinton, Mauro Racca, Aldo Montano, Renzo Nostini
3. U.S.A., Norman Armitage, George Worth, Tibor Nyilas, Dean Cetrulo, Miguel De Capriles, James Flynn

1936

1. Hungary, Endre Kabos, Aladar Gerevich, Tibor Berczelly, Pal Kovacs, Laszlo Rajcsanyi, Imre Rajczy
2. Italy, Vincenzo Pinton, Giulio Gaudini, Aldo Masciotta, Gustavo Marzi, Aldo Montano, Athos Tanzini
3. Greece, Richard Wahl, Julius Eisenecker, Erwin Casmir, August Heim, Hans Esser, Hans Jorger

1932

1. Hungary, Gyorgy Piller, Endre Kabos, Attila Petschauer, Erno Nagy, Gyula Glykais, Aladar Gerevich
2. Italy, Renato Anselmi, Arturo De Vecchi, Emilio Salafia, Ugo Pignotti, Gustavo Marzi, Giulio Gaudini
3. Poland, Adam Papee, Tadeusz Friedrich, Wladyslaw Segda, Leszek Lubicz-Nycz, Wladyslaw Dobrowolski, Marian Suski

1928

1. Hungary, Odon Terstyanszky, Dr. Sandor Gombos, Attila Petschauer, Janos Garay, Jozsef Rady, Gyula Glykais
2. Italy, Bino Bini, Renato Anselmi, Gustavo Marzi, Oreste Puliti, Emilio Salafia, Giulio Sarrocchi
3. Poland, Adam Papee, Tadeusz Friedrich, Kazimierz Laskowski, Wladyslaw Segda, Aleksander Malecki, Jerzy Zabielski

1924

1. Italy, Renato Anselmi, Guido Balzarini, Marcello Bertinetti, Bino Bini, Vincenzo Cuccia, Oreste Moricca, Oreste Puliti, Giulio Sarrocchi
2. Hungary, Laszlo Berti, Janos Garay, Sandor Posta, Jozsef Rady, Zoltan Schenker, Laszlo

Szechy, Odon Terstyanszky, Jeno Uhlyarik
3. Netherlands, Adrianus E. W. de Jong, Jetze
   Doorman, Hendrik D. Scherpenhuizen, Jan
   van der Wiel, Maarten H. van Dulm, Henri J.
   M. Wijnoldij-Daniels

1920
1. Italy, Nedo Nadi, Aldo Nadi, Oreste Puliti,
   Baldo Baldi, Francesco Gargano, Giorgio
   Santelli, Dino Urbani
2. France, Georges Trombert, J. Margraff, Marc
   Perrodon, Henri de Saint Germain
3. Netherlands, Jan van der Wiel, Adrianus E. W.
   de Jong, Jetze Doorman, Willem P. Hubert
   van Blijenburgh, Louis A. Delaunoij, Salomon
   Zeldenrust, Henri J. M. Wijnoldij-Daniels

1912
1. Hungary, Dr. Jeno Fuchs, Laszlo Berti, Ervin
   Meszaros, Dr. Dezso Foldes, Dr. Oszkar
   Gerde, Zoltan Schenker, Dr. Peter Toth,
   Lajos Werkner
2. Austria, Richard Verderber, Dr. Otto
   Herschmann, Rudolf Cvetko, Friedrich
   Golling, Andreas Suttner, Albert Bogen,
   Reinhold Trampler
3. Netherlands, Willem P. Hubert vanBlijenburgh,
   George van Rossem, Adrianus E. W. de Jong,
   Jetze Doorman, Dirk Scalongne, Hendrik de
   Jongh

1908
1. Hungary, Dr. Jeno Fuchs, Oszkar Gerde, Peter
   Toth, Lajos Werkner, Dezso Foldes
2. Italy, Riccardo Nowak, Alessandro Pirzio-
   Biroli, Abelardo Olivier, Marcello Bertinetti,
   Santi Ceccherini
3. Bohemia, Vilem Goppold von Lobsdorf,
   Jaroslav Tucek, Vlastimil Lada-Sazavsky,
   Otakar Lada, Bedrich Schejbal

1906
1. West Germany, Gustav Casmir, Jacob
   Erckrath de Bary, August Petri, Emil Schon
2. Greece, Jean Georgiadis, Menelaos
   Sakorraphos, Ch Zorbas, Triantaphylos
   Kordogiannis
3. Netherlands, James Melvill van Carnbee,
   Johannes F. Osten, George van Rossem,
   Maurits J. van Loben Sels

1896–1904
Not held

Fencing—Women's Individual Foil
1992
1. Giovanna Trillini, Italy
2. Wang Huifeng, China
3. Tatiana Sadovskaia, Russia

1988
1. Anja Fichtel, West Germany
2. Sabine Bau, West Germany
3. Zita Funkenhauser, West Germany

1984
1. Jujie Luan, China
2. Cornelia Hanisch, West Germany
3. Dorina Vaccaroni, Italy

1980
1. Pascale Trinquet-Hachin, France
2. Magdolina Maros, Hungary
3. Barbara Wysoczanska, Poland

1976
1. Ildiko Schwarzenberger-Tordasi, Hungary
2. Marta C. Collino, Italy
3. Yelena Belova-Novikova, Soviet Union

1972
1. Antonella Lonzi-Ragno, Italy
2. Ildiko Bobis, Hungary
3. Galina Gorokhova, Soviet Union

1968
1. Yelena Novikova, Soviet Union
2. Pilar Roldan, Mexico
3. Ildiko Ujlaki-Rejto, Hungary

1964
1. Ildiko Ujlaki-Rejto, Hungary
2. Helga Mees, West Germany
3. Antonella Ragno, Italy

1960
1. Heidi Schmid, West Germany
2. Valentina Rastvorova, Soviet Union
2. Maria Vicol, Romania

1956
1. Gillian Sheen, Great Britain
2. Olga Orban, Romania
3. Renee Garilhe, France

1952
1. Irene Camber, Italy
2. Ilona Elek, Hungary
3. Karen Lachmann, Denmark

1948
1. Ilona Elek, Hungary
2. Karen Lachmann, Denmark
3. Ellen Muller-Preis, Austria

1936
1. Ilona Elek, Hungary
2. Helene Mayer, Germany
3. Ellen Preis, Austria

1932
1. Ellen Preis, Austria

2. J. Heather Guinness, Great Britain
3. Erna Bogen, Hungary

1928
1. Helene Mayer, Germany
2. Muriel Freeman, Great Britain
3. Olga Oelkers, Germany

1924
1. Ellen Osiier, Denmark
2. Gladys Davis, Great Britain
3. Grete Heckscher, Denmark

1896–1920
Not held

Fencing—Women's Team Foil

1992
1. Italy, Giovanna Trillini, Margherita Zalaffi, Francesca Bortolozzi, Diana Bianchedi, Dorina Vaccaroni
2. Germany, Sabine Christiane Bau, Zita-Eva Funkenhauser, Annette Dobmeier, Anja Fichtel-Mauritz, Monika Weber-Koszto
3. Romania, Reka Szabo, Claudia Grigorescu, Elisabeta Tufan, Laura Badea, Roxana Dumitrescu

1988
1. West Germany, Anja Fichtel, Sabine Bau, Zita Funkenhauser, Annette Klug, Christiane Weber
2. Italy, Margherita Zalaffi, Dorina Vaccaroni, Annapia Gandolfi, Francesca Bortolozzi, Lucia Traversa
3. Hungary, Zsuzsanna Janosi, Gertrud Stefanek, Zsuz Sanna Szocs, Katalin Tuschak, Edit Kovacs

1984
1. West Germany, Christiane Weber, Cornelia Hanisch, Sabine Bischoff, Zita Funkenhauser
2. Romania, Aurora Dan, Koszto Veber, Rozalia Oros, Marcela Zsak, Elisabeta Guzganu
3. France, Laurence Modaine, Pascale Trinquet-Hachin, Brigitte Gaudin, Veronique Brouquier

1980
1. France, Brigitte, Latrille-Gaudin, Pascale Trinquet-Hachin, Isabelle Regard, Veronique Brouquier, Christine Muzio
2. Soviet Union, Valentina Sidorova, Nailia Giliazova, Yelana Belova-Novikova, Irina Ushakova, Larisa Tsagaraeva
3. Hungary, Ildiko Bobis-Schwarczenberger, Magdolna Maros, Gertrud Stefanek, Zsuz Sanna Szocs, Edit Kovacs

1976
1. Soviet Union, Yelena Belova-Novikova, Olga Kniazeva, Valentina Sidorova, Nailia Guiliazova, Valentina Nikonova
2. France, Brigitte Latrille, Brigitte Dumont-Gapais, Christine Muzio, Veronique Trinquet, Claudie Josland
3. Hungary, Ildiko Schwarczenberger-Tordasi, Edit Kovacs, Maga Magdolna Maros, Ildiko Sagi-Ujlaki-Rejto, Ildiko Bobis

1972
1. Soviet Union, Yelena Belova-Novikova, Aleksandra Zabelina, Galina Gorokhova, Tatiane Samusenko, Svetlana Chirkova
2. Hungary, Ildiko Sagi-Ujlaki-Rejto, Ildiko Tordasi, Maria Szolnoki, Ildiko Bobis, Ildiko Matuscsak
3. Romania, Olga Szabo, Ileana Gyulai-Drimba, Ana Passcu-Ene, Ecaterina Stahl

1968
1. Soviet Union, Aleksandra Zebelina, Yelena Novikova, Galina Gorokhova, Tatiane Samusenko, Svetlana Chirkova
2. Hungary, Ildiko Bobis, Lidia Sakovics, Ildiko Ujlaki-Rejto, Maria Gulacsy, Paula Marosi
3. Romania, Clara Iencic, Ileana Drimba, Olga Szabo, Maria Vicol, Ana Ene-Dersidan

1964
1. Hungary, Ildiko Ujlaki-Rejto, Katalin Juhasz-Nagy, Lidia Sakovics-Domolky, Judit Mendelenyi-Agoston, Paula Marosi
2. Soviet Union, Galina Gorokhova, Valentina Prudskova, Tatiane Samusenko-Petrenko, Ljudmila Schishova, Valentina Rastvorova
3. West Germany, Heidi Schmid, Helga Mees, Rosemarie Scherberger, Gudrun Theuerkauff

1960
1. Soviet Union, Tatiane Petrenko, Valentina Rastvorova, Ljudmila Schishova, Valentina Prudskova, Aleksandra Zabelina, Galina Gorokhova
2. Hungary, Gyorgyi Szekely, Ildiko Rejto, Magdolna Kovacs-Nyari, Katalin Iuhasz-Nagy, Lidia Domolky
3. Italy, Irene Camber, Welleda Cesari, Antonella Ragno, Bruna Colombetti, Claudia Pasini

1896–1956
Not held

Trivia Quiz

1. Fencing has been included in the Olympic program
  a. Only in years when the Modern Pentathlon is part of the Olympic roster
  b. In every Games since 1896
  c. Since the 1988 Seoul Games, before which it was a demonstration sport

2. Which of the following fencing events has *not* been included in the Olympics?
  a. Three-weapon events **b.** Outdoor fencing **c.** Four-weapon events

3. Electrical scoring was introduced to épée events in
  a. 1935 **b.** 1955 **c.** 1984

4. Men's Olympic fencing matches end
  a. When a fencer touches the tip of his sword to the middle of his opponent's chest
  b. When a fencer has been touched five times
  c. When a fencer draws a "Z" on his opponent's chest

5. Women first competed in Olympic fencing
  a. In 1896 **b.** In 1924 **c.** In 1988

6. The only American ever to win a gold medal in Olympic fencing was
  a. Albertson Van Zo Post **b.** Franz Bibfeldt **c.** Caitlin Bilodeaux

7. Which Olympic personality was a former fencer?
  a. Avery Brundage **b.** Baron Pierre de Coubertin
  c. Juan Antonio Samaranch

8. The modern épée evolved from swords that were used
  a. In military combat **b.** In dueling contests
  c. In Erroll Flynn movies

9. Until the mid-1960s, Olympic sabre competition was dominated by
  a. Italy **b.** Hungary **c.** Jamaica

10. Officials stop Olympic fencing bouts when
  a. A fencer scores an off-target hit
  b. A competitor steps off the fencing "strip"
  c. A fencer swings from a chandelier or slides down a stair rail

Answers: 1-b; 2-c; 3-a; 4-b; 5-b; 6-a; 7-b; 8-b; 9-b; 10-a and -b

FIELD HOCKEY

Warm-up

Historically a game of the upper classes, field hockey is now one of the most popular team sports in the world, with more than 100 national associations claiming membership in the Fédération Internationale de Hockey (FIH), the world governing body for the sport. When played by the experts, the game is a blend of power, speed, and agility.

The earliest record of field hockey is a drawing dated more than 4000 years ago decorating a tomb at Beni-Hasan in Egypt's Nile Valley. The mural shows two men holding sticks with curved ends that are similar to those used by early 20th-century field hockey players. As if in a faceoff (or, as they say in field hockey, a push back), the men stand over a small hoop or ball, immersed in a moment of strategic thinking.

Historians believe that ancient Greeks and Persians were also adept at field hockey. During the Middle Ages, the Araucano Indians of Argentina invented a game similar to hockey, called **cheuca.** The Araucanos believed that the game, played with sticks curved at one end, would make them better warriors. Needless to say, high sticking was fairly common.

Evidence also suggests that Native American tribes played a vigorous form of field hockey for several thousand years, although the game was somewhat different from today's. For instance, the goals were several miles apart, the game lasted from sunrise to sunset (no doubt in order to negotiate the distance), and a team might consist of 1000 players or so. Halftime was more a state of mind and Gatorade had not yet been invented.

Modern field hockey evolved in the British Isles. No doubt the ancient Irish game of hurling is the grand daddy of several related games, including field hockey, shinty in Scotland, and bandy in Wales. In the Canterbury Cathedral, the colored glass in a 600-year-old window shows a boy striking a round ball with a crooked stick. The oldest hockey club still in existence is Blackheath, England, with records dating back to 1860. The game grew in popularity throughout the British Empire, particularly in India and Pakistan, where field hockey is considered a national pastime. In 1886, the Hockey Association was formed in Britain and shortly thereafter, the rules were standardized.

Women began playing the game during the second half of the 19th century. For a time, field hockey was considered the only proper team sport for women. The first women's club was started in Surrey, England, in 1887, and the first national association, the Irish Ladies Hockey Union, sprang up in Dublin seven years later. By the end of the 19th century, women's field hockey had spread to New Zealand, South Africa, the Netherlands, Germany, Switzerland, and elsewhere. In 1927, the International Federation of Women's Hockey Associations (IFWHA) was formed.

The game was introduced in the United States by Constance M. K. Applebee, a British physical education teacher who staged an exhibition of the sport at Harvard the summer of 1901. During the next two years, Applebee taught the game to women at Smith, Wellesley, Mt. Holyoke, and other colleges in the region.

> "By the time the Olympics begin, we want to feel like the Olympic venue is really our home field."
> —U.S. women's coach Pam Hixon, explaining why she transplanted her team to Atlanta in July 1995

Although the sport has long welcomed active female participation, as an Olympic event women's field hockey did not debut until more than 70 years after the initial men's competition. Men's field hockey was added to the Olympic Games in 1908, but it wasn't until 1980 that women's teams were invited as well.

England, ever the stronghold for the sport, won that first Olympics handily, beating Ireland in the finals. In 1920, when hockey was next included on the Olympic program, Great Britain again won. The Fédération Internationale de Hockey was formed in 1924, without British participation, since those in the British field hockey community opposed competitions involving medals and prizes. This controversy affected the Olympics, as again in 1924 the Games did not feature field hockey.

In 1932, the U.S. fielded its first men's team, losing to gold medalist India, then the dominant team in the world, by a score of 24–1, followed by a 9–2 defeat at the hands of silver medalist Japan. As luck would have it, however, the U.S. managed to win the bronze, being the third team in a three-team field. It was to be the first and last medal ever collected by the U.S. men's team, as the game continues to be dominated by India, Pakistan, Great Britain, and Germany.

Spectator's Guide

Although the objective of the game is to score more goals than your opponent, defensive strategy is the key to field hockey. Similar to soccer, the game features a fast pace and demands individual coordination, skills, fitness, and finesse as well as team work.

Field hockey consists of two 35-minute halves; two teams of 11 players each armed with hardwood sticks that resemble ice hockey sticks, though smaller; a field roughly the size of a football field; two umpires; one timekeeper; and a smooth, seamless ball, slightly larger than a baseball and weighing about 5.5 ounces. The head of the stick is flat on one side and rounded on the other, and only the flat side (which is always on the left) may be used to hit the ball. With a proper hit, the ball travels around the field at up to 100 miles per hour. Players wear shin guards to protect against the occasional wicked stick slapped at the knees and the more frequent accidental pitch to the turf.

The goals are twelve feet wide and seven feet high. The front of the goal posts touches the outer edge of the goal line, across which the attacker must propel the ball in order for a point to be gained. A **shooting circle** is placed 16 yards from the goal.

Only within this circle may an attacker shoot for a goal. It is not uncommon for a team to pull its forwards back until an almost impenetrable wall of bodies is formed in front of the goal. Quick, accurate passing is the most efficient method for evading the defense and scoring a goal. While teams such as India have favored short, crisp passes, the continental style has been to try to hit to the open person with a long pass.

The goalkeeper, who wears a face mask and heavy padding from foot to neck, is allowed to use any part of his or her body to stop the ball. The goalkeeper can kick the ball, the only person on the field who may do so. Unlike ice hockey, the goalie's stick is the same as the other players'.

At the start of each half and after each goal, play begins with a **push back.**

Within the 25-yard line, an attacking player must either have the ball or at least two opponents (one may be the goalkeeper) between him or her and the goal line. Otherwise, **offside** is called.

When you watch a field hockey match, you may notice the umpire whistling a foul called **obstruction.** In every other team sport, shielding the ball or puck with one's body is an integral part of the game's strategy. But not in field hockey. A player may not use his or her body to prevent an opponent from playing the ball. All players have an equal chance to gain control of the ball as it is dribbled and passed down the field.

For any breach of rules, an umpire may award a free hit, a penalty corner, or a penalty stroke to the opposing team. The **free hit** must be taken at the site of the foul. At a free hit, no player may stand within five yards of the player with the ball; any stroke, except a scoop or a flick into the air (which may lead to dangerous play), is permissible.

If a player puts the ball over the sideline, a free hit is awarded to the opposing team and is taken on the line where the ball went out. If the ball deflects off a defender's stick and goes over the end line, the attacking team is awarded a **corner hit.** The corner hit may be taken from the sideline or from the end line within five yards of the corner.

If the ball is hit over the end line by the attacking team, the defenders are given a free hit within 16 yards of the end line and in line with the point where it went out.

If the ball is hit over the end line by the defenders, the attacking team is awarded a penalty corner.

Since goals may only be scored from within the shooting circle, penalties are more severe for fouls committed in that area. Penalty corners are generally awarded to the other team for infractions that occur within the shooting circle as well as deliberate fouls within 25 yards of the end line. A **penalty corner** is essentially a free hit by the attackers from a point on the goal line that is at least ten yards from the goal. To begin the penalty corner, no attacking players may be within the circle. Six defenders are behind the end line and five behind the midfield. As an attacking player puts the ball into play from a point ten yards from the goal, both attackers and defenders may enter the circle to play the ball.

If an intentional foul is committed by a defender within the circle or a defender stops a sure goal by committing a foul, a **penalty stroke** is awarded. A push or flick shot from seven yards out is taken by one attacking player with only the goalkeeper in the goal to defend.

In 1996, twelve men's teams and eight women's teams will compete in field hockey at Morris Brown College and Clark Atlanta University. For the women's competition, one pool of eight teams will compete in a round-robin tournament, progressing to medal-round matches. The men will compete in two pools of six teams, progressing to semifinal, classification, and medal-round matches.

Hopefuls

There is little doubt which four teams will dominate men's field hockey in Atlanta. It will likely be the same four that have traded the sports' top prizes for years: Pakistan, Australia, the Netherlands, and Germany.

The question is, who will take home the Olympic gold medal?

The Pakistanis were good enough to win a bronze medal at the 1992 Olympics. They are even better now, under former Dutch national coach Hans Jorritsma. Pakistan had never had a European coach, but finally bucked tradition to get one of the world's best. Jorritsma's influence has paid off.

The men in green won the prestigious Champions Trophy and the World Cup in 1994. Veteran Shahbaz Ahmed is Pakistan's best-known player, but fans should keep their eyes on less-heralded Tahir Zaman and K. M. Junaid.

If anyone can give Pakistan trouble, it is the Netherlands. Though the Dutch failed to win a medal in Barcelona, and managed only a bronze at the 1994 Champions Trophy, they remain one of the world's most talented teams. The Dutch went unbeaten through six games at the Amsterdam seven-nations tournament in the summer of 1994, thanks largely to corner-specialist Floris Jan Bovelander. They finished runner-up to Pakistan in the World Cup, and are determined to make up for their disappointing 1992 Olympic performance with a medal in Atlanta.

Australia also enters the Olympics with an impressive resume: bronze medal at 1994 World Cup, silver at seven-nations tournament, and silver at the 1992 Olympics. Warren Birmingham, aging legs and all, remains the man to watch on this squad.

The Germans are consistently in the medal hunt, and it will be no different this time. Captain Christian Blunck leads a talent-packed roster that has survived the retirements of Carsten Fischer and Volker Fried. Germany reached the semi-finals in seven of the past eight World Cups, and they won't go down easy in Atlanta.

Don't rule out India, a historically successful team in turmoil as of late. Field hockey is the most popular sport in India, and the Indian team won seven of eight Olympic gold medals from 1928 to 1964. But India has not fared as well in the modern Games, winning only one medal (gold in 1980) since 1972. They were seventh in Barcelona in 1992, and fifth at the 1994 World Cup.

India has talented players, like Dhanraj Pillay and Mukesh Kumar, but team politics keep the squad from reaching its potential.

The surprise team of the Olympics could be South Korea, which burst onto the world scene with a 4-0 victory over Pakistan in the 1994 Asia Cup. The Koreans are, perhaps, the quickest team in the world and their work ethic is unrivaled.

Team USA, while improving, is not expected to make the medal podium. U.S. players have been living and training at the Olympic Training Center in San Diego since 1995, and hope to have a respectable showing. The U.S. men are led by forward Marq Mellor, of Mount Vernon, New York.

On the **women**'s side, the American team is expecting more than a good showing. Australia is the team to beat, and youthful Argentina is a close second. But host United States, which did not even qualify for the 1992 Olympics and finished last at the 1988 Games, is the team to watch.

The U.S. women were seeded 11th for the 1994 World Cup in Dublin, Ireland, and surprised everyone—themselves included—with a bronze medal behind perennial powers Australia and Argentina.

Team USA has four holdovers from the 1992 Olympic squad, and captain Barb Marois has been around since the 1988 Games in Seoul. Coach Pam Hixon, who took over in January 1994 after 15 years at University of Massachusetts, is credited with the team's turnaround.

The Americans raised eyebrows at the 1995 Pan American Games in Argentina, where they outscored opponents 28-1 on the way to the gold medal match. They played tough against the Argentines in the final in front of a partisan sellout crowd before losing, 3-2.

The Pan Am Games final was such a big event in Argentina that large-screened televisions were erected in shopping areas so that fans could watch the match live.

Australia remains the Olympic favorite, after beating Argentina in the 1994 World Cup. Though the Argentines are younger and possess great ball-handling skills, the Aussies have remarkable precision and a dangerous attacking style. The Australian style has become the yardstick by which other teams measure themselves.

Most teams have a star player. Argentina has Karina Masotta, the Michael Jordan of field hockey. Germany has Britta Becker. Australia has no stars. All 16 players are equally talented, and essential to the team's success.

Aussie coach Ric Charlesworth has said time and again that his goal was to create a team whose opposition doesn't know whom to mark.

Argentina's success is largely due to a youth movement introduced in 1990 by coach Rodolpho Mendoza. He replaced six veterans with 17-year-olds, a controversial move at the time, but one that is celebrated heading into the Olympic Games.

"It was an important decision, and now we are reaping the harvest," the coach said.

South Korea will also be a team to keep an eye on. The "Red Bees," as their speedy players are nicknamed, wear out opponents who are not accustomed to running at full speed the entire match.

FACT: In 1995, the U.S. women's team was ranked number 3 in the world—its highest world ranking since the team bagged a bronze medal at the LA Games in 1984.

For every nation whose field hockey reputation is intact or rising going into the Olympics, there is another struggling to regain respect.

Reigning Olympic-champion Spain finished eighth at the 1994 Cup, and the defending world champion Dutch could do no better than sixth. Dutch coach Bert Wentink resigned days after the World Cup.

Women's field hockey, introduced into the Olympics in 1980, has gotten so popular that organizers increased the number of games in the 1996 Olympic tournament from 20 to 30.

—*Michelle Kaufman*

Schedule

The tentative field hockey schedule is:

Saturday, July 20
Women's pool 1–4
Men's pool 1–3

Sunday, July 21
Men's pool 4–6
Women's pool 5 & 6

Monday, July 22
Men's pool 7–9
Women's pool 7 & 8

Tuesday, July 23
Women's pool 9–12
Men's pool 10–12

Wednesday, July 24
Men's pool 13–15

Thursday, July 25
Women's pool 13–16
Men's pool 16–18

Friday, July 26
Men's pool 19–21
Women's pool 17 & 18

Saturday, July 27
Men's pool 22–24
Women's pool 19 & 20

Sunday, July 28
Women's pool 21–24
Men's pool 25–27

Monday, July 29
Men's pool 28–30

Tuesday, July 30
Women's pool 25–28

Wednesday, July 31
Men's classification 1–4
Men's semifinal 1 & 2

Thursday, August 1
Men's final 7–10
Men's final 11 & 12
Women's bronze & gold medal

Friday, August 2
Men's final 5 & 6
Men's bronze & gold medal

Highlights

Field hockey first appeared in the Games in 1908, when only the British Isles competed: England beat Ireland, followed by Scotland and Wales. The sport was next included in the Games in 1920, when Great Britain, this time with competition from other countries—two, to be exact—again took first place; Denmark and Belgium finished second and third. Omitted from the 1924 Olympics, field hockey permanently returned to the program in 1928, the year that marked the beginning of India's participation in the sport in the Olympic arena—and, consequently, the beginning of India's nearly 30-year spate of gold medals. India won its first of six consecutive gold medals in 1928.

During India's tenure as the Olympic field hockey "masters," the U.S. team entered its first Games in 1932, fortuitously winning its first and only medal. They also enjoyed the dubious honor of having lost to the highest-ever score in an international match. India was accompanied by a number of other countries on the victory stand during its six-Games reign: in 1928, the Netherlands took silver, Germany gold; in 1932, Japan took silver; in 1936, Germany stood above the Netherlands; in 1948 Great Britain placed before the Netherlands—and vice versa in 1952. Interestingly, 1948 was the year that marked India's independence from Britain, and their first-ever competition together at the Olympics.

In 1956, Pakistan took silver, while the Federal Republic of Germany took bronze, a year that ended a chapter in Olympic field hockey history. India's hegemony ended in Rome in 1960, when Pakistan became heir to the gold in the final match, winning 1–0. The India-Pakistan rivalry continued through the next couple of Games: India reappropriated the gold in 1964 only to lose it again in 1968, when the Indian team placed third behind Australia. India's bronze medal lacked some of its luster since the Indian team had gained their place by forfeit: during a preliminary match with India, the Japanese team, in protest of a penalty stroke awarded to their opponents, walked off the field, forfeiting the match.

At the Munich Games, the West German team stunned the public and its competitors with its emergence as a major contender, and managed to keep the gold at home. The Indian team settled for bronze, but the silver-medaling Pakistani team and its fans were less than pleased at the host country's upset victory; they so thoroughly misbehaved, they were suspended from the Games for four years. Eleven of the Pakistani players were permanently barred from the Olympics.

At the Montreal Games in 1976, yet another contender emerged: New Zealand took the gold while Australia took silver in a closely contested 1–0 final. Pakistan, the heavy favorite after its four-year absence, won only bronze. In 1980—for the first time since 1964—India returned to victory, followed this time by Spain and the Soviet Union. Also in 1980, women competed in field hockey for the first time in the Games; Zimbabwe placed first, followed by Czechoslovakia and the Soviet Union.

At the 1984 Games, the once-victorious British team returned to the victory stand, this time to accept a bronze medal. Rematched again with a German team in the final, Pakistan turned the tables on the Federal Republic of Germany's team, to take the gold it had so ungraciously lost in Munich. In the women's field, the

Netherlands placed first, followed by the Federal Republic of Germany, and the U.S. women's team brought home the bronze.

In 1988, Great Britain fully realized its comeback, winning a gold medal in a final against the Federal Republic of Germany. The Netherlands, a sometime runner-up, won the bronze. The Australians placed first among the women, followed by South Korea and the Netherlands.

Highlights from Barcelona

India, the most gilded nation in the history of Olympic field hockey, failed to capture a single medal in the stick-and-ball sport at the Barcelona Games. And the erstwhile champions' ill luck didn't stop there: Indian athletes returned home from the Games without a single medal to show for their trouble. The situation was so bleak, in fact, that on August 8, the penultimate day of the XXVth Olympiad, it was reported that opposition members of parliament had introduced measures to mourn the death of sports in their nation.

"In 1992, Spain won the gold medal. In 1988, the South Korean women came out of nowhere to play for a medal. There must be something to this home-field advantage stuff."

—U.S. women's coach Pam Hixon on her team's Atlanta prospects

The host country, on the other hand, had much cause to celebrate. The Spanish women, competing in their first Olympic tournament, had trained intensively for their debut. Ranked a distant eleventh in the world in 1988, the 1992 Olympic squad first competed as an ensemble in 1989, earning a third-place finish in the New Delhi Intercontinental Cup. And in 1991, the team placed fourth in the Champions Trophy and sixth in the European Cup.

Almost 12,000 ecstatic fans watched as the home team knocked out the Australians, 1988's gold medalists, en route to cheating the German team of the chance to improve on their 1984 silver-medal finish. At the last minute, the Spanish women mysteriously replaced their phenomenal goalkeeper, Marivi Gonzalez, allowing her substitute to join the team on the podium as they collected the first Spanish team gold at the Games.

On the men's field, the German players were the odds-on favorites, having won the 1991 European Cup and a second consecutive Champions Trophy earlier in the Olympic year. In a savage battle with the Australian team—who had already dispatched the reigning champion Brits—the German squad pulled ahead before half-time in the final, never losing their lead before closing with a 2–1 victory.

The thrice-titled Pakistani team, meanwhile, had a score to settle, having finished a disappointing fifth at the Seoul Games. Losing a game 2–1 to the Germans, the Pakistani players gained momentum, eventually beating the Dutch team to a bronze-worthy finish.

Medalists

Field Hockey—Men's Team

1992

1. Germany, Michael Knauth, Chritopher Reitz, Jan-Peter Tewes, Carsten Fischer, Christian Blunck, Stefan Saliger, Michael Metz, Christian Mayerhofer, Sven Meinhardt, Andreas Keller, Michael Hilgers, Andreas Becker, Stefan Tewes, Klaus Michler, Volker Fried, Oliver Michael Kurtz

2. Australia, Warren Birmingham, David Wansbrough, John Roderick Bestall, Lee Bodimeade, Ashley Carey, Stephen Davies, Damon Diletti, Lachlan Dreher, Lachlan Elmer, Dean Evans, Gregory Corbitt, Paul Snowden Lewis, Graham Reid, Jay Stacey, Kenneth Wark, Michael York

3. Pakistan, Ali Khan Shahid, Mujahid Ali Rana, Bashsir Khalid, Saeed Anjum, Hasan Khan Farhat, Muhammad Junaid Khawaja, Qamar Ibrahim Muhammad, Zaman Tahir, Asif Bajwa Muhammad, Ahmed Shahbaz, Feroz Wasim, Ahmed Mansoor, Ikhlaq Muhammad, Khalid Muhammad, Hussain Musadduq, Shehbaz Muhammad

1988

1. Great Britain, Paul Barber, S. Batchelor, Dulbir Bhaura, Robert Clift, Richard Dodds, David Faulkner, Russell Garcia, Martyn Grimley, Sean Kerly, James Kirkwood, Richard Leman, Stephen Martin, Veryan Pappin, Jon Potter, Imran Sherwani, Ian Taylor

2. West Germany, Stefan Bloecher, Dirk Brinkmann, T. Brankman, Heiner Dopp, H. Fastrich, Carsten Fischer, Tobias Frank, Volker Fried, Ulrich Haenel, Michael Hilgers, Andreas Keller, Michael Metz, A. Mollandin, Thomas Reck, C. Schiliemann, E. Schmidt-Opper

3. Netherlands, Marc Benninga, F. Bove Lander, J. Brinkman, Maurits Crugg, Marc Delissen, C. Diepeveen, Patrick Faber, Ronald Jansen, Rene Klaassen, H. Kooijman, J. Kruize, Prank Leistra, Erik Parlevliet G. Schlatmann, Tim Steens, Van Den Honert

1984

1. Pakistan, G. Moinuddin, Qasim Zia, Nasir Ali, A. Rashid, Ayaz Mehmood, Naeem Akhtar, Kaleemullah, Manzoor Hussain, Hasan Sardar, Hanir Khan, Khlid Hameed, Shahid Ali Khan, Tauqeer Dar, Ishtiaq Ahmen, Salleem Sherwani, Mushtaq Ahmad

2. West Germany, Christian Bassemir, Yobias Frank, Ulrich Hanel, Carsten Fischer, Joachim Hurter, Ekkhard Schmidt-Oppet, Reinhard Krull, Michael Peter, Stefan Blocher, Andreas Keller, Thomas Reck, Maekku Slawyk, Thomas Gunst, Heiner Dopp, Volker Fried, Dirk Brinkmann

3. Great Britain, Ian Taylor, Veryan Pappin, Stephen Martin, Paul Barber, Robert Cattrall, Jonathan Potter, Richard Dodds, William McConnell, Norman Hughes, David Westcott, Richard Leman, Stephen Batchelor, Sean Kerly, James Duthie, Kulbir Bhaura, Mark Precious

1980

1. India, Allan Schofield, Chettri Bir Bhadur, Dung Dung Sylvanus, Rajinder Singh, Davinder Singh, Gurmail Singh, Ravinder Pal Singh, Vasudevan Baskaran, Somaya Maneypanda, Marahaj Krishon Kaushik, Charanjit Kumar, Mervyn Fernandis, Amarjit Rana Singh, Shahid Mohamed, Zafar Iqbal, Surinder Singh

2. Spain, Jose Garcia, Juan Amat, Santiago Malgosa, Rafael Garralda, Francisco Fabregas, Juan Luis Coghen, Ricardo Cabot, Jaimes Arbos, Carlos Roca, Juan Pellon, Miguel de Paz, Miguel Chavez, Juan Arbos, Javier Cabot, Paulino Monsalve, Jaime, Zumalacarregui

3. Soviet Union, Vladimir Pleshakov, Vyacheslav Lampeev, Leonid Pavlovsky, Sos Airapetyan, Farit Zigangirov, Valeri Belyakov, Sergei Klevtsov, Oleg Zagoroonev, Aleksandr Gusev,

Sergei Pleshakov, Mikhail Nichepurenko, Minneula Azizov, Aleksandr Sytchev, Aleksandr Myasnikov, Viktor Deputatov, Aleksandr Goncharov

1976

1. New Zealand, Paul Ackerley, Jeff Archibald, Thur Borren, Alan Chesney, John Christensen, Greg Dayman, Tony Ineson, Alan McIntyre, Neil McLeod, Barry Maister, Selwyn Maister, Trevor Manning, Arthur Parkin, Mohan Patel, Ramesh Patel, Les Wilson
2. Australia, Robert Haigh, Richard Charlesworth, David Bell, Gregory Browning, Ian Cooke, Barry Dancer, Douglas Golder, Wayne Hammond, James Irvine, Malcolm Poole, Robert Proctor, Graham Reid, Ronald Riley, Trevor Smith, Terry Walsh
3. Pakistan, Saleem Sherwani, Manzoor Hassan, Munawaruz Zaman, Saleem Nazim, Rasool Akhtar, Iftikhar Syed, Islah Islahuddin, Manzoor Hussain, Abdul Rashid, Shanaz Skeikh, Samiulah Khan, Qamar Zia, Arshad Mahmood, Arshad Ali Chaudry, Mudassar Asghar, Haneef Khan

1972

1. West Germany, Peter Kraus, Michael Peter, Dieter Freise, Michael Krause, Eduard THelen, Horst Drose, Carsten Keller, Ulrich Klaes, Wolfgang Baumgart, Uli Vos, Peter Trump, Wolfgang Rott, Detlef Kittstein, Werner Kaessmann, Fritz Schmidt, Wolfgang Strodter, Edkart Suhl, and Rainer Siefert
2. Pakistan, Saleem Sherwani, Akhtarul Islam, Manawarux Zaman, Saeed Anwar, Riaz Ahmed, Fazalur Rehman, Islahud Din, Mudassar Asghar, Abdul Rashid, Mohammad Asad Malik, Mohammad Shahnaz, Jahangir Ahmad Butt, Rasool Akhtar, Iftikhar Ahmed, Mohammad Zahid
3. India, Cornelius Charles, Mukhbain Singh, Kindo Michael, Krishnamurty Perumal, Ajitpal Singh, Harmik Singh, Ganesh Mollerapoovayya, Harbinder Singh, Govin Billimogaputtaswamy, Ashok Kumar, Harcharan Singh, Manuel Frederick, Kulwant Singh, Virinder Singh

1968

1. Pakistan, Zakir Hussain, Tanvir Ahmad Dar, Tariq Aziz, Saeed Anwar, Riaz Ahmed, Gulrez Akhtar, Khalid Mahmood Hussain, Mohammad Ashfaq, Abdul Rashid, Mohammad Asad Malik, Jahangir Ahmad Butt, Riaz-ud-Din, Tariq Niazi
2. Australia, Paul Dearing, James Mason, Brian Glencross, Gordon Pearce, Julian Pearce, Robert Haigh, Donald Martin, Raymond Evans, Ronald Riley, Patrick Nilan, Donald Smart, Desmond Piper, Eric Pearce, Frederick Quinn
3. India, Rajendra A. Christy, Gurbux Singh, Prithipal Singh, Balbir Singh II, Ajitpal Singh, Krishnamurty Perumal, Balbir Singh III, Balbir Singh I, Harbinder Singh, Inamur Rehman, Inder Singh, Munir Sait, Harmik Singh, Jagjit Singh, John V. Peter, Tarsem Singh

1964

1. India, Shankar Laxman, Prithipal Singh, Dharam Singh, Mohinder Lal, Charanjit Singh, Gurbux Singh, Joginder Singh, John V. Peter, Harbinder Singh, Kaushik Haripal, Darshan Singh, Jagjit Singh, Bandu Patil, Udham Singh, Ali Sayeed
2. Pakistan, Abdul Hamid, Munir Ahmad Dar, Manzur Hussain Atif, Saeed Anwar, Anwar Ahmad Khan, Muhammad Rashid, Khalid Mahmood, Zaka-ud-Din, Muhammad Afzal Manna, Mohammad Asad Malik, Mutih Ullah, Tariq Niazi, Zafar Hayat, Khurshid Azam, Khizar Nawaz, Tariq Aziz
3. Australia, Paul Dearing, Donald McWatters, Brian Glencross, John McBryde, Julian Pearce, Graham Wood, Robin Hodder, Raymond Evans, Eric Pearce, Patrick Nilan, Donald Smart, Antony Waters, Mervyn Crossman, Desmond Piper

1960

1. Pakistan, Abdul Rashid, Bashir Ahmad, Manzur Hussain Atif, Ghulam Rasul, Anwar Ahmad Khan, Habib Ali Kiddi, Noor Alam, Abdul Hamid, Abdul Waheed, Nasir Ahmad, Mutih Ullah, Mushtaq Ahmad, Munir Ahmad Dar, Kurshid Aslam
2. India, Shankar Laxman, Prithipal Singh, Jaman Lal Sharma, Leslie W. Claudius, Joseph Antic, Mohinder Lal, Joginder Singh, John V. Peter, Jaswant Singh, Udham Singh, Raghbir Singh Bhola, Charanjit Singh, Govind Savant
3. Spain, Pedro Amat Fontanals, Francisco Caballer Soteras, Juan Angel Calzado de Castro, Jose Colomer Rivas, Carlos Del Coso Iglesias, Jose Antonio Dinares Massague, Eduardo Dualde Santos de Lamadrid, Joaquin Dualde Santos de Lamadrid, Rafael

Egusquiza Basterra, Ignacio Macaya Santos de Lamadrid, Pedro Murua Leguizamon, Pedro Roig Juyent, Luis Maria Usoz Qintana, Narciso Ventallo Surralles

1956

1. India, Shankar Laxman, Bakshish Singh, Randhir Singh Gentle, Leslie W. Claudius, Amir Kumar, Govind Perumal, Raghbir Lal, Gurdev Singh, Balbir Singh, Udham Singh, Raghbir Singh Bhola, Charles Stephen, Ranganandhan Francis, Balkishan Singh, Amit Singh Bakshi, Kaushik Haripal, Hardyal Singh
2. Pakistan, Zakir Hussain, Munir Ahmad Dar, Manzur Hussain Atif, Ghulam Rasul, Answar Ahmad Khan, Hussain Mussarat, Noor Alam, Abdul Hamid, Habibur Rehman, Nasir Ahmad, Mutih Ullah, Latifur Rehman, Husein Akhtar, Habib Ali Kiddi
3. West Germany, Alfred Lucker, Helmut Nonn, Gunther Ullerich, Gunther Brennecke, Werner Delmes, Eberhard Ferstl, Hugo Dollheriser, Heinz Radzikowski, Wolfgang Nonn, Hugo Budinger, Werner Rosenbaum

1952

1. India, Ranganandhan Francis, Dharam Singh, Randhir Singh Gentle, Leslie Claudius, Keshava Datt, Govind Perumal, Raghbir Lal, Kunwar Digvijai Singh, Balbir Singh, Udham Singh, Muniswamy Rajgopal, Chinadorai Deshmutu, Meldric St. Clair Daluz, Grahanandan Singh
2. Netherlands, Laurentz S. Mulder, Henri J. J. Derckx, Johan F. Drijver, Julius T. Ancion, Hermanus P. Loggere, Edouard H. Tiel, Willem van Heel, Rius T. Esser, Jan H. Kruize, Andries C. Boerstra, Leonard H. Wery
3. Great Britain, Graham B. Dadds, Roger K. Midgley, Denys J. Carnill, John A. Cockett, Dennis M. R. Eagan, Anthony J. B. Robinson, Anthony S. Nunn, Robin A. Fletcher, Richard O. A. Norris, John V. Conroy, John P. Taylor, Derek M. Day, Neil A. Nugent

1948

1. India, Leo Pinto, Trilochan Singh, Randhir Singh Gentle, Keshava Datt, Amir Kumar, Maxie Vaz, Kishan Lal, Kunwar Digvijai Singh, Grahanandan Singh, Patrick Jansen, Lawrie Fernandes, Ranganandhan Francis, Akhtar Hussain, Leslie Claudius, Jaswant Rajput, Reginald Rodrigues, Latifur Rehman, Balbir Singh, Walter D'Souza, Gerry Glacken

2. Great Britain, David L. S. Brodie, George B. Sime, William L. C. Lindsay, Michael Walford, Frank Reynolds, Robin Lindsay, John M. Peake, Neil White, Robert E. Adlard, Norman Borrett, William S. Griffiths, Ronald Davies
3. Netherlands, Antonius M. Richter, Henri J. J. Derckx, Johan F. Drijver, Jenne Langhout, Hermanus P. Loggere, Edouard H. Tiel, Willem van Heel, Andries C. Boerstra, Pieter M. J. Bromberg, Jan H. Kruize, Ruis Theo Esser, Henricus N. Bouwman

1936

1. India, Richard J. Allen, Carlyle C. Tapsell, Mohomed Hussain, Baboo Narsoo Nimal, Earnest J. Cullen, Joseph Galibardy, Shabban Shahab ud Din, Dara Singh, Dhyan Chand, Roop Singh, Sayed M. Jaffar, Cyril J. Michie, Fernandes P. Peter, Joseph Phillip, Garewal Gurcharan Singh, Ahsan Mohomed Khan, Ahmed Sher Kahn, Lionel C. Emmett, Mirza Nasir ud Din Masood
2. Germany, Karl Drose, Herbert Kemmer, Dr. Erich Zander, Alfred Gerdes, Erwin Keller, Heinz Schmalix, Harald Huffmann, Werner Hamel, Kurt Weiss, Hans Scherbart, Fritz Messner, Tito Warnholtz, Detlef Okrent, Hermann Auf der Heide, Heinrich Peter, Carl Menke, Heinz Raack, Paul Mehlitz, Ludwig Beisiegel, Karl Ruck, Erich Cuntz, Werner Kubitzki
3. Netherlands, Jan de Looper, Reindert B. J. de Waal, Max Westerkamp, Hendrik C. de Looper, Rudolf J. van der Haar, Antoine R. van Lierop, Pieter A. Gunning, Henri C. W. Schnitger, Ernst W. van den Berg, Agathon de Roos, Rene Sparenberg, Carl E. Heybroek

1932

1. India, Arthur C. Hind, Carlyle C. Tapsell, Leslie C. Hammond, Masud Minhas, Broome E. Pinniger, Lal Shah Bokhari, Richard J. Carr, Gurmit Singh, Dhyan Chand, Roop Singh, Sayed M. Jaffar
2. Japan, Shumkichi Hamada, Akio Sohda, Sadayoshi Kobayashi, Katsumi Shibata, Yoshio Sakai, Eiichi Nakamura, Haruhiko Kon, Hiroshi Nagata, Kenichi Konishi, Toshio Usami, Junzo Inohara
3. U.S.A., Harold Brewster, Samuel Ewing, Leonard O'Brien, Henry Greer, James Gentle, Horace Disston, Lawrence Knapp, Charles Shaeffer, Amos Deacon, William

Boddington, David McMullin, Frederick
Wolters

1928

1. India, Richard J. Allen, Leslie C. Hammond,
   Michael E. Rocque, Sayed M. Yusuf, Broome
   E. Pinniger, Rex A. Norris, William J. Cullen,
   Frederic S. Seaman, Dhyan Chand, George E.
   Marthins, Maurice A. Gateley, Jaipal Singh,
   Shaukat Ali, Feroze Khan
2. Netherlands, Adriaan J. L. Katte, Reindert B. J.
   de Waal, Albert W. Tresling, Jan G.
   Ankerman, Emil P. J. Duson, Johannes W.
   Brand, August J. Kop, Gerrit J. A. Jannink,
   Paulus van de Rovaert, Robert van der Veen,
   Hendrik P. Visser t'Hooft
3. Germany, Georg Brunner, Heinz Woltje,
   Werner Proft, Erich Zander, Theo Haag,
   Werner Freyberg, Herbert Kemmer, Herbert
   Hobein, Bruno Boche, Herbert Muller,
   Friedrich Horn, Erwin Franzkowiak, Hans
   Haussmann, Karl Heinz Irmer, Aribert
   Heymann, Kurt Haverbeck, Rolf Wollner,
   Gerd Strantzen, Heinz Forstendorf

1924
Not held

1920

1. Great Britain, Harry Haslam, John Bennett,
   Charles Atkin, Harold Cooke, Eric Crockford,
   Cyril Wilkinson, William Smith, George
   McGrath, John McBryan, Stanley Shoveller,
   Rex Crummack, Arthur Leighton, Harold K.
   Cassels, Colin Campbell, Charles Marcom
2. Denmark, Andreas Rasmussen, Hans C.
   Herlak, Frans Faber, Erik Husted, Henning
   Holst, Hans J. Hansen, Hans A. Bjerrum,
   Thorvald Eigenbrod, Svend Blach, Steen Due,
   Ejvind Blach
3. Belgium, Charles Delelienne, Maurice van
   den Bempt, Raoul Daufresne de la
   Chevalerie, Rene Strauwen, Fernand de
   Montigny, Adolphe Goemaere, Pierre
   Chibert, Andre Becquet, Raymond Keppens,
   Pierre Valcke, Jean van Nerom, Robert
   Gevers, Louis Diercxsens

1912
Not held

1908

1. Great Britain (England), H. I. Wood, Harry S.
   Freeman, L. C. Baillon, John Robinson, Edgar
   Page, Alan Noble, Percy Rees, Gerald Logan,
   Stanley Shoveller, Reginald Pridmore, Eric
   Green
2. Great Britain (Ireland), E. P. C. Holmes,

Henry Brown, Walter Peterson, William
Graham, Walter Campbell, Henry Murphy, C.
F. Power, G. S. Gregg, Eric Allman-Smith,
Frank Robinson, Robert L. Kennedy, W. G.
McCormick

3. Great Britain (Wales), Bruce Turnbull,
   E. W. G. Richards, Llewellyn Evans,
   C. W. Shephard, R. Lyne, F. Connah, F.
   Gordon Phillips, A. A. Law, P. B. Turnbull, J.
   Ralph Williams, W. J. Pallott
3. Great Britain (Scotland), John Burt, Hugh
   Neilson, Charles H. Foulkes, Hew Fraser,
   AlexanderBurt, Andrew Dennistoun, Norman
   Stevenson, Ivan Laing, John Harper-Orr,
   Hugh Walker, William Orchardson

1896–1906
Not held

Field Hockey—Women's Team

1992

1. Spain, Maria V. Gonzalez Laguillo, Natalia
   Dorado Gomez, Virginia Ramirez Merino,
   Maria Del Carme N. Barea Cobos, Silvia
   Manrique Perez, Nagore Gabellanes Marieta,
   Marida D. Rodriguez Suarez, Sonia Barrio
   Gutierrez, Celia Corres Giner, Elisabeth
   Maragall Verge, Teresa Motos Iceta, Maider
   Telleria Goni, Mercedes Coghen Alberdingo,
   Nuria Olive Vancells, Ana Maiques Dern, M.
   Martinez de Murguia
2. Germany, Susanne Wollschlaeger, Bianca
   Margot Weiss, Tanja Roswitha
   Dickenscheid, Susanne Muller, Nadine
   Ernsting, Simone Heike Thomaschinski, Irina
   Kuhnt, Anke Wild, Franziska Hentschel,
   Kristina Peters, Eva Hagenbaumer, Britta
   Becker, Caren Jungjohann, Christina
   Stephanie Ferneck, Heike Latzsch, Katrin
   Kauschke
3. Britain, Joanne Sarah Thompson, Helen Jane
   Morgan, Lisa Jayne Bayliss, Karen Brown,
   Mary Elizabeth Nevill, Gillian Atkins,
   Victoria Jane Dixon, Wendy Katrina Fraser,
   Sandra Lister, Jane Theresa Sixsmith,
   Alison Gail Ramsay, Jackie Amanda
   McWilliams, Tammy Kelly Miller, Mandy
   Nicholls, Kathryn Louise Johnson, Susan
   Barbara Fraser

1988

1. Australia, Tracey Belbin, Deborah Bowman,
   Lee Capes, Michelle Capes, Sally Carbon,
   Elspeth Clement, Loretta Dorman, Maree
   Fish, Rechelle Hawkes, Lorraine Hillas, K.
   Partridge, Sharon Patmore, I. Pereira,

Sandra Pisani, Kim Small, Liane Tooth

2. South Korea, Eun-Jung Chang, Ki-Hyang Cho, Choon-Ok Choi, Eun-Kyung Chung, Sang-Hyun Chung, Keum-Sil Han, Ok-Kyung Han, Keum-Sook Hwang, Won-Sim Jin, Mi-Sun Kim, Soon-Duk Kim, Young-Sook Kim, Kye-Sook Lim, Soon-ja Park, Hyo-Sun Seo, Kwang-Mi Seo

3. Netherlands, W. Aardenburg, Carina Benninga, M. Bolhuis, Yvonne Buter, B. De Beus, Annemieke Fokke, Noor Holsboer, I. Lejeune, A. Nieuwenhuizen, Martine Ohr, H. Van Der Ben, M. Van Doorn, A. Van Manen, S. Von Weiler, L. Willemse, Ingrid Wolff

1984

1. Netherlands, Bernadette De Beus, Alette Pos, Margnet Zegers, Laurien Willemse, Marjolein Eysvogel, Josephine Boekhorst, Carina Benninga, Alexandra Le Poole, Francisca Hillen, Marieke Van Doom, Sophie Von Weiler, Arlette Van Manen, Irene Hendriks, Elisabeth Sevens, Martine Ohr, Anneloes Nieuwenhuizen

2. West Germany Ursula Thielemann, Elke Drull, Beate Deininger, Christina Moser, Hella Roth, Dagmar Breiken, Birgit Hagen, Birgit Hahn, Gabriele Appel, Andrea Weiermann-Lietz, Corinna Lingnau, Martina Koch, Gabriele Schley, Patricia Ott, Susanne Schmid, Sigrid Landgraf

3. U.S.A., Gwen Cheeseman, Beth Anders,

Kathleen McGahey, Anita Miller, Regina Buggy, Christine Larson-Mason, Beth Beglin, Marcella Place, Julie Staver, Diane Moyer, Sheryl Johnson, Charlene Morett, Karen Shelton, Brenda Stauffer, Leslie Milne, Judy Strong

1980

1. Zimbabwe, Sarah English, Ann Mary Grant, Brenda Phillips, Patricia McKillop, Sonia Robertson, Patricia Davies, Maureen George, Linda Watson, Susan Huggett, Gillian Cowley, Elizabeth Chase, Sandra Chick, Helen Volk, Christine Prinsloo, Arlene Boxall, Anthea Stewart

2. Czechoslovakia, Jamila Krachckova, Berta Hruba, Iveta Srankova, Lenda Vymazalova, Jirina Krizova, Jirina Kadlecova, Jirina Cermakova, Marta Urbanova, Kveta Petrickova, Marie Sykorova, Ida Hubackova, Milada Blazkova, Jana Lahodova, Alena Kyselicova, Jirina Hajkova, Viera Podhanyiova

3. Soviet Union, Galina Inzhuvatova, Nelli Gorbatkova, Valentina Zazdravnykh, Nadezhda Ovechkina, Natella Krasnikova, Natalya Bykova, Lydia Glubokova, Galina Vyuzhanina, Natalya Buzunova, Lyailya Akhmerova, Nadezhda Filippova, Yelena Gureva, Tatiana Yembakhtova, Tatiana Shvyganova, Alina Kham, Ljudmila Frolova

Trivia Quiz

1. The earliest record of field hockey is

a. In Canterbury Cathedral, where a 600-year old window shows a boy striking a ball

b. A Welsh notice that dates to the eighteenth century

c. A drawing that decorates a tomb at Beni-Hasen in the Nile Valley

2. Native American tribes played a form of field hockey that featured

a. Goals that were several miles apart

b. Teams of 1,000 or more players

c. Day-long matches

3. Field hockey was first popular

a. In India and Pakistan, from where it was imported to the British Isles

b. The British Isles, from where it spread to the British Empire

c. In Greenland, from where it spread to the Aleutian Islands

4. When women started playing field hockey in the latter half of the nineteenth century
   a. It caused public outcry because the sport was considered unladylike
   b. It was considered to be the only team sport appropriate for women
   c. It was considered to be a surefire route to an athletic scholarship and professional career

5. A shooting circle is placed
   a. 12 yards from the goal.   **b.** 16 yards from the goal
   c. 15 yards from the goal.

6. A well hit ball travels at speeds up to
   a. 55 mph   **b.** 100 mph   **c.** 32 mph

7. To stop the ball, the goalkeeper is allowed to use
   a. His or her stick only   **b.** The stick and any part of his or her body
   c. The stick and his or her lower body, below the waist

8. When field hockey was first included in the Olympics in 1908
   a. 12 nations competed   **b.** The British Isles and India competed
   c. Only the British Isles competed

9. The U.S. won its only field hockey medal
   a. In its first Olympic entry, in 1932   **b.** In Barcelona in 1992
   c. The U.S. has never won a field hockey medal

10. In 1980, when women competed in Olympic field hockey for the first time, the championship title went to
   a. Great Britain   **b.** Pakistan   **c.** Zimbabwe

Answers: 1-c; 2-a, -b, and -c; 3-b; 4-b; 5-b; 6-b; 7-b; 8-c; 9-a; 10-c

GYMNASTICS

Warm-up

Gymnastics has become an Olympic favorite in the U.S., bolstered by the televised drama of photogenic teenagers such as Olga Korbut (1972), Nadia Comaneci (1976), and Mary Lou Retton (1984) ascending to the gold. And who can forget watching the great (or at least the over-achieving) 1984 American men's team led by veteran Bart Conner? Gymnastics is truly an event made for television, the athletes commanding the screen as they tumble, twist, leap, and vault within camera range. But the history of gymnastics stretches back beyond television, past ancient Greece, to our earliest acrobatic ancestors.

The art was developed by ancient Chinese, Persians, Indians, and Greeks, who all practiced a form of gymnastics as a means of readying young men for battle. The word gymnastics derives from the Greek word *gymnos,* meaning naked. The exercises were performed in the nude at *gymnasia,* which were public exercise facilities.

Although gymnastics were included in the ancient Olympics, and the wooden horse used in vaulting and the pommel horse both date back to the height of the Roman Empire, gymnastics was largely a forgotten sport for many centuries. Acrobats of all sorts continued to use gymnastics techniques, but the modern resurrection of gymnastics began in Germany during the 18th century.

John Basedow introduced the sport to schools in that country, while Johann Guts Muth published the first major tome on the sport, called *Gymnastics for Youth,* in which he encouraged the use of climbing poles, ropes, balance beams, and ladders. Yet another German of that period, Friederich Jahn, introduced the parallel bars and rings along with routines for the horizontal bars.

Toward the end of the 19th century, gymnastic clubs sprang up in Germany and elsewhere in Europe. In 1881, the International Gymnastics Federation/Fédération Internationale de Gymnastique (FIG) was formed (then called the Bureau of the European Gymnastics Federation), opening the way for international competition. The first large-scale meeting of gymnasts was the 1896 Olympics, where Germany virtually swept the medal parade. Seventy-five gymnasts from five countries competed in the men's horizontal bar, parallel bars, pommel horse, still rings, and horse vault events.

At the 1900 Games in Paris, only one gymnastic event was held, an individual combined exercise. The first international gymnastics competition outside of the Olympics was held in 1903 in Antwerp, Belgium, and gymnasts from Belgium, France, Luxembourg, and the Netherlands competed in what is now considered the first world championship. At St. Louis in 1904, the men's team combined competition was added to the Olympic program.

"You must understand, it is just a form of theater."
— Yuri Titov, president of the International Gymnastics Federation

An interesting side note to the gymnastics world championships is that in 1922, swimming and track and field events were added to the competition in Antwerp. Soon after this experiment, the sport's leaders agreed that swimming had no business in a gymnastics competition. But at the ninth world championship in 1930 at Luxembourg, the competition included the pole vault, broad jump, shot put, rope climb, and a 100-meter sprint. Track and field did not fully disappear from the world championship gymnastics circuit until the 1954 competition.

At the 1924 Games in Paris, the basis of modern Olympic gymnastic competition was firmly established. The athletes (men) began to compete for individual Olympic titles on apparatuses, as well as in combined individual and team exercises. The 1928 Games witnessed the debut of the first women's event, the team combined exercise, won by the Netherlands. A quarter of a century after that breakthrough, five individual events for women were added in 1952: the combined, balance beam, floor exercise, uneven bars, and horse vault. The women's rhythmic individual all-around was added in 1984.

Through 1960, the Olympics (and world championships) were dominated by European teams, with the Italians (and in the 1950s, the Soviets) reigning supreme. In the 1960s and 1970s, the Japanese ruled as the number-one men's team, while the Soviets held forth as the women's team to beat. With the exception of the

U.S. men's team stunning upset in the Eastern-bloc boycotted 1984 Games, the Soviets continued to produce the world's best men's and women's gymnastics teams. In 1992 the athletes from the former Soviet Union competed as members of the Unified Team and they again dominated the gymnastics competition.

Spectator's Guide

Two types of gymnastics are performed at the Olympics: artistic and rhythmic. The men compete in eight artistic events, while the women vie for medals in six artistic events and one rhythmic event. The events for men include: team competition, individual all-around, floor exercise, pommel horse, still rings, vault, parallel bars, and horizontal bars. Women's events include team competition, individual all-around, vault, uneven bars, balance beam, floor exercise, and the rhythmic individual all-around.

The chief difference between artistic and rhythmic gymnastics is that while artistic events are performed *on* an apparatus, such as balance beams, parallel bars, and vaults, rhythmics are performed *with* apparatuses, such as 20-foot ribbons, hoops, and ropes. The rhythmic props are rolled along the ground, jumped through, and wound around the body, with emphasis on grace, beauty, and coordination of movement between prop and athlete. The event, a combination of gymnastics and ballet, is performed to music.

FACT: The "new life" rules adopted in 1989 allow gymnasts to enter the all-around with a clean slate.

Artistic gymnastics competition is divided into compulsory and optional movements. For each routine, the gymnast begins with less than a perfect score (for women, 9.40, and for men 9.00). In awarding their scores, judges take into consideration the degree of difficulty of a gymnast's program, along with aesthetic appeal. Points are deducted for such faults as poor execution, lack of control, falling, missing requirements, or exceeding the time limit. Judges may award up to 0.60 bonus points for women and up to 1.00 for men. The "perfect 10.00" score was first awarded in world-class competition to Nadia Comaneci at the 1976 Olympic Games.

The individual all-around (combined) champions for men and women are determined by totaling scores on all the apparatuses. For the men's and women's team combined, the total of the top six scores on each apparatus is the team's score.

In 1996 a whopping 304 athletes are expected to compete in gymnastics events at the Georgia Dome and the University of Georgia Coliseum.

What to Look for on Each Apparatus

Floor Exercise: Today's floor exercise routines for men consist of dynamic tumbling skills that only a few years ago were performed solely on the trampoline. Multiple saltos (flips or somersaults) and twists are increasingly common. The best will incorporate three or four tumbling passes of substantial difficulty, performing twisting double saltos on the second or third passes. Unlike the women's competition, the men's floor exercise is not performed to music.

Always a crowd favorite, women's floor exercise is best identified with Nadia Comaneci's perfect precision and Mary Lou Retton's powerful tumbling. The most important aspect to the floor exercise is grace. Look for dancer-like command of music, rhythm, and space. The gymnastics elements should flow freely into each other—the leaps covering impressive distances; the pirouettes and turns adding excitement to the music; the displays of strength, flexibility and balance all complementing each other. Difficult tumbling, ranging from triple twists to double-back somersaults with a full twist, are expected.

Vault: Men's and women's vaults begin with a strong, accelerated run. The best vaulters explode off the board, getting their feet up over their head with tremendous quickness during the first flight phase of the vault—from the springboard to contact with the horse. The judges are looking for proper body, shoulder, and hand position and instantaneous repulsion. The second flight phase and the landing are critical. Watch for height and distance of travel, as well as the number of saltos and twists—usually the more of each, the higher the difficulty value of the vault. The sudden impact of a no-step, "stuck" landing creates a favorable impression. Note that male gymnasts are not allowed to perform the round-off vault, or Yurchenko, named after the Soviet woman who invented the maneuver. The women's horse is set perpendicular to the approach while the men's horse is set in line with the launching board.

Pommel Horse (men only): Considered by many to be the most difficult of all men's gymnastics events, the pommel horse is also the most subtle. Each move is defined by complex hand placements and body positions. The difficulty stems from two factors. First, the gymnast is performing moves that differ from the swinging and tumbling skills of the other five events. Second, he spends most of each routine on only one arm, as the free hand reaches for another part of the horse to begin the next move. Look for a long series of moves in which the gymnast reaches his hands behind his back, or places both hands on a single pommel. The hand placements should be quick, quiet, and rhythmic.

Rings (men only): The rings are the least stable of the men's apparatuses. Stillness is paramount and those with the best command of the event will display extraordinary skill in arriving at all holds with absolute precision. The rings should not wobble or swing, the body should not sag or twist, and the arms should not waver or shake.

Parallel Bars (men only): Although not a requirement, some of the better gymnasts move outside the two rails, performing handstands, presses, kips, and hip circles on only one bar. The most difficult skills require the gymnast to lose sight of the bars for a moment, as in front and back saltos.

Horizontal Bar (men only): Watch for blind releases, in which the gymnast loses sight of the bar while executing a salto or twist. One-arm giants are extremely difficult, and if the gymnast performs several in succession as he changes directions, or if he performs a blind release out of one-arm giants, he has performed admirably.

Uneven Bars (women only): The most spectacular of the women's events. Watch for the big swings that begin in handstands on the high bar—two, three, or four in succession, incorporating multiple hand changes, pirouettes, and release/flight elements.

Balance Beam (women only): The overall execution should give the impression that the gymnast is performing on a floor, not on a strip four inches wide. (The beam is sixteen feet, three inches long, four inches wide, and almost four feet off the floor.) Watch for variations in rhythm, changes in level (from sitting on the beam to jumping head-height above it) and the harmonious blend of gymnastics and acrobatic elements.

Jumping Gymnastics: A Glossary

Aerial: A stunt in which the gymnast turns completely over in the air without touching the apparatus with his or her hands.

Flip-Flop: A back handspring; a jump backward from the feet through the handstand position and back to the feet again.

Giant: A swing in which the body is fully extended and moving through a 360-degree rotation around the bar.

Half-in, Half-out: A double salto with a full twist—the complete twist performed during the first salto.

Kip: Movement from a position below the equipment to a position above.

Kovac: Performed on men's horizontal bar; involves a swing forward with a back salto traveling backward over the bar to recatch the bar.

Pike Position: Body bent forward more than 90 degrees at the hips while the legs are kept straight out.

Pirouettes: When the gymnast changes direction while being supported by the hands and arms; twists while in the handstand position.

Planche: A balance position on the hands in which the body is held at an angle with shoulders forward of hands.

Salto: Flip or somersault, with the feet coming up over the head and the body rotating around the waist.

Tkatchev: Giant circle backward to a straddle release backward over the bar to a hang on the bar.

Tsukahara: Vault with a one-half turn onto the horse followed by a backward one and one-half salto; named for its innovator, Japanese gymnast Mitsuo Tsukahara.

Thomas Flairs: Straddle leg circles on pommel horse in similar fashion as "helicopter swings"; named for its innovator, U.S. gymnast Kurt Thomas.

Tuck: A position in which the knees and hips are bent and drawn into the chest, the body folded at the waist.

Valdez: Backward walkover with alternate hand placement originating from a seated position.

Yurchenko: A vault that is preceded by a round-off onto the board, a flip-flop onto the horse, and a back one and one-half salto off; named for its innovator, Soviet gymnast Natalia Yurchenko.

Hopefuls—Men's

Mihai Bagiu

Even back in his home country of Romania, gymnastics coaches could see Mihai Bagiu's potential.

Of course, that was back when Bagiu was five, and swinging from the same bar in the yard that his mother used for draping rugs when she beat the dust out of them. A group of national team coaches visited Bagiu's school looking for prospects.

"First, the coaches look at your body type," Bagiu (pronounced *BAH-joo;* b. March 3, 1970), told the *St. Louis Post-Dispatch.* "Then, they look at your strength and flexibility, which is important to gymnastics. And I guess they liked the way I looked, my strength."

The examination won Bagiu a trip to the prestigious Sports School No. 10.

"You'd go to the gym and play around and flip around and swing on the bars," Bagiu recalls. "When you're a kid, that's fun. It's still fun, just in a different way. I got my basics there."

It could have evolved into a very good deal.

"If you're an athlete (in Romania), you have a better life," he says.

Instead, Bagiu's parents—his mother a hairdresser, his father a carpenter—emigrated to the U.S. (California) when Mihai was eight.

And there is nothing in his story to indicate that neither Bagiu's eastern European lineage, nor his home country's gymnastics successes, won Bagiu a free pass to gymnastics stardom here. Far from it. His development, in fact, has been more like a steady, arduous climb.

Bagiu finished 34th all-around as recently as the 1992 U.S. Championships and 24th at the 1992 Winter Nationals. Two years later, things finally began coming together. In 1994, Bagiu finished second all-around at the Winter Nationals. In the Nationals in Nashville, Tenn., he finished 5th all-around—first in the pommel horse, second on the parallel bars, and third on the high bar.

FACT: Gymnastics coaches look for a particular body type. Since a girl's mother is the best predictor of how she will mature physically, coaches often examine pictures of the mothers of aspiring gymnasts that were taken during her teenage years.

Bagiu, married and the father of toddler Gabriela, lists pommel horse as his favorite event.

"Coming to the United States was a dream," says Bagiu, who currently calls Albuquerque, N.M., his home. "I am very Americanized now." Indeed, Bagiu, who still speaks Romanian and who is learning to speak Italian, lists motorcycles as his favorite hobby, and alternative music (his favorite band is New Order) and pizza as other favorites.

Bagiu continues: "What Americans take for granted is when you walk into a grocery store, you have aisles and aisles of fruits and vegetables. [In Romania], it's like if you got oranges or bananas, something like that—they never imported anything—it was like a delicacy."

At about 5-feet-10 and 160 pounds, Bagiu is known more for a peaceful, easy elegance than for explosive movements.

Part of that may be traced to his eastern European roots, says his coach, Ed Burch.

"They take a more artistic approach to gymnastics over there," Burch says of the Romanians. "In this country, you don't find many artists. We don't try to develop that at a young age. Our system doesn't concentrate on that. We teach a lot of big-time tricks, rather than technique. What Mihai does, he does nicely, with very nice lines, with very good execution."

With some cause for consternation, sometimes.

"It takes him a long time to learn a move," Burch says with a touch of exasperation tinged with a dash of wonder. "But when he learns it, he learns it very well. By God, when he learns something, he just doesn't miss it."

Bagiu is also laid back, Burch says. Almost to a fault—or at least to a coach's worry.

"Sometimes, he gets you nervous that he's so laid back."

Bagiu trains six hours a day, six days a week in Albuquerque, sometimes under the watchful eye of wife Kris, a former gymnast who also doubles as a trainer—packing her husband in ice, switching on the Jacuzzi, or massaging his sore muscles after tough workouts.

"His focus is probably his best quality," Kris, whose mother is a gymnastics coach, told the *Post-Dispatch*. "I can see it when he trains."

His coach, Ed Burch, concurs.

"It's different working with a married man," says Burch, who has trained previous Olympians. "Mihai is married with a child. His priorities are somewhat different. He's more focused. It's not that other U.S. gymnasts aren't focused, but he's got tunnel vision. He understands his responsibilities. He wants to medal for the U.S."

"It's a dream, of course," says Bagiu who tells stories of seeing himself standing alone on an Olympic medal stand with his arms raised high. "Hopefully, it will come true. When you compete and you do well, you get this great feeling that you've accomplished something. Especially at the Olympic level. If you win the gold medal, you're the best in the world. It's very gratifying."

Says Burch: "He can medal in two events—pommel horse and high bar. What you need to do is be hitting on the days that you need to hit. Make a mistake and you're out. But if he has a good meet, he should be able to medal."

What Burch is basically saying is that he concurs with the Romanian bird dogs.

Bagiu has the potential.

—Eric Kinkopf

Chainey Umphrey

Gymnast Chainey Umphrey looks like a "running back," his gymnastics coach, Art Shurlock, says.

What's the secret to the impressive musculature?

Albert Chainey Umphrey III, 26 (b. August 2, 1970), UCLA team captain in 1991 and 1993, a native of Albuquerque and resident of Los Angeles, doesn't credit ESPN-TV's *Body Shaping* crew for getting him all pumped up. He points, instead, to a pair of broken feet.

"During my freshman year at UCLA, I broke my right foot and then as a junior, I broke the left one," says Umphrey, a powerful 5-feet-6 and 165 pounds. "Each time it happened, I grew bigger and stronger because of the crutches. Our campus has a lot of hills and it takes a lot of work to get around."

Umphrey, whose strongest event is the parallel bars, credits an *un*breakable spirit for his entry into gymnastics.

That was back when he was 10, and his mother, Martha, an elementary school music teacher, enrolled her son in a ballet class.

"I remember bouncing around in class and the teacher kicked me out," Umphrey says.

The next door down from the ballet class was an acrobatics class.

And a home.

"I started acrobatics and never stopped," says Umphrey, the second of six children of Martha and Albert, a junior high math teacher.

Indeed, Umphrey's list of accomplishments fills almost two pages of a U.S.A. Gymnastics handout. The highlights began in 1985, when Umphrey finished first in the all-around competition at the junior nationals.

Chainey Umphrey (U.S.) is expected to be a medalist in '96. *Dave Black/U.S. Gymnastics*

An ankle injury kept him from competing in the 1992 U.S. championships and subsequent Olympic Games, but Umphrey, a six-year veteran of the U.S. national team, won the 1993 Hilton Bounce Back Award for his tremendous recovery from the injury, won an award at the 1994 Goodwill Games for Most Impressive Performance, and copped the 1995 all-around competition at the Winter Cup Challenge in Colorado Springs.

Obviously, his mettle goes much deeper than the plating on his trophies and medals.

"My success is attributable to many people—coach Sherlock, my parents, family, teachers. I'm a culmination of all their efforts."

But much has to do, of course, with the young man's character.

To wit: "If you give a kid something and he thinks he can be the best at it," Umphrey says, "it gives him something to shoot for. So, all the work didn't seem hard to me because I loved it.

"But you have to give your all every day. You can't measure progress day to day. After one to two years, you realize where you are and where you came from. There are injuries and setbacks. Sometimes you want to quit. But then some days, you feel like an angel—creative, wonderful. The feeling of being the best is incredible. When I compete, I'm carrying America's hopes. It's difficult, but definitely an honor. I want to be the best because I want the American gymnastics team to be the best. I want every flag raised to be an American flag."

Sherlock has first-hand experience of Umphrey's ethic.

"He works incredibly hard and does everything to the maximum," the UCLA gymnastics coach says.

Indeed, Olympics teammate Scott Keswick is certain that Umphrey is the strongest gymnast in the world.

Despite his physical attributes, Umphrey's body has betrayed him. In addition to the broken feet, he has been slowed by a broken leg, injured ankles, and a few years ago by an inner ear infection that scuttled his chances at the nationals.

His balance was so out of whack, he "couldn't find the floor," he said. The pommel horse was bucking like one of those electronic barroom bulls.

His resiliency, says Umphrey, whose body fat hovers around four percent, "is a gift from God and my parents."

So, too, is his personality.

Umphrey, who favors TV shows *Martin* and *Fresh Prince*, remote-control cars, and lists his mother's waffles as his favorite food ("I'm a breakfast man," he says) has an extremely likeable manner. Indeed, he has been asked to ride on a Rose Bowl float on New Year's Day and has appeared on the *Mister Roger's Neighborhood* TV show in—typically—a "hard work" segment.

He graduated UCLA with a pre-med degree in 1994 and plans to enter medical school after the Atlanta Olympics, perhaps developing a career as an orthopedic surgeon.

FACT: As gymnastics routines become more complex and difficult, the maximum score of 10 does not mean perfection so much as it means a better and harder performance than the previous competitor's. For that reason, the order in which gymnasts compete is crucial: coaches send out their lineups of six team members in inverse order of accomplishment. The weakest competitor in an event goes first, and her score becomes the base against which the rest are compared. If the first scores well and the second a bit better, the judges' scores escalate until, finally, the top performer goes out last in hopes of building on a base now escalated to 9.90 or 9.95.

Few questions have lingered about Chainey Umphrey's dedication or personality.

Then, again, there is that . . . name.

When asked about it, the gymnast tells a story of his great, great grandfather, Albert Umphrey, who lived in a rough part of Indianapolis. While returning home from a movie one night, Albert Umphrey found himself cornered by a group of men in an alley.

"He found a chain and managed to survive," Umphrey explains.

The symbolism is appropriate. The great-great-grandson is a battler, too. It also is his gift.

"For the U.S. to do well, I need to be in Atlanta," Umphrey says. "My experience will help the team."

His strength will help, too. As will his character. Ballet's loss. Gymnastic's gain.

—*Eric Kinkopf*

Hopefuls—Women's

Amy Chow

Susan Chow grew up in Hong Kong dreaming of becoming a dancer. Her parents made her quit.

"It was more than disappointing," Susan Chow recalled to the *San Jose Mercury News*. "It was really painful."

"Back then, it was a priority thing," said Nelson Chow, a test engineering manager for a California computer company, who grew up in Canton, China, moved to Hong Kong when he was 10, and imigrated to San Jose when he was 20, where he met his wife. "Girls were supposed to be nice to their mother and parents and stay home. Even education was not an absolute must for girls. Parents sometimes suppressed a child's need to do some things."

So, it would come as no surprise, really, that Nelson and Susan Chow would give their daughter the gift of freedom.

Amy Chow, 18 (b. May 15, 1978), of San Jose, Calif., one of the budding stars of the U.S. women's gymnastics team, has made the most of it—but on her own terms.

Which wasn't *exactly* what Susan Chow had in mind.

Susan Chow's dream was for Amy to be the ballet dancer she never was. Problem was, that at three, Amy was too small to enroll in ballet schools. So, Susan enrolled her in gymnastics classes, just to pass the time. When Amy was five, Susan took her back to the ballet schools. But it was already too late. Amy didn't like ballet. She wanted gymnastics.

And she proved it.

At age eight, she was the first elite-level gymnast produced by San Jose's West Valley Gymnastics club.

"Amy's the fastest kid I've ever worked with," West Valley coach Mark Young said.

Not that Amy Chow is an automaton in tights. Not by a long shot.

Chow, who wants to study medicine in college and become a pediatrician, dives, plays classical piano, and managed a 4.0 GPA in high school, while taking such challenging classes as pre-calculus, psychology, American literature, and chemistry. All this, while training before *and* after school at a pace approximating a 40-hour-a-week job.

FACT: Most of the best U.S. gymnasts are college students who must follow NCAA guidelines, which limit their training to 20 hours per week. Most of the U.S. team's women gymnasts are still in high school, and can train in private gyms with no restrictions.

Okay, so she put off getting her driver's license to concentrate on gymnastics. What's a little sacrifice?

"I just don't have time," Chow says. "I just don't really have time."

Though some have labeled Chow's national rise a surprise—from a 23rd all-around ranking at the 1993 Coca-Cola National Championships to fifth in 1994—legendary gymnastics coach Bela Karolyi offered this: "She may be a surprise to many people, but not to me. She is one of the most promising girls leading up to the 1996 Olympic games."

"Amy Chow isn't just an Olympic hopeful," said Steve Nunno, head of the Pan American Games women's team. "She's a super-contender."

Chow's routines are marked by high-difficulty moves. When working on the bars, she dismounts with her signature double-twisting double back. On the beam, she does a standing pike full twist.

If there is a single flaw, it is in her demeanor. Observers say that if she develops a personality to match her skill and perseverance, Chow truly will blossom.

Indeed, in an effort to communicate some of her inner joy, Chow has worked with noted gymnastics coach Geza Pozsar, a Karolyi colleague who choreographed routines for Nadia Comaneci and Mary Lou Retton. (Chow was six when she watched Retton on TV in 1984.)

Chow says of Retton's influence: "It was her spirit. Some gymnasts look so concerned. They look nervous. She looked calm and ready to go. She looked like she was having fun."

Chow's stoicism is part of her personality. Her high school classmates, she says, are "always trying to pry what I'm doing out of me."

Her reticence can even extend to her coaches.

In 1993, Amy injured her ankle on her beam dismount—a round-off flip-flop triple twist, which has been described as "more difficult to perform than to describe."

The injury ruined Chow's season and was blamed for her 22nd-place all-around finish at her first senior national championships. Once healed, Chow spent weeks working with her coach, Diane Amos, to simplify the dismount—but not without frustration. Amos spent hours trying to get Chow to verbalize what she was broiling inside.

Chow finally did, saying simply, "I want to do *my* dismount."

"Amy couldn't tell me what was bothering her because I was her teacher," Amos said. "The way she saw it, I'm supposed to tell her *what* to do, not ask her what she *wants* to do. But it was her dismount, and there was no way she was going to do anything else."

Chow's piano teacher, Steva Goff, who has taught Chow since she was four, says that determination is what makes Amy special.

"When students are recording pieces for competitions, they'll usually do it once," Goff said. "When I ask Amy if she's done, she'll always say, 'No, I'll do it again.' She records each piece several times.

"I think it's a quality she was born with. It has nothing to do with environment or anything like that. It's the quality that makes people succeed," added Goff.

Amy Chow says: "It's an honor to compete for your country, but I don't think I feel any more pressure because of that. When I compete, I tell myself to be calm. It's not something that's the rest of your life. You're in gymnastics for the fun."

And the freedom.

—Eric Kinkopf

Dominique Dawes

Got your *Jeopardy* caps on? The category is: "Adjectives for $500." Question: What word best describes the female athlete who: won a 1995 national citizenship award; swept a 1994 national championships competition, becoming the first competitor to do so since 1969; was a finalist for the prestigious Sullivan Award, given the best amateur athlete in the U.S; was selected a 1994 sportswoman of the year; has been profiled in *People, Harper's Bazaar, Jet,* and *Seventeen* magazines; was a member of her Gaithersburg, Md., high-school honor roll, *and* was her school's senior prom queen . . . and won a scholarship to Stanford University?

Answer: What is the word, awesome?

Just awesome?

It'll have to do, until a better word comes along.

Or until U.S. gymnast Dominique "Awesome Dawesome" Dawes, 19 (b. November 20, 1976) who fancies Stephen King novels, Boyz II Men soul ballads, hip-hop, rap, Janet Jackson, horror movies, Jean-Claude Van Damme, Bruce Willis, Demi Moore, a blue-gray 1988 Ford Escort, and who is considering an acting career (Goldie Hawn is a Gaithersburg High alum), becomes a full-fledged legend.

Got all that?

Too good to be true? Maybe it's just because we're moving a bit too quickly.

What you basically need to know is that Dawes, who, at 16, became the first African-American gymnast to win a pair of

1994 National Champion Dominique Dawes on the beam. Look for her in Atlanta. *Dave Black/U.S. Gymnastics*

silver medals at a world championships, and who won a bronze medal as a member of the 1992 U.S. Olympic gymnastics team, "is just a real neat kid," says Luan Peszak of U.S.A. Gymnastics, the sport's governing body.

"She's a real '90s gymnast, explosive and athletic. Nobody does it like her," Mary Lou Retton, the 1984 Olympic all-around gold medalist, told *USA Weekend.* "Dominique's also very genuine. And I believe that's why she's been blessed; because her heart's in the right place. She's not in it for the exposure. She's true."

Like most success stories, Dawes's had an unremarkable beginning. When Dominique was six, Loretta Dawes dragged her hyper-energetic daughter to a local gym, looking for a place for Dominique to burn off some excess energy.

"We knew right away that she was very, very talented," Kelli Hill, the coach of a gymnastics club—Hill's Angels—told *USA Weekend.* "Right off the bat she wanted to try stuff other kids were doing. 'No, you can't do that,' we'd say. 'You're not ready yet.' Then you'd turn around and there she'd be—'Watch me! Watch me! Watch me!—trying the stuff the older kids were doing, kamikaze-style. It was a little scary."

Actually the genesis goes back even a bit further.

All the way to the stairs at the Dawes home in Silver Springs, Md., just north of Washington, D.C.—the house with the brown aluminum awning over the front door and the sea horse birdbath in the yard.

What Dominique would do—like her father, Don, and his siblings did before her—was belly slide as fast as she could down the stairs to the small landing, torquing her body into a final, hard, right turn and coming to rest in a heap by the fireplace.

The best guess from Don is that she ended up there one day while the 1984 Olympic gymnastics competition was flashing on the TV. The rest is history.

Shortly thereafter, Dawes started "jumping from one couch to another, flipping around, doing cartwheels," Loretta Dawes says.

At age 9, Don Dawes found his daughter psyching herself up for a gymnastics meet by taking a crayon and writing and rewriting the same word—over and over again—on her bedroom mirror.

The word, Don Dawes says, was "determination."

"I was amazed that she even knew how to spell it," he said.

When she blitzed the national competition at Nashville in 1994 by taking the floor exercise, the balance beam, the uneven bars, vault, and all-around, Dominique established herself as the most dominating national champion of all time.

Olympic teammate Shannon Miller almost blocked the sweep with a 9.912 score in the floor exercise, but Dawes won over the judges when she opened her floor routine with an up-and-back-pass, during which she tumbled diagonally across the mat from corner to corner without pause. The standard performance virtually always includes only one trip across the mat at a time.

"It was a challenge and she did it," Hill said.

Dawes's response? "It was just one competition. I just don't think of me as being No. 1 in the U.S." And: "My goal really wasn't to go out and beat Shannon. I just wanted to go out and do well. I don't think I've broken any barrier. I just feel very good about it."

Pressed in a later interview, Dawes finally acceded at least to her drive to succeed. "Oh, yeah, I do have something I say to my-self: 'D^3—determination, dedication, dynamics.'"

Not that all of this has exactly been a walk in the park. In fact, Dawes faced serious doubts and challenges while fashioning her Olympic encore. A virtual *grand dame* in a sport identified with prepubescence, Dawes is a rare two-time female Olympic gymnast. Still petite at a chiseled five-feet and 98 pounds, Dawes's boyish build has given way to young womanhood. In female gymnastics, that sort of transition is not often welcome. Womanly physical developments realign a young girl's center of gravity. That can be trouble.

But Dawes has adapted. Noted early in her career for her power and aggressiveness and the difficulty of her routines, she has been rediscovered for her grace and elegance.

Loretta Dawes, the mother of two other children, is almost as amazed as everyone else at what has happened. "You wouldn't imagine that one child who started out tumbling steps at home would be famous, and that one child could do all this," she says. "I never thought it would come to this."

And it's not over, yet. Awesome? Yes. And maybe . . . understated.

—Eric Kinkopf

Dominique Moceanu

Her facial features remind people of Nadia Comaneci, who captured the hearts of the world at the 1976 Games in Montreal. Her expressiveness evokes images of Mary Lou Retton, the similarly seductive star of the 1984 Olympics in Los Angeles.

Her father, Dumitru, was a member of the Romanian junior gymnastics team as a youngster, until his mother made him give up the sport to concentrate on schoolwork. Dumitru planned from her birth to make his daughter the best in the world.

Is there a movie, here, or what?

Wait, there's more.

When his daughter was a little more than three years old, dad, who defected from Romania in 1979 (mom followed a year later), called legendary gymnastics coach Bela Karolyi in Houston. He already wanted to enroll his child. Karolyi urged a little patience—about six years' worth.

"I told him to let the kid grow up," Karolyi told the *Baltimore Sun.*

When the daughter said she was ready at age 9—specifically to train with Karolyi—dad, daughter, and mom moved lock, stock, and barrel to Houston.

The result? Today, diminutive Dominique Moceanu, 14 (b. September 30, 1981), is on the cusp of international stardom.

Then, again, what would you expect from someone born in Hollywood, Calif.?

"In a couple of years, she could be the best the in world," says former all-around world champion, Svetlana Boguinskaia, who trains with Moceanu at Karolyi's gym.

Boguinskaia made that prediction in the spring of 1995. Most observers figure the veteran gymnast left the "give or take a year" part of her prediction unsaid, which would put Moceanu smack dab in the spotlight at the 1996 Olympic Games.

That may be no stretch at all.

After the 1995 Visa Challenge at George Mason University in Fairfax, Va., in which Moceanu placed first overall while competing against former champions Boguinskaia, Kim Zmeskal, and 1996 Olympic teammate Dominique "Awesome Dawesome" Dawes—not to mention the top gymnasts from Belarus and China—*Sports Illustrated*'s E.M. Swift wrote:

"Dominique performs older than she looks. Her hand movements on the beam, for example, are not those of a 13-year-old. The way she carries her head, her facial expressions, her swagger, if you will, all conspire to convince us there is an older person inside that tiny body. And as she proved . . . while pretending to play *Let's Twist Again* on the piano during her winning floor exercise routine, she knows how to preen for the crowd."

Gymnastics magazine's Dwight Normile gave more technical evaluation:

"It looked like fun. Moceanu smiled through four spectacular events with difficulty and amplitude to match. She . . . sailed three releases on bars, railed balance beam and airmailed her tumbling on floor. Anyone struggling to master a front-full on floor might study Moceanu's technique. She twists late, then pops an effortless front layout. In Fairfax, she bounded two feet in the air on landing. For sure, Moceanu is Bela Karolyi's ace right now, and he knows how to mold a winner."

Karolyi credits part of Moceanu's maturation to her training with Boguinskaia and Zmeskal.

"She is going to be one of the great ones," he told the *Baltimore Sun.*

And the Visa Challenge was only the second competition at the senior level for Moceanu, the 1994 U.S. junior national champion and the youngest member ever of the national junior team.

"It was nice," Moceanu said of the Visa competition, in which she finished second in the vault, second (to Dawes) in the uneven bars, third in the balance beam, and first in the floor exercise. "It was fun competing."

At the Visa competition, Comaneci served as Moceanu's ringside mentor, often calling out encouragement to the youngster.

In fact, Comaneci is Moceanu's idol.

"She calls me 'alternate mother,'" Comaneci told the *Nashville Banner.* "When I first met her, I didn't know she was Romanian. I didn't know anything about her past. I got to talking to her. I met her parents, and we are just very close. Her mom says that she idolizes me. She wants to know everything about me. She calls me. She tells me what she did, what she's working on. It is a very, very close relationship. She is very ambitious."

And, of course, Karolyi sees lots of Retton in his budding star.

"She's an outgoing kid, like Mary Lou," Karolyi told *SI*'s Swift. "She's not a hidden personality. She can laugh one minute and cry the next—an open book. This is a good kind to coach."

The coach also credits Boguinskaia's influence.

"Dominique's matured so fast next to Svetlana. All of a sudden, this little thing, her head is up. She smiling. It's very promising."

Says Moceanu: "I want people to remember me for being happy and for my smile. I don't fake smile." She adds: "Svetlana's so elegant and expressive (and) Kim's so powerful. I try to take that with me. . . ."

Karolyi smiles. "This is a good age," he says. "At 13, they don't get psycho yet over the pressure."

Says Moceanu, with a maturity beyond her years: "You can't get anywhere in life without hard work. I want to be somebody."

"She has to build her confidence and her strength," says Boguinskaia of Moceanu, who'd been called "Shorty" by former schoolmates. "She's just so little." In stature. Only.

—Eric Kinkopf

Schedule

The tentative gymnastics schedule for podium training events is:

July 15
Men's podium training -compulsory

July 16
Women's podium training -compulsory

July 17
Men's podium training -optional

July 18
Women's podium training -optional

The tentative gymnastics schedule for artistic events is:

Saturday, July 20
Men's team compulsories

Sunday, July 21
Women's team compulsories

Monday, July 22
Men's team optionals & final

Tuesday, July 23
Women's team optionals & final

Wednesday, July 24
Men's individual all-around final

Thursday, July 25
Women's individual all-around final

Sunday, July 28
Men's floor exercise final
Women's vault final
Men's pommel horse final
Women's uneven bars final
Men's rings final

Monday, July 29
Men's vault final
Women's balance beam final
Men's parallel bars final
Women's floor exercise final
Men's high bars final

Tuesday, July 30
Gymnastics exhibition

The tentative gymnastics schedule for rhythmic events is:

Thursday, August 1
individual preliminaries
group preliminaries

Friday, August 2
individual preliminaries
group finals

Saturday, August 3
individual semifinals

Sunday, August 4
individual finals

MEN'S GYMNASTICS EVENTS

Highlights

Long dominated by Europeans, especially the Soviets, gymnastics until the 1980s stressed grace and style as much as athletic power. Japanese gymnasts began to make their mark in the 1960s with exceptional smoothness and elegance. In the 1980s innovations in the sport's equipment allowed gymnasts to emphasize physical power; for instance, instead of functioning as padding, the tumbling mats are now mounted on springs, affording athletes extra hang time for aerial maneuvers.

U.S. men won gold medals in 1904 and 1932, including golds at the 1932 Los Angeles Games for rope climb, Indian clubs, and tumbling. Among notable medal winners, Japan's Akinori Nakayama earned six gold medals, two silver, and two bronze in the late 1960s; he was followed by his countryman Sawao Kato, who captured six gold, two silver, and one bronze. The male record for individual gymnastics gold medals is six each for Boris Shakhlin, competing in the 1960s, and Nikolai Andrianov, competing in 1976 and 1980, both of the U.S.S.R. Shakhlin also won a team gold medal, and four silver and two bronze. Andrianov set a record for the most medals by a male competitor in any sport, winning a total of 15.

At the Moscow Games in 1980 Aleksandr Dityatin was the first male gymnast to gain medals in all eight categories open to him at a single Games. The U.S.'s first black Olympic gymnast, Charles Lakes, competed in 1988.

Individual All-Around Combined Exercises: This competition was not held for men in 1896 but has been part of every Olympiad since 1900. Men's combined exercises include the horse vault, the side (pommel) horse, the horizontal bar, parallel bars, rings, and floor exercises.

Gustave Sandras of France was the first men's all-around champion, leading a French sweep of the competition at the Paris Games. In 1904 the title was won by Julius Lenhardt, competing for the U.S. team. France's Pierre Payssé won two individuals (a five- and a six-event competition) in the unofficial Olympics of 1906, both times besting Italy's Alberto Braglia. Braglia was the first gymnast to win two consecutive Olympic medals in the individual combined exercises, in 1908 and 1912.

More than four decades later the Soviet Union's Victor Chukarin achieved the same feat when he won his second medal

Italy's Alberto Braglia was the first gymnast to win two consecutive Olympic gold medals in the individual combined exercises, in 1908 and 1912. *AP/Wide World Photos*

in this event in 1956, defeating Japan's Takashi Ono by only 0.05 points. Ono was again beaten by a Soviet in 1960, again by only 0.05 points. Behind Ono both times was Soviet gymnast Yury Titov.

In 1972 Japan's Sawao Kato became the third man to win the all-round gold medal twice, leading the Japanese to a sweep of this event. Japan's Akinori Nakayama took the bronze in 1968 and 1972. At the Montreal Games Kato came back for a silver in the all-around, behind Soviet Nikolai Andrianov and ahead of Japan's Mitsuo Tsukahara. Andrianov settled for silver behind teammate Aleksandr Dityatin in 1980.

The U.S.A.'s Peter Vidmar was silver medalist in this competition in 1984, ceding gold by a mere 0.025 of a point to Japan's Koji Gushiken, the smallest men's margin of victory. In 1988 this event was swept by the Soviets.

Team Combined Exercises: The Swedish team captured the gold in 1908, then Italy won the men's team championships four times between 1912 and 1932. After Germany and Finland each won once, the U.S.S.R. captured the team gold in 1952 and 1956. Finland's bronze medal-winning team in 1952 included 44-year-old Heikki Savolainen, who set a record by competing in five Games from 1928 to 1952. Starting in 1960, Japan claimed the team title five times in a row. The 1960 Japanese team included 40-year-old Masao Takemoto, the oldest gold-medaling gymnast. In 1976 the Japanese team won on the strength of Mitsuo Tsukahara's performance on the horizontal bar.

The Soviet team captured the gold in the boycott year of 1980. Going into the 1984 Games, needless to say, American men had endured a long drought in gymnastics. In fact, before 1984, no American gymnast had won a gold since the 1932 Games, when male gymnasts also climbed ropes and juggled Indian clubs. But in 1984, albeit with the Eastern bloc countries absent, the U.S. men's team took the gold, winning a close contest against China, to Japan's bronze. In 1988 the Soviet men, led by all-around champion Vladimir Artemov, won the team gold medal ahead of East Germany, with Japan again claiming the bronze.

Floor Exercise: Swiss competitor Georges Miez enthralled the Berlin crowd in 1936, when he placed first in this event. Miez had won the all-around gold in 1928, and by 1936 his Olympic medal total came to four gold, three silver, and one bronze. K. William Thoresson of Sweden captured the floor exercise gold in 1952 and was part of a unique three-way tie for the silver in 1956, sharing the medal with Viktor Chukarin of the Soviet Union and Japan's Nobuyuki Aihara, who returned in 1960 to claim the gold.

Italy's Franco Menichelli took a bronze before the home crowd at the 1960 Rome Games and four years later was awarded the gold. Akinori Nakayama of Japan silver medaled in 1968 and 1972. A surprise bronze came for U.S. gymnast Peter Kormann in this event in 1976. Chinese gymnasts captured the two top spots in 1984, and the Soviets did likewise in Seoul.

Horizontal Bar: Yugoslavia's Leon Stukelj struck gold in 1924, the year that Swiss competitor Georges Miez placed fourth; four years later, Miez was good as gold. Heikki Savolainen, competing for Finland, took a silver on the horizontal bar in 1932 and, twenty years later, placed fifth.

Another elder gymnast, Japan's Masao Takemoto, earned a silver medal on the horizontal bar in 1960 at the age of 40. Mitsuo Tsukahara won the gold in 1972 and 1976. Japanese gymnasts claimed the gold and bronze in 1984, while two Soviets tied for gold four years later.

Parallel Bars: U.S. gymnast George Eyser took the gold in 1904 (not hampered by a wooden leg). He ultimately won another gold, two silver, and a bronze at the St. Louis Games. The next American to capture the gold in the parallel bars was Bart Conner, in 1984; his teammate, Mitch Gaylord, claimed the bronze. In 1988 Soviet gymnasts took the top two spots.

Pommel Horse (or Sidehorse): This event was not held from 1908 to 1920. Heikki Savolainen of Finland captured the bronze in the pommel horse in 1928 and twenty years later, in 1948. Zoltán Magyar of Hungary claimed the gold twice, in 1976 and 1980. In 1984 U.S. gymnast Peter Vidmar tied with China's Li Ning for the gold, and Timothy Daggett of the U.S. brought in the bronze. A three-way tie for the gold resulted in 1988, with Dmitri Bilozertchev of the Soviet Union, Hungary's Zsolt Borkai, and Lyubomir Gueraskov of Bulgaria sharing the top honor.

Still Rings: Ioannis Mitropolos won the gold in 1896, the Modern Olympics' first announced Greek champion. Yugoslavia's Leon Stukelj took fourth place in 1924, then moved up for the gold in 1928; he was 37 when he won the silver on the rings in 1936, adding to the three gold and two bronze medals he'd won at previous games over a dozen years, including the all-around gold in 1924.

Japan's Akinori Nakayama repeated for the gold on the rings in 1968 and 1972. Aleksandr Dityatin of the U.S.S.R. followed his silver in this event in 1976 with a gold in 1980. In 1984 Mitch Gaylord of the U.S. captured a bronze, behind Li Ning of China and Koji Gushiken of Japan, who tied for the gold. Holger Behrendt of East Germany and Dmitri Bilozertchev of the Soviet Union also shared the gold at Seoul.

Horse (or Longhorse) Vault: The event's first gold medalist was German Carl Schuhmann in 1896. In 1964 Haruhiro Yamashita of Japan won the gold with a handspring in a pike position, and the maneuver was subsequently named the Yamashita. In 1972, East Germany's Klaus Köste won the title with a Yamashita and a forward somersault, claiming the first gold for his country in men's gymnastics. The U.S.S.R.'s Aleksandr Dityatin was the first male gymnast to receive a 10.0 score from judges in Olympic competition, accorded for a horse vault in 1980. Four years later U.S. gymnast Mitch Gaylord settled for a quarter share of the silver, as he tied with Koji Gushiken and Shninji Morisue of Japan and China's Li Ning. Alone at the top was Yun Lou of China.

The 1984 U.S.A. Men's Gymnastics Team

"Say hello to the 1984 equivalent of the 1980 U.S. hockey team," *Miami Herald* sports columnist Edwin Pope wrote from the Los Angeles Olympic Games. The U.S. men's gymnastic team had just won its first gold medal in eight decades of competition—and its first team medal of *any* kind since a silver in 1932.

"Winning a gold as a team—it's a miracle," U.S. gymnast Scott Johnson affirmed.

"It's pretty amazing," teammate Bart Conner acknowledged then. "If you'd taken a poll of the world gymnastic community on our chances, we wouldn't have gotten very many votes a week ago."

But voting had nothing to do with anything in LA. What won the gold—an untarnished medal (though the Soviets and many Eastern bloc countries boycotted the games, the U.S. defeated the reigning world champion Chinese)—were incredible performances by all members of the team: Conner, Tim Daggett, Peter Vidmar, Mitch Gaylord, James Hartung, and Scott Johnson.

"We got 'em on depth," Conner explained.

Indeed. The U.S. earned a passel of perfect 10s, from performances by team captain Vidmar, as well as Daggett, Gaylord, and Conner, and strong ninth and 16th overall finishes from Hartung and Johnson respectively.

"Those 'lows,' " Pope wrote of Hartung and Johnson's finishes, "actually were remarkably high in overall competition."

And the highs didn't end there, though after sweating and straining in relative obscurity for years, the gymnasts found their newfound celebrity could be something more difficult to balance. Vidmar complained of the apparent arrogance of having to wear sunglasses in public to avoid recognition.

"I'm just uncomfortable with it," he revealed a few months after the Games. "You walk by and people look at you and their mouths hit the floor and it scares you, almost. You back up not knowing what to do."

Things had truly changed.

Before the 1984 triumph, the U.S. gymnastic team would go to the Olympics to "meet Dwight Stones and to see Harvey Glance run and to talk with the security guards in the Olympic Village," Conner recalled. "When you swim for the United States, you go to the Games with the idea that you can win a medal. That wasn't the case in gymnastics."

Wasn't. Past tense.

Their popularity—temporary matinee-idol status, in some instances—turned out to be a catapult, too.

Vidmar, born on June 30, 1961, completed a Mormon missionary assignment in the Los Angeles area after the Games. He developed a TV analyst/motivational speaking career.

Mitch Gaylord, born on March 10, 1961, appeared in *Super-Teen* magazine, gave his name to a gymnastic maneuver (the *Gaylord II,* a one-and-one-half flip on the high bar), and competed in the 1988 Games. He appeared in numerous TV shows and some films: a 1986 production, *American Anthem,* and a 1990 film, *American Tiger,* a supernatural thriller about a college student who is drawn into a web of intrigue after taking a part-time job as a rickshaw puller in Miami.

Conner, born on March 28, 1958, is a three-time Olympian from the University of Oklahoma. He parlayed his increased visibility into further development of his career as a TV analyst. Conner signed to appear in some TV series and movies; competed in celebrity road-racing events; was chosen one of the top-10 best-dressed short men in 1990 (in company with actor Michael J. Fox and novelist Tom Wolfe); and has become engaged to former Romanian Olympic gymnast Nadia Comaneci, who helps him run the Bart Conner Gymnastics Academy in Norman, Oklahoma.

Daggett went on to run a gym in Massachusetts and provide analysis for network TV.

Only Hartung, who joined the board of the U.S. Gymnastics Federation and has also done some coaching, and Scott Johnson, who went into management for McDonald's Hamburgers in Florida, were able to dodge that ever-searching spotlight.

—*Eric Kinkopf*

FACT: When U.S. gymnasts Bart Conner and Mary Lou Retton won individual golds in 1984, they were the first individual gold medals for American gymnasts since 1932 when Dallas Bixler took top honors in the men's horizontal bar and George Gulack won the still rings event.

Highlights from Barcelona

All the world was watching as athletes from the last generation of the Soviet sports machine performed their swan song at the Olympic Games. Between 1952 and 1988, gymnastic hegemony seemed to be written into the constitution of the various incarnations of the Soviet state. Excluding the boycotted 1984 Games, Soviet women medaled in *every* event, in *every* year, except one (the 1976 uneven bars). The Soviet men, too, draped themselves in precious metals, failing only nine times, over the same period, to mount the victory podium.

> "Obviously, I'm thrilled. I certainly didn't expect this to happen. It seemed to me it would be impossible to win so many gold medals."
> — *The Unified Team's Vitali Chtcherbo, who nabbed six gold medals in Barcelona — more than any gymnast had ever won in an Olympics*

Barcelona was no exception. The Unified Team dominated men's gymnastics, grabbing the team title and sweeping the individual all-around for the second consecutive Olympics. First, the Unified men dispatched their Chinese rivals with a handsome five-point margin. Settling for silver, the Chinese team pocketed their third-ever team medal, while Japanese athletes repeated their bronze-medal performance of the previous Games.

Next, the Unified teammates mounted a charge for the all-around individual medals, this time competing against one another, under the flags of their individual republics. Clearly, the erstwhile teammates were destined to stand together on the victory podium; but no one knew in what order. It was any man's game until the final event, when Vitali Chtcherbo's 9.9 on the rings struck gold for Belarus. Behind him, Grigori Misioutine collected a silver for Ukraine, while Valeri Belenki took a bronze for Azerbaijan.

There was more gold to come, and most of it fell to Belarus, thanks to the record-breaking winning streak of Chtcherbo. Dominating the parallel bars, the pommel horse, the rings, and the vault, the 20-year-old newlywed culled six gold medals at the 1992 Games — an Olympic record for a gymnast. Receding into Olympic history was Nikolai Andrianov's record of four golds, set in Montreal in 1976.

Not to be overlooked, U.S. gymnasts staged a proud day for Old Glory. Trent Dimas — a college-deferring 21-year-old who made the U.S. team by the skin of his teeth — grabbed a surprise victory in the horizontal bar. It was the U.S. men's team's first medal at Barcelona. More importantly, it was the first time any American gymnast — male or female — had managed a gold in the presence of Soviet-trained athletes.

Unified Team gymnast Vitali Chtcherbo nabbed six gold medals in Barcelona — more golds than any gymnast had ever won in an Olympics. *AP/Wide World Photos*

Medalists

Gymnastics, Artistic—Men's Individual All-Around (Combined Exercises)

1992
1. Vitali Chtcherbo, Belarus, 59.025
2. Grigori Misioutine, Ukraine, 58.925
3. Valeri Belenki, Azerbaijan, 58.625

1988
1. Vladimir Artemov, Soviet Union, 119.125
2. Valeri Lioukine, Soviet Union, 119.025
3. Dmitri Bilozertchev, Soviet Union, 118.975

1984
1. Koji Gushiken, Japan, 118.700
2. Peter Vidmar, U.S.A., 118.675
3. Li Ning, China, 118.575

1980
1. Aleksandr Dityatin, Soviet Union, 118.650
2. Nikolai Andrianov, Soviet Union, 118.225
3. Stoian Delchev, Bulgaria, 118.000

1976
1. Nikolai Andrianov, Soviet Union, 116.650
2. Sawao Kato, Japan, 115.650
3. Mitsuo Tsukahara, Japan, 115.575

1972
1. Sawao Kato, Japan, 114.650
2. Eizo Kenmotsu, Japan, 114.575
3. Akinori Nakayama, Japan, 114.325

1968
1. Sawao Kato, Japan, 115.90
2. Mikhail Voronin, Soviet Union, 115.85
3. Akinori Nakayama, Japan, 115.65

1964
1. Yukio Endo, Japan, 115.95
2. Viktor Lisitski, Soviet Union, 115.40
2. Boris Shakhlin, Soviet Union, 115.40
2. Shuji Tsurumi, Japan, 115.40

1960
1. Boris Shakhlin, Soviet Union, 115.95
2. Takashi Ono, Japan, 115.90
3. Yuri Titov, Soviet Union, 115.60

1956
1. Viktor Chukarin, Soviet Union, 114.25
2. Takashi Ono, Japan, 114.20
3. Yuri Titov, Soviet Union, 113.80

1952
1. Viktor Chukarin, Soviet Union, 115.70
2. Grant Shaginyan, Soviet Union, 114.95
3. Josef Stalder, Switzerland, 114.75

1948
1. Veikko Huhtanen, Finland, 229.70

2. Walter Lehmann, Switzerland, 229.00
3. Paavo Aaltonen, Finland, 228.80

1936
1. Alfred Schwarzmann, Germany, 113.100
2. Eugen Mack, Switzerland, 112.334
3. Konrad Frey, Germany, 111.532

1932
1. Romeo Neri, Italy, 140.625
2. Istvan Pelle, Hungary, 134.925
3. Heikki Savolainen, Finland, 134.575

1928
1. Georges Miez, Switzerland, 247.500
2. Hermann Hanggi, Switzerland, 246.625
3. Leon Stukelj, Yugoslavia, 244.875

1924
1. Leon Stukelj, Yugoslavia, 110.340
2. Robert Prazak, Czechoslovakia, 110.323
3. Bedrich Supcik, Czechoslovakia, 106.930

1920
1. Giorgio Zampori, Italy, 88.35
2. Marco Torres, France, 87.62
3. Jean Gounot, France, 87.45

1912
1. Alberto Braglia, Italy, 135.0
2. Louis Segura, France, 132.5
3. Serafino Mazzarochi, Italy, 131.5

1908
1. Alberto Braglia, Italy, 317.0
2. S. W. Tysal, Great Britain, 312.0
3. Louis Segura, France, 297.0

1906
1. Pierre Paysse, France, 116 (five apparatuses)
1. Pierre Paysse, France, 97 (six apparatuses)
2. Alberto Braglia, Italy, 115 (five apparatuses)
2. Alberto Braglia, Italy, 95 (six apparatuses)
3. Georges Charmoille, France, 113 (five apparatuses)
3. Georges Charmoille, France, 94 (six apparatuses)

1904
1. Julius Lenhart, Austria, 69.80
2. Wilhelm Weber, Germany, 69.10
3. Adolf Spinnler, Switzerland, 67.99

1900
1. Gustave Sandras, France, 302
2. Noel Bas, France, 295
3. Lucien Demanet, France, 293

1896
Not held

Gymnastics, Artistic—Men's Team (Combined Exercises)

1992

1. Unified Team, 585.450, Vitali Chtcherbo, Valeri Belenki, Grigori Misioutine, Igor Korobtchinski, Aleksei Voropaev, Roustam Charipov
2. China, 580.375, Li Xiaosahuang, Li Chunyang, Guo Linyao, Li Jing, Li Dashuang, Li Ge
3. Japan, 578.250, Yukio Iketani, Yoshiaki Hatakeda, Takashi Chinen, Daisuke Nishikawa, Yutaka Aihara, Masayuki Matsunaga

1988

1. Soviet Union, 593.350, Vladimir Gogoladze, Vladimir Nouvikov, Serguei Kharikov, Dmitri Bilozertchev, Vladimir Artemov, Valeri Lioukine
2. East Germany, 588.450, Ulf Hoffman, Andreas Wecker, Sven Tippelt, Ralf Buechner, Holger Behrendt, Sylvio Kroll
3. Japan, 585.600, Hiroyuki Konishi, Takahiro Yamada, Toshiharu Sato, Daisuke Nishikawa, Koichi Mizushima, Yukio Iketani

1984

1. U.S.A., 591.40, Scott Johnson, James Hartung, Timothy Daggett, Bart Conner, Peter Vidmar, Mitchell Gaylor
2. China, 590.80, Yuejiu Li, Xiaoping Li, Yun Lou, Zhigiang Xu, Fei Tong, Ning Li
3. Japan, 586.70, Shinji Morisue, Noritoshi Hirata, Nobuyuki Kajitani, Kyoji Yamawaki, Koji Sotomura, Koji Gushiken

1980

1. Soviet Union, 589.60, Nikolai Andrianov, Eduard Azaryan, Bogdan Makuts, Vladimir Markelov, Aleksandr Dityatin, Aleksandr Tkachov
2. East Germany, 581.15, Lutz Mack, Ralf-Peter Hemman, Lutz Hoffmann, Michael Nikolay, Andreas Bronst, Roland Brueckner
3. Hungary, 575.00, Ferenc Donath, Gyorgy Guczoghy, Zoltan Keleman, Peter Kovacs, Istvan Vamos, Dr. Zoltan Magyar

1976

1. Japan, 576.85, Sawao Kato, Hiroshi Kajiyama, Eizo Kenmotsu, Hisato Igarashi, Shun Fujimoto, Mitsuo Tukahara
2. Soviet Union, 576.45, Nikolai Andrianov, Vladimir Markelov, Aleksandr Dityatin, Gennady Kryssin, Vladimir Marchenko, Vladimir Tikhonov
3. East Germany, 564.65, Lutz Mack, Bernd Jaeger, Michael Nikolay, Roland Brueckner, Wolfgang Klotz, Rainer Hanschke

1972

1. Japan, 571.25, Sawao Kato, Eizo Kenmotsu, Shigeru Kasamatsu, Akinori Nakayama, Mitsuo Tsukahara, Teruichi Okamura
2. Soviet Union, 564.05, Nikolai Andrianov, Mickail Voronin, Viktor Klimenko, Edvard Mikhaelyan, Aleksandr Maleyev, Vladimir Shukin
3. East Germany, 559.70, Klaus Koste, Matthias Brehme, Wolfgang Thune, Wolfgang Klotz, Reinhard Rychly, Jurgen Paeke

1968

1. Japan, 575.90, Sawao Kato, Akinori Nakayama, Eizo Kenmotsu, Takeshi Kato, Yukio Endo, Mitsuo Tsukahara
2. Soviet Union, 571.10, Mikhail Voronin, Sergei Diomidov, Viktor Klimenko, Valeri Karassev, Viktor Lisitski, Valeri Ilyinykh
3. East Germany, 557.15, Matthias Brehme, Klaus Koste, Siegfried Fulle, Peter Weber, Gerhard Dietrich, Gunter Beier

1964

1. Japan, 577.95, Yukio Endo, Shuji Tsurumi, Haruhiro Yamashita, Takuji Hayata, Takashi Mitsukuri, Takashi Ono
2. Soviet Union, 575.45, Boris Shakhlin, Viktor Lisitsky, Viktor Leontyer, Yuri Tsapenko, Yuri Titov, Sergei Diomidov
3. West Germany, 565.10, Siegfried Fulle, Klaus Koste, Erwin Koppe, Peter Weber, Philipp Furst, Gunter Lyhs

1960

1. Japan, 575.20, Takashi Ono, Shuji Tsurumi, Yukio Endo, Masao Takemoto, Nobuyuki Aihara, Takashi Mitsukuri
2. Soviet Union, 572.70, Boris Shakhlin, Yuri Titov, Albert Azaryan, Vladimir Portnoi, Nikolai Miligulo, Valeri Kerdemelidi
3. Italy, 559.05, Franco Menichelli, Giovanni Carminucci, Angelo Vicardi, Pasquale Carminucci, Orlando Polmonari, Gianfranco Marzolla

1956

1. Soviet Union, 568.25, Viktor Chukarin, Yuri Titov, Valentin Muratov, Albert Azaryan, Boris Shakhlin, Pavel Stolbov
2. Japan, 566.40, Takashi Ono, Masao Takemoto, Masami Kubota, Nobuyuki Aihara, Shinsaku Tsukawaki, Akira Kono
3. Finland, 555.95, Kalevi Suoniemi, Berndt Lindfors, Martti Mansikka, Onni Lappalainen, Olavi Leimuvirta, Raimo Heinonen

1952

1. Soviet Union, 574.40, Viktor Chukarin, Grant Shaginyan, Valentin Muratov, Yergeny Korolkov, Vladimir Belyakov, Josif Berdijev, Mikhail Perelman, Dmitri Leonkin
2. Switzerland, 567.50, Josef Stalder, Hans Eugster, Jean Tschabold, Jack Gunthard, Melchior Thalmann, Ernst Gebendinger, Hans Schwarzentruber, Ernst Fivian
3. Finland, 564.20, Onni Lappalainen, Berndt Lindfors, Paavo Aaltonen, Kaino Lempinen, Heikki Savolainen, Kalevi Laitinen, Kalevi Viskari, Olavi Rove

1948

1. Finland, 1358.30, Veikko Huhtanen, Paavo Aaltonen, Kalevi Laitinen, Olavi Rove, Einari Terasvirta, Heikki Savolainen
2. Switzerland, 1356.70, Walter Lehmann, Josef Stalder, Christian Kipfer, Emil Studer, Robert Lucy, Michael Reusch
3. Hungary, 1330.85, Lajos Toth, Dr. Lajos Santha, Laszlo Baranyai, Ferenc Pataki, Janos Mogyorosi-Klencs, Ferenc Varkoi

1936

1. Germany, 657.430, Alfred Schwarzmann, Konrad Frey, Matthias Volz, Willi Stadel, Franz Beckert, Walter Steffens
2. Switzerland, 654.802, Eugen Mack, Michael Reusch, Edi Steinemann, Walter Bach, Albert Bachmann, Georges Miez
3. Finland, 638.468, Martti Uosikkinen, Heikki Savolainen, Mauri Noroma-Nyberg, Aleksanteri Saarvala, Esa Seeste, Veikko Pakarinen

1932

1. Italy, 541.850, Romeo Neri, Mario Lertora, Savino Guglielmetti, Oreste Capuzzo
2. U.S.A., 522.275, Frank Haubold, Frederick Meyer, Alfred Jochim, Frank Cumiskey
3. Finland, 509.995, Heikki Savolainen, Mauri Noroma-Nyberg, Veikko Pakarinen, Einari Terasvirta

1928

1. Switzerland, 1718.625, Georges Miez, Hermann Hanggi, Eugen Mack, Melchior Wetzel, Edi Steinemann, August Guttinger, Hans Grieder, Otto Pfister
2. Czechoslovakia, 1712.250, Ladislav Vacha, Emanuel Loffler, Jan Gajdos, Josef Effenberger, Bedrich Supcik, Vaclav Vesely, Jan Koutny, Ladislav Tikal
3. Yugoslavia, 1648.750, Leon Stukelj, Josip Primozic, Anton Malej, Eduard Antosiewicz,

Boris Gregorka, Ivan Porenta, Stane Derganc, Dragutin Ciotti

1924

1. Italy, 839.058, Ferdinando Mandrini, Mario Lertora, Vittorio Lucchetti, Francesco Martino, Luigi Cambiaso, Giuseppe Paris, Giorgio Zampori, Luigi Maiocco
2. France, 820.528, Jean Gounot, Leon Delsarte, Albert Seguin, Eugene Cordonnier, Francois Gangloff, Arthur Hermann, Andre Higelin, Joseph Huber
3. Switzerland, 816.661, August Guttinger, Jean Gutweniger, Hans Grieder, Georges Miez, Josef Wilhelm, Otto Pfister, Carl Widmer, Antoine Rebetez

1920

1. Italy, 359.855, Arnaldo Andreoli, Pietro Bianchi, Ettore Bellotto, Luigi Cambiaso, Luigi Contessi, Carlo Costigliolo, Luigi Costigliolo, Fernando Bonatti, Giuseppe Domenichelli, Roberto Ferrari, Carlo Fregosi, Romualdo Ghiglione, Ambrogio Levati, Francesco Loy, Vittorio Lucchetti, Luigi Maiocco, Fernando Mandrini, Gianni Mangiante, Renzo Mangiante, Antonio Marovelli, Michele Mastromarino, Giuseppe Paris, Manlio Pastorini, Ezio Roselli, Paolo Salvi, Giovan Battista Tubino, Giorgio Zampori, Angelo Zorzi
2. Belgium, 346.785, Eugenius Auwerkerken, Theophile Bauer, Francois Claessens, Auguste Cootmans, Frans Gibens, Jean Van Guysse, Albert Haepers, Dominique Jacobs, Felicien Kempeneers, Jules Labeeu, Hubert Lafortune, Auguste Landrieu, Charles Lannie, Constant Loriot, Alphonse Van Mele, Ferdinand Minnaert, Nicolas Moerloos, Louis Stoop, Francois Verboven, Jean Verboven, Julien Verdonck, Joseph Verstraeten, Georges Vivex, Julianus Wagemans
3. France, 340.100, Emile Bouches, Paul J. Durin, Paulin A. Lemaire, Georges Berger, Leon Delsarte, Georges Duvant, Louis Kempe, Lucien Demanet, Auguste Hoel, Rene Boulanger, Fernand Fauconnier, Albert Hersoy, Georges Lagouge, Ernest Lespinasse, Jules Pirard, Julien Wartelle, Paul Wartelle, Emile Martel, Georges Thurnherr, Alfred Buyenne, Eugene Cordonnier, Arthur Hermann, Andre Higelin, Eugene Pollet

1912

1. Italy, 265.75, Guido Boni, Giuseppe Domenichelli, Luciano Savorini, Guido Romano, Angelo Zorzi, Giorgio Zampori,

Gianni Mangiante, Renzo Mangiante, Adolfo Tunesi, Pietro Bianchi, Paolo Salvi, Alberto Braglia, Alfredo Gollini, Serafino Mazzarocchi, Francesco Loy, Carlo Fregosi
2. Hungary, 227.25, Jozsef Bittenbinder, Imre Erdody, Samu Foti, Imre Gellert, Gyozo Haberfeld, Otto Hellmich, Istvan Herezeg, Jozsef Keresztessy, Lajos Kmetyko, Janos Krizmanich, Elemer Paszty, Arpad Pedery, Jeno Rittich, Ferene Szuts, Odon Tery, Geza Tuli
3. Great Britain, 184.50, Albert E. Betts, Harry Dickason, Samuel Hodgetts, Alfred W. Messenger, Edward E. Pepper, Charles A. Vigurs, Samuel John Walker, John Whitaker, Sidney Cross, Bernard W. Franklin, Edward W. Potts, Reginald H. Potts, George J. Ross, Henry A. Oberholzer, Charles Simmons, Arthur George Southern, Ronald G. McLean, Charles James Luck, Herbert J. Drury, William MacKune, William Titt, William Cowhig, Leonard Hanson

1908
1. Sweden, 438, Gosta Asbrink, Carl Bertilsson, Andreas Cervin, Hjalmar Cedercrona, Rudolf Degermark, Carl W. Folcker, Sven Forssman, Erik G. Granfelt, Carl Harleman, Nils E. Hellsten, Gunnar Hojer, Arvid Holmberg, Carl Holmberg, Osvald Holmberg, Hugo Jahnke, John Jarlen, Harald Jonsson, Rolf Jonsson, Nils G. Kantzow, Sven Landberg, Olle Lanner, Axel Ljung, Ossvald Moberg, Carl M. Norberg, Erik Norberg, Thor Norberg, Axel Norling, Daniel Norling, Gosta Olsson, Leonhard Peterson, Sven Rosen, Gustaf Rosenquist, Axel Sjoblom, Birger Sorvik, Haakon Sorvik, Karl-Johan Svensson, Karl-Gustaf Vingqvist, Nils Widforss
2. Norway, 425, Arthur Amundsen, Carl A. Andersen, Otto Authen, Hermann Bohne, Trygve Boysen, Oskar W. Bye, Conrad Carlsrud, Sverre Groner, Harald Halvorsen, Harald Hansen, Petter Hol, Eugen Ingebretsen, Ole Iversen, Mathias Jespersen, Sigge Johannesen, Nicolai Kior, Karl Klaeth, Thor Larsen, Rolf Lefdahl, Hans Lem, Anders Moen, Fridtjof Olsen, Carl A. Pedersen, Paul Pedersen, John Skrataas, Harald Smedvik, Sigvard Sivertsen, Andreas Strand, Olaf Syvertsen, Thomas Thorstensen
3. Finland, 405, Eino Forsstrom, Otto Granstrom, Johan Kemp, Jivari Kyykoski, Heikki Lehmusto, John Lindroth, Yrjo Linko, Edvard Linna, Matti Markanen, Kalle Mikkolainen, Veli Nieminen, Kalle K. Paasia,

Arvi Pohjanpaa, Aarne Pohjonen, Eino Railio, Heikki Riipinen, Arno Saarinen, Einari V. Sahlstein, Arne Salovaara, Kaarlo Sandelin, Elias Sipila, Viktor Smeds, Kaarlo Soinio, Kurt E. Stenberg, Vaino Tiiri, Magnus Wegelius

1906
1. Norway, 19.00, Carl A. Andersen, Oskar W. Bye, Conrad Carlsrud, Harald A. Eriksen, Osvald Falch, Christian Fjeringen, Yngvar Fredriksen, Karl J. Haagensen, Harald Halvorsen, Petter Hol, Andreas Hagelund, Eugen Ingebretsen, Mathias Jespersen, Finn Munster, Fridtjof Olsen, Carl A. Pedersen, Rasmus Pettersen, Thorleif Pettersen, Thorleif Rehn, Johan Stumpf
2. Denmark, 18.00, Carl Andersen, Halvor Birch, H. Bukdahl, K. Gnudtzmann, Knud Holm, Erik Klem, Harald Klem, R. Kraft, Edvard Larsen, J. Lorentzen, Robert Madsen, C. Manicus-Hansen, Oluf Olsen, Christian Petersen, Hans Pedersen, Niels Petersen, Viktor Rasmussen, M. K. Skram-Jensen, Marius Thuesen
3. Italy, 16.71, Manlio Pastorini, Spartaco Nerozzi, Federico Bertinotti, Vitaliano Masotti, Raffaello Giannoni, Quintillo Mazzoncini, Azeglio Innocenti, Filiberto Innocenti, Ciro Civinini, Maurizio Masetti

1904
1. Philadelphia, 374.43, Julius Lenhart, Philipp Kassel, Anton Heida, Max Hess, Ernst Reckeweg, John Grieb
2. New York, 356.37, Otto Steffen, John Bissinger, Emil Beyer, Max Wolf, Julian Schmitz, Arthur Rosenkampf
3. Chicago, 349.69, George Mayer, John Duha, Edward Siegler, Phillip Schuster, Robert Mayack, Charles Krause

1896–1900
Not held

Gymnastics, Artistic—Men's Floor Exercise

1992
1. Li Xiaosahuang, China, 9.925
2. Yukio Iketani, Japan, 9.787
2. Grigori Misioutine, Ukraine, 9.787

1988
1. Serguei Kharikov, Soviet Union, 19.925
2. Vladimir Artemov, Soviet Union, 19.900
3. Yukio Iketani, Japan, 19.850
3. Yun Lou, People's Republic of China, 19.850

1984
1. Ning Li, China, 19.925
2. Yun Lou, China, 19.775
3. Koji Sotomura, Japan, 19.700
3. Philippe Vatuone, France, 19.700

1980
1. Roland Bruckner, East Germany, 19.750
2. Nikolai Andrianov, Soviet Union, 19.725
3. Aleksandr Dityatin, Soviet Union, 19.700

1976
1. Nikolai Andrianov, Soviet Union, 19.450
2. Vladimir Marchenko, Soviet Union, 19.425
3. Peter Kormann, U.S.A., 19.300

1972
1. Nikolai Andrianov, Soviet Union, 19.175
2. Akinori Nakayama, Japan, 19.125
3. Shigeru Kasamatsu, Japan, 19.025

1968
1. Sawao Kato, Japan, 19.475
2. Akinori Nakayama, Japan, 19.400
3. Takeshi Kato, Japan, 19.275

1964
1. Franco Menichelli, Italy, 19.450
2. Yukio Endo, Japan, 19.350
2. Viktor Lisitski, Soviet Union, 19.350

1960
1. Nobuyuki Aihara, Japan, 19.450
2. Yuri Titov, Soviet Union, 19.325
3. Franco Menichelli, Italy, 19.275

1956
1. Valentin Muratov, Soviet Union, 19.20
2. Nobuyuki Aihara, Japan, 19.10
2. Viktor Chukarin, Soviet Union, 19.10
2. William Thoresson, Sweden, 19.10

1952
1. William Thoresson, Sweden, 19.25
2. Tadao Uesako, Japan, 19.15
3. Jerzy Jokiel, Poland, 19.15

1948
1. Ferenc Pataki, Hungary, 38.70
2. Janos Magyorosi-Klencs, Hungary, 38.40
3. Zdenek Ruzicka, Czechoslovakia, 38.10

1936
1. Georges Miez, Switzerland, 18.666
2. Josef Walter, Switzerland, 18.500
3. Konrad Frey, Germany, 18.466
3. Eugen Mack, Switzerland, 18.466

1932
1. Istvan Pelle, Hungary, 9.60
2. Georges Miez, Switzerland, 9.47
3. Mario Lertora, Italy, 9.23

1896–1928
Not held

Gymnastics, Artistic—Men's Horizontal Bar

1992
1. Trent Dimas, U.S.A., 9.875
2. Andreas Wecker, Germany, 9.837
2. Grigori Misioutine, Ukraine, 9.837

1988
1. Vladimir Artemov, Soviet Union, 19.90
1. Valeri Lioukine, Soviet Union, 19.90
2. No award
3. Holger Behrendt, East Germany, 19.800
3. Marius Gherman, Romania, 19.800

1984
1. Shinji Morisue, Japan, 20.000
2. Tong Fei, China, 19.975
3. Koji Gushiken, Japan, 19.950

1980
1. Stoian Delchev, Bulgaria, 19.825
2. Aleksandr Dityatin, Soviet Union, 19.750
3. Nikolai Andrianov, Soviet Union, 19.675

1976
1. Mitsuo Tsukahara, Japan, 19.675
2. Eizo Kenmotsu, Japan, 19.500
3. Henri Boerio, France, 19.475
3. Eberhard Gienger, West Germany, 19.475

1972
1. Mitsuo Tsukahara, Japan, 19.725
2. Sawao Kato, Japan, 19.525
3. Shigeru Kasamatsu, Japan, 19.450

1968
1. Akinori Nakayama, Japan, 19.550
1. Mikhail Voronin, Soviet Union, 19.550
3. Eizo Kenmotsu, Japan, 19.375

1964
1. Boris Shakhlin, Soviet Union, 19.625
2. Yuri Titov, Soviet Uhion, 19.550
3. Miroslav Cerar, Yugoslavia, 19.500

1960
1. Takashi Ono, Japan, 19.600
2. Masao Takemoto, Japan, 19.525
3. Boris Shakhlin, Soviet Union, 19.475

1956
1. Takashi Ono, Japan, 19.60
2. Yuri Titov, Soviet Union, 19.40
3. Masao Takemoto, Japan, 19.30

1952
1. Jack Gunthard, Switzerland, 19.55
2. Alfred Schwarzmann, Germany, 19.50
2. Josef Stalder, Switzerland, 19.50

1948
1. Josef Stalder, Switzerland, 39.70
2. Walter Lehmann, Switzerland, 39.40
3. Veikko Huhtanen, Finland, 39.20

1936
1. Aleksanteri Saarvala, Finland, 19.367
2. Konrad Frey, Germany, 19.267
3. Alfred Schwarzmann, Germany, 19.233

1932
1. Dallas Bixler, U.S.A., 18.33
2. Heikki Savolainen, Finland, 18.07
3. Einari Terasvirta, Finland, 18.07

1928
1. Georges Miez, Switzerland, 19.17
2. Romeo Neri, Italy, 19.00
3. Eugen Mack, Switzerland, 18.92

1924
1. Leon Stukelj, Yugoslavia, 19.730
2. Jean Gutweniger, Switzerland, 19.236
3. Andre Higelin, France, 19.163

1906–1920
Not held

1904
1. Anton Heida, U.S.A., 40
1. Edward Hennig, U.S.A., 40
3. George Eyser, U.S.A., 39

1900
Not held

1896
1. Hermann Weingartner, Germany
2. Alfred Flatow, Germany

Gymnastics, Artistic—Men's Parallel Bars

1992
1. Vitali Chtcherbo, Belarus, 9.900
2. Li Jing, China, 9.812
3. Igor Korobtchinski, Ukraine, 9.800
3. Guo Linyao, China, 9.800
3. Masayuki Matsunaga, Japan, 9.800

1988
1. Vladimir Artemov, Soviet Union, 19.925
2. Valeri Lioukine, Soviet Union, 19.900
3. Sven Tippelt, East Germany, 19.750

1984
1. Bart Conner, U.S.A., 19.950
2. Nobuyuki Kajitani, Japan, 19.925
3. Mitchell Gaylord, U.S.A., 19.850

1980
1. Aleksandr Tkachyov, Soviet Union, 19.775
2. Aleksandr Dityatin, Soviet Union, 19.750

3. Roland Bruckner, German Democratic Repubilc, 19.650

1976
1. Sawao Kato, Japan, 19.675
2. Nikolai Andrianov, Soviet Union, 19.500
3. Mitsuo Tsukahara, Japan, 19.475

1972
1. Sawao Kato, Japan, 19.475
2. Shigeru Kasamatsu, Japan, 19.375
3. Eizo Kenmotsu, Japan, 19.250

1968
1. Akinori Nakayama, Japan, 19.475
2. Mikhail Voronin, Soviet Union, 19.425
3. Vladimir Klimenko, Soviet Union, 19.225

1964
1. Yukio Endo, Japan, 19.675
2. Shuji Tsurumi, Japan, 19.450
3. Franco Menichelli, Italy, 19.350

1960
1. Boris Shakhlin, Soviet Union, 19.400
2. Giovanni Carminucci, Italy, 19.375
3. Takashi Ono, Japan, 19.350

1956
1. Viktor Chukarin, Soviet Union, 19.20
2. Masami Kubota, Japan, 19.15
3. Takashi Ono, Japan, 19.10
3. Masao Takemoto, Japan, 19.10

1952
1. Hans Eugster, Switzerland, 19.65
2. Viktor Chukarin, Soviet Union, 19.60
3. Josef Stalder, Switzerland, 19.50

1948
1. Michael Reusch, Switzerland, 19.75
2. Veikko Huhtanen, Finland, 19.65
3. Christian Kipfer, Switzerland, 19.55
3. Josef Stalder, Switzerland, 19.55

1936
1. Konrad Frey, Germany, 19.067
2. Michael Reusch, Switzerland, 19.034
3. Alfred Schwarzmann, Germany, 18.967

1932
1. Romeo Neri, Italy, 18.97
2. Istvan Pelle, Hungary, 18.60
3. Heikki Savolainen, Finland, 18.27

1928
1. Ladislav Vacha, Czechoslovakia, 18.83
2. Josip Primozic, Yugoslavia, 18.50
3. Hermann Hanggi, Switzerland, 18.08

1924
1. August Guttinger, Switzerland, 21.63
2. Robert Prazak, Czechoslovakia, 21.61
3. Giorgio Zampori, Italy, 21.45

1908–1920
Not held

1904
1. George Eyser, U.S.A., 44
2. Anton Heida, U.S.A., 43
3. John Duha, U.S.A., 40

1900
Not held

1896
1. Alfred Flatow, Germany
2. Louis Zutter, Germany
3. Hermann Weingartner, Germany

Gymnastics, Artistic—Men's Pommel Horse

1992
1. Vitali Chtcherbo, Belarus, 9.925
1. Pae Gil-Su, North Korea, 9.925
3. Andreas Wecker, Germany, 9.887

1988
1. Dmitri Bilozertchev, Soviet Union, 19.950
1. Zsolt Borkai, Hungary, 19.950
1. Lyubomir Gueraskov, Bulgaria 19.950
2. No award
3. No award

1984
1. Ning Li, China, 19.950
1. Peter Vidmar, U.S.A., 19.950
3. Timothy Daggett, U.S.A., 19.825

1980
1. Zoltan Magyar, Hungary, 19.925
2. Aleksandr Dityatin, Soviet Union, 19.800
3. Michael Nikolay, East Germany, 19.775

1976
1. Zoltan Magyar, Hungary, 19.700
2. Eizo Kenmotsu, Japan, 19.575
3. Nikolai Andrianov, Soviet Union, 19.525
3. Michael Nikolay, East Germany, 19.525

1972
1. Viktor Klimenko, Soviet Union, 19.125
2. Sawao Kato, Japan, 19.000
3. Eizo Kenmotsu, Japan, 18.950

1968
1. Miroslav Cerar, Yugoslavia, 19.325
2. Olli E. Laiho, Finland, 19.225
3. Mikhail Voronin, Soviet Union, 19.200

1964
1. Miroslav Cerar, Yugoslavia, 19,525
2. Shuji Tsurumi, Japan, 19.325
3. Yuri Tsapenko, Soviet Union, 19.200

1960
1. Eugen Ekman, Finland, 19.375
1. Boris Shakhlin, Soviet Union, 19.375
3. Shuji Tsurumi, Japan, 19.150

1956
1. Boris Shakhlin, Soviet Union, 19.25
2. Takashi Ono, Japan, 19.20
3. Viktor Chukarin, Soviet Union, 19.10

1952
1. Viktor Chukarin, Soviet Union, 19.50
2. Yevgeny Korolkov, Soviet Union, 19.40
3. Grant Shaginyan, Soviet Union, 19.40

1948
1. Paavo Aaltonen, Finland, 38.70
1. Veikko Huhtanen, Finland, 38.70
1. Heikki Savolainen, Finland, 38.70
2. Luigi Zanetti, Italy, 38.30
3. Guido Figone, Italy, 38.20

1936
1. Konrad Frey, Germany, 19.333
2. Eugen Mack, Switzerland, 19.167
3. Albert Bachmann, Switzerland, 19.067

1932
1. Istvan Pelle, Hungary, 19.07
2. Omero Bonoli, Italy, 18.87
3. Frank Haubold, U.S.A., 18.57

1928
1. Hermann Hanggi, Switzerland, 19.75
2. Georges Miez, Switzerland, 19.25
3. Heikki Savolainen, Finland, 18.83

1924
1. Josef Wilhelm, Switzerland, 21.23
2. Jean Gutweniger, Switzerland, 21.13
3. Antoine Rebetez, Switzerland, 20.73

1906–1920
Not held

1904
1. Anton Heida, U.S.A., 42
2. George Eyser, U.S.A., 33
3. William Merz, U.S.A., 29

1900
Not held

1896
1. Louis Zutter, Switzerland
2. Hermann Weingartner, Germany

Gymnastics, Artistic—Men's Still Rings

1992
1. Vitali Chtcherbo, Belarus, 9.937
2. Li Jing, China, 9.875

3. Andreas Wecker, Germany, 9.862
3. Li Xiaosahuang, China, 9.862

1988
1. Holger Behrendt, East Germany, 19.925
1. Dmitri Bilozertchev, Soviet Union, 19.925
2. No award
3. Sven Tippelt, East Germany, 19.875

1984
1. Koji Gushiken, Japan, 19.850
1. Li Ning, China, 19.850
3. Mitchell Gaylord, U.S.A., 19.825

1980
1. Aleksandr Dityatin, Soviet Union, 19.875
2. Aleksandr Tkachyov, Soviet Union, 19.725
3. Jiri Tabak, Czechoslovakia, 19.600

1976
1. Nikolai Andrianov, Soviet Union, 19.650
2. Aleksandr Dityatin, Soviet Union, 19.550
3. Danut Grecu, Romania, 19.500

1972
1. Akinori Nakayama, Japan, 19.350
2. Mikhail Voronin, Soviet Union, 19.275
3. Mitsuo Tsukahara, Japan, 19.225

1968
1. Akinori Nakayama, Japan, 19.450
2. Mikhail Voronin, Soviet Union, 19.325
3. Sawao Kato, Japan, 19.225

1964
1. Takuji Hayata, Japan, 19.475
2. Franco Menichelli, Italy, 19.425
3. Boris Shacklin, Soviet Union, 19.400

1960
1. Albert Azaryan, Soviet Union, 19.725
2. Boris Shakhlin, Soviet Union, 19.500
3. Welik Kapsazow, Bulgaria, 19.425
3. Takashi Ono, Japan, 19.425

1956
1. Albert Azaryan, Soviet Union, 19.35
2. Valentin Muratov, Soviet Union, 19.15
3. Masami Kubota, Japan, 19.10
3. Masao Takemoto, Japan, 19.10

1952
1. Grant Shaginyan, Soviet Union, 19.75
2. Viktor Chukarin, Soviet Union, 19.55
3. Hans Eugster, Switzerland, 19.40
3. Dmitri Leonkin, Soviet Union, 19.40

1948
1. Karl Frei, Switzerland, 39.60
2. Michael Reusch, Switzerland, 39.10
3. Zdenek Ruzicka, Czechoslovakia, 38.50

1936
1. Alois Hudec, Czechoslovakia, 19.433

2. Leon Stukelj, Yugoslavia, 18.867
3. Matthias Volz, Germany, 18.667

1932
1. George Gulack, U.S.A., 18.97
2. William Denton, U.S.A., 18.60
3. Giovanni Lattuada, Italy, 18.50

1928
1. Leon Stukelj, Yugoslavia, 19.25
2. Ladislav Vacha, Czechoslovakia, 19.17
3. Emanuel Loffler, Czechoslovakia, 18.83

1924
1. Francesco Martino, Italy, 21.553
2. Robert Prazak, Czechoslovakia, 21.483
3. Ladislav Vacha, Czechoslovakia, 21.430

1906–1920
Not held

1904
1. Hermann Glass, U.S.A., 45
2. William Merz, U.S.A., 35
3. Emil Voigt, U.S.A., 32

1900
Not held

1896
1. Ioannis Metropoulos, Greece
2. Hermann Weingartner, Germany
3. Petros Persakis, Greece

Gymnastics, Artistic—Men's Horse Vault

1992
1. Vitali Chtcherbo, Belarus, 9.856
2. Grigori Misioutine, Ukraine, 9.781
3. Yoo Ok Ryul, South Korea, 9.762

1988
1. Yun Lou, People's Republic of China, 19.875
2. Sylvio Kroll, East Germany, 19.862
3. Jong-hoon Park, South Korea, 19.775

1984
1. Yun Lou, China, 19.950
2. Mitchell Gaylord, U.S.A., 19.825
2. Koji Gushiken, Japan, 19.825
2. Shinji Morisue, Japan, 19.825
2. Li Ning, China, 19.825

1980
1. Nikolai Andrianov, Soviet Union, 19.825
2. Aleksandr Dityatin, Soviet Union, 19.800
3. Roland Bruckner, East Germany, 19.775

1976
1. Nikolai Andrianov, Soviet Union, 19.450
2. Mitsuo Tsukahara, Japan, 19.375
3. Hiroshi Kajiyama, Japan, 19.275

1972
1. Klaus Koste, East Germany, 18.850
2. Viktor Klimenko, Soviet Union, 18.825
3. Nikolai Andrianov, Soviet Union, 18.800

1968
1. Mikhail Voronin, Soviet Union, 19.000
2. Yukio Endo, Japan, 18.950
3. Sergei Diomidov, Soviet Union, 18.925

1964
1. Haruhiro Yamashita, Japan, 19.600
2. Viktor Lisitski, Soviet Union, 19.325
3. Hannu Rantakari, Finland, 19.300

1960
1. Takashi Ono, Japan, 19.350
1. Boris Shakhlin, Soviet Union, 19.350
3. Vladimir Portnoi, Soviet Union, 19.225

1956
1. Helmut Bantz, West Germany, 18.85
1. Valentin Muratov, Soviet Union, 18.85
3. Yuri Titov, Soviet Union, 18.75

1952
1. Viktor Chukarin, Soviet Union, 19.20
2. Masao Takemoto, Japan, 19.15
3. Takashi Ono, Japan, 19.10
3. Tadao Uesako, Japan, 19.10

1948
1. Paavo Aaltonen, Finland, 39.10
2. Olavi Rove, Finland, 39.00
3. Janos Mogyorosi-Klencs, Hungary, 38.50

3. Ferenc Pataki, Hungary, 38.50
3. Leo Sotornik, Czechoslovakia, 38.50

1936
1. Alfred Schwarzmann, Germany, 19,200
2. Eugen Mack, Switzerland, 18.967
3. Matthias Volz, Germany, 18.467

1932
1. Savino Guglielmetti, Italy, 18.03
2. Alfred Jochim, U.S.A., 17.77
3. Edward Carmichael, U.S.A., 17.53

1928
1. Eugen Mack, Switzerland, 9.58
2. Emanuel Loffler, Czechoslovakia, 9.50
3. Stane Derganc, Yugoslavia, 9.46

1924
1. Frank Kriz, U.S.A., 9.98
2. Jan Koutny, Czechoslovakia, 9.97
3. Bohumil Morkovsky, Czechoslovakia, 9.93

1906–1920
Not held

1904
1. George Eyser, U.S.A., 36
1. Anton Heida, U.S.A., 36
3. William Merz, U.S.A., 31

1900
Not held

1896
1. Carl Schuhmann, Germany
2. Louis Zutter, Switzerland

WOMEN'S GYMNASTICS EVENTS

Highlights

Gymnastics competition for women was introduced in 1928, but awards were only presented for the team combined exercises. The individual events, added in 1952, were soon dominated by Eastern Europeans, especially the Soviets. Until the 1980s, women's (and men's) gymnastics stressed grace and style as much as athletic power, which is now the trend in the sport.

Larissa Latynina of the Soviet Union won a record-setting 18 medals between 1956 and 1964, including nine golds (a women's Olympics record), five silvers, and four bronzes. She was followed by Czech gymnast Vera Cáslavská, who won seven individual golds

Lavinia Milosovici waves in triumph after scoring a perfect 10 in the Olympics to win the gold medal in the floor exercise. The Romanian gymnast also picked up a gold in the horse vault, a silver in the combined, and a bronze in the individual all-around during the XXVth Olympic Games. *AP/Wide World Photos*

in 1964 and 1968 (also a record) to add to four silver medals. Hungary's Ágnes Keleti won ten Olympic medals from 1948 through 1956, including five gold, four silver, and one bronze.

Individual All-Around Combined Exercises, Artistic: For women the individual all-around (combined exercises) event was first held in 1952. Women's combined exercises include the balance beam, the horse vault, uneven bars, and floor exercises. In 1960 the Soviet Union's Larissa Latynina won her second medal for individual combined exercises.

> "All of the girls are upset the team will be broken up. This is like breaking up a family."
> — The 1992 Unified Team's women's coach, Aleksandr Aleksandrov, commenting on the dissolution of the former Soviet team

Czechoslovakia's Vera Cáslavská dominated the women's competitions in 1964 and again in 1968. Four years later Soviet gymnast Olga Korbut won fans around the world without placing in this event; her teammate Lyudmila Tourischeva captured the 1972 gold, settling for bronze four years later behind her teammate, silver-medalist Nelli Kim. In 1976 Romania's Nadia Comaneci had become the new darling, taking a gold in this event; she came back, missing the gold by 0.075 points, to tie for the silver in 1980.

Continuing the tradition of pixie-like television favorites, Mary Lou Retton became the first American to win this event in 1984. Retton beat Romanian rival Ecaterina Szabo by only 0.05 points for the individual gold, the closest women's margin. Part of what helped her win that score was her unique (among women) mastery of the full-twisting layout double Tsukahara on the vault, a maneuver only a few men in the world could manage in 1984. Retton also defied gender in the type of floor exercises she could pull off, including a layout double back somersault.

Elena Shoushounova edged Romanian Daniela Silivas for the all-around title in 1988. The decision came down to the final vault, in which Shoushounova performed her trademark full-twisting Yurchenko.

Team Combined Exercises: The American women's best results in Olympic gymnastics before 1984 was a team bronze in 1948, when the judging was held to be highly questionable. That year the Czech team lost one of its members to infantile paralysis while in London and still managed to win the gold. Soviet women dominated this competition beginning in 1952, retaining the title until the 1984 boycott. That year Romania claimed the gold by one point over the U.S. team, with China earning a bronze.

In 1988 Elena Shoushounova led the Soviet women's team to the team gold ahead of the Romanians. A questionable ruling cost the U.S. women's team the bronze medal, when East German official Ellen Berger assessed a harsh penalty of 0.5 point for an arguable infraction; the U.S. lost their medal to East Germany by 0.3 point. Two days after the decision, gymnastics rules were changed to prevent similar actions in the future.

Balance Beam: Eva Bosáková of the Soviet Union took the silver in 1956 and returned four years later for the gold in Rome, where Czech Vera Cáslavská placed sixth. The Czech was back for the gold in 1964 and the silver in 1968. The darling of the 1972 Games, Soviet gymnast Olga Korbut, was the first Olympic competitor ever to perform a backflip on the balance beam, and her daring earned her the gold. In Montreal she settled for silver behind the next sensation, Romania's Comaneci, who again captured the gold in 1980.

The U.S. recorded a medal in 1984, as Kathy Johnson took a bronze. She trailed two Romanians, Simona Pauca and Ecaterina Szabo. U.S. gymnast Phoebe Mills was her country's only medalist in 1988, claiming a bronze on the beam behind silver medalist Elena Shoushounova of the Soviet Union and gold keeper Daniela Silivas of Romania.

Floor Exercise: Agnes Keleti of Hungary swept the first two golds in 1952 and 1956, followed by back-to-back golds in 1960 and 1964 for the Soviet Union's Larissa Latynina. Czech gymnast Vera Cáslavská tied for the gold in 1968 with Soviet gymnast Larissa Petrik.

Olga Korbut of the U.S.S.R. captured the floor exercise gold in 1972, ahead of Lyudmila Tourischeva of the U.S.S.R. Tourischeva took second again in 1976, behind teammate Nelli Kim. Kim captured the floor exercise gold that year with a perfect 10.0 score, then silver medaled in 1980 behind Romania's Comaneci. Kim was officiating gymnastics at the Seoul Games in 1988.

In 1984 Ecaterina Szabo of Romania triumphed in the floor exercise, ahead of U.S. gymnast Julianne McNamara and her teammate, Mary Lou Retton. Daniela Silivas of Romania reigned in Seoul.

Uneven Bars: 35-year-old Hungarian Agnes Keleti defied age and won the gold in 1956. A younger Polina Astakhova of the Soviet Union captured the gold in 1960 and 1964. East German Karin Janz warmed up with the

FACT: The U.S. women's 1984 silver medal was the first team medal that Uncle Sam's distaff gymnasts had captured since 1948.

silver in 1968 before taking the gold in 1972. She placed ahead of silver medalist Olga Korbut of the U.S.S.R., who captured the world's hearts instead.

In 1976 Romanian Nadia Comaneci on the uneven bars posted the first perfect 10.0 scores ever in Olympic competition, becoming the story of the Games; she was only 14 years old when she captured the gold in this event.

Three tied for bronze at the Moscow Games, as Maria Filatova of the Soviet Union, Steffi Kraeker of East Germany, and Melita Ruhn of Romania settled for thirds. In 1984 Yanhong Ma of China tied with Julianne McNamara of the U.S. for the gold, ahead of bronze medalist Mary Lou Retton. In Seoul, Romanian Silivas struck gold again and Soviet Elena Shoushounova nabbed the bronze behind East German Dagmar Kersten.

Horse Vault: Czech gymnast Vera Cáslavská grabbed the gold in 1964 and 1968. Nelli Kim of the U.S.S.R. earned perfect 10.0 scores vaulting the horse in 1976. In 1983 Soviet Natalia Yurchenko displayed the round-off vault, now called the Yurchenko, a highly risky move that paralyzed U.S. gymnast Juliss Gomez in 1988. Men are not allowed to perform this maneuver. Mary Lou Retton of the U.S. brought a full-twisting layout double Tsukahara to the vault in 1984, a maneuver only a few men in the world could manage at the time; it earned her a silver behind Romania's Ecaterina Szabo. Soviet vaulter Svetlana Boguinskaia triumphed in Seoul.

Individual All-Around Combined Exercises, Rhythmic: This event was introduced in 1984, when Lori Fung earned a rare gold for Canada. Marina Lobatch of the Soviet Union captured the gold in 1988.

Olga, Nadia, and Mary Lou

Together they transformed the entire philosophy of Olympic gymnastics—Olga Korbut, the teenaged Soviet pixie who wept on the sidelines after a crucial mistake; poker-faced Nadia Comaneci, a Romanian and the first gymnast to score a perfect 10.0; and bouncy Mary Lou Retton, a native of West Virginia who braved injury and pressure to win a gold medal in 1984. Before these talented teenagers happened into the sport, gymnastics was the province of older women who performed less like athletes than like ballerinas.

Korbut changed all of that in 1972, when she injected new daring and dash into the sport. Comaneci followed suit with her flawless work on the uneven parallel bars and the balance beam.

Olga Korbut won three medals and fans the world over during the 1972 Games. The teenaged Soviet gymnast was the first Olympic competitor ever to perform a back flip on the balance beam. *AP/Wide World Photos*

Fifteen-year-old Nadia Comaneci flies out of the uneven bars to score a perfect 10 at the Olympics in Montreal, 1976. It was the first 10 in Olympic history. *AP/Wide World Photos*

Retton, watching these performances on television as a child, vowed to do the very same thing.

Olga Korbut was perhaps the first notable example of a changing trend in women's gymnastics. As international competitions intensified during the 1960s, coaches began to look for younger and younger children who could be trained to perform daring stunts before natural fear processes set in. Korbut, born in 1955, was nine when she began to work out at a gymnastics club in Grodno, near the Polish border. A mere five years later she was a national star, the first athlete ever to perform a back flip on the balance beam. She became the entire world's darling at the 1972 Olympics, earning gold medals for Soviet team victory, balance beam, and floor exercises, and a silver medal for her performance on the uneven bars.

Korbut's return to the 1976 Games was overshadowed by a powerhouse from Romania, fourteen-year-old Nadia Comaneci. Comaneci had literally *lived* gymnastics for years, having been plucked from a classroom by coach Bela Karolyi for his fledgling National Institute of Gymnastics. As a resident of Karolyi's institute, Comaneci received an education, free meals and lodging, training, equipment, and coaching, all paid for by the Romanian government. She developed slowly but showed a willingness to try moves no one had done before.

"We are not in the gym to be having fun. The fun comes in the end, with the winning of the medals."
—Bela Karolyi, whose coaching is credited for much of the U.S. women's team's success

It was this daring that led her to the Olympics in 1976, where her work on the uneven bars and balance beam made history with the first perfect scores ever awarded. Comaneci left Montreal that year with two gold medals, a silver for team finish, and a bronze for floor exercise. As Walter Bingham put it in *Sports Illustrated,* the youngster compiled routines "that had the audience first gasping, then roaring with applause."

From the sidelines in Montreal, Olga Korbut viewed Comaneci's commanding performance. Mary Lou Retton watched it on television at her home in Fairmont, West Virginia. Born in 1968, Retton was a natural athlete who was galvanized into action by the 1976 Olympics. She began gymnastics classes in nearby Morgantown, but as she progressed she realized that the training facilities in West Virginia simply were not adequate. She had formulated decisive goals, as she told *Sports Illustrated:* "I had it timed perfectly in my head. I'd be 16 [in 1984] and in my prime."

Reluctantly, Retton decided that, in order to develop into a medal-calibre athlete, she would have to leave home. Taking her high school courses by correspondence, she moved to Houston and placed herself under the tutelage of none other than Bela Karolyi, Comaneci's former coach. Karolyi had defected to the United States and was working at a private gym called Sundance. There Retton reduced her weight from 100 pounds to 92 and completely re-vamped her technique. She recalled: "I'd do a routine I thought was good . . . and he'd say 'no, no, no.' It felt good to me but it just wasn't good enough for him."

Retton's showdown in the 1984 Olympics was one of the closest ever. With her scores hovering within .10 of opponent Ecaterina Szabo—and coming off knee and wrist injuries—Retton earned her own medals. She won the all-around gold, silver in team and vault, and bronze in uneven bars and floor exercise, earning a place in the record books next to the champions who had inspired her.

Youth is an absolute premium now in gymnastics, thanks to the exploits of Korbut, Comaneci, Retton, and their peers. It is no coincidence that each of the three champions retired before the age that most people go to work. As Retton declared in 1989: "I just can't do it [anymore]. My body's strong enough, but I don't have the discipline. The girl who won those medals was a machine. Gymnastics was her life. I've found other things now—that you actually can go to a movie on a Thursday night, and it can be very nice. Just go to a movie."

Retton is now married and tours the country giving motivational speeches. She is also a corporate spokesperson and in August 1995 began hosting the syndicated television show *American Sportswomen*. In April 1995 she gave birth to her first child. *USA Today* capitalized on Retton's experience as an Olympian to comment on the Games in Barcelona in 1992.

Recent years have not been so kind to Korbut and Comaneci. Korbut married a well-known Soviet rock star and had a son who is now in his early teens. The family visited America in 1991, not to discuss gymnastics, but to have themselves tested for exposure to radiation from the 1986 Chernobyl nuclear disaster. Fortunately, tests showed no immediate signs that the nuclear accident has caused Korbut, her son, or her husband health problems. Korbut now coaches gymnastics in Atlanta, Georgia, where she lives with her family, and heads the Belarus American Child Health Foundation, an organization that raises money for the victims of the Chernobyl disaster.

Comaneci's life since the Olympics has been rife with melodrama. In the spring of 1990 she escaped Romania with the help of an American, Constantin Panait. The tabloids jumped on the story, especially when reporters discovered that Panait was married and the father of four. Her reputation tarnished by allegations of a romantic attachment to Panait, Comaneci retreated to Montreal. "I want to let the time prove that I am the same person that America knew when I was a gold winner at the Olympic Games," she told the *Chicago Tribune*. Comaneci plans to marry Bart Conner. Together they operate the Bart Conner Gymnastics Academy in Norman, Oklahoma.

Their offstage exploits notwithstanding, Korbut, Comaneci, and Retton pioneered a new style of Olympic woman gymnast—one who is physically daring and agile as well as graceful and balletic. Future generations of Olympians will remember these three women as the first crest of a wave that will take gymnastics in a different direction as the new century dawns.

—Mark Kram

Highlights from Barcelona

The women's competition at the Palau Saint Jordi provided a fitting final chapter to the Soviet legacy. Uniformly strong, the Unified women scored 15 out of 24 at 9.9 or higher. Only two of the team's gymnasts made a false step in any routine. And many were as good as gold. Collecting the team title with 0.587 points to spare, the Unified women one-upped the Romanians as they had at every Games since 1976, bar LA. Only 0.962 behind, the U.S. women posted their best team finish since 1912, apart form their 1984 silver.

"We have such an organized system. In the future, it will be dispersed to the various republics. It is a pity. The main point for the future is that I will try to perform for a sport, not an emblem or country. What really matters is that you represent a sport, not a country."
—Tatiana Lyssenko, the Unified Team's 1992 dual gold medalist in the balance beam and team event

The women's individual events held more than a few surprise victories and unlooked-for defeats. As the rules have it, each team is allowed to advance only the leading three gymnasts to the all-around competition. Earning top marks on the Unified Team, Svetlana Boguinskaia, Tatiana Lyssenko, and Roza Galieva, proceeded to the all-around, leaving Tatiana Goutsou on the sidelines. Although trumpeted as an Olympic contender, Goutsou had, in the qualifying routines, slipped off a balance beam and out of the medals; or so it seemed.

Then Galieva developed a mysterious knee ailment, allowing Goutsou to step in as her replacement. Concluding her routine with a near-flawless vault, Goutsou scored a victory for the Ukraine, with 79.737 points. Perennially cast in the shadow of teammate Kim Zmeskal, Shannon Miller, with a second-place finish, scored the first U.S. medal in the women's all-around in a non-boycotted Olympics. Having entered the Games as the heavily favored all-around champion, Zmeskal slipped on a balance beam and out of contention on her first day of Olympic competition.

Medalists

Gymnastics, Artistic—
Women's Individual All-Around
(Combined Exercises)

1992
1. Tatiana Goutsou, Ukraine, 39.737
2. Shannon Miller, U.S.A., 39.725
3. Lavinia Milosovici, Romania, 39.687

1988
1. Elena Shoushounova, Soviet Union, 79.662
2. Daniela Silivas, Romania, 79.637
3. Svetlana Boguinskaia, Soviet Union, 79.400

1984
1. Mary Lou Retton, U.S.A., 79.175
2. Ecaterina Szabo, Romania, 79.125
3. Simona Pauca, Romania, 78.675

1980
1. Yelena Davydova, Soviet Union, 79.150
2. Maxi Gnauck, East Germany, 79.075
3. Nadia Comaneci, Romania, 79.075

1976
1. Nadia Comaneci, Romania, 79.275
2. Nelli Kim, Soviet Union, 78.675
3. Lyudmila Tourischeva, Soviet Union, 78.625

1972
1. Lyudmila Tourischeva, Soviet Union, 77.025
2. Karin Janz, East Germany, 76.875
3. Tamara Lakakovitch, Soviet Union, 76.850

1968
1. Vera Caslavska, Czechoslovakia, 78.25
2. Zinaida Voronina, Soviet Union, 76.85
3. Natalia Kuchinskaya, Soviet Union, 76.75

1964
1. Vera Caslavska, Czechoslovakia, 77.564
2. Larissa Latynina, Soviet Union, 76.998
3. Polina Astakhova, Soviet Union, 76.965

1960
1. Larissa Latynina, Soviet Union, 77.031
2. Sofia Muratova, Soviet Union, 76.696
3. Polina Astakhova, Soviet Union, 76,164

1956
1. Larissa Latynina, Soviet Union, 74.933
2. Agnes Keleti, Hungary, 74.633
3. Sofia Muratova, Soviet Union, 74.466

1952
1. Maria Gorokhovskaya, Soviet Union, 76.78
2. Nina Bocharova, Soviet Union, 75.94
3. Margit Korondi, Hungary, 75.82

1896–1948
Not held

Gymnastics, Artistic—Women's Team
(Combined Exercises)

1992
1. Unified Team, 395.666, Oksana Tchoussovitina, Tatiana Lyssenko, Elena Groudneva, Svetlana Boguinskaia, Roza Galieva, Tatiana Goutsou
2. Romania, 395.079, Gina Gogean, Maria Neculita, Mirela Pasca, Cristina Bontas, Vanda Hadarean, Lavinia Milosovici
3. U.S.A., 394.704, Wendy Bruce, Kerri Strug, Kim Zmeskal, Betty Okino, Shannon Miller, Dominique Dawes

1988
1. Soviet Union, 395.475, Svetlana Baitova, Elena Chevtchenko, Olga Strajeva, Svetlana Boguinskaia, Natalia Lachtchenova, Elena Schoushounova
2. Romania, 394.125, Camelia Voinea, Eugenia Golea, Celestina Popa, Gabriela Potorac, Daniela Silivas, Aurelia Dobre

3. East Germany, 390.875, Martina Jentsch, Gabriele Faehnrich, Ulrike Klotz, Bettina Schieferdecker, Doerte Thuemmler, Dagmar Kersten

1984

1. Romania, 392.20, Simona Pauca, Mihaela Stanulet, Cristina Grigoras, Laura Cutina, Lavinia Agache, Escaterina Szabo
2. U.S.A., 391.20, Michelle Dusserre, Pamela Bileck, Kathy Johnson, Julianne MacNamara, Tracee Talavera, Mary Lou Retton
3. People's Republic of China, 388.60, Qun Huang, Qiuri Zhou, Yanhong Ma, Yongyan Chen, Ping Yhou, Jiani Wu

1980

1. Soviet Union, 394.90, Yelena Davydova, Marija Filatova, Nelli Kim, Yelena Naimuschina, Natalia Shaposhnikova, Stella Zakharova
2. Romania, 393.50, Nadia Comenici, Rodica Dunca, Emilia Eberle, Melita Ruhn, Dumitrita Turner, Cristina Elena Grigoras
3. East Germany, 392.55, Maxi Gnauck, Silvia Hindorff, Katharina Rensch, Karola Sube, Steffi Kraeker, Birgit Suess

1976

1. Soviet Union, 390.35, Svetlana Grozdova, Elvira Saadi, Marija Filatova, Olga Korbut, Ljudmila Tourischeva, Nelli Kim
2. Romania, 387.15, Nadia Comaneci, Teodora Ungureanu, Mariana Constantin, Anca Grigoras, Gabriela Trusca, Georgeta Gabor
3. East Germany, 382.10, Gitta Sommer-Escher, Marion Kische, Kerstin Kurrat-Gerschau, Angelica Keilig-Hellman, Steffi Kraeker, Carola Dombeck

1972

1. Soviet Union, 380.50, Ljudmila Tourischeva, Olga Korbut, Tamara Lazakovitsch, Lyubow Burda, Elvira Saadi, Antonina Koshel
2. East Germany, 376.55, Karin Janz, Erika Zuchold, Angelika Hellmann, Irene Abel, Christine Schmitt, Richarda Schmeisser
3. Hungary, 368.25, Ilona Bekesi, Monika Csaszar, Krisztina Medveczky, Aniko Kery, Marta Kelemen, Zsuzsa Nagy

1968

1. Soviet Union, 382.85, Sinaida Voronina, Natalia Kuchinskaya, Larissa Petrik, Olga Karasseva, Ljudmila Tourischeva, Lyubow Burda
2. Czechoslovakia, 382.20, Vera Caslavska, Bohumila Rimnacova, Miroslava Sklenickova, Maria Krajcirova, Hana Liskova, Jana Kubickova
3. East Germany, 379.10, Erika Zuchold, Karin Janz, Maritta Bauerschmidt, Ute Starke, Marianne Noack, Magdalena Schmidt

1964

1. Soviet Union, 380.890, Larissa Latynina, Polina Astakhova, Yelena Volchetskaya, Tamara Zamotailova-Lyukhina, Tamara Manina, Ljudmila Gromova
2. Czechoslovakia, 379.989, Vera Caslavska, Hana Ruzickova, Jaroslava Sedlackova, Adolfina Tkacikova, Maria Krajcirova, Jana Posnerova
3. Japan, 377.889, Keiko Ikeda-Tanaka, Toshiko Aihara-Shirasu, Kiyoko Ono, Taniko Nakamura, Ginko Chiba-Abukawa, Hiroko Tsuji

1960

1. Soviet Union, 382.320, Larissa Latynina, Sofia Muratova, Polina Astakhova, Margarita Nikolayeva, Lydia Ivanova-Kalinina, Tamara Lyukhina
2. Czechoslovakia, 373.323, Vera Caslavska, Eva Bosakova, Ludmila Svedova, Adolfina Tacova, Matylda Matouskova-Sinova, Hana Ruzickova
3. Romania, 372.053, Sonia Iovan, Elena Leustean, Emilia Lita, Atanasia Ionesia, Uta Poreceanu, Elena Niculescu

1956

1. Soviet Union, 444.80, Larissa Latynina, Sofia Muratova, Tamara Manina, Ljudmila Yegorova, Polina Astakhova, Lydia Kalinina
2. Hungary, 443.50, Agnes Keleti, Olga Tass, Margit Korondi, Andrea Molnar-Bodo, Erzsebet Gulyas-Koteles, Aliz Kertesz
3. Romania, 438.20, Elena Leustean, Sonia Iovan, Georgeta Hurmuzachi, Emilia Vatasoiu, Elena Margarit, Elena Sacalici

1952

1. Soviet Union, 527.03, Maria Gorokhovskaya, Nina Bocharova, Galina Minaicheva, Galina Urbanowich, Pelageya Danilova, Galina Schamrai, Medeja Dzugeli, Yekaterina Kalinchuk
2. Hungary, 520.96, Margit Korondi, Agnes Keleti, Edit Perenyi-Vasarhelyi, Olga Tass, Erzsebet Gulyas-Koteles, Maria Zalai-Kovi, Andrea Bodo, Iren Daruhazi-Karpati
3. Czechoslovakia, 503.32, Eva Vechtova, Alena Chadimova, Jana Rabasova, Bozena Srncova, Hana Bobkova, Matylda Sinova, Vera Vancurova, Alena Reichova

1948
1. Czechoslovakia, 445.45, Zdenka Honsova, Miloslava Misakova, Vera Ruzickova, Bozena Srncova, Milena Mullerova, Zdenka Vermirovska, Olga Silhanova, Marie Kovarova
2. Hungary, 440.55, Edit Vasarhelyi, Maria Kovi, Iren Karpati-Karcsics, Erzsebet Gulyas, Erzsebet Balazs, Olga Tass, Anna Feher, Maria Sandor
3. U.S.A., 422.63, Helen Schifano, Clara Schroth, Meta Elste, Marian Berone, Ladislava Bakanic, Consetta Lenz, Anita Simonis, Dorothy Dalton

1936
1. Germany, 506.50, Trudi Meyer, Erna Burger, Kathe Sohnemann, Isolde Frolian, Anita Barwirth, Paula Pohlsen, Friedl Iby, Julie Schmitt
2. Czechoslovakia, 503.60, Vlasta Foltova, Vlasta Dekanova, Zdenka Vermirovska, Matylda Palfyova, Anna Hrebrinova, Bozena Dobesova, Marie Vetrovska, Jaroslava Bajerova
3. Hungary, 499.00, Margit Csillik, Judit Toth, Margit Nagy, Gabriella Meszaros, Eszter Voit, Olga Toros, Ilona Madary, Margit Kalocsai

1932
Not held

1928
1. Netherlands, 316.75, Petronella P.J. Van Randwijk, Jacomina E.S. Van Den Berg, Ans Polak, Helena Nordheim, Alida J. Van Den Bos, Hendrika A. Van Rumt, Anna M. Van Der Vegt, Elly De Levie, Jacoba C. Stelma, Estella Agsteribbe, Petronella Burgerhof, Jud Simons
2. Italy, 289.00, Bianca Ambrosetti, Lavinia Gianoni, Luigina Perversi, Diana Pizzavini, Luigina Giavotti, Anna Tanzini, Carolina Tronconi, Ines Vercesi, Rita Vittadini, Virginia Giorgi, Germana Malabarba, Clara Marangoni
3. Great Britain, 258.25, Margaret Hartley, E. Carrie Pickles, Annie Broadbent, Amy C. Jagger, Ada Smith, Lucy Desmond, Doris Woods, Jessie T. Kite, Queenie Judd, Midge Moreman, Ethel Seymour, Hilda Smith

1896–1924
Not held

Gymnastics, Artistic—Women's Balance Beam

1992
1. Tatiana Lyssenko, Ukraine, 9.975

2. Lu Li, China, 9.912
2. Shannon Miller, U.S.A., 9.912

1988
1. Daniela Silivas, Romania, 19.924
2. Elena Shoushounova, Soviet Union, 19.875
3. Phoebe Mills, U.S.A., 19.837
3. Gabriela Potorac, Romania, 19.837

1984
1. Simona Pauca, Romania, 19.800
1. Ecaterina Szabo, Romania, 19.800
3. Kathy Johnson, U.S.A., 19.650

1980
1. Nadia Comaneci, Romania, 19.800
2. Yelena Davydova, Soviet Union, 19.750
3. Natalia Shaposhnikova, Soviet Union, 19.725

1976
1. Nadia Comaneci, Romania, 19.950
2. Olga Korbut, Soviet Union, 19.725
3. Teodora Ungureanu, Romania, 19.700

1972
1. Olga Korbut, Soviet Union, 19.400
2. Tamara Lazakovitch, Soviet Union, 19.375
3. Karin Janz, East Germany, 18.975

1968
1. Natalia Kutschinskaya, Soviet Union, 19.650
2. Vera Caslavska, Czechoslovakia, 19.575
3. Larissa Petrik, Soviet Union, 19.250

1964
1. Vera Caslavska, Czechoslovakia, 19.449
2. Tamara Manina, Soviet Union, 19.399
3. Larissa Latynina, Soviet Union, 19.382

1960
1. Eva Bosakova, Czechoslovakia, 19.283
2. Larissa Latynina, Soviet Union, 19.233
3. Sofia Muratova, Soviet Union, 19.232

1956
1. Agnes Keleti, Hungary, 18.800
2. Eva Bosakova, Czechoslovakia, 18.633
2. Tamara Manina, Soviet Union, 18.633

1952
1. Nina Bocharova, Soviet Union, 19.22
2. Maria Gorokhovskaya, Soviet Union, 19.13
3. Margit Korondi, Hungary, 19.02

1896–1948
Not held

Gymnastics, Artistic—Women's Floor Exercise

1992
1. Lavinia Milosovici, Romania, 10.000
2. Henrietta Onodi, Hungary, 9.950
3. Shannon Miller, U.S.A., 9.912

3. Cristina Bontas, Romania, 9.912
3. Tatiana Goutsou, Ukraine, 9.912

1988
1. Daniela Silivas, Romania, 19.937
2. Svetlana Boguinskaia, Soviet Union, 19.887
3. Diana Doudeva, Bulgaria, 19.850

1984
1. Ecaterina Szabo, Romania, 19.975
2. Julianne McNamara, U.S.A., 19.950
3. Mary Lou Retton, U.S.A., 19.775

1980
1. Nelli Kim, Soviet Union, 19.875
2. Nadia Comaneci, Romania, 19.875
3. Maxi Gnauck, East Germany, 19.825
3. Natalia Shaposhnikova, Soviet Union, 19.825

1976
1. Nelli Kim, Soviet Union, 19.850
2. Lyudmila Tourischeva, Soviet Union, 19.825
3. Nadia Comaneci, Romania, 19.750

1972
1. Olga Korbut, Soviet Union, 19.575
2. Lyudmila Tourischeva, Soviet Union, 19.550
3. Tamara Lazakovitch, Soviet Union, 19.450

1968
1. Vera Caslavska, Czechoslovakia, 19.675
1. Larissa Petrik, Soviet Union, 19.675
3. Natalia Kuchinskaya, Soviet Union, 19.650

1964
1. Larissa Latynina, Soviet Union, 19.599
2. Polina Astakhova, Soviet Union, 19.500
3. Aniko Janosi, Hungary, 19.300

1960
1. Larissa Latynina, Soviet Union, 19.583
2. Polina Astakhova, Soviet Union, 19.532
3. Tamara Lyukhina, Soviet Union, 19.449

1956
1. Agnes Keleti, Hungary, 18.733
1. Laarissa Latynina, Soviet Union, 18.733
3. Elena Leustean, Romania, 18.700

1952
1. Agnes Keleti, Hungary, 19.36
2. Maria Gorokhovskaya, Soviet Union, 19.20
3. Margit Korondi, Hungary, 19.00

1896–1948
Not held

Gymnastics, Artistic—Women's Uneven Bars

1992
1. Lu Li, China, 10.000
2. Tatiana Goutsou, Ukraine, 9.975
3. Shannon Miller, U.S.A., 9.962

1988
1. Daniela Silivas, Romania, 20.000
2. Dagmar Kersten, East Germany, 19.987
3. Elena Shoushounova, Soviet Union, 19.962

1984
1. Yanhong Ma, China, 19.950
1. Julianne McNamara, U.S.A., 19.950
3. Mary Lou Retton, U.S.A., 19.800

1980
1. Maxi Gnauck, East Germany, 19.875
2. Emilia Eberle, Romania, 19.850
3. Maria Filatova, Soviet Union, 19.775
3. Steffi Kraeker, East Germany, 19.775
3. Melita Ruhn, Romania, 19.775

1976
1. Nadia Comaneci, Romania, 20.000
2. Teodora Ungureanu, Romania, 19.800
3. Marta Egervari, Hungary, 19.775

1972
1. Karin Janz, East Germany, 19.675
2. Olga Korbut, Soviet Union, 19.450
3. Erika Zuchold, East Germany, 19.450

1968
1. Vera Caslavska, Czechoslovakia, 19.650
2. Karin Janz, East Germany, 19.500
3. Zinaida Voronina, Soviet Union, 19.425

1964
1. Polina Astakhova, Soviet Union, 19.332
2. Katalin Makray, Hungary, 19.216
3. Larissa Latynina, Soviet Union, 19.199

1960
1. Polina Astakhova, Soviet Union, 19.616
2. Larissa Latynina, Soviet Union, 19.416
3. Tamara Lyukhina, Soviet Union, 19.399

1956
1. Agnes Keleti, Hungary, 18.966
2. Larissa Latynina, Soviet Union, 18.833
3. Sofia Muratova, Soviet Union, 18.800

1952
1. Margit Korondi, Hungary, 19.40
2. Maria Gorokhovskaya, Soviet Union, 19.26
3. Agnes Keleti, Hungary, 19.16

1896–1948
Not held

Gymnastics, Artistic—Women's Horse Vault

1992
1. Henrietta Onodi, Hungary, 9.925
1. Lavinia Milosovici, Romania, 9.925
3. Tatiana Lyssenko, Ukraine, 9.912

1988
1. Svetlana Boguinskaia, Soviet Union, 19.905
2. Gabriela Potorac, Romania, 19.830
3. Daniela Silivas, Romania, 19.818

1984
1. Ecaterina Szabo, Romania, 19.875
2. Mary Lou Retton, U.S.A., 19.850
3. Lavinia Agache, Romania, 19.750

1980
1. Natalia Shaposhnikova, Soviet Union, 19.725
2. Steffi Kraeker, East Germany, 19.675
3. Melita Ruhn, Romaina, 19.650

1976
1. Nelli Kim, Soviet Union, 19.800
2. Lyudmila Tourischeva, Soviet Union, 19.650
3. Carola Dombeck, East Germany, 19.650

1972
1. Karin Janz, East Germany, 19.525
2. Erika Zuchold, East Germany, 19.275
3. Lyudmila Tourischeva, Soviet Union, 19.250

1968
1. Vera Caslavska, Czechoslovakia, 19.775
2. Erika Zuchold, East Germany, 19.625
3. Zinaida Voronina, Soviet Union, 19.500

1964
1. Vera Caslavska, Czechoslovakia, 19.483
2. Larissa Latynina, Soviet Union, 19.283
2. Birgit Radochla, East Germany, 19.283

1960
1. Margarita Nikolayeva, Soviet Union, 19.316

2. Sofia Muratova, Soviet Union, 19.049
3. Larissa Latynina, Soviet Union, 19.016

1956
1. Larissa Latynina, Soviet Union, 18.833
2. Tamara Manina, Soviet Union, 18.800
3. Ann-Sofi Colling, Sweden, 18.733
3. Olga Tass, Hungary, 18.733

1952
1. Yekaterina Kalinchuk, Soviet Union, 19.20
2. Maria Gorokhovskaya, Soviet Union, 19.19
3. Galina Minaicheva, Soviet Union, 19.16

1896–1948
Not held

Gymnastics, Rhythmic—Women's Individual All-Around

1992
1. Alexandra Timoshenko, Ukraine, 59.037
2. Carolina Pascual Garcia, Spain, 58.100
3. Oksana Skaldina, Ukraine, 57.912

1988
1. Marina Lobatch, Soviet Union, 60.00
2. Adriana Dounavska, Bulgaria, 59.950
3. Alexandra Timochenko, Soviet Union, 59.875

1984
1. Lori Fung, Canada, 57.950
2. Doina Staiculescu, Romania, 57.900
3. Regina Weber, West Germany, 57.700

Trivia Quiz

1. **Gymnastic events at the 1896 Olympics—the first large-scale meeting of gymnasts—were dominated by**
   a. The U.S.   **b.** Russia   **c.** Germany

2. **The first gymnastics world championship was held**
   a. In 1897, the year after the first Modern Games
   b. In 1903, in Antwerp, Belgium   **c.** In 1926, in Paris, France

3. **The 1930 world championship gymnastics competition did not include**
   a. The pole vault and shot put   **b.** The 100m dash
   c. The 100m butterfly

4. **The basis for Modern Olympic gymnastic competition was established**
   a. At the 1924 Games, where athletes competed for individual titles on apparatuses, as well as in combined individual and team exercises

b. At the 1896 Games, when the gymnastic events were essentially the same as they are today

c. At the 1956 Games, when team exercises were added to the program

5. The first Olympic women's event was

a. The team combined exercise, added in 1928

b. The balance beam, added in 1924

c. The individual all-around, added in 1960

6. The first "perfect 10.00" score awarded in world-class gymnastic competition went to

a. Olga Korbut   **b.** Nadia Comaneci   **c.** Mary Lou Retton

7. The Yurchenko

a. Is a vault named after Soviet gymnast Natalia Yurchenko

b. Is also known as the round-off vault

c. Is not allowed in the men's routines

8. The balance beam, used by women only in Olympic competition, is

a. Sixteen feet, three inches long and four inches wide

b. Sixteen feet, three inches long and six inches wide

c. A vertiginous experience for most mortals

9. The first U.S. woman to win an all-around world gymnastics competition was

a. Mary Lou Retton   **b.** Kim Zmeskal   **c.** Kathy Johnson

10. George Eyser, the 1904 gold medalist in the parallel bars

a. Won every individual event that year

b. Captured the gold medal in that event for three consecutive Games

c. Had one wooden leg

JUDO

Warm-up

Derived from *jiu-jitsu*, a hand-to-hand combat technique favored by the *samurai* warriors of ancient Japan, judo (literally, "soft way") was developed by Dr. Jigoro Kano in the 1880s. Many of the *samurai* elements, designed to subdue an enemy fighter, survive in the modern sport: a contest is still won after a fighter either throws an opponent forcibly on his back, strangles or arm locks him into submission, or holds him immobile on his back for thirty seconds.

Seeking to develop a sport not quite as dangerous as *jiu-jitsu*, Dr. Kano studied *jiu-jitsu* and other martial arts. Kano's objective was a sport/self defense technique in which the opponent's own moves were used to pull the opponent off balance and into a throw. Kano selected various elements of jiu-jitsu, combining them with self-defense techniques of his own, and called his new sport Kodokan judo. In 1882 he opened the Kodokan School of Judo, and popularized the sport in Japan by winning a series of matches against proponents of other martial arts techniques. The philosophy of judo proposes that training should produce a mind and body in a state of harmony and balance.

During the next 50 years, disciples of Kano began judo schools in countries around the world. In 1902, the first U.S. school opened, and three years later, the Paris police were taught judo. The first club in Europe, The Budokwai, was founded by Gunji Koizumi in 1918, and became a mecca for the sport on that continent. Shinzo Takagaki took judo to Australia in 1928 and Africa in 1931.

Although Japan instituted its All-Japan Championships in 1930, it was not until after World War II that international competition flourished. In 1948, the European Judo Union was founded in London and the first European Championships were held three years later. The International Judo Federation was established in 1951 and organized the first world championships in Tokyo in 1956.

Weight classes became part of the sport with the arrival of Antonius Geesink, who placed third in the first world championship. Proponents of the sport had always claimed that it was possible for a big skilled fighter to be beaten by an equally skillful smaller man, since the key ingredients are leverage and timing. Hence, one competition for everyone was the rule of the sport through the 1950s. But the success of Geesink, a 6½-foot, 253-pound Dutchman, against smaller opponents helped hasten the arrival of weight classes. In 1961 during one of the last open-weight competitions, Geesink won the world championship, beating three Japanese in consecutive rounds.

FACT: At the 1972 Munich Games, it took Japan's gold medalist, Toyokazu Nomura, only ten minutes and 49 seconds to subdue his five opponents.

Back to Kano for a moment. In 1909, Kano became the first Oriental member of the International Olympic Committee, becoming known as the "Father of Japanese Olympics." More than 50 years later, as a tribute to Kano, judo was added to the 1964 Olympic program at the insistence of the host country, Japan. For the Tokyo Olympic Games, four divisions were established: lightweight, middleweight, heavyweight, and open class. Japan took three of the categories, with big Geesink reigning as king of the open category.

In the 1968 Olympics at Mexico City, judo was not included on the program, although a year later Mexico City hosted the world championships. Since the 1972 Games at Munich, judo has been a regular part of the Olympic program, with seven weight classifications. In 1988, the open category, which often drew the best athletes, was discontinued. Women's events were added for Barcelona: in 1992, seven full-medal competitions (by weight class) for women were held for the first time.

Spectator's Guide

Judo contestants are called *judokas* and compete wearing traditional baggy white pants and wrap-around coats tied by a belt that signifies their rank, white being the lowest and black the highest. They compete on a 20-foot-square mat.

After a ceremonial bow, the contestants await the referee's command of "*hajme*," which means "begin fighting." Olympic matches last 10 minutes and are won by a single point, which may be scored if one contestant throws his or her opponent to the mat so that the opponent's back strikes the canvas. If the throw is executed with perfect form, a point is awarded and the match is over. If the form is not perfect, half a point may be awarded; another half can be gained by holding the opponent on the mat 20 seconds. Thirty seconds of holding is worth a full point as well.

If no point is scored in the full 10 minutes, the decision is up to the referee and judges. An extra three minutes of competition may be held at the judges' request. As with boxing, two bronze medals are awarded, one to each losing semifinalist.

Events for men include: extra lightweight (up to 60 kg); half lightweight (60 kg to 65 kg); lightweight (65 kg to 71 kg); half middleweight (71 kg up to 78 kg); middleweight (78 kg to 86 kg); half heavyweight (86 kg to 95 kg); and heavyweight (over 96 kg).

Women's events include extra lightweight (up to 48 kg); half lightweight (48 kg to 52 kg); lightweight (52 kg to 56 kg); half middleweight (56 kg to 61 kg); middleweight (61 kg to 66 kg); half heavyweight (66 kg to 72 kg); and heavyweight (over 72 kg).

Within each weight class, athletes compete in an elimination format with double repechage. Four hundred men and women will compete in the 14 medal events in the Georgia World Congress Center.

The Five Forms of Throwing an Opponent

Tewaza, or hand technique.

Koshiwaza, or hip method.

Ashiwaza, or foot-and-leg system.

Masutemi Waza, or throwing with one's back on the mat.

Yokosutemi Waza, or throwing with one's side on the mat.

Hopefuls

If you can't beat 'em, join 'em—or at least, train with 'em.

That is what U.S. judo champions Jim Pedro (71 kg.) and Cliff Sunada (60 kg.) were thinking when they moved to Tokyo,

Japan, in 1995 to train at Nihon University. It meant sleeping on rice-filled pillows and tatami mats. It meant waking at 6 a.m., and training beyond nightfall in a gymnasium that is neither air-conditioned nor heated.

There is little question where the best judo players in the world come from—Japan and Korea. Nearly six million people practice judo in Japan. The sport is taught in every school and sports club.

The sport has grown over the years in France, Italy, Hungary, Brazil, and even, Israel. But it is still the Japanese and Korean judokas that are most feared.

Watch for legend Naoya Ogawa in the over 95 kg. category., Toshihiko Koga at 71 kgs., and Hidehiko Yoshida at 78 kg. Ryoko Tamura is a threat in the women's competition.

Pedro and Sundada hope Japanese training translates to success in Atlanta.

Pedro, of Danvers, Mass., was the 1995 Pan American Games gold medalist, and he finished fifth at the 1993 World Championships. He is a four-time U.S. champion.

Another top American judoka is Jason Morris, who won a silver medal at the 1992 Olympics in Barcelona, a bronze at the 1993 World Championships, and a silver at the 1995 Pan American Games.

The U.S. men are coached by four-time Olympian Mike Swain, a bronze medalist at the 1988 Games in Korea.

On the women's side, teenager Hillary Wolf leads Team USA. Wolf, who will be 19 by Summer 1996, is better-known as Macauley Culkin's obnoxious sister in the *Home Alone* movies. Wolf, of Chicago, won the 1995 world junior championship at 48 kgs. and is considered a rising star in the sport. Wolf spent much of 1995 training in Europe.

Other top U.S. women are Liliko Ogasawara (66 kg.), two-time Olympian Lynn Roethke (56 kg.), Corrina Broz (56 kg.), 1992 Olympian Grace Jividen (72 kg.), and Jo Anne Quiring (52 kg.). Broz is a three-time national champion in judo and a U.S. silver medalist in wrestling.

The U.S. judo teams did well at the 1995 Pacific Rim Championships, winning bronze medals in the men's and women's competitions. Brian Olson won a silver medal at 86 kg.

—Michelle Kaufman

Schedule

The tentative judo schedule is:

Saturday, July 20
Women's & Men's heavyweight (+72kg &
+95kg) preliminaries & repechages
Women's & Men's heavyweight (+72kg &
+95kg) final rounds & medal matches

Sunday, July 21
Women's & Men's half heavyweight
(72kg & 95kg) preliminaries &
repechages
Women's & Men's half heavyweight
(72kg & 95kg) final rounds & medal
matches

Monday, July 22
Women's & Men's middleweight (66kg &
86kg) preliminaries & repechages
Women's & Men's middleweight (66kg &
86kg) final rounds & medal matches

Tuesday, July 23
Women's & Men's half middleweight
(61kg & 78kg) preliminaries & repechages

Women's & Men's half middleweight
(61kg & 78kg) final rounds & medal
matches

Wednesday, July 24
Women's & Men's lightweight (56kg &
71kg) preliminaries & repechages
Women's & Men's lightweight (56kg &
71kg) final rounds & medal matches

Thursday, July 25
Women's & Men's half lightweight
(51kg & 65kg) preliminaries &
repechages
Women's & Men's half lightweight
(51kg & 65kg) final rounds & medal
matches

Friday, July 26
Women's & Men's extra-lightweight
(48kg & 60kg) preliminaries & repechages
Women's & Men's extra-lightweight
(48kg & 60kg) final rounds & medal
matches

Highlights

The year was 1964 when Tokyo hosted the Olympics; under the IOC's rules, the host country was permitted to select a sport of its choosing to be added to that year's program. Japan chose judo, and four weight divisions were established: lightweight, middleweight, heavyweight, and an open class.

Japan's Takehide Nakatani won the first gold medal, in the lightweight class, and two other golds remained in the host country. However, a 6'6" Dutchman, Anton Geesink, created quite an upset in the open class, in which the Japanese were again heavily favored. In Nippon Budokan Hall—with 15,000 witnesses—Geesink defeated Akio Kami-

FACT: Korea's 1988 judo squad underwent some unusual training rituals. The team's regimen included occasional visits to the cemetery, where athletes were required to sit alone in the wee hours of the morning before returning home to view videotapes of competitors.

naga, the three-time All-Japan champion. And he did so twice. The Soviet Union, another surprise contender, earned four bronze medals. James Bregman of the U.S. won the bronze in the middleweight category. It was clear from the start that judo would attract an international cast of medalists in the Games.

Omitted from the Mexico City Games, judo reappeared on the program in Munich, thanks to the 1966 IOC ruling to include three new sports in 1972. Each country was allowed one competitor in each of the six divisions. Although the Japanese were favored in most of the categories, other countries proved their mettle in the sport. Even though Japan took home a few medals that year, after the team's performance in the judo events, all the team's trainers were fired.

Willem Ruska, another Dutchman, won the first category on the program, the heavyweight division, devastating Japan's hopes of an opening-day medal. In the light-heavyweight division, Japanese favorite Fumio Sasahara—the two-time world champion—was soundly beaten by Soviet Shota Khokhoshvili, who went on to defeat Britain's Dave Starbrook in the final. Although Japan earned gold medals in the lightweight, half middleweight and middleweight categories, not a single medal went to them in the open category; Ruska, the sport's first double gold-medalist, placed first, followed by Soviet Viatli Kuznetsov. Ruska was 32 at the time.

FACT: East Germany's Dietmar Lorenz, who won the gold medal in the 1980 open category (which has since been eliminated from Olympic competition), was the shortest competitor in that category. He was 5 feet 11 inches tall.

Third place was shared between Jean-Claude Brondani of France, and nineteen-year-old Angelo Parisi, who entered for Britain. Parisi went on to win three more medals in the Games: next representing France, Parisi won a gold and two silvers in 1980 and 1984. Also in 1972, Mongolian Bakhaavaa Buidaa, the lightweight silver medalist, was the first competitor to be disqualified for failing a drug test in any international competition in the sport.

In Montreal, Japan took three of the six gold medals, while the Soviets earned two and Cuba—taking its first medal in the sport—captured one gold. Fifteen countries won medals at Moscow in 1980, when Japan was absent from the Games: the Soviet Union and France claimed two golds apiece, while the gold rush continued with East Germany, Italy, Hungary, Switzerland, and Belgium. Mongolia won a silver and a bronze (half of the medals it won in Moscow). Cuba, West Germany, the Netherlands, Bulgaria, Czechoslovakia, Yugoslavia, and Great Britain also medaled in Moscow.

In 1984—even with Japan competing—judo again featured an international array of medalists. Medals went to traditional and surprise victors: Japan, West Germany, Korea, Great Britain, Italy, France, Brazil, Romania, Iceland, Canada, and Egypt all medaled. Robert Berland became the first American silver medalist and his country's second medalist overall.

The Seoul Games were unusual in a number of respects: Japan captured only one gold medal, the open category was not included on the program, and women's judo was introduced as a demonstration sport. Gold medals went to Poland, Austria, Brazil, France, and South Korea. The U.S. medaled twice: Michael Swain earned a bronze in the lightweight division, while Kevin Asana finessed his way to the silver as an extra lightweight.

Highlights from Barcelona

Women's judo—a demonstration event in 1988—made its first official Olympic appearance at the Barcelona Games. Having had no judoka in a top-three spot in any category at the Seoul Olympics, the home team managed to snag two gold medals, bringing Spain its first-ever gold in the sport. The French women, too, struck Spanish gold twice. In the 48-kg final, Cécile Nowak, the world and European champion, thwarted 16-year-old dervish Ryoko Tamura's bid for the title, while Catherine Fleury, the world and European champion in the 61-kg category, managed a grand slam by outpointing Israel's Yael Arad.

Settling for silver on a less-than-unanimous referee's decision, Arad, a 25-year-old judoist from Tel Aviv, nevertheless captured the first Olympic medal in her nation's history. Entering the Games with a third-place world championship finish under her belt, Arad stopped en route to Barcelona to visit the families of the Israeli athletes killed by Palestinian terrorists during the Munich Games. In one of the most touching moments of the Barcelona Games, she dedicated her medal to the 11 slain members of Israel's 1972 Olympic team. "Maybe now we can say we have avenged this murder," she told an interviewer. "We'll never forget it, but maybe today it is something that will close the circle."

FACT: When women's judo debuted as a medal sport at the Barcelona Games, Spain captured the title in both the 48-kg and 56-kg categories. In 1988, when women's judo was a demonstration event, there had been no Spaniards in the top three of any event.

Later, Shay Smadga—a 21-year-old longshot who was not expected to shine until 1996—nailed a third-place finish in the men's 71-kg category, bringing Israel its second medal ever at the Games.

More than half of the men's bouts, although generally less aggressive than the women's, finished before the time limit, with "ippons," or victory points—judo's equivalent to a knock-out. With looser kimonos and better penalties for passivity, the new rules in 1992 favored attack. The Unified Team's David Khakhaleichvili, for example, thumped Naoya Ogawa's golden aspirations, grabbing the Japanese judoist's belt to throw him down for an ippon. This came as a rude blow to the Japanese fans who had turned out en masse to see the three-time world champion claim his rightful place at the head of the over 95-kg category.

Nevertheless, before Games' end, Japanese judoists were duly decorated, as Toshihiko Koga beat Hungary's Bertalan Hajtos to the 71-kg title, and teammate Hidehiko Yoshida defeated American Jason Morris in his second bid for a 78-kg victory. Also claiming their share in the spoils were the Hungarians, who—with Antal Kovacs's victory over the Commonwealth champion from Britain in the 95-kg category—captured judo gold. And Rogerio Cardoso, as the 65-kg champ, became the second Brazilian to land a judo gold.

FACT: The 1992 French women's judo team, which snagged two gold medals, was led by a former world champion, Jean-Luc Rougé.

Medalists

Judo—Men's Extra Lightweight (Up to 60 kg)

1992
1. Nazim Gousseinov, Azerbaijan
2. Yoon Hyun, South Korea
3. Richard Trautmann, Germany
3. Tadanori Koshino, Japan

1988
1. Jae-Yup Kim, Republic of Korea
2. Kevin Asano, U.S.A.
3. Shinji Hosokawa, Japan
3. Amiran Totikachvili, Soviet Union

1984
1. Shinji Hosokawa, Japan
2. Jae-Yup Kim, Republic of Korea
3. Neil Eckersley, Great Britain
3. Felice Mariani, Italy

1980
1. Thierry Rey, France
2. Rafael Rodriguez, Cuba
3. Aramby Emizh, Soviet Union
3. Tibor Kincses, Hungary

1896–1976
Not held

Judo—Men's Half Lightweight (Up to 65 kg)

1992
1. Rogerio Cardoso, Brazil
2. Jozsef Csak, Hungary
3. Udo Quellmalz, Germany
3. Israel Hernandez Planas, Cuba

1988
1. Kyung-Keun Lee, South Korea

2. Janusz Pawlowski, Poland
3. Bruno Carabetta, France
3. Yosuke Yamamoto, Japan

1984
1. Yoshiyuki Matsuoka, Japan
2. Jung-Oh Hwang, Republic of Korea
3. Marc Alexandre, France
3. Josef Reiter, Austria

1980
1. Nikolai Solodukhin, Soviet Union
2. Tsendying Damdin, Mongolia
3. Ilian Nedkov, Bulgaria
3. Janusz Pawlowski, Poland

1896–1976
Not held

Judo—Men's Lightweight
(Up to 71 kg)

1992
1. Toshihiko Koga, Japan
2. Bertalan Hajtos, Hungary
3. Chung Hoon, South Korea
3. Shay Smadga, Israel

1988
1. Marc Alexandre, France
2. Sven Loll, East Germany
3. Michael Swain, U.S.A.
3. Gueorgui Tenadze, Soviet Union

1984
1. Byeng-Keun Ahn, Korea
2. Ezio Gamba, Italy
3. Kerrith Brown, Great Britain
3. Luis Onmura, Brazil

1980
1. Ezio Gamba, Italy
2. Neil Adams, Great Britain
3. Ravdan Davaadalai, Mongolia
3. Karl-Heinz Lehmann, East Germany

1976
1. Hector Rodriguez, Cuba
2. Eunkung Chang, Republic of Korea
3. Felice Mariani, Italy
3. Marian Standowicz, Poland

1972
1. Takao Kawaguchi, Japan
3. Yong-ik Kim, Democratic People's Republic of Korea
3. Jean-Jacques Mounier, France

1968
Not held

1964
1. Takehide Nakatani, Japan
2. Eric Hanni, Switzerland
3. Aron Bogolyubov, Soviet Union
3. Oleg Stepanov, Soviet Union

1896–1960
Not held

Judo—Men's Half Middleweight
(Up to 78 kg)

1992
1. Hidehiko Yoshida, Japan
2. Jason Morris, U.S.A.
3. Bertrand Damaisin, France
3. Kim Byung-Joo, South Korea

1988
1. Waldemar Legien, Poland
2. Frank Wieneke, West Germany
3. Torsten Brechot, East Germany
3. Bachir Varaev, Soviet Union

1984
1. Frank Wieneke, West Germany
2. Neil Adams, Great Britain
3. Mireca Fratica, Romania
3. Michel Nowak, France

1980
1. Shota Khabareli, Soviet Union
2. Juan Ferrer, Cuba
3. Harald Heinke, East Germany
3. Bernard Tchoullauyan, France

1976
1. Vladimir Nevzorov, Soviet Union
2. Koji Kuramoto, Japan
3. Marion Talaj, Poland
3. Patrick Vial, France

1972
1. Toyokazu Nomura, Japan
2. Antoni Zajkowski, Poland
3. Dietmar Hotger, East Germany
3. Antoli Novikov, Soviet Union

1896–1968
Not held

Judo—Men's Middleweight
(Up to 86 kg)

1992
1. Waldemar Legien, Poland
2. Pascal Tayot, France
3. Hirotaka Okada, Japan
3. Nicolas Gill, Canada

1988
1. Peter Seisenbacher, Austria
2. Vladimir Chestakov, Soviet Union
3. Akinobu Osako, Japan
3. Ben Spijkers, Netherlands

1984
1. Peter Seigenbacher, Austria
2. Robert Berland, U.S.A.
3. Walter Carmona, Brazil
3. Seiki Nose, Japan

1980
1. Jurg Rothlisberger, Switzerland
2. Isaac Azcuy, Cuba
3. Detlef Ultsch, East Germany
3. Aleksandr Yatskevich, Soviet Union

1976
1. Isamu Sonoda, Japan
2. Valery Dvoinikov, Soviet Union
3. Slavko Obadov, Yugoslavia
3. Youngchul Park, Republic of Korea

1972
1. Shinobu Sekine, Japan
2. Seung-lip Oh, Republic of Korea
3. Jean-Paul Coche, France
3. Brian Jacks, Great Britain

1968
Not held

1964
1. Isao Okano, Japan
2. Wolfgang Hofmann, West Germany
3. James Bregman, U.S.A.
3. Ui-tae Kim, Republic of Korea

1896–1960
Not held

Judo—Men's Half Heavyweight
(Up to 95 kg)

1992
1. Antal Kovacs, Hungary
2. Raymond Stevens, Britain
3. Dmitri Sergeev, Russia
3. Theo Meijer, Netherlands

1988
1. Aurelio Miguel, Brazil
2. Marc Meiling, West Germany
3. Dennis Stewart, Great Britain
3. Robert van de Walle, Belgium

1984
1. Hyoung-Zoo Ha, Korea
2. Douglas Vieira, Brazil

3. Bjarni Fridriksson, Iceland
3. Gunter Neureuther, West Germany

1980
1. Robert van de Walle, Belgium
2. Tengiz Khubuluri, Soviet Union
3. Dietmar Lorenz, East Germany
3. Henk Numan, Netherlands

1976
1. Kazuhiro Ninomiya, Japan
2. Ramaz Harshiladze, Soviet Union
3. Jurg Rothlisberger, Switzerland
3. David Starbrook, Great Britain

1972
1. Schota Chochoshvili, Soviet Union
2. David Starbrook, Great Britain
3. Paul Barth, West Germany
3. Chiak Ishii, Brazil

1896–1968
Not held

Judo—Men's Heavyweight
(Over 95 kg)

1992
1. David Khakhaleichvili, Georgia
2. Naoya Ogawa, Japan
3. David Douillet, France
3. Imre Csosz, Hungary

1988
1. Hitoshi Saito, Japan
2. Henry Stoehr, East Germany
3. Yong-Chul Cho, South Korea
3. Grigori Veritchev, Soviet Union

1984
1. Hitoshi Saito, Japan
2. Angelo Parisi, France
3. Mark Berger, Canada
3. Yong-Chul Cho, Republic of Korea

1980
1. Angelo Parisi, France
2. Dimitr Zaprianov, Bulgaria
3. Vladimir Kocman, Czechoslovakia
3. Radomir Kovacevic, Yugoslavia

1976
1. Sergei Novikov, Soviet Union
2. Gunter Neureuther, West Germany
3. Allen Coage, U.S.A.
3. Sumio Endo, Japan

1972
1. Wim Ruska, Netherlands
2. Klaus Glahn, West Germany
3. Motoki Nishimura, Japan
3. Givi Onashvili, Soviet Union

1968
Not held

1964
1. Isao Inokuma, Japan
2. Alfred Rogers, Canada
3. Parnaoz Chikviladze, Soviet Union
3. Ansor Kiknadse, Soviet Union

1896–1960
Not held

Judo—Men's Open Category

1992
Not held

1988
Not held

1984
1. Yasuhiro Yamashita, Japan
2. Mohamed Rashwan, Egypt
3. Mihai Cioc, Romania
3. Arthur Schnabel, West Germany
4. Andras Ozsvar, Hungary

1980
1. Dietmar Lorenz, East Germany
2. Angelo Parisi, France
3. Arthur Mapp, Great Britain

1976
1. Haruko Uemura, Japan
2. Keith Remfry, Great Britain
3. Jeaki Cho, Republic of Korea
3. Jean Luc Rouge, France

1972
1. Wim Ruska, Netherlands
2. Vitali Kuznetsov, Soviet Union
3. Jean-Claude Brondani, France
3. Angelo Parisi, Great Britain

1968
Not held

1964
1. Antonius Geesink, Netherlands
2. Akio Kaminaga, Japan
3. Theodore Boronovskis, Australia
3. Klaus Glahn, West Germany

1896–1960
Not held

Judo—Women's Extra Lightweight (Up to 48kg)

1992
1. Cécile Nowak, France
2. Ryoko Tamura, Japan

3. Hulya Senyurt, Turkey
3. Amarilis Savon Carmenaty, Cuba

Judo—Women's Half Lightweight (Up to 52kg)

1992
1. Almudena Martinez, Spain
2. Noriko Mizoguchi, Japan
3. Li Zhongyun, China
3. Sharon Rendle, Britain

Judo—Women's Lightweight (Up to 56kg)

1992
1. Miriam Blasco Soto, Spain
2. Nicola Fairbrother, Britain
3. Chiyori Tateno, Japan
3. Driulis Gonzalez, Cuba

Judo—Women's Half Middleweight (Up to 61kg)

1992
1. Catherine Fleury, France
2. Yael Arad, Israel
3. Zhang Di, China
3. Elena Petrova, Russia

Judo—Women's Middleweight (Up to 66kg)

1992
1. Odalis Reve Jimenez, Cuba
2. Emanuela Pierantozzi, Italy
3. Heidi Rakels, Belgium
3. Kate Howey, Britain

Judo—Women's Half Heavyweight (Up to 72kg)

1992
1. Kim Mi-Jung, South Korea
2. Yoko Tanabe, Japan
3. Irene De Kok, Netherlands
3. Laetitia Meignan, France

Judo—Women's Heavyweight (Over 72kg)

1992
1. Zhuang Xiaoyan, China
2. Estela Rodriguez Villanueva, Cuba
3. Yoko Sakaue, Japan
3. Natalia Lupino, France

Judo

Trivia Quiz

1. The Japanese word *judo* means
a. "To dance in combat " **b.** The "soft way " **c.** "Pajama sport "

2. Judo is derived from
a. Aikido **b.** Jiu-jitsu **c.** *The Teenage Mutant Ninja Turtles*

3. The first U.S. judo school opened
a. In 1870, two years after the Japanese shogunate was abolished
b. In 1902, three years before the Parisian police were schooled in Judo
c. In 1918

4. Weight classes were added to international competition
a. In 1951, when the International Judo Federation was established
b. In Tokyo in 1956, at the first world championships
c. Shortly after a six-and-a-half-foot 253-pound Dutchman claimed the world championship title

5. A judo contestant is called
a. A *judoka* b. A *tatami* **c.** An *anago*

6. Judo has been a regular part of the Olympic program
a. Since it was first included in Tokyo, in 1964
b. Since the 1972 Games at Munich
c. Since the 1972 Games at Sapporo

7. The first Asian member of the IOC, who became known as the "Father of Japanese Olympics" was
a. Gunji Koizumi **b.** Jigoro Kano **c.** Toshiro Mifune

8. Women's judo events
a. Have never been a part of the Olympic Games
b. Were included as exhibition events at the 1960 Rome Games
c. Were added as full-medal events in 1992 after having had demonstration status in Seoul

9. After the 1972 Games in Munich
a. The U.S., French, and West German teams hired Japanese coaches
b. The Japanese national team fired all of the team trainers
c. Judo became the national sport of the Netherlands

10. The open category in judo competition
a. Has seen only two Japanese champions in Olympic competition
b. Was discontinued in 1988, even though it often drew the best athletes
c. Has included one Egyptian silver medalist

Answers: 1-b; 2-b; 3-b; 4-c; 5-a; 6-b; 7-b; 8-c; 9-b; 10-a, -b, and -c

338

MODERN PENTATHLON

Warm-up

Modern pentathlon is one of the older Olympic sports, having been introduced at the 1912 games in Stockholm, where 42 men participated in the competition. The Swedish Olympic Committee devised the five events for this competition, which may account for the Swedish pentathletes placing in six of the seven top places. The fifth-place finisher, the lone non-Swede, was a U.S. Army lieutenant by the name of George S. Patton, Jr., who went on to greater fame in his military career. Patton would have finished much higher had he been able to shoot straighter; he finished sixth in riding, fourth in fencing, seventh in swimming, and third in the run. But he could only manage 21st in the pistol shoot, ironic considering the mythic portrait of Patton during World War II, two pearl-handled revolvers slung on his hips.

Pentathlon was introduced in ancient Olympic competition at the 18th Olympic Games in 708 BC, as officials catered to the whims of whining Spartans. The Spartans, known for their war-mongering demeanor and eschewing of the normal materialistic possessions, complained that the Games were slanted toward the civilian competition, with nothing of interest or help to bold warriors.

The pentathlon was therefore designed for the soldier athlete and included discus, spear or javelin throwing, broad jumping, running, and wrestling. Unlike modern pentathlon, in which every person competes to the end, the original pentathlon was an elimination contest. All participants took part in the broad jumping contest. Those who jumped a certain distance entered the second event, spear or javelin throwing. The four best in that event qualified for the sprint. The top three in the sprint entered the discus throw, and the two surviving athletes wound up the grueling competition in a grunt and groan session—wrestling each other to a finish. The exhausted winner was crowned the Olympic pentathlon champion.

When the Modern Olympics were introduced in 1896, the pentathlon was not included because of the crowded program. But in 1912, it was felt that a modern pentathlon event—one with a military background—should be added to attract soldier-athletes. Baron Pierre de Courbertin, the Frenchman who revived the modern-day Olympics, was personally responsible for the return of pentathlon in 1912. He felt that better world relations and peace might occur if soldiers of the world's armies could meet in friendly competition, rather than the battlefield. And he wanted to attract top athletes by creating a sport combining some of the most difficult competitions of the Olympic Games. Some consider modern pentathlon to be the supreme test of the all-around athlete.

True to its warrior spirit, modern pentathlon is based upon the duties of an unlucky 19th-century military courier assigned to deliver a message to his commander across enemy lines. First, the courier mounts an unfamiliar horse, riding over uneven terrain and varied obstacles. He is challenged by an enemy soldier who draws a sword. Winning the duel, the messenger remounts his horse, only to have it shot out from under him by another enemy soldier. The messenger fires one shot from his pistol and kills the enemy. Unfortunately, his horse is now dead as well. Undeterred, the messenger runs great distances, swims rivers and streams, shoots his way through enemy ranks, and repels any remaining opposition with his sword. Arriving at his destination, soggy message hanging limply from his hand, he collapses at the feet of his commander, who mumbles a brief, "What took you?"

FACT: In an effort to improve the sport's "perceived obscure image" to become "one of the glamour events of the 1996 Games," in 1995, the US federation made movie star Dolph Lundgren the team's appointment official.

Thus, five events comprise the modern pentathlon: equestrian, fencing, pistol shooting, swimming, and cross-country running. The only event of the five that has changed significantly from the 1912 format is the equestrian, which was changed from a 5000-meter cross-country course to a 350-to-450-meter stadium-jumping course. The scoring system has been completely revised to produce a points award for each individual performance, so that the highest point total after five events is the winner. Both individual and team competitions have traditionally been held, but only the individual competition survives for the 1996 Games.

Women's pentathlon was officially introduced in 1977, when the first major competition was conducted in San Antonio, Texas, in conjunction with the World Championships. It was slated to be a part of the 1996 Olympics, but in spite of the lobbying of the U.S. federation for the modern pentathlon, international officials vetoed the idea. Some sources speculate that Olympic officials want to drop the sport from the Olympic program without affecting Olympic opportunities for women in the process. This decision must have dashed the hopes of Lori Norwood, 1989 world champion. Around the time of the 1992 Olympics, when it looked like women would be able to participate in '96, she said "I'm incredibly excited, I've achieved most of my goals, but without the Olympics, there wouldn't have been that much more to fight for."

Spectator's Guide

In Atlanta, 32 athletes from as many as 25 countries are expected to participate in the modern pentathlon. In a drastic move to reduce costs and make the sport more spectator-friendly, the Olympic competition was shortened from two days to one. The order of events in the modern pentathlon is shooting, fencing, swimming, riding, and cross-country running.

The team competition has been dropped for the Atlanta Games, where only one gold medal will be awarded. Individual athletes are awarded points for their performances in each of the five disciplines. With the exception of the fencing contest, all of the competitions pit the athlete against the clock.

Modern Pentathlon Event-o-rama Guide

Shooting: Competitors fire air pistols. The targets, 10 meters away, face the shooter for three seconds, then rotate away for seven seconds. During the three seconds, the contestant must raise the pistol, aim, and fire one shot. After four rounds of five shots each, the scores are totaled. Each bullet is worth up to 10 points, with the highest possible target score being 200 points. Only twice in Olympic history has a perfect score been achieved.

Fencing: This is the only event of the five in which the athletes engage in one-on-one competition. The dueling sword, or épée, is used in one-hit, sudden death bouts, which are limited to two minutes but often end in a matter of seconds. Scoring is determined by percentage of wins.

Swimming: A three-hundred-meter freestyle heat, during which athletes are swimming against the clock; the faster his time, the more points the pentathlete earns.

Riding: On horses selected by random draw immediately before the competition, the riders are allowed a maximum of 20 minutes to practice with their mount. Horse and rider take on a 350- to-450-meter course of 15 obstacles. Points are taken off for refusals, falls, knockdowns, and for riding too slowly.

Running: A 4000-meter cross-country course is run, which begins with a staggered start: competitors take their places according to their standings going into this final event. Whoever crosses the finish line first is the winner of the entire Pentathlon event.

Hopefuls

Who will be the most exhausted athletes at the 1996 Olympic Games?

Probably the modern pentathletes. In an effort to reduce costs and make the sport more spectator-friendly, the five-event competition was shortened from two days to one. Four years ago, the event took place over four days.

Athletes will have 12 hours to fence, swim 300 meters, shoot four rounds with a pistol, run 4000 meters, and ride a 600-meter jumping course on an unfamiliar horse. To make matters worse, they'll be doing it in the Atlanta heat and humidity.

If anyone can survive the brutal event it's Dmitri Svatkovsky, the reigning world champion from Russia, who scored 5,583 points at the 1995 world championships. Others to watch are: Sebastien Deleigne of France, Imre Tidemann of Estonia, Peter Steinmann of Switzerland, and Per Olov Danielsson of Sweden.

In the relay, reigning Olympic champion and 1995 world champion Poland will be the team to beat. Because the modern pentathlon is a military-oriented sport, many Scandinavian and central European countries have strong teams. Hungary, France and Italy are particularly good.

Also watch for Mexico.

That's right. Mexico.

The Mexican team won the bronze medal at the 1995 world championships, and two of its pentathletes finished in the top 20 in the individual competition. Mexico placed fifth at the 1984 Olympics in Los Angeles and eighth at the 1988 Games in Seoul; though the team did not place in the top eight at the 1992 Olympics in Barcelona.

Three-time Olympian Rob Stull and two-time Olympian Michael Gostigan lead the U.S. team. Stull, an especially talented fencer, competed in épée fencing and modern pentathlon at the 1988 Olympics in Seoul. He scored 5,580 points at the 1995 Czech Championships, a score that likely would win an Olympic medal in Atlanta. Stull's training was put on hold for several months in 1995 when he broke his leg in a freak accident on his horse. He missed the world championships.

Gostigan, especially strong at swimming and running, placed 13th at the 1995 world championships.

—Michelle Kaufman

Schedule

The tentative modern pentathlon schedule is:

Tuesday, July 30
Men's shooting, fencing, swimming, riding & running

Highlights

Modern Pentathlon was dominated by Sweden during its first decade at the Games; the first non-Swedish modern pentathlon medalist came in 1928, when Germany's Helmuth Kahl won a bronze medal. Although the Swedes swept the 1912 competition, the sport's most famous participant—George S. Patton, Jr.—came in fifth. Then a twenty-six-year-old army lieutenant, Patton was in the running for the gold until the shooting competition; insisting that he use a non-standard issue pistol, he shot his way to 21st place (with 150 target points) in a field of 32, putting him out of the running for the gold, or any medal, for that matter. Patton's results are interesting to look at: he received 0 time faults and 0 riding faults, with a 10:42 riding time, to give him 100 points, or 6th place in the riding event; 20 victories in fencing put him in 4th place; a 5:55 time put him in 7th place in the swimming event, and a 20:01 running time put him in his best standing, third, in running. Patton never competed again in the Olympics, but gained more than little fame as a general during WWII.

The Swede who actually won the 1912 competition—Gosta Lilliehook—totalled only 27 points

"Pentathlon is the Edsel of Olympic sports—it'll be long gone before anyone appreciates it."
—Rob Stull, fourth-place finisher at the Barcelona Games

on individual finishes of 4th, 5th, 3rd, 10th and 5th, in the order of the events. Interestingly, each of the competitors placing in the final four spots behind Lilliehook actually finished better than the gold medalist in three of the five events, but Lilliehook's consistency created the crucial margin for victory.

The sport's first non-military medalist came in 1952, when Lars Hall, a twenty-five-year-old Swede, won the gold. Hall's medal, it turns out, resulted from a couple of fortuitous events: when the horse he was assigned was discovered to be lame, he was reassigned a horse considered to be the best mount in Norway, and later in the event, he escaped being disqualified for arriving twenty minutes late to the pistol-shooting event, thanks to a Soviet protest that was still in progress. That year also marked the introduction of the team event, in which the Swedes placed second behind the first-place Hungarian team; the Finnish team took third place.

FACT: Sweden's Lars Hall, who captured the individual title in 1952 and 1956, is modern pentathlon's only repeat winner.

The assignment of a horse has affected the outcome of more than one pentathlete's scores. In 1968 in Mexico City, Hans-Jürgen Todt was allotted an intransigent—albeit handsome—horse named Ranchero, who three times balked at one of the obstacles. Dismayed at the horse's contribution to his poor score, Todt attacked the animal, and had to be restrained by his teammates.

Drugs and alcohol have a couple of times been an issue in Olympic pentathlon competition. In the 1972 Games, drug tests caused quite a scandal, but no disqualifications, when at least fourteen pentathletes were revealed to have taken tranquilizers prior to the shooting event—apparently a fairly common practice, to steady the athlete's aim. Since the drugs—valium and lithium—were then banned by the International Pentathlon Union but not by the IOC, the athletes were spared disqualification. The previous Games' would-be bronze medalist hadn't been so lucky, though: traces of alcohol in his blood after the shooting event left Swede Hans-Gunnar Liljenvall—who claimed to have imbibed only two beers—disqualified from the team event. The entire Swedish team, with a total of 14,188 points, was disqualified, allowing the French team, with 13,289 points, to take the bronze.

Scandals haven't been limited to drug and alcohol abuse, either. Perhaps the most infamous event occurred in 1976, when the Soviet team was disqualified because one of its members—1972's individual silver medalist, Boris Onischenko—was discovered to have tampered with the electrical parts of his épée so that he could, at will, register a hit without actually touching his opponent. Onischenko's épée scores prior to the 1976 Games (which had begun an upward climb beginning in 1970) have since been viewed with not a little suspicion.

The U.S. has never earned a gold medal in the individual or the team event, and hasn't medaled in the individual since Robert Beck won a bronze medal in 1960; his medal was preceded by a U.S. bronze in 1932, a silver in 1936, and a silver in 1948. The U.S. team took a bronze medal home from the 1960 Games (with Robert Beck on their team), and three times placed second, most recently in the 1984 Games. Italy finished first, and France third in the team event in 1984. The U.S. failed to place in either the individual or the team event in 1988, while Italy this time took second place to Hungary; Great Britain took home the bronze medal.

Highlights from Barcelona

Just when it looked like the U.S. team would walk away from Barcelona with its first individual pentathlon medal since the 1979 World Championships, fate reared its head—and Rob Stull's mount, Canario, shied. On the final day of competition, only one jump stood between Stull and the third tier of the podium. But at the 13th gate, his medal hopes were bucked as Canario balked.

FACT: At the 1984 Games, the shooting portion of the modern pentathlon was moved to the morning of the final day—five hours before the cross-country run—in an effort to discourage athletes from taking nerve-calming sedatives and beta-blockers to improve their shooting scores.

But fate smiled kindly on the Poles, who pulled off a double, winning both the individual and team events. With over one thousand points in each of the five individual events, Arkadiusz Skrzypaszek outscored Hungary's Attila Mizser, whose fencing and riding fell short of perfection. The Unified Team's Edouard Zenovka, who enjoyed a brief tenure in first place, settled for a bronze finish, in spite of his excellent scores in running, shooting, and swimming. Again, the horse was at fault. (In Olympic competition, riders draw lots to determine their mounts.)

In the team event, tension was high, as the Italian team failed to defend their claim to the second position on the podium, having pocketed a silver medal in Seoul. Edging out the Italians by a slim margin of 164 points, the Unified Team—with individual bronze medalist Zenovka in their ranks—staked its claim to the silver medal.

Medalists

Modern Pentathlon—Individual

1992
1. Arkadiusz Skrzypaszek, Poland, 5,559
2. Attila Mizser, Hungary, 5,446
3. Edouard Zenovka, Russia, 5,361

1988
1. Janos Martinek, Hungary, 5,404
2. Carlo Massullo, Italy, 5,379
3. Vakhtang Iagorachvili, Soviet Union, 5,367

1984
1. Daniele Masala, Italy, 5,469
2. Svante Rasmuson, Sweden, 5,456
3. Carlo Massullo, Italy, 5,406

1980
1. Anatoli Starostin, Soviet Union, 5,568
2. Tamas Szombathelyi, Hungary, 5,502
3. Pavel Lednev, Soviet Union, 5,382

1976
1. Janusz Pyciak-Peciak, Poland, 5,520
2. Pavel Lednev, Soviet Union, 5,485
3. Jan Bartu, Czechoslovakia, 5,466

1972
1. Andras Balczo, Hungary, 5,412
2. Boris Onischenko, Soviet Union, 5,335
3. Pavel Lednev, Soviet Union, 5,328

1968
1. Bjorn Ferm, Sweden, 4,964
2. Andras Balczo, Hungary, 4,953
3. Pavel Lednev, Soviet Union, 4,795

1964
1. Ferenc Torok, Hungary, 5,116
2. Igor Novikov, Soviet Union, 5,067
3. Albert Mokeyev, Soviet Union, 5,039

1960
1. Ferenc Nemeth, Hungary, 5,024
2. Imre Nagy, Hungary, 4,988
3. Robert Beck, U.S.A., 4,981

1956
1. Lars Hall, Sweden, 4,843
2. Olavi Mannonen, Finland, 4,774.5
3. Vaino Korhonen, Finland, 4,750

1952
1. Lars Hall, Sweden, 32
2. Gabor Benedek, Hungary, 39
3. Istvan Szondy, Hungary, 41

1948
1. William Grut, Sweden, 16
2. George Moore, U.S.A., 47
3. Gosta Gardin, Sweden, 49

1936
1. Gotthard Handrick, Germany, 31.5
2. Charles Leonard, U.S.A., 39.5
3. Silvano Abba, Italy, 45.5

1932
1. Johan Oxenstierna, Sweden 32
2. Bo Lindman, Sweden, 35.5
3. Richard Mayo, U.S.A., 38.5

1928
1. Sven Thofelt, Sweden, 47
2. Bo Lindman, Sweden, 50
3. Helmuth Kahl, Germany, 52

1924
1. Bo Lindman, Sweden, 18
2. Gustaf Dyrssen, Sweden, 39.5
3. Bertil Uggla, Sweden, 45

1920
1. Gustaf Dyrssen, Sweden, 18
2. Erik de Laval, Sweden, 23
3. Gosta Runo, Sweden, 27

1912
1. Gosta Lilliehook, Sweden, 27
2. Gosta Asbrink, Sweden, 28
3. Georg de Laval, Sweden, 30

1896–1908
Not held

Modern Pentathlon—Team

1992
1. Poland, 16,018, Maciej Czyzowicz, Arkadiusz Skrzypaszek, Dariusz Gozdziak
2. Unified Team, 15,924, Anatoli Starostine, Dmitri Svatkovski, Edouard Zenovka
3. Italy, 15,760, Gianluca Tiberti, Carlo Massullo, Roberto Bomprezzi

1988
1. Hungary, 15,886, Janos Martinek, Attila Mizser, Laszlo Fabian
2. Italy, 15,571, Carlo Massullo, Daniele Masala, Gianluca Tiberti
3. Great Britain, 15,276, Richard Phelps, Dominic Mahony, Graham Brookhouse

1984
1. Italy, 16,060, Daniele Masala, Carlo Massullo, Pierpaolo Cristofori
2. U.S.A., 15,568, Michael Storm, Robert Gregory Losey, Dean Glenesk
3. France, 15,565, Paul Four, Didier Boube, Joel Bouzou

1980

1. Soviet Union, 16,126, Anatoli Starostin, Pavel Lednev, Yevgeny Lipeev
2. Hungary, 15,912, Tamas Szombathelyi, Tibor Maracsko, Laszlo Horvath
3. Sweden, 15,845, Svante Rasmuson, Lennart Pettersson, George Horvath

1976

1. Great Britain, 15,559, Adrian Parker, Robert Nightingale, Jeremy Fox
2. Czechoslovakia, 15,451, Jan Bartu, Bohumil Starnovsky, Jiri Adam
3. Hungary, 15,395, Tamas Kancsa, Tibor Maracsko, Svetiszlar Sasics

1972

1. Soviet Union, 15,968, Boris Onischenko, Pavel Lednev, Vladimir Schmelyov
2. Hungary, 15,348, Andras Balczo, Zsigmond Villanyi, Pal Bako
3. Finland, 14,812, Risto Hurme, Veikko Salminen, Martti Ketela

1968

1. Hungary, 14,325, Andras Balczo, Istvan Mona, Ferenc Torok
2. Soviet Union, 14,248, Pavel Lednev, Boris Onischenko, Stasis Schaparnis
3. France, 13,289, Raoul Gueguen, Lucien Guiguet, Jean Pierre Giudicelli

1964

1. Soviet Union, 14,961, Igor Novikov, Albert Mokeyev, Viktor Mineyev
2. U.S.A., 14,189, James Moore, David Kirkwood,Paul Pesthy
3. Hungary, 14,173, Ferenc Torok, Imre Nagy, Otto Torok

1960

1. Hungary, 14,863, Ferenc Nemeth, Imre Nagy, Andras Balczo
2. Soviet Union, 14,309, Igor Novikov, Nikolai Tatarinov, Hanno Selg
3. U.S.A., 14,192, Robert Beck, Jack Daniels, George Lambert

1956

1. Soviet Union, 13,690.5, Igor Novikov, Aleksandr Tarassov, Ivan Derjugin
2. U.S.A., 13,482, George Lambert, William Andre, Jack Daniels
3. Finland, 13,185.5, Olavi Mannonen, Vaino Korhonen, Berndt Katter

1952

1. Hungary, 166, Gabor Benedek, Istvan Sandy, Aladar Kovacsi
2. Sweden, 182, Lars Hall, Torsten Lindqvist, Claes Egnell
3. Finland, 213 Olavi Mannonen, Lauri Vilkko, Olavi Rokka

1896–1948

Not held

Trivia Quiz

1. The Modern Pentathlon first appeared in the Olympics

   a. In 1912, in Stockholm   **b.** In 1948, in London

   c. In 708 BC, at the 18th Olympic Games

2. The fifth-place finisher in the first Olympic Modern Pentathlon was

   a. Teddy Roosevelt   **b.** George S. Patton, Jr   **c.** Franz Bibfeldt

3. The pentathlon in the Ancient Olympic Games included

   a. Wrestling, boxing, sword fighting, running, and spear throwing

   b. Discus, spear or javelin throwing, broad jumping, running and wrestling

   c. Lute playing, poetry reading, a cookie bake-off, rhythmic spear throwing, and basket weaving

4. The person responsible for introducing Modern Pentathlon to the Olympic program was

   a. George S. Patton   **b.** Baron Pierre de Coubertin   **c.** Oliver North

5. Of the Modern Pentathlon's five events, the only one to change significantly since the sport was introduced at the Olympics is
   a. The equestrian event, which was changed from a 5,000-m cross-country course to a 600-m stadium-jumping course
   b. The swimming event, which was changed from a 1-mile open-water swim to a 300-m freestyle against the clock
   c. The pistol shooting, which did away with live targets

6. A perfect shooting score
   a. Has never been achieved in Modern Pentathlon's Olympic history
   b. Has been achieved twice in Modern Pentathlon's Olympic history
   c. Is a prerequisite for an Olympic gold medal

7. The horses used in Olympic competition
   a. Are a critical part of the competition; each athlete chooses his mount well before the competition
   b. Are selected by random draw immediately before the competition
   c. Are selected from the top performers in the Olympic equestrian events

8. The drug scandal at the 1972 Games involved
   a. Anabolic steroids   **b.** Tranquilizers
   c. A Modern Pentathlon subculture known as Dead-heads

9. Women's Modern Pentathlon
   a. Has never been a part of the Olympic program
   b. Was officially introduced in 1977, in San Antonio, Texas
   c. Was supposed to be part of the 1996 Olympic program

10. The first decade of Modern Pentathlon events at the Olympic Games was dominated by
   a. Swiss athletes   **b.** Swedish athletes   **c.** U.S. athletes

Answers: 1-a; 2-b; 3-b; 4-b; 5-a; 6-b; 7-b; 8-b; 9-a, -b, and -c; 10-b

Rowing

Warm-up

Rowing became an Olympic event at the 1900 Paris Games, introducing five events. By the second Olympic regatta in Stockholm, the modern 2000m (about 1½ mile) course had been established. Other wrinkles needed smoothing in Stockholm, however, such as a hazard in the form of a midstream "bathing shed" that had to be negotiated around in mid-race.

The sport of rowing, however, precedes its Olympic debut by several thousand years. The earliest boats were propelled by paddles held entirely in the boatmans' hands. About two thousand years ago the Greeks decided to try mounting their paddles to the side of their boat at a fulcrum point, to increase the efficiency of their stroke: the rowboat resulted. Earlier evidence suggests that the Egyptians were rowboat enthusiasts. The rowing prowess of King Amenophis II is illuminated in an inscription on his tomb dating from 1430 BC.

Throughout history, all kinds of boats have been rowed, from small workboats and fishing boats to large ships of commerce and war. The galleys of the Roman Empire could be as long as 150 feet and were driven by the efforts of 50 or more captive oarsmen (usually slaves, convicts, prisoners of war, or other unfortunates who got on the wrong side of the guys with whips). In fact, the Roman poet Virgil includes an account of a rowing race in his epic *Aeneid.*

Racing has been a part of rowing from the start. Evidence indicates that racing of longboats was a pastime in prehistoric China and Southeast Asia, and oared barges competed on the Nile as early as 2500 BC. In modern times, rowboat racing has been embraced wherever rowboats plied the waters commercially. One of the longest-running continuous sporting events in the world began in

1715 among boatmen on the Thames in England. Thomas Doggett, a popular Irish actor, offered a prize to the winner of a race from the London Bridge to Chelsea. The event is known today by the quaint, if puzzling, name of the Doggett's Coat and Badge rowing race.

In the U.S., boatmen in New York Harbor in the 1880s could row for fun and profit in professional racing. At that time it was possible to sustain a handsome livelihood as a professional rower, vying for prizes up to $6000. But the *really* big earnings were going to the gamblers whose shady behavior, such as rigging races and sabotaging boats, sullied the reputation of the sport and caused the popularity of professional rowing to fade.

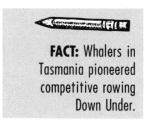

FACT: Whalers in Tasmania pioneered competitive rowing Down Under.

The amateur branch of the sport, however, flourished in America and England. In the United States, rowing became popular among Ivy League colleges and universities. The country's first inter-collegiate athletic event, the Harvard/Yale boat race, was held for the first time in 1852. The body governing amateur rowing, the International Federation of Rowing Societies (Fédération Internationale des Sociétés d'Aviron, or FISA) was formed in 1892.

Technologically, the development of the rowing shell, as the boat is called, underwent many refinements and a couple of quantum leaps in the mid-nineteenth century. The first major change came with the invention of the outrigger by Britain's Henry Clasper. Prior to this development, the oarlock, which is the fulcrum point of the oar, was mounted on the gunwale of the boat. (The gunwale is the upper edge of the side of the boat. If you inverted a rowboat and placed it on sawhorses, it would be resting on its gunwales.) The width of the boat was necessarily constrained by considerations of oarlock location. To make a fast hull design, a narrow beam (beam: the boat's width at its widest part) is desired. But as the beam becomes narrower, the span between the oarlocks on the gunwales becomes smaller, until the oarlocks are too far inboard to function properly. The solution offered by the outrigger, or "rigger," was to suspend the oarlocks by means of rigid metal frameworks *outboard* of the boat's gunwales. By using riggers, a boat designer could craft as narrow a boat as was desired for speed's sake. Indeed, modern shells can be as narrow as 10 inches at the beam.

Boat designs evolved into longer and narrower dimensions, and into these longer boats rowers began putting longer seats. Rowers could slide forward and back on these broad seats, thus somewhat lengthening their stroke and adding leg power to the rowing motion. The oarsmen at Harvard, putting their superior educations to good purpose, realized that greasing their leather rowing pants would facilitate this sliding motion. Yale's contribution to the burgeoning technology was to try oatmeal as a lubricant; they sure earned their sheepskin in those days. Finally someone did it right when in 1857 J.C. Babcock of New York invented a seat on rollers, which maximized the sliding motion and allowed the rower to use as many muscle groups as possible to propel the boat.

Once the outriggers and sliding seats were incorporated, further developments consisted of gradual fine-tuning: smoothing the hull, lightening it, and adjusting hull design. Interestingly, even though FISA, the governing body of the sport, imposes very few limitations on boat design for competition, today's racing shells show very little variation from one boat to another. The design's evolution has arrived at the point of seeming near-perfection for rowing fast in flat water.

Spectator's Guide

The Boats

Simply keeping the terminology straight in the world of rowing should be considered an athletic pursuit. Many terms are obscure, and some items are called by more than one name, depending on who's doing the calling. First, there's the matter of rowing itself. Rowing is not paddling. The paddler of a canoe or kayak sits or kneels facing forward and uses an unsupported paddle. A person rowing a boat wields an oar—not a paddle—and sits facing the rear of the boat. The oar pivots in an oarlock, which acts as a fulcrum, for mechanical advantage. An oar with a wider blade is easier to grip the water with, but feels heavier to the oarsman, especially at the beginning of the stroke. The boats in competitive rowing are called shells. Within that main group is the subclassification of sculls. All sculls are shells, but all shells are not sculls.

Whether a shell is a scull or not depends on the arrangement of the oars. In a scull, each crew member rows with two oars—one on either side—called sculling oars. Competitive sculls can be made for a single rower, two rowers, or four. A shell that is *not* a scull is set up with one oar—a sweep oar—per crew member. The sweep rower pulls his oar with both hands as he rows on one side of the boat; the rower next in line rows on the opposite side.

This keeps the boat's propulsion balanced so that the shell can track a straight line. This sweep-oar type of shell comes in versions for crews of two, four, or eight rowers.

To confuse matters more, certain crew configurations may or may not include an extra member, called a coxswain (pronounced *cox'n),* who does not row but who uses a rudder to steer and also coaches the rowers. The coxswain observes the progress from his vantage point, usually in the back of the boat, and directs the crew in matters of cadence and form. Altogether, eight different boat arrangements result, and each goes by at least a couple of different names.

The **sculls** (people who row sculls are scullers and they use sculling oars) are:

- the single scull (1×), or "the single," rowed by one person;

- the double scull (2×), or "the double," rowed by two people; and

- the quadruple scull (4×), or "the quad," rowed by four people.

Not too bad so far, but it gets dicier with the next group. **The shells that are not sculls** (the rowers of these boats each pull one oar, a sweep oar) are:

- a pair without coxswain (2−), or a "straight pair," or a "pair without," or a "coxless pair," crewed by two rowers only;

- a pair with coxswain (2+), or a "pair with," or a "coxed pair," crewed by two rowers plus a coxswain;

- a four without coxswain (4−), or a "straight four," or a "four without," or a "coxless four," crewed by four rowers only;

- a four with coxswain (4+), or a "coxed four," or a "four with," crewed by four rowers plus a coxswain; and

- an eight (8+), or a "coxed eights" or "eight oars," crewed by eight rowers plus a coxswain.

FACT: The pair with coxswain event is unofficially termed "the floating leg press" in recognition of its huge demand on thigh muscle power

The shells themselves range in length from 26 feet for a single scull to about 58 feet for an eight. They can be built of high-tech materials such as kevlar and graphite fiber, but some of the most competitive boats are still made of ultra-thin plywood. Some shells are constructed with hulls only 1/16-inch thick.

The Races

Olympic races, like other international competition in rowing, are run on a 2000m course (about 1½ miles). A system of heats, semifinals, and repêchages is used to determine who will be in the finals. The top finishers in each heat go to the semifinals while the remaining crews go into a repêchage, or "second chance," round to try to get back into the semifinals. The top three crews of each of the two semifinal races then go on to the final, where medalists and final 4th, 5th, and 6th place are determined. Meanwhile the 4th, 5th, and 6th place finishers of each semifinal go into a petit final to determine final rankings of 7th through 12th place finishers. Added to the Olympic program for 1996 is the lightweight men's double sculls and the lightweight women's double sculls events. The adjective applies not to the boats but to the weight of the athletes.

The Times

Speeds attained by the various classes of shells can range from about 10½ miles per hour for a single scull to more than 13 miles per hour for an eight. That kind of speed may not seem too impressive to someone living in the age of internal combustion, but for a human-powered watercraft it's truly remarkable. The speed of a racing shell is not constant, however, and the spectator or television viewer will observe that the motion of the hull through the water is jerky. The reason, of course, is that the power being applied through oar strokes is intermittent. The superlight shells accelerate rapidly but don't have the mass to carry their speed like a heavier boat would. What's interesting is that the point in the rowing cycle where hull speed is highest is not when the oars are pulling through the water. It is on the oars' return, when the crew members slide on their sliding seats back toward their feet—and toward the back of the boat (remember the rower sits facing backward). Suddenly moving the relatively large mass of the crew toward the back of the boat results in a brief forward burst of speed. This effect will be most noticeable when a camera shot is perpendicular to the direction of the shell's travel, or sideways to the boat.

FACT: According to their US Rowing athlete profiles, sweep rowers Betsy and Mary McCagg are, at six feet two inches each, "one of the tallest sets of twin women in elite athletics."

Hopefuls

The Olympic rowing competition for 1996 will take place at Lake Lanier, in Gainesville, Georgia. With an investment of ten

Canada's women's coxed eights team display their gold medals after winning the Olympic rowing finals in 1992. Canadian women medaled in four of six events in the XXV Games and are expected to be a force to be reckoned with again in 1996.
AP/Wide World Photos

million dollars from the Atlanta Committee for the Olympic Games, the site was specially altered to accommodate rowing. The flatwater canoe/kayak events will also be held at Lake Lanier, bringing the total number of athletes competing at the venue to about one thousand.

Canada, Germany, France and the Ukraine are floating favored competitors in the rowing events, while the U.S. men's eights are widely expected to take the gold in their event in 1996. A surprise contender in men's single sculls is U.S. rower Cyrus Beasley, who took up the sport in 1994 at the age of twenty-two and is described as a "surfer/lifeguard/free spirit." His silver medal at the Pan Am Games in 1995 underscored his swift climb to serious contention and caused rowers around the world to watch him closely as Atlanta approached.

A talent to watch in 1996, Canada's Silken Laumann was the story of the Barcelona Games in women's rowing. In May of 1992, just a few short months before the Olympic competition, another boat crashed into Laumann's shell. The severe leg injuries that Laumann sustained as a result seemed certain to end her career in rowing. Laumann was nonetheless entered in the women's single sculls event at Barcelona, where the medal favorites were Elisabeta Lipa of Romania, Beate Schramm of Germany, and Annelies Bredael of Belgium. Not only did Laumann row the event, she powered her boat to a bronze behind Lipa and Bredael, upsetting Schramm and inspiring the world. Laumann looks to be back stronger than ever for Canada in 1996.

U.S. women's rowers Lindsay Burns and Teresa Zarzeczny, competing in the lightweight women's double sculls, look strong for medals in Atlanta. The U.S. women's eight is expected to be in gold medal contention, having silvered behind Germany in the 1994 Worlds and consistently beaten Germany in 1995. That very stable crew is expected to take the gold in Atlanta. Among them is Amy Fuller, who crewed on the female-dominated America's Cup sailing yacht, *America*[3], along with Jennifer Dore, Catriona Fallon, Yasmin Farooq, Anne Kakela, Laurel Korholz, twins Betsy and Mary McCagg, and Monica Tranel.

FACT: When Silken Laumann's shell was struck by another boat in May 1992, the Canadian's leg injuries threatened to put an end to her rowing career. But in Barcelona, Laumann came back from her injuries to nab a bronze medal in single sculls.

The tentative rowing schedule is:

Sunday, July 21
Men's & Women's heats

Monday, July 22
Men's & Women's heats

Tuesday, July 23
Men's & Women's repechages

Wednesday, July 24
Men's & Women's repechages

Thursday, July 25
Men's & Women's semifinals

Friday, July 26
Men's & Women's semifinals

Saturday, July 27
Men's & Women's finals

Sunday, July 28
Men's & Women's finals

MEN'S ROWING EVENTS

Highlights

America's John Kelly may be best known as the father of film star Grace Kelly, the late Princess Grace of Monaco, but he also has the distinction of having won three Olympic gold medals in rowing. His victory in single sculls at Antwerp was one of 126 consecutive races he won during 1919 and 1920. He also teamed with his cousin, Paul Costello, to win the double sculls in both 1920 and 1924. Costello's Olympic golds also totalled three, the last in 1928 with partner Charles McIlvaine.

Kelly's son, John Jr., was also an Olympic competitor in single sculls. At the 1948 Games in London he failed to make the finals, and four years later at Helsinki he was overtaken in the stretch and finished fourth. Shortly before his last Olympics, at Melbourne, he promised to bring back a medal as a wedding gift to his sister, who was about to marry Prince Rainier of Monaco. Kelly didn't say which medal he would bring, but he did deliver, and Princess Grace wound up with some bronze of tremendous sentimental value for the royal coffers.

Rowing was first included in the Olympics at Paris in 1900, although Greek crews had given several demonstrations at Athens four years earlier. The German crew in the coxed fours event in 1900 included three brothers, Oskar, Gustav, and Carl Gossler

(Carl as coxswain). At Paris the U.S. won the first of many gold medals in the eights event. British rowers dominated at the 1908 Games in London and again in Stockholm, where Germany also picked up a medal.

Among the British medalists in 1908 was Guy Nickalls, Sr., who won an eights gold at the age of 42; Guy Nickalls, Jr., won eights silvers in 1920 and 1928. Another gold medalist on Britain's eights team in 1908, Charles Burnell, sired a rowing son, Richard, who triumphed in the double sculls with B. Herbert Bushnell in 1948. On the team for Britain in 1912 was Julius Beresford, who took a silver in the coxed fours event; his son Jack was also a successful Olympic rower, capturing three gold medals between 1920 and 1936, as well as two silvers.

FACT: The 1906 Games in Athens included two events that have never again been contested at the Olympics. The Intercalated Games included a 2,000-m six-man naval rowing boat event and a 3,000-m sixteen-man naval rowing boat race.

After World War I the U.S. came to the fore in rowing. A U.S. crew from Yale that included medical student Benjamin Spock won the eights event in 1924. Between 1920 and 1956 crews from different American universities and clubs won the eights event eight straight times. In the single sculls, U.S. rowers William Garrett Gilmore, Ken Myers, and Bill Miller won three consecutive silvers between 1924 and 1932. Canada, Britain, Australia, and Germany also floated strong rowers in those years.

Standouts into the 1950s included Britons Jack Beresford (son of Julius), W.G. "Ran" Laurie, and Jack Wilson and Australians Bob (Henry Robert) Pearce and Mervyn Wood. Pearce was known for letting a family of ducks pass before finishing his gold-medal performance in the single sculls in 1928; he relocated to Canada but still rowed for Australia in 1932.

The Soviet Union and East Germany dominated rowing beginning in the 1950s. Soviet rower Yuri Tyukalov grabbed the single sculls in 1952, and his countryman, Vyacheslav Ivanov, stroked to an unprecedented three straight gold medals in the single sculls from 1956 to 1964. Ivanov was a master of the come-from-behind finish.

Robert Zimonyi was 46 when he coxed the U.S. eights to a gold in 1964; in 1948, competing for Hungary, he had coxed a pair to a bronze medal. Canada also captured some rare gold, in 1956 in the coxless fours, and in 1964, in the coxless pairs, to go with an eights silver won in Rome.

At the Mexico City Games in 1968 the two Germanies captured three gold and two silver medals, including an eights gold for East Germany in a much lighter boat, while U.S. rowers claimed a silver and a bronze. At Munich the U.S. managed only a silver in the eights event behind New Zealand's eight (who were funded by a series of bingo games and a "dream kitchen" raffle), and otherwise in 1972 the two Germanies were dominant. The double sculls race in 1972 featured a spectacularly close finish in which a Soviet crew barely bested a Norwegian crew.

East German Siegfried Brietzke captured three gold medals from 1972 to 1980, in the coxless pairs and coxless fours events. Norwegian brothers Frank and Alf Hansen won the double sculls event in 1976, and U.S. coxless pairs Calvin Coffey and Michael Staines drew a silver medal. But the real powerhouse at the Montreal Games was East Germany, taking four of the eight men's gold medals awarded. In 1980 at the Moscow Games East Germans made off with seven men's gold medals. In the coxless pairs event in 1980 the East German Landvoight twins outstroked the Soviet Pimenov twins. Canada took the gold from a favored U.S. crew in the men's eights in 1984. That year Romanian rower Ivan Patzaichin competed in his fifth Olympics.

Finnish single-sculler Pertti Karppinen, a fireman, won the gold in 1976, 1980, and 1984. Karppinen had developed a long-standing rivalry with West German Peter-Michael Kolbe, who took a silver behind Karppinen in 1976 and 1984 (having boycotted the Moscow Games). Karppinen didn't make the finals in 1988, however, and Kolbe settled for silver once again, almost 5 seconds behind East German Thomas Lange, eleven years Kolbe's junior.

Andrew Sudduth was a member of the American eight that took a silver medal in 1984, and competed as a single sculler in 1988. In Seoul U.S. men stroked to a silver in the men's four without coxswain and a bronze in the men's eight.

Highlights from Barcelona

Spain captured a record in Barcelona by floating the youngest competitor at the 1992 Games, 11-year-old Carlos Front, who served as coxswain for Spain's men's eight. His father,

FACT: Spain's last-finishing eight-oared shell at the Barcelona Games managed to make its way into Olympic history. Carlos Front, the boat's 11-year-old coxswain, was Barcelona's youngest competitor. Front, who was training with an eye toward the Atlanta Games, gained a berth in the 1992 Olympics when the team's former coxswain outgrew his post.

Canada's Silken Laumann strains at the oars on her way to winning the Olympic women's singles sculls semi-finals in Banyoles, Spain, in 1992. Laumann, a world-champion sculler whose leg was severely injured the May before, made a remarkable comeback, winning the bronze. *AP/Wide World Photos*

359

Bienvenido Front, was technical director of the Catalonia Rowing Federation, and had initiated Carlos into the sport when he was six.

Germany, Romania, and the Netherlands looked strong in men's rowing going into the 1992 Games. When the medals were tallied, Germany had captured two gold, two silver, and one bronze medal; Britain and Australia had each garnered two gold medals; and Canada and Romania rowed to one gold medal each. The U.S. earned a silver medal in men's coxless fours, in a boat powered by Doug Burden, Jeff McLaughlin, Thomas Bohrer, and Patrick Manning.

No rowing event looked more like a lock in Barcelona than the men's pair with coxswain, which had been dominated in the previous two Games by the gold-medal-winning performances of Italy's Giuseppe and Carmine Abbagnale, along with coxswain Giuseppe DiCapua. The Abbagnale brothers had won seven of nine world championships going into Barcelona, and seemed sure of the gold there. Instead they were upset by another pair of brothers, Britain's Jonathan and Greg Searle, with coxswain Garry Herbert. Romania took the bronze behind Italy in that event.

Medalists

Rowing—Men's Single Sculls

1992
1. Thomas Lange, Germany, 6:51.40
2. Vaclav Chalupa, Czechoslovakia, 6:52.93
3. Kajetan Broniewski, Poland, 6:56.82

1988
1. Thomas Lange, East Germany, 6:49.86
2. Peter Michael Kolbe, West Germany, 6:54.77
3. Eric Verdonk, New Zealand, 6:58.66

1984
1. Pertti Karppinen, Finland, 7:00.24
2. Peter-Michael Kolbe, West Germany, 7:02.19
3. Robert Mills, Canada, 7:10.38

1980
1. Pertti Karppinen, Finland, 7:09.61
2. Vassili Yakusha, Soviet Union, 7:11.66
3. Peter Kersten, East Germany, 7:14.88

1976
1. Pertti Karppinen, Finland, 7:29.03
2. Peter-Michael Kolbe, West Germany, 7:31.67
3. Joachim Dreifke, East Germany, 7:38.03

1972
1. Yuri Malishev, Soviet Union, 7:10.12

2. Alberto Demiddi, Argentina, 7:11.53
3. Wolfgang Guldenpfennig, East Germany, 7:14.45

1968
1. Henri Jan Wienese, Netherlands, 7:47.80
2. Jochen Meissner, West Germany, 7:52.00
3. Alberto Demiddi, Argentina, 7:57.19

1964
1. Vyacheslav Ivanov, Soviet Union, 8:22.51
2. Achim Hill, East Germany, 8:26.24
3. Gottfried Kottmann, Switzerland, 8:29.68

1960
1. Vyacheslav Ivanov, Soviet Union, 7:13.96
2. Achim Hill, East Germany, 7:20.21
3. Teodor Kocerka, Poland, 7:21.26

1956
1. Vyacheslav Ivanov, Soviet Union, 8:02.5
2. Stuart Mackenzie, Australia, 8:07.7
3. John Kelly, Jr., U.S.A., 8:11.8

1952
1. Yuri Tyukalov, Soviet Union, 8:12.8
2. Mervyn Wood, Australia, 8:14.5
3. Teodor Kocerka, Poland, 8:19.4

1948

1. Mervyn Wood. Australia, 7:24.4
2. Eduardo Risso, Uruguay, 7:38.2
3. Romolo Catasta, Italy, 7:51.4

1936

1. Gustav Schafer, Germany, 8:21.5
2. Josef Hasenohrl, Austria, 8:25.8
3. Daniel Barrow, U.S.A., 8:28.0

1932

1. Henry Pearce, Australia, 7:44.4
2. William Miller, U.S.A., 7:45.2
3. Guillermo Douglas. Uruguay, 8:13.6

1928

1. Henry Pearce, Australia, 7:11.0
2. Kenneth Myers, U.S.A., 7:20.8
3. T. David Collet, Great Britain, 7:19.8

1924

1. Jack Beresford, Jr., Great Britain, 7:49.2
2. William E. Garrett Gilmore, U.S.A., 7:54.0
3. Josef Schneider, Switzerland, 8:01.1

1920

1. John Kelly Sr., U.S.A., 7:35.0
2. Jack Beresford, Jr., Great Britain, 7:36.0
3. D. Clarence Hadfield d'Arcy, New Zealand, 7:48.0

1912

1. William Kinnear, Great Britain, 7:47.6
2. Polydore Veirman, Belgium
3. Everard B. Butler, Canada
3. Maximilian Kusik, Soviet Union

1908

1. Harry Blackstaffe, Great Britain, 9:26.0
2. Alexander McCulloch, Great Britain
3. Karoly Levitzkty, Hungary
3. Bernhard von Gaza, Germany

1906

1. Gaston Delaplane, 5:53.4
2. Joseph Larran, France, 6:07.2

1904

1. Frank Greer, U.S.A., 10:08.5
2. James Juvenal, U.S.A
3. Constance Titus U.S.A

1900

1. Henri Barrelet, France, 7:35.6
2. Andre Gaudin, France, 7:41.6
3. George St. Ashe, Great Britain, 8:15.6

1896

Not held

Rowing—Men's Double Sculls

1992

1. Australia, Stephen Hawkins, Peter Antonie , 6:17.32
2. Austria, Arnold Jonke, Christoph Zerbst, 6:18.42
3. Netherlands, Henk-Jan Zwolle, Nico Rienks, 6:22.82

1988

1. Netherlands, 6:21.13, Ronald Florijn, Nicolaas Rienks
2. Switzerland, 6:22.59, Beat Schwerzmann, Ueli Bodenmann
3. Soviet Union, 6:22.87, Alexandre Martchenko, Vassily Iakoucha

1984

1. U.S.A., 6:36.87, Bradley Lewis, Paul Enquist
2. Belgium, 6:38.19, Pierre-Marie Deloof, Dirk Crois
3. Yugoslavia, 6:39.59, Zoran Pancic, Milorad Stanulov

1980

1. East Germany, 6:24.33, Joachim Dreifke, Kroppelien Klaus
2. Yugoslavia, 6:26.34, Zoran Pancic, Milorad Stanulov
3. Czechoslovakia, 6:29.07, Zdenek Pecka, Vaclav Vochoska

1976

1. Norway, 7:13.20, Frank Hansen, Alf Hansen
2. Great Britain, 7:15.26, Christopher Baillieu, Michael Hart
3. East Germany, 7:17.45, Hans-Ulrich Schmied, Jurgen Bertow

1972

1. Soviet Union, 7:01.77, Aleksandr Timoshinin, Gennady Korshikikov
2. Norway, 7:02.58, Frank Hansen, Svein Thogersen
3. East Germany, 7:05.55, Joachim Bohmer, Hans-Ulrich Schmied

1968

1. Soviet Union, 6:51.82, Anatoli Sass, Aleksandr Timoschinin
2. Netherlands, 6:52.80, Leendert F. van Dis, Henricus A. Droog
3. U.S.A., 6:54.21, William Maher, John Nunn

1964

1. Soviet Union, 7:10.66, Oleg Tyurin, Boris Dubrovski
2. U.S.A., 7:13.16, Seymour Cromwell, James Storm

3. Czechoslovakia, 7:14.23, Vladimir Andrs, Pavel Hofman

1960

1. Czechoslovakia, 6:47.50, Vaclav Kozak, Pavel Schmidt
2. Soviet Union, 6:50.49, Aleksandr Berkutov, Yuri Tyukalov
3. Switzerland, 6:50.59, Ernst Hurlimann, Rolf Larcher

1956

1. Soviet Union, 7:24.0, Aleksandr Berkutov, Yuri Tyukalov
2. U.S.A., 7:32.2, Bernard Costello Jr., James Gardiner
3. Australia, 7:37.4, Murray Riley, Mervyn Wood

1952

1. Argentina, 7:32.2, Tranquilo Cappozzo, Eduardo Guerrero
2. Soviet Union, 7:38.3, Georgi Zhilin, Igor Yemchuk
3. Uruguay, 7:43.7, Miguel Seijas, Juan Rodriguez

1948

1. Great Britain, 6:51.3, Richard Burnell, B. Herbert Bushnell
2. Denmark, 6:55.3, Ebbe Parsner, Aage Ernst Larsen
3. Uruguay, 7:12.4, William Jones, Juan Rodriguez

1936

1. Great Britain, 7:20.8, Jack Beresford, Jr., Leslie Southwood
2. Germany, 7:26.2, Willy Kaidel, Joachim Pirsch
3. Poland, 7:36.2, Roger Verey, Jerzy Ustupski

1932

1. U.S.A., 7:17.4, Kenneth Myers, William E. Garrett Gilmore
2. Germany, 7:22.8, Herbert Buhtz, Gerhard Boetzelen
3. Canada, 7:27.6, Charles Pratt, Noel de Mille

1928

1. U.S.A., 6:41.4, Paul Costello, Charles McIlvaine
2. Canada, 6:51.0, Joseph Wright, John Guest
3. Austria, 6:48.8, Leo Losert, Viktor Flessl

1924

1. U.S.A., 6:34.0, Paul Costello, John Kelly, Sr.

2. France, 6:38.0, Marc Detton, Jean-Piere Stock
3. Switzerland, Rudolf Bosshard, Heini Thoma

1920

1. U.S.A., 7:09.0, John Kelly, Sr., Paul Costello
2. Italy, 7:19.0, Erminio Dones, Pietro Annoni
3. France, 7:21.0, Alfred Ple, Gaston Giran

1906–1912

Not held

1904

1. U.S.A., 10:03.2, John Mulcahy, William Varley
2. U.S.A., James McLoughlin, John Hoben
3. U.S.A., Joseph Ravanack, John Wells

1896–1900

Not held

Rowing—Men's Coxless Pairs

1992

1. Britain, Steven Redgrave, Matthew Pinsent, 6:27.72
2. Germany, Peter Hoeltzenbein, Colin Von Ettingshausen, 6:32.68
3. Slovenia, Iztok Cop, Denis Zvegelj, 6:33.43

1988

1. Great Britain, 6:36.84, Andrew Holmes, Steven Redgrave
2. Romania, 6:38.06, Dragos Neagu, Danut Dobre
3. Yugoslavia, 6:41.01, Bojan Presern, Sadik Mujkic

1984

1. Romania, 6:45.39, Petru Iosub, Valer Toma
2. Spain, 6:48.44, Fernando Climent, Luis Lasurtegui
3. Norway, 6:51.81, Hans Magnus Grepperud, Sverre Loken

1980

1. East Germany, 6:48.01, Bernd Landvoigt, Jurgen Landvoigt
2. Soviet Union, 6:50.50, Yuri Pimenov, Nikolai Pimenov
3. Great Britain, 6:51.47, Charles Wiggin, Malcom Carmichael

1976

1. East Germany, 7:23.31, Jurgen Landvoigt, Bernd Landvoigt
2. U.S.A., 7:26.73, Calvin Coffey, Michael Staines
3. West Germany, 7:30.03, Peter Van Roye, Thomas Straub

1972

1. East Germany, 6:53.16, Siegfried Brietzke, Wolfgang Meyer
2. Switzerland, 6:57.06, Heinrich Fischer, Alfred Bachmann
3. Netherlands, 6:58.70, Roelof Luynenburg, Ruud Stokvis

1968

1. East Germany, 7:26.56, Jorg Lucke, Heinz-Jurgen Bothe
2. U.S.A., 7:26.71, Lawrence Hough, Philip Johnson
3. Denmark, 7:31.84, Peter Fich Christiansen, Ib Ivan Larsen

1964

1. Canada, 7:32.94, George Hungerford, Roger Ch. Jackson
2. Netherlands, 7:33.40, Steven Blaisse, Ernst W. Veenemans
3. West Germany, 7:38.63, Michael Schwan, Wolfgang Hottenrott

1960

1. Soviet Union, 7:02.01, Valentin Boreiko, Oleg Golovanov
2. Austria, 7:03.69, Alfred Sageder, Josef Kloimstein
3. Finland, 7:03.80, Veli Lehtela, Toimi Pitkanen

1956

1. U.S.A., 7:55.4, James Fifer, Duvall Hecht
2. Soviet Union, 8:03.9, Igor Buldakov, Viktor Ivanov
3. Austria, 8:11.8, Alfred Sageder, Josef Kloimstein

1952

1. U.S.A., 8:20.7, Charles Logg, Thomas Price
2. Belgium, 8:23.5, Michel Knuysen, Robert Baetens
3. Switzerland, 8:32.7, Kurt Schmid, Hans Kalt

1948

1. Great Britain, 7:21.1, John Wilson, W. George Laurie
2. Switzerland, 7:23.9, Hans Kalt, Josef Kalt
3. Italy, 7:31.5, Felice Fanetti, Bruno Boni

1936

1. Germany, 8:16.1, Willi Eichhorn, Hugo Strauss
2. Denmark, 8:19.2, Richard Olsen, Harry Julius Larsen
3. Argentina, 8:23.0, Horacio Podesta, Julio Curatella

1932

1. Great Britain, 8:00.0, H.R. Arthur Edwards, Lewis Clive
2. New Zealand, 8:02.4, Cyril Stiles, Frederick Thompson
3. Poland, 8:08.2, Henryk Budzynski, Janusz Mikolajczyk

1928

1. Germany, 7:06.4, Bruno Muller, Kurt Moeschter
2. Great Britain, 7:08.8, Terence O'Brien, R. Archibald Nisbet
3. U.S.A., 7:20.4, Paul McDowell, John Schmitt

1924

1. Netherlands, 8:19.4, Antonie C. Beijnen, Wilhelm H. Rosingh
2. France, 8:21.6, Maurice Bouton, Georges Piot

1912–1920

Not held

1908

1. Great Britain, 9:41.0, J. R. K. Fenning, Gordon Thomson
2. Great Britain, 2.5 Lengths, George Fairbairn, Philip Verdon

1896–1906

Not held

Rowing—Men's Coxed Pairs

1992

1. Britain, Jonathan Searle, Greg Searle, Garry Herbert, 6:49.83
2. Italy, Carmine Abbagnale, Giuseppe Abbagnale, Giuseppe Di Capua, 6:50.98
3. Romania, Dimitrie Popescu, Nicolaie Taga, Dumitru Raducanu, 6:54.58

1988

1. Italy, 6:58.79, Carmine Abbagnale, Giuseppe Abbagnale, Giuseppe DiCapua
2. East Germany, 7:00.63, Mario Streit, Detlef Kirchhoff, Rene Rensch
3. Great Britain, 7:01.95, Andrew Holmes, Steven Redgrave, Patrick Sweeney

1984

1. Italy, 7:05.99, Carmine Abbagnale, Giuseppe Abbagnale, Giuseppe Di Capua
2. Romania, 7:11.21, Dimitrie Popescu, Vasile Tomoiaga, Dumitru Raducanu
3. U.S.A., 7:12.81, Kevin Still, Robert Espeseth, Douglas Herland

1980

1. East Germany, 7:02.54, Harald Jahrling, Friedrich-Wilhelm Ulrich, Georg Spohr
2. Soviet Union, 7:03.35, Viktor Pereverzev, Gennady Kriuchkin, Aleksandr Lukianov
3. Yugoslavia, 7:04.92, Dusko Mrduljas, Zlatko Celent, Josip Reic

1976

1. East Germany, 7:58.99, Harald Jahrling, Friedrich-Wilhelm Ulrich, Georg Spohr
2. Soviet Union, 8:01.82, Dimitri Bekhterev, Yuri Shurkalov, Yuri Lorentsson
3. Czechoslovakia, 8:03.28, Oldrich Svojanovsky, Pavel Svojanovsky, Ladislav Vebr

1972

1. East Germany, 7:17.25, Wolfgang Gunkel, Jorg Lucke, Klaus-Dieter Neubert
2. Czechoslovakia, 7:19.57, Oldrich Svojanovsky, Pavel Svojanovsky, Vladimir Petricek
3. Romania, 7:21.36, Stefan Tudor, Petre Ceapura, Ladislau Lowrenschi

1968

1. Italy, 8:04.81, Primo Baran, Renzo Sambo, Bruno Cipolla
2. Netherlands, 8:06.80, Herman J. Suselbeek, Hadriaan van Nees, Roderick Rijnders
3. Denmark, 8:08.07, Jorn Krab, Harry Jorgensen, Preben Krab

1964

1. U.S.A., 8:21.23, Edward Ferry, Conn Findlay, Henry K. Mitchell
2. France, 8:23.15, Jacques Morel, Georges Morel, Jean-Claude Darouy
3. Netherlands, 8:32.42, Jan Jaspers Bos, Herman J. Rouwe, Frederik Hartsuiker

1960

1. West Germany, 7:29.14, Bernhard Knubel, Heinz Renneberg, Klaus Zerta
2. Soviet Union, 7:30.17, Antanas Bogdanavichus, Sigmas Yukna, Igor Rudakov
3. U.S.A., 7:34.58, Richard Draeger, Conn Findlay, Henry K. Mitchell

1956

1. U.S.A., 8:26.1, Arthur Ayrault, Conn Findlay, Armin K. Seifert
2. West Germany, 8:29.2, Karl-Heinrich von Groddeck, Horst Arndt, Rainer Borkowsky
3. Soviet Union, 8:31.0, Igor Yemtschuk, Georgi Schilin, Vladimir Petrov

1952

1. France, 8:28.6, Raymond Salles, Gaston Mercier, Bernard Malivoire

2. Germany, 8:32.1, Heinz Manchen, Helmut Heinhold, Helmut Noll
3. Denmark, 8:34.9, Svend Pedersen, Poul Svendsen, Jorgen Frandsen

1948

1. Denmark, 8:00.5, Finn Pedersen, Tage Henriksen, Carl Ebbe Andersen
2. Italy, 8:12.2, Giovanni Steffe, Aldo Tarlao, Alberto Radi
3. Hungary, 8:25.2, Antal Szendey, Bela Zsitnik, Robert Zimonyi

1936

1. Germany, 8:36.9, Gerhard Gustmann, Herbert Adamski, Dieter Arend
2. Italy, 8:49.7, Almiro Bergamo, Guido Santin, Luciano Negrini
3. France, 8:54.0, Georges Tapie, Marceau Fourcade, Noel Vandernotte

1932

1. U.S.A., 8:25.8, Joseph Schauers, Charles Kieffer, Edward Jennings
2. Poland, 8:31.2, Jerzy Braun, Janusz Slazak, Jerzy Skolimowski
3. France, 8:41.2, Anselme Brusa, Andre Giriat, Pierre Brunet

1928

1. Switzerland, 7:42.6, Hans Schochlin, Karl Schochlin, Hans Bourquin
2. France, 7:48.4, Armand Marcelle, Edouard Marcelle, Henri Preaux
3. Belgium, 7:59.4, Leon Flament, Francois De Coninck, Georges Anthony

1924

1. Switzerland, 8:39.0, Edouard Candeveau, Alfred Felber, Emile Lachapelle
2. Italy, 8: 39.1, Ercole Olgeni, Giovanni Scatturin, Gino Sopracordevole
3. U.S.A., 3 Lengths, Leon Butler, Harold Wilson, Edward Jennings

1920

1. Italy, 7:56.0, Ercole Olgeni, Giovanni Scatturin, Guido De Filip
2. France, 7:57.0, Gabriel Poix, Maurice Bouton, Ernest Barberolle
3. Switzerland, Edouard Candeveau, Alfred Felber, Paul Piaget

1908–1912

Not held

1906

1. Italy, 7:32.4, Enrico Bruna, Emilio Fontanella, Giorgio Cesana
1. Italy, 4:23.0, Enrico Bruna, Emilio Fontanella, Giorgio Cesana

2. Italy, 4:30.0, Luigi Diana, Francesco Civera, Emilio Cesarana

2. Belgium, 8:03.0, Max Orban, Remy Orban, Th. Psiliakos

3. France, 8:08.6, Adolphe Bernard, Joseph Halcet, Jean-Baptiste Mathieu

3. France, Gaston Delaplane, Charles Delaporte, Marcel Freibourg

1904
Not held

1900

1. Netherlands, 7:34.2, Francois A. Brandt, Roelof Klein, Dr. Hermanus Brockmann

2. France, 7:34.4, Louis Martinet, Waleff

3. France, 7:57.2, Carlos Deltour, Antoine Vedrenne, Paoli

1896
Not held

Rowing—Men's Quadruple Sculls

1992

1. Germany, Andre Willms, Andreas Hajek, Stephan Volkert, Michael Steinbach, 5:45.17

2. Norway, Lars Bjonness, Rolf Thorsen, Kjetil Undset, Per Saetersdal, 5:47.09

3. Italy, Gianluca Farina, Rossano Galtarossa, Alessandro Corona, Filippo Soffici, 5:47.33

1988

1. Italy, 5:53.37, Piero Poli, Gianluca Farina, Davide Tizzano, Agostino Abbagnale

2. Norway, 5:55.08, Lars Bjonness, Vetle Vinje, Rolf Bernt Thorsen, Alf Hansen

3. East Germany, 5:56.13, Steffan Bogs, Steffan Zuehlke, Heiko Habermann, Jens Koeppen

1984

1. West Germany, 5:57.55, Albert Hedderich, Raimund Hormann, Dieter Wiedenmann, Michael Dursch

2. Australia, 5:57.98, Paul Reedy, Gary Gullock, Timothy Mclaren, Anthony Lovrich

3. Canada, 5:59.07, Doug Hamilton, Mike Hughes, Phil Monckton, Bruce Ford

1980

1. East Germany, 5:49.81, Frank Dundr, Karsten Bunk, Uwe Heppner, Martin Winter

2. Soviet Union, 5:51.47, Yuri Shapochka, Yevgeny Barbakov, Valeri Kleshnev, Nikolai Dovgan

3. Bulgaria, 5:52.38, Mincho Nikolov, Liubomir Petrov, Ivo Rusev, Bogdan Dobrev

1976

1. East Germany, 6:18.65, Wolfgang Gueldenpfennig, Rudiger Reiche, Michael Wolfgramm, Karl-Heinz Bussert

2. Soviet Union, 6:19.89, Yevgeny Duleyev, Yuri Yakimov, Aivar Lazdenieks, Vatautas Butkus

3. Czechoslovakia, 6:21.77, Jaroslav Helebrand, Vaclav Vochoska, Zdenek Pecks, Vladek Lacina

Rowing—Men's Coxless Fours

1992

1. Australia, Andrew Cooper, Michael McKay, Nicholas Green, James Tomkins, 5:55.04

2. U.S.A., Doug Burden, Jeff McLaughlin, Thomas Bohrer, Patrick Manning, 5:56.68

3. Slovenia, Janez Klemencic, Saso Mirjanic, Milan Jansa, Sadik Mujkic, 5:58.24

1988

1. East Germany, 6:03.11, Roland Schroeder, Thomas Greiner, Ralf Brudel, Olaf Foerster

2. U.S.A., 6:05.53, Raoul Rodriguez, Thomas Bohrer, David Krmpotich, Richard Kennelly, Jr.

3. West Germany, 6:06.22, Norbert Kesslau, Volker Grabow, Jorg Puttliz, Guido Grabow

1984

1. New Zealand, 6:03.48, Leslie O'Connell, Shane O'Brien, Conrad Robertson, Keith Trask

2. U.S.A., 6:06.10, David Clark, Jonathan Smith, Philip Stekl, Alan Forney

3. Denmark, 6:07.72, Michael Jessen, Lars Nielsen, Per H. S. Rasmussen, Erik Christiansen

1980

1. East Germany, 6:08.17, Jurgen Thiele, Andreas Decker, Stefan Semmler, Siegfried Brietzke

2. Soviet Union, 6:11.81, Aleksei Kamkin, Valeri Dolinin, Aleksandr Kulagin, Vitali Yeliseyev

3. Great Britain, 6:16.58, John Beattie, Ian McNuff, David Townsend, Martin Cross

1976

1. East Germany, 6:37.42, Siegfried Brietzke, Stefan Semmler, Andreas Decker, Wolfgang Mager

2. Norway, 6:41.22, Ole Nafstad, Arne Bergodd, Finn Tveter, Rolf Andreasson

3. Soviet Union, 6:42.52, Raul Arnemann, Nikolai Kuznetsov, Valeri Dolinin, Anushavan Gasan-Dzhalolov

1972

1. East Germany, 6:24.27, Frank Forberger, Frank Ruhle, Dieter Grahn, Dieter Schubert

2. New Zealand, 6:25.64, Dick Tonks, Dudley Storey, Ross Collinge, Noel Mills

3. West Germany, 6:28.41, Joachim Ehrig, Peter Funnekotter, Franz Held, Wolfgang Plottke

1968

1. East Germany, 6:39.18, Frank Forberger, Dieter Grahn, Frank Ruhle, Dieter Schubert
2. Hungary, 6:41.18, Zoltan Melis, Gyorgy Sarlos, Jozsef Csermely, Antal Melis
3. Italy, 6:44.01, Renato Bosatta, Tullio Baraglia, Pier Angelo Conti Manzini, Abramo Albini

1964

1. Denmark, 6:59.30, John O. Hansen, Bjorn Haslov, Erik Petersen, Kurt Helmudt
2. Great Britain, 7:00.47, John M. Russell, Hugh Wardell-Yerburgh, William Barry, John James
3. U.S.A., 7:01.37, Geoffrey Picard, Richard Lyon, Theodore Mittet, Ted Nash

1960

1. U.S.A., 6:26.26, Arthur Ayrault, Ted Nash, John Sayre, Richard Wailes
2. Italy, 6:28.78, Tullio Baraglia, Renato Bosatta, Giancarlo Crosta, Giuseppe Galante
3. Soviet Union, 6:29.62, Igor Akhremchik, Yuri Bachurov, Valentin Morkovkin, Anatoli Tarabrin

1956

1. Canada, 7:08.8, Archibald McKinnon, Lorne Loomer, I. Walter D'Hondt, Donald Arnold
2. U.S.A., 7:18.4, John Welchli, John McKinlay, Arthur McKinlay, James McIntosh
3. France, 7:20.9, Rene Guissart, Yves Delacour, Gaston Mercier, Guy Guillabert

1952

1. Yugoslavia, 7:16.0, Duje Bonacic, Velimir Valenta, Mate Trojanovic, Petar Segvic
2. France, 7:18.9, Pierre Blondiaux, Jacques Guissart, Marc Bouissou, Roger Gautier
3. Finland, 7:23.3, Veikko Lommi, Kauko Wahlsten, Oiva Lommi, Lauri Nevalainen

1948

1. Italy, 6:39.0, Giuseppe Moioli, Elio Morille, Giovanni Invernizzi, Franco Faggi
2. Denmark, 6:43.5, Helge Halkjaer, Askel B. Hansen, Helge Schroder, Ib Storm Larsen
3. U.S.A., 6:47.7, Frederick J. Kingsbury, Stuart Griffing, Gregory Gates, Robert Perew

1936

1. Germany, 7:01.8, Rudolf Eckstein, Anton Rom, Martin Karl, Wilhelm Menne
2. Great Britain, 7:06.5, Thomas Bristow, Alan Barrett, Peter Jackson, John D. Sturrock
3. Switzerland, 7:10.6, Hermann Betschart, Hans Homberger, Alex Homberger, Karl Schmid

1932

1. Great Britain, 6:58.2, John C. Badcock, Hugh R.A. Edwards, Jack Beresford, Rowland D. George
2. Germany, 7:03.0, Karl Aletter, Ernst Gaber, Walter Flinsch, Hans Maier
3. Italy, 7:04.0, Antonio Ghiardello, Francesco Cossu, Giliante D'Este, Antonio Provenzani

1928

1. Great Britain, 6:36.0, John G. H. Lander, Michael H. Warriner, Richard Beesly, Edward V. Bevan
2. U.S.A., 6:37.0, Charles Karle, William Miller, George Heales, Ernest Bayer
3. Italy, 6:31.6, Cesare Rossi, Pietro Freschi, Umberto Bonade, Paolo Gennari

1924

1. Great Britain, 7:08.6, Charles R. M. Eley, James A. MacNabb, Robert E. Morrison, Terrence R.B. Sanders
2. Canada, 1 Length, Colin H. B. Finlayson, Archibald C. Black, George F. Mackay, William Wood
3. Switzerland, 2 Lengths, Emile Albrecht, Alfred Probst, Eugen Sigg, Hans Walter

1912–1920

Not held

1908

1. Great Britain, 8:34.0, C. Robert Cudmore, James A. Gillan, Duncan McKinnon, Robert Somers-Smith
2. Great Britain, 1.5 Lengths, Philip R. Filleul, Harold R. Barker, J. R. K. Fenning, Gordon L. Thomson

1906

Not held

1904

1. U.S.A., 9:53.8, George Dietz, August Erker, Albert Nasse, Arthur Stockhoff
2. U.S.A., Charles Aman, Michael Begley, Martin Fromanack, Frederick Suerig

1896–1900

Not held

Rowing—Men's Coxed Fours

1992

1. Romania, Viorel Talapan, Iulica Ruican, Dimitrie Popescu, Nicolaie Taga, Dumitru Raducanu, 5:59.37
2. Germany, Uwe Kellner, Ralf Brudel, Thoralf Peters, Karsten Finger, Hendrik Reiher, 6:00.34
3. Poland, Jacek Streich, Wojciech Jankowski, Tomasz Tomiak, Maciej Lasicki, Michal Cieslak, 6:03.27

1988

1. East Germany, 6:10.74, Frank Klawonn, Bernd Eichwurzel, Bernd Niesecke, Karsten Schmeing, Hendrick Reiher
2. Romania, 6:13.58, Dimitrie Popescu, Ioan Snep, Valentin Robu, Vasile Tomoiaga, Ladislau Lovrenski
3. New Zealand, 6:15.78, George Keys, Ian Wright, Gregory Johnston, Christopher White, Andrew Bird

1984

1. Great Britain, 6:18.64, Martin Cross, Richard Budgett, Andrew Holmes, Steven Redgrave, Adrian Ellison
2. U.S.A., 6:20.28, Thomas Kiefer, Gregory Springer, Michael Bach, Edward Ives, John Stillings
3. New Zealand, 6:23.68, Kevin Lawton, Donald Symon, Barrie Vlabbott, Ross Tong, Brett Hollister

1980

1. East Germany, 6:14.51, Dieter Wendisch, Ullrich Diessner, Walter Diessner, Gottfried Dohn, Andreas Gregor
2. Soviet Union, 6:19.05, Artur Garonskis, Dimant Krishianis, Dzintars Krishianis, Zhorzh Tikmers, Yuris Berzynsh
3. Poland, 6:22.52, Grzegorz Stellak, Adam Tomasiak, Grzegorz Nowak, Ryszard Stadniuk, Ryszard Kubiak

1976

1. Soviet Union, 6:40.22, Vladimir Yeshino, Nikolai Ivanov, Mikhail Kuznetsov, Aleksandre Klepikov, Aleksandr Lukianov
2. East Germany, 6:42.70, Rudiger Kunze, Walter Diessner, Ullrich Diessner, Johannes Thomas
3. West Germany, 6:46.96, Ralph Kubail, Hans-Johann Faerber, Siegfried Fricke, Peter Niehusen, Hartmut Wenzel

1972

1. West Germany, 6:31.85, Peter Berger, Hans-Johann Farber, Gerhard Auer, Alois Bierl, Uwe Benter
2. East Germany, 6:33.30, Dietrich Zander, Reinhard Gust, Eckhard Martens, Rolf Jobst, Klaus-Dieter Ludwig
3. Czechoslovakia, 6:35.64, Otakar Marecek, Karel Neffe, Vladimir Janos, Frantisek Provaznik, Vladimir Petricek

1968

1. New Zealand, 6:45.62, Richard J. Joyce, Dudley L. Storey, Ross H. Collinge, Warren J. Cole, Simon Ch. Dickie

2. East Germany, 6:48.20, Peter Kremtz, Roland Gohler, Manfred Gelpke, Klaus Jacob, Dieter Semetzky
3. Switzerland, 6:49.04, Denis Oswald, Hugo Waser, Peter Bolliger, Jakob Grob, Gottlieb Frohlich

1964

1. West Germany, 7:00.44, Peter Neusel, Bernhard Britting, Joachim Werner, Egbert Hirschfelder, Jurgen Oelke
2. Italy, 7:02.84, Renato Bosatta, Emilio Trivini, Giuseppe Galante, Franco De Pedrina, Giovanni Spinola
3. Netherlands, 7:06.46, Alex Mullink, Jan van de Graaf, Frederick R. van de Graaf, Robert van de Graaf, Marius Klumperbeek

1960

1. West Germany, 6:39.12, Gerd Cintl, Horst Effertz, Klaus Riekemann, Jurgen Litz, Michael Obst
2. France, 6:41.62, Robert Dumontois, Claude Martin, Jacques Morel, Guy Nosbaum, Jean Klein
3. Italy, 6:43.72, Fulvio Balatti, Romano Sgheiz, Franco Trincavelli, Giovanni Zucchi, Ivo Stefanoni

1956

1. Italy, 7:19.4, Alberto Winkler, Romano Sgheiz, Angelo Vanzin, Franco Trincavelli, Ivo Stefanoni
2. Sweden, 7:22.4, Olof Larsson, Gosta Eriksson, Ivar Aronsson, Sven E. Gunnarsson, Bertil Goransson
3. Finland, 7:30.9, Kauko Hanninen, Reino Poutanen, Veli Lehtela, Toimi Pitkanen, Matti Niemi

1952

1. Czechoslovakia, 7:33.4, Karle Mejta, Jiri Havlis, Jan Jindra, Stanislav Lusk, Miroslav Koranda
2. Switzerland, 7:36.5, Enrico Bianchi, Karl Weidmann, Heinrich Scheller, Emile Ess, Walter Leiser
3. U.S.A., 7:37.0, Carl Lovested, Alvin Ulbrickson, Richard Wahlstrom, Matthew Leanderson, Albert Rossi

1948

1. U.S.A., 6:50.3, Warren Westlund, Robert Martin, Robert Will, Gordon Giovanelli, Allen Morgan
2. Switzerland, 6:53.3, Rudolf Reichling, Erich Schriever, Emile Knecht, Pierre Stebler, Andre Moccand

3. Denmark, 6:58.6, Erik Ch. Larsen, Borge R. Nielsen, Henry C. Larsen, Harry M. Knudsen, Jorgen Ib Olsen

1936

1. Germany, 7:16.2, Hans Maier, Walter Volle, Ernst Gaber, Paul Sollner, Fritz Bauer
2. Switzerland, 7:24.3, Hermann Betschart, Hans Homberger, Alex Homberger, Karl Schmid, Rolf Spring
3. France, 7:33.3, Fernand Vandernotte, Marcel Vandernotte, Marcel Cosmat, Marcel Chauvigne, Noel Vandernotte

1932

1. Germany, 7:19.0, Hans Eller, Horst Hoeck, Walter Meyer, Joachim Spremberg, Karlheinz Neumann
2. Italy, 7:19.2, Bruno Vattovaz, Giovanni Plazzer, Riccardo Divora, Bruno Parovel, Giovanni Scherl
3. Poland, 7:26.8, Jerzy Braun, Janusz Slazak, Stanislaw Urban, Edward Kobylinski, Jerzy Skolimovski

1928

1. Italy, 6:47.8, Valerio Perentin, Giliante D'Este, Nicolo Vittori, Giovanni Delise, Renato Petronio
2. Switzerland, 7:03.4, Ernst Haas, Joseph Meyer, Dr. Otto Bucher, Karl Schwegler, Fritz Bosch
3. Poland, 7:12.8, Franciszek Bronikowski, Edmund Jankowski, Leon Birkholc, Bernard Ormanowski, Bronislaw Drewek

1924

1. Switzerland, 7:18.4, Emile Albrecht, Alfred Probst, Eugen Sigg, Hans Walter, Emile Lachapelle
2. France, 7:21.6, Eugene Constant, Louis Gressier, Georges Lecointe, Raymond Talleux, Marcel Lepan
3. U.S.A., Robert Gerhardt, Sidney Jelinek, Edward Mitchell, Henry Welsford, John Kennedy

1920

1. Switzerland, 6:54.0, Willy Bruderlin, Max Rudolf, Paul Rudolf, Hans Walter, Paul Staub
2. U.S.A., 6:58.0, Kenneth Meyers, Carl Otto Klose, Franz Federschmidt, Erich Federschmidt, Sherman Clark
3. Norway, 7:02.0, Birger Var, Theodor Klem, Henry Larsen, Per Gulbrandsen, Thoralf Hagen

1912

1. Germany, 6:59.4, (Ludwigshafener R.V.), Albert Arnheiter, Otto Fickeisen, Rudolf Fickeisen, Hermann Wilker, Otto Maier

2. Great Britain, (Thames R.C.), Julius Beresford sen., Charles G. Vernon, Charles Rought, Bruce Logan, Geoffrey Carr
3. Denmark, (Polyteknik R.C.), Erik Bisgaard, Rasmus P. Frandsen, Magnus Simonsen, Paul Thymann, Eigil Clemmensen

1908
Not held

1906

1. Italy, 8:13.0, (Bucintoro), Enrico Bruna, Emilio Fontanella, Riccardo Zardinoni, Giuseppe Poli, Giorgio Cesana
2. France, (Societe Nautique de la Basse Seine), Gaston Delaplane, Charles Delaporte, Leon Delignieres, Paul Echard, Marcel Frebourg
3. France, (Societe Nautique de Bayonne), Adolphe Bernard, Joseph Halcet, Jean-Baptiste Laporte, Jean-Baptiste Mathieu, Pierre Sourbe

1904
Not held

1900

1. France, 7:11.0, (Cercle de l'Aviron de Roubaix) Emile Delchambre, Jean Cau, Henri Boukaert, Henri Hazebroucq, . . .Charlot
1. Germany, 5:59.0, (Germania R.C. Hamburg), Oskar Gossler, Walter Kartzenstein, Waldemar Tietgens, Gustav L. Gossler, Carl Heinrich Gossler
2. France, 7:18.0, (Club Nautique de Lyon) Charles Perrin, Daniel Soubeyran, Emile Wegelin, Georges Lumpp
2. Netherlands, 6:33.0, (Minerva Amsterdam), Gerhard O. Lotsy, Gerhard Hiebendaal, Paulus J. Lotsy, Johannes H. Terwogt, Dr. Hermanus Brockmann
3. Germany, 6:35.0, (Ludwigshafener R.V.), Carl Lehle, Ernst Felle, Herman Wilker, Otto Fickeisen, Franz Krowerath
3. Germany, 7:18.2, (R.C. Favorite Hammonia, Hamburg), Hugo Ruster, Wilhelm Carstens, Julius Korner, Adolf Moller, Max Ammermann

1896
Not held

Rowing—Men's Eight Oars

1992

1. Canada, John Wallace, Bruce Robertson, Michael Forgeron, Darren Barber, Robert Marland, Michael Rascher, Andrew Crosby, Derek Porter, Terrence Paul, 5:29.53
2. Romania, Ioan Iulian Vizitiu, Danut Dobre, Claudiu Gabriel Marin, Iulica Ruican, Viorel

Talapan, Vasile Dorel Nastase, Valentin Robu, Vasile Ionel Mastacan, Marin Gheorghe, 5:29.67

3. Germany, Frank Richter, Thorsten Streppelhoff, Detlef Kirchhoff, Armin Eichholz, Bahne Rabe, Hans Sennewald, Ansgar Wessling, Roland Baar, Manfred Klein, 5:31.00

1988

1. West Germany, 5:46.05, Thomas Moellenkamp, Matthias Mellinghaus, Eckhardt Schultz, Ansgar Wessling, Armin Eichholz, Thomas Domian, Wolfgang Maennig, Bahne Rabe, Manfred Klein
2. Soviet Union, 5:48.01, Vinea Mine Bout, Nikolai Komarov, Vassili Tikhanov, Alexandre Doumtchev, Pavel Gourkovsky, Victor Didouk, Victor Omelianovitch, Andrei Vassiliev, Alexandre Loukianov
3. U.S.A., 5:48.26, Doug Burden, Jeff McLaughlin, Peter Nordell, Edward Patton, John Pescatore, John Rusher, John Smith, Michael Teti

1984

1. Canada, 5:41.32, Pat Turner, Kevin Neufield, Mark Evans, Grant Main, Paul Steele, Mike Evans, Dean Crawford, Blair Horm, Brian McMahon
2. U.S.A., 5:41.74 , Walter Lubsen, Jr., Andrew Sudduth, John Terwilliger, Christopher Penny, Thomas Darling, Earl Borchelt, Charles Clapp III, Bruce Ibbetson, Robert Jaugstetter
3. Australia, 5:43.40, Craig Muller, Clyde Hefer, Sam Patten, Timothy Willoughby, Ian Edmunds, James Battersby, Ion Popa, Steve Evans, Gavin Thredgold

1980

1. East Germany, 5:49.05, Bernd Krauss, Hans-Peter Koppe, Ulrich Kons, Jorg Friedrich, Jens Doberscheutz, Ulrich Karnatz, Uwe Duehring, Bernd Hoing, Klaus-Dieter Ludwig
2. Great Britain, 5:51.92, Duncan McDougall, Allan Whitwell, Henry Clay, Chris Mahoney, Andrew Justice, John Pritchard, Malcolm McGowan, Richard Stanhope, Colin Moynihan
3. Soviet Union, 5:52.66, Viktor Kakoschin, Andrei Tishchenko, Alexandr Tkatschenko, Jonas Pinskus, Jonas Narmontas, Andrei Lugin, Aleksandr Mantsewitsch, Igor Maistrenko, Grigori Dmitrenko

1976

1. East Germany, 5:58.29, Bernd Baumgart, Gottfried Doehn, Werner Kalatt, Hans-

Joachim Lueck, Dieter Wendisch, Roland Kostulski, Ulrich Karnatz, Karl-Heinz Prudoehl, Karl-Heinz Danielowski

2. Great Britain, 6:00.82, Richard Lester, John Yallop, Timothy Crooks, Hugh Matheson, David Maxwell, James Clark, Frederick Smallbone, Leonard Robertson, Patrick Sweeney
3. New Zealand, 6:03.51, Ivan Sutherland, Lindsay Wilson, Athol Earl, Trevor Coker, Dave Roger, Alex McLean, Peter Dignan, Tony Hurt, Simon Ch. Dickie

1972

1. New Zealand, 6:08.94, Tony Hurt, Wybo Veldman, Richard "Dick" Joyce, John Hunter, Lindsay Wilson, Athol Earl, Trevor Coker, Gary Robertson, Simon Dickie
2. U.S.A., 6:11.61, Lawrence Terry, Fritz Hobbs, Peter Raymond, Timothy Mickelson, Eugene Clapp, William Hobbs, Cleve Livingston, Michael Livingston, Paul Hoffman
3. East Germany, 6:11.67, Hans-Joachim Borzym, Jorg Landvoigt, Harold Dimke, Manfred Schneider, Hartmut Schreiber, Manfred Schmorde, Bernd Landvoigt, Heinrich Mederow, Dietmar Schwarz

1968

1. West Germany, 6:07.00, Horst Meyer, Dirk Schreyer, Rudiger Henning, Wolfgang Hottenrott, Lutz Ulbricht, Egbert Hirschfelder, Jorg Siebert, Nico Ott, Gunther Tiersch
2. Australia, 6:07.98, Alfred Duval, Michael Morgan, Joseph Fazio, Peter Dickson, David Douglas, John Ranch, Gary Pearce, Robert Shirlaw, Alan Grover
3. Soviet Union, 6:09.11, Zigmas Yukna, Antanas Bogdanavichus, Vladimir Sterlik, Yosanas Yagelavichus, Aleksandr Martyschkin, Vitautas Briedis, Valentin Kravchuk, Viktor Suslin, Yuri Lorentsson

1964

1. U.S.A., 6:18.23, Joseph Amlong, Thomas Amlong, Harold Budd, Emory Clark, Stanley Cwiklinski, Hugh Foley, William Knecht, William Stowe, Robert Zimonyi
2. West Germany, 6:23.29, Klaus Aeffke, Klaus Bittner, Karl-Heinrich von Groddeck, Hans-Jurgen Wallbrecht, Klaus Behrens, Jurgen Schroder, Jurgen Plagemann, Horst Meyer, Thomas Ahrens
3. Czechoslovakia, 6:25.11, Petr Cermak, Jiri Lundak, Jan Mrvik, Julius Tocek, Josef

Ventus, Ludek Pojezny, Bohumil Janousek, Richard Novy, Miroslav Konicek

1960
1. West Germany, 5:57.18, Manfred Rulffs, Walter Schroder, Frank Schepke, Kraft Schepke, Karl-Heinrich von Groddeck, Karl-Heinz Hopp, Klaus Bittner, Hans Lenk, Willi Padge
2. Canada, 6:01.52, Donald Arnold, Walter D'Hondt, Nelson Kuhn, John Lecky, Lorne Loomer, Archibald McKinnon, William McKerlich, Glen Mervyn, Sohen Biln
3. Czechoslovakia, 6:04.84, Bohumil Janousek, Jan Jindra, Jiri Lundak, Stanislav Lusk, Vaclav Pavkovic, Ludek Pojezny, Jan Sveda, Josef Ventus, Miroslav Konicek

1956
1. U.S.A., 6:35.2, Thomas Charlton, David Wight, John Cooke, Donald Beer, Caldwell Esselstyn, Charles Grimes, Richard Wailes, Robert Morey, William Becklean
2. Canada, 6:37.1, Philip Kueber, Richard McClure, Robert Wilson, David Helliwell, Donald Pretty, William McKerlich, Douglas McDonald, Lawrence West, Carlton Ogawa
3. Australia, 6:39.2, Michael Aikman, David Boykett, Angus Benfield, James Howden, Garth Manton, Walter Howell, Adrian Monger, Bryan Doyle, Harold Hewitt

1952
1. U.S.A., 6:25.9, Franklin Shakespeare, William Fields, James Dunbar, Richard Murphy, Robert Detweiler, Henry Proctor, Wayne Frye, Edward Stevens, Charles Manring
2. Soviet Union, 6:31.2, Yevgeny Brago, Vladimir Rodimuskin, Aleksei Komarov, Igor Borisov, Slava Amiragov, Leonid Gissen, Yevgeny Samsonov, Vladimir Krukov, Igor Polyakov
3. Australia, 6:33.1, Robert Tinning, Ernest Chapman, Nimrod Greenwood, Mervyn Finlay, Edward Pain, Phiip Cayzer, Thomas Chessel, David Anderson, Geoffrey Williamson

1948
1. U.S.A., 5:56.7, Ian Turner, David Turner, James Hardy, George Ahlgren, Lloyd Butler, David Brown, Justus Smith, John Stack, Ralph Purchase
2. Great Britain, 6:06.9, Christopher Barton, Maurice Lapage, Guy Richardson, Paul Bircher, Paul Massey, Charles B. Lloyd, David Meyrick, Andrew Mellows, Jack Dearlove
3. Norway, 6:10.3, Kristoffer Lepsoe, Torstein Krakenes, Hans E. Hansen, Halfdan Gran Olsen, Harald Krakenes, Leif Naess, Thor

Pedersen, Carl H. Monssen, Sigurd Monssen

1936
1. U.S.A., 6:25.4, Herbert Morris, Charles Day, Gordon Adam, John White, James McMillin, George Hunt, Joseph Rantz, Donald Hume, Robert Moch
2. Italy, 6:26.0, Guglielmo Del Bimbo, Dino Barsotti, Oreste Grossi, Enzo Bartolini, Mario Checcacci, Dante Secchi, Ottorino Quaglierini, Enrico Garzelli, Cesare Milani
3. Germany, 6:26.4, Alfred Rieck, Helmut Radach, Hans Kuschke, Heinz Kaufmann, Gerd Vols, Werner Lockle, Hans-Joachim Hannemann, Herbert Schmidt, Wilhelm Mahlow

1932
1. U.S.A., 6:37.6, Edwin Salisbury, James Blair, Duncan Gregg, David Dunlap, Burton Jastram, Charles Chandler, Harold Tower, Winslow Hall, Norris Graham
2. Italy, 6:37.8, Vittorio Cioni, Mario Balleri, Renato Bracci, Dino Barsotti, Roberto Vestrini, Guglielmo Del Bimbo, Enrico Garzelli, Renato Barbieri, Cesare Milani
3. Canada, 6:40.4, Earl Eastwood, Joseph Harris, Stanley Stanyar, Harry Fry, Cedric Liddell, William Thoburn, Donald Boal, Albert Taylor, George MacDonald

1928
1. U.S.A., 6:03.2, Marvin Stalder, John Brinck, Francis Frederick, William Thompson, William Dally, James Workman, Hubert Caldwell, Peter Donlon, Donald Blessing
2. Great Britain, 6:05.6, James Hamilton, Guy O. Nickalls, John Badcock, Donald Gollan, Harold Lane, Gordon Killick, Jack Beresford, Harold West, Arthur Sulley
3. Canada, 6:03.8, Frederick Hedges, Frank Fiddes, John Hand, Herbert Richardson, Jack Murdock, Athol Meech, Edgar Norris , William Ross, John Donnelly

1924
1. U.S.A., 6:33.4, Leonard Carpenter, Howard Kingsbury, Daniel Lindley, John Miller, James Rockefeller, Frederick Sheffield, Benjamin Spock, Alfred Wilson, Laurence Stoddard
2. Canada, 6:49.0, Arthur Bell, Robert Hunter, William Langford, Harold Little, John Smith, Warren Snyder, Norman Taylor, William Wallace, Ivor Campbell
3. Italy, Antonio Cattalinich, Francesco Cattalinich, Simeone Cattalinich, Giuseppe Crivelli, Latino Galasso, Pietro Ivanov, Bruno Sorich, Carlo Toniatti, Vittorio Gliubich

1920

1. U.S.A., 6:02.6, Virgil Jacomini, Edwin Graves, William Jordan, Edward Moore, Allen Sanborn, Donald Johnston, Vincent Gallagher, Clyde King, Sherman Clark
2. Great Britain, 6:05.0, Ewart Horsfall, Guy O. Nickalls, Richard Lucas, Walter James, John Campbell, Sebastian Earl, Ralph Shove, Sidney Swann, Robin Johnstone
3. Norway, 6:36.0, Theodor Nag, Conrad Olsen, Adolf Nilsen, Haakon Ellingsen, Thore Michelsen, Arne Mortensen, Karl Nag, Tollef Tollefsen, Thoralf Hagen

1912

1. Great Britain, 6:15.0, (Leander Club), Edgar Burgess, Sidney Swann, Leslie Wormald, Ewart Horsfall, James Gillan, Arthur Garton, Alister Kirby, Philip Fleming, Henry Wells
2. Great Britain, (New College), William Fison, William Parker, Thomas Gillespie, Beaufort Burdekin, Frederick Pitman, Arthur Wiggins, Charles Littlejohn, Robert Bourne, John Walker
3. Germany, (Berliner R.V. 1876), Otto Liebing, Max Broeske, Max Vetter, Willi Bartholomae, Fritz Bartholomae, Werner Dehn, Rudolf Reichelt, Hans Matthiae, Kurt Runge

1908

1. Great Britain, 7:52.0, (Leander Club), Albert Gladstone, Frederick Kelly, Banner Johnstone, Guy Nickalls, Charles Burnell, Ronald Sanderson, Raymond Etherington-Smith, Henry Bucknall, Gilchrist MacLagan
2. Belgium, (Royal C.N., Gand), Oscar Taelman, Marcel Morimont, Remy Orban, Georges Mijs, Francois Vergucht, Polydore Veirman, Oscar De Somville, Rodolphe Poma, Alfred Valandeghem
3. Canada, (Argonaut R.C.), Irvine Robertson, George F. Wright, Julius A. Thomson, Walter A. Lewis, Gordon B. Balfour, Becher R. Gale, Charles Riddy, Geoffrey Taylor, Douglas E. Kertland
3. Great Britain, (Cambridge University B.C.), Frederick Jerwood, Eric Powell, Guy Carver, Edward Williams, Henry Goldsmith, Harold Kitching, John Burn, Douglas Stuart, Richard Boyle

1906

Not held

1904

1. U.S.A., 7:50.0, (Vesper B.C.), Louis Abell, Joseph F. Dempsey, M.D. Gleason, Frank Schell, James Flanigan, Charles E. Armstrong, Harry H. Lott, Frederick Cresser, John Exley
2. Canada (Argonaut R.C., Toronto), Joseph Wright, Donald MacKenzie, William Wadsworth, George Strange, Phil Boyd, C.R. "Pat" Reiffenstein, Colonel W. Rice, R. Bailey, Thomas Loudon

1900

1. U.S.A., 6:09.8, (Vesper B.C., Philadelphia), Louis Abell, Harry DeBaecke, William Carr, John Exley, John Geiger, Edward Hedley, James Juvenal, Roscoe Lockwood, Edward Marsh
2. Belgium, 6:13.8, (Royal Club Nautique de Gand), Marcel van Crombrugghe, Maurice Hemelsoet, Oscar De Cock, Maurice Verdonck, Prospere Bruggeman, Oscar De Somville, Frank Odberg, Jules De Bisschop, Alfred Vanlandeghem
3. Netherlands, 6:23.0, (Minerva Amsterdam), Walter Mejer Timmerman-Thijssen, Ruurd G. Leegstra, Johannes W. van Dijk, Henricus Tromp, Hendrik K. Offerhaus, Roelof Klein, Francois A. Brandt, Walter Middelberg, Dr. Hermanus Brockmann

1896

Not held

WOMEN'S ROWING EVENTS

Highlights

Rowing events for women were finally included in the Olympic program in 1976. In its short history, women's Olympic rowing has been dominated by Eastern Europeans, including East Germans, Bulgarians, Romanians, and Soviets.

The U.S. women's eights captured a bronze in 1976 ahead of the Canadian eight and behind East Germany and the U.S.S.R. And U.S. single sculler Joan Lind brought a silver medal home from the Montreal Games.

In 1984 the Romanian women stroked to five gold medals and one silver in their six races. That year the U.S. eights team took the gold medal, U.S. single-sculler Charlotte Geer brought home a silver in her event, and the U.S. quadruple sculls crew also rowed to a silver. The Netherlands and Canada medaled in double sculls in 1984, and Canada picked up silvers in the coxless pairs and coxed four, while the Netherlands captured a bronze in the eights.

U.S. single-sculler Anne Marden took the silver medal behind Jutta Behrendt of East Germany in 1988. East Germany pulled away with most of the women's rowing gold in Seoul, except the coxless pair, which went to a Romanian crew.

Highlights from Barcelona

In women's rowing likely medalists for 1992 included athletes from Germany, the Unified Team, Canada, and Romania. When the last bow crossed the line, Canada had captured three gold medals and a bronze. Germany tallied up two gold medals, one silver, and two bronze; Romania picked up one gold and three silver; and the U.S. garnered a silver in women's coxless fours—earned by Shelagh Donohoe, Cindy Eckert, Amy Fuller, and Carol Feeney—and a bronze in coxless pairs—compliments of Anna Seaton and Stephanie Pierson.

Double gold winners on Canada's women's team included Marnie McBean and Kathleen Heddle, besting the field in both coxless pairs and coxed eights, and Kirsten Barnes, Brenda Taylor, Jessica Monroe, and Kay Worthington, taking the top spot in both coxless fours and coxed eights. Also turning in golden performances on Canada's women's coxed eights were Megan Delehanty and Shannon Crawford. Canada's bronze medal came in women's single sculls, in a stunning comeback-from-injury upset by Silken Laumann.

Medalists

Rowing—Women's Single Sculls

1992
1. Elisabeta Lipa, Romania, 7:25.54
2. Annelies Bredael, Belgium, 7:26.64
3. Silken Laumann, Canada, 7:28.85

1988
1. Jutta Behrendt, East Germany, 7:47.19
2. Anne Marden, U.S.A., 7:50.28
3. Magdalena Gueorguieva, Bulgaria, 7:53.65

1984
1. Valeria Racila, Romania, 3:40.68
2. Charlotte Geer, U.S.A., 3:43.89
3. Ann Haesebrouck, Belgium, 3:45.72

1980
1. Sanda Toma, Romania, 3:40.69
2. Antonina Makhina, Soviet Union, 3:41.65
3. Martina Schroeter, East Germany 3:43.54

1976
1. Christine Scheiblich, East Germany, 4:05.56
2. Joan Lind, U.S.A., 4:06.21
3. Elena Antonova, Soviet Union, 4:10.24

Rowing—Women's Double Sculls

1992
1. Germany, Kerstin Koeppen, Kathrin Boron, 6:49.00
2. Romania, Veronica Cochelea, Elisabeta Lipa, 6:51.47
3. China, Gu Xiaoli, Lu Huali, 6:55.16

1988
1. East Germany, 7:00.48, Birgit Peter, Martina Schroeter
2. Romania, 7:04.36, Elisabeta Lipa, Veronica Cogeanu
3. Bulgaria, 7:06.03, Violeta Ninova, Stefka Madina

1984
1. Romania, 3:26.75, Manoara Popescu, Elisabeta Oleniuc
2. Netherlands, 3:29.13, Greet Hellemans, Nicolette Hellemans
3. Canada, 3.29.82, Daniele Laumann, Silken Laumann

1980
1. Soviet Union, 3:16.27, Yelena Khloptseva, Larissa Popova
2. East Germany, 3:17.63, Cornelia Linse, Heidi Westphal
3. Romania, 3:18.91, Olga Homeghi, Valeria Rosca

1976
1. Bulgaria, 3:44.38, Svetla Ozetova, Zdravko Yordanova-Barboulova
2. East Germany, 3:47.86, Sabine Jahn, Petra Boesler
3. Soviet Union, 3:49.93, Leonora Kaminskaite, Genovaite Ramoshkene

Rowing—Women's Coxless Pairs

1992
1. Canada, Marnie McBean, Kathleen Heddle, 7:06.22
2. Germany, Stefani Werremeier, Ingeburg Schwerzmann, 7:07.96
3. U.S.A., Anna Seaton, Stephanie Pierson, 7:08.11

1988
1. Romania, 7:28.13, Rodica Arba, Olga Homeghi
2. Bulgaria, 7:31.95, Radka Stoyanova, Lalka Berberova
3. New Zealand, 7:35.68, Nicola Payne, Lynley Hannen

1984
1. Romania, 3:32.60, Rodica Arba, Elena Horvat
2. Canada, 3:36.06, Betty Craig, Tricia Smith
3. West Germany, 3:40.50, Ellen Becker, Iris Volkner

1980
1. East Germany, 3:30.49, Ute Steindorf, Cornelia Klier
2. Poland, 3:30.95, Malgorzata Dluzewska, Czeslawa Koscianska
3. Bulgaria, 3:32.39, Siika Barboulova, Stoianka Kurbatova

1976
1. Bulgaria, 4:01.22, Siika Kelbecheva-Barboulova, Stoyanka Grouicheva
2. East Germany, 4:01.64, Angelica Noack, Sabine Daehne
3. West Germany, 4:02.35, Edith Eckbauer, Thea Einoeder

Rowing—Women's Coxless Fours

1992
1. Canada, Kirsten Barnes, Brenda Taylor, Jessica Monroe, Kay Worthington, 6:30.85
2. U.S.A., Shelagh Donohoe, Cindy Eckert, Amy Fuller, Carol Feeney, 6:31.86
3. Germany, Antje Frank, Gabriele Mehl, Birte Siech, Annette Hohn, 6:32.34

Rowing—Women's Quadruple Sculls

1992
1. Germany, Kerstin Mueller, Sybille Schmidt, Birgit Peter, Kristina Mundt, 6:20.18
2. Romania, Constanta Pipota, Doina Ignat, Veronica Cochelea, Anisoara Dobre, 6:24.34
3. Unified Team, Ekaterina Khodotovitch, Antonina Zelikovitch, Tatiana Oustioujanina, Elena Khloptseva, 6:25.07

1988
1. East Germany, 6:21.06, Kerstin Foerster, Kristina Mundt, Beate Schramm, Jana Sorgers
2. Soviet Union, 6:23.47, Irina Kalimbet, Svetlana Mazyi, Inna Frolova, Antonina Doumtcheva
3. Romania, 6:23.81, Anisoara Balan, Anisoara Minea, Veronica Cogeanu, Elisabeta Lipa

1984

1. Romania, 3:14.11, Maricica Taran, Anisoara Sorohan, Ioana Badea, Sofia Corban, Ecaterina Oancia
2. U.S.A., 3:15.57, Anne Marden, Lisa Rohde, Joan Lind, Virginia Gilder, Kelly Rickon
3. Denmark, 3:16.02, Hanne Mandsf Eriksen, Birgitte Hanel, Charlotte Koefoed, Bodil Steen Rasmussen, Jette Hejli Soerensen

1980

1. East Germany, 3:15.32, Sybille Reinhardt, Jutta Ploch, Jutta Lau, Roswietha Zobelt, Liane Buhr-Weigelt
2. Soviet Union, 3:15.73, Antonina Pustovit, Yelena Matievskaya, Olga Vasilchenko, Nadezhda Lyubimova, Nina Cheremisina
3. Bulgaria, 3:16.10, Mariana Serbezova, Roumeliana Boneva, Dolores Nakova, Ani Bakova, Stanka Georgieva

1976

1. East Germany, 3:29.99, Anke Borchmann, Jutta Lau, Viola Kowalschek-Poley, Roswietha Zobelt, Liane Buhr-Weigelt
2. Soviet Union, 3:32.49, Anna Kondrachina, Mira Bryunina, Larissa Aleksandrova, Galina Ermolaeva, Nadezhda Chernyscheva
3. Romania, 3:32.76, Ioana Tudoran, Maria Micsa, Felicia Afrasiloaia, Elisabeta Lazar, Elena Giurca

Rowing—Women's Coxed Fours

1992

Not held

1988

1. East Germany, 6:56.00, Martina Walther, Gerlinde Doberschuetz, Carola Hornig, Birte Siech, Sylvia Rose
2. People's Republic of China, 6:58.78, Zhang Xianghua, Hu Yadong, Yang Xiao, Zhou Shouying, Li Ronghua
3. Romania, 7:01.13, Marioara Trasca, Veronica Necula, Herta Anitas, Doina Iilian Balan, Escatering Oancia

1984

1. Romania, 3:19.30, Florica Lavric, Maria Fricioiu, Chira Apostol, Olga Bularda, Viorica Ioja
2. Canada, 3:21.55, Marilyn Brain, Angie Schneider, Barbara Armbrust, Jane Tregunno, Lesley Thompson
3. Australia, 3:23.29, Robyn Grey-Gardner, Karen Brancourt, Susan Chapman, Margot Foster, Susan Lee

1980

1. East Germany, 3:19.27, Ramona Kapheim, Silvia Frohlich, Angelika Noack, Romy Saalfeld, Kirsten Wenzel
2. Bulgaria, 3:20.75, Ginka Gurova, Mariika Modeva, Rita Todorova, Iskra Velinova, Nadezhda Filipova
3. Soviet Union, 3:20.92, Maria Fadeyeva, Galina Sovetnikova, Marina Studneva, Svetlana Semyonova, Nina Cheremisina

1976

1. East Germany, 3:45.08, Karin Metze, Bianka Borrman-Schwede, Gavrielle Koehn-Lohs, Andrea Kurth-Sredzki, Sabine Schubert-Hess
2. Bulgaria, 3:48.24, Guinka Guiourova, Liliana Vasseva, Reni Yordahova, Mariika Modeva, Kapka Georguieva-Panayotova
3. Soviet Union, 3:49.38, Nadezhda Sevostyanova, Ljudmila Korkhina, Galina Mishenina, Anna Pasokha, Lydia Krylova

1896–1972

Not held

Rowing—Women's Eight Oars

1992

1. Canada, Kirsten Barnes, Brenda Taylor, Megan Delehanty, Shannon Crawford, Marnie McBean, Kay Worthington, Jessica Monroe, Kathleen Heddle, Lesley Thompson, 6:02.62
2. Romania, Doina Snep, Doina Robu, Ioana Olteanu, Victoria Lepadatu, Iulia Bobeica, Viorica Neculai, Adriana Bazon, Maria Padurariu, Elena Georgescu, 6:06.26
3. Germany, Annegret Strauch, Sylvia Doerdelmann, Kathrin Haacker, Dana Pyritz, Cerstin Petersmann, Ute Wagner, Christiane Harzendorf, Judith Zeidler, Daniela Neunast, 6:07.80

1988

1. East Germany, 6:15.17, Annegret Strauch, Judith Zeidler, Kathrin Haacker, Ute Wild, Anja Kluge, Beatrix Schroer, Ramona Balthasar, Uta Stange, Daniela Neunast
2. Romania, 6:17.44, Doina Lilian Balan, Marioara Trasca, Veronica Necula, Herta Anitas, Adriana Bazon, Mihaela Armasescu, Rodica Arba, Olga Homeghi, Ecaterina Oancia
3. People's Republic of China, 6:21.83, Xiuhua Zhou, Yali Zhang, Yanwen He, Yaqin Han, Xianghua Zhang, Shouhging Zhou, Xiao Yang, Yadong Hu

1984
1. U.S.A., 2:59.80, Shyril O'Steen, Harriet Metcalf, Caroll Bower, Carie Graves, Jeanne Flanagan, Kristine Norellus, Kristen Thorsness, Kathryn Keeler, Betsy Beard
2. Romania, 3:00.87, Doina Balan, Marioara Trasca, Aurora Plesca, Aneta Mihaly, Adriana Chelariu, Mihaela Armasescu, Camelia Diaconescu, Lucia Sauca, Viorica Ioja
3. Netherlands, 3:02.92, Nicolette Hellemans, Lynda Cornet, Harriet Van Ettekoven, Greet Hellemans, Marieke Van Drogenbroek, Anne Marie Quist, Catharina Neelissen, Willemien Vaandrager, Martha Laurijsen

1980
1. East Germany, 3:03.32, Martina Boesler, Kersten Neisser, Christiane Kopke, Birgit Schutz, Gabriele Kuhn, Ilona Richter, Marita Sandig, Karin Metze, Marina Wilke
2. Soviet Union, 3:04.29, Olga Pivovarova, Nina Umanets, Nadezhda Prishchepa, Valentina Zhulina, Tatyana Stetsenko, Yelena Tereshina, Nina Preobrazhenskaya, Mariya Pazyun, Nina Frolova
3. Romania, 3:05.63, Angelica Aposteanu, Marlena Zagoni, Rodica Frintu, Florica Bucur, Rodica Puscatu, Ana Illiuta, Maria Constantinescu, Elena Bondar, Elena Dobritoiu

1976
1. East Germany, 3:33.32, Viola Landroight-Goretzki, Christiane Koepe-Knetsch, Ilona Doerfel-Richter, Brigitte Ahrenholz, Monika Leschhorn-Kallies, Henrietta Ebert, Helma Lehmann, Irina Weisse-Mueller, Marina Jaehrling-Wilke
2. Soviet Union, 3:36.17, Lyubov Talalayeva, Nadezhda Roshchina, Klavdiya Kozenkova, Elena Zubko, Olga Kolkova, Nelli Tarakanova, Nadezhda Rozgon, Olga Guzenko, Olga Pugovskaya
3. U.S.A., 3:38.68, Jacqueline Zoch, Anita DeFrantz, Carie Graves, Marion Greig, Anne Warner, Peggy McCarthy, Carol Brown, Gail Ricketson, Lynn Silliman

Trivia Quiz

1. The first U.S. inter-collegiate event, the Harvard/Yale boat race, was held
a. In 1895, the year before the first Olympic Games
b. In 1892, the year the International Federation of Rowing Societies was formed
c. In 1852, the year of the second Burmese war

2. Before J.C. Babcock invented a seat on rollers in 1857, rowers
a. Greased their pants to facilitate sliding on the seat
b. Used oatmeal to facilitate sliding on the seat
c. Used WD-40 to facilitate sliding on the seat

3. All boats in competitive rowing are called shells, and whether or not a shell is a scull depends on
a. Who you're talking to   b. The arrangement of the oars
c. The hull design

4. The coxswain's role is
a. To steer by means of a rudder and coach the rowers
b. To steer by means of a sweep-oar and coach the rowers
c. To sing lullabies to the crew

5. Olympic races are run on
a. A 2,000m course   b. A 1,500m course   c. Courses of varying lengths

6. A scull powered by eight rowers can travel

a. At speeds up to 18 mph   **b.** At speeds up to 13 mph

c. At speeds equal to those of recreational jet-skis

7. Three-time Olympic rowing gold medalist John Kelly was also

a. The mayor of New York, later in life

b. A silver medalist in the bobsled   **c.** The father of Grace Kelly

8. Rowing first appeared in the Olympics

a. As a demonstration event in 1896

b. As a full-medal sport at the Stockholm Games in 1912

c. As an exhibition event at the London Games in 1908

9. The 1924 U.S. eights crew, which won that year's gold medal, included

a. Linus Pauling, the 1954 Nobel laureate

b. Benjamin Spock, a Yale medical student

c. Franz Bibfeldt, a University of Chicago divinity student

10. The sweep rower

a. Pulls the oar with both hands as he or she rows on one side of the boat

b. Sits in the rear of the boat, just ahead of the coxswain

c. Dusts off the boat before competition

Answers: 1-c; 2-a and -b; 3-b; 4-a; 5-a; 6-b; 7-c; 8-a; 9-b; 10-a.

SHOOTING

Warm-up

Shooting competitions began in the fourteenth century. Not so coincidentally, the firearm was invented during this period as well. The first documented shooting contest was held in 1477 in Eichstadt, Germany, using blunderbusses. After pistols were developed, handguns became standard equipment in the military, and competitions eventually involved both rifles and handguns.

Shooting is a traditional Olympic event. In the 1896 Games in Athens, five shooting events were included among the nine sports on the program. Also included in the 1900 Games at Paris, these first Olympic shooting contests served as a prelude to the emergence and organization of shooting as an international sport. Shooting is also part of the Biathlon, a Winter Games event, and the Modern Pentathlon, another Summer Games event.

In 1907, eight countries established the Union Internationale de Tir (UIT), which became the governing body of the sport, at the Swiss Federal Shooting Festival in Zurich. The founding nations were Argentina, Austria, Belgium, France, Greece, Italy, the Netherlands, and Switzerland. Annual world championships were developed under the guidance of this organization, with programs devoted exclusively to rifle shooting at 300 meters and pistol matches at 50 meters.

By 1913, eleven nations took part in a World Championship event at Camp Perry, near Port Clinton, Ohio. Shooting contests involving many more contestants (known as World Wars I and II) interrupted the World Championships and temporarily disrupted the UIT, which remains the ruling body of international shooting competitions.

Although shooting is a traditional Olympic event, the sport has changed a great deal over the years. International, or Olympic-style, shooting combines aspects of its military origins with a more leisurely and European aristocratic tradition. Over the years, preparation and training has moved away from shooting's original military orientation to an emphasis today placed entirely on shooting as a sport.

From the five original events included in the 1896 Olympic Games to the 13 events scheduled for the 1996 Games in Atlanta, the number of events as well as the number of competitors has changed constantly. For example, while nine shooting events were held at the 1972 Games at Munich, a reduction to seven was made at the 1976 Montreal and 1980 Moscow Games. In Los Angeles in 1984, the number of events shot up to 11, including the air rifle for men.

An historic first was created at LA, when three women-only events were added: standard rifle, air rifle, and pistol match. In 1976 at Montreal, women were allowed to compete in the men's events, and Margaret Murdock of the United States won a silver medal in the three-position competition. The 1968 Games were also notable for the addition of skeet shooting to the program, an event that traces its origins to the United States.

Adding to the continual change and development of the sport are technical improvements to guns, ammunition, and equipment. Modern forms of training and the steady increase in the number of participating nations ensure that the sport continues to evolve.

FACT: A banner year, the 1992 Games saw Olympic record performances in every event except the men's free pistol. The Unified Team's Iouri Fedkine set a final Olympic record in the air rifle, the first for the newly introduced air target. Michael Jakosits offered Germany a berth in the record books, setting an Olympic record of 580 in the preliminaries and another final record of 673 to capture the running game target gold.

Spectator's Guide

The 1996 Olympic Games will include 15 medal events in four disciplines: Rapid-fire pistol, trap, skeet, and running target competitions offer viewers the most exciting experience. Time, distance, and precision are the key factors in shooting.

Medal winners in each event are determined in a final-round. The top eight finishers in rifle and pistol events, and the top six in running target, fire a 10-shot final round under strict time limits. In the shotgun events, the top six compete in a 25-target final round.

In all finals except shotgun events, each competitor's score is announced to spectators, and aggregate place-standings are tabulated after every shot. In rifle and pistol events, targets are scored in tenths of a point, with 10.9 being a perfect shot.

If scores are tied at the end of a final, then a sudden-death shoot-off is fired.

In Atlanta, 430 athletes are expected to compete in the shooting competition at Wolf Creek Shooting Range.

Air Pistol: Separate men's and women's events are held with air or gas-powered .177 caliber pistols from 10 meters. One shot is fired per target, a bullseye with a one-half inch ten-ring. The course of fire is 60 shots in one hour and 45 minutes for men; 40 shots in one hour and 15 minutes for women. A perfect score is 600 for men (585 is considered a world-class score); 400 for women (385 is considered world-class).

Free Pistol: This men's event is shot with a .22 caliber pistol. Regulations require only that it be a .22 caliber pistol with metallic sights. This is the only Olympic-style pistol event fired at 50 meters, and shooters fire five shots per target, a bullseye with a two-inch 10-ring. The course of fire is 60 shots in two hours. A perfect score is 600, with 565 as world class.

Rapid-fire Pistol: Using a .22 caliber pistol from 25 meters, men fire one shot at each of five adjacent targets. The targets, a bullseye with a four-inch center, begin on edge and then turn to face the competitor for either eight, six, or four seconds. As an added difficulty, competitors must hold their pistols downward at a 45-degree angle until the targets turn to face them. The course of fire is 60 shots, fired in two courses of 30 shots; in each course, competitors twice fire five shots in eight seconds, six seconds, then four seconds. A perfect score is 600, with 592 as world class.

Sport Pistol: Women fire .22 caliber standard pistols from 25 meters. The course of fire is 60 shots, divided into a 30-shot precision phase and a 30-shot rapid-fire stage. The precision, or slow-fire stage, is fired in six series of five shots, and competitors are allowed six minutes per series. In the 30-shot rapid-fire stage, the target, a bullseye with a four-inch center for duel (and a two-inch center for precision), begins on edge, turns to face the shooter for three seconds, then turns away for seven seconds. A perfect score is 600, with 585 as world class.

Men's Smallbore Free Rifle Prone: This event is shot at 50 meters with .22 caliber rifles weighing up to 17.6 pounds. Athletes fire one shot per target, a bullseye with a 10.4 millimeter center (roughly the size of a dime), from the prone (lying down) position. As with all rifle events described, metallic sights are used.

The course of fire is 60 shots in one hour and 30 minutes. A perfect score is 600, with 597 as world class. Smallbore competition flourished during the Depression—between the World Wars—when smallbore ammunition was the easiest to afford.

Three-Position: Separate events are fired for men and women. Men use .22 caliber free rifles not weighing more than 17.6 pounds. Women fire .22 caliber standard rifles not exceeding 12 pounds. The target, a bullseye with a 10.4 millimeter center, is fired upon from the prone, standing, and kneeling positions. Athletes fire one shot per target from 50 meters. The course of fire is 120 shots for men—40 shots per position with the following time limits: one and one-quarter hour for prone, one hour and 45 minutes for standing, and one and one-half hours for kneeling. 60 shots for women—20 per position. Women are allowed a total of two and one-half hours for all three positions. A perfect score is 1200 for men, with 1165 as world class; 600 for women, with 580 as world class.

Air Rifle: Separate events are fired for men and women, with all competitors firing air- or gas-powered .177 caliber rifles weighing up to 12 pounds. Competitors fire one shot per target, a bullseye with a one-half millimeter center (roughly the size of the head of a pin), from a standing position at a distance of 10 meters. The course of fire is 60 shots in one hour and 45 minutes for men; 40 shots in one hour and 15 minutes for women. A perfect score is 600 for men, with 590 as world class; 400 for women, with 393 as world class.

Running Target: Men shoot .177 caliber air rifles with telescopic sights (not exceeding four-power) at paper targets moving across a track ten meters away. The target has two bullseyes spaced roughly six inches apart; an aiming dot placed between them aids the shooter in tracking. The course of fire is 60 shots divided into 30 slow runs (5 seconds to track, aim, and fire) and 30 fast runs (2.5 seconds to track, aim, and fire). A perfect score is 600, with 575 as world class.

Trap: Along with skeet, trap is a men-only event for the 1996 Games. In trap breakable four-inch clay targets are thrown from an underground bunker a minimum distance of 70 meters and at speeds of up to 65 miles per hour. Competitors mount their shotguns on their shoulders before calling for the target and are allowed two shots per target. The course of fire is 125 targets in five rounds of 25. Three rounds are fired on day one; two rounds plus the 25 target final are fired on day two. A perfect score is 125, with 121 as world class.

Skeet: Skeet will be a men-only competition in 1996, with competitors using 12-gauge shotguns. Single or double clay targets are thrown at least 65 meters from the high or low house on either side of the semicircular field. Competitors fire one shot per target from each of eight stations. Unlike international trap, the competitor must hold the shotgun at hip level until the target appears, which can be anywhere from 0–3 seconds after called. The course of fire is same as trap. A perfect score is same as trap.

Double Trap: The men's and women's double trap events are first-time additions to the Olympic program in 1996. Competitors fire 12-gauge shotguns from each of five adjacent shooting stations. At each station, four-inch clay targets are thrown two at a time— at speeds of up to 50 miles per hour—from an underground bunker. Competitors get one shot per target. Men fire three rounds of 50 for a total of 150 targets. Women shoot three rounds of 40 for a 120-target total. For men, 135 is world-class; for women, it's 100.

In both events, the top six competitors advance to a final— 50 targets for men, 40 for women. Medals are awarded based on aggregate (match plus final) scores. The perfect aggregate score is 200 for men and 160 for women.

For all events, medal winners in each event are determined by match score plus finals score. The top eight finishers in rifle and pistol events and the top six in running target fire a 10-shot final round under strict time limits. In the shotgun events, the top six compete in a 25-target final round.

Them's Shootin' Words

Airgun: A gun that discharges lead pellets through compressed air or carbon dioxide.

Bore: The interior diameter of a gun barrel.

Bull: The central blackened portion of a target that appears as a dot to the shooter who is taking aim. The center ring is a ten or "bullseye."

Bunker (in trapshooting): The underground "dugout" in front of the firing line that houses the clay target throwing machine.

Caliber: The interior diameter of a rifle or pistol barrel.

Cartridge: The complete unit of ammunition, including the projectile, case, powder, and primer.

Challenge: A shooter's petition that a target be rescored.

Chamber: The rear portion of the gun barrel into which a cartridge is inserted for firing.

Crossfire: A shot accidentally fired on a target assigned to another competitor.

Firing Line: The line from which competitors position themselves to shoot their targets.

Free Pistol: A .22 caliber pistol relatively "free" of restrictions.

Free Rifle: A smallbore or centerfire rifle used in international competition that is relatively "free" of restrictions.

Metallic Sight: Includes the devices on the front and rear ends of a gun barrel used to assist aim.

Offhand: Another term for the standing shooting position.

Pits: In .22 caliber firing ranges, are the man-made berms or walls rising behind the targets to absorb bullets.

Sighters: Are practice shots fired at the beginning of a match to check sight adjustments; they do not count in the match score.

String: A series of shots, normally five or ten.

Stock: The wooden, metal, plastic, or fiberglass portion of a rifle or shotgun, to which the barrel, action, trigger assembly, etc., are seated.

Ten-ring: The innermost ring of the black section of the target.

Hopefuls

Deena Wigger

Lones Wigger, a rifle gold-medalist at the 1964 and 1972 Olympics knew early on that his daughter, Deena, a Comeback Kid candidate in Atlanta, had a golden eye.

"The first time we put her on the sandbag—she laid the rifle on a sandbag to shoot—she took a long time getting set up," he told the *Denver Post*. "She wouldn't shoot the shot until everything was perfect."

After Deena, then 12, squeezed off five shots, Lones took a look at the results.

"The five-shot group looked like one hole," he said. "That was a pretty good indication that she was going to do well."

She did, in fact. Deena, now 29 (b. August 27, 1966), went on to win a spot in rifle on the 1988 Olympic team.

What followed for Wigger, whose shooting résumé ripples with gold, silver, and bronze medals earned at various national and international competitions, was disappointment—and perhaps her first serious brush with one of the realities of shooting:

In shooting, your body generally doesn't betray you, but your mind might.

With her father along as team manager, Wigger finished ninth at the Seoul Olympics.

"I was real nervous before I went to the '88 Games and I didn't know how to deal with it," Wigger says. "I shot safe. I didn't shoot to win. I was real disappointed and started thinking, 'Here my dad did it so many times and I was too scared to do it.' I started thinking it wasn't natural for me. I didn't shoot (after that) for quite a while."

"Disappointment is the toughest thing to learn," says Wigger, who won a gold medal at the 1983 Pan Am Games in her first international competition, then led her college team at Murray State University to the NCAA championships in 1987. "I was in the top two nationally for awhile. It wasn't difficult for me to make a team, to win a medal. But once you get into the leading position, you have more to lose. When you're first starting out, all you can see is what's ahead. You don't look back."

That analysis underscores the real mystique of the sport, says Bob Foth, a U.S. silver medalist at the Barcelona Games.

The truth of the matter is that shooting is a sport that doesn't discriminate. You don't need height, power, weight. You don't need speed, incredible acceleration or some sort of astronomical vertical jump. Women and men compete side-by-side in collegiate competitions.

"But it's a very personal challenge," Foth says. "It's a very difficult sport to compete in at the highest level."

That goes along with an old shooting bromide that takes various shapes, but generally goes something like this:

"The rifle has the firepower, the mind has the winning power."

Add to that mental challenge the fact that the targets, Foth says, "are so small that your heartbeat can move you out of contention."

Indeed, shooters wear several layers of clothing to insulate their heartbeats.

It is ironic, then, that Wigger, who failed to make the 1992 Olympic team in another disappointment finally decided to listen to hers.

Wigger, who earned a marketing degree from Murray State, while winning eight collegiate All-American honors, later became a resident athlete at the Olympic Training Center in Colorado Springs. She later questioned that decision.

"I don't think it was the answer for me because all I did was shoot all the time," she told the *Fort Benning Leader*. "I was shooting seven hours a day and that became my life. Before, I had things going on and my main priority was school. And I think shooting should be a priority, but I don't think it should be the only thing you have going. I think that when that happens and you don't have a good competition, you seem to put all your self-worth into the competition."

Says Foth: "Kids just starting out can get tired of it. You really have to watch the training levels, because most of it is mental."

In fact, Wigger's entire life felt affected. She also told the *Benning Leader* that it was hard for her to feel good about herself while training, because she wasn't making any money. "You're almost stagnant for those years when you're training for the Olympics," she said. "It's like you're not making progress in other areas of your life."

Wigger eventually took action to remedy that feeling. She enlisted in the Wyoming Air National Guard in 1994, then entered active duty in the Air Force last summer (1995). While in the Air Force, she will serve as an assistant coach for the Air Force Academy Rifle Team, with an eye on training hopefuls for the Olympics. She has further plans for either officer candidate school or a master's degree.

And, oh yes, she won a gold medal in the 1995 Pan Am Games, earning the U.S. a rifle slot in the Olympics, which seems to indicate that Deena Wigger is right back on track. Or, better, yet, on *target*.

—Eric Kinkopf

Schedule

The tentative shooting schedule is:

Saturday, July 20
Women's 10m air rifle preliminaries & final
Men's trap preliminaries
Men's 10m air pistol preliminaries & final

Sunday, July 21
Men's trap preliminaries & final
Women's 10m air pistol preliminaries & final

Monday, July 22
Men's 10m air rifle preliminaries & final

Tuesday, July 23
Men's 50m free pistol preliminaries & final

Women's double trap preliminaries & final

Wednesday, July 24
Women's 50m 3x20 rifle preliminaries & final
Men's double trap preliminaries & final
Men's 25m rapid-fire pistol preliminaries

Thursday, July 25
Men's 50m prone rifle preliminaries & final
Men's 10m run target preliminaries
Men's 25m rapid-fire pistol preliminaries & final

Friday, July 26
Women's 25m sport pistol preliminaries &
final
Men's 10m run target preliminaries &
final
Men's skeet preliminaries

Saturday, July 27
Men's 50m 3x40 rifle preliminaries &
final
Men's skeet preliminaries & final

Highlights

Shooting events were sure to be included among the nine original sports in the Olympics, since Baron de Coubertin, the founder of the Modern Games, had been a pistol-shooter in his youth. The first Olympic gold medalist was Pantelis Karasevdas, from Greece, in the free rifle event. Greece took two other golds in 1896, and America won the two remaining events.

Perhaps the most memorable—if somewhat distasteful—victory in 1900 was that of Léon de Lunden, from Belgium, who became an Olympic victor for slaying a record 21 pigeons in the one-and-only live pigeon shooting event. France—who entered 173 participants—and Switzerland dominated the other events that year.

Shooting was omitted from the program in 1904, but returned for the London Games in 1908, when seventy competitors from the host country participated. The Russians, who had alerted officials that they would be competing, arrived in time to help with the clean-up. Following the Julian calendar, rather than the Gregorian calendar—which the Games followed—they arrived twelve days late. In the Russians' absence, Oscar Swahn won his first Olympic gold medal, in running deer shooting, a discontinued event. The sixty-year-old Swede hadn't experienced his last Olympic victory. Swahn medaled in the same event in 1920 and again in 1924, the final time this event was held.

In 1908, the U.S. dominated the military revolver teams event, which was later discontinued. The 1912 and 1920 Games were an exercise in déjà vu: American Alfred Lane and marine Sergeant Morris Fisher won more than one gold . . . at both Games. Also in 1912, the ten-time Russian pistol champion, Nikolai Kolomenkin, placed eighth in the free pistol event; not as impressive as his gold medal as a figure skater in the 1908 Games. The 1920 free pistol event was marked by good sportsmanship: Brazilian Alfranio da Costa won silver with a pistol lent to him by the American team. Alfred Lane, who had given da Costa his ammunition, came in third.

Perhaps the most noteworthy shooting event of the 1924 Games was the rapid-fire shooting event. When 8 of the 55 competitors achieved perfect scores, another round was called; this, too, produced eight perfect scores. Yet another round was called. This went on until the sixth round, when two shooters still maintained perfect scores. In the final round, Henry Bailey, a U.S. Marine Corps sergeant, lost part of his eight seconds removing a cartridge from his .22, which had malfunctioned. Nevertheless, his five remaining shots were on target—enough to earn him the 1924 gold medal.

No shooting events appeared in the 1928 Games, but the sport returned—although with only two events—in 1932. Yet another good sportsman brightened the 1932 LA Games: Hungarian Antonius Lemberkovits hit a bullseye in the smallbore rifle, prone event, but was credited with a complete miss because he alerted judges that he had aimed at the wrong target. In the same event in the 1936 Games, Norwegian Willy Rögeberg captured the gold with a perfect-300 score, the first such score to be recorded in international competition.

In 1948, Hungarian Károly Tákacs—the European pistol champion of the 1930s—won the rapid-fire pistol event, and won it again in 1952, becoming one of only five competitors to have defended an Olympic shooting title successfully. What is most unusual about Tákacs, though, is that he won the event left-handed; originally a right-handed shooter, he lost the use of his right arm when a grenade exploded in his hand in 1938, during army training.

In 1952, Canadian George Généreux won the gold medal in the trap shooting event by one point; Swede Knut Holmquist, who missed the penultimate shot of his last round, earned the silver medal, while his compatriot, Hans Liljedahl, won the bronze. Winning the event at age seventeen, Généreux became the youngest gold medalist in the sport of shooting. Also at the Helsinki Games, Huelet Benner became the first American in 32 years to win a pistol event.

At the 1956 Games, Gerald Ouellette won the smallbore, prone event and set a world record—they thought—with a perfect-600 score. When the course was discovered to measure $48\frac{1}{2}$m instead of the standard 50m, Ouellette's record was disallowed.

In 1960, American William McMillan won the rapid-fire pistol event, and went on to a record of competing in six games. Swede Torsten Ullman, who had won the free pistol event in Berlin, placed in the top ten of the event in every Games up to and including the Rome Games, where he finished fourth at the age of 52. Finland's Pentti Linnosvuo won the gold medal in the rapid-fire pistol event; having won the free pistol event in 1956, he became the second shooter in the history of the Games to win the gold in both events.

Women competed in shooting for the first time in 1968, albeit without separate categories. Poland, Peru, and Mexico each entered one woman in the men's events; the first to compete, Nuria Ortiz of Mexico finished thirteenth in the skeet event. The 1972 smallbore, prone event winner, Ho Jun Li, from North Korea, made history not so much for his medal as for his professed secret to success: he claimed to pretend to aim at a capitalist.

In the year 1976 the sport of shooting inducted a member into the Hall of Shame: Paul Cerutti of Monaco—who finished 43rd out of 44 competitors—was disqualified for drug use. At 65 years old, Cerutti is the oldest Games competitor, as far as records indicate, to have been disqualified for drug use. Also that year, American Margaret Murdock became the first woman to medal in shooting.

The U.S.S.R. and East Germany swept the Moscow Games: the Soviets took three golds, a silver, and a bronze, while the East Germans took five silvers and a bronze. In the smallbore rifle, prone event, Hungarian Károly Varga captured the gold despite having broken his shooting hand just prior to the Games.

In 1984, the U.S. cultivated a bumper crop in terms of medals: two gold, one silver, and one bronze medal went to the U.S. men's team, while a gold and a bronze went to the U.S. women—who, at long last, competed in their own classes. China boasted an even better year: Xu Heifing captured the gold medal for pistol shooting, and five other medals went to the Chinese team, including two more golds.

1988 produced the first Olympic shooter to win consecutive medals in the men's smallbore rifle, three position event. Malcolm Cooper, from Great Britain, outshot his countryman Alister Allan by 3.7 points, in his second victory over Allan, who had placed third in 1984. The U.S. men's team took home only one medal from Seoul—Edward Etzel's smallbore free rifle, prone—and the U.S. women failed to medal at all.

Highlights from Barcelona

Olympic history was made in Barcelona as skeet shooter Zhang Shan set an Olympic record by notching 223 points out of a possible 225, having nailed a perfect score of 200 in the preliminary rounds. But that wasn't the only Olympic first the Shanghai student scored. Zhang, at 24, is the first woman ever to beat a man to an Olympic shooting title. Pity is, she's also the last. Since not many women qualify against men for the big shootouts, the International Shooting Union has since ruled to do away with mixed meets.

Competing in her first international competition, air rifle shooter Kab-Soon Yeo landed Korea's first gold in women's shooting when she beat Bulgarian veteran Vesela Letcheva in the final. Both shared a claim in an Olympic record, having tied at 396 in the preliminary round. Aranka Binder, who competed as an Independent Olympic Participant, settled for bronze, only 0.2 points behind Letcheva.

The U.S. women fared well in Barcelona, thanks to Launi Meili's three-position win against the heavily favored European shooters. With a 683.4-point total that included a perfect 200 prone, Meili bagged the nation's first gold in that event (missing the world record by 0.6 points).

FACT: Until 1992, shooting, equestrian, and yachting were the only international sports to allow mixed-gender competition. The International Shooting Union, the sport's governing body, has since ruled to drop mixed meets.

Meanwhile, with six shooters in the finals, and three in the semifinals, the U.S. men collected only one medal. Avenging his disappointing performance in the air rifle event, Robert Foth captured the silver in the men's three-position smallbore rifle, having led the event until the last of the ten shots. And Darius "Doc" Young settled for a fourth-place finish in the men's free pistol—out of the medals, but right on the mark for the best U.S. men's performance in the event since 1968.

Medalists

Shooting—Men's Air Pistol

1992
1. Wang Yifu, China, 684.8 (FOR)
2. Serguei Pyjianov, Russia, 684.1
3. Sorin Babii, Romania, 684.1

1988
1. Taniou Kiriakov, Bulgaria, 687.9
2. Erich Buljung, U.S.A., 687.9 (EWR)
3. Haifeng Xu, People's Republic of China, 684.5

Shooting—Men's Free Pistol

1992
1. Konstantine Loukachik, Belarus, 658
2. Wang Yifu, China, 657
3. Ragnar Skanaker, Sweden, 657

1988
1. Sorin Babii, Romania, 660

2. Ragnar Skanaker, Sweden, 657
3. Igor Bassinski, Soviet Union, 657

1984
1. Haifeng Xu, China, 566
2. Ragnar Skanaker, Sweden, 565
3. Yifu Wang, China, 564

1980
1. Aleksandr Melentiev, Soviet Union, 581 (WR)
2. Harald Vollmar, East Germany, 568
3. Lubcho Diakov, Bulgaria, 565

1976
1. Uwe Potteck, East Germany, 573 (WR, OR)
2. Harald Vollmar, East Germany, 567
3. Rudolf Dollinger, Austria, 562

1972
1. Ragnar Skanaker, Sweden, 567 (OR)
2. Dan Iuga, Romania, 562
3. Rudolf Dollinger, Austria, 560

1968
1. Grigori Kossykh, Soviet Union, 562/30 (OR)
2. Heinz Mertel, West Germany, 562/26 (OR)
3. Harald Vollmar, East Germany, 560

1964
1. Vaino Markkanen, Finland, 560 (EOR)
2. Franklin Green, U.S.A., 557
3. Yoshihisa Yoshikawa, Japan, 554/26

1960
1. Aleksei Gustchin, Soviet Union, 560 (OR)
2. Makhmud Umarov, Soviet Union, 552/26
3. Yoshihisa Yoshikawa, Japan, 552/20

1956
1. Pentti Linnosvuo, Finland, 556/26 (OR)
2. Makhmud Umarov, Soviet Union, 556/24 (OR)
3. Offutt Pinion, U.S.A., 551

1952
1. Huelet Benner, U.S.A., 553 (OR)
2. Angel Leon De Gozalo, Spain, 550
3. Ambrus Balogh, Hungary, 549

1948
1. Edwin Vasquez Cam, Peru, 545
2. Rudolf Schnyder, Switzerland, 539/60/21
3. Torsten Ullman, Sweden, 539/60/16

1936
1. Torsten Ullman, Sweden, 559 (WR)
2. Erich Krempel, Germany, 544
3. Charles Des Jammonieres, France, 540

1924–1932
Not held

1920
1. Karl Frederick, U.S.A., 496
2. Afranio Da Costa, Brazil, 489
3. Alfred Lane, U.S.A., 481

1912
1. Alfred Lane, U.S.A., 499
2. Peter Dolfen, U.S.A., 474
3. Charles E. Stewart, Great Britain, 470

1908
Not held

1906
1. Georgios Orphanidis, Greece, 221
2. Jean Fouconnier, France, 219
3. Aristides Rangavis, Greece, 218

1904
Not held

1900
1. Conrad Roderer, Switzerland, 503
2. Achille Paroche, France, 466
3. Konrad Staheli, Switzerland, 453

1896
1. Sumner Paine, U.S.A., 442

2. Holger Nielsen, Denmark, 285
3. Nikoalos Morakis, Greece

Shooting—Men's Rapid-Fire Pistol
1992
1. Ralf Schumann, Germany, 885 (FOR)
2. Afanasijs Kuzmins, Latvia, 882
3. Vladimir Vokhmianine, Kazakhstan, 882

1988
1. Afanasi Kouzming, Soviet Union, 698 (WR)
2. Ralf Schumann, East Germany, 696
3. Zoltan Kovacs, Hungary, 693

1984
1. Takeo Kamachi, Japan, 595
2. Corneliu Ion, Romania, 593
3. Rauno Bies, Finland, 591/146

1980
1. Corneliu Ion, Romania, 596/148/147/148
2. Jurgen Wiefel, East Germany, 596/148/
   147/147
3. Gerhard Petritsch, Austria, 596/146

1976
1. Norbert Klaar, East Germany, 597 (OR)
2. Jurgen Wiefel, East Germany, 596
3. Roberto Ferraris, Italy, 595

1972
1. Jozef Zapedzki, Poland, 595 (OR)
2. Ladislav Falta, Czechoslovakia, 594
3. Viktor Torshin, Soviet Union, 593

1968
1. Jozef Zapedzki, Poland, 593 (OR)
2. Marcel Rosca, Romania, 591/147
3. Renart Suleimanov, Soviet Union, 591/146

1964
1. Pentti Linnosvuo, Finland, 592 (OR)
2. Ion Tripsa, Romania, 591
3. Lubomir Nacovsky, Czechoslovakia, 590

1960
1. William McMillan, U.S.A., 587/147 (EOR)
2. Pentti Linnosvuo, Finland, 587/139
3. Aleksandr Zabelin, Soviet Union, 587/135

1956
1. Stefan Petrescu, Romania, 587 (OR)
2. Yergeny Cherkassov, Soviet Union, 585
3. Gheorghe Lichiardopol, Romania, 581

1952
1. Karoly Takacs, Hungary, 579
2. Szilard Kun, Hungary, 578
3. Gheorghe Lichiardopol, Romania, 578

1948
1. Karoly Takacs, Hungary, 580 (WR)
2. Carlos E. Diaz Saenz Valiente, Argentina, 571
3. Sven Lundqvist, Sweden, 569

1936
1. Cornelius Van Oyen, Germany, 36
2. Heinz Hax, Germany, 35
3. Torsten Ullman, Sweden, 34

1932
1. Renzo Morigi, Italy, 36
2. Heinz Hax, Germany, 36
3. Domenico Matteucci, Italy, 36

1928
Not held

1924
1. H. M. Bailey, U.S.A., 18
2. Vilhelm Carlberg, Sweden, 18
3. Lennart Hannelius, Finland, 18

1920
1. Guilherme Paraense, Brazil, 274
2. Raymond Bracken, U.S.A., 272
3. Fritz Zulauf, Switzerland, 269

1912
1. Alfred Lane, U.S.A., 287
2. Paul Palen, Sweden, 286
3. Johan Hubner Von Holst, Sweden, 283

1908
1. Paul Van Asbroeck, Belgium, 490
2. Reginald Storms, Belgium, 487
3. James E. Gorman, U.S.A., 485

1906
1. Maurice Lecoq, France, 250
2. Leon Moreaux, France, 249
3. Aristides Rangavis, Greece, 245

1904
Not held

1900
1. Maurice Larrouy, France, 58
2. Leon Moreaux, France, 57
3. Eugene Balme, France, 57

1896
1. Jean Phrangoudis, Greece, 344
2. Georgios Orphanidis, Greece, 249
3. Holger Nielsen, Denmark

Shooting—Men's Running Game Target

1992
1. Michael Jakosits, Germany, 673.0 (FOR)
2. Anatoli Asrabaev, Uzbekistan, 672.0
3. Lubos Racansky, Czechoslovakia, 670.0

1988
1. Tor Heiestad, Norway, 689 (OR)
2. Shiping Huang, People's Republic of China, 687
3. Guennadi Avramenko, Soviet Union, 686

1984
1. Yuwei Li, China, 587
2. Helmut Bellingrodt, Colombia, 584
3. Shiping Huang, China, 581

1980
1. Igor Sokolov, Soviet Union, 589 (WR)
2. Thomas Pfeffer, East Germany, 589
3. Aleksandr Gazov, Soviet Union, 587

1976
1. Aleksandr Gazov, Soviet Union, 579 (WR)
2. Alexandr Kedyrov, Soviet Union, 576
3. Jerzy Greszkiewicz, Poland, 571

1972
1. Yakov Zhelezniak, Soviet Union, 569 (WR)
2. Helmut Bellingrodt, Colombia, 565
3. John Kynoch, Great Britain, 562

1904–1968
Not held

1900
1. Louis Debray, France, 20
2. P. Nivet, France, 20
3. Comte De Lambert, France, 19

1896
Not held

Shooting—Men's Air Rifle

1992
1. Iouri Fedkine, Russia, 695.3 (FOR)
2. Franck Badiou, France, 691.9
3. Johann Riederer, Germany, 691.7

1988
1. Goran Maksimovic, Yugoslavia, 695.6 (OR)
2. Nicolas Berthelof, France, 694.2
3. Johann Reiderer, West Germany, 694.0

1984
1. Philippe Heberle, France, 589
2. Andreas D. I. Kronthaler, Austria, 587
3. Barry Dagger, Great Britain, 587

1896–1980
Not held

Shooting—Men's Smallbore Free Rifle, Prone

1992
1. Eun-Chul Lee, South Korea, 702.5 (FOR)
2. Harald Stenvaag, Norway, 701.4
3. Stevan Pletikosic, Yugoslavia, 701.1

1988
1. Miroslav Varga, Czechoslovakia, 703.9 (EWR)
2. Young-Chul Cha, South Korea, 702.8
3. Attila Zahonyi, Hungary, 701.9

1984
1. Edward Etzel, U.S.A., 599
2. Michel Bury, France, 596
3. Michael Sullivan, Great Britain, 596

1980
1. Karoly Varga, Hungary, 599 (EWR)
2. Hellfried Heilfort, East Germany, 599 (EWR)
3. Petur Zaprianov, Bulgaria, 598

1976
1. Karlheinz Smieszek, West Germany, 599 (WR,OR)
2. Ulrich Lind, West Germany, 597
3. Gennady Lushnikov, Soviet Union, 595

1972
1. Ho-Jun Li Democratic People's Republic of Korea, 599 (WR)
2. Victor Auer, U.S.A., 598
3. Nicolae Rotaru, Romania, 598

1968
1. Jan Kurka, Czechoslovakia, 598 (EWR)
2. Laszlo Hammerl, Hungary, 598 (EWR)
3. Ian Ballinger, New Zealand, 597

1964
1. Laszlo Hammerl, Hungary, 597 (WR)
2. Lones Wigger, U.S.A., 597 (WR)
3. Tommy Pool, U.S.A., 596

1960
1. Peter Kohnke, West Germany, 590
2. James Hill, U.S.A., 589
3. Enrico Forcella Pelliccioni, Venezuela, 587

1956
1. Gerald R. Ouellette, Canada, 600
2. Vassili Borissov, Soviet Union, 599
3. Gilmour S. Boa, Canada, 598

1952
1. Iosif Sirbu, Romania, 400/33 (EWR)
2. Boris Andreyev, Soviet Union, 400/28 (EWR)
3. Arthur Jackson, U.S.A., 399

1948
1. Arthur Cook, U.S.A., 599/43 (WR)
2. Walter Tomsen, U.S.A., 599/42 (WR)
3. Jonas Jonsson, Sweden, 597

1936
1. Willy Rogeberg, Norway, 300 (WR)
2. Ralf Berzsenyi, Hungary, 296
3. Wladyslaw Karas, Poland, 296

1932
1. Bertil Ronnmark, Sweden, 294
2. Gustavo Huet, Mexico, 294
3. Zoltan Hradetzky-Soos, Hungary, 293

1928
Not held

1924
1. Pierre Coquelin De Lisle, France, 398 (prone)
2. Marcus Dinwiddie, U.S.A., 396 (prone)
3. Josias Hartmann, Switzerland, 394 (prone)

1920
1. Lawrence A. Nuesslein, U.S.A., 391 (standing)
2. Arthur Rothrock, U.S.A., 386 (standing)
3. Dennis Fenton, U.S.A., 385 (standing)

1912
1. Frederick Hird, U.S.A., 194 (any position)
2. William Milne, Great Britain, 193 (any position)
3. Harry Burt, Great Britain, 192 (any position)

1908
1. A. A. Carnell, Great Britain, 387 (any position)
2. Harry R. Humby, Great Britain, 386 (any position)
3. G. Barnes, Great Britain, 385 (any position)

1896–1906
Not held

Shooting—Men's Smallbore Rifle, Three-Position

1992
1. Gratchia Petikian, Armenia, 1267.4 (FOR)
2. Robert Foth, U.S.A., 1266.6
3. Ryohei Koba, Japan, 1265.9

1988
1. Malcolm Cooper, Great Britain, 1279.3
2. Alister Allan, Great Britain, 1275.6
3. Kirill Ivanov, Soviet Union, 1275.0

1984
1. Malcolm Cooper, Great Britain, 1173
2. Daniel Nipkow, Switzerland, 1163
3. Alister Allan, Great Britain, 1162

1980
1. Viktor Vlasov, Soviet Union, 1173 (WR)
2. Bernd Hartstein, East Germany, 1166
3. Sven Johansson, Sweden, 1165

1976
1. Lanny Bassham, U.S.A., 1162
2. Margaret Murdock, U.S.A., 1162
3. Rainer Seibold, West Germany, 1160

1972
1. John Writer, U.S.A., 1166 (WR)
2. Lanny Bassham, U.S.A., 1157
3. Werner Lippoldt, East Germany, 1153

1968
1. Bernd Klingner, West Germany, 1157
2. John Writer, U.S.A., 1156
3. Vitali Parkhimovich, Soviet Union, 1154

1964
1. Lones Wigger, U.S.A., 1164 (WR)
2. Velitschko Christov, Bulgaria, 1152
3. Laszlo Hammerl, Hungary, 1151

1960
1. Viktor Shamburkin, Soviet Union, 1149 (EWR)
2. Marat Niyasov, Soviet Union, 1145
3. Klaus Zahringer, West Germany, 1139

1956
1. Anatoli Bogdanov, Soviet Union, 1172 (OR)
2. Otakar Horinek, Czechoslovakia, 1172 (OR)
3. John Sundberg, Sweden, 1167

1952
1. Erling Kongshaug, Norway, 1164/53
2. Vilho Ylonen, Finland, 1164/49
3. Boris Andreyev, Soviet Union, 1163

1896–1948
Not held

Shooting—Olympic Trap (Open)

1992
1. Petr Hrdlicka, Czechoslovakia, 219 (FOR)
2. Kazumi Watanabe, Japan, 219 (FOR)
3. Marco Venturini, Italy, 218

1988
1. Dmitri Monakov, Soviet Union, 222
2. Miloslav Bednarik, Czechoslovakia, 222
3. Frans Peeters, Belgium, 219

1984
1. Luciano Giovannetti, Italy, 192/24
2. Francisco Boza, Peru, 192/23
3. Daniel Carlisle, U.S.A., 192/22

1980
1. Luciano Giovannetti, Italy, 198
2. Rustam Yambulatov, Soviet Union, 196/24/25
3. Jorg Damme, East Germany, 196/24/24

1976
1. Donald Haldeman, U.S.A., 190
2. Armando Silva Marquese, Portugal, 189
3. Ubaldesco Baldi, Italy, 189

1972
1. Angelo Scalzone, Italy, 199 (WR)
2. Michel Carrega, France, 198
3. Silvano Basagni, Italy, 195

1968
1. John R. Braithwaite, Great Britain, 198 (EWR)
2. Thomas Garrigus, U.S.A., 196/25/25
3. Kurt Czekalla, East Germany, 196/25/23

1964
1. Ennio Mattarelli, Italy, 198 (OR)
2. Pavel Senichev, Soviet Union, 194/25
3. William Morris, U.S.A., 194/24

1960
1. Ion Dumitrescu, Romania, 192
2. Galliano Rossini, Italy, 191
3. Sergei Kalinin, Soviet Union, 190

1956
1. Galliano Rossini, Italy, 195 (OR)
2. Adam Smelczynski, Poland, 190
3. Alessandro Ciceri, Italy, 188

1952
1. George P. Genereux, Canada, 192
2. Knut Holmqvist, Sweden, 191
3. Hans Liljedahl, Sweden, 190

1928–1948
Not held

1924
1. Gyula Halasy, Hungary, 98/8 (OR)
2. Konrad Huber, Finland, 98/7 (OR)
3. Frank Hughes, U.S.A., 97

1920
1. Mark Arie, U.S.A., 95
2. Frank Troeh, U.S.A., 93
3. Frank Wright, U.S.A., 87

1912
1. James Graham, U.S.A., 96
2. Alfred Goeldel, Germany, 94
3. Harry Blau, Russia, 91

1908
1. Walter H. Ewing, Canada, 72
2. George Beattie, Canada, 60
3. Alexander Maunder, Great Britain, 57
3. Anastasios Metaxas, Greece, 57

1906
1. Gerald Merlin, Great Britain, 24 (single shot)
1. Sidney Merlin, Great Britain, 15 (double shot)
2. Anastasios Metaxas, Greece, 13 (double shot)
2. Ioannis Peridis, Greece, 23 (single shot)
3. Gerald Merlin, Great Britain, 12 (double shot)
3. Sidney Merlin, Great Britain, 21 (single shot)

1904
Not held

1900
1. Roger De Barbarin, France, 17
2. Rene Guyot, France, 17
3. Justinien De Clary, France, 17

1896
Not held

Shooting—Olympic Skeet (Open)

1992
1. Zhang Shan, China, 223 (FOR)
2. Juan Jorge Giha Yarur, Peru, 222
3. Bruno Rossetti, Italy, 222

1988
1. Axel Wegner, East Germany, 222 (EOR)
2. Alfonso De Iruarrizaga, Chile, 221 (EOR)
3. Jorge Guardiola, Spain, 220

1984
1. Matthew Dryke, U.S.A., 198
2. Ole Riber Rasmussen, Denmark, 196/25
3. Luca Scribani Italy, 196/23

1980
1. Hans Kjeld Rasmussen, Denmark, 196/25/25
2. Lars-Goran Carlsson, Sweden, 196/25/24
3. Roberto Castrillo, Cuba, 196/25/23

1976
1. Josef Panacek, Czechoslovakia, 198 (EOR)
2. Eric Swinkels, Netherlands, 198 (EOR)
3. Wieslaw Gwalikowski, Poland, 196

1972
1. Konrad Wirnhier, West Germany, 195/25
2. Yevgeny Petrov, Soviet Union, 195/24
3. Michael Buchheim, East Germany, 195/23

1968
1. Yevgeny Petrov, Soviet Union, 198/25 (EWR)
2. Romano Garagnani, Italy, 198/25 (EWR)
3. Konrad Wirnhier, West Germany, 198/24/23 (EWR)

1896–1964
Not held

Shooting—Women's Air Pistol

1992
1. Marina Logvinenko, Russia, 486.4 (FOR)
2. Jasna Sekaric, Yugoslavia, 486.4 (FOR)
3. Maria Grozdeva, Bulgaria, 481.6

1988
1. Jasna Sekaric, Yugoslavia, 489.5 (WR)
2. Nino Saloukvadze, Soviet Union, 487.5
3. Marina Dobrantcheva, Soviet Union, 485.2

Shooting—Women's Sport Pistol

1992
1. Marina Logvinenko, Russia, 684 (FOR)
2. Li Duihong, China, 680
3. Dorzhsuren Munkhbayar, Mongolia, 679

1988
1. Nino Salukvadze, Soviet Union, 690.0 (OR)
2. Tomoko Hasegawa, Japan, 686.0
3. Jasna Sekaric, Yugoslavia, 686.0 (OR)

1984
1. Linda Thom, Canada, 585/198
2. Ruby Fox, U.S.A., 585/197
3. Patricia Dench, Australia, 583/196

1896–1980
Not held

Shooting—Women's Air Rifle

1992
1. Kab-Soon Yeo, South Korea, 498.2 (FOR)
2. Vesela Letcheva, Bulgaria, 495.3
3. Aranka Binder, Yugoslavia, 495.1

1988
1. Irina Chilova, Soviet Union, 498.5 (OR)
2. Silvia Sperber, West Germany, 497.5
3. Anna Maloukhina, Soviet Union, 495.8

1984
1. Pat Spurgin, U.S.A., 393
2. Edith Gufler, Italy, 391
3. Xiao Xuan Wu, China, 389

1896–1980
Not held

Shooting—Women's Smallbore Rifle, Three-Position

1992
1. Launi Meili, U.S.A., 684.3 (FOR)
2. Nonka Matova, Bulgaria, 682.7
3. Malgorzata Ksiazkiewicz, Poland, 681.5

1988
1. Silvia Sperber, West Germany, 685.6 (OR)
2. Vessela Letcheva, Bulgaria, 683.2
3. Valentina Tcherka Ssova, Soviet Union, 681.4

1984
1. Xiao Xuan Wu, China, 581
2. Ulrike Holmer, West Germany, 578
3. Wanda Jewel, U.S.A., 578

1896–1980
Not held

Trivia Quiz

1. The first documented shooting contest was held
   a. In 1477, in Germany   **b.** In the year 1,000, in China
   c. In 1313, in Germany

2. Shooting is a part of
a. No other Olympic sport   b. One other Olympic sport
c. Two other Olympic sports

3. Which of the following nations was not one of the eight countries involved in the founding of the Union Internationale de Tir (UIT), the sport's governing body?
a. Switzerland   b. Argentina   c. Germany

4. The shooting events that were included in the 1896 Olympic Games
a. Were the same as those on the program today, with the exception of women's events
b. Allowed women to compete among the men
c. Were military in origin and included only five events

5. In 1900, Belgium's Léon de Lunden captured a shooting gold medal
a. In the Open Trap event   b. In the Running Game Target event
c. In the live pigeon shooting event

6. The youngest Olympic gold medalist in the sport of shooting was
a. 17 years old at the time he won the title
b. 15 years old at the time he won the title
c. 19 years old at the time he won the title

7. Gerald Ouellette's 1956 world record in the smallbore prone event was disallowed because
a. He tested positive for tranquilizers
b. He was not shooting from a fully prone position
c. The course was discovered to be only 4½m, rather than the standard 50m

8. Russian shooters did not compete in the 1908 London Games
a. Because the competition overlapped with Foreign Minister Izvolski's London conference
b. To protest the results of the previous Olympic competition
c. Because the Russian team arrived 12 days late, following the Julian calendar

9. Nikolai Kolomenkin, Russia's 10-time pistol champion, placed eighth in the 1912 free pistol event and also
a. Won a bronze medal in that year's Modern Pentathlon
b. Captured a gold medal in the event in the 1920 Games
c. Won a gold medal as a figure skater in the 1908 Games

10. The 1992 Open Skeet competition was noteworthy because
a. A woman captured first place for the first time in the history of the event
b. It was the event's final appearance in the Olympic Games
c. The gold medalist equaled the world record and set a new Olympic record

Answers: 1-a; 2-c; 3-c; 4-c; 5-c; 6-a; 7-c; 8-c; 9-c; 10-a, -b, and -c

Soccer

Warm-up

Today, it is the world's most popular sport, thanks to successful 18th- and 19th-century British Empire expansion. Yet soccer, or *futbol* (football) as it is known in all parts of the world outside the U.S. and Canada, has been around in one form or another for thousands of years. And so, likewise, has the violence associated with the sport.

In 80 BC China, a popular game of the day involved one goal, formed with two bamboo poles thirty or more feet high, with an opening one-foot in diameter. Players took turns trying to kick a ball through the opening, scoring points for each success.

In ancient Greece and Rome, several types of balls were used in games. One, the *follis*, was a large ball filled with hair and otherwise similar to a modern soccer ball. In the Roman game of *follis*, the object was to toss the ball in the air and keep it up by using the hands. A smaller ball, the *harpastum*, was used in another game played with the hands. Participants tossed the ball to one another while others tried to intercept it or tackle the player who caught it. But neither the *follis* or *harpastum* was ever kicked on purpose.

In ancient Florence, a game called *calcio* was very big. *Calcio* involved 27 players on a side and one ball. The object was to pass, kick, or carry the ball across the goal. The game was more like the English version of mob football, in which the real goal was to kick your neighbor.

Legend has it that Roman legionnaires would celebrate a victory by kicking around the severed heads of their foes. Apparently villagers in Britain witnessed this great fun and decided they had the basis of a game. Using an inflated bladder for a ball and village streets for a field, *futbol* was born. Or another legend: around 1050, workmen digging in an old battlefield came across the skull of a Dane. How they knew it was the skull of a Dane, we do not know. The workmen, angered at Danes in general for occupying England during the period, began kicking the skull around the battlefield and at some point, directed it at targets for points. Interestingly enough, "heading" is a big part of the game now, although you don't necessarily have to lose one to be effective.

Football's first mention in English literature appeared in a history of London written in 1174. During the 12th and 13th centuries, a game loosely resembling modern soccer, but involving more physical violence among participants, was played throughout England. The object was to advance the ball to the opponent's goal, playing on an ad hoc field that often wove through the middle of a town. At any given moment, a football game might rush through town, damaging storefronts and homes. Players used arms, legs, heads, and brute force to move the ball forward. With its potential for mayhem, the game attracted the thug element (which apparently in Old England was rather profuse), so authorities sought to shut it down. In 1314, King Edward II of England outlawed football, on the basis that it was a waste of people's time. Similar actions were later taken by Richard II and Henry VIII (who, incidentally, chose better ways of wasting his time).

But regardless of what the authorities did, the game continued to flourish. Eventually, it was confined to a preestablished field, which appeased the town dwellers who did not embrace spontaneous soccer action exploding in front of their homes or businesses. Standardized rules were adopted, so that by the end of the 15th century the game was described as one in which the ball was propelled by striking it with the feet. In 1580, the game appeared on British college campuses as an intramural sport, and 40 years later as an intercollegiate event.

In the 1800s, football was introduced in Britain's public schools, where it became further refined. But the question of hand use during the game was still open. At the schools, such as Westminster, where the playgrounds were smaller, the kicking version of soccer dominated. At Rugby School, however, the wide open spaces of the campus invited carrying the ball. It was left to William Webb Elias to turn fantasy into reality, as he elected during a football game to run with the ball, creating another game in the process, rugby.

The modern game started with the foundation of the Football Association (of England) in 1863. There is record of soccer being played under the evening floodlights in 1878. By 1883, England, Ireland, Scotland, and Wales had founded the International

Board, which has become the game's sole rule-making council. The term soccer stems from 1890s British University slang; derived from association football, the term takes the *soc* and adds an *-er* suffix. In 1904, the Fédération Internationale de Football Associations (FIFA) was founded, becoming soccer's worldwide administrative body.

Soccer was the first team sport added to the Olympics. Great Britain dominated the early tournaments, winning three of the first four. Although the sport made its medal debut in 1900, it was not until 1908 that the tournament attracted reasonable international representation.

After World War I, as the sport grew internationally, British dominance ended, while the South American style came into vogue, with Uruguay taking the 1924 and 1928 Olympics (the only tournaments at which a non-European team has won). The BBC began broadcasting live soccer commentary in 1927. At the same time, controversy increased over what constituted a professional or amateur player, a debate that has dogged the Olympic tournament for years. In 1932, soccer was pulled from the program at Los Angeles as the issue of pseudo-amateurs in the Games reached the boiling point.

In 1930, the first World Cup was held, coming two years after the Olympics, and the two events have followed this staggered four-year sequence ever since. Held in Uruguay, 13 countries participated, including the U.S. and four teams from Europe: France, Belgium, Romania, and Yugoslavia. The U.S. slipped into the semifinals (its highest placement to date in the World Cup) before losing 6–1 to the Argentines, the bronze medal winners in the 1928 Olympics. The host Uruguayans became the first World Cup world champions.

Although America has never taken the World Cup and has not won an Olympic medal since 1904, the popularity of the game continues to increase in the United States. In 1991, the U.S. women's team won the inaugural Women's World Championship. And according to a 1993 survey released by the Soccer Industry Council of America, approximately 17 million Americans over the age of six played soccer at least once during 1993. The sport is administered by the U.S. Soccer Federation, founded in 1913. In 1994, the U.S. hosted the World Cup, an event that many in the soccer community believed would greatly increase the popularity of the sport in America; time will tell. In its fourth appearance in World Cup play, the U.S. men's team advanced to the second round, where they lost to Brazil.

Spectator's Guide

Let's talk kicking, shall we? The basic soccer kick is made with the foot turned sideways, using the instep rather than the toe. The technique assures greater accuracy because more of the foot is in contact with the ball. This comes as no surprise to the National Football League, in which many teams employ a soccer-style kicker for that very reason. The best kickers can make the ball travel more than 70 miles per hour. Lateral passing, or flick passing, can be accomplished by kicking the ball with the outside of the foot.

Games are divided into 45-minute halves. The game begins with a coin toss; the winner elects either to pick which goal to defend or to take the kickoff. The kickoff has little meaning in soccer, so the winner of the coin toss usually elects to choose which goal to defend.

While goals are few and far between (perhaps the chief reason for the still dispassionate American view of the game), scoring opportunities are frequent. Tempo is one of the keys to watch—which team is completing more passes, who is getting off the most shots on goal, which side is controlling the ball at midfield with the most consistency.

Ball control is a fundamental part of soccer. In addition to the feet, soccer players use their heads and chests for passing and controlling the ball. A popular strategy during corner kicks is for one or more players to hang in front of the net hoping to get a piece of the ball with his head and jam it past the goalie.

As a player moves up the field with the ball, he often resorts to dribbling. Dribbling is accomplished via a series of short kicks as the player alternately hits the ball with first one instep and then the other. Attackers take much of their running diagonally across the field, rather than straight down, since this creates more problems for the defense.

The field on which all that dribbling occurs is somewhat larger than an American football field, about 120 yards long and 75 yards wide. The goals are eight feet high and 24 feet wide, with a six by 20 foot penalty area in front. The ball is 8.5 inches in diameter and weighs between 14 and 16 ounces.

Each team fields 11 players. Of these 11, only the goalie is allowed to use his hands during play, and only when he occupies his penalty area. When in possession of the ball, the goalie is allowed four steps before he must get rid of it.

Soccer allows one exception to the no-hands rule, and that is on **throw-ins**, when the ball is put in play from out-of-bounds (note that a ball on a line is considered in play). If the ball crosses either sideline, a player on the team that did not knock it out must throw the ball back into play, holding the ball with both hands and throwing it over his head while both feet are planted.

The clock can only be stopped at the referee's discretion, usually for serious injuries. The single referee is joined by two linesmen, who together police the game, watching for the ball bounding over the sidelines, players streaking offside, and the presence of one of the nine deadly fouls.

The nine serious fouls in soccer include dangerous charging, charging from behind, holding, striking, pushing, tripping, kicking or jumping at an opponent, and handling the ball (for a foul to be called, the handling must be judged by the referee or linesman to be intentional). These offenses will result in a direct free kick against the guilty team, or a penalty kick if the foul occurred in the penalty area. During a penalty kick, the ball is placed 12 yards from the goal, and the player taking the kick has only the goalkeeper to beat. The goalie must stand on his goal line and is not allowed to move his feet until the ball is kicked.

Under international rules, penalty-kick shootouts are not held to break ties. A team is permitted two substitutes during a match, and once a player is removed, he or she cannot return.

At the Olympics, 16 men's teams compete for the gold in a single elimination tournament. The defending champion and the host country receive automatic berths, while the other 14 teams are survivors of a worldwide qualifying tournament. At the 1996 Atlanta Games, the men's teams will enforce an under-23 rule, although each team will be allowed three "wild card" players over the age of 23. Also at the Atlanta Games, the first women's Olympic tournament will be played. The women's teams have no age restrictions. The eight best women's teams in the world will compete.

FIFA asked the Atlanta Organizing Committee to test a system that could lower field temperatures by 15 degrees. A system of large fans that blow a fine mist over the field's surface was slated for testing during an A-League match between Atlanta and Montreal in August 1995, in the midst of a particularly hot summer throughout the U.S.

Banana shot: A hard shot at goal in which the ball is kicked off center, giving it a spin the makes it curve in flight; usually used on free kicks near the goal.

Bend: To kick the ball off center, so that it curves in flight.

Boot: To kick the ball awkwardly.

Box: The penalty area (the 18-yard box); also, less frequently, the goal area (the six-yard box).

Cannonball shot: Any very fast and powerful shot on goal.

Center circle: A circle of ten yard's radius marked out around the center spot of the field; at the moment of kickoff, players on the team not taking the kick must be outside the circle. Kickoffs also start the second half and follow scores, with the team that gave up the goal taking the kick.

Challenge: To approach a player who has possession of the ball in order to force the player to commit to either a pass or a run.

Charge: Physical contact of the shoulder-to-shoulder variety with an opponent in an attempt to force him off the ball; can result in a foul call if contact is excessive.

Clogger: A player who tackles in a physical way.

Corner kick: What the attacking side is awarded when a defending player kicks the ball over his own goal line (other than into the goal). The ball is placed in the corner area and kicked, usually in the air, so that it will reach the opposing goal mouth, where the attackers gather, hoping to head or kick it into the goal.

Free kick: Two kinds of free kicks are awarded—**indirect** (from which a goal cannot be scored unless the ball has been played or touched by a player other than the kicker before passing through the goal) and **direct** (from which a goal can be scored directly from the kicker's foot). Opposing players must stand at least 10 yards away from the ball while the kick is being taken.

Goal area: A rectangular area, marked by a line, in front of each goal, measuring twenty yards wide and six yards deep; inside this area the goalie cannot be charged.

Goal kick: When the attacking team plays the ball over the opponent's goal line, play is restarted by the defending team receiving a chance to kick it out of there; the ball is then placed at the edge of the goal area and kicked by the goalie or a defender.

Mark: In man-to-man coverage, the defender is said to mark the attacker; the closer he plays to him, the tighter the marking.

Offside: The offside rule requires than an attacker must have at least two opponents (one of whom can be the goalie) between himself and the opposing goal line when the ball is passed to him and he is on the defender's half of the field. If the attacker is running toward the opposing goal and the ball is front of him, he cannot be called for offside.

Overhead kick: Also called a somersault or bicycle kick; useful when a player finds himself facing the wrong way with no time to turn around. The player flips into the air, throwing his feet up and his torso down. When contact is made with the ball, the body is parallel to the ground and some three or four feet above it.

Penalty area: An area at each end of the field bounded by two lines drawn at right angles to the goal line, 18 yards from each goalpost, that extend into the field of play for a distance of 18 yards and are met by a line running parallel with the goal line.

Stopper: Denotes a defender who is tightly marking a striker.

Striker: Any of the central attacking players in the 4–2–4, 4–3–3, and 4–4–2 formations.

Touchline: Also called sideline; the line at each side of the field. A ball going over the touchline is said to have gone into touch.

Hopefuls—Men's

Tom Dooley

Thomas Dooley, a roving defender with an instinct for goal, is the linchpin of the U.S. national soccer team. Dooley, like a few other members of the American team, comes from abroad. He was born in West Germany in 1961, the year before his father, an American G.I., returned to the United States and effectively abandoned the family. In his teens Dooley trained as a toolmaker, but he eventually set for himself the twin goals of undertaking collegiate study and playing regularly for any third-division squad. By his mid-twenties Dooley had succeeded on both counts, for he was studying architecture at the University of Kaiserslautern and playing regularly with third-division F.C. Hamburg.

In the ensuing few years, Dooley's soccer prowess improved sufficiently to merit him a defensive post with F.C. Kaiserslautern in the highly competitive German Bundesliga. A call up to the

German national team seemed inevitable, but then fate intervened. An ankle injury necessitated an operation that rendered him inactive. He then suffered a chest injury, including broken ribs and a punctured lung, that sidelined him.

By this time, the early 1990s, American soccer officials had discovered Dooley's American connection as the son of a serviceman, U.S. interest was related to Dooley, who responded affirmatively. Thus by 1992, with considerable assistance from U.S. officials, Dooley was an American citizen and, moreover, a starter with the U.S. national team.

In the initial U.S. Cup of 1992, Dooley quickly established himself as an exciting player with a multiple capacity to defend close to goal, direct attack from the midfield, or dash forward in search of goals. He made a stunning debut for the U.S. in an equally stunning triumph over an Irish team that had been quarterfinalists at the World Cup two years earlier.

Against Ireland Dooley repeatedly charged into the attack, and he largely created two of the team's scoring maneuvers. Throughout that brief tournament, which the U.S. team narrowly won over a powerhouse Italian squad, Dooley continually showed himself to be a formidable, and versatile, player.

In the next year's U.S. Cup Dooley again enjoyed great personal success, though the U.S. team fared rather less well. The highlight of that event, at least from an American perspective, was certainly the surprising, and decisive, 2–0 victory over England. Dooley scored the first goal in that convincing triumph. The Americans closed U.S. Cup 1995 in exciting fashion, losing 4-3 to the world champions and tournament winners, Germany. In that contest, Dooley scored two more goals.

Dooley continued to shine for the United States in the 1994 World Cup, where the U.S. team was eliminated only by eventual winners, Brazil. After a personally inconsistent start against Switzerland, in a 1–1 draw, Dooley, as well as his American teammates, regained their strength and defeated the highly touted Colombians more significantly than the 2–1 score indicates. By virtue of this victory the U.S. team reached the second round of the tournament. Their achievement was, thus, a successful one, even though they were then put out by the Brazilians.

During the 1994–95 Bundesliga season, Dooley played for Bayer Leverkusen, whose roster included fellow American Claudio Reyna. The team, despite the presence of colorful Bern Schuster and goal-scoring great Rudi Voller, finished in only the middle of the table. Greater success awaited Dooley back in the states, though, when U.S. Cup 1995 commenced in June. In that tournament, which the United States contested with Mexico, Colombia, and African champions Nigeria, Dooley once again showed his versatility in both preventing and attempting goals, particularly in a spirited 4–0 triumph over a vaunted Mexico squad. The U.S. team won the U.S. Cup in June, 1995, and immediately traveled south to vie for the Copa America championship held in Uruguay. And though Dooley is now in his mid-thirties, it seems likely that he will remain an integral part of the American team, at least into the qualifying games for World Cup 1998 in France.

—Les Stone

Kasey Keller

Kasey Keller ranks among the most impressive of the younger players likely to emerge as pivotal performers with the United States soccer team in the forthcoming Olympics and World Cup events. Keller, who is still in his mid-twenties, was born near Olympia, Washington, and he served as goaltender at the University of Portland. Since 1992 he has played in England, where he is the regular goaltender for Millwall in the country's first division. In a nation notorious for its soccer hooliganism, Millwall's fans nonetheless stand out as, rather proudly, the most notorious. On various occasions, notably the closing of the club's old, ominous ground in a particularly unappealing area of the city, the Millwall faithful have seen fit to invade the pitch and strip the players of their playing clothes. Keller has also witnessed frequent fisticuffs in the stands and, on at least one occasion, between a fan and an opposing player!

Such vehement support often proves fickle, however, and Millwall fans have been known to turn quickly against home players guilty of allegedly disgracing the Millwall uniform. Goaltenders are often the most immediate targets of fan abuse. But Keller, by virtue of an extraordinary work rate and equally extraordinary results, has utterly won over the Millwall supporters. During his debut season of 1992–93, Keller played in fifty-one straight games and posted sixteen shutouts. For his achievements, he was selected by the home supporters as Millwall's most valuable player.

Unfortunately for Keller, club success did not carry over into equal time with the United States national team. He hardly helped his own cause by bluntly stating, prior to America's hosting of the 1994 World Cup, that he felt himself deserving of the starting position for team U.S.A. Such a candid expression of self-confidence, though justifiable, apparently served to alienate Keller from his prospective U.S. teammates, not the least of which was Tony Meola, the team's starting goaltender and, moreover, its captain. Perhaps more damaging, however, was the effect Keller's candor seemingly had on the team's rather inscrutable coach, Bora Milutinovic, whose handling of Keller's comments served to emphasize his own considerable authority with the U.S. team. Milutinovic responded to Keller's comments by reaffirming, justifiably enough, his support of Meola as goalkeeper number one. Less justifiable, though, was Milutinovic's consequent disregard of Keller as even a number two keeper. Ultimately, Milutinovic accorded Keller little opportunity to obtain a regular place with the national team prior to the World Cup games.

But home support—fueled, no doubt, by consideration of his achievements in England—remained strong for Keller, who is likely the most fundamentally sound of the U.S. goalkeeping prospects. In 1995, at the U.S. Cup contested with Nigeria, Mexico, and Colombia, Keller once again showed why he is particularly valuable. He played in only one of the United States's three games, but in that game he yielded no goals to a talented Mexico team, losing finalists at the Copa America games two years earlier. Keller demonstrated, in the process, both raw athleticism, so necessary for making reflex saves, and a keen awareness of goaltending fundamentals, including the ability to swiftly reduce opponents' shooting angles.

With all respect to Brad Friedel, the former college star now playing for Brondby in the Danish League, Keller is probably the fans favorite to succeed Tony Meola on the U.S. team. It remains to be seen, though, whether he will become the preferred keeper for the U.S. Olympic soccer team coaching staff.

—*Les Stone*

Claudio Reyna

Claudio Reyna is perhaps the most promising of the younger players on the U.S. soccer team. A New Jersey native, Reyna showed considerable talent at an early age, and by the time that he was in high school he was also playing for the American Under-16 squad. He was also a star collegiate player, leading his University of Virginia team to three straight NCAA titles in the early

1990s and being named a first-team All-American for three years in a row. During his time at Virginia, Reyna was an integral member of the U.S. Under-20 team. He also played for the United States in qualifying games for the 1992 Olympics and won a gold medal the year prior as a member of the 1991 Pan-Am soccer champions.

Only a hamstring injury kept Reyna out of the 1994 World Cup, in which the U.S. team bowed out to the eventual champions, Brazil. Since that tournament, Reyna has regained match fitness and has joined U.S. teammate Tom Dooley at Bayer Leverkusen in the German Bundesliga. He has also gained a starting position with the American team. Although Reyna had been playing as a midfielder with the American team, it was as a forward that he distinguished himself at the 1995 U.S. Cup, which the U.S. squad won convincingly. In the U.S. team's 4–0 routing of Mexico, Reyna scored one goal and created two others. If Reyna can sustain the quality of play he exhibited in that game, he will likely remain a key part of the U.S. national team for several years to come.

—Les Stone

Romario

Romario is among the soccer elite's most explosive forwards. He was still a teenager when he began playing for Vasco da Gama in Brazil's Rio de Janeiro league. He continued to draw attention as a twenty-two-year-old with Brazil's team at the 1988 Olympic games in Seoul. Brazil lost the final game of that tournament 2–1 to the Soviet Union. Romario scored Brazil's lone goal.

After the Olympics Romario left Brazil for the more lucrative leagues in western Europe. He signed with P.S.V. Eindhoven in the Netherlands and promptly led the team to the Dutch title. During his five years in the Netherlands Romario ranked among the league's top scorers. His tally read ninety-eight goals. But though there was no denying Romario's skill as a creative, opportunistic striker with a deadly kick, there was also no avoiding his reputation as a temperamental, outspoken player, and he sometimes prompted disciplinary action from the Eindhoven management.

Still, Romario was considered among soccer's most deadly attackers, and when he departed from Eindhoven in 1993 he left for the weighty sum of $4.5 million. Romario's new club was Barcelona, which had regularly won European trophies and several league titles and was generally considered to be the top team in the Spanish league. Barcelona was managed by Dutchman

Johan Cruyff, who ranks among the game's all-time greatest players. Cruyff was himself a rather volatile player, but as a manager he had already proven himself capable of working with temperamental stars, notably the great Bulgarian player Hristo Stoichkov.

With Cruyff as his club manager and Stoichkov as a teammate, Romario promptly led the Spanish league in scoring, and Barcelona once again captured the league crown. It was clear that Romario, regardless of the competition, was a truly lethal scorer. At this time it was also clear in South America that the Brazilian national team lacked significant scoring punch. In 1993 Brazil suffered its first ever loss in a World Cup qualifier, against Bolivia, and the unlikely seemed at least possible: Brazil, three-time world champions, actually had to consider elimination from the World Cup at the qualifying stage.

Yielding to the demands of fans and players, Brazilian coach Carlos Alberto Parreira called Romario back to international duty. The recall immediately yielded results, for Romario scored both goals against Uruguay in the victory that sent Brazil into the World Cup. In that tournament, Romario once again distinguished himself as an enterprising scorer. In Brazil's seven games Romario talled five goals, including an unlikely header that decided the semi-final against Sweden, and Brazil regained the World Cup.

Since that highlight, Romario has again been involved in controversy. He returned late to the Barcelona training grounds and was promptly fined. He was then slow to show the scoring form that had made him so dangerous in the World Cup only a few months earlier. It was eventually revealed that Romario was homesick for Brazil, whereupon a deal was made sending the unhappy striker home to Flamengo in the Rio de Janeiro league.

Romario was rather slow to regain his touch with Flamengo, too, but by late spring he was once again scoring at a more expectable pace. For the 1995–96 season Romario will be paired in attack with another highly productive and highly temperamental forward, Edmundo. This volatile partnership will probably generate some outstanding goals and some disturbing behavior. Flamengo fans are hoping, no doubt, that that the former greatly exceeds the latter.

Romario chose to abstain from playing in the 1995 Copa America championship held in Uruguay. But he said that he would return to the Brazilian squad in order to again vie for the Olympic gold. His presence on an already strong squad assures Brazil's status among the favorites in soccer at the 1996 Olympic games.

—Les Stone

Hopefuls—Women's

Michelle Akers

Michelle Akers is the star of the U.S. women's soccer team, and she is arguably the greatest female player in the world today. Hers is a career rich in triumphs and personal honors. As a high-schooler she was three times named an All-American, and as a player at the University of Central Florida in Orlando she became the first recepient of the prestigious Hermann Trophy.

Akers began playing for the United States in 1985, and she scored in each of her first two games. In the ensuing years she has continued to produce for the U.S. team at an impressive rate: by the end of 1994 she had tallied a phenomenal seventy goals in seventy four international appearances. Her tallies at club level have been equally impressive. As a forward for Tyreso in Sweden's women's league, Akers has been particular productive, scoring forty-three goals in 1992 alone.

As a U.S. player, Akers enjoyed outstanding success at the first Women's World Championship, which was held in China in 1991. In that tournament Akers scored ten goals and led the U.S. team to the top prize. That same year, she became the first player to twice win the U.S. Soccer Federation's Female Athlete of the Year award.

Akers seemed likely to continue her international success in 1995 when the U.S. team defended the world championship in Sweden. But an injury in the first contest sidelined Akers through-out most of the remaining games. She managed another appear-ance in the U.S. team's thrilling semifinal contest against Norway, which the Norwegians won 1–0. Barring another injury, Akers will likely continue with the U.S. team through the 1996 Olympics. Her presence guarantees that the United States will rank among the strongest contenders in that tournament.

—Les Stone

Mia Hamm

Mia Hamm ranks among the U.S. team's most accomplished scorers. That should come as little surprise to anyone who fol-lowed Hamm's collegiate career at the University of North Car-olina, which won the NCAA championship during each of Hamm's four years at the school. By the time her college days were done in 1993, Hamm was the Atlantic Coast Conference's all-time leading scorer, with 103 goals.

Hamm began playing for the United States in 1987, but it was not until 1990 that she got on the scoreboard by tallying against Norway. Since then she has produced regularly for the U.S. team, and her international total now exceeds thirty goals.

Though only nineteen years old, Hamm was an integral member of the U.S. squad that won the world championship in 1991. She started five of the team's six games and contributed two goals. Two years later, she led all players with six goals at the World University Games, where the United States won the silver medal. And in 1994, during the qualifying tournament to determine World Cup finalists, Hamm scored six more goals. That year, she was named Female Athlete of the Year by the U.S. Soccer Federation.

Hamm continued to shine for the U.S. at the World Championship in 1995, where the U.S. team bowed out only after a thrilling 1–0 defeat in the semifinal against Norway. For Hamm, and the remainder of the Americans, the Olympics provide an opportunity to regain top honors.

—Les Stone

FACT: In 1995, the 20 members of the U.S. women's soccer team received salaries between $24,000 and $40,000, plus housing and bonuses. The five members who retained their college eligibility received no salaries, although their housing and expenses were paid by U.S. Soccer, the sport's governing body.

Briana Scurry

Goalkeeper Briana Scurry is a recent addition to the U.S. women's team, having begun her international career in 1994. Prior to joining the American team, Scurry had played at the University of Massachusetts, which lost only three times during her tenure. In her time at Massachusetts Scurry posted thirty-seven shutouts in sixty-five games for a goals-against-average of 0.56! And during her junior year, she also made three appearances as a forward.

In 1994 Scurry was named Most Valuable Player at the Chiquita Cup, where the United States destroyed arch-rivals Norway 4–1. Scurry also starred for the United States at the 1994 tournament to determine qualifiers for the 1995 world championship in Sweden. At the championship she continued to play well, but a single goal yielded against the Norwegians was enough to see the Scandinavians avenge the Chiquita Cup defeat and end the U.S. team's hopes at the semifinal stage.

The 1996 Olympics afford Scurry and her American teammates an excellent opportunity to make amends for their loss of the world championship. Is another U.S.-Norway duel pending?

—Les Stone

Schedule

The tentative soccer schedule is:

Saturday, July 20
Men's matches 1–4

Sunday, July 21
Men's matches 5–8
Women's matches 1–4

Monday, July 22
Men's matches 9–12

Tuesday, July 23
Women's match 5–8
Men's matches 13–16

Wednesday, July 24
Men's matches 17–20

Thursday, July 25
Men's match 21–24
Women's match 9–12

Saturday, July 27
Men's quarterfinal 1 & 2

Sunday, July 28
Women's semifinal 1 & 2
Men's quarterfinal 3 & 4

Wednesday, July 31
Men's semifinal 1 & 2

Thursday, August 1
Women's bronze & gold medal

Friday, August 2
Men's bronze medal

Saturday, August 3
Men's gold medal

Highlights

Although at the time not officially recognized as an Olympic sport, two soccer matches were played in 1896 at Athens: a Greek team from Smyrna was defeated in the final by a Danish team by a score of 15–0. Soccer was considered a demonstration sport at Paris in 1900, when London defeated the host city's team with a score of 4–0. The host city's team in the St. Louis Games, too, was defeated, this time by the Galt Football Club of Canada. The third place team, also from the U.S., scored one goal . . . for the opposing team.

Finally, in 1908, the host city's team claimed a victory: Britain outscored Denmark, who in turn soundly beat the two French teams. Ten of Denmark's 17 goals in their match against the French B team—which scored once—were netted by Sophus Nielsen. Britain successfully defended the title in Stockholm in 1912; their opponents, a Danish team, were forced to play with only ten men when the eleventh was sidelined by injury.

1920 produced the first of what would be a series of incidents in the field: the Belgian team was awarded the victory when a

Czech player—who had kicked a Belgian player rather than the ball—was ejected from the game. His teammates followed, and the gold went to Belgium.

Uruguay, the only non-European team to win the final up until then, took the gold medal home in both 1924 and in 1928; oddly, they never participated in Olympic soccer again. In the 1924 match, Uruguay played against Switzerland, with a French referee. Initially, the game was assigned a Dutch referee; Uruguay promptly protested, having beaten the Dutch team, amid some controversy, in the semifinals. Some 60,000 people jammed the stadium to watch the final match, and the 5000 would-be spectators outside the stadium sustained a number of injuries.

Uruguay's 1928 victory over Argentina was less turbulent, although the final had to be replayed because of a tied score in the first match. Conspicuous by its absence, Great Britain entered neither the 1924 nor the 1928 Games because of its grudges with the Football Association and with the FIFA.

Soccer was omitted from the 1932 Games, and reintroduced itself at the Berlin Games with little aplomb. Two Americans were injured in the first match between the U.S. and Italy, who played with a full complement of players, despite the fact that the referee had ordered one of the Italians to leave the game.

What came later in the tournament was mayhem: in the second overtime in the quarterfinal match between Peru and Austria, Peruvian fans stormed the field and attacked an Austrian player; the Peruvian team seized the opportunity to score two goals, and, not surprisingly, the results were protested. Officials ordered a rematch between Peru and Austria—to be played under lock and key, with no crowds to interfere—and the Peruvian team refused to play. In fact, all of Peru's athletes withdrew from the Games, and the Colombians followed. Meanwhile, in Lima, demonstrators were hurling insults and stones at the German consulate. With the Peruvians absent, the final was contested between the Austrians and the Italians, who, in overtime, won the gold.

The 1948 final match turned out to be a firemen's ball: the Swedish team—which included three brothers and three firemen—won the match over Yugoslavia. By 1952, soccer had become such a popular Olympic sport that pre-Games tournaments were held to decide which 16 teams would compete. In Helsinki, Hungary won the first of three victories, defeating Yugoslavia in 1952, Czechoslovakia in 1964, and Bulgaria in 1968. The Soviets won in Melbourne against the Yugoslavian team, 1−0, thanks to a disallowed Yugoslavian goal.

Yugoslavia—who until 1960 had always been the bridesmaid and never the bride, and whose team made the quarterfinal by virtue of a coin toss—enjoyed its day in the sun at the Rome Games. Yugoslavia defeated Denmark in the final match—even though their team captain had been expelled from the game for having insulted a referee.

The 1964 match has become infamous not because of the ultimate resolution of the tournament—in which Hungary defeated Czechoslovakia—but for the tragic outcome of one of the qualifying matches. The match between Peru and Argentina—held in Lima—was suspended when unruly crowds protested the referee's decision to disallow the Peruvian team's tying goal because of rough play. The rioting that followed was so violent that the Peruvian government declared a state of siege; 328 people were left dead, and another 500 were injured.

Crowds in the final match in Mexico City were tame compared to the Lima debacle, but were unruly nonetheless, throwing cushions at the field to express their lack of sympathy with the referees. When a Bulgarian player was expelled for rough play, a domino effect seemed to take place, and two other Bulgarian expulsions followed, leaving a skeleton team of only 8 players. Eight was not enough, and the Hungarians won the final with a score of 4−1.

Although the U.S. was one of the first teams eliminated from the Munich Games, they had at least qualified. 1972 provided a rainy day for Hungary—who had lost only one Olympic match since 1960—when rainstorms and windy weather turned the tables on them in the second half of the final. The Polish team, with the wind at their backs during the final half, scored two goals against Hungary, winning the gold.

Attempting to defend their title in Montreal, the Polish team was defeated by the East Germans, when the latter scored their third and final goal with six minutes to go. The Moscow Games were not entirely up to snuff—seven of the sixteen qualifying teams declined to participate—and only one goal was scored in the final match, allowing the Czechs a victory over the East Germans; for third place, the Soviets defeated the Yugoslavs.

In the boycott year of 1984, for the first time since the Swedish team had won in 1948, a non-Communist country won the gold:

The home
team won the
gold at
Barcelona:
Spain's men's
soccer team
medaled for
the first time
since 1920.
*AP/Wide
World Photos*

In a final match against Brazil, the French team took the first-place medal. The Yugoslavian team won the bronze.

By the 1988 Olympics, the U.S. had won only two of thirteen matches, and had been outscored by as much as 53–8. In Seoul, however, they made it up to the quarterfinal: having tied with the South Korean team, they proceeded to take on the Soviets, who ultimately beat them 4–2. In the finals, the Soviets outscored the Brazilian team. The bronze-medaling team in 1988 was from Germany—this time from the West.

Highlights from Barcelona

For the tenth time in ten appearances, the U.S. team was eliminated from Olympic soccer competition in the first round of matches. On the day before the Games officially opened, before a modest crowd of 18,000, the Italians stomped the U.S. team 2–0, thanks to Demetrio Albertini. Three days later, scoring three goals at Zaragoza, U.S. players dominated the Kuwaitis 3–1. And finally, on their last day of play, the U.S. squad—whose sweeper Alexi Lalas was playing with a broken left foot—tied the soon-to-be-medaled Polish team 2–2 in group play. Still, it was a good year for the U.S. team, which had earned three points in the first round, matching its best Olympic performance.

Although Australia, like the U.S., does not have a strong soccer tradition, the Aussie team staged a brief but valiant coup. After qualifying for the Games by beating the Dutch, the Australian squad proceeded to knock out Sweden 2–1 to reach the semifinals. Although soundly clocked by the Poles in their final match, the Aussies nevertheless managed a creditable fourth place behind the podium-bound African squad.

It was a better year still for the Spanish team. Playing before King Juan Carlos and a crowd of 95,000 delirious spectators, the Spanish squad romped to its first-ever Olympic soccer victory. In the matches leading up to the final, Spain scored eleven times without conceding a single goal, thanks to 20-year-old striker Francisco Narvaex-Kiko. Buoyed by their quarterfinal victory over arch-rival Italy, the Spaniards faced off against Ghana in the semi's, scoring twice without giving up a goal. By now guaranteed a silver-medal finish, the home team marched into battle with Poland, who had beaten Australia 6–1 in the semi-final. And the rest was history: with a last-minute goal by Albert Ferrer, Spain wrested victory from the Poles, ensuring that the title would rest with the home team.

Medalists

Men's Soccer (Football)

1992

1. Spain, Jose Santiago Cañizares Ruiz, Albert Ferrer Llopis, Mikel Lasa Goicoechea, Roberto Solozabal Villanueva, Juan M. Lopez Martinez, David Villabona Etxaleku, Jose Amavisca Garate, Luis Enrique Martinez Garcia, Josep Guardiola Sala, Abelardo Fernandez Antuña, Javier Manjarin Pereda, Francisco Veza Fragoso, Antonio Jimenez Sistachs, Gabriel Vidal Nova, Francisco Soler Atencis, Miguel Hernandez Sanchez, Rafael Berges Marin, Antonio Pinilla Miranda, Quico Narvaez, Alfonso Perez Muñoz

2. Poland, Aleksander Klak, Marcin Jalocha, Tomasz Lapinski, Marek Kozminski, Tomasz Waldoch, Dariusz Adamczuk, Grzegorz Mielcarski, Jerzy Brzeczek, Andrzej Juskowiak, Arkadiusz Onyszko, Ryszard Staniek, Marek Bajor, Andrzej Kobylanski, Miroslaw Waligora, Dariusz Szubert, Tomasz Wieszczycki, Dariusz Kosela, Wojciech Kowalczyk

3. Ghana, Simon Addo, Sammi Adjei, Mamood Amadu, Frank Amankwah, Bernard Nii Aryee, Isaac Asare, Kwame Ayew, Ibrahim Dossey, Mohammed Gargo, Mohammed Dramani Kalilu, Maxwell Konadu, Osei Kuffuor, Samuel Ablade Kumah, Nii Odartey Lamptey, Anthony Mensah, Alex Nyarko, Yaw Preko, Shamo Quaye, Oli Rahman

1988

1. Soviet Union, A. Borodiouk, I. Dovrosvolski, Serguei Fokine, S. Gorloukovitch, Arvidas Ianonis, E. Iarovenko, G. Ketachvili, Dmitri Kharine, E. Kouznetsov, V. Lioutyi, Victor Lossev, Mikhailitchenko, A. Narbekovas, Igor Ponomarev, A. Proundnikov, Iouri Savitchev, Igor Skliarov, V. Tatartchouk, A. Cherednik, V. Tichtchenko

2. Brazil, Aloisio Alves, Jose Araujo, Jorge Campos, Valdo Candido, Andre Cruz, Romario Farias, Jose Ferreira, Ademir Kaefer, I. Nascimento, Sergio Luiz, Jose Oliveira, R. Raimundo, Edmar Santos, Joao Santos, Geovani Silva, Jorge Silva, Hamilton Souza, Milton Souza, C. Taffarel, Luiz Winck

3. West Germany, Rudi Bommer, Holger Fach, Wolfgang Funkel, Armin Goertz, R. Grahammer, Thomas Haessler, Thomas Hoerster, Olaf Janssen, Uwe Kamps, G. Kleppinger, J. Klinsmann, Frank Mill, Oliver Reck, K. Riedle, Gunnar Sauer, C. Schreier, Michael Schulz, Ralf Sievers, Fritz Walter, Wolfram Wuttke

1984

1. France, Albert Rust, William Ayache, Michel Bibard, Dominique Bijotat, Francois Brisson, Patrick Cubaynes, Patrice Garande, Phillipe Jeannol, Guy Lacombe, Jean-Claude Lemoult, Jean-Phillipe Rohr, Didier Senac, Jean-Christoph Thouvenel, Jose Toure, Daniel Xuereb, Jean-Louis Zanon, Michel Bensoussan

2. Brazil, Gilmar Rinaldi, Ronaldo Silva, Jorge Luiz Brum, Mauro Galvao, Ademir Rock Kaeser, Andre Luiz Ferreira, Paulo Santos, Carlos Verri, Joao Leiehardt Neto, Augilmar Oliveira, Silvio Paiva, Luiz Dias, Luiz Carlos Winck, Davi Cortez Silva, Antonio Jose Gil, Francisco Vidal, Milton Cruz

3. Yugoslavia, Ivan Pudar, Vlado Capljic, Mirsad Baljic, S. Katanec, Marko Elsner, Ljubomir Radanovic, Admir Smajic, Nenad Gracan, Milko Djurovski, Mehmed Basdarevic, Borislav Cvetkovic, Tomislav Ivkovic, Jovica Nikolic, Stjepan Devec, Branko Miljus, Dragan Stojkovic, Mitar Mrkela

1980

1. Czechoslovakia, Stanislav Seman, Ludek Macela, Josef Mazura, Libor Radimec, Zdenek Rygel, Petr Nemec, Ladislav Vizek, Jan Berger, Jindrich Svoboda, Lubos Pokluda, Werner Licka, Rostislav Vaclavicek, Jaroslav Netolicka, Oldrich Rott, Frantisek Stambacher, Frantisek Kunzo

2. East Germany, Bodo Rudwaleit, Artur Ullrich, Lothar Hause, Frank Uhlig, Frank Baum, Rudiger Schnuphase, Frank Terletzki, Wolfgang Steinbach, Jurgen Bahringer, Werner Peter, Dieter Kuhn, Norbert Trieloff, Matthias Liebers, Bernd Jakubowski, Wolf-Ridiger Netz, Matthias Muller

3. Soviet Union, Rinat Dasaev, Tengiz Sulakvelidze, Aleksandr Chivadze, Vigaz Khidiyatullin, Oleg Romantsev, Sergei Shavlo, Sergei Andreev, Vladimir Bessonov, Yuri Gavrilov, Fyodor Cherenkov, Valeri Gazzaev, Vladimir Pilguj, Sergei Baltacha, Sergei Nikulin, Khoren Oganesyan, Aleksandr Prokopenko

1976

1. East Germany, Jurgen Croy, Gerd Weber, Hans-Jurgen Dorner, Konrad Weise, Lothar Kurbjuweit, Reinhard Lauck, Gert Heidler, Reinhard Hafner, Hans-Jurgen Riediger, Bernd Bransch, Martin Hoffman, Gerd Kische, Wolfram Lowe, Hartmut Schade, Dieter Riedel, Hans-Ullrich Grapenthin, Wilfried Grobner

2. Poland, Jan Tomaszewski, Antoni Szymanowski, Jerzy Gorgon, Wojciech Rudy, Wladyslaw Zmuda, Zygmunt Maszczyk, Grzegroz Lato, Henryk Kasperczak, Kazimierz Deyna, Andrzej Szarmach, Kazimierz Kmiecik, Piotr Mowlik, Henryk Wawrowski, Henryk Wieczorek, Leslaw Cmikiewicz, Jan Beniger, Roman Ogaza

3. Soviet Union, Vladimir Astapovskiy, Anatoli Konkov, Viktor Matvienko, Mikhail Fomenko, Stefan Reshko, Vladimir Troshkin, David Kipiani, Vladimir Onishenko, Viktor Kolotov, Vladimir Veremeev, Oleg Blochin, Leonid Buriak, Vladimir Feodorov, Aleksandr Minayev, Viktor Zyiaginchev, Leonid Nazarenko, Aleksandr Prokhorov

1972

1. Poland, Hubert Kostka, Zbigniew Gut, Jerzy Gorgon, Zygmunt Maszczyk, Jerzy Kraska, Kazimierz Dejna, Ryszard Szymczak, Zygfryd Szoltysik, Wlodzimierz Lubanski, Robert Gadocha, Antoni Szymanowski, Marian Ostafinski, Kazimierz Kmiecik, Joachim Marx, Grzegorz Lato, Zygmunt Anczok, Leslaw Cmikiewicz

2. Hungary, Istvan Geczi, Peter Vepi, Miklos Pancsics, Laszlo Balint, Peter Juhasz, Ede Dunai, Lajos Ku, Lajos Szucs, Mihaly Kozma, Antal Dunai, Bela Varadi, Kalman Toth, Lajos Kocsis, Jozsef Kovacs, Laszlo Branikovits, Csaba Vidats, Adam Rothermel

3. East Germany, Jurgen Croy, Frank Ganzera, Lothar Kurbjuweit, Konrad Weise, Manfred Zapf, Bernd Bransch, Jurgen Pommerenke, Wolfgang Seguin, Eberhard Vogel, Hans-Jurgen Kreische, Jurgen Sparwasser, Peter Ducke, Joachim Streich, Ralf Schulenberg, Reinhard Hafner, Harald Irmscher, Siegemar Watzlich

3. Soviet Union, Oleg Blochin, Murtaz Hurcilava, Yuri Istomin, Vladimir Kaplichnyi, Viktor Kolotov, Yevgeny Lovchev, Sergei Olshanskiy, Yevgeny Rudakov, Vyacheslav Semenov, Gennady Yevrushikhin, Oganes Zanazanian, Andrei Yakubik, Arkadiy Andriasian

1968

1. Hungary, Karoly Fater, Dezso Novak, Lajos Dunai, Miklos Pancsics, Ivan Menczel, Lajos Szucs, Laszlo Fazekas, Antal Dunai, Laszlo Nagy, Erno Nosko, Istvan Juhasz, Lajos Kocsis, Istvan Basti, Laszlo Keglovich, Istvan Sarkozi

2. Bulgaria, Stojan Jordanow, Atanas Gerow, Georgi Christakijew, Milko Gaidarski, Kiril Iwkow, Iwailo Georgijew, Tswetan Dimitrow, Jewgeni Jantschowski, Petar Schekow, Atanas Christow, Asparuch Donew, Kiril Christow, Todor Nikolow, Michail Gionin, Jantscho Dimitrow, Georgi Iwanow, Iwan Safirow, Georgi Wassiljew

3. Japan, Kenzo Yokoyama, Hiroshi Katayama, Yoshitada Yamaguchi, Mitsuo Kamata, Takaji Mori, Aritatsu Ogi, Teruki Miyamoto, Masashi Watanabe, Kunishige Kamamoto, Ikuo Matsumoto, Ryuichi Sugiyama, Masakatsu Miyamoto, Yasuyuki Kuwahara, Shigeo Yaegashi

1964

1. Hungary, Antal Szentmihalyi, Dezso Novak, Kalman Ihasz, Gusztav Szepesi, Arpad Orban, Ferenc Nogradi, Janos Farkas, Tibor Csernai, Ferenc Bene, Imre Komora, Sandor Katona, Jozsef Gelei, Karoly Palotai, Zoltan Varga

2. Czechoslovakia, Frantisek Schmucker, Anton Urban, Karel Z. Picman, Josef Vojta, Vladimir Weiss, Jan Geleta, Jan Brumovsky, Ivan Mraz, Karel Lichtnegl, Vojtech Masny, Frantisek Vlosek, Anton Svajlen, Karel Knesl, Stefan Matlak, Karel Nepomucky, Frantisek Knebort, Ludevit Cvetler

3. East Germany, Hans Jurgen Heinsch, Peter Rock, Manfred Geisler, Herbert Pankau, Manfred Walter, Gerhard Korner, Otto Frassdorf, Henning Frenzel, Jurgen Noldner, Eberhard Vogel, Horst Weigang, Klaus Urbanczyk, Bernd Bauchspress, Klaus-Dieter Sechaus, Werner Unger, Wolfgang Barthels, Klaus Lisiewicz, Dieter Engelhardt, Hermann Stocker

1960

1. Yugoslavia, Blagoje Vidinic, Novak Roganovic, Fahrudin Jusufi, Zeljko Perusic, Vladimir Durkovic, Ante Zanetic, Andrija Ankovic, Zeljko Matus, Milan Galic, Tomislav Knez, Borivoje Kostic, Milutin Soskic, Velimir Sombolac, Aleksandar Kozlina, Silvester Takac, Dusan Maravic

2. Denmark, Henry From, Poul Andersen, Poul
Jensen, Bent Hansen, Hans C. Nielsen,
Flemming Nielsen, Poul Pedersen, Tommy
Troelsen, Harald Nielsen, Henning Enoksen,
Jorn Sorensen, John Danielsen
3. Hungary, Gabor Torok, Zoltan Dudas, Jeno
Dalnoki, Erno Solymosi, Pal Varhidi, Ferenc
Kovacs, Imre Satori, Janos Gorocs, Florian
Albert, Pal Orosz, Janos Dunai, Lajos
Farago, Dezso Novak, Oszkar Vilezsal, Gyula
Rakosi, Laszlo Pal, Tibor Pal

1956

1. Soviet Union, Lev Yashin, Anatoli Bashashkin,
Mikhail Ogognikov, Boris Kuznyetsov, Igor
Netto, Anatoli Maslyonkin, Boris Tatushin,
Anatoli Issayev, Nikita Simonyan, Sergei
Salnikov, Anatoli Ilyun, Nikolai Tichenko,
Aleksei Paramonov, Eduard Streltsov,
Valentin Ivanov, Vladimir Ryjkin, Yosif
Betsa, Boris Rasinsky
2. Yugoslavia, Petar Radenkovic, Mladen
Koscak, Nikola Radovic, Ivan Santek,
Ljubisa Spajic, Dobroslav Krstic, Dragoslav
Sekularac, Zlatko Papec, Sava Antic, Todor
Veselinovic, Muhamed Mujic, Blagoje
Vidinic, Ibrahim Biogradlic, Luka Liposinovic
3. Bulgaria, Josif Josifow, Kiril Rakarow,
Nikola Kowatschew, Stefan Stefanow, Mnaol
Manolow, Gawril Stojanow, Dimiter
Milanow, Georgi Dimitrow, Panajot
Panajotow, Iwan Kolew, Todor Dijew, Georgi
Naydenow, Miltscho Goranow, Krum Janew

1952

1. Hungary, Gyula Grosics, Jeno Buzanszky,
Mihaly Lantos, Jozsef Bozsik, Gyula Lorant,
Jozsef Zakarias, Nandor Hidegkuti, Sandor
Kocsis, Peter Palotas, Ferenc Puskas, Zoltan
Czibor, Jeno Dalnoki, Imre Kovacs I, Laszlo
Budai II , Lajos Csordas
2. Yugoslavia, Vladimir Beara, Branislav
Stankovic, Tomislav Crnkovic, Zlatko
Cajkovski, Ivan Horvat, Vujadin Boskov,
Tihomir Ognjanov, Rajko Mitic, Bernard
Vukas, Stjepan Bobek, Branko Zebec
3. Sweden, Karl Svensson, Lennart Samuelsson,
Erik Nilsson, Olof Ahlund, Bengt Gustavsson,
Gosta Lindh, Sylve Bengtsson, Gosta
Lofgren, Ingvar Rydell, Yngve Brodd, Gosta
Sandberg, Holger Hansson

1948

1. Sweden, Torsten Lindberg, Knut Nordahl,
Erik Nilsson, Birger Rosengren, Bertil
Nordahl, Sune Andersson, Kjell Rosen,
Gunnar Gren, Gunnar Nordahl, Henry
Carlsson, Nils Liedholm, Borje Leander
2. Yugoslavia, Ljubomir Lovric, Miroslav
Brozovic, Branislav Stankovic, Zlatko
Cajkovski, Miodrag Jovanovic, Aleksandar
Atanackovic, Zvonko Cimermancic, Rajko
Mitic, Stjepan Bobek, Zeljko Cajkovski,
Bernard Vukas, Franjo Sostaric, Prvoslav
Mihajlovic, Franjo Wolfl, Kosta Tomasevic
3. Denmark, Eigil Nielsen, Viggo Jensen, Knud B.
Overgaard, Axel Pilmark, Dion Ornvold, Ivan
Jensen, Johannes Ploger, Knud Lundberg,
Carl A. Praest, John Hansen, Jorgen
Sorensen, Holger Seebach, Karl A. Hansen

1936

1. Italy, Bruno Venturini, Alfredo Foni, Pietro
Rava, Giuseppe Baldo, Achille Piccini, Ugo
Locatelli, Annibale Frossi, Libero Marchini,
Sergio Bertoni, Carlo Biagi, Francesco
Gabriotti, Luigi Scarabello, Giulio Cappelli,
Alfonso Negro
2. Austria, Eduard Kainberger, Ernst Kunz,
Martin Kargl, Anton Krenn, Karl Wahlmuller,
Max Hofmeister, Walter Werginz, Adolf
Laudon, Klement Steinmetz, Karl Kainberger,
Franz Fuchsberger, Franz Mandl, Josef
Kitzmuller
3. Norway, Henry Johansen, Nils Eriksen,
Oivind Holmsen, Frithjof Ulleberg, Jorgen
Juve, Rolf Holmberg, Magdalon Monsen,
Reidar Kvammen, Alf Martinsen, Odd
Frantzen, Arne Brustad, Fredrik Horn, Sverre
Hansen, Magnar Isaksen

1932

Not held

1928

1. Uruguay, Andres Mazali, Jose Nasazzi, Pedro
Arispe, Jose L. Andrade, Lorenzo Fernandez,
Juan Piriz, Alvaro Gestido, Santos
Urdinaran, Hector Castro, Pedro Petrone,
Pedro Cea, Antonio Campolo, Adhemar
Canavesi, Juan Arremon, Rene Borjas, Hector
Scarone, Robert Figueroa
2. Argentina, Angel Bosio, Fernando Paternoster,
Ludovico Bidoglio, Juan Evaristo, Luis F.
Monti, Segundo Medici, Raimundo Orsi,
Enrique Gainzarain, Manuel Ferreyra,
Domingo Tarasconi, Adolfo Carricaberry,
Feliciano A. Perducca, Octavio Diaz, Robert
Cherro, Rodolfo Orlandini, Saul Calandra
3. Italy, Giampiero Combi, Delfo Bellini,
Umberto Caligaris, Alfredo Pitto, Fulvio
Bernardini, Pietro Genovesi, Adolfo

Baloncieri, Elvio Banchero, Angelo Schiavio, Mario Magnozzi, Virgilio F. Levratto, Giovanni Depra, Virginio Rosetta, Silvio Pietroboni, Antonio Janni, Enrico Rivolta, Gino Rossetti

1924

1. Uruguay, Andres Mazali, Jose Nasazzi, Pedro Arispe, Jose L. Andrade, Jose Vidal, Alfredo Ghierra, Santos Urdinaran, Hector Scarone, Pedro Petrone, Pedro Cea, Angel Romano, Umberto Tomasina, Jose Naya, Alfredo Zibechi, Antoni o Urdinaran
2. Switzerland, Hans Pulver, Adolphe Reymond, Rudolf Ramseyer, August Oberhauser, Paul Schmiedlin, Aron Pollitz, Karl Ehrenbolger, Robert Pache, Walter Dietrich, Max Abegglen, Paul Fassler, Felix Bedouret, Adolphe Mengotti, Paul Sturzenegger, Edmond Kramer
3. Sweden, Sigfrid Lindberg, Axel Alfredsson, Fritjof Hillen, Gunnar Holmberg, Sven Friberg, Harry Sundberg, Evert Lundqvist, Sven Rydell, Per Kaufeldt, Tore Keller, Rudolf Kock, Gustaf Carlson, Charles Brommesson, Thorsten Svensson, Albin Dahl, Konrad Hirsch, Sven Lindqvist, Sten Mellgren

1920

1. Belgium, Jan De Bie, Armand Swartenbroeks, Oscar Verbeeck, Joseph Musch, Emile Hanse, Andre Fierens, Louis van Hege, Henri Larnoe, Mathieu Bragard, Robert Coppee, Desire Bastin, Felix Balyu, Fernand Nisot, Georges Hebdin
2. Spain, Ricardo Zamora, Pedro Vallana, Mariano Arrate, Jose Samitier, Jose M. Belausteguigoitia, Agustin Sancho, Ramon Eguiazabal, Felix Sesumaga, Patricio Arabolaza, Rafael Moreno, Domingo Acedo, Juan Artola, Francisco Pagazaurtundua, Louis Otero, Joaquin Vasquez, Ramon Moncho Gil, Sabino Bilbao, Silverio Izaguirre
3. Netherlands, Robert McNeill, Henri L. B. Denis, Bernard W. J. Verweij, Leonard F. G. Bosschart, Frederik C. Kuipers, Hermanus H. Steeman, Oscar E. van Rappard, Jan L. van Dort, Bernardus Groosjohan, Herman C. F. van Heijden, Jacob E. Bulder, Johannes D. de Natris, Evert J. Bulder, Adrianus G. Bieshaar

1912

1. Great Britain, Ronald Brebner, Thomas Burn, Arthur Knight, Douglas McWhirter, Henry C. Littlewort, Joseph Dines, Arthur Berry, Vivian Woodward, Harold Walden, Gordon Hoare, Ivan Sharpe, Edward Hanney, Gordon Wright, Harold Stamper
2. Denmark, Sophus Hansen, Nils Middelboe, Harald Hansen, Charles Buchwald, Emil Jorgensen, Paul Berth, Oscar Nielsen-Norlund, Axel Thufason, Anton Olsen, Sophus Nielsen, Vilhelm Wolffhagen, Hjalmar Christoffersen, Aksel Petersen, Ivar Lykke Seidelin, Poul Nielsen
3. Netherlands, Marius J. Gobel, David Wijnveldt, Piet Bouman, Gerardus Fortgens, Constant W. Feith, Nicolaas de Wolf, Dirk N. Lotsy, Johannes W. Boutmy, Jan G. van Breda Kolff, Huug de Groot, Caesar H. ten Cate, Jan van der Sluis, Jan Vos, Nico Bouvy, Johannes M. de Korver

1908

1. Great Britain, Horace B. Bailey, William Corbett, Herbert Smith, Kenneth Hunt, Frederick W. Chapman, Robert Hawkes, Arthur Berry, Vivian Woodward, Hubert Stapley, Claude Purnell, Harold Hardman
2. Denmark, Ludvig Drescher, Charles Buchwald, Harald Hansen, Harald Bohr, Kristian Middelboe, Nils Middelboe, Oscar Nielsen-Norland, August Lindgreen, Sophus Nielsen, Vilhelm Wolffhagen, Bjorn Rasmussen, Marius Andersen, Johannes Gandil
3. Netherlands, Reinier B. Beeuwkes, Karel Heijting, Lou Otten, Johan W. E. Sol, Johannes M. de Korver, Emil G. Mundt, Jan H. Welcker, Edu Snethlage, Gerard S. Reeman, Jan Thomee, Georges F. de Bruyn Kops, Johan A. F. Kok

1906

1. Denmark, Viggo Andersen, Peter Petersen, Charles Buchwald, Parmo Ferslew, Stefan Rasmussen, Aage Andersen, Oscar Nielsen-Norland, Carl F. Petersen, Holger Fredriksen, August Lundgreen, Henry Rambusch, Hjalmar Heerup
2. International (Smyrna), Edwin Charnaud, Zareck Couyoumdzian, Edouard Giraud, Jacques Giraud, Henri Joly, Percy de la Fontaine, Donald Whittal, Albert Whittal, Godfrey Whittal, Herbert Whittal, Edward Whittal
3. Greece (Thessaloniki), Georgios Vaporis, Nicolaos Pindos, A. Tegos, Nicolaos Pentzikis, Ioannis Kyrou, Georgios Sotiriadis, V. Zarkadis, Dimitrios Michitsopoulos, A. Karangonidis, Ioannis Abbot, Ioannis Saridakis

1904

1. Canada, (Galt F. C. Ontario), Ernest Linton, George Ducker, John Gourley, John Fraser, Albert Johnson, Robert Lane, Tom Taylor, Frederick Steep, Alexander Hall, Gordon McDonald, William Twaits
2. U.S.A., (Christian Brothers College), Louis Menges, Oscar B. Brockmyer, Thomas T. January, John H. January, Charles January, Peter J. Ratican, Warren G. Brittingham, Alexander Cudmore, Charles A. Bartliff, Joseph P. Lydon, Raymond Lawler
3. U.S.A., (St. Rose. St. Louis), Frank Frost, George Crook, Henry W. Jameson, Joseph Brady, Dierkes, Martin T. Dooling, Cormic F. Cosgrove, O'Connell, Claude Jameson, Harry Tate, Thomas Cooke, Johnson

1900

1. Great Britain, J. H. Jones, Grosling, Claude Percy Buckenham, W. Quash, T. E. Burridge, A. Chalk, Haslam, J. Zealley, J. Nicholas, Spackman, R. P. Turner
2. France, Huteau, Bach, Pierre Allemane, Gaillard, Bloch, Macaire, Fraysse, Garnier, Lambert, Grandjean, Fernand Canelle, Dupare, Peltier
3. Belgium, Marcel Leboutte, R. Kelecom, Ernest Moreau, Alphonse Renier, Georges Pelgrims, E. Neefs, Erich Thornton, Albert Delbecque, H. Spannoghe, van Heuckelum, Londot

1896

Not held

Trivia Quiz

1. In 1314, King Edward II of England outlawed soccer because

a. Competitions routinely escalated into violent brawls

b. His royal highness was too fond of betting

c. He considered the sport to be an unforgivable waste of time

2. Soccer first appeared as an intramural sport

a. In the late nineteenth century, on Ivy league campuses

b. In the early twentieth century, at British boarding schools

c. In 1580, on British college campuses

3. A relative of soccer, in which players were allowed to run with the ball, was developed in the 1800s at

a. Notre Dame   **b.** Exeter Academy   **c.** Rugby School

4. Soccer was pulled from the 1932 Olympic program because

a. Spectators at the 1928 Olympic match had gotten into an uncontrollable brawl

b. Officials could not resolve a controversy concerning amateurism

c. The competition conflicted with that year's World Cup tournament

5. In 1930, the first World Cup was held in

a. England   **b.** Uruguay   **c.** Pontiac, Michigan

6. The United States team

a. Captured the bronze medal at the 1932 Games

b. Has never won an Olympic medal in soccer or taken the World Cup

c. Dominated the first ten years of Olympic soccer

7. Women's soccer
a. Was included as an exhibition event at the 1984 Games in LA
b. Will be a full-medal event for the first time in Atlanta
c. Shows no signs of being included on the Olympic roster

8. In Olympic competition, an automatic berth is not awarded to
a. The host country   **b.** The defending Olympic champion
c. The previous year's Pan American champion

9. The U.S. team's only goal in the 1900 Games was noteworthy because
a. It was scored as the result of a somersault kick
b. It was booted past a daydreaming goalie
c. It was scored for the opposing team

10. After capturing the 1924 and 1928 Olympic titles, Uruguay
a. Dominated the Olympic event for another twelve years
b. Never participated in Olympic soccer again
c. Caught the next boat to Disneyworld

SOFTBALL—WOMEN'S FAST PITCH

Warm-up

Whether you call it Mush Ball, Big Ball, Kitten Ball, or Twilight Ball, softball is America's favorite national sport. Really. According to a 1990 Gallup poll, almost 40 million Americans were playing the nostalgic summer game; by contrast, only 24.9 million Americans stepped up to the plate to play baseball. That makes softball the most popular team participation sport in the U.S.; it's so popular, in fact, that it has more participants than baseball and football *combined*.

And it's still growing. Between 1972 and 1990, softball participation in the United States leapfrogged from 27.2 million to 39.8 million participants.

One of the few sports in which there is near parity among the numbers of men and women participating, softball has drawn increasing numbers of girls and women. "When girls were given the right to equal opportunities in sports [with the passage of Title IX], fast pitch softball was one of the sports that really took off," Bill Redmer, the editor of *FastPitch World* magazine told the *LA Times*. "Softball is probably the most prominent example of where women have made dramatic gain."

And these women aren't just playing for fun. According to figures the NCAA released in 1995, softball continues to be one of the fastest growing women's sports on the collegiate level. And figures provided by the National Federation of State High School Associations indicate that fast pitch softball easily registered the top increase in school sponsorships among girls' sports.

These figures add up to one thing: Competition. Young girls are now playing softball the way boys have traditionally played baseball and a handful of other mainstream sports. They're playing a high-stakes game whose rewards include athletic scholarships, professional positions, and even some measure of fame. Not to mention precious medals.

Softball's Olympic status was a long time in coming. In 1968, then IOC President Avery Brundage had a few words of wisdom for Don E. Porter—the Executive Director of the Amateur Softball Association—who was lobbying to have the sport included on the Olympic roster. "Be patient," the IOC legend counseled, "and your sport's time will come."

You have heard of the patience of Job. On June 13, 1991, at an Executive Board meeting in Birmingham, England, the IOC accepted softball as a medal sport—for Atlanta only. Whether or not the sport will be a part of future Games is a question that will be resolved after the 1996 Olympics. In this respect, the sport's prospects look good: the Columbus, Georgia matches should draw large, enthusiastic crowds, and Australia—the host country for the next Summer Games—has a deep field of very strong women softball players.

FACT: Softball is the third most popular women's collegiate sport. Track and basketball top the list of the top 10 women's collegiate sports.

Women weren't always a part of softball's history, which began in November, 1887, inside the Farragut Boat Club in Chicago, when a number of ivy league alumni were impatiently waiting to hear the results of a Harvard-Yale football skirmish. When the news of Yale's victory came, a Yalie lobbed a boxing glove at a nearby Harvard alum, who attempted to hit the soft "ball" with a stick.

George Hancock, a reporter for the Chicago Board of Trade, took the idea and ran with it. Tying together the laces of the boxing glove for a ball, and marking off a playing area with chalk, the ivy leaguers, under Hancock's supervision, divided into two teams to play "indoor U.K." The Farragut team soon challenged other gyms to games, and the sport eventually moved outdoors, to fields that weren't quite big enough for U.K.

By 1889, the Mid Winter Indoor U.K. League of Chicago officially adopted a set of 19 rules that Hancock had adapted from the outdoor game. The sport gradually spread throughout the country, becoming especially popular in Minneapolis, where Louis Rober, a Fire Department lieutenant, decided the game would help keep his firemen fit. Playing with a bat two inches in diameter, Rober's firefighters tried to hit a small medicine ball that the pitcher lobbed from a distance of 35 feet. In no time, other fire companies caught softball fever. When Rober transferred to another company in 1895, he organized a team called the Kittens, and the firemen's game was soon known as "Kitten League Ball" (and later "Kitten Ball").

By 1933, two Chicago businessmen saw an opportunity to capitalize on the game's popularity. Leo Fischer and Michael J. Pauley, a Chicago Sporting goods salesman, decided to organize thousands of local softball teams into cohesive state organizations; these state organizations, in turn, were to be organized into a national organization.

Fischer and Pauley invited 55 teams—divided into three classes: fastballers, slow pitch, and women—to participate in a tournament that was staged in conjunction with the 1933 World's Fair in Chicago. On the tournament's opening day, where 70,000 spectators attended the first round of play, the Chicago *American* effused, "it is the largest and most comprehensive tournament ever held in the sport which has swept the country like wildfire."

Shortly thereafter, during the 1934 National Recreation Congress, the Amateur Softball Association (ASA) was admitted as a member of the Joint Rules Committee. The ASA brought order to the game, which, at the time, was at sixes and sevens; with no clearly defined rules, the length of the bases and pitcher's box had never been the same from one game to the next.

The following year, the *Playground Association Softball Guide* boasted that "the years of persistent effort, constant promotion and unchanging faith of believers in softball proved to have not been in vain for in 1934 softball came into its own. . . . The battle for recognition of this splendid game is over. Softball has won a place among America's foremost sports."

Sixty-some years later, with the sport's first Olympic appearance, the years of persistent effort, constant promotion, and unchanging faith of believers in softball proved once again to have not been in vain. Like the man said: "Be patient and your sport's time will come."

FACT: Although softball officials would like to have slow pitch added to the Olympic menu, the sport must first be accepted as a medal sport at the Pan American Games.

Spectator's Guide

The rules of softball are very similar to those of baseball. The ball is larger—between $11\frac{7}{8}$ and $12\frac{1}{8}$ inches in diameter—and weighs $6\frac{1}{4}$ to 7 ounces. Originally a cork-and-yarn ball, many leagues use a kapok ball or a solid polyurethane sphere that is anything but soft. But it is fast: Michele Granger, college softball's sultana of strikeouts, has an underhanded "riseball" that blasts over home plate somewhere in the mid-70s. (The pitching rubber in softball is closer to the plate than it is in baseball; that puts Granger's pitch somewhere in the neighborhood of a 96-mile-per-hour major league fastball.)

Bases in a fast pitch softball diamond are placed 60 feet apart, with the **pitcher's mound** 40 feet from home plate. (In men's fast pitch and both men's and women's slow pitch—none of which currently has Olympic status—the pitcher's mound is placed 46 feet from home.) The **outfield fence** is 200 feet from home plate in women's fast pitch (and 225–250 feet for men's).

Each team consists of **nine players**, whose positions are the same as in baseball: pitcher, catcher, first baseman, second baseman, third baseman, shortstop, left fielder, center fielder, and right fielder. Softball is played in only **seven innings**, with **three outs per inning**. A **tied game** continues for additional innings until one side has scored more runs at the end of a completed inning.

The pitcher stands with both feet on the rubber pitcher's plate, facing the batter, with her shoulders in line with first and third bases. The **pitch** must be delivered underhand, and the hand must be below the hip, with the wrist no further from the body than the elbow. The pitcher is allowed one step forward—in the direction of the batter and simultaneous with delivery. The ball's release and the follow-through must both be in a forward direction.

Pitchers can use any kind of **wind-up** with a few guidelines:

- there can be only one revolution in a "windmill" pitch
- one hand cannot be removed from the ball and then returned after the swing
- there must not be any halt or reverse in the forward motion
- the ball must be pitched immediately after the pitching motion.

The **strike zone** in fast pitch covers any part of home plate that is between the batter's arm pits and the top of her knees. Any ball pitched outside the strike zone is a **ball** (as long as the batter doesn't swing). In fast pitch, a ball the batter doesn't swing at is **live**. After four balls, the batter walks to first.

After hitting the ball into fair territory, the batter becomes a runner. A player scores a **run** by rounding all three bases—making sure to touch each one. Players are not allowed to score a run ahead of a preceding runner. Runners who are on base are permitted to move to the next base when the ball is in play; they may also run when the ball leaves the pitcher's hand on a pitch, and when it is dropped during the wind-up or backswing.

The object of the game, as in baseball, is simple: the team that scores the most points at the end of seven innings wins.

Hopefuls

Eight teams will compete at the 8,500-seat Golden Park Stadium in Columbus, an hour and a half outside of Atlanta. The first five countries—Australia, Canada, China, Chinese Taipei, and the U.S.—were chosen by their order of finish in the International Softball Federation championships in St. John's, Newfoundland, while the remaining three countries — Japan, Netherlands, and Puerto Rico — were selected in Olympic qualifying tournaments.

The U.S. women, with a phenomenal string of victories, are expected to take no prisoners in Atlanta. At the start of the 1995 season, the Women's National Team had won every competition entered; *and* every game. Between 1986 and the first quarter of 1995, they had racked up an astonishing 105–0 record in international play, including three consecutive ISF World Championships. Entering the Pan Am Games as the odds-on favorites, the U.S. women pulled a three-peat, making Pan Am history with their third consecutive gold medal performance.

And these weren't even the same women who had rousted all 15 opponents at the qualifying games earlier that year in Guatemala: None of the 18 women who dominated the Guatemalan qualifying games took part in the ruthless dissection of Pan Am pretenders.

Coaching the U.S. squad will be Ralph Raymond, who has a pretty impressive record of his own. As head coach of U.S.A. Softball Women's National Teams, he produced five gold medals in ISF World Championship play for a combined record of 55–0. He also led U.S. players to 10 other gold medals in competitions including the Pan Am Games, World Games, International Cup, Intercontinental Cup, World Cup, Challenger Cup, and South Pacific Classic.

"We have an abundance of talented players in the United States," Raymond told *Olympian* magazine. "But, individuals—great as they may be—working as individuals, do not make a

FACT: More than 3,700 women are scheduled to compete in the 1996 Olympics—about 600 more than in 1992—the largest number of women ever in Olympic medal competition.

"I want a hard-nosed kid who is willing to go all out and do the job, who believes that we can do it, and who will work their butts off to get that piece of gold."
—*Ralph Raymond, coach of the U.S. women's softball team*

team. It is my challenge to take the best of these and turn them into a cohesive unit, a family if you will."

Raymond's family includes some of the best women fast pitch softball players in the world. Ever. Pitcher Michele Granger presides as the NCAA all-time strikeout leader. "She throws like a baseball pitcher," her father told *Sports Illustrated*, "except underhanded." Infielder Laura Espinoza is considered to be the Babe Ruth of fast pitch; with 74 career home runs at the start of the 1995 season, she blasted the previous NCAA record of 34 right out of the ballpark.

And shortstop Dot Richardson was already a phenom by the age of 13, when she became the youngest player ever in the national Women's Major Fast Pitch league. A former UCLA star, she played on three Pan Am Games teams and in three ISF world championships. "This is one of the most phenomenal players to come down the pike," Raymond claims.

"What has occurred in the last 15 to 20 years is the American culture accepting and embracing girls and women in sports and respecting their athleticism and their involvement. That was not the case when I played in the earlier league."
—Rayla J. Allison, vice president and league director of the Women's Professional Fastpitch League (WPF)

And then there's Lisa Fernandez, who, many people say, is the best athlete ever to play the game. "She's got it all," says teammate Kelly Inouye. "It's scary." Finishing her college career in 1993 with a 93–7 record and a 0.22 earned-run average, Fernandez went 1–0 as pitcher for the gold-medaling U.S. team at the 1994 ISF World Championship at St. John's, Newfoundland. And she pitched a no-hitter with an ERA of 0.000 at the 1995 Pan Am qualifier in Guatemala.

The U.S. team's toughest competition will probably come from the Chinese women, who placed second at the ISF World Championship. (China doesn't compete in the Pan Am Games.) The Chinese National Women's Softball Team draws from a handful of municipal and provincial teams that are comprised of only a couple hundred athletes; with such a small pool of players to build on, it's no small miracle that the Chinese women have consistently nipped at the heels of the U.S. women's softball machine.

Recruiting athletes from other disciplines, Chinese coaches don't reap the benefits of a grassroots movement in the sport. What's more, because they have access to such a limited number of players, the odds are stacked against fortuitously discovering a once-in-a-lifetime natural. The secret to the success of the Chinese women's team is simple: They train maniacally, relying on preternatural conditioning and flawless defense.

—Marie J. MacNee

Schedule

The tentative softball schedule is:

Sunday, July 21
games 1–4

Monday, July 22
games 5–8

Tuesday, July 23
games 9–12

Wednesday, July 24
games 13–16

Thursday, July 25
games 17–20

Friday, July 26
games 21–24

Saturday, July 27
games 25–28

Monday, July 29
semifinals 1 & 2

Tuesday, July 30
bronze & gold medal

Trivia Quiz

1. **In the sport's early days, softball was known as**
   a. Mush Ball **b.** Kitten Ball **c.** Big Ball

2. **The IOC accepted softball as a full medal sport in**
   a. 1991 **b.** 1992 **c.** 1994

3. **Prior to the 1996 Games, softball**
   a. Was included in one Olympics, as a men's event
   b. Was included in two Olympics, as a demonstration sport
   c. Was never a part of the Olympic Games

4. **Former IOC President Avery Brundage**
   a. Was vehemently opposed to including softball in the Olympics
   b. Lobbied tirelessly to have softball included on the Olympic program
   c. Will not be throwing out the first pitch in Atlanta

5. **Softball was serendipitously invented in**
   a. The Farragut Boat Club in Chicago
   b. The YMCA in Holyoke, Massachusetts
   c. The dugout at Yankee stadium

6. **In the 1930s, softball gained national popularity thanks to**
   a. A team of Massachusetts players who traveled around the country to play
   b. Two Midwestern sporting goods salesmen **c.** The mayor of New York

7. **In Olympic softball, the windup of a windmill pitch may include**
   a. Only one revolution **b.** Up to three revolutions
   c. No fewer than two revolutions

8. Olympic softball is played in
   a. Seven innings   **b.** Eight innings   **c.** Nine innings

9. Which material is *not* used in the manufacture of softballs?
   a. Kapok   **b.** Kevlar   **c.** Polyurethane

10. Slow pitch softball
   a. Is slated to appear in the Olympics in the year 2000
   b. Is not currently included in the Pan American Games
   c. Will be a demonstration sport in Atlanta

Answers: 1-a, -b, and -c; 2-a; 3-c; 4-c; 5-a; 6-b; 7-a; 8-a; 9-b; 10-b

Swimming

Warm-up

Although the English generally are credited with introducing swimming as a sport in the late 1830s, races were held in Japan nearly two thousand years earlier. And in 1603 the Japanese formed the first national swimming organization.

But long before the first races were held, people went swimming. Plato remarked that anyone who couldn't swim lacked education. Julius Caesar, Alexander the Great, and Charlemagne were known for their swimming prowess, as well as their ability to conquer large parts of the world. The Old Testament describes people swimming in the Nile, and Greek mythology relates the tale of Leander swimming the Hellespont to enjoy the company of his lover. Lord Byron later crossed the same Hellespont in 1810 and the Tagus in 1818, both significant feats of swimming endurance.

Since the first human encountered a body of water blocking his or her way, people have been swimming (or perhaps first, drowning). Swimming for speed probably began when a waterborne human first encountered a large aquatic creature with dinner on its mind. But swimming didn't become a competitive sport resembling its modern form until the 19th century. In one of the first races on record, two Native Americans were brought to London in 1844 to compete for a silver medal offered by the National Swimming Society in England. The transatlantic competitors introduced the overhand (crawl) stroke to Britain, although the stuffy English clung to the slower breaststroke for another 40 years, insisting that endurance, not speed, was the issue.

In 1878, an Englishman by the name of Frederick Cavill moved to Australia. There he built that country's first swimming pool. But for pool building he's not remembered. On a trip through the South Seas, Cavill observed some natives swimming, and particularly noted the leg action that provided them with an extra kick. Returning to Australia, he demonstrated the leg kick to other swimmers, who appreciated the additional power that the kick provided. At the turn of the century, the leg kick was introduced to the U.S. and England by two of Cavill's sons, and the resulting stroke became known as the Australian crawl, revolutionizing swimming competitions.

A little more than 20 years after Captain Matthew Webb's pioneering swim across the English Channel (using the breaststroke), swimming was included on the initial Olympic Games program in 1896. Six countries sent 18 swimmers to compete for swimming titles in the 100, 500, and 1200 meter races, plus a special 100-meter race for sailors only. The events were restricted to men; women entered the Olympic swimming fray in 1912, taking part in three events: the 100-meter freestyle, the 4 × 100-meter relay, and high diving.

Following the 1896 debut, the next two Olympics were rather disorganized affairs, featuring programs essentially crafted by the host cities. At the 1900 Games, swimming events were held in the Seine, while an underwater race was held at the 1904 Games in St. Louis. The pool in St. Louis was in the middle of an artificial lake, making good seats scarce for spectators.

The 1908 Games in London were much better organized, providing the swimmers with a specially built pool 100 meters long and 17 meters wide. At this Olympiad, the Fédération Internationale de Natation Amateur (FINA), the governing body for competitive swimming, diving, water polo, and synchronized swimming, was formed. Under FINA's leadership, the sport became better organized and more popular, and now reigns as one of the dominant Olympic attractions.

Spectator's Guide

In the Olympics, swimmers compete in 32 medal events. The events are held in a 50-meter pool, also called the long course. A competitive pool must contain a minimum of eight lanes, each lane seven to nine feet wide. Additionally the water temperature must be between 78 and 80 degrees Fahrenheit (25.5 to 26.6 degrees Celcius).

Many races are lost in poor starts and turns. In the start, the swimmer is called to starting position by the starter, who visually checks that all swimmers are down and still. Then, once the starter is satisfied, the race is started by either a gun or an electronic tone. If the starter believes that one of the swimmers has jumped early, the race will be recalled and the offending swimmer disqualified.

Quick turns are essential. In all events the swimmer must touch the wall, but in the freestyle and the backstroke, the swimmer may somersault as he or she reaches the wall, touching only with the feet. In the other two competitive strokes, the swimmer must touch the wall with one or both hands before executing the turn.

The sprint races (50m and 100m) are all-out scrambles from start to finish. The slightest mistake can cost precious hundredths of seconds and, ultimately, the race.

The 200m events are a controlled sprint, as the swimmers pace themselves during the first part of the race.

The 400m, 800m, and 1500m freestyles require the swimmers to remain constantly aware of where they are and how tired they are becoming. Swimming the first portion of the race at too fast a pace can sap a swimmer's strength and cause a poor finish. Swimming the first portion of the race too slowly can separate the swimmer from the leading pack and make catching up impossible.

Two methods are used by swimmers for the distance races. They may elect to swim the race evenly (which is the preferred method of Janet Evans, who captured gold medals in the 1988 and 1992 Games and is expected to appear in the 1996 Games in Atlanta), holding the same pace throughout the race. Or they may "negative split" the race, covering the second half faster than the first, the most popular method in the early 1980s.

In the **freestyle**, competitors may use any strokes they wish, and their wish is usually the Australian crawl, characterized by the alternate overhand motion of the arms. Individual freestyle events for men and women include 50m, 100m, 200m, and 400m. Women also swim an 800m individual race, while the men engage in a 1500m event. Additionally, both women and men swim 400m and 800m freestyle relays, in which no individual may swim more than one leg of the race.

The **butterfly** features the simultaneous overhead stroke of the arms combined with the dolphin kick, and both the arms and legs move up and down together. No flutter kicking is allowed. The butterfly, perhaps the most beautiful and physically demanding stroke, was developed in the early 1950s as a loophole in the breaststroke rules and in 1956 became an Olympic event at the Melbourne Games. Butterfly races include a men's and women's 100m and 200m.

Popularized by Harry Hebner of the United States in the 1912 Olympics, the **backstroke** requires the swimmer to remain on his or her back at all times. The backstroke is the only race in which the competitors are in the water at the start, taking a handgrip on the edge of the pool while resting on their back. The stroke is an alternating motion of the arm, resembling an upside-down crawl. Starting in 1991, a swimmer no longer must touch the wall with his or her hand before executing the turn maneuver, a change that may cause many Olympic backstroke records to fall. Backstroke events include the men's and women's 100m and 200m races.

One of the most difficult strokes to master is the **breaststroke**, which requires simultaneous movements of the arms on the same horizontal plane. The hands are pushed forward from the breast or under the surface of the water and brought backward in the propulsive stage of the stroke simultaneously.

The kick is a simultaneous thrust of the legs called a "frog" or breaststroke kick. No flutter or dolphin kicking is allowed. At each turn a swimmer must touch with both hands at the same time. The breaststroke races include a men's and women's 100m and 200m.

The **individual** medley features all four competitive strokes. The swimmer begins with the butterfly, changes to the backstroke for another quarter, then breastroke, and finally finishes with the freestyle. The new "no-touch" backstroke turn may not be used in the backstroke to breaststroke exchange in an individual medley race. Both men and women swim 200m and 400m individual medleys.

And then we have the **medley relay**: all four strokes are swum by four different swimmers, covering 100m each. No swimmer may swim more than one leg of the relay, which is swum in backstroke, breaststroke, butterfly, then freestyle order. The men and women each compete in their own 400m race. An important part of any relay race is the exchange between the swimmer in the water and the next swimmer on the relay team. In a perfect exchange, the finishing swimmer's hand will alight on the touch pad at the same time as the starting swimmer's feet are still just touching the starting block, with the body extended over the water in the last instant before takeoff.

The first leg of a relay can be counted for a record, because while swimming an individual event or the lead-off leg of a relay, a swimmer cannot move on the blocks. To do so is called **rolling**, and constitutes a false start. On the subsequent legs of a relay, a swimmer can roll, as long as the person does not leave the block before the swimmer in the water touches the wall. As a result, relay splits tend to be faster than corresponding individual times and are not eligible for record consideration.

Swim Speak

Banana heat: Slang term for the consolation final of an event.

Blocks: The starting blocks from which the swimmer dives into the pool to begin the race; the front edge of the block is 30 inches above the surface of the water.

Gravity wave: Wave action caused by the swimmers' bodies moving through the water. Gravity waves move down and forward from the swimmer, bounce off the bottom of the pool, and return to the surface in the form of turbulence.

Lane: The area of the pool in which each swimmer competes during a race.

Lanelines: The dividers used to delineate the individual lanes. These are made of individual finned disks strung on a cable, rotating on the cable when hit by a wave. The rotating disks dissipate surface tension waves in a competitive pool.

Negative split: A race strategy in the distance freestyle events, in which a swimmer covers the second half of the race faster than the first half.

Relay exchange: The exchange between the swimmer in the water and the next swimmer on the relay team. In a perfect exchange, the finishing swimmer's hand will alight on the touch pad at the same time as the starting swimmer's feet are still just touching the starting block, with the body extended over the water in the last instant before takeoff.

Roll: To move on the blocks prior to the starting signal. A roll is usually caught by the starter, but swimmers will often try to guess the starter's cadence and get a good start. Similar to illegal procedure in football.

Shave: With a haircut, formerly two bits. Prior to a major competition, a swimmer will shave his or her entire body, lessening the resistance between skin and water.

Split: A swimmer's intermediate time in a race; splits are registered every 50 meters and are used to determine if a swimmer is on a record pace.

Touchpad: The area at the end of each lane in the pool where a swimmer's time is registered and sent electronically to the timing system.

Hopefuls—Men's

Gary Hall

Swimming has to be fun for Gary Hall, Jr., or he just won't do it. A likely Olympic contender in 1996, Hall is the fourth-fastest American in history—and a national champion—in the

100-meter freestyle. He won silver medals in both the 100-meter and the 50-meter freestyles at the 1994 World Championships and promises to improve his times in preparation for the 1996 Summer Games. An easygoing fellow who loves the sunny weather in his native Arizona, Hall tries to keep his swimming in proper perspective. "It's a sport, and I take it as a sport," he told the *Phoenix Gazette* on November 12, 1994. "It should always be fun. If I don't get an Olympic medal, it's not the end of the world."

At least some of Hall's considerable talent has been inherited from his forebears. His father, Gary Sr., qualified for the U.S. Olympic Team in 1968, 1972, and 1976. His maternal grandfather, Charles Keating, was an All-American collegiate swimmer who is better known for having been jailed in a federal prison after the $3.4 billion failure of Lincoln Savings & Loan in 1993. Whatever Hall might have reaped as a genetic benefit, however, has been countered by the anxiety he has felt over his grandfather's trial and imprisonment. "He always did a lot for me," Hall told the *Phoenix Gazette* when asked about his grandfather. "It was like losing a father. High school is hard enough without that. A lot of times I wonder how I kept swimming through high school."

Hall earned his first recognition as a junior at Brophy College Preparatory School, when he won the 50-meter and 100-meter freestyle races in record times at the Long Course Junior National Championships. That same year he swept all of the shorter freestyle races at the Arizona state high school championships. After graduating from Brophy Prep in 1993, Hall won an athletic scholarship to the University of Texas. There he moved out of his father's shadow for good, anchoring his Texas team to a record-breaking NCAA title in the 400-yard free relay. His success notwithstanding, Hall was unhappy in Texas. "I just had a hard time relating to the climate, the people and the atmosphere," he explained in the *Phoenix Gazette*. "I missed home and the sunny days."

Hall transferred to the University of Arizona, but after the 1994 World Championships he decided to forego his remaining years of college eligibility in favor of a more rigorous training schedule. The 1994 Worlds was Hall's first international meet, and he stunned more established swimmers by walking away with the silver medals in the 50-meter and 100-meter freestyles and two gold medals, for the 400-meter freestyle and medley relays. With a monthly stipend from U.S. Swimming and the prize money he can earn at events, Hall is supporting himself and preparing for the 1996 Olympics. He hopes to add ten pounds of muscle to his six-foot-eight, 183-pound frame by 1996. Eric Hansen, Hall's coach at the Phoenix Swim Club, told the *Phoenix Gazette:* "[Gary] needs to pull more water with each stroke. He needs to take pride in lifting and say, 'I want to be big for awhile.' "

Most observers agree that the amiable Hall was more highly motivated by his international experience than by his collegiate competition. Hall admits to having a fair share of unmotivated workouts. In this respect he has been helped by his principal international opponent, the Russian Alexandre Popov, who beat Hall at the 1994 World Championships. Interviewed after the meet, Popov bragged that he could win "on good days and bad," and he completely discounted Hall as a serious contender. The Russian couldn't have done his rival a bigger favor. "In practice sometimes it's easier to think about the competition," Hall told the *Phoenix Gazette*. "I keep him [Popov] in mind. My goal [at the World Championships] was to let him know I'm coming up and going to be there in '96. I accomplished that." He added: "It's a lot more motivating if the person beating you is bad mouthing you. It's like teasing an aggravated dog. It bothers me to see people be intimidated by [Popov]. I'm not at all."

> "It's a lot more motivating if the person beating you is bad mouthing you. It's like teasing an aggravated dog."
> —*Gary Hall, Jr.*

Hall, who likes to display the 1962 Volkswagon Microbus he restored himself two years ago, has made a fan even of his famous father. Gary Sr., now an eye surgeon in Paradise Valley, Arizona, described his son in the *Phoenix Gazette* as "a little bit of a [Grateful] Dead Head." The father added: "Gary is an artist. He's like a spaceman." Perhaps a future mission will take him to Atlanta.

—*Mark Kram*

Mel Stewart

Melvin Stewart enters the 1996 Olympics as a legitimate—and embattled—contender for the gold medal in the 200-meter butterfly race. Stewart, who held the world record in the 200-meter butterfly from early in 1991 until 1995, is a two-time Olympic team member and the holder of the 1992 Olympic gold medal in the event. He has been beaten only twice since 1988 and—thanks to a controversial style that keeps him under water for much of the race—is expected to dominate the Summer Games in Atlanta. On June 19, 1995, Stewart told *USA Today:* "My training is focused toward peaking next year. The time to swim fast is 1996."

Outgoing and a bit of a prankster, Stewart has had an unconventional life, to say the least. He was a nationally-ranked swimmer as a pre-teen who won races against older and larger

Mel Stewart (U.S.) medaled in Barcelona and plans to be back for the Games in Atlanta. *AP/Wide World Photos*

opponents. He lived with his family on the grounds of Heritage U.S.A., the "village" owned and run by the now-defunct and scandalized PTL Ministry. His career as a swimmer was helped immensely by his enrollment at the prestigious Mercersburg Academy in Pennsylvania, an opportunity made possible by the generous donations of a wealthy alumnus, George Baxter. "I guess you could say I've had some interesting . . . years," Stewart told *Sports Illustrated* on July 4, 1988. "Changing schools, becoming a world-class swimmer, traveling to Russia, having a father who works for an evangelical ministry that got involved in the biggest religious scandal in history. I don't know—is all that good or bad?"

For Stewart the news has almost always been good. Born and raised in Gastonia and Charlotte, North Carolina, he began swimming as a preschooler. He was in serious training by the age of seven, working with coach Frankie Bell who taught him to breathe to the side when doing the butterfly stroke. At ten he was ranked among the top ten in the nation in his age group in a phenomenal 16 events— he was number one in four of them. "Every time I fell into the water, it seemed I set a record," he recalled in a July 6, 1992 *Sports Illustrated* profile. "It was great." With personality to match his swimming prowess, Stewart attracted significant media attention. He proclaimed at every turn that he planned to win Olympic medals some day.

"I was counting down, 50 more meters, 40 more meters and then this nightmare is over."
—*Mel Stewart, who captured the 1992 200m butterfly title in Olympic record time*

When Stewart was 14, his parents moved to the Heritage U.S.A. community, where his father took the job of recreation director for PTL and athletic director of its school. Although employed by the ministry, the elder Stewart was skeptical about its leader, Jim Bakker, so Melvin and his sister attended the local public school, Fort Mill High. There Stewart suffered from a lack of academic motivation, but he was completely devoted to his sport. "I worked hard," he told *Sports Illustrated*. "Swimming was a release. I *had* to get away."

The chance to get even further away came early in Stewart's junior year at Fort Mill High. He was offered a place at Mercersburg Academy, a private preparatory school that had produced 15 Olympic swimmers in the past. Stewart wanted to go, but his family could not afford the $13,900 tuition. Help arrived in the form of a special scholarship donated by Baxter, a wealthy businessman who has served as friend and mentor for Stewart ever since. Stewart graduated from Mercersburg in 1988, two years after his international ranking in the 200 meter butterfly had soared from 33rd to second.

Possibly the biggest disappointment of Stewart's career occurred in the 1988 Olympics in Seoul. He was favored to win the gold in his event but finished a distant fifth. "My stomach felt sick," he recalled in *Sports Illustrated*. "I knew it would be the longest time until 1992." Thus began what Stewart has since described as a "four-year nightmare." He enrolled in the University of Tennessee and concentrated on his swimming, mentally racing against his principal opponents over and over again. When the National Collegiate Athletic Association (NCAA) tightened restrictions on practice time for college swimmers, Stewart decided to give up his final year of eligibility. That meant that he could start earning money from product endorsements and stipends from U.S. Swimming. He spent the summers of 1990 and 1991 training in Las Vegas—the very antithesis of the pious and pristine Heritage U.S.A.

> "People in the swimming community are looking for an easy way out, a way to decrease the amount of time they spend in the water. But in years to come we're going to see athletes doing much more work. You've got to feel pain every day."
> —*Mel Stewart, in* Sports Illustrated

Mel Stewart has been forthright about his acceptance of money and sponsorship throughout his recent career. "The future of the Olympic Games and something called Olympic spirit—intangible but priceless—will depend on corporate support," he told *USA Today* on May 26, 1993. ". . . I can say for sure that money is not the motivation when you're at the Games. There, it's all about competition. The money is only a motivation when the alarm goes off at 5:30 in the morning and you realize you have to go to practice again. Then it helps."

On January 12, 1991, Stewart set a new world record for the 200-meter butterfly with a mark of 1:55.69. His years of "nightmare" did not end, however, until the 1992 Summer Olympics. In Barcelona he finally earned his gold medal, winning decisively with an Olympic record-setting time of 1:56.26. The delighted swimmer gave his medal to his benefactor, George Baxter. "When I finished fifth in Seoul, everyone was nice to me," he explained in *Sports Illustrated*. "All my coaches, friends. They patted me on the back and said I'd done a good job. Mr. Baxter said, 'This is fuel for the fire.' He was the one who knew. I knew exactly what he meant. I started working again."

In preparation for his third Olympics, Stewart has been perfecting an under water style that has led to new American records in the 100-meter (short-course) and 200-meter butterfly. "I'm totally excited. It's so fast it's scary," he enthused to *USA Today* on December 20, 1994. New challenges await the champion, however. His world record was broken in the summer of 1995 by Russian Denis Pankratov—probably his most serious rival for the gold medal in 1996. Asked for his reaction to the news of this latest competitor, the affable Stewart told *USA Today:* "All I can say is this makes life a lot more interesting. . . . I like things that raise the emotions."

—Mark Kram

Up and Comers

A number of up-and-coming swimmers will challenge for the chance to represent the U.S. at the 1996 Olympics. **Tom Dolan**, named U.S. Swimming's Swimmer of the Year in 1994, is one who knows well how tough it can be to win a medal. The world record holder and world champion in the grueling 400-meter individual medley, Dolan suffers from asthma, allergies, and a restricted esophagus—"it's like having *no* air," he explained in the *Kansas City Star* on October 1, 1994. His physical limitations notwithstanding, the six-foot-six Dolan is a five-time U.S. National Champion and former Sullivan Award nominee. He is also the first man since Mark Spitz in 1972 to win four events at the Phillips 66 Spring Nationals.

A Virginia native, Dolan was born September 15, 1975. He suffered from allergies as a child but did not let them deter him from the physical activities that he loved so much. A talented swimmer as a youth, he was told at age 13 that he had exercise-induced asthma. He persisted nevertheless, taking care to rest well before meets. Today he battles the condition by using watered-down inhaler sprays—just about the only medication allowed under the strict rules of competition. Dolan told the *Kansas City Star* that he sought the help of a pulmonary specialist for the condition. "They stuck a tiny little black tube with a camera in it down the back of my throat to my larynx," he said. "What they saw was the size of my esophagus was too small."

Has his health made a difference? Not at all. Dolan won the silver medal in the 400-meter individual medley at the 1993 Pan Pacific Game. A freshman at the University of Michigan, he was named Big Ten Swimmer of the Year and Big Ten Freshman of the Year. The following summer he improved even further, setting an American record in the 400-meter individual medley at the Phillips 66 Spring Nationals and then setting a new world record in the same event at the World Championships. Legend has it that Dolan's performance at the 1994 P66 Spring Nationals caused former record holder Tamas Darnyi to announce his retirement.

Long and lean, Dolan is one of those charmed individuals who can eat anything without gaining weight. His best events are the 400-meter individual medley, the 800-meter freestyle, and the 1,500-meter freestyle.

Chad Carvin, born on April 13, 1974, in Laguna Hills, California, may look and sound like a Southern California native. His work ethic, however, is more in line with the New England Calvinists. "I've always liked to train. I've never been the type to go, 'Oh no, we've got a hard set coming up. I don't want to do it,'" Carvin told the *Orange County Register* on August 10, 1994. The American record holder in the 50-yard and 1,650-yard freestyle races, Carvin has yet to prove himself in international competition. At the 1994 World Championships he finished eighth in the 200-meter freestyle, 12th in the 400-meter freestyle and 10th in the 1,500-meter freestyle—and then came home and had his appendix removed within days of the event. It is fair to say he might have done better in full health.

Carvin, who was a triple gold medal winner with the 1992 Junior National team (200-meter, 400-meter, and 1,500-meter freestyles) is trying to make his mark in a crowded field of American freestyle sprinters. He told the *Orange County Register* that he has had to face down his fiercest opponent: himself. "I can remember races where I'd be thinking, 'That guy ahead of me, he's pretty tough, he'll probably beat me and that's OK,'" he recalled. "Now, if I do get beat, it makes me so mad. It's like, 'Next time I won't let that happen.'"

One of those guys ahead of Carvin might turn out to be **David Fox**, a 1993 graduate of North Carolina State. Fox owned the shorter freestyle events at the 1995 U.S. Spring Nationals in Minneapolis. He won gold medals in the 50-meter, 100-meter, and 200-meter freestyle races, turning in the third-fastest time in U.S. history in the 50-meter sprint. Later he called the event "the best total performance I've ever put in."

Born on February 25, 1971, Fox has been swimming since he was four years old. As a teen he was the Y.M.C.A. national champion in the 50-meter and 100-meter freestyle in 1988, as well as the national champion in the 50-meter freestyle, 100-meter freestyle, and 100-meter butterfly in 1989. He enrolled at North Carolina State in 1989 and, after being set back by a bout of mononucleosis, set the Atlantic Coast Conference record in both the 50-yard and 100-yard freestyles in 1992. Fox earned his bachelor's degree in civil engineering in 1993, the same year that he won his first national title—a 50-meter freestyle sprint at the Phillips 66 Summer Nationals. That same year he took four gold medals (50-meter, 100-meter, 400-meter freestyle, 400-meter medley relay) at the World University Games. He also broke Matt Biondi's 1987 National Collegiate Athletic Association record in the 50-yard freestyle by a miniscule one one-hundredth of a second.

Having finished college, Fox moved to Fort Lauderdale, Florida and tried to combine his swimming pursuits with a part-time job. The result was a dismal failure. He finished dead last in the 200-meter freestyle at the 1994 Spring Nationals and finished a dismal 29th in the 50-meter race. "I got hammered," he told *Sports Illustrated* on May 1, 1995. "It showed me that if I was going to keep swimming, I had to give it 100 percent of my time. I had to decide what was important to me. This is it."

Since then Fox has been in Colorado Springs, Colorado, working with U.S. Swimming's resident national team. The sixth-fastest man ever in the 50-meter freestyle hopes to make a big return to his sport in time for the Summer Games. "I like the purity of this sport," Fox concluded. "It's just me, the lane, the clock . . ." and possibly the medal stand.

—Mark Kram

Hopefuls—Women's

Janet Evans

Janet Evans is viewing the 1996 Olympic Games as a chance to have fun. The world record holder in the 400-meter, 800-meter, and 1500-meter freestyle, Evans is the only American woman ever to win four Olympic gold medals in swimming and the rare competitor who has won gold at two consecutive Olympics. She was the darling of the 1988 Games in Seoul, and now she is swimming's *grande dame*, racing against rivals who were just little girls when she won her first Olympic gold.

Fame has been particularly kind to Evans. William A. Henry III noted in a *Time* magazine profile on July 27, 1992 that, as "the world's most famous woman swimmer," Evans has "cashed in." Product endorsements, motivational speeches, and a perennial berth on the U.S. Swimming national team have provided the athlete with a comfortable income and the freedom to train vigorously for the longer-distance events in which she so excels. If she is no longer quite as fast as she was in 1988, neither is anyone else—all three of her world records were recorded in the 1980s and have yet to be surpassed.

U.S. swimmer Janet Evans waves to the crowd after winning the gold in the 800-meter freestyle in 1992. Evans also picked up a silver in the 400-meter freestyle, adding to her three golds from Seoul. *AP/Wide World Photos*

Evans was born on August 28, 1971 in Placentia, California. She grew up there, learning to swim soon after she learned to walk. At five she competed in her first race. By the age of 15 she had earned a national ranking, winning the Phillips Performance Award at the U.S. Open Swim Meet for breaking Tracy Caulkins's 400-meter individual medley meet record. She was a junior in high school when she set national high school records for the 200-yard individual medley and the 500-yard freestyle. Even then Evans was something of a celebrity, although she tried to keep her life away from the pool as normal as possible. She signed her first autograph at 15. "It was really weird when that started," she recalled in a March 26, 1990 *Sports Illustrated* profile, "because I thought *I* was one of those little kids."

"Little" might be one way of describing Evans as she easily qualified for her first Olympics in 1988. At the time she was just five feet, 5½ inches tall and weighed 102 pounds. A *Sports Illustrated* reporter who watched her climb the block for her gold medal 800-meter freestyle race—surrounded on both sides by enormous, muscled East German rivals—described her as looking like "an age-group swimmer who had somehow stumbled into the wrong race." In fact, Evans's lithe figure proved a significant asset. She won the Olympic gold in the 400-meter individual medley, set a world record in the 400-meter freestyle in a gold medal performance three days later, and capped the Summer Games by taking the gold medal in the 800-meter freestyle. Evans was the only American woman who won individual gold medals in swimming that year, and her perky personality and obvious youth charmed the viewers at home. "Evans was the bright spot for the U.S. women swimmers," wrote Bruce Anderson in *Sports Illustrated* on October 3, 1988. ". . . And she beamed and bubbled and giggled with delight at winning."

"My body has changed, and if I never swim an 8:16 in my life again, I'm not going to consider it the end of the world."
—Janet Evans

The reality of celebrity began to affect Evans's life when she returned home after Seoul. She enrolled in Stanford University in 1989 but stayed only two years, relinquishing her eligibility when the National Collegiate Athletic Association set new rules reducing the amount of practice time for collegiate swimmers. Freed from her academic duties—she had been an "A" student—Evans accepted product endorsements and moved to Austin, Texas to train with coach Mark Schubert. By 1990 she was ranked in the top three in the world in an astonishing five events.

Summer Sanders swims for the gold medal in the 200-meter butterfly race in Barcelona. She plans to compete again in Atlanta. *AP/Wide World Photos*

Try as she might, Evans could never duplicate her world record-setting times in the 400-meter, 800-meter, and 1,500-meter freestyle. The 400-meter and 1,500-meter records were set in 1988 and the 800-meter in 1989, when Evans was at her "little" and lithesome best. She found, as she entered her twenties, that she had to compensate for changes in her figure and weight. She was able to do this, and she returned to the 1992 Summer Games in Barcelona favored to win gold again in her two best races, the 800-meter freestyle and the 400-meter freestyle. She did win the gold in the 800-meter, but she had to settle for a silver in the 400-meter freestyle—and she did not qualify for the relay team.

The Janet Evans of the 1992 Summer Games was no longer a giggling teenager. In retrospect, she told *USA Today* on July 7, 1995, she was not even happy. "Swimming was the be-all and end-all of my life," she recalled. "I listened to all the stuff about why I wasn't as fast as before. I felt the pressure, and it made me a little bitter. And that kept me from going as fast as I might have." Still her achievements were nothing to take lightly. Evans is the first American woman to win four Olympic gold medals in swimming, and she has five medals overall going into yet another Olympic year.

As if to prove her naysayers wrong, Evans has been particularly dominating in the 800-meter freestyle since 1993. She owns back-to-back world championship medals in the event, for 1993 and 1994, and her strongest competition may come not from abroad but from American Brooke Bennett, who, at 15 herself, is being described as "the next Janet Evans." Asked about facing competitors who were in grade school when she won her first Olympic gold, Evans told *USA Today:* "I'm looking forward to it. . . . I like the competition." She added that the 1996 Summer Games will give her an opportunity to enjoy the "fun" of the Olympics again as she really has nothing left to prove. "My body has changed, and if I never swim an 8:16 (her 800-meter world record) in my life again, I'm not going to consider it the end of the world. I was able to swim more than 10 seconds off that and still win a world championship. The way I look at that now, that just tells me it was a pretty amazing thing when I did it."

—*Anne Janette Johnson*

Summer Sanders

One of the most visible and popular athletes from the 1992 Olympics, Summer Sanders will attempt the comeback of her life in 1996. Sanders, an eight-time United States national champion and the winner of four medals in Barcelona, still holds American records in the 200- and 400-meter individual medleys. Older now but newly dedicated to her training regime, she will try to qualify for the Olympic team in the 200-meter butterfly and the 200-meter individual medley, her two strongest events. If she manages to win a berth on the team headed for Atlanta, Sanders will defy the prevailing view that teenagers have a competitive edge in the demanding field of race swimming.

On March 16, 1992, Leigh Montville wrote in *Sports Illustrated:* "Summer Sanders. Could there be a name that is more American? More golden?" The swimmer received her unusual first name in an odd way. Her parents' first child was due on June 21, the first day of summer. They decided to use the name "Summer" because of the date. However, the baby that arrived on June 21 was a boy. He earned the name Trevor, and Summer got the original name even though she was born in October of 1972. Sanders once joked about the whole scenario in *Sports Illustrated.* "The first question always is, 'Were your parents hippies?' The answer is no. The second question always is, 'Do you come from California?' The answer is yes. The third question always is, 'What's your brother's name? Winter?' I hate the third question. It's so stupid."

> "Once, I swam because it was habit, it was something I'd always done. Now, it's my risk and my decision, and that makes life a lot more interesting."
> — *Summer Sanders*

When Sanders was a toddler, her father had a swimming pool built in the family's backyard. Little Summer did not seem interested in learning to swim at all, and her worried parents hovered around her whenever she went near the pool. Then one day, when their backs were turned, she leaped in and swam with her older brother. At three she could swim a standard 25-yard lap, and at four she was winning races against seven-year-olds. At the tender age of 15 she earned times in the 200- and 400-meter individual medleys and the 100- and 200-meter breaststrokes that won her the opportunity to swim in the 1988 Olympic qualifying meet.

Everyone—including Sanders—was astonished by her performance at the 1988 Olympic trials. She qualified for the finals in the 400-meter individual medley (she finished eighth), and she missed making the Olympic team by a mere .27 second in the 200-meter individual medley. She had never before even qualified for a national final. Elated by her strong showing, Sanders returned home to Roseville, California determined to make the 1992 Olympic team.

An honors student in high school, Sanders won an athletic scholarship to Stanford University. She was named National Collegiate Athletic Association Swimmer of the Year in both 1991 and 1992, even though she relinquished her NCAA eligibility to pursue endorsement opportunities as the 1992 Olympics approached. At the Olympic trials in March of 1992, she established herself as the ascendant star in women's swimming, winning the 200- and 400-meter individual medleys and the 200-meter butterfly, and finishing second in the 100-meter butterfly. In all, she qualified for five Olympic events and was considered a serious contender in all of them. "This is the payoff for all the tears, the pain, the frustration," she told *Sports Illustrated*. "You work so hard. You sit in a little room and wait for your coach to come in with the workout cards, these blue cards that tell who you have to do, and you're scared about what the cards will say. You see the cards, and you know the pain that is in them. You need the payoff somewhere."

Sanders's "payoff" at the Olympics in Barcelona was spectacular. The 19-year-old with the odd name became an American hero of the Summer Games, earning the gold medal in the 200-meter butterfly, another gold in the 400-meter medley relay preliminaries, a silver in the 200-meter individual medley, and a bronze in the 400-meter individual medley. Sanders was the first woman swimmer since 1976 to compete in four individual events and the first since 1984 to win four medals at one Olympiad. Asked to describe her feelings as she accepted her awards, Sanders admitted in an August 10, 1992 *Sports Illustrated* piece: "I just want to sit down and relax. I want to enjoy the feeling that nobody expects me to do anything great tomorrow."

Pretty and engaging, Sanders found that her Olympic fame opened many doors in the public arena. She won lucrative product endorsements and appeared as a guest star on her favorite daytime drama, *All My Children*. She also became an MTV host and earned still more money as a motivational speaker. As for her swimming, however, she was never able to better her times from the summer of 1992. She announced her retirement in January of 1994.

After a 17-month hiatus Sanders returned to competitive swimming in April of 1995 when she was accepted to the United States Swimming Resident National Team. She joined the team in Colorado Springs and was dismayed to find that the coach, Jonty Skinner, had reserved a separate lane of the pool for her to use. She was "segregated" because she could not keep up with the other swimmers, and Skinner did not want her to become discouraged. Over a period of weeks she performed the most demanding workouts that Skinner could devise, and by June she was allowed to join the group. In her first competition, the Charlotte Ultraswim on June 18, 1995, she finished seventh in the 100-meter butterfly, in a tie for sixth in the 200-meter butterfly, and fifth in the 200-meter individual medley.

Sanders faces a considerable challenge as she ponders an attempt to make the 1996 Olympic team. She will have to compete against younger rivals who have been swimming consistently over the past two years. She will have to guard against injuries and ignore the evidence that women's swimming is a sport best performed by teenagers. On the other hand, Sanders knows how it feels to be the best and to win gold medals and national championships. Her very presence in competition is expected to add depth to the field, especially in the 200-meter butterfly. Sanders herself views her future swimming career with the cool presence of mind that has marked all her years of competition. "Once, I swam because it was habit, it was something I'd always done," she told *USA Today* on June 14, 1995. "Now, it's my risk and my decision, and that makes life a lot more interesting."

—Anne Janette Johnson

Jenny Thompson

Olympic double gold medalist Jenny Thompson will attempt to repeat her winning ways at the 1996 Summer Games. Thompson, the first American woman in 59 years to set a world record in the 100-meter freestyle, is one of the most decorated athletes in the history of the National Collegiate Athletic Association. She also holds the American records for both the 100-meter freestyle and the 100-yard freestyle. Unlike the majority of Olympic-caliber swimmers, she chose to complete her college education rather than give up her eligibility early in favor of swimming stipends and product endorsements—and thus burned a hole in the NCAA while earning a bachelor's degree. "I like to think of myself as a well-rounded person," Thompson told the *Contra Costa Times* on March 21, 1995. "I think I would go crazy if I was just thinking about athletics all day long."

"I would like to recapture the 100 free world record, because I feel it's mine and that it was unfairly broken."
—Jenny Thompson, whose 100 free record was lowered from 54.48 to 54.01 by Chinese swimmer Le Jingyi at the 1994 World Championships in Rome

Although she is no stranger to international competition, one feat has eluded Thompson: she has never won an *individual* gold medal in a world competition. Both of her Olympic golds were awarded for relay work. In individual races, she has been beaten by Chinese swimmers, including Le Jingyi, Zhuang Yong, and Lu Bin. It was Le Jingyi who stole Thompson's world record in the 100-meter freestyle at the 1994 World Championships in Rome. Far from feeling defeated, however, Thompson is on a personal quest to unseat her Chinese rivals, preferably at the 1996 Olympic Games. Since the Chinese program has been tainted by the discovery of ten positive drug tests among their top swimmers, Thompson has made much of the fact that she performs drug-free.

The youngest child and only daughter in her family, Thompson was born in Georgetown, Massachusetts on February 26, 1993. Growing up with three older brothers, she was more or less forced to assert herself, a practice that she has since adopted in her swimming style. Thompson's parents divorced when she was two, and she grew up in a single-parent household. Her mother worked as a medical technologist, but the family still had to count their pennies at every turn. Thompson recalled in a March 28, 1994 *Sports Illustrated* profile that she and her mother often shared a brown-bag lunch at swim meets while other swim families dined in restaurants. The money saved on meals helped fund her lessons at the Seacoast Swimming Association in Dover, New Hampshire. Recalling those times in a July 1995 *Swimming World and Junior Swimmer* profile, Thompson admitted: "My mom has a real high credit card bill to this day."

Thompson showed swimming prowess early and continued to improve throughout her high school years. She was world-ranked in the 50-meter freestyle as a 12-year-old. In 1987 she became the youngest U.S. swimming gold medalist ever when she won the 50-meter free at the Pan American Games, and in 1991 she was named Swimmer of the Meet at the High School All-Star meet after winning both the 50-meter and 100-meter freestyle.

Thompson accepted a scholarship to Stanford University and there began an amateur career that has never been equalled in NCAA swimming history. In four years with Stanford, she won an unprecedented 19 NCAA titles (individual and relay) and led her university's celebrated team to four consecutive national championships. She also excelled at Pan Pacific meets, in 1993 alone winning six gold medals at that event. She was named United States Swimming "Swimmer of the Year" in 1993 after taking five U.S. national titles, five NCAA titles, and the six Pan Pac gold medals.

The determined Thompson accomplished all her victories between 1991 and 1995 within the NCAA's stringent guidelines for practice time and personal behavior. She set a high priority upon earning her college degree—and keeping her swimming in proper perspective. "I wanted to experience college like it's supposed to be experienced, for the full period of time. I didn't want to give any of it up," she explained in the *Contra Costa Times*. In 1995 Thompson was just one quarter short of earning her degree in human biology. She plans to attend graduate school in the public health field.

Thompson's 1992 posting of a 54.48 time in the 100-meter freestyle at the U.S. Olympic Trials set a new world record that held for three years. She was also a highly visible member of the 1992 U.S. Olympic Team. At the Summer Games in Barcelona she earned two gold medals, in the 400-meter freestyle relay and the 400-meter medley relay, and a silver in the 100-meter freestyle. In the ensuing years she has become a vocal champion of drug testing for Olympic athletes. As she told *Sports Illustrated*, "I want the play in my pool to be fair."

Thompson broke her arm in May of 1994 but returned to win two gold medals in the national championships in August of that year. At the 1994 World Championships she saw her 100-meter freestyle record fall, but undaunted she surged through 1995, winning three individual events (100-yard butterfly, 100-yard freestyle, and 200-yard individual medley) and anchoring two winning relay teams at the 1995 NCAA Championships. Richard Quick, who coached Thompson at Stanford and who will also head the coaching duties for the 1996 women's Olympic swimming team, told *Swimming World and Junior Swimmer* that his star athlete has been galvanized by the competition she is facing on the international front. "I think Jenny could be a successful athlete in another sport if she had chosen to," he said. "She's a very powerful woman. She's improved through the years because she's willing to work on her weaknesses and takes to coaching very well." He added: "The world record was Jenny's greatest accomplishment. The greatest frustration is I feel like cheaters took it away. I don't think there is any question about it. I think Jenny is going to swim better than she ever has in Atlanta. She will swim her lifetime best performances. Her goal is to win the races, regardless of what happens with the Chinese."

Outside of the pool, Thompson is as down-to-earth and easygoing as any native of rural

> "There are a lot of factors that go into being successful: enough sleep, nutrition, being consistent in the weight room and staying focused and believing in yourself."
> —Jenny Thompson, in Swimming World and Junior Swimmer

New England. Friends joke about her collection of flags and clothing featuring the American flag pattern. Lea Loveless, Thompson's teammate at Stanford, told *Swimming World* and *Junior Swimmer* that the preference for red, white, and blue "is not just an Olympic thing. You could say [Jenny's] model is Wonder Woman." Like her comic book heroine, Thompson is dreaming of victory over a set of international foes. She says she is ready to win. "I compare (Barcelona) to my first Olympic Trials in 1988 when I choked as a nervous 15-year-old," she concluded in *Swimming World and Junior Swimmer*. "But I came back in the 1992 Olympic Trials with much more confidence. So I look at the Olympics as a learning experience, and I know what to do in Atlanta."

—Anne Janette Johnson

Up and Comers

Watch out, Janet Evans. Some new rising stars are threatening your hold on the longer freestyle races.

Sixteen-year-old **Christina Teuscher** is one competitor who may well outperform some of America's established women's swimming champions in 1996. A four-time visitor to the World Championships, Teuscher is ranked sixth in the world in both the 200-meter freestyle and the 400-meter freestyle. Surprising even her coaches, she has been showing strength in the sprint as well as the longer swim. Teuscher's best events are those that have been dominated by Evans for so long—the 400-meter and 800-meter freestyle. Even the reigning champion Evans had to admit, in an August 18, 1994 *New York Times* article, that Teuscher "has got a lot of speed."

Christina Teuscher (pronounced TOY-cher) was born in America to parents who are citizens of Argentina. Her father, Enrique Teuscher, is a psychiatrist at St. Barnabas Hospital in the Bronx. Christina, who was born on March 12, 1978, lives in New Rochelle, New York, where she attends public school. She has trained since her youth at the Badger Swim Club with John Collins, a noted coach who has turned out such medalists as Rick Carey and Lea Loveless. During the warm summer months, Teuscher and her Badger teammates train in Collins's 50-yard concrete pool of 1930s vintage, located in Larchmont, New York. In the winter they work out at the indoor pool at Manhattanville College. Either place, Teuscher shines.

As a high school freshman in 1993 Teuscher received a world ranking of 8th in the 1500-meter freestyle. In 1994 she improved significantly, winning the silver medal in the 400-meter freestyle at the World Championships in Rome. The gold medalist in that event, Aihua Yang of China, tested positive for steroids one month after the competition, earning the scorn not only of Teuscher but of American swimmers in general. Teuscher also won the World Championship silver medal in the 800-meter freestyle—finishing just behind Evans—and a bronze in the 800-meter freestyle relay. Coaches and fans concur that the spirited New Yorker is a likely candidate for the 1996 U.S. Olympic Team, at which time she will join some of the women who served as "role models" in her youth.

FACT: Aihua Yang (China), a dual medalist at the 1994 Worlds, will be ineligible to compete in Atlanta because she tested positive for testosterone, an anabolic steroid. Training with the steroid, Yang was able to maintain a grueling workout schedule, in which she swam 20,000 meters—or 12.5 miles—every day.

A collector of antique Coca-Cola bottles and fluent in Spanish, Teuscher is delighted with her progress as a world-class swimmer. "I'm happy," she told the *New York Times*. "... It's a fantasy, a dream, but it's becoming more reality as the days go by."

A native of Plant City, Florida, **Brooke Bennett** was in grade school when Evans won three gold medals in Seoul in 1988. "I was 8 and was just starting to get into swimming more when I saw her swim in Seoul," Bennett recalled in a July 7, 1995 *USA Today* profile. "And when I saw it, I said, 'I want to do what she's doing.'" In May of 1995, Bennett finished 2.12 seconds ahead of Evans at the Alamo Challenge in the 400-meter freestyle, earning the title "the new Janet Evans" in the process.

Born on May 6, 1980, Bennett is still in the early years of her high school education. Nonetheless she has managed to win a bronze medal in the 800-meter freestyle at the 1994 World Championships, and that same year she won both the 400-meter and the 800-meter freestyle races at the U.S. Open. In 1994 she was ranked fourth in the world for the 800-meter freestyle.

The idea that she may be a clone of Evans rather rankles Bennett. She would rather be taken on her own terms. However, her five-foot-three-inch height and slender 109-pound build are distinctly reminiscent of the young Evans who won all those gold medals in Seoul. Bennett is also known as a tough opponent who turns on the speed late in races, discouraging and disheartening her rivals. "I like to get out and control the race," she told *USA Today*. "I want people to think I'm the person to beat."

—Anne Janette Johnson

Schedule

The tentative swimming schedule is:

Saturday, July 20
Women's 100 free preliminaries
Men's 100 breast preliminaries
Women's 400 im preliminaries
Men's 200 free preliminaries
Women's 100 free final
Men's 100 breast final
Women's 400 im final
Men's 200 free final

Sunday, July 21
Women's 200 free preliminaries
Men's 400 im preliminaries
Women's 100 breast preliminaries
Men's 4 × 200 free relay preliminaries
Women's 200 free final
Men's 400 im final
Women's 100 breast final
Men's 4 × 200 free relay final

Monday, July 22
Women's 400 free preliminaries
Men's 100 free preliminaries
Women's 100 back preliminaries
Men's 200 fly preliminaries
Women's 4 × 100 free relay
  preliminaries
Women's 400 free final
Men's 100 free final
Women's 100 back final
Men's 200 fly final
Women's 4 × 100 free relay final

Tuesday, July 23
Men's 400 free preliminaries
Women's 200 breast preliminaries
Men's 100 back preliminaries
Women's 100 fly preliminaries
Men's 4 × 100 free relay preliminaries
Men's 400 free final

Women's 200 breast final
Men's 100 back final
Women's 100 fly final
Men's 4 × 100 free relay final

Wednesday, July 24
Men's 200 breast preliminaries
Women's 200 im preliminaries
Men's 100 fly preliminaries
Women's 4 × 100 medley relay
  preliminaries
Women's 800 free preliminaries
Men's 200 breast final
Women's 200 im final
Men's 100 fly final
Women's 4 × 100 medley relay final

Thursday, July 25
Men's 50 free preliminaries
Women's 200 back preliminaries
Men's 200 medley preliminaries
Women's 4 × 200 free preliminaries
Men's 1500 free preliminaries
Women's 800 free final
Men's 50 free final
Women's 200 back final
Men's 200 medley final
Women's 4 × 200 free final

Friday, July 26
Women's 200 fly preliminaries
Men's 200 back preliminaries
Women's 50 free preliminaries
Men's 4 × 100 medley preliminaries
Women's 200 fly final
Men's 200 back final
Women's 50 free final
Men's 1500 free final
Men's 4 × 100 medley final

Men's Swimming Events

Highlights

In 1896, when only four swimming events were included in the Games, Alfréd Hajós became the first swimmer to win an Olympic title, winning first the 100m freestyle and then the 1200m as well. Twenty-eight years later, in Paris, Hajós won a silver Olympic medal, this time for a more sedentary adventure, stadium architecture.

Britain's John Jarvis was a double winner in 1900, when he took the 1000m and 4000m events, while the Australian Frederick Lane captured the 200 meters. Four years later, in St. Louis, the home team scored its first victory, as Charlie Daniels swam his way to five medals. Zoltán von Halmay, a Hungarian, beat out Daniels, the medium-distance title holder, in the sprint. Daniels is also credited with evolving the American crawl from the Australian two-beat crawl.

In 1908, Daniels returned—to swim in water that was neither heated nor filtered—this time to win the 100m sprint, while von Halmay placed second. Daniels had become the leading proponent of the new crawl stroke. The 1912 Games introduced Duke Kahanamoku and his brother Samuel, descendants of a Hawaiian chief, as prominent U.S. swimmers. Duke, the older of the two, swam to a 100m first place, which he managed to defend in Antwerp in 1920, where the Americans won five gold medals.

1924 marked the Olympic debut of a tall, slim, and shy Johnny Weissmuller, who won three of the six gold medals awarded to the U.S. in Paris: he captured the 100m and 400m freestyles, and swam a leg of the winning 800m relay team. The now-veteran Kahanamoku brothers came in second and third in the 100m freestyle, giving the U.S. a clean sweep of the event. Although soon-to-be-Tarzan-the-ape-man Weissmuller did manage to win another two gold medals at Amsterdam in 1928—again for the 100m freestyle and the 800m relay team—Japan was moving ahead as a dominant power, and Yoshiyuki Tsuruta won the 200m breaststroke.

By 1932, the American supremacy was thoroughly undermined, when the Japanese men won five of the six races, along with various other lesser wins. Winning four individual medals, the young Japanese team also lowered the freestyle relay record by 38 seconds. Buster Crabbe, another Tarzan-to-be, won the only U.S. medal by defeating world record holder Jean Taris of France in the 400m freestyle.

It wasn't much better for the Yanks in 1936, although they doubled their gold haul with Jack Medica winning the 400m freestyle and Adolph Kiefer the backstroke. Japan, in the meantime, won yet another four races, including the relay. After the war, the Americans enjoyed another moment in the sun (with the Japanese absent from the Games), when they captured six golds at London in 1948, including a sweep of the three freestyle races. That same year, almost all the Olympic records—and some world records—were broken.

Freestyle again proved to be the primary vein of gold for the U.S. in 1952 when Clarke Scholes won the 100m; Ford Konno won the 1500, lowering the Olympic record by 42 seconds, later swimming on the successful relay team. Australia, which had won a total of only three medals since the very beginning of the Games, captured a gold when John Davies outswam American Bowen Stassforth in the 200m breaststroke.

The 1956 Games, held in Melbourne, were ruled by the newly established Australians. With Murray Rose sweeping both the 400m and 1500m freestyles, the Aussies captured five gold medals; for the first time since 1900 America was shut out in the freestyle, as Australia also captured the relay and Jon Henricks took the 100 meters. In fact, all that prevented the U.S. from being totally wiped out was the introduction that year of the butterfly to the Olympic program. Bill Yorzyk began the American domination of that stroke by winning at 200 meters.

Good fortune—not to mention skill—followed the Australians to Rome in 1960. John Devitt was declared winner of the 100m freestyle even though the electronic timer caught American Lance Larson in a faster time, allowing Australia to sweep the individual freestyle races once again, as Rose made a successful defense of the 400m and John Konrads won the 1500m. But the U.S. salvaged both relays, including the 400m medley, conducted for the first time. The latter event has been the exclusive property of the U.S. in the Olympics, with the obvious exception of 1980, when an Australian won the event; Americans have also been unbeaten in the 800m freestyle relay since 1960, and in the 400m freestyle relay since it was introduced in 1960.

In 1964, when the men's program had grown to 10 events, America indisputably reclaimed its position as the No. 1 power. Don Schollander became the first Olympian to win four gold medals in a single Olympics, and his teammates added three more victories. When a minor controversy developed over the third place in the 100m freestyle, the unofficial electronic timers provided by the Japanese were consulted; although Germany's Hans-Joachim

Klein and America's Gary Ilman had stopped the clock together at the same hundredth of a second, Klein had finished one one-thousandth of a second sooner, thus earning the bronze medal.

The Americans went to Mexico City as heavy favorites in 1968, and indeed they won 10 of 15 swimming events. Mike Burton and Charley Hickcox each won two individual events, Burton taking the 400m and 1500m freestyles and Hickcox the 200m and 400m individual medleys. That year, however, the 100m freestyle victory went to Australian Michael Wenden, who landed the most decisive 100m victory in 40 years. In third place in that same race, Mark Spitz quietly earned one of the first of his Olympic medals.

Limited to two gold medals for his work on the 1968 relay teams, Spitz stormed the 1972 Games in Munich, capturing four individual races (the freestyle sprints and both butterfly events) and swimming on three successful relay teams. As if that weren't enough, all seven events broke world record times. While Mike Burton successfully defended his 1500m title, America's final gold went to John Hencken in the 200m breaststroke; one of America's principal antagonists, Swede Gunnar Larsson, won both medleys this time around. And sixteen-year-old Rick DeMont, swimming for the U.S., finished first in the 400m freestyle, but was disqualified because the prescription medicine he was taking for asthma was ruled to be illegal.

In Montreal in 1976, the U.S. conducted a near-shutout, taking 12 of the 13 gold medals and 10 of the 11 silvers. The only man to foil both sweeps was British breaststroker David Wilkie (who happened to have attended school in the U.S.). Of the 27 men on the U.S. team, 19 earned individual medals, and the Americans set 18 world records, seven times setting a mark in the heats and then lowering it again in the finals. Unlike 1972, when Mark Spitz hogged the limelight, the 1976 performance was more a team effort; the big winner of the Games, however, was John Naber, who won four golds (in the 100m and 200m backstroke, and two medleys), and a silver (in the 200m freestyle).

In the absence of the U.S. at Moscow, it was the host country who dominated the men's swimming program, capturing seven gold, seven silver, and three bronze. Prior to 1980, the Soviet men had never won a swimming gold. Vladimir Salnikov led the way with three gold and compatriot Sergei Kopliakov took two gold and a silver. With a time of 14 minutes, 58.27 seconds for the 1500m freestyle, Salnikov became the first person to break the 15-minute barrier. Whereas American men accounted for 11 world records in 1976 at Montreal, Salnikov's 1500m mark was the only world standard to fall in what was considered to be a "fast pool" at Moscow.

American swimmer Rowdy Gaines, hurt by the 1980 boycott, won three golds at age 25 in 1984. His 1980 teammate, Steve Lunquist, also came back in 1984, for a pair of golds in the 100m breaststroke and the 400m medley relay. That year the Canadians, who hadn't won a gold in swimming since 1912, picked up seven medals on the men's team, including golds for Alex Baumann and Victor Davis, as well as two silvers and two bronzes. Australian swimmers earned 13 medals that year, the most since 1960, when the team from Down Under also won 13. These included men's medals in the 100m freestyle (silver), the 100m breaststroke (bronze), the 200m breaststroke (silver), the 100m butterfly (bronze), and the 200m butterfly (gold), to name but a few.

Another swimming phenomenon of 1984, West Germany's Michael Gross, entered the Games as the only male swimmer since Mark Spitz to hold world records in two strokes at the same time. His countryman, Thomas Fahrner, failed to qualify for the 400m freestyle and was so angry with himself that in the consolation race he broke the just-set Olympic record in the event; record, but no medal.

In 1988, U.S. butterflyer/freestyler Matt Biondi burst on the scene to set or help to set four world records, piling up a total of five gold medals, one silver, and one bronze, the best performance in swimming since Mark Spitz's haul in 1972. He added these to the gold medal he'd won as a member of the 4 × 100 freestyle relay in 1984. Meanwhile, the American men relayers shattered world records.

Other swimming greats competing in 1988 included West German Michael Gross, who won the 200m butterfly, Artur Wojdat of Poland, who took third in the 400m freestyle, Anders Holmertz of Sweden, who took second in the 200m freestyle, and Australian Duncan Armstrong, who won the 200m freestyle, and placed second in the 400m. Tamas Darnyi of Hungary swept the 200m and 400m individual medleys, smashing his own world records in those events; he also competed in the 200m backstroke, his strongest discipline.

U.S. backstroker David Berkoff adapted an underwater maneuver for the start of his race after seeing U.S. swimmer Jesse Vassallo experiment with the innovation in 1984; he stayed underwater for 35 meters after the start of the race, then surfaced half a body length ahead of the rest of the pool. Berkoff's silver in the 100m backstroke heralded a new direction for backstrokers worldwide.

From Poolside to Film Stardom

Three U.S. swimmers during the 1920s and 1930s won Olympic medals, then launched film careers.

Duke Paoa Kahanamoku was named for the Duke of Edinburgh, who happened to be in Honolulu when the future swimmer was born August 24, 1890. He won the 100m freestyle in 1912 and 1920, surviving a re-swim after an apparent lane violation by another competitor (this was before lane markers were used). At the 100m freestyle in Paris in 1924, he and brother Samuel flanked Johnny Weissmuller, who feared they would team up against him. Instead, Duke told Johnny the most important goal was getting the "American flag up there three times." Weissmuller won; the brothers placed second and third. Kahanamoku, who often played Hawaiian kings in the movies, also helped popularize surfing. The Duke died in Honolulu on January 22, 1968.

As an infant, **Johnny Weissmuller**, born on June 2, 1904, was thought to have heart trouble, a condition that seems not to have held him back. Just before the 1924 Paris Olympics, Weissmuller became the first man ever to swim 100 meters in under one minute, at 57.4 seconds. Just 20, Weissmuller won four medals in Paris, and two more four years later in Amsterdam. His style was then unique: riding high in the water and alternating sides when lifting his head to breathe—the better to see his opponents. He held 52 U.S. titles and 28 world records. Weissmuller never lost a race in 10 years of amateur swimming at distances from 50 yards to 1/2 mile. Later, Weissmuller became one of Hollywood's Tarzans (and probably the most popular one), debuting in *Tarzan, the Ape Man,* in 1932 and starring in 18 other Tarzan flicks. He died in Acapulco on January 20, 1984.

Clarence "Buster" Crabbe credits his discovery by Hollywood moguls to his one-tenth of a second victory over France's Jean Taris in the 400m freestyle at the 1932 Los Angeles Olympics. Crabbe also won a bronze in the 1500m freestyle in 1928. Like Weissmuller, Crabbe starred as Tarzan; he then went on to play Flash Gordon and Buck Rodgers. He died April 23, 1983, in Scottsdale, Arizona.

—Harvey Dickson

Mark Spitz

In his heyday he was unchallenged as the best swimmer in the world: Mark Spitz, winner of seven gold medals and holder of seven world records at the 1972 Olympics in Munich. Not only was Spitz, then in his early twenties, considered the greatest

U.S. swimmer Mark Spitz won a record seven gold medals swimming at the Munich Games in 1972. *AP/Wide World Photos*

Olympic swimmer ever, he was an ideal celebrity, an all-American hero "who happened to look like a cross between Omar Sharif and the Marlboro Man," to quote the *Chicago Tribune*. Posters of the handsome Spitz with his medals splayed across his chest became the best-selling Olympic souvenir item ever.

When he was contemplating a comeback for Barcelona, Spitz looked back at those years as if they passed in a dream. "As a kid, I ended up in the sport of swimming through osmosis," he told the *Washington Post*. "I went out, sort of swam, was on a team, I got better, I got good, I got great, then I held world records. I never had a chance to sit back and reflect: What would I be doing if I wasn't doing this?"

Spitz never reflected on his talent because it came almost naturally. He was born February 10, 1950, in Modesto, California, and began swimming competitively at age eight. He spent the next ten years roaming Northern California in search of top-flight swim clubs where he could hone his abilities. He continued his swimming in college at the University of Indiana and quickly gained a national reputation, although he quietly assured fans that he wanted to study to be a dentist.

Ron Ballatore, swimming coach at the University of California, Los Angeles, remembered that as a young Olympic hopeful, Spitz showed tremendous potential. He could deceive his trainers by swimming far faster in meets than in practice, he tested better than any other United States swimmer on stroke efficiency, and both his hands and legs worked flawlessly to propel him forward in a variety of strokes. Ballatore said: "It is hard to explain. He's like an artist in the water. Many people can copy his stroke, but it doesn't mean it is going to work for them."

Spitz suffered a disappointing—if you can call it that—outing in the 1968 Olympics in Mexico City. During that meet, he earned only two gold medals, both for relays. His day to shine came in 1972, in Munich, where he entered seven events and won all seven of them in record-setting times. His victories came in the 100m freestyle, the 200m freestyle, the 100m butterfly, the 200m butterfly, the 400m freestyle relay, the 800m freestyle relay, and the 400m medley relay. His success was arguably one of America's finest moments in Olympic history.

At the height of his fame, Spitz stopped swimming and opened a real estate development business with the money he earned on product endorsements. He drifted slowly back into obscurity as, one by one, his records fell at subsequent Olympic Games. Then, in 1990, the forty-year-old Spitz announced that he would train for a spot on the 1992 Olympic team. Battling a

U.S. swimmer Matt Biondi took home two more medals from Barcelona—bringing the grand total to ten. *AP/Wide World Photos*

back injury and years of inactivity, he strove to regain his old form, at least in short-distance butterfly sprints. "There aren't that many skeptics," he told the *Atlanta Constitution* of his proposed comeback. "Deep down inside they all kind of wish and hope I can do it. They're kind of reliving my past and their own past. It's sort of like all the couch potatoes united."

The comeback was not a success but Spitz is slated to return to the Olympics in 1996—this time as a participant in the closing or opening ceremonies.

—*Mark Kram*

Matt Biondi

As a child, Matt Biondi admired Olympic champions, never dreaming that one day he would become one himself. Yet the six-foot-seven, 210-pound University of California graduate rose to stardom during the 1988 Summer Games, walking off with five gold, one silver, and one bronze medal—a haul eclipsed only by the 1972 performance of Mark Spitz.

Most Olympic swimmers begin preparing for the games as mere youngsters, practicing endlessly at childhood swim meets. Biondi—who was born in Moraga, California, on October 8, 1965—began swimming competitively at the comparatively late age of fifteen. Three years later, in 1984, he made the Olympic team. A graduate of Campolinda High in Moraga, Biondi played basketball and water polo in addition to swimming races. He was almost a well-kept secret when he earned a spot on the team that went to Los Angeles.

It was in Los Angeles in 1984 that Biondi earned his first gold medal, as part of the 400m freestyle relay team. He entered the University of California and continued his cross-training as a race swimmer and water polo player, helping his school to win several NCAA water polo championships even as he was breaking records in 100- and 200-yard freestyle races.

Biondi was considered one of the most promising stars of the 1988 Olympic team, and he lived up to his advance billing. He earned golds in the 4 × 200m freestyle relay, the 100m freestyle, the 4 × 100m freestyle relay, the 50m freestyle, and the 400m medley relay. In the process he also set or helped to set four world records. His silver medal came in the 100m fly, and he earned a bronze in the 200m freestyle. Afterwards, he told the *Charlotte Observer:* "One time, I wanted to show the world at a meet like this what Matt Biondi is about."

U.S. women's swim team won the gold medal in the 4 × 100-meter freestyle relay, setting a world record with a time of 3:39.46; the U.S. women also took the gold and set *another* world record in the 4 × 100-meter medley relay, with a time of 4:02.54. *Duomo Photography*

The Unified Team's Alexandre Popov stroked to the 50m title at a rate of one stroke to his opponents' every one-and-a-half—in Olympic record-breaking time.
AP/Wide World Photos

And swim he did in Barcelona. Biondi picked up a silver in the 50m freestyle and a team gold in the 4 × 100 freestyle relay to bring his total number of Olympic medals to 10, thus joining the ranks of the most-medaled U.S. Olympians. Biondi believes his most valuable lessons as a swimmer came from dolphins he swam among in the Bahamas. "Watching them made me aware of how water moves across my body," he says. "The best swimmers are the ones who know how to swim through the water, to feel the water. Watching the dolphins heightened my awareness."

—Mark Kram

Highlights from Barcelona

"I started thinking again that nobody expected me to win, and that got me going," U.S. medalist Nelson Diebel recalled. "It's a spiteful, childish thing to do, but it works." And how. Diebel—the so-called "rebel with a medal"—swam away from a drug-addled petty-criminal past to nab the first U.S. medal at the Barcelona Games. In so doing, he became the first U.S. swimmer since 1976 to win the 100m breaststroke.

Barcelona was full of surprises. The 50m freestyle, first reintroduced in 1988, had always been a marquee event for U.S. swimmers: at Games' start, the U.S. team—dubbed by the Spanish press "Los tiburones yanqui," "The Yankee sharks"—reigned undefeated in international competition. Matinee idols Matt Biondi and Tom Jager—1988's gold and silver medalists—were expected to stage a play-it-again-Sam in the Spanish theater. Anticipating a touch-out 1–2 finish in 1992, they promoted their rivalry like a Reebok commercial.

"He [Alexandre Popov, who nailed the 1992 men's 50m freestyle] had the courage to stand up to Matt Biondi and Tom Jager and take them down. He's the first person to do that in this event."

– Tom Jager, bronze medalist in the 1992 50m freestyle

Auditioning for a minor part in the sprint was Alexandre Popov—until recently known as "Alexander 'Who?'"—a boyishly handsome 6′6″ rising star in a cast of chlorinated characters. No one expected a Unified Team swimmer to grab top billing in any piscine event: with only four golds since 1956 (excluding the boycotted Moscow Games), the Soviet machine seemed to stall in the pool.

But Popov had his own script, and it wasn't a Western. Elegantly stroking to the 50m title—at a rate of one stroke to his

Hungarian Krisztina Egerszegi swims to an Olympic record and gold medal for the women's 100-meter backstroke in Barcelona. *AP/Wide World Photos*

In Barcelona U.S. swimmer Nelson Diebel set an Olympic record in the 100-meter breaststroke—good enough for the gold. *AP/Wide World Photos*

opponents' every one-and-a-half—Popov unseated the American duo in Olympic record-breaking time. His understudy, Biondi, the erstwhile goldenboy, settled for silver, while Jager placed a distant third.

Not to be upstaged, Biondi—who, with Popov's help, failed to make the curtain call in the 400, an event he hadn't lost since 1984—staged an encore golden performance in the 4 × 100 freestyle ensemble. With an eleventh medal draped around his swimmerly shoulders, Biondi joined swimming legend Mark Spitz and shooter Carl Osburn as the most-medaled U.S. Olympians.

"It was like a drug. A great rush. The best high you could ever get. It was happy. It was sad. You wanted to keep doing it. You really had to be there."

Medalists

Swimming—Men's 50-Meter Freestyle

1992
1. Alexandre Popov, Russia, 21.91 (OR)
2. Matthew Biondi, U.S.A., 22.09
3. Tom Jager, U.S.A., 22.30

1988
1. Matthew Biondi, U.S.A., 22.14 (WR)
2. Thomas Jager, U.S.A., 22.36
3. Gennadi Prigoda, Soviet Union, 22.71

1906–1984
Not held

1904
1. Zoltan von Halmay, Hungary, 28.0
2. J. Scott Leary, U.S.A., 28.6
3. Charles Daniels, U.S.A.

1896–1900
Not held

Swimming—Men's 100-Meter Freestyle

1992
1. Alexandre Popov, Russia, 49.02
2. Gustavo Borges, Brazil, 49.43
3. Stephan Caron, France, 49.50

1988
1. Matthew Biondi, U.S.A., 48.63 (OR)
2. Christopher Jacobs, U.S.A., 49.08
3. Stephan Caron, France, 49.62

1984
1. Ambrose Gaines, U.S.A., 49.80 (OR)
2. Mark Stockwell, Australia, 50.24
3. Per Johansson, Sweden, 50.31

1980
1. Jorg Woithe, East Germany, 50.40
2. Per Holmertz, Sweden, 50.91
3. Per Johansson, Sweden, 51.29

1976
1. Jim Montgomery, U.S.A., 49.99 (WR, OR)
2. Jack Babashoff, U.S.A., 50.81
3. Peter Nocke, West Germany, 51.31

1972
1. Mark Spitz, U.S.A., 51.22 (WR)
2. Jerry Heidenreich, U.S.A., 51.65
3. Vladimir Bure, Soviet Union, 51.77

1968
1. Michael Wenden, Australia, 52.2 (WR)
2. Ken Walsh, U.S.A., 52.8
3. Mark Spitz, U.S.A., 53.0

1964
1. Don Schollander, U.S.A., 53.4 (OR)
2. Robert McGregor, Great Britain, 53.5
3. Hans-Joachim Klein, West Germany, 54.0

1960
1. John Devitt, Australia, 55.2 (OR)
2. Lance Larson, U.S.A., 55.2 (OR)
3. Manuel Dos Santos, Brazil, 55.4

1956
1. Jon Henricks, Australia, 55.4 (OR)
2. John Devitt, Australia, 55.8
3. Gary Chapman, Australia, 56.7

1952
1. Clarke Scholes, U.S.A., 57.4
2. Hiroshi Suzuki, Japan, 57.4
3. Goran Larsson, Sweden, 58.2

1948
1. Walter Ris, U.S.A., 57.3 (OR)
2. Alan Ford, U.S.A., 57.8
3. Geza Kadas, Hungary, 58.1

1936
1. Ferenc Csik, Hungary, 57.6
2. Masanori Yusa, Japan, 57.9
3. Shigeo Arai, Japan, 58.0

1932
1. Yasuji Miyazaki, Japan, 58.2
2. Tatsugo Kawaishi, Japan, 58.6
3. Albert Schwartz, U.S.A., 58.8

1928
1. John Weissmuller, U.S.A., 58.6 (OR)
2. Istvan Barany, Hungary, 59.8
3. Katsuo Takaishi, Japan, 1:00.0

1924
1. John Weissmuller, U.S.A., 59.0 (OR)
2. Duke Paoa Kahanamoku, U.S.A., 1:01.4
3. Samuel Kahanamoku, U.S.A., 1:01.8

1920
1. Duke Paoa Kahanamoku, U.S.A., 1:01.4 (WR)
2. Pua Kela Kealoha, U.S.A., 1:02.2
3. William Harris, U.S.A., 1:03.2

1912
1. Duke Paoa Kahanamoku, U.S.A., 1:03.4
2. Cecil Healy, Australia, 1:04.6
3. Kenneth Huszagh, U.S.A., 1:05.6

1908
1. Charles Daniels, U.S.A., 1:05.6 (WR)

2. Zoltan von Halmay, Hungary, 1:06.2
3. Harald Julin, Sweden, 1:08.0

1906
1. Charles Daniels, U.S.A., 1:13.4 (WR)
2. Zoltan von Halmay, Hungary, 1:14.2
3. Cecil Healy, Australia

1904
1. Zoltan von Halmay, Hungary, 1:02.8
2. Charles Daniels, U.S.A.
3. J. Scott Leary, U.S.A.

1900
Not held

1896
1. Alfred Hajos, Hungary, 1:22.2 (OR)
2. Efstathios Choraphas, Greece, 1:23.0
3. Otto Herschmann, Austria

Swimming—Men's 200-Meter Freestyle

1992
1. Evgueni Sadovyi, Russia, 1:46.70 (OR)
2. Anders Holmertz, Sweden, 1:46.86
3. Antti Kasvio, Finland, 1:47.63

1988
1. Duncan Armstrong, Australia 1:47.25 (WR)
2. Anders Holmertz, Sweden, 1:47.89
3. Matthew Biondi, U.S.A., 1:47.99

1984
1. Michael Gross, West Germany, 1:47.44
2. Michael Heath, U.S.A., 1:49.10
3. Thomas Fahrner, West Germany, 1:49.69

1980
1. Sergei Kopliakov, Soviet Union, 1:49.81 (OR)
2. Andrei Krylov, Soviet Union, 1:50.76
3. Graeme Brewer, Australia, 1:51.60

1976
1. Bruce Furniss, U.S.A., 1:50.29 (WR, OR)
2. John Naber, U.S.A., 1:50.50
3. Jim Montgomery, U.S.A., 1:50.58

1972
1. Mark Spitz, U.S.A., 1:52.78 (WR)
2. Steven Genter, U.S.A., 1:53.73
3. Werner Lampe, West Germany, 1:53.99

1968
1. Michael Wenden, Australia, 1:55.2 (OR)
2. Don Schollander, U.S.A., 1:55.8
3. John Nelson, U.S.A., 1:58.1

1906–1964
Not held

1904
1. Charles Daniels, U.S.A., 2:44.2
2. Francis Gailey, U.S.A., 2:46.0
3. Emil Rausch, Germany, 2:56.0

1900
1. Frederick C. V. Lane, Australia, 2:25.2 (OR)
2. Zoltan von Halmay, Hungary, 2:31.4
3. Karl Ruberl, Austria, 2:32.0

1896
Not held

Swimming—Men's 400-Meter Freestyle

1992
1. Evgueni Sadovyi, Russia, 3:45.00 (WR)
2. Kieren Perkins, Australia, 3:45.16
3. Anders Holmertz, Sweden, 3:46.77

1988
1. Uwe Dassler, East Germany, 3:46.95 (WR)
2. Duncan Armstrong, Australia, 3:47.15
3. Artur Wojdat, Poland, 3:47.34

1984
1. George Dicarlo, U.S.A., 3:51.23 (OR)
2. John Mykkanen, U.S.A., 3:51.49
3. Justin Lemberg, U.S.A., 3:51.79

1980
1. Vladimir Salnikov, Soviet Union, 3:51.31 (OR)
2. Andrei Krylov, Soviet Union, 3:53.24
3. Ivar Stukolkin, Soviet Union, 3:53.95

1976
1. Brian Goodell, U.S.A., 3:51.93 (WR, OR)
2. Tim Shaw, U.S.A., 3:52.54
3. Vladimir Raskatov, Soviet Union, 3:55.76

1972
1. Bradford Cooper, Australia, 4:00.27 (OR)
2. Steven Genter, U.S.A., 4:01.94
3. Tom McBreen, U.S.A., 4:02.64

1968
1. Michael Burton, U.S.A., 4:09.0 (OR)
2. Ralph Hutton, Canada, 4:11.7
3. Alain Mosconi, France, 4:13.3

1964
1. Don Schollander, U.S.A., 4:12.2 (WR)
2. Frank Wiegand, East Germany, 4:14.9
3. Allan Wood, Australia, 4:15.1

1960
1. Murray Rose, Australia, 4:18.3 (OR)
2. Tsuyoshi Yamanaka, Japan, 4:21.4
3. John Konrads, Australia, 4:21.8

1956
1. Murray Rose, Australia, 4:27.3 (OR)
2. Tsuyoshi Yamanaka, Japan, 4:30.4
3. George Breen, U.S.A., 4:32.5

1952
1. Jean Boiteux, France, 4:30.7 (OR)
2. Ford Konno, U.S.A., 4:31.3
3. Per-Olof Ostrand, Sweden, 4:35.2

1948
1. William Smith, U.S.A., 4:41.0 (OR)
2. James McLane, U.S.A., 4:43.4
3. John Marshall, Australia, 4:47.4

1936
1. Jack Medica, U.S.A., 4:44.5 (OR)
2. Shumpei Uto, Japan, 4:45.6
3. Shozo Makino, Japan, 4:48.1

1932
1. Clarence Crabbe, U.S.A., 4:48.4 (OR)
2. Jean Taris, France, 4:48.5
3. Tsutomu Oyokota, Japan, 4:52.3

1928
1. Alberto Zorilla, Argentina, 5:01.6 (OR)
2. Andrew Charlton, Australia, 5:03.6
3. Arne Borg, Sweden, 5:04.6

1924
1. John Weissmuller, U.S.A., 5:04.2 (OR)
2. Arne Borg, Sweden, 5:06.6
3. Andrew Charlton, Australia, 5:06.6

1920
1. Norman Ross, U.S.A., 5:26.8
2. Ludy Langer, U.S.A., 5:29.0
3. George Vernot, Canada, 5:29.6

1912
1. George Hodgson, Canada, 5:24.4
2. John Hatfield, Great Britain, 5:25.8
3. Harold Hardwick, Australia, 5:31.2

1908
1. Henry Taylor, Great Britain, 5:36.8
2. Frank Beaurepaire, Australia, 5:44.2
3. Otto Scheff, Austria, 5:46.0

1906
1. Otto Scheff, Austria, 6:23.8
2. Henry Taylor, Great Britain, 6:24.4
3. John Jarvis, Great Britain, 6:27.2

1904
1. Charles Daniels, U.S.A., 6:16.2
2. Francis Gailey, U.S.A., 6:22.0
3. Otto Wahle, Austria, 6:39.0

1900
Not held

1896
1. Paul Neumann, Australia, 8:12.6
2. Antonios Pepanos, Greece, 30 m behind
3. Efstathios Choraphas, Greece

Swimming—Men's 1,500-Meter Freestyle

1992
1. Kieren Perkins, Australia, 14:43.48 (WR)
2. Glen Housman, Australia, 14:55.29
3. Joerg Hoffmann, Germany, 15:02.29

1988
1. Vladimir Salnikov, Soviet Union, 15:00.40
2. Stefan Pfeiffer, West Germany, 15:02.69
3. Uwe Dassler, East Germany, 15:06.15

1984
1. Michael O'Brien, U.S.A., 15:05.20
2. George DiCarlo, U.S.A., 15:10.59
3. Stefan Pfeiffer, West Germany, 15:12.11

1980
1. Vladimir Salnikov, Soviet Union, 14:58.27 (WR)
2. Aleksandr Chaev, Soviet Union, 15:14.30
3. Maxwell Metzker, Australia, 15:14.49

1976
1. Brian Goodell, U.S.A., 15:02.40 (WR, OR)
2. Bobby Hackett, U.S.A., 15:03.91
3. Stephen Holland, Australia, 15:04.66

1972
1. Michael Burton, U.S.A., 15:52.58 (WR)
2. Graham Windeatt, Australia, 15:58.48
3. Douglas Northway, U.S.A., 16:09.25

1968
1. Michael Burton, U.S.A., 16:38.9 (OR)
2. John Kinsella, U.S.A., 16:57.3
3. Gregory Brough, Australia, 17:04.7

1964
1. Robert Windle, Australia, 17:01.7 (OR)
2. John Nelson, U.S.A., 17:03.0
3. Allan Wood, Australia, 17:07.7

1960
1. John Konrads, Australia, 17:19.6 (OR)
2. Murray Rose, Australia, 17:21.7
3. George Breen, U.S.A., 17:30.6

1956
1. Murray Rose, Australia, 17:58.9
2. Tsuyoshi Yamanaka, Japan, 18:00.3
3. George Breen, U.S.A., 18:08.2

1952
1. Ford Konno, U.S.A., 18:30.3 (OR)

2. Shiro Hashizume, Japan, 18:41.4
3. Tetsuo Okamoto, Brazil, 18:51.3

1948
1. James McLane, U.S.A., 19:18.5
2. John Marshall, Australia, 19:31.3
3. Gyorgy Mitro, Hungary, 19:43.2

1936
1. Noboru Terada, Japan, 19:13.7
2. Jack Medica, U.S.A., 19:34.0
3. Shumpei Uto, Japan, 19:34.5

1932
1. Kusuo Kitamura, Japan, 19:12.4 (OR)
2. Shozo Makino, Japan, 19:14.1
3. James Cristy, U.S.A., 19:39.5

1928
1. Arne Borg, Sweden, 19:51.8 (OR)
2. Andrew Charlton, Australia, 20:02.6
3. Clarence Crabbe, U.S.A., 20:28.8

1924
1. Andrew Charlton, Australia, 20:06.6 (WR)
2. Arne Borg, Sweden, 20:41.4
3. Frank Beaurepaire, Australia, 21:48.4

1920
1. Norman Ross, U.S.A., 22:23.2
2. George Vernot, Canada, 22:36.4
3. Frank Beaurepaire, Australia, 23:04.0

1912
1. George Hodgson, Canada, 22:00.0 (WR)
2. John Hatfield, Great Britain, 22:39.0
3. Harold Hardwick, Australia, 23:15.4

1908
1. Henry Taylor, Great Britain, 22:48.4 (WR)
2. Thomas Battersby, Great Britain, 22:51.2
3. Frank Beaurepaire, Australia, 22:56.2

1906
1. Henry Taylor, Great Britain, 28:28.0
2. John Jarvis, Great Britain, 30:07.6
3. Otto Scheff, Austria, 30:53.4

1904
1. Emil Rausch, Germany, 27:18.2
2. Geza Kiss, Hungary, 28:28.2
3. Francis Gailey, U.S.A., 28:54.0

1900
1. John Jarvis, Great Britain, 13:40.2
2. Otto Wahle, Austria, 14:53.6
3. Zoltan von Halmay, Hungary, 15:16.4

1896
1. Alfred Hajos, Hungary, 18.22.2 (OR)
2. Jean Andreou, Greece, 21:03.4
3. Efstathios Choraphas, Greece

Swimming—Men's 100-Meter Backstroke

1992
1. Mark Tewksbury, Canada, 53.98 (OR)
2. Jeff Rouse, U.S.A., 54.04
3. David Berkoff, U.S.A., 54.78

1988
1. Daichi Suzuki, Japan, 55.05
2. David Berkoff, U.S.A., 55.18
3. Igor Polianski, Soviet Union, 55.20

1984
1. Richard Carey, U.S.A., 55.79
2. David Wilson, U.S.A., 56.35
3. Mike West, Canada, 56.49

1980
1. Bengt Baron, Sweden, 56.53
2. Viktor Kuznetsov, Soviet Union, 56.99
3. Vladimir Dolgov, Soviet Union, 57.63

1976
1. John Naber, U.S.A., 55.49 (WR, OR)
2. Peter Rocca, U.S.A., 56.34
3. Roland Matthes, East Germany, 57.22

1972
1. Roland Matthes, East Germany, 56.58 (OR)
2. Mike Stamm, U.S.A., 57.70
3. John Murphy, U.S.A., 58.35

1968
1. Roland Matthes, East Germany, 58.7 (OR)
2. Charles Hickcox, U.S.A., 1:00.2
3. Ron Mills, U.S.A., 1:00.5

1964
Not held

1960
1. David Theile, Australia, 1:01.9 (OR)
2. Frank McKinney, U.S.A., 1:02.1
3. Robert Bennett, U.S.A., 1:02.3

1956
1. David Theile, Australia, 1:02.2 (OR)
2. John Monckton, Australia, 1:03.2
3. Frank McKinney, U.S.A., 1:04.5

1952
1. Yoshinobu Oyakawa, U.S.A., 1:05.4 (OR)
2. Gilbert Bozon, France, 1:06.2
3. Jack Taylor, U.S.A., 1:06.4

1948
1. Allen Stack, U.S.A., 1:06.4
2. Robert Cowell, U.S.A., 1:06.5
3. Georges Vallerey, France, 1:07.8

1936
1. Adolf Kiefer, U.S.A., 1:05.9 (OR)
2. Albert Van de Weghe, U.S.A., 1:07.7
3. Masaji Kiyokawa, Japan, 1:08.4

1932
1. Masaji Kiyokawa, Japan, 1:08.6
2. Toshio Irie, Japan, 1:09.8
3. Kentaro Kawatsu, Japan, 1:10.0

1928
1. George Kojac, U.S.A., 1:08.2 (WR)
2. Walter Laufer, U.S.A., 1:10.0
3. Paul Wyatt, U.S.A., 1:12.0

1924
1. Warren Paoa Kealoha, U.S.A., 1:13.2 (OR)
2. Paul Wyatt, U.S.A., 1:15.4
3. Karoly Bartha, Hungary, 1:17.8

1920
1. Warren Paoa Kealoha, U.S.A., 1:15.2
2. Ray Kegeris, U.S.A., 1:16.2
3. Gerard Blitz, Belgium, 1:19.0

1912
1. Harry Hebner, U.S.A., 1:21.2
2. Otto Fahr, Germany, 1:22.4
3. Paul Kellner, Germany

1908
1. Arno Bieberstein, Germany, 1:24.6 (WR)
2. Ludvig Dam, Denmark, 1:26.6
3. Herbert Haresnape, Great Britain, 1:27.0

1906
Not held

1904
1. Walter Brack, Germany, 1:16.8
2. Georg Hoffmann, Germany
3. Georg Zacharias, Germany

1896–1900
Not held

Swimming—Men's 200-Meter Backstroke

1992
1. Martin Lopez-Zubero, Spain, 1:58.47 (OR)
2. Vladimir Selkov, Russia, 1:58.87
3. Stefano Battistelli, Italy, 1:59.40

1988
1. Igor Polianski, Soviet Union, 1:59.37
2. Frank Baltrusch, East Germany, 1:59.60
3. Paul Kingsman, New Zealand, 2:00.48

1984
1. Richard Carey, U.S.A., 2:00.23
2. Frederic Delcourt France, 2:01.75
3. Cameron Henning, Canada, 2:02.37

1980

1. Sandor Wladar, Hungary, 2:01.93
2. Zoltan Verraszto, Hungary, 2:02.40
3. Mark Kerry, Australia, 2:03.14

1976

1. John Naber, U.S.A., 1:59.19 (WR, OR)
2. Peter Rocca, U.S.A., 2:00.55
3. Dan Harrigan, U.S.A., 2:01.35

1972

1. Roland Matthes, East Germany, 2:02.82 (EWR)
2. Mike Stamm, U.S.A., 2:04.09
3. Mitchell Ivey, U.S.A., 2:04.33

1968

1. Roland Matthes, East Germany, 2:09.6 (OR)
2. Mitchell Ivey, U.S.A., 2:10.6
3. Jack Horsley, U.S.A., 2:10.9

1964

1. Jed Graef, U.S.A., 2:10.3 (WR)
2. Gary Dilley, U.S.A., 2:10.5
3. Robert Bennett, U.S.A., 2:13.1

1904–1960

Not held

1900

1. Ernst Hoppenberg, Germany, 2:47.0
2. Karl Ruberl, Austria, 2:56.0
3. Johannes Drost, Netherlands, 3:01.0

1896

Not held

Swimming—Men's 100-Meter Breaststroke

1992

1. Nelson Diebel, U.S.A., 1:01.50 (OR)
2. Norbert Rozsa, Hungary, 1:01.68
3. Philip Rogers, Australia, 1:01.76

1988

1. Adrian Moorhouse, Great Britain, 1:02.04
2. Karoly Guttler, Hungary, 1:02.05
3. Dmitri Volkov, Soviet Union, 1:02.20

1984

1. Steve Lundquist, U.S.A., 1:01.65
2. Victor Davis, Canada, 1:01.99
3. Peter Evans, Australia, 1:02.97

1980

1. Dunkan Goodhew, Great Britain, 1:03.34
2. Arsen Miskarov, Soviet Union, 1:03.82
3. Peter Evans, Australia, 1:03.96

1976

1. John Hencken, U.S.A., 1:03.11 (WR, OR)

2. David Wilkie, Great Britain, 1:03.43
3. Arvidas Iuozaytis, Soviet Union, 1:04.23

1972

1. Nobutaka Taguchi, Japan, 1:04.94 (WR)
2. Tom Bruce, U.S.A., 1:05.43
3. John Hencken, U.S.A., 1:05.61

1968

1. Donald McKenzie, U.S.A., 1:07.7 (OR)
2. Vladimir Kossinsky, Soviet Union, 1:08.0
3. Nikolai Pankin, Soviet Union, 1:08.0

1896–1964

Not held

Swimming—Men's 200-Meter Breaststroke

1992

1. Mike Barrowman, U.S.A., 2:10.16 (WR)
2. Norbert Rozsa, Hungary, 2:11.23
3. Nick Gillingham, Britain, 2:11.29

1988

1. Jozsef Szabo, Hungary, 2:13.52
2. Nick Gillingham, Great Britain, 2:14.12
3. Sergio Lopez, Spain, 2:15.21

1984

1. Victor Davis, Canada, 2:13.34 (WR)
2. Glenn Beringen, Australia, 2:15.79
3. Etienne Dagon, Switzerland, 2:17.41

1980

1. Robertas Zulpa, Soviet Union, 2:15.85
2. Alban Vermes, Hungary, 2:16.93
3. Arsen Miskarov, Soviet Union, 2:17.28

1976

1. David Wilkie, Great Britain, 2:15.11 (WR, OR)
2. John Hencken, U.S.A., 2:17.26
3. Rick Colella, U.S.A., 2:19.20

1972

1. John Hencken, U.S.A., 2:21.55 (WR)
2. David Wilkie, Great Britain, 2:23.67
3. Nobutaka Taguchi, Japan, 2:23.88

1968

1. Felipe Munoz, Mexico, 2:28.7
2. Vladimir Kossinsky, Soviet Union, 2:29.2
3. Brian Job, U.S.A., 2:29.9

1964

1. Ian O'Brien, Australia, 2:27.8 (WR)
2. Georgy Prokopenko, Soviet Union, 2:28.2
3. Chester Jastremski, U.S.A., 2:29.6

1960

1. William Mulliken, U.S.A., 2:37.4
2. Yoshihiko Osaki, Japan, 2:38.0
3. Wieger Mensonides, Netherlands, 2:39.7

1956
1. Masaru Furukawa, Japan, 2:34.7 (OR)
2. Masahiro Yoshimura, Japan, 2:36.7
3. Charis Yunichev, Soviet Union, 2:36.8

1952
1. John Davies, Australia, 2:34.4 (OR)
2. Bowen Stassforth, U.S.A., 2:34.7
3. Herbert Klein, West Germany, 2:35.9

1948
1. Joseph Verdeur, U.S.A., 2:39.3 (OR)
2. Keith Carter, U.S.A., 2:40.2
3. Robert Sohl, U.S.A., 2:43.9

1936
1. Tetsuo Hamuro, Japan, 2:41.5 (OR)
2. Erwin Sietas, Germany, 2:42.9
3. Reizo Koike, Japan, 2:44.2

1932
1. Yoshiyuki Tsuruta, Japan, 2:45.4
2. Reizo Koike, Japan, 2:46.6
3. Teofilo Yldefonzo, Philippines, 2:47.1

1928
1. Yoshiyuki Tsuruta, Japan, 2:48.8 (OR)
2. Erich Rademacher, Germany, 2:50.6
3. Teofilo Yldefonzo, Philippines, 2:56.4

1924
1. Robert Skelton, U.S.A., 2:56.6
2. Joseph De Combe, Belgium, 2:59.2
3. William Kirschbaum, U.S.A., 3:01.0

1920
1. Hakan Malmroth, Sweden, 3:04.4
2. Thor Henning, Sweden, 3:09.2
3. Arvo Aaltonen, Finland, 3:12.2

1912
1. Walther Bathe, Germany, 3:01.8 (OR)
2. Willy Lutzow, Germany, 3:05.0
3. Kurt Malisch, Germany, 3:08.0

1908
1. Frederick Holman, Great Britain, 3:09.2 (WR)
2. William Robinson, Great Britain, 3:12.8
3. Pontus Hanson, Sweden, 3:14.6

1896–1906
Not held

Swimming—Men's 100-Meter Butterfly

1992
1. Pablo Morales, U.S.A., 53.32
2. Rafal Szukala, Poland, 53.35
3. Anthony Nesty, Suriname, 53.41

1988
1. Anthony Nesty, Suriname, 53.00 (OR)
2. Matthew Biondi, U.S.A., 53.01
3. Andy Jameson, Great Britain, 53.30

1984
1. Michael Gross, West Germany, 53.08 (WR)
2. Pedro Pablo Morales, U.S.A., 53.23
3. Glenn Buchanan, Australia, 53.85

1980
1. Par Arvidsson, Sweden, 54.92
2. Roger Pyttel, East Germany, 54.94
3. David Lopez, Spain, 55.13

1976
1. Matt Vogel, U.S.A., 54.35
2. Joe Bottom, U.S.A., 54.50
3. Gary Hall, U.S.A., 54.65

1972
1. Mark Spitz, U.S.A., 54.27 (WR)
2. Bruce Robertson, Canada, 55.56
3. Jerry Heidenreich, U.S.A., 55.74

1968
1. Douglas Russell, U.S.A., 55.9 (OR)
2. Mark Spitz, U.S.A., 56.4
3. Ross Wales, U.S.A., 57.2

1896–1964
Not held

Swimming—Men's 200-Meter Butterfly

1992
1. Mel Stewart, U.S.A., 1:56.26 (OR)
2. Danyon Loader, New Zealand, 1:57.93
3. Franck Esposito, France, 1:58.51

1988
1. Michael Gross, West Germany, 1:56.94 (OR)
2. Benny Nielsen, Denmark, 1:58.24
3. Anthony Mosse, New Zealand, 1:58.28

1984
1. Jon Sieben, Australia, 1:57.04 (WR)
2. Michael Gross, West Germany, 1:57.40
3. Rafael Vidal Castro, Venezuela, 1:57.51

1980
1. Sergei Fesenko, Soviet Union, 1:59.76
2. Philip Hubble, Great Britain, 2:01.20
3. Roger Pyttel, East Germany, 2:01.39

1976
1. Mike Bruner, U.S.A., 1:59.23 (WR,OR)
2. Steven Gregg, U.S.A., 1:59.54
3. Bill Forrester, U.S.A., 1:59.96

1972
1. Mark Spitz, U.S.A., 2:00.70 (WR)
2. Gary Hall, U.S.A., 2:02.86
3. Robin Backhaus, U.S.A., 2:03.23

1968
1. Carl Robie, U.S.A., 2:08.7
2. Martin Woodroffe, Great Britain, 2:09.0
3. John Ferris, U.S.A., 2:09.3

1964
1. Kevin Berry, Australia, 2:06.6 (WR)
2. Carl Robie, U.S.A., 2:07.5
3. Fred Schmidt, U.S.A., 2:09.3

1960
1. Michael Troy, U.S.A., 2:12.8 (WR)
2. Neville Hayes, Australia, 2:14.6
3. J. David Gillanders, U.S.A., 2:15.3

1956
1. William Yorzyk, U.S.A., 2:19.3 (OR)
2. Takashi Ishimoto, Japan, 2:23.8
3. Gyorgy Tumpek, Hungary, 2:23.9

1896–1952
Not held

Swimming—Men's 200-Meter Individual Medley

1992
1. Tamas Darnyi, Hungary, 2:00.76
2. Greg Burgess, U.S.A., 2:00.97
3. Attila Czene, Hungary, 2:01.00

1988
1. Tamas Darnyi, Hungary, 2:00.17 (WR)
2. Patrick Kuehl, East Germany, 2:01.61
3. Vadim Iarochtchouk, Soviet Union, 2:02.40

1984
1. Alex Baumann, Canada, 2:01.42 (WR)
2. Pedro Pablo Morales, U.S.A., 2:03.05
3. Neil Cochran, Great Britain, 2:04.38

1976–1980
Not held

1972
1. Gunnar Larsson, Sweden, 2:07.17 (WR)
2. Tim McKee, U.S.A., 2:08.37
3. Steven Furniss, U.S.A., 2:08.45

1968
1. Charles Hickcox, U.S.A., 2:12.0 (OR)
2. Gregory Buckingham, U.S.A., 2:13.0
3. John Ferris, U.S.A., 2:13.3

1896–1964
Not held

Swimming—Men's 400-Meter Individual Medley

1992
1. Tamas Darnyi, Hungary, 4:14.23 (OR)
2. Eric Namesnik, U.S.A., 4:15.57
3. Luca Sacchi, Italy, 4:16.34

1988
1. Tamas Darnyi, Hungary, 4:14.75 (WR)
2. David Wharton, U.S.A., 4:17.36
3. Stefano Battistelli, Italy, 4:18.01

1984
1. Alex Baumann, Canada, 4:17.41 (WR)
2. Richardo Prado, Brazil, 4:18.45
3. Robert Woodhouse, Australia, 4:20.50

1980
1. Aleksandr Sidorenko, Soviet Union, 4:22.89 (OR)
2. Sergei Fesenko, Soviet Union, 4:23.43
3. Zoltan Verraszto, Hungary, 4:24.24

1976
1. Rod Strachan, U.S.A., 4:23.68 (WR, OR)
2. Tim McKee, U.S.A., 4:24.62
3. Andrei Smirnov, Soviet Union, 4:26.90

1972
1. Gunnar Larsson, Sweden, 4:31.98 (OR)
2. Tim McKee, U.S.A., 4:31.98 (OR)
3. Andras Hargitay, Hungary, 4:32.70

1968
1. Charles Hickcox, U.S.A., 4:48.4
2. Gary Hall, U.S.A., 4:48.7
3. Michael Holthaus, West Germany, 4:51.4

1964
1. Richard Roth, U.S.A., 4:45.4 (WR)
2. Roy Saari, U.S.A., 4:47.1
3. Gerhard Hetz, West Germany, 4:51.0

1896–1960
Not held

Swimming—Men's 4 × 100-Meter Freestyle Relay

1992
1. U.S.A., 3:16.74, Joseph Hudepohl, Matthew Biondi, Tom Jager, Jon Olsen
2. Unified Team, 3:17.56, Pavel Khnykine, Guennadi Prigoda, Iouri Bashkatov, Alexandre Popov
3. Germany, 3:17.90, Christian Troeger, Dirk Richter, Steffen Zesner, Mark Pinger

1988

1. U.S.A., 3:16.53, (WR), Christopher Jacobs
   Troy Dalbey, Thomas Jager, Matthew Biondi
2. Soviet Union, 3:18.33, Gennadi Prigoda,
   Iouri Bachkatov, Nikolai Evseev, Vladimir
   Tkashenko
3. East Germany, 3:19.82, Dirk Richter, Thomas
   Flemming, Lars Hinneburg, Steffen Zesner

1984

1. U.S.A., 3:19.03 (WR), Christopher Cavanaugh,
   Michael Heath, Matthew Biondi, Ambrose
   Gaines
2. Australia, 3:19.68, Gregory Fasala, Neil
   Brooks, Michael Delany, Mark Stockwell
3. Sweden, 3:22.69, Thomas Leidstrom, Bengt
   Baron, Mikael Orn, Per Johansson

1976–1980

Not held

1972

1. U.S.A., 3:26.42 (WR), David Edgar, John
   Murphy, Jerry Heidenreich, Mark Spitz
2. Soviet Union, 3:29.72, Vladimir Bure, Viktor
   Mazanov, Viktor Aboimov, Igor Grivennikov
3. East Germany, 3:32.42, Roland Matthes,
   Wilfried Hartung, Peter Bruch, Lutz Unger

1968

1. U.S.A., 3:31.7, Zachary Zorn, Stephen
   Rerych, Mark Spitz, Kenneth Walsh (WR)
2. Soviet Union, 3:34.2, Semyon Belits-
   Geiman, Viktor Mazanov, Georgy Kulikov,
   Leonid Ilyichev
3. Austria, 3:34.7, Gregory Rogers, Robert
   Windle, Robert Cusack, Michael Wenden

1964

1. U.S.A., 3:33.2 (WR), Stephen Clark, Michael
   Austin, Gary Ilman, Don Schollander
2. East Germany, 3:37.2, Horst Loffler, Frank
   Wiegand, Uwe Jacobsen, Hans-Joachim Klein
3. Austria, 3:39.1, David Dickson, Peter Doak,
   John Ryan, Robert Windle

1896–1960

Not held

Swimming—Men's 4 × 100-Meter Medley Relay

1992

1. U.S.A., 3:36.93 (WR), Jeff Rouse, Nelson
   Diebel, Pablo Morales, Jon Olsen
2. Unified Team, 3:38.56, Vladimir Selkov,
   Alexandre Popov, Pavel Khnykine, Vassili
   Ivanov

3. Canada, 3:39.66, Mark Tewksbury, Jonathan
   Cleveland, Stephen Clarke, Marcel Gery

1988

1. U.S.A., 3:36.93, (WR), David Berkoff, Richard
   Schroeder, Matthew Biondi, Christopher Jacobs
2. Canada, 3:39.28, Mark Tewksbury, Victor Davis,
   Thomas Ponting, Donald Alexander Goss
3. Soviet Union, 3:39.96, Igor Polianski, Dmitri
   Volkov, Vadim Iarochtchouk, Gennadi Prigoda

1984

1. U.S.A., 3:39.30 (WR,OR), Richard Carey,
   Steve Lundquist, Pedro Pablo Morales,
   Ambrose Gaines
2. Canada, 3:43.23, Mike West, Victor Davis,
   Thomas Ponting, Sandy Goss
3. Australia, 3:43.25, Mark Kerry, Peter Evans,
   Glenn Buchanan, Mark Stockwell

1980

1. Australia, 3:45.70, Mark Kerry, Peter Evans,
   Mark Tonelli, Neil Brooks
2. Soviet Union, 3:45.92, Viktor Kuznetsov,
   Arsen Miskarov, Yevgeny Seredin, Sergei
   Kopliakov
3. Great Britain, 3:47.71, Gary Abraham,
   Dunkan Goodhew, David Lowe, Martin Smith

1976

1. U.S.A., 3:42.22 (WR, OR), John Naber, John
   Hencken, Matt Vogel, Jim Montgomery
2. Canada, 3:45.94, Stephen Pickell, Graham
   Smith, Clay Evans, Gary MacDonald
3. West Germany, 3:47.29, Klaus Steinbach,
   Walter Kusch, Michael Kraus, Peter Nocke

1972

1. U.S.A., 3:48.16 (WR), Mike Stamm, Tom
   Bruce, Mark Spitz, Jerry Heidenreich
2. East Germany, 3:52.12, Roland Matthes,
   Klaus Katzur, Hartmut Flockner, Lutz Unger
3. Canada, 3:52.26, Eric Fish, William Mahony,
   Bruce Robertson, Robert Kasting

1968

1. U.S.A., 3:54.9 (WR), Charles Hickcox, Donald
   McKenzie, Douglas Russell, Kenneth Walsh
2. East Germany, 3:57.5, Roland Matthes, Egon
   Henninger, Horst-Gunter Gregor, Frank Wiegand
3. Soviet Union, 4:00.7, Yuri Gromak, Vladimir
   Kossinsky, Vladimir Nemshilov, Leonid
   Ilyichev

1964

1. U.S.A., 3:58.4 (WR), H. Thompson Mann,
   William Craig, Fred Schmidt, Stephen Clark

2. West Germany, 4:01.6, Ernst-Joachim Kuppers, Egon Henninger, Horst-Gunter Gregor, Hans-Joachim Klein
3. Australia, 4:02.3, Peter Reynolds, Ian O'Brien, Kevin Berry, David Dickson

1960
1. U.S.A., 4:05.4 (WR), Frank McKinney, Paul Hait, Lance Larson, F. Jeffrey Farrell
2. Australia, 4:12.0, David Theile, Terry Gathercole, Neville Hayes, Geoffrey Shipton
3. Japan, 4:12.2, Kazuo Tomita, Koichi Hirakida, Yoshihiko Osaki, Keigo Shimizu

1896–1956
Not held

Swimming—Men's 4 × 200-Meter Freestyle Relay

1992
1. Unified Team, 7:11.95 (WR), Dmitri Lepikov, Vladimir Pychnenko, Veniamin Taïanovitch, Evgueni Sadovyi
2. Sweden, 7:15.51, Christer Wallin, Anders Holmertz, Tommy Werner, Lars Frolander
3. U.S.A., 7:16.23, Joe Hudepohl, Mel Stewart, Jon Olsen, Doug Gjertsen

1988
1. U.S.A., 7:12.51 (WR), Troy Dalbey, Matt Cetlinski, Doug Gjertser, Matthew Biondi
2. East Germany, 7:13.68, Uwe Dassler, Sven Lodziewski, Thomas Flemming, Steffen Zesner
3. West Germany, 7:14.35, Erik Hochstein, Thomas Fahrner, Rainer Henkel, Michael Gross

1984
1. U.S.A., 7:15.69 (WR), Michael Heath, David Larson, Jeffrey Float, Lawrence Bruce Hayes
2. West Germany, 7:15.73, Thomas Fahrner, Dirk Korthals, Alexander Schowtka, Michael Gross
3. Great Britain, 7:24.78, Neil Cochran, Paul Easter, Paul Howe, Andrew Astbury

1980
1. Soviet Union, 7:23.50, Sergei Kopliakov, Vladimir Salnikov, Ivar Stukolkin, Andrei Krylov
2. East Germany, 7:28.60, Frank Pfutze, Jorg Woithe, Detlev Grabs, Rainer Strohbach
3. Brazil, 7:29.30, Jorge Luiz Fernandes, Marcus Laborne Mattioli, Ciro Marques Delgado, Djan Garrido Madruga

1976
1. U.S.A., 7:23.22 (WR, OR), Bruce Furniss, Mike Bruner, John Naber, Jim Montgomery

2. Soviet Union, 7:27.97, Vladimir Raskatov, Andrei Bogdanov, Sergei Kopliakov, Andrei Krylov
3. Great Britain, 7:32.11, Alan MacClatchey, David Dunne, Gordon Downie, Brian Brinkley

1972
1. U.S.A., 7:35.78 (WR), John Kinsella, Frederick Tyler, Steven Genter, Mark Spitz
2. West Germany, 7:41.69, Klaus Steinbach, Werner Lampe, Hans-Gunter Vosseler, Hans Fassnacht
3. Soviet Union, 7:45.76, Igor Grivennikov, Viktor Masanov, Georgy Kulikov, Vladimir Bure

1968
1. U.S.A., 7:52.33, John Nelson, Stephen Rerych, Mark Spitz, Donald Schollander
2. Australia, 7:53.77, Gregory Rogers, Graham White, Robert Windle, Michael Wenden
3. Soviet Union, 8:01.66, Vladimir Bure, Semyon Belits-Geiman, Georgy Kulikov, Leonid Ilyichev

1964
1. U.S.A., 7:52.1 (WR), Stephen Clark, Roy Saari, Gary Ilman, Don Schollander
2. West Germany, 7:59.3, Horst-Gunter Gregor, Gerhard Hetz, Frank Wiegand, Hans-Joachim Klein
3. Japan, 8:03.8, Makoto Fukui, Kunihiro Iwasaki, Toshio Shoji, Yukiaki Okabe

1960
1. U.S.A., 8:10.2 (WR), George Harrison, Richard Blick, Michael Troy, F. Jeffrey Farrell
2. Japan, 8:13.2, Makoto Fukui, Hiroshi Ishii, Tsuyoshi Yamanaka, Tatsuo Fujimoto
3. Australia, 8:13.8, David Dickson, John Devitt, Murray Rose, John Konrads

1956
1. Australia, 8:23.6 (WR), Kevin O'Halloran, John Devitt, Murray Rose, Jon Henricks
2. U.S.A., 8:31.5, Richard Hanley, George Breen, William Woolsey, Ford Konno
3. Soviet Union, 8:34.7, Vitali Sorokin, Vladimir Strushanov, Gennady Nikolayev, Boris Nikitin

1952
1. U.S.A., 8:31.1 (OR), Wayne Moore, William Woolsey, Ford Konno, James McLane
2. Japan, 8:33.5, Hiroshi Suzuki, Yoshihiro Hamaguchi, Toru Goto, Teijiro Tanikawa
3. France, 8:45.9, Joseph Bernardo, Aldo Eminente, Alexandre Jany, Jean Boiteux

1948

1. U.S.A., 8:46.0 (WR), Walter Ris, James McLane, Wallace Wolf, William Smith
2. Hungary, 8:48.4, Elemer Szathmary, Gyorgy Mitro, Imre Kadas Geza Kadas
3. France, 9:08.0, Joseph Bernardo, Henri Padou, Jr., Rene Cornu, Alexandre Jany

1936

1. Japan, 8:51.5 (WR), Masanori Yusa, Shigeo Sugiura, Masaharu Taguchi, Shigeo Arai
2. U.S.A., 9:03.0, Ralph Flanagan, John Macionis, Paul Wolf, Jack Medica
3. Hungary, 9:12.3, Arpad Lengyel, Oszkar Abay-Nemes, Odon Grof, Ference Csik

1932

1. Japan, 8:58.4 (WR), Yasuji Miyazaki, Masanori Yusa, Takashi Yokoyama, Hisakichi Toyoda
2. U.S.A., 9:10.5, Frank Booth, George Fissler, Marola Kalili, Manuella Kalili
3. Hungary, 9:31.4, Andras Wannie, Laszlo Szabados, Andras Szekely, Istvan Barany

1928

1. U.S.A., 9:36.2, Austin Clapp, Walter Laufer, George Kojac, John Weissmuller (WR)
2. Japan, 9:41.4, Hiroshi Yoneyama, Nobuo Arai, Tokuhei Sada, Katsuo Takaishi
3. Canada, 9:47.8, F. Munro Bourne, James Thompson, Garnet Ault, Walter Spence

1924

1. U.S.A., 9:53.4 (WR), Wallace O'Connor, Harry Glancy, Ralph Breyer, John Weissmuller
2. Australia, 10:02.2, Maurice Christie, Ernest Henry, Frank Beaurepaire, Andrew Charlton
3. Sweden, 10:06.8, Georg Werner, Orvar Trolle, Ake Borg, Arne Borg

1920

1. U.S.A., 10:04.4 (WR), Perry McGillivray, Pua Kela Kealoha, Norman Ross, Duke Paoa Kahanamoku
2. Australia, 10:25.4, Henry Hay, William Herald, Ivan Stedman, Frank Beaurepaire
3. Great Britain, 10:37.2, Leslie Savage, E. Percy Peter, Henry Taylor, Harold E. Annison

1912

1. Australia, 10:11.6 (WR), Cecil Healy, Malcolm Champion, Leslie Boardman, Harold Hardwick
2. U.S.A., 10:20.2, Kenneth Huszagh, Harry Hebner, Perry McGillivray, Duke Paoa Kahanamoku
3. Great Britain, 10:28.2, William Foster, Thomas Battersby, John Hatfield, Henry Taylor

1908

1. Great Britain, 10:55.6 (WR), John Derbyshire, Paul Radmilovic, William Foster, Henry Taylor
2. Hungary, 10:59.0, Jozsef Munk, Imre Zachar, Bela von Las Torres, Zoltan von Halmay
3. U.S.A., 11:02.8, Harry Hebner, Leo Goodwin, Charles Daniels, Leslie G. Rich

1906

1. Hungary, 16:52.4, Jozsef Onody, Henrik Hajos, Geza Kiss, Zoltan von Halmay
2. Germany, 17:16.2, Ernst Bahnmeyer, Oscar Schiele, Emil Rausch, Max Pape
3. Great Britain, William Henry, John Derbyshire, Henry Taylor, John Jarvis

1896–1904

Not held

WOMEN'S SWIMMING EVENTS

Highlights

Women were first allowed to swim in the Olympics in 1912, and Australia's Fanny Durack—wearing a long woollen swimsuit with a skirt—won the 100m freestyle to become the first female champion in the Games; impressively, her time was the same as the men's winner's. The U.S. was a consistent power almost from the start: in 1920, Ethelda Bleibtrey achieved a personal sweep by winning both individual races and joining the successful relay team. During the period from 1920 to 1936, the Americans collected a total of 31 of a possible 59 medals. American women took all the swimming titles in 1924, except for the breaststroke, which British Lucy Morton captured.

Four years later, in Amsterdam, a German woman won the 200m breaststroke, while Dutch swimmer Marie Braun, whose mother trained her and other swimmers, won the 100m backstroke. The U.S. placed well, taking the 100m and 400m freestyle and the 400m freestyle relay. Faring a little better than the men in 1932, the American women were led by Helene Madison, and managed to win the 100m and 400m freestyle, the backstroke event, and the 400m freestyle relay.

In Berlin in 1936, the Dutch team proved to be America's nemesis, with a star performer in Rie Mastenbroek, who won the 100m and 400m freestyle. The second-place finisher, Ragnhild Hveger, was only fifteen and a half, and later went on to set all freestyle records except the 100m; in fact, between 1936 and 1942, Hveger demolished forty-two world records. U.S. backstroker Eleanor Holm, a gold medalist in 1932, was disqualified from the Berlin Games "for sipping champagne with officials."

In London, in 1948, Denmark's Greta Andersen won the 100m freestyle, and later turned professional, swimming the English Channel six times; at the age of 36, she set the England-to-France record in 13 hours, 14 minutes. The U.S. came from behind in the 400m freestyle relay, thanks to Ann Curtis, whose unofficial time bettered the 12-year-old world record time for the 100 meters.

The American women were hardly able to place in 1952, when Hungarian women took most of the titles, except the 100m backstroke, which South African Joan Harrison won.

In Melbourne in 1956, Australian Dawn Fraser was nineteen years old; she dominated the freestyle sprints until her retirement in 1964, after becoming the first woman to freestyle a sub-minute 100 meters. While Fraser won the 100m freestyle, she placed second in the 400m to fellow countrywoman Lorraine Crapp, who had just before the Games become the first woman to swim the 400 meters in less than 5 minutes. The first butterfly event was swept by the U.S., whose first-place finisher, Shelly Mann, had taken up swimming as therapy for childhood polio.

An American resurgence began in 1960, when Chris von Saltza led a group of so-called "water babies" who averaged 16 years old. Von Saltza finished second to Dawn Fraser in the 100m freestyle, then upset the Australian in the 400m, and then swam on two winning relay teams. Fraser captured the 100m for the third consecutive time at Tokyo in 1964, but Ginny Duenkel led an American 1–2–3 sweep in the 400m freestyle and Donna deVarona did likewise in the individual medley. Cathy Ferguson won the backstroke and the U.S. captured both relays. In 1965 deVarona was the first woman to break into network television in the sports broadcasting field.

In 1968, the American women captured 11 of the 14 events, and 16-year-old Debbie Meyer, who won three golds that year in the 200m, 400m, and 800m freestyles, was named the U.S.A. amateur athlete for 1968. Claudia Kolb, Kaye Hall, and Sue Pedersen each came away with two gold medals. Kolb won the new 200m medley as well as the 400m, Hall won the 100m backstroke and swam on the medley relay, and Pedersen took a leg on both relay teams. The 1968 Games were also marked by Jan Henne's victory in the 100m freestyle, the first American to win that event since Helene Madison in 1932. The events not taken that year by the Americans were awarded to Yugoslavia, in the 100m breaststroke, Australia, in the 100m butterfly, and the Netherlands, in the 200m butterfly; a pair of second-place finishes in the two backstrokes marked the first silver medals ever won by a Canadian woman swimmer.

Between them, the U.S. and Australia won 13 of the 14 women's events at Munich in 1972. The individual star was Australia's Shane Gould, who competed in a record 12 races, including heats and finals. For her effort, she took home three gold (the 200m and 400m freestyle and the 200m individual medley), a silver, and a bronze. Keena Rothhammer, a 15-year-old Californian, thwarted Gould in the 800m freestyle with a world-record time of 8:53.7, and Sandra Neilson and Shirley Babashoff both beat out the dynamic Aussie in the 100m freestyle. Melissa Belote, another 15-year-old, won both backstroke races for the U.S.

As successful as the U.S. men swimmers were at Montreal in 1976, their female counterparts were struggling to remain competitive; while the men lost only one race, the women won only one. East Germany took the 1976 events by a landslide (as it were), winning 11 of 13 events, establishing what would become a long term of East German domination. The only U.S. success came in the final race, the 400m freestyle relay. Meanwhile, the American camp put forth insinuations that the muscular East Germans looked more like men and that their training methods were too autocratic. Kornelia Ender was the outstanding performer with four gold medals, barely missing a fifth in the relay; with a total of five medals, she and Shirley Babashoff share the distinction of being the only women to medal five times in swimming in a single Games. She also provided the media with a sentimental story because of a reunion with her grandmother, who had defected to the U.S. in 1959. Two of Ender's victories came within the space of 26 minutes, as she first tied the world record in the 100m butterfly, then came back to set a world record in the 200m freestyle.

It was the same old story in 1980, although this time the Americans weren't around to have their faces pushed into the water. For the second Olympics in a row, the East Germans captured 11 of 13 events, and at Moscow they swept all of the medals in six of the 11 individual races. Freestyler Barbara Krause, who had missed the 1976 Games because of illness, backstroke specialist Rica Reinisch, only 15 years old at the time, and Caren Metschuck each won three gold medals. The East German women set six world records, with Reinisch helping to account for half of them, two in the backstroke events and one in the 400m medley relay.

In 1984 U.S. swimmer Nancy Hogshead was the big winner in women's swimming, earning four medals. Her teammate, Tracy Caulkins, had been hurt by the 1980 U.S. boycott of the Games, but held on to claim three gold medals at the 1984 Games. Another swimmer affected by the 1980 boycott, butterflyer Mary T. Meagher, won three gold medals in 1984 and captured the 200m butterfly bronze in 1988. But 1984 was the first since 1952 that the Olympics failed to produce at least one women's swimming world record. And for the first time ever, two gold medals were awarded in a single Olympic swimming race, in the women's 100-meter freestyle, the first-place time shared by Americans Hogshead and Carrie Steinseifer, Olympic bunkmates. Also that year, Canada's first swimming medals since 1912 included three medals for the women's team: a gold and a silver captured by Anne Ottenbrite and a relay bronze. While their male counterparts earned the most medals since the 1960 Games, the Australian women contributed their share, winning the silver in the 200m butterfly and the 400m individual medley, along with the bronze in the 200m individual medley.

FACT: Astrid Strauss, of the former East Germany, won the silver medal in the women's 800m freestyle at the 1988 Games. In out-of-competition tests, she tested positive for steroids, and was banned from competition for 18 months.

In 1988 East German Kristin Otto accumulated swimming medals as has no woman in Olympic history, taking the 100m freestyle, the 100m backstroke, the 100m butterfly, and the 50m freestyle, then leading her relay teams to gold medals in the 4 × 100 freestyle and the 4 × 100 medley.

The East German women might have swept the Seoul Games if it hadn't been for U.S. triple-gold medalist Janet Evans. She triumphed in the 400m individual medley, the 400m freestyle, and the 800m freestyle, becoming the fifth woman to win three or more individual swimming gold medals at one Olympics. In fact, she was the only American woman to win any individual gold. Evans's mark in the 400m freestyle beat the record Mark Spitz set in that event in 1968, and her 800m freestyle time would have won any men's race until 1973.

Also swimming strong in 1988 were Tania Dangalakova of Bulgaria in the 100m breaststroke and Krisztina Egerszegi of Hungary in the 200m backstroke, both of whom took home the gold.

Shane Gould

When Shane Gould got home from the 1972 Munich Summer Olympics, she said, "I'm tired. I'm looking forward to school. I wish to be an ordinary teenager." Not an easy order when, at 15, you've won five Olympic medals, including three golds that set world-record times. The young Australian phenomenon had American women swimmers so spooked at Munich, they wore t-shirts that read: "All that glitters is not Gould." It didn't help much.

Gould, born September 4, 1956 in Brisbane, Queensland, could swim underwater with her eyes closed at the age of three. At six she began professional lessons and at thirteen started the serious training that would bring her to international acclaim and the amazingly low heart rate of 40 beats per minute. By 1971, she held every women's freestyle record up to 1500 meters.

Her 1972 Olympic victories came in the 200m and 400m freestyles, and the 200m individual medley. She took a silver medal in the 800m and a bronze in the 100m freestyle races, which were her first freestyle losses in two years. Gould's parents were nearly as big a presence as their daughter at the Games. Her mother, Shirley Gould, had already written a book, *Swimming the Shane Gould Way*.

Tired of the regimen, Gould announced her retirement the following year. Three years after the Olympics, Gould, then 18, married 25-year-old Bible student Neil Innes. After the outdoor wedding, Gould said, "Instead of saying the formal vows, we made up our own. It seemed to be in line with what we believe. We like the open air and surfing."

—Harvey Dickson

Tracy Caulkins

Few people "retire" at the age of twenty-one, but that is exactly what Tracy Caulkins has done. The University of Florida swimming great who won three gold medals at the 1984 Summer Olympics is an athlete who is content these days to watch her own records fall as a new generation prepares for future Games.

Caulkins was born on January 11, 1963, in Winona, Minnesota. She grew up in Nashville, Tennessee, and attended Harpeth Hall Academy, a private school. She began swimming competitively as a youngster. In 1981 she enrolled at the University of Florida, where, over a period of four years, she turned in a stunning record as an amateur athlete. Her achievements include 48 national long and short course titles—the most won by any swimmer in U.S. history—62 American records, 15 individual American records, and participation in 11 American record-setting relay teams. From 1980 until 1984 she was widely considered the best and fastest woman swimmer in America.

Caulkins actually earned a position on the Olympic team in 1980, even before she entered college. That year the United States boycotted the games. All of the Olympic athletes were disappointed, but none more so than Caulkins. She has said that she trained even harder during her college years so that she could prove herself beyond any doubt at the 1984 Games in Los Angeles.

While at Florida, Caulkins won the Broderick Cup as outstanding collegiate woman athlete of the year in both 1983 and 1984. Although she was a consistent winner throughout her college years—and a winner in the 200m and 400m individual medleys at the 1982 Pan American Games—her best year as an NCAA swimmer came in 1984. That year she set NCAA records in all four of her individual events (the 200m individual medley, or IM, 400m IM, 100m breaststroke, and 200m fly). She also helped the Florida team to win the 800m freestyle relay and the 400m freestyle relay, both in NCAA record-setting times.

In preparation for the 1984 Olympic trials, Caulkins swam five hours a day, six days per week. The intense practice and long record of first place finishes paid off handsomely during the Games, where she won the 400m IM, setting an American record, and the 200m IM, establishing an Olympic record. Her third gold medal came as part of a victorious 400m relay team. After the Games ended, the United States Olympic Committee recognized Caulkins as "female athlete of the year," a fitting tribute.

For some time several of Caulkins's records remained unbroken, especially the 200-yard individual medley. That record was only recently bested by Summer Sanders, winner of two gold medals in the 1992 Games. Caulkins expresses no regrets as her successors in competitive swimming gradually beat her in the numbers game. She told the Associated Press. "I thought, 'Why are [my] records not falling?' It shows a lot of progress when they do. The women . . . are not satisfied with just winning."

Caulkins was inducted into the International Swimming Hall of Fame in 1990. The University of Florida has also honored her accomplishments by naming a double swimming scholarship after her and by awarding a Tracy Caulkins Award to Florida's best female swimmer each year.

—*Mark Kram*

Highlights from Barcelona

Making a splash at the Barcelona Games were the amazonian Chinese women, who nailed four golds and five silvers in 15 events. Records fell, rivals' hopes were dashed, and rumors of performance-enhancing pharmacology were numerous. Even with a reputation for ruthlessly training in the pool as well as the body shop, the mesomorphic Chinese squad still managed to surprise opponents with their formidable presence. Having lost the 100m butterfly, an event she historically owned, to Qian Hong of China, the U.S. team's Crissy Ahmann-Leighton lamented, "I wasn't used to someone swimming next to me. In all of my races, I've been out there alone. When I saw someone come up next to me, I thought, 'There she is.'"

FACT: One month after nabbing 12 of 16 medals at the World Championships in Rome, three of China's top women swimmers tested positive for a banned performance-enhancing drug. After failing more drug tests, Chinese swimmers were banned from pre-Olympic competition in 1995.

And they were there. Whether or not the Chinese women were ergonomically suped-up versions of lesser mortals, there was no denying it: the Mainland's intensive eight-year preparations for an all-out assault on the medals podium had paid off. From their very first race, they were a presence to be reckoned with, routinely knocking out many of the U.S. team's most golden girls. Summer Sanders was upset in the 100m free by Lin Li in world-record time. Jenny Thompson and Angel Marino were rousted in the 50m free by Yang Wenyi—in record time, again. And world-record holder Thompson took yet another thumping as Zhuang Yong confiscated the 100m freestyle title. Clearly, the Chinese women had a mission. "Whether Yang [Wenyi] wins or I win," Zhuang Yong later explained, "it's the same, a win for China over the United States. The United States is not that terrifying."

Not terrifying, perhaps, but not to be taken lightly. In spite of the Chinese juggernaut, the U.S. women hung on to five gold medals. Drafting in the wake of Germany's inexperienced Franziska Van Almsick, Nicole Haislett darted from behind to capture her team's first Spanish gold. Summer Sanders grabbed a 200m butterfly win. Janet Evans, losing her first 400 since 1986, atoned for the loss by becoming the first woman to win consecutive Olympic 800s. And then there were the relays: the U.S. women won both, and in world record time.

Fading in her world-record event—the 200m breaststroke—Anita Nall settled for a bronze, allowing Japan's 14-year-old phenom, Kyoko Iwasaki, to become the youngest swimmer to win an Olympic gold. The Hungarian women, too, left Barcelona with precious metals, thanks mostly to Krisztina Egerszegi. Claiming both backstroke events in Olympic record time; the 17-year-old also captured the 400m individual medley gold.

Medalists

Swimming—Women's 50-Meter Freestyle

1992
1. Yang Wenyi, China, 24.79 (WR)
2. Zhuang Yong, China, 25.08
3. Angel Martino, U.S.A., 25.23

1988
1. Kristin Otto, East Germany, 25.49 (OR)
2. Yang Wenyi, People's Republic of China, 25.64
3. Katrin Meissner, East Germany, 25.71
3. Jill Sterkel, U.S.A., 25.71

Swimming—Women's 100-Meter Freestyle

1992
1. Zhuang Yong, China, 54.64 (OR)
2. Jenny Thompson, U.S.A., 54.84
3. Franziska Van Almsick, Germany, 54.94

1988
1. Kristin Otto, East Germany, 54.93
2. Yong Zhuang, People's Republic of China, 55.47
3. Catherine Plewinski, France, 55.49

1984
1. Nancy Hogshead, U.S.A., 55.92
1. Carrie Steinseifer, U.S.A., 55.92
3. Annemarie Verstappen, Netherlands, 56.08

1980
1. Barbara Krause, East Germany, 54.79 (WR)
2. Caren Metschuck, East Germany, 55.16
3. Ines Diers, East Germany, 55.65

1976
1. Kornelia Ender, East Germany, 55.65 (WR, OR)
2. Petra Priemer, East Germany, 56.49
3. Enith Brigitha, Netherlands, 56.65

1972
1. Sandra Neilson, U.S.A., 58.59 (OR)
2. Shirley Babashoff, U.S.A., 59.02
3. Shane Gould, Australia, 59.06

1968
1. Jan Henne, U.S.A., 1:00.0
2. Susan Pedersen, U.S.A., 1:00.3
3. Linda Gustavson, U.S.A., 1:00.3

1964
1. Dawn Fraser, Australia, 59.5 (OR)
2. Sharon Stouder, U.S.A., 59.9
3. Kathleen Ellis, U.S.A., 1:00.8

1960
1. Dawn Fraser, Australia, 1:01.2 (OR)
2. Christine Von Saltza, U.S.A., 1:02.8
3. Natalie Steward, Great Britain, 1:03.1

1956
1. Dawn Fraser, Australia, 1:02.0 (WR)
2. Lorraine Crapp, Australia, 1:02.3
3. Faith Leech, Australia, 1:05.1

Swimming

1952
1. Katalin Szoke, Hungary, 1:06.8
2. Johanna Termeulen, Netherlands, 1:07.0
3. Judit Temes, Hungary, 1:07.1

1948
1. Greta Andersen, Denmark, 1:06.3
2. Ann Curtis, U.S.A., 1:06.5
3. Marie-Louise Vaessen, Netherlands, 1:07.6

1936
1. Hendrika Mastenbroek, Netherlands, 1:05.9 (OR)
2. Jeanette Campbell, Argentina, 1:06.4
3. Gisela Arendt, Germany, 1:06.6

1932
1. Helene Madison, U.S.A., 1:06.8 (OR)
2. Willemijntje den Ouden, Netherlands, 1:07.8
3. Eleanor Saville-Garatti, U.S.A., 1:08.2

1928
1. Albina Osipowich, U.S.A., 1:11.0 (OR)
2. Eleanor Garatti, U.S.A., 1:11.4
3. M. Joyce Cooper, Great Britain, 1:13.6

1924
1. Ethel Lackie, U.S.A., 1:12.4
2. Mariechen Wehselau, U.S.A., 1:12.8
3. Gertrude Ederle, U.S.A., 1:14.2

1920
1. Ethelda Bleibtrey, U.S.A., 1:13.6 (WR)
2. Irene Guest, U.S.A., 1:17.0
3. Frances Schroth, U.S.A., 1:17.2

1912
1. Fanny Durack, Australia, 1:22.2
2. Wilhelmina Wylie, Australia, 1:25.4
3. Jennie Fletcher, Great Britain, 1:27.0

1896–1908
Not held

Swimming—Women's 200-Meter Freestyle

1992
1. Nicole Haislett, U.S.A., 1:57.90
2. Franziska Van Almsick, Germany, 1:58.00
3. Kerstin Kielgass, Germany, 1:59.67

1988
1. Heike Friedrich, East Germany, 1:57.65 (OR)
2. Silvia Poll, Costa Ria, 1:58.67
3. Manuela Stellmach, East Germany, 1:59.01

1984
1. Mary Wayte, U.S.A., 1:59.23
2. Cynthia Woodhead, U.S.A., 1:59.50
3. Annemarie Verstappen, Netherlands, 1:59.69

1980
1. Barbara Krause, East Germany, 1:58.33 (OR)
2. Ines Diers, East Germany, 1:59.64
3. Carmela Schmidt, East Germany, 2:01.44

1976
1. Kornelia Ender, East Germany, 1:59.26 (WR, OR)
2. Shirley Babashoff, U.S.A., 2:01.22
3. Enith Brigitha, Netherlands, 2:01.40

1972
1. Shane Gould, Australia, 2:03.56 (WR)
2. Shirley Babashoff, U.S.A., 2:04.33
3. Keena Rothhammer, U.S.A., 2:04.92

1968
1. Debbie Meyer, U.S.A., 2:10.5 (OR)
2. Jan Henne, U.S.A., 2:11.0
3. Jane Barkman, U.S.A., 2:11.2

1896–1964
Not held

Swimming—Women's 400-Meter Freestyle

1992
1. Dagmar Hase, Germany, 4:07.18
2. Janet Evans, U.S.A., 4:07.37
3. Hayley Lewis, Australia, 4:11.22

1988
1. Janet Evans, U.S.A., 4:03.85 (WR)
2. Heike Friedrich, East Germany, 4:05.94
3. Anke Moehring, East Germany, 4:06.62

1984
1. Tiffany Cohen, U.S.A., 4:07.10 (OR)
2. Sarah Hardcastle, Great Britain, 4:10.27
3. June Croft, Great Britain, 4:11.49

1980
1. Ines Diers, East Germany, 4:08.76 (OR)
2. Petra Schneider, East Germany, 4:09.16
3. Carmela Schmidt, East Germany, 4:10.86

1976
1. Petra Thuemer, East Germany, 4:09.89 (WR,OR)
2. Shirley Babashoff, U.S.A., 4:10.46
3. Shannon Smith, Canada, 4:14.60

1972
1. Shane Gould, Australia, 4:19.04 (WR)
2. Novella Calhgaris, Italy, 4:22.44
3. Gudrun Wegner, East Germany, 4:23.11

1968
1. Debbie Meyer, U.S.A., 4:31.8 (OR)
2. Linda Gustavson, U.S.A., 4:35.5
3. Karen Moras, Australia, 4:37.0

1964
1. Virginia Duenkel, U.S.A., 4:43.3 (OR)
2. Marilyn Ramenofsky, U.S.A., 4:44.6
3. Terri Lee Stickles, U.S.A., 4:47.2

1960
1. Christine Von Saltza, U.S.A., 4:50.6 (OR)
2. Jane Cederqvist, Sweden, 4:53.9
3. Catharina Lagerberg, Netherlands, 4:56.9

1956
1. Lorraine Crapp, Australia, 4:54.6 (OR)
2. Dawn Fraser, Australia, 5:02.5
3. Sylvia Ruuska, U.S.A., 5:07.1

1952
1. Valeria Gyenge, Hungary, 5:12.1 (OR)
2. Eva Novak, Hungary, 5:13.7
3. Evelyn Kawamoto, U.S.A., 5:14.6

1948
1. Ann Curtis, U.S.A., 5:17.8 (OR)
2. Karen-Margrete Harup, Denmark, 5:21.2
3. Catherine Gibson, Great Britain, 5:22.5

1936
1. Hendrika Mastenbroek, Netherlands, 5:26.4 (OR)
2. Ragnhild Hveger, Denmark, 5:27.5
3. Lenore Wingard-Kight, U.S.A., 5:29.0

1932
1. Helene Madison, U.S.A., 5:28.5 (WR)
2. Lenore Kight, U.S.A., 5:28.6
3. Jennie Makaal, South Africa, 5:47.3

1928
1. Martha Norelius, U.S.A., 5:42.8 (WR)
2. Maria Johanna Braun, Netherlands, 5:57.8
3. Josephine McKim, U.S.A., 6:00.2

1924
1. Martha Norelius, U.S.A., 6:02.2 (OR)
2. Helen Wainwright, U.S.A., 6:03.8
3. Gertrude Ederle, U.S.A., 6:04.8

1920
1. Ethelda Bleibtrey, U.S.A., 4:34.0 (WR)
2. Margaret Woodbridge, U.S.A., 4:42.8
3. Frances Schroth, U.S.A., 4:52.0

1896–1912
Not held

Swimming—Women's 800-Meter Freestyle

1992
1. Janet Evans, U.S.A., 8:25.52
2. Hayley Lewis, Australia, 8:30.34
3. Jana Henke, Germany, 8:30.99

1988
1. Janet Evans, U.S.A., 8:20.20 (OR)
2. Astrid Strauss, East Germany, 8:22.09
3. Julie McDonald, Australia, 8:22.93

1984
1. Tiffany Cohen, U.S.A., 8:24.95 (OR)
2. Michele Richardson, U.S.A., 8:30.73
3. Sarah Hardcastle, Great Britain, 8:32.60

1980
1. Michelle Ford, Australia, 8:28.90 (OR)
2. Ines Diers, East Germany, 8:32.55
3. Heike Dahne, East Germany, 8:33.48

1976
1. Petra Thuemer, East Germany, 8:37.14 (WR, OR)
2. Shirley Babashoff, U.S.A., 8:37.59
3. Wendy Weinberg, U.S.A., 8:42.60

1972
1. Keena Rothhammer, U.S.A., 8:53.68 (WR)
2. Shane Gould, Australia, 8:56.39
3. Novella Calligaris, Italy, 8:57.46

1968
1. Debbie Meyer, U.S.A., 9:24.0 (OR)
2. Pamela Kruse, U.S.A., 9:35.7
3. Maria Teresa Ramirez, Mexico, 9:38.5

1896–1964
Not held

Swimming—Women's 100-Meter Backstroke

1992
1. Krisztina Egerszegi, Hungary, 1:00.68 (OR)
2. Tunde Szabo, Hungary, 1:01.14
3. Lea Loveless, U.S.A., 1:01.43

1988
1. Kristin Otto, East Germany, 1:00.89
2. Krisztina Egerszegi, Hungary, 1:01.56
3. Cornelia Sirch, East Germany, 1:01.57

1984
1. Theresa Andrews, U.S.A., 1:02.55
2. Betsy Mitchell, U.S.A., 1:02.63
3. Jolanda de Rover, Netherlands, 1:02.91

1980
1. Rica Reinisch, East Germany, 1:00.86 (WR)
2. Ina Kleber, East Germany, 1:02.07
3. Petra Riedel, East Germany, 1:02.64

1976
1. Ulrike Richter, East Germany, 1:01.83 (OR)
2. Brigit Treiber, East Germany, 1:03.41
3. Nancy Garapick, Canada, 1:03.71

1972
1. Melissa Belote, U.S.A., 1:05.78 (OR)
2. Andrea Gyarmati, Hungary, 1:06.26
3. Susie Atwood, U.S.A., 1:06.34

1968
1. Kaye Hall, U.S.A., 1:06.2 (WR)
2. Elaine Tanner, Canada, 1:06.7
3. Jane Swagerty, U.S.A., 1:08.1

1964
1. Cathy Ferguson, U.S.A., 1:07.7 (WR)
2. Christine Caron, France, 1:07.9
3. Virginia Duenkel, U.S.A., 1:08.0

1960
1. Lynn Burke, U.S.A., 1:09.3 (OR)
2. Natalie Steward, Great Britain, 1:10.8
3. Satoko Tanaka, Japan, 1:11.4

1956
1. Judith Grinham, Great Britain, 1:12.9 (OR)
2. Carin Cone, U.S.A., 1:12.9
3. Margaret Edwards, Great Britain, 1:13.1

1952
1. Joan Harrison, South Africa, 1:14.3
2. Geertje Wielema, Netherlands, 1:14.5
3. Jean Stewart, New Zealand, 1:15.8

1948
1. Karen Margrete Harup, Denmark, 1:14.4 (OR)
2. Suzanne Zimmerman, U.S.A., 1:16.0
3. Judy Davies, Australia, 1:16.7

1936
1. Dina W. Senff, Netherlands, 1:18.9
2. Hendrika Mastenbroek, Netherlands, 1:19.2
3. Alice Bridges, U.S.A., 1:19.4

1932
1. Eleanor Holm, U.S.A., 1:19.4
2. Philomena Mealing, Australia, 1:21.3
3. E. Valerie Davies, Great Britain, 1:22.5

1928
1. Maria Johanna Braun, Netherlands, 1:22.0
2. Ellen E. King, Great Britain, 1:22.2
3. M. Joyce Cooper, Great Britain, 1:22.8

1924
1. Sybil Bauer, U.S.A., 1:23.2 (OR)
2. Phyllis Harding, Great Britain, 1:27.4
3. Aileen Riggin, U.S.A., 1:28.2

1896–1920
Not held

Swimming—Women's 200-Meter Backstroke

1992
1. Krisztina Egerszegi, Hungary, 2:07.06 (OR)

2. Dagmar Hase, Germany, 2:09.46
3. Nicole Stevenson, Australia, 2:10.20

1988
1. Krisztina Egerszegi, Hungary, 2:09.29 (OR)
2. Kathrin Zimmermann, East Germany, 2:10.61
3. Cornelia Sirch, East Germany, 2:11.45

1984
1. Jolanda De Rover, Netherlands, 2:12.38
2. Amy White, U.S.A., 2:13.04
3. Aneta Patrascoiu, Romania, 2:13.29

1980
1. Rica Reinisch, East Germany, 2:11.77 (WR)
2. Cornelia Polit, East Germany, 2:13.75
3. Brigit Treiber, East Germany, 2:14.14

1976
1. Ulrike Richter, East Germany, 2:13.43. (OR)
2. Brigit Treiber, East Germany, 2:14.97
3. Nancy Garapick, Canada, 2.15.60

1972
1. Melissa Belote, U.S.A., 2:19.19 (WR)
2. Susie Atwood, U.S.A., 2:20.38
3. Donna Marie Gurr, Canada, 2:23.22

1968
1. Pokey Watson, U.S.A., 2:24.8 (OR)
2. Elaine Tanner, Canada, 2:27.4
3. Kaye Hall, U.S.A., 2:28.9

1896–1964
Not held

Swimming—Women's 100-Meter Breaststroke

1992
1. Elena Roudkovskaïa, Belarus, 1:08.00
2. Anita Nall, U.S.A., 1:08.17
3. Samantha Riley, Australia, 1:09.25

1988
1. Tania Dangalakova, Bulgaria, 1:07.95 (OR)
2. Antoaneta Frenkeva, Bulgaria, 1:08.74
3. Silke Hoerner, East Germany, 1:08.83

1984
1. Petra Van Staveren, Netherlands, 1:09.88 (OR)
2. Anne Ottenbrite, Canada, 1:10.69
3. Catherine Poirot, France, 1:10.70

1980
1. Ute Geweniger, East Germany, 1:10.22
2. Elvira Vasilkova, Soviet Union, 1:10.41
3. Susanne Schultz Nielsson, Denmark, 1:11.16

1976
1. Hannelore Anke, East Germany, 1:11.16

2. Liubov Rusanova, Soviet Union, 1:13.04
3. Marina Koshevaia, Soviet Union, 1:13.30

1972
1. Catherine Carr, U.S.A., 1:13.58 (WR)
2. Galina Stepanova-Prozumenshikova, Soviet Union, 1:14.99
3. Beverly Whitfield, Australia, 1:15.73

1968
1. Djurdjica Bjedov, Yugoslavia, 1:15.8 (OR)
2. Galina Prozumenshikova, Soviet Union, 1:15.9
3. Sharon Wichman, U.S.A., 1:16.1

1896–1964
Not held

Swimming—Women's 200-Meter Breaststroke

1992
1. Kyoko Iwasaki, Japan, 2:26.65 (OR)
2. Lin Li, China, 2:26.85
3. Anita Nall, U.S.A., 2:26.88

1988
1. Silke Hoerner, East Germany, 2:26.71 (WR)
2. Xiaomin Huang, People's Republic of China, 2:27.49
3. Antoaneta Frenkeva, Bulgaria, 2:28.34

1984
1. Anne Ottenbrite, Canada, 2:30.38
2. Susan Rapp, U.S.A., 2:31.15
3. Ingrid Lempereur, Belgium, 2:31.40

1980
1. Lina Kochushite, Soviet Union, 2:29.54 (OR)
2. Svetlana Varganova, Soviet Union, 2:29.61
3. Yulia Bogdanova, Soviet Union, 2:32.39

1976
1. Marina Koshevaia, Soviet Union, 2:33.35 (WR, OR)
2. Marina Iurchenia, Soviet Union, 2:36.08
3. Liubov Rusanova, Soviet Union, 2:36.22

1972
1. Beverly Whitfield, Australia, 2:41.71 (OR)
2. Dana Schoenfield, U.S.A., 2:42.05
3. Galina Stepanowa-Prozumenshikova, Soviet Union, 2:42.36

1968
1. Sharon Wichman, U.S.A., 2:44.4 (OR)
2. Djurdjica Bjedov, Yugoslavia, 2:46.4
3. Galina Prozumenshikova, Soviet Union, 2:47.0

1964
1. Galina Prozumenshikova, Soviet Union, 2:46.4 (OR)

2. Claudia Kolb, U.S.A., 2:47.6
3. Svetlana Babanina, Soviet Union, 2:48.6

1960
1. Anita Lonsbrough, Great Britain, 2:49.5 (WR)
2. Wiltrud Urselmann, West Germany, 2:50.0
3. Barbara Gobel, East Germany, 2:53.6

1956
1. Ursula Happe, West Germany, 2:53.1 (OR)
2. Eva Szekely, Hungary, 2:54.8
3. Eva-Maria Ten Elsen, East Germany, 2:55.1

1952
1. Eva Szekely, Hungary, 2:51.7 (OR)
2. Eva Novak, Hungary, 2:54.4
3. Helen Gordon, Great Britain, 2:57.6

1948
1. Petronella van Vliet, Netherlands, 2:57.2
2. Beatrice Lyons, Australia, 2:57.7
3. Eva Novak, Hungary, 3:00.2

1936
1. Hideko Maehata, Japan, 3:03.6
2. Martha Geneger, Germany, 3:04.2
3. Inge Sorensen, Denmark, 3:07.8

1932
1. Claire Dennis, Australia, 3:06.3 (OR)
2. Hideko Maehata, Japan, 3:06.4
3. Else Jacobsen, Denmark, 3:07.1

1928
1. Hilde Schrader, Germany, 3:12.6
2. Mietje Baron, Netherlands, 3:15.2
3. Lotte Muhe, Germany, 3:17.6

1924
1. Lucy Morton, Great Britain, 3:33.2 (OR)
2. Agnes Geraghty, U.S.A., 3:34.0
3. Gladys Carson, Great Britain, 3:35.4

1896–1920
Not held

Swimming—Women's 100-Meter Butterfly

1992
1. Qian Hong, China, 58.62 (OR)
2. Crissy Ahmann-Leighton, U.S.A., 58.74
3. Catherine Plewinski, France , 59.01

1988
1. Kristin Otto, East Germany, 59.00 (OR)
2. Birte Weigang, East Germany, 59.45
3. Hong Qian, People's Republic of China, 59.52

1984
1. Mary T. Meagher, U.S.A., 59.26
2. Jenna Johnson, U.S.A., 1:00.19
3. Karin Seick, West Germany, 1:01.36

1980
1. Caren Metschuck, East Germany, 1:00.42
2. Andrea Pollack, East Germany, 1:00.90
3. Christiane Knacke, East Germany, 1:01.44

1976
1. Kornelia Ender, East Germany, 1:00.13 (EWR)
2. Andrea Pollack, East Germany, 1:00.98
3. Wendy Boglioli, U.S.A., 1:01.17

1972
1. Mayumi Aoki, Japan, 1:03.34 (WR)
2. Roswitha Beier, East Germany, 1:03.61
3. Andrea Gyarmati, Hungary, 1:03.73

1968
1. Lynette McClements, Australia, 1:05.5
2. Ellie Daniel, U.S.A., 1:05.8
3. Susan Shields, U.S.A., 1:06.2

1964
1. Sharon Stouder, U.S.A., 1:04.7 (WR)
2. Ada Kok, Netherlands, 1:05.6
3. Kathleen Ellis, U.S.A., 1:06.0

1960
1. Carolyn Schuler, U.S.A., 1:09.5 (OR)
2. Marianne Heemskerk, Netherlands, 1:10.4
3. Janice Andrew, Australia, 1:12.2

1956
1. Shelley Mann, U.S.A., 1:11.0 (OR)
2. Nancy Ramey, U.S.A., 1:11.9
3. Mary Sears, U.S.A., 1:14.4

1896–1952
Not held

Swimming—Women's 200-Meter Butterfly

1992
1. Summer Sanders, U.S.A., 2:08.67
2. Wang Xiaohong, China, 2:09.01
3. Susan O'Neill, Australia, 2:09.03

1988
1. Kathleen Nord, East Germany, 2:09.51
2. Birte Weigang, East Germany, 2:09.91
3. Mary T. Meagher, U.S.A., 2:10.80

1984
1. Mary T. Meagher, U.S.A., (OR) 2:06.90
2. Karen Phillips, Australia, 2:10.56
3. Ina Beyermann, West Germany, 2:11.91

1980
1. Ines Geissler, East Germany, 2:10.44 (OR)
2. Sybille Schonrock, East Germany, 2:10.45
3. Michelle Ford, Australia, 2:11.66

1976
1. Andrea Pollack, East Germany, 2:11.41 (OR)
2. Ulrike Tauber, East Germany, 2:12.50
3. Rosemarie Gabriel, East Germany, 2:12.86

1972
1. Karen Moe, U.S.A., 2:15.57 (WR)
2. Lynn Colella, U.S.A., 2:16.34
3. Ellie Daniel, U.S.A., 2:16.74

1968
1. Ada Kok, Netherlands, 2:24.7 (OR)
2. Helga Lindner, East Germany, 2:24.8
3. Ellie Daniel, U.S.A., 2:25.9

1896–1964
Not held

Swimming—Women's 200-Meter Individual Medley

1992
1. Lin Li, China, 2:11.65 (WR)
2. Summer Sanders, U.S.A., 2:11.91
3. Daniela Hunger, Germany, 2:13.92

1988
1. Daniela Hunger, East Germany, 2:12.59 (OR)
2. Elena Dendeberova, Soviet Union, 2:13.31
3. Noemi Ildiko Lung, Romania, 2:14.85

1984
1. Tracy Caulkins, U.S.A., 2:12.64 (OR)
2. Nancy Hogshead, U.S.A., 2:15.17
3. Michele Pearson, Australia, 2:15.92

1976–1980
Not held

1972
1. Shane Gould, Australia, 2:23.07 (WR)
2. Kornelia Ender, East Germany, 2:23.59
3. Lynn Vidali, U.S.A., 2:24.06

1968
1. Claudia Kolb, U.S.A., 2:24.7 (OR)
2. Susan Pedersen, U.S.A., 2:28.8
3. Jan Henne, U.S.A., 2:31.4

1896–1964
Not held

Swimming—Women's 400-Meter Individual Medley

1992
1. Krisztina Egerszegi, Hungary, 4:36.54
2. Lin Li, China, 4:36.73
3. Summer Sanders, U.S.A., 4:37.58

1988
1. Janet Evans, U.S.A., 4:37.76
2. Noemi Ildiko Lung, Romania, 4:39.46
3. Daniela Hunger, East Germany, 4:39.76

1984
1. Tracy Caulkins, U.S.A., 3:39.24
2. Suzanne Landells, Australia, 4:48.30
3. Petra Zindler, West Germany, 4:48.57

1980
1. Petra Schneider, East Germany, 4:36.29 (WR)
2. Sharron Davies, Great Britain, 4:46.83
3. Agnieszka Czopek, Poland, 4:48.17

1976
1. Ulrike Tauber, East Germany, 4:42.77 (WR, OR)
2. Cheryl Gibson, Canada, 4:48.10
3. Becky Smith, Canada, 4:50.48

1972
1. Gail Neall, Australia, 5:02.97 (WR)
2. Leslie Cliff, Canada, 5:03.57
3. Novella Calligaris, Italy, 5:03.99

1968
1. Claudia Kolb, U.S.A., 5:08.5 (OR)
2. Lynn Vidali, U.S.A., 5:22.2
3. Sabine Steinbach, East Germany, 5:25.3

1964
1. Donna De Varona, U.S.A., 5:18.7 (OR)
2. Sharon Finneran, U.S.A., 5:24.1
3. Martha Randall, U.S.A., 5:24.2

1896–1960
Not held

Swimming—Women's 4 × 100-Meter Freestyle Relay

1992
1. U.S.A., 3:39.46 (WR), Dara Torres, Jenny Thompson, Angel Martino, Nicole Haislett
2. China, 3:40.12, Zhuang Yong, Yang Wenyi, Lu Bin, Le Jingyi
3. Germany, 3:41.60, Franziska Van Almsick, Manuela Stellmach, Simone Osygus, Daniela Hunger

1988
1. East Germany, 3:40.63 (OR), Kristin Otto, Katrin Meissner, Daniela Hunger, Manuela Stellmach
2. Netherlands, 3:43.39, Marianne Muis, Mildred Muis, Connie Van Bentum, Karin Brienesse
3. U.S.A., 3:44.25, Mary Wayte, Mitzi Kremer, Laura Walker, Dara Torres

1984
1. U.S.A., 3:43.43, Jenna Johnson, Carrie Steinseifer, Dara Torres, Nancy Hogshead
2. Netherlands, 3:44.40, Annemarie Verstappen, Elles Vosles, Desi Reijers, Connie Van Bentum
3. West Germany, 3:45.56, Iris Zscherpe, Suzanne Schuster, Christiane Pielke, Karin Seick

1980
1. East Germany, 3:42.71 (WR), Barbara Kruase, Caren Metschuck, Ines Diers, Sarina Hulsenbeck
2. Sweden, 3:48.93, Carina Ljungdahl, Tina Gustafsson, Agneta Maartensson, Agneta Eriksson
3. Netherlands, 3:49.51, Connie Van Bentum, Wilma van Velsen, Reggie de Jong, Annelies Maas

1976
1. U.S.A., 3:44.82, (WR), Kim Peyton, Wendy Boglioli, Jill Sterkel, Shirley Babashoff
2. East Germany, 3:34.50, Kornelia Ender, Petra Priemer, Andrea Pollack, Claudia Hempel
3. Canada, 3:48.81, Gail Amundrud, Barbara Clark, Becky Smith, Anne Jardin

1972
1. U.S.A., 3:55.19 (WR), Sandra Neilson, Jennifer Kemp, Jane Barkman, Shirley Babashoff
2. East Germany, 3:55.55, Gabriele Wetzko, Andrea Eife, Elke Sehmisch, Kornelia Ender
3. West Germany, 3:57.93, Jutta Weber, Heidemarie Reineck, Gudrun Beckmann, Angela Steinbach

1968
1. U.S.A., 4:02.5 (OR), Jane Barkman, Linda Gustavson, Susan Pedersen, Jan Henne
2. East Germany, 4:05.7, Martina Grunert, Uta Schmuck, Roswitha Krause, Gabriele Wetzko
3. Canada, 4:07.2, Angela Coughlan, Marilyn Corson, Elaine Tanner, Marion Lay

1964
1. U.S.A., 4:03.8 (WR), Sharon Stouder, Donna De Varona, Lillian "Pokey" Watson, Kathleen Ellis
2. Australia, 4:06.9, Robyn Thorn, Janice Murphy, Lynette Bell, Dawn Fraser
3. Netherlands, 4:12.0, Pauline van der Wildt, Catharina Beumer, Winnie van Weerdenburg, Erica Terpstra

1960

1. U.S.A., 4:08.9 (WR), Joan Spillane, Shirley Stobs, Carolyn Wood, Susan Christine Von Saltza
2. Australia, 4:11.3, Dawn Fraser, Ilsa Konrads, Lorraine Crapp, Alva Colqhoun
3. West Germany and East Germany, 4:19.7, Christel Steffin, Heidi Pechstein, Gisela Weiss, Ursula Brunner

1956

1. Australia, 4:17.1 (WR), Dawn Fraser, Faith Leech, Sandra Morgan, Lorraine Crapp
2. U.S.A., 4:19.2, Sylvia Ruuska, Shelley Mann, Nancy Simons, Joan Rosazza
3. South Africa, 4:25.7, Jeanette Myburgh, Susan Roberts, Natalie Myburgh, Moira Abernathy

1952

1. Hungary, 4:24.4 (WR), Ilona Novak, Judit Temes, Eva Novak, Katalin Szoke
2. Netherlands, 4:29.0, Marie-Louise Linssen-Vaessen, Koosje van Voorn, Johanna Termeulen, Irma Heijting-Schuhmacher
3. U.S.A., 4:30.1, Jacqueline La Vine, Marilee Stepan, Joan Alderson, Evelyn Kawamoto

1948

1. U.S.A., 4:29.2 (OR), Marie Corridon, Thelma Kalama, Brenda Helser, Ann Curtis
2. Denmark, 4:29.6, Eva Riise, Karen-Margrete Harup, Greta Andersen, Fritze Carstensen
3. Netherlands, 4:31.6, Irma Schuhmacher, Margot Marsman, Marie-Louise Vaessen, Johanna Termeulen

1936

1. Netherlands, 4:36.0 (OR), Johanna Selbach, Catherina Wagner, Willemijntje den Ouden, Hendrika Mastenbroek
2. Germany, 4:36.8, Ruth Halbsguth, Leni Lohmar, Ingeborg Schmitz, Gisela Arendt
3. U.S.A., 4:40.2, Katherine Rawls, Bernice Lapp, Mavis Freeman, Olive McKean

1932

1. U.S.A., 4:38.0 (WR), Josephine McKim, Helen Johns, Eleanor Saville-Garatti, Helene Madison
2. Netherlands, 4:47.5, Maria Vierdag, Maria Oversloot, Cornelia Ladde, Willemijntje den Ouden
3. Great Britain, 4:52.4, E. Valerie Davies, Helen Varcoe, M. Joyce Cooper, Edna Hughes

1928

1. U.S.A., 4:47.6 (WR), Adelaide Lambert, Eleanor Garatti, Albina Osipowich, Martha Norelius

2. Great Britain, 5:02.8, M. Joyce Cooper, Sarah Stewart, I. Vera Tanner, Ellen E. King
3. South Africa, 5:13.4, Kathleen Russell, Rhoda Rennie, Marie Bedford, Frederica J. van der Goes

1924

1. U.S.A., 4:58.8 (WR), Gertrude Ederle, Euphrasia Donnelly, Ethel Lackie, Mariechen Wehselau
2. Great Britain, 5:17.0, Florence Barker, Grace McKenzie, I. Vera Tanner, Constance Jeans
3. Sweden, 5:35.6, Aina Berg, Vivian Pettersson, Gulli Everlund, Hjordis Topel

1920

1. U.S.A., 5:11.6 (WR), Margaret Woodbridge, Frances Schroth, Irene Guest, Ethelda Bleibtrey
2. Great Britain, 5:40.6, Hilda James, Constance Jeans, Charlotte Radcliffe, Grace McKenzie
3. Sweden, 5:43.6, Aina Berg, Emy Machnow, Carin Nilsson, Jane Gylling

1912

1. Great Britain, 552.8 (WR), Bella Moore, Jennie Fletcher, Annie Speirs, Irene Steer
2. West Germany, 6:04.6, Vally Dressel, Louise Otto, Hermine Stindt, Grete Rosenberg
3. Austria, 6:17.0, Margarete Adler, Klara Milch, Josephine Sticker, Berta Zahourek

1896–1908

Not held

Swimming—Women's 4 × 100-Meter Medley Relay

1992

1. U.S.A., 4:02.54 (WR), Lea Loveless, Anita Nall, Crissy Ahmann-Leighton, Jenny Thompson
2. Germany, 4:05.19, Dagmar Hase, Jana Doerries, Franziska Van Almsick, Daniela Hunger
3. Unified Team, 4:06.44, Nina Jivanevskaïa, Elena Roudkovskaïa, Olga Kiritchenko, Natalia Mechtcheriakova

1988

1. East Germany, 4:03.74 (OR), Kristin Otto, Silke Hoerner, Birte Weigang, Katrin Meissner
2. U.S.A., 4:07.90, Beth Barr, Tracey McFarlane, Janel Jorgensen, Mary Wayte
3. Canada, 4:10.49, Lori Melien, Allison Higson, Jane Kerr, Andrea Nugent

1984

1. U.S.A., 4:08.34, Theresa Andrews, Tracy Caulkins, Mary T. Meagher, Nancy Hogshead

2. West Germany, 4:11.97, Svenja Schlicht, Ute Hasse, Ina Beyermann, Karin Seick
3. Canada, 4:12.98, Reema Abdo, Anne Ottenbrite, Michele McPherson, Pamela Rai

1980
1. East Germany, 4:06.67 (WR), Rica Reinisch, Ute Geweniger, Andrea Pollack, Caren Metschuck
2. Great Britain, 4:12.24, Helen Jameson, Margaret Kelly, Ann Osgerby, June Croft
3. Soviet Union, 4:13.61, Yelena Kruglova, Elvira Vasilkova, Alla Grishchenkova, Natalia Strunnikova

1976
1. East Germany, 4:07.95 (WR, OR), Ulrike Richter, Hannelore Anke, Andrea Pollack, Kornelia Ender
2. U.S.A., 4:14.55 Linda Jezek, Lauri Siering, Camille Wright, Shirley Babashoff
3. Canada, 4:15.22, Wendy Hugg, Robin Corsiglia, Susan Sloan, Anne Jardin

1972
1. U.S.A., 4:20.75 (WR), Melissa Belote, Catherine Carr, Deena Deardurff, Sandra Neilson
2. East Germany, 4:24.91, Christine Herbst, Renate Vogel, Roswitha Beier, Kornelia Ender
3. West Germany, 4:26.46, Silke Pielen, Verena Eberle, Gudrun Beckmann, Heidemarie Reineck

1968
1. U.S.A., 4:28.3 (OR), Kaye Hall, Catie Ball, Ellie Daniel, Susan Pedersen
2. Australia, 4:30.0, Lynette Watson, Lynette McClements, Judy Playfair, Janet Steinbeck
3. West Germany, 4:36.4, Angelika Kraus, Uta Frommater, Heike Hustede, Heidemarie Reineck

1964
1. U.S.A., 4:33.9 (WR), Cathy Ferguson, Cynthia Goyette, Sharon Stouder, Kathleen Ellis
2. Netherlands, 4:37.0, Cornelia Winkel, Klena Bimolt, Ada Kok, Erica Terpstra
3. Soviet Union, 4:39.2, Tatyana Savelyeva, Svetlana Babanina, Tatyana Devyatova, Natalia Ustinova

1960
1. U.S.A., 4:41.1 (WR), Lynn Burke, Patty Kempner, Carolyn Schuler, Susan Christine Von Saltza
2. Australia, 4:45.9, Marilyn Wilson, Rosemary Lassig, Janice Andrew, Dawn Fraser
3. East Germany and West Germany, 4:47.6, Ingrid Schmidt, Ursula Kuper, Barbel Fuhrmann, Ursel Brunner

1896–1956
Not held

Trivia Quiz

1. The 100m swim in the 1896 Olympics at Athens was limited to
a. Swimmers who had successfully swum across the English Channel
b. The top medalists of that year's three other events
c. Sailors

2. The swimming events at the 1900 Olympics in Paris were held
a. In a 25m indoor pool **b.** In a 50m outdoor pool **c.** In the Seine

3. The water temperature in competitive pools must be between
a. 78 and 80 degrees Fahrenheit
b. 72 and 76 degrees Fahrenheit
c. 70 and 72 degrees Fahrenheit

4. Swimmers competing in Olympic backstroke competition
a. Must touch the wall with one hand before exiting the turn maneuver
b. May use the "no touch" backstroke turn

5. Swimmers in the medley relay
a. May swim any or all of the four legs of the race

b. May swim as many as two legs of the race

c. May only swim one leg of the race

6. "Banana heat" refers to
a. A preliminary qualifying heat **b.** The consolation final of an event

c. The smell of mildewed Speedos

7. The swimming events at the 1904 Games in St. Louis included
a. An underwater race **b.** A synchronized swimming competition

c. A bathing suit contest

8. The swimmer to win a gold medal was
a. Pablo Morales, who came back from retirement to compete in Barcelona.

b. Duke Kahanamoku, the descendant of a Hawaiian chief

c. Charlie Daniels, a vintage competitor

9. U.S. swimmer Johnny Weismuller
a. Was thought to have heart trouble as a child, but won six Olympic medals

b. Was the first athlete to swim 100 meters in under 1 minute and set 28 world records

c. Played Tarzan in 18 movies

10. Before winning three gold medals at the 1988 Olympics, Janet Evans
a. Was a couch potato **b.** Was a competitive triathlete

c. Was the world record holder in the 800m and 1500m freestyles

Answers: 1-c; 2-c; 3-a; 4-b; 5-c; 6-b; 7-a; 8-b; 9-a, -b, and -c; 10-c

SYNCHRONIZED SWIMMING

Warm-up

Described as a cross between Esther Williams movies and advanced figure skating, synchronized swimming is a sport requiring overall body strength and agility, grace and beauty, split-second timing, musical interpretation, and a bit of the dramatic. You also have to know how to hold your breath underwater.

Added to the Olympics menu in 1984, synchro competitions were first held in England at the turn of the century. In the U.S., Katherine Curtis, a swimmer at the University of Wisconsin in the early 1920s, is credited with developing the modern version of the sport, then called water ballet. The term *synchronized swimming* was first used by a radio announcer at the 1934 World's Fair in Chicago. And following the popularity of Billy Rose's Aquacade at the New York World's Fair in 1939, Hollywood created the first synchronized-swimming movie star, Esther Williams.

In 1945, the Amateur Athletic Union recognized synchronized swimming as a sport, and a year later, the first National Synchronized Swimming Championships were held. In the 1950s, the Pan American Games offered synchro events, and soon world championships were held. The 1952 Olympic Games offered synchro as a demonstration sport, the same year that it was recognized by the Fédération Internationale de Natation Amateur (FINA), the governing body for swimming competitions.

Today, three events are internationally recognized in synchronized swimming: solo, duet (two swimmers), and team (eight swimmers). For the 1992 Olympics, solo and duet competitions were held. In 1996, however, the team competition will replace the solo and duet features. "The team event is the premier event in synchronized swimming," asserts Betty Watanabe, executive director of the program commission of the International Olympic Committee. "Synchronizing eight individuals together is what synchronized swimming is all about."

Spectator's Guide

Contestants have to hold their breath for long periods, with up to 60 percent of the 3.5-minute routine performed underwater. Tracie Ruiz-Conforto, silver medalist in the 1988 solo competition (and gold in the solo and duet in 1984), explains that to score well, "You have to have charisma, enthusiasm, and flair. You have to be dynamic. The judges look at 50 performances, and you want to do something so they don't get bored."

Synchronized swimming consists of technical and free routine competitions (which correspond to the short and long programs in figure skating), accounting for 35 percent and 65 percent of the final score, respectively. The rules are similar to the sports' counterparts, figure skating and gymnastics, and comprehending the scoring system is on the same level of difficulty. During a routine, the swimmer cannot touch the side or bottom of the pool.

For the **free competition**, swimmers choose their own music and choreography. Routines are enhanced by the use of original and expressive movements, patterns, rhythms, and audience contact. In 1996, two panels of five judges will award points from 0 to 10 in one-tenth point increments; one panel judges technical merit while the other rates artistic impression. *Technical merit* includes execution, the ability of the swimmers to match each other's moves (synchronization), and degree of difficulty, which covers such items as time underwater, amount of body weight extended above the water surface, and complexity of the routine. *Artistic impression* covers creativity of the choreography, the use of movement to interpret the music, and the poise and confidence with which the routine is presented (called "manner of presentation").

The highest and lowest of the scores awarded by the judges in the two categories are canceled and the remaining scores averaged. The technical merit total is multiplied by six and the artistic impression score by four. The total of these two equals the routine score.

In the **technical competition**, each athlete is required to perform seven required elements—in the same order—before a panel of judges. With such exotic names as alba, aurora, gaviata, nova, catalina, flamingo, swordfish, and heron, the figures are designed to determine the swimmer's ability to control movement and demonstrate balance, flexibility, and timing. Judges award points from 0 to 10 in one-tenth point increments (e.g., 7.3 or 8.1), based on the accuracy of the performance, as well as the timing, height, stability, and control demonstrated. Solo technical routines are two minutes; duet, two minutes and twenty seconds; and team, two minutes and fifty seconds.

To determine the overall figure score for each competitor, the judges' awards are multiplied by the varying degrees of difficulty and are then combined for a total figure score. The scores are added to the routine totals to determine a final composite score. For duet and team events, the figure scores of the competitors actually performing the routine are averaged before adding the routine score. The scoring system is identical for both the preliminaries and the finals.

Eight teams—a total of 80 swimmers—will compete in synchronized swimming at the new Aquatic Center.

Basic Synchro Positions

Ballet leg: Body and one leg horizontal, with the foot and face at the surface. The hips as close to the surface as possible. One leg perpendicular to the surface.

Bent Knee/vertical: In front layout, back layout, vertical, or arched position. One leg is bent with the toe of that leg at the inside of the other leg, at or above the knee. In the bent knee used to raise or lower a ballet leg, only the knee shall be bent until the thigh of this leg is perpendicular to the surface, the toe remaining at the inside of the other leg.

Crane: Head downward, with the head, body, and one leg vertical and the other leg horizontal and parallel to the surface.

Flamingo: One leg vertical, perpendicular to the surface; the other leg is drawn toward the chest, with its mid-calf opposite the vertical leg, and its foot at the surface. The face is at the surface, and horizontal, with the hips as close to the surface as possible.

Front pike: The trunk and head are vertical, head downward. The heels, thighs, and buttocks are at the surface, with the legs perpendicular to the body.

Split: Legs evenly split forward and backward with both feet and hips as near the surface as possible. Back arches, with shoulders, head, and hip as close to a vertical line as possible.

Tuck: Body as compact as possible, with the back rounded, heels close to buttocks, face close to the knees, with the knees together.

Vertical: Body vertical, head downward. Head, hips, and ankle(s) in line.

Hopefuls

Becky Dyroen-Lancer

Becky Dyroen-Lancer will be just one of the girls in Atlanta. And with the world finally watching for her, that will be a terrible shame.

With a rules change for 1996, synchronized swimming will no longer be a solo or duet Olympic event. Competition will be limited to teams of eight women. Which means that Dyroen-Lancer, arguably the greatest performer in the history of the event, will have to share the spotlight with seven other teammates.

Which would've been like putting Mary Lou Retton in a gymnastics chorus line at the 1984 Games in Los Angeles.

Just how individually dominating has Dyroen-Lancer been?

Like Babe Ruth, she specializes in grand slams. At least eight times in her career, Dyroen-Lancer, 25 (b. February 19, 1971), has swept the individual, duet, and figures events at competitions and shared in team gold medals.

"She will go down as one of the most incredible athletes in the sport ever," said Kristen Babb-Sprague, who won the 1992 Olympic gold medal in Barcelona, after edging out Dyroen-Lancer for the only solo berth on the team.

Even more incredible than what Dyroen-Lancer has done is, perhaps, where she's come from.

The San Jose native, married to a former ballet dancer, Kevin, who helps with her choreography, was born with a hole in her heart. At age 5 she underwent open heart surgery to repair the birth defect.

It's a bit ironic, then, that Dyroen-Lancer's heart is perhaps her greatest asset.

First, aerobically.

"What Becky does in the water is a combination of what a gymnast or figure skater does," U.S. National Team coach Charlotte Davis told *USA Today.* "But for a skater, the ice is always firm. Becky has to do the same moves, but in a constantly changing medium."

> "The toughest thing is the hours and day-to-day commitment. We probably spend more hours training than a lot of sports do physically. You can't spend nine hours shooting arrows in archery. There are so many different aspects to this sport. It's like gymnastics training in different disciplines day after day after day."
> —Becky Dyroen-Lancer, winner of the 1994 World Aquatics Championships

Says Chris Carver, Dyroen-Lancer's personal coach: "You need the aerobic base of a swimmer, and you have to tread water as well or better than a water polo player—and you'd better be able to make it look easy."

Then there are the intangibles of the heart.

"Becky is a sweet person out of the water," Davis says. "But if I were an opponent watching her, I'd be very intimidated."

Adds Carver: "Just when I think she has run out of things, she seems to pull out something else. I always knew that Becky was good, but you never know about the mind. She has that, too. She's amazing, because she continues to grow. That's a coach's dream."

None of this comes easy, of course. Dyroen-Lancer practices six to eight hours a day, six days a week.

"That's the toughest thing," she says. "We probably spend more hours training then I think a lot of sports do physically. You can't spend eight hours shooting arrows in archery. There are so many different aspects to this sport. It's like gymnastics training in different disciplines, day after day after day."

Except on Sundays. Then, Dyroen-Lancer, known as a last-out-of-the-water perfectionist, rests.

"I take Sundays off and do nothing but go to church and then relax the rest of the day," says Dyroen-Lancer, whose mother, Paula, was a synchronized swimmer. "There has never been a time in my life where I actually said to myself I want to retire. But there are times, of course, when I question it. If you're an athlete at this level in any sport, you would be insane or something if you didn't question it. I ask myself all the time, 'Why am I doing this?'"

That introspection is one of Dyroen-Lancer's best qualities, Carver says.

"This is a person who can really take a realistic look at her own performance. She can look at her mistakes, and not let that affect her image of herself. It's very unusual to be so easygoing and at the same time so goal-oriented."

Dyroen-Lancer got involved in the sport recreationally at age 10 with a friend.

"It looked like loads of fun. It was so entertaining. Everyone was together in costumes doing the same routine. When you're that age, you don't see any of the hard work that goes into it."

That realization wasn't far behind, however.

"About age 13, I stared to realize the demand synchronized swimming had on my time," Dyroen-Lancer says. "It was always work, but I never took it serious at that age, because it was so natural for me. I was pretty self-motivated. I remember in the beginning I was getting some pretty low scores. I didn't place very well. But I just kept setting high goals and kept going after them. It's hard for me to believe what I've accomplished. Sometimes it seems like a dream.

"But it does seem that the better you get, the more of a sacrifice it becomes. I guess that's true in sports and life in general. A lot of it is keeping up the motivation and the drive. All I can do is compete against myself, within myself, and hope for the best."

And it keeps coming out the same way—the best.

"Her upside-down movements and interpretation—she can do moves with her legs that nobody else can do," says Babb-Sprague. "She can basically make her legs sing the music."

As for missing out to Babb-Sprague on the trip to Barcelona?

"I'm glad I didn't go," Dyroen-Lancer says. "It wasn't my time. Kristen had put in the work and time and 1992 was her time."

There might be a twinge of disappointment, however, that the competition has been changed for Atlanta, just in time for *her* time.

"In a way, I feel bad," Dyroen-Lancer says. "But it will be a lot less work for me. And I really like the feeling of working with a group. I think that's more exciting."

She's willing to share the spotlight. After all, she does say, "I don't look at myself as some big historical figure."

Which is fine. Mainly because she doesn't have to.

Those that know about her already do.

—*Eric Kinkopf*

Schedule

The tentative synchronized swimming schedule is:

Tuesday, July 30
team preliminaries

Friday, August 2
team final

Highlights

First included as an official event in the LA Games, synchronized swimming did not receive entirely unanimous support from IOC officials. Nonetheless, it was so successful in 1984 that it continues to be part of the Olympic program.

The American team performed exceptionally well in 1984, when both the individual and duet gold medals stayed in the States: Tracie Ruiz won the individual event with a score of 198.467, followed by Canada's Carolyn Waldo, with 195.300 points, and Miwako Motoyoshi, from Japan, with 187.050 points. In the duet event, the U.S. team—which included Ruiz—took another gold medal, with a score of 195.584, followed by the Canadian team, with 194.234, and the Japanese team, with 187.992.

In 1988, Canada and the U.S. traded places, this time with the Maple Leaf team taking both golds. Carolyn Waldo, of Canada, scored an unprecedented 200.150 in the individual event, followed by the now-married American, Tracie Ruiz-Conforto, with 197.633, a little below her previous year's score. Japan, the perennial bronze medalist, came in third with Mikako Kotani's score of 191.850. In the duet event, the Canadian team outscored the U.S., while yet another bronze went to the Japanese team.

Highlights from Barcelona

Two sets of arms, two pairs of legs, all moving in a cosmic synchronicity; you'd swear you were seeing double. The gold-medaling duet didn't just move alike; they *looked* alike. And with good reason: the U.S. gold medalists, Karen and Sarah Josephson, are twins. Determined to improve on their second-place finish in Seoul, the identical sisters concentrated on building a lead in the compulsories. The judges approved: team Josephson earned eight 10s—four in technical and four in artistic impression—with a total of 192.175 points.

Behind them, in mirror image, were Canadian twins Penny and Vicky Vilagos, with 189.394. "It is true that being twins means the bodies are more in harmony," they jointly opined, "but errors are seen more easily."

FACT: By winning the solo, duet, and team titles for the U.S. at the 1994 World Aquatics Championships, Becky Dyroen-Lancer became the first American in over 20 years to strike a grand slam at the world championships. And no U.S. synchro swimmer had won the solo event since Tracie Ruiz captured the title in 1982.

In the solo event, U.S. swimmer and 1991 world championship runner-up, Kristen Babb-Sprague, squeaked into first place—with a micro-margin of 0.131—to turn the tables on Canadian titlist Sylvie Frechette. Well behind them, with 187.056, was Fumiko Okuno, who added a Barcelona medal to Japan's growing collection of bronze necklaces—which includes one for each solo and duet since synchronized swimming was added to the Olympic roster.

Medalists

Synchronized Swimming—Solo

1992
1. Kristen Babb-Sprague, U.S.A., 191.848
2. Sylvie Frechette, Canada, 191.717
3. Fumiko Okuno, Japan, 187.056

1988
1. Carolyn Waldo, Canada, 200.150
2. Tracie Ruiz-Conforto, U.S.A., 197.633
3. Mikako Kotani, Japan, 191.850

1984
1. Tracie Ruiz, U.S.A., 198.467
2. Carolyn Waldo, Canada, 195.300
3. Miwako Motoyoshi, Japan, 187.050

1896–1980
Not held

Synchronized Swimming—Duet

1992
1. U.S.A., 192.175, Karen Josephson, Sarah Josephson
2. Canada, 189.394, Penny Vilagos, Vicky Vilagos
3. Japan, 186.868, Fumiko Okuno, Aki Takayama

1988
1. Canada, 197.717, Michelle Cameron, Carolyn Waldo
2. U.S.A., 197.284, Sarah Josephson, Karen Josephson
3. Japan, 190.159 Miyako Tanaka, Mikako Kotani

1984
1. U.S.A., 195.584, Candy Costie, Tracie Ruiz
2. Canada, 194.234, Sharon Hambrook, Kelly Kryczka
3. Japan, 187.992, Saeko Kimura, Miwako Motoyoshi

Trivia Quiz

1. The term "synchronized swimming" was first used by
a. Esther Williams **b.** Ginger Rogers
c. A radio announcer at the 1934 Word's Fair

2. The Amateur Athletic Union
a. Has never recognized synchronized swimming as a sport
b. First recognized synchronized swimming as a sport in 1982
c. Recognized synchronized swimming as a sport in 1945

3. Synchronized swimming made its first Olympic appearance
a. In 1952, as a demonstration sport   **b.** In 1984, as a full medal sport
c. In the Ancient Games, as part of the pankration

4. In synchro competitions, swimmers
a. Spend up to 60 percent of the 3.5 minute routine under water
b. Spend up to 40 percent of the 3.5 minute routine underwater
c. Hold their breath a lot

5. Synchro rules dictate that swimmers
a. Cannot touch the sides of the pool
b. Cannot touch the sides or bottom of the pool
c. Cannot use snorkeling gear

6. The internationally recognized synchronized swimming events include
a. Solo, duet, and team **b.** Duet and team **c.** Solo and duet

7. The 1996 Olympics will include
a. Team competition only   **b.** Solo and duet competition only
c. Duet and team competition only

8. In the figure competition
a. Swimmers perform a routine set to music
b. Swimmers must perform four figures without music
c. Swimmers must calculate difficult math problems

9. The United States team
a. Has never medaled in synchronized swimming
b. Has four Olympic gold medals in synchronized swimming
c. Has always been defeated by Canada in Olympic synchronized swimming

10. The degree of difficulty of a routine does not take into account
a. The amount of time spent underwater
b. The amount of body weight extended above the water surface
c. The depth at which underwater moves are performed

Answers: 1-c; 2-c; 3-a; 4-a and -c; 5-b; 6-a; 7-a; 8-b; 9-b; 10-c

TABLE TENNIS

Warm-up

The most popular racket sport in the world (and the world's second largest participation sport) made its debut as a full medal sport in the 1988 Summer Olympic Games in Seoul. More than 10 million players annually participate in sanctioned tournaments worldwide.

Table tennis began around the turn of the century as a genteel parlor game, a far cry from today's blitzkrieg smash-o-rama. Although there is little evidence to suggest it, table tennis likely started on college campuses and in military recreational halls.

In the 1890s, Parker Brothers, a sports equipment manufacturer in Salem, Massachusetts, marketed a game called "Indoor Tennis." While mildly received in the U.S., the game was exported to England, where it became popular. The game was played with small rackets and a firm light ball covered with a knitted web. The small net could be stretched across a dining room table, or between chairs if played on the floor.

An Englishman by the name of James Gibb added a celluloid ball (that he had bought in America) to the game. A game called "Gossima" was manufactured in England, and soon came to be known by the onomatopoeic tag of *Ping Pong*. Ping for when the racket hit the ball; Pong for the ball striking the table. The name was patented in England and the U.S. by Parker Brothers.

In 1903, another Englishman, E. C. Goode, improvised a new racket by sticking a piece of pimpled rubber to the standard type of wooden paddle. In addition to wood, early paddles were made of cork, vellum, and cardboard, and covered with cloth, leather, or sandpaper. The game caught on extremely well in Britain, particularly among the upper class. Soon, however, the craze subsided and Ping Pong became something of a forgotten recreation.

In the 1920s, groups in several European countries revived the game, reintroducing it as table tennis due to Parker's proprietary interest in the trademark Ping Pong. In 1923, the English Table Tennis Association formed, and in 1926 the International Table Tennis Federation (ITTF) was founded in Berlin, with Austria, Czechoslovakia, Denmark, England, Germany, Hungary, India, Sweden, and Wales as members. By the 1930s, table tennis had evolved into a highly competitive international sport, and had captured a large U.S. audience. As a result, the United States Table Tennis Association (USTTA) was formed in 1933. The international game did not involve the Soviet Union, however; table tennis was banned there from around 1930 to 1950, allegedly because it was harmful to the eyes.

By 1936, the United States was the first country to win both the Swaythling and Corbillon Cups, awarded to the world's best men's and women's teams, respectively. The USTTA remains the national governing body for the sport in the United States and is affiliated with the International Table Tennis Federation (ITTF).

The game is thought to have been introduced to Japan in the early part of this century by an English cleric. The Japanese Ping Pong Association, founded in the 1920s, joined the ITTF in 1929. From the 1920s to the 1950s, international play was dominated by Hungary in particular, as well as by Austria, Czechoslovakia, England, and Germany. In 1954, however, the Asian era of ping pong began. Between 1952 and 1971, for instance, the Japanese won the Swaythling Cup seven times, the Corbillon Cup eight times, the men's singles six times, the men's doubles three times, and the mixed doubles seven times. During the 1960s, the Chinese began to challenge Japanese supremacy on the green table, and today more than four million Chinese play the game. The Koreans have also become formidable in international play.

FACT: South Korea's Yoo Nam-Kyu holds the most Olympic table tennis medals, with one gold and two bronze, from the 1988 and 1992 Games.

Table tennis has been a part of the Pan American Games since 1979, when it was a demonstration sport. The U.S. team dominated the 1983 Pan Am Games, winning five gold medals and one bronze in seven events. A very young 1987 U.S. Pan American team won three gold and three silver medals, once again dominating the competition.

Spectator's Guide

Table tennis has undergone constant change throughout its history. Today's players are indeed playing a different game from that played in the 1930s. Past world championship games sometimes lasted for several hours. Today, the average match at the top levels of competition lasts about 30 minutes, as players smash the ball past each other at speeds exceeding 100 miles per hour.

Four events are on the 1996 table tennis Olympic program—men's and women's singles and doubles.

The table is nine feet in length, five feet in width, and two and one-half feet high. The net is six inches high. The ball is made of celluloid and approximately 1.5 inches in diameter and weighs roughly 2.5 grams.

Each player whacks at the ball with a small racket. A racket may be of any size, shape, or weight. Its surface must be dark colored and matte, and the blade made of wood. The blade may be covered with plain ordinary pimpled rubber of a total thickness of 2mm, or with "sandwich" consisting of a layer of cellular rubber surfaced by pimpled rubber with pimples either inward or outward with a total thickness of not more than 4mm.

The rules of the game are fairly straightforward. Generally, the first player to score 21 points (one point at a time) wins. In the event of a deuce at 20, the players alternate serves until one scores two consecutive points. A match is two games out of three or three games out of five. The player winning the toss has choice of service or end of table. The first player serves five times, then receives five times, and so on. On the serve, the ball must be thrown straight up at least six inches from a flat, open palm and cannot be hit until it begins to descend.

The period when the ball is in play is called a "rally." Volleying, or striking the ball in play before it has touched the playing surface on the player's side of the table, is not allowed. The ball is deemed out of play once it has touched any object other than the net, its supports, the playing surface, the racquet, or the racquet hand below the wrist.

Players display a variety of styles in the hotly competitive game. The **defender** pushes, chops, and blocks to let his opponent make a mistake. Relying on his ability to return every ball, the defender literally wears down his opponent. The **pick hitter** is basically a defender but occasionally hits the ball past his opponent when there is an opening. The **all-out attacker** hits every ball and tries to kill as many as he can, hoping to win by overpowering his opponent. The benevolent-sounding **looper** is the offensive counterpart to the pick hitter. He uses the loop until the ball pops up enough to kill.

And tactics? **Short serves** to the forehand are very difficult to return. Against a top player, a very short, very low serve is the safest way to get the ball into play. **Three- and five-ball attack** strategies attempt to end the point by the third or fifth ball over the net. In a three-ball attack the server attempts to kill the serve return. A typical five-ball attack begins with a serve, then a return, then a loop, return, then kill. Psychological ploys are often used in table tennis. Watch for players toweling themselves off, tying their shoes, or in some other way attempting to change the pace of the game.

In Atlanta, about 192 athletes will compete in four medal events in table tennis at the Georgia World Congress Center. As host country, the U.S. is assured one berth in singles and one in doubles.

Strokes and Grips

The Push is used to return a ball that has underspin on it or when balls are too low or too far over the table. It is seldom used by experts.

The Block is used to return a hard shot or when a player is out of position.

The Kill is the fastest shot in table tennis and almost impossible to return. Kill shots average 80 miles per hour and may reach 105 mph.

The Hit (or counterdrive) is a slower version of the kill shot.

The Loop is relatively new. With a long sweeping upward motion, the looper just grazes the ball and puts a tremendous amount of topspin on it. A good loop goes straight up if it strikes a vertical paddle. The main use of the loop is as a set-up shot for the kill shot.

The Chop is used to force a player to hit the ball into the net. The downward stroke puts underspin on the ball and makes it difficult to return.

The Shakehands is the most popular grip. The player basically "shakes hands" with the racket.

The Penhold gives a good forehand but a weaker backhand. The racket is held as if holding a pen, with the racket tip pointing downward.

The Seemiller is an unorthodox grip used successfully by five-time U.S. National Champion Danny Seemiller. It is a version of the shakehands grip, with the racket rotated so that the forehand side of the racket can be used on the backhand side. The grip enables the player to switch surfaces for any given shot.

Hopefuls

Hopefuls

Amy Feng

Not fair.

The complaint resurfaces like clockwork just about every four years. And it generally comes from U.S. fans who have watched U.S. athletes compete against opponents raised and educated in state-supported sports schools.

Amy Feng, the No. 1-ranked female table tennis player in the U.S. and its top hope in Atlanta, has a different take on the topic.

Born near Beijing, and selected for a special sports school at age 11, Feng became disgruntled with the sport-as-a-life approach of her native country and emigrated to the U.S. in 1992.

"Table tennis in China takes so much time," says Feng, 27 (b. April 9, 1969), who currently resides in Wheaton, Maryland, and trains in Augusta, Georgia. "When you are 18 or 19, maybe you want to try some other things. I didn't want to stop playing table tennis, but I wanted a little more time to try other things. I didn't have enough time. Table tennis in China—it's your life."

Feng, who began playing the game with her father, a high school teacher, just for fun as a young child, tells stories of the sports school days that began at 6 a.m. with an hour of running and calisthenics. After breakfast, she says, students were trained in table tennis for almost six hours. Two hours of studies followed.

"Table tennis was not easy for me," Feng says. "But I worked very hard. I hoped one day to be in the Olympics."

When she arrived at the school, Feng was No. 3 out of 12 girls. After two years, she was No. 1.

"But five hours of table tennis a day is too much," she says. "You cannot think for that long. After a while, you are just playing, not thinking *how* you are playing. I loved to play, at first. After a while, I had no choice. They make you play."

Not that the strategy didn't pay dividends.

From 1985 to 1990, Feng was women's champion of the Chinese state of Tianjin, placing fifth or higher each time in the Chinese national championships. In 1986, she was ranked No. 26 in the world and placed second in the Chinese National Championships.

Feng was succeeding. But there were disappointments. As Feng tells it, the precise—and stultifying—objectivity of the sports schools was laced with subjectivity.

"When I finished second in China, I felt I should go to the worlds, " said Feng, whose play features a quick serve and explosive attack. "But the coach did not like me, so he did not choose me to go. In China, if the coach likes you, you can do anything. You can play on the world team—*anything*. Because there are so many good players in China, anyone from No. 1 to No. 20 can go to the worlds and win."

Feng's career—and life—took a major turn in 1991 when she met Andrew Tan, a U.S. citizen and amateur table tennis buff, who'd taken a vacation to China to train. As Tan tells it, the excursion was sort of like one of those baseball fantasy camps for the ping-pong set.

Feng and Tan met at the sports school. They scrimmaged.

"Me against her? It's like a normal tennis player against Pete Sampras," Tan says with a smile.

Feng kept in touch with Tan after he left. They married in 1992.

Feng apparently has found the U.S. system of athletics more to her liking, though, of course, far from perfect.

When comparing the two systems, she first refers back to the disappointment of being left off the Chinese national team a decade ago.

"Here, it is better," she says. "Here, any person can go to world competition or the Olympics. They don't give everyone an even chance in China. This is a very fair country. Here, there's more freedom."

And also more difficulty.

Although Feng is at the top of the U.S. ladder, her international ranking suffers. She was ranked No. 40 in the world in 1995, down from that 26th ranking in the late '80s.

"Now, she really needs to train full-time," Tan says, understanding the apparent irony. "She only gets to play, now, a couple of times a week. All the top players in the world play four to five hours a day."

There is also the problem of finding top competition.

"It *is* harder to train," says Feng, who was selected as one of 109 U.S. Olympic Committee Athletes of the Year in 1993 and was featured in *Sports Illustrated's* "Faces in the Crowd" section in January 1994.

Says Tan: "Here, you just grab someone (to practice with) whenever you can."

There is also the cost of training.

"It's mostly all at our own expense," says Tan, a computer programmer who supports Feng's sport. "Amy earns a little bit in table tennis and we get some help from the U.S. Table Tennis Association for winning the national title. That helps offset some of the cost, but not much."

Indeed, Tan says that he and Feng select the tournaments in which she plays by the amount of prize money available.

Feng says a big tournament could offer as much as $1,000.

"If it's a small tournament, Amy doesn't go," Tan says.

Still, things have managed to work. Feng is taking classes to improve her English and coaches children and takes other part-time jobs to support her career—and an Olympic-sized dream.

"I know everybody who plays in China," she says. "I could end up playing someone from my old country. Before, they didn't give me the chance to go to the worlds. Right now, I would just like to beat them."

—Eric Kinkopf

Schedule

The tentative table tennis schedule is:

Tuesday, July 23
Women's & Men's doubles preliminaries

Wednesday, July 24
Women's singles preliminaries
Women's & Men's doubles preliminaries

Thursday, July 25
Women's & Men's singles preliminaries
Men's & Women's doubles preliminaries
Men's singles preliminaries

Friday, July 26
Men's & Women's singles preliminaries
Women's doubles quarterfinal
Men's singles preliminaries

Saturday, July 27
Men's singles preliminaries
Women's singles octos

Men's doubles quarterfinal
Women's doubles semifinal

Sunday, July 28
Men's singles octos

Monday, July 29
Women's doubles final
Women's singles quarterfinal
Men's doubles semifinal

Tuesday, July 30
Men's doubles final
Men's singles quarterfinal
Women's singles semifinal

Wednesday, July 31
Women's singles final
Men's singles semifinal

Thursday, August 1
Men's singles final

Highlights

Although first recognized by the IOC as an Olympic sport in 1977, table tennis was not included in the Games—even as a demonstration sport—until 1988. The host country was victorious in a number of events: South Korea won the gold in the women's doubles, both gold and silver in the men's singles, and the bronze in men's doubles. China captured the most medals at Seoul, sweeping the medals in women's singles, taking a silver in women's doubles, and grabbing a gold in the men's doubles, but they failed to medal in the men's singles, where the bronze was taken by a Swedish player. The remaining medals—a silver in the men's doubles and a bronze in the women's doubles—went to Yugoslavia.

FACT: When table tennis debuted at the Seoul Games, none of the men's top-seeded players advanced to the semifinals.

The field of competitors was limited to 64 men and 48 women, which included three American players: Insook Bhushan, Sean O'Neill, and Diana Gee. With only one man among them, the U.S. team did not compete in men's doubles. In women's singles, Bhushan completed the competition with a 2–3 record and came in fourth in her grouping, while Diana Gee finished fifth. Seeded third in her six-player group, Bhushan beat an Australian, a Tunisian, and a Dominican woman. In the women's doubles, Bhushan and Gee finished with a record of 1–5 to take sixth place. Sean O'Neill, with a 2–5 win/loss record, finished sixth in his grouping in men's singles.

Highlights from Barcelona

"I can't explain the difference between a world championship and the Olympic Games, but the truth is, they're nothing to do with each other," Steffen Fetzner, half of Germany's world champion duo, lamented after having been beaten to the gold by China's Lin Lu and Tao Wang.

"Playing with my regular training partner had no influence on the match."
— Yaping Deng, upon beating her teammate Hong Qiao at the 1992 Games

Jean-Phillippe Gatien, the world's top seed, probably felt the same way. Matching wits against Sweden's Jan-Ove Waldner, France's gold medal hopeful was excused from the table only thirty minutes into the final. Having rallied after a poor first set of 10–21, he had no reply to Waldner's cunning serve, losing the next two sets 18–21, 23–25. Nam Kyu Yoo, the 1988 Olympic champ, had already succumbed to the

Swede's relentless table manner in a taut five setter that ended 21–19, allowing Wenge Ma of China and Taek Soo Kim of Korea to share the bronze medal between them.

In the women's events, China's Yaping Deng became the first Olympic double individual gold medalist by defeating her teammate Hong Qiao in a thrilling final. "If it's true we know each other very well, far from being an advantage it was rather the opposite," she confessed after the match.

But it was definitely an advantage to compete as a team. Combining forces in the doubles competition, Hong and Yaping dismissed teammates Zihe Chen and Jun Gao. Picking up the team bronze, Sun-Bok Yu doubled the prodigal Korea's first-ever table tennis medal haul.

Medalists

Table Tennis—Men's Singles

1992
1. Jan Waldner, Sweden
2. Jean-Philippe Gatien, France
3. Ma Wenge, China
3. Taek Soo Kim, South Korea

1988
1. Nam-Kyu Yoo, South Korea
2. Ki-Taik Kim, South Korea
3. Erik Lindh, Sweden

Table Tennis—Men's Doubles

1992
1. China, Lu Lin, Wang Tao
2. Germany, Steffen Fetzner, Jorg Rosskopf
3. South Korea, Hee Chan Kang, Chul Seung Lee
3. South Korea, Taek Soo Kim, Nam-Kyu Yoo

1988
1. People's Republic of China, Longcan Chen, Qingguang Wei
2. Yugoslavia, Ilija Lupulesku, Zoran Primorac
3. South Korea, Jae-Hyung Ahn, Nam-Kyu Yoo

Table Tennis—Women's Singles

1992
1. Deng Yaping, China
2. Qiao Hong, China
3. Jung Hwa Hyun, South Korea
3. Bun Hui Li, North Korea

1988
1. Jing Chen, People's Republic of China
2. Huifen Li, People's Republic of China
3. Zhimin Jiao, People's Republic of China

Table Tennis—Women's Doubles

1992
1. China, Deng Yaping, Qiao Hong
2. China, Chen Zihe, Gao Jun
3. North Korea, Bun Hui Li, Sun Bok Yu
3. South Korea, Cha Ok Hong, Jung Hwa Hyun

1988
1. South Korea, Jung-Hwa Hyun, Young-Ja Yang
2. People's Republic of China, Jing Chen, Zhimin Jiao
3. Yugoslavia, Jasna Fazlic, Gordana Perkucin

Trivia Quiz

1. Table tennis was originally known as
a. Gossima.   **b.** Looper   **c.** Dining room tennis

2. The International Table Tennis Federation (ITTF), founded in Berlin in 1926, did not originally include
a. Hungary   **b.** Sweden   **c.** The U.S.

3. The 1983 Pan Am Games were dominated by
  a. The United States **b.** Japan **c.** England

4. Parker Brothers, a Massachusetts sports equipment manufacturer,
  a. Published a rules book for Table Tennis
  b. Manufactured the celluloid balls used in Table Tennis
  c. Patented the "Ping Pong" name in England and the U.S.

5. In 1936, both the Swaythling and the Corbillon Cups were won by
  a. England **b.** Germany **c.** The United States

6. Competitive players hit the ping pong ball at speeds exceeding
  a. 100 mph **b.** 32 mph **c.** 65 mph

7. From the 1920s to the 1950s, international play was dominated by
  a. Hungary **b.** The U.S. **c.** Japan

8. Psychological ploys
  a. Are frowned on in table tennis **b.** Are often used in table tennis
  c. Are what makes the world go 'round

9. The Seemiller is
  a. A return that puts a lot of topspin on the ball **b.** An unorthodox grip
  c. A women's tournament

10. Table tennis was banned in the Soviet Union from around 1930 to 1950, allegedly because
  a. It was harmful to the eyes **b.** It cultivated unnecessary skills
  c. It was fun

Answers: 1-a; 2-c; 3-a; 4-c; 5-c; 6-a; 7-a; 8-b; 9-b; 10-a

TEAM HANDBALL

Warm-up

To U.S. Olympic fans, team handball is not one of the glamour sports of the Games, although more than three million players worldwide are registered with the international handball association. Adding to the apparent nonchalance is the confusion about what team handball is; it is not at all like the "handball" sport played in a small room by four people.

In Europe the game is called "handball," while in the U.S. it goes by the moniker "team handball," due to the existence of that other, four-wall, game. Team handball combines elements of other, better-known games: it's been called ice hockey without sticks and ice, water polo without water, and indoor soccer without kicking. Although it's never been called baseball without bats or tennis without rackets, team handball does incorporate many elements of basketball, but not the basket.

Though team handball as we know it is a modern game, a fourth-century mosaic in Sicily's Piazza Armerina depicts women playing what looks like a form of handball. But the team handball we know was invented about the same time as basketball—in the 1890s—by a group of Danish track and field athletes looking for an effective indoor exercise during the cold Scandinavian winter. They placed two soccer balls at each end of a gymnasium floor and began playing a soccer-type game using the hands instead of the feet. In 1906, Danish teacher Holger Nielsen formalized the first rules and organized competitions.

Germans tried the same sort of game outdoors that summer, as did members of several other European countries. The Scandinavian version called for an indoor court and six players a side, plus a goalkeeper; elsewhere, teams used 10 or 11 players per side in the great outdoors.

In 1924, the many variations of the game were standardized by the International Handball Federation (IHF). In 1928, representatives of 11 handball nations met at the Olympic Games, formed the International Amateur Handball Federation and printed the first official international rules. In 1936 at Berlin, team handball, with 11 to a team playing on a soccer field, officially became an Olympic sport, with Germany, Austria, Switzerland, Hungary, Romania, and the United States competing.

Meanwhile, the Scandinavians continued to refine indoor, seven-a-side handball. The first world championship for handball (both seven and 11 a side) was held in 1938.

At the 1948 Games, however, handball was taken off the program. The 11-a-side game was waning in popularity, while seven-a-side was still becoming established as an international sport. Basketball tactics and jargon were integrated into the sport during this period, reflected in such handball/basketball terms as dribble, pivot, post, and man-to-man.

The formation of the U.S. Team Handball Federation (USTHF) in 1959 marked the beginning of team handball in the United States. Men's team handball was reintroduced to the Olympic program in 1972, and the women's event followed four years later.

FACT: Permitted to add one sport to the Olympic roster, the Germans selected handball — a descendant of field handball, which evolved in Germany — as the their addition to the 1936 Berlin Games.

Spectator's Guide

Team handball combines the skills of running, jumping, catching, and throwing into a fast-moving game. The basic objective of the game is to score a goal by using passing and good teamwork. A successful scoring attempt results in a point, and the final scores in the game run in the high teens or low twenties. Twelve teams compete in the men's tournament and eight in the women's.

The court is slightly larger than a basketball court, measuring 40 meters in length (131 feet) and 20 meters from sideline to sideline (65.5 feet). The goal is 2 meters by 3 meters (about 7 feet high by ten feet wide). The most significant line on the court is the six-meter line, or **goal area line**. The area enclosed by the line is called the goal area, or **circle**. Only the goalie is allowed to stand inside the goal area. However, an offensive or defensive player may be in the air over the circle as long as they take off from outside of the goal area line. Once they land in the circle, players cannot interfere with play in any way and must exit as quickly as possible. If a goal is scored while the goal scorer or a teammate is in the circle, the goal does not count. If the defense gains an advantage by being in the circle, a penalty throw is awarded to the offense.

The men's ball is some 60 centimeters (23 inches) in circumference and weighs 16 ounces. The women's ball is slightly smaller at 56 centimeters (22 inches), but that is the only difference between the men's and women's games.

The game is played in 30-minute halves, with no timeouts except for injuries or other major interruptions, as determined by the referees. Each team fields seven players (six court players and one goalie). All players may roam over the entire court. The essential line-up includes a player at left backcourt, center, and right backcourt. Forward positions include a left wing, a circle runner, and a right wing.

The backcourt players are usually tall and good leapers who shoot from the backcourt over the defense. The center is a play maker who directs the offense. The wings are smaller, quicker players who shoot from difficult angles. And the circle runners are large, aggressive tight-end types who screen and pick to disorganize the defense, awaiting the opportunity of blasting a shot from the six-meter line.

The offense usually runs set plays, but free-lance play is encouraged, particularly in quick or fast-break situations. The pace of the game runs the gamut from "slow down and set up" to "run and gun."

A coin flip determines the first possession of the ball, and the game begins with a throw-off, or pass, at center court. The same procedure is followed after each goal. Before passing or shooting, a player is permitted to run three steps with the ball or hold it for three seconds. They also may dribble as much as they like, although the game is not as dribble-oriented as basketball. Double dribbling results in a free throw for the opposing team. A player cannot kick the ball.

A player is allowed to use the body to obstruct an opponent either with or without the ball. However, using the arms or legs to obstruct, push, hold, trip, or hit is not allowed. A free throw is awarded if an offensive player charges into a defensive player. As in hockey, excessive roughness can result in a yellow card (warning) or in a two-minute penalty.

On the occasion of a third two-minute penalty, the offending player is issued a red card, signaling his/her disqualification. Teams play short for the duration of each two-minute penalty.

A **throw-in** is awarded to an opponent when one team loses the ball out of bounds. The defense must be three meters away when the ball is thrown in.

Free throws are awarded for minor infringements of the rules, similar to a free kick in soccer. The free throw is taken immediately, without the referee handling the ball, from the place where the violation occurred. The defense must remain three meters away. The thrower must keep one foot continuously in contact with the court, and must make a throw or pass within three seconds. A goal may be scored directly from a free throw. If a minor foul occurs between the goal line and the free throw line (nine meters from the goal line), the free throw is taken from the free throw line just opposite from where the foul took place.

For more serious fouls, such as those that occur while a player is shooting, a **penalty throw** is awarded. When the penalty throw is taken, one foot must remain in contact with the floor behind the seven-meter penalty line until the ball is released. The penalty throw is in essence a one-on-one between goalie and shooter.

Hopefuls

If there is one team handball player fans should see, it's Jackson Richardson of France. Dreadlocks flop over his head as he weaves his way across the court, creating chaos for defenders. Richardson, one of the most popular players in the world, is a key reason France is the team to beat at the 1996 Olympics.

The French were surprise bronze medalists in 1992, and their team has improved each year. They are the reigning world champions. Opponents have a hard time getting through the unique French lineup, which uses five defenders, while Richardson roams alone. "The French game revolves around Richardson, his quickness, and his judgement," said U.S. coach Rick Oleksyk. "He is just so good."

Right up there with France is Croatia, which will be competing under its own flag for the first time in Olympic history. The Croats were banned from the 1992 Games because of the political strife that plagued Eastern Europe. Croatia, which won the silver medal at the 1995 World Championships, uses finesse and a well-balanced attack led by right wing Irfan Smajlagic.

When it comes to goaltending, there is no team like Sweden. Tomas Svenssen recently reached terms with a Spanish club for the largest professional contract ever offered a handball goalie. And when Svenssen doesn't play, Mats Olsen, another top-notch goalie fills in. The Swedes, who finished fourth at the 1995 world championships, are also known for their difficult-to-defend fast-break offense. They have been compared to the Los Angeles Lakers basketball teams of the 1980s.

Another team in the Olympic medal hunt will be Germany, which boasts a back line that measures 6-feet-10, 6-feet-6, and 6-feet-4. Much to the dismay of their opponents, the Germans are as physical as they are tall. No team in the world matches their power and size. German goaltender Andreas Thiel, a lawyer by trade, made the all-star team at the 1995 world championships and is considered as good as Svenssen.

Russia, Spain, and Korea are longshots for a medal, but all have strong squads. Spain is led by center Tolen Dujshebaev, a Mongolian native who used to play for the Soviet team and emigrated to Spain.

As for Team U.S.A., expect to see athleticism and bold style of play, but do not count on a medal. Most of the U.S. players learned the sport as adults, and they lack the handball intuition shared by the rest of the world.

The U.S. Team Handball Federation recruits many of its athletes from collegiate football, basketball, soccer, baseball, softball and track. Letters are sent to Division I, II, and III colleges asking for soon-to-be graduating athletes who are tall (6-feet-4 for men, 5-feet-10 for women) and have speed, arm strength and agility.

Among the top American players are: John Keller, a former tight end for the University of North Carolina football team; Derek Brown, a former basketball player and track star at LaSalle University; Tony Dave, a former basketball player at the University of New Mexico; and Thomas Fitzgerald, a former basketball standout at St. Bonaventure. Chris Havlicek, son of Boston Celtics great John Havlicek, is one of the sport's up-and-comers.

Also in the past few years, there has been an effort to recruit Native American athletes for handball. Mike Jones, a 6-foot-7 left back, was spotted at the Native American Basketball Championships in Oklahoma, and recruited for a tryout. His mother is a member of the Tolowa tribe.

New York, California, Oklahoma, and Colorado have become hotbeds for the men's game. The women's game is thriving in Pennsylvania, Minnesota, and Wisconsin.

The U.S. women's team is among the top six in the world, and a longshot for a medal. Eight women are back from the 1992 sixth-place Olympic team, and three players will be competing in their third Olympics—Laura Coenen, Kim Clarke, and Carol Paterka.

Like the men, several women on the U.S. team got their start on the basketball court. Coenen had her jersey retired at the University of Minnesota, and captain Chrys Watts played basketball and ran track at the University of North Carolina.

If the U.S. women are to reach the medal podium, they'll have to tangle with Norway, Denmark, Germany, Austria, and Korea.

The Danes won the 1995 European championship, and have emerged as the team to beat.

Two-time Olympic champion Korea plays an unorthodox style that has been nicknamed "circus handball". It is an acrobatic style that relies on speed, agility and discipline. The Koreans jumped into the world scene in 1986, with an 11th-place finish at the world championships. Two years later, they won the Olympic gold. They took home gold again in 1992, and are looking for a three-peat.

Both U.S. teams have been based in Atlanta since March 1994. The players relocated, many of them giving up jobs, for the sake of team unity and a chance to practice together daily. Time will tell if the sacrifice paid off.

—*Michelle Kaufman*

Schedule

The tentative team handball schedule is:

Wednesday, July 24
Men's preliminaries 1–6

Thursday, July 25
Men's preliminaries 7–12

Friday, July 26
Women's preliminaries 1–4

Saturday, July 27
Men's preliminaries 13–18

Sunday, July 28
Women's preliminaries 5–8

Monday, July 29
Men's preliminaries 19–24

Tuesday, July 30
Women's preliminaries 9–12

Wednesday, July 31
Men's preliminaries 25–30

Thursday, August 1
Women's finals 5–6, 7–8 & semifinals 1 & 2

Friday, August 2
Men's final 5–6, 7–8, 9–10, 11–12 & semifinals 1 & 2

Saturday, August 3
Women's bronze & gold medal

Sunday, August 4
Men's bronze & gold medal

Highlights

Team handball first appeared and later reappeared in Games held in Germany. In the 1936 Olympics, the host country—

which had opted to include the sport in the Berlin Games—easily defeated the opposition: the U.S. was beaten 29–1, and only Austria managed to close the score a little with a losing score of 8–6. Absent from the Games until Munich, the seven-man event was no longer dominated by Germany—with Yugoslavia taking the gold, Czechoslovakia the silver, and Romania the bronze; East Germany came in fourth while West Germany finished sixth.

Romania, whose team held the world championship title in 1972 and 1976, improved their 1972 bronze with a 1976 silver, still shy of the gold. The Soviets, who had placed fifth in 1972, captured the 1976 gold; they dominated the final from halftime on, winning with a score of 19–15. In the first women's handball match, the Soviets dominated as well, defeating East Germany; Hungary came in third, while the Romanian women's team came in fourth.

At the Moscow Games the women's gold medal was taken by the host country, while East Germany took the men's gold. The last point of the game was scored by East German Hans-Georg Beyer, who came from an Olympic family: Also during the Moscow Games, his brother, Udo, medaled in the shot put, and his sister, Gisela, took fourth place in the discus. On the bronze-medaling East German women's team, Roswitha Krause competed in her second Games, having captured a silver medal in the freestyle swimming relay in Mexico City.

Yugoslavia dominated the 1984 Games, taking both the men's and women's gold. The West German men's team came in second, while the Romanians placed third. In the women's events, the Republic of Korea captured the silver medal, while the People's Republic of China took the bronze.

In 1988, the host country again kept a gold medal: South Korea won the gold in the women's event. In the same event, a new player entered the Hall of Olympic medalists in handball: The Norwegian women's team took second place ahead of the Soviets. The men's event featured a familiar cast of medalists: While the host country won the silver, the Soviets took the gold and the Yugoslavian team earned the bronze.

The U.S. men's team suffered a number of disappointments through its six matches. In the initial match against Iceland, the U.S. team lost 15–22; the following match, the U.S. went up

FACT: At the 1984 LA Games, the Yugoslavian women's team trounced the U.S. thanks in part to 27-year-old Jasna Kolar-Merdan, who scored 17 goals—an Olympic record.

against the previous year's gold medalist, Yugoslavia. Most interestingly, the U.S. coach was not only Yugoslavian-born, but had coached the winning 1984 team. The U.S. started off well but slipped in the second half, losing with a score of 23–31. No one was surprised by the Soviets' 26–14 victory in the next match, but the round with Sweden—which the U.S. had hoped to win—produced a stunning loss, with a score of 26–12. Having lost their fifth match against Algeria, the U.S. incurred its most devastating loss, in a 21–24 match against Japan, whose team they had considered to be eminently beatable.

Highlights from Barcelona

In a 22–20 victory over the world champion Swedes, the triple-threat Unified Team reaped their final handball gold. But not without a fight. To the casual observer, the handball remnant of the great Soviet sports machine seemed to be running out of steam; the Swedish squad, on the other hand, was vaunted as the team most likely to bank gold. Both blessed with unusually peripatetic goalkeepers, the Soviet collective and the Swedes battled neck-and-neck until the second half, when the Unified athletes seemed to gather momentum.

FACT: The gold-medal-winning 1988 Soviet team towered over the competition, literally: the average height of the Soviet players was nearly 6 feet 4 inches.

Mounting an unflagging defense, the Unified Team began to inch away from the persistent Swedish players, who continued their heel-nipping until the final hour. Adding a fourth gold medal to the Unified Team's collection, coach Spartak Mironovitch made a point of thanking the players from Belarus and Ukraine for joining his patchwork confederation of athletes.

Surprising everyone—not least of all themselves—was the there-by-the-skin-of-their-teeth French team. First was a hot-and-heavy *mano a mano* with the prepossessing German squad; a roust-about with the Romanians followed, and again the French emerged unscathed. Edging out the Icelanders—who stepped in to replace the excommunicated Yugoslavs—the French team grabbed their first-ever Olympic handball medal.

On the women's court, it was déjà vu all over again. The 1992 goldengirls from South Korea again outscored vice-champion Norway—and by the same point spread. There was little doubt how the match would end: with six goals in ten minutes, the Korean women built up a yawning 16–8 lead by half time. With Siri

Eftedal busting some excellent moves, Norway managed to rally again, but nothing could weaken the Koreans' stranglehold. In third place again was the Unified team, who romped through the German squad en route to their medals.

Medalists

Team Handball—Men's Team

1992
1. Unified Team, Andrei Lavrov, Igor Vassiliev, Iouri Gavrilov, Andrei Barbachinski, Andrei Minevski, Viacheslav Gorpishin, Serguei Bebechko, Valeri Gopine, Vassili Koudinov, Talant Douichebaev, Dmitri Filioppov, Mikhail Iakimovitch, Oleg Grebnev, Oleg Kiselev, Igor Tchoumak
2. Sweden, Mats Olsson, Robert Hedin, Magnus Wislander, Anders Backegren, Ola Lindgren, Per Carlem, Erik Hajas, Magnus Cato, Axel Sjöblad, Robert Andersson, Pierre Thorsson, Patrik Liljestrand, Steffan Olsson, Magnus Andersson, Tommy Suoraniemi, Tomas Svensson
3. France, Philippe Medard, Gilles Derot, Pascal Mahe, Philippe Debureau, Frederic Volle, Philippe Schaaf, Denis Lathoud, Denis Tristant, Gael Monthurel, Alain Portes, Eric Quintin, Jean-Luc Thiebaut, Philippe Gardent, Thierry Perreux, Laurent Munier, Frederic Perez, Jackson Richardson, Stephane Stoecklin

1988
1. Soviet Union, V. Atavin, K. Charovarov, Youri Chevtson, L. Dorochenko, Vareli Gopin, A. Karchakevish, Andrei Lavrov, Youri Nesterov, V. Novitski, A. Rymanov, G. Sviridenko, Igor Tcooumak, A. Tioumentsev, A. Toutchkine, M. Vassiliev
2. South Korea, Suk-Jae Choi, Jae-Won Kang, Jae-Hwan Kim, Man-Ho Kim, Suk-Chang Koh, Kyung-Mo Lee, Sang-Hyo Lee, Jin-Suk Lim, Youg-Li Oh, Do-Hun Park, Young-Dae Park, Hyun-Suk Roh, Jae-Hong Shim, Young-Suk Sin, Tae-Il Yoon
3. Yugoslavia, Mirko Basic, Jozef Holpert, Boris Jarak, S. Kuzmanovski, Muhamed Memic, A. Nacinovic, Goran Perkovac, Zlatko Portner, Iztok Puc, Rolando Pusnik, Momir Rnic, Z. Saracevic, Irfan Smajlagic, Ermin Velic, Veselin Vujovic

1984
1. Yugoslavia, Zlatan Arnautovic, Momir Rnic, Veselin Vukovic, Milan Kalina, Jovan Elezovic, Zdravko Zovko, Branko Strbac, Pavo Jurina, Veselin Vujovic, Slobodan Kuzmanovski, Mirko Basic, Dragan Mladenovic, Zdravko Radjenovic, Mile Isakovic, Rolando Pusnik
2. West Germany, Andreas Thiel, Arnulf Meffle, Rudiger Neitzel, Martin Schwalb, Dirk Rauin, Michael Paul, Michael Roth, Thomas Happe, Erhard Wunderlich, Thomas Springel, Klaus Woller, Jochen Fraatz, Uwe Schwenker, Siegfried Roch, Ulrich Roth
3. Romania, Nicolae Munteanu, Marian Dumitru, Iosif Boros, Maricel Voinea, Vasile Stinga, George Dogarescu, Gheorghe Covaciu, Cornel Durau, Dumitru Berbece, Alexandru Folker, Neculai Vasilca, Alexandru Buligan, Vasile Oprea, Mircea Bedivan, Adrain Simion

1980
1. East Germany, Siegfried Voigt, Gunter Dreibrodt, Peter Rost, Klaus Gruner, Hans-Georg Beyer, Dietmar Schmidt, Hartmut Kruger, Lothar Doering, Ernst Gerlach, Frank-Michael Wahl, Ingolf Wiegert, Wieland Schmidt, Rainer Hoft, Hans-Georg Jaunich
2. Soviet Union, Mikhail Ishchenko, Viktor Makhorin, Sergei Kushniryuk, Aleksandr Karshakevich, Vladimir Kravzov, Vladimir Belov, Anatoli Fedyukin, Aleksandr Anpilogov, Yevgeny Chernyshov, Aleksei Zhuk, Nikolai Tomin, Yuri Kidyaev, Vladimir Repiev, Valdemar Novitsky
3. Romania, Nicolae Munteanu, Marian Dumitru, Iosif Boros, Maricel Vionea, Vasile Stinga, Radu Voina, Cezar Draganita, Cornel Durau, Stefan Birtalan, Alexandru Folker, Neculai Vasilca, Lucian Vasilache, Adrian Cosma, Claudiu Eugen Ionescu

1976
1. Soviet Union, 19, 18:20, Mikhail Ishchenko, Anatoli Fedyukin, Vladimir Maximov, Segei Kushniryuk, Vassili Ilyin, Vladimir Kravzov,

Yuri Klimov, Yuri Lagutin, Aleksandr Anpilogov, Yevgeny Chernyshov, Valeri Gassiy, Anatoli Tomin, Yuri Kidyaev, Aleksandr Rezanov

2. Romania, 15, 18:20, Cornel Penu, Gavril Kicsid, Cristian Gatu, Cezar Draganita, Radu Voina, Roland Gunesch, Alexandru Folker, Stefan Birtalan, Adrian Cosma, Constantin Tudosie, Nicolae Munteanu, Werner Stockl, Mircea Grabovschi, Ghita Licu

3. Poland, 21, 23:22, Andrzej Szymczak, Piotr Ciesla, Zdzislaw Antczak, Zygfryd Kuchta, Jerzy Klempel, Janusz Brzozowski, Ryszard Przbysz, Jerzy Melcer, Andrzej Sokolowski, Jan Gmyrek, Henryk Rozmiarek, Alfred Kaluzinski, Wlodzimierz Zielinski, Mieczyslaw Wojczak

1972

1. Yugoslavia, Zoran Zivkovic, Abaz Arslanagic, Miroslav Pribanic, Petar Fajfric, Milorad Karalic, Djoko Lavrnic, Slobodan Miskovic, Hrvoje Horvat, Branislav Pokrajac, Zdravko Miljak, Milan Lazarevic, Nebojsa Popvic, Zdenko Zorko, Albin Vidovic

2. Czechoslovakia, Frantisek Kralik, Petr Pospisil, Ivan Satrapa, Vladimir Jary, Jiri Kavan, Andrej Lukosik, Vladimir Haber, Jindrich Krepindl, Ladislav Benes, Vincent Lafko, Jaroslav Konecny, Pavel Mikes, Frantisek Bruna, Zdenek Skara, Jaroslav Skarvan, Arnost Klimcik

3. Romania, Cornel Penu, Alexandru Dinca, Gavril Kicsid, Ghita Licu, Christian Gatu, Roladn Gunesch, Radu Voina, Simion Schobel, Gheorghe Gruia, Werner Stockl, Dan Marin, Adrian Cosma, Valentin Samungi, Constantin Tudose, Stefan Birtolan

1956–1968
Not held

1952
Demonstration game only.
(Sweden 19, Denmark 11)

1948
Not held

1936

1. Germany, Heinz Korvers, Arthur Knautz, Willy Bandholz, Hans Keiter, Wilhelm Brinkmann, Gerog Dascher, Erich Herrmann, Hans Theilig, Helmut Berthold, Alfred Klinger, Fritz Fromm, Karl Kreutzberg, Heinrich Keimig, Wilheim Muller, Kurt Dossin, Rudolf Stahl, Hermann Hansen, Fritz Sengler, Edgar Reinhardt, Gunther Ortmann, Wilhelm Baumann, Helmut Braselmann

2. Austria, Alois Schnabel, Franz Bartl, Johann Tauscher, Otto Licha, Emil Juracka, Leopold Wohlrab, Jaroslav Volak, Alfred Schmalzer, Ludwig Schubert, Ferdinand Kiefler, Anton Perwein, Fritz Maurer, Franz Brunner, Fritz Wurmbock, Siegfried Purner, Hans Zehetner, Hans Houska, Franz Bistricky, Franz Berghammer, Walter Reisp, Josef Krejci, Siegfried Powolny

3. Switzerland, Willi Gysi, Robert Studer, Erich Schmitt, Rolf Faes, Erland Herkenrath, Burkhard Gantenbein, Werner Meyer, Max Streib, Georg Mischon, Ernst Hufschmid, Eugen Seiterle, Edy Schmid, Max Blosch, Werner Scheurmann, Willy Schafer, Willy Hufschmid, Rudolf Wirz

1896–1932
Not held

Team Handball—Women's Team

1992

1. South Korea, Hyang-Ja Moon, Eun-Young Nam, Ho-Youn Lee, Sun-Hee Hwang, Mi-Young Lee, Jeong-Ho Hong, O-Kyung Lim, Hye-Sook Min, Jeong-Lim Park, Sung-Ok Oh, Hyun-Sook Han, Ri-Ra Jang, Sun-Hi Han, Hwa-Sook Kim, Kap-Sook Park, Jae-Kyung Cha

2. Norway, Hege Kirsti Froseth, Tonje Sagstuen, Hanne Hogness, Heidi Sundal, Susann Goksor, Cathrine Svendsen, Mona Dahle, Siri Ettedal, Henriette Henriksen, Ingrid Steen, Karin Pettersen, Annette Skotvoll, Kristine Duvholt, Hege Kristine Luno Kvitsand, Anne Brit Skarstein, Heidi Marie Tjugum

3. Unified Team, Svetlana Bogdanova, Natalia Deriouguina, Galina Onoprienko, Tatiana Gorb, Elina Gousseva, Larissa Kisseleva, Marina Bazanova, Natalia Morskova, Lioudmila Goudz, Svetlana Priahina, Natalia Anissimova, Svetlana Rozintseva, Raissa Verakso, Galina Borzenkova, Tatiana Djandjgava

1988

1. South Korea, Hyun-Sook Han, Mi-Sook Ki, Choon-Rye Kim, Hyun-Mee Kim, Kyung-Soon Kim, Myung-Soon Kim, Young-Sook Kim, Ki-Soon Lee, Mi-Young Lee, Mi-Kyung Lim, Hyun-Sook Park, Mi-Na Son, Ji-Hyun Song, Min-Hee Suk, Kyung-Hwa Sung

2. Norway, K. Andersen, Berit Digre, Marte Eliasson, Susann Goksor, Trine Haltvik, Hanne Hegh, Hanne Hogness, Vibeke Johnsen, Kristin Midthun, Karin Pettersen,

Karin Singstao, A. Skottvoll, Ingrid Steen, Heidi Sundal, C. Svendsen

3. Soviet Union, Imova N. Aniss, Marina Bazanova, T. Djandagava, Elina Gouszeva, Larissa Karlova, N. Lapitskaia, S. Mankova, N. Mitruiuk, N. Morskova, E. Nemachkalo, N. Rousnatchenko, Olga Semenova, Z. Tourtchina, E. Tovstogan, Tatiana Gorb

1984

1. Yugoslavia, Jasna Ptujec, Mirjana Ognjenovic, Ljubinka Jankovic, Svetlana Anastasovski, Svetlana Dasic-Kitic, Alenka Cuderman, Svetlana Mugosa, Mirjana Djunca, Biserka Visnjic, Slavica Djukic, Jasna Kolar-Merdan, Ljiljana Mugosa

2. Republic of Korea, Kyung-Soon Kim, Soon-Ei Lee, Hyoi-Soon Jeong, Mi-Sook Kim, Hwa-Soo Han, Ok-Hwa Kim, Choon-Yei Kim, Soon-Bok Jeung, Byung-Soon Yoon, Young-Ya Lee, Kyung-Hwa Sung, Soo-Kyung Youn

3. People's Republic of China, Xingjiang Wu, Jianping He, Juefeng Zhu, Weihong Zhang, Xiumin Gao, Linwei Wang, Liping Liu, Xiulan Sun, Yumei Liu, Lan Li, Mingxing Wang, Zhen Chen

1980

1. Soviet Union, Natalia Timoshkina, Larissa Karlova, Irina Palchikova, Zinaida Turchina, Tatiana Kochergina Makerez, Ljudmila Poradnik Bobrus, Larissa Savkina, Aldona Nenenene-Chesaitite, Yulia Safina, Olga Zubareva, Valentina Lutaeva, Lyubov Odinokova-Berechnaya, Sigita Strechen

2. Yugoslavia, Ana Titlic, Slavica Jeremic, Zorica Vojinovic, Radmila Drljaca, Katica Iles, Mirjana Ognjenovic, Svetlana Anastasovski, Rada Savic, Svetlana Kitic, Mirjana Djurica, Biserka Visnjic, Vesna Radovic, Jasna Merdan, Vesna Milosevic

3. East Germany, Hannelore Zober, Katrin Kruger, Evelyn Matz, Roswitha Krause, Christina Rost, Petra Uhlig, Claudia Wunderlich, Sabine Rother, Kornelia Kunisch, Marion Tietz, Kristina Richter, Waltraud Kertzschmar, Birgit Heinecke, Renate Rudolph

1976

1. Soviet Union, Natalia Sherstyuk, Rafiga Shabanova, Lyubov Berezhnaya, Zinaida Turchina, Tatiana Makarez, Maria Litoshenko, Ljudmila Bobrus, Tatiana Gluschenko, Ljudmila Shubina, Galina Zakharova, Aldona Chesaitite, Nina Lobova, Ljudmila Pantchuk, Larissa Karlova

2. East Germany, Hannelore Zober, Gabriele Badorek, Evelyn Matz, Roswitha Krause, Christina Rost, Petra Uhlig, Christina Voss, Liane Michaellis, Silvia Siefert, Marion Tietz, Kristina Richter, Eva Paskuy, Waltraud, Kretzschmar, Hannelore Burosch

3. Hungary, Agota Bujdoso, Marta Magyeri, Borbala Toth-Harsanyi, Katalin Laki, Amalia Sterbinszky, Ilona Nagy, Klara Csik, Rozalia Lelkes, Maria Vadasz, Erzsebet Nemeth, Eva Angyal, Maria Berzsenyi, Marianna Nagy, Zsuzsanna Kezi

Trivia Quiz

1. Team handball was invented in the 1890s by
   a. A New York fireman
   b. A group of Danish track and field athletes
   c. A Yale alumnus

2. In team handball, excessive roughness is
   a. To be expected
   b. Penalized with a two-minute penalty
   c. Grounds for immediate forfeit

3. The sport of team handball has borrowed a lot of tactics and terms from
   a. Baseball   **b.** Synchronized swimming   **c.** Basketball

4. At the 1936 Berlin Games, team handball was played
   a. In the gymnasium   **b.** On a soccer field   **c.** Under the bleachers

5. Double dribbling results in
a. A throw-in awarded to the opposing team
b. A free throw for the opposing team
c. A firing squad at dawn

6. The first women's Olympic handball match was dominated by
a. The Soviets   b. The U.S.   c. Jamaica

7. Which nation has not won an Olympic team handball medal?
a. Italy   b. Switzerland   c. Norway

8. First possession of the ball is determined by
a. Each team's points standings   b. A coin flip   c. A ouija board

9. The team handball court is
a. Slightly larger than a basketball court
b. About half the size of a basketball court
c. No place to try out your new spandex shorts

10. East Germany's Hans-Georg Beyer, who medaled at the Moscow Games
a. Had a brother, Udo, who medaled in the shot put in Moscow
b. Had a sister, Gisela, who took fourth place in the discus in Moscow
c. Had a twin, Georg-Hans, who medaled in ballroom dancing at the Workers Olympics

TENNIS

Warm-up

Reestablished as an Olympic sport in 1988 after a 64-year siesta, tennis is a grand old game with roots that go back to the Stone Age, when human beings first discovered the thrill of hitting rocks with a club over dirt and stone barricades. Even further along in the history of human development, a person on the other side returned the rock. Soon, the volley was invented.

It was the French who gave shape to the semi-modern game of tennis. The word tennis may be derived from the French *tenez,* meaning "take it" or "play." Tennis is derivative of a game similar to handball, which was played in ancient Greece, Rome, Egypt, Persia, and Arabia. During the 10th century or so, legend has it, a wandering minstrel introduced the game to the French Court. Evidence also suggests that it was a recreation in monastic cloisters as early as the 11th century. The game was amenable to either outdoor or indoor play. Indoors, a rope cord stretched across the room served as the net, while outdoors, a mound of dirt served to divide the court.

Players used their open hands to swat a cloth bag stuffed with hair back and forth. The game became known as *jeu de paume,* or "sport of the hands" (or palm). Outside France, it was known as *real* (royal) tennis.

Although Louis IV (who ruled what was considered France during the 10th century) banned tennis as undignified (much as the English kings attempted to do so with soccer), the sport continued to attract interest. Throughout the Middle Ages, ecclesiastical bans were imposed by bishops and so forth, in the hope of inhibiting tennis-crazed monks. "Born to serve" had taken on an entirely new meaning.

By the 14th century, tennis had swum the channel to the British Isles, where first it may have washed up in Scotland and was known as *caitchspeel*. Within a hundred years it was established as a royal game, although it was not to Richard II's tastes. Richard the Deuce, who thought that soccer was a great waste of time, felt likewise about tennis, believing that his soldiers were misplacing their priorities. England, he reckoned, could be invaded while his army was playing tennis. And a soldier did not improve upon his bow and arrow technique while swatting a small ball around a court. Henry VII and Henry VIII, however, both enthusiastically embraced the game. The court that Henry VIII had built at Hampton is the oldest of the 17 ancient tennis courts surviving in England.

An all-wood racket, similar to a table tennis racket, was added to the game as it became fashionable throughout Europe in the later Middle Ages. By 1500, a racket with a wooden handle and a head strung with sheep gut had been developed. In 16th-century France, tennis became the national game. Nearly every town featured a tennis court (or several), and Paris boasted more than 1000.

But by 1600, interest in the game had dissipated, for reasons unknown. For the next two hundred years, tennis was a seldom-played game. Then in the 19th century, the sport was rediscovered in England.

In 1858, Major T.H. Gem and J.B. Perera marked out a tennis court at Edgbaston, Birmingham, England. There they began to adapt real tennis to an open-air court on grass. The modern game took another giant leap forward in 1873, when Major Walter Wingfield introduced a game called *sphairistike* (the Greek root for "ball.") in England. Only the server could score and a game was 15 points, played on an hourglass-shaped court divided by a net seven feet high. Wingfield had the foresight to patent his equipment, which essentially consisted of tape that he used to mark out the court.

The All-England Croquet Club took an interest in the sport, and club officials, always short of funds, decided to hold a championship to raise money for the club. Three members drew up the rules, and the first Wimbledon lawn tennis championships were held in 1877 on the original ground at Worple Road.

In 1874, the game was introduced in the United States by Mary Outerbridge, who was initiated in the game while vacationing in Bermuda. Upon her return she brought with her two rackets, a ball, and a net, and began the long search for a singles partner. Through her efforts, the first court was established on the lawn of the Staten Island Cricket and Baseball Club.

The game caught on quickly in the States, leading to the formation of the U.S. Lawn Tennis Association in 1881. One of the oldest international competitions, the Davis Cup, traces its roots to the United States. In 1900, Dwight Filley Davis, then a 21-year-old just graduated from Harvard College and a leading American player, started the International Lawn Tennis Challenge Trophy. He envisioned a yearly team tournament for men that would advance friendship and goodwill internationally among sportsmen who visited one another's countries for matches. The endeavor succeeded, and the sterling silver bowl became known as the Davis Cup. In the spirit of the Davis Cup, the Federation Cup—now called the Fed cup—was launched in 1963 by the International Lawn Tennis Federation as a worldwide team competition for women.

In 1923, the Wightman Cup was established, providing an arena for teams of British and American women to compete against one another. Coincidentally, the first captain of the American team was Hazel Wightman (Hazel Hotchkiss), one of the better players in the world then (and an Olympic champion in 1924), who led the U.S. squad to victory. Currently the United States leads in the series, 51 matches to 10.

During the first modern Olympics in 1896, men's singles and doubles events were on the program. In 1900, a mixed event and women's singles were added, and in 1904, subtracted. Tennis disappeared from the Olympic menu after the 1924 Paris Games until its revival as a demonstration sport at Mexico in 1968. The game was dropped after the Paris Olympics due to the ongoing problem (in many sports besides tennis) of deciding where to draw the line between amateur and professional players. Before reaching full-medal status at Seoul, tennis was again a demonstration event in LA in 1984.

FACT: The women's singles title at the 1988 Games was won by the demonstration sport's youngest competitor. At the age of 15, Germany's Steffi Graf added an Olympic gold to her mounting collection of trophies: just one week before the Games began, Graf had become the fifth player in history to nail a tennis Grand Slam victory.

Today, in addition to Wimbledon, the major international individual championships include the U.S. Open Championships, with the first tournament held in 1881; the French Open Championships, dating from 1891; and the Australian Open Championships, which were first held in 1905.

To win all of these championships in a single season is known as a Grand Slam. The first to achieve one was California's Don Budge in 1938.

Other Grand Slammers include Maureen Connolly of San Diego in 1953, Australians Rod Laver in 1962 and 1969 and Margaret Smith Court in 1970, and Germany's Steffi Graf in 1988.

Spectator's Guide

Four Olympic events are held: men's and women's singles and doubles. Both men's and women's events allow a maximum of 96 competitors, and after playing on clay in Barcelona, competitors return to a hard court surface in Atlanta. Play consists of a series of elimination rounds.

The equipment consists of a racket, ball, court, and net. The court measures 36 feet wide (10.97m) by 78 feet long (23.77m). For singles play, the sideline boundaries are pinched in at the 27 foot mark (8.23m). The height of the net is three feet at center court. Rackets, made of metal or wood, weigh between 12 and 15 ounces and are approximately 27 inches long. Tennis balls, the favorite chewing toy of puppies everywhere, are made from rubber molded into two cups that are cemented together and covered with wool felt. The ball is inflated with compressed air or gas, is approximately 2.5 inches in diameter, and weighs two ounces. When dropped from 100 feet, it should bounce 55 feet. By comparison, a watermelon dropped by David Letterman from 100 feet will only bounce some five feet.

The rules of tennis are relatively simple. The server starts play by sending the ball over the net into the service court. A player will serve for an entire game, upon which the service goes to his or her opponent, so that the server becomes the receiver and the receiver the server. Players may use underhand or overhand serves at their discretion. The server may stand anywhere in back of the baseline between the imaginary extensions of the center mark and the singles sideline.

For the service to be good, the ball must cross the net without bouncing and pitch into the service court diagonally opposite. If the service or server infringes any rule, a fault is called and the server is permitted a second serve. If the second serve is a fault, the server loses a point.

A player wins a point when the opponent fails to return the ball over the net before it touches the ground twice on the opponent's side of the net. Points are also won when the opponent returns the ball so that it first hits the ground outside of the boundaries of the court or a permanent fixture outside the court (umpire stand, etc.) or goes into the net. The ball cannot be hit twice with a racket on any return. A return is good if it bounces within the opponent's court after crossing the net. A ball hit on any portion of the sidelines or baselines is considered in bounds. The ball may touch the net or cross outside the post as long as it lands in the correct court.

In doubles, the order of service is decided this way: the pair who have to serve in the first game of each set shall decide which partner shall do so, and the opposing pair shall decide similarly for the second game. The partner of the player who served in the first game shall serve in the third; and the partner of the player who served in the second game shall serve in the fourth, and so on for all subsequent games of the set.

A match is scored in games and sets. The first point is 15, the second 30, the third 40, and the fourth wins the game unless there is a deuce, which is called at the score of 40-all. After deuce, the next point won is scored as an advantage to the player who won it, and if he or she wins the following point, he or she wins the game. Should the opponent redress the balance, the score returns to deuce and the game continues.

A player must win a set by two games, and the first player to win six games wins the set. If each player has won five games, two scenarios are possible: one player can win the next two games and win the set, or they can tie at six-all and play a tiebreaker. In a tiebreaker, the first player to reach seven points (again being ahead by two) wins the tiebreaker and the set.

Players change ends after every odd numbered game in each set.

Through the 1992 Games, men's doubles and singles players won all matches by dominating three out of five sets. In 1996, all men's matches will be determined by two out of three sets, with the exception of the singles and doubles gold-medal matches, which will be determined by three out of five sets. Women's events will continue to be decided by two out of three sets.

Also for the first time at the 1996 Games, competitors will play off for the bronze medal. Whereas the losers in the two semi-final matches for each event were awarded bronze medals in previous Games, losing semifinalists will now compete in a semifinal round for third place.

Tennis Talk

Ace: A ball that is served so excellently that the opponent fails to touch it with the racket.

All: Score all tied up.

Back Court: The area between the service line and the baseline.

Backhand: The stroke used to return balls hit to the left of a right-handed player, and to the right of a left-handed player.

Baseline: The end boundary line of a tennis court, located 39 feet from the net.

Deuce: A score of 40–40.

Dink: A ball hit so that it floats back really soft.

Drop Shot: A softly hit shot that barely crosses the net.

Earned Point: A point won by skillful playing rather than by a player's mistake.

Error: A point that ends by an obvious mistake rather than by skillful playing.

Fault: A serve error.

Forecourt: The area between the net and the service line.

Ground Strokes: Strokes made after the ball has bounced, either forehand or backhand.

Hold Serve: To serve and win the game.

Kill: To smash the ball down very hard, usually resulting in a point.

Let: A serve that hits the top of the net or an interruption that forces a replay of the point.

Lob: A ball hit high enough in the air to pass over the head of the player at the net.

Love: Zero or no score.

Match point: The point that, if won, wins the match for a player.

Poach: A strategy whereby the net player in doubles moves over to his serving partner's side of the court to make a volley.

Service line: The line that outlines the base of the service court; parallel to the baseline and 21 feet from the net.

Set: That part of a match that is completed when one player or side wins at least six games and is ahead by at least two games, or has won the tie break.

Set point: The point that, if won, wins the set.

Smash: A hard, overhead shot.

Straight sets: Winning a match without the loss of a set.

Volley: To hit the ball before it bounces.

Hopefuls

The wealth of publicity surrounding the basketball Olympic Dream Team has made it easy to overlook another, equally impressive "Dream Team" in the making—the 1996 U.S. Olympic tennis team. Since tennis returned to the Olympics as a medal sport in 1988, America has always fielded an impressive roster of tennis stars in the competition. This year will be no exception. Some of the players who have expressed interest in the Olympics include Andre Agassi, Pete Sampras, Michael Chang, Martina Navratilova, and Monica Seles.

Tennis was one of the original Olympic sports at the first Games in Athens in 1896. The sport was included in the Olympics until 1925, when the International Tennis Federation and the Olympic Committee disagreed over the definition of amateurism. For more than 60 years the Summer Games went on without tennis as an official medal sport, although demonstrations were mounted at the 1968 Games in Mexico City and the 1984 Games in Los Angeles. Tennis returned officially in 1988 with new rules that allow professional players to compete. This reversal was a boon for the United States, which has always had its share of the top-ranked tennis talent.

"I'm very proud for Puerto Rico. I'm very proud for the U.S. I'm very proud."

—Gigi Fernandez, a Puerto Rican native who played for the U.S. and shares the 1992 doubles medal with Mary Joe Fernandez

The American women were big winners at the 1992 Summer Games in Barcelona. Sixteen-year-old Jennifer Capriati scored a stunning upset victory in the women's singles final, beating Steffi Graf of Germany for the gold medal. The tandem of Mary Joe Fernandez and Gigi Fernandez (no relation) captured the gold in the doubles competition. Less successful were the male team members, Sampras, Jim Courier, and Michael Chang, none of whom advanced to the finals round.

Sampras and Chang will seek to return to the 1996 Summer Games, but all eyes on the flamboyant Agassi, who was the reigning U.S. Open tennis champion until Sampras edged him out in 1995. Agassi won Wimbledon in 1992 but saw his ranking slip the following year while he underwent wrist surgery. His game—and his celebrated image—have undergone a resurgence since then, and he is actively challenging Sampras for the number one ranking. Viewers can expect to see Agassi as one of three American singles contenders and possibly also as half of a doubles unit.

Other American men's tennis stars who want to participate in the Olympics include Olympic veteran Jim Courier, who was last ranked at number one in 1993, and African American star MaliVai Washington. Boris Becker will likely return on the German team as a principal opponent, either in singles or doubles play.

A touching story is unfolding on the American women's team as well. In 1995, Monica Seles announced her return to professional tennis after a two-year absence from the sport. Seles was stabbed in the back on April 30, 1993, by an unemployed German named Guenther Parche, during a lull in a tennis match in Hamburg. Parche, who received a two-year suspended sentence for the attack, was trying to remove Seles from competition so his favorite, Steffi Graf, would return to the number one ranking. Seles was 19 at the time and the winner of seven of the last eight Grand Slam events she had attended. Since the assault, she has struggled to regain her composure and the fierce competitive drive that once fueled her.

In order for Seles to qualify for the Olympic team she must meet a set of requirements that are the same for both men and women. All eligible professional tennis players who want to make the Olympics must make themselves available for the Davis Cup (men) or the Fed Cup (women) in two years between 1993 and 1996. One of the years has to be either 1995 or 1996. Seles, who missed 1993 and 1994, must play a Fed Cup event in 1995 and compete in a sanctioned match in Austria in April of 1996 in order to qualify for the Summer Games. The same requirements hold true for recent retiree Martina Navratilova, who has also expressed interest in the 1996 Olympics. Fed Cup coach Billie Jean King told the press in 1995 that Seles would be added to the Fed Cup roster if she performed well at the U.S. Open—an event that Seles has dominated in the past. In 1995 Seles made it to the finals where she was defeated by Steffi Graf.

While former Olympians Mary Joe Fernandez and Gigi Fernandez stand a good chance of returning to the Summer Games, Seles is without a doubt the sentimental favorite for singles competition. Seles—who will almost certainly face Steffi Graf again at some point—knows that her assailant is still free and still obsessed with his evil purpose. She has had to adjust mentally to the fear and frustration. "The one place I felt safe was a tennis court— and that was taken away from me," she told *Sports Illustrated* on July 17, 1995. "That's the place where I'd have no worries, whatever was going on in my private life or in my school. I felt comfortable. And now, this is the place I feel least safe."

The U.S. Olympic tennis team is allowed no more than three singles performers of each sex and no more than one doubles team of each sex. It is likely, however, that some of the singles participants will also participate as doubles players. All events *except* the gold medal finals will be the best two of three sets—the final will be a best three of five match. For the first time in 1996, the losers of each semifinal will compete against each other for the bronze medal.

Final selections for the American team will occur in May of 1996 and will be made jointly between the Olympic tennis coaches and United States Tennis Association president Les Snyder. The matches will be held at a state-of-the-art facility in Stone Mountain, Georgia, with a seating capacity of 27,000.

—Mark Kram

Schedule

The tentative tennis schedule is:

Tuesday, July 23
Men's & Women's singles preliminaries

Wednesday, July 24
Men's & Women's singles preliminaries

Thursday, July 25
Men's & Women's singles & doubles preliminaries

Friday, July 26
Men's & Women's singles & doubles preliminaries

Saturday, July 27
Men's & Women's singles & doubles preliminaries

Sunday, July 28
Men's singles & doubles preliminaries

Monday, July 29
Women's singles quarterfinal
Men's doubles quarterfinal

Tuesday, July 30
Men's singles quarterfinal
Women's doubles quarterfinal

Wednesday, July 31
Women's singles semifinal
Women's & Men's doubles semifinal

Thursday, August 1
Men's singles semifinal
Women's & Men's doubles bronze medal

Friday, August 2
Women's singles bronze medal and gold medal
Men's doubles gold medal

Saturday, August 3
Men's singles bronze medal and gold medal
Women's doubles gold medal

Highlights

Prior to tennis' reappearance at the Games in 1988, the sport was played in every Games from Athens in 1896 to Paris in 1924. Irish-born John Pius Boland won the first gold medal, for Great

Britain, in singles. What is perhaps most interesting about his performance is that he had traveled from Oxford to attend the Games . . . as a spectator. Winning the men's doubles as well—with a German partner, Fritz Traun—Boland protested when the English flag was raised for his victory, and an Irish flag was raised in its stead.

When, in 1900, the women's singles event was added, Charlotte Cooper, from Great Britain, became the first woman to medal in tennis—or any sport, for that matter. 1912 was hardly a banner year, since the events were held—albeit on indoor courts—at the same time as Wimbledon.

FACT: Jeu de paume, an ancestor of modern tennis, was played once at the Olympic Games—in 1908, when U.S. player Jay Gould captured the court tennis title.

Impressive performances were the order of the 1920 Games, however: Suzanne Lenglen from France—one of the all-time greatest women tennis players ever—captured the gold medal by losing only four games in the ten sets it took to win the singles title. That same year, the women's doubles event was added, and Great Britain took both the gold and silver. The U.S. made a dazzling show at the 1924 Games, winning the gold for both the men's singles and doubles, the gold and silver in mixed doubles, and the gold in both women's events, before the sport went on hiatus from the Games.

When tennis returned to the official program in 1988, the U.S. fared well—though perhaps not quite so well as it had in 1924. The U.S. captured two golds—in the men's and women's doubles, a silver and bronze in the men's singles, and a bronze in the women's singles. Ken Flack and Robert Seguso made up the men's doubles, while Pam Shriver and Zina Garrison paired for the women's event. West German Steffi Graf beat out Argentinean Gabriela Sabatini in the women's singles, in which Garrison took third. The other medals were divided among a smattering of countries, including Czechoslovakia, Spain, Sweden, Bulgaria, and Australia.

Steffi Graf

Achievement comes early in some sports, a bit later in others. Distance runners often don't reach their peak until their late twenties or early thirties. Athletes well into their forties have competed in events such as the discus. On the other hand, tennis players start young. Case in point: Steffi Graf, born in Bruhl, Germany, in 1969. Only the fifth player in history to win tennis's coveted Grand Slam (with victories in the Australian, French, and U.S. Opens and at Wimbledon in the same year), Graf started swinging a racket at the tender age of three, while her contemporaries continued to lounge in the sandbox of their choice.

Her father, Peter Graf, a nationally ranked West German semiprofessional tennis player, thought his toddler daughter only wanted to emulate him. But her insistence eventually won him over. He cut off one of his tennis rackets and showed her how to hit the ball. After that, Steffi's mother, Heidi, reports, "we broke a lot of lamps."

But Steffi progressed quickly under her father's tutelage. She won her first tournament at six, dominated her age group for several years, and at 13 won the German junior championship in the 18-and-under division. She quit school in 1982 and joined the professional tour, becoming the second-youngest player to receive an international ranking. At the 1984 Olympics in Los Angeles, where tennis was still a demonstration sport, Graf won the women's gold medal, even though at the age of 15 she was the youngest competitor in the event.

In 1987 Graf defeated Martina Navratilova and captured her first professional tournament—the French Open—becoming the youngest player to do so. By mid–1987, she had achieved the number-one ranking. Thus was the table set for Graf in 1988, a year that many experts have called the finest ever for any tennis player.

In January 1988, Graf captured the Australian Open, defeating Chris Evert in the finals, then in March Graf volleyed to victory in the French Open. Prior to Wimbledon, she practiced with a male left-hander in preparation for an expected finals match against the formidable Navratilova, who was competing for a record ninth Wimbledon title. As expected, the two faced off at center court in the final round. After a somewhat shaky start, Graf settled her game, taking the match by winning 12 of the last 13 games. She concluded the Grand Slam in September with a hard-fought victory over Gabriela Sabatini at the U.S. Open.

Only a few days later, Graf was in Seoul, South Korea, where tennis was to be played as a full medal Olympic sport for the first time in 64 years. Again she started slowly, struggling in her early-round matches. Perhaps Graf suffered from an emotional and physical letdown following the Grand Slam quest. But she recovered for the semifinals, in which she played an inspired match against American Zina Garrison, and went into the gold-medal round pitted, once again, against Sabatini. This time, Graf quickly found her rhythm and Sabatini discovered the blues, losing 6–3, 6–3. A year shy of 20, Graf had grabbed the gold.

In an upset, Jennifer Capriati (U.S.) beat Steffi Graf (Germany) in the women's finals. *Duomo Photography*

German tennis players Boris Becker and Michael Stich won gold medals for their performance in the men's doubles in 1992. *Duomo Photography*

The U.S.A.'s Gigi Fernandez screams and Mary Joe Fernandez laughs after winning the women's doubles at Barcelona. *AP/Wide World Photos*

In an upset at the 1992 Games, Graf was defeated , 3–6, 6–3, 6–4, by 16-year-old Jennifer Capriati, who took home the gold. Steffi Graf continues to be a dominant force in her sport. She enjoys all-around ability that has allowed her to remain a strong contender. Her topspin forehand may be the best in the history of women's tennis, and her powerful serve and lightning speed give her tremendous edges against opponents. As Navratilova has said, "I think she can do pretty much anything."

In July 1995 she introduced her own line of casual clothing—the Steffi Graf Collection—amid news of trouble from back home: Her father, Peter Graf, was charged with—and later was jailed for—tax evasion in Germany and many reports indicated that Steffi, too, might be investigated. Nevertheless, Graf's game remained strong, beating Monica Seles in the finals of the 1995 U.S. Open.

—Paul Green

Highlights from Barcelona

With Arantxa Sanchez Vicario paired with Conchita Martínez in doubles, the home team seemed poised to seize the day. Anticipation hung in the humid Catalan air; the ebullient crowd hung on the players' every move. There was no mistaking it, Spain had high expectations, and everywhere, banners and signs proclaimed their medal aspirations: boldly, they announced, "Arantxa-Conchita, Catalunya vol l'or"— "Arantxa-Conchita, Catalonia wants gold."

But tennis gold was not to be part of Spain's Olympic destiny. Pitted against the U.S. doubles team of Mary Joe Fernandez and Gigi Fernandez (a Puerto Rican player who elected to play for the United States protectorate), the two Barcelonans were no match for their opponents—except in the second set when, at 2–1 down, the arrival of King Juan Carlos and Queen Sophia seemed to rejuvenate their play. Miraculously, they took five games in a row to level the set, just as suddenly losing their momentum. In the eleventh hour, team Fernandez subdued the Spanish duo with a 6–2 victory, good enough for gold.

It was a golden year for the U.S. women's team, as sixteen-year-old Jennifer Capriati unseated longtime nemesis Steffi Graf to claim the individual title. Sometime after the second serve, Graf began a downward spiral, and Capriati was

FACT: Wayne Ferreira and Piet Norval's silver medal in men's doubles was South Africa's first medal at the Barcelona Games. Competing in the Olympics for the first time since 1960, the South African team consisted of 85 whites and 12 nonwhites—approximately a 7-to-1 ratio. Nonwhites outnumber whites in South Africa by a ratio of 4 to 1.

there on the line. The crowd began to chant, "U.S.A., U.S.A." Then, Capriati—who had never, in four attempts, beaten the number-two ranked Graf—scored a 3–6, 6–3, 6–4 upset over the two-time defending gold medalist. "I had chills the whole time. I just can't believe it," she later reported. "All week I watched the other athletes up there and I was with them and I thought, 'Wow, that would be so cool.'"

The slow red clay of the Teixonera courts in Vall d'Hebron was anything but cool, and many of the men's top seeds had a hard time battling the heat and slow courts. One by one, the world's top seeds fell out of contention. Absent from the gold-medal match were number-one ranked Jim Courier, 1988 bronze medalist Stefan Edberg, Pete Sampras, Emilio Sanchez, and Boris Becker—leaving two players ranked 30th and 43rd in the world to cross racquets for the Olympic title. Valiantly fighting to guard the host country's claim to the spoils, Jordi Arrese eventually fell to the where'd-he-come-from Swiss player, who served 33 aces, eventually breaking the young Spaniard at match point.

In men's doubles, the German team compensated for their thankless experience at the 1988 Games, as Boris Becker and Michel Stich captured the title. Having given the Germans a good run in a four setter with two tie-breaks, Wayne Ferreira and Piet Norval collected the first South African Olympic medal in over three decades, leaving the bronze medals to Argentina (the nation's second tennis medal since Gabriela Sabatini's silver in 1988) and to Croatia.

Medalists

Tennis—Men's Singles

1992
1. Marc Rosset, Switzerland
2. Jordi Arrese, Spain
3. Goran Ivanisevic, Croatia
3. Andrei Cherkasov, Russia

1988
1. Miloslav Mecir, Czechoslovakia
2. Tim Mayotte, U.S.A.
3. Stefan Edberg, Sweden
3. Brad Gilbert, U.S.A.

1928–1984
Not held

1924
1. Vincent Richards, U.S.A.
2. Henri Cochet, France
3. Umberto De Morpurgo, Italy

1920
1. Louis Raymond, South Africa
2. Ichiya Kumagae, Japan
3. Charles Winslow, Great Britain

1912
1. Charles Winslow, South Africa, outdoor
1. Andre Govert, France, indoor
2. Harold Kitson, South Africa, outdoor
2. Charles Dixon, Great Britain, indoor
3. Oscar Kreuzer, Germany, outdoor
3. Anthony Wilding, New Zealand, indoor

1908
1. Josiah Ritchie, Great Britain, outdoor
1. Wentworth Gore, Great Britain, indoor
2. Otto Froitzheim, Germany, outdoor
2. George Caridia, Great Britain, indoor
3. Wilberforce Eves, Great Britain, outdoor
3. Josiah Ritchie, Great Britain, indoor

1906
1. Max Decugis, France
2. Maurice Germot, France
3. Zdenek Zemia, Bohemia (Czech)

1904
1. Beals Wright, U.S.A.
2. Robert LeRoy, U.S.A.

1900
1. Hugh Doherty, Great Britain
2. Harold Mahony, Great Britain
3. Reginald Doherty, Great Britain
3. A.B. Norris, Great Britain

1896
1. John Boland, Great Britain
2. Demis Kasdaglis, Great Britain

Tennis—Men's Doubles
1992
1. Germany, Boris Becker, Michael Stich
2. South Africa, Wayne Ferreira, Piet Norval
3. Croatia, Goran Ivanisevic, Goran Prpic
3. Argentina, Javier Frana, Christian Carlos Miniussi

1988
1. U.S.A., Ken Flach, Robert Seguso
2. Spain, Emilio Sanchez, Sergio Casal
3. Sweden, Stefan Edberg, Anders Jarryd
3. Czechoslovakia, Miloslav Mecir, Milan Srejber

1928–1984
Not held

1924
1. U.S.A.
2. France
3. France

1920
1. Great Britain
2. Japan
3. France

1912
1. South Africa, outdoor
1. France, indoor
2. Austria, outdoor
2. Sweden, indoor
3. France, outdoor
3. Great Britain, indoor

1908
1. Great Britain, outdoor
1. Great Britain, indoor
2. Great Britain, outdoor
2. Great Britain, indoor

3. Great Britain, outdoor
3. Sweden, indoor

1906
1. France
2. Greece
3. Bohemia (Czech)

1904
1. U.S.A.
2. U.S.A.

1900
1. Great Britain
2. U.S.A./France
3. France
3. Great Britain

1896
1. Great Britain/Germany
2. Greece

Tennis—Women's Singles
1992
1. Jennifer Capriati, U.S.A.
2. Steffi Graf, Germany
3. Mary Joe Fernandez, U.S.A.
3. Arantxa Sanchez Vicario, Spain

1988
1. Steffi Graf, West Germany
2. Gabriela Sabatini, Argentina
3. Zina Garrison, U.S.A.
3. Manuela Maleeva, Bulgaria

1928–2984
Not held

1924
1. Helen Wills, U.S.A.
2. Julie Vlasto, France
3. Kitty McKane, Great Britain

1920
1. Suzanne Lenglen, France
2. Dorothy Holman, Great Britain
3. Kitty McKane, Great Britain

1912
1. Maarguerite Broquedis, France, outdoor
1. Ethel Hannam, Great Britain, indoor
2. Dora Koring, Germany, outdoor
2. Thora Castenschiold, Denmark, indoor
3. Molla Bjurstedt, Norway, outdoor
3. Mabel Parton, Great Britain, indoor

1908
1. Dorothea Chambers, Great Britain, outdoor
1. Gwen Eastlake-Smith, Great Britain, indoor
2. Dorothy Boothby, Great Britain, outdoor

2. Angela Greene, Great Britain, indoor
3. Martha Adlerstrahle, Sweden, outdoor
3. Molla Bjurstedt, Norway, indoor

1906
1. Esmee Simiriotou, Greece
2. Sophia Marinou, Greece
3. Euphrosine Paspati, Greece

1904
Not held

1900
1. Charlotte Cooper, Great Britain
2. Helene Prevost, France
3. Marion Jones, U.S.A.
3. Hedwiga Rosenbaumova, Bohemia (Czech)

Tennis—Women's Doubles

1992
1. U.S.A., Gigi Fernandez, Mary Joe Fernandez
2. Spain, Conchita Martinez, Arantxa Sanchez-Vicario
3. Australia, Rachel McQuillan, Nicole Provis
3. Unified Team, Leila Meskhi, Natalia Zvereva

1988
1. U.S.A., Zina Garrison, Pam Shriver
2. Czechoslovakia, Jana Novotna, Helena Sukova
3. West Germany, Steffi Graf, Claudia Kohde-Kilsch
3. Australia, Elizabeth Smylie, Wendy Turnbull

1928–1984
Not held

1924
1. U.S.A.
2. Great Britain
3. Great Britain

1920
1. Great Britain
2. Great Britain
3. France

1896–1912
Not held

Trivia Quiz

1. Olympic tennis events allow a maximum of
   a. 62 competitors   **b.** 96 competitors   **c.** 78 competitors

2. When dropped from 100 feet, a tennis ball should bounce
   a. 32 feet   **b.** 55 feet   **c.** To Uranus and back

3. An early relative of tennis, in which players used their hands to swat a cloth bag filled with hair, was called
   a. Tenez   **b.** Jeu de paume   **c.** Hairball

4. The first player to win a Grand Slam was
   a. Manuel Orantes   **b.** Jimmy Connors   **c.** Don Budge

5. In the 10th century, Louis IV banned tennis because
   a. It was popular in England   **b.** It was undignified   **c.** He never won

6. Bishops in the Middle Ages imposed ecclesiastical bans on tennis because
   a. Parishioners were playing tennis instead of attending church
   b. Tennis was considered to be the devil's work
   c. Too many monks had tennis fever

7. In the sixteenth century, Paris, France
a. Had civil laws against tennis playing
b. Had more than 1,000 tennis courts
c. Opened a museum called the Jeu de Paume

8. From 1600 to the mid-eighteenth century, tennis
a. Was the national game of both France and England
b. Fell out of favor and was seldom played
c. Began to spread to South America

9. Prior to being accepted as a full-medal sport for the 1988 Olympics, tennis
a. Had been exhibited at the 1928 Olympics
b. Had been a full-medal sport in eight other Games
c. Had never been included on the Olympic roster

10. Which nation has not been awarded an Olympic tennis medal?
a. South Africa.   **b.** India.   **c.** Bohemia

Answers: 1-b; 2-b; 3-b; 4-c; 5-b; 6-c; 7-b; 8-b; 9-b; 10-b

545

TRACK AND FIELD
(ATHLETICS)—JUMPING

Warm-up

As soon as humans began jumping, running, and throwing things, they began jumping, running, and throwing things higher, faster, and farther than (and occasionally at) each other. Well, actually, they probably first developed those skills to obtain or avoid becoming food, but individual competition surfaced early on and remains the heart of the modern Olympic Games. Today track and field accounts for more U.S. Olympic medals than any other sport.

The long jump became one of five sports that made up the pentathlon in 708 BC during the ancient Greek Olympics in Peloponnesus. Greek long jumpers used jumping weights, called halters. Artwork representing the Games shows the weights being swung backwards by athletes, apparently to gain a better landing position. (English long jumpers in the 19th century jumped carrying dumbbells, which they released when airborne to change mass, oddly enough.)

Evidence suggests that one Greek Olympian named Chionis jumped to a distance of 23 feet, 1.5 inches in 656 BC.

Not bad for his day. Contemporary long jumpers are floating to just over 29 feet.

The Greeks, including Chionis, also recorded some jumps in the 50-foot (15–16 meter) range, which leads sports historians to believe these were a series of jumps, perhaps an ancient version of the triple jump or standing broad jumps. It is not clear if the Greeks practiced a running jump or a standing one. Some ancient vases with scenes depicting the games show both standing jumps and running jumpers carrying halters.

Jumping events are believed to stem from Celtic roots as well. Vaulting, which apparently sprang from the use of small sticks or poles to jump streams, was part of the ancient Irish Tailteann Games that took place in 1829 BC.

Jumping continued in competitions in Ireland and in the Highland Games of Scotland. When English track and field organizers set minimum standards for performances in 1834, athletes had to long jump at least 20 feet and high jump at least five feet, seven inches to qualify.

At the first modern Olympic Games in 1896, pole vault, long jump, high jump, and triple jump were among the six field events. The long jump was one of two field events added for women in the 1928 Olympics. Before that, standing jumping events (for men) were included in addition to the running versions. The standing high jump and long jump were held 1900–12, and the standing triple jump took place in the 1900 and 1904 Games. American Ray Ewery dominated the three events. He won 10 gold medals in four different Olympics, having overcome polio as a child to become a superb athlete.

Innovation led to improved performances in the jumping events, especially the pole vault and high jump. In vaulting it was changes to the pole, and in high jump, new styles of jumping.

The first vaulting poles were probably large sticks or tree limbs. Vaulters in the 19th century used wooden poles, and bamboo was even better until World War II interrupted (among other things) bamboo supplies from Japan. Metal poles were used for about a decade, though aluminum is less flexible than bamboo.

FACT: Unimpressed with Dick Fosbury's revolutionary high-jumping technique, Oregon State University college coaches asked the engineering major to practice the conventional Western roll. But after setting an OSU record as a sophomore, Fosbury was permitted to flop full-time.

Fiberglass poles were introduced in the mid–1950s, and soon vaulters were soaring higher than ever. The fiberglass pole permitted handholds of 15 feet (4.57m) and this made vaults of 18 feet (5.48m) possible.

Early high jumpers favored the scissors style, with the legs moving and the torso remaining vertical to the bar. In 1912, American George Horine broke a record with his western roll, in which the jumper passes over the bar lying on his side with knees together. That was refined further to the belly roll, with the jumper going over the bar face down. Another roll change was the straddle. In this style, the jumper's arm and leading leg crossed over the bar and started down as the other arm and leg were still rising. Two straddler style jumpers were Charles Dumas, an American who in 1956 was first to clear seven feet, and Valeri Brumel, a Soviet who dominated high jumping in the 1960s.

American jumper Dick Fosbury won an Olympic gold in 1968 and won over most fellow jumpers with his Fosbury flop. Fosbury used a circular run to approach the bar, then leapt head first and cleared the height with his back facing the bar and his legs trailing. Javier Sotomayor of Cuba cleared eight feet with a flop in 1989.

Foam landing pads replaced those made of sand and allowed jumpers and vaulters to land on their back without injury.

Spectator's Guide

High Jump: In the high jump, the athlete tries to propel his or her body over a bar that rests across two uprights. The approach can be from any angle along a semi-circular runway. If the jumper hits the bar and causes it to fall, that jump is scored a miss. A contestant can pass, or decline to jump, at any height. Three successive misses, even at different heights, eliminates the jumper.

In case of ties, the high jumper with the fewest misses at the last height cleared wins. If there is still a tie, the competitor with the fewest total misses wins. If there is still a tie, the athlete who has taken the fewest attempts, successful or not, wins. If there is still a tie, excepting a tie for first place, each athlete is given an extra jump. If the deadlock is still not resolved, then the bar is raised or lowered and the contestants jump until the tie is broken.

Another rule is that jumpers must take off from one foot. There have been some challenges to this rule. In 1954, American gymnastics tumbler Dick Browning is reported to have somersaulted over a bar set at seven feet six inches (2.28m). In 1962, another jumper did a back handspring with a back flip over a bar set at seven feet four inches (2.23m). He landed on his feet.

There are also limits on the thickness of a jumper's shoe and sole ever since, in the 1950s, contestants began breaking records with the aid of built-up shoes, using a vaulting effect.

Olympic officials have had to struggle to keep up with the varying styles of high jumpers. In 1932, they objected to the diving style—head and shoulders first—of American Mildred

"Babe" Didrikson. She finished first but was awarded the silver because of this unorthodoxy. She did win golds in the javelin and 80m hurdles that year.

Much of the emphasis in style changes has been on finding a lower center of gravity, thus more control over movement. With the upright scissors style of the earlier part of the century, a jumper's center of gravity passed over the bar and offered little control. The western roll of 1912 and related belly roll improved control better still.

Dick Fosbury's famous flop allowed the jumper's center of gravity to actually pass under the bar. More than 25 years later, the Fosbury Flop is still popular.

Psyching out one's opponent is not uncommon in field events, mostly because the wait between jumps or throws can toy with the fragile and frayed nerves of athletes. A winner is one who can avoid being rattled by the pressure from any source. Likewise, the power of positive thinking is important. As world high jump recordholder Dwight Stones has said, "The body doesn't know it has limits. It's your brain that screws everything up."

Pole Vault: In the pole vault, an athlete uses a long flexible pole to push himself, as if catapulted, over a bar three times his size. The vaulter sprints along a short runway track and jams the pole into a box beneath the bar. He raises the pole and his forward running speed shifts into upward motion. He hangs upside down as he rises off the ground at the end of a bending pole. He turns and pushes off the pole with his arms and, if the vault is successful, passes over the bar legs first and face down before landing in a pit of foam. When the vaulter is only halfway between take-off and the bar, and the pole is bent and ready to snap back, the vaulter's body must be curled completely upside down in perfect alignment with the pole, or the force from the pole's upward swing will be lost.

Sounds gravity-defying, doesn't it?

Contestants are allowed three tries at each height, which is gradually increased. Three misses at any height disqualifies a pole vaulter. A miss is charged if an athlete knocks over the bar, passes to the side or underneath it, touches the ground beyond with the pole, switches his hands on the pole, or moves his upper hand on the pole after leaving the ground. A vaulter who takes more than two minutes after getting clearance to begin an attempt is also charged with a miss.

Vaulters are usually fast runners with powerful upper bodies and good all-around gymnastics ability.

During WWII, when bamboo poles were not available, pole vaulters used steel or aluminum poles, which lacked the flexibility of bamboo but were more consistent. Poles made of fiberglass were introduced as early as 1956, though it was several years before vaulters learned properly how to use them. When they did, vaults mounted higher and higher.

Fiberglass offers both consistency and flexibility. Fiberglass poles bend several feet, then snap back when the athlete's feet are pointed up while approaching the pole. The flexibility of a pole determines the height at which it can be gripped. The stiffer the pole, and the lighter the vaulter, the greater the whip and potential for height. Still, it takes strength to bend the pole sufficiently.

Sergei Bubka, a Soviet pole vaulter who won the Olympic gold medal in 1988, has said that the speed of the take-off and strength in the jump are all-important.

Long jump: Formerly called a broad jump, a valid one must be made from behind the far edge of a take-off board, which is about eight inches (20cm) wide, and level to the ground. The jump is measured from the nearest impression in the sand made by the jumper's body to the nearest edge of the board. Jumpers approach the board along a runway. The board contains a strip of plasticine four inches (10cm) wide on the runway side of the board so judges can detect fouls. The plasticine is raised about one-third inch (7mm) above the board and will show any contact by the jumper's shoe.

The competition begins with a qualifying round, the results from which are not carried over to the final. In the final, each contestant is allowed three jumps, then the best eight jumpers are allowed three more jumps. If a jump is aided by wind of more than two meters per second (4.473 miles per hour), the jump counts but is not recognized as a record.

Americans have dominated the Olympic men's long jump. They have won it 20 of 23 times, losing once because of a boycott. (In both 1988 and 1992, a U.S. triumvirate swept the long jump medals.) Bob Beamon's 29ft, 2.5in jump in the 1968 Olympics is considered one of the greatest track and field performances ever. That world record leap, which took place in the "rare air" Olympics in Mexico City, was tops for 23 years.

In the early part of the 20th century, long jumpers were speedsters with great spring. Jumpers now have added strength training to their repertoire to increase distance.

FACT: Ukraine's Sergei Bubka left Barcelona empty-handed, having failed to make any height in the pole vault. But a little over a month later, in Tokyo, Bubka vaulted 20′1½″— his third outdoor record of 1992 and 32nd world record overall.

Triple Jump: This is similar to the long jump except for the mechanics of the actual jump. It's also known as the hop, step and jump because the athlete makes a running start, hops, lands on the same foot from which he took off, takes one step onto the other foot, then jumps. The leap is ruled a foul if a trailing foot touches the ground.

Jumpers sprint down a runway and must jump before reaching a takeoff line, same as in the long jump. The final maneuver of the triple jump leaves the athlete in the sand pit, from which the distance is measured.

Japanese jumpers dominated this men-only event through the 1930s, while a Brazilian named Adhemar Ferreira da Silva won gold medals in the event in 1952 and 1956. Eastern Europeans then ruled the event through the 1960s, led by the Soviet jumper Viktor Saneyev.

Hopefuls

Carl Lewis

Frederick Carleton Lewis is, without doubt, the greatest track and field athlete of all time.

No one else is even close.

Lewis has won eight Olympic gold medals in three different Olympiads and dozens of other medals and awards. Now, he has his sights set on Atlanta.

Has had.

"I believe the most golds anyone's won are 10," he said, coyly, in a 1994 interview in *Sports Illustrated*, already pointing toward Atlanta. (Turn-of-the-century jumper Ray Ewery won the 10 in the now-defunct standing jump.)

Lewis also is fully aware that with a gold medal in the long jump in Atlanta he could match the record set by discus thrower Al Oerter of four straight gold medals in the same event.

He also is fully aware that he is getting older. Lewis will be 35 (b. July 1, 1961) by the time the flame is lit in Georgia.

In fact, he's already been written off by some competitors.

Olympic 100-meter champion Linford Christie pointed out back in 1994, that it had been three years since Lewis had broken 10 seconds in the 100-meter dash without the aid of a tailwind.

Another competitor has said, "The other sprinters in the world aren't worried about Carl at all."

Not that Lewis has exactly recast a spike of fear to imbed into the hearts of his opponenents. Lewis did not qualify for the 1995 World Championships in the 100, but did make the U.S. team in the long jump, finishing second to Mike Powell.

After that meet, Lewis said: "It's another year to the Olympics. You're going to see a more committed performer than you've ever seen before."

Does that mean that Lewis will be cutting back on his signature bag of extra-curriculars—reporting for radio shows; writing biographies; taking acting lessons; recording songs; drumming for his *King Carl* hats and T-shirts in Europe and Asia, and posing for ads, such as the one for Pirelli tire billboards that has him on the starting blocks attired in a one-piece sprinter's suit and red high heels? (Lewis deadpans: "I can't believe a little ad we did got all that attention. It's nice to know you can still get attention." The billboard, which netted Lewis $100,000, was used in Great Britain and Italy, but not the U.S. It was deemed too controversial.)

It's hard to say if King Carl will become a bit more pedestrian—Carl Lewis *being* Carl Lewis.

The safe bet is that Lewis will in fact be ready for Atlanta. Most assuredly in the long jump.

Lewis, in fact, gives short shrift to those who continue to measure his readiness by using results from individual meets.

"When you've been to 14 of this relay or 13 of this meet or 11 of this, you don't approach it the same way," he says. "I have a difficult time getting focused for some of the meets I've been to so many times. But the one thing I've kept is my enthusiasm for training for major meets."

Not that even that is always easy.

Lewis explained the flip side of his successes in an interview with *Runner's World.*

"Challenging myself isn't the same anymore. When I was younger, I was always trying to achieve a certain goal. Now, I know what I can do, and I challenge myself to see if I can do more of it. For example, I've won four gold medals in one Olympiad. That's not a big deal anymore. But now, can I do it when everyone's running faster and jumping better?

"What's nice is that I've gotten past the point of having to prove anything, having to achieve anything. I can just plan to do what I was born to do. For whatever reasons—my tenacity, my athletic ability, my vision—I've outlasted a lot of people. And now I feel like I'm reaping the benefits."

If Atlanta is Lewis' curtain call—and that might be the case. He will be missed.

For antics/events such as the Pirelli ad.

"People all around the world can bring out psychologist Joyce Brothers and whatever to read my mind all they want. They can do handwriting analysis and all that stuff. Geraldo can have a mock trial. But when it all comes down, I did the ad for two reasons. No. 1, it's a commercial and they paid me to do that. Secondly, I like working with photographer Annie Liebowitz."

He will be more sorely missed for what he has given the world of sport.

Gary Smith wrote in *Sports Illustrated:*

"The mark of genius, the stamp of an original, does not come to a man simply by performing his craft better than any of his contemporaries. It comes when a man reivents a form. The sprinter, before Lewis (and perhaps even after him), was a prisoner of time; his career, like his race, a bang and a blur . . . and then nothing. The great ones have exploded upon us for one Olympics, then either dropped to the ground with twisted faces—thoroughbreds faster than their tendons or ligaments could bear—or lost half a finger snap of speed and vanished from sight. Long jumpers aren't much different. Six leaps a night, 1.4 seconds each time in the air, 8.4 seconds of life upon our retinas . . . But Lewis has transcended the trap of time, staved off the death inherent in any great burst of speed—a saxophonist who had not only discoverd a new, pure note, but also a way not to let go of it."

Can King Carl play it again in Atlanta?

Who would bet against him?

—Eric Kinkopf

Javier Sotomayor

Since 1988 the high jump has been owned by one man: Javier Sotomayor of Cuba, the world record holder and only person ever to jump eight feet in competition. Sotomayor made his record-shattering eight-foot jump in August of 1989. He has never bested that mark, but neither has anyone else, including a host of determined Americans. Sotomayor was also the gold medalist in high

Cuba's Javier Sotomayor took home the gold for the men's high jump in Barcelona. *Duomo Photography*

jump at the 1992 Olympics, finally earning the international recognition that had eluded him when Cuba boycotted both the 1984 and 1988 Summer Games. Known affectionately as "Soto" in his homeland, Sotomayor is proud to be a representative of Cuba's athletic excellence. His achievements in the Olympics and other events, he told the *Los Angeles Times* on August 3, 1992, serve as "clear evidence that in spite of our current problems we [in Cuba] are still capable of great things."

Sotomayor was capable of "great things" from an early age. He was born in Limonar, Cuba, a small town east of Havana. As a boy he set dried sugar cane sticks across empty oil drums so he could practice high-jumping. He also excelled in other sports and was so tall that he was admitted to one of Cuba's elite sports schools as a basketball player. He might have made the Cuban national team in that sport, but he was encouraged to return to the high jump by Alberto Juantorena, Cuba's well-known middle distance runner.

Training with track coach Luis Godoy, Sotomayor showed steady improvement in the high jump. At the age of 16 in 1984 he broke the Cuban record with a jump of 2.33 meters (7 feet, 7¾ inches), thereby announcing his arrival on the international stage. By 1988 he was favored to win the gold medal at Seoul after breaking the world high jump record just days before the Olympics were set to begin. Unfortunately for Sotomayor, Cuba's leader, Fidel Castro, decided that his country's athletes would boycott the 1988 Summer Games in a show of support to North Korea. Sotomayor was disappointed, but in the spirit of patriotism that drives so many of Cuba's athletes he agreed to the boycott without comment. He was one of many Cuban athletes who was awarded a special government gold medal by Castro in lieu of competing in the Olympics.

One year after Seoul, Sotomayor made his most spectacular jump, at the Caribbean Zone Track and Field Championships. On his second attempt, he cleared a bar set at 2.44 meters, just a fraction above eight feet. More than 33 years had passed since an American, Charles Dumas, had set a world record with a seven-foot jump, and Sotomayor's achievement left many observers wondering if a human being could ever possibly leap nine feet over a bar. Watching Sotomayor clear the eight-foot barrier, Puerto Rican decathlete Liston Bochette told *Sports Illustrated* on August 7, 1989: "No one in the foreseeable future is going to put it at nine feet. I have to feel like I not only saw a record, I saw the beginning of the end."

Sotomayor's fabulous jump might have been the beginning of the end of his own career. Although still a world-class jumper, he has suffered injuries and setbacks that might be expected of an athlete in such a demanding event. He missed most of the 1990 outdoor track season after having surgery on his knee and heel. By 1991, however, he had returned to form and won the high jump gold medal at the Pan American Games in front of a hometown crowd in Havana. "For me, the most important thing was to win a gold medal for my people," he said in the *Chicago Tribune* on August 11, 1991.

The affable Sotomayor got his first chance to win Olympic gold in 1992 at Barcelona. There he turned in a performance that, while not spectacular, was good enough for the gold—he was the first competitor to clear seven feet, eight inches in the contest and thus won the medal even though other jumpers cleared the same height. As he watched the high jump competition wind down and realized that he had won, Sotomayor buried his head in his hands and cried. "It was a great moment that I hoped to come," he told the *Los Angeles Times*. "But I didn't think it would necessarily happen."

It might happen again. Sotomayor has battled through injuries, is still in prime shape and, at 27, can still hope to compete strongly in Atlanta. A hero in his homeland, he is one of the first Cuban athletes to receive permission to participate in track meets for a fee. Nevertheless, he lives modestly in a home near Havana and does little to promote his financial interests. "In Cuba, it is true that athletes live by a philosophy that is not like what you find in other countries," he explained in the *Chicago Tribune* on November 12, 1992. "Sports is for the soul, not the wallet." The world record-holder added that his most prized possession is not his shelf of gold medals, but rather a small portable television given to him by Castro as a wedding present. "He is like a friend," Sotomayor said of Cuba's controversial leader.

> "In Cuba, it is true that athletes live by a philosophy that is not like what you find in other countries. Sports is for the soul, not the wallet."
> —Javier Sotomayor

All politics aside, Javier Sotomayor has set the standard that athletes will be chasing for the next decade. By being the first jumper over the eight-foot barrier, he has earned his own spot in the record books—and he may hold it for 33 years.

—Mark Kram

The tentative track & field (athletics)—jumping schedule is:

Friday, July 26
Men's high jump, qualifying

Saturday, July 27
Women's triple jump, qualifying
Men's triple jump, qualifying

Sunday, July 28
Men's high jump, final
Women's triple jump, final

Monday, July 29
Men's triple jump, final

Wednesday, July 31
Men's long jump, qualifying

Thursday, August 1
Women's high jump, qualifying
Women's long jump, qualifying
Men's long jump, final

Friday, August 2
Women's long jump, final

Saturday, August 3
Women's high jump, final

MEN'S JUMPING EVENTS

Highlights

Long jump: The Athens games provided an American shutout in the long jump, then known as the broad jump: Ellery Clark won the gold, while teammates Robert Garrett and James Connolly took the silver and bronze. The star of the 1900 long jump, Alvin Kraenzlein, is distinguished as the athlete who received the most individual titles (four) at a single Games. 1900's second-place finisher, Meyer Prinstein, also an American, went on to win the long jump at the St. Louis Games and again in 1906.

The London and Stockholm Games set new Olympic records, with Americans Francis "Frank" Irons winning the gold at London, and Albert Gutterson at Stockholm. The Antwerp Games marked the first non-American gold medalist, when William Petersen of Sweden leapt 23ft, 5.5in, to beat out American Carl Johnson.

The Paris Games marked yet another Olympic first when American William De Hart Hubbard became the first black to win an individual Olympic gold medal. In second place, American Edward Gourdin jumped only 23ft, 10.25in—short of the world record-setting mark he had posted prior to the Games, when he broke the twenty-year record of Peter O'Connor.

Although American Edward Hamm won the 1928 competition and set a new Olympic record in the long jump, it was Haiti's second-place finisher, Silvio Cator, who went on to be the first long jumper to surpass the 26-foot benchmark. A number of Americans distinguished themselves in track and field at the Games in 1932, including Edward Gordon, whose long jump won the gold.

Everyone knew the name of Jesse Owens by the time of the 1936 Berlin Games, since he had set a new world record the previous year. What they didn't know was that it would take twenty-five years for that record to be surpassed—pretty remarkable considering the short life of many of the other world records. Although Owens's Olympic jump fell short of his world record distance, he easily set a new Olympic record and won the gold medal.

Continuing the American domination of long jumping, the U.S. won the gold in four more Games: Willie Steele won in 1948, Jerome Biffle in 1952, Gregory Bell in 1956, and Ralph Boston in 1960. It was Boston who finally broke Jesse Owens's seemingly immortal record jump, just two weeks before the Rome Games began. Boston set a new Olympic record at 26ft, 7.75in, while fellow American Irvin "Bo" Roberson followed close on his heels with a 26ft, 7.25in jump; Soviet bronze medalist Igor Ter-Ovanesyan also surpassed the 26-foot mark by 4.5 inches. The Rome meet marked the first time that four men had outjumped the 26-foot mark.

FACT: At the 1936 Berlin Olympics, gold medal winners were presented with one-year-old potted oak seedlings, adorned with the motto, "Grow to the honor of victory! Summon to further achievement!" A few of the oaks are still alive, including one of the three brought back by Jesse Owens.

In Tokyo in 1964, Great Britain's Lynn Davies stole the title from the previous Games' gold and silver medalists, much to everyone's surprise, making him the first Welshman to capture a gold medal at the Games.

The 1968 meet featured a star-studded lineup: Ralph Boston, Lynn Davies, and Igor Ter-Orvanesyan, all of whom had medaled in 1964, were there, and they were all in top form. And then there was Bob Beamon—on suspension from the University of Texas at El Paso for refusing to compete against

Brigham Young University because of their racial policies—who was informally receiving advice from Boston. Known for fouling often, Beamon managed a perfect takeoff on his first jump, thanks to advice from Boston. Clearly Beamon's jump was a good one, even to the naked eye. Not relying on the high-tech measuring apparatus at their disposal, officials used a measuring tape to confirm that Beamon had, indeed, jumped 29ft 2.5in (21.75 inches beyond the world record) and when the magnitude of what he had done finally sunk in, Beamon suffered what is called a "cataplectic seizure"—that is, he fell to his knees in shock.

Beamon's jump is still considered to be one of the greatest of all track and field accomplishments, remaining unsurpassed until Mike Powell jumped 29ft 4.5in in 1991.

In Munich, American Randy Williams's 27ft, 0.5in might have seemed anti-climatic in the long jump pit; nonetheless, Williams won a gold medal, followed by German Hans Baumgartner in second place and American Arnie Robinson in third. Robinson returned four years later to win the gold, marking the tenth time in a dozen Games that an African-American had won the event, and he did so in the first round, marking the third consecutive Olympics in which the long jump had been won in the first round.

1980 was yet another benchmark year. No one—including Bob Beamon—had ever long jumped 28 feet in an Olympic meet: Beamon had sailed right past the 28 foot mark. Lutz Dombrowski, East Germany's gold medalist at the Moscow Games, was the first man to achieve an Olympic jump in the 28-foot range, jumping 28ft, 0.25in. His countryman, Frank Paschek, placed second with a 26ft, 11.25in leap, followed by the Soviet Valery Podluzhniy.

Carl Lewis took the gold in Los Angeles in 1984 and successfully defended his title in Seoul four years later, when the Americans again swept the medals: Mike Powell earned a silver medal while Larry Myricks picked up a bronze.

Triple jump: Irish-American James Connolly became the first thoroughly modern Olympic champion when he won the triple jump—then known as the hop, step, and jump—on April 6, 1896. The last to jump, Connolly threw his cap down a yard beyond the leading jumper's mark and, lucky for him, proceeded to best Frenchman Alexandre Tuffere's mark of 42ft, 8in with a jump of 44ft, 11.75in.

Meyer Prinstein increased his medal haul by winning the 1900 and 1904 triple jump events (while James Connolly placed second in Paris); by the end of his Olympic career, Prinstein had earned a silver and two gold medals in the long jump, in addition to his two triple jump golds.

Despite American domination in other jumping events, the U.S. would not receive another gold medal in the triple jump until 1984. The 1908 London Games triple jump winner was an Irishman, Timothy Ahearne, who set a new Olympic record of 48ft, 11.25in. The Swedes shut out the competition, taking all the medals in the event in 1912, but took only a silver and bronze away from the Antwerp Games, where a Finn captured the gold medal. Australian Anthony Winter established a world record in Paris with a 50ft, 11.25 jump, and Japanese Mikio Oda became the first Asian to win a gold medal when he won the triple jump at the Amsterdam Games.

Another Japanese jumper captured the gold in Los Angeles, setting a world record with his 51ft, 7in jump; Chuhei Nambu had the added distinction of being the world record holder in the long jump as well.

Once again, in Berlin, Japanese jumpers captured the gold and silver medals, and Naoto Tajima's world record of 52ft, 6in withstood the 1948 Olympic meet, in spite of Japan's absence. However, Japan has not regained its prominence in the Olympic triple jump event.

Brazil's Adhemar Ferreira da Silva went into the Helsinki Games as the world record holder, and left with a gold medal and a new world record—during his six jumps, he had broken his world record four times. The bronze medalist, Arnoldo Devonish, was the first Venezuelan athlete to earn an Olympic medal.

Da Silva earned a second gold medal in the triple jump at Melbourne, resetting the Olympic record, and when Icelander Vilhjálmur Einarsson won the silver medal at Melbourne, he became the first medalist from his country. The Rome meet proved to be no contest when Poland's Józef Schmidt—who had been the first man to break the 55-foot barrier—leapt 55ft, 2in. Schmidt recaptured the gold in Tokyo in 1964, setting a new Olympic record at 55ft, 3.5in, despite having undergone knee surgery less than two months before the Games.

Schmidt's world record stood at the start of the Mexico City Games, but it was to fall more than once during the course of the 1968 triple jump event. Soviet Viktor Saneyev vaulted to a new world record of 57ft, 0.75in, while Brazilian Nelson Prudencio and Italian Giuseppe Gentile took second and third place. Saneyev reigned as the king of the triple jump in Munich and Montreal, making him one of a select few track and field athletes to have earned three or more individual gold medals in a single event.

In second place at the Moscow Games, Saneyev just missed winning his fourth consecutive gold medal. Another Soviet, Jaak

Uudmäe, made the gold-medaling jump, while Brazilian Joao Carlos de Oliveira—whose world record remained unchallenged—won the bronze.

For the first time since 1904, the U.S. won the triple jump gold medal in 1984, thanks to Al Joyner, whose name was splashed throughout Olympic records. Joyner's teammate, Mike Conley, added to the U.S. medals, taking the silver as well. 1984 didn't prove to initiate a winning streak for the U.S., though, and the American team was shut out from medaling at the Seoul Games: Bulgarian Hristo Markov won the event, followed by Soviets Igor Lapchine and Alexandre Kovalenko.

High jump: A noteworthy medal haul was taken by America's Robert Garrett in 1896, when he added silvers in the high and long jumps to his golds in the shot and discus. Tied for second place was his teammate James Connolly, the winner of the triple jump. Ellery Clark, also from the States, won the event with a 5ft, 11.25in jump, making him a double-gold medalist in the high and long jump. Clark is still the only person to have won those two events at the same Summer Games.

The Americans continued to dominate the long jump for the next several Games: Irving Baxter set a new Olympic record in 1900 at 6ft, 2.75in; Samuel Jones set no record but won the gold medal in 1904; Harry Porter lifted the Olympic record to 6ft, 3in in 1908, and Alma Richards raised the record yet another inch in 1912—the year Jim Thorpe tied for fourth place.

The 1920 gold went to Richmond Landon, and 1924's went to decathlon silver medalist Harold Osborn. In Paris in 1924, the U.S. matched the Finns' distance-running ability with its field-event strength. American Harold Osborn—who won the 1924 decathlon—won the high jump competition using the back layout version of the Western roll at the Paris Games, and consequently sparked a controversy that resulted in a rule change.

American Robert King posted the best jump of 1928; interestingly, the next four jumpers behind King all leapt 6ft, 3.25in, and places had to be decided by a jump-off.

Not until LA, ironically, in 1932, did a non-American win the high jump—but not by much. Canadian Duncan McNaughton won the gold, thanks to a jump-off, although the top four jumpers all leapt exactly 6ft, 5.5in. Under current tie-breaking rules, McNaughton would have received only a bronze medal, and the second-place finisher, American Robert Van Osdel, would have won the gold.

When the U.S. swept the high jump medals in 1936, Nazi leader Adolf Hitler—who was already in trouble with the IOC for summoning the German shot-put winner for a special tribute, against Olympic protocol—had already left the stadium. Cornelius Johnson, in first place, set an Olympic record, which lasted until another American, Walter Davis, broke it in 1952.

An Australian, John Winter, won the 1948 high jump, and the silver and bronze medals—both awarded to athletes who had jumped 6ft, 4.75in—were decided by calculating the number of misses, rather than by a jump-off. In Helsinki, American Walter Davis jumped a half-inch higher than his height to win the gold medal and set a new Olympic record at 6ft, 8.5in. It wasn't much of a surprise when this record was broken by American Charlie Dumas, who won the gold and set a new Olympic record in Melbourne, since he had managed to clear the seemingly unbeatable 7-foot mark in the U.S. Olympic trials. (Les Steers's world record jump of 6ft, 11in stood from 1941 until 1953, when Walt Davis still fell a half inch short of the seven-foot mark.)

By 1960, the mystical barrier had utterly lost its spell, and the field included a number of athletes who had cleared 7 feet. All three medalists surpassed the seven-foot mark, with Soviets Robert Shavlakadze and Valeri Brumel placing first and second, and American John Thomas third. Charles Dumas, with a 6ft, 8in jump, managed only to place sixth.

John Thomas improved his position in Tokyo, earning the silver medal and sharing the Olympic record with Soviet Valery Brumel. While both had jumped 7ft, 1.75in, Brumel was awarded the gold since he had fewer misses. The 1960 gold medalist, Shavlakadze, managed only to place fifth, and American John Rambo earned a bronze.

FACT: Between 1972 and 1992, 13 of the 15 men's Olympic high jumping medalists used the Fosbury Flop.

Mexico City's rarified air sparked a number of rare achievements: the "Fosbury flop" became the talk of the town of the 1968 Games when American Dick Fosbury won the gold medal with an Olympic record-breaking jump of 7ft, 4.25in. Soviet Yuri Tarmak won the gold in Munich, but still fell one inch short of Fosbury's mark. At Montreal in 1976, Dwight Stones, who had placed third in the Munich Games, managed only to place third again, although the world record he had set prior to the 1976 Games remained untouched. Poland's Jacek Wszola set a new Olympic record that year with his gold-winning 7ft, 4.5in jump.

Wszola was considered a prime candidate for the gold in Moscow, but a relatively unknown East German by the name of Gerd Wessig—who had made the East German team two weeks before the Games—upset the competition. Wessig easily won the gold medal with a 7ft, 8.75in jump—a full 1.75in above Wszola's second-place jump—and he became the first man to establish a high jump world record at the Games.

Dietmar Moegenburg won the 1984 event for West Germany, followed by Patrik Sjoberg of Sweden, and, in an unusual showing, Zhu Jianhua of China took the bronze. Sjoberg managed only to tie for third in Seoul, with Soviet Roudolf Povarnitsyne, while Hollis Conway of the U.S. captured the silver medal. Soviet Guennadi Avdeenko set an Olympic record as he vaulted to the gold in Seoul.

Pole vault: The first pole vault competition was won by American William Welles Hoyt, and it was another seventy-six years before a non-American would win the event in the Olympics. Irving Baxter won the pole vault in Paris in 1900 amid much controversy: a number of the competitors objected to the fact that the event was being held on a Sunday, and they refused to participate. And two of the U.S. team's best vaulters had been misinformed that the event would be rescheduled and consequently missed the competition. When a consolation competition was staged, Baxter's teammate, D.S. Horton, bettered his jump by 5.75 inches.

Charles Dvorak, the other American who had been misinformed of a rescheduled event by the Olympic officials, went on to win the 1904 event in Saint Louis. The Americans swept the event that year, taking first through sixth place. In the following Games, Edward Cooke and Alfred Gilbert managed to establish an Olympic record despite having to compete amid the havoc that the marathon finish had created; both shared first place with a 12ft, 2in jump. Gilbert went on to post-Olympic fame to create the ubiquitous Erector set.

Harry Babcock set an Olympic record in Stockholm, while his teammates Frank Nelson and Marcus Wright helped America sweep the medals again. Then, in Antwerp, Frank Foss set a new world record with a 13ft, 5in jump—giving him the largest margin of victory in Olympic history. Denmark's Henry Petersen managed only 12ft, 1.5in for second place.

The U.S. made a clean sweep of the Paris and Amsterdam Games, and was expected to do so again in LA when a surprise contender from Japan, Shuhei Nishida, jumped just a half inch less than the American gold medalist, William Miller. The following Games, in Berlin, Nishida was again awarded silver, and another Japanese vaulter, Sueo Oe, was given the bronze, despite the fact that both had vaulted 13ft, 11.25in. Back in Japan, the two winners had their medals re-worked so that each was half silver and half bronze.

In Barcelona, Unified Team pole vaulter Sergei Bubka stunned everyone when he no-heighted in the pole vault event after setting an Olympic record and winning the gold in Seoul. *AP/Wide World Photos*

The U.S. hegemony remained unchallenged for the next few years, with O. Guinn Smith winning the event at London, and Robert Richards at Helsinki and again at Melbourne, which made him the only man to win two gold medals—three medals, in total—for pole vaulting. In recognition of his accomplishments, Richards was pictured on the front of Wheaties cereal boxes.

Almost nine hours of grueling vaulting decided the Tokyo competition, which made a gold medalist out of the world record holder, Texan Frederick Hansen. Though Hansen established a new Olympic record, his world record—which marked the seventeenth time the world record had been broken since the Rome Games—remained intact. The Tokyo Games marked the first time flexible fiberglass poles were used. The U.S. went home from Mexico City with another gold medal, but clearly the Americans were not unchallenged: American Robert Seagren, West German Claus Schiprowski, and East German Wolfgang Nordwig all shared the Olympic record at 17ft, 8.5in, and medals were determined based on the number of misses.

Wolfgang Nordwig, who had won the bronze in 1968, returned to the Munich Games to win the first pole vaulting gold medal ever awarded to a non-American, while Robert Seagren and Jan Johnson kept the U.S. in the medals by winning the silver and bronze. The U.S. managed only a bronze medal in Montreal, when David Roberts jumped 18ft, 0.5in—as had the Polish gold medalist and the Finnish silver medalist; once again, places were determined by the number of misses. As fate would have it, had Roberts not missed his first attempt at 17ft, 6.75in, he would have won the gold medal.

When the 1980 Games began, a new two-week-old world record of 18ft, 11in existed; set by Philippe Houvion of France, the record was short lived. Poland's Wladyslaw Kozakiewicz jumped an extra half inch to set another world record—the second pole vaulting world record to be established during an Olympics—allowing erstwhile world record holder Houvion to place only fourth, with a jump of 18ft, 6.5in, by virtue of number of misses.

The 1984 Games introduced a new gold medalist when Pierre Quinon of France out-vaulted the competition; Americans Mike Tully and Earl Bell placed second and third. The Seoul Games proved to be a total sweep for the Soviets: Grigori Egorov captured the bronze, Radion Gataoulline the silver, and Sergei Bubka—who grips the fiberglass pole closer to the end than any other pole vaulter—set an Olympic record to win the Seoul gold medal.

Carl Lewis (U.S.) flies through the air in Barcelona: His best jump was 8.67 feet, winning him a gold medal for the third straight Olympiad. *AP/Wide World Photos*

Highlights from Barcelona

Carl Lewis, at the well-ripened age of 31, entered his third Olympic Games as the long shot to win the long jump. In Seoul, Lewis relegated Mike Powell to a second-place finish with a jump of 8.72—.23 ahead of his teammate's best effort. But in 1991, the tables had turned: with an astonishing 29'4½" jump, Powell leapt beyond Lewis's best flight, straight into the record books. Obliterated was Bob Beamon's 23-year-old world record. Then, as if to drive home his point, Powell again bested his erstwhile nemesis at the Olympic trials.

Barcelona was to be the battlefield of Hatfield versus McCoy. Powell, the world record holder, had no intention of settling for a second Olympic vice championship. Lewis, on the other hand, was gunning for a three-peat. Having failed to qualify for either the 100-m or 200-m dash, he needed a fastest-highest-strongest performance in the long jump if he was to leave Barcelona with an individual gold.

Soaring 28'5½" inches in his first jump, Lewis reclaimed his title as the greatest long jumper of all time. Powell's best and last effort, at 28'4¼", earned him second spot on the podium, again in the shadow of the athlete who has come to be known as a latter-day Jesse Owens. "I've said it all along," Mel Rosen, head coach of the U.S. men's track and field team asserted, "Carl is the greatest athlete I have ever seen, and he proves it time and again." Fresh from his gold-medal performance in the long jump, Lewis proceeded to bag another in the 4 × 100 relay, bringing his gold-medal tally to eight—a record that only four Olympians have surpassed.

In the triple jump, the U.S. team's Mike Conley was determined to grab top honors, having been second-bested by Al Joyner in the 1984 Games. On his second jump, he exploded to an Olympic-record distance of 57'10½", nearly one foot better than Bahamian Frank Rutherford's best effort. Then he turned on the afterburners. In his sixth and final jump, Conley sailed 59'7½", nearly three feet beyond Rutherford's second-place leap. And eight inches further than Willie Banks's seven-year old world record.

But Conley had to settle for a gold medal. With 4.7 mile-per-hour trailing wind, the young American's record flight was not recognized as a world record. "I came here to win the gold medal," Conley later philosophized. "To sit here and be disappointed about the world record would be absolutely greedy, and I'm not a greedy person."

If anyone was disappointed in Barcelona, it was the Ukraine's Sergei Bubka. Having captured the 1988 pole vaulting title with an Olympic record height, the legendary flyer strode into the

Barcelona Games as the overwhelming favorite. Holding title to some 30 world records in the pole vault, Bubka stunned the Barcelona crowds not by vaulting to a thirty-first record, but by no-heighting. Capturing the title for the Unified Team was teammate Maksim Tarasov, with 19'1/4", who settled for a gold without Bubka's congratulations: the vertically challenged erstwhile champion had already left the stadium in disgust.

Medalists

Track and Field—Men's High Jump

1992
1. Javier Sotomayor Sanabria, Cuba, 2.34
2. Patrik Sjöeberg, Sweden, 2.34
3. Artur Partyka, Poland, 2.34
3. Timothy Forsythe, Australia, 2.34
3. Hollis Conway, U.S.A., 2.34

1988
1. Guennadi Avdeenko, Soviet Union, 2.38 (OR)
2. Hollis Conway, U.S.A., 2.36
3. Roudolf Povarnitsyne, Soviet Union, 2.36
3. Patrik Sjoberg, Sweden, 2.36

1984
1. Dietmar Moegenburg, FRG, 2.35
2. Patrik Sjoberg, Sweden, 2.33
3. Zhu Jianhua, China, 2.31

1980
1. Gerd Wessig, East Germany, 2.36 (WR)
2. Jacek Wszola, Poland, 2.31
3. Jorg Freimuth, East Germany, 2.31

1976
1. Jacek Wzsola, Poland, 2.25 (OR)
2. Greg Joy, Canada, 2.23
3. Dwight Stones, U.S.A., 2.21

1972
1. Yuri Tarmak, Soviet Union, 2.23
2. Stefan Junge, G.D.R., 2.21
3. Dwight Stones, U.S.A., 2.21

1968
1. Dick Fosbury, U.S.A., 2.24 (OR)
2. Ed Caruthers, U.S.A., 2.22
3. Valentin Gavrilov, Soviet Union, 2.20

1964
1. Valeri Brumel, Soviet Union, 2.18 (OR)
2. John Thomas, U.S.A. 2.18 (OR)
3. John Rambo, U.S.A., 2.16

1960
1. Robert Shavlakadze, Soviet Union, 2.16 (OR)
2. Valeri Brumel, Soviet Union, 2.16
3. John Thomas, U.S.A., 2.14

1956
1. Charles Dumas, U.S.A., 2.12 (OR)
2. Charles Porter, Australia, 2.10
3. Igor Kashkarov, Soviet Union, 2.08

1952
1. Walter Davis, U.S.A., 2.04 (OR)
2. Kenneth Wiesner, U.S.A., 2.01
3. Jose Telles da Conceicao, Brazil, 1.98

1948
1. John Winter, Australia, 1.98
2. Bjorn Paulson, Norway, 1.95
3. George Stanich, U.S.A., 1.95

1936
1. Cornelius Johnson, U.S.A., 2.03 (OR)
2. David Albritton, U.S.A., 2.00
3. Delos Thurber, U.S.A., 2.00

1932
1. Duncan McNaughton, Canada, 1.97
2. Robert Van Osdel, U.S.A., 1.97
3. Simeon Toribio Philippines, 1.97

1928
1. Robert King, U.S.A., 1.94
2. Benjamin Hedges, U.S.A., 1.91
3. Claude Menard, France, 1.91

1924
1. Harold Osborn, U.S.A., 1.98 (OR)
2. Leroy Brown, U.S.A., 1.95
3. Pierre Lewden, France, 1.92

1920
1. Richmond Landon, U.S.A., 1.935 (OR)
2. Harold Muller, U.S.A., 1.90
3. Bo Ekelund, Sweden, 1.90

1912
1. Alma Richards, U.S.A., 1.93 (OR)
2. Hans Liesche, Germany, 1.91
3. George Horine, U.S.A., 1.89

1908
1. Harry Porter, U.S.A., 1.905 (OR)
2. Geo Andre, France, 1.88
2. Con Leahy, Great Britain/Ireland, 1.88
2. Istvan Somodi, Hungary, 1.88

1906
1. Con Leahy, Great Britain/Ireland, 1.775
2. Lajos Gonczy, Hungary, 1.75
3. Themistoklis Diakidis, Greece, 1.725
3. Herbert Kerrigan, U.S.A., 1.725

1904
1. Samuel Jones, U.S.A., 1.803
2. Garrett Serviss, U.S.A., 1.778
3. Paul Weinstein, Germany, 1.778

1900
1. Irving Baxter, U.S.A., 1.90 (OR)
2. Patrick Leahy, Great Britain/Ireland, 1.78
3. Lajos Gonczy, Hungary, 1.75

1896
1. Ellery Clark, U.S.A., 1.81
2. James Connolly, U.S.A., 1.65
3. Robert Garrett, U.S.A., 1.65

Track and Field—Men's Pole Vault
1992
1. Maxim Tarassov, Russia, 5.80
2. Igor Trandenkov, Russia, 5.80
3. Javier Garcia Chico, Spain, 5.75

1988
1. Sergei Bubka, Soviet Union, 5.90 (OR)
2. Radion Gataoulline, Soviet Union, 5.85
3. Grigori Egorov, Soviet Union, 5.80

1984
1. Pierre Quinon, France, 5.75
2. Mike Tully, U.S.A., 5.65
3. Earl Bell, U.S.A., 5.60

1980
1. Wladyslaw Kozakiewicz, Poland, 5.78 (WR)
2. Tadeusz Slusarski, Poland, 5.65
3. Konstantin Volkov, Soviet Union, 5.65

1976
1. Tadeusz Slusarski, Poland, 5.50 (EOR)
2. Antti Kalliomaki, Finland, 5.50 (EOR)
3. Dave Roberts, U.S.A., 5.50 (EOR)

1972
1. Wolfgang Nordwig, East Germany, 5.50 (OR)
2. Bob Seagren, U.S.A., 5.40
3. Jan Johnson, U.S.A., 5.35

1968
1. Bob Seagren, U.S.A., 5.40 (OR)

2. Claus Schiprowski, West Germany, 5.40 (OR)
3. Wolfgang Nordwig, East Germany, 5.40 (OR)

1964
1. Fred Hansen, U.S.A., 5.10 (OR)
2. Wolfgang Reinhardt, West Germany, 5.05
3. Klaus Lehnertz, West Germany, 5.00

1960
1. Donald Bragg, U.S.A., 4.70 (OR)
2. Ronald Morris, U.S.A., 4.60
3. Eeles Landstrom, Finland, 4.55

1956
1. Robert Richards, U.S.A., 4.56 (OR)
2. Robert Gutowski, U.S.A., 4.53
3. Georgios Roubanis, Greece, 4.50

1952
1. Robert Richards, U.S.A., 4.55 (OR)
2. Donald Laz, U.S.A., 4.50
3. Ragnar Lundberg, Sweden, 4.40

1948
1. Guinn Smith, U.S.A., 4.30
2. Erkki Kataja, Finland, 4.20
3. Robert Richards, U.S.A., 4.20

1936
1. Earle Meadows, U.S.A., 4.35 (OR)
2. Shuhei Nishida, Japan, 4.25
3. Sueo Oe, Japan, 4.25

1932
1. William Miller, U.S.A., 4.315 (OR)
2. Shuhei Nishida, Japan, 4.30
3. George Jefferson, U.S.A., 4.20

1928
1. Sabin Carr, U.S.A., 4.20 (OR)
2. William Droegemuller, U.S.A., 4.10
3. Charles McGinnis, U.S.A., 3.95

1924
1. Lee Barnes, U.S.A., 3.95
2. Glenn Graham, U.S.A., 3.95
3. James Brooker, U.S.A., 3.90

1920
1. Frank Foss, U.S.A., 4.09 (WR)
2. Henry Petersen, Denmark, 3.70
3. Edwin Myers, U.S.A., 3.60

1912
1. Harry Babcock, U.S.A., 3.95 (OR)
2. Frank Nelson, U.S.A., 3.85
2. Marcus Wright, U.S.A., 3.85
3. William Happenny, Canada, 3.80
3. Frank Murphy, U.S.A., 3.80
3. Bertil Uggla, Sweden, 3.80

1908
1. Edward Cooke, U.S.A., 3.71 (OR)
1. Alfred Gilbert, U.S.A., 3.71 (OR)
3. Edward B. Archibald, Canada, 3.58
3. Charles Jacobs, U.S.A., 3.58
3. Bruno Soderstrom, Sweden, 3.58

1906
1. Fernand Gonder, France, 3.50
2. Bruno Soderstrom, Sweden, 3.40
3. Ernest Glover, U.S.A., 3.35

1904
1. Charles Dvorak, U.S.A., 3.505
2. LeRoy Samse, U.S.A., 3.43
3. Louis Wilkins., U.S.A., 3.43

1900
1. Irving Baxter, U.S.A., 3.30
2. Michael Colket, U.S.A., 3.25
3. Carl-Albert Andersen, Norway, 3.20

1896
1. William Hoyt, U.S.A., 3.30
2. Albert Tyler, U.S.A., 3.25
3. Evangelos Damaskos, Greece, 2.85

Track and Field—Men's Long Jump

1992
1. Carl Lewis, U.S.A., 8.67
2. Mike Powell, U.S.A., 8.64
3. Joe Greene, U.S.A., 8.34

1988
1. Carl Lewis, U.S.A., 8.72
2. Mike Powell, U.S.A., 8.49
3. Larry Myricks, U.S.A., 8.27

1984
1. Carl Lewis, U.S.A., 8.54
2. Gary Honey, Australia, 8.24
3. Giovanni Evangelisti, Italy, 8.24

1980
1. Lutz Dombrowski, East Germany, 8.54
2. Frank Paschek, East Germany, 8.21
3. Valeri Podluzhnyi, Soviet Union, 8.18

1976
1. Arnie Robinson, U.S.A., 8.35
2. Randy Williams, U.S.A., 8.11
3. Frank Wartenberg, East Germany, 8.02

1972
1. Randy Williams, U.S.A., 8.24
2. Hans Baumgartner, West Germany, 8.18
3. Arnie Robinson, U.S.A., 8.03

1968
1. Bob Beamon, U.S.A., 8.90 (WR)

2. Klaus Beer, East Germany, 8.19
3. Ralph Boston, U.S.A., 8.16

1964
1. Lynn Davies, Great Britain, 8.07
2. Ralph Boston, U.S.A., 8.03
3. Igor Ter-Ovanesyan, Soviet Union, 7.99

1960
1. Ralph Boston, U.S.A., 8.12 (OR)
2. Irvin Roberson, U.S.A., 8.11
3. Igor Ter-Ovanesyan, Soviet Union, 8.04

1956
1. Greg Bell, U.S.A., 7.83
2. John Bennett, U.S.A., 7.68
3. Jorma Valkama, Finland, 7.48

1952
1. Jerome Biffle, U.S.A., 7.57
2. Meredith Gourdine, U.S.A., 7.53
3. Odon Foldessy, Hungary, 7.30

1948
1. Willie Steele, U.S.A., 7.825
2. Thomas Bruce, Australia, 7.555
3. Herbert Douglas, U.S.A., 7.545

1936
1. Jesse Owens, U.S.A., 8.06 (OR)
2. Luz Long, Germany, 7.87
3. Naoto Tajima, Japan, 7.74

1932
1. Edward Gordon, U.S.A., 7.64
2. C. Lambert Redd, U.S.A., 7.60
3. Chuhei Nambu, Japan, 7.45

1928
1. Edward Hamm, U.S.A., 7.73 (OR)
2. Silvio Cator, Haiti, 7.58
3. Alfred Bates, U.S.A., 7.40

1924
1. William DeHart Hubbard, U.S.A., 7.445
2. Edward Gourdin, U.S.A., 7.275
3. Sverre Hansen, Norway, 7.26

1920
1. William Petersson, Sweden, 7.15
2. Carl Johnson, U.S.A., 7.095
3. Eric Abrahamsson, Sweden, 7.08

1912
1. Albert Gutterson, U.S.A., 7.60 (OR)
2. Calvin Bricker, Canada, 7.21
3. Georg Aberg, Sweden, 7.18

1908
1. Francis Irons, U.S.A., 7.48 (OR)
2. Daniel Kelly, U.S.A., 7.09
3. Calvin Bricker, Canada, 7.085

1906

1. Meyer Prinstein, U.S.A., 7.20
2. Peter O'Connor, Great Britain/Ireland, 7.025
3. Hugo Friend, U.S.A., 6.96

1904

1. Meyer Prinstein, U.S.A., 7.34 (OR)
2. Daniel Frank, U.S.A., 6.89
3. Robert Stangland, U.S.A., 6.88

1900

1. Alvin Kraenzlein, U.S.A., 7.185 (OR)
2. Meyer Prinstein, U.S.A., 7.175
3. Patrick Leahy, Great Britain/Ireland, 6.95

1896

1. Ellery Clark, U.S.A., 6.35
2. Robert Garrett, U.S.A., 6.18
3. James Connolly, U.S.A., 6.11

Track and Field—Men's Triple Jump

1992

1. Mike Conley, U.S.A., 18.17 (OR)
2. Charles Simpkins, U.S.A., 17.60
3. Frank Rutherford, Bahamas, 17.36

1988

1. Hristo Markov, Bulgaria, 17.61
2. Igor Lapchine, Soviet Union, 17.52
3. Alexandre Kovalenko, Soviet Union, 17.42

1984

1. Al Joyner, U.S.A., 17.26
2. Mike Conley, U.S.A., 17.18
3. Keith Connor, Great Britain, 16.87

1980

1. Jaak Uudmae, Soviet Union, 17.35
2. Viktor Saneyev, Soviet Union, 17.24
3. Joao Carlos de Oliveira, Brazil, 17.22

1976

1. Viktor Saneyev, Soviet Union, 17.29
2. James Butts, U.S.A., 17.18
3. Joao Carlos de Oliveira, Brazil, 16.90

1972

1. Viktor Saneyev, Soviet Union, 17.35
2. Jorg Drehmel, East Germany, 17.31
3. Nelson Prudencio, Brazil, 17.05

1968

1. Viktor Saneyev, Soviet Union, 17.39 (WR)
2. Nelson Prudencio, Brazil, 17.27
3. Giuseppe Gentile, Italy, 17.22

1964

1. Jozef Schmidt, Poland, 16.85 (OR)
2. Oleg Fyedoseyev, Soviet Union, 16.58
3. Viktor Kravchenko, Soviet Union, 16.57

1960

1. Jozef Schmidt, Poland, 16.81
2. Vladimir Goryayev, Soviet Union, 16.63
3. Vitold Kreyer, Soviet Union, 16.43

1956

1. Adhemar Ferreira da Silva, Brazil, 16.35 (OR)
2. Vilhjalmur Einarsson, Iceland, 16.26
3. Vitold Kreyer, Soviet Union, 16.02

1952

1. Adhemar Ferreira da Silva, Brazil, 16.22 (WR)
2. Leonid Sherbakov, Soviet Union, 15.98
3. Arnoldo Devonish, Venezuela, 15.52

1948

1. Arne Ahman, Sweden, 15.40
2. George Avery, Australia, 15.365
3. Ruhi Sarialp, Turkey, 15.025

1936

1. Naoto Tajima, Japan, 16.00 (WR)
2. Masao Harada, Japan, 15.66
3. John Metcalfe, Australia, 15.50

1932

1. Chuhei Nambu, Japan, 15.72 (WR)
2. Erik Svensson, Sweden, 15.32
3. Kenkichi Oshima, Japan, 15.12

1928

1. Mikio Oda, Japan, 15.21
2. Levi Casey, U.S.A., 15.17
3. Vilho Tuulos, Finland, 15.11

1924

1. Anthony Winter, Australia, 15,525 (WR)
2. Luis Bruneto, Argentina, 15.425
3. Vilho Tuulos, Finland, 15.37

1920

1. Vilho Tuulos, Finland, 14.505
2. Folke Jansson, Sweden, 14.48
3. Eric Almlof, Sweden, 14.27

1912

1. Gustaf Lindblom, Sweden, 14.76
2. Georg Aberg, Sweden, 14.51
3. Eric Almlof, Sweden, 14.17

1908

1. Timothy Ahearne, Great Britain/Ireland, 14.92 (OR)
2. J. Garfield MacDonald, Canada, 14.76
3. Edvard Larsen, Norway, 14.395

1906

1. Peter O'Connor, Great Britain/Ireland, 14.075
2. Con Leahy, Great Britain/Ireland, 13.98
3. Thomas Cronan, U.S.A., 13.70

1904
1. Meyer Prinstein, U.S.A., 14.35
2. Frederick Englehardt, U.S.A., 13.90
3. Robert Stangland, U.S.A., 13.365

1900
1. Meyer Prinstein, U.S.A., 14.47 (OR)

2. James Connolly, U.S.A., 13.97
3. Lewis P. Sheldon, U.S.A., 13.64

1896
1. James Connolly, U.S.A., 13.71
2. Alexandre Tuffere, France, 12.70
3. Ioannis Persakis, Greece, 12.52

WOMEN'S JUMPING EVENTS

Highlights

High jump: Not until Amsterdam in 1928 were women permitted to compete in jumping events at the Games; the high jump was added to the women's program in 1928, but the long jump would not be added for another two decades. The first women's high jump gold was awarded to Canadian Ethel Catherwood, aka "The Saskatoon Lily," who was an eighteen-year-old beauty known for facing the bar smiling before she launched a successful jump. Asked whether she would pursue a career in Tinseltown, she responded, "I'd rather gulp poison than try my hand at motion pictures."

American Mildred "Babe" Didriksen—later known for her golfing prowess as Babe Zaharias—captured a unique assortment of medals in 1932 when she won the silver for the high jump, in addition to golds in the 80m hurdles and javelin. Both she and fellow American Jean Shiley jumped 5ft, 5.25in—after already having tied in the LA Olympic trials—at which point the judges ruled her technique illegal. The rule that penalized her "diving" technique in the high jump—which relegated her to second place—was rescinded in 1937. While Babe had to settle for the silver medal, she was recognized in the world record.

While Ibolya Csák of Hungary was awarded the 1936 gold medal, Great Britain's Dorothy Odam—who had matched her jump—was forced to settle for second place after a jump-off. Had current tie-breaking rules been applied, the 16-year-old Odam would have taken the gold. Germany's Dora Ratjen placed fourth in the 1936 high jump but was barred from further competition in 1938, when she was discovered to be the wrong gender.

The odds were against Dorothy Odam—now Dorothy Tyler—again in the 1948 London Games when she lost a tie with Alice Coachman, even though she had fewer misses. Coachman, the first black woman to win an Olympic gold, shared an Olympic record with Tyler. That same year, French concert pianist Micheline Ostermeyer added a bronze in the high jump to her golds in the discus and shot in 1948.

After placing fifth in Melbourne, Romanian Iolanda Balas leapt over the competition in Rome in 1960 by jumping an Olympic record-setting 6ft, 0.75in. The first woman to jump over 6 feet, Balas set 14 world records in the following ten and a half years. The year after the Rome Games, Balas bounded 6ft, 3.25in, a benchmark that wouldn't be approached for another decade.

When Ulrike Meyfarth of West Germany won the high jump in 1972, she became the youngest Olympic individual event champion. Jumping 2.75 inches higher than she ever had, Meyfarth equaled the world record at Munich.

In Montreal, Meyfarth, along with three other women who had 6ft, 3in jumps in their repertoire, were eliminated from the qualifying rounds. Three hours into the competition, eighteen women had jumped six feet—a feat that hadn't been achieved before 1960. Rosemarie Ackermann, from East Germany, won the gold, becoming the first woman to jump two meters over her own height.

Jumping just shy of an inch less than she had in Montreal, Ackermann managed only to place fourth in Moscow, where Italian Sara Simeoni earned a gold with an Olympic record-breaking jump of 6ft, 5.5in. Shortly before the Games, Soviet Marina Sysoyeva had reset the women's world record for jumping over one's height, setting the mark at 10.25 inches.

For the first time since 1956, the U.S. was in the money when Joni Huntley captured a bronze medal in 1984; Sara Simeoni of Italy took the silver, while West Germany's Ulrike Mayfarth set an Olympic record for first place. Finally, in Seoul, American women took home another gold medal when Louise Ritter re-set the Olympic record. Also that year, Bulgarian Stefka Kostavinova captured the silver, while Soviet Tamara Bykova won the bronze.

Long jump: When women were finally permitted to compete in the Olympics in the long jump in 1948, the number of events in which they were allowed to compete at a single Games was still limited. So Fanny Blankers-Koen, the Dutch world-record holder in the long jump, competed in other events at the London Games. 1948's winner, Hungarian Olga Gyarmati, jumped 18ft, 8.25in—almost two feet shy of Blankers-Koen's world record.

New Zealand's Yvette Williams set a new Olympic record— still considerably shy of the Blankers-Koen's world record—at

20ft, 5.75in. The second place finisher, Soviet Aleksandra Chudina, also took the silver in the javelin, and the bronze in the high jump.

Willye White was the first American woman to medal in the long jump, winning the silver medal at the 1956 Melbourne Games with a jump of 19ft, 11.75in. Jumping more than a foot farther than White, Poland's Elzbieta Krzesinska set a new world record at 20ft, 10in. Her record was bested in Rome, where she managed only a 20ft, 7in jump for second place; Soviet Vyera Krepkina set a new Olympic record at 20ft, 10.75in, earning the gold but falling shy of the new women's world record of 21ft. Still not bad for someone better known as a sprinter: Krepkina was the co-holder of the women's world record for the 100m.

Until 1964, no British woman had ever won an Olympic gold medal in track and field. Great Britain's Mary Rand, however, left Tokyo with the long jump gold medal—not to mention a pentathlon silver and a 4 × 100m relay bronze. Jumping into a 1.69m-per-second wind, Rand managed to break the world record with a 22ft, 2.25in flight.

That was far, but not far enough to stand through the next Olympiad, in which Romanian Viorica Viscopoleanu added another 2.25in to the world record, easily winning the gold medal with her 22ft, 4.5in jump—nine inches better than she had ever jumped. Behind her, Sheila Sherwood won another medal for Great Britain, taking a silver for her 21ft, 11in jump.

The Munich crowds jumped for joy when Heidemarie Rosendahl leapt for the host country's first gold medal of 1972; Rosendahl tripled her medal haul later in Munich with a pentathlon silver and a 4 × 100m relay gold. In second place that year, Diana Yorgova won Bulgaria's first track and field medal.

The U.S. earned its second women's long jump medal in 1976 when Kathy McMillan earned the silver with a 21ft, 10.25in leap; East Germany's Angela Voigt won the gold that year. The 1980 Olympic long jump competition provided quite an upset when the third-string Soviet jumper, Tatiana Kolpakova, bested her compatriots—not to mention herself—by setting a new Olympic record of 23ft, 2in—nine inches further than she had ever jumped.

1984 proved to be a good year for the Romanian women, who stole both first and second place, while Great Britain's Susan Hearnshaw captured the bronze. And finally, in Seoul, the Joyner name appeared again on Olympic records, this time when Jackie Joyner-Kersee—Florence Griffith Joyner's sister-in-law and Al Joyner's sister—set a new Olympic benchmark to win the gold, while East Germans Heike Drechsler and Galina Tchistiakova trailed in second and third place.

Highlights from Barcelona

Having relegated East Germany's Heike Drechsler to second place in Seoul with an Olympic record long jump of 7:40, Jackie Joyner-Kersee was in for a rude surprise. In Barcelona, under windy conditions, the German long jumper nailed her first major win over decathlon legend Joyner-Kersee. Outdistancing Inessa Kravets of the Ukraine by two short centimeters, Drechsler grabbed top honors, leaving the 1988 champion to settle for bronze. Even so, Joyner-Kersee's third-place win earned her kudos; having also collected the heptathlon gold, she was the only athlete in Barcelona to nab individual medals in both track and field events.

The German women fared well in the high jump as well, as another Heike—Heike Henkel—bested the field with her first successful jump (having missed her first two attempts). Settling for the role of runner-up was Romania's world junior champion Galina Astafei, while Joanet Quintero Alvarez, with a bronze, grabbed the Cuban women's first medal in the event.

Medalists

Track and Field—Women's High Jump

1992
1. Heike Henkel, Germany, 2.02
2. Galina Astafei, Romania, 2.00
3. Joanet Quintero Alvarez, Cuba, 1.97

1988
1. Louise Ritter, U.S.A., 2.03 (OR)
2. Stefka Kostavinova, Bulgaria, 2.01
3. Tamara Bykova, Soviet Union, 1.99

1984
1. Ulrike Mayfarth, West Germany, 2.02 (OR)
2. Sara Simeoni, Italy, 2.00
3. Joni Huntley, U.S.A., 1.97

1980
1. Sara Simeoni, Italy, 1.97 (OR)
2. Urszula Kielan, Poland, 1.94
3. Jutta Kirst, East Germany, 1.94

1976
1. Rosemarie Ackermann, East Germany, 1.93 (OR)
2. Sara Simeoni, Italy, 1.91
3. Yordanka Blagoyeva, Bulgaria, 1.91

1972
1. Ulrike Meyfarth, West Germany, 1.92 (EWR)
2. Yordanka Blagoyeva, Bulgaria, 1.88
3. Ilona Gusenbauer, Austria, 1.88

1968
1. Miloslava Rezkova, Czechoslovakia, 1.82
2. Antonina Okorokova, Soviet Union, 1.80
3. Valentina Kozyr, Soviet Union, 1.80

1964
1. Iolanda Balas, Romania, 1.90 (OR)
2. Michele Brown-Mason, Australia, 1.80
3. Taisiya Chenchik, Soviet Union, 1.78

1960
1. Iolanda Balas, Romania, 1.85
2. Jaroslawa Jozwiakowska, Poland, 1.71
2. Dorothy Shirley, Great Britain, 1.71

1956
1. Mildred McDaniel, U.S.A., 1.76 (WR)
2. Thelma Hopkins, Great Britain, 1.67
2. Maria Pissaryeva, Soviet Union, 1.67

1952
1. Esther Brand, South Africa, 1.67
2. Sheila Lerwill, Great Britain, 1.65
3. Aleksandra Chudina, Soviet Union, 1.63

1948
1. Alice Coachman, U.S.A., 1.68 (OR)
2. Dorothy Tyler-Odam, Great Britain, 1.68 (OR)
3. Micheline Ostermeyer, France, 1.61

1936
1. Ibolya Csak, Hungary, 1.60
2. Dorothy Odam, Great Britain, 1.60
3. Elfriede Kaun, Germany, 1.60

1932
1. Jean Shiley, U.S.A., 1.657 (WR)
2. Mildred "Babe" Didrikson, U.S.A., 1.657 (WR)
3. Eva Dawes, Canada, 1.60

1928
1. Ethel Catherwood, Canada, 1.59
2. Carolina Gisolf, Netherlands, 1.56
3. Mildred Wiley, U.S.A., 1.56

1896–1924
Not held

Track and Field—Women's Long Jump

1992
1. Heike Drechsler, Germany, 7.14
2. Inessa Kravets, Ukraine, 7.12
3. Jackie Joyner-Kersee, U.S.A., 7.07

1988
1. Jackie Joyner-Kersee, U.S.A., 7.40 (OR)
2. Heike Drechsler, East Germany, 7.22
3. Galina Tchistiakova, Soviet Union, 7.11

1984
1. Anisoara Cusmir-Stanciu, Romania, 6.96
2. Vali Ionescu, Romania, 6.81
3. Susan Hearnshaw, Great Britain, 6.80

1980
1. Tatiana Kolpakova, Soviet Union, 7.06 (OR)
2. Brigitte Wujak, East Germany, 7.04
3. Tatiana Skachko, Soviet Union, 7.01

1976
1. Angela Voigt, East Germany, 6.72

2. Kathy McMillan, U.S.A., 6.66
3. Lydia Alfeyeva, Soviet Union, 6.60

1972
1. Heidemarie Rosendahl, West Germany, 6.78
2. Diana Jorgova, Bulgaria, 6.77
3. Eva Suranova, Czechoslovakia, 6.67

1968
1. Viorica Viscopoleanu, Romania, 6.82 (WR)
2. Sheila Sherwood, Great Britain, 6.68
3. Tatyana Talisheva, Soviet Union, 6.66

1964
1. Mary Rand, Great Britain, 6.76 (WR)
2. Irena Kirszenstein, Poland, 6.60
3. Tatyana Schelkanova, Soviet Union, 6.42

1960
1. Vyera Krepkina, Soviet Union, 6.37 (OR)
2. Elzbieta Krzesinska, Poland, 6.27
3. Hildrun Claus, East Germany, 6.21

1956
1. Elzbieta Krzesinska, Poland, 6.35 (EWR)
2. Willye White, U.S.A., 6.09
3. Nadezhda Dvalischvili, Soviet Union, 6.07

1952
1. Yvette Williams, New Zealand, 6.24 (OR)
2. Aleksandra Chudina, Soviet Union, 6.14
3. Shirley Cawley, Great Britain, 5.92

1948
1. Olga Gyarmati, Hungary, 5.695
2. Noemi Simonetto De Portela, Argentina, 5.60
3. Ann-Britt Leyman, Sweden, 5.575

1896–1936
Not held

Trivia Quiz

1. The long jump world record set by Jesse Owens the year before the 1936 Games
a. Has never been surpassed
b. Was broken at the 1936 Games—by Owens
c. Stood unchallenged for 25 years

2. Track and Field represents
a. More U.S. medals than any other sport
b. The second most U.S. medals of any sport
c. The most U.S. men's medals of any sport

3. The first Modern Games in 1896 included
a. No field events   **b.** Three field events   **c.** Six field events

4. In the Ancient Olympics, long jumpers used
a. Launching pads to lengthen their jumps
b. Jumping weights to lengthen their jumps
c. Anabolic steroids to improve their performance

5. Records indicate that an ancient Greek named Chionis jumped
a. 32 feet, 1.5 inches   **b.** 23 feet, 1.5 inches   **c.** 30 feet, 1.5 inches

6. American George Horine broke the high jumping record in 1912 using
a. The belly roll   **b.** The western roll   **c.** The jelly roll

7. When English track and field organizers set minimum standards for athletes in 1834, athletes were required to
a. Long jump at least 20 feet and high jump at least five feet seven inches to qualify
b. Long jump at least 17.5 feet and high jump at least five feet seven inches to qualify
c. Long jump at least 30 feet while whistling Dixie

8. The high and long jump have
a. Never been won at the same Olympics by one person
b. Been won by one person at the same Olympics, only once, in 1896
c. Been won by one person at the same Olympics three times; once by Carl Lewis

9. Women's field events were added to the Olympic program in
a. 1928   **b.** 1956   **c.** 1976

10. The Fosbury flop refers to
a. A head-first run preceded by a circular run
b. A crash landing   **c.** An ice cream sundae

Answers: 1-c; 2-a; 3-c; 4-b; 5-b; 6-b; 7-a; 8-b; 9-a; 10-a

TRACK AND FIELD
(ATHLETICS)—RUNNING

Warm-up

The games of ancient Greece, held at Olympia in Peloponnesus every four years, began with running races, drawing contestants and spectators from surrounding city-states. For variety, the Greeks occasionally required the runners to dress in infantry armor and compete over a two-stadium course, though this was later modified so runners carried only a soldier's shield.

The first recorded Olympic champion was named Coroebus, a sprinter who competed in 776 BC and won the stadion, a race run over a course of 630 feet (about 193 meters).

A few centuries later, in 394 AD, the Olympic Games were banned as unchristian, and little record survives of formal running contests for the next 800 years. Undoubtedly, though, a few heathens managed to sneak in some clandestine contests, and soldiers probably continued to compete in races to test speed and endurance.

Track and field as a sport was revived in England in the 12th century, and much later—in 1871—the first modern athletic club was formed in Suffolk, England. The first college track meet had already taken place in 1864, pitting Oxford versus Cambridge.

Some English athletic enthusiasts set minimum standards for athletes in 1834, which included a five-minute mile and a 10-minute, two-mile run.

The first Greek tracks were banked and earthen, probably with holes in the ground for blocks. In longer races, runners turned around a pillar at the halfway mark before heading for the finish line.

The first English running tracks were turnpike roads or horse racing tracks. These running tracks eventually became circular and were made of cinder. England boasted more running tracks than all of Europe combined by 1896, and it was an Englishman who designed the track at Athens used in the first modern Olympics held that year.

The 1896 Olympic Games included 100m, 400m, 800m, and 1500m runs, the 110m hurdle event, and a marathon. Though not part of the ancient Games, the marathon commemorates the 25-mile run by Greek soldier and Olympic star Pheidippides. He'd run from Marathon to Athens with news of the Athenian victory over the Persians. "Rejoice, we conquer," he announced. Then, according to legend, he fell over dead.

The conquering Athenians rejoiced following the 1896 Olympic marathon as well—along with the winner himself, Spyridon Louis, whose post-race fate was much less dire than that of Pheidippides. As Louis entered the stadium on the final lap, Greek princes Constantine and George ran from their seats to the track to accompany him.

It was not until 1928 that Olympic Games organizers allowed women to compete in track and field events. (Until then, swimming and tennis were the only women's events.) Five events were added that year: the 100m and 800m runs, high jump, discus, and a 4 × 100m relay.

Controversy, emerged though, over the 800m race. The distance was considered dangerously long for women. A 17-year-old German, Lina Radke, won in just over two minutes, but several racers collapsed after the race and Olympic officials banned the race from future games. Amazingly, the ban lasted 32 years.

The women's 800m did not return until Rome in 1960, and its absence may have slowed the development of women distance runners. More recently, a women's 10,000m was added in 1988, and the marathon in 1984.

The winning time in the 100 meters in 1896 was 12 seconds. World record time is now about 9.9 seconds. Runners are stronger, faster, and better conditioned, and their track equipment is better. Starting blocks have replaced holes dug in the ground for sprinters. Racing spikes are lighter, and times are recorded electronically. The synthetic track surface, first featured in the 1968 Olympics, is more consistent than cinder and helps yield better running times. Called Tartan, the surface was originally developed for racehorse training during inclement weather.

Spectator's Guide

Races begin at the sound of a starter's pistol. When runners are ready, the starter calls, "On your marks." In races of 400m or less, the starter calls, "Set." Then the pistol fires. A runner who jumps the gun causes a false start, and two false starts disqualify a runner.

Runners in races over one lap are notified of the last lap by a bell. A runner finishes when any part of the body other than the head or limbs crosses the vertical plane of the finish line.

Weather affects both the runner and the race. In sprints, warm weather is preferable to cold because it keeps muscles looser. Hot weather can add to the difficulties of a marathon runner. A sprint race is considered wind-aided if the breeze blows at the competitors' backs at more than two meters per second.

Sprints: A sprint is a race run at full speed over a short distance, such as the 100m and 200m dashes. A quick start is as important as speed in running a successful race. Before the race begins, runners set their feet against metal starting blocks in a kneeling position. They raise their knees at the "Set" command. When the gun sounds, they push off hard and lengthen their strides as they reach full speed. Runners generally lean into the finish line to try to gain an advantage on competitors.

"When you line up in the 100 meters in the Olympics, look left and right, be satisfied. You're one of the eight best in the world."
—Dr. LeRoy Walker, USOC president

The 200-meter dash features a staggered start. Runners start several meters apart in adjoining lanes to compensate for running around a curve. Most sprinters prefer the middle lanes, which keep them away from the tighter turn of inside lanes while allowing them to see opponents. The larger the runner physically, the more likely she is to prefer a lane toward the outside, where turns aren't as sharp to negotiate.

Middle distance events: For these 400m, 800m, and 1500m races, runners must have speed and endurance. The 400m features a staggered start, and runners go one lap around the track, remaining in their assigned lanes for the entire race. Runners must set their own pace rather than marking their speed against a competitor's.

The 800m and 1500m involve kick, or speed, versus steady-pace tactics. Jim Ryun preferred to finish strong. But Filbert Bayi began to change the style of middle distance running by setting a very fast pace early, then holding on with amazing strength. The increased strength of Bayi and others, like Alberto Juantorena of Cuba, have begun to make 800m similar to the 400m—more like a sprint than a middle distance run. These improved runners don't wait around for a strong finishing kick; they start early.

In the 400m, runners circle the track twice and must stay in their lanes for the first half-lap. Thereafter, runners converge in a pack. Position becomes important because every inch or centimeter from the inside curve adds distance to the race. In 1968, American Lee Evans set a record in this event, 43.86, which lasted 10 years.

In 1960, New Zealander Peter Snell's training regimen began to be widely copied after he won the 800m despite relative inexperience. Under coach Arthur Lydiard, Snell ran 100 miles a week. This was considered revolutionary. Until then, middle distance training consisted of a series of much shorter runs. The new methods helped improve both middle distance and distance performances.

The 1500m is 110 meters or 120 yards shorter than a mile. Roger Bannister's sub-four-minute mile preceded several other runners' equally barrier-breaking performances in the 1500m race.

Distance events: Women compete in a 3000m run, men compete in a 5000m run, and both compete in the 10,000m event. The 10,000m, which is equal to 6.2 miles, has been a men's event since 1912 but only became a women's Olympic event in 1988.

> "You can't be a champion in a week or a year. You must accept a time of suffering."
> —Algeria's Hassiba Boulmerka, winner of the 1992 women's 1500m title

In longer distances like the 10,000m, unnecessary motion is avoided. Knee action is slight, arm movements are reduced to a comfortable minimum, and strides are much shorter than those used by sprinters or middle distance runners. When in full stride, the distance runner lands on the ball of his or her foot, lowers the heel briefly, then drives forward off the toes.

Dominant runners are able to shatter their opponents with sudden bursts of speed at various stages of the race. They can run an extremely fast lap, then cruise for a while, then run another fast lap, while still holding back strength for a finishing kick.

Marathon: This is the longest Olympic running race, 26 miles, 385 yards. It is one of the most grueling as well. The race starts and finishes inside the stadium. In between, it is a road race and runners must contend with hills and concrete rather than a consistent, flat oval track.

Though the first women's Olympic marathon didn't take place until 1984, the first men's marathon was in 1896, from the Greek city of Marathon to Athens. Twelve years later, at the Games in London, the race's distance was extended slightly so British royalty could watch the start in front of Windsor Castle.

The marathon requires competitors to run hard when necessary while conserving strength for any possible difficulties ahead. As in all distance races, pace is important. Runners must also be able to ascend hills with efficient strides, and descend them evenly.

Weather can be a factor. Some runners can handle warm temperatures, or cool ones, better than others. But a temperature above 70 degrees Fahrenheit is considered difficult on any runner.

Steeplechase: This challenging event covers 3000 meters. Runners must contend with a course full of obstacles, among them 28 hurdles and seven water jumps. The hurdles are three feet (91.4cm) high and solid—they can't be knocked over. The top surface of the hurdles is five inches wide so runners can step on them, though most do not. The water jumps are preceded by a hurdle. Beyond the hurdle is a pool of water 12 feet (3.7m) square and, at the deepest point closest to the hurdle, 27 inches (70cm) deep. The bottom of the pool slopes up, and runners often use the water's surface to soften their landings.

Steeplechasers are distance runners and, because of the uniqueness of the event, specialists. They generally don't compete in other events, though there have been exceptions. The Finn Ville Ritola and the Kenyan Kip Keino, both runners but novice steeplechasers, won the event in 1924 and 1972, respectively.

Hurdles: These are basically sprint races made tougher with a series of barriers. Women run the 100m and 400m hurdles, the latter only since 1984. The hurdles stand two feet, nine inches in the shorter race and two feet, six inches in the longer. For men, the barriers stand three feet in the 400m, and three feet, six inches in the 110m.

FACT: Pyambuu Tuul, a one-eyed Mongolian runner, finished the men's marathon in just over four hours. The last person to finish the run, Tuul was shooed away from the finish line because the Olympic stadium was busy with the closing ceremony.

Hurdlers start their race like sprinters, getting up to speed as quickly as possible. In approaching a hurdle they jump and lean forward, trying to clear the barrier without breaking their running stride. The first leg over the hurdle hits the ground sharply while the second clears the hurdle at almost a right angle to the body.

Runners are not penalized for pushing over hurdles, though contact with the uprights often slows them. There are 10 hurdles in each race. High hurdlers take three steps between, and runners in the 400m take 13 to 15, the longer the stride the better. It takes dexterity and great timing to be a hurdler, and not all sprinters are successful hurdlers.

The hurdles themselves are made of wood and metal, and they can be knocked over with a force of eight pounds (four kilograms).

Relays: Track teams are often made up of sprinters and middle distance runners who can also run relays or the hurdles. So countries with medal-winning sprinters will often field a strong relay team as well. The events for both men and women are the 4 × 100 meters and the 4 × 400 meters.

Four runners make up a relay team, and each runs a leg, a quarter of the race's distance. When each runner finishes a leg, he or she passes a hollow tube called the baton to the next runner. A key to winning a relay race is an efficient and effective baton passage. The two runners must exchange the baton within a passing zone, and the team is disqualified if the exchange takes place outside the zone, or for failing to carry the baton across the finish line.

Ideally, the baton passer and baton receiver should be in full stride when the hand-off takes place. The receiver needs to reach full speed quickly. Typically, the receiver will be facing forward with his or her hand outstretched behind. Though speed is important, a team skilled in passing the baton can often beat a faster team that exchanges poorly.

Walking: This is one of the most unheralded of Olympic track events. A women's 10k (10,000m) walk was added to the Olympic program in 1992. The walking race makes for an unusual spectacle as well, with men and women sashaying down the street, seemingly half-walking and half-running, shoulders pumping and hips rolling.

There is a reason for this display, of course. It is to prove the competitors are walking and not running, the latter being faster but illegal. The rules require the walker's front foot to touch the ground before his or her rear foot leaves the ground. Also, while the foot is on the ground, the leg must be bent for a moment. If it is not, the walker is warned the first time, then disqualified by a judge. The offense is called "lifting."

This, then, leads to the odd form. Walking is much less popular than marathon running, but it undoubtedly takes the same endurance and stamina.

Great Britain's Linford Christie wins the men's 100-meter race in 9.96 seconds during the Olympic Games in Barcelona. At far left is U.S.A.'s Dennis Mitchell, who placed second in 10.02. *AP/Wide World Photos*

The 1908 Olympics featured a 10,000m and a 10-mile walk, and currently three walking events are staged: the men's 20,000m and the 50,000m walk, and the women's 10,000m (or 10k) walk. The 50,000m walk was dropped from the 1976 Olympics, then added again after competitors complained.

Official world records in walking races can be set only on a track. Olympic races take place on the road, so they are not eligible for world record consideration.

Walking rules are difficult to judge, and walkers are believed to have generally increased the amount of unbroken contact with the ground. Times have increased significantly over the years—20 percent during the last 40 years in the 50,000m walk, compared to about 5.5 percent in the marathon run.

Hopefuls—Men's Events

Linford Christie

If you enjoy a little theater with your sports, you have to hope that Great Britain's Linford Christie, considered by some as the greatest, big-event sprinter in the world as late as the summer of 1995, shows up in the starting blocks at the 100-meter dash in Atlanta.

What are the odds of that?

Hard to tell. Christie, the defending Olympic champion in the 100-meter dash, tearfully announced his decision not to compete in the 1996 Games during an appearance on British television in June 1995.

"Athletics isn't my life," said the sprinter who will be 36 when the Games begin in Atlanta.

A month later at the British National Championships, Christie, slowed by a sore knee, finished fourth in his qualifying heat, failing to make the final. That was his out. He could have quit right there and been done with it. Instead, he requested a "guest" spot in the final from British track officials, got it—"a gesture to the crowd and Linford," a spokesman said—and won.

Shortly after that, Christie, who at age 32 in Barcelona was the oldest man to win the 100-meter dash in Olympic history, won the 100-meter race at the Bislett Games, defeating, among others, Canada's Donovan Powell, 11 years his junior.

Before that race, Christie had said, "I love athletics dearly."

And after? "In the beginning all I wanted to do was be the fastest in the world for one year," he said. "Now, I think it's best if I get out on top."

Still, doubts abound. Call British track and field officials and ask the odds of Christie, who won a silver medal in the 100 in Seoul, competing in Atlanta and they throw up their arms and refer you to Christie's agent.

She doesn't return phone calls.

In fact, like most athletes who manage to succeed at ages once considered far past the prime—"People have said I was too old since I was 26," Christie has said—the great Brit has toyed with the idea of retirement before. That was back in 1991, when Christie ran a personal best of 9.92 at the world championships in Tokyo—and lost.

"Can you imagine," he asked, "running a 9.92 and finishing fourth?"

Perhaps more perplexing—and tiresome—than age is the treatment Christie receives in the British tabloids.

"If (the media) don't write about me," he has said, "they don't eat."

According to one report, shortly after Christie's mother passed away from cancer, not long after Christie's retirement announcement, Christie's father received a call from a photographer from a London tabloid requesting a shot of Mabel Christie's body. The sprinter, who has a brother who has been in and out of trouble with the law, figures that retirement from the sport would get him off the front page.

FACT: Carl Lewis is the only track and field athlete to capture a gold medal in each of the past three Olympic Games.

Christie, a native of Jamaica, moved with his family to London at age seven, where his father worked as a porter for the BBC. The sprinter, who didn't become totally involved in athletics until age 25, trains at West London Stadium, next to Wormwood Scrubs, a notorious prison for hard-core criminals. Before running, he worked with troubled youths. He is as recognizable around the world as his long-time rival and foil, Carl Lewis, and, like Lewis—the Ali to Christie's Joe Frazier—Christie is known for flamboyant running costumes and his candor.

Lewis, whom Christie defeated in a much-ballyhooed $150,000 head-to-head race in 1993, and who also has managed to stretch his career, mostly through the long jump and the relays, "has that gift of gab," Christie told *Sports Illustrated*. "He keeps fooling everybody, making people believe that he's on top. He thinks he's immortal. But no one lives forever."

"Mentally it's all very taxing," Christie says. "Because at the end of the day, no matter how many athletes have broken 10 seconds, or set world records, I am The Guy out there. I'm the Olympic champion. I'm always the only European going against four or five Americans. It's like me versus all the rest. And it's very, very lonely. Sprinters are very aggressive people. Hurdlers, for example, can talk to each other; sprinters cannot. Hurdlers go against barriers, but sprinters go against each other."

Even before his retirement announcement, Christie said publicly that he would run in Atlanta only if he feels he can win another gold medal.

"At a certain point it becomes like boxing," he said. "You see the young fighters coming up, sparring partners start to hurt you, pretty soon someone punches you flat out in the face and you think, 'Why am I doing this?' Look at Foreman and Ali. I'm not going out like that."

Problem is, first, no one's quite landed that knockout punch just yet.

And, second, when Christie did announce his retirement, it came with a fusillade aimed toward British track and field officials for spending money to import foreign athletes to British meets instead of supporting him.

"I turn up for my club and run for free," he said. "But the British Athletic Federation is paying the top Americans to bring them here."

All of that notwithstanding, the real question remains:

Is Linford Christie certain he can't slip one by Father Time one more time?

Or, is Linford Christie just making noise?

An Olympic sprint champion at age 36?

Absurd.

But that's what they said about the same possibility at age 32.

Stay tuned.

—Eric Kinkopf

Mark Croghan

OK, so you won't see this on an MTV special. But it's still one good spring-break tale.

It's 1991, and Mark Croghan, currently the top U.S. hopeful in the 3,000-meter steeplechase, is a 1,500- and 3,000-meter distance runner at Ohio State University. Plain track. Which means no water hazards, no hurdles.

Croghan's performances are also rather plain. Which means that he doesn't qualify for the Buckeye track team's spring-break trip for competition in Florida.

So Croghan hooks up with a pair of buddies and heads for the sunshine anyway. On his own. A *real* vacation. But once in Florida, he takes a flier and decides to enter a pair of races as an open athlete, unaffiliated with his OSU team. He enters the steeplechase, which he's never run.

And he wins—twice.

And qualifies for the NCAA Championships.

And, quite incredibly, another Olympic athlete is born.

How did his Ohio State coaches react to Croghan's feat?

"They were surprised to see me win," says the former choirboy with the choirboy looks. "I had gone on the previous two spring-break trips with the Ohio State team, but we had just gotten a new coach and his philosophy was to leave behind those runners who weren't performing. And being left behind was the sort of motivation I needed."

As for the event, Croghan says that he'd had a former teammate who ran the steeplechase. His marriage to the event? Just managed to find something he was good at, he says. It wasn't exactly love at first sight, but more something he's learned to like.

"It's sort of an event I've adapted to," he says.

"Mark was a competitive runner at Ohio State, but nothing outstanding," his father, Dan, says. "He hadn't really distinguished himself. He found something he really enjoyed."

"It just kind of came easy to me," Croghan told the *Canton Repository.* "I had been at Ohio State almost three years and I wasn't running the way I wanted to. Things just seemed to come together for me in the steeplechase."

Croghan, 28 (b. January 8, 1968), a native of Akron, Ohio, and the former cross-country coach at his alma mater, is now being heralded as one of the best young American distance runners to come along in years. The last four years he's been ranked either No. 1 or No. 2 nationally in the steeplechase. He was ranked No. 4 in the world both in 1994 and 1995.

His trademarks are boldness and versatility. He likes to go against the best in the world. And he can push the pace and lead from the gun, run with the lead pack, or lay off the lead and kick hard at the finish.

"He's also smart," Dan Croghan says. "Mark agonizes about races. He'll sit back and reflect on what he needs to do in a race or against a certain set of runners. When Mark gets beat, it's never because he did something dumb. It's tough to outthink Mark."

"Mark's always had the potential and the mental toughness," said his college coach, Lee LaBadie.

Plans are fine, Mark says, "but you also have to be able to adapt."

Croghan began making a name for himself in 1991 at the NCAA Outdoor Championships in a race against Samuel Kibiri, a Kenyan who was competing for Washington State University. Like his father says, Croghan had his strategy planned, his mind set. Kibiri had outkicked Croghan in the steeplechase two months earlier at the Penn Relays, leaving the Buckeye gasping in the dust. During the championships at the University of Oregon's Hayward Field, Kibiri was trailing Croghan, but running so close to him that *Sports Illustrated's* Kenny Moore wrote, "Sometimes (Kibiri) seemed to be steering Croghan with a hand on his elbow."

(Or, as Dave Kuehls wrote a bit more colorfully in *Runner's World:* "Kibiri was perched on his outside shoulder like a guilty conscience.")

"I think the Kenyans do that," Croghan later said, "to get you distracted, to take some energy out of you."

A less disciplined runner might have panicked. Croghan did not. His plan was to sprint for home early.

"I wanted to run the next-to-last lap so hard that from then on it would be survival," Croghan said.

Croghan more than survived, running, at that time, the fastest time in the world for 1991.

As *SI's* Moore observed. "Croghan will surely run faster. No man can run harder."

"That was definitely a big race for me," Croghan said. "No one expected me to win. Kibiri had beaten me twice. He'd blown me away at the Penn Relays."

Croghan, who made the 1992 Olympic team but failed to qualify for the steeplechase final, *has* run faster. In 1993, he ran a personal best of 8:09.76 at the World Championships, missing the American record by 59 hundredths of a second.

Dan Croghan smiles when he recalls his son's early years, which gave no indication of running prowess.

"Mark always had a lot of energy. It didn't dawn on us that he had that kind of stamina until he began running competitively."

Dan Croghan said football was his younger son's first love. (Mark has an older brother and a younger sister.) It turned out to be unrequited. It's tough to develop a relationship with that sport when you weigh less than 100 pounds entering high school.

The NFL's loss is the U.S. track team's gain.

"He's very well organized and extremely disciplined," Dan Croghan says of Mark, who now checks in at 5-feet-9 and a whopping 135 pounds. "Most distance runners have to be. They have to get themselves out of bed to train, no matter what the weather is. When Mark puts his mind to do something, no one can talk him out of it. He puts a plan together."

And Mark Croghan's planning on a medal in Atlanta.

You doubt him?

Just ask Sam Kibiri.

—Eric Kinkopf

Darnell Hall

Darnell Hall stands on an asphalt track at a middle school. He is being interviewed by a reporter from the *Detroit Free Press*.

Hall, dubbed a "quote machine" by some reporters, is in his elements—plural.

"I come out here because it's the only place I find peace and quiet," says Hall, an emerging 400-meter star and a member of the reigning Olympic champion 4 × 400-meter relay team. "This is my safety zone. No matter what problems I have away from this track, when I come here, I can clear my mind and think straight. For me, stepping on the track is like walking into a church."

Hall, 24 (b. September 26, 1971), a Detroit native and the youngest Olympian on the 1992 U.S. track team, was born and raised in a Detroit housing project, and still calls his old neighborhood home. Few recognize him as a world-class athlete. When he visits the bank to open his safe-deposit box and touch his gold medal, the tellers have no idea what he's there to see.

"I've worked real hard to get where I am," he says. "Sometimes it bothers me. I see athletes complain about having to sign autographs and do interviews and I'd love to do that. I'm not saying I need to be a celebrity and live in a $2 million house, but it would be nice to be recognized for being an Olympian."

Recognition could be closer than Hall thinks. At the 1995 U.S. Track and Field Championships in Sacramento, Calif., he took a bronze medal in the 400, behind world champion Michael Johnson and world-record holder Butch Reynolds.

"I knew I was up with the big boys. I just had to prove it at a national meet," Hall said. "I used to be afraid to run against the best. Now, I get revved up. I'm right on pace for 1996, and I promise you, I will not fade."

Hall, who adorned his left shoulder after the 1992 Olympics with a now-trademark tattoo of the five Olympic rings, had earlier won the 1995 World Indoor title.

His life wasn't always so grand.

Hall began life as a sickly, three-pound, seven-ounce baby. But his family was always at his side.

So was the Detroit community. When the word got out in 1992 that Hall's parents, Nelson, a factory worker, and Dana, at the time an unemployed nurse, couldn't attend the U.S. Olympic trials in New Orleans, a pair of local small businessmen and a group of Hall's relatives pitched in to cover the airfare and hotel costs.

Hall, who usually travels alone because of the expense, was extremely grateful.

"It means so much to have my parents by my side," Hall said afterwards in gratitude for the generosity. "I have a chance to be something and I want [my father] to be something right along with me. My dad was a great athlete who never had a chance and I'd like to share with him this beautiful experience."

Hall, who grew up in a neighborhood that mainly knows defeat, knew from the time he was in grade school that he wanted to be something special.

Calvin Johnson, who began coaching Hall in 1993, set out to make some adjustments in Hall's technique. Yes, even a gold-medal Olympian can use an overhaul every now and then.

"Darnell was getting by on pure strength and endurance," says Johnson, who figures that Hall might not reach his peak until the 2000 Olympics in Sydney, Australia. "That will work if all you want to be is world-class. But he wants to be up there with the elite, and that means picking up his foot speed in the first 200 meters and changing his entire racing philosophy."

Says Hall: "I had to change the whole way I approach a race, and that was hard. I'd have a bad race and then I'd dwell on it for three or four days. Calvin taught me to relax, correct my mistakes and be a man. I've matured so much since meeting him."

After the 1995 race in Sacramento, he said: "My heart is stronger than anybody's. If I'm with somebody in the last few meters, my heart is bigger. I don't care who it is; it can be Carl Lewis or Michael Johnson. I'm gonna give it all I've got. I showed I belong among the best. I made a statement that I'm not a coward—I won't run fast one time, then fall back into the crowd. I'll do whatever it takes to be a threat."

And like the tweaks to his technique, Hall's motivation also undergoes changes.

To wit: He wasn't talking quite so bravely before the 1992 trials. Coming out of Blinn Junior College in Brenham, Texas, he went to New Orleans just hoping to be noticed.

"I want people to ask, 'Who's that guy? A quarter-miler from Detroit?'" he said. "I want to show that a guy from Detroit can make it if he really tries. I control my destiny, and I can be a champion. When I step on that line, that's what I'll be thinking. I'm going to be hungrier than those big-name guys."

Those big-name guys?

After Atlanta, Darnell Hall may be one of them.

Or just, *the* one.

Period.

—Eric Kinkopf

Michael Johnson

Michael Johnson could use one of those old American Express commercials. You know the script.

"Do you know me? I'm Michael Johnson, greatest 200- and 400-meter sprinter in the history of the world."

Huh?

Exactly.

"I do feel underappreciated at times," Johnson says. "People don't understand the magnitude of what I've done."

FACT: Michael Johnson is the only person ever to have run both the 400 under 44 seconds and the 200 under 20 seconds.

Simply put, Johnson, perhaps the fastest human alive, and the favorite in both the 200- and 400-meter races at Atlanta, is the only athlete to be ranked number one in the world during the same year in both the 200- and 400-meter dashes.

Ever.

Repeat—ever.

At the 1994 U.S. Championships in Sacramento, he won both the 200 and 400. It was the first time that someone captured both national titles at the same time since Maxie Long did it in 1899.

But Johnson, 28 (b. September 13, 1967), a Dallas native, is used to a certain facelessness.

In grade school, where he won a running ribbon or two, Johnson was "a short, fat little fellow," his father, Paul, a truck driver, says.

Johnson's high school track coach remembers him as a kid who, "with his glasses, looked like a little squirrel."

Joel Ezar, the coach at Skyline High, told the *Dallas Morning News,* "One day he came out and said he wanted to run track, and I said, 'Great.' Of course, we never turn anyone down."

Johnson left high school without a state track title.

His college track coach at Baylor University, Clyde Hart, says, "I'd like to say I was a genius for recruiting him, but really, all I knew was that we had a kid who could help our relay teams. I never projected him to be even a conference champion."

And now?

After the championships in Sacramento, the executive director of U.S.A. Track and Field compared Johnson to Jesse Owens. European sports reporters have all but literally given Johnson the crown formerly worn by Carl Lewis, as king of the oval.

What happened?

Easy. Michael Johnson got fast. *Very* fast.

He also started to get serious. *Very* serious.

"I had no idea what I was doing in high school," he told the *Dallas Morning News.* "I was running off raw talent. I never really got in shape in high school. I never practiced that much. I never matured as a runner. I regret that now."

Ezar says Johnson started tapping more than just his physical potential. "He's got a killer instinct that you can't coach. He's got an inner burn that you never see."

Johnson, who speaks in a basso rumble and has been described as "reserved, almost to the point of being dull," says: "Off the track, I'm mellow and I don't really worry too much. But on the track, I'm very aggressive. On the track, that's where I'm an athlete."

In fact, Johnson so finely tuned his talents that he says he can tell the difference between a 19.9 and 20-flat—without a stopwatch. "Yeah, I know pretty close." Johnson arrived at the 1992 Games in Barcelona as the favorite in both the 200- and 400-meter races. He went home emptyhanded.

He didn't attempt the 400. He didn't even qualify for the 200 final, after suffering a bout of food poisoning brought on by a bad pan of paella.

"This is the Olympic Games, the one I wanted," a distraught Johnson said after the '92 races.

"That's it," he says, three years later. "The Olympics is going to be the big show." So, he's gearing up for Atlanta, big time.

Not so much in his track workouts. A millionaire from appearance fees, Johnson still lives in an off-campus apartment in Waco, Texas, and still trains with Clyde Hart.

"He's treated the same as he was as a freshman," Hart says. "Trains the same as ever. No secret workouts, here."

Johnson, 6-feet-1 and about 183 pounds, now has gone after it in the weight room. He added about 10 pounds to his upper body—and he's running faster.

"That is strange," Johnson says about the apparent contradiction of adding weight but moving faster. "But everything I put on is muscle in the upper body. The stronger I am in my upper body, the better I'm able to hold my form. That's one reason my 400 time has improved."

Has that made him the world's fastest human?

"That depends," he told the *Dallas Morning News*. "Usually, it's the 100-meter guy who is called the fastest man in the world, although if you moved him to the 200, he might not be the fastest. If you're talking in terms of miles per hour, that title has to go to the 200-meter man."

At the World Track and Field Championships in August 1995, Johnson won three gold medals: In addition to his unprecedented double in the 200 and 400, he anchored the winning 4 × 400 relay team.

Johnson, who fancies junk food and chocolate and, naturally, fast cars—he has a 1991 Corvette convertible—has been busy off the track, too. He's petitioned international track officials to alter the race schedule in Atlanta so that he can compete in both the 200- and 400-meter races.

Johnson has said that he definitely would not try to run both races unless he could run all four rounds of the 400 before beginning the 200-meter rounds.

Although negotiations are still ongoing, International Amateur Athletics Federation president Primo Nebiolo began some juggling.

"I wrote to him," Nebiolo said. "I wrote, 'Be tranquil. The schedule is good and you can be the hero of athletics in Atlanta.'"

Two races. Two golds?

"I'm capable," Johnson says, "of winning an Olympic double."

Then what more would a guy have to do to get a little recognition?

—*Eric Kinkopf*

Bob Kennedy

Bob Kennedy is not bashful. "I'm not in this sport to make the national team every year or merely make another Olympic team," the 5,000-meter specialist told *Runner's World.* "I want to win the gold medal. That's the pinnacle of any runner's career. To win Olympic gold, you have to beat the best in the world on the one day when (the other runners) are most likely to be at their best."

Robert Owen Kennedy, Jr., 26 (b. August 18, 1970), was marked as a runner to watch after finishing fifth in the 1987 National Junior Championships as a 16-year-old junior at North High in Westerville, Ohio. This summer, Kennedy carries the U.S. hopes in the 5,000 meters, a race no U.S. Olympian has medaled in since 1964, when Bob Schul and Bill Dellinger placed first and third, respectively.

Recently, the distance events have been dominated by Kenyans, Ethiopians, Moroccans, and Algerians. Quatar and Burundi runners have recently been added to the list.

America has produced women distance champions—Mary Decker Slaney, Joan Samuelson, and Lynn Jennings, to name a few. A pair of transplanted South Africans—Sydney Maree and Mark Plaatjes—have fashioned a few international highlights for the red, white, and blue in the 5,000 and marathon, respectively. But American kids?

The last two are simply fond memories—Steve Prefontaine in the mid-'70s and Craig Virgin in the early '80s.

"We could produce quarterbacks," wrote *Track & Field News* reporter Marc Bloom. "Where were the distance runners?"

Well, Bob Kennedy is one. And he is here—now.

While showing up is part of the equation, it isn't the answer, especially when the main competition comes from a bottomless resource of Kenyan runners.

To bring home the gold, Kennedy, who qualified for the final heat in 1992 at Barcelona but finished a disappointing twelfth, will need to be faster, quicker, and stronger than the Kenyans. He has an answer for that challenge, too.

"The mystique of the Kenyan athletes is not there for me any longer," he told *Track & Field News* after training with a group of the always-fabled runners. "They're just men. They're beatable. An Olympic medal is a legitimate goal for me."

Said Kennedy: "Early on, I did have an inferiority complex. As soon as opponents heard that you were an American, they figured that you were average or no good at all. And that was true. Now, I have no inferiority complex."

Kennedy, the only child of Bob, Sr., who set a New Jersey two-mile record in high school and a three-mile mark at Indiana University, and Barbara, who runs 10Ks, says, "My father told me, whether it be baseball or running or playing the saxophone, make sure you go 100 percent."

Kennedy junior settled on track after testing his talents in football, basketball, and soccer.

Kennedy the elder says: "Bob was always allowed to make his own decisions. We sometimes talked about running at the dinner table, but I tried to bite my tongue and let him come along naturally."

And he did.

And although a more relaxed attitude toward his development probably cost him a shot at a sub-four-minute mile in high school, it paid off big at Indiana with 23 Big Ten titles, a pair of NCAA cross-country championships, an NCAA indoor mile title, and an NCAA outdoor title in the 1,500 meters.

"My high school coaches exercised great patience," Kennedy says. "They expected that I would move on to an even higher level after I left them."

Indeed, he has. At Indiana, Kennedy came under the tutelage of legendary track coach Sam Bell.

"What I'll always remember about Bob, is his victory in the NCAA cross-country race as a freshman (in 1988)," Bell told *Track & Field News.* "As we were leaving the course, he said, 'I've got to forget about this and look ahead.'"

And what about that, lately?

Kennedy ended 1994 with personal records in the 5,000 (13:02.93), the 3,000 (7:53.33, an American record), and the mile (3:56.21). *Track & Field News* ranked him No. 4 in the world, the highest placing by an American runner since 1985.

Noted running author Hal Higdon describes Kennedy's running style as both otherworldly and earthly.

"Bob Kennedy runs with an economy of motion that seems mystical. His knees rise and fall rapidly (and) his arms move in rhythm, but his torso remains still . . . no expression on his face. His eyes stare straight ahead. (And) because Kennedy doesn't have the same snap as the better kickers, he's developed a style built around setting a punishing pace and surging relentlessly, frequently, almost foolishly, until those in his wake refuse to pay the cost of staying near."

Fellow 5,000-meter hopeful Reuben Reina gives a slightly different analysis. "Bob showed us Americans that we can run with anyone."

Ten-thousand meter hopeful Todd Williams echoes the sentiment. "That's one thing I learned from Bob. I don't let the Kenyans intimidate me. Once you're beat mentally, you might as well not even go to the line."

Says Kennedy: "A lot of my speed comes from muscle memory. If you repeat something often enough, you become adept at it."

Repeat this all ye Kenyans: Bob Kennedy, U.S. threat. Then, commit it to memory. (No fools, there. They probably already have.)

—Eric Kinkopf

The Kenyans

When asked which runners he fears most, Noureddine Morcelli, a middle-distance runner from Algeria, never hesitates.

"The *new* Kenyans," Morcelli says. "There are *always* new Kenyans."

Hyperbole?

Hardly.

Consider this: When the dust settled after the 1992 Kenyan Olympic trials in Nairobi, 1988 gold medalists Paul Ereng, Peter Rono, Julius Kariuki, and John Ngugi, reigning world champions Billy Konchellah, Moses Tanui, Moses Kiptanui, and world-record-holding steeplechaser Peter Koech had failed to make the team.

The Kenyan contingent in Barcelona still won two golds, three silvers, and a pair of bronze medals, including a medals sweep in the 3,000-meter steeplechase.

More recently, Kenyan 5,000-meter hopeful Josephat Kapkory was asked about his chances of making the Kenyan Olympic team. He had just defeated three countrymen in a 5,000-meter road race in San Francisco.

"There are so many great Kenyan runners," Kapkory said. "But I'll give it a try."

In previewing the 1996 Olympics in the summer of 1995, *Runner's World* predicted that the race for the 10,000-meter gold medal would come down to Morocco's Khalid Shah—who won the 10,000-meter gold in Barcelona in a duel with Kenya's Richard Chelimo—versus . . . "the Kenyans."

Kenya is a land of 17 million people. Sometimes it just seems as though every one was born a brilliant distance runner.

The Kenyan mystique was born in the late 1960s and early 1970s when Kenyan police inspector Kip Keino won gold and silver medals at the 1968 and 1972 Olympics, leading Kenyan contingents that won an astounding eight distance medals at the 1968 games and six in 1972 (and seven in Seoul). Keino attributed his successes to training in the thin air and mountain terrain of his native country, saying that it translated into stamina and strength in flatland races.

Former Kenya national coach Mike Kosgei has said, "It's attitude, not altitude."

Richard Chelimo's younger brother, Ismael Kirui, the 1993 world champion in the 5,000 meters, says, "Nothing is easy in this life."

(Nonetheless, Finland's Annemarie Sandell flew to Kenya to train before winning the 1995 junior world cross country title. Sandell did everything the Kenyans did, including eating *ugali*, the cornmeal-mush staple of Kenyan runners. Interestingly enough, Sandell kicked away from three Kenyans to win the race.)

Altitude or attitude, the only thing you need to validate the Kenyans' continued distance and middle-distance successes is the agate page of your local sports section. These entries were included in 1995 spring and summer editions:

- Cosmas Ndeti wins his third straight Boston Marathon, becoming the youngest of seven three-time Boston Marathon winners. Ndeti, who again ran the second—and more difficult—half of the race faster than the first half, was 23 at the time. None of the other six three-time winners had won their third Boston Marathon before age 30.

- Led by Paul Tergat and Ismael Kirui, Kenya places four runners in the top ten in the World Cross-Country Championships in Durham, England.

- Kirui wins a 10-mile road race in Washington, D.C., breaking the 10-mile road-race mark set by countryman William Sigei a year earlier.

- Kirui, again, sets a 5,000-meter road-race mark in California. (His girlfriend, Rose Cheruiyot, also of Kenya, wins—and sets a women's record.)

- Joseph Kimani, running his second ever 10,000-meter race, sets a course record in Mobile, Ala. Countrymen Ondoro Osoro and Steve Nyamu finished second and third, respectively.

- Josephat Machuka sets a 12,000-meter world record at a race in Spokane, Wash., eclipsing a mark set by Kirui, who wins a 10K in Cleveland, while countryman Boniface Merande is winning the marathon.

- John Kagwe destroys a 10-year-old Pittsburgh Marathon course record, with a 2:10.24 and could have, some say, run two minutes faster on a flat course. Countryman Patrick Maturi is second.

- Joseph Kamau wins a 10-miler in Philadelphia.

Want a few more names?

The one that's on the tip of everyone's tongue is Daniel Komen, a double champion at the 1994 Junior World Championships, who is being hailed as the next superstar Kenyan, and five-time world cross-country champion John Ngugi, who was recently reinstated by the Kenyan track federation after a four-year ban in 1993 for refusing to take a drug test. Ngugi, the 1988 Olympic 5,000-meter champion, is shedding some 50 extra pounds and is targeting the Atlanta Olympics 5,000-meter race as his goal.

Want to bet against him?

Consider this: British bookies, who will take bets on anything from Princess Di to Hugh Grant, refused to make book on the 1995 World Cross-Country Championships, the first to be staged in England in more than a dozen years. Why? Everyone figured the Kenyans would win, so why bother wagering?

In light of all that, Kenya's competition is putting on a brave, new face. Or at least talking tougher.

American 5,000-meter hopeful Steve Kennedy says that he doesn't fear the Kenyans anymore.

"They're just men," Kennedy says.

There are, after all, some cracks in what used to be perceived as an invincible Kenyan solidarity.

Members of the Kenyan national team threatened to boycott the 1995 World Championships unless there were mass resignations by Kenyan track federation officials. The threat came after the firing of national team coach Kosgei.

"They think we are here to serve them instead of them serving us," said Yobes Ondieki, a former 5,000-meter world champion. "Some of the biggest thieves in our country are in the federation."

"A boycott is a sure way to get heard," said Moses Tanui, 10,000-meter world champ in 1991.

Kosgei worries that athlete discontent could affect Kenyan performances. He points out that Kenya won seven individual and team gold medals out of eight at the 1994 World Cross-Country Championships in Budapest, Hungary, but only five in England.

Only five.

Maybe it *is* attitude.

—Eric Kinkopf

Paul McMullen

Hello, Paul McMullen, world-famous . . . *runner?*

"In high school, you want to be separated from the runners, because you think they're wimpy," the Cadillac, Mich., native told *Track & Field News.* "I was a football man. I didn't want to be recognized as a runner."

As a senior at Cadillac High School, McMullen, at 6-feet-2 and 210 pounds, and a three sport letter-winner—basketball, track and football—filled in rather nicely as tight end, scoring six touchdowns (including an 87-yarder on a kickoff return in the homecoming game, at which he was crowned, naturally, King).

Now, almost 40 pounds lighter, McMullen, a 1,500-meter specialist, doesn't mind one bit being recognized as a thinclad. In fact, the way he came on in 1995, you would almost think he was looking for a little of that attention.

First, he finished third at the NCAA Indoor Championships behind a pair of Canadians. Then, he beat heavily favored Steve Holman in the U.S. National Championships in Sacramento in 3:43.90, to win a spot on the U.S. National Team. Finally, he ran a personal best at the Bislett Games in Oslo, Norway, with a 3:36.96, good for fifth place.

Suddenly, Paul McMullen, 24 (b. February 19, 1972), was more than just another runner. Suddenly, he was a U.S. hopeful in the metric mile.

All this from a less than auspicious start.

On McMullen's first day of track practice at Eastern Michigan University in Ypsilanti, Mich., in the fall of 1989, world-class times were the furthest thing from his mind.

"I just wanted to make it through practice," he told the *Cadillac Evening News.* "I went from never running over five miles a day in high school to 10 miles my first day of cross-country practice."

McMullen's recent surge up the ladder of U.S. milers is no accident. Mostly, it's a result of a rededication.

"Over Christmas in 1994, I put in a lot of extra work," he says. "Normally, that's the time I take it easy. This time, I made the decision to prepare myself better. There are a lot of things motivating me. For one thing, I'm motivated just to run faster. And I want to compete on the global level."

Bob Parks, McMullen's coach at Eastern Michigan, agrees with his student's assessment.

"Paul changed his attitude," Parks said, "not that it was bad. But the new attitude is what has taken him to another level. He's a great kid and a great competitor."

Motivation is one thing McMullen apparently understands.

Runner Jill Stamison, an 800-meter specialist whom McMullen was to marry in September 1995, was on the verge of hanging up her spikes when McMullen finally got through to her.

"He just never gives up," says Stamison, who'd never even placed in a conference meet until she started listening to McMullen. "I never thought that I was anything. He told me that I was and I started to believe it."

Last year, Stamison finished fourth in the NCAAs.

"In every aspect of his life he's like that," she says—'Never give up, don't get down about anything.' It can't help but be contagious."

McMullen downplays some of that.

"Jill and I are a team," he says. "It is really nice for both of us to do really good."

McMullen will, however, admit to understanding strategy and tactics—and he'll tell you so.

"I'm a true racer," he says. "You have to be able to adjust, because every race is unpredictable."

The race against Holman in the U.S. meet was a perfect example—and perhaps McMullen's real breakthrough.

The pace of that race was extremely slow, so slow that the usually laid-back Californians began booing. Through the first 400 meters the pace lagged behind the pace set by the women. McMullen soon took control, however, upping the tempo, then giving up the lead to Holman and another runner and drafting off them.

"Through the bell lap I took a deep breath and told myself, 'Paul, relax and start to build momentum,'" McMullen said. "When they came flying down the backstretch, I was still drafting off them and they were working a lot harder than me."

When Holman pulled to the outside to hold off the runner in second pace, McMullen dove for the hole.

"I took advantage of it," he said. "I took the most direct route to the finish line. Everyone sprinted and I hauled right down the pike. It was like a gift from heaven."

As for the Olympics, McMullen—who graduated from Eastern Michigan with a degree in accounting, is in training to become a certified financial planner, and still drives an '89 Omni—says: "I like to think that nobody scares me, that I have the ability to run with the best."

That attitude notwithstanding, he's managed to keep his humility.

"One thing I miss when I'm competing in a race in a city is the stars at night," says McMullen, who still cherishes his rural Michigan roots. "The stars help me bring everything into perspective because I feel so insignificant. You look up at a billion stars and you just feel what really goes on on Earth doesn't really matter that much. You are just a small speck of dust in a huge universe. Feeling insignificant releases the pressure."

The stars.

One day you're looking at them.

The next, you're reaching for them.

It's Paul McMullen's story.

—Eric Kinkopf

U.S.A.'s Quincy Watts races to an Olympic record time of 43.71 in the second heat of the men's 400-meter semifinals in Barcelona. He went on to win the gold with another Olympic record of 43.50. *AP/Wide World Photos*

Quincy Watts

The Q.

That what friends call defending Olympic 400-meter champion Quincy Watts.

"He's just a normal guy who likes to hang with his friends," Watts told the *Los Angeles Times*. "He doesn't sweat and bleed track. When he's competing, though, that's when he becomes the Q. Then he's taking care of business."

Which is exactly what Watts, 26 (b. June 17, 1970), who also won a gold medal in the 4 × 400-meter relay, did in Barcelona in 1992, in what some consider one of the greatest 400-meter races ever.

Watts passed runners down the backstretch and crossed the finish line in an Olympic-record 43.50 seconds, beating 1988 gold medal winner Steve Lewis by nearly three-fourths of a second.

"I was a little nervous because this was my first Olympic Games," Watts said. "But I was pretty pleased."

Suddenly, The Q, described as easy-going and soft-spoken, was arguably the fastest man in the world.

Which was no surprise to his father, Rufus. Quincy had told his dad eight years earlier, as a precocious 14-year-old, while watching Carl Lewis at the Los Angeles Olympics, that just that would happen.

Not that getting there was a simple matter.

Two years before that piece of innocent bravado, Quincy Watts was living in Detroit and headed for trouble. He was hanging around with the wrong crowd, cutting classes, getting suspended from school. His mother, Allitah Hunt, decided that her son needed male guidance. She sent him to Los Angeles to live with his father, Rufus Watts, a postal clerk.

"It took a lot of guts for her to make that decision," Quincy told the *Detroit Free Press*.

"Quincy was giving her so many problems," Rufus Watts said. "I just said, 'Send him to me. I'll turn him around.'"

Rufus Watts did.

When Quincy Watts came home with a poor grade, Rufus Watts held him out of basketball games. When Quincy Watts needed tutoring for the SAT test, Rufus Watts squeezed the money out of his salary. He also inundated his kid with inspirational messages:

"To succeed, you need backbone, not wishbone.

"Being the best means doing the things you hate to do when you need to do them.

"It's cloudy right now, but if you work hard, the sun will shine again."

The Q took it all to heart—eventually. He got himself straightened out.

"If I hadn't gotten out of Detroit, you would never have heard of Quincy Watts," Quincy told the *Los Angeles Times*. "I'm sure I would've fallen by the wayside."

The Q's biggest test of heart, however, came with a string of hamstring injuries beginning in the spring of his senior year of high school, when he tore his right hamstring. As a freshman sprinter at the University of Southern California he tore it again. As a sophomore, he strained his left hamstring, returned, and strained it again.

People were beginning to wonder if The Q was a *Mis-Q*— and at the tender age of 19.

"That was the low point," Rufus Watts says. "Quincy's been through a lot of adversity, but that was the worst. He really had to dig down deep that time."

When the track coach suggested that Watts abandon the sprints for the 400, Watts turned to football for a time, walking onto the USC team, regaining his competitive edge and building leg strength. He never caught a pass, never even played in a game. But he did regain his confidence.

"Football helped Q a lot," a USC teammate told the *Los Angeles Times*. "Football showed him how tough he could be."

In the spring of 1991, Watts turned back to track, and began focusing full-time on the 400.

"I ran away from the 400, at first, like most sprinters would," he says. "It's a grueling race. It hurts. Sprinters never experience that kind of hurt, and I was afraid. I began dreading coming to practice. But I was putting up some pretty good numbers, and I knew I could do even better."

He began to see himself becoming the world's fastest human. And he leaned on one of his father's proverbs: "Being the best means doing the things you hate to do when you need to do them."

"Once I did that," Watts says, "I stopped hating the 400."

At the 1992 Olympic Trials in New Orleans, Watts ran a 43.97-seconds race in the semis, the fastest 400 time in the world since the 1988 Olympics.

"When Quincy was young, he just ran off God's gift," Watts' coach, John Smith, said before the 1992 Olympics. "He didn't know about training or preparation or pressure. He just ran. And let me tell you, he was a beautiful runner. He was the *stuff.*"

Smith and Watts devised a strategy for Barcelona. The Q would use his sprinting mentality to build a lead in the first 200 meters and use his strength to finish off the race.

"I just told Quincy to fly like a bird and jump on someone early," Smith said after Watts' gold-medal effort in Spain. "He probably went out a little too fast and paid for it in the end. But I knew he could win the gold. It's a feeling I had."

Rufus Watts had spent countless hours holding stopwatches for Quincy, meeting with his son's teachers, watching The Q practice, motivating him. ("It's cloudy now, but if you work hard. . . . ")

"The sun is shining, now," the elder Watts told the *Los Angeles Times* before the 1992 Games.

Well, it certainly shone in Barcelona.

Most expect the forecast to be the same for Atlanta.

—*Eric Kinkopf*

Todd Williams

Todd Williams, former little fish in a fast pond, runs in anonymity.

While he was cruising with the leaders at the World Cross-Country Championships in April 1995, the track announcer in Durham, England, kept calling him Bob Kennedy, the better-known U.S. 5,000-meter runner and a close friend.

"That made me push harder," Williams said after the race. "I thought, 'I've got to make a name for myself.' "

Williams, 27 (b. March 7, 1969), of Monroe, Michigan, and a member of a so-called new breed of U.S. distance hopefuls that includes Kennedy and a handful of others, did just that.

Williams's ninth-place finish was the best by a U.S. runner since 1987. Pal Kennedy, who finished 14th, says, "Todd is the toughest of the [new breed] as far as pushing himself twice a day, seven days a week."

Williams—the same 5-feet-9 and 140 pounds he was in ninth grade—ran collegiately for the University of Tennessee. He trains alone in Knoxville, epitomizing the cliche of the loneliness of the long-distance runner.

"I do everything by myself so I don't have to worry about somebody else taking the pace," Williams told *Track & Field News.* "Then, when I get into a race, it's almost like practice. A race is always a harder effort, but mentally I'm so used to being out at practice clicking it off. For me, it's a big help mentally to train alone.

"People ask me why I don't move to a place like Boulder or Albuquerque [to train with other runners]. But the motivation I have is right here. If I can pull this off by myself—and I'm definitely driven, self-motivated; nobody has to push me out the door to do anything—then I'll feel that much more accomplished."

And, it's worked so far.

Williams won the Olympic trials 10K in 1992 and finished 10th in Barcelona, rated as the top American. A year later, he was ranked 10th internationally. The progression bodes well for Williams, who never placed higher than sixth in the NCAA Cross-Country Championships, but was the top U.S. runner at the world competition twice.

Williams credits experience for his improved quality.

"It's mainly a matter of you figuring out exactly what you have to go through and how much more you have to do to get to that level," he says. "It's just a process you have to go through in your mind. It's impossible to do that overnight."

Indeed, even when incredible progress comes, the other running shoe can clatter thunderously to the ground.

At the 1993 Bislett Games in Oslo, Williams recorded a 10K time of 27:40.37, slicing 22 seconds off his previous best. He still finished 300 meters behind the leader, Yobes Ondieki of Kenya.

"It was great to lower my PR [personal record]," Williams said. "But you can also look at the results and realize, 'I just cut my PR by 22 seconds and still got beaten by 300 meters.' On the other hand—and this is good—you stay humble. There's no overconfidence. So, you pat yourself on the back a little for the PR, but you also realize how much more work you have to do."

The race also helped Williams realize that he's ready for the next level. Which means a corresponding change in tactics.

"I can't go out slow, then catch people at the end," he says. "When the break is made, those guys are too damn good to catch in the last 220. To medal, you have to be smarter and run a lot closer to the front."

To accomplish those goals, Williams takes inspiration from fabled U.S. distance runner Steve Prefontaine, whose career was cut short by a fatal traffic accident.

"After reading so much about him, I realized that you only go through your career one time—and it's a short time. I think a lot of athletes just let races go by. It's an attitude of 'I'll do something different in the next one.' But Steve never looked at it like that. Each race to him was almost like his last one. I'd like to think I'm starting to run like that."

Though so intensely driven, Williams manages to keep things in perspective. He knows he has a tough job, but not one that is boring, confining, or mind-numbing.

"This is a heck of a job to have. The next 10–12 years seem like they'll be the best of my life. Traveling to different countries, competing, meeting people—and getting paid on top of that. It's pretty much a dream come true."

(The only thing he hates about training is wind: "I hate it. It seems the day I really want to pump one out, I'll wake up and the trees are touching the ground.)

All Todd Williams needs is a little honing to trim another 20–25 seconds off his time. That would put the former little fish at what he calls "shark level."

Which brings to mind a story Todd's father, Dave, tells. The elder Williams says that he knew his kid was going to be something special the day Todd asked him to go to the hardware store to buy an ax. Todd was just then getting interested in distance running and had figured that some backyard wood-chopping would help get him in shape.

"A few too many 'Rocky' movies, I guess," the junior Williams said a bit sheepishly in an interview with the *Detroit Free Press*. "I wanted to do anything to get an edge."

—*Eric Kinkopf*

Hopefuls—Women's Events

Gail Devers

Miraculous—that's the only way to describe Gail Devers's career. Devers has won gold medals in the 100-meter sprint at both the Olympics and the World Championships. She also has gone gold over the 100-meter hurdles as recently as 1995. That's not a bad résumé for someone who once thought her feet would have to be amputated.

A promising athlete in college, Devers became stricken with Graves' disease—a serious thyroid disorder—in 1988. She literally went from an appearance at the Seoul Olympics to being so ill that she could only crawl or be carried. Devers has estimated that she came within 48 hours of having her feet surgically removed due to the rigors of the radiation treatment she underwent for her condition. Saved by a change in therapy, she has mounted possibly the greatest comeback in track history. A former Olympic and world gold medalist in the 100-meter sprint, she will probably concentrate on the 100-meter hurdles in Atlanta. She won a gold medal in that event at the 1993 World Championships in Stuttgart, Germany.

Devers was born and raised in San Diego, the daughter of a Baptist minister. "We were a *Leave It to Beaver* family," she recalled in a May 10, 1993, *Sports Illustrated* profile. Her strict parents imposed all sorts of rules on Devers and her brother, and Devers never seemed to mind. She dreamed of becoming a school teacher, using her girlfriends as model "pupils." She began running track in high school, first as a distance runner and only later as a sprinter. By her senior year of high school she had won the 100-meter sprint and the 100-meter hurdles at the California High School Track Championships. She was offered a scholarship to the University of California, Los Angeles.

FACT: Take a ruler and mark off about two and a half inches. That's how much track separated runner-up Juliet Cuthbert from 1992 100m gold medalist Gail Devers.

The naive and sheltered Devers arrived at UCLA with great curiosity about her new college track coach, Bob Kersee. In the *Sports Illustrated* profile, she remembered that she expected him to be "an old white man." Instead she met a dynamic young individual who sized up her potential in an instant. After only a few practices, Kersee informed Devers that she would some day break the U.S. record in the 100-meter hurdles and that she would make the 1988 Olympic team. As if he were reading a crystal ball, Kersee predicted gold medals in Devers's future. "Regardless of whether his predictions were going to turn out to be true or whether he was just trying to motivate me, I liked them," Devers admitted in *Sports Illustrated*. "I hadn't run track until high school. I started as a distance runner. I hadn't had much coaching. So I thought that if he had all this faith in me, he'd coach me well. For quite a while Bobby believed in me more than I believed in myself."

As a senior at UCLA Devers set a new American record for the 100-meter hurdles. She easily qualified for the 1988 Olympics in that event, but when she got to Seoul her performance was inexplicably stale. Returning from the Summer Games, she began to experience strange weight fluctuations, fits of shaking, memory loss, migraine headaches, and temporary loss of vision in one eye. At times she menstruated without stopping, and the slightest scratch could cause her skin to bleed profusely. Doctors found a cyst on her thyroid gland, and the radiation treatments prescribed to correct the problem completely destroyed her thyroid. Worse, the treatments caused her feet to swell and ooze. She had to be carried around her apartment and could do virtually nothing on her own.

The condition of Devers's feet became so severe that her doctors thought they would have to amputate. As a last measure they changed her medication, and she began a dramatic recovery. In a month she was able to walk, and a year later, at the 1991 World Championships in Tokyo, she won a silver medal in the 100-meter hurdles.

The 1992 Olympics brought both triumph and disappointment. Devers won the 100-meter sprint in the closest finish ever recorded in an Olympic race—a mere one-hundredth of a second. In the hurdles, she jumped out to a commanding lead, only to trip over the final barrier and slide on her knees to a fifth-place finish. When fellow American Gwen Torrence suggested that some of the 100-meter competitors were using performance-enhancing drugs—without naming names—Devers did not involve herself in the controversy, even though Torrence seemed to be pointing a finger at her. "All I take is Cynthroit," she explained in *The New York Times* on August 2, 1992. "It fools my body into thinking I have a thyroid." Coach Kersee was a bit more emphatic in his defense of his star sprinter. "I'm tired of all these sour grapes," he complained to *The New York Times*. "Anybody who believes Gail has ever taken performance-enhancing drugs can kiss my butt."

> "Every hurdler in the world has got to be intimidated by Gail because they all know rule No 1: remove the hurdles and there's no way they can outsprint her."
> —*Bob Kersee on 100-meter hurdler Gail Devers*

Indeed, Gail Devers has never failed a drug test, and she emphatically denies using anything but the medicines she needs to combat her thyroid condition.

A different kind of controversy awaited Devers at the 1993 World Championships. There, once again, she raced to a photo finish in the 100-meter sprint, this time beating Jamaican Merlene Ottey by only several one-hundredths of a second. The finish was so close that Devers and Ottey were both given the same time on the scoreboard—only later did the judges announce that

Devers had won. The decision was not popular with the crowd at the event in Stuttgart, and in the ensuing media crush Devers was almost reduced to tears. She finally rallied, however, and stood up for herself. "I'm leaving this meet happy," she concluded, as reported by *Track & Field News* in November of 1993. "I believe everything happens for a reason, and this was just my time."

More chances await Devers at the 1996 Summer Games. Since 1994, when her world ranking in the 100-meter sprint dropped to ninth, she has been concentrating on the hurdles. She won the 100 hurdles at the 1995 U.S. Track Championship and holds the American record in the event. The athlete has admitted that she once considered herself "too small" to run hurdles, but her years of training with Kersee have given her confidence. It's no wonder. Asked about Devers's chances as a hurdler, Kersee told *Track & Field News* in May of 1993: "It's obvious there is no hurdler in the world as fast as Gail. The matter of control between hurdles, and how much time she spends in the air from takeoff to touchdown, will be the difference in how fast she runs the hurdles. But every hurdler in the world has got to be intimidated by Gail because they all know rule No. 1: remove the hurdles and there's no way they can outsprint her."

FACT: The Scan-o-Vision camera, which captures photo finishes of events, will be in use for the first time at the Atlanta Games. The camera shows a picture of time rather than space and the image it produces can determine a winner even if the athletes' times are identical.

Devers credits at least a part of her success to the lessons she learned from her long illness. "I'm stronger as a person; it's not hard for me to concentrate on the job at hand," she told *Track & Field News*. "I've said before that there's nothing that can come up in my life that I can't get over after going through what I did." She added of her experience: "I wouldn't wish it on anyone, but I'm happy I went through it. I think back . . . to March of 1991, when I was wondering if I would ever walk again, let alone run."

—*Anne Janette Johnson*

Meredith Rainey

Meredith Rainey skipped running track from seventh grade right through high school. She attended Harvard University, that bastion of academia, and graduated *cum laude*. Now she is on her way to her second Olympic appearance and will be a featured performer in the grueling 800-meter race. Rainey's career is a case of talent and desire overcoming a wealth of obstacles, from the demands of an Ivy League education to the dislocation of training three thousand miles from home. She will be an athlete to watch probably through the year 2000.

Born October 15, 1968, in New York City, Rainey grew up in the Crown Heights section of Brooklyn. Hers was a family of educated and socially-conscious parents and grandparents—her maternal great-grandfather had been burnt out of his house in Charleston, South Carolina, for daring to stand up to white people, and her grandmother was a respected civic leader in Brooklyn. The younger daughter of a school teacher and a police officer, Rainey attended private schools and began running track at age eight for the Atoms Track Club.

At twelve she abandoned track completely. Although she had been a winning sprinter, athletics never presented themselves as a high priority in her household—a premium was placed on education and getting into a top-ranked college. Rainey certainly accomplished that goal. She was accepted at Harvard University and enrolled in the autumn of 1986. In November of her freshman year she sought out the Harvard track coach and returned to competition. "I felt like I was coming home," she recalled in a June, 1993, *Runner's World* profile.

Despite the demands of her Harvard studies, Rainey soon excelled on the Ivy League track circuit. She began with the 400-meter race and then moved up to the 800 with gratifying results. In her junior year she won the event at the National Collegiate Athletic Association Championships—the first time an Ivy League woman had ever won a national collegiate track title. As a Harvard senior she not only turned in an honors thesis on the history of inner city settlement houses, she also won the 800-meter race at the U.S. Nationals.

"I came back to running with no expectations other than to have fun, meet people and get in shape. The idea that I would get to this level, make an Olympic team, was the furthest thought from my mind."
—*Meredith Rainey, in* Runner's World

Rainey graduated from Harvard in 1990 and developed a two-year plan that would take her to the Olympics. She finished third at the 1992 Olympic Trials and qualified for the U.S. team, but her experience in Barcelona was a great disappointment—she placed third in the first heat she ran and thus did not even qualify for the semifinals. "After working so hard to get there, having my whole Olympic experience amount to 2 minutes was a real emotional letdown," she admitted in *Runner's World.* "At the Trials, finishing third was as good as finishing first. In the Olympics, finishing third in my heat was as bad as finishing last."

In the wake of the 1992 Olympics, Rainey sought the help of coach Brooks Johnson, a former Olympic track coach and currently the director of track and field at Cal Poly San Luis Obispo. Working with Brooks meant that Rainey would have to leave New York City and live in California—a major sacrifice for someone who describes herself as an "East Coast person." Rainey spent two years in California with Johnson and still structures her workouts around his suggestions. For his part, coach Johnson told *Runner's World* that Rainey has true championship potential. "Meredith has the bloodlines of a true thoroughbred," he said. "She comes from one of the more accomplished, committed black families in America. She's very cerebral, but she doesn't trip herself up by the wrong kind of thinking. As far as running goes, she has done her studying and knows what's out there in terms of talent. She knows that hers is at the very top level. If she hadn't come to that assessment, she would have already taken her honors degree from Harvard and be well on her way in a career in public policy."

The career in public policy will have to wait. Now training primarily in Silver Spring, Maryland, with frequent visits to San Luis Obispo, Rainey has consistently improved her times in the 800-meter event. She was the 1995 U.S. champion with a time of 2:00.07 and is preparing to challenge in Atlanta. Rainey plans to continue her track career at least until the 2000 Olympics and then return to her scholarly pursuits. "I just don't think it takes a narrow-minded athlete to win," she explained in *Runner's World.* "It's the narrow-minded people who most often burn out. Running is fun for me because I know I can be better. Also, it's fun because it's not a life-or-death thing for me. It's an option. I'm doing it because I want to."

—*Anne Janette Johnson*

Mary Decker Slaney

Middle-distance running legend Mary Decker Slaney wants to end an Olympic jinx that has dogged her since 1976, and win a medal in 1996. Never mind that she has had almost two dozen rounds of surgery on her legs and will be pushing 40 at the next Summer Games—the feisty Slaney says she still has the will to compete and win. "Now that the Games are going to be in Atlanta in 1996, I'd like to be there—healthy and fit," she told *People* magazine on October 17, 1994. "I dream about being healthy. That's all I need to be."

When Slaney is healthy, she is great. In her prime years in the early 1980s she was competing against no one but the clock, compiling 36 American and 17 world records. In 1982 alone she was the fastest woman at *every distance* between 800 and 10,000 meters. She was also the first woman to run 880 yards in less than two minutes, and her American record in the 1,500-meter race (3:57.12) still stands. She won the 1982 Sullivan Award as best amateur athlete of the year and took home the Jesse Owens award as well. In the first-ever World Track and Field Championships in 1983, she cruised to gold medal finishes in both the 1,500-meter and the 3,000-meter races.

Olympic victories have been another matter. The determined runner, born on August 4, 1958, in Bunnvale, New Jersey, was a record-setter as a teen in the 800-meter and 1,000-yard distances. As a high school senior she was expected to attend the 1976 Olympic Games but was sidelined by painful stress fractures in her legs. The following year she underwent surgery for compartment syndrome, a muscle condition, and returned to championship form. Beginning in 1980, she broke records—both indoor and out—in such events as the mile, the 1,500-meter, the 2,000-meter, and the 3,000-meter. Once again Olympic glory eluded her in 1980, however. President Jimmy Carter decided that the Americans should boycott the Games that year because of the Soviet invasion of Afghanistan. Mary Decker buried her disappointment by competing in other international track and field events—and she began to prepare for 1984.

Even casual Olympics observers will remember the fateful 3,000-meter race Mary Decker ran at the 1984 Olympics in Los Angeles. As the race neared its end, she was tripped by South African Zola Budd and fell flat onto the track in obvious pain. A decade later, the runner recalled her disappointment in *People*. "Even though I had people telling me [Budd] did it intentionally, I never thought she did," Slaney said. "I don't hate her. I hated the fact that it was an opportunity for me that got messed up."

> "I dream about being healthy. That's all I need to be."
> —Mary Decker Slaney

Slaney—who married in 1985—kept running, grimly determined to outlast her injuries and outrace her opponents. She set a new world mile record in 1985 and qualified for the Olympics in 1988 with Olympics Trials victories in the 1,500-meter and the 3,000-meter. The injuries kept coming, however, and she was not a featured performer in either the 1988 or the 1992 Summer Games.

With a new round of Achilles tendon and heel surgery behind her, Slaney plans to make one last attempt at joining the

Olympic team. "I think women reach their peak in their mid-30's," she told *Sports Illustrated* on July 29, 1991. "If I can just stay healthy for one whole year, I know I can run better."

Slaney will celebrate her 38th birthday in 1996. She has a daughter who will be ten years old. Age is not necessarily a barrier in middle distance races, though. The top-ranked 1,500-meter racer of 1994 was Russian Yekaterina Podkopayeva, who was 42 at the time. Injuries are a more perplexing problem for Slaney—and the American competition has only gotten better.

One opponent who stands a good chance of stealing Slaney's thunder is Regina Jacobs, the 1995 American champion at 1,500-meters. Jacobs too is a seasoned veteran of Olympic competition, having qualified for both the 1988 and 1992 Summer Games. In both of her previous Olympic appearances, Jacobs failed to advance to the finals, but she has since been diagnosed and treated for a chronic iron deficiency. Her strength and endurance restored, she has returned to the middle distance races with a vengeance, capturing four U.S. outdoor 1,500-meter titles and the 1995 World Indoor 1,500-meter championship. Jacobs told *Runner's World* in August, 1995, that she has a "road map" planned for the Olympics and she is "more structured, more purposeful" than ever before.

To get to the Olympics, Mary Decker Slaney will have to beat the 32-year-old Jacobs, who says she has learned how to psych out her opponents before the running even begins. "Competition shouldn't be something to fear," Jacobs concluded in *Runner's World*. "It should be something exciting that we like to engage in." She added: "I love pushing myself to that point where it's really painful but it's also really great. I see myself winning medals and going on and on."

> "Competition shouldn't be something to fear. . . . I see myself winning medals and going on and on."
> —*Regina Jacobs*

That's certainly not good news for Mary Decker Slaney.

—*Anne Janette Johnson*

Gwen Torrence

"Everyone wants to be the world's fastest woman," Gwen Torrence told *Sports Illustrated* on June 26, 1995. Everyone might want the title, but Torrence has a fair chance of winning it during the Olympics. A returning medal-winner and the 1995 national champion in both the 100-meter and 200-meter sprints, Torrence will seek to cap an amazing—and at times controversial—career with

U.S. runner Gwen Torrence jubilates as she crosses the finish to win the women's 200-meter race in Barcelona. *AP/Wide World Photos*

double gold medals in Atlanta. Formerly an unmotivated trainer with an affection for soap operas and junk food, Torrence has more recently dedicated herself thoroughly to her sport and has seen her determination pay off in major victories. In 1996 she especially wants the gold medal in the 100-meter race. "People tell me I'm better suited to the 400, but there's something about that 100 title," she confided to *Sports Illustrated.*

Torrence will have a distinct advantage over all of her opponents in the 1996 Summer Games—she will be performing virtually in her own backyard. She was born in Atlanta on June 12, 1965, and she still lives in nearby Lithonia, Georgia. No cottage in an Olympic Village awaits this runner. On race day she'll arrive from the comfort of her own home, which she shares with husband/coach Manley Waller and their son, Manley, Jr. Needless to say, the hometown crowds will treat her like their conquering hero.

One of five children born into a working-class family in Atlanta, Gwen Torrence was seven years younger than her nearest sibling and was thus doted upon by her older brothers and sisters. Her family lived in a housing project when she was a baby, but by the time she was ready for school they had moved to a better home in Decatur, a suburb of Atlanta. There she attended Columbia High School and found the eye of physical education teacher Ray Bonner. Bonner had to do quite a bit of coaxing to get Torrence to run, and when he finally convinced her, she refused to wear athletic shorts or running shoes. "I felt [spikes] were too hot for my skinny little legs," she explained in a February 15, 1988, *Sports Illustrated* profile.

FACT: When she was in tenth grade, Torrence set an unofficial state record in the 220-yard dash while wearing low-heeled patent leather pumps.

Thus, during a gym class when she was in tenth grade, Torrence set an unofficial state record in the 220-yard dash while wearing low-heeled patent leather pumps. After that, Bonner insisted that she train properly in the right clothing and shoes. He told her that God would be angry with her if she wasted such natural talent.

The lecture worked. Despite embarrassment about her "skinny little legs," Torrence became a high school All-America and three-time state champion at the 100 and 200-meter races. She took double gold medals in those events at the TAC Junior Olympics during her senior year of high school, and in 1984 she qualified for the U.S. Olympic Trials. At 19 she had such misgivings about her ability to make the Olympic team that she refused to participate in the trials. Her time was yet to come.

Torrence attended the University of Georgia on an athletic scholarship and began her college career in the controversial developmental studies program, a remedial course of study. She was given four quarters to move out of that program and into the standard university curriculum, and she did so, eventually earning dean's list grades.

The athlete often cites 1986 as the turning point in her running career. That year she beat 1984 Olympic gold medalist Evelyn Ashford in the 55-meter dash at the Millrose games. Her winning time of 6.57 seconds was a meet record. In 1987 she won National Collegiate Athletic Association championships at 55, 100, and 200 meters, and she also took gold medals in the 100- and 200-meter races at the World University Games in Zagreb, Yugoslavia.

Torrence attended her first Olympic Games in 1988. In Seoul she finished fifth in the 100-meter and sixth in the 200-meter finals. For a time she thought that was the closest she would ever get to an Olympic medal. She became pregnant in 1989 and suffered complications that kept her bedridden for three months. She lost the muscle tone, strength, and stamina that are essential parts of any world class athlete's arsenal. After her son was born late in 1989, she realized how much conditioning she had lost. "I had to learn how to run all over again," she recalled in *Women's Sports and Fitness*.

Through all of 1990 Torrence didn't win a single race. She realized, however, that her layoff from running had filled her with new determination and the will to train. Gradually she regained her form, and in 1991 she finished second in both the 100- and 200-meter races at the World Championships. The only woman who beat her, Katrin Krabbe of Germany, later tested positive for the banned drug clenbuterol.

Torrence's performance at the 1992 Olympics is remembered less for her success there than for a remark she made that caused a scandal. After finishing a disappointing fourth in the 100-meter sprint final, she commented that she thought three other performers in that race had been using performance-enhancing drugs. When the remark was repeated in the press, some observers dismissed her accusations as a case of "sour grapes." The controversy would not die, however. Even though Torrence did not "name names," the other runners in the race complained loudly about the remark, and she later issued a formal apology. Then, while being hounded by press and public, she went out and won the gold medal in the 200-meter sprint, took another gold in the 4 × 100-meter relay, and a silver in the 4 × 400-meter relay.

The days of controversy are behind Torrence now, and as a defending Olympic champion she has been methodically preparing for the next Summer Games. She has suffered injuries to her right hamstring and knee, but she ran through the pain at the 1995 U.S. Outdoor Championships and won both the 100- and the 200-meter sprints. She plans to keep a light schedule of competitions until just prior to the Olympic Trials in order to minimize her risks for further injury.

Torrence's main opponent in 1996 will probably be Merlene Ottey of Jamaica, who beat Torrence in the 200-meter sprint at the 1993 World Championships. Ottey will be a long way from home, however, and Gwen Torrence—who ran her first race in pumps—will be right at home in a city that has rejoiced in her stellar career. "The Games' being here [in Atlanta] are a gift from God," Torrence commented in the June 1994 issue of *Track & Field News*. "He didn't like what happened to me in '92, so He's trying to make up for that by bringing the Games here." She added: "Now I just have to make that team. There are three spots to be earned and I always feel, not that I'm *the* best but certainly *one* of the best. But I still have to train as hard as ever, because nothing is guaranteed in this sport."

—*Anne Janette Johnson*

Schedule

The tentative track & field (athletics)—running schedule is:

Friday, July 26
Men's 20km walk
Men's & Women's 100m, 1st & 2nd rnd
Men's & Women's 800m, 1st rnd
Women's 5,000m, 1st rnd
Men's 10,000m, qualifying

Saturday, July 27
Men's & Women's 400m, 1st rnd
Men's & Women's 100m, semifinal, final
Men's 800m, 2nd rnd
Women's 800m, semifinal
Women's 10,000m, 1st rnd

Sunday, July 28
Women's marathon
Men's 110m hurdles, 1st & 2nd rnd
Men's & Women's 400m, 2nd rnd
Women's 400m hurdles, 1st rnd

Men's 800m, semifinal
Women's 5,000m, final

Monday, July 29
Women's 10km walk
Men's & Women's 200m, 1st rnd
Men's 1,500m, 1st rnd
Men's 400m hurdles, 1st rnd
Men's 110m hurdles, semifinal, final
Men's & Women's 200m, 2nd rnd
Men's & Women's 400m, semifinal
Women's 800m, final
Men's 3,000m steeplechase, 1st rnd
Women's 400m hurdles, semifinal
Men's 10,000m, final

Wednesday, July 31
Women's 1,500m, 1st rnd
Women's 100m hurdles, 1st & 2nd rnd

Men's & Women's 200m, semifinal
Men's 400m hurdles, semifinal
Women's 400m hurdles, final
Men's 3,000m steeplechase, semifinal
Men's & Women's 400m, final
Men's 800m, final
Men's 5,000m, 1st rnd

Thursday, August 1
Men's 1,500m wheelchair, final
Women's 800m wheelchair, final
Women's 100m hurdles, semifinal and
    final
Men's & Women's 200m, final
Men's 400m hurdles, final
Men's & Women's 1,500m, semifinal
Men's 5,000m, semifinal

Friday, August 2
Men's 50k walk
Men's & Women's 4 × 100m, 1st rnd
Men's & Women's 4 × 400m, 1st rnd
Men's & Women's 4 × 100m, semifinal
Men's 4 × 400m, semifinal
Men's 3,000m steeplechase, final
Women's 10,000m, final

Saturday, August 3
Men's & Women's 4 × 100m, final
Men's & Women's 1,500m final
Men's 5,000m, final
Men's & Women's 4 × 400m, final

Sunday, August 4
Men's marathon

MEN'S RUNNING EVENTS

Highlights

Sprints, 400 Meters, and Relays

Thomas Burke of the U.S. won the first 100m race of the Modern Olympics; four years later the U.S. came in 1–2 in the 100m, with Frank Jarvis and John Walter Tewksbury ahead of Australian Stanley Rowley; Rowley also won bronze medals in the 60m and 200m.

Tewksbury (who also medaled in the 60m sprint and two hurdle events) grabbed the 200m gold ahead of India's Norman Pritchard. U.S. sprinter Archie Hahn won three gold medals in 1904, including the 100m and 200m, in which he led U.S. sweeps. Hahn later wrote the book *How to Sprint.*

Born in Ireland, Robert Kerr represented Canada in the 200m at the 1908 Games, where he ran away with the 100m bronze and the 200m gold ahead of two U.S. sprinters. The 400m in 1908 was total chaos, resulting in protests, disqualifications, and a lone medalist. The U.S. swept the 100m again in 1912, then took the event 1–2 in 1920; the U.S. also took the 200m 1–2, with Charley Paddock accepting the silver behind Allen Woodring. In an American 3000m steeplechase championship shortly before the 1920 Olympics, Percy Hodge lost the heel of his shoe during the second lap, removed, readjusted, and retied his shoe, and proceeded to win by 60 yards. He also reached gold at the Antwerp Games.

The story of the 1924 Olympics was Harold Abrahams, England's storied winner in the 100m, recalled in the vivid, if not entirely accurate, film *Chariots of Fire*. Abrahams faced stiff competition in U.S. runners Charley Paddock (the world-record holder and defending Olympic champion), Jackson Scholz, and Loren Murchison. The field was even at first, but when Abrahams pulled away for the gold, New Zealand's Arthur Porritt—who went on to serve as that country's Governor-General—took the bronze behind Scholz.

Also featured as a character in *Chariots of Fire* was the winner of the 400m in 1924, Eric Liddell, a rugby champion from Scotland who changed the way the race was run by setting out at a blistering pace for the race's first half. Liddell also won the 200m bronze in 1924; Charley Paddock was back for the 200m silver behind Jackson Scholz, and Abrahams came in sixth.

At the Amsterdam Games in 1928 Canadian Percy Williams became a national hero with his gold medals in the 100m and 200m. That year, sprinter Ray Barbuti's victory in the 400m was the only individual gold won by the U.S.; James Ball of Canada took the 400m silver. But American sprinter Frank Wykoff won the first of his three relay gold medals in 1928; in 1936 he became the first sprinter to win gold medals in three Games.

> "You're really talented. You're a little guy but you beat all the big guys."
>
> —Jesse Owens, upon presenting a track meet long-jump medal to a 10-year-old athlete named Carl Lewis

U.S. sprinter Eddie Tolan won double gold in 1932, setting records in the 100m and 200m. A master of the late-race spurt, U.S. runner Ralph Metcalfe silver medaled in the 100m behind Tolan, but the finish was so close, the call could really have gone either way. The U.S. swept the 200m, with Tolan taking the gold and Metcalfe the bronze behind George Simpson; Metcalfe may have started three of four feet too far back in his lane. Teammate Bill Carr also claimed a gold and a record in the 400m, then added another gold in the 4 × 100 relay. Carr's chief rival, Benjamin Eastman, settled for the 400m silver, and Canadian Alexander Wilson took home the bronze. That was also the year Volmari Iso-Hollo of Finland won the 3000m steeplechase with a time of 10:33.4, even though it was later discovered he ran an extra lap because of a lap counter's error. Stanislawa Walasiewicz won the women's 100m gold, setting a world-record time of 11.9, which would not be beaten until 1952.

Metcalfe again took the silver in the 100m in 1936, behind an American legend. The Berlin Games of 1936, Hitler notwithstanding, belonged to U.S. athlete Jesse Owens, who cleaned up in the 100m, the 200m, and the 4 × 100m relay, as well as the broad jump (now called the long jump). Owens's Olympic marks proved their greatness by their staying power: his 100m record lasted until 1952, his 200m record until 1956, his long jump record until 1960. Silver medalist behind Owens in the 200m was Matthew "Mack" Robinson, older brother of baseball great Jackie Robinson. British sprinter Arthur Godfrey Brown also made a good showing at the Berlin Games in the 400m and the 4 × 400m relay. Finland's Volmari Iso-Hollo won another gold medal in the steeplechase with a time of 9:03.8.

At the London Games in 1948, U.S. hurdler Harrison Dillard entered the 100m when he failed to qualify for his main event. Dillard found inspiration in Jesse Owens, who had presented Dillard with the pair of running shoes that he wore at the Berlin Games. Dillard duly ran off with the 1948 100m gold ahead of all of the favorites, including Melvin Patton; his teammate, H. Norwood "Barney" Ewell, initially thought he had the gold, but happily settled for silver in a sportsmanlike demonstration that impressed onlookers. The third-place runner, Lloyd LaBeach, became Panama's first Olympic medalist. Patton and Ewell won 1–2 in the 200m, with LaBeach gaining another bronze for Panama. Jamaican Arthur Wint took the 400m title in 1948, ahead of his countryman, Herbert McKenley, who was favored.

McKenley repeated his silver medal in the 400m, 18 inches behind another Jamaican, and also captured a surprise silver in the 100m in 1952, when two of the favorites were unable to compete. McKenley almost ran away with the 100m gold, but a photo-finish awarded the title to American unknown Lindy Remigino. The favorite, Emmanuel McDonald Bailey of Great Britain, took the 100m bronze. The 200m at Helsinki was swept by the U.S., with Andrew Stanfield, W. Thane Baker, and Jamer Gathers coming in 1–2–3; Stanfield and Baker were on board for another U.S. sweep of the 200m in 1956. That year the U.S. took the 100m 1–2, with the bronze going to Australian champion Hector Hogan; gold medalist in the 100m and 200m in Melbourne was Bobby Morrow. The U.S. picked up another gold in the 400m, earned by Charles Jenkins.

The U.S. relay team was disappointed in Rome when sprinter Ray Norton messed up a

FACT: The last gold medal of the Barcelona Games was won by South Korean runner Hwang Young-Cho, who hammered up "suicide hill" to grab the marathon title. Kitei Son, the only other Korean to ever win the marathon, was forced to compete under the Japanese flag in the 1936 Berlin Games.

baton pass; he also finished last in the sprint events he was expected to win. The 1960 100m title went to Armin Hary, the first German male to win an Olympic track gold; he was known for a "blitz start" that carried him to victory. The 200m title was captured for the ecstatic home crowd by Italian Livio Berruti. Otis Davis of the U.S. claimed the 400m gold.

U.S. sprinters Bob Hayes and Henry Carr made their mark at the 1964 Tokyo Games, when electronic timing was used for the first time. Hayes took the gold in the 100m, ahead of Cuba's first-time track medalist Enrique Figuerola Camue, who beat out Hayes's teammate Harry Jerome. Carr struck gold in the 200m ahead of teammate Otis Drayton and bronze medalist Edwin Roberts from Trinidad and Tobago. Injured in 1960, U.S. runner Michael Larrabee kicked to a gold finish in the 400m.

Sprinters may have been helped by the high altitude at the Mexico City Games, setting world records in many events. Jimmy Hines took the 100m (ahead of Jamaica's Lennox Miller and U.S. runner Charles Greene), Tommie Smith the 200m, and Lee Evans (leading a U.S. sweep) the 400m, all in record time, all for the U.S. The 100m race in 1968 was the first all-black final in Olympic history.

It was also in 1968 that Smith and American bronze-medalist sprinter John Carlos, both members of the Olympic Project for Human Rights, stirred controversy when they stood barefoot on the medal podium, black-gloved fists silently raised in the black power salute. They were ousted from the Olympic Village and removed from the U.S. team. Pre-war track star Jesse Owens initially backed the USOC in this controversy, but in 1972 reversed his support. Sports journalist Brent Musburger, then a columnist in Chicago, reportedly called Smith and Carlos "black-skinned storm troopers." Some reconciliation must have occurred over time: in 1984 John Carlos worked for the Los Angeles Olympic Organizing Committee preparing for the Summer Games.

At the Munich Games of 1972, two favored American sprinters failed to show up for their 100m trials when their coach apparently relied on the wrong time schedule. U.S. runners Vince Matthews and Wayne Collett, after finishing 1–2 in the 400m, displayed their own variation of the civil rights demonstration by chatting and moving about on the victory stand during their medal ceremony, instead of standing at attention. The IOC instantly banned them "for life," and the U.S. was left without enough runners to compete in the 4 × 400 relay.

Jamaica's Lennox Miller was back for the 100m bronze in 1972. That year the Soviet Union fielded its first sprinting hero,

Valery Borzov, who streaked off with the gold in the 100m and the 200m events, and later married solid-gold Soviet gymnast Lyudmila Turischeva. Bronze medalist in the 200m at Munich, Pietro Mennea exposed the crowd to his jockstrap while donning his running shorts; he competed in the 200m without medaling in 1976, then came back for the gold in that event in 1980.

The Soviet Borzov was back for the 100m bronze in 1976, behind Trinidad's Hasely Crawford and Jamaican silver medalist Donald Quarrie. Quarrie took the gold in the 200m ahead of two U.S. runners. Two U.S. runners also finished the 400m behind Cuban runner Alberto Juantorena, who also took a gold in the 800m. The Cuban athlete's stride measured nine feet.

Scottish sprinter Allan Wells ignored the boycott of the Moscow Games to take the 100m for Great Britain ahead of Cuba's Silvio Leonard; Wells had only begun using starting blocks that year. In the 200m Wells took the silver ahead of Jamaica's defending champ, Donald Quarrie. The 400m title was won by a Soviet unknown, Viktor Markin. In the 1980 4 × 100 relay French twins Patrick and Pascal Barré sprinted their team to a bronze medal.

In 1984 U.S. sprinter Carl Lewis took the 100m gold ahead of teammate Sam Graddy; the bronze medalist that year was Canada's Ben Johnson. Lewis also broke Tommie Smith's 1968 Olympic record in the 200m, and that year for the fifth time the U.S. swept the event, winning all three Olympic medals. Italy's Pietro Mennea ran the 200m for his fourth straight Olympics in 1984; defending the title he won in 1980, he placed seventh. In the 400m, the U.S. captured the gold and bronze, leaving the silver to Gabriel Tiacoh of the Côte d'Ivoire. The only track and field world record established at the 1984 Games came in the 4 × 100 relay.

FACT: When asked by an Albuquerque, New Mexico, schoolboy to name his favorite Olympian, IOC president Juan Antonio Samaranch picked Carl Lewis.

Up to 1988, no man had ever successfully defended an Olympic 100m title, and at first Carl Lewis watched as Canada's Ben Johnson crossed the finish-line ahead of him. But Lewis was ultimately to retain the 100m gold, when Johnson was disqualified for illegal drug use. Lewis finished ahead of Britain's Linford Christie; 1988 bronze medalist Calvin Smith turned in a time equal to Lewis's 1984 gold time. Lewis lost his 200m Olympic title, taking the silver medal in the 200m in Seoul behind teammate Joe DeLoach; Brazil's Robson de Silva captured the bronze. Steven Lewis led a U.S. sweep of the 400m at Seoul.

Middle Distance, Long Distance, and Cross Country

Australian Eddie Flack won the first 800m race of the modern Games, and put together a winning sprint at the end of the 1500m to capture that event as well. British runner Alfred Tysoe captured the 800m title in 1900. Four years later the U.S. swept the event, led by James Lightbody in a come-from-behind victory. Lightbody also led a U.S. sweep of the 1500m.

U.S. runner Mel Sheppard, who not long before the 1908 Games had been rejected by the New York City police as being physically unfit, won the 1500m in Olympic record time, and took the 800m in world record time. In 1912, 18-year-old American Ted Meredith won the 800m gold, just edging Sheppard, who came in for the silver; Ira Davenport completed the U.S. 800m sweep. British runner Arnold Jackson passed the field in the 1500m in a final burst that prevented an American sweep of the event in 1912. Another British runner, Albert Hill, mined double gold in 1920 with the 800m and 1500m titles.

The first "flying Finn," Hannes Kolehmainen, flew in to the 1912 Games, where he took golds in the 5000m and the 10,000m, as well as the 8,000m cross-country. He was back in 1920 to win the marathon. But his memory is overshadowed by that of Finland's emerging legend, Paavo Nurmi, a bony man with receding hairline, high cheekbones, a sour expression or, at best, no expression at all. At the 1920 Games he was the prototype Flying Finn, winning the 10,000-meter cross-country race and the 10,000-meter track race.

In the decade between 1921 and 1931 Nurmi broke the world outdoor record 16 times at races from 1500 meters up to 20,000 meters. He won nine gold medals and three silvers in the Olympics from 1920 through 1928; he was tossed out of the 1932 Games after the Germans protested that he had taken excessive expenses the year before.

In 1924 Nurmi was at his peak, winning the 1500m, the 5000m, the 10,000m cross-country and the 3000m team races. That year Finland won every race of 1500 meters or longer, and Nurmi's teammate, Ville Ritola, ran 39,000 meters in heats and finals during one week on his way to victories in the 10,000m flat race and 3000m steeplechase, plus second-place finishes in the 5000m, the 10,000 cross-country, and the 3000m team race. The 1924 800m race was won by British runner Douglas Lowe, who successfully defended his title in 1928. Nurmi won his last Olympic gold in 1928, in the 10,000.

Italy's Luigi Beccali stood out in the 1500m race in 1932, besting such notables as Glenn Cunningham of the U.S. and Jack

Lovelock of New Zealand. Canadians Alexander Wilson and Philip Edwards (who was bronze medalist in the 1500m) took the silver and bronze in the 800m in 1932 behind Britain's Thomas Hampson; Edwards defended his 800m bronze successfully in Berlin, while Beccali had to settle for bronze in the 1500m in 1936. That year's 1500m winner was New Zealand's John Lovelock.

Swedish runners finished 1–2 in the 1500m in London, while U.S. runner Malvin Whitfield pulled ahead of Jamaica's Arthur Wint for the 800m title in 1948. The pair finished 1–2 in the half-mile in Helsinki as well, with Whitfield matching his 1948 time, and Wint bettering his.

Versatile Czech runner Emil Zátopek made his first appearance at the 1948 Games in London; he claimed the gold in the 10,000m and a silver in the 5000m. Zátopek's wife, Dana, won the women's javelin that year, making the first husband-wife double gold in track and field. Zátopek was the biggest story of the 1952 Games, claiming the gold in the 5000m, the 10,000m, and the marathon, a monumental triple.

British runner Roger Bannister competed in the 1500m at Helsinki but did not medal; the first-place finisher in that race, Josy Barthel of Luxembourg, claimed his country's first Olympic medal. Bannister was spurred by his defeat to train harder, and two years later broke the four-minute mile. The first Olympic encounter of sub-four-minute milers was staged in the 1500m at the Melbourne Games, with Ireland's Ron Delany claiming the gold.

Soviet runners exploded on the scene in 1956, and in the 5000m and 10,000m races the gold medals went to Vladimir Kuts, the first Soviet male to win a track and field gold medal. That year U.S. runner Tom Courtney twice lost his lead in the stretch of the 800m, and regained it twice to win; he was so exhausted by the effort that he was unable to claim his medal four hours later.

The 1960 Games saw the surprise victory of New Zealand's Peter Snell in the 800m, thanks in part to a rigorous training program, then experimental, that included up to 100 miles of running per week. Silver medaling behind Snell was world record-holder Roger Moens of Belgium. In the 1500m it was Australian favorite Herb Elliott ahead of France's Michel Jazy. Snell took the 800m and the 1500m in 1964, the first runner to achieve a double gold since 1920; behind him in the 800m was Canadian William Crothers, and bronze medalist Wilson Kiprugut (claiming Kenya's first medal), while silver medaling in the 1500m was Czech Josef Odlozil.

In the 10,000m race at the Tokyo Games, favorite Ron Clarke of Australia was shocked when Billy Mills of the U.S. triumphed, coming seemingly out of nowhere. "Hell, I never heard of Mills," Clarke remarked. Tunisia's Mohamed Gammoudi slipped ahead of Clarke for the silver that year. Another American upset came in the 5000m, where Bob Schul ran off with the gold.

Runners in the longer-distance events were handicapped by the high altitude at the Mexico City Games, where they went into oxygen deficit in the thin air. Kenya's Wilson Kiprugut was edged out of the 800m gold by Australian Ralph Doubell. U.S. runner Jim Ryun, the dominant miler for three years prior to the Games, was done in by both thin air and shrewd teamwork on the part of Kenyans Ben Jipcho and Kip Keino during the 1500m. Jipcho, unheralded at the time, set a searing pace, with the intent of sapping Ryun's strength early, thus allowing Keino to relax during the early stages of the race, then cruise past the weary Ryun at the end. Ryun won a medal—a silver—and was hounded by the press and public, who craved more precious metal. Ryun, back for more in 1972, seemed cursed by the Olympic gods; he tripped and fell in the 1500m first-round heat at Munich, and Keino successfully defended his title.

Ryun's teammate, Rick Wohlhuter, was favored to win the 800m in 1972 but fell in his trial heat; relatively unknown Dave Wottle, wearing his trademark white golf cap, showed a devastating kick to salvage the 800m gold for the U.S. team that year, besting the favorite, Soviet Yevgeny Arzhanov. Finland's Lasse Viren ran off with double gold in the 5000m and 10,000m, in Munich, despite taking a fall early in the 10,000m final.

The Montreal Games were boycotted by African nations protesting the participation of New Zealand, who had played rugby against South Africa (during the height of apartheid). The great match-up between milers John Walker of New Zealand and Filbert Bayi of Tanzania was not to be; Walker took the 1500m gold at a dreadfully plodding pace. Lasse Viren provided excitement, mining double gold again in the 5000m and 10,000m; he even competed in the marathon, but did not medal. Cuba's massive Alberto Juantorena barreled to a unique double win in the 400m, as favorite, and the 800m, as upset.

With the absence of U.S. athletes from the 1980 Games, the only closely watched track events were the 800m and 1500m races, where British greats Sebastian Coe and Steve Ovett at last met head on, partly because they were among a handful of British athletes who went against their Olympic association's request that they, too, boycott Moscow.

At the time, the two shared the world 1500m record and Ovett had recently broken Coe's world mile record. And an additional element was the way the two avoided each other in competition—not to mention on the sidelines. They didn't speak to each other, they were strikingly different personalities, Coe the good guy, Ovett the villain. Coe was the speed man, Ovett the strength man, so that Coe was favored in the 800m, Ovett in the 1500m. But the 800m was run first, and Ovett won. Then they ran the 1500m, and Coe won. Those two races were the emotional high point of the Moscow Games.

In 1984 Coe became the first man ever to win two Olympic 1500m races, capturing the title ahead of countryman Steve Cram. Coe also silver medaled in the 800m behind Brazil's Joaquim Cruz. Moroccan Said Aouita captured the 5000m in 1984, while Italy's Alberto Cova triumphed in the 10,000m.

Defending his 800m title, Brazil's Joaquim Cruz settled for silver behind Kenya's Paul Ereng in Seoul. Kenya's Peter Rono captured the 1500m ahead of Britain's Peter Elliott. Kenya took yet another gold in the 5000m when John Ngugi posted the winning time ahead of two Germans, but had to settle for a Kenyan bronze in the 10,000m, where Morocco's Brahim Boutaib excelled.

Marathon and Walking

At the first Games in 1896, the Greeks cheered local hero Spiridon Loues, who won his country's only track and field gold medal that year in a most fitting event, the marathon. In 1904 the apparent winner of the marathon, Fred Lorz, mentioned that he had experienced part of the race from an automobile, and the gold was awarded to U.S. runner Tommy Hicks.

The marathon distance was standardized during the London Olympics of 1908. The English royal family wanted to watch the start of the race, and the distance from the private lawns of Windsor Castle to the Olympic stadium finish line was 26 miles, 385 yards. The marathon's distance was thus fixed.

That year the marathon was again dramatic, as 22-year-old Dorando Pietri, a candy maker from Italy, took the lead from South Africa's Charles Hefferon with some two miles remaining. Half of the field of 56 had dropped out. U.S.A.'s Johnny Hayes was in the process of catching Hefferon. Pietri triumphantly entered the stadium and then—yikes!—turned the wrong way. Suddenly the heat and the race's toll grabbed Pietri all at once. An invisible bear had jumped out of an invisible forest and landed on his back, as distance runners used to say. Pietri staggered, fell, got up, turned around, and staggered again. He fell again, only yards from the finish line. The spectators leaned forward as the action mounted, and trackside officials moved in, propping up the tiny runner as he wobbled across the finish line. Hayes, meanwhile, was striding toward the finish himself. After a lengthy discussion, officials decided Pietri had been unfairly aided across the line, giving the victory to Hayes.

The 1920 marathon title went to Hannes Kolehmainen, a triple-gold medalist in 1912. Fifty years later Czech runner Emil Zátopek also claimed a triple gold with a victory in the marathon, an event he'd never run before, as well as the 5000m and the 10,000m. For his marathon feat Zátopek became known as the Iron Czech.

Korea's great marathoner Sohn Kee Chung was forced to accept a gold medal for Japan at the Games of 1936, when Korea was under Japanese colonial rule; at age 76 he carried the Olympic flame into the stadium at the opening of the Seoul Games in 1988.

Ethiopia's Abebe Bikila ran barefoot down the Appian Way at the Rome Games of 1960, attaining the Arch of Constantine ahead of the field for a marathon gold. Bikila was back, with shoes on, to repeat for the gold in Tokyo.

Of the Americans' performances in 1972 at the Munich Games, none had the overall impact of that turned in by Frank Shorter, a Yale man who had dabbled in medical school and law school while training 20 miles a day. Shorter's marathon victory pulled an entire nation with it; television beamed almost every step back to the U.S., where thousands apparently decided to see how far *they* could run. And within five years, distance running became the most fashionable of American leisure-time sports. Shorter was back for the marathon silver in 1976 at the Montreal Games, and several months later began producing his own line of running gear.

In Moscow Frank Shorter's 1976 silver-medal time would have been good as gold in the marathon, an unimpressive event at the boycotted games. Portugal's Carlos Lopes was 37 when he won the gold in the marathon in 1984. He had narrowly missed a gold in the 10,000 meters in 1976 when Finland's Lasse Viren outsprinted him in the last lap. Ireland's John Treacy took the silver in 1984. The 1988 marathon title went to Gelindo Bordin of Italy, ahead of runners from Kenya and Djbouti.

The oldest track gold medalist was Tebbs Lloyd Johnson of Great Britain, who was 48 when he walked off with the 1952 gold in the 3500m walk, the only time that event was held.

Hurdles and Steeplechase

U.S. hurdler Alvin Kraenzlein won two golds at the 1900 Games, in high and low hurdles, to add to two other golds he won in the 60m dash and the long jump. In 1904 U.S. hurdler Harry Hillman won three golds in three hurdle events.

Lord Burghley, the sixth marquess of Exeter, won the gold medal in the 1928 Olympics in Amsterdam; he later served as a member of the IOC, turning up as a character in the film *Chariots of Fire*.

U.S. hurdler George Saling leaped for gold in the 110m event in 1932, while teammate Glenn Hardin lost the gold by two feet in the 400m hurdles to Ireland's Robert Tisdall, who knocked over the last hurdle (and thus under the old rules could not set a record); Hardin's second-place performance was good for an Olympic record but only a silver medal.

Top-ranked U.S. hurdler Harrison Dillard fell in his Olympic trials' race and failed to make the U.S. team in 1948; he competed in the 100m sprint that year instead, claiming the gold. Dillard was able to come back for his event, the 110m hurdles, in 1952 and claim that gold, too.

The hurdler to beat in 1968 was Great Britain's David Hemery, who looked like he'd invented hurdles winning the 400m event. In 1972 Uganda's John Akii-Bua set a world record in the 400m hurdles.

U.S. hurdler Edwin Moses cruised to his first gold in the 400m hurdles at Montreal in 1976, sat out the 1980 Games, then repeated for gold in 1984.

Amadou Dia Ba of Senegal claimed the 400m silver medal in 1988, behind Andre Phillips of the U.S. and ahead of then legendary Moses. Moses's record, set in 1976, was broken by Phillips in 1988. In fact, Moses ran faster for the bronze in 1988 than he had for either of his gold medals.

In the high hurdles, Lee Calhoun of the U.S. was the first man to win two golds in that event, in 1956 and 1960. U.S. hurdler Roger Kingdom repeated that feat, taking the event in Los Angeles by 0.03 seconds over his teammate Greg Foster, then in 1988 setting an Olympic record, winning by an amazing three meters over the U.K.'s Colin Jackson and U.S. hurdler Tonie Campbell.

Steeplechase distance wasn't standardized in the early Games. At one time there was a 5000m team steeplechase, and then a

Finnish distance runner Paavo Nurmi, who earned Olympic medals from 1920 to 1928, lit the
Olympic flame to open the Helsinki Games in 1952. *AP/Wide World Photos*

3000m team steeplechase. In 1904 U.S. runner James Lightbody won three golds in three steeplechase events. In 1952 Russian steeplechaser Vladimir Kazantsen was leading until the last water jump of the race, when U.S. FBI agent Horace Ashenfelter caught him and went on to win in world-record time.

Paavo Nurmi

The "Flying Finn" may be the most famous, most innovative, most stubborn runner of all time. He won nine Olympic gold medals, set 29 world records and competed in three separate Olympics: 1920, 1924, and 1928.

Nurmi legends make for some of the best Olympic lore. In Paris in 1924, "The Phantom Finn" (as he was also known) had only half an hour to rest between the finals of the 1500m and 5000m races. He won them both.

Finnish athletic officials, facing an embarrassment of riches in the 1924 Games, barred Nurmi from defending his 10,000m title of 1920 to give countryman Ville Ritola a crack at the gold. Ritola won. But, according to legend, Nurmi, carrying a stopwatch, ran a one-man exhibition on a nearby track, beating Ritola's time by 40 seconds.

Nurmi, born June 13, 1897, in Turku, Finland, habitually ran with a stopwatch, both while training and competing. He was one of the first to practice pacing in a scientific manner. Nurmi began a self-imposed running regimen at age 12, loping through Finnish forests for endurance. He entered the Finnish military in 1919 and was known to run entire 20-kilometer marches with full pack and rifle plus an 11-pound sack of sand.

Nurmi's last public appearance on a track came in 1952 at the age of 55, when he carried the Olympic torch into the arena for the Helsinki Games. The appearance came 20 years after he was banned from competing in the 1932 Games by the International Amateur Athletic Foundation because of supposed professionalism. Having become financially secure through real estate investing, he died in Helsinki on October 2, 1973. The great Finn is commemorated with a bronze statue that stands outside the Helsinki Olympic stadium.

—Harvey Dickson

Chariots of Fire: Abrahams and Liddell, Coe and Ovett

Chariots of Fire is a inspirational movie, with Vangelis's mythic soundtrack providing some of the best running-on-the-beach music

After training intensely for four years, British sprinter Harold Abrahams captured the 100m gold medal at the 1924 Games; his story inspired the movie *Chariots of Fire*. *AP/Wide World Photos*

ever. Even if you don't usually trot on the beach, you'll want to after listening to this. But as literal track history, portraying the life and times of Olympians Harold Abrahams and Eric Liddell, the movie puts forth the usual cinematic discrepancies. Some events are compressed, others fabricated. What the movie does stay truthful to, however, is the complex and separate visions that drove Abrahams and Liddell at the 1924 Paris Games.

Abrahams, who was Jewish, surely did feel the sting of anti-Semitism. But he was also competing against the memory of his older brothers' achievements, including one who competed in Stockholm in 1912. Abrahams ran at the Antwerp Games in 1920 but lost in the quarterfinals of the 100m. During the next four years he worked relentlessly at his sprinting style; he carried a piece of string to measure where his first step should fall after the start. At the 100m in Paris, the training helped him defeat the favored American runners.

Liddell had been born in China to missionary parents of Scottish origin. He was as natural at athletics—training was only a sometime thing for the former rugby star—as he was at preaching. At Paris, he declined the opportunity to run three races, including two relays, because they fell on Sundays and conflicted with his religious beliefs. That allowed him to focus on the 400m race, which he won by the wide margin of five meters. He also won a bronze in the 200m sprint. But he was loudly criticized by countrymen for denying Scotland a rare shot at more Olympic medals.

Abrahams was forced into retirement not long after the 1924 Games when he injured his thigh during a long jump. He became a lawyer, worked in radio, and served as president of the British Amateur Athletic Association. Abrahams died in 1978.

A year after winning his medals, Liddell went back to China to help his father's missionary work. He was imprisoned during World War II and died of a brain tumor in a Japanese internment camp on February 21, 1945. A six-foot column of Scottish granite was erected near the site of his death in 1991.

Let's take another listen to that *Chariots of Fire* soundtrack. Fifty-six years after Paris, two more British subjects were linked again by the urge to run in the Olympics. The 800m race in Moscow was to be a classic match-up between Steve Ovett and Sebastian Coe. Ovett had won their last head-to-head encounter in 1978, but the two runners had avoided each other ever since. Coe was one of the great runners of the period. The media hyped the battle between the two track stars, and anticipation was high that a classic duel was in the making.

Scots runner Eric Liddell also figured into the movie *Chariots of Fire*. His performance at the 1924 Games brought him a gold medal in the 400m and a bronze in the 200m. *AP/Wide World Photos*

But the 800m race was anticlimactic. The pace was plodding, though Ovett eventually broke away from the pack to win. Coe put himself in poor positions in outside lanes before ending with a sprint for the silver medal. In a book he later wrote about the Olympic games, Coe revealed, "I still can't watch the 800 meters final on video, even after all this time, without kicking myself. I clearly lost concentration."

But in the 1500m race, Coe found a measure of revenge. Ovett should have been the favorite, having won 42 straight races in that distance range. But Coe was determined not to repeat the mistakes he made in the 800m. This time, Coe stayed near the front, finally passing East German Jürgen Straub 200 meters before the finish. Ovett placed third.

Coe defended his title in the 1500m four years later in Los Angeles, defeating another Brit, Steve Cram. Ovett enjoyed less luck repeating. Battling bronchitis, he was the last to qualify for the 800m final, and then placed eighth out of eight runners. He collapsed after the race and spent two days in hospital.

—*Harvey Dickson*

Edwin Moses

When he attended the 1976 Summer Olympics in Montreal, Edwin Moses was a twenty-year-old physics major at Morehouse

Another great U.K. match-up: At the 1980 Games Sebastian Coe (c.) captured the gold in the 1500m, ahead of arch-rival and Steve Ovett (#279). In the 800m that year it was Ovett for the gold and Coe for the silver. *AP/Wide World Photos*

College who had pretty much taught himself to run hurdles. In those Games, Moses set a world record of 47.64 seconds in his event, winning a gold medal and beginning a legendary career as an Olympic athlete. While other athletes—amateur and professional—came and went, Moses endured as *the* star of the 400m hurdles, at one point winning a staggering 107 consecutive races.

Ironically, Moses was attending Morehouse on an academic, rather than an athletic, scholarship, and the college did not even have a track. Running hurdles was a hobby for him, a way to keep fit while he earned his physics degree. After Montreal, which was his first international meet, he began to devote himself wholeheartedly to the sport. For ten years he was nearly untouchable.

Moses developed a 13-step rhythm between each hurdle that he was able to maintain throughout the course. While his competitors would tire in the stretch and begin to take 15 or 16 steps, Moses remained in what seemed like an effortless flow from jump to jump. He was highly favored to win the 400m hurdles in the 1980 Olympics in Moscow, but the U.S. boycott kept him sidelined from the event. Other international competitions remained open to him, however, and he attended almost all of them, winning with a consistency that confounded his opponents. His 1983 world record of 47.02 seconds was considered unbeatable.

Moses arrived at the 1984 Olympics a heavy favorite. In Los Angeles he hurdled to a second gold medal, despite a poor start and—by his standards—a mediocre pace. At that time he was in the midst of a winning streak that stretched to 107 before the 1984 silver medalist Danny Harris did the undoable, beating Moses at a race in Madrid. After that loss Moses came back with 10 more consecutive victories, for a total of 117 wins in 119 starts from 1977 until 1987.

The statistics are tarnished somewhat by the fact that, as he aged, Moses picked and chose his races carefully. Some observers contended that he was avoiding the other top-level hurdlers— such as Harris—but Moses answered that he was pacing himself, saving his strength for the most important matches. However, as the 1988 Games approached, and Moses found himself over 30, the athlete "began to think of himself less as a competitor than as conservator of the [winning] streak," to quote *Sports Illustrated* correspondent Pat Butcher. At any rate, Moses settled for the bronze in Seoul, behind teammate Andre Phillips and suprise silver medalist El Hedj Dia Ba of Senegal.

But another sport beckoned Edwin Moses—bobsledding. He told *Sports Illustrated* that he "got the fever" to try bobsledding after attending the 1988 Winter Games in Calgary. He teamed up with Brian Shimer. The pair were the only Americans to win a medal at the 1991 World Cup bobsled competition. They earned their prize—a bronze—in Winterberg, Germany, but failed to make the U.S. Olympic team for 1992.

Moses told *Sports Illustrated* that he planned to make a comeback as a hurdler for the 1992 Summer Games. But it was in Barcelona that Kevin Young (of the U.S.) broke the 47-second barrier in the 400m hurdles, setting a world record that even outdid Moses's track record. In 1994, Edwin Moses was honored by his alma mater, Morehouse College, at the school's "A Candle in the Dark" awards presentation.

—*Mark Kram*

Highlights from Barcelona

Even with medal magnet Carl Lewis sidelined in the 100m and 200m dash, the U.S. men had a banner year in Barcelona, grabbing 11 medals in running, of which 5 were gold. Kevin Young, who placed 4th in the Seoul Games and in the 1991 World Championships, lowered his personal best by nearly one second in the 400m hurdles. In so doing, he set a world record, obliterating one of the oldest records in the sport, Edwin Moses's nearly nine-year-old mark of 47.02. Finishing the race in 46.78, the

U.S. hurdler Edwin Moses won his first gold medal in the 400m at the 1976 Olympics, then had to sit out for the Moscow Games. He recaptured the gold in 1984, and in 1988 outdid his previous winning times, but the performance was only good for the bronze that year. *AP/Wide World Photos*

25-year-old Young—who had taped sub-47 times to the walls of his Olympic Village room—became the first man in history to break the 47-second barrier in the 400 hurdles (even though he raised his right arm 7 meters from the finish).

Also breaking barriers was the U.S. men's 4 × 100 relay team, anchored by much-gilded Carl Lewis. It took only 37.40 seconds of Olympic history-making for Mike Marsh, Leroy Burrell, Dennis Mitchell, and Lewis to smash the reigning world record. The other U.S. men's relay team—the 4 × 400—also had the Midas touch, annihilating the sport's oldest record with a time of 2:55:74; set in 1968, the 2:56:16 previous world record had only been tied once, in 1988. Sharing in the relay gold was Quincy Watts, who, three days earlier, had dominated the open 400 by the largest margin ever with the second-fastest time in the race's 68-year history.

Entering the 100m dash, the U.S. team's Leroy Burrell was the odds-on favorite, having reeled in Great Britain's Linford Christie in the semifinals less than two hours before the final. Carl Lewis, the world record holder in the 100, was conspicuously absent, having failed to make the U.S. team in the event by placing a distant sixth at the Olympic trials. And Ben Johnson, who was stripped of his 1988 gold medal after testing positive for steroids, also failed to qualify for the finals.

Unfazed by nerve-racking delays and a false start, Christie blazed to the finish in 9.96—half a meter ahead of Namibia's Frank Fredericks (10.02) and the U.S.'s Dennis Mitchell (10.04). At the age of 32, Christie became the oldest Olympic champion in the event.

Probably the year's most heartrending performance took place in a 400m heat, in which British runner Derek Redmond suddenly felt a piercing pain in his right leg. He collapsed on the track, and, with his hamstring pulled, struggled to continue the race. He limped around the track, obviously in excruciating pain. Then, seemingly out of nowhere, Redmond's father leapt out of the stands to help his son around the track. "They weren't going to carry me off that track on a stretcher," the runner later told reporters; and they didn't.

Medalists

Track and Field—Men's 100 Meters

1992
1. Linford Christie, Britain, 9.96
2. Frank Fredericks, Namibia, 10.02
3. Dennis Mitchell, U.S.A., 10.04

1988
1. Carl Lewis, U.S.A., 9.92 (OR). (Ben Johnson, Canada, ran 9.79 but was disqualified.)
2. Linford Christie, Great Britain, 9.97
3. Calvin Smith, U.S.A., 9.99

1984
1. Carl Lewis, U.S.A., 9.99
2. Sam Graddy, U.S.A., 10.19
3. Ben Johnson, Canada, 10.22

1980
1. Allan Wells, Great Britain, 10.25
2. Silvio Leonard, Cuba, 10.25
3. Peter Petrov, Bulgaria, 10.39

1976
1. Hasely Crawford, Trinidad and Tobago, 10.06
2. Donald Quarrie, Jamaica, 10.08
3. Valeri Borzov, Soviet Union, 10.14

1972
1. Valery Borsov, Soviet Union, 10.14
2. Robert Taylor, U.S.A., 10.24
3. Lennox Miller, Jamaica, 10.33

1968
1. Jim Hines, U.S.A., 9.95 (WR)
2. Lennox Miller, Jamaica, 10.0
3. Charles Greene, U.S.A., 10.0

1964
1. Robert Hayes, U.S.A., 10.0 (EWR)
2. Enrique Figuerola, Cuba, 10.2
3. Harry Jerome, Canada, 10.2

1960
1. Armin Hary, West Germany, 10.2 (OR)
2. David Sime, U.S.A., 10.2
3. Peter Radford, Great Britain, 10.3

1956
1. Robert Morrow, U.S.A., 10.5
2. Thane Baker, U.S.A., 10.5
3. Hector Hogan, Australia, 10.6

1952
1. Lindy Remigino, U.S.A., 10.4
2. Herbert McKenley, Jamaica, 10.4
3. Emmanuel McDonald Bailey, Great Britain, 10.4

1948
1. Harrison Dillard, U.S.A., 10.3 (EOR)
2. Norwood Ewell, U.S.A., 10.4
3. Lloyd LaBeach, Panama, 10.4

1936
1. Jesse Owens, U.S.A., 10.3
2. Ralph Metcalfe, U.S.A., 10.4
3. Martinus Osendarp, Netherlands, 10.5

1932
1. Eddie Tolan, U.S.A., 10.3 (OR)
2. Ralph Metcalfe, U.S.A., 10.3
3. Arthur Jonath, Germany, 10.4

1928
1. Percy Williams, Canada, 10.8
2. Jack London, Great Britain, 10.9
3. Georg Lammers, Germany, 10.9

1924
1. Harold Abrahams, Great Britian, 10.6 (OR)
2. Jackson Scholz, U.S.A., 10.7
3. Arthur Porritt, New Zealand, 10.8

1920
1. Charles Paddock, U.S.A., 10.8
2. Morris Kirksey, U.S.A., 10.8
3. Harry Edward, Great Britain, 11.0

1912
1. Ralph Craig, U.S.A., 10.8
2. Alvah Mayer, U.S.A., 10.9
3. Donald Lippincott, U.S.A., 10.9

1908
1. Reginald Walker, South Africa, 10.8 (OR)
2. James Rector, U.S.A., 10.9
3. Robert Kerr, Canada, 11.0

1906
1. Archie Hahn, U.S.A., 11.2
2. Fay Moulton, U.S.A., 11.3
3. Nigel Barker, Australia, 11.3

1904
1. Archie Hahn, U.S.A., 11.0
2. Nathaniel Cartmell, U.S.A., 11.2
3. William Hogenson, U.S.A., 11.2

1900
1. Francis Jarvis, U.S.A., 11.0
2. John Walter Tewksbury, U.S.A. 11.1
3. Stanley Rowley, Australia, 11.2

1896
1. Thomas Burke, U.S.A., 12.0
2. Fritz Hofmann, Germany, 12.2
3. Alajos Szokolyi, Hungary, 12.6

Track and Field—Men's 200 Meters

1992
1. Mike Marsh, U.S.A., 20.01
2. Frank Fredericks, Namibia, 20.13
3. Michael Bates, U.S.A., 20.38

1988
1. Joe DeLoach, U.S.A., 19.75 (OR)
2. Carl Lewis, U.S.A., 19.79
3. Robson de Silva, Brazil, 20.04

1984
1. Carl Lewis, U.S.A., 19.80 (OR)
2. Kirk Baptiste, U.S.A., 19.96
3. Thomas Jefferson, U.S.A., 20.26

1980
1. Pietro Mennea, Italy, 20.19
2. Allan Wells, Great Britain, 20.21
3. Donald Quarrie, Jamaica, 20.29

1976
1. Donald Quarrie, Jamaica, 20.23
2. Millard Hampton, U.S.A., 20.29
3. Dwayne Evans, U.S.A., 20.43

1972
1. Valery Borsov, Soviet Union, 20.00
2. Larry Black, U.S.A., 20.19
3. Pietro Mennea, Italy, 20.30

1968
1. Tommie Smith, U.S.A., 19.83 (WR)
2. Peter Norman, Australia, 20.0
3. John Carlos, U.S.A., 20.0

1964
1. Henry Carr, U.S.A., 20.3 (OR)
2. Otis Drayton, U.S.A., 20.5
3. Edwin Roberts, Trinidad and Tobago, 20.6

1960
1. Livio Berruti, Italy, 20.5 (EWR)
2. Lester Carney, U.S.A., 20.6
3. Abdoulaye Seye, France, 20.7

1956
1. Robert Morrow, U.S.A., 20.6 (OR)
2. Andrew Stanfield, U.S.A., 20.7
3. Thane Baker, U.S.A., 20.9

1952
1. Andrew Stanfield, U.S.A., 20.7
2. Thane Baker, U.S.A., 20.8
3. James Gathers, U.S.A., 20.8

1948
1. Mel Patton, U.S.A., 21.1
2. Norwood Ewell, U.S.A., 21.1
3. Lloyd LaBeach, Panama, 21.2

1936
1. Jesse Owens, U.S.A., 20.7 (OR)
2. Matthew Robinson, U.S.A., 21.1
3. Martinus Osendarp, Netherlands, 21.3

1932
1. Eddie Tolan, U.S.A., 21.2 (OR)
2. George Simpson, U.S.A., 21.4
3. Ralph Metcalfe, U.S.A., 21.5

1928
1. Percy Williams, Canada, 21.8
2. Walter Rangeley, Great Britain, 21.9
3. Helmut Kornig, Germany, 21.9

1924
1. Jackson Scholz, U.S.A., 21.6

2. Charles Paddock, U.S.A., 21.7
3. Eric Liddell, Great Britain, 21.9

1920
1. Allen Woodring, U.S.A., 22.0
2. Charles Paddock, U.S.A., 22.1
3. Harry Edward, Great Britain, 22.2

1912
1. Ralph Craig, U.S.A., 21.7
2. Donald Lippincott, U.S.A., 21.8
3. William Applegarth, Great Britain, 22.0

1908
1. Robert Kerr, Canada, 22.6
2. Robert Cloughen, U.S.A., 22.6
3. Nathaniel Cartmell, U.S.A., 22.7

1906
Not held

1904
1. Archie Hahn, U.S.A., 21.6 (OR)
2. Nathaniel Cartmell, U.S.A., 21.9
3. William Hogenson, U.S.A.

1900
1. John Walter Tewksbury, U.S.A., 22.2
2. Norman Pritchard, India, 22.8
3. Stanley Rowley, Australia, 22.9

1896
Not held

Track and Field—Men's 400 Meters

1992
1. Quincy Watts, U.S.A., 43.50 (OR)
2. Steve Lewis, U.S.A., 44.21
3. Samson Kitur, Kenya, 44.24

1988
1. Steven Lewis, U.S.A., 43.87
2. Butch Reynolds, U.S.A., 43.93
3. Danny Everett, U.S.A., 44.09

1984
1. Alonzo Babers, U.S.A., 44.27
2. Gabriel Tiacoh, Cote d'Ivorie, 44.54
3. Antonio McKay, U.S.A., 44.71

1980
1. Viktor Markin, Soviet Union, 44.60
2. Richard Mitchell, Australia, 44.84
3. Frank Schaffer, East Germany, 44.87

1976
1. Alberto Juantorena, Cuba, 44.26
2. Frederick Newhouse, U.S.A., 44.40
3. Herman Frazier, U.S.A., 44.95

1972
1. Vincent Matthews, U.S.A., 44.66
2. Wayne Collett, U.S.A., 44.80
3. Julius Sang, Kenya, 44.92

1968
1. Lee Evans, U.S.A., 43.86 (WR)
2. Larry James, U.S.A., 43.9
3. Ronald Freeman, U.S.A., 44.4

1964
1. Michael Larrabee, U.S.A., 45.1
2. Wendell Mottley, Trinidad and Tobago, 45.2
3. Andrzej Badenski, Poland, 45.6

1960
1. Otis Davis, U.S.A., 44.9 (WR)
2. Carl Kaufmann, West Germany, 44.9 (WR)
3. Malcolm Spence, South Africa, 45.5

1956
1. Charles Jenkins, U.S.A., 46.7
2. Karl-Friedrich Haas, West Germany, 46.8
3. Voitto Hellsten, Finland, 47.0
3. Ardalion Ignatyev, Soviet Union, 47.0

1952
1. George Rhoden, Jamaica, 45.9 (OR)
2. Herbert McKenley, Jamaica, 45.9
3. Ollie Matson, U.S.A., 46.8

1948
1. Arthur Wint, Jamaica, 46.2
2. Herbert McKenley, Jamaica, 46.4
3. Malvin Whitfield, U.S.A., 46.9

1936
1. Archie Williams, U.S.A., 46.5
2. A. Godfrey Brown, Great Britain, 46.7
3. James LuValle, U.S.A., 46.8

1932
1. William Carr, U.S.A., 46.2 (WR)
2. Benjamin Eastman, U.S.A. 46.4
3. Alexander Wilson, Canada, 47.4

1928
1. Raymond Barbuti, U.S.A., 47.8
2. James Ball, Canada, 48.0
3. Joachim Buchner, Germany, 48.2

1924
1. Eric Liddell, Great Britain, 47.6 (OR)
2. Horatio Fitch, U.S.A., 48.4
3. Guy Butler, Great Britain, 48.6

1920
1. Bevil Rudd, South Africa, 50.0
2. Guy Butler, Great Britain, 49.9
3. Nils Engdahl, Sweden, 50.0

1912
1. Charles Reidpath, U.S.A., 48.2 (OR)
2. Hanns Braun, Germany, 48.3
3. Edward Lindberg, U.S.A., 48.4

1908
1. Wyndham Halswelle, Great Britain, 50.0

1906
1. Paul Pilgrim, U.S.A., 53.2
2. Wyndham Halswelle, Great Britain, 53.8
3. Nigel Barker, Australia, 54.1

1904
1. Harry Hillman, U.S.A., 49.2 (OR)
2. Frank Waller, U.S.A., 49.9
3. Herman Groman, U.S.A., 50.0

1900
1. Maxwell Long, U.S.A.,, 49.4 (OR)
2. William Holland, U.S.A., 49.6
3. Ernst Schulz, Denmark, 15m behind

1896
1. Thomas Burke, U.S.A., 54.2
2. Herbert Jamison, U.S.A., 14m behind
3. Charles Gmelin, Great Britain

Track and Field—Men's 800 Meters

1992
1. William Tanui, Kenya, 1:43.66
2. Nixon Kiprotich, Kenya, 1:43.70
3. Johnny Gray, U.S.A., 1:43.97

1988
1. Paul Ereng, Kenya, 1:43.45
2. Joaquim Cruz, Brazil, 1:43.90
3. Said Aouita, Morocco, 1:44.06

1984
1. Joaquim Cruz, Brazil, 1:43.00 (OR)
2. Sebastian Coe, Great Britain, 1:43.64
3. Earl Jones U.S.A., 1:43.83

1980
1. Steven Ovett, Great Britain, 1:45.4
2. Sebastian Coe, Great Britain, 1:45.9
3. Nikolai Kirov, Soviet Union, 1:46.0

1976
1. Alberto Juantorena, Cuba, 1:43.50 (WR, OR)
2. Ivo Van Damme, Belgium, 1:43.86
3. Richard Wohlhuter, U.S.A., 1:44.12

1972
1. David Wottle, U.S.A., 1:45.9
2. Yevgeny Arzhanov, Soviet Union, 1:45.9
3. Mike Boit, Kenya, 1:46.0

1968
1. Ralph Doubell, Australia, 1:44.3 (EWR)
2. Wilson Kiprugut, Kenya, 1:44.5
3. Thomas Farrell, U.S.A., 1:45.4

1964
1. Peter Snell, New Zealand, 1:45.1 (OR)
2. William Crothers, Canada, 1:45.6
3. Wilson Kiprugut, Kenya, 1:45.9

1960
1. Peter Snell, New Zealand, 1:46.3 (OR)
2. Roger Moens, Belgium, 1:46.5
3. George Kerr, Antilles, 1:47.1

1956
1. Tom Courtney, U.S.A. 1:47.7 (OR)
2. Derek Johnson, Great Britain, 1:47.8
3. Audun Boysen, Norway, 1:48.1

1952
1. Malvin Whitfield, U.S.A., 1:49.2 (EOR)
2. Arthur Wint, Jamaica, 1:49.4
3. Heinz Ulzheimer, Germany 1:49.7

1948
1. Malvin Whitfield, U.S.A., 1:49.2 (OR)
2. Arthur Wint, Jamaica, 1:49.5
3. Marcel Hansenne, France, 1:49.8

1936
1. John Woodruff, U.S.A., 1:52.9
2. Mario Lanzi, Italy, 1:53.3
3. Philip Edwards, Canada, 1:53.6

1932
1. Thomas Hampson, Great Britain, 1:49.7 (WR)
2. Alexander Wilson, Canada, 1:49.9
3. Philip Edwards, Canada, 1:51.5

1928
1. Douglas Lowe, Great Britain, 1:51.8 (OR)
2. Erik Bylehn, Sweden, 1:52.8
3. Hermann Engelhard, Germany, 1:53.2

1924
1. Douglas Lowe, Great Britain, 1:52.4
2. Paul Martin, Switzerland, 1:52.6
3. Schuyler Enck, U.S.A., 1:53.0

1920
1. Albert Hill, Great Britain, 1:53.4
2. Earl Eby, U.S.A., 1:53.6
3. Bevil Rudd, South Africa, 1:54.0

1912
1. James Meredith, U.S.A., 1:51.9 (WR)
2. Melvin Sheppard, U.S.A., 1:52.0
3. Ira Davenport, U.S.A., 1:52.0

1908
1. Melvin Sheppard, U.S.A., 1:52.8 (WR)

2. Emilio Lunghi, Italy, 1:54.2
3. Hanns Braun, Germany, 1:55.2

1906
1. Paul Pilgrim, U.S.A., 2:01.5
2. James Lightbody, U.S.A., 2:01.6
3. Wyndham Halswelle, Great Britain, 2:03.0

1904
1. James Lightbody, U.S.A., 1:56.0 (OR)
2. Howard Valentine, U.S.A., 1:56.3
3. Emil Breitkreutz, U.S.A., 1:56.4

1900
1. Alfred Tysoe, Great Britain, 2:01.2
2. John Cregan, U.S.A., 2:03.0
3. David Hall, U.S.A.

1896
1. Edwin Flack, Australia, 2:11.0
2. Nandor Dani, Hungary, 2:11.8
3. Dimitrios Golemis, Greece, 90m behind

Track and Field—Men's 1,500 Meters

1992
1. Fermin Cacho Ruiz, Spain, 3:40.12
2. Rachid El-Basir, Morocco, 3:40.62
3. Mohamed Ahmed Sulaiman, Qatar, 3:40.69

1988
1. Peter Rono, Kenya, 3:35.96
2. Peter Elliott, Great Britain, 3:36.15
3. Jens-Peter Herold, East Germany, 3:36.21

1984
1. Sebastian Coe, Great Britain, 3:32.53 (OR)
2. Steve Cram, Great Britain, 3:33.40
3. Jose Abascal, Spain, 3:34.30

1980
1. Sebastian Coe, Great Britain, 3:38.4
2. Jurgen Straub, Great Britain, 3:38.8
3. Steven Ovett, Great Britain, 3:39.0

1976
1. John Walker, New Zealand, 3:39.17
2. Ivo Van Damme, Belgium, 3:39.27
3. Paul-Heinz Wellmann, West Germany, 3:39.33

1972
1. Kipchoge Keino, Kenya, 3:36.8
1. Pekkha Vasala, Finland, 3:36.3
3. Rod Dixon, New Zealand, 3:37.5

1968
1. Kipchoge Keino, Kenya, 3:34.9 (OR)
2. Jim Ryun, U.S.A., 3:37.8
3. Bodo Tummler, West Germany, 3:39.0

1964
1. Peter Snell, New Zealand, 3:38.1

2. Josef Odlozil, Czechoslovakia, 3:39.6
3. John Davies, New Zealand, 3:39.6

1960
1. Herbert Elliott, Australia, 3:35.6 (WR)
2. Michel Jazy, France, 3:38.4
3. Istvan Rozsavolgyi, Hungary, 3:39.2

1956
1. Ron Delany, Ireland, 3:41.2 (OR)
2. Klaus Richtzenhain, East Germany, 3:42.0
3. John Landy, Australia, 3:42.0

1952
1. Josef Barthel, Luxembourg, 3:45.1 (OR)
2. Robert McMillen, U.S.A., 3:45.2
3. Werner Lueg, Germany, 3:45.4

1948
1. Henry Eriksson, Sweden, 3:49.8
2. Lennart Strand, Sweden, 3:50.4
3. Willem Slijkhuis, Netherlands, 3:50.4

1936
1. John Lovelock, New Zealand, 3:47.8 (WR)
2. Glenn Cunningham, U.S.A., 3:48.4
3. Luigi Beccali, Italy, 3:49.2

1932
1. Luigi Beccali, Italy, 3:51.2 (OR)
2. John Cornes, Great Britain, 3:52.6
3. Philip Edwards, Canada, 3:52.8

1928
1. Harri Larva,, Finland, 3:53.2 (OR)
2. Jules Ladoumegue, France, 3:53.8
3. Eino Purje-Borg, Finland, 3:56.4

1924
1. Paavo Nurmi, Finland, 3:53.6 (OR)
2. Willy Scharer, Switzerland, 3:55.0
3. Henry Stallard, Great Britain, 3:55.6

1920
1. Albert Hill, Great Britain, 4:01.8
2. Philip Baker, Great Britain, 4:02.4
3. Lawrence Shields, U.S.A., 4:03.1

1912
1. Arnold Jackson, Great Britain, 3:56.8 (OR)
2. Abel Kiviat, U.S.A., 3:56.9
3. Norman Taber, U.S.A., 3:56.9

1908
1. Melvin Sheppard, U.S.A., 4:03.4 (OR)
2. Harold Wilson, Great Britain, 4:03.6
3. Norman Hallows, Great Britain, 4:04.0

1906
1. James Lightbody, U.S.A., 4:12.0
2. John McGough, Great Britain/Ireland, 4:12.6
3. Kristian Hellstrom, Sweden, 4:13.4

1904
1. James Lightbody, U.S.A., 4:05.4 (WR)
2. W. Frank Verner, U.S.A., 4:06.8
3. Lacey Hearn, U.S.A.

1900
1. Charles Bennett, Great Britain, 4:06.2 (WR)
2. Henri Deloge, France, 4:06.6
3. John Bray, U.S.A., 4:07.2

1896
1. Edwin Flack, Australia, 4:33.2
2. Arthur Blake, U.S.A., 4:34.0
3. Albin Lermusiaux, France, 4:36.0

Track and Field—Men's 5,000 Meters
1992
1. Dieter Baumann, Germany, 13:12.52
2. Paul Bitok, Kenya, 13:12.71
3. Fita Bayisa, Ethiopia, 13:13.03

1988
1. John Ngugi, Kenya, 13:11.70
2. Dieter Baumann, West Germany, 13:15.52
3. Hansjoerg Kunze, East Germany, 13:15.73

1984
1. Said Aouita, Morocco, 13:05.59 (OR)
2. Markus Ryffel, Switzerland, 13:07.54
3. Antonio Leitao, Portugal, 13:09.20

1980
1. Miruts Yifter, Ethiopia, 13:21.0
2. Suleiman Nyambui, Tanzania, 13:21.6
3. Kaarlo Maaninka, Finland, 13:22.0

1976
1. Lasse Viren, Finland, 13:24.76
2. Dick Quax, New Zealand, 13:25.16
3. Klaus-Dieter Hildenbrand, West Germany, 13:25.38

1972
1. Lasse Viren, Finland, 13:26.4 (OR)
2. Mohamed Gammoudi, Tunisia, 13:27.4
3. Ian Stewart, Great Britain, 13:27.6

1968
1. Mohamed Gammoudi, Tunisia, 14:05.0
2. Kipchoge Keino, Kenya, 14:05.2
3. Naftali Temu, Kenya, 14:06.4

1964
1. Robert Schul, U.S.A., 13:48.8
2. Harald Norpoth, West Germany, 13:49.6
3. William Dellinger, U.S.A., 13:49.8

1960
1. Murray Halberg, New Zealand, 13:43.4
2. Hans Grodotzki, East Germany, 13:44.6
3. Kazimierz Zimmy, Poland, 13:44.8

1956
1. Vladimir Kuts, Soviet Union, 13.39.6 (OR)
2. Gordon Pirie, Great Britain, 13:50.6
3. Derek Ibbotson, Great Britain, 13.54.4

1952
1. Emil Zatopek, Czechoslovakia, 14:06.6 (OR)
2. Alain Mimoun O'Kacha, France, 14:07.4
3. Herbert Schade, West Germany, 14:08.6

1948
1. Gaston Reiff, Belgium, 14:17.6 (OR)
2. Emil Zatopek, Czechoslovakia, 14:17.8
3. Willem Slijkhuis, Netherlands, 14:26.8

1936
1. Gunnar Hockert, Finland, 14:22.2 (OR)
2. Lauri Lehtinen, Finland, 14:25.8
3. Henry Jonsson, Sweden, 14:29.0

1932
1. Lauri Lehtinen, Finland, 14:30.0 (OR)
2. Ralph Hill, U.S.A., 14:30.0
3. Lauri Virtanen, Finland, 14:44.0

1928
1. Ville Ritola, Finland, 14:38.0
2. Paavo Nurmi, Finland, 14:40.0
3. Edvin Wide, Sweden, 14:41.2

1924
1. Paavo Nurmi, Finland, 14:31.2
2. Ville Ritola, Finland, 14:31.4
3. Edvin Wide, Sweden, 15:01.8

1920
1. Joseph Guillemot, France, 14.55.6
2. Paavo Nurmi, Finland, 15:00.0
3. Eric Backman, Sweden, 15:13.0

1912
1. Johannes Kolehmainen, Finland, 14:36.6 (WR)
2. Jean Bouin, France, 14:36.7
3. George Hutson, Great Britain, 15:07.6

1896–1908
Not held

Track and Field—Men's 10,000 Meters

1992
1. Khalid Skah, Morocco, 27:46.70
2. Richard Chelimo, Kenya, 27:47.72
3. Addis Abebe, Ethiopia, 28:00.07

1988
1. Brahim Boutaib, Morocco, 27:21.46 (OR)
2. Salvatore Antibo, Italy, 27:23.55
3. Kipkemboi Kimeli, Kenya, 27:25.16

1984
1. Alberto Cova, Italy, 27:47.54

2. Michael McLeod, Great Britain, 28:06.22
3. Michael Musyoki, Kenya, 28:06.46

1980
1. Miruts Yifter, Ethiopia, 27:42.7
2. Kaarlo Maaninka, Finland, 27:44.3
3. Mohammed Kedir, Ethiopia, 27:44.7

1976
1. Lasse Viren, Finland, 27:40.38
2. Carlos Lopez, Portugal, 27:45.17
3. Brendan Foster, Great Britain, 27:54.92

1972
1. Lasse Viren, Finland, 27:38.4 (WR)
2. Emiel Puttemans, Belgium, 27:39.6
3. Miruts Yifter, Ethiopia, 27:41.0

1968
1. Naftali Temu, Kenya, 29:27.4
2. Mamo Wolde, Ethiopia, 29:28.0
3. Mohamed Gammoudi, Tunisia, 29:34.2

1964
1. William Mills, U.S.A., 28:24.4 (OR)
2. Mohamed Gammoudi, Tunisia, 28:24.8
3. Ronald Clarke, Australia, 28:25.8

1960
1. Pyotr Bolotnikov, Soviet Union, 28:32.2 (OR)
2. Hans Grodotzki, East Germany, 28:37.0
3. David Power, Australia, 28:38.2

1956
1. Vladimir Kuts, Soviet Union, 28:45.6 (OR)
2. Jozsef Kovacs, Hungary, 28:52.4
3. Allan Lawrence, Australia, 28:53.6

1952
1. Emil Zatopek, Czechoslovakia, 29:17.0 (OR)
2. Alain Mimoun O'Kacha, France, 29:32.8
3. Aleksandr Anufriev, Soviet Union, 29:48.2

1948
1. Emil Zatopek, Czechoslovakia, 29:59.6 (OR)
2. Alain Mimoun O'Kacha, France, 30:47.4
3. Bertil Albertsson, Sweden, 30:53.6

1936
1. Ilmari Salminen, Finland, 30:15.4
2. Arvo Askola, Finland, 30:15.6
3. Volmari Iso-Hollo, Finland, 30:20.2

1932
1. Janusz Kusocinski, Poland, 30:11.4 (OR)
2. Volmari Iso-Hollo, Finland, 30:12.6
3. Lauri Virtanen, Finland, 30:35.0

1928
1. Paavo Nurmi, Finland, 30.18.8 (OR)
2. Ville Ritola, Finland, 30:19.4
3. Edvin Wide, Sweden, 31:00.8

1924
1. Ville Ritola, Finland, 30:23.2 (WR)
2. Edvin Wide, Sweden, 30:55.2
3. Eero Berg, Finland, 31:43.0

1920
1. Paavo Nurmi, Finland, 31:45.8
2. Joseph Guillemot, France, 31:47.2
3. James Wilson, Great Britain, 31:50.8

1912
1. Johannes Kolehmainen, Finland, 31:20.8
2. Louis Tewanima, U.S.A., 32:06.6
3. Albin Stenroos, Finland, 32:21.8

1896–1908
Not held

Track and Field—Men's Marathon

1992
1. Hwang Young-Cho, South Korea, 2:13.23
2. Koichi Morishita, Japan, 2:13.45
3. Stephan Freigang, Germany, 2:14.00

1988
1. Gelindo Bordin, Italy, 2:10:32
2. Douglas Wakiihuri, Kenya, 2:10:47
3. Houssein Ahmed Saleh, Djibouti, 2:10:59

1984
1. Carlos Lopez, Portugal, 2:09:21 (OR)
2. John Treacy, Ireland, 2:09:56
3. Charles Spedding, Great Britain, 2:09:58

1980
1. Waldemar Cierpinski, East Germany, 2:11:03.0
2. Gerard Nijboer, Netherlands, 2:11:20.0
3. Setymkul Dzhumanazarov, Soviet Union, 2:11:35.0

1976
1. Waldemar Cierpinski, East Germany, 2:09:55.0 (OR)
2. Frank Shorter, U.S.A., 2:10:45.8
3. Karel Lismont, Belgium, 2:11:12.6

1972
1. Frank Shorter, U.S.A., 2:12:19.8
2. Karel Lismont, Belgium, 2:14:31.8
3. Mamo Wolde, Ethiopia, 2:15:08.4

1968
1. Mamo Wolde, Ethiopia, 2:20:26.4
2. Kenji Kimihara, Japan, 2:23:31.0
3. Michael Ryan, New Zealand, 2:23:45.0

1964
1. Abebe Bikila, Ethiopia, 2:12:11.2 (WB)
2. Basil Heatley, Great Britain, 2:16:19.2
3. Kokichi Tsuburaya, Japan, 2:16:22.8

1960
1. Abebe Bikila, Ethiopia, 2:15:16.2 (WB)
2. Rhadi Ben Abdesselam, Morocco, 2:15:41.6
3. Barry Magee, New Zealand, 2:17:18.2

1956
1. Alain Mimoun O'Kacha, France, 2:25:00.0
2. Franjo Mihalic, Yugoslavia, 2:26:32.0
3. Veikko Karvonen, Finland, 2:27:47.0

1952
1. Emil Zatopek, Czechoslovakia, 2:23:03.2 (OR)
2. Reinaldo Gorno, Argentina, 2:25:35.0
3. Gustaf Jansson, Sweden, 2:26:07.0

1948
1. Delfo Cabrera, Argentina, 2:34:51.6
2. Thomas Richards, Great Britain, 2:35:07.6
3. Etienne Gailly, Belgium, 2:35:33.6

1936
1. Kitei Son, Japan/Republic of Korea, 2:29:19.2 (OR)
2. Ernest Harper, Great Britain, 2:31:23:2
3. Shoryu Nan, Japan/Republic of Korea, 2:31:42.0

1932
1. Juan Zabala, Argentina, 2:31:36.0 (OR)
2. Samuel Ferris, Great Britain, 2:31:55:0
3. Armas Toivonen, Finland, 2:32:12.0

1928
1. Boughera El Ouafi, France, 2:32:57.0
2. Miguel Plaza, Chile, 2:33:23.0
3. Martti Marttelin, Finland, 2:35:02.0

1924
1. Albin Stenroos, Finland, 2:41:22.6
2. Romeo Bertini, Italy, 2:47:19.6
3. Clarence DeMar, U.S.A., 2:48:14.0

1920
1. Johannes Kolehmainen, Finland, 2:32:35.8 (WB)
2. Juri Lossman, Estonia, 2:32:48.6
3. Valerio Arri, Italy, 2:36:32.8

1912
1. Kenneth McArthur, South Africa, 2:36:54.8
2. Christian Gitsham, South Africa, 2:37:52.0
3. Gaston Strobino, U.S.A., 2:38:42.4

1908
1. John Hayes, U.S.A., 2:55:18.4 (OR)
2. Charles Hefferon, South Africa, 2:56:06.0
3. Joseph Forshaw, U.S.A., 2:57:10.4

1906
1. W. John Sherring, Canada, 2:51:23.6
2. John Svanberg, Sweden, 2:58:20.8
3. William Frank, U.S.A., 3:00:46.8

1904
1. Thomas Hicks, U.S.A., 3:28:53
2. Albert Coery, U.S.A., 3:34:52
3. Arthur Newton, U.S.A., 3:47:33

1900
1. Michel Theato, France, 2:59:45
2. Emilie Champion, France, 3:04:17
3. Ernst Fast, Sweden, 3:37:14

1896
1. Spyridon Louis, Greece, 2:58:50
2. Charilaos Vasilakos, Greece, 3:06:03
3. Gyula Kellner, Hungary, 3:06:35

Track and Field—Men's 110-Meter Hurdles

1992
1. Mark McKoy, Canada, 13.12
2. Tony Dees, U.S.A., 13.24
3. Jack Pierce, U.S.A., 13.26

1988
1. Roger Kingdom, U.S.A., 12.98 (OR)
2. Colin Jackson, Great Britain, 13.28
3. Tonie Campbell, U.S.A., 13.38

1984
1. Roger Kingdom, U.S.A., 13.20 (OR)
2. Greg Foster, U.S.A., 13.23
3. Arto Bryggare, Finland, 13.40

1980
1. Thomas Munkelt, East Germany, 13.39
2. Alejandro Casanas, Cuba, 13.40
3. Aleksandr Puchkov, Soviet Union, 13.44

1976
1. Guy Drut, France, 13.30
2. Alejandro Casanas, Cuba, 13.33
3. Willie Davenport, U.S.A., 13.38

1972
1. Rod Milburn, U.S.A., 13.24 (EWR)
2. Guy Drut, France, 13.34
3. Thomas Hill, U.S.A., 13.48

1968
1. Willie Davenport, U.S.A., 13.3 (OR)
2. Erv Hall, U.S.A., 13.4
2. Ervin Hall, U.S.A., 13.4
3. Eddy Ottoz, Italy, 13.4

1964
1. Hayes Jones, U.S.A., 13.6
2. H. Blaine Lindgren, U.S.A., 13.7
3. Anatoli Mikhailov, Soviet Union, 13.7

1960
1. Lee Calhoun, U.S.A., 13.8

2. Willie May, U.S.A., 13.8
3. Hayes Jones, U.S.A., 14.0

1956
1. Lee Calhoun, U.S.A., 13.5 (OR)
2. Jack Davis, U.S.A., 13.5
3. Joel Shankle, U.S.A., 14.1

1952
1. Harrison Dillard, U.S.A., 13.7 (OR)
2. Jack Davis, U.S.A., 13.7
3. Arthur Barnard, U.S.A., 14.1

1948
1. William Porter, U.S.A., 13.9 (OR)
2. Clyde Scott, U.S.A., 14.1
3. Craig Dixon, U.S.A., 14.1

1936
1. Forrest Towns, U.S.A., 14.2
2. Donald Finlay, Great Britain, 14 4
3. Frederick Pollard, U.S.A., 14.4

1932
1. George Saling, U.S.A., 14.6
2. Percy Beard, U.S.A., 14.7
3. Donald Finlay, Great Britain, 14.8

1928
1. Sydney Atkinson, South Africa, 14.8
2. Stephen Anderson. U.S.A., 14.8
3. John Collier, U.S.A., 14.9

1924
1. Daniel Kinsey, U.S.A., 15.0
2. Sydney Atkinson, South Africa, 15.0
3. Sten Pettersson, Sweden, 15.4

1920
1. Earl Thomson, Canada, 14.8 (WR)
2. Harold Barron, U.S.A., 15.1
3. Frederick Murray, U.S.A., 15.2

1912
1. Frederick Kelly, U.S.A., 15.1
2. James Wendell, U.S.A., 15.2
3. Martin Hawkins, U.S.A., 15.3

1908
1. Forest Smithson. U.S.A., 15.0 (WR)
2. John Garrels, U.S.A., 15.7
3. Arthur Shaw, U.S.A.

1906
1. Robert Leavitt, U.S.A., 16.2
2. A. H. Healey, Great Britain, 16.2
3. Vincent Duncker, South Africa, 16.3

1904
1. Frederick Schule, U.S.A., 16.0
2. Thaddeus Shideler, U.S.A., 16.3
3. Lesley Ashburner, U.S.A., 16.4

1900

1. Alvin Kraenzlein, U.S.A., 15.4 (OR)
2. John McLean, U.S.A., 15.5
3. Fred Moloney, U.S.A.

1896

1. Thomas Curtis, U.S.A., 17.6
2. Grantley Goulding, Great Britain, 17.7

Track and Field—Men's 400-Meter Hurdles

1992

1. Kevin Young, U.S.A., 46.78 (WR)
2. Winthrop Graham, Jamaica, 47.66
3. Kriss Akabusi, Britain, 47.82

1988

1. Andre Phillips, U.S.A., 47.19 (OR)
2. El Hedj Dia Ba, Senegal, 47.23
3. Edwin Moses, U.S.A., 47.56

1984

1. Edwin Moses, U.S.A., 47.75
2. Danny Harris U.S.A., 48.13
3. Harald Schmid, FRG, 48.19

1980

1. Volker Beck, East Germany, 48.70
2. Vasili Arkhipenko, Soviet Union, 48.86
3. Gary Oakes, Great Britain, 49.11

1976

1. Edwin Moses, U.S.A., 47.64 (WR, OR)
2. Michael Shine, U.S.A., 48.69
3. Yevgeny Gavrilenko, Soviet Union, 49.45

1972

1. John Akii-Bua, Uganda, 47.82 (WR)
2. Ralph Mann, U.S.A., 48.51
3. David Hemery, Great Britain, 48.52

1968

1. David Hemery, Great Britain, 48.1 (WR)
2. Gerhard Hennige, West Germany, 49.0
3. John Sherwood, Great Britain, 49.0

1964

1. Warren Cawley, U.S.A., 49.6
2. John Cooper, Great Britain, 50.1
3. Salvatore Morale, Italy, 50.1

1960

1. Glenn Davis, U.S.A., 49.3 (OR)
2. Clifton Cushman, U.S.A., 49.6
3. Richard Howard, U.S.A., 49.7

1956

1. Glenn Davis, U.S.A., 50.1 (OR)
2. Eddie Southern, U.S.A., 50.8
3. Josh Culbreath, U.S.A., 51.6

1952

1. Charles Moore, U.S.A., 50.8 (OR)
2. Juri Lituyev, Soviet Union, 51.3
3. John Holland, New Zealand, 52.2

1948

1. Roy Cochran, U.S.A., 51.1 (OR)
2. Duncan White, Ceylon, 51.8
3. Rune Larsson, Sweden, 52.2

1936

1. Glenn Hardin, U.S.A., 52.4
2. John Loaring, Canada, 52.7
3. Miguel White, Philippines, 52.8

1932

1. Robert Tisdall, Ireland, 51.7
2. Glenn Hardin, U.S.A., 51.9 (WR)
3. F. Morgan Taylor, U.S.A., 52.0

1928

1. David Burghley, Great Britain, 53.4 (OR)
2. Frank Cuhel, U.S.A., 53.6
3. F. Morgan Taylor, U.S.A., 53.6

1924

1. F. Morgan Taylor, U.S.A., 52.6
2. Erik Vilen, Finland, 53.8 (OR)
3. Ivan Riley, U.S.A., 54.2

1920

1. Frank Loomis, U.S.A., 54.0 (WR)
2. John Norton, U.S.A., 54.3
3. August Desch, U.S.A., 54.5

1912

Not held

1908

1. Charles Bacon, U.S.A., 55.0 (WR)
2. Harry Hillman, U.S.A., 55.3
3. Leonard Tremeer, Great Britain, 57.0

1906

Not held

1904

1. Harry Hillman, U.S.A., 53.0
2. Frank Waller, U.S.A., 53.2
3. George Poage, U.S.A.

1900

1. John Walter Tewksbury, U.S.A., 57.6
2. Henri Tauzin, France, 58.3
3. George Orton, Canada

1896

Not held

Track and Field—3,000-Meter Steeplechase

1992
1. Mathew Birir, Kenya, 8:08.84
2. Patrick Sang, Kenya, 8:09.55
3. William Mutwol, Kenya, 8:10.74

1988
1. Julius Kariuki, Kenya, 8:05.51 (OR)
2. Peter Koech, Kenya, 8:06.79
3. Mark Rowland, Great Britain, 8:07.96

1984
1. Julius Korir, Kenya, 8:11.80
2. Joseph Mahmoud, France, 8:13.31
3. Brian Diemer, U.S.A., 8:14.06

1980
1. Bronislav Malinovski, Poland, 8:09.7
2. Filbert Bayi, Tanganyika, 8:12.5
3. Eshetu Tura, Ethiopia, 8:13.6

1976
1. Anders Garderud, Sweden, 8:08.2 (WR, OR)
2. Bronislav Malinovski, Poland, 8:09.2
3. Frank Baumgartl, East Germany, 8:10.4

1972
1. Kipchoge Keino, Kenya, 8:23.6 (OR)
2. Benjamin Jipcho, Kenya, 8:24.6
3. Tapio Kantanen, Finland, 8:24.8

1968
1. Amos Biwott, Kenya, 8:51.0
2. Benjamin Kogo, Kenya, 8:51.6
3. George Young, U.S.A., 8:51.8

1964
1. Gaston Roelants, Belgium, 8:30.8 (OR)
2. Maurice Herriott, Great Britain, 8:32.4
3. Ivan Belyayev, Soviet Union, 8:33.8

1960
1. Zdzislaw Krzyszkowiak, Poland, 8:34.2 (OR)
2. Nikolai Sokolov, Soviet Union, 8:36.4
3. Semyon Rzhischin, Soviet Union, 8:42.2

1956
1. Christopher Brasher, Great Britain, 8:41.2 (OR)
2. Sandor Rozsnyoi, Hungary, 8:43.6
3. Ernst Larsen, Norway, 8:44.0

1952
1. Horace Ashenfelter, U.S.A., 8:45.4 (WR)
2. Vladimir Kazantsev, Soviet Union, 8:51.6
3. John Disley, Great Britain, 8:51.8

1948
1. Thore Sjostrand, Sweden, 9:04.6
2. Erik Elmsater, Sweden, 9:08.2
3. Gote Hagstrom, Sweden, 9:11.3

1936
1. Volmari Iso-Hollo, Finland, 9:03.8 (WR)
2. Kaarlo Tuominen, Finland, 9:06.8
3. Alfred Dompert, Germany, 9:07.2

1932
1. Volmari Iso-Hollo, Finland, 10:33.4
2. Thomas Evenson, Great Britian, 10:46.0
3. Joseph McCluskey, U.S.A., 10:46.2

1928
1. Toivo Loukola, Finland, 9:21.8 (WR)
2. Paavo Nurmi, Finland, 9:31.2
3. Ove Andersen, Finland, 9:35.6

1924
1. Ville Ritola, Finland, 9:33.6 (EWR)
2. Elias Katz, Finland, 9:44.0
3. Paul Bontemps, France, 9:45.2

1920
1. Percy Hodge, Great Britain, 10:00.4 (OR)
2. Patrick Flynn, U.S.A., 100m behind
3. Ernesto Ambrosini, Italy, 130m behind

1912
Not held

1908
1. Arthur Russell, Great Britain, 10:47.8
2. Archie Robertson, Great Britain, 10:48.4
3. John Eisele, U.S.A., 20m behind

1906
Not held

1904
1. James Lightbody, U.S.A., 7:39.6
2. John Daly, Great Britain/Ireland, 7:40.6
3. Arthur Newton, U.S.A., 25m behind

1900
1. George Orton, Canada, 7:34.4
2. Sidney Robinson, Great Britain, 7:38.0
3. Jacques Chastanie, France

1896
Not held

Track and Field—Men's 4 × 100-Meter Relay

1992
1. U.S.A., 37.40 (WR), Mike Marsh, Leroy Burrell, Dennis Mitchell, Carl Lewis
2. Nigeria, 37.98, Oluyemi Kayode, Chidi Imoh, Olapade Adeniken, Davidson Ezinwa
3. Cuba, 38.00, Andres Simon Gomez, Joel Lamela Loaces, Joel Isasi Gonzalez, Jorge Luis Aguilera Ruiz

1988

1. Soviet Union, 38.19, Victor Bryzgine, Vladimir Krylov, Vladimir Mouraviev, Vitali Savine
2. Great Britain, 38.40, Elliot Bunney, John Regis, Michael McFarlane, Linford Christie
3. France, 38.47, Bruno Marie-Rose, Daniel Sangouma, Gilles Queneherve, Max Moriniere

1984

1. U.S.A., 37.83, (WR,OR) Sam Graddy, Ron Brown, Calvin Smith, Carl Lewis
2. Jamaica, 38.62, Albert Lawrence, Gregory Meghoo, Donald Quarrie, Ray Stewart
3. Canada, 38.70, Ben Johnson, Tony Sharpe, Desai Williams, Sterling Hinds

1980

1. Soviet Union, 38.26, Vladimir Muraviov, Nikolai Sidorov, Aleksandr Aksinin, Andrei Prokofiev
2. Poland, 38.33, Krzysztof Zwolinski, Zenon Licznerski, Leszek Dunecki, Marian Woronin
3. France, 38.53, Antoine Richard, Pascal Barre, Patrick Barre, Herman Panzo

1976

1. U.S.A., 38.33, Harvey Glance, John Jones, Millard Hampton, Steven Riddick
2. East Germany, 38.66, Manfred Kokot, Joerg Pfeifer, Klaus-Dieter Kurrat, Alexander Thieme
3. Soviet Union, 38.78, Aleksandr Aksinin, Nikolai Kolesnikov, Yuri Silvos, Valeri Borzov

1972

1. U.S.A., 38.19, (WR) Larry Black, Robert Taylor, Gerald Tinker, Eddie Hart
2. Soviet Union, 38.50, Aleksandr Kornelyuk, Vladimir Lovetski, Yuri Silvos, Valeri Borzov
3. West Germany, 38.79, Jobst Hirscht, Karlheinz Klotz, Gerhard Wucherer, Klas Ehl

1968

1. U.S.A., 38.2, (WR) Charles Greene, Melvin Pender, Ronnie Ray Smith, Jim Hines
2. Cuba, 38.3, Hermes Ramirez, Juan Morales, Pablo Montes, Enrique Figuerola
3. France, 38.4, Gerard Fenouil, Jocelyn Delecour, Claude Piquemal, Roger Bambuck

1964

1. U.S.A., 39.0, (WR) O. Paul Drayton, Gerald Ashworth, Richard Stebbins, Robert Hayes
2. Poland, 39.3, Andrzej Zielinski, Wieslaw Maniak, Marian Foik, Marian Dudziak

3. France, 39.3, Paul Genevay, Bernard Laidebeur, Claude Piquemal, Jocelyn Delecour

1960

1. East Germany, 39.5, (EWR) Bernd Cullmann, Armin Hary, Walter Mahlendorf, Martin Lauer
2. Soviet Union, 40.1, Gusman Kosanov, Leonid Bartenyev, Yuri Konovalov, Edvin Ozolin
3. Great Britain, 40.2, Peter Radford, David Jones, David Segal, Neville Whitehead

1956

1. U.S.A., 39.5, (WR) Ira Murchison, Leamon King, Thane Baker, Robert Morrow
2. Soviet Union, 39.8, Boris Tokaryev, Vladimir Sukharyev, Leonid Bartenyev, Yuri Konovalov
3. East Germany, 40.3, Lothar Knorzer, Leonhard Pohl, Heinz Futterer, Manfred Germar

1952

1. U.S.A., 40.1, Dean Smith, Harrison Dillard, Lindy Remigino, Andrew Stanfield
2. Soviet Union, 40.3, Boris Tokaryev, Levan Kalyayev, Levan Sanadze, Vladimir Sukharyev
3. Hungary, 40.5, Laszlo Zarandi, Geza Varasdi, Gyorgy Csanyi, Bela Goldovanyi

1948

1. U.S.A., 40.6, Norwood Ewell, Lorenzo Wright, Harrison Dillard, Mel Patton
2. Great Britain, 41.3, John Archer, John Gregory, Alistair McCorquodale, Ken Jones
3. Italy, 41.5, Michele Tito, Enrico Perucconi, Antonio Siddi, Carlo Monti

1936

1. U.S.A., 39.8, (WR) Jesse Owens,, Ralph Metcalfe, Foy Draper, Frank Wykoff
2. Italy, 41.1, Orazio Mariani, Gianni Caldana, Elio Ragni, Tullio Gonnelli
3. Germany, 41.2, Wilhelm Leichum, Erich Borchmeyer, Erwin Gillmeister, Gerd Hornberger

1932

1. U.S.A., 40.0, (WR) Robert Kiesel, Emmett Toppino, Hector Dyer, Frank Wykoff
2. Germany, 40.9, Helmut Kornig, Friedrich Hendrix, Erich Borchmeyer, Arthur Jonath
3. Italy, 41.2, Giuseppe Castelli, Ruggero Maregatti, Gabriele Salviati, Edgardo Toetti

1928

1. U.S.A., 41.0, (EWR) Frank Wykoff, James Quinn, Charles Borah, Henry Russell
2. Germany, 41.2, Georg Lammers, Richard Corts, Hubert Houben, Helmut Kornig
3. Great Britain, 41.8, Cyril Gill, Ellis Smouha, Walter Rangeley, Jack London

1960
1. Vladimir Golubnichi, Soviet Union, 1:34:07.2
2. Noel Freeman, Australia, 1:34:16.4
3. Stanley Vickers, Great Britain, 1:34:56.4

1956
1. Leonid Spirin, Soviet Union, 1:31:27.4
2. Antanas Mikenas, Soviet Union, 1:32:03.0
3. Bruno Junk, Soviet Union, 1:32:12.0

1896–1952
Not held

Track and Field—Men's 50 km Walk

1992
1. Andrey Perlov, Russia, 3:50.13
2. Carlos Mercenario Carbajal, Mexico, 3:52.09
3. Ronald Weigel, Germany, 3:53.45

1988
1. Viacheslav Ivanenko, Soviet Union, 3:38:29 (OR)
2. Ronald Weigel, East Germany, 3:28:56
3. Hartwig Gauder, East Germany, 3:39:45

1984
1. Raul Gonzalez, Mexico, 3:47:26
2. Bo Gustafsson, Sweden, 3:53:19
3. Alessandro Belluci, Italy, 3:53:45

1980
1. Hartwig Gauder, East Germany, 3:49:24.0 (OR)
2. Jorge Llopart, Spain, 3:51:25.0
3. Yevgeny Ivchenko, Soviet Union, 3:56:32.0

1976
Not held

1972
1. Bernd Kannenberg, West Germany, 3:56:11.6 (OR)
1. Veniamin Soldatenko, Soviet Union, 3:58:24.0
3. Larry Young, U.S.A., 4:00:46.0

1968
1. Christoph Hohne, East Germany, 4:20:13.6
2. Antal Kiss, Hungary, 4:30:17.0
3. Larry Young, U.S.A., 4:31:55.4

1964
1. Abdon Pamich, Italy, 4:11:12.4 (OR)
2. Paul Nihill, Great Britain, 4:11:31.2
3. Ingvar Pettersson, Sweden, 4:14:17.4

1960
1. Donald Thompson, Great Britain, 4:25:30.0 (OR)
2. John Ljunggren, Sweden, 4:25:47.0
3. Abdon Pamich, Italy, 4:27:55.4

1956
1. Norman Read, New Zealand, 4:30:42.8
2. Yevgeny Maskinskov, Soviet Union, 4:32:57.0
3. John Ljunggren, Sweden, 4:35:02.0

1952
1. Giuseppe Dordoni, Italy, 4:28:07.8 (OR)
2. Josef Dolezal, Czechoslovakia, 4:30:17.8
3. Antal Roka, Hungary, 4:31:27.2

1948
1. John Ljunggren, Sweden, 4:41:52
2. Godel Gaston, Switzerland, 4:48:17
3. Tebbs Lloyd-Johnson, Great Britain, 4:48:31

1936
1. H. Harold Whitlock, Great Britain, 4:30:41.4 (OR)
2. Arthur Schwab, Switzerland, 4:32:09.2
3. Adalberts Bubenko, Latvia, 4:32:42.2

1932
1. Thomas Green, Great Britain, 4:50:10
2. Janis Dalinsch, Latvia, 4:57:20
3. Ugo Frigerio, Italy, 4:59:06

1896–1928
Not held

WOMEN'S RUNNING EVENTS

Highlights

Sprints, 400 Meters, and Relays

In 1928 the 100m, the initial Olympic women's track and field event, was won by Elizabeth Robinson of the U.S.A. few years after the Amsterdam Games, Robinson was severely injured in a plane crash, and her prospects of returning to competition were bleak. Astonishingly, she managed a comeback and went on to capture another gold medal in Berlin as a member of the American 4 × 100 relay team.

A poignant Olympic story relates that the German women's relay team of 1936 couldn't lose; that is, until Marie Dollinger and a teammate dropped the baton. The world was watching, and so was Hitler. The American team—anchored by 1928's 100m winner Betty Robinson and 1936's 100m winner Helen Stephens—seized the golden opportunity, winning by eight yards. Dollinger's daughter, Brunhilde Hendrix, ran the relay final in 1960 for Germany, and happily brought home a silver medal.

Polish-born Stella Walasiewicz (later Walsh, as an American citizen), won the 100m gold in 1932 and the 100m silver in 1936, and minced no words when she referred to the young American upstart, Helen Stephens, who beat her in the 1936 Games, calling her a "greenie from the sticks." Walsh's story came to a tragic end—and her record was amended—when she was caught in the middle of a holdup; the post-shooting autopsy revealed that Stella Walsh was a man.

Fanny Blankers-Koen was the belle of the ball in 1948; having been on the 1936 Dutch team, Blankers had married, had two children, and established six world records in the 12-year interim. Some thought she was too old to compete well in London, but her four-medal haul—that's almost half of that year's women's track and field medals—soon silenced them. Blankers-Koen won the 100m, the 80m hurdles, the 200m, and the 4 × 100m relay. Too bad she wasn't allowed to compete in her strongest event, the long jump: her best jump beat the gold medal distance by twenty inches. Blankers-Koen also held the world record in the high jump.

Fifteen-year-old U.S. sprinter Barbara Jones ran a leg in 1952's 4 × 100 relay team, becoming the youngest track gold medal winner. Also that year, Australian Marjorie Jackson tied the 17-year-old record for the 200m that had been set by Stella Walsh. Jackson tied his-or-her record in the first round, and broke it in the first semifinal; in the final, having no more record to challenge, she left her competition in the dust four yards back.

Australia's Betty Cuthbert struck gold in 1956 at the tender age of 18, winning the 100m and 200m, and helping her team to the relay gold. 1956 was the first time in the history of the Games that the first and second place finisher of the 100m were in the same person and the same order as for the 200 meters, as Christa Stubnick of East Germany took the silver in both races. At the wizened age of 22, Cuthbert triumphed again in the 400m in 1960.

Wilma Rudolph was 1960's champion, winning a total of three gold medals, at that time the most ever by a U.S. woman. Touted as the world's fastest woman, Rudolph was clocked in the final at 11.0 flat. Although she had beaten the world record time, her time was disallowed because the favoring wind was .752 meters per second above the acceptable limit.

Rudolph was followed by sprint champion Wyomia Tyus, who captured the 100m in Tokyo. Tyus was the first athlete, man or woman, to win back-to-back titles in the 100m in the Olympics when she defended her gold in 1968.

Poland's Irena Szewinska-Kirszenstein captured a silver medal in the 200m in 1964, came back for the gold in 1968—setting a world record in the 200 with a time of 22.5—then completed the set with a bronze in 1972. She also shared in the team gold of the Polish 4 × 100m relay team in 1964, won the silver medal in 1964's long jump, and dashed to a bronze in the 100m in 1968. In 1976, she capped her very successful Olympic career with a gold in the 400m. Szewinska-Kirszenstein was the first woman to win medals at three successive Games, and also in five different events.

East Germany's Bärbel Eckert, later competing as Bärbel Wöckel, captured four gold medals from 1976 to 1980, in the 200m and the 4 × 100m relay. Competing in 1976 at the age of 21 as a third-string sprinter, she surprised everyone when—after equaling her personal best in the quarterfinals—she won the final with an Olympic record for the 200 meters. In 1980, even though Wöckel had not won a single heat, she made it to the 200m finals, and sprinted to the front in the final turn to take another gold.

Wilma Rudolph's 1960 performance was matched in 1984 by Valerie Brisco-Hooks. Brisco-Hooks became the only 200m and 400m double winner of either gender in all Olympic history. Evelyn Ashford set an Olympic record in the 100m in 1984; Florence Griffith Joyner broke that record in 1988 in the preliminaries, and ran even faster in the finals, but Griffith Joyner's time didn't count for the record because the tail wind was above the allowable maximum. Griffith Joyner nonetheless won the gold, while Ashford took home the silver in 1988.

In 1988, the U.S.A.'s 4 × 100m relay team of Alice Brown, Sheila Echols, Griffith Joyner, and Ashford claimed the gold, followed by the East German and Soviet teams. In the 4 × 400m race, the Soviet Union ran for the gold and the U.S.A. (Brisco-Hooks, Griffith Joyner, Denean Howard-Hill, and Diane Dixon) settled for silver, trailing the Soviets by less than half a second.

Middle Distance, Long Distance, and Cross Country

The women's 800m was run at the first Games to admit women for track events, in 1928. The sight of ill-trained women staggering toward the finish of the 800m caused the event to be banished from the Olympic program until 1960. Even in 1960, Australian Dixie Willis, who had led the race until the final 150 meters, staggered off the track, allowing Soviet Lyudmila Shevtsova to sprint to the gold and an Olympic record. British runner Ann Packer took the gold in that event in 1964, even though the 800 was not her event; she had already captured the 400m silver that year.

The 1968 800m was best remembered for the unfortunate story of the Yugoslavian record holder, Vera Nikolic´. Apparently on the verge of suicide because of the pressure of being Yugoslavia's only hope for a track and field medal, Nikolic´ was rumored to have been prevented from jumping off a bridge by her coach. American Madeline Manning won the event that year.

Thirteen women beat the pre-Olympic world record in the 1972 semifinals for the 1500m. Twenty-nine-year-old Soviet Lyudmila Bragina maintained a 12-meter lead over the pack during the entire final lap, winning the gold and setting a world record.

At the Montreal Games, Bragina managed only fifth place in the 1500m. Fellow Soviet Tatayana Kazankina, who had broken Bragina's world record the previous month, ran a tactical race to capture the gold, but set no record.

In 1984 Romanian Maricica Puica won the gold in the 3000m race and a bronze in the 1500m. The International Olympic Committee finally allowed the women's 10,000m race for the 1988 Games, and Olga Bondarenko of the Soviet Union promptly ran for the gold, setting an Olympic record in the process.

Marathon and Walking

The U.S.A.'s Joan Benoit won the first Olympic women's marathon in 1984. That year, Switzerland's Gabriela Andersen Schiess staggered to the finish line, unaided and obviously in trouble, sparking debate about whether someone should have gone out and saved her from those last agonizing steps, when she seemed not only near collapse, but possibly near death. She reeled over the line in 37th place. In 1988 Portugal's Rosa Mota, bronze medalist in 1984, won the gold but did not break Benoit's Olympic record.

Track and Field (Athletics)—Running

Hurdles

In 1932, at the second Olympics open to women, U.S. hurdler Babe Didrikson won a gold in the hurdles to add to her gold in the javelin and a silver in the high jump (changed from gold when her style was ruled illegal).

Didrikson's multiple-medaling performance seemed to foreshadow things to come. Holland's Fanny Blankers-Koen earned a hurdling gold in 1948 to complement her other Olympic spoils. With four firsts, she became distinguished as the woman with the most gold medals earned at a single Games.

Australian Shirley Strickland took the bronze in the hurdles in 1948, then competing as Shirley de la Hunty captured the hurdles gold in 1952 and 1956, to add to a 1956 relay gold, a 1948 relay silver, and two bronzes in the 100m (1948 and 1952). Photo studies show that Strickland also came in third in the 200m event of 1948, but the result has not yet been officially changed.

In 1960 Soviet hurdler Irina Press captured the 80m gold, while her sister, Tamara, won the shot put title, giving the two the impressive distinction of being the Olympics' most successful sisters.

At Munich in 1972, Israeli Esther Shakhamorov cherished hopes of becoming her country's first Olympic finalist by competing in the 100m hurdles. When she withdrew following the shocking terrorist attack on Israeli athletes, East Germany's Annelie Ehrhardt had no real competition, and proceeded to set a world record in the hurdles.

Having married in the interim, Shakhamorov competed in Montreal as Esther Rot, and managed to become Israel's first Olympic finalist by placing fifth in the 100m hurdles competition. An imbroglio during the second heat had Soviet Lyubov Kononova bumping into Romanian Valeria Stefanescu in the lane next to her. It was Johanna Schaller, from East Germany, however, who won the race in 12.77.

U.S.A.'s Benita Fitzgerald-Brown won the 100m hurdles in 1984, while Bulgaria's Jordanka Donkova took the gold in 1988. Casablanca native Nawal El Moutawakel leaped to gold in 1984's 400m hurdles, setting an Olympic record and giving Morocco its first gold medal of the modern Olympics; this was thought to be the only medal ever won by an Arab woman. U.S.A.'s Judi Brown trailed for silver. In the 1988 400m hurdles, Debra Flintoff-King of Australia set an Olympic record and claimed the gold, although she was a scant one one-hundredth of a second ahead of Tatiana Ledovskaia of the Soviet Union.

Joan Benoit Samuelson

In April 1979, on the way to compete in her first Boston Marathon, Joan Benoit found herself caught in a traffic jam. She jumped out of her friend's car, ran two miles to the starting line, and 26 miles later won the race with a record-setting time of 2:35:15.

This same determination drove her to enter a marathon in September 1982, just months after surgery on both Achilles tendons. She won that race in 2:26:11, breaking the record for American women by two minutes. And she ran to victory in the 1984 U.S. Olympic trials with a time of 2:31:04, just 17 days after undergoing arthroscopic surgery on her knee.

The diminutive Joan Benoit Samuelson—she stands 5 feet, 3 inches, and weighs 105 pounds—has set new standards of both speed and courage for long-distance runners with her victories in the 1979 and 1983 Boston Marathons. And she secured her place in history by winning the gold medal in the first women's Olympic marathon at the Los Angeles Games in 1984, in an incredible 2:24:52.

The Olympic marathon started off slowly—too slowly, thought Benoit. She took the lead at the three-mile mark and wondered why she was so outpacing her competitors. Toward the end, she maintained a more comfortable pace, conserving energy in case she needed to repel a last-minute challenge. That never happened: Benoit entered the Los Angeles Coliseum to the thunderous ovation of 77,000 spectators.

Asked later to recall her thoughts during the final yards of the marathon, she said: "I couldn't believe no one had challenged me. . . . I couldn't imagine that it was almost over." Her time was the third-fastest ever run by a woman in a marathon.

The daughter of Andre (who runs an apparel store in Portland, Maine) and Nancy Benoit, Joan Benoit Samuelson was born on May 16, 1957. She became a dedicated athlete, concentrating primarily on skiing until she broke her leg in a slalom race. As part of her rehabilitation program, she began running, eventually turning in a 5:15 mile in her senior year of high school. At Bowdoin College, where she earned a bachelor's degree in 1979, and North Carolina State University, she was highly ranked as a distance runner, which ultimately led to her outstanding performance in numerous marathons and culminated in her Olympic victory.

On September 29, 1984, Joan Benoit married Scott Samuelson. They have two children, Abigail and Anders. She ran the 1987 Boston Marathon while three months pregnant with her first child and competed in that event in 1991 one month after she had stopped nursing her second. Since giving birth to Abigail in 1987 she has been plagued with chronic lower back pain. But as she says, "I'm learning to work with it. I make the best of what I have."

Although she has had to contend with a long list of injuries, Samuelson still runs occasionally. In 1995 her book *Joan Samuelson's Running for Women* was published.

—Paul Green

Highlights from Barcelona

If anything captured the global character of the Barcelona Games—where 172 nations and fragments of nations participated in the opening ceremony—it was the women's track and field events. Clinching the 10,000m, Ethiopia's Derartu Tulu became the second African woman to earn an Olympic gold medal. In the 100m hurdles, Paraskevi Patoulidou captured the first Greek track and field gold in 80 years. And Algeria's Hassiba Boulmerka defied Islamic fundamentalist criticism to grab the 1,500m title.

Not that this was to the detriment of American athletes: the U.S. women's team scored 8 medals in running—3 gold, 3 silver, and 2 bronze. In what was perhaps the most poignant of the American victories, Gail Devers came back from a debilitating hyperthyroid condition to capture the 100m victory in a too-close-for-the-naked-eye photo finish. Having set an American record in the 100 hurdles in 1988, Devers's performance began inexplicably to fall off before the Seoul Games, where she didn't even make it to the finals. Her health began to deteriorate. She had mysterious shaking bouts, lost the vision in one eye, and put up with three menstrual cycles each month.

FACT: With a 30-medal harvest from Barcelona, U.S. track and field athletes scored their highest total in a non-boycotted Games since 1956.

Two years of physical hell passed before doctors finally diagnosed Devers with Graves' disease, a condition that can be easily controlled with medication—medication that's on the IOC's list of banned substances. Choosing radiation therapy over medication, Devers suffered side effects that left her unable to walk, and nearly forced her to have both feet amputated. After changing her therapy, Devers eased into workouts—the first of which was a painful, shoe-less walking lap around the track—and signed up Bob Kersee to coach her to the Games.

Among the 8 athletes at the starting line of the 1992 100m dash were Gwen Torrence, the U.S. Olympic trials champ, and

Merlene Ottey, who had nailed 57-straight finals in the four years leading up to her defeat at the hands of Katrin Krabbe in the 1991 World Championships. As Devers approached the final, Florence Griffith Joyner had some words of advice: "You worked hard for this," she told Devers, "you better get it." Edging out Jamaica's Juliet Cuthbert and Russia's Irina Privalova, Devers fought a one-meter-per-second win to pocket the gold. Taking stock of the wind, only one other woman—Flo Jo, the world record holder—had ever run the sprint faster.

Adding to the growing roster of women's Olympic track and field events, a 10km walk debuted in Barcelona. Although the Unified Team's Alina Ivanova finished first, she was deposed as champion for "lifting," or removing one foot from the ground as she walked. With Ivanova out of the way, Chen Yueling moved into first place to become China's first track and field champ. In second place was Russia's Elena Nikolaeva, followed by Li Chunxia of China. The women's marathon finish, meanwhile, was the closest ever at the Games, as Russia's Valentina Yegorova finished only eight seconds ahead of Yuko Arimori of Japan.

Medalists

Track and Field—Women's 100 Meters

1992
1. Gail Devers, U.S.A., 10.82
2. Juliet Cuthbert, Jamaica, 10.83
3. Irina Privalova, Russia, 10.84

1988
1. Florence Griffith Joyner, U.S.A., 10.54 (OR)
2. Evelyn Ashford, U.S.A., 10.83
3. Heike Drechsler, East Germany, 10.85

1984
1. Evelyn Ashford, U.S.A., (OR) 10.97
2. Alice Brown, U.S.A., 11.13
3. Merlene Ottey-Page, Jamaica, 11.16

1980
1. Lyudmila Kondratyeva, Soviet Union, 11.06
2. Marlies Gohr, East Germany, 11.07
3. Ingrid Auerswald, East Germany, 11.14

1976
1. Annegret Richter, West Germany, 11.08
2. Renate Stecher, East Germany, 11.13
3. Inge Helten, West Germany, 11.17

1972
1. Renate Stecher, East Germany, 11.07

2. Raelene Boyle, Australia, 11.23
3. Silvia Chibas, Cuba, 11.24

1968
1. Wyomia Tyus, U.S.A., 11.0 (WR)
2. Barbara Ferrell, U.S.A., 11.1
3. Irena Szewinska-Kirzenstein, Poland, 11.1

1964
1. Wyomia Tyus, U.S.A., 11.4
2. Edith McGuire, U.S.A., 11.6
3. Ewa Klobukowska, Poland, 11.6

1960
1. Wilma Rudolph, U.S.A., 11.0
2. Dorothy Hyman, Great Britain, 11.3
3. Giuseppina Leone, Italy, 11.3

1956
1. Betty Cuthbert, Australia, 11.5
2. Christa Stubnick, East Germany, 11.7
3. Marlene Matthews, Australia, 11.7

1952
1. Marjorie Jackson, Australia, 11.5 (EWR)
2. Daphne Hasenjager-Robb, South Africa, 11.8
3. Shirley De La Hunty-Strickland, Australia, 11.9

1948
1. Francina Blankers-Koen, Netherlands, 11.9

2. Dorothy Manley, Great Britain, 12.2
3. Shirley Strickland, Australia, 12.2

1936

1. Helen Stephens, U.S.A., 11.5
2. Stanislawa Walasiewicz, Poland, 11.7
3. Kathe Krauss, Germany, 11.9

1932

1. Stanislawa Walasiewicz, Poland, 11.9 (EWR)
2. Hilda Strike, Canada, 11.9
3. Wilhelmina Von Bremen, U.S.A., 12.0

1928

1. Elizabeth Robinson, U.S.A., 12.2 (EWR)
2. Fanny Rosenfeld, Canada, 12.3
3. Ethel Smith, Canada, 12.3

1896–1924

Not held

Track and Field—Women's 200 Meters

1992

1. Gwen Torrence, U.S.A., 21.81
2. Juliet Cuthbert, Jamaica, 22.02
3. Merlene Ottey, Jamaica, 22.09

1988

1. Florence Griffith Joyner, U.S.A., 21.34 (WR)
2. Grace Jackson, Jamaica, 21.72
3. Heike Drechsler, East Germany, 21.95

1984

1. Valerie Brisco-Hooks, U.S.A., 21.81 (OR)
2. Florence Griffith, U.S.A., 22.04
3. Merlene Ottey-Page, Jamaica, 22.09

1980

1. Barbel Eckert Wockel, East Germany, 22.03 (OR)
2. Natalya Bochina, Soviet Union, 22.19
3. Merlene Ottey, Jamaica, 22.20

1976

1. Barbel Eckert, East Germany, 22.37 (OR)
2. Annegret Richter, West Germany, 22.39
3. Renate Stecher, East Germany, 22.47

1972

1. Renate Stecher, East Germany, 22.40 (EWR)
2. Raelene Boyle, Australia, 22.45
3. Irena Szewinska-Kirszenstein, Poland, 22.74

1968

1. Irena Szewinska-Kirszenstein, Poland, 22.5 (WR)
2. Raelene Boyle, Australia, 22.7
3. Jennifer Lamy, Australia, 22.8

1964

1. Edith McGuire, U.S.A., 23.0 (OR)
2. Irena Kirszenstein, Poland, 23.1
3. Marilyn Black, Australia, 23.1

1960

1. Wilma Rudolph, U.S.A., 24.0
2. Jutta Heine, West Germany, 24.4
3. Dorothy Hyman, Great Britain, 24.7

1956

1. Betty Cuthbert, Australia, 23.4 (EOR)
2. Christa Stubnick, East Germany, 23.7
3. Marlene Matthews, Australia, 23.8

1952

1. Marjorie Jackson, Australia, 23.7
2. Bertha Brouwer, Netherlands, 24.2
3. Nadezhda Khnykina, Soviet Union, 24.2

1948

1. Francina Blankers-Koen, Netherlands, 24.4
2. Audrey Williamson, Great Britain, 25.1
3. Audrey Patterson, U.S.A., 25.2

1896–1936

Not held

Track and Field—Women's 400 Meters

1992

1. Marie-José Pérec, France, 48.83
2. Olga Bryzgina, Ukraine, 49.05
3. Ximena Restrepo Gaviria, Colombia, 49.64

1988

1. Olga Bryzguina, Soviet Union, 48.65 (OR)
2. Petra Mueller, East Germany, 49.45
3. Olga Nazarova, Soviet Union, 49.90

1984

1. Valerie Brisco-Hooks, U.S.A., 48.83 (OR)
2. Chandra Cheeseborough, U.S.A., 49.05
3. Kathryn Cook, Great Britain, 49.42

1980

1. Marita Koch, East Germany, 48.88 (OR)
2. Jarmila Kratochvilova, Czechoslovakia, 49.46
3. Christina Lathan, East Germany, 49.66

1976

1. Irena Szewinska-Kirszenstein, Poland, 49.29 (WR, OR)
2. Christina Brehmer, East Germany, 50.51
3. Ellen Streidt, East Germany, 50.55

1972

1. Monika Zehrt, East Germany, 51.08 (OR)
2. Rita Wilden, West Germany, 51.21
3. Kathy Hammond, U.S.A., 51.64

1968

1. Colette Besson, France, 52.0 (EOR)
2. Lillian Board, Great Britain, 52.1
3. Natalja Pechenkina, Soviet Union, 52.2

1964

1. Betty Cuthbert, Australia, 52.0 (OR)
2. Ann Packer, Great Britain, 52.2
3. Judith Amoore, Australia, 53.4

1896–1960

Not held

Track and Field—Women's 800 Meters

1992

1. Ellen Van Langen, Netherlands, 1:55.54
2. Lilia Nurutdinova, Russia, 1:55.99
3. Ana Fidelia Quirot Moret, Cuba, 1:56.80

1988

1. Sigrun Wodars, East Germany, 1:56.10
2. Christine Wachtel, East Germany, 1:56.64
3. Kim Gallagher, U.S.A., 1:56.91

1984

1. Doina Melinte, Romania, 1:57.60
2. Kim Gallagher, U.S.A., 1:58.63
3. Fita Lovin, Romania, 1:58.83

1980

1. Nadezhda Olizarenko, Soviet Union, 1:53.42 (WR)
2. Olga Mineyeva, Soviet Union, 1:54.9
3. Tatyana Providokhina, Soviet Union, 1:55.5

1976

1. Tatyana Kazankina, Soviet Union, 1:54.94 (WR, OR)
2. Nikolina Shtereva, Bulgaria, 1:55.42
3. Elfi Zinn, East Germany, 1:55.60

1972

1. Hildegard Falck, West Germany, 1:58.55 (OR)
2. Niole Sabaite, Soviet Union, 1:58.65
3. Gunhild Hoffmeister, East Germany, 1:59.19

1968

1. Madeline Manning, U.S.A., 2:00.9 (OR)
2. Ileana Silai, Romania, 2:02.5
3. Maria Gommers, Netherlands, 2:02.6

1964

1. Ann Packer, Great Britain, 2:01.1 (OR)
2. Maryvonne Dupureur, France, 2:01.9
3. Ann Chamberlain, New Zealand, 2:02.8

1960

1. Lyudmila Shevtsova, Soviet Union, 2:04.3 (EWR)

2. Brenda Jones, Australia, 2:04.4
3. Ursula Donath, East Germany, 2:05.6

1932–1956

Not held

1928

1. Lina Radke, Germany, 2:16.8 (WR)
2. Kinue Hitomi, Japan, 2:17.6
3. Inga Gentzel, Sweden, 2:17.8

1896–1924

Not held

Track and Field—Women's 1,500 Meters

1992

1. Hassiba Boulmerka, Algeria, 3:55.30
2. Lyudmila Rogacheva, Russia, 3:56.91
3. Qu Yunxia, China, 3:57.08

1988

1. Paula Ivan, Romania, 3:53.96 (OR)
2. Lailoute Baikauskaite, Soviet Union, 4:00.24
3. Tatiana Samolenko, Soviet Union, 4:00.30

1984

1. Gabriella Dorio, Italy, 4:03.25
2. Doina Melinte, Romania, 4:03.76
3. Maricica Puica, Romania, 4:04.15

1980

1. Tatyana Kazankina, Soviet Union, 3:56.6 (OR)
2. Christiane Wartenberg, East Germany, 3:57.8
3. Nadezhda Olizarenko, Soviet Union, 3:59.6

1976

1. Tatyana Kazankina, Soviet Union, 4:05.48
2. Gunhild Hoffmeister, East Germany, 4:06.02
3. Ulrike Klapezynski, East Germany, 4:06.09

1972

1. Ljudmila Bragina, Soviet Union, 4:01.4 (WR)
2. Gunhild Hoffmeister, East Germany, 4:02.8
3. Paola Cacchi-Pigni, Italy, 4:02.9

1896–1968

Not held

Track and Field—Women's 3,000 Meters

1992

1. Elena Romanova, Russia, 8:46.04
2. Tatiana Dorovskikh, Ukraine, 8:46.85
3. Angela Chalmers, Canada, 8:47.22

1988

1. Tatiana Samolenko, Soviet Union, 8:26.53 (OR)
2. Paula Ivan, Romania, 8:27.15
3. Yvonne Murray, Great Britain, 8:29.02

1984
1. Maricica Puica, Romania, 8:35.96 (OR)
2. Wendy Sly, Great Britain, 8:39.47
3. Lynn Williams, Canada, 8:42.14

1896–1980
Not held

Track and Field—Women's 10,000 Meters

1992
1. Derartu Tulu, Ethiopia, 31:06.02
2. Elana Meyer, South Africa, 31:11.75
3. Lynn Jennings, U.S.A., 31:19.89

1988
1. Olga Bondarenko, Soviet Union, 31:05.21 (OR)
2. Elizabeth McColgan, Great Britain, 31:08.44
3. Elena Joupieva, Soviet Union, 31:19.82

1896–1984
Not held

Track and Field—Women's Marathon

1992
1. Valentina Yegorova, Russia, 2:32.41
2. Yuko Arimori, Japan, 2:32.49
3. Lorraine Moller, New Zealand, 2:33.59

1988
1. Rosa Mota, Portugal, 2:25.40
2. Lisa Martin, Australia, 2:25.53
3. Kathrin Doerre, East Germany, 2:26.21

1984
1. Joan Benoit, U.S.A., 2:24.52
2. Grete Waitz, Norway, 2:26.18
3. Rosa Mota, Portugal, 2:26.57

1896–1980
Not held

Track and Field—Women's 100-Meter Hurdles

1992
1. Paraskevi Patoulidou, Greece, 12.64
2. LaVonna Martin, U.S.A., 12.69
3. Yordanka Donkova, Bulgaria, 12.70

1988
1. Jordanka Donkova, Bulgaria, 12.38 (OR)
2. Gloria Siebert, East Germany, 12.61
3. Claudia Zackiewicz, West Germany, 12.75

1984
1. Benita Fitzgerald-Brown, U.S.A., 12.84
2. Shirley Strong, Great Britain, 12.88

3. Michele Chardonnet, France, 13.06
3. Kim Turner, U.S.A., 13.06

1980
1. Vera Komisova, Soviet Union, 12.56 (OR)
2. Johanna Klier, East Germany, 12.63
3. Lucyna Langer, Poland, 12.65

1976
1. Johanna Schaller, East Germany, 12.77
2. Tatiana Anisimova, Soviet Union, 12.78
3. Natalia Lebedeva, Soviet Union, 12.80

1972
1. Annelie Ehrhardt, East Germany, 12.59 (OR)
2. Valeria Bufanu, Romania, 12.84
3. Karin Balzer, East Germany, 12.90

1968 (80m hurdles, 1932-68)
1. Maureen Caird, Australia, 10.3 (OR)
2. Pamela Kilborn, Australia, 10.4
3. Chi Cheng, Taiwan, 10.4

1964
1. Karin Balzer, East Germany, 10.5
2. Teresa Ciepla, Poland, 10.5
3. Pamela Kilborn, Australia, 10.5

1960
1. Irina Press, Soviet Union, 10.8
2. Carol Quinton, Great Britain, 10.9
3. Gisela Birkemeyer-Kohler, East Germany, 11.0

1956
1. Shirley De La Hunty-Strickland, Australia, 10.7 (OR)
2. Gisela Kohler, East Germany, 10.9
3. Norma Thrower, Australia, 11.0

1952
1. Shirley De La Hunty-Strickland, Australia, 10.9 (WR)
2. Maria Golubnichaya, Soviet Union, 11.1
3. Maria Sander, West Germany, 11.1

1948
1. Francina Blankers-Koen, Netherlands, 11.2 (OR)
2. Maureen Gardner, Great Britain, 11.2
3. Shirley Strickland, Australia, 11.4

1936
1. Trebisonda Valla, Italy, 11.7
2. Anni Steuer, Germany, 11.7
3. Elizabeth Taylor, Canada, 11.7

1932
1. Mildred "Babe" Didrikson, U.S.A., 11.7 (WR)
2. Evelyne Hall, U.S.A., 11.7
3. Marjorie Clark, South Africa, 11.8

1896–1928
Not held

Track and Field—Women's 400-Meter Hurdles

1992
1. Sally Gunnell, Britain, 53.23
2. Sandra Farmer-Patrick, U.S.A., 53.69
3. Janeene Vickers, U.S.A., 54.31

1988
1. Debra Flintoff-King, Australia, 53.17 (OR)
2. Tatiana Ledovskaia, Soviet Union, 53.18
3. Ellen Fiedler, East Germany, 53.63

1984
1. Nawal El Moutawakel, Morocco, 54.61 (OR)
2. Judi Brown, U.S.A., 55.20
3. Christina Cojocaru, Romania, 55:41

1896–1980
Not held

Track and Field—Women's 4 × 100-Meter Relay

1992
1. U.S.A., 42.11, Evelyn Ashford, Esther Jones, Carlette Guidry, Gwen Torrence
2. Unified Team, 42.16, Olga Bogoslovskaya, Galina Malchugina, Marina Trandenkova, Irina Privalova
3. Nigeria, 42.81, Beatrice Utondu, Faith Idehen, Christy Thompson, Mary Onyali

1988
1. U.S.A., 41.98, Alice Brown, Sheila Echols, Florence Griffith Joyner, Evelyn Ashford
2. East Germany, 42.09, Silke Moeller, Kerstin Behrendt, Ingrid Lange, Marlies Goehr
3. Soviet Union, 42.75, Lyudmila Kondrayeva, Galina Maltchougina, Marina Jirova, Natalia Pomochtchnikova

1984
1. U.S.A., 41.65, Alice Brown, Jeannette Bolden, Chandra Cheeseborough, Evelyn Ashford
2. Canada, 42.77, Angella Bailey, Marita Payne, Angella Taylor, France Gareau
3. Great Britain, 43.11, Simone Jacobs, Kathryn Cook, Beverley Callender, Heather Oakes

1980
1. East Germany, 41.60, (WR) Romy Muller, Barbel Wockel Eckert, Ingrid Auerswald, Marlies Gohr
2. Soviet Union, 42.10, Vera Komisova, Lyudmila Maslakova-Zharkova, Vera Anisimova, Natalya Bochina
3. Great Britain, 42.43, Heather Hunte, Kathryn Smallwood, Beverley Goddard, Sonia Lannaman

1976
1. East Germany, 42.55 (OR), Marlies Oelsner, Barbel Eckert Wockel Renate Stecher Meissner, Carla Bodendorf
2. West Germany, 42.59, Elvira Possekel, Inge Helten, Annegret Richter, Annegret Kroninger
3. Soviet Union, 43.09, Tatyana Prorochenko, Lyudmila Maslakova-Zharkova, Nadezhda Besfamilnaya, Vera Anisimova

1972
1. West Germany, 42.81, (EWR) Christiane Krause, Ingrid Mickler, Annegret Richter, Heidemarie Rosendahl
2. East Germany, 42.95, Evelyn Kaufer, Christina Heinich, Barbel Struppert, Renate Stecher
3. Cuba, 43.36, Marlene Elejarde, Carmen Valdes, Fulgencia Romay, Silvia Chibas

1968
1. U.S.A., 42.8, (WR) Barbara Ferrell, Margaret Bailes, Mildrette Netter, Wyomia Tyus
2. Cuba, 43.3, Marlene Elejarde, Fulgencia Romay, Violetta Quesada, Miguelina Cobian
3. Soviet Union, 43.4, Lyudmila Zharkova, Galina Bukharina, Vyera Popkova, Lyudmila Samotysova

1964
1. Poland, 43.6 Teresa Ciepla-Wieczorek, Irena Kirszenstein, Halina Gorecka-Richter, Ewa Klobukowska
2. U.S.A., 43.9, Willye White, Wyomia Tyus, Marilyn White, Edith McGuire
3. Great Britain, 44.0, Janet Simpson, Mary Rand, Daphne Arden, Dorothy Hyman

1960
1. U.S.A., 44.5, Martha Hudson, Lucinda Williams, Barbara Jones, Wilma Rudolph
2. West Germany, 44.8, Martha Langbein, Anni Biechl, Brunhilde Hendrix, Jutta Heine
3. Poland, 45.0, Teresa Wieczorek, Barbara Janiszewska, Celina Jesionowska, Halina Richter

1956
1. Australia, 44.5, (WR) Shirley De La Hunty-Strickland, Norma Croker, F leur Mellor, Betty Cuthbert
2. Great Britain, 44.7, Anne Pashley, Jean Scrivens, June Paul-Foulds, Heather Armitage
3. U.S.A., 44.9, Mae Faggs, Margaret Matthews, Wilma Rudolph, Isabelle Daniels

Hammer throwing was popular for centuries in Britain. Like the shot put, it remains part of the modern Scottish Highland Games. Its popularity carried over to America, where the hammer evolved from a clumsy, wood-shafted implement to a clumsy, metallic implement. Americans also experimented in building a hammer from shafts of knotted grape vines.

The first few modern Olympic Games featured several throwing events long since discontinued. There was stone throwing, in which athletes used a javelin toss-like technique to propel a 14-pound rock, and there were two-handed versions of the shot, discus, and javelin throws. Contestants threw with their left and right hands, and were scored based on an aggregate total of the two.

Discus was the only throwing event included when women began competing in track and field sports during the 1928 Olympics. The first female track and field gold medalist was Halina Konopacka of Poland, the discus winner.

In the 1988 Olympic Games, Eastern European athletes won every men's throwing event except the javelin, which was won by a Finn.

Some observers believe that anabolic steroids, now illegal in Olympic competition, were widely used by athletes in "heavy" sports like the throwing events and weightlifting as far back as the mid-1960s to stimulate muscle growth and increase work capacity. If true, the drugs no doubt helped to increase record performances.

Throwing events were combined with running and jumping events early on. The Greeks held the first known pentathlon in 708 BC, which included javelin and discus throws, wrestling, long jump, and foot racing. Ireland staged all-around athletic competitions in the mid-19th century, and the Americans began the same in 1884. A decathlon (not as we know it today) was added to the 1904 Olympics in St. Louis as a men's event. It disappeared until 1912, when the events were reestablished. The women's pentathlon was added in 1964, and in 1980 two more events were added and it became the heptathlon. The Scandinavians organized a decathlon that included the same 10 events as in modern Olympic competition.

"You've got to be a bit of an animal to be a decathlete. Being poor helps, too."
—Daley Thompson, two-time gold medalist

Bill Toomey, an American, won the decathlon in 1968 after stressing training for every event. His lead was followed by most decathletes who followed. Daley Thompson, a Briton, set four world records and won the decathlons of 1980 and 1984. German and Soviet women dominated the pentathlon until 1980. World-wide, decathlon and heptathlon winners are considered the best of the best.

Spectator's Guide

Discus: Today's discus is made from wood and metal and shaped like a flying saucer. It has a metal rim and metal center for added weight. The men's discus is about 22 centimeters (0.66 inches) and weighs two kilograms (4 pounds, 6.5 ounces). The women's discus weighs one kilogram and measures 18 centimeters (7.13 inches).

The athlete holds the discus flat against the palm and forearm while standing in the 2.5m (eight foot, 2.25-inch) throwing circle. The throw begins with one and a half spins that leads to a sidearm release.

The discus spins through the air at an upward angle, the spin helping to propel it farther. Throws with a strong wind will carry the discus farther, but there is no rule against wind-aided throws. This makes it difficult to compare the distances of throws.

Once the athlete enters the throwing circle, he or she must not leave until the discus has landed. Throws are measured from the landing point to the inside edge of the circle.

Too much spin on the thrower's part causes an uneven launch. Early discus throwers were strong but slow athletes who depended on pure power for throw length. Smaller but quicker athletes began to get better results by concentrating on form and spin. The winning distance for the discus has more than doubled since the modern Games began in 1896, when the winning throw was 95 feet, 7.5 inches.

Al Oerter is probably the greatest discus thrower of modern times. He favored a controlled spin in his throws, and he won four Olympic gold medals, beginning in 1956 at age 20.

Shot put: The shot is a ball of solid metal that weighs 16 pounds for men, and eight pounds, 13 ounces for women. The goal of this event is to "put" the shot as far as possible.

Because shots lose weight in use—tiny particles get chipped off when they land—the balls are weighed before each use. Additional tungsten chips can be added through a plugged hole to bring the shot back up to legal weight.

The shot must be pushed, or put, not thrown. The shot must not drop during the put below the athlete's shoulder. The putting technique begins with the contestant holding the shot in his or her hand, which rests against the shoulder. This is followed by a series of hops inside the putting circle, which is seven feet (2.1m) in diameter. The athlete then springs powerfully from a near-crouch, unleashes his or her arm, and lets loose the shot with a powerful push.

The athlete must remain within the circle during the throw. The ring is bounded by a board four inches (10cm) high at the top of the circle. The purpose is to allow the competitor's foot to hit the board without pushing beyond the circle to be disqualified.

Measurement is from the point of impact to the inside circumference of the putting circle.

Like discus throwers, shot putters were originally physically powerful athletes who lacked technique. That changed as speed became important and as weight training improved performances. Additionally, shot putters were among the first athletes to abuse steroids, and many performances improved accordingly.

Up until the early 20th century, most shot putters used the side-on hop favored by Scottish athletes since the beginning of the 19th century. A new putting technique was developed by American Parry O'Brien, who started with his back to the putting field to give more momentum before releasing the shot. He won gold medals in 1952 and 1956. And some putters use a relatively new technique of making one complete spin in the ring before putting.

Hammer throw (men only): The hammer is a 16-pound metal ball attached to nearly four feet (121.5cm) of a spring steel wire that leads to grips. The name apparently derives from the Scottish and English sport of sledgehammer throwing.

The throwing circle is seven feet (2.1m) in diameter. Inside the circle, with his feet stationary, the thrower grasps the handle in both hands and begins to swing the hammer. He swings the hammer in an arc so it passes below his knees and above his head several times. Before releasing the hammer he swings his body around to build up even more force, up to 500 pounds (227kg). Measurement of the throw is from the dent in the ground where the hammer landed to the inside circumference of the circle. A cage protects spectators from wild throws. Throws that land outside a marked field are not allowed.

Irish Americans won the hammer toss at the Olympics from 1896–1924. John Flanagan, a New York City policeman and Irish emigrant, won three golds, and Matt McGrath, also a policeman, won a gold and a silver.

Europeans dominated the sport then until the mid–1950s. Soviet hammer throwers swept the event in the 1976, 1980, and 1988 Olympics, and again as the Unified Team in 1992.

Javelin: A men's javelin must weigh at least 800 grams (one pound, 12.25 ounces) and measure 2.6–2.7 meters (eight feet, 6.25 inches and eight feet, 10.25 inches). A women's javelin weighs at least 600 grams (26.16 ounces) and measures 2.2–2.3 meters (seven feet, 2.66 inches and seven feet, 6.5 inches).

The shaft can be either wood or metal, though the tip is always steel. For a throw to be counted, the metal tip must break the turf, and the distance is measured from the first touch-down point to a scratch line at the end of the thrower's runway.

Unlike competitors in other throwing events, javelin throwers wear spikes. They begin with a sprint down the runway, carrying the spear-like instrument by a grip in the shaft's center. (Spinning before throwing the javelin is illegal because it endangers spectators.) As they near the line, throwers turn to one side, pull back the javelin and throw. Crossing the scratch line disqualifies the throw.

In the Middle Ages, the javelin was thrown for accuracy. Throwing for distance was developed in Hungary and Germany in the mid-1800s. Most modern developments in the sport came in Sweden and Finland. Throwers from these two countries won all the Olympic competitions in javelin until 1936.

Franklin Held, an American, helped develop a more aerodynamic javelin. It floated farther but sometimes landed flat rather than at the point. He used this javelin to extend the world record to 263 feet. An East German athlete threw the javelin 16 feet, eight inches beyond the world record at the time, and in 1986 an amateur sports federation placed limits on the javelin that emphasize aerodynamics over distance.

Mixed or combined events: Both the decathlon and the heptathlon are two-day competitions that stress stamina and versatility.

The decathlon is the men's event and consists of the 100m dash, long jump, shot put, high jump, and 400m run in the first day. Day two continues with the 110m hurdles, discus throw, pole vault, javelin throw, and 1500m run.

The heptathlon for women includes the following on day one: 200m run, 100m hurdles, high jump, and shot put. Day two sports are the long jump, javelin throw, and 800m run.

Points are scored according to a set of tables approved by the International Amateur Athletic Federation. Athletes do not have to win every event, but rather finish well in the largest number of sports.

Hopefuls—Men's Events

Lance Deal

The hammer throw, virtually ignored by public and press, may finally earn its share of the spotlight at the 1996 Olympic Games. The event could very well bring a medal to Lance Deal, the United States champion and a serious contender in this era of strict drug testing. Deal finished seventh in the hammer throw at the 1992 Olympics and was ranked fourth in the world in 1994. He has since improved his world best three times and has earned the Grand Prix title as the highest point-getter in the 1995 indoor track and field season.

Any kind of publicity will be warmly welcomed by Deal. Never having enjoyed the high profile of a runner, swimmer, or gymnast, he has worked in the shadows of sports for years, patiently and consistently improving his talents without the help of anabolic steroids or other performance-enhancing drugs. At times he has had to pay his coach's salary in order to continue to train, and in 1993 he spent more than $5,000 to fly opponents to events so his specialty would qualify for Grand Prix points. Deal sees the measures he has taken as a matter of self-preservation. "If the [hammer throw] event fades away, I'm out of a vocation and an avocation," he explained in a March 13, 1995 *Sports Illustrated* profile. "I got into this because I love it. I don't want to see it disappear."

Lance Deal grew up in Casper, Wyoming and was an All-America linebacker in high school. Even then he loved throwing the discus and the shot put. "I just loved watching the thing fly," he recalled of his discus days in *Sports Illustrated*. He won a track-football scholarship to Montana State University, but he quickly determined that he preferred to concentrate on discus. During a summer break from college in 1980, he discovered a throwing hammer hanging on the wall at the sporting goods store where he was working. He paid six dollars for the weight, began to practice throwing it, and found a lifelong calling.

After graduating from college in 1985, Deal moved to Eugene, Oregon, where track and field coach Stewart Togher was offering weekend hammer-throwing clinics. The working relationship between Togher and Deal has been strong ever since. When U.S.A. Track and Field eliminated the salary for hammer coach in 1993, Deal paid Togher out of track meet winnings so they could continue to train together. The results have been satisfying for both. In these days of more rigorous drug testing, Deal—at six-foot-two, 260 pounds—competes drug-free and has helped spark an American comeback in the hammer throw.

No American has won a medal in hammer since 1956, but Deal has a very good chance. At the 1994 Goodwill Games in St. Petersburg, Russia, he finished in first place ahead of a Russian team that has dominated the event in the past. Since then he has improved his world best record three times and has taken the U.S. national championship. Still under 35, he is not considered old for his sport.

Deal approaches the rigors of hammer and weight throwing with a philosophy that is almost reminiscent of Zen Buddhism. Asked by *Sports Illustrated* how he prepares for his event, the affable Wyoming native replied: "Basically, instead of worrying about how strong you are and what you can do to the hammer, it's how much you can get back out of the hammer." Perhaps in Atlanta, the hammer will be happy to oblige.

—Anne Janette Johnson

John Godina

Can a likable athlete from Big Sky country find a way to restore the tarnished image of American shot-putting? UCLA's John Godina will certainly try. Ranked seventh nationally in both the shot put and the discus throw in 1994, Godina has since improved his personal records in both events. His all-time best shot throw of 72 feet, two inches gives him a clear chance at making the Olympic team and medaling in other international events. Throwing expert Art Venegas, Godina's most recent coach, told *Track & Field News:* "[John] knows he's the man—not because you guys say it, but because he knows it, and that's important."

Godina finds himself competing in events that have lost a great deal of prestige due to drug abuse among the competing athletes. At the 1992 Olympics, for instance, all three shot put medalists had previously served suspensions for drug use. Rather than being praised for their gold-silver finish in the event, Americans Mike Stulce and Jim Doehring found themselves faced with a skeptical press corps that quizzed them about steroids and training practices. World record holder Randy Barnes missed the Olympics completely because he was serving a two-year suspension for testing positive for a testosterone derivative. The discus and hammer throws have faced similar problems.

The perception that shot put and drugs are linked is so common that, in the early 1990s, a world-class shot putter said, off the record, that he believed everyone who had thrown 70 feet or better had used drugs. It is in this atmosphere of suspicion that John Godina has begun his double-event career.

Born May 31, 1972, in Fort Sill, Oklahoma, Godina grew up in Cheyenne, Wyoming. He was an All-American football player at Central High in Cheyenne, as well as a nationally ranked discus and shot thrower. "It was about three weeks after my senior football season that I decided to concentrate only on track," Godina joked in the *Los Angeles Times* on April 15, 1993. Whatever led him to the decision, Godina has never regretted it. The six-foot-four, 260-pound athlete won a scholarship to the University of California, Los Angeles and quickly established himself as one of the best collegiate throwers in the country.

As a UCLA freshman, Godina placed second in the shot and third in the discus at the Pacific 10 Championships. He was ninth in the discus at the 1992 Olympic Trials. From 1993 until his graduation Godina dominated the PAC-10 as a throwing doubler. The truly big marks in both events did not come until after he graduated from college, however. Under Venegas's direction, he reduced his weightlifting schedule with dramatic effects. As a college senior he had ranked seventh nationally with a personal best shot put of 65 feet, $8\frac{3}{4}$ inches and a discus throw of 204 feet. In 1995 he achieved a shot put of 72 feet, two inches and a discus throw of 213 feet. Those numbers put him in world class just a year before the Olympics.

The National Collegiate Athletic Association (NCAA) champion in shot and discus in 1994, Godina is preparing for his ascent into international competition. His appeal as a double-event threat has drawn comment both in America and abroad as the throwing athletes try to restore their events' reputations. Nice-looking and personable, Godina seems poised to lead his sport back to respectability. "It's kind of strange to get attention like that when you're a thrower," he noted in *Track & Field News*, "but it's not something I'm going to turn down, by any means."

—*Anne Janette Johnson*

Dave Johnson

Enjoy your final go-round with Dave Johnson, America. Atlanta 1996 is the decathlete's final event.

By now, even the most casual track and field fan knows at least bits and pieces of Dave Johnson's life story.

Johnson grew up a burgeoning hoodlum in Missoula, Mont., taking on all comers with a chain wrapped around his wrist, then discovered athletics, then became a Christian, then a top-ranked decathlete. Then he became part of the "Dan or Dave" Reebok marketing strategy/story, blossoming into a living example of courage and determination, as he limped home to a bronze medal at Barcelona on an ankle split with not one, but two fractures.

It, quite simply, Johnson says, is time for different challenges.

"After the Olympics, I'm definitely going to retire from the decathlon," Johnson, 33 (b. April 7, 1963), told *Track & Field News* last July. "I'll enjoy the (Olympics), (then) walk away from the decathlon as a success, as a mountain climbed, and be able to look down on it seeing a lot of experiences that have propelled me to the next mountains I have to climb."

Johnson has been training hard for Atlanta, but not against Dan O'Brien, his former Reebok marketing mate and current decathlon world-record holder. This time, Johnson has a different opponent at his shoulder.

This time, it's Father Time. The past four years have not been easy. Johnson lost all of 1993 to rehabilitation of his ankle and '94 was a mixed bag, with some successes marred by a 16th-place finish at the nationals and knee surgery.

Recovery has been a little slower, too. Johnson is feeling a little more pain than he did in his youth.

"My right ankle feels a little bit sore still because there are pins in the bone," he says of some everyday aches and pains. "It's a little bit arthritic, but once I start running, I don't feel anything at all in my ankles. I had surgery on my right knee . . . and that still feels a little sore once in a while. But these are all little aches and pains. Once I get warmed up a bit, they go away. To feel a little bit of pain when I'm warming up and have it go away when I'm running—it gives me that much more confidence."

And Johnson's confidence is his bread and butter. It grows during the competition. Just when his opponents are beginning to wind down, Johnson, author of the autobiography *Aim High: An Olympic Decathlete's Inspiring Story,* is usually just getting started.

Johnson, who lacks the spectacular speed and style of some decathletes, developed himself into what has been characterized as a "second-day wonder." When most other athletes start feeling a bit weary in the last two events—the javelin and the 1,500-meter race—Johnson is just hitting his stride.

The resiliency, grit, and gumption are testaments to Johnson's determination.

"Dave told me his first year competing in the decathlon that he could score with the best decathletes in the country," Terry Franson, his Azusa Pacific University coach, told *Time* magazine.

"I thought he was crazy, then, but the key to Dave's winning record is that he has always been able to visualize success. He has continued to stun everyone, including me.

"He's a committed risk-taker, which is just what you need when a competition comes down to the crunch."

Johnson also—no surprise, here—trains his butt off.

A typical day includes breakfast and "goof-off" time with his two daughters; knee and ankle therapy; warmup on the stationary bike; stretching; lunch with his coaches; another warm up; concentrated work on at least two events; running, and a weight workout. He's usually home by 7 p.m.

In his free time, Johnson plays golf, does a lot of mountain biking, and takes correspondence courses.

"I eventually want to do something else with my life," he says. "Sports psychology and marriage/family counseling is the direction I want to take."

Former Olympic gold-medal winner Bruce Jenner says: "What makes Dave Johnson stand out is that he knows how to win. That is crucial. You've got to be the best you can be on that given day—and know it."

Johnson puts it another way. "I've learned to always be aggressive," he says. "It even carries over (for example) to when I'm driving on the freeway. I want to be in front of every car that I see. It's a very tense situation. I've got to calm myself down or I end up getting a ticket. When I mountain bike or golf, there's a competitive side. I want to beat the guy next to me."

It carries, of course, over to the decathlon: "When there's points to be had, that's when the most courageous guy comes out in me."

A big part of Johnson's life is his religion.

"I'm pretty competitive," he told *T&FN*. "I've learned to do things as Christ would. So, I try to give 100 percent of myself, as He did. I mean, He died on the cross—that's 100 percent, no doubt about it. When I give 100 per cent, the outcome is always a winning situation."

Throughout his successes, Johnson has managed to keep things in perspective. The father of two daughters, Johnson and wife, Sheri, lost their first child to miscarriage.

"The true meaning of life is kids," he says.

Terry Franson adds: "Athletics is kind of silly when you think about it. It's a question of who can run around a track faster." But not forever. What will Dave Johnson do after the 1996 Olympic games? "I might," he says, "just throw the javelin for the fun of it."

—Eric Kinkopf

Dan O'Brien

Dan O'Brien is no longer affiliated with Reebok. He no longer is linked with fellow U.S. decathlete Dan Johnson.

In fact, unknown to most, the fadeout scene of the athletic shoe campaign—*Dan or Dave?*—didn't take place at the Olympic Decathlon Trials in New Orleans in 1992, when O'Brien failed to clear the pole vault in three tries, thus failing to qualify for the Olympic team and scuttling the ad strategy.

Nor did it take place at a track in Stockholm, a month after the 1992 Olympics, when O'Brien no-heighted in the high jump and failed to finish the competition.

The last scene—*"Dan Can't Take The Heat"*—was written almost a year later, when a fiberglass statue of O'Brien, purchased at a salvage auction by a Georgia U-Haul dealer, melted outside the dealership on its Reebok-logoed pedestal in Conyers, Georgia.

O'Brien, 30 (b. July 18, 1966), out of view of all but the most fervent track and field fan, had actually redeemed himself months earlier.

A month after Stockholm, with the failure at New Orleans still all too fresh in his mind, O'Brien set a world decathlon record at a meet in Talence, France, with 8,891 points.

In fact, although most experts describe O'Brien's most impressive talent as his "ballistic" speed, Rick Sloan, who coaches O'Brien in the field events, said before the Talence meet that his decathlete's greatest asset is his "ability to forget."

It seems sort of odd, then, that Dan O'Brien's main opponent has always been himself.

"The only guy we ever really compete against," Sloan says, "is this O'Brien kid."

FACT: Within a year of his Olympic debacle, Dan O'Brien scored a whopping 8,891, besting Daley Thompson's decathlon record by 44 points.

O'Brien, whose past includes bouts with alcohol, has told countless stories of problems with self-discipline. He has admitted responsibility for collegiate academic ineligibilities, habitual tardiness, and problems with basic social graces, such as returning phone calls and answering mail.

He told *U.S. News & World Report* that he once spent a Christmas alone in an apartment in Idaho, drinking up to a dozen beers a day. "I had no job and no money, then," O'Brien recalled. "I would wake up every day thinking I was a loser."

Dan O'Brien, a *loser?*

In fact, O'Brien was in the lifelong throes of what has been described as almost paralyzing bouts of anxiety and self-doubt. Some later even attributed O'Brien's failure in New Orleans to what has been diagnosed as an attention deficit problem.

The New Orleans disappointment was a result of O'Brien's "immaturity and focus," Mike Keller, another O'Brien coach, told the *New York Times.* "Dan sat on his butt for an hour and didn't get warmed up properly."

Keller, however, began suspecting that O'Brien's problem was more than simple irresponsibility. Keller began to suspect that O'Brien was having some of the same problems that Keller's son, Travis, was having.

"I was reading a book about (attention deficit disorder with hyperactivity)," Keller told *Sports Illustrated.* "On every page I was writing Dan-Travis, Travis-Dan in the margin."

It was a drinking problem, however, that finally pushed O'Brien to seek help.

In January of 1994, O'Brien was scheduled to fly from his hometown of Moscow, Idaho, to New York for a press conference. The night before he was scheduled to leave, he bumped into friends and. . . .

"One drink led to another," O'Brien said. "I got wasted. I was too sick for days to travel anywhere. I knew it was time to do something."

O'Brien turned to former discus thrower-turned counselling psychologist Jim Reardon, who ran some tests on O'Brien and came to the conclusion that the decathlete was "hyperdistractible."

O'Brien was subsequently put on medication. The effects were eye-opening.

Before taking the medicine "I couldn't read an article to the end," he said. "I couldn't sit in one place for five minutes. I can think so clearly, now."

That wasn't the end of the story, however. Side effects of the medication—headaches and insomnia—caused him to give up on the medicine. He now relies on deep-breathing techniques and massage therapy to keep his focus.

Which is, of course, a gold medal at the 1996 Olympics.

"It doesn't matter what I do (record-wise)," O'Brien told the *New York Times*, "if I don't win a gold medal, I'm never going to be placed in the same group with Bob Mathias, Milt Campbell, Rafer Johnson, Bill Toomey and Bruce Jenner."

Despite his past troubles, O'Brien has always been described as disarmingly candid, with childlike charm. In the wake of the New Orleans debacle, Tim Sullivan, a sports reporter for the *Moscow-Pullman Daily News*, wrote:

"We cheer for O'Brien because he is just that normal guy on the street. His athletic talent surpasses just about everyone in the world of sport, yet he's still the same guy who walks down Main Street in Moscow. The guy you say 'Hi!' to, and end up talking to for 20 minutes."

Normal or not, once-troubled or not, the potential of the former all-stater in track *and* football is what most educated observers see.

"He can be anything he wants to be," says Daley Thompson, who set a decathlon record at the Los Angeles Olympics in 1984. "I see him as a 9,500-point man."

Says O'Brien: "I don't think of (winning a gold medal) as redeeming myself. I think of it as taking my place in history. If I don't get it in '96, you're going to see an old man going for it in 2000."

—*Eric Kinkopf*

Hopefuls—Women's Events

Jackie Joyner-Kersee

If amateur athletics has a queen, that monarch would have to be Jackie Joyner-Kersee. Described everywhere as the greatest multi-event track and field athlete of all time, Joyner-Kersee has won three Olympic gold medals, one silver, and one bronze, and has competed in every Summer Olympics since 1984. Her list of accomplishments is impressive: the first American woman to win a gold medal in the long jump, the first woman in history to earn more than 7,000 points in the seven-event heptathlon, the world record holder in the heptathlon since 1986, and the first athlete in 64 years to win gold medals in both a multi-event and a single

U.S.A.'s Jackie Joyner-Kersee competes in the first heat of the women's heptathlon 100-meter hurdles in the 1992 Games. She finished with a time of 12.85 for 1147 points and later took the gold in the women's heptathlon event. *AP/Wide World Photos*

682

event in track and field. Going into the 1996 Olympics she is still a force to be reckoned with, and she shows no signs of slowing down.

America loves Jackie Joyner-Kersee. Not only has she been a stand-out Olympian, she has also dazzled fans and opponents alike with her winning personality, her grace and intelligence, and her commitment to the community. She has never let success go to her head but has instead worked to promote physical fitness among young people, especially in urban environments. In the February, 1995 issue of *Women's Sports & Fitness,* she said: "I find it touching, in a sense, that people want my autograph and they're in tears. I think, my God! I'm just happy that I'm in the position I'm in and that people would even take the time to talk to me. . . . I understand the position I'm in, but I also know that tomorrow there's going to be someone else. So I try to keep things in perspective."

Joyner-Kersee was born March 3, 1962 in East St. Louis, Illinois, a poverty-stricken city on the Mississippi River. The younger of two children of teenaged parents, she grew up dreaming of a better life for herself and her brother Al. Together the young Joyner siblings took part in sports activities at the publicly funded Mayor Brown Community Center in East St. Louis. It was there that Jackie Joyner was introduced to track events. After watching the 1976 Olympics on television, she became determined to try to make the U.S. team herself one day.

Almost immediately the versatile young athlete began laying the foundations for her big dreams. At the age of 14 she won the first of four straight national junior pentathlon championships. She also played basketball and volleyball and earned honor roll grades. Recruited by many top flight colleges, she accepted a scholarship to the University of California, Los Angeles. She chose well: a coach was waiting there to help her achieve her fullest potential.

Bob Kersee met Jackie Joyner in 1980, when she was still playing basketball as a primary sport. He convinced Jackie—and the athletic brass at UCLA—that she should concentrate on multi-event track. She was already a good long jumper and a winner at the 200-meter sprint. Her brother Al Joyner helped her to learn to run hurdles and throw the javelin and shot put. By 1982 Jackie had chosen the demanding heptathlon as her event, and the following year she qualified for the World Championships. Her

FACT: Competing with a painful hamstring injury, Jackie Joyner-Kersee settled for a silver medal in the heptathlon in 1984, only 5 points behind the Australian winner. If she had competed in top form, she probably would have clinched the gold medal, as she did in 1988 and 1992.

first international competition ended in disappointment when she pulled a hamstring muscle and had to withdraw.

She has had few disappointments since. At her first Olympic appearance in 1984 she won a silver medal in the heptathlon, missing the gold by only .06 seconds in her final event, the 800-meter run. At the 1986 Goodwill Games in Moscow she set a new world record in the heptathlon with 7,148 points. She broke that record three weeks later in Houston on a day when temperatures reached 100 degrees. It was those two performances that earned Jackie Joyner the 1986 Sullivan Award and the Jesse Owens Award. That same year she married Bob Kersee, and the two have worked closely together ever since.

Joyner-Kersee's performance at the 1988 Olympics was one of the outstanding accomplishments of those games. She won gold medals in both the heptathlon and the long jump and set yet another world record in the heptathlon, with 7,291 points. These were the Summer Games that were marked by the enthusiasm and affection of Joyner-Kersee and her sister-in-law Florence Griffith Joyner as they congratulated each other on their medal-winning races.

More glory awaited Joyner-Kersee in the 1992 Olympics in Barcelona. There she won the heptathlon gold medal again and added a bronze in the long jump. She further endeared herself to her fans by being a gracious "loser" in the long jump to her friend Heike Drechsler of Germany. Asked if she planned to retire after the Games in Barcelona, the animated Joyner-Kersee declared that she fully intended to stay in competition until 1996, so she could begin and end her Olympic career with appearances in Summer Games on American soil.

"You would think it would be easier to focus now, but because of all the things I've already accomplished, sometimes it's harder. I can't think I'm going to go out there and win just because I'm Jackie Joyner-Kersee."

—Jackie Joyner-Kersee

Another Olympics looms, and Jackie Joyner-Kersee says she is ready. Her stamina has never flagged, but she has suffered from injuries in her Achilles tendon, hamstring, and groin. No one, male or female, has ever won a multi-event medal at 34, the age Joyner-Kersee will be at the next Olympics. She is undaunted, though. "That's the ultimate challenge—to do something nobody has been able to do," she told *Women's Sports & Fitness*. "I would love that." To win, Joyner-Kersee will have to earn points for a 200-meter sprint, a 100-meter hurdles, the high jump, the long jump, the shot put, the javelin, and the 800-meter run. Needless to say, she will be facing much younger competitors both from the U.S. and abroad.

Asked the secret of her longevity in a January, 1993 *Women's Sports & Fitness* profile, Joyner-Kersee replied: "A lot of it has to do with how you take care of your body while you're young, and I've always taken care of myself. One good thing about multievent is that I don't have to compete every weekend, like sprinters do. The most heptathlons I do in a year is two, and then I break the events up and work on them at different meets." She admitted that her advancing age may be a liability. "You would think it would be easier to focus now, but because of all the things I've already accomplished, sometimes it's harder," she said. "I can't think I'm going to go out there and win just because I'm Jackie Joyner-Kersee."

One of the only African American women athletes to win lucrative product endorsement contracts, Joyner-Kersee is conscious of her status as a role model. "I feel that as an African American woman the only thing I can do is continue to better myself, continue to perform well, continue to make sure that I'm a good commodity," she concluded in *Women's Sports & Fitness*. "If doors aren't opened for me, then maybe it will happen for someone else."

—Anne Janette Johnson

Schedule

The tentative track & field (athletics)—throwing & mixed events schedule is:

Friday, July 26
Men's shot put, qualifying
Women's javelin, qualifying
Men's shot put, final

Saturday, July 27
Women's heptathlon (100m hurdles, high jump)
Men's hammer throw, qualifying
Women's heptathlon (shot put, 200m)
Women's javelin, final

Sunday, July 28
Women's heptathlon (long jump)
Women's discus, qualifying
Men's hammer throw, final
Women's heptathlon (javelin, 800m)

Monday, July 29
Men's discus, qualifying
Women's discus, final

Wednesday, July 31
Men's decathlon (100m, long jump, shot put)
Men's pole vault, qualifying
Women's shot put, qualifying
Men's decathlon (high jump, 400m)
Men's discus, final

Thursday, August 1
Men's decathlon (110m hurdles, discus)
Men's decathlon (javelin, 1500m, pole vault)

Friday, August 2
Men's javelin, qualifying
Men's pole vault, final
Women's shot put, final

Saturday, August 3
Men's javelin, final

MEN'S THROWING AND MIXED EVENTS

Highlights

Shot Put

Everyone knows Johnny Weissmuller as Tarzan, and a lot of people know Buster Crabbe as the apeman, but not only swimmers make good Tarzans. In Amsterdam in 1928, American shotputter Herman Brix finished second in his event, and went on to be the first of many Olympic athletes to play Tarzan on the silver screen. You won't find the name Brix in the credits, though: look for his tinseltown name, Bruce Bennet.

It was a shot-putter that got Hitler in trouble with the IOC in Berlin in 1936 . . . sort of. When a tall, blond German shotputter won the event on the first day of the Games, Hitler summoned the athlete to congratulate him, or tell him he thought it was mighty Aryan of him to win the first medal, or something like that; the IOC frowned on such behavior, advising Hitler that it wasn't protocol for him to greet winners, but if he did he would have to greet them all. The message didn't seem to hit home, though: Hitler failed to congratulate African American athletes, including Jesse Owens.

U.S. shot putter Randy Matson claimed the gold in 1968. Twenty years later Randy Barnes of the U.S. produced a magnificent come-through throw of 73′5½″ to momentarily take the lead, but East German Ulf Timmermann summoned a historic throw of 73′8¾″ to regain the lead and the gold.

Hammer Throw

American policeman John J. Flanagan was the first Olympic hammer throw champion; competing in the 1900 Games in Paris, he won his second gold medal, even though the event was marred by the insouciant treatment the track and field events had been given by the Parisian organizers; many of the athletes' throws wound up in the trees that year, due to poor planning of the field. Flanagan won his third consecutive hammer throw in London in 1908. The following year, at the age of 41, he threw the hammer 184 feet 4 inches to become the oldest world record breaker in track and field history.

When Harold Connolly hammered the competition at Melbourne in 1956, he became the first American to win the hammer throw since 1924 (when Frederick Tootell had won). What's even more interesting, though, is that he married the women's discus champion, Olga Fikotova of Czechoslovakia, who was allowed to emigrate for the marriage. Connolly went on to participate in four Games, but divorced his Czech wife in 1975, later marrying another Olympian, Pat Daniels.

Soviet hammer thrower Uri Sedykh is the only man to win the event twice; his characteristic performance produced his best throw on his first try. Sedykh was going for his third gold in 1988, but had to accept the silver behind teammate Sergei Litvinov; Uri Tamm completed a Soviet sweep of the event.

Discus

American Robert Garrett became the first discus champion of the modern Games when he won the event in Athens in 1896. He was also the first shot put champion. In his spare time, he silvered in the high and long jumps. That guy really knew how to throw his weight around.

In Melbourne, in 1956, American Al Oerter won the gold medal for throwing the discus a record distance; earning another three gold medals in the event, Oerter has the unique distinction of winning four successive gold medals in the discus. And, by the way, he won the 1964 event despite a ruptured muscle.

Based on world rankings just prior to the Moscow Games in 1980, the U.S. boasted the best four discus throwers, in addition to a variety of other frustrated track and field hopefuls. Soviet Viktor Rashchupkin was the victor that year. 1984's gold medalist, West German Rolf Danneberg, came back for a bronze in Seoul in '88.

Decathlon

The decathlon gets little attention between Olympic years, and then suddenly it becomes the test to see who's the world's best all-around athlete. In Stockholm in 1912, no doubt existed about who the world's best all-around athlete was. By the time the Stockholm Games were over, King Gustav V of Sweden had told American decathlete Jim Thorpe: "You, sir, are the greatest athlete in the world." Thorpe won the 10-event decathlon, finishing an astounding 700 points ahead of the runner-up. And that's not all: he won the five-event pentathlon as well—winning four of the five events. Thorpe's timing wasn't bad, either: many heads wearing crowns were in the audience, including those from Russia, Germany, Austria-Hungary, Greece, and Italy, not to mention Thorpe's buddy, Gustav.

There was this one hitch, though: Olympic officials declared Thorpe a professional and stripped him of all his medals. Seventy years later, when the IOC decided that playing a little summer

U.S. decathlete Jim Thorpe was called "the greatest athlete in the world" when he captured the gold in 1912. *AP/Wide World Photos*

baseball for a few dollars didn't make you a professional ringer, Thorpe's medals were restored in a posthumous presentation to the Thorpe family.

Bob Mathias of Tulare, California, was a babe of seventeen when he competed in London in 1948 in the decathlon. He finished the first day of the decathlon in third place, behind Enrique Kistenmacher of Argentina and Ignace Heinrich of France. Not bad for someone who had learned two of the events—the pole vault and javelin—only months before the competition. But Mathias hadn't competed in his best events yet; his 110m hurdles time and his discus distance pulled him into the lead, and by the time he finished the javelin, pole vault, and 1500 meters, he'd won himself a gold necklace. As if there weren't enough drama in the ten-event sport, Mathias finished in rain and darkness, and officials had to use flashlights to mark his javelin throws. Mathias—who later became a U.S. congressman—was the youngest Olympic gold medalist to date. He repeated his decathlon gold performance in 1952.

Decathlon drama heated up in Rome in 1960, when two UCLA teammates, American Rafer Johnson and Taiwan's C.K. Yang, tried to best each other ten times over. Yang bested Johnson in six running and jumping events, but Johnson, silver medalist in 1956, had finished so far ahead of the smallish Yang in the weight events that Johnson needed only to stay within 10 seconds of Yang in the final event, the 1500 meters, to win. Johnson finished a second and a half behind Yang to earn the gold. And that wouldn't be the last time Johnson would run in the Olympics: he served as the final torchbearer in 1984, lighting the Olympic flame to start the Los Angeles Games.

British decathlete Daley Thompson began competing in 1977 and won every decathlon he entered through 1984; Thompson describes the decathlon as "nine Mickey Mouse events and a 1500m." Earning Olympic gold medals in 1980 and 1984, Thompson tried again in 1988; however, when his pole-vault broke in half during the competition, he re-injured an adductor muscle. All hopes of a medal in Seoul were dashed.

Several decathletes have gone on to acting performances, or politics—not to mention cereal celebrity in the guise of Wheaties-box fame. Such cereal athletcs include Jim Thorpe, Bob Mathias, Rafer Johnson, C.K. Yang, Dennis Weaver, and Bruce Jenner.

Al Oerter

Al Oerter's feat will almost certainly never be surpassed in the annals of Olympic history. Oerter—a discus thrower—is the only athlete who has ever won four gold medals in four consecutive Olympiads. *Philadelphia Inquirer* correspondent Frank Dolson notes that Oerter's accomplishment represents "what many consider—with good reason—the greatest athletic achievement of our time. Not the most highly publicized. And certainly not the most highly rewarded in monetary terms. But to an athlete who epitomizes the amateur spirit, surely the most satisfying."

Born in 1936, Alfred Oerter competed in his first Olympics in Melbourne in 1956. At the time he was a sophomore at the University of Kansas, although he had grown up in West Babylon, New York. During those Games, the favorite for the gold was world record-holder Fortune Gordien. When Oerter's turn came to throw, his three turns outstripped all of his competitors by five feet. It was the beginning of a long period of dominance for the determined Oerter.

He won the gold again in Rome in 1960, again in Tokyo in 1964, and again in Mexico City in 1968. Injuries from automobile accidents and muscle pulls never seemed to daunt him, even though his glory years came before the advent of sophisticated sports medicine. Amazingly, his best official discus throw came not during these years but in 1980, when he posted a 227-foot, 11-inch hurl.

In 1968 Oerter retired from the Games. He was married and raising children and held a full-time job in a computer business. The lure of competition proved irresistible, however, and in 1980—at the age of 44—he qualified once again for the Olympic trials. He announced that he would try again in 1984. Once again he qualified for the trials, but a torn Achilles' tendon ruined his chances.

FACT: Beating heavily favored Werner Gunthor of Switzerland to the 1992 shot put title, Mike Stulce was the first American to win the event since 1968.

The best he could do in 1984 was to help carry the giant flag into the Los Angeles Arena as part of the opening ceremonies. He also presented the discus throwers with their medals. "Being around good, intense competition really started fueling this interest in 1988," he told the *Philadelphia Daily News* soon after the Games.

At the age of fifty, and a grandfather, Oerter was still training regularly with the hopes of gaining yet another Olympic berth. The fact that he was unable to do so does not detract from his extraordinary Olympic achievement. As Dolson puts it, "The Games have changed in many ways since Oerter won his first gold medal. . . . They're bigger and more political and more commercial. . . . The sports-for-sports-sake attitude of yesterday has turned, in too many cases, into the take-the-money-and-run attitude of today. But just when you begin to doubt whether there's really a place for the Olympic Games and the Olympic ideals in today's world, you run into an Al Oerter and you realize that the spirit that feeds the Olympic flame hasn't burned out yet."

—Mark Kram

Highlights from Barcelona

In the weeks leading up to the Barcelona Games, dueling decathletes "Dave" and "Dan" could have been the poster boys for Olympic commercialism. Having dropped a tidy sum to hype the impending showdown between Dave Johnson and Dan O'Brien, Reebok aspired to punch up its sales by associating its name with the pumped-up decathletes.

But no one expected Dan O'Brien to appear in Barcelona as a color commentator for NBC. On June 27, at the Olympic trials in New Orleans, Dan stunned his opponents, himself, and not least of all his corporate sponsors—who lavished a reported $30 million on the Dave-versus-Dan campaign—by no-heighting the pole vault. Three times failing to clear his opening height of 15'9", O'Brien was grounded from Olympic competition, having lost his shot at a berth on the U.S. team.

But Dan wasn't the only one to have a bout of bad karma. Two weeks before the Games were to begin, while training for the 1500 meters at Azusa Pacific University in California, Johnson felt something "go pop" in his right ankle, and the condition persisted through the Games. "All along," he later recounted, "it felt like a small knife in my ankle. After the pole vault, it felt like a sledgehammer."

What's more, he was hardly playing to a sympathetic crowd. It all started with the shot put, the third event of the first day, when Johnson unmistakably fouled his first two tries. His third put, too, received the red flag, but his dumbfounded reaction inspired a second official to rescind the call. On his fourth try, Johnson tossed his best put ever, which kept him in contention—but out of favor with the booing Barcelona bystanders.

"In Prague, not many knew him," a Slovak National Television commentator said of even-

FACT: Czech decathlete Robert Zmelik won an Olympic gold medal, only to lose it in a Barcelona cab. Lucky for him, he'd had an honest driver, who returned his Olympic jewelry unscathed.

tual gold medalist Robert Zmelik. "Now, probably, they will. Who doesn't like gold medals?" Taking the lead in the first event of the second day of the decathlon, the soft-spoken 23-year-old Czech never looked back, outscoring Spain's silver medaling Antonio Peñalver by nearly 200 points. His golden aspirations bronzed, his ego and his ankle bruised, world record holder Johnson settled for a third-place showing.

Medalists

Track and Field—Men's Shot Put

1992
1. Michael Stulce, U.S.A., 21.70
2. James Doehring, U.S.A., 20.96
3. Vyacheslav Lykho, Russia, 20.94

1988
1. Ulf Timmerman, East Germany, 22.47 (OR)
2. Randy Barnes, U.S.A., 22.39
3. Werner Guenthoer, Switzerland, 21.99

1984
1. Alessandro Andrei, Italy, 21.26
2. Michael Carter, U.S.A., 21.09
3. David Laut, U.S.A., 20.97

1980
1. Vladimir Kiselyov, Soviet Union, 21.35 (OR)
2. Aleksandr Baryshnikov, Soviet Union, 21.08
3. Udo Beyer, East Germany, 21.06

1976
1. Udo Beyer, East Germany, 21.05
2. Yevgeny Mironov, Soviet Union, 21.03
3. Alexsandr Baryshnikov, Soviet Union, 21.00

1972
1. Wladyslaw Komar, Poland, 21.18 (OR)
2. George Woods, U.S.A., 21.17
3. Hartmut Briesenick, East Germany, 21.14

1968
1. Randy Matson, U.S.A., 20.54
2. George Woods, U.S.A., 20.12
3. Eduard Gushchin, Soviet Union, 20.09

1964
1. Dallas Long, U.S.A., 20.33 (OR)
2. Randy Matson, U.S.A., 20.20
3. Vilmos Varju, Hungary, 19.39

1960
1. William Nieder, U.S.A., 19.68 (OR)
2. Parry O'Brien, U.S.A., 19.11
3. Dallas Long, U.S.A., 19.01

1956
1. Parry O'Brien, U.S.A., 18.57 (OR)
2. William Nieder, U.S.A., 18.18
3. Jiri Skobla, Czechoslovakia, 17.65

1952
1. Parry O'Brien, U.S.A., 17.41 (OR)
2. Darrow Hooper, U.S.A., 17.39
3. James Fuchs, U.S.A., 17.06

1948
1. Wilbur Thompson, U.S.A., 17.12 (OR)
2. F. James Delaney, U.S.A., 16.68
3. James Fuchs, U.S.A., 16.42

1936
1. Hans Woellke, Germany, 16.20 (OR)
2. Sulo Barlund, Finland, 16.12
3. Gerhard Stock, Germany, 15.66

1932
1. Leo Sexton, U.S.A., 16.005 (OR)
2. Harlow Rothert, U.S.A., 15.675
3. Frantisek Douda, Czechoslovakia, 15.61

1928
1. John Kuck, U.S.A., 15.87 (WR)
2. Herman Brix, U.S.A., 15.75
3. Emil Hirschfeld, Germany, 15.72

1924
1. Clarence Houser, U.S.A., 14.995
2. Glenn Hartranft, U.S.A., 14.895
3. Ralph Hills, U.S.A., 14.64

1920
1. Ville Porhola, Finland, 14.81
2. Elmer Niklander, Finland, 14.155
3. Harry Liversedge, U.S.A., 14.15

1912
1. Patrick McDonald, U.S.A., 15.34 (OR)
2. Ralph Rose, U.S.A., 15.25
3. Lawrence Whitney, U.S.A., 13.93

1908
1. Ralph Rose, U.S.A., 14.21

2. Dennis Horgan, Great Britain, 13.62
3. John Garreis, U.S.A., 13.18

1906
1. Martin Sheridan, U.S.A., 12.325
2. Mihaly David, Hungary, 11.83
3. Eric Lemming, Sweden, 11.26

1904
1. Ralph Rose, U.S.A., 14.81 (WR)
2. William Coe, U.S.A., 14.40
3. Leon Feuerbach, U.S.A., 13.37

1900
1. Richard Sheldon, U.S.A. 14.10 (OR)
2. Josiah McCracken, U.S.A., 12.85
3. Robert Garrett,. U.S.A., 12.37

1896
1. Robert Garrett, U.S.A., 11.22
2. Miltiades Gouskos, Greece, 11.20
3. Georgios Papasideris, Greece, 10.36

Track and Field—Men's Discus Throw

1992
1. Romas Ubartas, Lithuania, 65.12
2. Jurgen Schult, Germany, 64.94
3. Roberto Moya, Cuba, 64.12

1988
1. Jurgen Schult, East Germany, 68.82 (OR)
2. Romas Oubartas, Soviet Union, 67.48
3. Rolf Danneberg, West Germany, 67.38

1984
1. Rolf Danneberg, West Germany, 66.60
2. Mac Wilkins, U.S.A., 66.30
3. John (Boog) Powell, U.S.A., 65.46

1980
1. Viktor Rashchupkin, Soviet Union, 66.64
2. Imrich Bugar, Czechoslovakia, 66.38
3. Luis Delis, Cuba, 66.32

1976
1. Mac Wilkins, U.S.A., 67.50
2. Wolfgang Schmidt, East Germany, 66.22
3. John (Boog) Powell, U.S.A., 65.70

1972
1. Ludvik Danek, Czechoslovakia, 64.40
2. Jay Silvester, U.S.A., 63.50
3. Rickard Bruch, Sweden, 63.40

1968
1. Al Oerter, U.S.A., 64.78 (OR)
2. Lothar Milde, East Germany, 63.08
3. Ludvik Danek, Czechoslovakia, 62.92

1964
1. Al Oerter, U.S.A., 61.00 (OR)

2. Ludvik Danek, Czechoslovakia, 60.52
3. David Weill, U.S.A., 59.49

1960
1. Al Oerter, U.S.A., 59.18 (OR)
2. Richard Babka, U.S.A., 58.02
3. Richard Cochran, U.S.A., 57.16

1956
1. Al Oerter, U.S.A., 56.36 (OR)
2. Fortune Gordien, U.S.A., 54.81
3. Desmond Koch, U.S.A., 54.40

1952
1. Sim Iness, U.S.A., 55.03 (OR)
2. Adolfo Consolini, Italy, 53.78
3. James Dillion, U.S.A., 53.28

1948
1. Adolfo Consolini, Italy, 52.78 (OR)
2. Giuseppe Tosi, Italy, 51.78
3. Fortune Gordien, U.S.A., 50.77

1936
1. Kenneth Carpenter, U.S.A., 50.48 (OR)
2. Gordon Dunn, U.S.A., 49.36
3. Giorgio Oberweger, Italy, 49.23

1932
1. John Anderson, U.S.A., 49.49 (OR)
2. Henry Laborde, U.S.A., 48.47
3. Paul Winter, France, 47.85

1928
1. Clarence Houser, U.S.A., 47.32 (OR)
2. Antero Kivi, Finland, 47.23
3. James Corson, U.S.A., 47.10

1924
1. Clarence Houser, U.S.A., 46.15 (OR)
2. Vilho Niittymaa, Finland, 44.95
3. Thomas Lieb, U.S.A., 44.83

1920
1. Elmer Niklander, Finland, 44.685
2. Armas Taipale, Finland, 44.19
3. Augustus Pope, U.S.A., 42.13

1912
1. Armas Taipale, Finland, 45.21 (OR)
2. Richard Byrd, U.S.A., 42.32
3. James Duncan, U.S.A., 42.28

1908
1. Martin Sheridan, U.S.A., 40.89 (OR)
2. Merritt Griffin, U.S.A., 40.70
3. Marquis Horr, U.S.A., 39.445

1906
1. Martin Sheridan, U.S.A., 41.46
2. Nicolaos Georgantas, Greece, 38.06
3. Werner Jarvinen, Finland, 36.82

1904
1. Martin Sheridan, U.S.A., 39.28 (OR)
2. Ralph Rose, U.S.A., 39.28
3. Nicolaos Georgantas, Greece, 37.68

1900
1. Rudolf Bauer, Hungary, 36.04 (OR)
2. Frantisek Janda-Suk, Bohemia, 35.25
3. Richard Sheldon, U.S.A., 34.60

1896
1. Robert Garrett, U.S.A., 29.15
2. Panagiotis Paraskevopoulos, Greece, 28.955
3. Sotirios Versis, Greece, 28.78

Track and Field—Men's Hammer Throw

1992
1. Andrey Abduvaliyev, Tadzhikstan, 82.54
2. Igor Astapkovich, Belarus, 81.96
3. Igor Nikulin, Russia, 81.38

1988
1. Serguei Litvinov, Soviet Union, 84.80 (OR)
2. Yuriy Sedykh, Soviet Union, 83.76
3. Iouri Tamm, Soviet Union, 81.16

1984
1. Juha Tiainen, Finland, 78.0
2. Karl-Hans Riehm, West Germany, 77.9
3. Klaus Ploghaus, West Germany, 76.68

1980
1. Yuriy Sedykh, Soviet Union, 81.80 (WR)
2. Sergei Litvinov, Soviet Union, 80.64
3. Iouri Tamm, Soviet Union, 78.96

1976
1. Yuriy Sedykh, Soviet Union, 77.52 (OR)
2. Aleksei Spiridonov, Soviet Union, 76.08
3. Anatoli Bondarchuk, Soviet Union, 75.48

1972
1. Anatoli Bondarchuk, Soviet Union, 75.50 (OR)
2. Jochen Sachse, East Germany, 74.96
3. Vasily Khmelevski, Soviet Union, 74.04

1968
1. Gyula Zsivotzky, Hungary, 73.36 (OR)
2. Romuald Klim, Soviet Union, 73.28
3. Lazar Lovasz, Hungary, 69.78

1964
1. Romuald Klim, Soviet Union, 69.74 (OR)
2. Gyula Zsivotzky, Hungary, 69.09
3. Uwe Beyer, West Germany, 68.09

1960
1. Vasily Rudenkov, Soviet Union, 67.10 (OR)

2. Gyula Zsivotzky, Hungary, 65.79
3. Tadeusz Rut, Poland, 65.64

1956
1. Harold Connolly, U.S.A., 63.19 (OR)
2. Mikhail Krivonosov, U.S.A., 63.03
3. Anatoly Samotsvetov, Soviet Union, 62.56

1952
1. Jozsef Csermak, Hungary, 60.34 (WR)
2. Karl Storch, West Germany, 58.86
3. Imre Nemeth, Hungary, 57.74

1948
1. Imre Nemeth, Hungary, 56.07
2. Ivan Gubijan, Yugoslavia, 54.27
3. Robert Bennett, U.S.A., 53.73

1936
1. Karl Hein, Germany, 56.49 (OR)
2. Erwin Blask, Germany, 55.04
3. Fred Warngard, Sweden, 54.83

1932
1. Patrick O'Callaghan, Ireland, 53.92
2. Ville Porhola, Finland, 52.27
3. Peter Zaremba, U.S.A., 50.33

1928
1. Patrick O'Callaghan, Ireland, 51.39
2. Ossian Skiold, Sweden, 51.29
3. Edmund Black, U.S.A., 49.03

1924
1. Frederick Tootell, U.S.A., 53.295
2. Matthew McGrath, U.S.A., 50.84
3. Malcolm Nokes, Great Britain, 48.875

1920
1. Patrick Ryan, U.S.A., 52.875
2. Carl Johan Lind, Sweden, 48.43
3. Basil Bennet, U.S.A., 48.25

1912
1. Matthew McGrath, U.S.A., 54.74 (OR)
2. Duncan Gillis, Canada, 48.39
3. Clarence Childs, U.S.A., 48.17

1908
1. John Flanagan, U.S.A., 51.92 (OR)
2. Matthew McGrath, U.S.A., 51.18
3. Cornelius Walsh, U.S.A., 48.51

1906
Not held

1904
1. John Flanagan, U.S.A., 51.23 (OR)
2. John DeWitt, U.S.A., 50.265
3. Ralph Rose, U.S.A., 45.73

1900
1. John Flanagan, U.S.A., 49.73

2. Truxton Hare, U.S.A., 49.13
3. Josiah McCracken, U.S.A., 42.46

1896
Not held

Track and Field—Men's Javelin Throw

1992
1. Jan Zelezny, Czechoslovakia, 89.66 (OR)
2. Seppo Raty, Finland, 86.60
3. Steve Backley, Britain, 83.38

1988
1. Tapio Korjus, Finland, 84.28
2. Jan Zelezny, Czechoslovakia, 84.12
3. Seppo Raty, Finland, 83.26

1984
1. Arto Harkonen, Finland, 86.76
2. David Ottley, Great Britain, 85.74
3. Kenth Eldebrink, Sweden, 83.72

1980
1. Dainis Kula, Soviet Union, 91.20
2. Aleksandr Makarov, Soviet Union, 89.64
3. Wolfgang Hanisch, East Germany, 86.72

1976
1. Miklos Nemeth, Hungary, 94.58 (WR, OR)
2. Hannu Siitonen, Finland, 87.92
3. Gheorghe Megelea, Romania, 87.16

1972
1. Klaus Wolfermann, West Germany, 90.48 (OR)
2. Janis Lusis, Soviet Union, 90.46
3. William Schmidt, U.S.A., 84.42

1968
1. Janis Lusis, Soviet Union, 90.10 (OR)
2. Jorma Kinnunen, Finland, 88.58
3. Gergely Kulcsar, Hungary, 87.06

1964
1. Pauli Nevala, Finland, 82.66
2. Gergely Kulcsar, Hungary, 82.32
3. Janis Lusis, Soviet Union, 80.57

1960
1. Viktor Tsibulenko, Soviet Union, 84.64
2. Walter Kruger, East Germany, 79.36
3. Gergely Kulcsar, Hungary, 78.57

1956
1. Egil Danielsen, Norway, 85.71 (WR)
2. Janusz Sidlo, Poland, 79.98

3. Viktor Tsibulenko, Soviet Union, 79.50

1952
1. Cyrus Young, U.S.A., 73.78 (OR)
2. William Miller, U.S.A., 72.46
3. Toivo Hyytiainen, Finland, 71.89

1948
1. Tapio Rautavaara, Finland, 69.77
2. Steve Seymour, U.S.A., 67.56
3. Jozsef Varszegi, Hungary, 67.03

1936
1. Gerhard Stock, Great Britain, 71.84
2. Yrjo Nikkanen, Finland, 70.77
3. Kalervo Toivonen, Finland, 70.72

1932
1. Matti Jarvinen, Finland, 72.71 (OR)
2. Matti Sippala, Finland, 69.80
3. Eino Penttila, Finland, 68.70

1928
1. Erik Lundkvist, Sweden, 66.60 (OR)
2. Bela Szepes, Hungary, 65.26
3. Olav Sunde, Norway, 63.97

1924
1. Jonni Myyra, Finland, 62.96
2. Gunnar Lindstrom, Sweden, 60.92
3. Eugene Oberst, U.S.A., 58.35

1920
1. Jonni Myyra, Finland, 65.78 (OR)
2. Urho Peltonen, Finland, 63.50
3. Pekka Johansson-Jaale, Finland, 63.095

1912
1. Eric Lemming, Sweden, 60.64 (WR)
2. Julius Saaristo, Finland, 58.66
3. Mor Koczan, Hungary, 55.50

1908
1. Eric Lemming, Sweden, 54.825 (WR)
2. Arne Halse, Norway, 50.57
3. Otto Nilsson, Sweden, 47.105

1906
1. Eric Lemming, Sweden, 53.90 (WR)
2. Knut Lindberg, Sweden 45.17
3. Bruno Soderstrom, Sweden, 44.92

1896
Not held

Track and Field—Men's Decathlon

1992
1. Robert Zmelik, Czechoslovakia, 8,611

2. Antonio Peñalver, Spain, 8,412
3. Dave Johnson, U.S.A., 8,309

1988
1. Christian Schenk, East Germany, 8,488
2. Torsten Voss, East Germany, 8,399
3. Dave Steen, Canada, 8,328

1984
1. Daley Thompson, Great Britain, 8,798 (EWR)
2. Jurgen Hingsen, West Germany, 8,673
3. Siegfried Wentz, West Germany, 8,412

1980
1. Daley Thompson, Great Britain, 8,495
2. Yuri Kutsenko, Soviet Union, 8,331
3. Sergei Zhelanov, Soviet Union, 8,135

1976
1. Bruce Jenner, U.S.A., 8,618 (WR)
2. Guido Kretschmer, West Germany, 8,411
3. Nikolai Avilov, Soviet Union, 8,369

1972
1. Nikolai Avilov, Soviet Union, 8,454 (WR)
2. Leonid Litvinenko, Soviet Union, 8,035
3. Ryszard Katus, Poland, 7,984

1968
1. Bill Toomey, U.S.A., 8,193 (OR)
2. Hans-Joachim Walde, West Germany, 8,111
3. Kurt Bendlin, West Germany, 8,064

1964
1. Willi Holdorf, West Germany, 7,887
2. Rein Aun, Soviet Union, 7,842
3. Hans-Joachim Walde, West Germany, 7,809

1960
1. Rafer Johnson, U.S.A., 8,001 (OR)
2. Chuan-Kwang Yang, Taiwan, 7,930
3. Vassily Kuznyetsov, Soviet Union, 7,624

1956
1. Milton Campbell, U.S.A., 7,708 (OR)
2. Rafer Johnson, U.S.A., 7,568
3. Vassily Kuznyetsov, Soviet Union, 7,461

1952
1. Robert B. Mathias, U.S.A., 7,731 (WR)
2. Milton Campbell, U.S.A., 7,132
3. Floyd Simmons, U.S.A., 7,069

1948
1. Robert B. Mathias, U.S.A., 6,826

2. Ignace Heinrich, France, 6,740
3. Floyd Simmons, U.S.A., 6,711

1936
1. Glenn Morris, U.S.A., 7,421 (WR)
2. Robert Clark, U.S.A., 7,226
3. Jack Parker, U.S.A., 6,918

1932
1. James Bausch, U.S.A., 6,896 (WR)
2. Akilles Jarvinen, Finland, 7,038
3. Wolrad Eberle, Germany, 6,830

1928
1. Paavo Yrjola, Finland, 6,774 (WR)
2. Akilles Jarvinen, Finland, 6,815
3. J. Kenneth Doherty, U.S.A., 6,593

1924
1. Harold Osborn, U.S.A., 6,668 (WR)
2. Emerson Norton, U.S.A., 6,340
3. Alexander Klumberg, Estonia, 6,260

1920
1. Helge Lovland, Norway, 5,970
2. Brutus Hamilton, U.S.A., 5,940
3. Bertil Ohlson, Sweden, 5,825

1912
1. James Thorpe, U.S.A., 6,765 (WR)
   (previously disqualified, Jim Thorpe's
   medals were restored in 1982)
2. Hugo Wieslander, Sweden, 6,161
3. Charles Lomberg, Sweden, 5,943
4. Gosta Holmer, Sweden, 5,956

1906–1908
Not held

1904
1. Thomas Kiely, Great Britain/Ireland, 6,036
2. Adam Gunn, U.S.A., 5,907
3. Truxton Hare, U.S.A., 5,813

1896–1900
Not held

WOMEN'S THROWING AND MIXED EVENTS

Highlights

Javelin

A woman of many talents, America's Babe Didriksen added a javelin gold to her 80m hurdle gold and her high jump silver in 1932. Although her medal haul eclipsed other performances that year (no other woman holds triple medals in running, jumping, and throwing events), a number of notable American field performances occurred among both men and women, including James Bausch in the decathlon, John Anderson in the discus, Lillian Copeland in the women's discus, and Leo Sexton in the shot put.

In Helsinki in 1952, while runner Emil Zátopek, a Czech army officer, won the gold in the 10,000m and the gold in the 5000m, Dana Zátopek, Emil's wife, won the women's javelin. Dana and Emil thus marched into history as the first husband-wife Olympic double in track and field. And if that didn't earn them a place in the Twilight Zone: they were born on the same day.

Shot Put

The women's shot put boasts an Olympic first: in Rome, 1960, Soviet sisters Irina Press and Tamara Press won golds in their events, becoming the first sisters to win the Olympic gold. While Irina won the 80m hurdles, sister Tamara pressed for gold in the shot put. Between the two of them, the two Leningrad lasses set 26 world records and won five Olympic golds, and one silver. There seems to be some dispute about their hormonal makeup. Nevertheless their record as Olympic siblings would probably still stand.

The first Bulgarian track and field gold medal was awarded to Ivanka Hristova, who, at the age of 34, set an Olympic record. And the competitors that year were no slouches: there was one world record holder and three former record holders. In second place, Soviet Nadezhda Chizhova completed the necklace, adding the silver to the gold and bronze she already owned.

Discus

When women's track and field events were finally added to the Olympic program in 1928 Poland's Halina Konopacka earned the double honor of winning the discus event and becoming the first woman to win an Olympic gold medal in track and field.

Frenchwoman Micheline Ostermeyer earned an unusual assortment of medals when she won the shot put and the discus, and took a bronze medal in the high jump in 1948. Not bad for a concert pianist.

The discus knows no limits, it seems: the oldest female Olympic champion threw the discus in Mexico City in 1968: Rumanian Lia Manoliu was 36 when she treated herself to a gold. A glutton for the Games, she is a co-holder of the record for female attendance, having attended six Games (1952–1968).

And the women's discus event has contributed its share of infamy to the Olympic Hall of Shame: in 1976, Poland's discus champ Danuta Rosani was the first Olympic athlete to be DQ'd because she didn't "just say no." Anabolic steroids have probably been present in athletics since the mid–1960s, and heavy throwers have historically been big fans of improperly pumping up; without the ready-made hormones, the record books might have told a different story.

Heptathlon

The women's heptathlon's previous incarnation, the pentathlon, boasts a record for the shortest time that an athlete has held an Olympic record. In 1980, Soviet pentathlete Olga Rukavishnikova enjoyed four-tenths of a second of fame. Wonder what Andy Warhol would say about that.

U.S. athlete Jackie Joyner-Kersee missed winning the heptathlon—which in 1984 replaced the pentathlon—in Los Angeles by a mere five points. That year, Glynnis Nunn of Australia won the inaugural event, and West Germany's Sabine Everts took home the bronze. In 1988, however, Joyner-Kersee proved her mettle when she posted a world-record heptathlon score of 7291 points. In second place, East German Sabine John trailed with only 6897 points, while her compatriot Anke Behmer followed with 6858 for the bronze.

U.S. athlete Babe Didriksen medaled in running, throwing, and jumping events at the 1932 Games. She took golds in the 80m hurdles and the javelin but had to settle for silver in the high jump due to her unorthodox style. *AP/Wide World Photos*

Babe Didriksen

Mildred "Babe" Didriksen even typed fast: 85 words per minute for a Dallas insurance company before she became an American icon. Her only complaint about the 1932 Los Angeles Games was that she was permitted to enter just three events, even though she had qualified at U.S. trials for five. After she arrived, the thin 18-year-old from Port Arthur, Texas, told reporters, "I came out here to beat everybody in sight, and that is exactly what I'm going to do." Confidence was never a problem for Babe, and she was nearly as good as her word.

Didriksen defeated two German favorites in the javelin throw, set a world record in the 80m hurdles and tied for first with countrywoman Jean Shiley in the high jump. But—to break the tie—judges ruled that Didriksen's technique had been illegal. She was awarded the silver, even though her jump matched Shiley's world record.

Didriksen quickly turned professional everything, touring America playing harmonica, telling jokes, posing in auto ad campaigns, pitching for the House of David baseball team, and throwing an inning in an exhibition game for the St. Louis Cardinals against the Philadelphia Athletics. She became the most successful female golfer ever, winning 14 consecutive tournaments at one point. Romance entered her life in the person of wrestler George Zaharias, whom she later married.

In 1950, the Associated Press named her the greatest female athlete of the first half-century. But in 1953, Didriksen was diagnosed with cancer. Doctors performed an emergency colostomy. Displaying the colossal drive that made her a champion, Didriksen returned to the golf circuit three months later. The next year she again accomplished the improbable, winning the U.S. Open by 12 strokes. But soon the cancer returned, this time inoperable. On September 17, 1956, the amazing athletic career and life of Babe Didriksen ended at the age of 42.

—Harvey Dickson

Highlights from Barcelona

"She is going to be the best athlete in history, out of men and women," 1976 decathlon champ Bruce Jenner opined. "She," of course, is Jackie Joyner-Kersee.

Entering the Barcelona Games as the 1988 Olympic champion, Joyner-Kersee had a hard act to follow. Scoring 7,291 points in Seoul, she established a world record that even she would have trouble matching. Although she racked up only 7,044 points—her sixth-best score yet—Joyner-Kersee's Barcelona performance was no less astonishing.

From start to finish, she dominated every one of the seven events, accumulating a 199-point margin over the Unified Team's silver medalist, Irina Belova; and she was an incredible 395 points ahead of Germany's Sabine Braun, who was third in line behind the 30-year-old heptathlete.

Capturing her second consecutive gold medal, Joyner-Kersee became the first woman ever to win matching gold medals in a multisport event. (Husband/trainer Bob Kersee had only to utter the hallowed name of Bob Mathias, the only decathlete to win consecutive Olympic titles in non-boycotted Olympics, to inspire his wife to another Olympic win.)

With a silver from the 1984 Games, Joyner-Kersee is one of a handful of women who have captured medals at three Olympics. And her 1992 score, although 247 points below her world record, is nearly unrivaled; only one other woman—Russia's Larisa Nikitina, in 1989—has ever accumulated more than 7,000 points. Joyner-Kersee exceeded 7,000 points no fewer than six times.

By the end of the javelin throw, the sixth event, Joyner-Kersee was as good as gold. All that remained was the 800m sprint. "Only one thing matters," Bob Kersee said: "running fast enough around the track to bring home the gold. Everything else is just statistics." She needed to run the 800 in 2 minutes 15 seconds; she finished with full seconds to spare.

> "I know other people see me as invincible, but I can't let what I have accomplished control what I'm trying to do."
> —Two-time decathlon gold medalist Jackie Joyner-Kersee

FACT: Athletics (track and field) has a well-established presence at the games: It was the first Olympic sport and has been a staple of Olympic competition ever since. In 1996, more than 1,800 athletes will compete in track & field events in Atlanta.

Medalists

Track and Field—Women's Shot Put

1992
1. Svetlana Kriveleva, Russia, 21.06
2. Huang Zhihong, China, 20.47
3. Kathrin Neimke, Germany, 19.78

1988
1. Natalia Lisovskaya, Soviet Union, 22.24
2. Kathrin Neimke, East Germany, 21.07
3. Meisu Li, People's Republic of China, 21.06

1984
1. Claudia Losch, West Germany, 20.48
2. Mihaela Loghin, Romania, 20.47
3. Gael Martin, Australia, 19.19

1980
1. Ilona Slupianek, East Germany, 22.41
2. Svetlana Krachevskaya, Soviet Union, 21.42
3. Margitta Pufe, East Germany, 21.20

1976
1. Ivanka Hristova, Bulgaria, 21.16 (OR)
2. Nadezhda Chizhova, Soviet Union, 20.96
3. Helena Fibingerova, Czechoslovakia, 20.67

1972
1. Nadezhda Chizhova, Soviet Union, 21.03 (WR)
2. Margitta Gummel-Helmbolt, East Germany, 20.22
3. Ivanka Hristova, Bulgaria, 19.35

1968
1. Margitta Gummel-Helmbolt, East Germany, 19.61 (WR)
2. Marita Lange, East Germany, 18.78
3. Nadezhda Chizhova, Soviet Union, 18.19

1964
1. Tamara Press, Soviet Union, 18.14 (OR)
2. Renate Garisch-Culmberger, East Germany, 17.61
3. Galina Zybina, Soviet Union, 17.45

1960
1. Tamara Press, Soviet Union, 17.32 (OR)
2. Johanna Luttge, East Germany, 16.61
3. Earlene Brown, U.S.A., 16.42

1956
1. Tamara Tyshkevich, Soviet Union, 16.59 (OR)
2. Galina Zybina, Soviet Union, 16.53
3. Marianne Werner, West Germany, 15.61

1952
1. Galina Zybina, Soviet Union, 15.28 (WR)
2. Marianne Werner, West Germany, 14.57

3. Klaudia Tochenova, Soviet Union, 14.50

1948
1. Micheline Ostermeyer, France, 13.75
2. Amelia Piccinini, Italy, 13.09
3. Ine Schaffer, Austria, 13.08

1896–1936
Not held

Track and Field—Women's Discus

1992
1. Maritza Marten Garcia, Cuba, 70.06
2. Tzvetanka Khristova, Bulgaria, 67.78
3. Daniela Costian, Australia, 66.24

1988
1. Martina Hellmann, East Germany, 72.30 (OR)
2. Diana Gansky, East Germany, 71.88
3. Tzvetanka Hristova, Bulgaria, 69.74

1984
1. Ria Stalman, Netherlands, 65.36
2. Leslie Deniz, U.S.A., 64.86
3. Florenta Craciunescu, Romania, 63.64

1980
1. Evelin Jahl-Schlaak, East Germany, 69.96 (OR)
2. Maria Petkova, Bulgaria, 67.90
3. Tatiana Lesovaya, Soviet Union, 67.40

1976
1. Evelin Schlaak, East Germany, 69.00 (OR)
2. Maria Vergova, Bulgaria, 67.30
3. Gabriele Hinzmann, East Germany, 66.84

1972
1. Faina Melnik, Soviet Union, 66.62 (OR)
2. Argentina Menis, Romania, 65.06
3. Wassilka Stoeva, Bulgaria, 64.34

1968
1. Lia Manoliu, Romania, 58.28
2. Liesel Westermann, West Germany, 57.76
3. Jolan Kleiber, Hungary, 54.90

1964
1. Tamara Press, Soviet Union, 57.27 (OR)
2. Ingrid Lotz, East Germany, 57.21
3. Lia Manoliu, Romania, 56.97

1960
1. Nina Ponomaryeva-Romaschkova, Soviet Union, 55.10 (OR)
2. Tamara Press, Soviet Union, 52.59
3. Lia Manoliu, Romania, 52.36

1956
1. Olga Fikotova, Czechoslovakia, 53.69 (OR)

2. Irina Beglyakova, Soviet Union, 52.54
3. Nina Ponomaryeva-Romaschkova, Soviet Union, 52.02

1952
1. Nina Romaschkova, Soviet Union, 51.42 (OR)
2. Yelisaveta Bagryantseva, Soviet Union, 47.08
3. Nina Dumbadze, Soviet Union, 46.29

1948
1. Micheline Ostermeyer, France, 41.92
2. Edera Gentile-Cordiale, Italy, 41.17
3. Jacqueline Mazeas, France, 40.47

1936
1. Gisela Mauermeyer, Germany, 47.63 (OR)
2. Jadwiga Wajsowna, Poland, 46.22
3. Paula Mollenhauer, Germany, 39.80

1932
1. Lillian Copeland, U.S.A., 40.58 (OR)
2. Ruth Osburn, U.S.A., 40.12
3. Jadwiga Wajsowna, Poland, 38.74

1928
1. Halina Konopacka, Poland, 39.62 (WR)
2. Lillian Copeland, U.S.A., 37.08
3. Ruth Svedberg, Sweden, 35.92

1896–1924
Not held

Track and Field—Women's Javelin

1992
1. Silke Renk, Germany, 68.34
2. Natalia Shikolenko, Belarus, 68.26
3. Karen Forkel, Germany, 66.86

1988
1. Petra Felke, East Germany, 74.68 (OR)
2. Fatima Whitbread, Great Britain, 70.32
3. Beate Koch, East Germany, 67.30

1984
1. Tessa Sanderson, Great Britain, 69.56 (OR)
2. Tiina Lillak, Finland, 69.00
3. Fatima Whitbread, Great Britain, 67.14

1980
1. Maria Colon, Cuba, 68.40 (OR)
2. Saida Gunba, Soviet Union, 67.76
3. Ute Hommola, East Germany, 66,56

1976
1. Ruth Fuchs, East Germany, 65.94 (OR)
2. Marion Becker, West Germany, 64.70
3. Kathy Schmidt, U.S.A., 63.96

1972
1. Ruth Fuchs, East Germany, 63.88 (OR)

2. Jaqueline Todten, East Germany, 62.54
3. Kathy Schmidt, U.S.A., 59.94

1968
1. Angela Nemeth, Hungary, 60.36
2. Mihaela Penes, Romania, 59.92
3. Eva Janko, Austria, 58.04

1964
1. Mihaela Penes, Romania, 60.54
2. Marta Rudas, Hungary, 58.27
3. Yelena Gorchakova, Soviet Union, 57.06

1960
1. Elvira Ozolina, Soviet Union, 55.98 (OR)
2. Dana Zatopkova, Czechoslovakia, 53.78
3. Birute Kalediene, Soviet Union, 53.45

1956
1. Inese Jaunzeme, Soviet Union, 53.86 (OR)
2. Marlene Ahrens, Chile, 50.38
3. Nadezhda Konyayeva, Soviet Union, 50.28

1952
1. Dana Zatopkova, Czechoslovakia, 50.47 (OR)
2. Aleksandra Chudina, Soviet Union, 50.01
3. Yelena Gorchakova, Soviet Union, 49.76

1948
1. Herma Bauma, Austria, 45.57 (OR)
2. Kaisa Parviainen, Finland, 43.79
3. Lily Carlstedt, Denmark, 42.08

1936
1. Tilly Fleischer, Germany, 45.18 (OR)
2. Luise Kruger, Germany, 43.29
3. Maria Kwasniewska, Poland, 41.80

1932
1. Mildred "Babe" Didrikson, U.S.A., 43.68 (OR)
2. Ellen Braumuller, Germany, 43.49
3. Tilly Fleischer, Germany, 43.00

1896–1928
Not held

Track and Field—Women's Pentathlon

1984–1992
Not held

1980
1. Nadezhda Tkachenko, Soviet Union, 5083 (WR)
2. Olga Rukavishnikova, Soviet Union, 4937
3. Olga Kuragina, Soviet Union, 4875

1976
1. Siegrun Siegl, East Germany, 4745
2. Christine Laser, East Germany, 4745
3. Burglinde Pollak, East Germany, 4740

1972
1. Mary Peters, Great Britain, 4801 (WR)
2. Heidemarie Rosendahl, West Germany, 4791
3. Burglinde Pollak, East Germany, 4768

1968
1. Ingrid Becker, West Germany, 5098
2. Liese Prokop, Austria, 4966
3. Annamaria Toth, Hungary, 4959

1964
1. Irina Press, Soviet Union, 5246 (WR)
2. Mary Rand, Great Britain, 5035
3. Galina Bystrova, Soviet Union, 4956

1896–1960
Not held

Track and Field—Women's Heptathlon

1992
1. Jackie Joyner-Kersee, U.S.A., 7,044
2. Irina Belova, Russia, 6,845
3. Sabine Braun, Germany, 6,649

1988
1. Jackie Joyner-Kersee, U.S.A., 7,291 (WR)
2. Sabine John, East Germany, 6,897
3. Anke Behmer, East Germany, 6,858

1984
1. Glynis Nunn, Australia, 6,390 (OR)
2. Jackie Joyner, U.S.A., 6,385
3. Sabine Everts, West Germany, 6,363

Trivia Quiz

1. The IOC stripped legendary American multisport athlete Jim Thorpe of his medals because
   a. He had once played summer baseball for money
   b. He wasn't recognized as a member of the U.S. team
   c. He hadn't followed the proper registration procedures

2. In the discus throw, the ancient Greeks probably used
   a. A ceramic disk   **b.** A bronze plate   **c.** A frisbee

3. Athletes in the Ancient Games threw the javelin
   a. For distance   **b.** For accuracy   **c.** At their mothers-in-law

4. Anabolic steroids
   a. Have never been a problem among field athletes
   b. Were probably widely used by athletes in the "heavy" sports as far back as the mid–1960s
   c. Have only become a problem among field athletes in the last decade

5. The first women's throwing event to be included in the Modern Games was
   a. The hammer throw   **b.** The discus throw   **c.** The skillet toss

6. The Modern Games have *never* included
   a. Stone throwing.
   b. A combination of left- and right-handed throws   **c.** Spear fishing

7. Before the women's heptathlon was added to the Olympics in 1980, women
   a. Had competed in the heptathlon as a demonstration sport
   b. Had never competed in Olympic mixed field events
   c. Had competed for pentathlon medals

8. The winning distance for the discus has

a. Remained about the same since the 1896 Games

b. More than doubled since the 1896 Games

c. Declined since the 1896 Games

9. British athlete Daley Thompson

a. Set four world records but never won an Olympic decathlon

b. Won two Olympic decathlons but never approached a world record

c. Set four world records and won two Olympic decathlons

10. The first Olympic athlete to portray Tarzan was

a. Buster Crabbe   **b.** Johnny Weissmuller   **c.** Herman Brix

Answers: 1-a; 2-b; 3-b; 4-b; 5-b; 6-c; 7-c; 8-b; 9-c; 10-c

VOLLEYBALL

Warm-up

"Awesome serve, dude!"

Whether played on the beach, the gym, or the Olympic stage, volleyball carries a made-in-the-USA tag. Volleyball was invented in 1895 by William G. Morgan, the athletic director of the YMCA training school in Holyoke, Massachusetts. The game, known then as minonette, spread quickly to other YMCAs in the region, where it competed with that other new-fangled sport, basketball. In fact, Morgan invented the game as an alternative for middle-aged fitness fans who found basketball too strenuous.

Via the international YMCA network, the game spread slowly throughout the world, with the exception of Asia, where volleyball enjoyed its most enthusiastic reception. By 1896 the game was played five a side in the U.S., while in Japan each team fielded nine members, creating havoc in the backcourt. By 1918 the current six-a-side game was established, as was the clockwise rotation on service.

In 1923, the first All-USA Championship was held, and national organizations for the game were founded in Russia and Japan during the next five years.

Exported overseas by American servicemen, volleyball became popular throughout the world by the end of World War II. The game required little organization and minimal equipment, and followed simple rules. It could be played outdoors and indoors, with as few as two people to a side. Responding to the increasing awareness of the sport worldwide, the Federation Internationale de Volleyball (FIVB) was organized in 1948. A year later, the initial World Championships were held in Prague, Czechoslovakia. Buoyed by the general public's acceptance of the game, the FIVB began lobbying to add volleyball to the Olympic Games, a dream that came true in Tokyo 15 years later.

is not allowed to touch the ball two times consecutively, a blocker may make first contact with the ball after the attempted block.

Setting is a pass used to "set up" a point-winning shot. The player making the second hit in a three-hit sequence lofts the ball softly into the air with little spin toward a teammate by the net, who spikes the ball at its apex toward the opposing team. The softness and trajectory of a good set permit the player receiving the pass to place the ball more accurately between defenders on the opposing side to negate the return.

A team is permitted six player-substitutions during a game. The substitutions may be made before any point for any position on the floor. A substitute can only be substituted into a game once. A starting player may leave the game once and re-enter only in his or her starting position.

How to Lose the Serve or Give up a Point

A team gives up a point or loses the serve under the following conditions:

- A player initiates contact with the ball before it crosses the plane of the net.
- A player crosses the vertical plane of the net and touches the court or an opponent.
- The ball touches the ground on that team's side of the court, within the boundaries.
- A player hits the ball so that it lands out of bounds. If the ball is on the line, the ball is in play.
- A player serving hits the ball out of bounds or into the net.
- A team makes more than three contacts with the ball in succession.
- A player touches the ball twice consecutively, except in the case of a blocker.
- A player touches the net.
- A player steps over the center line during play.
- A backline player in the attack area returns the ball from above net height. The players in the backcourt cannot spike the ball unless they are at least 10 feet behind the net.

Hopefuls—Men's

If the U.S. men's volleyball team is to win a medal at the 1996 Olympics, it will need strong performances from **Bryan Ivie** and **Bob Ctvrtlik**. Ivie and Ctvrtlik are two of four returning starters who represented the U.S. in volleyball at the 1992 Summer Games in Barcelona. Ctvrtlik, the 1995 U.S. national volleyball captain, also played with the 1988 gold medal-winning squad. These two key players are expected to direct a young team with many members who have seen little international competition. They hope to keep alive a string of Olympic medal finishes that began with a gold at the 1984 Los Angeles Games.

For both athletes, participation on the U.S. team has meant a significant loss of income—their commitment to the national team precludes playing in the lucrative beach volleyball tournaments and European professional leagues that have stolen some of America's most talented volleyball stars. Ctvrtlik told the *San Jose Mercury News* on February 26, 1995, that he figures the decision to play for the national team cost him about $250,000. Nevertheless, he and Ivie are hardly in reduced straits. Both of them have signed contracts that keep them with the national team through 1996—Ivie's alone is estimated to be in six figures. Besides, Ctvrtlik added, playing on an Olympics-bound team is a sacrifice anyone could afford to make. "People just don't understand what being an Olympic medalist really means," he said. "It's kind of like being on top of the world—you can't put a price on that."

The most seasoned veteran on the U.S. men's team, Ctvrtlik began his stint as an Olympic volleyball player when such great American stars as Karch Kiraly, Dusty Dvorak, and Steve Timmons were still in the amateur game. Ctvrtlik, a Long Beach, California, native whose teammates call him "Four Star," joined the U.S. men's team after guiding Pepperdine University to the 1985 National Collegiate Athletic Association championship. The youngest member of the 1988 Olympic squad, he was named outstanding passer at the Games in Seoul, where the American men won a gold medal.

In those days the United States did not support a resident national volleyball team year-round, so Ctvrtlik was free to seek his fortune between Olympic stints. An outside hitter, he has played in Croatia, on the beach volleyball circuit, and in Italy. In 1992 he returned to the Olympic team roster and helped the Americans win a bronze medal at Barcelona by recording 122 kills, 12 blocks, and five service aces in eight games. Ctvrtlik played professionally until 1994, when he signed a two-year contract with the resident U.S. team. "The whole reason I returned was to win a gold medal in Atlanta," Ctvrtlik told the *Boston Globe* on March 18, 1995. "I definitely think this team can win. I think we'll be good enough at that point—but who knows?"

Success may rest on Ivie's shoulders. The middle blocker, who is ranked sixth in the world among attackers, was captain of the U.S. men's team in 1994. Another return star from the 1992 Olympic roster, Ivie likes to say that he gravitated to volleyball when he grew too tall for his first love—surfing. "I used to play beach volleyball only between surfing," the Manhattan Beach, California, native explained in the *Akron Beacon Journal* on March 14, 1993. "It was when I got to high school that I made the transition and started to take volleyball more seriously. Now I concentrate on volleyball, but I still do both. I use surfing as a way to get away . . . to relax."

> "The whole reason I returned was to win a gold medal in Atlanta. I definitely think this team can win. I think we'll be good enough at that point."
>
> —Bob Ctvrtlik

At six-feet-seven and 215 pounds, Ivie has proven an imposing figure on the volleyball court since his college days. Twice named National Collegiate Athletic Association player of the year, he led the University of Southern California Trojans to the NCAA title in 1990 and also came off the bench to help the United States win a gold medal at the 1990 Goodwill Games. The first collegian to break the 2,000-kill barrier, he was one of the youngest members of the 1992 Olympic volleyball team at 23. Unlike Ctvrtlik, who came of age in a different era, Ivie has done very little touring as a professional. Instead he signed a contract with the U.S. Volleyball Association that has kept him with the resident national team from 1992 until the present—at an estimated $100,000 salary per year. That sum might seem like fantastic compensation, but a performer of Ivie's caliber could make far more than that on the beaches or in Europe. Instead, it's the game itself, not the riches, that motivates Ivie. "Volleyball has so many elements," he mused in the *Akron Beacon Journal*. "It has a combination of both power and finesse. It's also a team sport but there is also an individual side to it."

American domination of men's volleyball remains seriously in question as the 1996 Summer Games approach. Although the team won a respectable silver medal at the 1995 Pan American Games—being beaten only by an Argentinean team in Argentina—the same U.S. team finished a dismal fourth in the 1995 World League Group A, behind Brazil, Cuba, and Spain. The sad fact is that volleyball's increasing popularity worldwide has eroded Team U.S.A.'s ability to attract top talent and keep players together until they develop consistency and performance as a unit. Ivie told the *Los Angeles Times* on July 9, 1993, that the U.S. Volleyball Association's decision to sign players to contracts and pay them stipends might help to attract a stable roster. "I think it was just a matter of [the U.S. Volleyball Association] deciding, really deciding, where they wanted their program to head," he said. "To show the players that they want to build a team." Ivie concluded that the Americans have only one ambition: to win the gold medal in Atlanta. "That is the goal," he affirmed.

—Mark Kram

Hopefuls—Women's

Nothing beats experience. At least that's the philosophy of Terry Liskevych, coach of the U.S. women's national volleyball team. In preparation for the 1996 Olympics, Liskevych has recruited three veterans of former Olympic volleyball teams, **Paula Weishoff, Caren Kemner,** and **Keba Phipps**. These three international stars will combine with a group of up-and-coming collegians to form the nucleus of a team that will have to work hard to win a medal.

Bronze medalists at the 1992 Olympics, the U.S. national team will face extremely tough competition from Cuba and Brazil, both powerhouses on the international volleyball circuit. How good is the opposition? Team U.S.A. was beaten by Cuba in the finals of the 1995 Pan American Games and dropped four of five matches to Brazil during a May, 1995, tour of the American Midwest. Coach Liskevych believes that sustained practice—the art of getting to know one another on the court—will prepare the women's team for medal contention in Atlanta. Having a starting rotation full of former Olympic medalists like Kemner, Weishoff, Tammy Liley, and Lori Endicott will certainly help.

At six feet, one inch, Paula Weishoff is a middle blocker who brings a wealth of experience to the Team U.S.A. roster. Born May 1, 1962, in Torrance, California, she established her potential even before she made her national team debut in 1981. As a Junior Olympian, she helped an American team win a silver medal at the U.S. Olympic Festival in 1979 and then earned all-America and MVP citations at the 1980 U.S. Junior Olympics. She attended the University of Southern California for one year, just long enough to lead the Trojans to a national championship. Named Outstanding Collegiate Player of the Year in 1980, she left college to pursue volleyball full time in 1981.

Weishoff was a starring player on the bronze medal-winning American team at the 1982 World Championships. Her time to shine came in the 1984 Olympics, however. There she helped Team U.S.A. win a silver medal and was awarded the U.S. Most

Valuable Player award. After that she left the national team to play professional volleyball in Italy, but she returned in time to train for, and participate in, the 1992 Summer Games. Once again she turned in a fine performance, compiling 96 kills and nine blocks in six matches as the Americans took the bronze medal. This time Weishoff's personal honors included an Outstanding Player of the 1992 Olympics citation. An internationally-recognized pro star in Brazil and Japan, she rejoined Team U.S.A. in the summer of 1995, specifically to prepare for the next Olympics.

Kemner has also seen action in two Olympics tournaments. The six-foot-one-inch outside hitter was born in Quincy, Illinois, on April 16, 1965, and was 20 when she joined the national team in 1985. A six-time recipient of the U.S. Olympic Committee's Female Volleyball Athlete of the Year award, she turned in 66 kills, 18 blocks, and passed a team-leading 119 serves in five matches at the 1988 Olympics. In 1991, after a particularly strong showing in international competition, she was named Most Valuable Woman Player in the World by the Federation Internationale de Volley-Ball (FIVB). She was also nominated for the Sullivan Award in both 1990 and 1991.

Kemner's contributions to the 1992 bronze medal-winning team included a team-high 127 kills and seven aces, a performance that led her to be named to FIVB's 1992 "Super Four." She has also played professionally in Brazil, Japan, and Italy.

"Caren and Paula have been two of the finest players I have coached in my tenure with the U.S.A. women's team," Liskevych said at a press conference on June 9, 1995. "They will be a big factor in our becoming the best team in the world."

If Weishoff and Kemner are the proven commodities, Keba Phipps might be considered the wild card. Even Phipps herself agrees that her career with the national team in the 1980s was a disappointment, probably because she rushed into top-level competition before she was quite ready. She joined Team U.S.A. while still in high school, leaving home at 17 to live and train in San Diego. At 19 she turned in an uneven performance at the 1988 Olympics, a year in which the American women failed to advance out of the early rounds.

Worse troubles awaited Phipps in 1990. She was kicked off the national team after a positive drug test. Today Phipps will not reveal the drug involved, but she maintains that her minimal use of the substance was something she deeply regrets. "It was stupid, and I paid for it," she told the *St. Paul Pioneer Press Dispatch* on April 28, 1990. "I'm sorry I did it. I'd tell other people to just say no, period. . . . It isn't worth it."

Deprived of the opportunity to compete in the 1992 Olympics, Phipps moved to Italy and carved out a successful professional career there. She is a three-time Most Valuable Player of the Italian indoor professional league, and her salary has been estimated at $250,000 to $300,000 per year. The best U.S.A. Volleyball can offer Phipps is $70,000, a mere pittance compared to what she could earn abroad. Nevertheless, she wants to return, to vindicate her own reputation and to help the Americans win another medal. "She really wants to play in the U.S. again," coach Liskevych told *USA Today* on June 23, 1995.

Asked by the *Los Angeles Times* on June 26, 1995, how he thought Team U.S.A. might fare against the competition in Atlanta, Liskevych was optimistic. "We're not that far behind," he concluded. "We might have the right blend of players now."

Time will tell.

—Anne Janette Johnson

Schedule

The tentative volleyball schedule is:

Saturday, July 20
Women's preliminaries, matches 1–6

Sunday, July 21
Men's preliminaries, matches 1–6

Monday, July 22
Women's preliminaries, matches 7–12

Tuesday, July 23
Men's preliminaries, matches 7–12

Wednesday, July 24
Women's preliminaries, matches 13–18

Thursday, July 25
Men's preliminaries, matches 13–18

Friday, July 26
Women's preliminaries, matches 19–24

Saturday, July 27
Men's preliminaries, matches 19–24

Sunday, July 28
Women's preliminaries, matches 25–30

Monday, July 29
Men's preliminaries, matches 25–30

Tuesday, July 30
Women's quarterfinals 1–4

Wednesday, July 31
Men's quarterfinals 1–4

Thursday, August 1
Women's finals 5–8 places
Women's semifinals 1 & 2

Friday, August 2
Men's finals 5–8 places
Men's semifinals 1 & 2

Saturday, August 3
Women's bronze & gold medal

Sunday, August 4
Men's bronze & gold medal

Highlights

Between the introduction of volleyball into the Games in 1964 and the LA Games, the Soviet/Japanese-shared hegemony of the sport was hardly challenged: the Soviets took a total of ten medals, and the Japanese took eight, while the next-closest competitor, Poland, counted only three medals to its name. In fact, the Soviet domination was so thoroughgoing that the men lost only four of 39 matches, and their women's team lost only two of 28 matches during that time span.

FACT: In 1976 Poland's men's team was well prepared for their grueling two-and-a-half-hour final against a vertically gifted Soviet team. The Polish players' daily training routine included jumping over a four-and-a-half-foot barrier 392 times—while wearing 20- to 30-pound weights.

During the Soviet absence from the LA Games, a new reign was in the making. The U.S., which until 1984 had not even been able to qualify a team—despite the sport's American origins—won its first medals ever: a silver in the women's event, and a gold in the men's. The name of Karch Kiraly, the U.S. team's standout setter-hitter, has become synonymous with the LA Games.

The U.S. team, which had been led in 1984 by head coach Doug Beal, enjoyed an auspicious between-Games period: the men's 1985 World Cup, the 1986 World Championship, the 1987 Pan Am gold. In 1988, under head coach Marv Dunphy, the U.S. team was primed for another victory.

The Japanese team, however, had set its sights on the gold, and was ahead of the U.S. early in the first game, by a score of 11−7. Coming from behind, the U.S. managed victory by a two-point margin, defeating the Japanese in the next two matches by a decisive score of 15−2. The U.S. team, with Karch Kiraly—by then proclaimed the world's greatest player—earned its second gold medal, even with the Soviets present. The U.S. women's team, however, didn't fare so well: medals were taken by the Soviet Union, Peru, and the People's Republic of China.

Highlights from Barcelona

The U.S. squad entered the 1992 Games looking to pull off a three-peat. But they returned home from Barcelona—looking much like a collection of poster boys for a Bald is Beautiful campaign—with their egos bruised and their medal bronzed.

U.S. Volleyball player Bob Samuelson takes a tough loss to Brazil in semifinal action in Barcelona. The loss ended the U.S. team's bid to become the first team to win three gold medals in a row in the event. *AP/Wide World Photos*

Olympic Cuban volleyball players celebrate their win over the Unified Team at Barcelona. *AP/Wide World Photos*

It all started in an opening game against the Japanese. The U.S. team's youngest player, twenty-six-year-old Bob Samuelson, was exercising his claim to the title The Man Who Loves to Be Hated. The young American quibbled with referees; the referees responded with a yellow card. He quibbled some more; a second yellow card ensued. The U.S. team nevertheless marched blithely to victory.

That is, until the Japanese team filed a protest. It seems the second yellow card should have been a red card, which carried with it certain penalties. Had the proper card been issued, Samuelson would have been expelled—although it's hard to say which team that would penalize—the U.S. would have incurred a penalty point, and Japan, ahead at that time, would have won the game.

The FIVB sided with the Japanese, and the U.S. team was aced out of a win. Disgruntled, the U.S. players shaved their heads to express solidarity with their vociferous teammate, who, as luck would have it, was sporting the cue-ball look. It wasn't just your average bad hair day: with that early defeat, the U.S. team bid *adios* to the probability of striking Spanish gold.

FACT: The 1992 U.S. men's team was the oldest volleyball squad at the Barcelona Games.

Ultimately, Brazil shut the U.S. out of the final, upsetting medal-round favorite Cuba in pool play as well. The world-champion Italians, who had enjoyed a four-year reign as absolute rulers, were also knocked out before the final go-round; and by the underdog out-of-the-money-in-Seoul Dutch team, no less (who happened to be coached by former U.S. women's coach Arie Selinger).

The Dutch outsized their opponents, but the Brazilian team was a well-oiled machine. With impeccable teamwork, they subdued the Dutch team three sets to one (15-12, 15-8, 15-5), pocketing the Olympic title, having been ranked only fifth in pre-Olympics predictions. The sixth-ranked Dutch team nabbed the silver, forcing a disappointed band of American boys to settle for the low tier on the podium.

The reigning women's Olympic champions were forced to step down as well. Unable to fend off a Cuban assault, the 1988 gold-medaling Unified Team—which had three other gold medals in its coffers—settled for a silver medal. In a grueling match with five sets, it was clear that returning Seoul-mates Irina Smirnova, Valentina Ogiendo et al. were not as full of vim and vigor as they once had been.

Beaten by the Cubans, the U.S. women held their own thanks to Caren Kemner's blocks at the net, which kept them ahead in a three-set match against Brazil. Sliding into a third-place finish, the U.S. team collected their second medal, having pocketed a silver in 1984, without Soviet competition.

Medalists

Volleyball—Men's Team

1992

1. Brazil, Marcelo Negrao, Jorge De Brito, Giovane Gavio, Paulo Silva, Mauricio Lima, Janelson Carvalho, Douglas Chiarotti, Antonio Gouveia, Talmo De Oliveira, Andre Ferreira, Alexandre Samuel, Amauri Ribeiro
2. Netherlands, Martin Teffer, Henk-Jan Held, Ron Boudrie, Marko Klok, Ronald Zwerver, Avital Selinger, Edwin Benne, Olof Van Der Meulen, Peter Blange, Jan Posthuma, Martin Van Der Host, Ronald Zoodsma
3. U.S.A., Carlos Briceno, Daniel Greenbaum, Nick Becker, Robert Ctvrtlik, Bryan Ivie, Stephen Timmons, Brent Hilliard, Scott Fortune, Robert Samuelson, Jeffrey Stork, Eric Sato, Robert Parti

1988

1. U.S.A., Craig Buck, Robert Ctvrtlik, Scott Fortune, Charles "Karch" Kiraly, Ricci Luyties, Robert Doug Partie, Jon Root, Eric Sato, David Saunders, Jeff Stork, Troy Tanner, Steve Timmons
2. Soviet Union, I. Antonov, V. Chkourikhine, A. Kouzentsov, E. Krasilnikov, Valeri Lossev, I. Pantchenko, Igor Rounov, Iouri Sapega, A. Sorokolet, I. Tcherednik, Raimond Vilde, V. Zaitsev
3. Argentina, D. Castellani, Daniel M. Colla, H. Conte, J. Cuminetti, E. De Palma, Alejandro Diz, W. Kantor, E. Martinez, R. Quiroga, J. Uriarte, Carlos J. Weber, C. Zulianello

1984

1. U.S.A., Dusty Dvorak, Dave Saunders, Steve Salmons, Paul Sunderland, Rich Duwelius, Steve Timmons, Craig Buck, Marc Waldie, Chris Marlowe, Aldis Berzins, Pat Powers, Karch Kiraly
2. Brazil, Bernardo Rezende, Mario Xando Oliveria Neto, Antonio Ribeiro, Jose Junior Montanaro, Ruy Campos Nascimento, Renan Dal Zotto, William Silva, Amauri Ribeiro, Marcus Freire, Domingos Lamapariello Neto, Bernard Rajzman, Fernando D'Avila
3. Italy, Marco Negri, Pier Paolo Lucchetta, Gian Carlo Dametto, Franco Bertoli, Francesco Dall'Olio, Piero Rebaudengo, Giovanni Errichiello, Guido De Luigi, Fabio Vullo, Giovanni Lanfranco, Paolo Vecchi, Andrea Lucchetta

1980

1. Soviet Union, Yuri Panchenko Vyacheslav Zaitsev, Aleksandr Savin, Vladimir Dorokhov, Aleksandr Yermilov, Pavel Selivanov, Oleg Moliboga, Vladimir Kondra, Vladimir Chernyshev, Fyodor Lashchenov, Valeri Krivov, Vilyar Loor
2. Bulgaria, Stoyan Gounchev, Hristo Stoyanov, Dimitar Zlatanov, Dimitar Dimitrov, Petko Petkov, Mitko Todorov, Kaspar Simeonov, Emil Vulchev, Hristo Illiev, Yordan Angelov, Tsano Tsanov, Stefan Dimitrov
3. Romania, Corneliu Oros, Laurentiu Dumanoiu, Dan Girleanu, Nicu Stoian, Sorin Macavei, Constantin Sterea, Neculae Vasile Pop, Gunter Enescu, Valter-Korneliu Chifu, Marius Chata-Chitiga

1976

1. Poland, Wlodzimierz Stefanski, Bronslaw Bebel, Lech Lasko, Edward Skorek, Tomasz Wojtowicz, Wieslaw Gawlowski, Mieczyslaw Rybaczewski, Zbigniew Lubiejewski, Ryszard Bosek, Wlodzimierz Sadalski, Zbigniew Zarzycki, Marek Karbarz
2. Soviet Union, Anatoli Polishuk, Vyacheslav Zaitsev, Efim Chulak, Vladimir Dorohov, Aleksandr Ermilov, Pavel Selivanov, Oleg Moliboga, Vladimir Kondra, Yuri Starunski, Vladimir Chernyshev, Vladimir Ulanov, Aleksandr Savin, Yuri Chesnokov, Vladimir Patkin

3. Cuba, Leonel Marshall, Victoriano Sarmientos, Ernesto Maritnez, Victor Garcia, Carlosy Salas, Raul Virches, Jesus Savigne, Lorenzo Martinez, Diego Lapera, Antonio Rodriguez, Alfredo Figueredo, Jorge Perez

1972

1. Japan, Katsutoshi Nekoda, Kenji Kimura Yoshihide Fukao, Jungo Morita, Tadayoshi Yokota, Seiji Oko, Kenji Shimaoka, Yuzo Nakamura, Masayuki Minami, Tetsuo Sato, Yasuhiro Noguchi, Tetsuo Nishimoto
2. East Germany, Arnold Schulz, Wolfgang Webner, Siegfried Schneider, Wolfgang Weise, Rudi Schumann, Eckehard Pietzsch, Wolfgang Lowe, Wolfgang Maibohm, Rainer Tscharke, Jurgen Maune, Horst Peter, Horst Hagen
3. Soviet Union, Victor Borsch, Vyacheslav Domani, Vladimir Patkin, Leonid Zaiko, Yuri Starunski, Aleksandr Saprykine, VLadimir Kondra, Efim Chulak, Vladimir Poutiatov, Valeri Kravchenko, Yevgeny Lapinsky, Yuri Poyarkov

1968

1. Soviet Union, Eduard Sibiryakov, Valeri Kravchenko, Vladimir Belyayev, Yevgeny Lapinsky, Oleg Antropov, Vasiliyus Matuschevas, Viktor Mikhalchuk, Vladimir Ivanov, Yvan Bugayenkov, Georgi Mondzolevsky
2. Japan, Masayuki Minami, Katsutoshi Nekoda, Mamoru Shiragami, Isao Koizumi, Kenji Kimura, Yasuaki Mitsumori, Jungo Morita, Tadayoshi Yokota, Seiji Oko, Tetsuo Sato, Kenji Shimaoka
3. Czechoslovakia, Antonin Prochazka, Jiri Svoboda, Lubomir Zajicek, Joserf Musil, Josef Smolka, Wladimir Petlak, Petr Kop, Frantisek Sokol, Bohumil Golian, Zdenek Groessl, Pavel Schenk, Drabomir Koudelka

1964

1. Soviet Union, Yvan Buagyenkov, Nikolai Burobin, Yuri Chesnokov, Vascha Kacharava, Valeri Kalatschikhin, Vitali Kovalenko, Stanislav Lyugaylo, Gerogy Mondzolevsky, Yuri Poyarkov, Fduard Sibiryakov, Yuri Vengerovsky, Dmitri Voskoboynikov
2. Czechoslovakia, Milan Cuda, Bohumil Golian, Zdenek Humhal, Petr Kop, Josef Labuda, Josef Musil, Karel Paulus, Boris Perusic, Pavel Schenk, Vaclav Smidl, Josef Sorm, Ladislav Toman

3. Japan, Yutaka Demachi, Tsutomu Koyama, Sadatoshi Sugahara, Naohiro Ikeda, Yasutaka Sato, Toshiaki Kosedo, Tokihiko Higuchi, Masayuki Minami, Takeshi Tokutomi, Teruhisa Moriyama, Yuzo Nakamura, Katsutoshi Nekoda

1896–1960

Not held

Volleyball—Women's Team

1992

1. Cuba, Tania Calvo, Marleny Blanco, Alejandrina Hernandez, Lilia Aguirre, Idalmis Moya, Raisa Bolaños, Regla McKenzie, Regla Herrera, Norka Daudinot, Mercedes Martinez, Ana Valle, Magaly Rivera
2. Unified Team, Valentina Ogienko, Natalia Morozova, Marina Nikoulina, Elena Batoukhtina, Irina Smirnova, Tatiana Sidorenko, Tatiana Menchova, Evguenia Artamonova, Galina Lebedeva, Svetlana Vassilevskaïa, Elena Tcheboukina, Svetlana Koritova
3. U.S.A., Tonya Sanders, Yoko Zetterlund, Kimberly Oden, Lory Endicott, Paula Weishoff, Caren Kemner, Tammy Liley, Elaina Oden, Janet Cobbs, Tara Cross-Battle, Liane Sato, Ruth Lawanson

1988

1. Soviet Union, Olga Chkournova, S. Korytova, Marina Koumych, T. Krainova, O. Krivocheeva, M. Nikoulina, V. Oguienko, E. Ovtchinnikova, I. Parkhomtchouk, T. Sidorenko, Irina Smirnova, Elena Volkova
2. Peru, Luisa Cervera, A. De La Guerra, Demisse Fajardo, Miriam Gallardo, Rosa Garcia, Isabel Heredia, Katherine Horny, Natalia Malaga, Gabriela Perez Del Solar, Cecilia Tilt, Gina Torrealva, Cenaida Uribe
3. People's Republic of China, Yongmei Cui, Yuzhu Hou, Ying Jiang, Guojun Li, Yueming Li, Huijuan Su, Yajun Wang, Dan Wu, Xiaojun Yang, Xilan Yang, Hong Zhao, Meizhu Zheng

1984

1. People's Republic of China, Ping Lang, Yan Liang, Ling Zhu, Yuzhu Hou, Xiaolan Zhou, Xilan Yang, Huijuan Su, Ying Jiang, Yanjun Li, Xiaojun Yang, Meizhu Zheng, Rongfang Zhang

2. U.S.A., Paula Weishoff, Susan Woodstra, Riat Crockett, Laurie Flachmeier, Carolyn Becker, Flora Hyman, Rose Magers, Julie Vollertsen, Debbie Green, Kimberly Ruddins, Jeanne Beauprey, Linda Chisholm

3. Japan, Yumi Egami, Kimie Morita, Yuko Mitsuya, Miyoko Hirose, Kyoko Ishida, Yoko Kagabu, Norie Hiro, Kayoko Sugiyama, Sachiko Otani, Keiko Miyajima, Emiko Odaka, Kumi Nakada

1980

1. Soviet Union, Nadazhda Radzevich, Natalia Razumova, Olga Solovova, Yelena Akhaminova, Larissa Pavlova, Yelena Andreyuk, Irina Makagonova, Lyubov Kozyreva, Svetlana Nikishina, Ljudmila Chernysheva, Svetlana Badulina, Lydia Loginova

2. East Germany, Ute Kkostrzewa, Andrea Heim, Annette Schultz, Christine Mummhardt, Hieke Lehmann, Barbara Czekalla, Karla Roffeis, Martina Schmidt, Anke Westendorf, Karin Puschel, Brigitte Fetzer, Katharina Bullin

3. Bulgaria, Tania Dimitrova, Valentina Ilieva, Galina Stancheva, Silva Petrunova, Anka Hristolova, Verka Borisova, Margarita Gherasimova, Roumiana Kaicheva, Maya Georgieva, Tania Gogova, Tzvetana Bozhurina, Rossitza Dimitrova

1976

1. Japan, Takako Iida, Mariko Okamato, Echiko Maedo, Noriko Matsuda, Takako Shirai, Kiyomi Kato, Yuko Arakida, Katsuko Kanesaka, Mariko Yoshida, Shoko Takayanagi, Hiromi Yano, Juri Yokoyama

2. Soviet Union, Anna Rostova, Lyudmila Shetinina, Lilia Osadchaya, Natalya Kushnir, Olga Kozakova, Nina Smoleeva, Lyubov Rudovskaya, Larisa Bergen, Inna Ryskal, Lyudmila Chernysheva, Zoya Iusova, Nina Muradian

3. Republic of Korea, Soon-Bok Lee, Jung-Hye Yu, Kyung-Ja Byon, Soo-Nok Lee, Myung-Sun Baik, Hee-Sook Chang, Kum-Ja Ma, Young-Nae Yun, Kyung-Hwa Yu, Mi-Kum Park, Soo-Nok Jung, Jea-Jung Jo

1972

1. Soviet Union, Inna Ryskal, Vera Douiounova, Tatiana Tretiakova, Nina Smoleeva, Roza Salikhova, Ljudmila Buldakova, Tatiana Gonobobleva, Lyubov Turina, Galina Leontieva, Tatiana Sarycheva

2. Japan, Sumie Oinuma, Noriko Yamashita, Seiko Shimakage, Makiko Furukawa, Takako Iida, Katsumi Matsumura, Michiko Shiokawa, Takako Shirai, Mariko Okamoto, Keiko Hama, Yaeko Yamazaki, Toyoko Iwahara

3. Democratic People's Republic of Korea, Chun-Ok Ri, Myong-Suk Kim, Zung-Bok Kim, Ok-Sun Kang, Yeun-Ja Kim, He-Suk Hwang, Ok-Rim Jang, Myong-Suk Paek, Chun-ja Ryom, Su-Dae Kim, Ok-Jin Jong

1968

1. Soviet Union, Ljudmila Buldakova, Ljudmila Mikhailovskaya, Vera Lantratova, Vera Galushka, Tatiana Sarycheva, Tatiana Ponyayeva, Nina Smoleeeva, Inna Ryskal, Galina Leontieva, Roza Salikhova, Valentina Vinogradova

2. Japan, Setsuko Yoshida, Suzue Takayama, Toyoko Iwahara, Yukiyo Kojima, Sachiko Fukunaka, Kunie Shishikura, Setsuko Inoue, Sumie Oinuma, Keiko Hama

3. Poland, Krystyna Czajkowska, Jozefa Ledwigowa, Elzbieta Porzec, Wanda Wiecha, Zofia Szczesniewska, Krystyna Jakubowska, Lidia Chmielnicka, Barbara Niemczyk, Halina Aszkielowicz, Krystyna Krupowa, Jadwiga Ksiazek, Krystyna Ostromecka

1964

1. Japan, Masae Kasai, Emiko Miyamoto, Kinuko Tanida, Yuriko Handa, Yoshiko Matsumura, Sata Isobe, Katsumi Matsumura, Yoko Shinozaki, Setsuko Sasaki, Yuko Fujimoto, Masako Kondo, Ayano Shibuki

2. Soviet Union, Nelly Abramova, Astra Biltauer, Ljudmila Buldakova, Lyudmila Gureyeva, Valentina Kamenek, Marita Katusheva, Ninel Lukanina, Valentina Mishak, Tatiana Roschina, Inna Ryzkal, Antonina Ryschova, Tamara Tikhonina

3. Poland, Krystyna Czajkowska, Maria Golimowska, Krystyna Jakubowska, Danuta Kordaczuk, Krystyna Krupowa, Jozefa Ledwigowa, Jadwiga Marko, Jadwiga Rutkowska, Maria Sliwkowa, Zofia Szczesniewska

1896–1960

Not held

Trivia Quiz

1. Volleyball was invented in 1895 by
a. The athletic director of the YMCA in Holyoke, Massachusetts
b. A college trainer in Kyoto, Japan
c. Karch Kiraly.

2. The six-a-side game
a. Has always been the most popular indoor game
b. Was adopted by 1918
c. Was first adopted by Japanese teams

3. The Japanese men's team
a. Has medaled in almost every Olympics since 1964
b. Has not medaled since 1972
c. Has never medaled

4. Volleyball was first known as
a. Minonette
b. Set-ball
c. Kiraly-ball

5. The first volleyball World Championships were held in 1949 in
a. Japan
b. The United States
c. Czechoslovakia

6. The rolling receive was first introduced by
a. Hirofumi Diamatsu, the coach of Japan's 1964 women's team
b. Soviet players in the 1980s
c. Karch Kiraly

7. Competitive players can spike the ball at speeds
a. In excess of 62 mph
b. In excess of 100 mph
c. That make you want to say "ouch"

8. Volleyball became a full-medal Olympic sport
a. At the Montreal Games in 1976
b. At the LA Games in 1984
c. At the Tokyo Games in 1964

Volleyball

9. Which of the following countries has *not* won an Olympic volleyball medal?

a. The Netherlands

b. Peru

c. Canada

10. Women's volleyball

a. Was added to the Olympic program at the same time as men's volleyball

b. Will debut at the Atlanta Games

c. Was added to the Olympic program in 1964

Volleyball—Beach

Warm-up

O nce a sport played by bronzed beach bums searching for beer, babes, and a bodacious win, beach volleyball has changed a lot since its early days on the sandy beaches of southern California.

Well, sort of. There's still the beer: all but four of the Association of Volleyball Professionals (AVP) tournaments are sponsored by Miller Lite. Anheuser-Busch has its own four-man Bud Light Pro league, and Coors Light created a venue for women to bump and block against a backdrop of ocean vistas and corporate logos.

But today's top players, no longer playing for brewskies, rake in corporate sponsorships and tournament purses that send their salaries out of the six-digit orbit. And now, thanks to a September 23, 1993, IOC ruling, the discipline of beach volleyball will have full medal status at the Atlanta Games.

How it got there is a story that plays like a cross between *Gidget* and *Wall Street*. A cult sport played on Golden State beaches since the 1940s, beach volleyball spawned its first beach tour in 1976—when most of the current pro tour's top players were still in diapers. Players made their own travel arrangements and financed their own expenses for a crack at a victory on the circuit. The spoils were modest: a pitcher of suds, small-scale celebrity, and eventually a $5,000 pot.

By 1987, an international assortment of beach pros competed in Rio de Janeiro in the first World Championships of Beach Volleyball. Teams from eight countries played before a crowd of bikini-clad good-time-having Brazilian baby boomers. And live TV captured the moment.

Enter, stage left: The Miller Brewing Company, eager to tap the thirsty beach crowd, and willing to spend big money to do so. Corporate sponsors flocked to the sport like moths to a flame. In 1991, ten years after Miller's first beach venture, the AVP circuit landed its first network deal, in the form of three live telecasts with NBC.

Meanwhile, back at the Federation Internationale de Volleyball, the beach game was beginning to take on some semblance of official stature. In 1987, through a circuit comprised of a handful of tournaments, the federation began to position the highly watchable sport as a contender for Olympic acceptance.

Six years later—thanks to the indefatigable PR work of federation head Ruben Acosta and leading AVP players—beach volleyball will have its moment in the sun at the Olympic Games in 1996.

Spectator's Guide

A 1947-issue USVBA official publication explains that "beach volley ball develop[s] excellent coordination and ball-handling. . . ." That about sums it up. Played in the great al fresco, against a background of azure skies and rolling surf, the game is markedly different from the indoor version. Competing barefoot in the sand, players can't explode as high or as fast as they can on an indoor court. The sand forces players to begin their approach sooner, and places more demands on the athletes' conditioning. The wind, too, changes the protocol of outdoor games: volleying into fickle winds, players are forced to keep the ball low, whether they're passing or setting.

With only two members per team, beach volleyball forces players to master every skill: just as the game showcases individual performance, it accentuates a player's weaknesses and faults. While the indoor game, with six players, allows athletes to specialize, the beach game develops all-around players who can serve, set, dig, and block with equal ability. (With each side divided in half, down the middle, beach players sometimes specialize on the right side or left.)

FACT: Beach volleyball, which has never been an exhibition sport at the Olympics, has been granted full medal status for the Atlanta Games only.

Serving strategies take into account the wind and the sun. High serves (also known as skyballs) can force opponents to look directly into the sun; they can also force the other team to guess where the wind will carry the ball. Beach players also tend to serve hard, looking for aces (a point scored on a serve); this is why you'll probably see a lot of jump-serving.

Beach defense is much less complicated than the indoor game. Defending players have the option to:

- block the line
- block the angle
- block the middle
- fake the block
- stay back and dig

Beach players set the ball just as an indoor player would, except for one significant difference: With only one teammate, players don't try to fool their opponents by faking a set. Accurate setting is especially important in the beach game since the sand makes it difficult to run for the ball.

Verbal cues between teammates are important. You may hear players shouting "Angle!" and "Line!" to inform a teammate how to direct a shot; "Nobody!," on the other hand, indicates that the opposition has no one at the net—an ideal moment to spike the ball. Not surprisingly, the most successful two-player teams have a long history together, which allows them to capitalize on each other's abilities.

Beach Talk

Ace a Point: Scored as a result of a serve; the ball usually hits the sand before the other team can touch it.

Block: An above-the-net defensive move that prevents the ball from crossing the net

Bump: The receiving team's first contact with the ball after it's been served

Cut Shot: A shot that causes the ball to leave a player's hand at a sharp angle

Deep Dish: To hold on to the ball too long in order to take the spin off

Dig: A defensive move; most often the successful return of a ball that's been spiked

Dink: A gentle shot placed near or above the opposing blockers

Jump Serve: A serve in which the server hits the ball after having taken a running jump from behind the endline

Kill: An offensive move that the opposing team can't return

Kong Block: Randy Stoklos's signature one-armed blocking style

Rainbow: A gentle shot over the opposing players to the back line

Shank: A bad pass or dig

Sideout: The receiving team earns a sideout (and the serve) after preventing the opposing team from scoring on a serve

Spike: To hit the ball as forcefully as possible into the other team's side

Tweener: A player who is both an excellent blocker and digger

Hopefuls

Over the course of 1995 and 1996, men and women from over 50 different countries will compete in tournaments staged by the FIVB World Series for more than $3.6 million in prize money—and the opportunity to represent their country in the 1996 Olympic Games. The final rankings of this series will determine which countries and players will qualify to play at Atlanta Beach, where 24 men's and 16 women's teams will compete.

If early tournament results are an accurate predictor of Olympic success, Brazilian beach volleyballers should fare well in Atlanta. The world's top-ranked combo of Roberto Lopes Da Costa and Franco Neto Vieira had early-season success, as did the Brazilian women's duo pairing Sandra Pires and Jacqui Silva.

Not everyone, however, was happy with the Olympic selection process. One year before the Games were scheduled to begin, top U.S. male pros locked horns with the international volleyball federation over the rules that determined which players would qualify. By tying Olympic qualification to the results of an FIVB-promoted tour, the federation forced U.S. pros between a rock and a hard place: players either had to skip some lucrative AVP tournaments, or risk losing out on an Olympic berth.

Asked to play lesser teams outside of the U.S., many of the pro players were incensed. The federation's demand, AVP chief Jon Stevenson argued, was "like telling the NBA that Michael Jordan has to play in a tourn'ament in Belgrade to qualify." The pro men decided to boycott the FIVB series, jeopardizing their chances to compete in Atlanta; if the AVP players and federation officials don't manage to work out their differences, the 1996 U.S. men's team could turn out to be a low-profile assembly of lesser stars.

The U.S. women's team, on the other hand, had no problem following the FIVB qualifying procedures. "If the NBA worked

Karch Kiraly, U.S. volleyball captain in 1984, hopes to return to the Games in 1996, this time playing beach volleyball. *AP/Wide World Photos*

with the Olympic organizations, don't tell me the AVP can't," Lori Forythe, a top women's player told the *Wall Street Journal.* "Michael Jordan worked it out . . . Karch Kiraly can work it out."

Karch Kiraly and Kent Steffes

"Kiraly and Steffes," *The New York Times* announced in April of 1995, "are the logical favorites—barring a collapse at the Olympic trials, à la Dan O'Brien—for 1996 gold."

The AVP's stand-off with the volleyball federation could turn out to be just such a collapse. But if Kiraly and Steffes do make it to the Olympic showdown, the duo may preside as Kings of Atlanta Beach.

First paired together in the summer of 1990, the two share similarly sunny southern California upbringings. Kiraly, seven-and-a-half years Steffes's senior, grew up as a first-generation Santa Barbaran. His father, Laszlo—a member of the Hungarian Junior National Voleyball Team—fled Budapest in 1956, under a hail of bullets. Leaving the Soviet invasion and most of his worldly possessions behind, the elder Kiraly (pronounced kuh-RYE) arrived in America with a will to succeed and a love for his game.

At the age of six, Karch moved with his father—now a physician—and mother, Toni, to the West Coast. There, father Kiraly taught his obviously gifted son the fundamentals of Hungarian v-ball. Soon, the father-son duo were competing together. In 1972, the eleven-year-old rising star entered his first beach tournament with his father, and by 1976 they clinched a third-place showing in a B tournament at Muscle Beach.

FACT: In 1995, Karch Kiraly was the AVP's all-time highest earner, with more than $2 million in career winnings.

Soon thereafter, son Kiraly led Santa Barbara High School to a state championship and undefeated season—not exactly a walk on the beach in southern California. From there, he was off to UCLA, where, as a solid 3.5 student in biochemistry, he starred on the championship-winning volleyball team.

Right about that time, Kent Steffes was playing the stock market. Twelve years old and already demonically driven, the youthful dynamo managed his own $1,000 portfolio while scurrying between appointments; playing on a handful of basketball and baseball teams, a soccer squad, and a volleyball team, he also supervised a gaggle of eight-year-old Little Leaguers.

Like his senior partner, Steffes grew up in a middle-class neighborhood in the Golden State, and he, too, came from a long line of athletic achievers. Like Kiraly, his father is still a competitive jock, having staked his claim to a world record in the 4 x 100 relay for men over 50. And, like the Olympic veteran, he was a hot volleyball commodity when he graduated from high school.

That's where the two life stories diverge. "I was a pompous ass," Steffes told *Volleyball* magazine, referring to his short tenure at Stanford. Many are still inclined to agree. Having transferred to Kiraly's alma mater, Steffes continued to ruffle feathers and step on toes, finally losing his NCAA eligibility because his beach partner (UCLA's assistant volleyball coach), wasn't playing for free.

"I always thought I could play both," Steffes later told *Outside* magazine, "but when they told me I couldn't play one, I just went and played on the beach, and that was that." Just then, as Karma would have it, Kiraly—with two Olympic gold medals to his credit—had decided to retire from the indoor game, and was casting about for a suitable mate.

In the summer of 1990, Steffes proposed, and Kiraly was swayed by the younger man's swagger. "Kent came to me and said, 'I think we can win at least 17 of 22 tournaments,'" Kiraly told *The New York Times*, "[and] I said, 'I like your confidence.'"

The partnership didn't last. Disillusioned by their 3–9 record against Sinjin Smith and Randy Stoklos, Kiraly left Steffes for his former partner, Brent Frohoff. "I was bummed. I was bitter," Steffes confided to *Sports Illustrated*. "I knew he was the best partner for me."

FACT: *People* magazine named beach player Kent Steffes one of the 50 most beautiful people of 1995.

Eventually, Kiraly would agree. After more than a season apart, the seasoned veteran—who had recently spent a lucrative stint in an indoor six-man league in Italy—returned to find a more mature version of his erstwhile partner. The new, improved Steffes was downright Olympian, able to run, dig, and spike faster, higher, and stronger. Soon, partnered again, Kiraly and Steffes were on a roll, galloping to a 16-out-of-19 victory streak that included a 13-consecutive-win run. Ruthlessly dominating the sport since their 1992 reunion, the May–December duo seemed destined to stand together on the Olympic victory podium—the seasoned veteran, a gentleman player with two Olympic gold medals to his credit, and the brash, business-minded takeover artist, eager to roust all pretenders to the Olympic title.

There's no doubt: Steffes and Kiraly are the logical favorites to strike gold in the sand at the Atlanta Games. But life on the beach is sometimes illogical.

—Marie J. MacNee

Schedule

The tentative volleyball—beach schedule is:

Tuesday, July 23
Women's & Men's eliminations

Wednesday, July 24
Women's & Men's eliminations

Thursday, July 25
Women's & Men's eliminations

Friday, July 26
Women's & Men's eliminations
Women's semifinal

Saturday, July 27
Men's semifinal
Women's bronze medal and gold medal

Sunday, July 28
Men's bronze medal and gold medal

Trivia Quiz

1. **Beach Volleyball will be**
   a. A demonstration sport at the 1996 Games
   b. A full-medal sport at the 1996 Games
   c. A beer commercial at the 1996 Games

2. **The first beach tour took place in California in**
   a. 1968   b. 1976   c. 1980

3. **The first World Championships of Beach Volleyball were held**
   a. In Venice Beach, California   b. In Rio de Janeiro   c. In Belmar, New Jersey

4. **The Federation Internationale de Volleyball was organized in**
   a. 1948   b. 1967   c. 1926

5. **Olympic beach volleyball teams consist of**
   a. Two players   b. Four players   c. Four or six players

6. **In beach volleyball, the ball tends to be played**
   a. Higher than in the indoor game   b. Lower than in the indoor game
   c. The same as in the indoor game

7. **A "tweener" refers to**
   a. A ball that lands between two players
   b. A player who is an excellent blocker and digger
   c. An athlete on anabolic steroids

8. **AVP rules require men**
   a. To wear tank tops   b. To play shirtless   c. None of the above

9. **A "Kong block" refers to a move popularized by**
   a. Beach King Kiraly   b. Gabrielle Reece   c. Randy Stoklos

10. **Top U.S. players like Karch Kiraly and Kent Steffes**
    a. Automatically qualified for the 1996 Games
    b. Competed in the AVB tour for an Olympic berth
    c. Initially refused to participate in the Olympic qualifying tournaments

Answers: 1-b; 2-b; 3-b; 4-a; 5-a; 6-a; 7-b; 8-c; 9-c; 10-c

WATER POLO

Warm-up

Known as "football in the water," or "aquatic soccer" or "hockey without sticks or skates or ice" (wait! that's team handball!), water polo has a history similar to soccer's, in that the early games of both sports were invitations for mayhem and violence. Invented in England during the 1870s by resort owners as a means of attracting guests, water polo first found favor with goons hellbent on discovering the quiet, novel joy of pulverizing an opponent in the water, as opposed to the usual roughhousing on land. Participants straddled wooden barrels and slapped at a ball with kayak paddles. The game grew so physical and dangerous that it was once barred from U.S. collegiate competition.

Soon enough, paddles and barrels were dropped as equipment, leaving the ball, the water, and the object of desire: the goal. Although many of the early players were unable to swim, this did not greatly impede their game. Water polo was played in waters fit for advanced wading; the chief talent of a good player was knowing how to protect himself below the water line. Inasmuch as the water presented a natural screen, much of the unauthorized activity and near drownings could be negotiated out of sight of the referee.

Although on the Olympic program by 1900, the sport was slow in developing in Europe and the United States. The first U.S. national champion was recognized in 1906 when the sport was known as softball polo, a version that put a premium on rough, unethical conduct. It was eventually discarded in favor of hardball polo, the basis for the current game.

Two key developments occurred in the 1920s that introduced the need for more skill, thereby helping water polo mature into a legitimate sport. The first was the use of larger and deeper pools, creating a need for players to acquire swimming ability, and the other was the development in Hungary of a method of passing the ball from player to player without allowing it to touch the water.

In the U.S., the game is still a California phenomenon, with much of the Olympic squad usually hailing from that state. The University of California, for instance, has won eight NCAA titles in the last two decades, and in 1994, Stanford University captured its second consecutive NCAA title. And the U.S. has been a power at the Olympic level, winning the silver medal in 1984 and 1988; in 1992, however, the U.S. team failed to advance beyond the semi-final.

Spectator's Guide

Water polo is similar to soccer, in that the basic object is to put the ball into the other team's net. Good passing technique is a necessity. The ball is advanced by passing or dribbling, and shots on goal are generally taken with brutal speed. A player is not allowed to touch the ball with both hands simultaneously. Goals can be scored off any part of the body, except a clenched fist. Also prohibited are striking the ball with a clenched fist and holding the ball underwater when tackled.

The water in the pool must be at least 5 feet, 11 inches in depth, and the distance between goal lines is just under 100 feet. The width of the playing area is 65 feet, seven inches. A team consists of the goalkeeper and six others, playing a game with four periods of seven minutes each, allowing a two-minute interval between periods for changing ends.

Minor offenses, such as splashing water in the face of an opponent (take that, you dirty animal), pushing, punching the ball, playing the ball with both hands, or wasting time, result in a free throw being awarded to the opposing team. A major foul results in a free throw and the exclusion of the guilty player from the pool for 45 seconds or until a goal is scored (much like the ice hockey power play). Major fouls include kicking or striking an opponent, holding, sinking, and unwarranted brutality.

A team earns two points for a victory and one for a tie. In the event of a deadlock in the standings, the first tie-breaker is goal difference. The event consists of preliminary rounds, semifinals, and the final.

Hopefuls

Chris Duplanty

Goalie Chris Duplanty hopes to be water polo's Steve Young.

For the good times.

He already knows the bad.

Most sports fans know Steve Young's story—San Francisco 49er quarterback with Super Bowl potential spends what seems like a lifetime backing up the best NFL quarterback that ever was, Joe Montana.

Until Montana moved on.

And Young won Most Valuable Player awards.

And a Super Bowl ring.

Well, Duplanty's personal Joe, Craig Wilson, considered by most to be the best water polo goalie to ever play the game, has finally hung up his Speedo.

That's FINALLY.

Capital letters.

Bold-faced.

Duplanty, 30 (b. October 21, 1965), a native of Honolulu and a veteran of both the Seoul and Barcelona Olympics, with less than two minutes Olympic game time in eight years—*total*—is finally getting his chance.

"The first Olympics in Seoul in 1988 was a dream come true," Duplanty told the *Los Angeles Times*. "I'd only been on the team for six months. I was the youngest guy there. I was just blown away. And I still had one more year of college."

Indeed, Duplanty, who spent the Seoul Olympics riding the bench for all but 34 seconds, serving mainly as team cheerleader and accepting a silver medal, returned to the University of California-Irvine after the Games and led the Anteaters to the 1989 NCAA championship.

Four years later, Duplanty was back on the Olympic team—but so was Wilson.

Duplanty played in one game in Barcelona—against France. The U.S., which ended up a disappointing fourth in the tournament, had an 11–1 lead.

When Duplanty returned to Hawaii after Barcelona, he had some serious thinking to do.

"I wanted to re-evaluate my life," he told the *Los Angeles Times.* "There's always a period of depression after the Olympics and I was into the riding-the-pine syndrome. What had I learned the past four years? That I can sit attentively? That I'm very patient?

"It's hard to sit, no matter who you are. I try to train just like everybody else. I feel like I'd be letting the team down if I took advantage of the situation of (just) being a cheerleader."

He wasn't thrilled, either, that the former U.S. National Team coach, Bill Barnett, had said that because of Wilson's presence, Duplanty was "there basically as a cheerleader."

"That certainly wasn't what my goals were," Duplanty responded. "One goal was certainly to be on the team, but they go beyond that. If I just practiced my yelling and screaming and towel waving, I think that I would be letting the team down. I almost have to prepare for the worst scenario, and I think a Steve Young or any other backup would do the same."

After eight years, however, it began to seem to Duplanty that the worst scenario would be a career backup. And the clock was ticking.

After Barcelona, Duplanty went home to think. He took a job as a substitute teacher and assistant water polo coach at his high school alma mater. He eventually decided to stick it out on the U.S. team for four more years.

As it turns out, Duplanty is one of the cornerstones of a new, rejuvenated U.S. team.

"I had to test the water (by remaining on the team)," he said. "I couldn't quit without really knowing how good I could've been. Could I have been the best in the world? I wouldn't know and that would haunt me for the rest of my life. If I went out and fell on my face, at least I could walk away knowing I gave it my best shot. That's what has kept me going.

"When you sit as much as I have, you can't help but wonder, 'Am I any good?' You lose confidence and you can't help but question yourself. I realized that I had been behind the world's best goal keeper, undeniably, in everyone's mind. You know where you stand. That part is very clear. But then there's the question of, 'How far behind (him) am I?'"

The early assessment was . . . a bit.

When Duplanty first took over full-time, new coach Rich Corso said, "Chris is making the same kinds of blocks and saves and the same kinds of mistakes that Wilson made . . . when he first came on the national team. I think Chris has the potential to be a fine goalkeeper at this level, but he's been a chair general for such a long time and now he has to be a field general. He needs to learn when to relax, when to focus on the ball and when to move and make adjustments."

He's learned, of course.

And through everything, he's kept a sense of humor.

After the Barcelona Olympics, Duplanty was approached by a professional team in Italy.

"I guess they liked the way I sat at attention on the bench," he said.

And when someone brings up Wilson's name?

"Craig is a great person and he's always been very supportive," Duplanty says. "He says he really enjoys what he's doing now, but we still joke about him coming back. Well, *he* jokes about it."

Duplanty also, quite obviously, understands fully the assessment of another goalkeeper, this one on the ice.

Ron Tugnutt, a National Hockey League veteran who's served as a backup in Edmonton, Anaheim, and Montreal, says that the job of backup goaltender "sort of stinks."

Well, the aroma has finally changed for Chris Duplanty.

Everything's coming up roses.

Finally.

—Eric Kinkopf

Alex Rousseau, Rick McNair, and Eriks Krumins

What makes the U.S. water polo team so interesting as a whole are the individual stories.

For example: Troy Barnhart raised and showed market sheep and swine for stock shows in high school. Jack Bowen's grandfather, Fred Zihlman, invented the landing craft used on the moon. Danny Leyson's father, Leon, was one of the thousands of workers saved by Oskar Schindler during the Holocaust. Eriks Krumins's father was an immigrant of Latvia and former captain of the Rutgers University soccer team. Kirk Everist learned to swim at the age of three with Kristen Babb-Sprague, the 1992 Olympic gold medalist in synchronized swimming.

Even more interesting, perhaps, in light of the team concept, are the diverse approaches various U.S. Water Polo players take toward the sport and the Olympic Games.

Alex Rousseau, 28 (b. November 4, 1967), has dedicated his life to the Olympics. Period.

Rick McNair, 27 (b. September 4, 1968), is more or less trying to squeeze a normal existence into a life dominated by the sport.

Eriks Krumins, 27 (b. May 18, 1969), is simply trying to do everything possible at once.

And it all somehow comes together.

"I read some stories before 1992 about those people who mortgaged their houses and just did anything and everything to be in one more Olympics," said Rousseau, who is 6-feet-3, 200 pounds, owns a B.A. in economics from UCLA, was a member of the fourth-place team in Barcelona, and is one of the cornerstones of the rebuilt 1996 U.S. team.

> "I read some of the stories before 1992 about those people who mortgaged their houses and just did everything to be in one more Olympics, and after experiencing '92, I found [the Olympics] very, very addictive."
> —*Alex Rousseau, member of the 1992 US water polo team*

He shares a house with two other national team players a block and a half from the beach and 10 minutes by car to the team's training center at Belmont Plaza Olympic Pool in Long Beach.

McNair, 6-feet-5 and 195 pounds, a 1991 Stanford University economics graduate and investment manager and Wall Street analyst, has worked for one of the largest institutional money management houses in the U.S. He continues to work part-time in the field while practicing and traveling with the U.S. team.

"I don't think I've given up the business career just yet," says McNair, who alternates early morning workouts between weightlifting and swimming, works a mostly 9-to-5 business shift, then practices with the team from 6–9 p.m. "Hopefully, I can do enough work in order to allow me to step right back into it when I'm done playing. I have very little time. I have a very regimented schedule. But I would prefer not to have a lot of idle time, and I'm doing something I like."

Then, there's Krumins.

"What Krumins is trying to accomplish are four surmountable goals: make an Olympic team, medal at an Olympics, attend law school and study for the bar," says U.S. Men's National Team coach Rich Corso. "For most, just achieving one of those would be an accomplishment of a lifetime. He's taking it all on at once."

Says Krumins: "Sometimes I think I might have bitten off more than I can chew. It's like fighting a war on two fronts. As the Germans found out, it's not too easy. I don't have a break from either water polo or law school. It can thin you out in terms of the time, emotional stamina and physical sleep."

Rousseau, who was the final player selected for the 1992 Olympic team, speaks French, Spanish, and Italian and lived in Canada for a time and played ice hockey. He's been nicknamed Mr. Continental because of the way he handles himself on trips with the team—he's come in handy at many a foreign hotel or restaurant.

He's almost grown up with the Olympics.

His mother, Nicole, was a hostess at the 1976 Summer Olympics in Montreal, where Alex took advantage of his mother's position and hung out in the athlete's village. In 1980, the Rousseau's drove from their new home in Vermont to Lake Placid for the 1980 Winter Games, where Alex watched Ingemar Stenmark and the brothers Mahre ski.

"I guess I have a passion for the Olympics," says Rousseau, who also prides himself on remembering just about every joke he's ever heard.

Krumins has a passion for the Games and for music, too. The 6-foot-6, 190-pound driver, who carries law books and his ever-present lap-top computer on team trips and who observed in person the jury *voirdire* process—the questioning of potential jurors—during the O.J. Simpson double-murder trial as part of a law school class, wants to move someday into entertainment law.

"Utopia for me would be to be a lawyer who manages and takes a band from ground-zero and up," says the former three-time All-American and two-time NCAA champion, who owns a degree in political economy from the University of California-Berkeley.

Says McNair of his out-of-pool experiences in the business world: "Sometimes it's a pure adrenaline rush, kind of like a sports competition."

Indeed, what you keep coming back to with all the water polo players is the ethic, the desire to succeed at no matter what.

"After experiencing '92, I found the Olympics very, very addictive," says Rousseau. "You know you are sacrificing, but you know it's worth everything and it's definitely gold—all the memories. It's something you can't pass up."

It is, perhaps, the one common thread.

It makes the individuals into the team.

—Eric Kinkopf

The Sports Illustrated Connection

The topic was so hot that U.S. Water Polo dedicated four pages of its 1994–95 media guide to it.

The discovery of a water polo *wunderkind?*

Revolutionary rules changes?

Nope. Not even close.

Give up?

The topic was the 1994 *Sports Illustrated* swimsuit edition, which featured five members of the U.S. Water Polo Senior Men's National Team—Troy Barnhart, Chris Duplanty, Kirk Everist, Rick McNair, and Alex Rousseau. It was the first time men shared the spotlight with the traditional array of supermodels in the magazine's special edition.

The idea was born 10 years previous, in 1984, when Julie Campbell, *SI*'s senior editor of fashion and travel, received a beefcake poster of the 1984 U.S. Olympic Water Polo Team. (The poster, unofficially declared by the *Los Angeles Times* as the "pin-up poster" of the Los Angeles Games, became so popular that an 800 number was established to handle the demand.) As the years passed, the story goes, Campbell's poster eventually came down, but the picture remained in her thoughts.

For years, editors of the magazine—the swimsuit edition reaches an estimated 50 million adult readers—have received complaints about the lack of males in the special edition. Well, Julie Campbell finally answered the critics. She called U.S. Water Polo officials. They were only to happy to oblige.

"The toughest decision was the selection of the five players," said U.S. Water Polo Executive Director Bruce Wigo. "Our entire men's national team is a fine bunch of men blessed with good looks. The sport seems to attract fine-looking athletes who are extremely bright."

Indeed, Olympian Terry Schroeder posed for the bronze statue at the gateway to the Los Angeles Coliseum for the 1984 Games. And *USA Today* once ran a story entitled "Bod-watching: A sport unto itself," recognizing Schroeder's physique, among others. Water polo Olympians have modeled in *GQ, Men's Fitness, Muscle & Fitness Magazine, U Man,* and *Orange Coast Magazine* and have appeared in television commercials for the Milk Council, Wheaties, and the Atlanta Committee for the Olympic Games.

"The poster, and that they are good-looking, healthy and a team—that's what made me think of water polo," Campbell said.

Olympian Alex Rousseau, who appeared on five pages of the magazine, was playing professionally in Marseilles, France, when he received a call from U.S. Water Polo officials. "I told my coach in France, 'It's either I go do this, or I quit.' It was pretty simple."

The theme for the 30th anniversary issue was "Some of the Most Beautiful Swimming Pools in the World." That also worked in the team's favor.

"There is something to be said for competition pools and their beauty," *SI* reporter Julie Stern said. "Julie Campbell thought that one of the best ways to show competition pools would be to shoot a water sport. I don't think we could have asked for a better on-set relationship between the models, the players and crew. Although the players aren't professional models, they came off like them. We couldn't have gotten a better shoot from male models."

Not that there weren't some doubts.

"We were definitely nervous about how the guys would look," Stern said. "Would they photograph well? Well, every single one was attractive and photographs well. Athletes have something in common with models, because they are comfortable with their bodies and have good physiques."

They were tall, too, which is something that lanky supermodel Elle Macpherson noticed.

"Being around a lot of tall, good-looking, strong athletes is always nice—especially when you are six feet tall," she said.

FACT: Alex Rousseau, a 6' 3" 200-pound member of the U.S. water polo team, was one of the first men ever to be featured in *Sports Illustrated's* swimsuit issue. He appears on five pages of the magazine's 1994 edition—a record matched only by supermodel Stacey Williams.

Said model Stacey Williams: "It was so different from anything we'd done before. I was genuinely excited to do the shoot. The Julies (Campbell and Stern) are always trying to fix me up with someone. They said, 'Maybe you'll meet your husband, so make sure to wear some makeup.'"

And the reaction from the players?

"In the initial shoot, it was thrilling to be on the pool deck with them," said Troy Barnhart. "I'd known the models for about half and hour and they were already whistling at me and calling my name out for a shot. Definitely having Elle and Kathy Ireland and Olympic swimmer Dara Torres-Gowen whistling and carrying on like they were was something. I'll cherish that moment. It was fun to reverse roles and feel that degraded."

"That was huge," Rick McNair said. "I couldn't concentrate on my work. I kept asking myself, 'What am I doing?' It was unbelievable. It was an opportunity of a lifetime. Buddies of mine kept calling to ask what it was like and I couldn't help but make it sound even better than it was."

Rousseau was skeptical "until the actual morning of the shoot, when we saw the models. That's when I realized, 'Oh, my God, this is going to happen.' After that, it was just total giddiness. It was hilarious. The first day, all five of us were total fools. Every time we had a moment alone, we'd just look at each other, smile and laugh. After that, we had a great time and got to know the models. They are actually really nice people."

The final product, especially one photo that had Macpherson perched on Rousseau's shoulders, prompted *The Tonight Show's* Jay Leno to ask a national television audience:

"How do you get that job?"

Rousseau just shakes his head. He still isn't quite sure which lucky star he was sitting beneath when his name was picked.

In fact, he's only sure of one thing:

"I'd do it again," Rousseau says with a boyish smile. "I'll tell you that much."

—Eric Kinkopf

Schedule

The tentative water polo schedule is:

Saturday, July 20
preliminaries games 1–6

Sunday, July 21
preliminaries games 7–12

Monday, July 22
preliminaries games 13–18

Tuesday, July 23
preliminaries games 19–24

Wednesday, July 24
preliminaries games 25–30

Friday, July 26
classification games 1 & 2
quarterfinal games 1–4

Saturday, July 27
classification games 3–6
semifinals 1 & 2

Sunday, July 28
finals games 5–12
bronze final & gold final

Highlights

Water polo medals have traditionally been dominated by the Hungarians — who have mined a total of 12 medals, seven of them gold — while the next-in-line medalist, the U.S., has a total of seven, with one gold. The Hungarian Olympic presence has been marked by a variety of standout performances and interesting sidelights. A number of the Hungarian victories were awarded simply by virtue of a higher goal differential: in Berlin in 1936, Hungary and Germany were tied 2–2; in Helsinki in 1952, Yugoslavia and Hungary were tied 2–2; and again in Tokyo in 1964, the two were tied ... and each time Hungary made away with the gold because of the goal differential.

Some of Hungary's more notable players include Dezsö Gyarmati, who medaled in five different Games (and whose wife, Eva, won a gold and silver in swimming events in 1952 and 1956), and Oliver Halassy, who played on three Olympic water polo teams (including two gold-medaling teams) — despite the fact that one of his legs had been amputated below the knee due to a childhood accident.

Hungarian sportsmanship hasn't always been impeccable. In the 1972 Munich Games, in a match between Hungary and Italy, eight Hungarian players were suspended in a mere 38 seconds. That must be some kind of record. A much more serious imbroglio developed in the pool in 1956 when the Hungarian team competed against the Soviets. The match began with not a little acrimony: 200,000 Soviet troops had invaded Hungary just over one month prior to the match-not-made-in-heaven. Hailed as an underwater boxing match, the subaquatic war was called with Hungary in the lead 4–0; the Hungarian team was proclaimed victorious, and police were summoned to prevent rioting among the 5500 Soviet-unsympathetic spectators.

FACT: After Great Britain defeated the Belgian team at the 1920 Antwerp Games, Belgian spectators attacked the British players. The U.K.'s team was forced to leave the Olympic venue under armed guard.

The Hungarian presence has not been felt in recent Games: Yugoslavia captured the gold in the 1984 and 1988 Games, while the U.S. took silver both times. America's first medals came in 1904, when the U.S. team literally swept the pool, taking gold, silver, and bronze. The victory is somewhat tarnished, however, by the fact that because the Americans insisted on playing the American way — using a soft, underinflated ball — at the St. Louis Games, no other countries participated. Paris in 1924 produced

America's most famous water polo player (albeit best known for his swimming prowess): as a member of the U.S. water polo team, the soon-to-be-known-as-Tarzan Johnny Weissmuller collected a bronze medal to add to his three swimming golds.

Highlights from Barcelona

Between 1952 and 1988, Yugoslavian athletes mounted the medal podium in all but three Olympics; and in recent years, they occupied the highest tier. But the U.S. team was coming on strong; in 1991, at the FINA World Cup in Barcelona, the U.S. squad roughhoused the Yugoslavs to capture the championship title.

Barcelona was to be a grudge match. Chafing to roust their American protagonists, the Yugoslav team was dealt a stinging blow. They were grounded, banished from the Games, under the authority of a United Nations sanction.

FACT: Although both the U.S. and Yugoslavian teams finished with the same record at the 1984 Games, Yugoslavia won the match because they had a greater goal differential in the final round. Before the 1988 Games, the FINA changed the rules to allow six-minute overtime periods in the medal round.

So the Barcelona Games proceeded without them. But not without their coaches: it was old home week at the Catalonian pool as the final match between Italy and Spain pitted Ratko Rudic—the erstwhile coach of Yugoslavia's 1984 and 1988 Olympic teams—against Dragan Matutinovic.

It was a seemingly endless 46 minutes before the Italians finally eclipsed the Spanish team 9–8. The Italians were dominant; the Spaniards, persistent. Down 4–2 after the second quarter, the homeboys managed a throw-in every time, racking up a nail-biting tally of seven-all with only 34 seconds before the end of normal time.

Then came three six-minute periods of extra time; the score crept to 8–8. Finally, Italy's Ferdinando Gandolfi drove the winning goal past the Spanish team's unsuspecting defense. Settling for the bronze medal was the Unified Team, who had won all their matches in this tournament. And they'd beaten the American team, as had the Spanish in the semifinal, forcing the U.S. players to skip the finals for the first time since they boycotted the Games in 1980.

Meanwhile, Hungary—the winningest nation in Olympic competition, with a record six gold medals—came up dry. Unable to break through the tough Italian defense in a tooth-and-nail preliminary match, the one-time champions fell out of contention.

Medalists

Water Polo

1992

1. Italy, Francesco Attolico, Marco Altrui, Alessandro Bovo, Giuseppe Porzio, Alessandro Campagna, Paolo Caldarella, Mario Fiorillo, Francesco Porzio, Amedeo Pomilio, Ferdinando Gandolfi, Massimiliano Ferretti, Carlo Silipo, Gianni Averaimo
2. Spain, Jesus Prada, Sergio Cavalle, Marco Junquera, Ruben Jover, Manuel Duocastella, Daniel Sans, Jose Llado, Ricardo Alarcon, Jordi Juan, Salvador Aguera, Miguel Gaia, Manuel Sanchez, Pedro Aguado
3. Unified Team, Evgueni Charonov, Alexandre Ogorodnikov, Alexei Vdovine, Nikolai Kozlov, Serguei Naoumov, Andrei Belofastov, Alexandre Kolotov, Dmitri Apanassenko, Dmitri Gorchkov, Serguei Markotch, Andrei Kovalenko, Vladimir Karaboutov, Alexandre Tchiguir

1988

1. Yugoslavia, Dragan Andric, M. Bezmalinovic, Perica Bukic, Veselin Djuho, Igor Gocanin, Deni Lusic, Igor Milanovic, T. Paskvalin, R. Posinkovic, G. Radjenovic, Dubravko Simenc, A. Sostar, Mirko Vicevic
2. U.S.A., James Bergeson, Greg Boyer, Jeff Campbell, Jody Campbell, Peter Campbell, Chris DuPlanty, Mike Evans, Doug Kimball, Craig Klass, Alan Mouchawar, Kevin Robertson, Terry Schroeder, Craig Wilson
3. Soviet Union, D. Apanasenko, V. Berendiouga, E. Charonov, M. Giorgadze, Evgeni Grichine, Mikhail Ivanov, Serguei Kotenko, S. Markotch, G. Mchvenieradze, N. Mendygaliev, Sergei Naoumov, Nikolai Smirnov

1984

1. Yugoslavia, Milorad Krivokapic, Deni Lusic, Zoran Petrovic, Bozo Vuletic, Veselin Djuho, Zoran Roje, Milivoj Bebic, Perica Bukic, Goran Sukno, Tomislav Paskvalin, Igor Milanovic, Dragan Andric, Andrija Popovic
2. U.S.A., Craig Wilson, Kevin Robertson, Gary Figueroa, Peter Campbell, Douglas Burke, Joseph Vargas, Jon Svendsen, John Siman, Andrew McDonald, Terry Schroeder, Jody Campbell, Timothy Shaw, Christopher Dorst
3. West Germany, Peter Rohle, Thomas Loebb, Frank Otto, Rainer Hoppe, Armando Fernandez, Thomas Huber, Jurgen Schroeder, Rainer Osselmann, Hagen Stamm, Roland Freund, Dirk Theismann, Santiago Chalmovsky, Werner Obschernikat

1980

1. Soviet Union, Yevgeny Sharonov, Sergei Kotenko, Vladimir Akimov, Yevgeny Grishin, Mait Riysman, Aleksandr Kabanov, Aleksei Barkalov, Erkin Shagaev, Georgi Mshvenieradze, Mikhail Ivanov, Vyacheslav Sobchenko
2. Yugoslavia, Luka Vezilic, Zoran Gopcevic, Damir Polic, Ratko Rudic, Zoran Mustur, Zoran Roje Milivoj Bebic, Slobodan Trifunovic, Bosko Lozica, Predrag Manojlovic, Milorad Krivokapic
3. Hungary, Endre Molnar, Istvan Szivos, Attila Sudar, Gyorgy Gerendas, Gyorgy Horkai, Gabor Csapo, Istvan Kiss, Istvan Udvardi, Laszlo Kuncz, Tamas Farago, Karoly Hauszler

1976

1. Hungary, Endre Molnar, Istvan Szivos, Tamas Farago, Laszlo Sarosi, Gyorgy Horkai, Gabor Csapo, Attila Sudar, Gyorgy Kenex, Gyorgy Gerendas, Ferenc Konrad, Tibor Cservenyak
2. Italy, Alberto Alberani, Rolando Simeoni, Silvio Baracchini, Sante Marsili, Marcello Del Duca, Gianni De Magistris, Alessandro Ghibellini, Luigi Castagnola, Riccardo De Magistris, Vincenzo D'Angelo, Umberto Panerai
3. Netherlands, Evert Kroon, Nico Landweerd, Jan Evert Veer, Hans van Zeeland, Ton Buunk, Piet de Zwarte, Hans Smits, Rik Toonen, Gyze Stroboer, Andy Hoepelman, Alex Boegschoten

1972

1. Soviet Union, Vadim Gulyaev, Anatoly Akimov, Aleksandr Dreval, Aleksandr Dolgushin, Vladimir Shmudski, Aleksandr Kabanov, Aleksei Barkalov, Aleksandr Shidlovsky, Nikolai Melnikov, Leonid Osipov, Vyacheslav Sobchenko
2. Hungary, Endre Molnar, Tibor Cservenyak, Dr. Andras Bodnar, Istvan Gorgenyi, Zoltan Kasas, Tamas Farago, Laszlo Sarosi, Istvan Szivos, Istvan Magas, Denes Pocsik, Dr. Ferenc Konrad
3. U.S.A., James Slatton, Stanley Cole, Russell Webb, Barry Weitzenberg, Gary Sheerer, Bruce Bradley, Peter Asch, James Ferguson, Steven Barnett, John Parker, Eric Lindroth

1968

1. Yugoslavia, Karlo Stipanic, Ivo Trumbic, Ozren Bonacic, Uros Marovic, Ronald Lopatny, Zoran Jankovic, Miroslav Poljak, Dejan Dabovic, Djordje Perisic, Mirko Sandic, Zdravko Hebel
2. Soviet Union, Vadim Gulyaev, Givi Chikvanaya, Boris Grishin, Aleksandr Dolgushin, Aleksei Barkalov, Yuri Grigorovsky, Vladimir Semyonov, Aleksandr Shidlovsky, Vyacheslav Skok, Leonid Osipov, Oleg Bovin
3. Hungary, Endre Molnar, Mihaly Mayer, Istvan Szivos, Janos Konrad II, Laszlo Sarosi, Laszlo Felkai, Ferene Konrad III, Denes Pocsik, Andras Bodnar, Zoltan Domotor, Janos Steinmetz

1964

1. Hungary, Miklos Ambrus, Laszlo Felkai, Janos Konrad, Zoltan Domotor, Tivadar Kanizsa, Peter Rusoran II, Gyorgy Karpati, Otto Boros, Mihaly Mayer, Denes Pocsik, Andras Bodnar, Dezso Gyarmati
2. Yugoslavia, Milan Muskatirovic, Ivo Trumbic, Vinko Rosic, Zlatko Simenc, Bozidar Stanisic, Ante Nardeli, Zoran Jankovic, Mirko Sandic, Ozren Bonacic, Frane Nonkovic, Karlo Stipanic
3. Soviet Union, Igor Grabovsky, Vladimir Kuznyetsov, Boris Grishin, Boris Popov, Nikolai Kalashnikov, Zenon Bortkevich, Nikolai Kuznetsov, Viktor Ageyev, Leonid Osipov, Vladimir Semyonov, Eduard Yegorov

1960

1. Italy, Dante Rossi, Giuseppe D'Altrui, Eraldo Pizzo, Gianni Lonzi, Franco Lavoratori, Rosario Parmegiani, Danio Bardi, Brunello Spinelli, Salvatore Gionta, Amadeo Ambron, Giancarlo Guerrini, Luigi Mannelli
2. Soviet Union, Leri Gogoladze, Givi Chikvanaya, Vyacheslav Kurennoi, Anatoly Kartashov, Yuri Grigorovsky, Pyotr Mshvenieradze , Vladimir Semyonov, Boris Goikhman, Yevgeny Salzyn, Viktor Ageyev, Vladimir Novikov
3. Hungary, Otto Boros, Istvan Hevesi, Mihaly Mayer, Dezso Gyarmati, Tivadar Kanizsa, Zoltan Domotor, Laszlo Felkai, Laszlo Jeney, Andras Katona, Kalman Markovits, Peter Rusoran II, Gyorgy Karpati, Janos Konrad, Andras Bodnar

1956

1. Hungary, Otto Boros, Istvan Hevesi, Dezso Gyarmati, Kalman Markovits, Antal Bolvari, Mihaly Mayer, Gyorgy Karpati, Laszlo Jeney, Istvan Szivos, Tivadar Kanizsa, Ervin Zador
2. Yugoslavia, Zdravko Kovacic, Ivo Cipci, Hrvoje Kacic, Marjan Zurej, Zdravko Jezic, Lovro Radonjic, Tomislav Franjkovic, Vladimir Ivkovic
3. Soviet Union, Boris Goikhman, Viktor Ageyev, Yuri Schlyapin, Vyacheslav Kurennoi, Pyotr Breus, Pyotr Mshvenieradze, Nodar Gyakharia, Mikhail Ryschak, Valentin Prokopov, Boris Markarov

1952

1. Hungary, Laszlo Jeney, Gyorgy Vizvari, Dezso Gyarmati, Kalman Markovits, Antal Bolvari, Istvan Szivos, Gyorgy Karpati, Robert Antal, Dezso Fabian, Karoly Szittya, Dezso Lemhenyi, Istvan Hasznos, Miklos Martin
2. Yugoslavia, Zdravko Kovacic, Veljko Bakasun, Ivo Stakula, Ivo Kurtini, Bosko Vuksanovic, Zdravko Jezic, Lovro Radonjic, Marko Brainovic, Vlado Ivkovic
3. Italy, Raffaello Gambino, Vincenzo Polito, Cesare Rubini, Carlo Peretti, Ermenegildo Arena, Maurizio Mannelli, Renato De Sanzuane, Renato Traiola, Geminio Ognio, Salvatore Gionta, Lucio Ceccarini

1948

1. Italy, Pasquale Buonocore, Emilio Bulgarelli, Cesare Rubini, Geminio Ognio, Ermenegildo Arena, Aldo Ghira, Gianfranco Pandolfini, Mario Maioni, Tullio Pandolfini
2. Hungary, Endre Gyorfi, Miklos Holop, Dezso Gyarmati, Karoly Szittya, Oszkar Csuvik, Istvan Szivos, Dezso Lemhenyi, Laszlo Jeney, Dezso Fabian, Jeno Brandi
3. Netherlands, Johannes J. Rohner, Cornelis Korevaar, Cor Braasem, Hans Stam, Albert F. Ruimschotel, Rudolph van Feggelen, Fritz Smol, Pieter J. Salomons, Hendrikus Keetelaar

1936

1. Hungary, Gyorgy Brody, Kalman Hazai, Marton Homannai, Oliver Halassy, Jeno Brandi, Janos Nemeth, Mihaly Bozsi, Gyorgy Kutasi, Miklos Sarkany, Sandor Tarics, Istvan Molnar
2. Germany, Paul Klingenburg, Bernhard Baier, Gustav Schurger, Fritz Gunst, Josef Hauser, Hans Schneider, Hans Schulze, Fritz Stolze, Heinrich Krug, Alfred Kienzle, Helmuth Schwenn
3. Belgium, Henri Disy, Joseph De Combe, Henri Stoelen, Fernand Issele, Albert Casteleyns, Gerard Blitz, Pierre Coppieters, Henri De Pauw, Edmond Michiels

1932

1. Hungary, Gyorgy Brody, Sandor Ivady, Marton Homonnai, Oliver Halassy, Jozsef Vertesy, Janos Nemeth, Ferenc Keseru I, Alajos Keseru II, Istvan Barta, Miklos Sarkany
2. Germany, Erich Rademacher, Fritz Gunst, Otto Cordes, Emil Benecke, Joachim Rademacher, Heiko Schwartz, Hans Schulze, Hans Eckstein
3. U.S.A., Herbert Wildman, Calvert Strong, Charles Finn, Harold McAlister, Philip Daubenspeck, Austin Clapp, Wallace O'Connor

1928

1. Germany, Erich Rademacher, Otto Cordes, Emil Benecke, Fritz Gunst, Joachim Rademacher, Karl Bahre, Max Amann, Johann Blank
2. Hungary, Istvan Barta, Sandor Ivady, Alajos Keseru II, Marton Homonnai, Ferenc Keseru I, Jozsef Vertesy, Oliver Halassy
3. France, Paul Dujardin, Jules Keignaert, Henri Padou, Emile Bulteel, Achille Tribouillet, Henri Cuvelier, Albert Vandeplancke, Ernest Rogez, Albert Thevenon

1924

1. France, Paul Dujardin, Noel Delberghe, Georges Rigal, Henri Padou, Robert Desmettre, Albert Mayaud, Albert Delborgies
2. Belgium, Albert Durant, Joseph De Combe, Maurice Blitz, Joseph Pletincx, Pierre Dewin, Gerard Blitz, Joseph Cludts, Georges Fleurix, Paul Gailly, Jules Thiry, Pierre Vermetten
3. U.S.A., Frederick Lauer, Oliver Horn, Clarence Mitchell, George Schroth, Herbert Vollmer, John Weissmuller, Arthur Austin, John Norton, Wallace O'Connor

1920

1. Great Britain, Charles Smith, Noel Purcell, Christopher Jones, Charles Bugbee, William Dean, Paul Radmilovic, William Peacock
2. Belgium, Albert Durant, Paul Gailly, Pierre Nijs, Joseph Pletincx, Maurice Blitz, Rene Bauwens, Gerard Blitz, Pierre Dewin
3. Sweden, Theodor Naumann, Pontus Hanson, Max Gumpel, Vilhelm Anderson, Nils Backlund, Robert Andersson, Erik Andersson, Harald Julin, Erik Bergqvist

1912

1. Great Britain, Charles Smith, George Cornet, Charles Bugbee, Arthur Hill, George Wilkinson, Paul Radmilovic, Isaac Bentham

2. Sweden, Torsten Kumfeldt, Harald Julin, Max Gumpel, Pontus Hanson, Vilhelm Anderson, Robert Andersson, Erik Bergqvist
3. Belgium, Albert Durant, Herman Donners, Victor Boin, Joseph Pletincx, Oscar Gregoire, Herman Meyboom, Felicien Courbet, Jean Hoffmann, Pierre Nijs

1908

1. Great Britain, Charles Smith, George Nevinson, George Cornet, Thomas Thould, George Wilkinson, Paul Radmilovic, Charles Forsyth
2. Belgium, Albert Michant, Herman Meyboom, Victor Boin, Joseph Pletincx, Fernand Feyaerts, Oscar Gregoire, Herman Donners
3. Sweden, Torsten Kumfeldt, Axel Runstrom, Harald Julin, Pontus Hanson, Gunnar Wennerstrom, Robert Andersson, Erik Bergvall

1906

Not held

1904

1. U.S.A. (New York Athletic Club), David Bratton, George Van Cleef, Leo "Budd" Goodwin, Louis Handley, David Hesser, Joseph Ruddy, James Steen
2. U.S.A. (Chicago Athletic Club), R. E. Breach, James Steever, Swatek, Charles Healy, Frank Kehoe, David Hammond, William Tuttle
2. U.S.A. (Missouri Athletic Club), John Meyers, Manfred Toeppen, Gwynne Evans, Amadee Reyburn, Fred Schreiner, A. M. Goessling, W. R. Orthwein

1900

1. Great Britain, (Osborne Swimming Club, Manchester), Arthur Robertson, Thomas Coe, Eric Robinson, Peter Kemp, George Wilkinson, John H. Derbyshire, William Lister
2. Belgium, (Club de Natation de Bruxelles), Albert Michant, Fernand Fayaerts, Henri Cohen, Victor De Behr, Oscar Gregoire, Victor Sonnemans, Jean De Backer
3. France (II), (Pupilles de Neptune de Lille), Coulon, Fardelle, Favier, Loriche, Louis Martin, Charles Treffel, Desire Merchez
3. France (I), (Libellule de Paris), Henri Peslier, Thomas Burgess, Decuyper, Pesloy, Paul Vasseur, Devenot, Louis Lauffray

1896

Not held

Trivia Quiz

1. Water polo was invented in the 1870s
   a. By ivy league college swim coaches   **b.** By English resort owners
   c. By a team of Canadian hockey players looking for a summer activity

2. Early matches involved
   a. Wooden barrels and kayak paddles   **b.** Hockey sticks   **c.** Wooden rafts

3. The first water polo matches
   a. Required players to be expert swimmers
   b. Did not require players to swim   **c.** Were held on croquet lawns.

3. After captaining the 1984 and 1988 U.S. water polo teams, Terry Schroeder
   a. Competed in a 1992 Olympic relay
   b. Played professional beach volleyball
   c. Posed nude for a statue in Los Angeles

4. Water polo was once barred from U.S. collegiate competition because
   a. It was considered frivolous   **b.** It was considered dangerous
   c. Nobody would pay to see it

5. Water polo was first included on the Olympic program in
   a. 1900   **b.** 1956   **c.** 1980

6. The current game of water polo was based on
   a. Softball polo   **b.** Harball polo   **c.** Aroz con pollo

7. When water polo moved to larger and deeper pools in the 1920s, players were for the first time required to
   a. Play without shoes   **b.** Get wet.   **c.** Learn how to swim

8. The method of passing the ball from player to player without allowing it to touch the water was developed in
   a. California. b. Hungary   **c.** Great Britain

9. In 1992, the Yugoslavian team
   a. Won its third consecutive Olympic gold medal
   b. Was eliminated before the final   **c.** Was not allowed to compete

10. In the 1972 Munich Games, eight Hungarian players
   a. Withdrew because of the flu
   b. Were disqualified for using performance-enhancing drugs
   c. Were suspended in a matter of 38 seconds

Answers: 1-b; 2-a; 3-c; 4-b; 5-a; 6-b; 7-c; 8-b; 9-c; 10-c

WEIGHTLIFTING

Warm-up

Strong men lifting unbelievable weights are the stuff of myth and legend. Atlas, Hercules, and Samson were legendary men of remarkable strength. Together, strength and virtue have created unforgettable ideals.

Legends also indicate that competitions between strong men go back for thousands of years. Weightlifting was part of the regimen of the classical Greek athlete, who used stone or lead weights that were held in one hand and later came to be known as dumbbells.

Weightlifting as a competitive sport may have begun in the eighteenth century in countries such as Germany, France, Switzerland, and Austria, as well as the Scandinavian countries. Widely regarded as showmen, weightlifters often performed in sideshows and music halls.

Athletic clubs for strong men first appeared in the 1860s. Early competitors did not enjoy the advantage of adjustable weights, so rankings were determined by lifting a certain weight several times. The first form of two-handed weight was a metal bar with balls at each end made of solid iron or filled with sand, pebbles, lead shot, or pieces of metal.

Weightlifting became a respected sport with its inclusion in the Olympic program of 1896. The first official World Championships involving one- and two-hand events were held in Vienna in 1898.

The International Weightlifting Federation (IWF) was founded in Paris in 1920 with 14 members. Prior to 1920, weightlifting was governed by the International Gymnastics Federation (FIG).

Weightlifting took its modern-day form of competition in 1928, when the excercises done with one hand were abolished and the disc barbells appeared. The 1928 Olympics at Amsterdam included the press, the snatch, and the jerk, all done with two hands.

With the exception of the 1900, 1908, and 1912 Olympic Games, weightlifting has always been a part of the Olympic program. Before the current rule of determining the winner of a tie by placing the lighter competitor first, two gold medals were awarded for ties. This happened in 1928 and 1936 in the lightweight event.

The press was eliminated from Olympic competition for the 1972 Games in Munich. The event had proved difficult to adjudicate, and controversies arose over deviations between the valid lay-back style and the "Military Press."

Results in weightlifting are increasingly dramatic, and year after year new records are established. The United States dominated the weightlifting events from 1948 through 1956. The Soviet Union dominated the 1960 Games at Rome and continued their dominance through 1988. The weightlifters did well again in 1992, when they competed as members of the Unified Team.

Spectator's Guide

Two lift events are contested in the Olympics, the snatch and the clean-and-jerk. A lifter's total represents the combined weight of his best snatch and clean-and-jerk. Only the heaviest successful snatch and clean-and-jerk are used when tabulating the final score. Medals are awarded for totals only in ten different bodyweight classifications, which for 1996 are as follows: 54kg (119lb), 59kg (130lb), 64kg (141lb), 70kg (154lb), 76kg (168lb), 83kg (183lb), 91kg (201lb), 99kg (218lb), 108kg (238lb), and over 108kg. For the 1996 Games, the IOC has ruled to impose a 250-athlete limit.

The snatch is the more technical and more explosive of the two lifts. It is performed in one continuous movement: the bar is brought from the platform to a position overhead using one fluid motion. The lifter pulls the bar to about chest height and then, in the moment before the bar starts to descend, pulls his body into a squat position under the bar, securing it overhead with arms held straight. The lifter must stand and wait for the referee's signal, called a "down" signal, to lower the bar.

More weight is lifted in the clean-and-jerk than in the snatch. Two separate efforts are involved. First, in the "clean," the lifter must pull the weight from the platform to his shoulders in one motion. The bar is pulled to about waist level, keeping it close to the body and even close enough to brush the thighs. Then, before the bar starts to descend, the lifter pulls his body beneath the bar, secures the bar on his shoulders or chest, and then stands erect. The "jerk" then follows in which the lifter thrusts the bar from his shoulders to a position overhead, again in one motion, and splits his legs front and back. The lifter then brings his feet together and awaits the signal from the referee to lower the bar.

In both events, the down signal is given once the lifter is motionless.

Each lifter is allowed three chances to perform each lift successfully. If a lifter misses all three opportunities in the snatch, he is allowed to continue in the clean-and-jerk but is ineligible for final placing.

The starting weight is up to each individual lifter. Since each contestant is limited to three lifts in the snatch and three in the clean-and-jerk, he must choose carefully. In some cases, lifters will pass on the lower weights, but this strategy can backfire if the lifter is not able to make a lift at his first weight.

The lifting order for the competition is determined by the weight each individual lifter chooses to start with. In the case of identical weight requests, the order is determined by lot number.

The weight lifted for each attempt must increase by a minimum of 2.5 kg. In the case of attempting to break a record, a fourth attempt may be granted, and the weight increase may be as little as 0.5 kg.

Each lifter is accorded a 90-second time limit in which to mount the platform and begin the lift. If the lifter is making consecutive attempts, then three minutes are allowed between lifts.

If upon completion of a weight class, two lifters have identical totals, the lifter with the lower bodyweight is awarded the higher place.

Three referees judge each lift, a head referee and two side referees. Referees watch carefully for incorrect movements and rules violations. When officials disagree, the majority rules.

A judgement of "no lift" may occur when the bar touches the legs; during any unfinished attempt in which the bar has arrived at the height of the knees; when any part of the body except the feet touches the platform; if the bar stops in its upward path before arriving at the shoulders in the snatch or arm's length in the clean-and-jerk; when the bar is placed on the chest before the turning over of the elbows.

Common errors causing bad lifts include the press out, which occurs when the lifter bends his arms while holding the bar overhead and then presses out to make them straight; touching the platform with any part of the body except the feet; failure to control the bar; and touching the arm or elbow on the knee or leg in the clean part of the clean-and-jerk.

Hopefuls

Mark Henry

Barbara Moss bought her youngest son, Mark Henry, a set of weights when he was a kid to keep him and his brother Patrick busy.

That's the sanitized version. Actually, she purchased the bodybuilding equipment "to keep them from destroying each other." Another Olympic hopeful was born.

FACT: Placing tenth in the superheavyweight category at the Barcelona Games, U.S. weightlifter Mark Henry was the bulkiest weightlifter in Olympic history, at 365 pounds. In 1995, at 6' 3" and 400 pounds, Henry boasted a 24" neck, 62" chest, 48" waist, 38" thighs, 23" calves and biceps—and size 16EEE feet.

Not Patrick, who at a mere 6-feet-2 and 285 pounds, excelled on the defensive line for Texas A&M University, but Mark, 25 (b. June 12, 1971), who, at last sighting, was 6-feet-3, and tipped the scales at 400 pounds.

"You should have seen Uncle Chudd," says Henry, whose father died when Mark was 13, and whose Uncle Chudd was 6-feet-5 and 420 pounds. "He picked me up when I was a boy and I cried. He was just so damn big."

U.S. weightlifting officials are hoping that Henry, raised in the piney east Texas town of Silsbee, can bring tears to the eyes of his Olympic opponents in Atlanta. It could happen. It is said that if Henry, who owns all the U.S. records in his weight class—475 pounds clean-and-jerk, 390 pounds snatch, and 855 pounds total—develops the technique to match his brawn, he could become the first American superheavyweight to win an Olympic gold medal since Paul Anderson in 1956.

He's obviously what you would call a *strong* contender.

Henry's story, as you can tell, is already pretty weighty.

Although a mere seven pounds at birth, Henry was eating mashed potatoes and rice at six weeks. By age 10, he weighed 220 pounds. His shoe size today is 16EEE. His jacket size is 62 inches, his waist measures four feet, his biceps almost two feet, and his thighs 38 inches. His hands are so big, he can't find gloves to fit. He weighed in at the 1992 Olympics, where he placed 10th in his weight class, at 366 pounds, making him the largest weightlifter in the history of the Games.

Today, he downs 5,000 calories a day and puts away as many as five baked potatoes at one sitting with little effort. And he's still developing stamina. While many of his weightlifting buddies visit those all-you-can eat places and down 70 ounces of steak, Henry says he has to stop at 50 ounces, because his face "gets tired."

Oddly enough, he skips breakfast.

"I'm in perfect health," Henry told *USA Today.* "I have 18 percent body fat, which is incredibly good for my size. Doctors always want to check my blood pressure three or four times. It's normal, and they find it hard to believe."

And, yes, he can dunk a basketball. He placed third at the 1994 Foot Locker SlamFest, one spot ahead of fellow Olympian and long jump world-record holder Mike Powell.

And, yes, he does have a sense of humor. He calls Dallas Cowboy 325-pound guard Nate Newton a "little guy," and he trains in a T-shirt that reads: *West Virginia Gymnastics.*

FACT: No American superheavyweight has won an Olympic gold medal since Paul Anderson captured the 1956 title.

Henry's Achilles heel obviously isn't size and strength. It's ambition. It's not that Henry doesn't have any. It may be that he has too much.

Jere Longman wrote in the *New York Times:* "Does he want to win a gold medal? Or does he want an acting career? Will he flirt with professional football? Will he gravitate toward strongman exhibitions? He thinks he could draw a crowd by lifting a table laden with 15 kids, or tossing beer kegs like Frisbees, or lifting cars by the bumper as he once did to his aunt's Pinto, leaving two wheels spinning in the air as she tried to drive home."

For the time being, Henry seems pretty well focused on Atlanta.

"I'd like to win a medal at the Olympics," Henry told Longman. "You can be a movie star, but if you don't get any more roles, then you 'used' to be a movie star. You get an Olympic medal, you've always got an Olympic medal."

"Of all the top 10 lifters in the world, Mark is the strongest," said Dragomir Cioroslan, who won a bronze medal for Romania at the 1984 Olympics and who will coach the U.S. weightlifting team in Atlanta. "If he's healthy, he's definitely a medal candidate at any major international competition. I've never seen anyone with Mark's raw talent."

Nor, perhaps, his exuberance.

Unlike his stoical competitors, Henry has often celebrated successful lifts by firing, then holstering, an imaginary six-shooter.

And no matter where he competes, Henry attracts children. The kids gravitate to him.

"They know I'm one of 'em," he told *Sports Illustrated.* "I'm the biggest kid of them all."

In a sport beset with rumors of steroid use, Henry even has an anti-drug motive.

"I'm already strong enough without drugs," Henry says. "My goal is to lift a weight so high, that people on drugs can't even do it."

Says Cioroslan: "Mark likes to talk, he likes to share. He wants to play golf and dunk basketballs."

Then, the coach smiles. It is all he can do.

"We are very fortunate to have Mark," he says. "He makes our sport a show."

—Eric Kinkopf

Tim McRae

Tim McRae has come to grips with his height.

"I really don't care about being bigger any more," he says. "I've just got my mind on getting an Olympic gold medal."

It wasn't always that way. In fact, McRae, 26 (b. August 4, 1970), 5-feet-3 and 154 pounds, began lifting in high school to get bigger—*taller*, actually.

It didn't work, of course.

"I started lifting when I played football, like everyone else," he told the *San Antonio Express News.* "I was too small. It was something to try to be bigger. I wanted to get taller, really. I just wanted to grow. It didn't work."

Not as planned.

"I told him, 'You may get bigger, but you're not going to get any taller,'" said his father, Herbert.

The experience did, however, open McRae's eyes to weightlifting as more than a means to an end. When he began lifting, McRae didn't know weightlifting was an Olympic sport.

Today, the Daytona Beach native, who placed eighth in his weight class in Barcelona and who holds eight American records in three different weight classes—and personal bests of 314 pounds in the snatch and 385 pounds in the clean-and-jerk in his current weight class—is considered by many to be the strongest lifter, pound-for-pound, in the U.S. weightlifting arsenal—and a solid bet for a medal in Atlanta.

"I think the Barcelona Olympics made me more of a fighter," said McRae, the U.S. Weightlifting Federation's Men's Athlete of the Year for both 1993 and 1994. "I'm on a different level, now. My mind has moved up to a different level. I want to be the best in the world. The only place you can beat the best is in (world competition). I know it sounds funny, but being the best in the United States doesn't mean that much to me anymore."

"Tim has risen to the top rapidly," says U.S. national team coach Dragomir Cioroslan. "He can be in the medal ceremony in Atlanta. He is young, but very talented. He is an athlete with exceptional qualities. He pushes himself beyond his limits on almost a daily basis."

If McRae, who left Florida in 1989 to live at the U.S. Olympic Training Center in Colorado Springs, does medal in Atlanta, he can credit some of his success to his experiences in Barcelona.

"I just gained from watching the other competitors," he said. "They make it look so easy. There's so much concentration in it. You have to be so focused to lift weights. When I was in high school, I didn't know your mind had to be so much into it. Your mind has to get stronger, just like your body. I'm still learning that."

McRae, who is studying to become a phsyical therapist, says that mental strength—toughness—is the difference between winning a medal and finishing out of the top three.

"Sometimes, it scares you—'Am I really going to lift this much?' But when you go up there, you can't have any second thoughts. You tell yourself that you did it before, that this is nothing new to you."

Says Cioroslan: "Tim grew up in Barcelona the way all coaches hope their athletes grow up."

McRae had a few other eye-opening experiences in Barcelona. For one thing, he got to meet up with basketball's Dream Team, comprised of Magic Johnson, Michael Jordan, Larry Bird, and others.

"I was intimidated at first, then I realized they're just like me—I'm just like them," he said. "I just don't get paid like them."

McRae was, however, disappointed by the turnout for the weightlifting competition.

"I was thinking that it would be more of a big crowd," he said. "When I walked out there, I was expecting a gym full of people. It was only half full."

Especially for his weight class. Most observers, he says, want to see the big guys lift.

"At competitions, everyone notices the big guys," he says. "I'll give the big guys credit. It's great to watch the big guys lift big weights."

The disappointment, however, didn't stop McRae from equalling a pair of American records for his weight class in Barcelona. It did put into perspective, however, the reception he got when he arrived home.

"He felt like a hero, then," Herbert McRae says.

McRae expected only to see his mother and father at the Daytona Beach Regional Airport terminal. More than 60 people were waiting.

"There were people I didn't even recognize," he said. "That was better than the opening ceremonies."

McRae is hoping a few of the faithful can make it to Atlanta.

"The thing it takes for us to get more support is winning medals," he says. "And when I know that my family is behind me, I'm not afraid of anything. That's when I'll be able to do what I've never done before. That's what keeps me going."

And coming from Tim McRae, you can be sure that that's no tall story.

—Eric Kinkopf

Schedule

The tentative weightlifting schedule is:

Saturday, July 20
54 kg group B
54 kg group A finals

Sunday, July 21
59 kg group B
59 kg group A finals

Monday, July 22
64 kg group B
64 kg group A finals

Tuesday, July 23
70 kg group B
70 kg group A finals

Wednesday, July 24
76 kg group B
76 kg group A finals

Friday, July 26
83 kg group B
83 kg group A finals

Saturday, July 27	Monday, July 29
91 kg group B	108 kg group B
91 kg group A finals	108 kg group A finals

Sunday, July 28	Tuesday, July 30
99 kg group B	over 108 kg group B
99 kg group A finals	over 108 kg group A finals

Highlights

In weightlifting's first appearance at the Athens Games, Viggo Jensen of Denmark and Launceston Eliot of Great Britain both lifted the same weight in the two-arm competition. Viggo, however, was awarded the gold medal—thus becoming the first Olympic weightlifting champion—by virtue of the fact that Eliot had shuffled one of his feet during the lift. This would hardly be the last time such a fortuitous detail would be the criterion for victory.

During the Golden Age of American domination, the U.S. earned four gold medals in each of the 1948, 1952, and 1956 Games, in addition to various silver and bronze medals. But America's Golden era quickly grew lackluster at the 1960 Rome Games, where the Soviets captured five of the six gold medals, initiating a trend of Eastern European domination.

FACT: In 1936, Egypt's Khadr Sayed El Touni stunned spectators at the Berlin Games by lifting a world record Middleweight division total of 387.5 kilograms—15 kilograms more than that year's Light Heavyweight champion lifted.

Weightlifting, it seems, is as much weight watching as anything: the difference between 300-odd pound athletes as measured in ounces can mean the difference between victory and defeat, or even between being allowed to compete or not. In the Melbourne Games in 1956, American Charles Vinci—who stood 4'10"—weighed 1½ pounds more than his category allowed. He was able to compete after an hour of perspiration-inducing running—and a last-minute haircut. In the 1968 Games in Mexico City, Iran's Seresht Mohammed Nassiri and Hungarian Imre Földi both lifted a total of exactly 367.5 kg; Nassiri, however, snatched the gold because he weighed ten ounces less than Földi. Ironically, this had happened in Berlin in 1936, and, when the decision was protested, both athletes received gold medals.

Perhaps one of the most interesting weightwatching stories is that of American Tamio "Tommy" Kono—the archetypal wimpy-kid-turned-muscleman—who, depending on the needs of the U.S. weightlifting squad, bulked up and down to compete in lighter or heavier categories. If the U.S. needed a heavyweight, he ate seven meals a day, if they needed a lightweight, he dieted on three. Kono won two Olympic golds in 1952 and 1956, and a silver in 1960, all in different weight categories.

Recent Games have continued to be dominated by non-Western musclemen. The U.S. managed to lift two medals at the LA Games: a bronze for Guy Carlton in the 110kg category, and a silver for Mario Martinez in the over 110kg category. Romania and China took most of the medals in 1984, with Romania garnering eight and China six.

FACT: The Soviet boycott of the 1984 LA Games affected weightlifting more than any other sport. Ninety-four of the world's top 100 ranked lifters were absent from the Games, as were 29 of the 30 medalists from the last world championships. And all of the defending world champions in the ten weight categories were absent.

Drugs have for a long time been a problem among those who are improperly pumped up. 1988 produced another doping debacle, this time involving the heavily favored Bulgarian team: after Mitko Grabley and Angel Guenchev were stripped of their gold medals for failing a test revealing probable steroid use, the entire Bulgarian team pulled out of the Seoul Games.

Turkish weightlifter Naim Sulemanoglu, the "Pocket Hercules," became a favorite of the 1988 Games for a host of reasons. Ethnically Turkish, in 1986 he defected from Bulgaria, where his parents and two brothers were still trapped when he captured the gold in Seoul. His performance in the 132¼-pound division would have won him a silver medal in the heavyweight division in the 1960 Games, and in 1956 it would have earned him a victory over Olympic heavyweight champ Paul Anderson, who weighed more than 300 pounds. Sulemanoglu was the first man to lift 2½ times his weight in the snatch lift; with a herculean 342.5kg lift, he made clean away with the gold in his weight class: the Bulgarian silver medalist, Stefan Topourov, lifted only 312.5 kg.

Highlights from Barcelona

It was old home week at the Pavello L' Espanya Industrial in Barcelona, where 65 of the 261 competitors were repeat Olympians. But unlike Seoul, where four world records fell, Barcelona posted no world's best performances. World records maintained their foothold, as did many of the reigning champi-

Unified Team's Israel Militossian lifts 155.0kg to take Olympic gold in Barcelona. His lift equaled the Olympic record he set in 1988. *AP/Wide World Photos*

ons. Turkey's Naim Suleymanoglu, for instance, held on to his 60kg pocket Hercules title with an iron fist, outlifting Bulgaria's silver medalist by a weighty margin of 15 points. And Alexandre Kourlovitch of Belarus—a 110kg-plus Goliath of a man—snatched his second consecutive title by outmuscling his teammate, Leonid Taranenko, by a hefty 25-point margin.

Thanks to Germany's Ronny Weller, the Unified Team had to settle for five golds, one shy of their six-gold harvest in Seoul. Beating Russia's Artour Akoev in his final 240kg clean and jerk, Weller, who collected a bronze medal in 1992, clinched first place in the 110kg category. Competing individually, Unified athletes were allowed to represent their republics, and medals ceremonies became a patchwork of unfamiliar banners as athletes from Moldova, Belarus, and Uzbekistan mounted the medals podium.

1992 also saw some mighty close calls. Cuba's Pablo Lara Rodriguez lifted every kilogram of Fedor Kassapu's 357.5kg total, but had to settle for silver in the 75kg category because he weighed in heavier than his Moldovan opponent. The 82.5kg category's three-way tie wasn't so easy to settle: Greece's Pyrros Dimas and Poland's Krzysztof Siemion both tipped the scales at exactly the same weight. Dimas collected the gold since he had been first to hoist the weight. In third place, because he was 50 grams heavier than his opponents, was Russia's Ibragim Samadov. He was not a happy camper. Samadov refused the bronze medal, which the IWF and IOC agreed to withdraw, leaving the 1992 Games bereft of a bronze medalist in the 82.5kg category.

A handful of lifters came close to world-record performances. Armenia's Israel Militossian added a gold medal to his 1988 silver by matching the Olympic record in the snatch in the 67.5kg category. Bulgaria's three-time flyweight world champion, Ivan Ivanov Ivanov, also equaled a standing Olympic record with his 115kg snatch in the 52kg category. And Russia's Victor Tregoubov, too, matched the 100kg Olympic snatch record kilogram-for-kilogram.

Only two athletes posted new Olympic records. South Korea's Chun Byung-Kwan—who collected a silver in the 52kg class in Seoul—ran away with an Olympic record and a gold medal when he moved up to 56kg category in Barcelona. And Sergei Syrtsov, from Uzbekistan, settled for a silver medal in the 90kg class, even though his 190kg snatch established a new Olympic record. Just ahead of Syrtsov, Russia's Kakhi Kakhiachvili was the only competitor to come anywhere near a world-record performance, with a 235kg clean and jerk.

Weightlifting—52 kg

1992
1. Ivan Ivanov, Bulgaria, 265.0
2. Lin Qisheng, China, 262.5
3. Traian Ciharean, Romania, 252.5

1988
1. Sevdalin Marinov, Bulgaria, 270.0 kg (WR)
2. Byung-Kwan Chun, South Korea, 260.0 kg
3. Zhuoqiang He, People's Republic of China, 257.5 kg

1984
1. Guoqiang Zeng, People's Republic of China, 235.0 kg
2. Peishun Zhou, People's Republic of China, 235.0 kg
3. Kazushito Manabe, Japan, 232.5 kg

1980
1. Kanybek Osmonaliev, Soviet Union, 245.0 kg (OR)
2. Bong Chol Ho, Democratic People's Republic of Korea, 245.0 kg
3. Gyong Si Han, Democratic People's Republic of Korea, 245.0 kg

1976
1. Alexander Voronin, Soviet Union, 242.5 kg (EWR)
2. Gyorgy Koszegi, Hungary, 237.5 kg
3. Mohammad Nassiri, Iran, 235.0 kg

1972
1. Zygmunt Smalcerz, Poland, 337.5 kg
2. Lajos Szucs, Hungary, 330.0 Kg
3. Sandor Holczreiter, Hungary, 327.5 Kg

1896–1968
Not held

Weightlifting—56 kg

1992
1. Chun Byung-Kwan, South Korea, 287.5
2. Liu Shoubin, China, 277.5
3. Luo Jianming, China, 277.5

1988
1. Oxen Mirzoian, Soviet Union, 292.5 kg (OR); Mitko Grablev of Bulgaria won but was disqualified.
2. Yingqiang He, People's Republic of China, 287.5 kg
3. Shoubin Liu, People's Republic of China, 267.5 kg

1984
1. Shude Wu, People's Republic of China, 267.5 kg
2. Runming Lai, People's Republic of China, 265.0 kg
3. Masahiro Kotaka, Japan, 252.5 kg

1980
1. Daniel Nunez, Cuba, 275.0 kg (WR)
2. Yurik Sarkisian, Soviet Union, 270.0 kg
3. Tadeusz Dembonczyk, Poland, 265.0 kg

1976
1. Norair Nourikian, Bulgaria, 262.5 kg (WR)
2. Grzegorz Cziura, Poland, 252.5 kg
3. Kenkichi Ando, Japan, 250.0 kg

1972
1. Imre Foldi, Hungary, 377.5 kg (WR)
2. Mohammad Nassiri, Iran, 370.0 kg
3. Gennady Chetin, Soviet Union, 367.5 kg

1968
1. Mohammad Nassiri, Iran, 367.5 kg (EWR)
2. Imre Foldi, Hungary, 367.5 kg (EWR)
3. Henryk Trebicki, Poland, 357.5 kg

1964
1. Aleksei Vakhonin, Soviet Union, 357.5 kg (WR)
2. Imre Foldi, Hungary, 355.0 kg
3. Shiro Ichinoseki, Japan, 347.5 kg

1960
1. Charles Vinci, U.S.A., 345.0 kg (EWR)
2. Yoshinobu Miyake, Japan, 337.5 kg
3. Esmail Elm Khan, Iran, 330.0 kg

1956
1. Charles Vinci, U.S.A., 342.5 kg (WR)
2. Vladimir Stogov, Soviet Union, 337.5 kg
3. Mahmoud Namdjou, Iran, 332.5 kg

1952
1. Ivan Udodov, Soviet Union, 315.0 kg (OR)
2. Mahmoud Namdjou, Iran, 307.5 kg
3. Ali Mirzai, Iran, 300.0 kg

1948
1. Joseph De Pietro, U.S.A., 307.5 kg (WR)
2. Julian Creus, Great Britain, 297.5 kg
3. Richard Tom, U.S.A., 295.0 Kg

1896–1936
Not held

Weightlifting—60 kg

1992
1. Naim Suleymanoglu, Turkey, 320.0
2. Nikolai Peshalov, Bulgaria, 305.0
3. He Yingqiang, China, 295.0

1988
1. Naim Suleymanoglu, Turkey, 342.5 kg (WR)
2. Stefan Topourov, Bulgaria, 312.5 kg
3. Huenming Ye, People's Republic of China, 287.5 kg

1984
1. Weiqiang Chen, People's Republic of China, 282.5 kg
2. Gelu Radu, Romania, 280.0 kg
3. Wen-Yee Tsai, Taiwan, 272.5 kg

1980
1. Viktor Mazin, Soviet Union, 290.0 kg (OR)
2. Stefan Dimitrov, Bulgaria, 287.5 kg
3. Marek Seweryn, Poland, 282.5 kg

1976
1. Nikolai Kolesnikov, Soviet Union, 285.0 kg (EWR)
2. Georgi Todorov, Bulgaria, 280.0 kg
3. Kazumasu Hirai, Japan, 275.0 kg

1972
1. Norair Nurikjan, Bulgaria, 402.5 kg (EWR)
2. Dito Shanidze, Soviet Union, 400.0 kg
3. Janos Benedek, Hungary, 390.0 kg

1968
1. Yoshinobu Miyake, Japan, 392.5 kg
2. Dito Shanidze, Soviet Union, 387.5 kg
3. Yoshiyuki Mijake, Japan, 385.0 kg

1964
1. Yoshinobu Miyake, Japan, 397.5 kg (WR)
2. Isaac Berger, U.S.A., 382.5 kg
3. Mieczyslaw Nowak, Poland, 377.5 kg

1960
1. Yevgeny Minayev, Soviet Union, 372.5 kg (EWR)
2. Isaac Berger, U.S.A., 362.5 kg
3. Sebastiano Mannironi, Italy, 352.5 kg

1956
1. Isaac Berger, U.S.A., 352.5 kg (WR)
2. Yevgeny Minayev, Soviet Union, 342.5 kg
3. Marian Zielinski, Poland, 335.0 kg

1952
1. Rafael Chimishkyan, Soviet Union, 337.5 kg (WR)
2. Nikolai Saksonov, Soviet Union, 332.5 kg
3. Rodney Wilkes, Trinidad and Tobago, 322.5 kg

1948
1. Mahmoud Fayad, Egypt, 332.5 kg (WR)
2. Rodney Wilkes, Trinad and Tobago, 317.5 kg
3. Jaffar Salmasi, Iran, 312.5 kg

1936
1. Anthony Terlazzo, U.S.A., 312.5 kg (WR)
2. Saleh M. Soliman, Egypt, 305.0 kg
3. Ibrahim H. Shams, Egypt, 300.0 kg

1932
1. Raymond Suvigny, France, 287.5 kg (EOR)
2. Hans Wolpert, Germany, 282.5 kg
3. Anthony Terlazzo, U.S.A., 280.0 kg

1928
1. Franz Andrysek, Austria, 287.5 kg
2. Pierino Gabetti, Italy, 282.5 kg
3. Hans Wolpert, Germany, 282.5 kg

1924
1. Pierino Gabetti, Italy, 402.5 kg
2. Andreas Stadler, Austria, 385.0 kg
3. Artur Reinmann, Switzerland, 382.5 kg

1920
1. Frans De Haes, Belgium, 220.0 kg
2. Alfred Schmidt, Estonia, 212.5 kg
3. Eugene Ryther, Switzerland, 210.0 kg

1896–1912
Not held

Weightlifting—67.5 kg

1992
1. Israel Militossian, Armenia, 337.5
2. Yoto Yotov, Bulgaria, 327.5
3. Andreas Behm, Germany, 320.0

1988
1. Angel Guenchev, Bulgaria (disqualified)
1. Joachim Kunz, East Germany, 340.0 kg
2. Israel Militossian, Soviet Union, 337.5 kg
3. Jinhe Li, People's Republic of China, 325.0 kg

1984
1. Yao Jingyuan, People's Republic of China, 320.0 kg
2. Andrei Socaci, Romania, 312.5 kg
3. Jouni Gronman, Finland, 312.5 kg

1980
1. Yanko Rusev, Bulgaria, 342.5 kg (WR)
2. Joachim Kunz, East Germany, 335.0 kg
3. Mincho Pashev, Bulgaria, 325.0 kg

1976
1. Zbigniew Kaczmarek, Poland, 307.5 kg
2. Piotr Korol, Soviet Union, 305.0 kg
3. Daniel Senet, France, 300.0 kg

1972

1. Muckarbi Kirzhinov, Soviet Union, 460.0 kg (WR)
2. Mladen Kutschew, Bulgaria, 450.0 kg
3. Zbigniew Kaczmarek, Poland, 437.5 kg

1968

1. Waldemar Baszanowski, Poland, 437.5 kg (OR)
2. Parviz Jalayer, Iran, 422.5 kg
3. Marian Zielinski, Poland, 420.0 kg

1964

1. Waldemar Baszanowski, Poland, 432.5 kg (WR)
2. Vladimir Kaplunov, Soviet Union, 432.5 kg (WR)
3. Marian Zielinski, Poland, 420.0 kg

1960

1. Viktor Buschuyev, Soviet Union, 397.5 kg (WR)
2. Howe-Liang Tan, Singapore, 380.0 kg
3. Abdul Wahid Aziz, Iraq, 380.0 kg

1956

1. Igor Rybak, Soviet Union, 380.0 kg (OR)
2. Rafael Khabutdinov, Soviet Union, 372.5 kg
3. Chang-hee Kim, Republic of Korea, 370.0 kg

1952

1. Tamio "Tommy" Kono, U.S.A., 362.5 kg (OR)
2. Yevgeny Lopatin, Soviet Union, 350.0 kg
3. Verne Barberis, Australia, 350.0 kg

1948

1. Ibrahim H. Shams, Egypt, 360.0 kg (OR)
2. Appia Hamouda, Egypt, 360.0 kg (OR)
3. James Halliday, Great Britain, 340.0 kg

1936

1. Robert Fein, Austria, 342.5 (WR)
1. Anwar M. Mesbah, Egypt, 342.5 kg (WR)
3. Karl Jansen, Germany, 327.5 kg

1932

1. Rene Duverger, France, 325.0 kg (EWR)
2. Hans Haas, Austria, 307.5 kg
3. Gastone Pierini, Italy, 302.5 kg

1928

1. Hans Haas, Austria, 322.5 kg
1. Kurt Helbig, Germany, 322.5 kg
3. Fernand Arnout, France, 302.5 kg

1924

1. Edmond Decottignies, France, 440.0 kg
2. Anton Zwerina, Austria, 427.5
3. Bohumil Durdis, Czechoslovakia, 425.0 kg

1920

1. Alfred Neuland, Estonia, 257.5
2. Louis Williquet, Belgium, 240.0 kg
3. Florimond Rooms, Belgium, 230.0 kg

1896–1912

Not held

Weightlifting—75 kg

1992

1. Fedor Kassapu, Moldavia, 357.5
2. Pablo Lara Rodriguez, Cuba, 357.5
3. Kim Myong Nam, North Korea, 352.5

1988

1. Borislav Guidikov, Bulgaria, 375.0 kg
2. Ingo Steinhoefel, East Germany, 360.0 kg
3. Alexander Varbanov, Bulgaria, 357.5 kg

1984

1. Karl-Heinz Radschinsky, West Germany, 340.0 kg
2. Jacques Demers, Canada, 335.0 kg
3. Dragomir Cioroslan, Romania, 332.5 kg

1980

1. Assen Zlatev, Bulgaria, 360.0 kg (WR)
2. Aleksandr Pervy, Soviet Union, 357.5 kg
3. Nedelcho Kolev, Bulgaria, 345.0 kg

1976

1. Yordan Mitkov, Bulgaria, 335.0 kg (OR)
2. Vartan Militosyan, Soviet Union, 330.0 kg
3. Peter Wenzel, East Germany, 327.5 kg

1972

1. Yordan Bikow, Bulgaria, 485.0 kg (WR)
2. Mohamed Trabulsi, Lebanon, 472.5 kg
3. Anselmo Silvino, Italy, 470.0 kg

1968

1. Viktor Kurentsov, Soviet Union, 475.0 kg (OR)
2. Masashi Ouchi, Japan, 455.0 kg
3. Karoly Bakos, Hungary, 440.0 kg

1964

1. Hans Zdrazila, Czechoslovakia, 445.0 kg (EWR)
2. Viktor Kurentsov, Soviet Union, 440.0 kg
3. Masashi Ouchi, Japan, 437.5 kg

1960

1. Aleksandr Kurynov, Soviet Union, 437.5 kg (WR)
2. Thomas Kono, U.S.A., 427.5 kg
3. Gyozo Veres, Hungary, 405.0 kg

1956

1. Fyodor Bogdanovsky, Soviet Union, 420.0 kg (WR)
2. Peter George, U.S.A., 412.5 kg
3. Ermanno Pignatti, Italy, 382.5 kg

1952

1. Peter George, U.S.A., 400.0 kg (OR)
2. Gerard Gratton, Canada, 390.0 kg
3. Sung-jip Kim, Republic of Korea, 382.5 kg

1948

1. Frank Spellman, U.S.A., 390.0 kg (OR)
2. Peter George, U.S.A., 382.5 kg
3. Sung-jip Kim, Republic of Korea, 380.0 kg

1936

1. Khadr Sayed El Touni, Egypt, 387.5 kg (WR)
2. Rudolf Ismayr, Germany, 352.5 kg
3. Adolf Wagner, Germany, 352.5 kg

1932

1. Rudolf Ismayr, Germany, 345.0 kg
2. Carlo Galimberti, Italy, 340.0 kg
3. Karl Hipfinger, Austria, 337.5 kg

1928

1. Roger Francois, France, 335.0 kg (WR)
2. Carlo Galimberti, Italy, 332.5 kg
3. August Scheffer, Netherlands, 327.5 kg

1924

1. Carlo Galimberti, Italy, 492.5 kg
2. Jaan Kikkas, Estonia, 450.0 kg
2. Alfred Neuland, Estonia, 455.0 kg

1920

1. Henri Gance, France, 245.0 kg
2. Pietro Bianchi, Italy, 237.5 kg
3. Albert Pettersson, Sweden, 237.5 kg

1896–1912

Not held

Weightlifting—82.5 kg

1992

1. Pyrros Dimas, Greece, 370.0
2. Krzysztof Siemion, Poland, 370.0
3. None awarded (Ibragim Samadov of Russia refused medal)

1988

1. Israil Arsamakov, Soviet Union, 377.5 kg
2. Istvan Messzi, Hungary, 370.0 kg
3. Hyung-Kun Lee, South Korea, 367.5 kg

1984

1. Petre Becheru, Romania, 355.0 kg
2. Robert Kabbas, Australia, 342.5 kg
3. Ryoji Isaoka, Japan, 340.0 kg

1980

1. Yurik Vardanjan, Soviet Union, 400.0 kg
2. Blagoi Blagoev, Bulgaria, 372.5 kg
3. Dusan Poliacik, Czechoslovakia, 367.5 kg

1976

1. Valeri Shary, Soviet Union, 365.0 kg (OR)
2. Blagoi Blagoev, Bulgaria, 362.5 kg
3. Trendafil Stoichev, Bulgaria, 360.0 kg

1972

1. Leif Jenssen, Norway, 507.5 kg (OR)
2. Norbert Ozimek, Poland, 497.5 kg
3. Gyorgy Horvath, Hungary, 495.0 kg

1968

1. Boris Selitsky, Soviet Union, 485.0 kg (EWR)
2. Vladimir Belyayev, Soviet Union, 485.0 kg (EWR)
3. Norbert Ozimek, Poland, 472.5 kg

1964

1. Rudolf Plukfelder, Soviet Union, 475.0 kg (OR)
2. Geza Toth, Hungary, 467.5 kg
3. Gyozo Veres, Hungary, 467.5 kg

1960

1. Ireneusz Palinski, Poland, 442.5 kg
2. James George, U.S.A., 430.0 kg
3. Jan Bochenek, Poland, 420.0 kg

1956

1. Tamio "Tommy" Kono, U.S.A., 447.5 kg (WR)
2. Vassili Stepanov, Soviet Union, 427.5 kg
3. James George, U.S.A., 417.5 kg

1952

1. Trofim Lomakin, Soviet Union, 417.5 kg (EOR)
2. Stanley Stanczyk, U.S.A., 415.0 kg
3. Arkadi Vorobyov, Soviet Union, 407.5 kg

1948

1. Stanley Stanczyk, U.S.A., 417.5 kg (OR)
2. Harold Sakata, U.S.A., 380.0 kg
3. Gosta Magnusson, Sweden, 375.0 kg

1936

1. Louis Hostin, France, 372.5 kg (OR)
2. Eugen Deutsch, Germany, 365.0 kg
3. Ibrahim Wasif, Egypt, 360.0 kg

1932

1. Louis Hostin, France, 365.0 kg (EWR)
2. Svend Olsen, Denmark, 360.0 kg
3. Henry Duey, U.S.A., 330.0 kg

1928

1. El Sayed Nosseir, Egypt, 355.0 kg (WR)
2. Louis Hostin, France, 352.5 kg
3. Johannes Verheijen, Netherlands, 337.5 kg

1924
1. Charles Rigoulot, France, 502.5 kg
2. Fritz Hunenberger, Switzerland, 490.0 kg
3. Leopold Friedrich, Austria, 490.0 kg

1920
1. Ernest Cadine, France, 290.0 kg
2. Fritz Hunenberger, Switzerland, 275.0 kg
3. Erik Pettersson, Sweden, 272.5 kg

1896–1912
Not held

Weightlifting—90 kg

1992
1. Kakhi Kakhiachvili, Russia, 412.5
2. Sergei Syrtsov, Uzbekistan, 412.5
3. Sergiusz Wolczaniecki, Poland, 392.5

1988
1. Anatoli Khrapatyi, Soviet Union, 412.5 kg
2. Nail Moukhamediarov, Soviet Union, 400.0 kg
3. Slawomir Zawada, Poland, 400.0 kg

1984
1. Nicu Vlad, Romania, 392.5 kg (OR)
2. Dumitru Petre, Romania, 360.0 kg
3. David Mercer, Great Britain, 352.5 kg

1980
1. Peter Baczako, Hungary, 377.5 kg
2. Roumen Aleksandrov, Bulgaria, 375.0 kg
3. Frank Mantek, East Germany, 370.0 kg

1976
1. David Rigert, Soviet Union, 382.5 kg (OR)
2. Lee James, U.S.A., 362.5 kg
3. Atanas Shopov, Bulgaria, 360.0 kg

1972
1. Andon Nikolov, Bulgaria, 525.0 kg (OR)
2. Atanas Schopov, Bulgaria, 517.5 kg
3. Hans Bettembourg, Sweden, 512.5 kg

1968
1. Kaarlo Kangasniemi, Finland, 517.5 kg (OR)
2. Jan Talts, Soviet Union, 507.5 kg
3. Marek Golab, Poland, 495.0 kg

1964
1. Vladimir Golovanov, Soviet Union, 487.5 kg (WR)
2. Louis Martin, Great Britain, 475.0 kg
3. Ireneusz Palinski, Poland, 467.5 kg

1960
1. Arkadi Vorobyov, Soviet Union, 472.5 kg (WR)
2. Trofim Lomakin, Soviet Union, 457.5 kg
3. Louis Martin, Great Britain, 445.0 kg

1956
1. Arkadi Vorobyov, Soviet Union, 462.5 kg (WR)
2. David Sheppard, U.S.A., 442.5 kg
3. Jean Debuf, France, 425.0 kg

1952
1. Norbert Schemansky, U.S.A., 445.0 kg (WR)
2. Grigori Novak, Soviet Union, 410.0 kg
3. Lennox Kilgour, Trinidad and Tobago, 402.5 kg

1896–1948
Not held

Weightlifting—100 kg

1992
1. Victor Tregoubov, Russia, 410.0
2. Timour Taimazov, Ukraine, 402.5
3. Waldemar Malak, Poland, 400.0

1988
1. Pavel Kouznetsov, Soviet Union, 425.0 kg (OR) (Andov Szanyi was disqualified)
2. Nicu Vlad, Romania, 402.5 kg
3. Peter Immesberger, West Germany, 395.0 kg

1984
1. Rolf Milser, West Germany, 385.0 kg
2. Vasile Gropa, Romania, 382.5 kg
3. Pekka Niemi, Finland, 367.5 kg

1980
1. Ota Zaremba, Czechoslovakia, 395.0 kg (OR)
2. Igor Nikitin, Soviet Union, 392.5 kg
3. Alberto Blanco Fernandez, Cuba, 385.0 kg

Weightlifting—110 kg

1992
1. Ronny Weller, Germany, 432.5
2. Artour Akoev, Russia, 430.0
3. Stefan Botev, Bulgaria, 417.5

1988
1. Yuri Zakharevitch, Soviet Union, 455.0 kg (WR)
2. Jozsef Jacso, Hungary, 427.5 kg
3. Ronny Weller, East Germany, 425.0 kg

1984
1. Norberto Oberburger, Italy, 390.0 kg
2. Stefan Tasnadi, Romania, 380.0 kg
3. Guy Carlton, U.S.A., 377.5 kg

1980
1. Leonid Taranenko, Soviet Union, 422.5 kg (WR)
2. Valentin Hristov, Bulgaria, 405.0 kg.
3. Gyorgy Szalai, Hungary, 390.0 kg

1976
1. Valentin Khristov, Bulgaria, 400.0 kg
2. Yuri Zaitsev, Soviet Union, 385.0 kg
3. Krastic Sermedjiev, Bulgaria, 385.0 kg

1972
1. Jan Talts, Soviet Union, 580.0 kg (OR)
2. Aleksandr Kraichev, Bulgaria, 562.5 kg
3. Stefan Grutzner, East Germany, 555.0 kg

1968
1. Leonid Schabotinski, Soviet Union, 572.5 kg (EOR)
2. Serge Reding, Belgium, 555.0 kg
3. Joe Dube, U.S.A., 555.0 kg

1964
1. Leonid Zhabotinsky, Soviet Union, 572.5 kg (OR)
2. Yuri Vlassov, Soviet Union, 570.0 kg
3. Norbert Schemansky, U.S.A., 537.5 kg

1960
1. Yuri Vlassov, Soviet Union, 537.5 kg (WR)
2. James Bradford, U.S.A., 512.5 kg
3. Norbert Schemansky, U.S.A., 500.0 kg

1956
1. Paul Anderson, U.S.A., 500.0 kg (OR)
2. Humberto Selvetti, Argentina, 500.0 kg (OR)
3. Alberto Pigaiani, Italy, 452.5 kg

1952
1. John Davis, U.S.A., 460.0 kg (OR)
2. James Bradford, U.S.A., 437.5 kg
3. Humberto Selvetti, Argentina, 432.5 kg

1948
1. John Davis, U.S.A., 452.5 kg (OR)
2. Norbert Schemansky, U.S.A., 425.0 kg
3. Abraham Charite, Netherlands, 412.5 kg

1936
1. Josef Manger, Germany, 410.0 kg (WR)
2. Vaclav Psenicka, Czechoslovakia, 402.5 kg
3. Arnold Luhaar, Estonia, 400.0 kg

1932
1. Jaroslav Skobla, Czechoslovakia, 380.0 kg (OR)
2. Vaclav Psenicka, Czechoslovakia, 377.5 kg
3. Josef Strassberger, Germany, 377.5 kg

1928
1. Josef Strassberger, Germany, 372.5 kg (WR)
2. Arnold Luhaar, Estonia, 360.0 kg
3. Jaroslav Skobla, Czechoslovakia, 357.5 kg

1924
1. Giuseppe Tonani, Italy, 517.5 kg
2. Franz Aigner, Austria, 515.0 kg
3. Harald Tammer, Estonia, 497.5 kg

1920
1. Filippo Bottino, Italy, 270.0 kg
2. Joseph Alzin, Luxembourg, 255.0 kg
3. Louis Bernot, France, 250.0 kg

1908–1912
Not held

1906
1. Josef Steinbach, Austria -one-hand lift, 76.55 kg
1. Dimitrios Tofalos, Great Britain -two-hand lift, 142.5 kg
2. Tullio Camilotti, Italy -one-hand lift, 73.75 kg
2. Josef Steinbach, Austria -two-hand lift, 136.5 kg
3. Alexandre Maspoli, France -two-hand lift, 129.5 kg
3. Heinrich Rondi, Germany -two-hand lift, 129.5 kg
3. Heinrich Schneidereit, Germany -two-hand lift, 129.5 kg
3. Heinrich Schneidereit, Germany -one-hand lift, 70.75 kg

1904
1. Perikles Kakousis, Greece -two-hand lift, 111.70 kg
1. Oscar Paul Osthoff, U.S.A. -one-hand lift, 48 P.
2. Oscar Paul Osthoff, U.S.A. -two-hand lift, 84.37 kg
2. Frederick Winters, U.S.A. -one-hand lift, 45 P.
3. Frank Kungler, U.S.A. -two-hand lift, 79.61 kg
3. Frank Kungler, U.S.A. -one-hand lift, 10 P.

1900
Not held

1896
1. Launceston Elliott, Great Britain -one-hand lift, 71.0 kg
1. Viggo Jensen, Denmark -two-hand lift, 111.5 kg
2. Launceston Elliott, Great Britain -two-hand lift, 111.5 kg
2. Viggo Jensen, Denmark -one-hand lift, 57.2 kg
3. Alexandros Nikolopoulos, Greece -one-hand lift, 57.2 kg
3. Sotirios Versis, Greece -two-hand lift, 100.0 kg

Weightlifting—Over 110 kg

1992
1. Alexandre Kourlovitch, Belarus, 450.0
2. Leonid Taranenko, Belarus, 425.0
3. Manfred Nerlinger, Germany, 412.5

1988
1. Alexandre Kourlovitch, Soviet Union, 462.5 kg
2. Manfred Nerlinger, West Germany, 430.0 kg
3. Martin Zawieja, West Germany, 407.5 kg

1984
1. Dean "Dinko" Lukin, Australia, 412.5 kg
2. Mario Martinez, U.S.A., 410.0 kg
3. Manfred Nerlinger, West Germany, 397.5 kg

1980
1. Sultan Rakhmanov, Soviet Union, 440.0 kg
2. Jurgen Heuser, East Germany, 410.0 kg
3. Tadeusz Rutkowski, Poland, 407.5 kg

1976
1. Vassili Alekseyev, Soviet Union, 440.0 kg
2. Gerd Bonk, East Germany, 405.0 kg
3. Helmut Losch, East Germany, 387.5 kg

1972
1. Vassili Alekseyev, Soviet Union, 230.0 kg (OR)
2. Rudolf Mang, West Germany, 610.0 kg
3. Gerd Bonk, East Germany, 572.5 kg

1896–1968
Not held

Trivia Quiz

1. The first official World Championships in Vienna in 1898 involved
a. Two-handed events only **b.** One- and two-handed events
c. One-handed events only

2. Weightlifting first appeared in the Modern Games
a. In Athens in 1896 **b.** In Paris in 1900 **c.** In Antwerp in 1920

3. Weightlifting events
a. Have been included in every Olympics
b. Have been included in all but three Olympics
c. Have been included in every Olympics since 1920

4. To determine the winner of a tie, Olympic officials
a. Have always placed the lighter competitor first
b. Have sometimes awarded two gold medals **c.** Usually toss a coin

5. The United States team
a. Has never done well in Olympic competition
b. Dominated Olympic weightlifting events from 1948 through 1956

6. In Olympic competition, athletes lift
a. More weight in the clean-and-jerk **b.** More weight in the snatch
c. Equal weights in the snatch and clean-and-jerk

7. Each lifter is allowed
a. Only one chance to lift the weight
b. Three chances to lift the weight
c. As many chances as he wants to lift the weight

8. In the "clean," athletes must lift the weight
  a. From the platform to knee-level   **b.** From the platform to waist-level
  c. From the platform to shoulder-level

9. Viggo Jensen, who tied for first place, was awarded the first Olympic weightlifting gold medal because
  a. His opponent weighed less than he did
  b. His opponent shuffled his feet during the lift
  c. He winked at the judges

10. In order to make his weight category at the 1956 Games, American Charles Vinci
  a. Ate three whole chickens and five pounds of potatoes
  b. Ran for one hour and got a haircut
  c. Held his breath and prayed

Answers: 1-b; 2-a; 3-b; 4-b; 5-b; 6-a; 7-b; 8-c; 9-b; 10-b

WRESTLING

Warm-up

Statues, stone slabs, and wall paintings from ancient civilizations indicate that wrestling is as old as civilization itself. Bearing no relationship to the modern performance art of professional wrestling, it was once an honored pastime and practiced by royalty in ancient Japan, China, India, Babylon, Egypt, and elsewhere.

Wrestling as a competitive sport first appeared in ancient Greece. Records indicate that events between men were introduced in the 18th Olympic Games (708 BC). During the Middle Ages a typical prize for a victorious wrestler in England was a ram.

US president Abraham Lincoln (1809–65) was known as a first-class wrestler. Wrestling was a part of the first modern-day Olympic Games held in 1896. Only one category, heavyweight, was contested that year, and the sport was left out of the 1900 Games. However, wrestling grew in importance in the years prior to World War I.

Although wrestling is an ancient sport, it has known countless variations as different countries practice their own versions: sumo in Japan, sambo in Russia, kushti in Iran, yagli in Turkey, and schwingen in Switzerland.

The two forms of wrestling practiced in the Olympics are freestyle and Greco-Roman. Freestyle events in seven weight categories were contested in the 1904 Games. Greco-Roman was introduced at the 1908 London Games with competitions in four weight classes. The primary distinction between freestyle and Greco-Roman is that Greco-Roman wrestlers may not grasp the legs of their opponents nor use their legs in any aggressive action.

By 1912, when the Games were held in Stockholm, freestyle competition was dropped in favor of Greco-Roman, indicating that style's popularity in the Scandinavian countries. It was during the 1912 Games that the longest final ever staged in a combat sport occurred. The light-heavyweight match was called after nine hours of wrestling.

The International Amateur Wrestling Federation (FILA) was founded in 1912, and in the years following World War I wrestling became increasingly regulated. International rules were established, and World and European Championships were eventually held on an annual basis.

Wrestling expanded after World War II, with 266 competitors from 27 nations entering the 1948 Olympic Games at London. The U.S.S.R. wrestlers made their debut in 1952 and took most of the medals. Turkey and Japan made strong showings in subsequent Games, and in 1972, two weight categories were added to bring the total to ten. These new categories were a new weight group under 48kg (105.5lb) and a super-heavyweight category over 100kg (220lb).

Spectator's Guide

Recent rules changes have made wrestling a more interesting spectator sport. Starting in 1989, a match became a one-period, five-minute contest. Matches had previously consisted of two rounds of three minutes each, and prior to that were three rounds of three minutes each. By limiting the matches to shorter time periods, officials hoped to introduce more action to lessen the emphasis on endurance. Matches are refereed and one of the referee's jobs is to make sure the wrestlers' fingernails are cut short.

Wrestlers are arranged in ten weight categories, from under 48kg (105lb) to over 130kg (286lb). Wrestlers compete on a circular mat, including a nine-meter circular competition area and a two-meter passivity zone at the edge. Each bout starts with the wrestlers standing on their feet. They attempt to take their opponent down to score points. Wrestling also occurs with both wrestlers down on the mat; this is known as *par terre.*

The main objective in wrestling is to pin your opponent. This is achieved by holding his shoulder blades to the mat for one-half of one second. Automatically ending the match, the pin is similar to a knockout in boxing. A pin is also known as a fall.

Most matches are won on points, which are awarded for performing techniques or moves within the rules. If a wrestler earns

10 or more points than his opponent at any time, the bout is stopped. This is known as a technical fall and is similar to the TKO in boxing.

Points are scored in three basic ways. The first is through a takedown, when a wrestler takes his opponent to the mat. This is worth one point but can be worth more if the opponent is brought down on his back. A high amplitude takedown, where an opponent goes through the air to land on his back, is worth five points.

A second way to score points is to turn the opponent's shoulders to the mat. This is called exposure. Points are scored once the back area breaks a 90-degree angle.

A third scoring maneuver is called a reversal. A point is awarded when the man underneath completely reverses his position and comes to the top position.

FACT: In the ancient Olympic Games, simply touching the back or shoulders to the ground constituted a fall. The concept of pinning your opponent was foreign to ancient wrestlers.

The most popular takedown techniques in freestyle are the single-leg and double-leg takedowns. Popular throws include bodylocks and headlocks. The gut wrench is the most popular turning maneuver and involves rolling over the opponent's back after locking around his waist.

In Greco-Roman, popular takedowns include arm throws, arm drags, slidebys, and snapdowns. Body lifts and saltos are among the spectacular throws seen in Greco-Roman wrestling.

Hopefuls

Bruce Baumgartner

It's impossible not to smile at Bruce Baumgartner's story.

Here's a guy who lives down the road from Slippery Rock University, tends garden, and bakes Christmas cookies.

His dad is nicknamed "Big Bob," and Bruce met his wife Linda, a former student trainer at Indiana State University, where he wrestled as a collegian, when he limped into the training room with a bad ankle. ("It was love at first taping," she says.)

One of his collegiate wrestling victims was a grappler named Steve Williams, who later turned to professional wrestling as *Dr. Death*, which leads Bruce to say, "I killed Dr. Death. Is that possible?"

U.S. wrestler Bruce Baumgartner holds down the Unified Team's David Gobedjichvili during 130kg freestyle wrestling in Barcelona. Baumgartner defeated his opponent in the match, later taking the gold for the event while Gobedjichvili settled for the bronze. *AP/Wide World Photos*

He also has a cat named Lutte, which is French for "wrestling."

Mostly, it's impossible not to smile at Bruce Baumgartner's story, because, like the Energizer Bunny—a bit larger of course, at 6-feet-2 and 286 pounds—Bruce Baumgartner, 35 (b. November 1, 1960), the greatest freestyle heavyweight wrestler in U.S. history, just keeps on going.

The 1984 Olympics.

The 1988 Olympics.

The 1992 Olympics.

The 1996 Olympics.

He's even hinted at hanging around for the 2000 Games.

"If I wanted to," Baumgartner says with a smile. "That's the key—if I wanted to."

"If I wanted to," because Baumgartner, who already owns three Olympic medals—golds in 1984 and 1992 and a silver in Seoul in 1988—saw first-hand last Olympics in Barcelona, what happens when the flame dies.

Baumgartner was facing the Georgian wrestler, David Gobedjishvili, who had beaten him for the gold in Seoul. When the referee signaled for the men to compete, Baumgartner exploded, driving into Gobedjishvili, lifting him, then slamming him to the mat for the victory. Later, Baumgartner remarked that Gobedjishvili was not the same wrestler he had faced in Seoul.

"It seemed that he had lost his fire," Baumgartner said.

Well, the pilot still burns tight and blue in Baumgartner, the wrestling coach at tiny Edinboro College in northern Pennsylvania, though what he accomplished in Barcelona would be difficult to top. There, Baumgartner dispatched six opponents by a combined score of 35-1, which included an 11-second pin of China's Chungauang Wang.

If he medals at Atlanta, Baumgartner will tie four other U.S. Olympians with medals in four different games—Francis Conn Findlay, rowing/yachting; Al Oerter, discus; Michael Plumb, equestrian; and Norbert Schemansky, weightlifting.

A fourth Olympic medal would tie him for second with Hungary's Imre Polyak for most Olympic wrestling medals. (West Germany's Wilfried Dietrich won five medals between 1956 and 1972.)

Not bad for a kid who, unlike most top U.S. wrestlers, never won a state wrestling tournament in high school.

"Halfway through his sophomore year in college, Bruce started to realize his potential," said Fran McCann, Baumgartner's coach at ISU. "He worked harder than any heavyweight I ever saw."

Baumgartner matured at ISU in other ways, too, finishing up with a 3.77 GPA in industrial arts education (he later earned a Master's from Oklahoma State), and being named one of the NCAA's top scholar-athletes. That, from a kid who graduated high school with a C-minus average.

Baumgartner, the father of two sons, Bryan and Zachary, also earns high marks in citizenship. He's been a four-time finalist for the Sullivan Award, given to the top U.S. amateur athlete, and a teammate once said of him: "Bruce is a very unusual person. He doesn't drink, doesn't smoke, doesn't chase around. All those things your mother said you are supposed to do—Bruce does them.")

Robert "Big Bob" Baumgartner says all of that development—academically and athletically—is a tribute to his kid's dedication.

Bruce Baumgartner turns right around and says that he got the message from his dad. He tells this story:

Big Bob, a diesel mechanic for a bus company in Haledon, N.J., got a call to the bus barn one night when Bruce was a kid. A furnace had failed with the temperature in the single digits and the water pipes had broken, causing a flood. Big Bob, his coveralls wet from the water, held a blowtorch on a stuck valve for two hours until the water was shut off. That night Big Bob's leg swelled like a balloon.

"The leg had frozen," Bruce says. "But he never asked anyone to take the torch."

Bruce is also quick to name other contributors to his success, the main one being his wife, Linda.

"I don't think you could compete as long as I have without tremendous support from your family," he says. "You've either got to be single and live like a nomad, or have a real supportive wife like I do. When I'm training, sometimes I get ornery and grouchy. And the pressures of my work load get to me every once in awhile. And, when you're competing, you spend a lot of time away from home. So the support system has got to be there, and it has got to be strong."

Then there's the lifestyle to which an unsuspecting mate must get accustomed.

"You don't make any money wrestling," Baumgartner says. "You *spend* money."

Baumgartner credits some of his longevity to his job as wrestling coach.

"When you teach wrestling, you learn more about the sport. You look at things analytically. And by wrestling guys who are not world-caliber, you have an opportunity to work on techniques you otherwise wouldn't be able to try."

But the main drive is the sport, itself. "I still enjoy wrestling," Baumgartner says. "I like the one-on-one competition. It still has a lure for me."

Most of Baumgartner's ability to fool Father Time comes from inside, says U.S. freestyle coach Bruce Burnett.

"Bruce Baumgartner is a coach's dream," Burnett says. "He can coach himself. Physically he's a little slower, and eventually age does catch up to you. (But) he understands positions and where he wants to be."

Where he wants to be, again, this summer, is on the medal stand in Atlanta. After that? Maybe . . . Sydney. Why not?

—Eric Kinkopf

Schedule

The tentative wrestling schedule for freestyle events is:

Tuesday, July 30
48kg, 57kg, 68kg, 82kg & 100kg
preliminaries
48kg, 57kg, 68kg, 82kg & 100kg
classification

Wednesday, July 31
48kg, 57kg, 68kg, 82kg & 100kg
classification
48kg, 57kg, 68kg, 82kg & 100kg bronze
& gold

Thursday, August 1
52kg, 62kg, 74kg, 90kg & 130kg
preliminaries
52kg, 62kg, 74kg, 90kg & 130kg
classification

Friday, August 2
52kg, 62kg, 74kg, 90kg & 130kg
classification
52kg, 62kg, 74kg, 90kg & 130kg bronze
& gold

The tentative wrestling schedule for greco-roman events is:

Saturday, July 20
48kg, 57kg, 68kg, 82kg & 100kg
preliminaries
48kg, 57kg, 68kg, 82kg & 100kg
classification

Sunday, July 21
48kg, 57kg, 68kg, 82kg & 100kg
classification
48kg, 57kg, 68kg, 82kg & 100kg bronze
& gold

Monday, July 22
52kg, 62kg, 74kg, 90kg & 130kg
preliminaries
52kg, 62kg, 74kg, 90kg & 130kg
classification

Tuesday, July 23
52kg, 62kg, 74kg, 90kg & 130kg
classification
52kg, 62kg, 74kg, 90kg & 130kg bronze
& gold

Highlights

Carl Schuhmann, who stood a mere 64 inches tall, became the first wrestling victor of the modern Games in 1896; competing in an event with no bodyweight limit, the German defeated Great Britain's weightlifting champion Launceston Eliot in the preliminaries. The wrestling title was not Schuhmann's only Olympic victory: he was a gymnastics triple gold medalist as well.

The host Americans dominated the sport upon its return to the Games in St. Louis, taking literally every title in each of the seven freestyle weight categories that year. At the 1908 Games, the Americans had to share the medals, primarily with Great Britain, which took three of the five golds, and various other titles. The U.S. held on to two golds this time around, one of which was won by 63.5 inch Yale student George Dole in the featherweight division; he was the only non-British wrestler in that division.

When Greco-Roman events replaced freestyle events in the 1912 Games, the gold medals were shared between the Finns, who took three, and the Swedes, who claimed two. The longest match in Olympic history took place that year. In the Greco-Roman middleweight class, Estonian Martin Klein and Finn Alfred "Alpo" Asikáinen battled it out for 11 hours and 40 minutes, until Klein finally pinned Asikáinen. Claes Johanson of Sweden, however, won the gold, by default, because Klein was too exhausted to compete in the final.

At the 1920 Games, Sweden's Carl Westergren earned the first of his three gold medals—a feat only two other wrestlers, Ivar Johansson, also from Sweden, and Soviet Aleksandr Medved, have equalled. Westergren earned his 1920 gold in the Greco-Roman middleweight division, but went on to earn the other two titles in different divisions, in 1924 and 1932.

The 1924 Paris Games witnessed a number of repeat medalists. In the Greco-Roman events, Finn Kaarlo "Kalle" Anttila won his second Olympic gold, this time in the featherweight division (his 1920 gold was in the freestyle lightweight division); in the lightweight division, Finn Oskar Friman, who had won the featherweight title in the previous Games, earned his second gold, and Carl Westergren moved up to gold in the Greco-Roman light heavyweight division. In the freestyle events, Finn Kustaa Pihlajamäki won the first of his three Olympic medals in the bantamweight division; later his brother, Hermanni, won the featherweight gold in the 1932 Games.

In 1928, the U.S. managed a few titles in the freestyle events: Allie Morrison won the featherweight division, while Lloyd Appelton took second place in the welterweight division. In the Greco-Roman events, the U.S. failed to medal, while Germany, Estonia, Hungary, Finland, Sweden, and even Egypt took home gold. Also that year Hungarian Lajos Keresztes turned in a gold medal match in the lightweight division, having taken up wrestling on his doctor's advice as a cure for "prolonged neurosis."

Sweden's Ivar Johansson won a total of three gold medals, two of them at the 1932 Games: having won the freestyle middleweight division, he fasted and sweat it out in a sauna to be able to compete as a welterweight in the Greco-Roman competition. He lost eleven pounds, and gained a second gold medal. His third came in 1936, in the Greco-Roman middleweight division.

The only man to win a gold medal in both freestyle and Greco-Roman was heavyweight Kristjan Palusalu of Estonia in 1936, the year when American Frank Lewis won a gold medal in the welterweight division of the freestyle competition. In London in 1948, Turkey dominated, with a total of six gold medals in the two competitions, while Sweden continued to be a contender in the Greco-Roman events, winning five titles.

When the Turkish entry forms for the 1952 Games arrived late, the best athletes of their team were not allowed to compete, and Russian wrestlers captured most of the medals; Khalil Taha won a bronze medal for Lebanon that year. The Russians repeated their sweep definitively in Melbourne in 1956, where they took six gold, two silver and five bronze medals—even though their team did not include any World or Olympic champions. In fact, the Russians failed to place in the top three in only one event. One gold medal went to Hamit Kaplan of Turkey, in the freestyle heavyweight category; in 1960 he earned a silver medal in that event, and completed the set with a bronze in 1964.

The Turkish team swept seven gold medals at the 1960 Games. Turk Mustafa Dagistanli, who had won the freestyle bantamweight title in Melbourne, added a featherweight gold from Rome to his collection. Probably the most noteworthy performance, though, came from West Germany's Wilfried Dietrich, who took his second silver in freestyle wrestling and a gold in Greco-Roman in the super-heavyweight division; Dietrich was atypical of most wrestlers, who concentrate on one form or the other.

The 1964 Tokyo Games were dominated by the host country, whose sister sport of judo made Japanese athletes competitive in the lighter classes. The Japanese captured the most wrestling medals, earning five golds, three in freestyle and two in Greco-Roman. One of the freestyle medalists, Osamu Watanabe, a featherweight, won his 186th consecutive victory in taking the Olympic gold, and denied his opponents even a single point in any of his six Olympic matches. Also competing in Tokyo was Hungarian Greco-Roman featherweight Imre Polyak, who, after a string of three silver medals, finally pinned down the gold in 1964.

The U.S.S.R. primarily, and to some extent Turkey, dominated the 1968 Games, although other Eastern bloc countries put in their bids for medals. Hungarian Istvan "Pici" ("Tiny") Kozma successfully defended his heavyweight Greco-Roman title, only to lose his life two years later in a car accident. Japan contributed three champions, including Shigero Nakata, the freestyle flyweight world champion, who managed an upset defeat of American Dick Sanders.

The U.S.S.R. became a stronger force yet in the 1972 Games, taking a total of nine titles. Claiming his third gold, Soviet super-heavyweight freestyle wrestler Aleksandr Medved became the first to win wrestling gold medals in three consecutive Games. Also that year, Soviet heavyweight Ivan Yarygin managed to pin all of his opponents, a rare feat. Turkey was no longer a real contender, but the U.S. regained its form, taking three freestyle titles: lightweight Dan Gable, welterweight Wayne Wells and light heavyweight Ben Peterson all won their divisions. Another American, Chris Taylor, earned the distinction of becoming the heaviest competitor ever in any Olympic event, tipping the scales somewhere between 401 and 419 pounds. He also won the freestyle super-heavyweight bronze.

FACT: After making the 10,000-mile trek to the 1984 LA Games, Mauritania's Harouna Niang was disqualified from competing in the super heavyweight freestyle competition because he tipped the scales at only 216 pounds—less than five pounds shy of the minimum weight requirement.

Ben Peterson's brother, middleweight John Peterson, was the only U.S. gold medalist at Montréal, although the U.S. team did advance six of its 10 members to the finals. The Americans wound up with three silver medals, including one to Ben Peterson, and two bronzes. With some exceptions—such as Finland's Pertti Ukkola, Bulgaria's Hassan Issaev, South Korea's Yang Mo Yang, and Japan's Ijichiro Date and Yuki Takada—the Soviets continued to dominate gold-medaling performances in 1976. Mongolia claimed its only medal in the Games with a silver in the freestyle featherweight division captured by Zevegin Oydov.

1980 witnessed the first-ever "Greco" to win a Greco-Roman title at the Games; Greece's Stilianos Migiakis took the gold in the featherweight division. Other medalists included Romania, Hungary, Italy, and Bulgaria, although the Soviets outscored all others in their winnings. Bulgarian Valentin Angelov, who competed as a welterweight in the freestyle competition, won the gold by racking up five victories in a single day.

The 1984 Games were marked by a unique occurrence: two sets of brothers, Ed and Lou Banach and Dave and Mark Schultz—all Americans—won titles at the LA Games. The Greco-Roman competition, in the absence of most Eastern bloc countries, awarded medals far and wide: South Korea, Italy, Japan, West Germany, Yugoslavia, Finland, and Romania all took gold medals. The United States, typically weak in the Greco-Roman competition, took home two golds, thanks to Steven Fraser and Jeffrey Blatnick. Faring even better in the freestyle competition, the U.S. earned seven gold medals, thanks to Robert Weaver, Randy Lewis, the Schultz brothers, the Banach brothers, and Bruce Baumgartner.

In Seoul in 1988, the U.S. managed two more golds in the freestyle competition—won by John Smith, with his signature single-leg takedown, and Kenneth Monday—although they failed to win a Greco-Roman title. Bruce Baumgartner, the previous Games' super heavyweight winner, placed second to Soviet David Gobedjichvili. Apart from the eight Soviet golds, the medals were again fairly widespread: in freestyle, Japan, South Korea, and Romania took gold medals, while in the Greco-Roman competition, Italy, Norway, Hungary, South Korea, Bulgaria, and Poland all pinned down golds.

"We're in paradise now, but we came from hell." —Yugoslavian weightlifting coach Mlajan Talic, on arriving at the 1992 Games

John Smith

It takes a lot of world titles, more than a few prestigious awards, and a complete and sustained dominance over the competition for many years before a wrestler can assume the status of a national sports hero, and John Smith of Del City, Oklahoma, has earned the honor.

Arguably the greatest wrestler in American history, Smith became the first American in this tough, but underappreciated sport, to win four world titles when he ripped through his opponents in the 136.5-pound weight class at the 1990 World Championships by a combined total score of 58–4. Smith's performance that year in Tokyo was so impressive that FILA, the international wrestling federation, voted him the prestigious title of "Master of Technique."

In 1991 Smith earned further distinction when he outpolled the great Notre Dame football player Raghib "Rocket" Ismail and several others to win the 61st Sullivan Award as America's top amateur athlete.

But for Smith, a soft-spoken 26-year-old from a large, sports-oriented family, success is no reason to stop working. "Being the best at something, God, that's a great feeling," he admits. "You don't think about it too long, though. It's easy to let your priorities slip."

For the second-oldest son of Lee Roy Smith, a retired Oklahoma Transportation Department worker, and his wife Madalene, a down-to-earth, iron-willed mother, such humility came naturally. It also didn't hurt for young John to have an older brother to worship while growing up. The younger Lee Roy Smith was himself a multi-national title holder and has pushed John's career along as his brother's coach, mentor, and—sometimes—tormentor. "John learned to be fast wrestling Lee Roy," the boys' father said. "If he beat him, Lee Roy would hit him. John learned to take him down and take off running."

"I learned a lot from [Lee Roy] about how to prepare for competition," John has said. "I saw the fire in his eyes, the determination. . . . I started to wrestle because I wanted to be like him."

Smith wrestled well enough in high school to gain a scholarship to Oklahoma State, but it was not until he suffered his first major collegiate defeat that his career really began to blossom. As a sophomore wrestling in the 1985 NCAA championship finals, Smith was beaten 5–2 by Wisconsin's Jim Jordan, a quick, slick wrestler whose style Smith decided he would adopt for himself. Not as strong or muscular as most wrestlers, Smith began to play to his own strengths: speed, intelligence, and an attacking, unorthodox style that kept his opponents off-balance. The hard hours of practice eventually led to Smith's signature move, a lightning-fast single leg takedown that has proven virtually unstoppable.

FACT: Three world champions were defeated in the Greco-Roman finals in Barcelona. Rifat Yildiz (57kg, Germany), Sergei Marynov (62kg), and Islam Dougoutchiev (68kg, Unified Team) all left the Barcelona Games just a little bit humbler.

Since he first competed in international meets in 1986, Smith has added world titles in the 1986 and 1990 Goodwill Games, at the 1988 Olympics in Seoul he defeated the stocky Stephan Sarkissian of the Soviet Union 4–0 to win the gold, and in 1992 beat Asgari Mohammadian of Iran to again take home the gold.

Highlights from Barcelona

Dennis Koslowski, a 32-year-old hulk of a man, may not have won a gold medal in Barcelona, but he won a spot in the U.S. record books. After nabbing the bronze medal in the 100kg Greco-Roman weight class in Seoul, Koslowski bowed out of competition, spending his brief retirement as the national team coach. But in 1991, he realized he belonged back on the mat, and he began plotting a Barcelona comeback. "I just knew that if I could just get here again," he explained, "that in the back of my mind what I really wanted to do was give it all I had."

Koslowski gave it everything he had, and even came close to outpointing his younger Cuban opponent in the final. In a 2–1 decision in overtime, Hector Milian Perez was anointed as the 1992 champion—making him the first Latin American to snag a gold medal in Greco-Roman wrestling. Koslowski, with a silver medal, became the first U.S. Greco wrestler to nab two Olympic medals. Meanwhile, U.S. hopeful Shawn Sheldon, who was out of the medals in Greco competition because he failed to make weight in his lightweight category, was forced to put up with media jabs that suggested he enroll in a Nutrasystem regimen.

FACT: Only one wrestler—the U.S. team's Matt Ghaffari—has lasted a full five-minute regulation and a full three-minute overtime without being pinned or DQ'd in a match with Russian powerhouse Alexander Karelin.

In freestyle competition, the U.S. scored three gold medals. In a rerun of his starring appearance in Seoul in 1988, heavyweight Bruce Baumgartner collected a second gold medal. No one expected Baumgartner to mount a repeat performance since he had mustered only a seventh-place finish in the 1991 World Championships; then again, the wrestler's two-year-old son had sent dad to Spain with explicit instructions to "bring home the gold." Baumgartner also has one silver, from 1984, to round out his collection of Olympic medallions.

Three of 1988's freestyle champions successfully defended their titles in Barcelona. Five-time world champ Makharbek Khadartsev of Russia easily pummeled Turkey's Kenan Simsck into submission in the 90kg category. His teammate, six-time world champion Arsen Fadzaev showed no mercy to Valentin Getzov, whom he trounced 13–1 to win the 68kg division. And the U.S. team's John Smith repeated his 1988 62kg victory, defeating Iran's Asgari Mohammadian, who had pocketed a silver medal in Seoul—in the 57kg category.

Wrestling

Wrestling

Medalists

Wrestling, Freestyle—48 kg

1992
1. Kim Il, North Korea
2. Kim Jong-Shin, South Korea
3. Vougar Oroudjov, Belarus

1988
1. Takashi Kobayashi, Japan
2. Ivan Tzonov, Bulgaria
3. Serguei Karamtchakov, Soviet Union

1984
1. Robert Weaver, U.S.A.
2. Takashi Irie, Japan
3. Gab-Do Son, Republic of Korea

1980
1. Claudio Pollio, Italy
2. Se Hong Jang, Democratic People's Republic of Korea
3. Sergei Kornilaev, Soviet Union

1976
1. Hassan Issaev, Bulgaria
2. Roman Dmitriev, Soviet Union
3. Akira Kudo, Japan

1972
1. Roman Dmitriev, Soviet Union
2. Ognian Nikolov, Bulgaria
3. Ebrahim Javadi, Iran

1906–1968
Not held

1904
1. Robert Curry, U.S.A.
2. John Hein, U.S.A.
3. Gustav Thiefenthaler, U.S.A.

1896–1900
Not held

Wrestling, Freestyle—52 kg

1992
1. Li Hak-Son, South Korea
2. Zeke Jones, U.S.A.
3. Valentin Jordanov, Bulgaria

1988
1. Mitsuru Sato, Japan
2. Saban Trstena, Yugoslavia
3. Vladimir Togouzov, Soviet Union

1984
1. Saban Trstena, Yugoslavia

2. Jong-Kyu Kim, Republic of Korea
3. Yuji Takada, Japan

1980
1. Anatoli Beloglazov, Soviet Union
2. Wladyslaw Stecyk, Poland
3. Nermedin Selimov, Bulgaria

1976
1. Yuji Takada, Japan
2. Alexandr Ivanov, Soviet Union
3. Hae Sup Jeon, Republic of Korea

1972
1. Kiyomi Kato, Japan
2. Arsen Alkhverdiev, Soviet Union
3. Gwong-Hyong Kim, Democratic People's Republic of Korea

1968
1. Shigeo Nakata, Japan
2. Richard Sanders, U.S.A.
3. Surenjav Sukhbaatar, Mongolia

1964
1. Yoshikatsu Yoshida, Japan
2. Chang-sun Chang, Republic of Korea
3. Ali-Akbar Haydari, Iran

1960
1. Ahmet Bilek, Turkey
2. Masayuki Matsubara, Japan
3. Ebrahim Saifpour, Iran

1956
1. Mirian Tsalkalamanidze, Soviet Union
2. Mohamad-Ali Khojastehpour, Iran
3. Huseyin Akbas, Turkey

1952
1. Hasan Gemici, Turkey
2. Yushu Kitano, Japan
3. Mahmoud Mollaghassemi, Iran

1948
1. Lennart Viitala, Finland
2. Halit Balamir, Turkey
3. Thure Johansson, Sweden

1906–1936
Not held

1904
1. George Mehnert, U.S.A.
2. Gustave Bauers, U.S.A.
3. William Nelson, U.S.A.

1896–1900
Not held

Wrestling, Freestyle—57 kg

1992
1. Alejandro Puerto, Cuba
2. Serguei Smal, Belarus
3. Kim Yong Sik, North Korea

1988
1. Sergei Beloglazov, Soviet Union
2. Askari Mohammadian, Iran
3. Kyung-Sun Noh, South Korea

1984
1. Hideaki Tomiyama, Japan
2. Barry Davis, U.S.A.
3. Evi Kon Kim, Republic of Korea

1980
1. Sergei Beloglazov, Soviet Union
2. Ho Pyong Li, Democratic People's Republic of Korea
3. Dugarsuren Ouinbold, Mongolia

1976
1. Vladimir Umin, Soviet Union
2. Hans-Dieter Bruechert, East Germany
3. Masao Arai, Japan

1972
1. Hideaki Yanagida, Japan
2. Richard Sanders, U.S.A.
3. Laszlo Klinga, Hungary

1968
1. Yojiro Uetake, Japan
2. Donald Behm, U.S.A.
3. Abutaleb Talebi, Iran

1964
1. Yojiro Uetake, Japan
2. Huseyin Akbas, Turkey
3. Aydyn Ibragimov, Soviet Union

1960
1. Terrence McCann, U.S.A.
2. Nedschet Zalev, Bulgaria
3. Tadeusz Trojanowski, Poland

1956
1. Mustafa Dagistanli, Turkey
2. Mohamad Yaghoubi, Iran
3. Mikhail Chachov, Soviet Union

1952
1. Shohachi Ishii, Japan
2. Raschid Mamedbekov, Soviet Union
3. Kha-Shaba Jadav, India

1948
1. Nasuh Akar, Turkey
2. Gerald Leeman, U.S.A.
3. Charles Kouyos, France

1936
1. Odon Zombori, Hungary
2. Ross Flood, U.S.A.
3. Johannes Herbert, Germany

1932
1. Robert Pearce, U.S.A.
2. Odon Zombori, Hungary
3. Aatos Jaskari, Finland

1928
1. Kaarlo Makinen, Finland
2. Edmond Spapen, Belgium
3. James Trifunov, Canada

1924
1. Kustaa Pihlajamaki, Finland
2. Kaarlo Makinen, Finland
3. Bryant Hines, U.S.A.

1912–1920
Not held

1908
1. George Mehnert, U.S.A.
2. William Press, Great Britain
3. Aubert Cote, Canada

1906
Not held

1904
1. Isaac Niflot, U.S.A.
2. August Wester, U.S.A.
3. Z. B. Strebler, U.S.A.

1896–1900
Not held

Wrestling, Freestyle—62 kg

1992
1. John Smith, U.S.A.
2. Asgari Mohammadian, Iran
3. Lazaro Reinoso, Cuba

1988
1. John Smith, U.S.A.
2. Stepan Sarkissian, Soviet Union
3. Simeon Chterev, Bulgaria

1984
1. Randy Lewis, U.S.A.
2. Kosei Akaishi, Japan
3. Jung-Keun Lee, Republic of Korea

1980
1. Magomedgasan Abushev, Soviet Union
2. Mikho Dukov, Bulgaria
3. Georges Hajiioannidis, Greece

1976
1. Yang Mo Yang, Republic of Korea
2. Zevegin Oydov, Mongolia
3. Gene Davis, U.S.A.

1972
1. Sagalav Abdulbekov, Soviet Union
2. Vehbi Akdag, Turkey
3. Ivan Krastev, Bulgaria

1968
1. Masaaki Kaneko, Japan
2. Enyu Todorov, Bulgaria
3. Shamseddin Seyed-Abassy, Iran

1964
1. Osamu Watanabe, Japan
2. Stantcho Ivanov, Bulgaria
3. Nodar Khokhashvili, Soviet Union

1960
1. Mustafa Dagistanli, Turkey
2. Stantcho Ivanov, Bulgaria
3. Vladimir Rubashvili, Soviet Union

1956
1. Shozo Sasahara, Japan
2. Joseph Mewis, Belgium
3. Erkki Penttila, Finland

1952
1. Bayram Sit, Turkey
2. Nasser Guivehchi, Iran
3. Josiah Henson, U.S.A.

1948
1. Gazanfer Bilge, Turkey
2. Ivar Sjolin, Sweden
3. Adolf Muller, Switzerland

1936
1. Kustaa Pihlajamaki, Finland
2. Francis Millard, U.S.A.
3. Gosta Jonsson, Sweden

1932
1. Hermanni Pihlajamaki, Finland
2. Edgar Nemir, U.S.A.
3. Einar Karlsson, Sweden

1928
1. Allie Morrison, U.S.A.
2. Kustaa Pihlajamaki, Finland
3. Hans Minder, Switzerland

1924
1. Robin Reed, U.S.A.
2. Chester Newton, U.S.A.
3. Katsutoshi Naito, Japan

1920
1. Charles E. Ackerly, U.S.A.

2. Samuel Gerson, U.S.A.
3. P. W. Bernard, Great Britain

1912
Not held

1908
1. George Dole, U.S.A.
2. James Slim, Great Britain
3. William McKie, Great Britain

1906
Not held

1904
1. Benjamin Bradshaw, U.S.A.
2. Theodore McLear, U.S.A.
3. Charles Clapper, U.S.A.

1896–1900
Not held

Wrestling, Freestyle—68 kg
1992
1. Arsen Fadzaev, Russia
2. Valentin Getzov, Bulgaria
3. Kosei Akaishi, Japan

1988
1. Arsen Fadzaev, Soviet Union
2. Jang-Soon Park South Korea
3. Nate Carr, U.S.A.

1984
1. In-Tak Youh, Republic of Korea
2. Andrew Rein, U.S.A.
3. Jukka Rauhala, Finland

1980
1. Saipulla Absaidov, Soviet Union
2. Ivan Yankov, Bulgaria
3. Saban Sejdi, Yugoslavia

1976
1. Pavel Pinegin, Soviet Union
2. Lloyd Keaser, U.S.A.
3. Yasaburo Sugawara, Japan

1972
1. Dan Gable, U.S.A.
2. Kikuo Wada, Japan
3. Ruslan Ashuraliyev, Soviet Union

1968
1. Abdollah Movahed Ardabili, Iran
2. Enyu Waltschev, Bulgaria
3. Sereeter Danzandarjaa, Mongolia

1964
1. Enyu Waltschev, Bulgaria
2. Klaus-Jurgen Rost, West Germany
3. Iwao Horiuchi, Japan

1960
1. Shelby Wilson, U.S.A.
2. Vladimir Sinyavsky, Soviet Union
3. Enyu Dimov, Bulgaria

1956
1. Emamali Habibi, Iran
2. Shigeru Kasahara, Japan
3. Alimbeg Bestayev, Soviet Union

1952
1. Olle Anderberg, Sweden
2. J. Thomas Evans, U.S.A.
3. Djahanbakte Tovfighe, Iran

1948
1. Celal Atik, Turkey
2. Gosta Frandfors-Jonsson, Sweden
3. Hermann Baumann, Switzerland

1936
1. Karoly Karpati, Hungary
2. Wolfgang Ehrl, Germany
3. Hermanni Pihlajamaki, Finland

1932
1. Charles Pacome, France
2. Karoly Karpati, Hungary
3. Gustaf Klaren, Sweden

1928
1. Osvald Kapp, Estonia
2. Charles Pacome, France
3. Eino Leino, Finland

1924
1. Russell Vis, U.S.A.
2. Volmari Vikstrom, Finland
3. Arvo Haavisto, Finland

1920
1. Kalle Anttila, Finland
2. Gottfrid Svensson, Sweden
3. Peter Wright, Great Britain

1912
Not held

1908
1. George de Relwyskow, Great Britain
2. William Wood, Great Britain
3. Albert Gingell, Great Britain

1906
Not held

1904
1. Otto Roehm, U.S.A.
2. R. Tesing, U.S.A.
3. Albert Zirkel, U.S.A.

1896–1900
Not held

Wrestling, Freestyle—74 kg

1992
1. Park Jang-Soon, South Korea
2. Kenny Monday, U.S.A.
3. Amir Reza Khadem Azghadi, Iran 181.5 pounds

1988
1. Kenneth Monday, U.S.A.
2. Adlan Varaev, Soviet Union
3. Rakhmad Sofiadi, Bulgaria

1984
1. David Schultz, U.S.A.
2. Martin Knosp, West Germany
3. Saban Sejdi, Yugoslavia

1980
1. Valentin Raitchev, Bulgaria
2. Jamtsying Davaajav, Mongolia
3. Dan Karabin, Czechoslovakia

1976
1. Ijichiro Date, Japan
2. Mansour Barzegar, Iran
3. Stanley Dziedzic, U.S.A.

1972
1. Wayne Wells, U.S.A.
2. Jan Karlsson, Sweden
3. Adolf Seger, West Germany

1968
1. Mahmut Atalay, Turkey
2. Daniel Robin, France
3. Dagvasuren Purev, Mongolia

1964
1. Ismail Ogan, Turkey
2. Guliko Sagaradze, Soviet Union
3. Mohamad-Ali Sanatkaran, Iran

1960
1. Douglas Blubaugh, U.S.A.
2. Ismail Ogan, Turkey
3. Muhammed Bashir, Pakistan

1956
1. Mitsuo Ikeda, Japan
2. Ibrahim Zengin, Turkey
3. Vakhtang Balavadze, Soviet Union

1952
1. William Smith, U.S.A.
2. Per Berlin, Sweden
3. Abdullah Modjtabavi, Iran

1948
1. Yasar Dogu, Turkey
2. Richard Garrard, Australia
3. Leland Merrill, U.S.A.

1936
1. Frank Lewis, U.S.A.
2. Ture Andersson, Sweden
3. Joseph Schleimer, Canada

1932
1. Jack Van Bebber, U.S.A.
2. Daniel MacDonald, Canada
3. Eino Leino, Finland

1928
1. Arvo Haavisto, Finland
2. Lloyd Appleton, U.S.A.
3. Maurice Letchford, Canada

1924
1. Hermann Gehri, Switzerland
2. Eino Leino, Finland
3. Otto Muller, Switzerland

1906–1920
Not held

1904
1. Charles Erickson, U.S.A.
2. William Beckman, U.S.A.
3. Jerry Winholtz, U.S.A.

1896–1900
Not held

Wrestling, Freestyle—82 kg

1992
1. Kevin Jackson, U.S.A.
2. Elmadi Jabraijlov, Russia
3. Rasul Azghadi, Iran

1988
1. Myung-Woo Han, South Korea
2. Necmi Gencalp, Turkey
3. Josef Lohyna, Czechoslovakia

1984
1. Mark Schultz, U.S.A.
2. Hideyuki Nagashima, Japan
3. Chris Rinke, Canada

1980
1. Ismail Abilov, Bulgaria
2. Magomedhan Aratsilov, Soviet Union
3. Istvan Kovacs, Hungary

1976
1. John Peterson, U.S.A.
2. Viktor Novoyilov, Soviet Union
3. Adolf Seger, West Germany

1972
1. Levan Tediashvili, Soviet Union
2. John Peterson, U.S.A.
3. Vasile Iorga, Romania

1968
1. Boris Gurevitch, Soviet Union
2. Munkbat Jigjid, Mongolia
3. Prodan Gardschev, Bulgaria

1964
1. Prodan Gardschev, Bulgaria
2. Hasan Gungor, Turkey
3. Daniel Brand, U.S.A.

1960
1. Hasan Gungor, Turkey
2. Georgi Skhirtladze, Soviet Union
3. Hans Antonsson, Sweden

1956
1. Nikola Stantchev, Bulgaria
2. Daniel Hodge, U.S.A.
3. Georgi Skhirtladze, Soviet Union

1952
1. David Tsimakuridze, Soviet Union
2. Gholam-Reza Takhti, Iran
3. Gyorgy Gurics, Hungary

1948
1. Glen Brand, U.S.A.
2. Adil Candemir, Turkey
3. Erik Linden, Sweden

1936
1. Emile Poilve, France
2. Richard Voliva, U.S.A.
3. Ahmet Kirecci, Turkey

1932
1. Ivar Johansson, Sweden
2. Kyosti Luukko, Finland
3. Jozsef Tunyogi, Hungary

1928
1. Ernst Kyburz, Switzerland
2. Donald P. Stockton, Canada
3. Samuel Rabin, Great Britain

1924
1. Firtz Hagmann, Switzerland
2. Pierre Ollivier, Belgium
3. Vilho Pekkala, Finland

1920
1. Eino Leino, Finland
2. Vaino Penttala, Finland
3. Charles Johnson, U.S.A.

1912
Not held

1908
1. Stanley Bacon, Great Britain
2. George de Relwyskow, Great Britain
3. Frederick Beck, Great Britain

1896–1906

Not held

Wrestling, Freestyle—90 kg

1992
1. Makharbek Khadartsev, Russia
2. Kenan Simsek, Turkey
3. Chris Campbell, U.S.A.

1988
1. Makharbek Khadartsev, Soviet Union
2. Akira Ota, Japan
3. Tae-Woo Kim, South Korea

1984
1. Ed Banach, U.S.A.
2. Akira Ohta, Japan
3. Noel Loban, Great Britain

1980
1. Sanasar Oganesyan, Soviet Union
2. Uwe Neupert, East Germany
3. Aleksander Cichon, Poland

1976
1. Levan Tediashvili, Soviet Union
2. Ben Peterson, U.S.A.
3. Stelica Morcov, Romania

1972
1. Ben Peterson, U.S.A.
2. Gennady Strakhov, Soviet Union
3. Karoly Bajko, Hungary

1968
1. Ahmet Ayik, Turkey
2. Schota Lomidze, Soviet Union
3. Jozsef Csatari, Hungary

1964
1. Aleksandr Medved, Soviet Union
2. Ahmet Ayik, Turkey
3. Said Mustafov, Bulgaria

1960
1. Ismet Atli, Turkey
2. Gholam-Reza Takhti, Iran
3. Anatoli Albul, Soviet Union

1956
1. Gholam-Reza Takhti, Iran
2. Boris Kulayev, Soviet Union
3. Peter Blair, U.S.A.

1952
1. Wiking Palm, Sweden
2. Henry Wittenberg, U.S.A.
3. Adil Atan, Turkey

1948
1. Henry Wittenberg, U.S.A.

2. Fritz Stockli, Switzerland
3. Bengt Fahlkvist, Sweden

1936
1. Knut Fridell, Sweden
2. August Neo, Estonia
3. Erich Siebert, Germany

1932
1. Peter Mehringer, U.S.A.
2. Thure Sjostedt, Sweden
3. Eddie Scarf, Australia

1928
1. Thure Sjostedt, Sweden
2. Arnold Bogli, Switzerland
3. Henri Lefebre, France

1924
1. John Spellman, U.S.A.
2. Rudolf Svensson, Sweden
3. Charles Courant, Switzerland

1920
1. Anders Larsson, Sweden
2. Charles Courant, Switzerland
3. Walter Maurer, U.S.A.

1896–1912
Not held

Wrestling, Freestyle—100 kg

1992
1. Leri Khabelov, Georgia
2. Heiko Balz, Germany
3. Ali Kayali, Turkey

1988
1. Vasile Puscasu, Romania
2. Leri Khabelov, Soviet Union
3. Bill Scherr, U.S.A.

1984
1. Lou Banach, U.S.A.
2. Joseph Atiyeh, Syria
3. Vasile Puscasu, Romania

1980
1. Ilya Mate, Soviet Union
2. Slavcho Chervenkov, Bulgaria
3. Julius Strnisko, Czechoslovakia

1976
1. Ivan Yarygin, Soviet Union
2. Russell Hellickson, U.S.A.
3. Dimo Kostov, Bulgaria

1972
1. Ivan Yarygin, Soviet Union
2. Khorloo Baianmunkh, Mongolia
3. Jozsef Csatari, Hungary

1OK

1968
1. Aleksandr Medved, Soviet Union
2. Osman Duraliev, Bulgaria
3. Wilfried Dietrich, West Germany

1964
1. Aleksandr Ivanitsky, Soviet Union
2. Lyutvi Ahmedov, Bulgaria
3. Hamit Kaplan, Turkey

1960
1. Wilfried Dietrich, West Germany
2. Hamit Kaplan, Turkey
3. Savkus Dzarassov, Soviet Union

1956
1. Hamit Kaplan, Turkey
2. Hussein Mechmedov, Bulgaria
3. Taisto Kangasniemi, Finland

1952
1. Arsen Mekokischvili, Soviet Union
2. Bertil Antonsson, Sweden
3. Kenneth Richmond, Great Britain

1948
1. Gyula Bobis, Hungary
2. Bertil Antonsson, Sweden
3. Joseph Armstrong, Australia

1936
1. Kristjan Palusalu, Estonia
2. Josef Klapuch, Czechoslovakia
3. Hjalmar Nystrom, Finland

1932
1. Johan Richtoff, Sweden
2. John Riley, U.S.A.
3. Nikolaus Hirschl, Austria

1928
1. Johan Richtoff, Sweden
2. Aukusti Sihvola, Finland
3. Edmond Dame, France

1924
1. Harry Steele, U.S.A.
2. Henri Wenli, Switzerland
3. Andrew McDonald, Great Britain

1920
1. Robert Roth, Switzerland
2. Nathan Pendleton, U.S.A.
3. Frederick Meyer, U.S.A.
3. Ernst Nilsson, Sweden

1912
Not held

1908
1. George C. O'Kelly, Great Britain/Ireland

2. Jacob Gundersen, Norway
3. Edward Barrett, Great Britain/Ireland

1906
Not held

1904
1. B. Hansen, U.S.A.
2. Frank Kungler, U.S.A.
3. F. Charles Warmbold, U.S.A.

1896–1900
Not held

Wrestling, Freestyle—130 kg

1992
1. Bruce Baumgartner, U.S.A.
2. Jeff Thue, Canada
3. David Gobedjichvili, Georgia

1988
1. David Gobodjichvili, Soviet Union
2. Bruce Baumgartner, U.S.A.
3. Andreas Schroeder, East Germany

1984
1. Bruce Baumgartner, U.S.A.
2. Bob Moll, Canada
3. Ayhan Taskin, Turkey

1980
1. Soslan Andiev, Soviet Union
2. Jozsef Balla, Hungary
3. Adam Sandurski, Poland

1976
1. Soslan Andiev, Soviet Union
2. Jozsef Balla, Hungary
3. Ladislau Simon, Romania

1972
1. Aleksandr Medved, Soviet Union
2. Osman Duraliev, Bulgaria
3. Chris Taylor, U.S.A.

1896–1968
Not held

Wrestling, Greco-Roman—48 kg

1992
1. Oleg Koutherenko, Ukraine
2. Vincenzo Maenza, Italy
3. Wilber Sanchez, Cuba

1988
1. Vincenzo Maenza, Italy
2. Andrzej Glab, Poland
3. Bratan Tzenov, Bulgaria

1984

1. Vincenzo Maenza, Italy
2. Markus Scherer, West Germany
3. Ikuzo Saito, Japan

1980

1. Zaksylik Ushkempirov, Soviet Union
2. Constantin Alexandru, Romania
3. Ferenc Seres, Hungary

1976

1. Aleksei Shumakov, Soviet Union
2. Gheorghe Berceanu, Romania
3. Stefan Angelov, Bulgaria

1972

1. Gheorghe Berceanu, Romania
2. Rahim Aliabadi, Iran
3. Stefan Angelov, Bulgaria

1896–1968

Not held

Wrestling, Greco-Roman—52 kg

1992

1. Jon Ronningen, Norway
2. Alfred Ter-Mkrttchian, Russia
3. Min Kyung-Kap, South Korea

1988

1. Jon Ronningen, Norway
2. Atsuji Miyahara, Japan
3. Jae-Suk Lee, South Korea

1984

1. Atsuji Miyahara, Japan
2. Daniel Aceves, Mexico
3. Dae-Du Bang, Republic of Korea

1980

1. Vakhtang Blagidze, Soviet Union
2. Lajos Racz, Hungary
3. Mladen Mladenov, Bulgaria

1976

1. Vitali Konstantinov, Soviet Union
2. Nicu Ginga, Romania
3. Koichiro Hirayama, Japan

1972

1. Petar Kirov, Bulgaria
2. Koichiro Hirayama, Japan
3. Giuseppe Bognanni, Italy

1968

1. Petar Kirov, Bulgaria
2. Vladimir Bakulin, Soviet Union
3. Miroslav Zeman, Czechoslovakia

1964

1. Tsutomu Hanahara, Japan

2. Angel Keresov, Bulgaria
3. Dumitru Pirvulescu, Romania

1960

1. Dumitru Pirvulescu, Romania
2. Osman Sayed, United Arab Republic
3. Mohamed Paziraye, Iran

1956

1. Nikolai Solovyov, Soviet Union
2. Ignazio Fabra, Italy
3. Dursun Ali Egribas, Turkey

1952

1. Boris Gurevitch, Soviet Union
2. Ignazio Fabra, Italy
3. Leo Honkala, Finland

1948

1. Pietro Lombardi, Italy
2. Kenan Olcay, Turkey
3. Reino Kangasmaki, Finland

1896–1936

Not held

Wrestling, Greco-Roman—57 kg

1992

1. An Han-Bong, South Korea
2. Rifat Yildiz, Germany
3. Sheng Zetian, China

1988

1. Andras Sike, Hungary
2. Stoyan Balov, Bulgaria
3. Charalambos Holidis, Greece

1984

1. Pasquale Passarelli, West Germany
2. Masaki Eto, Japan
3. Charalambos Holidis, Greece

1980

1. Shamil Serikov, Soviet Union
2. Jozef Lipien, Poland
3. Benni Ljungbeck, Poland

1976

1. Pertti Ukkola, Finland
2. Ivan Frgic, Yugoslavia
3. Farhat Mustafin, Soviet Union

1972

1. Rustem Kazakov, Soviet Union
2. Hans-Jurgen Veil, West Germany
3. Risto Bjorlin, Finland

1968

1. Janos Varga, Hungary
2. Ion Baciu, Romania
3. Ivan Kochergin, Soviet Union

1964
1. Masamitsu Ichiguchi, Japan
2. Vladlen Trostyansky, Soviet Union
3. Ion Cernea, Romania

1960
1. Oleg Karavayev, Soviet Union
2. Ion Cernea, Romania
3. Petrow Dinko, Bulgaria

1956
1. Konstantin Vyrupayev, Soviet Union
2. Edvin Vesterby, Sweden
3. Francise Horvat, Romania

1952
1. Imre Hodos, Hungary
2. Zakaria Chihab, Lebanon
3. Artem Teryan, Soviet Union

1948
1. Kurt Pettersen, Sweden
2. Ali Mahmoud Hassan, Egypt
3. Halil Kaya, Turkey

1936
1. Marton Lorincz, Hungary
2. Egon Svensson, Sweden
3. Jakob Brendel, Germany

1932
1. Jakob Brendel, Germany
2. Marcello Nizzola, Italy
3. Louis Francois, France

1928
1. Kurt Leucht, Germany
2. Jindrich Maudr, Czechoslovakia
3. Giovanni Gozzi, Italy

1924
1. Eduard Putsep, Estonia
2. Anselm Ahlfors, Finland
3. Vaino Ikonen, Finland

1896–1920
Not held

Wrestling, Greco-Roman—62 kg

1992
1. M. Akif Pirim, Turkey
2. Serguei Martynov, Russia
3. Juan Maren, Cuba

1988
1. Kamander Madjidov, Soviet Union
2. Jivko Vanguelov, Bulgaria
3. Dae-Hyun An, South Korea

1984
1. Weon-Kee Kim, Republic of Korea

2. Kentolle Johansson, Sweden
3. Hugo Dietsche, Switzerland

1980
1. Stilianos Migiakis, Greece
2. Istvan Toth, Hungary
3. Boris Kramorenko, Soviet Union

1976
1. Kazimierz Lipien, Poland
2. Nelson Davidian, Soviet Union
3. Laszlo Reczi, Hungary

1972
1. Georgi Markow, Bulgaria
2. Heinz-Helmut Wehling, East Germany
3. Kazimierz Lipien, Poland

1968
1. Roman Rurua, Soviet Union
2. Hideo Fujimoto, Japan
3. Simeon Popescu, Romania

1964
1. Imre Polyak, Hungary
2. Roman Rurua, Soviet Union
3. Branislav Martinovic, Yugoslavia

1960
1. Muzahir Sille, Turkey
2. Imre Polyak, Hungary
3. Konstantin Vyrupayev, Soviet Union

1956
1. Rauno Makinen, Finland
2. Imre Polyak, Hungary
3. Roman Dzneladze, Soviet Union

1952
1. Jakov Punkin, Soviet Union
2. Imre Polyak, Hungary
3. Abdel Rashed, Egypt

1948
1. Mehmet Oktav, Turkey
2. Olle Anderberg, Sweden
3. Ferenc Toth, Hungary

1936
1. Yasar Erkan, Turkey
2. Aarne Reini, Finland
3. Einar Karlsson, Sweden

1932
1. Giovanni Gozzi, Italy
2. Wolfgang Ehrl, Germany
3. Lauri Koskela, Finland

1928
1. Voldemar Vali, Estonia
2. Erik Malmberg, Sweden
3. Gerolomo Quaglia, Italy

1924
1. Kalle Anttila, Finland
2. Aleksanteri Toivola, Finland
3. Erik Malmberg, Sweden

1920
1. Oskari Friman, Finland
2. Heikki Kahkonen, Finland
3. Fritiof Svensson, Sweden

1912
1. Kaarlo Koskelo, Finland
2. Georg Gerstacker, Germany
3. Otto Lasanen, Finland

1896–1908
Not held

Wrestling, Greco-Roman—68 kg

1992
1. Attila Repka, Hungary
2. Islam Dougoutchiev, Russia
3. Rodney Smith, U.S.A.

1988
1. Levon Djoulfalakian, Soviet Union
2. Sung-Moon Kim, South Korea
3. Tapio Sipila, Finland

1984
1. Vlado Lisjak, Yugoslavia
2. Tapio Sipila, Finland
3. James Martinez, U.S.A.

1980
1. Stefan Rusu, Romania
2. Andrzej Supron, Poland
3. Lars-Erik Skiold, Sweden

1976
1. Suren Nalbandyan, Soviet Union
2. Stefan Rusu, Romania
3. Heinz-Helmut Wehling, East Germany

1972
1. Schamil Khisamutdinov, Soviet Union
2. Stojan Apostolov, Bulgaria
3. Gian-Matteo Ranzi, Italy

1968
1. Munji Mumemura, Japan
2. Stevan Horvat, Yugoslavia
3. Petros Galaktopoulos, Greece

1964
1. Kazim Ayvaz, Turkey
2. Valeriu Bularca, Romania
3. David Gvantseladze, Soviet Union

1960
1. Avtandil Koridze, Soviet Union
2. Branislav Martinovic, Yugoslavia
3. Gustav Freij, Sweden

1956
1. Kyosti Lehtonen, Finland
2. Riza Dogan, Turkey
3. Gyula Toth, Hungary

1952
1. Schasam Safin, Soviet Union
2. Gustav Freij, Sweden
3. Mikulas Athanasov, Czechoslovakia

1948
1. Gustav Freij, Sweden
2. Aage Eriksen, Norway
3. Karoly Ferencz, Hungary

1936
1. Lauri Koskela, Finland
2. Josef Herda, Czechoslovakia
3. Voldemar Vali, Estonia

1932
1. Erik Malmberg, Sweden
2. Abraham Kurland, Denmark
3. Eduard Sperling, Germany

1928
1. Lajos Keresztes, Hungary
2. Eduard Sperling, Germany
3. Edvard Westerlund, Finland

1924
1. Oskari Friman, Finland
2. Lajos Keresztes, Hungary
3. Kalle Westerlund, Finland

1920
1. Eemil Vare, Finland
2. Taavi Tamminen, Finland
3. Frithjof Andersen, Norway

1912
1. Eemil Vare, Finland
2. Gustaf Malmstrom, Sweden
3. Edvin Matiason, Sweden

1908
1. Enrico Porro, Italy
2. Nikolai Orlov, Russia
3. Arvid Linden, Finland

1906
1. Rudolf Watzl, Austria
2. Karl Karlsen, Denmark
3. Ferenc Holuban, Hungary

1896–1904
Not held

Wrestling, Greco-Roman—74 kg

1992
1. Mnatsakan Iskandarian, Armenia
2. Jozef Tracz, Poland
3. Torbjorn Johansson, Sweden

1988
1. Young-Nam Kim, South Korea
2. Daoulet Tourlykhanov, Soviet Union
3. Josef Tracz, Poland

1984
1. Jouko Salomaki, Finland
2. Roger Tallroth, Sweden
3. Stefan Rusu, Romania

1980
1. Ferenc Kocsis, Hungary
2. Anatoli Bykov, Soviet Union
3. Mikko Huhtala, Finland

1976
1. Anatoli Bykov, Soviet Union
2. Vitezslav Macha, Czechoslovakia
3. Karl-Heinz Helbing, West Germany

1972
1. Vitezslav Macha, Czechoslovakia
2. Petros Galaktopoulos, Greece
3. Jan Karlsson, Sweden

1968
1. Rudolf Vesper, East Germany
2. Daniel Robin, France
3. Karoly Bajko, Hungary

1964
1. Anatoli Kolesov, Soviet Union
2. Kiril Petkov Todorov, Bulgaria
3. Bertil Nystrom, Sweden

1960
1. Mithat Bayrak, Turkey
2. Gunter Maritschnigg, West Germany
3. Rene Schiermeyer, France

1956
1. Mithat Bayrak, Turkey
2. Vladimir Maneyev, Soviet Union
3. Per Berlin, Sweden

1952
1. Miklos Szilvasi, Hungary
2. Gosta Andersson, Sweden
3. Khalil Taha, Lebanon

1948
1. Gosta Andersson, Sweden
2. Miklos Szilvasi, Hungary
3. Henrik Hansen, Denmark

1936
1. Rudolf Svedberg, Sweden
2. Fritz Schafer, Germany
3. Eino Virtanen, Finland

1932
1. Ivar Johansson, Sweden
2. Vaino Kajander, Finland
3. Ercole Gallegati, Italy

1896–1928
Not held

Wrestling, Greco-Roman—82 kg

1992
1. Peter Farkas, Hungary
2. Piotr Stepien, Poland
3. Daoulet Tourlykhanov, Kazakhstan

1988
1. Mikhail Mamiachvili, Soviet Union
2. Tibor Komaromi, Hungary
3. Sang-Kyu Kim, South Korea

1984
1. Ion Draica, Romania
2. Dimitrios Thanopoulos, Greece
3. Soren Claeson, Sweden

1980
1. Gennady Korban, Soviet Union
2. Jan Dolgowicz, Poland
3. Pavel Pavlov, Bulgaria

1976
1. Momir Petkovic, Yugoslavia
2. Vladimir Cheboksarov, Soviet Union
3. Ivan Kolev, Bulgaria

1972
1. Csaba Hegedus, Hungary
2. Anatoli Nazarenko, Soviet Union
3. Milan Nenadic, Yugoslavia

1968
1. Lothar Metz, East Germany
2. Valentin Olenik, Soviet Union
3. Branislav Simic, Yugoslavia

1964
1. Branislav Simic, Yugoslavia
2. Jiri Kormanik, Czechoslovakia
3. Lothar Metz, East Germany

1960
1. Dimiter Dobrev, Bulgaria
2. Lothar Metz, East Germany
3. Ion Taranu, Romania

1956

1. Givi Kartoziya, Soviet Union
2. Dimiter Dobrev, Bulgaria
3. Rune Jansson, Sweden

1952

1. Axel Gronberg, Sweden
2. Kalervo Rauhala, Finland
3. Nikolai Byelov, Soviet Union

1948

1. Axel Gronberg, Sweden
2. Muhlis Tayfur, Turkey
3. Ercole Gallegati, Italy

1936

1. Ivar Johansson, Sweden
2. Ludwig Schweickert, Germany
3. Jozsef Palotas, Hungary

1932

1. Vaino Kokkinen, Finland
2. Jean Foldeak, Germany
3. Axel Cadier, Sweden

1928

1. Vaino Kokkinen, Finland
2. Laszlo Papp, Hungary
3. Albert Kusnets, Estonia

1924

1. Edvard Westerlund, Finland
2. Artur Lindfors, Finland
3. Roman Steinberg, Estonia

1920

1. Carl Westergren, Sweden
2. Artur Lindfors, Finland
3. Matti Perttila, Finland

1912

1. Claes Johanson, Sweden
2. Martin Klein, Russia
3. Alfred Asikainen, Finland

1908

1. Frithiof Martensson, Sweden
2. Mauritz Andersson, Sweden
3. Anders Andersen, Denmark

1906

1. Verner Weckman, Finland
2. Rudolf Lindmayer, Austria
3. Robert Behrens, Denmark

1896–1904

Not held

Wrestling, Greco-Roman—90 kg

1992

1. Maik Bullmann, Germany

2. Hakki Basar, Turkey
3. Gogui Kogouachvili, Georgia

1988

1. Atanas Komchev, Bulgaria
2. Harri Koskela, Finland
3. Vladimir Popov, Soviet Union

1984

1. Steven Fraser, U.S.A.
2. Ilie Matei, Romania
3. Frank Andersson, Sweden

1980

1. Norbert Noevenyi, Hungary
2. Igor Kanygin, Soviet Union
3. Petre Dicu, Romania

1976

1. Valeri Rezantsev, Soviet Union
2. Stoyan Nikolov, Bulgaria
3. Czeslaw Kwiecinski, Poland

1972

1. Valeri Rezantsev, Soviet Union
2. Josip Corak, Yugoslavia
3. Czeslaw Kwiecinski, Poland

1968

1. Bojan Radev, Bulgaria
2. Nikolai Yakovenko, Soviet Union
3. Nicolae Martinescu, Romania

1964

1. Bojan Radev, Bulgaria
2. Per Svensson, Sweden
3. Heinz Kiehl, West Germany

1960

1. Tevfik Kis, Turkey
2. Krali Bimbalov, Bulgaria
3. Givi Kartoziya, Soviet Union

1956

1. Valentin Nikolayev, Soviet Union
2. Petko Sirakov, Bulgaria
3. Karl-Erik Nilsson, Sweden

1952

1. Kaelpo Grondahl, Finland
2. Chalva Chikhladze, Soviet Union
3. Karl-Erik Nilsson, Sweden

1948

1. Karl-Erik Nilsson, Sweden
2. Kaelpo Grondahl, Finland
3. Ibrahim Orabi, Egypt

1936

1. Axel Cadier, Sweden
2. Edwins Bietags, Latvia
3. August Neo, Estonia

1932
1. Rudolf Svensson, Sweden
2. Onni Pellinen, Finland
3. Mario Gruppioni, Italy

1928
1. Ibrahim Moustafa, Egypt
2. Adolf Rieger, Germany
3. Onni Pellinen, Finland

1924
1. Carl Westergren, Sweden
2. Rudolf Svensson, Sweden
3. Onni Pellinen, Finland

1920
1. Claes Johanson, Sweden
2. Edil Rosenqvist, Finland
3. Johannes Eriksen, Denmark

1912
2. Anders Ahlgren, Sweden
2. Ivar Bohling, Finland
3. Bela Varga, Hungary

1908
1. Verner Weckman, Finland
2. Yrjo Saarela, Finland
3. Carl Jensen, Denmark

1896–1906
Not held

Wrestling, Greco-Roman—100 kg

1992
1. Hector Milian Perez, Cuba
2. Dennis Koslowski, U.S.A.
3. Serguei Demiachkievitch, Belarus

1988
1. Andrzej Wronski, Poland
2. Gerhard Himmel, West Germany
3. Dennis Koslowski, U.S.A.

1984
1. Vasile Andrei, Romania
2. Greg Gibson, U.S.A.
3. Jozef Tertelje, Yugoslavia

1980
1. Georgi Raikov, Bulgaria
2. Roman Bierla, Poland
3. Vasile Andrei, Romania

1976
1. Nikolai Bolboshin, Soviet Union
2. Kamen Goranov, Bulgaria
3. Andrzej Skrzydlewski, Poland

1972
1. Nicolae Martinescu, Romania

2. Nikolai Iakovenko, Soviet Union
3. Ferenc Kiss, Hungary

1968
1. Istvan Kozma, Hungary
2. Anatoli Roshin, Soviet Union
3. Petr Kment, Czechoslovakia

1964
1. Istvan Kozma, Hungary
2. Anatoli Roshin, Soviet Union
3. Wilfried Dietrich, West Germany

1960
1. Ivan Bogdan, Soviet Union
2. Wilfried Dietrich, West Germany
3. Bohumil Kubat, Czechoslovakia

1956
1. Anatoli Parfenov, Soviet Union
2. Wilfried Dietrich, West Germany
3. Adelmo Bulgarelli, Italy

1952
1. Johannes Kotkas, Soviet Union
2. Josef Ruzicka, Czechoslovakia
3. Tauno Kovanen, Finland

1948
1. Ahmet Kirecci, Turkey
2. Tor Nilsson, Sweden
3. Guido Fantoni, Italy

1936
1. Kristjan Palusalu, Estonia
2. John Nyman, Sweden
3. Kurt Hornfischer, Germany

1932
1. Carl Westergren, Sweden
2. Josef Urban, Czechoslovakia
3. Nikolaus Hirschl, Austria

1928
1. Rudolf Svensson, Sweden
2. Hjalmar Nystrom, Finland
3. Georg Gehring, Germany

1924
1. Henri Deglane, France
2. Edil Rosenqvist, Finland
3. Rajmund Bado, Hungary

1920
1. Adolf Lindfors, Finland
2. Poul Hansen, Denmark
3. Marti Nieminen, Finland

1912
1. Yrjo Saarela, Finland
2. John Olin, Finland
3. Soren M. Jensen, Denmark

1908
1. Richard Weisz, Hungary
2. Aleksandr Petrov, Russia
3. Soren M. Jensen, Denmark

1906
1. Soren M. Jensen, Denmark
2. Henri Baur, Austria
3. Marcel Dubois, Belgium

1900–1904
Not held

1896
1. Carl Schuhmann, Germany
2. Georgios Tsitas, Greece
3. Stephanos Christopoulos, Greece

Wrestling, Greco-Roman—130 kg

1992
1. Alexander Karelin, Russia
2. Tomas Johansson, Sweden
3. Ioan Grigoras, Romania

1988
1. Alexandre Karelin, Soviet Union

2. Ranguel Guerovski, Bulgaria
3. Tomas Johansson, Sweden

1984
1. Jeffrey Blatnick, U.S.A.
2. Refik Memisevic, Yugoslavia
3. Victor Dolipshi, Romania

1980
1. Aleksandr Kolchinsky, Soviet Union
2. Aleksandr Tomov, Bulgaria
3. Hassan Bchara, Lebanon

1976
1. Aleksandr Kolchinsky, Soviet Union
2. Aleksandr Tomov, Bulgaria
3. Roman Codreanu, Romania

1972
1. Anatoli Roshin, Soviet Union
2. Aleksandr Tomov, Bulgaria
3. Victor Dolipshi, Romania

1896–1968
Not held

Trivia Quiz

1. The first Modern Olympics in 1896 included
a. Three categories of wrestling events   **b.** One wrestling event
c. No wrestling events

2. Greco-Roman wrestling was first included in the Modern Games
a. In 1896   **b.** In 1908   **c.** In 1976

3. The longest wrestling match in Olympic history lasted
a. 22 hours and 40 minutes   **b.** 11 hours and 40 minutes
c. It's still going

4. In 1972, the following two Olympic weight categories were added
a. Under 48kg and over 100kg   **b.** 48kg and 52kg   **c.** 68kg and 82kg

5. Greco-Roman wrestling differs from freestyle in that Greco-Roman wrestlers
a. May not grasp the legs of their opponents or use their legs in any aggressive action
b. May not pin their opponents with both their legs and arms
c. Wear Roman tunics

6. Current Olympic matches are
   a. One-period, five-minute contests
   b. Two-round, three-minute contests
   c. Endless free-for-alls

7. Abraham Lincoln was
   a. Never dishonest
   b. Known to be an good wrestler
   c. Elected U.S. president in 1860

8. Greek wrestlers
   a. Have always dominated the middleweight categories of Greco-Roman wrestling
   b. Took their first-ever Greco-Roman medal in 1980
   c. Have never medaled in Greco-Roman wrestling

9. Hungary's 1928 gold medalist took up wrestling on his doctor's advice as a cure for
   a. Hyperactivity   **b.** SADD   **c.** "Prolonged neurosis"

10. Wrestling events at the 1964 Tokyo Games were dominated by
   a. The host country   **b.** The U.S. team   **c.** The Soviet team

YACHTING

Warm-up

T he sailing of boats has been a preferred mode of water travel ever since people got tired of rowing, sculling, paddling, or punting their boats wherever they needed to go. The Dutch—maybe the first to tire—were particularly adept at the art of sailing.

By the 17th century they had colonized parts of the Americas, southern Africa, and the East Indies. Plenty of goods needed shipping to and from the colonies, and these overseas cargoes were vulnerable to piracy. To protect their cargo ships, the Dutch developed fast, agile sailing vessels called *jaghtschips;* the *jaght* part of the name means "to chase, hunt, or pursue"; the *schip* part just has an extra "c" to infuriate Anglophones. These *jaghtschips* proved to be excellent vehicles in which to run down pirates and also, as it turned out, very fun to sail. They were fast and easy to handle, and soon the aristocrats (who cornered the market on fun in those days) were sailing *jaghtschips* for sport.

In 1660 England's King Charles I lost his government to Oliver Cromwell and was beheaded in the process. His son fled to Holland, head intact, and it was there that he was introduced to the *jaghtschip,* probably because he needed a little fun in his life at that time. When he returned home to England as the reigning monarch, Charles II, he brought with him one of these boats, graciously given to him by the East India Company (schmoozing knows no era). The new sport caught on around the British Empire, and the English adapted the craft's name as yacht (which isn't a great improvement, frankly).

The first organized sailing club was the Water Club of the Harbour of Cork, established in Ireland in 1720. Yachting spread to the New World where, in 1811, the first American club, the Knickerbocker Boat Club, was formed on Long Island.

In 1851 the first international yachting event took place with the running of the Hundred Guineas Cup race, a 60-mile circuit around the Isle of Wight. The brand-new New York Yacht Club sent the 110-ton schooner *America* to sail across the ocean and represent them in the race. The Americans not only competed, they triumphed. They duly brought home their trophy, renamed it the America's Cup and proceeded to defend it for the next 132 years. In 1983 *Australia II* defeated the American yacht *Liberty* and sailed away with the cup, breaking the longest win streak in sports history.

Yachting has been an Olympic sport since the 1896 Games in Athens, although in that Olympiad the yacht racing events were all canceled due to foul weather. At the start of the century the classes of boats sailed at Olympic Games and other international competitions were meter classes. In this system, officials rated boats with an elaborate set of rules and formulae based on length, breadth, and sail area, in order to place them into categories bearing names such as 8-meter, 10-meter, etc.

> "We're trying to eliminate the term yachting from the Olympics and have them call it sailing. The connotation is that it's a rich man's sport, and it's not."
> —Hal Haenel, crew of the 1992 U.S. team's gold-medaling Star class boat

What's important to realize is that an 8-meter boat, for instance, is *not* eight meters long, wide, tall, or deep. Rather, its various pertinent dimensions, taken together and arranged according to a formula, give it the 8-meter rating, and it can race against other boats accorded the 8-meter rating. The problem that arose at the turn of the century in Olympic yachting was that not all the entered countries were using the same method of rating boat classes. Obviously this could lead to severe inequities, since boat designs from one country might be limited more stringently than those from another.

In 1904 (an Olympiad with no yachting events, incidentally) Britain and France agreed (amazingly!) on a rating system called the International Rule of Rating. Universal acceptance was not forthcoming, however, and in 1906 the International Yacht Racing Union was formed. This group, comprised of several European countries, produced the "International Rule of 1906," which became the standard for the 1908 Games.

Over the years many alterations have been made to the list of boat classes raced in the Olympics. In 1908 a 15-meter event was offered, but no one entered it; a 15-meter boat would be at least 75 feet long, and an amateur crew to race such a boat must have been difficult to assemble, the idle rich notwithstanding. That year also marked the one-time-only appearance of a motorboat in Olympic competition, a very temporary bout of insanity.

At the 1920 Antwerp Games, 12-foot and 18-foot dinghy classes were added, beginning a trend toward smaller boats with smaller crews. Another trend moved away from the meter classes to the so-called "one-design" classes, in which each boat is built from the same design, with tight restrictions on modifications, so that boats are virtually identical; this way the sailing skills of the crew are what's being tested in a race. Two one-design classes, the Olympiajolle and the Finn, were created especially for Olympic competition.

Spectator's Guide

In sailing, an old cliché states that the shortest distance between two points is a "Z." What this tepid witticism refers to is the sailor's practice of **tacking** in a zig-zag pattern in order to travel in a direction opposite to the wind. Primitive sailing rigs couldn't sail upwind (opposite the direction of the wind) at all. The early sails were simply big pieces of cloth, like a bedspread billowing on the clothesline or a rain poncho suspended between canoe paddles. These sails would simply catch the breeze and push the boat downwind. If the wind was blowing the same direction that early sailors wanted to go, everyone could take it easy and let the wind carry the boat. Otherwise, it was time to get the oars or paddles back out, or else wait for the wind to change.

FACT: The purpose of one-design class racing is to allow the best sailor—not the best boat—to win.

In modern times, however, this inconvenience is hardly acceptable. A recreational sailor needs to be able to get back to his or her starting place (i.e., where the car is parked), and can't wait for the wind to change; and no sailor wants to motor any great distance (providing motors were invented). With the development of modern sail design, sailing in an upwind direction is possible, and this is accomplished through **tacking**.

The main type of sail on a modern sailboat is usually of triangular configuration. One vertical spar, the **mast**, is mounted on the bottom of the boat somewhere forward of the boat's midpoint. The horizontal spar, or **boom**, is attached perpendicular to the mast, just above the point where the mast enters the deck of the boat. The sail is attached to this framework of spars, the mast and boom.

The key to sailing against the wind is the cut of the sail, which allows it to bag out a bit in the forward area, creating an airfoil shape reminiscent of the profile of an airplane wing. The force generated by air rushing around this curved surface pulls the boat forward. Now, so that sailing won't be too easy for those aristocrats to master, there are limits. A boat cannot aim directly into the wind and hope to move at all. In fact, the closest it can come to sailing into the wind is about 45 degrees, a **point** of sailing known as **beating**. So, if your destination is dead into the wind, what you must do is set a course 45 degrees off the wind's direction on one side, then turn, or **tack**, to sail 45 degrees off the wind's direction on the other side. Thus the Z-shaped path.

To help the boat keep from sliding sideways during this routine, some form of **centerboard** is used. The centerboard extends below the boat's **hull** on a longitudinal plane (from bow to stern) like a fin. It can take the form of a retractable centerboard, which can be pulled up out of the water, or a fixed **keel**, which also serves to add stability by means of **ballast**, or extra weight.

Points of sailing in addition to beating include **running**, which is sailing directly with the wind, and **reaching**, which generally accounts for every arrangement between the two extremes of beating and running.

In competitive sailing, such as the Olympic yachting events, courses are devised that require a crew to use all the points of sailing. The course is in the form of a circuit composed of several segments, or **legs**. The terminal point of each leg is defined by a **buoy** or **mark**. In sailing the course, the boat must round the marks in sequence, but the precise route followed is left up to the skipper. Many of the strategic decisions made in yacht racing involve choosing the best route to reach each mark. On an upwind leg, for example, beating as close to the wind direction as possible may seem expeditious, but higher speed may be achieved by sailing "off the wind" somewhat and reaching instead.

Courses for the Olympics are laid out in varying lengths; the faster classes of boats sail the longer courses. An average course length is about eleven miles. The courses are each composed of six legs. The first leg is upwind, followed by two reaching legs, another upwind leg, a run, and a final upwind leg. Some of the boat classes are allowed to add to their rig large balloon-like sails, called **spinnakers**, that are used during the downwind legs. This presents quite a colorful display to the spectator.

One of the most interesting aspects of yacht racing is the start of the race, or, rather, that portion just prior to the start. As the beginning of the race approaches, visual and audible warnings are given at five-minute intervals. In the vicinity of the starting line, boats maneuver for position. At the moment the starting gun sounds, each crew wants to be as close to the line as possible, without going over it (sort of like "The Price Is Right"). A boat over the line at the gun is disqualified. Rules concerning right-of-way add to the excitement in the pre-race jockeying.

One race is sailed each day in each class. The better a crew finishes, the fewer the points received. Point totals for all the races are added together, dropping the worst race, to determine final standings. The Soling class is an exception to this scheme. Here, an initial fleet race determines the six top boats, which then compete in a round-robin sequence of match races (one-on-one) to decide the three medal positions.

FACT: In Olympic yachting, sailors are permitted to throw out their worst race.

For 1996 there are eight one-design classes of yacht being sailed in ten events. The **Finn,** a 14-foot 9-inch, single-handed, cat-rigged centerboard dinghy, has been in continuous Olympic use longer than any other class. It was designed in 1949 expressly for the 1952 Games in Finland. Only men sail Finns in Olympic competition.

The **Europe** is an 11-foot, single-handed, cat-rigged centerboard dinghy, often referred to as a small Finn due to its similar design. Its size is suited for smaller sailors and thus the Europe is sailed as a women's event at the Olympics.

The **470** is a 15-foot 5-inch, two-handed, sloop-rigged centerboard dinghy. The rigging on a 470 includes trapeze hardware for hiking out. Its inventory of sails includes a spinnaker. Women and men compete in separate events in this class.

The **Laser,** a 13-foot 11-inch, single-handed, cat-rigged centerboard dinghy makes its Olympic debut in 1996. It's a very popular production sailboat with 150,000 copies in use around the world. Olympic competition in the Laser is open to men and women.

The **Mistral IMCO** (International Mistral Class Organization) is a 12-foot 2-inch windsurfer or sailboard. To sail this type of craft the single sailor stands on what is essentially a surfboard. The sail attaches to the board at a single point by means of a flexible joint and the sailor controls the sail by holding a wishbone-shaped boom. Control of the boat is achieved by manipulating the sail and shifting body weight on the board; there is no rudder. Windsurfers are very fast and their crews practice a very physical form of sailing. Separate men's and women's events are held in this class.

The **Soling** is a 26-foot 11-inch, three-handed, sloop-rigged keelboat (having a fixed, ballast keel). It is the largest and heaviest boat in the Olympic fleet. In 1996, as in 1992, Solings will

A 470 crew member hikes out in a trapeze rig; by using "human ballast" more sail power can be generated while maintaining the optimum angle of heel. *Onne Van der Wal/U.S. Sailing*

A pack of Solings race a downwind leg with spinnakers deployed. *Onne Van der Wal/U.S. Sailing*

compete in match racing. The Soling carries a spinnaker for downwind legs. Soling competition is open to men and women.

The **Star** is a 22-foot 8-inch, two-handed, sloop-rigged keelboat. The Star is the oldest one-design sailboat. Olympic Star competition is open to men and women.

The **Tornado** is a 20-foot, two-handed, sloop-rigged catamaran. A catamaran ties two narrow, widely spaced hulls together with cross members. The broad platform formed by the two hulls enables a catamaran to carry a great deal of sail for its comparatively small weight. As a result, catamarans are very fast sailboats. Tornadoes can reach speeds as high as 30 miles per hour. In addition to being fast, catamarans are prone to cataclysmic capsizes. To prevent this occurrence and to keep the boat sailing with both hulls on or near the water, crew members hike out over the water on the upwind side of the boat, hanging from trapeze harnesses. All this makes for some pretty flamboyant sailing when the breeze is up. The Tornado class event is open to men and women.

Salty Talk for Gilligan and Skipper, Too

Ballast: Extra weight carried for stability; usually lodged in the fixed **keel.**

Beat: Point of sailing most directly upwind or into the wind (about 45 degrees from wind direction); also considered a **close reach.**

Boom: Horizontal pole or spar that the bottom of the sail attaches to.

With one hull flying and crew members hiked out, the Tornado is a vision of forces in balance. *Onne Van der Wal/U.S. Sailing*

Cat Rig: Sail plan composed of a single sail.

Centerboard: Fin-shaped protrusion under the hull that prevents the boat from sliding sideways; unlike a fixed **keel, a centerboard can be pulled out of the water.**

Genoa: In a sloop-rigged boat, the large triangular forward sail (larger than a **jib**, but used in the same way).

Heeling: A boat's side-to-side leaning due to the wind's force on the sail.

Hike or Hike out: To use body weight of crew members as ballast by hanging all or parts of bodies over the side of the boat.

Jib: In a sloop-rigged boat, the smaller triangular forward sail (smaller than a **genoa**, but used in the same way).

Keel: A fixed, fin-shaped protrusion on the bottom of the hull that prevents the boat's sideways slippage; also contains **ballast** (weight) to enhance stability.

Leg: A segment of the yachting race course.

Mark: Buoy that defines the endpoint of a **leg** of a race; racers must "round the mark."

Mast: Vertical spar or pole that the front edge of the sail attaches to.

Reach: Any of the points of sailing between the extremes of **beat** and **run**.

Rudder: Vertical board hinged to the back of the boat that turns the craft.

Run: Point of sailing in which the boat sails directly downwind or with the wind.

Sloop Rig: Sail plan composed of two sails: a mainsail and a **jib** or **genoa**.

Tack: To change direction relative to the wind direction (e.g., changing from having the wind on your right to having the wind on your left; also the term for the technique of sailing zig-zags to travel upwind.

Trapeze: An apparatus to support a hiked-out sailor. A cable is attached at one end to a point high on the boat's mast and at the other end to a harness worn by the "human ballast," who, thus suspended, can hike out far over the water on the upwind side of the boat to counteract heeling forces.

Spinnaker: Large, billowing sail that can be used in place of or with a **jib** or **genoa**; used on downwind points of sailing only.

Tiller: Stick attached to the rudder used by the skipper (played by Alan Hale, Jr.) to control steering.

Hopefuls

The 1996 Olympic yachting events will take place in Savannah, Georgia's Wassaw Sound, where more than 400 competitors will vie in ten medal events. The venue's logistics and location were initially protested by the International Yacht Racing Union and environmentalists. The latter were concerned about damage to the vulnerable wetlands, wildlife, and barrier islands situated between the mainland and open racing waters. For racers, the temporary offshore marina arrangement raised issues about storing and towing boats.

FACT: The *America*[3] Foundation is providing funding for the U.S. sailing team, supplying money, technology, equipment, coaches, meteorologists, oceanographers, physiologists, and a sports psychologist.

The U.S. sailing team will have the advantage of competing on home waters, and comes to the 1996 Olympic Games leading in total Olympic yachting medals won. Of the 48 medals the U.S. has won at the Games, 21 have been earned in the last three Olympiads. An experienced U.S. team will once again raise its sails in 1996. Gold medalists in the Star class in 1992, U.S. sailors Mark Reynolds and Hal Haenel will once again compete. Also competing in that class will be countryman Jon Kostecki, the 1988 Soling class silver medalist. In the Finn class, 1992 Olympic silver medalist Brian Ledbetter looks likely to medal again for the U.S., as do men's 470 class sailors Morgan Reeser and Kevin Burnham, who also took silver in their class in 1992. Allison Jolly and Lynne Shore will try to repeat their 1988 gold medal performance for the U.S. in the women's 470 class. Men's Mistral sailor Mike Gebhardt of Ft. Pierce, Florida, will try to better the silver he had to settle for in Barcelona after being waylaid mid-race by a floating snag. Crewing for his wife, Pease Glaser, in the Tornado class will be 1984 Tornado class silver medalist Jay Glaser. Returning for a second Olympics on the U.S. team are boardsailor Lanee Butler and Tornado skipper Pete Melvin.

—Steve Carey

Schedule

The tentative yachting schedule is:

Monday, July 22
Men's & Women's Mistral
Men's & Women's 470, Star, Finn

Tuesday, July 23
Men's & Women's Mistral
Men's & Women's 470, Star, Finn

Wednesday, July 24
Men's & Women's Mistral
Men's & Women's 470, Star, Finn, Soling, Tornado

Thursday, July 25
Laser, Europe, Soling, Tornado

Friday, July 26
Laser, Europe, Star, Finn, Soling, Tornado

Saturday, July 27
Men's & Women's Mistral, Laser, Europe,
Star, Finn, Soling, Tornado

Sunday, July 28
Men's & Women's Mistral, 470
Star and Finn finals
Soling

Monday, July 29
Men's & Women's Mistral finals
Men's & Women's 470
Laser, Europe, Tornado

Tuesday, July 30
Men's & Women's 470 finals
Laser, Europe
Tornado finals

Wednesday, July 31
Soling match races
Laser, Europe finals

Thursday, August 1
Soling match race finals

Highlights

Although scheduled to be held in the Bay of Salmis in 1896, the first Olympic regattas were held at Meulan and Le Havre, with six nations participating, as part of the 1900 Paris Games. After the sport's eight-year Olympic hiatus, five nations competed in the London Games, but the winners in every class were British. Frances Clytie Rivett-Carnac, who won the seven-meter class with her husband, was the first woman to win in an event not restricted to women or mixed pairs in any sport. Also that year, the Olympic program featured two motorboating events, which were subsequently deep-sixed from the Games.

Four sailing events were held in 1912, the year when four Norwegian brothers—Henrik, Jan, Kristian, and Ole Östervold—won gold medals in the 12-meter class. By 1920 the total number of events had risen to 13, with a complicated scoring system that combined all the races for all the boats of each country. Norway won with 11 yachts sailing in 27 races. Sweden took two classes, the 30- and 40-meter classes; the crew of the larger boat included the Swedish designer Tore Holm.

> "Basically [winning at the Olympics is] a matter of putting more hours into it than the next guy. Preparing the bottom of your boat better."
>
> —Mark Reynolds, skipper of the 1992 U.S. team's gold-medaling Star class boat

Nineteen countries took part in the yachting events in Paris in 1924, when the competition was trimmed to three categories. The Dinghy class was won by the Belgians, while Norway sailed away with two medals in the meter classes: Eugen Lunde, whose son, grandson, and daughter-in-law medaled in the 1952 and 1960 Games, sailed the winning Norwegian six-meter in the Paris regatta, while the father-son crew of the two August Ringvolds sailed to victory in the eight-meter event.

The 1928 Olympic regatta hosted a number of celebrities. Twenty-three countries participated in three classes, and the Crown Prince of Norway—soon to be known as King Olav V—won the gold for the six-meter class in *Norna*, while his compatriot, Henrik Robert, won his second silver medal in the 12-foot Dinghy. The well-known French yachtswoman, Virginie Hériot, also made her appearance in the Amsterdam regatta, in a yacht chosen from her fleet named *L'Ailée VI*.

Only eleven countries entered the LA Games, where Tore Holm won his second gold medal, this time in the six-meter. The French captured the single-handed Dinghy, while gold in the Star class, appearing for the first time, was taken by the U.S. The host country also managed to keep the eight-meter gold at home. The number of participating countries climbed back to twenty-six in the Berlin Games, where the Kieler Förde was the site of the Olympic races. Twenty-five boats participated in the special class of the Olympiajolle, by far the most popular class of 1936; the Netherlands won that class, while the host country took the Star, Great Britain the six-meter, and Italy the eight-meter.

Twenty-three countries participated in the post-war regatta, which was held at Torbay, on the south coast of England. Denmark's Paul Elvstrom won the first of four consecutive one-design titles—from 1948 to 1960—making him the first man to hold on to a title through four quadrennia—in any sport. Also that year, Norwegian Magnus Konow matched the longest span of Olympic participation when he competed in the six-meter events four decades after he first competed in the eight-meter class of 1908, and Great Britain's Durward Knowles took part in the first of what would be a record of seven Olympic Games.

Rickard Sarby, a Swedish hairdresser, submitted the winning Firefly single-hander in the 1952 Games, and Sarby's Finn remained the Olympic single-hander in subsequent Games. Having come in fourth at Torbay, Sarby earned a bronze in the Firefly at the Helsinki Games. A total of 29 countries participated: Norwegian Thor Thorvladsen captured his second gold in the Dragon, and Italy won the gold in the Star. American Herman Whiton won his second gold in the six-meter, and his compatriot, Dr. Britton Chance—sailing the only American 5.5-meter of the day—took home the gold as well.

In 1956, 28 countries competed with a total of 71 boats, not least of which was the royally pedigreed *Bluebottle*, owned by Queen Elizabeth II and Prince Philip, and skippered by the Royal

Navy's Commander Graham Mann. While the *Bluebottle* took the bronze for the Dragon, Sweden's Folke Bohlin won on a tie breaker with Denmark's Ole Bernsten in that class. New Zealand took the 12-meter and the U.S. claimed gold in the Star, while Paul Elvstrom went on to his third gold medal, in the Finn class.

The Russians took their first yachting gold medal at Naples in 1960, in the Star class, albeit in an American boat with American sails. The U.S. took the 5.5-meter gold, while the Dragon gold this time went to the Crown Prince Constantine of the Hellenes, who would later become the King of Greece. Norwegian Peder Lunde, Jr.—part of the famous Lunde sailing clan—took the inaugural Flying Dutchman gold, while Paul Elvstorm won yet another gold in the single-handed Dinghy.

At Enoshima, in 1964, Denmark's Ole Berntsen this time succeeded in capturing the Dragon gold; the Flying Dutchman went to New Zealand, while the Bahamas captured the Star. Although East and West Germany entered a combined team, the IYRU authorized a West German helmsman, Willi Kuhweide, who took the Finn gold for Germany.

In Acapulco in 1968, 123 boats from 41 countries competed. The Soviets medaled again, this time in the Finn class. Great Britain's Flying Dutchman, *Super . . . docious*, helmed by Rodney Pattison, finished first in every race except one. Pattison not only won the Flying Dutchman, but set records as well; their record-setting boat is now in the Britain's National Maritime Museum in Greenwich, England.

In 1972, when the Soling and Tempest classes were introduced, 42 countries competed with 165 boats in six classes. Bud Melges, Bill Allen, and Bill Bensten won the gold medal for the U.S. in the Soling class, while Glen Foster and Peter Dean earned a silver in the Tempest; the crew of Don Cohan, Charles Horter, and John Marshall took the bronze in the Dragon class. Soviet Valentin Mankin won his second gold in the Finn class, Australia won the Star and the Dragon, while Serg Maury won the gold for France in the Finn class. Great Britain's Rodney Pattisson won his second Flying Dutchman gold in *Superdoso*, and Paul Elvstrom, who had attempted to become the first man to win gold medals at five different Games, finished only 13th overall in the Soling class.

The Danish Soling team won by such a narrow margin in 1976 that another eight seconds would have put them out of the running for medals. The U.S. team of John Kolius, Walter Glasgow, and Richard Hoepfner came in second, while the German Democratic Republic took third. The U.S. also took a silver in the

Tornado, and a bronze in the now discontinued Tempest class, with a crew of Dennis Conner and Conn Findlay.

At the age of 41, Valentin Mankin captured his third gold medal for the Soviets in the Star class in 1980, when the host country won an additional silver and bronze. Brazil took two golds at Moscow, in the Tornado and 470 classes, while Spain's victory in the Flying Dutchman class was its lone gold in the 1980 Games. Denmark, in the Soling class, and Finland, in the Finn class, were the other gold medalist nations. Also in 1980, a yachtsman competed from Botswana, a country so arid that it calls its money by the Botswanian word for "rain."

All 13 members of the U.S. team won either gold or silver medals at the 1984 Games: U.S. skippers captured three golds and four silvers in seven classes of boats. The most "weathered" sailor of 1984 was Denmark's Paul Elvstrom, at 59, whose fourth and last Olympic gold had come in 1960; his daughter Trine served as crew, flying on the boat-stabilizing trapeze of the Tornado catamaran class; the boat came in fourth. Also that year, Canadians and New Zealanders won three medals each. In the debut appearance of windgliding at the Games, the Netherlands won the gold medal while Randall Scott Steele of the U.S. took the silver; Bruce Kendall of New Zealand came in third.

1988 marked the inauguration of women's yachting events at the Games, and the team of Allison Jolly and Lynne Jewell won the women's 470 class for the U.S.; Sweden and the Soviet Union came in second and third; a French team won the men's 470. New Zealand's Bruce Kendall this time took first place in windgliding's second appearance at the Games, Spain took the Finn class gold— while the Virgin Islands took the silver—Denmark won the Flying Dutchman, East Germany the Soling, and Great Britain won the Star class, in which the U.S. took silver. France captured the Tornado class, while New Zealand and Brazil placed second and third, respectively.

Dennis Conner

Some sports fans know Dennis Conner as the first American in 132 years to lose the America's Cup, in 1983, and then reclaim it in 1987 with a controversial catamaran he entered in the competition through a loophole in the rules. And then lose it again in 1995 in a thrashing defeat.

Others know him as a man who is simply obsessed with winning—at any and all costs. "I think I'm abnormal, yes," Conner confessed to *The New York Times* in September, 1990.

Few know him as an Olympian. But bad boy Dennis Conner, 49, won a bronze medal for the United States during the 1976 Montreal Olympics, competing in the Tempest small-boat class, an event that Conner has characterized as "the America's Cup of small-boat racing."

Conner describes himself in his book, *No Excuse To Lose*, as a chubby, clumsy kid with a "bit of an inferiority complex," who hung out around the San Diego Yacht Club, a half block—five doors—from his house, "the way some kids hang around the local pool parlor."

The son of a commercial fisherman and factory worker, Conner had a paper route for the *San Diego Union* and a *TV Guide* route and was constantly doing boat chores for the club's sailors in exchange for rides.

He didn't so much develop a passion for sailing as he did a single-minded drive to succeed. "Sailing was one of the few things that I could do really well," Conner wrote in his book, "and since it was important for me to excel at something, I kept at it."

He told *Time* magazine in 1987: "I don't like to sail. I like to compete. I guess I don't *dislike* it, but my sailing is just the bottom line, like adding up the final score in bridge. My real interest is in the tremendous game of life."

He wrote in his book: "It's almost as though I'm addicted to the competition."

At Kingston, Ontario, in 1976, site of the small boat Olympic events, Conner and crewmate Conn Findlay were leading by almost four minutes at a stage in the fifth—and pivotal—of the seven races. Wind shifts and a flat calm dropped them to ninth and out of serious contention for a gold medal, the "one Olympic medal," he said heading into the race, "that really counts."

Conner and Findlay's bad luck was described by one racing expert as a "whim of the weather, something no one can predict. The wind just lightened up—he got shut out."

After the race, Conner, ever the competitor, said: "Winning the bronze medal was a lot better than winning no medal at all, but losing the chance at the gold because of that terrible fifth race was depressing."

Described as emotional, often less than articulate, and lacking in charisma—though highly intelligent and amazingly retentive—Conner was depicted by sailing competitors in *American Baby* magazine as someone with "an ability to judge time and distance with mechanical accuracy, a skill which is uncanny," and as a person "able to concentrate [a] highly technical mind for long periods on a single goal, to the exclusion of almost everything else."

No surprises there. Conner, who runs a wholesale and retail carpeting and drapery business in San Diego, postponed his wedding day twice because of sailboat races.

"Let me tell you how ambitious Dennis was," Conner's mother, Pamela, told *The New York Times*. "He would go [to the service station at the corner] and take the discarded oil cans . . . and he would drain the oil into a jar. He'd sell the oil back to the guys at the yacht club."

In the period leading up to the 1992 Games, Conner was competing *against* the Olympics. In trying to raise $27 million in corporate pledges for his May 1992 America's Cup defense in San Diego, he bucked up against fundraisers trying to woo some to the same sponsors—and money—for the Barcelona Games. Ultimately Conner raised only $15 million and had to settle for retrofitting an old boat for the 1992 Cup defense, for which race officials had stipulated altered boat specifications. Conner lost his chance to defend the America's Cup in 1992 to Bill Koch's *America³*, which retained the Cup for the U.S. against an Italian challenger.

Conner sailed some legs of the Whitbread 'Round the World race in 1993 while lining up sponsorship for his 1995 America's Cup bid. In the early rounds of the defender trials for that race Conner angered the all-female crew of the *America³*'s *Mighty Mary*— as well as the rest of the world—by reportedly referring to the contender as the "lesbo boat." His crew was observed to hurl insults and gesture obscenely at the women athletes. When Conner replaced his boat's keel partway through the defender trials, the repair drew a protest from the *America³* team, who claimed that the keel was illegally approved, illegally configured, and illegally positioned.

The defender finals came down to a three-way series of races between the *Mighty Mary*, Conner's *Stars & Stripes*, and PACT95's *Young America*. Over the course of the series' tight competition, Conner accused *Mighty Mary* and *Young America* of joining forces to stay alive in the three-way struggle and thereby violating fair play. Conner nonetheless emerged victorious, earning the right to defend the Cup against challenger Team New Zealand, sailing *Black Magic* under skipper Peter Blake. When Conner left the *Stars & Stripes* ashore and leased rival boat *Young America* (for a reported $300,000) to face New Zealand, some were stunned, perhaps none more so than *Stars & Stripes* designer David Pedrick, who issued a four-page news release questioning the wisdom and ethics of the switch. It was the first time a finalist had switched boats so late in the competition, but as *Time* magazine's Margot Hornblower reported, Conner would "do anything to prevent his worst nightmare: losing the Cup to Australia in 1983, which was the first time the Auld Mug had ever passed out of American hands."

Yet the nightmare recurred. Conner lost the America's Cup again on May 13, 1995, this time in the first 5-0 sweep in the 144-year history of the race. Some blamed the trouncing on the superior sailing skills of the Kiwi team. According to John Carey writing in *Business Week,* "the New Zealanders consistently read the wind shifts better, in part because of better seat-of-the-pants weather forecasting. And in the one race with stronger winds—conditions where the wider, more stable *Young America* had a predicted speed advantage—Conner blew it by picking the wrong mainsail."

But most yachting experts attributed Conner's defeat to boat design. In particular, the design enabled *Black Magic* to sail much closer to the wind than the other boats, so it gained time on the upwind legs of races. "The America's Cup is, after all, a design-driven competition," explained E.M. Swift in *Sports Illustrated.* "The fastest boat—as opposed to the best sailors— nearly always wins." Perhaps the experience has left Conner, an acknowledged master sailor, hankering for his Olympic days, when he was racing against identical boats and winning on skill and wits.

—*Eric Kinkopf with Steve Carey*

FACT: The first organized sailing club was the Water Club of the Harbour of Cork, established in Ireland in 1720. Yachting spread to the New World where, in 1811, the first American club, the Knickerbocker Boat Club, was formed on Long Island.

Highlights from Barcelona

Yachting at the 1992 Games was notable for the proximity of the courses to a topless beach and the condition of the venue's Mediterranean waters: horribly polluted. Sailors reported encountering all kinds of debris and sludge in the water. (The Besos, which flows into the Mediterranean not far from the Olympic port, was labeled Europe's dirtiest river in a report by the European community.) U.S. sailor Mike Gebhardt was headed for a gold medal in one sailboard race when a plastic garbage bag fouled his centerboard and killed his headway. By the time he untangled his craft, Gebhardt had to settle for a silver behind Franck David of France.

Competing in these notorious home waters, Spanish sailors pirated the most gold at the 1992 Games, winning four gold medals in addition to one silver. As expected, U.S. sailors compiled the highest medal tally, earning one gold, six silver, and two bronze medals. Apparently, the U.S. team's experience was of value in Barcelona, as four of the entries had seen prior Olympic competition. France captured two gold medals; New Zealand took one gold, two silver, and one bronze Down Under; Denmark vindicated the Vikings with a gold and a bronze, as did Norway with a lone gold; and Australia cast off with two bronze medals, while Britain and Canada each polished off a bronze as well.

Europe's royal House of Borbon has contributed many sailors to Olympic competition over the years: Spain's Queen Sofia sailed in the 1960 Rome Games along with Greece's King Constantine, who won the gold in the Dragon class. Spain's King Juan Carlos competed in the 1972 Munich Games, his daughter sailed in the 1988 Seoul Olympics, and his son (Crown Prince Felipe) crewed for Spain in the Soling class in Barcelona.

FACT: Spain's Crown Prince Felipe, who competed in the Soling class at the 1992 Olympics, carried the national flag in the athletes' procession at the Barcelona Games.

Medalists

Yachting—Men's 470

1992
1. Spain (Jordi Calafat, Francisco Sanchez)
2. U.S.A. (Morgan Reeser, Kevin Burnham)
3. Estonia (Tonu Toniste, Toomas Toniste)

1988
1. France, 34.70, Thierry Peponnet, Luc Pillot
2. Soviet Union, 46.00, Tynou Tyniste, Toomas Tyniste
3. U.S.A., 51.00, John Shadden, Charlie McKee

1984
1. Spain, 33.70, Jose Luis Doreste, Roberto Molina
2. U.S.A., 43.00, Stephen Benjamin, H. Christopher Steinfeld
3. France, 49.40, Thierry Peponnet, Luc Pillot

1980
1. Brazil, 36.4, Marcos Pinto Rizzo Soares, Eduardo Henrique Penido
2. East Germany, 38.7, Jorn Borowski, Egbert Swensson

3. Finland, 39.7, Jouko Lindgren, Georg Tallberg

1976
1. West Germany, 42.40, Frank Huebner, Harro Bode
2. Spain, 49.70, Antonio Gorostegui, Pedro Luis Millet
3. Australia, 57.00, Ian Brown, Ian Ruff

Yachting—Women's 470

1992
1. Spain (Theresa Zabell, Patricia Guerra)
2. New Zealand (Leslie Jean Egnot, Janet Shearer)
3. U.S.A. (J.J. Isler, Pam Healy)

1988
1. U.S.A., 26.70, Allison Jolly, Lynne Jewell
2. Sweden, 40.00, Marit Soderstrom, Birgitta Bengtsson
3. Soviet Union, 45.40, Larissa Moskalenko, Irina Tchounikhovskai

Yachting—Finn

1992
1. Jose Van Der Ploeg, Spain
2. Brian Ledbetter, U.S.A.
3. Craig Monk, New Zealand

1988
1. Jose Luis Doreste, Spain, 38.10
2. Peter Holmerg, Virgin Islands, 40.40
3. John Cutler, New Zealand, 45.00

1984
1. Russell Coutts, New Zealand, 34.70
2. John Bertrand, U.S.A., 37.00
3. Terry Neilson, Canada, 37.70

1980
1. Esko Rechardt, Finland, 36.7
2. Wolfgang Mayrhofer, Austria, 46.7
3. Andrei Balashov, Soviet Union, 47.4

1976
1. Jochen Schumann, East Germany, 35.40
2. Andrei Balashov, Soviet Union, 39.70
3. John Bertrand, Australia, 46.40

1972
1. Serge Maury, France, 58.0
2. Ilias Hatzipavlis, Greece, 71.0
3. Viktor Potapov, Soviet Union, 74.7

1968
1. Valentin Mankin, Soviet Union, 11.7
2. Hubert Raudaschl, Austria, 53.4
3. Fabio Albarelli, Italy, 55.1

1964
1. Wilhelm Kuhweide, West Germany, 7638
2. Peter Barrett, U.S.A., 6373
3. Henning Wind, Denmark, 6190

1960
1. Paul Elvstrom, Denmark, 8171
2. Aleksandr Chuchelov, Soviet Union, 6520
3. Andre Nelis, Belgium, 5934

1956
1. Paul Elvstrom, Denmark, 7509
2. Andre Nelis, Belgium, 6254
3. John Marvin, U.S.A., 5953

1952
1. Paul Elvstrom, Denmark, 8209
2. Charles Currey, Great Britain, 5449
3. Rickard Sarby, Sweden 5051

1948
1. Paul Elvstrom, Denmark, 5543
2. Ralph Evans, U.S.A., 5408
3. Jacobus H. de Jong, Netherlands, 5204

1936
1. Daniel M. J. Kagchelland, Netherlands, 163
2. Werner Krogmann, Germany, 150
3. Peter M. Scott, Great Britain, 131

1932
1. Jacques Lebrun, France, 87
2. Adriaan L. J. Maas, Netherlands, 85
3. Santiago Amat Cansino, Spain, 76

1928
1. Sven Thorell, Sweden
2. Henrik Robert, Norway
3. Bertil Broman, Finland

1924
1. Leon Huybrechts, Belgium, 2
2. Henrik Robert, Norway, 7
3. Hans Dittmar, Finland, 8

1896–1920
Not held

Yachting—Europe

1992
1. Linda Anderson, Norway
2. Natalia Via Dufresne, Spain
3. Julia Trotman, U.S.A.

Yachting—Flying Dutchman

1992
1. Spain (Luis Doreste, Domingo Manrique)
2. U.S.A. (Paul Foerster, Stephen Bourdow)
3. Denmark (Jorgen Bojsen, Jens Bojsen)

1988
1. Denmark, 31.40, Jorgen Bojsen-Moller, Christian Gronborg
2. Norway, 37.40, Olepetter Pollen, Erik Bjorkum
3. Canada, 48.40, Frank McLaughlin, John Millen

1984
1. U.S.A., 19.70, Jonathan McKee, William Carl Buchan
2. Canada, 22.70, Terry McLaughlin, Evert Bastet
3. Great Britain, 48.70, Jonathan Richards, Peter Allam

1980
1. Spain, 30.0, Alesandro Abascal, Miguel Noguer
2. Ireland, 30.0, David Wilkins, James Wilkinson
3. Hungary, 45.7, Szabolcs Detre, Zsolt Detre

1976

1. West Germany, 34.70, Jorg Diesch, Eckart Diesch
2. Great Britain, 51.70, Rodney Pattison, Julian Brooke Houghton
3. Brazil, 52.10, Reinaldo Conrad, Peter Ficker

1972

1. Great Britain, 22.7, Rodney Pattison, Christopher Davies
2. France, 40.7, Yves Pajot, Marc Pajot
3. West Germany, 51.1, Ullrich Libor, Peter Naumann

1968

1. Great Britain, 3.0 Rodney Pattison, Iain S. MacDonald-Smith
2. West Germany, 43.7, Ullrich Libor, Peter Naumann
3. Brazil, 48.4, Reinaldo Conrad, Burkhard Cordes

1964

1. New Zealand, 6255, Helmer Pedersen, Earle Wells
2. Great Britain, 5556, Franklyn Musto, Arthur Morgan
3. U.S.A., 5158, Harry Melges, William Bentsen

1960

1. Norway, 6774, Peder Lunde Jr., Bjorn Bergvall
2. Denmark, 5991, Hans Fogh, Ole Erik Petersen
3. West Germany, 5882, Rolf Mulka, Ingo von Bredow, Achim Kadelbach

1896–1956

Not held

Yachting—Division II Sailboard (Windgliding)

1992

1. Franck David, France
2. Mike Gebhardt, U.S.A.
3. Lars Kleppich, Australia

1988

1. Bruce Kendall, New Zealand, 35.40
2. Jan D. Boersma, Netherlands Antilles, 42.70
3. Michael Gebhardt, U.S.A., 48.00

1984

1. Stephan Van Den Berg, Netherlands, 27.70
2. Randall Scott Steele, U.S.A., 46.00
3. Bruce Kendall, New Zealand, 46.40

Yachting—Women's Sailboard

1992

1. Barbara Kendall, New Zealand
2. Zhang Xiaodong, China
3. Dorien De Vries, Netherlands

Yachting—Soling

1992

1. Denmark (Jesper Bank, Steen Secher, Jesper Seier)
2. U.S.A. (Kevin Mahaney, James Brady, Doug Kern)
3. Britain (Lawrence Smith, Robert Cruikshank, Simon Stewart)

1988

1. East Germany, 11.70, Jochen Schuemann, Thomas Flach, Bernd Jackel
2. U.S.A., 14.00, John Kostecki, William Baylis, Robert Billingham
3. Denmark, 52.70, Jesper Bank, Jesper Mathiasen, Steen Secher

1984

1. U.S.A., 33.70, Robert Haines Jr., Edward Trevelyan, Roderick Davis
2. Brazil, 43.40, Torben Grael, Daniel Adler, Ronaldo Senfft
3. Canada, 49.70, Hans Fogh, John Kerr, Steve Calder

1980

1. Denmark, 23.0, Paul R. H. Jensen, Valdemar Bandolowski, Erik Hansen
2. Soviet Union, 30.4, Boris Budnikov, Aleksandr Budnikov, Nikolai Poliakov
3. Greece, 31.1, Anastassios Boudouris, Anastassios Gavrilis, Aristidis Rapanakis

1976

1. Denmark, 46.70, Paul R. H. Jensen, Valdemar Bandolowski, Erik Hansen
2. U.S.A., 47.40, John Kolius, Walter Glasgow, Richard Hoepfner
3. East Germany, 47.40, Dieter Below, Michael Zachries, Olaf Engelhardt

1972

1. U.S.A., 8.7, Harry Melges, William Bentsen, William Allen
2. Sweden, 31.7, Stig Wennerstrom, Lennart Roslund, Bo Knape, Stefan Krook
3. Canada, 47.1, David Miller, John Ekels, Paul Cote

1896–1968

Not held

Yachting—Star

1992
1. U.S.A. (Mark Reynolds, Hal Haenel)
2. New Zealand (Roderick Davis, Donald Cowie)
3. Canada (D. Ross MacDonald, Eric Jespersen)

1988
1. Great Britain, 45.70, Michael McIntyre, Bryn Vaile
2. U.S.A., 48.00, Mark Reynolds, Hal Haenal
3. Brazil, 50.00, Torben Grael, Nelson Falcao

1984
1. U.S.A., 29.70, William E. Buchan, Stephen Erikson
2. West Germany, 41.40, Joachim Griese, Michael Marcour
3. Italy, 43.50, Giorgio Gorla, Alfio Peraboni

1980
1. Soviet Union, 24.7, Valentin Mankin, Aleksandr Muzychenko
2. Austria, 31.7, Hubert Raudaschl, Karl Ferstl
3. Italy, 36.1, Giorgio Gorla, Alfio Peraboni

1976
Not held

1972
1. Australia, 28.1, David Forbes,John Anderson
2. Sweden, 44.0, Pelle Pettersson, Stellan Westerdahl
3. West Germany, 44.4, Wilhelm Kuhweide, Karsten Meyer

1968
1. U.S.A., 14.4, Lowell North, Peter Barrett
2. Norway, 43.7, Peder Lunde, Per Olav Wiken
3. Italy, 44.7, Franco Cavallo, Camilo Gargano

1964
1. Bahamas, 5664, Durward Knowles, C. Cecil Cooke
2. U.S.A., 5585, Richard Stearns, Lynn Williams
3. Sweden, 5527, Pelle Pettersson, Holger Sundstrom

1960
1. Soviet Union, 7619, Timir Pinegin, Fyodor Shutkov
2. Portugal, 6665, Jose Quina, Mario Quina
3. U.S.A., 6269, William Parks, Robert Halperin

1956
1. U.S.A., 5876, Herbert Williams, Lawrence Low
2. Italy, 5649, Agostino Straulino, Nicolo Rode
3. Bahamas, 5223, Durward Knowles, Sloan Farrington

1952
1. Italy, 7635, Agostino Straulino, Nicolo Rode
2. U.S.A., 7126, John Reid, John Price
3. Portugal, 4903, Joaquim De Mascarenhas Fiuza, Francisco Rebelo De Andrade

1948
1. U.S.A., 5828, Hilary Smart, Paul Smart
2. Cuba, 4949, Carlos De Cardenas Culmell, Carlos De Cardenas, Jr.
3. Netherlands, 4731, Adriaan Maas, Edward Sutterheim

1936
1. Germany, 80, Peter Bischoff, Hans-Joachim Weise
2. Sweden, 64, Arvid Laurin, Uno Wallentin
3. Netherlands, 63, Willem de Vries-Lentsch, Adriaan Maas

1932
1. U.S.A., 46, Gilbert Gray, Andrew Libano
2. Great Britain, 35, Colin Ratsey, Peter Jaffe
3. Sweden, 28, Gunnar Asther, Danile Sunden-Cullberg

1896–1928
Not held

Yachting—Tornado

1992
1. France (Yves Loday, Nicolas Henard)
2. U.S.A. (Randy Smyth, Keith Notary)
3. Australia (Mitch Booth, John Forbes)

1988
1. France, 16.00, Jean-Yves Le Deroff, Nicolas Henard
2. New Zealand, 35.40, Christopher Timms, Rex Sellers
3. Brazil, 40.10, Lars Grael, Clinio Freitas

1984
1. New Zealand, Rex Sellers, Christopher Timms
2. U.S.A., Randy Smyth, Jay Glaser
3. Australia, Chris Cairns, John Anderson

1980
1. Brazil, 21.4, Alexandre Welter, Lars Sigurd Bjorkstrom
2. Denmark, 30.4, Peter Due, Per Kjergard
3. Sweden, 33.7, Goran Marstrom, Jorgen Ragnarsson

1976
1. Great Britain, 18.00, Reginald White, John Osborn
2. U.S.A., 36.00, David McFaull, Michael Rothwell

3. West Germany, 37.70, Jorg Spengler, Jorg Schmall

Yachting—Tempest

1976
1. Sweden, 14.0, John Albrechtson, Ingvar Hansson
2. Soviet Union, 30.4, Valentin Mankin, Vladislav Akimenko
3. U.S.A., 32.7, Dennis Conner, Conn Findlay

1972
1. Soviet Union, 28.1, Valentin Mankin, Vitali Dyrdyra
2. Great Britain, 34.4, Alan Warren, David Hunt
3. U.S.A., 47.7, Glen Foster, Peter Dean

1896–1968
Not held

Trivia Quiz

1. The first organized sailing club was the Water Club of
   a. Long Island, New York   **b.** Cork, Ireland   **c.** Baja, California

2. The America's Cup traces its roots to
   a. New York's Knickerbocker Boat Club
   b. The Hundred Guineas Cup race around the Isle of Wight
   c. The East India Company's boat club

3. Americans successfully defended the America's Cup for
   a. 53 years   **b.** 132 years   **c.** 72 years

4. In the 1896 Olympics in Athens, yachting events
   a. Were not included on the program
   b. Were canceled due to foul weather
   c. Attracted the most participants of any sport that year

5. A 10-meter boat is 10 meters
   a. Long   **b.** Wide   **c.** Deep   **d.** Tall   **e.** None of the above

6. The 1908 Olympics included
   a. A 15-meter event   **b.** A motor-boating event   **c.** A surfing event

7. "Genoa" refers to
   a. A sail plan composed of two sails
   b. The large triangular forward sail in a sloop-rigged boat
   c. Salami, the sailor's favorite lunchmeat.

8. The International Rule of 1906 was introduced
   a. To confuse spectators
   b. To establish rules governing the composition of boat crews
   c. To create a standard method of rating boat classes

9. Sailboarding

a. Has never been included in the Olympic program

b. Made its Olympic debut in 1984 in Los Angeles.

c. Was included as a demonstration sport at the 1980 Lake Placid Games.

10. The dragon class gold medal at the 1960 Rome Games went to

a. Bob Mathias, who later became a U.S. congressman.

b. Crown Prince Constantine, who later became King of Greece

c. Dennis Conner, who later became Dennis Conner.

OLYMPIC GAMES:
SCHEDULE OF EVENTS

Note: The Games are being broadcast in the United States by the NBC television network and in Canada by the CBC television network. Please check local listings for broadcast times and channels. (The following is a complete listing of events and their tentative times and dates. Many events may not be televised.)

July 15
11:00 a.m.–8:30 p.m.: Gymnastics, men's podium training—compulsory

July 16
12:00 p.m.–8:30 p.m.: Gymnastics, Women's podium training—compulsory

July 17
11:00 a.m.–8:30 p.m.: Gymnastics, men's podium training—optional

July 18
12:00 p.m.–8:30 p.m.: Gymnastics, Women's podium training—optional

July 19
8:30 p.m.–11:59 p.m.: Opening Ceremony

July 20
8:30 a.m.–1:00 p.m.: Field Hockey, Women's pool 1 & 2
9:00 a.m.–11:00 a.m.: Field Hockey, men's pool 1

9:00 a.m.–3:15 p.m.: Shooting, Women's 10m air rifle preliminaries & final, men's trap preliminaries
9:15 a.m.–11:11 a.m.: Gymnastics—Artistic, men's team compulsories
9:30 a.m.–1:23 p.m.: Judo, Women's & men's heavyweight (+72kg & +95kg) preliminaries & repechages
10:00 a.m.–1:00 p.m.: Baseball, game # 1
10:00 a.m.–1:30 p.m.: Basketball, men's preliminaries, games 1 & 2
10:00 a.m.–1:00 p.m.: Fencing, men's individual épée 1/32, 1/16, 1/8 & quarterfinals
10:00 a.m.–2:30 p.m.: Volleyball, Women's preliminaries, matches 1 & 2
10:00 a.m.–12:50 p.m.: Wrestling—Greco-Roman, 48kg, 57kg, 68kg, 82kg & 100kg preliminaries
10:05 a.m.–12:07 p.m.: Swimming, Women's 100 free preliminaries, men's 100 breaststroke preliminaries

821

11:00 a.m.–1:40 p.m.: Water Polo, preliminaries, games 1 & 2

12:30 p.m.–2:38 p.m.: Gymnastics—Artistic, men's team compulsories

12:30 p.m.–2:30 p.m.: Weightlifting, 54 kg group B

1:30 p.m.–5:00 p.m.: Boxing, first round session 1

3:00 p.m.–6:00 p.m.: Baseball, game # 2

3:00 p.m.–6:30 p.m.: Basketball, men's preliminaries, games 3 & 4

3:00 p.m.–4:40 p.m.: Fencing, men's individual épée semifinals 1 and 2, bronze & gold

3:00 p.m.–4:27 p.m.: Judo, Women's & men's heavyweight (+72kg & +95kg) final rounds & medal matches

3:00 p.m.–5:00 p.m.: Soccer, men's match 1

3:30 p.m.–6:10 p.m.: Water Polo, preliminaries, games 3 & 4

3:30 p.m.–6:00 p.m.: Weightlifting, 54 kg group A finals

3:30 p.m.–6:10 p.m.: Wrestling—Greco-Roman, 48kg, 57kg, 68kg, 82kg & 100kg classification

4:00 p.m.–8:30 p.m.: Volleyball, Women's preliminaries, matches 3 & 4

4:30 p.m.–9:00 p.m.: Field Hockey, Women's pool 3 & 4

4:30 p.m.–6:38 p.m.: Gymnastics—Artistic, men's team compulsories

5:30 p.m.–10:00 p.m.: Field Hockey, men's pool 2 & 3

6:30 p.m.–8:30 p.m.: Soccer, men's match 4

6:30 p.m.–8:30 p.m.: Soccer, men's match 2

6:30 p.m.–8:30 p.m.: Soccer, men's match 3

7:30 p.m.–11:59 p.m.: Volleyball, Women's preliminaries, matches 5 & 6

7:33 p.m.–9:07 p.m.: Swimming, Women's 100 free final, men's 100 breaststroke final

8:00 p.m.–11:00 p.m.: Baseball, game # 3

8:00 p.m.–11:30 p.m.: Basketball, men's preliminaries, games 5 & 6

8:00 p.m.–11:30 p.m.: Boxing, first round session 2

8:30 p.m.–11:10 p.m.: Water Polo, preliminaries, games 5 & 6

July 21

8:00 a.m.–12:50 p.m.: Fencing, Women's individual épée 1/32, 1/16, 1/8 & quarterfinals

9:00 a.m.–5:50 p.m.: Equestrian—three-day event, team dressage session 1

9:00 a.m.–11:00 a.m.: Field Hockey, men's pool 4

9:00 a.m.–12:40 p.m.: Rowing, men's & Women's heats

9:00 a.m.–3:25 p.m.: Shooting, men's trap preliminaries & final, Women's 10m air pistol preliminaries & final

9:00 a.m.–1:00 p.m.: Softball, games 1 & 2

9:30 a.m.–12:53 p.m.: Gymnastics—Artistic, Women's team compulsories

9:30 a.m.–1:23 p.m.: Judo, Women's & men's half-heavyweight (72kg & 95kg) preliminaries & repechages

10:00 a.m.–1:30 p.m.: Basketball, Women's preliminaries, games 1 & 2

10:00 a.m.–2:30 p.m.: Volleyball, men's preliminaries, matches 1 & 2

10:00 a.m.–1:00 p.m.: Wrestling—Greco-Roman, 48kg, 57kg, 68kg, 82kg & 100kg classification

10:05 a.m.–12:10 p.m.: Swimming, Women's 200 free preliminaries, men's 400 im preliminaries

11:00 a.m.–2:30 p.m.: Cycling—Road, Women's road race

11:00 a.m.–1:40 p.m.: Water Polo, preliminaries, games 7 & 8

12:30 p.m.–2:30 p.m.: Weightlifting, 59 kg group B

1:30 p.m.–5:00 p.m.: Boxing, first round session 3

1:30 p.m.–6:00 p.m.: Soccer, men's match 6 & Women's match 2

3:00 p.m.–6:00 p.m.: Baseball, game # 4

3:00 p.m.–6:30 p.m.: Basketball, Women's preliminaries, games 3 & 4

3:00 p.m.–6:00 p.m.: Fencing, Women's individual épée semifinals, bronze & gold

3:00 p.m.–6:28 p.m.: Gymnastics—Artistic, Women's team compulsories

3:00 p.m.–4:27 p.m.: Judo, Women's & men's half-heavyweight (72kg & 95kg) final rounds & medal matches

3:00 p.m.–7:30 p.m.: Soccer, men's match 5 & Women's match 1

3:30 p.m.–6:10 p.m.: Water Polo, preliminaries, games 9 & 10

3:30 p.m.–6:00 p.m.: Weightlifting, 59 kg group A finals

3:30 p.m.–6:20 p.m.: Wrestling—Greco-Roman, 48kg, 57kg, 68kg, 82kg & 100kg bronze & gold

4:00 p.m.–8:30 p.m.: Soccer, men's match 7 & Women's match 3

4:00 p.m.–8:30 p.m.: Soccer, men's match 8 & Women's match 4

4:00 p.m.–8:30 p.m.: Volleyball, men's preliminaries, matches 3 & 4

4:30 p.m.–9:00 p.m.: Field Hockey, men's pool 5 & 6

5:30 p.m.–10:00 p.m.: Field Hockey, Women's pool 5 & 6

6:30 p.m.–10:30 p.m.: Softball, games 3 & 4

7:30 p.m.–11:59 p.m.: Volleyball, men's preliminaries, matches 5 & 6

7:33 p.m.–9:12 p.m.: Swimming, Women's 200 free final, men's 400 im final

8:00 p.m.–11:00 p.m.: Baseball, game # 5

8:00 p.m.–11:30 p.m.: Basketball, Women's preliminaries, games 5 & 6

8:00 p.m.–11:30 p.m.: Boxing, first round session 4

8:30 p.m.–11:10 p.m.: Water Polo, preliminaries, games 11 & 12

July 22

8:00 a.m.–1:55 p.m.: Fencing, Women's & men's individual foil 1/32, 1/16, 1/8 & quarterfinals

8:30 a.m.–10:30 a.m.: Field Hockey, men's pool 7

9:00 a.m.–5:50 p.m.: Equestrian—three-day event, team dressage session 2

9:00 a.m.–1:00 p.m.: Field Hockey, Women's pool 7 & 8

9:00 a.m.–12:00 p.m.: Rowing, men's & Women's heats

9:00 a.m.–1:00 p.m.: Softball, games 5 & 6

9:15 a.m.–11:11 a.m.: Gymnastics—Artistic, men's team optionals

9:30 a.m.–1:23 p.m.: Judo, Women's & men's middleweight (66kg & 86kg) preliminaries & repechages

10:00 a.m.–1:00 p.m.: Baseball, game # 6

10:00 a.m.–1:30 p.m.: Basketball, men's preliminaries, games 7 & 8

10:00 a.m.–1:45 p.m.: Shooting, men's 10m air rifle preliminaries & final

10:00 a.m.–2:30 p.m.: Volleyball, Women's preliminaries, matches 7 & 8

10:00 a.m.–12:50 p.m.: Wrestling—Greco-Roman, 52kg, 62kg, 74kg, 90kg & 130kg preliminaries

10:05 a.m.–12:26 p.m.: Swimming, Women's 400 free preliminaries, men's 100 free preliminaries

11:00 a.m.–1:40 p.m.: Water Polo, preliminaries, games 13 & 14

12:30 p.m.–2:50 p.m.: Gymnastics—Artistic, men's team optionals

12:30 p.m.–2:30 p.m.: Weightlifting, 64 kg group B

1:00 p.m.–6:00 p.m.: Yachting, M & Women's Mistral, M & Women's 470, Star, Finn

1:30 p.m.–5:00 p.m.: Boxing, first round session 5

3:00 p.m.–6:00 p.m.: Baseball, game # 7

3:00 p.m.–6:30 p.m.: Basketball, men's preliminaries, games 9 & 10

3:00 p.m.–6:45 p.m.: Fencing, Women's & men's individual foil semifinals, bronze & gold

3:00 p.m.–4:27 p.m.: Judo, Women's & men's middleweight (66kg & 86kg) final rounds & medal matches

3:30 p.m.–6:10 p.m.: Water Polo, preliminaries, games 15 & 16

3:30 p.m.–6:00 p.m.: Weightlifting, 64 kg group A finals

3:30 p.m.–6:10 p.m.: Wrestling—Greco-Roman, 52kg, 62kg, 74kg, 90kg & 130kg classification

4:00 p.m.–8:30 p.m.: Volleyball, Women's preliminaries, matches 9 & 10

4:30 p.m.–7:13 p.m.: Gymnastics—Artistic, men's team optional final

5:00 p.m.–9:00 p.m.: Field Hockey, men's pool 8 & 9

6:30 p.m.–8:30 p.m.: Soccer, men's match 9

6:30 p.m.–10:30 p.m.: Softball, games 7 & 8

7:00 p.m.–9:00 p.m.: Soccer, men's match 11

7:00 p.m.–9:00 p.m.: Soccer, men's match 12

7:30 p.m.–9:30 p.m.: Soccer, men's match 10

7:30 p.m.–11:59 p.m.: Volleyball, Women's preliminaries, matches 11 & 12

7:33 p.m.–9:27 p.m.: Swimming, Women's 400 free final, men's 100 free final, Women's 100 back final

8:00 p.m.–11:00 p.m.: Baseball, game # 8

8:00 p.m.–11:30 p.m.: Basketball, men's preliminaries, games 11 & 12

8:00 p.m.–11:30 p.m.: Boxing, first round session 6

8:30 p.m.–11:10 p.m.: Water Polo, preliminaries, games 17 & 18

July 23

7:00 a.m.–6:00 p.m.: Equestrian—three-day event, team speed & endurance, individual dressage session 1

8:30 a.m.–1:00 p.m.: Field Hockey, Women's pool 9 & 10

9:00 a.m.–11:00 a.m.: Field Hockey, men's pool 10

9:00 a.m.–11:40 p.m.: Rowing, men's & Women's repechages

9:00 a.m.–3:25 p.m.: Shooting, men's 50m free pistol preliminaries & final, Women's double trap preliminaries & final

9:00 a.m.–1:00 p.m.: Softball, games 9 & 10

9:00 a.m.–12:45 p.m.: Volleyball—beach, Women's & men's eliminations

9:30 a.m.–12:53 p.m.: Gymnastics—Artistic, Women's team optionals

9:30 a.m.–1:23 p.m.: Judo, Women's & men's half-middleweight (61kg & 78kg) preliminaries & repechages

10:00 a.m.–1:00 p.m.: Baseball, game # 9

10:00 a.m.–1:30 p.m.: Basketball, Women's preliminaries, games 7 & 8

10:00 a.m.–1:45 p.m.: Fencing, men's team épée 1/8, quarterfinals, 5–12 places & semifinals

10:00 a.m.–7:30 p.m.: Tennis, men's & Women's singles preliminaries

10:00 a.m.–7:30 p.m.: Tennis, men's & Women's singles preliminaries

10:00 a.m.–2:30 p.m.: Volleyball, men's preliminaries, matches 7 & 8

10:00 a.m.–1:00 p.m.: Wrestling—Greco-Roman, 52kg, 62kg, 74kg, 90kg & 130kg classification

10:05 a.m.–12:22 p.m.: Swimming, men's 400 free preliminaries, Women's 200 breaststroke preliminaries

10:30 a.m.–1:10 p.m.: Table Tennis, Women's & men's doubles preliminaries

11:00 a.m.–1:40 p.m.: Water Polo, preliminaries, games 19 & 20

12:30 p.m.–2:30 p.m.: Weightlifting, 70 kg group B

1:00 p.m.–6:00 p.m.: Yachting, M & Women's Mistral, M & Women's 470, Star, Finn

1:30 p.m.–5:00 p.m.: Boxing, first round session 7

2:00 p.m.–5:45 p.m.: Volleyball—beach, Women's & men's eliminations

3:00 p.m.–6:00 p.m.: Baseball, game # 10

3:00 p.m.–6:30 p.m.: Basketball, Women's preliminaries, games 9 & 10

3:00 p.m.–5:00 p.m.: Fencing, men's team épée bronze & gold

3:00 p.m.–6:51 p.m.: Gymnastics—Artistic, Women's team optionals & final

3:00 p.m.–4:27 p.m.: Judo, Women's & men's half-middleweight (61kg &

78kg) final rounds &
medal matches

3:30 p.m.–6:10 p.m.: Water
Polo, preliminaries, games
21 & 22

3:30 p.m.–6:00 p.m.:
Weightlifting, 70 kg group
A finals

3:30 p.m.–6:20 p.m.:
Wrestling—Greco-Roman,
52kg, 62kg, 74kg, 90kg &
130kg bronze & gold

4:00 p.m.–8:30 p.m.: Volleyball, men's preliminaries,
matches 9 & 10

4:30 p.m.–9:00 p.m.: Field
Hockey, Women's pool 11
& 12

4:30 p.m.–9:00 p.m.: Soccer,
Women's match 5 & men's
match 13

5:30 p.m.–10:00 p.m.: Field
Hockey, men's pool 11 & 12

6:00 p.m.–10:30 p.m.: Soccer,
Women's match 8 & men's
match 16

6:00 p.m.–10:30 p.m.: Soccer,
Women's match 7 & men's
match 15

6:30 p.m.–11:00 p.m.: Soccer,
Women's match 6 & men's
match 14

6:30 p.m.–10:30 p.m.: Softball, games 11 & 12

7:30 p.m.–11:59 p.m.: Volleyball, men's preliminaries,
matches 11 & 12

7:33 p.m.–9:25 p.m.: Swimming, men's 400 free final,
Women's 200 breast final,
men's 100 back final

8:00 p.m.–11:00 p.m.: Baseball, game # 11

8:00 p.m.–11:30 p.m.: Basketball, Women's prelimi-
naries, games 11 & 12

8:00 p.m.–11:30 p.m.: Boxing, first round session 8

8:30 p.m.–11:10 p.m.: Water
Polo, preliminaries, games
23 & 24

July 24

8:00 a.m.–1:45 p.m.: Fencing, Women's team épée
1/8, quarterfinals, 5–12
places & semifinals

8:30 a.m.–3:25 p.m.: Shooting, Women's 50m 3x20
rifle preliminaries & final,
men's double trap preliminaries & final

9:00 a.m.–6:00 p.m.: Equestrian—three-day event,
team jumping & individual
dressage session 2

9:00 a.m.–11:00 a.m.: Field
Hockey, men's pool 13

9:00 a.m.–11:30 p.m.: Rowing, men's & Women's
repechages

9:00 a.m.–1:00 p.m.: Softball, games 13 & 14

9:00 a.m.–12:45 p.m.: Volleyball—beach, Women's
& men's eliminations

9:30 a.m.–1:23 p.m.: Judo,
Women's & men's light-
weight (56kg & 71kg) pre-
liminaries & repechages

10:00 a.m.–1:30 p.m.: Basketball, men's preliminaries, games 13 & 14

10:00 a.m.–1:00 p.m.: Team
Handball, men's prelimi-
naries 1 & 2

10:00 a.m.–6:30 p.m.: Tennis,
men's & Women's singles
preliminaries

10:00 a.m.–6:30 p.m.: Tennis,
men's & Women's singles
preliminaries

10:00 a.m.–2:30 p.m.: Volleyball, Women's prelimi-
naries, matches 13 & 14

10:05 a.m.–12:56 p.m.:
Swimming, men's 200
breast preliminaries,
Women's 200 im prelimi-
naries

10:30 a.m.–1:10 p.m.: Table
Tennis, Women's singles
preliminaries

11:00 a.m.–1:40 p.m.: Water Polo, preliminaries, games 25 & 26

12:30 p.m.–2:30 p.m.: Weightlifting, 76 kg group B

1:00 p.m.–6:00 p.m.: Yachting, M & Women's Mistral, M & Women's 470, Star, Finn, Soling, Tornado

1:30 p.m.–5:00 p.m.: Boxing, first round session 9

2:00 p.m.–4:30 p.m.: Track & Field, Women's & men's singles 1/32

2:00 p.m.–5:45 p.m.: Volleyball—beach, Women's & men's eliminations

2:30 p.m.–5:30 p.m.: Team Handball, men's preliminaries 3 & 4

3:00 p.m.–6:00 p.m.: Baseball, game # 12

3:00 p.m.–6:30 p.m.: Basketball, men's preliminaries, games 15 & 16

3:00 p.m.–7:10 p.m.: Fencing, Women's & men's team épée bronze & gold, men's team sabre bronze & gold

3:00 p.m.–4:27 p.m.: Judo, Women's & men's lightweight (56kg & 71kg) final rounds & medal matches

3:30 p.m.–6:10 p.m.: Water Polo, preliminaries, games 27 & 28

3:30 p.m.–6:00 p.m.: Weightlifting, 76 kg group A finals

4:00 p.m.–8:30 p.m.: Volleyball, Women's preliminaries, matches 15 & 16

4:15 p.m.–6:59 p.m.: Gymnastics—Artistic, men's individual all-around final

4:30 p.m.–6:55 p.m.: Cycling—Road, men's sprint qualifying (200m time trial), round 1 & repechages

5:00 p.m.–9:00 p.m.: Field Hockey, men's pool 14 & 15

6:30 p.m.–8:30 p.m.: Soccer, men's match 17

6:30 p.m.–10:30 p.m.: Softball, games 15 & 16

7:00 p.m.–9:00 p.m.: Soccer, men's match 19

7:00 p.m.–9:00 p.m.: Soccer, men's match 20

7:00 p.m.–9:40 p.m.: Table Tennis, Women's & men's doubles preliminaries

7:00 p.m.–10:00 p.m.: Team Handball, men's preliminaries 5 & 6

7:30 p.m.–9:30 p.m.: Soccer, men's match 18

7:30 p.m.–11:59 p.m.: Volleyball, Women's preliminaries, matches 17 & 18

7:33 p.m.–9:05 p.m.: Swimming, men's 200 breaststroke final, Women's 200 im final, men's 100 fly final

8:00 p.m.–11:00 p.m.: Baseball, game # 13

8:00 p.m.–11:30 p.m.: Basketball, men's preliminaries, games 17 & 18

8:00 p.m.–11:30 p.m.: Boxing, first round session 10

8:00 p.m.–11:00 p.m.: Track & Field, Women's & men's singles 1/32

8:30 p.m.–11:10 p.m.: Water Polo, preliminaries, games 29 & 30

July 25

7:30 a.m.–11:00 a.m.: Equestrian—three-day event, individual speed, endurance

8:00 a.m.–2:45 p.m.: Fencing, Women's & men's team foil 1/8, quarterfinals, 5–12 places & semifinals

8:30 a.m.–1:00 a.m.: Field Hockey, Women's pool 13 & 14

8:30 a.m.–3:25 p.m.: Shooting, men's 50m prone rifle preliminaries & final, men's 10m run target preliminaries

9:00 a.m.–12:10 p.m.: Cycling—Road, Women's ind pursuit qualifying, men's ind pursuit semifinal, men's sprint round 2

9:00 a.m.–11:00 a.m.: Field Hockey, men's pool 16

9:00 a.m.–11:40 p.m.: Rowing, men's & Women's semifinals

9:00 a.m.–1:00 p.m.: Softball, games 17 & 18

9:00 a.m.–12:45 p.m.: Track & Field, Women's doubles 1/16, men's doubles 1/16

9:00 a.m.–12:45 p.m.: Volleyball—beach, Women's & men's eliminations

9:30 a.m.–1:23 p.m.: Judo, Women's & men's half-lightweight (51kg & 65kg) preliminaries & repechages

10:00 a.m.–1:00 p.m.: Baseball, game # 14

10:00 a.m.–1:30 p.m.: Basketball, Women's preliminaries, games 13 & 14

10:00 a.m.–2:00 p.m.: Table Tennis, Women's & men's singles preliminaries

10:00 a.m.–1:00 p.m.: Team Handball, men's preliminaries 7 & 8

10:00 a.m.–6:30 p.m.: Tennis, men's & Women's singles & doubles preliminaries

10:00 a.m.–6:30 p.m.: Tennis, men's & Women's singles & doubles preliminaries

10:00 a.m.–2:30 p.m.: Volleyball, men's preliminaries, matches 13 & 14

10:05 a.m.–1:44 p.m.: Swimming, men's 50 free

preliminaries, Women's 200 back preliminaries

1:00 p.m.–6:00 p.m.: Yachting, Laser, Europe, Soling, Tornado

1:30 p.m.–4:30 p.m.: Boxing, second round session 11

2:00 p.m.–5:00 p.m.: Track & Field, men's doubles 1/16, men's singles 1/16

2:00 p.m.–5:45 p.m.: Volleyball—beach, Women's & men's eliminations

2:30 p.m.–5:30 p.m.: Team Handball, men's preliminaries 9 & 10

3:00 p.m.–6:00 p.m.: Baseball, game # 15

3:00 p.m.–6:30 p.m.: Basketball, Women's preliminaries, games 15 & 16

3:00 p.m.–7:10 p.m.: Fencing, Women's & men's team foil bronze & gold

3:00 p.m.–4:27 p.m.: Judo, Women's & men's half-lightweight (51kg & 65kg) final rounds & medal matches

4:00 p.m.–8:30 p.m.: Volleyball, men's preliminaries, matches 15 & 16

4:15 p.m.–7:07 p.m.: Gymnastics—Artistic, Women's individual all-around final

4:30 p.m.–9:00 p.m.: Field Hockey, Women's pool 15 & 16

5:30 p.m.–10:00 p.m.: Field Hockey, men's pool 17 & 18

5:30 p.m.–10:00 p.m.: Soccer, men's match 21 & Women's match 9

6:30 p.m.–11:00 p.m.: Soccer, men's match 24 & Women's match 12

6:30 p.m.–11:00 p.m.: Soccer, men's match 22 & Women's match 10

6:30 p.m.–11:00 p.m.: Soccer, men's match 23 & Women's match 11

6:30 p.m.–10:30 p.m.: Softball, games 19 & 20

7:00 p.m.–11:00 p.m.: Table Tennis, men's & Women's doubles preliminaries & men's singles preliminaries

7:00 p.m.–10:00 p.m.: Team Handball, men's preliminaries 11 & 12

7:30 p.m.–11:59 p.m.: Volleyball, men's preliminaries, matches 17 & 18

7:33 p.m.–9:43 p.m.: Swimming, Women's 800 free final, men's 50 free final, Women's 200 back final

8:00 p.m.–11:00 p.m.: Baseball, game # 16

8:00 p.m.–11:30 p.m.: Basketball, Women's preliminaries, games 17 & 18

8:00 p.m.–11:00 p.m.: Boxing, second round session 12

8:00 p.m.–10:15 p.m.: Track & Field, men's singles 1/16

July 26

8:00 a.m.–12:15 p.m.: Track & Field, men's 20km walk

8:30 a.m.–1:00 p.m.: Cycling—Road, men's team pursuit qualifying, Women's sprint qtr, men's sprint octos final

8:30 a.m.–3:25 p.m.: Shooting, Women's 25m sport pistol preliminaries & final, men's 10m run target prelims & final

9:00 a.m.–11:00 a.m. Field Hockey, men's pool 19

9:00 a.m.–11:30 a.m.: Rowing, men's & Women's semifinals

9:00 a.m.–1:00 p.m.: Softball, games 21 & 22

9:00 a.m.–12:30 p.m.: Track & Field, Women's singles 1/16, men's singles octos

9:30 a.m.–1:23 p.m.: Judo, Women's & men's extra-lightweight (48kg & 60kg) preliminaries & repechages

10:00 a.m.–1:30 p.m.: Basketball, men's preliminaries, games 19 & 20

10:00 a.m.–4:30 p.m.: Canoe Kayak—Slalom, official training runs

10:00 a.m.–2:00 p.m.: Table Tennis, men's & Women's singles preliminaries

10:00 a.m.–1:00 p.m.: Team Handball, Women's preliminaries 1 & 2

10:00 a.m.–6:30 p.m.: Tennis, men's & Women's singles & doubles preliminaries

10:00 a.m.–6:30 p.m.: Tennis, men's & Women's singles & doubles preliminaries

10:00 a.m.–2:30 p.m.: Volleyball, Women's preliminaries, matches 19 & 20

10:00 a.m.–12:15 p.m.: Volleyball—beach, Women's & men's eliminations

10:05 a.m.–11:47 a.m.: Swimming, Women's 200 fly preliminaries, men's 200 back preliminaries

11:00 a.m.–12:30 p.m.: Equestrian—three-day event, individual jumping

11:00 a.m.–1:40 p.m.: Water Polo, classification games 1 & 2

12:30 p.m.–2:30 p.m.: Weightlifting, 83 kg group B

1:00 p.m.–6:00 p.m.: Yachting, Laser, Europe, Star, Finn, Soling, Tornado

1:30 p.m.–4:30 p.m.: Boxing, second round session 13

2:00 p.m.–5:00 p.m.: Track & Field, men's singles octos, Women's singles 1/16

2:30 p.m.–5:30 p.m.: Team Handball, Women's preliminaries 3 & 4

2:30 p.m.–5:45 p.m.: Volleyball—beach, men's eliminations, Women's semifinal

3:00 p.m.–6:30 p.m.: Basketball, men's preliminaries, games 21 & 22

3:00 p.m.–5:30 p.m.: Diving, Women's platform preliminaries

3:00 p.m.–4:27 p.m.: Judo, Women's & men's extra-lightweight (48kg & 60kg) final rounds & medal matches

3:30 p.m.–6:00 p.m.: Weightlifting, 83 kg group A finals

4:00 p.m.–8:30 p.m.: Volleyball, Women's preliminaries, matches 21 & 22

4:00 p.m.–6:40 p.m.: Water Polo, quarterfinal games 1 & 2

4:30 p.m.–9:00 p.m.: Field Hockey, men's pool 20 & 21

5:30 p.m.–10:00 p.m.: Field Hockey, Women's pool 17 & 18

5:30 p.m.–10:15 p.m.: Track & Field, Women's javelin, qualifying

6:30 p.m.–10:30 p.m.: Softball, games 23 & 24

7:00 p.m.–9:20 p.m.: Table Tennis, Women's doubles quarterfinal & men's singles preliminaries

7:30 p.m.–11:59 p.m.: Volleyball, Women's preliminaries, matches 23 & 24

7:33 p.m.–9:47 p.m.: Swimming, Women's 200 fly final, men's 200 back final, Women's 50 free final

8:00 p.m.–11:30 p.m.: Basketball, men's preliminaries, games 23 & 24

8:00 p.m.–11:00 p.m.: Boxing, second round session 14

8:00 p.m.–11:59 p.m.: Track & Field, Women's singles 1/16, Mixed doubles 1/16

8:30 p.m.–11:10 p.m.: Water Polo, quarterfinal games 3 & 4

July 27

8:30 a.m.–3:05 p.m.: Equestrian, team dressage session 1

8:30 a.m.–10:30 a.m.: Field Hockey, men's pool 22

8:30 a.m.–3:15 p.m.: Shooting, men's 50m 3x40 rifle preliminaries & final, men's skeet preliminaries & final

9:00 a.m.–1:00 p.m.: Field Hockey, Women's pool 19 & 20

9:00 a.m.–12:35 p.m.: Rowing, men's & Women's finals

9:00 a.m.–1:00 p.m.: Softball, games 25 & 26

9:00 a.m.–1:00 p.m.: Track & Field, Women's singles octos, men's doubles octos

9:15 a.m.–2:30 p.m.: Track & Field, Women's heptathlon (100m hurdles, high jump)

10:00 a.m.–1:00 p.m.: Baseball, game # 17

10:00 a.m.–1:30 p.m.: Basketball, Women's preliminaries, games 19 & 20

10:00 a.m.–5:05 p.m.: Canoe Kayak—Slalom, K-1 Women's finals, C-1 men's finals

10:00 a.m.–2:40 p.m.: Table Tennis, men's singles preliminaries & Women's singles octos

10:00 a.m.–1:00 p.m.: Team Handball, men's preliminaries 13 & 14

10:00 a.m.–6:30 p.m.: Tennis, men's & Women's singles & doubles preliminaries

10:00 a.m.–6:30 p.m.: Tennis, men's & Women's singles & doubles preliminaries

10:00 a.m.–2:30 p.m.: Volleyball, men's preliminaries, matches 19 & 20

10:00 a.m.–12:45 p.m.: Volleyball—beach, men's semifinal, Women's bronze medal

11:00 a.m.–1:40 p.m.: Water Polo, classification games 3 & 4

11:15 a.m.–2:10 p.m.: Cycling—Road, men's sprint quarterfinal, Women's ind pursuit semifinal, men's team pursuit semifinal

11:30 a.m.–12:45 p.m.: Diving, Women's platform semifinal

12:30 p.m.–2:30 p.m.: Weightlifting, 91 kg group B

1:00 p.m.–6:00 p.m.: Yachting, men's & Women's Mistral, Laser, Europe, Star, Finn, Soling, Tornado

1:30 p.m.–4:30 p.m.: Boxing, second round session 15

2:00 p.m.–6:00 p.m.: Track & Field, men's doubles octos, Mixed doubles octos

2:00 p.m.–5:00 p.m.: Volleyball—beach, men's semifinal, Women's gold medal

2:30 p.m.–5:30 p.m.: Team Handball, men's preliminaries 15 & 16

3:00 p.m.–6:00 p.m.: Baseball, game # 18

3:00 p.m.–6:30 p.m.: Basketball, Women's preliminaries, games 21 & 22

3:30 p.m.–6:10 p.m.: Water Polo, classification game 5 & semifinal # 1

3:30 p.m.–6:00 p.m.: Weightlifting, 91 kg group A finals

4:00 p.m.–8:30 p.m.: Volleyball, men's preliminaries, matches 21 & 22

5:00 p.m.–9:00 p.m.: Field Hockey, men's pool 23 & 24

5:30 p.m.–10:20 p.m.: Track & Field, Women's heptathlon (shot put, 200m)

6:00 p.m.–8:00 p.m.: Soccer, men's quarterfinal 2

6:30 p.m.–8:30 p.m.: Soccer, men's quarterfinal 1

6:30 p.m.–10:30 p.m.: Softball, games 27 & 28

7:00 p.m.–10:00 p.m.: Table Tennis, men's doubles quarterfinal & Women's doubles semifinal

7:00 p.m.–10:00 p.m.: Team Handball, men's preliminaries 17 & 18

7:30 p.m.–11:59 p.m.: Volleyball, men's preliminaries, matches 23 & 24

8:00 p.m.–11:00 p.m.: Baseball, game # 19

8:00 p.m.–11:30 p.m.: Basketball, Women's preliminaries, games 23 & 24

8:00 p.m.–11:00 p.m.: Boxing, second round session 16

8:00 p.m.–11:00 p.m.: Track & Field, Women's doubles octos

8:30 p.m.–11:10 p.m.: Water Polo, semifinal # 2 & classification game 6

10:00 p.m.–11:15 p.m.: Diving, Women's platform final

July 28

7:30 a.m.–12:00 p.m.: Track & Field, Women's marathon

8:00 a.m.–10:30 a.m.: Water Polo, finals game 11, 12 & finals game 9, 10

8:30 a.m.–3:05 p.m.: Equestrian, team dressage session 2 & finals

8:30 a.m.–1:00 p.m.: Field Hockey, Women's pool 21 & 22

9:00 a.m.–11:00 a.m.: Field Hockey, men's pool 25

9:00 a.m.–12:35 p.m.: Rowing, men's & Women's finals

9:00 a.m.–12:00 p.m.: Track & Field, men's & Women's doubles quarterfinals

10:00 a.m.–1:00 p.m.: Baseball, game # 20

10:00 a.m.–1:30 p.m.: Basketball, men's preliminaries, games 25 & 26

10:00 a.m.–5:05 p.m.: Canoe Kayak—Slalom, C-2 men's finals, K-1 men's finals

10:00 a.m.–2:00 p.m.: Table Tennis, men's singles octos

10:00 a.m.–1:00 p.m.: Team Handball, Women's preliminaries 5 & 6

10:00 a.m.–4:30 p.m.: Tennis, men's singles & doubles preliminaries

10:00 a.m.–4:30 p.m.: Tennis, men's singles & doubles preliminaries

10:00 a.m.–2:30 p.m.: Volleyball, Women's preliminaries, matches 25 & 26

11:00 a.m.–1:30 p.m.: Water Polo, finals game 7, 8 & finals game 5, 6

11:15 a.m.–2:30 p.m.: Cycling—Road, Women's & men's points race final, men's sprint final, Women's individual pursuit final

11:30 a.m.–3:15 p.m.: Volleyball—beach, men's bronze medal, men's gold medal

12:30 p.m.–2:30 p.m.: Weightlifting, 99 kg group B

1:00 p.m.–6:00 p.m.: Yachting, men's & Women's Mistral, men's & Women's 470, Star finals, Finn finals, Soling

1:30 p.m.–4:30 p.m.: Boxing, second round session 17

2:30 p.m.–5:30 p.m.: Team Handball, Women's preliminaries 7 & 8

3:00 p.m.–6:00 p.m.: Baseball, game # 21

3:00 p.m.–7:30 p.m.: Soccer, Women's semifinal 1 & 2

3:00 p.m.–5:00 p.m.: Soccer, men's quarterfinal 3

3:00 p.m.–6:15 p.m.: Water Polo, bronze final & gold final

3:30 p.m.–9:50 p.m.: Track & Field, men's hammer throw, final

3:30 p.m.–6:00 p.m.: Weightlifting, 99 kg group A finals

4:00 p.m.–8:30 p.m.: Volleyball, Women's preliminaries, matches 27 & 28

4:30 p.m.–9:00 p.m.: Field Hockey, Women's pool 23 & 24

5:00 p.m.–8:30 p.m.: Basketball, men's preliminaries, games 27 & 28

5:30 p.m.–10:00 p.m.: Field Hockey, men's pool 26 & 27

6:00 p.m.–8:00 p.m.: Soccer, men's quarterfinal 4

7:30 p.m.–11:59 p.m.: Volleyball, Women's preliminaries, matches 29 & 30

8:00 p.m.–11:00 p.m.: Baseball, game # 22

8:00 p.m.–11:00 p.m.: Boxing, second round session 18

8:00 p.m.–11:59 p.m.: Diving, men's springboard preliminaries
8:00 p.m.–11:00 p.m.: Track & Field, Women's & men's singles quarterfinals
8:30 p.m.–11:59 p.m.: Basketball, men's preliminaries, games 29 & 30
9:30 p.m.–11:35 p.m.: Gymnastics—Artistic, men's floor exercise final, Women's vault final, men's pommel horse final

July 29
8:30 a.m.–1:00 p.m.: Equestrian, jumping first qualifier
8:30 a.m.–12:55 p.m.: Track & Field, Women's 10km walk
9:00 a.m.–12:20 p.m.: Archery, Women's 1/32 eliminations
9:00 a.m.–11:00 a.m.: Field Hockey, men's pool 28
9:00 a.m.–12:15 p.m.: Track & Field, Mixed doubles quarterfinal, Women's doubles semifinal
10:00 a.m.–1:00 p.m.: Baseball, game # 23
10:00 a.m.–1:30 p.m.: Basketball, Women's preliminaries, games 25 & 26
10:00 a.m.–1:00 p.m.: Team Handball, men's preliminaries 19 & 20
10:00 a.m.–2:30 p.m.: Volleyball, men's preliminaries, matches 25 & 26
11:00 a.m.–8:00 p.m.: Tennis, Women's singles & men's doubles quarterfinal
11:00 a.m.–8:00 p.m.: Tennis, Women's singles & men's doubles quarterfinal
11:30 a.m.–1:00 p.m.: Diving, men's springboard semifinal

12:30 p.m.–2:30 p.m.: Weightlifting, 108 kg group B
1:00 p.m.–2:15 p.m.: Table Tennis, Women's doubles final
1:00 p.m.–6:00 p.m.: Yachting, men's & Women's Mistral finals, men's & Women's 470, Laser, Europe, Tornado
2:00 p.m.–5:20 p.m.: Archery, Women's 1/16 eliminations
2:30 p.m.–5:30 p.m.: Team Handball, men's preliminaries 21 & 22
3:00 p.m.–6:00 p.m.: Baseball, game # 24
3:00 p.m.–6:30 p.m.: Basketball, Women's preliminaries, games 27 & 28
3:30 p.m.–6:00 p.m.: Weightlifting, 108 kg group A finals
4:00 p.m.–8:30 p.m.: Volleyball, men's preliminaries, matches 27 & 28
5:00 p.m.–9:00 p.m.: Field Hockey, men's pool 29 & 30
6:00 p.m.–10:30 p.m.: Track & Field, men's 110m hurdles, semifinal, final
6:30 p.m.–10:30 p.m.: Softball, semifinals 1 & 2
7:00 p.m.–10:00 p.m.: Table Tennis, Women's singles quarterfinal & men's doubles semifinal
7:00 p.m.–10:00 p.m.: Team Handball, men's preliminaries 23 & 24
7:30 p.m.–9:53 p.m.: Gymnastics—Artistic, men's vault final, Women's balance beam final, men's parallel bars final
7:30 p.m.–11:59 p.m.: Volleyball, men's preliminaries, matches 29 & 30

8:00 p.m.–11:00 p.m.: Baseball, game # 25

8:00 p.m.–11:30 p.m.: Basketball, Women's preliminaries, games 29 & 30

8:00 p.m.–11:45 p.m.: Track & Field, Women's & men's doubles semifinal

10:00 p.m.–11:30 p.m.: Diving, men's springboard final

July 30

7:30 a.m.–7:15 p.m.: Modern Pentathlon, men's shooting, fencing, swimming, riding & running

9:00 a.m.–12:20 p.m.: Archery, men's 1/32 eliminations

9:00 a.m.–12:30 p.m.: Canoe/ Kayak—Sprint, K-2 men's 1000 heats, C-1 men's 1000 heats, K-4 Women's 500 heats

9:00 a.m.–1:00 p.m.: Field Hockey, Women's pool 25 & 26

9:00 a.m.–11:45 a.m. Track & Field, Women's & men's singles semifinal

9:30 a.m.–12:20 p.m.: Wrestling—Freestyle, 48kg, 57kg, 68kg, 82kg & 100kg preliminaries

10:00 a.m.–1:00 p.m.: Baseball, game # 26

10:00 a.m.–1:30 p.m.: Basketball, men's quarterfinal, games 1 & 2

10:00 a.m.–4:00 p.m.: Mountain Bike Racing, Women's & men's individual cross country

10:00 a.m.–11:15 a.m.: Synchronized swimming, team preliminaries

10:00 a.m.–1:00 p.m.: Team Handball, Women's preliminaries 9 & 10

11:00 a.m.–8:00 p.m.: Tennis, men's singles & Women's doubles quarterfinal

11:00 a.m.–8:00 p.m.: Tennis, men's singles & Women's doubles quarterfinal

12:00 p.m.–4:30 p.m.: Volleyball, Women's quarterfinals 3 & 4

12:30 p.m.–2:30 p.m.: Weightlifting, over 108 kg group B

1:00 p.m.–2:15 p.m.: Table Tennis, men's doubles final

1:00 p.m.–6:00 p.m.: Yachting, men's & Women's 470 finals, Laser, Europe, Tornado finals

1:30 p.m.–4:30 p.m.: Boxing, quarterfinal session 1

2:00 p.m.–5:20 p.m.: Archery, men's 1/16 eliminations

2:00 p.m.–5:45 p.m.: Track & Field, men's singles semifinal, Mixed doubles semifinal

2:30 p.m.–4:50 p.m.: Canoe/ Kayak—Sprint, K-2 men's 1000 reps, C-1 men's 1000 reps, K-4 Women's 500 reps

2:30 p.m.–5:30 p.m.: Team Handball, Women's preliminaries 11 & 12

3:00 p.m.–6:00 p.m.: Baseball, game # 27

3:00 p.m.–6:30 p.m.: Basketball, men's classification, games 1 & 2

3:30 p.m.–6:00 p.m.: Weightlifting, over 108 kg group A finals

3:30 p.m.–6:10 p.m.: Wrestling—Freestyle, 48kg, 57kg, 68kg, 82kg & 100kg classification

4:00 p.m.–6:00 p.m.: Gymnastics—Artistic, Gymnastics exhibition

4:30 p.m.–10:45 p.m.: Softball, bronze & gold medal

5:00 p.m.–9:00 p.m.: Field Hockey, Women's pool 27 & 28

7:00 p.m.–10:00 p.m.: Table Tennis, men's singles quarterfinal & Women's singles semifinal

7:30 p.m.–11:59 p.m.: Volleyball, Women's quarterfinals 1 & 2

8:00 p.m.–11:00 p.m.: Baseball, game # 28

8:00 p.m.–11:30 p.m.: Basketball, men's quarterfinal, games 3 & 4

8:00 p.m.–11:00 p.m.: Boxing, quarterfinal session 2

8:00 p.m.–11:00 p.m.: Diving, Women's springboard preliminaries

8:00 p.m.–11:00 p.m.: Track & Field, Women's & men's doubles bronze medal

July 31

8:30 a.m.–1:00 p.m.: Field Hockey, men's classification 1 & 2

9:00 a.m.–12:20 p.m.: Archery, Women's 1/8 eliminations

9:00 a.m.–12:20 p.m.: Canoe/Kayak—Sprint, K-2 men's 500 heats, C-1 men's 500 heats, K-1 Women's 500 heats

9:00 a.m.–1:30 p.m.: Field Hockey, men's classification 3 & 4

9:00 a.m.–12:30 p.m.: Track & Field, Women's & men's doubles gold medal

9:00 a.m.–12:55 p.m.: Track & Field, men's decathlon (100m, long jump, shot put)

9:30 a.m.–12:30 p.m.: Wrestling—Freestyle, 48kg, 57kg, 68kg, 82kg & 100kg classification

10:00 a.m.–1:30 p.m.: Basketball, Women's classification, games 1 & 2

10:00 a.m.–3:40 p.m.: Equestrian, individual dressage final

10:00 a.m.–1:00 p.m.: Team Handball, men's preliminaries 25 & 26

11:00 a.m.–5:30 p.m.: Tennis, Women's singles semifinal & Women's & men's doubles semifinal

11:00 a.m.–5:30 p.m.: Tennis, Women's singles semifinal & Women's & men's doubles semifinal

11:30 a.m.–1:00 p.m.: Diving, Women's springboard semifinal

12:00 p.m.–4:30 p.m.: Volleyball, men's quarterfinals 3 & 4

1:00 p.m.–6:00 p.m.: Yachting, Soling match races, Laser finals, Europe finals

1:30 p.m.–4:30 p.m.: Boxing, quarterfinal session 3

2:00 p.m.–5:00 p.m.: Archery, Women's final

2:30 p.m.–4:50 p.m.: Canoe/Kayak—Sprint, K-2 men's 500 reps, C-1 men's 500 reps, K-1 Women's 500 reps

2:30 p.m.–5:30 p.m.: Team Handball, men's preliminaries 27 & 28

3:00 p.m.–6:30 p.m.: Basketball, Women's quarterfinal, games 1 & 2

3:00 p.m.–5:00 p.m.: Soccer, men's semifinal 1

3:30 p.m.–6:20 p.m.: Wrestling—Freestyle, 48kg, 57kg, 68kg, 82kg & 100kg bronze & gold

4:30 p.m.–5:45 p.m.: Table Tennis, Women's singles final

5:15 p.m.–11:00 p.m.: Track & Field, Women's shot put, qualifying

5:30 p.m.–10:00 p.m.: Field Hockey, men's semifinal 1 & 2

7:00 p.m.–9:00 p.m.: Table Tennis, men's singles semifinal

7:00 p.m.–10:00 p.m.: Team Handball, men's preliminaries 29 & 30

7:00 p.m.–11:30 p.m.: Track & Field, Women's & men's singles bronze medal, Mixed doubles bronze medal

7:30 p.m.–11:59 p.m.: Volleyball, men's quarterfinals 1 & 2

8:00 p.m.–11:30 p.m.: Basketball, Women's quarterfinal, games 3 & 4

8:00 p.m.–11:00 p.m.: Boxing, quarterfinal session 4

8:00 p.m.–10:00 p.m.: Soccer, men's semifinal 2

10:00 p.m.–11:15 p.m.: Diving, Women's springboard final

August 1

8:00 a.m.–11:35 a.m.: Track & Field, men's decathlon (110m hurdles, discus)

8:30 a.m.–6:30 p.m.: Equestrian, team jumping preliminary & final

8:30 a.m.–1:00 p.m.: Field Hockey, men's final 9–10 & 7–8

9:00 a.m.–12:20 p.m.: Archery, men's 1/8 eliminations

9:00 a.m.–11:10 a.m.: Canoe/Kayak—Sprint, K-2 men's 1000 semifinal, C-1

men's 1000 semifinal, K-4 Women's 500 semifinal

9:00 a.m.–11:30 a.m.: Field Hockey, men's final 11–12

9:00 a.m.–2:00 p.m.: Track & Field, Women's & men's singles gold medal, Mixed doubles gold medal

9:30 a.m.–12:20 p.m.: Wrestling—Freestyle, 52kg, 62kg, 74kg, 90kg & 130kg preliminaries

10:00 a.m.–1:30 p.m.: Basketball, men's classification, games 3 & 4

10:00 a.m.–12:50 p.m.: Gymnastics—Rhythmic, individual preliminaries

10:00 a.m.–1:00 p.m.: Team Handball, Women's final 7–8 & semifinal 1

11:00 a.m.–8:00 p.m.: Tennis, men's singles semifinal, Women's & men's doubles bronze medal

12:00 p.m.–4:30 p.m.: Volleyball, Women's finals 5–8 places

1:00 p.m.–6:00 p.m.: Yachting, Soling match race finals

2:00 p.m.–5:00 p.m.: Archery, men's final

2:00 p.m.–5:00 p.m.: Baseball, semifinal game # 1

2:00 p.m.–10:30 p.m.: Track & Field, men's decathlon (javelin, 1,500m, pole vault)

2:30 p.m.–5:30 p.m.: Team Handball, Women's final 5–6 & semifinal 2

3:00 p.m.–6:30 p.m.: Basketball, Women's classification, games 3 & 4

3:00 p.m.–4:40 p.m.: Gymnastics—Rhythmic, group preliminaries

3:30 p.m.–6:10 p.m.: Wrestling—Freestyle, 52kg, 62kg, 74kg, 90kg & 130kg classification

4:30 p.m.–5:45 p.m.: Table Tennis, men's singles final

5:30 p.m.–10:15 p.m.: Field Hockey, Women's bronze & gold medal

6:00 p.m.–10:45 p.m.: Soccer, Women's bronze & gold medal

7:00 p.m.–10:00 p.m.: Baseball, semifinal game # 2

7:30 p.m.–11:59 p.m.: Volleyball, Women's semifinals 1 & 2

8:00 p.m.–11:30 p.m.: Basketball, men's semifinals, games 1 & 2

8:00 p.m.–11:00 p.m.: Boxing, semifinal session 1

8:00 p.m.–11:59 p.m.: Diving, men's platform preliminaries

August 2

7:30 a.m.–11:05 a.m.: Track & Field, men's 50k walk

9:00 a.m.–12:00 p.m.: Archery, Women's & men's team 1/8 finals, quarterfinals & semifinals

9:00 a.m.–11:10 a.m. Canoe/Kayak—Sprint, K-2 men's & Women's 500 semifinal, C-1 men's 500 semifinal

9:00 a.m.–11:00 a.m.: Field Hockey, men's final 5–6

9:30 a.m.–12:30 p.m.: Wrestling—Freestyle, 52kg, 62kg, 74kg, 90kg & 130kg classification

10:00 a.m.–1:30 p.m.: Basketball, men's finals, games 7–8 & 5–6

10:00 a.m.–12:50 p.m.: Gymnastics—Rhythmic, individual preliminaries

10:00 a.m.–1:00 p.m.: Team Handball, men's final 11–12 & 9–10

10:00 a.m.–6:30 p.m.: Tennis, Women's singles bronze medal, Women's singles gold medal

11:30 a.m.–1:00 p.m.: Diving, men's platform semifinal

12:00 p.m.–4:30 p.m.: Volleyball, men's finals 5–8 places

1:30 p.m.–5:00 p.m.: Archery, Women's & men's team finals

2:00 p.m.–5:00 p.m.: Baseball, bronze medal game

2:30 p.m.–5:30 p.m.: Team Handball, men's final 7–8 & semifinal 1

3:00 p.m.–6:30 p.m.: Basketball, Women's semifinals, games 1 & 2

3:00 p.m.–4:35 p.m.: Gymnastics—Rhythmic, group finals

3:30 p.m.–6:40 p.m.: Wrestling—Freestyle, 52kg, 62kg, 74kg, 90kg & 130kg bronze & gold

5:00 p.m.–9:45 p.m.: Field Hockey, men's bronze & gold medal

5:00 p.m.–6:30 p.m.: Synchronized swimming, team final

6:00 p.m.–10:10 p.m.: Track & Field, men's pole vault, final

7:00 p.m.–10:20 p.m.: Baseball, gold medal game

7:00 p.m.–10:00 p.m.: Team Handball, men's final 5–6 & semifinal 2

7:30 p.m.–11:59 p.m.: Volleyball, men's semifinals 1 & 2

8:00 p.m.–11:30 p.m.: Basketball, men's finals 11–12 & 9–10 places

8:00 p.m.–11:00 p.m.: Boxing, semifinal session 2

8:00 p.m.–10:00 p.m.: Soccer, men's bronze medal

10:00 p.m.–11:30 p.m.: Diving, men's platform final

August 3

9:00 a.m.–11:20 a.m.: Canoe/Kayak—Sprint, K-2 men's 1000 final, C-1 men's 1000 final, K-4 Women's 500 final

9:00 a.m.–11:30 a.m. Equestrian, individual dressage freestyle final

10:00 a.m.–1:30 p.m.: Basketball, Women's finals 7–8 & 5–6 places

10:00 a.m.–12:50 p.m.: Gymnastics—Rhythmic, individual semifinals

10:00 a.m.–6:30 p.m.: Tennis, men's singles bronze medal, men's singles gold medal

12:00 p.m.–4:45 p.m.: Volleyball, Women's bronze & gold medal

1:30 p.m.–5:30 p.m.: Boxing, gold medal session 1

3:00 p.m.–6:30 p.m.: Basketball, Women's finals 11–12 & 9–10 places

3:30 p.m.–5:45 p.m.: Soccer, men's gold medal

3:30 p.m.–6:45 p.m.: Team Handball, Women's bronze & gold medal

6:30 p.m.–9:55 p.m.: Track & Field, Women's high jump, final

8:00 p.m.–11:30 p.m.: Basketball, men's bronze & gold medal games

August 4

9:00 a.m.–10:50 a.m.: Canoe/Kayak—Sprint, K-2 men's 500 final, C-1 men's 500 final, K-1 Women's 500 final

9:30 a.m.–1:00 p.m.: Basketball, Women's bronze & gold medal games

10:00 a.m.–3:30 p.m.: Equestrian, individual jumping final

12:00 p.m.–4:45 p.m.: Volleyball, men's bronze & gold medal

1:00 p.m.–3:15 p.m.: Gymnastics—Rhythmic, individual finals

1:30 p.m.–5:30 p.m.: Boxing, gold medal session 2

3:00 p.m.–6:15 p.m.: Team Handball, men's bronze & gold medal

6:30 p.m.–9:30 p.m.: Track & Field, men's marathon

9:00 p.m.–11:59 p.m.: Closing Ceremony

INDEX

C

Calhoun, Lee, 631
Calnan, George C., 244
Campbell, Ben Nighthorse, 80–81
Campbell, Julie, 740, 741
Campbell, Milt, 681
Campbell, Tonie, 631
Camue, Enrique Figuerola, 624
canoeing/kayaking, 11, 121–42; flat-water, 125–26; whitewater, 124, 125, 126
Capriati, Jennifer, 533, 538, 541–42
Caprilli, Federico, 205
Cardoso, Rogerio, 334
Carey, Rick, 451
Cariou, Jean, 219
Carlos, John, 624
Carlton, Guy, 758
Carpenter-Phinney, Connie, 19, 165, 168
Carr, Bill, 622
Carr, Henry, 624
Carter, Jimmy, 27
Cartwright, Alexander J., 59
Carver, Chris, 499
Carvin, Chad, 440–41
Cáslavská, Vera, 310, 312, 313, 314
Castarelli, Fabio, 171
Catherwood, Ethel, 573
Cator, Silvio, 559
Caulkins, Tracy, 443, 481, 483–84
Cavill, Frederick, 429–30
Cerutti, Paul, 387
Chance, Briton, 808
Chandler, Jennifer, 200
Chang, Michael, 533
Charles II, King of England, 797
Charlesworth, Ric, 263
Chelimo, Richard, 599
Chen Yueling, 661
Cheruiyot, Rose, 600
cheuca, 257
Chin-Ho Kim, 44
Chirinao, Jose, 106
Chizhova, Nadezhda, 697
Chladek, Dana, 129, 132
Chladek, Ema, 129
Chladek, Stan, 129
Cho Youn-Jeong, 36, 44
Chol Su Choi, 109
Chow, Amy, 284–88
Chow, Susan, 284, 285
Christie, Linford, 23, 552, 585, 586–88, 625, 640
Chtcherbo, Vitali, 26, 299, 300, 301
Chuhei Nambu, 561
Chukarin, Victor, 294, 296
Chun-gauang Wang, 773
Cioroslan, Dragomir, 753 54, 755
Clark, Ellery, 558, 562
Clark, Mary Ellen, 183–85
Clark, Ron, 628
Clark, Will, 64
Clarke, Kim, 519
Clasper, Henry, 350
Clay, Cassius *see* Ali, Muhammad
Cleitomachus 95
Clotworthy, Bob, 192

Coachman, Alice, 12, 573–74
Coakes, Marion, 219
Coe, Sebastian, 18, 628–29, 635–36, 637
Coenen, Laura, 519
Coffey, Calvin, 358
Cohan, Don, 809
Coimbra, Herlander, 83
Coleman, Georgia, 192, 198
Collett, Wayne, 624
Collins, John, 451
Comaneci, Nadia, 17, 273, 275, 276, 292, 312, 313, 314–19
Conley, Mike, 562, 568
Conner, Bart, 273, 297, 298, 299, 300, 319
Conner, Dennis, 810–13
Connolly, Harold, 686–87
Connolly, James, 3, 558, 560, 562
Constantine, King of Greece, 809, 814
Conway, Hollis, 564
Cooke, Edward, 564
Cooper, Charlotte, 536
Cooper, Malcolm, 387
Copeland, Lillian, 697
Coroebus, 579
Corso, Rich, 736–37, 738
Costa, Alfranio da, 385
Costello, Paul, 356
Coubertin, Pierre de Fredi, Baron de, 2, 5, 9, 231, 340
Courier, Jim, 533, 534, 542
Courtney, Tom, 627
Cova, Alberto, 629
Crabbe, Clarence "Buster," 454, 458, 686
Craig, Ralph, 8
Cram, Steve, 629, 636
Crapp, Lorraine, 479
Crawford, Hasely, 625
Crawford, Shannon, 372
cricket, 4
Croghan, Dan, 589, 590, 591
Croghan, Mark, 589–91
croquet, 4
Crothers, William, 627
Cruyff, Johan, 406
Cruz, Joaquim, 629
Csák, Ibolya, 573
Ctvrtlik, Bob, 710–11
Cunningham, Glenn, 626
Curtis, Ann, 479
Curtis, Katherine, 495
Cuthbert, Betty, 655
Cuthbert, Juliet, 610, 661
cycling, 155–78; individual pursuit, 159; individual road race, 160–61; individual time trial, 161; kilometer time trial, 160; match sprint, 158–59; points race, 160; team pursuit, 159–60; team time trial, 161; *see also* mountain biking

D

da Costa, Roberto Lopes, 728
Daggett, Timothy, 297, 298, 299

Index

851

On-Line Information

Once you've absorbed all the essential Olympic information in these pages, check out these Internet sites on the World Wide Web to find the late-breaking news on events leading up to the Olympic Games.

Atlanta Committee for the Olympic Games

http://www.atlanta.olympic.org
The official Web site for the 1996 Olympic Games. Lots of useful information, including sport-by-sport breakdowns, event schedules, and ticket and travel information.

NBC Sports

http://www.olympic.nbc.com
You're just a click away from NBC's 1996 Olympic site on the World Wide Web. Extensive coverage with features including every sport on the Olympic program, profiles of Olympic hopefuls and an athlete of the week, a detailed programming schedule, daily updates, press releases, history of the Games, Olympic quotes and photographs capturing Olympic moments.